Philosophy of Religion
宗教哲学经典选读

MELVILLE Y. STEWART　XING TAOTAO

北京大学西学影印丛书·哲学 | 北京大学出版社
PEKING UNIVERSITY PRESS

图书在版编目(CIP)数据

宗教哲学经典选读/(美)斯图尔特(Stewart, M.),邢滔滔选编.—北京:北京大学出版社,2005.9
(北京大学西学影印丛书)
ISBN 7-301-09572-4

Ⅰ.宗… Ⅱ.①斯…②邢… Ⅲ.宗教哲学-著作-选读-英文 Ⅳ.B920

中国版本图书馆 CIP 数据核字(2005)第 097852 号

书　　　名:宗教哲学经典选读
著作责任者:〔美〕斯图尔特(Melville Y. Stewart)　邢滔滔(Xing Taotao)
责 任 编 辑:王立刚
标 准 书 号:ISBN 7-301-09572-4/B·0333
出 版 发 行:北京大学出版社
地　　　址:北京市海淀区成府路 205 号　100871
网　　　址:http://cbs.pku.edu.cn　电子信箱:pkuwsz@yahoo.com.cn
电　　　话:邮购部 62752015　发行部 62750672　编辑部 62752025
排 版 者:北京军峰公司
印 刷 者:北京飞达印刷有限责任公司
经 销 者:新华书店
　　　　　787mm×960mm　16 开本　41.75 印张　800 千字
　　　　　2005 年 9 月第 1 版　2006 年 5 月第 2 次印刷
定　　　价:59.80 元

未经许可,不得以任何方式复制或抄袭本书之部分或全部内容。
版权所有,翻版必究

顾问委员会

(按姓氏拼音排序)

M.Stewart	韩水法	何怀宏
何兆武	靳希平	孙永平
万俊人	王一川	吴国盛
邢滔滔	章启群	张祥龙
张志刚	赵敦华	朱青生

DEDICATION

To our Friend and distinguished Scholar

PROFESSOR ZHAO DUNHUA

Chair of the Department of Philosophy
And Religious Studies

PEKING UNIVERSITY

TABLE OF CONTENTS

Preface .... v-viii

Forward ix

Introduction 1-12

PART I FAITH AND REASON

*1. Kierkegaard's Arguments Against Objective Reasoning
  in Religion*
   Robert Merrihew Adams 17-28
2. The Extended Aquinas/Calvin Model
   Alvin Plantinga 29-43
3. On Faith
   Thomas Aquinas 45-58
4. Jonathan Edwards and the Heart
   William J. Wainright 59-87
5. What Kinds of Religious Beliefs Are Worth Having?
   Richard Swinburne 89-99
6. Lectures on Religious Beliefs
   Ludwig Wittgenstein 101-112

PART II ARGUMENTS FOR GOD'S EXISTENCE

7. The Ontological Argument
   Anselm of Canterbury 117-118
8. The Cosmological Argument
   Bruce Reichenbach 119-135
9. An Examination of the Cosmological Argument
   William Rowe 137-147
10. The Argument to God from Laws of Nature
   Richard Swinburne 149-159
*11. A Scientific Argument for the Existence of God: The
   Fine-Tuning Design Argument*
   Robin Collins 161-180
12. Religious Experience as Self-Transcendence
   Merold Westphal 181-198
13. Religious Experience and Religious Belief
   William P. Alston 199-206

PART III PROBLEMS OF EVIL

14. *Evil and Omnipotence*
    John L. Mackie 211-219
15. *Can the Theist Refuse to Answer the Problem of Evil?*
    Robin Le Poidevin 221-225
16. *The Greater Good Defense*
    Keith Yandell 227-238
17. *The Free Will Defense*
    Alvin Plantinga 239-260
18. *The Soul Making Defense*
    John Hick 261-265
19. *O Felix Culpa, Redemption, and the Greater Good Defense*
    Melville Y. Stewart 267-282
20. *Resources to the Rescue*
    Marily McCord Adams 283-301
21. *The Inductive Argument From Evil and the Human Cognitive Condition*
    William P. Alston 303-326
22. *The Problem of Evil*
    Richard Swinburne 327-333

PART IV THE ATTRIBUTES OF GOD

23. *Some Puzzles Concerning Omnipotence*
    George I. Mavrodes 337-339
24. *Omnipotence and Almightiness*
    Peter Geach 341-351
25. *Middle Knowledge*
    William Hasker 353-374
26. *The Molinist Solution*
    Linda Zagzebski 375-397
27. *Eternity*
    Eleonore Stump and Norman Kretzmann 399-416
28. *A New Doctrine of Eternity*
    Alan Padgett 417-429

PART V MIRACLES

29. *Of Miracles*
    David Hume 433-444
30. *The Argument from Miracles*
    Michael Martin 445-463
31. *Miracles and the Laws of Nature*
    George I. Mavrodes 465-474

PART VI RELIGION AND SCIENCE

    32. *What Place, Then, for a Creator?: Hawking on God and Creation*
        William Lane Craig 479-493
    33. *Explanation from Physics to Theology*
        Philip Clayton 495-502
    34. *Quantum Theory and Free Will*
        Stephen M. Barr 503-508

PART VII RELIGION AND ETHICS

    35. *Kant on Recognizing Our Duties As God's Commands*
        John Hare 513-529
    36. *Divine Commands and the Social Nature of Obligation*
        Robert Merrihew Adams 531-540
    37. *Morality and God*
        Richard Swinburne 541-549

PART VIII DEATH AND IMMORTALITY

    38. *The Finality of Death*
        Bertrand Russell 553-555
    39. *Monism and Immortality*
        Bruce Reichenbach 557-570
    40. *The Possibility of Resurrection*
        Peter van Inwagen 571-574
    41. *What Makes Me Me?*
        Richard Swinburne 575-583

PART IX RELIGIOUS PLURALISM

    42. *Religious Pluralism and Salvation*
        John Hick 587-596
    43. *Plantinga, Pluralism and Justified Religious Belief*
        David Basinger 597-607
    44. *Pluralism*
        Alvin Plantinga 609-624

CONTRIBUTORS 625-630

GLOSSARY 631-644

INDEX 645-653

TABLE OF ILLUSTRATIONS

Part I Faith and Reason
Illustration 1, for **Reason & Faith**, picture of *Thomas Aquinas, The Angelic Doctor*, portrait by Justus of Leiden, the best claim to a likeness of Aquinas, who held to a complementary relationship between reason and faith, courtesy of Madame Vieillard, Ashmolean Museum, Oxford, England..

Part II Arguments for God's Existence
Illustration 2, for **Design,** digital picture of mechanical clock, purchased at the Pan Jia Yuan, Beijing, 2004, picture courtesy of Melville Y. Stewart.

Part III Problems of Evil and Defensive Strategies
Illustration 3 for **Evil**-Henri Rousseau (1844-1910), *War*, 1894, oil on canvas, courtesy of Muse de l'Impressionnisme, Paris, France.

Part IV The Attributes of God
Illustration 4 for **Eternity**, by William Blake (1757-1827), *The Ancient of Days* (Manchester Version), from 'Europa, before 1795, water color, courtesy of Whitworth Art Gallery, Manchester, England.

Part V Miracles
Illustration 5 for **Miracles**-Jacopo Tintoretto (1518-1594), The Miracle of St. Mark, 1548, oil on canvas, coutesy of Venice, Academia.

Part VI Religion and Science
Illustration 6 for **Religion**-Gérard Dou, A Hermit Praying, (1670), picture, courtesy of The William Hood Dunwoody Fund, The Minneapolis Institute of Art.

Illustration 7 for **Science**-picture of Kepler's Supernova Remnant. SN 1604, picture courtesy of NASA, ESA, R, Sankrit and W. Blair (Johns Hopkins University).

Part VII Religion and Ethics
Illustration 8 for **Ethics/Religion**-*Moses and the Tables of the Law*, Fresco, painted by Cosimo Rosselli (b. 1439, Firenze, d. 1507), courtesy of the Capella Sistina, Vatican.

Part VIII Death and Immortality
Illustration 9 for **Immortality/Resurrection**-*The Resurrection*, Mathis Neithardt-Gothardt Grűwald, the Isenheim Altarpiece, oil on wood, courtesy of the Isenheim Cathedral. Isenheim, Germany.

Part IX Religious Pluralism
Illustration 10 for **Chinese religion**, *The Temple of Heaven*, Beijing, China, P. R. China, picture courtesy of Melville Y. Stewart.

Illustration 11 for **Christianity**, *Roman Catholic Cathedral*, old campus, Shandong University, Jinan, P. R. China, picture courtesy of Melville Y. Stewart.

PREFACE

It has been with a special sense of pleasure that we have been able to work together in the production of this new anthology in philosophy of religion. Seven thousands miles separate us, but the computer world has helped shrink those miles for this exciting collaborative venture.

The range includes nine areas of specialty falling under the philosophy of religion rubric. Various key authors from the past are included so as to provide historical perspectives on issues and problems discussed.

The scholars enlisted are well recognized, and many have submitted their most recent contribution to their respective fields of specialty. We have had to work within certain space constraints but this has pushed us to include only the very best out there.

Philosophy of religion is of special interest to the current Chinese scholarly world. Universities in China are developing new religious studies departments attracting a whole new genre of students gifted to pursue issues relating to the religious. It has been the delight of both editors to sense that interest and excitement as it is found in the classroom.

Inquiry into the religious affects all other disciplines. The critical reflective processes of philosophical inquiry can aid the human spirit in this its most lofty of pursuits, namely, knowledge when available of the ultimate origin of things and their respective destinies.

We are very grateful to the editors of Peking University Press for the invitation and their interest in the project from the very beginning. We also want to thank the Press for allowing the inclusion of illustrations thereby signaling and enhancing each topic in the Collection.

Peking University Department Chair of Philosophy, Zhao Dunhua, is to be thanked for his supportive and affirmative role, as is also Bethel University Department Chair, Paul Reasoner for making the Copy Center facilities available for manuscript preparation.

Special thanks to our friend, Professor Bruce Reichenbach (Augsburg College), for his careful reading of various parts of the manuscript that led to needed refinements.

We want to thank five undergraduate students at Bethel University, Joshua D. Bau III, Daniel Farmer, Justin Marshall, Jason Markley, and Mike Nordin for their careful proofreading of the manuscript. They have thus contributed to the overall quality of the work.

But we especially want to thank Ms Marie Balsley Taylor for her masterful and artistic preparation of the manuscript. Without her careful attention to detail many errors and stylistic shortcomings would have otherwise gone unnoticed.

Our special thanks to Professor Richard Swinburne of Oxford University for writing the *Forward*, and for his contributions to several topics in the Collection.

We also want to thank various publishing houses in the West for making articles previously published accessible for inclusion in this work without fee, thereby allowing a potentially greater audience.

We look forward to the appearance and wide circulation of this English Edition venture.We wish all who read these pages a challenging and inspiring experience in the pursuit of wisdom in an area of inquiry so abundantly endowed with mystery, so rich with intriigue, and so lofty in respect to its subject matter. If and when truth shines forth, it is our hope that it will both exhilarate and liberate the human spirit.

Xing Taotao (Peking University)

Melville Y. Stewart (Bethel University)
Editors

FORWARD

Richard Swinburne

The early Greek philosophers of twenty five centuries ago gave philosophical form to those ultimate questions which should concern every human being-why does the world exist, what makes actions good and bad, are we really free when we make choices, what will happen to us after death? When Greek philosophy met the Christian religion, and the similar theistic (that is God-centered) religions of Judaism and Islam, these questions came to be expressed in ways which challenged those religions-did God make the world, does God's choice determine which actions are good or bad, does God cause humans to do what they do and if so do we deserve blame for doing wrong, is the essential part of each of us an immaterial soul to which (perhaps with a new body) God will give a new life after death?

These questions and all the other questions examined in this anthology were discussed in rigorous detail by the philosophers of the medieval West such as Anselm, Aquinas, and Duns Scotus; and again, with sensitivity to the developing modern science, by all the great philosophers of seventeenth and eighteenth century Europe-Descartes, Leibniz, Locke, Hume and Kant. But with the nineteenth and early twentieth century many philosophers of Europe and America no longer believed that religious answers had much plausibility. The late twentieth century however saw a considerable revival of interest among philosophers of the English speaking world in religious answers to these perennial questions. Philosophers began to apply their philosophical skills to the claims of religion, using in their work all the tools and theories being developed in branches of philosophy other than the philosophy of religion: the tools of deductive logic and the calculus of probability, and different theories of knowledge and justification, of morality and of meaning. Using these tools and theories, and sensitive to the latest developments in the sciences, they have put religious claims under a powerful philosophical microscope, asking what do these claims mean, are they true, and are we justified in holding them. This anthology contains examples of the very best of such work focussed on claims central to theistic religions. In order to bring out the historical background to modern discussions, it includes some extracts from classical works. But most of the papers are very recent, some published for the first time. Some of the authors favour the religious viewpoint, some attack it; but all think the issues to be of very great importance, and try to expound their own view with clarity and vigour. The final section of the anthology begins a philosophical examination of non-Western religions; and we can expect that much further philosophical work will in due course develop the approaches illustrated in this anthology to give the great religions of the East the thorough philosophical analysis which they deserve. It matters greatly which if any religious beliefs are true; and I congratulate the editors on producing a new large relevant anthology, covering different central topics and representative of different viewpoints, which will help philosophy students and the wider educated public to sort out their own views on these all-important questions.

FORWARD

INTRODUCTION

There is probably no area in contemporary Western philosophy more exciting and engaging than philosophy of religion. The plethora of books and articles on topics falling within its domain evidences unmistakably the avid interest of philosophers, both those disposed to religious belief as well as those inclined to reject it. This is partly due to the interconnectedness of the topics generally associated with philosophy of religion. Some find a never-ending fascination with trying to weave various initially discordant strands into a coherent meaningful whole, while others, contrariwise, see nothing but loose ends and disconnectedness. For example, some, notably atheists, view the existence of evil as incompatible with one or more of God's attributes. Others argue that the amount of evil in the world makes God's existence strongly improbable. Theists have tried to address the former problem with various consistency strategies and the latter with evidential arguments designed to hold the line for the probability of God's existence. There is also a cluster of troublesome and difficult questions relating to Christian theistic beliefs about God's sovereignty and how it relates to human freedom and responsibility. The questions are indeed multivarious and often perplexing if not daunting; the stakes are as high as any life presents.

But perhaps the chief reason for philosophy of religion's attraction is the fact that considerations having to do with the existence and nature of a Supreme Being raises issues of ultimate concern. No issue surpasses it in terms of importance, ramification and implication. All else one endeavors to affirm in philosophy pivots, and rightly so, on claims made regarding whether such a being exists, and what sort of beliefs properly follow from affirmation or denial of God's existence.

Two basic orientations prevail in the literature in the West, the analytic way of thinking, or as some prefer to call it, Anglo-American philosophy, and Continental philosophy. The latter finds some representation in this collection, but some readers no doubt may think it not enough. The analytic is given greater attention for a number of reasons, only a few of which are only briefly stated here. Scant if any attention is given to arguments for the existence of God by Continental authors. Other topics typically included in Western philosophy of religion texts are also sparsely covered if at all, such as miracles, and other evidential sorts of topics, like the problem of evil.

As for further representative balance, not only are the non-theists given a significant voice, authors from the three mainstream Christian traditions, Protestant, Roman Catholic, and Orthodox can be found in their respective distinctiveness. A choice is apparent with regard to numbers of authors. Wholeness of an essay has been an important criterion rather than numbers of authors. We've attempted to put together the best of the most recent materials available, some of which appears in book form for the first time.

The topics selected are something of an index to the bulk of the literature: faith and reason, arguments for the existence of God, the problem of evil, the attributes of God, miracles, religion and science, religion and ethics, death, identity, immortality and resurrection, and religious pluralism. Unlike my earlier anthology, *Philosophy of Religion, An Anthology of Contemporary Views* (also in a Chinese Edition), this new collection includes historical as well as contemporary authors. Philosophy can't be properly grasped apart from its historical context. One regret is that page constraints didn't allow a fuller historical panorama. The topics are briefly described below.

I. Faith and Reason

Six articles cover a spectrum of options ranging from the fideism of Søren Kierkegaard, the Reformed epistemological approach of Alvin Plantinga, the reason/faith model of Thomas Aquinas, the reason-of-the-heart slant of Jonathan Edwards, the probabilistic epistemic account of religious belief of Richard Swinburne, and finally Ludwig Wittgenstein's theology-of-grammar approach to the meaning of religious language. In no section should the order be viewed as an ascending scale from the least attractive to the most or as suggesting a progressive advance. These sorts of appraisals are left to the discretion of the reader.

The first, by Robbert Merrihew Adams, sets the stage for a consideration of fideism by critically examining three arguments offered by Kierkegaard in defense of his finely tuned fideism (the view that reason and argument are inappropriate to God's call to faith), the approximation, postponement, and passion arguments. Adams judges that while none of the arguments work—the first is faulty, and the second and third have an imbedded notion of religiousness Adams finds objectionable; he nonetheless concludes that Kierkegaard's case works with a more substantial logical structure than he is ordinarily viewed as having; moreover, he is judged as having more difficulty getting away from objective justification than he was willing to allow.

Having given an initial sketch of the Aquinas/Calvin model for warranted Christian belief in Chapter 6 (of *Warranted Christian Belief*), in this excerpt from Chapter 8, Alvin Plantinga expands on its chief aspects to show that Christian beliefs such as belief in God, the Trinity, the resurrection, etc., can be said to be *justified*, *rational* and *to have warrant*. God's rescue of humanity from fallenness is communicated via a three-tiered cognitive process as follows: (1) the production of the Scriptures; (2) the presence and action of the Holy Spirit; (3) a response of faith involving a cognitive component. The third, *faith* according to Aquinas and Calvin is a work of the Holy Spirit that also involves a "trio of processes," (1) the belief, (2) a divine teaching (content), and (3) a special divine activity. The model proposed means that a Christian can have *justification*, *internal* and *external rationality* and *warrant* for his beliefs. Basic Christian beliefs, on Plantinga's account can be and probably are (deontologically) *justified*. Such beliefs may also be *internally rational*, that is if they issue from a properly functioning belief-forming mechanism, and the believer has done his best to assist in their formulation. *Warrant* and *external rationality* may also be claimed providing four conditions are met: (1) the beliefs accepted by faith (a) are instigated of the Holy Spirit, and (b) are produced by a cognitive process working properly; (2) the cognitive environment is suited to the cognitive process; (3) the process is designed to produce true beliefs; (4) the beliefs produced are in fact true. Finally, regarding proper basicality and the Scriptures, as God's vehicle for communication of his message, the Scriptures are accepted because they are *self-authenticating*, that is, their acceptance does not rest upon the evidence of other beliefs.

In his article "On Faith," Thomas Aquinas examines the nature of faith, its corresponding gifts, knowledge and understanding, its opposing vices, and faith as a virtue. Faith is that which gives assent to the truth of God, and faith's object of knowledge is not a proposition, but the object which the proposition may be said to *describe*, the *heavenly vision*. The *light of faith* does not direct us to things that are seen, but to things which are above. He distinguishes two ways of knowing, the path of natural reason, and faith. Working with the former, one may come to give assent to first principles (by the natural light of reason), and following the mode of faith, one may perceive the *invisible things of God*. The latter is a complement to the former. There is a rational side to faith, if the believer is moved by the authority of God vindicated by the miraculous.

The piece by William J. Wainwright, "Jonathan Edwards and the Heart," treats the reader to one of America's greatest philosophers in the Christian tradition. Edwards falls within the Reformed tradition, and so contrary to Aquinas, he evidences a strong distrust of humanity's natural capacities, and hence of natural reason. At the same time, he is heir to the strong confidence in reason generally associated with the Continental rationalists and the British empiricists. Wainwright tries to show in a qualified way how Edwards weaves elements of these two traditions, the Reformed tradition, and English rational enlightenment confidence in rationality together in a reason-and-the-heart way, through a specially tuned evidentialism/foundationalism. Belief must rest on sufficient evidence. Edwards further insists that evidence must be met with a *passion* issuing from the *heart*.

In his article, "What Kinds of Religious Beliefs are Worth Having?," Richard Swinburne emphasizes that different philosophers provide different accounts of what makes belief *justified* or *warranted*. He is concerned with, not which of these accounts is correct (because such terms as *justified* or *warranted* are often used in very different senses in ordinary languages), but with what kind of justification or warrant do we need for our religious beliefs. He argues that we need beliefs which are probably true, since it would be silly, for example, to worship a God who almost certainly did not exist. He allows, by his *principle of credulity*, that anyone who has the evidence of a very strong personal experience of God has evidence which renders it probable that there is a God. But he considers that most people are not in this position and so they need arguments which start from publicly available evidence (such as the orderliness of the universe) to the existence of God, if their belief that there is a God is to be justified in a useful sense. He claims that such a theory of warrant as Plantinga's externalism, has the consequence that anyone whose beliefs are produced by a process such as Plantinga describes has no means of checking up on whether that process does yield true beliefs, and so no means of improving the quality of one's beliefs.

According to Ludwig Wittgenstein words do not have a fixed essential meaning (as he thought when he wrote the *Tractatus Logico-Philosophicus*), but are to be understood in the context of their use. Thus when it comes to religious terms and religious language games, he thought that the believer/theologian needs to pay attention to the sorts of things the rules of conversation permit one to say about such things as *angels*, *life after death* and *God*. His general proposal is thus a theology of grammar where religious expressions/utterances are to be understood in terms of their use.

The contemporary literature takes the reader well beyond the simple options of faith, or reason, or a simple combination of the two. Kierkegaard's fideism is presented from a non-favorable point of view. According to Plantinga's external epistemological model, a religious belief may be said to be *justified*, *rational* and *have warrant* just in case it meets certain specific criteria. Swinburne takes a probabilistic/internalism line, contending that beliefs worth having are those which are judged probably true because of the strength of the evidence of relevant personal experience. Aquinas crafts a reason/faith model which begins with natural reason and its limits, and moves beyond reason's limits by way of a faith expansion which accesses special revelation. There are of course other options, and multifarious fine tunings in the literature.

II. Arguments for the Existence of God

Regarding arguments for God's existence, pages giving account of them seem to go on without end.

Anselm's piece is the *locus classicus* of the ontological argument for God's existence. It proceeds from a definition of *God's being* as *that than which none greater can be conceived*.

From this definition he draws the conclusion that God exists, because if one hypothesizes that this being involves only mental existence, this leads to the absurdity that one can conceive of a greater than that than which nothing greater can be conceived, namely one which exists in the understanding and in reality. He concludes, God exists.

Bruce Reichenbach has provided the reader with the latest innovative formulations of Thomas Aquinas' cosmological proofs for God's existence, the Kalām form of the argument, and Swinburne's inductive cosmological argument. Reichenbach concludes that Swinburne's examination of the argument leaves us with questions as to what counts as an adequate explanation, of defining simplicity, and of determining prior probabilities. Another problem is examined, one that Aquinas was also aware of. Even if Aquinas' argument strategy works, he hasn't shown that the Uncaused Cause, the Unmoved Mover, the Necessary Being, is the God of Christian theism.

The piece by William Rowe, distinguishes the theist's task as having two parts, one which sets out to prove that a Necessary Being exists, and the other above, that of showing that this being is the God of Christian theism. Having drawn this distinction, he introduces his account of the principle of *Sufficient Reason*. He then proceeds to examine four objections to the argument, and comes to conclude that the major variant forms of the argument fail to achieve the objective of the first part, to show that there is a self-existent being.

Richard Swinburne in "The Argument from Laws of Nature," directs his discussion to the confirmatory force of the argument for God from the laws of nature. He concludes that the degree to which the universe is governed by simple laws of nature rather than being chaotic, adds to the probability of theism.

Robin Collins in his "Fine-Tuning Design Argument," appeals to recent findings of contemporary science which suggest that the universe is finely tuned in a way amazingly well-suited for human life, and that even slight variations from these regularities would mean that life as we know it would not have been able to exist. He examines a number of objections to his argument and responds in its defense.

The article by Merold Westphal, "Religious Experience and Self-Transcendence," is the first in this collection that works with the Continental method. His focus is upon religious experience: hence it is relevant to another argument for God's existence, the one from experience. This piece and the one that follows helps direct the reader along two tracks, the Continental and the Anglo-American.

Westphal begins by defining religious experience as *self-transcendence*. Considering various candidates for a proper sense of *self-transcendence*, he discounts both the *transcendence of intentionality* and contemplative or *ecstatic self-forgetfulness* because each retains the centrality of the self. An ethical move that refuses to grant center place to the will is taken as the final solution. He opines that only then can one encounter the *truly other*. But even this move does not absolve one from the possibility that true religion may generate self-deception about the presence of its substance. He finally sees self-transcendence as sometimes elusive and as a life-long pursuit if one is to experience a genuinely authentic Christian life.

William Alston in "Religious Experience and Religious Belief," argues that religious experience can serve as grounds for religious belief. His main contention is that the epistemology of religious experience is analogous to the epistemology of sense experience, even though there are disparities. The validity of sense experience is tied to *verifiability*, but because God is viewed as *wholly other*, these two categories are viewed as not applying to the epistemology of religious experience. His basic conclusion is that Christian Epistemic Practice (CP) has basically the same epistemic status as Perceptual Practice (PP) and furthermore, if one gives credence to the latter, then one should also see the propriety of the former.

Some of the main arguments on the scene today have been examined, the ontological, cosmological, the fine-tuning design argument, and the argument from experience. Once again, the reader is left to judge whether all, some combination, or none at all work or have value for the theistic apologist.

III. Problems of Evil and Defensive Strategies

There is an array of arguments against the theist based on evil, chief among which are the logical and probabilistic formulations. Various strategies have been formulated in response, ranging from a *defensive* scheme, which tends to be more modest than a *theodicy* because a *defense* is often intended only as a possible justification for allowing evil, whereas a *theodicy* may be tendered as a comprehensive justificatory scheme for all evils, sometimes with the added claim that the scheme is a close if not actual representation of God's reasons for allowing all of the evils that exist.

In his article, "Evil and Omnipotence," J. L. Mackie contends that Christian theists face a logical problem based on evil. It is his thesis that beliefs basic/central to the Christian faith, namely that (1) that God exists, (2) that he is omnipotent, omniscient, and omni-benevolent, and (3) that evil exists, together with two other propositions which are quasi-logical and boil down to (4) the God thus described in (2) above would eliminate every occurrence of evil, comprise a set that is logically inconsistent. He contends that the only way out for the theist is either to acknowledge that the system of Christian beliefs is inconsistent and so untenable, or to alter one of the basic beliefs, specifically (2), since (1) is essential to the Christian belief system, (3) is obviously true, and (4) is quasi-logical and so undeniably true. That part of (2) which he suggests needs to be altered is the claim that God is omnipotent. If theists somehow unpack this key attribute, say in a limited-God way, this would ease them out of the difficulty.

Robin Le Poidevin in "Can the Theist Refuse to Answer the Problem of Evil?", examines several alternatives for the believer. First is the approach which offers a full defense for the faith in the face of evil. The second avoids offering a justification for evil altogether. The fault Le Poidevin finds with the second is that it tends to make theism irrational or unintelligible.

In his piece, "The Greater Good Defense," Keith Yandell contends that because the God of Christian theism is all-good and all-powerful, these two beliefs *imply* some version of what he calls the *greater good defense*. That is, for every evil, there is at least a counterbalancing good, and the good in question logically requires the evil, or some evil like it, and there are some evils which are overbalanced by goods which logically require them or some evils like them. So on balance, the evil in the world is overbalanced by the goods.

Alvin Plantinga's "The Free Will Defense," is an updated modal version of Augustine's account of the same offered as a defense for God's allowing evil in his creation. That is, since God values *significant freedom* which involves choices between goods and evils, then if he wants creatures with this sort of freedom creating them brings about the possibility of evil in the world. Plantinga's modal version of the free will defense is developed in part as an answer to an objection raised by J. L. Mackie. Mackie contended that since God is all-knowing, even if he wanted creatures free, he could, since he is omniscient, bring about only those creatures whom he foreknew would choose only to do the good. Plantinga's counter to this is that while God is omnipotent, he can't bring about *just any* world that he *pleases*, *if* he wishes to bring about significantly free creatures. While he can (as the sole agent) *strongly actualize* such a world, following the mode of *weak actualization* (which involves both the divine and human agents), he cannot interfere with significantly free choices, and so he can't guarantee that the world he makes is free of evil. To clinch his case, Plantinga advances a transworld identity thesis, and adds that perhaps creatures across all possible worlds where they enjoy transworld identity are infected with *transworld depravity*, that is a depravity affecting human essences such that every human being eventually makes at least one choice that is evil. On this account, God could not have brought about a world without evil, even with foreknowledge.

John Hick, in "Evil and Soul-Making," gives account of human origins that is not Augustinian, but rather Irenaean. Humans were not created in a state of innocence. He distinguishes between humans being created in God's image, and their growing into his likeness. Accordingly, this world is viewed as a "veil of tears" that provides an ideal for soul-growth. To further enhance human freedom and growth God also absconds. Evils are thus God's tools, allowed to exist for the benefit of human development and growth into the likeness of God.

In "O Felix Culpa, Redemption, and the Greater-Good Defense," Melville Stewart contends that redemption is a specification of Yandell's greater good defense, in that redemption needs some sort of evil in order for it to be a meaningful act on the part of divinity. Without some sort of evil, God would not have to come to the rescue. So the fall is a happy event, not because it is intrinsically worthwhile, but because it is a necessary means to the end contemplated. Thus the fall which was divinely prohibited serves as a means, because it provides an opportunity for God to show love in a way he could not have otherwise.

Marilyn McCord Adams in "Resources to the Rescue," contends that there are evils in the world that are horrendous, so terrible as to appear completely incompatible with the Christian description of God as all-good and all-powerful. Her strategy involves going beyond general revelation and the natural light of reason. That is, the theist must appeal to the Scriptures as additional apologetic tools for dealing with horrendous evils. That is, Leibniz's best-of-all-possible worlds and Plantinga's modal free will defense are responses that yield small results at a tremendous expense. They fail to reckon with the real existential problem, the enormity of and horrendous character of evils in the real world. The only way to respond appropriately to these evils is to "better explain" how God can deal with these evils through richer principles derived from the Scriptures.

William P. Alston's "The Inductive Argument from Evil, and the Human Cognitive Condition," is a critical response to the probabilistic attack based on evils that assumes a "low estimate of the human cognitive capacities in a certain application." He has William Rowe specifically in mind. In his conclusion, he lists the cognitive limits that comprise "the backbone" of his argument: (1) lack of data; (2) complexity greater than we can handle; (3) difficulty of determining what is metaphysically possible or necessary; (4) ignorance of the full range of possibilities; (5) ignorance of the full range of values; (6) limits to our capacity to make well-considered value judgments. His argument is summed up as having established an agnostic thesis, by which he judges we are not able to justifiably assert that God does not have a sufficient reason for justifying or allowing human and animal suffering.

Richard Swinburne's "The Problem of Evil," is an attempt to show that God can be plausibly viewed as allowing evil for certain goods that could not (logically could not) occur in any other way. He includes as an example the experience of pain. He argues that God may provide circumstances so that for example persons may freely choose whether they will bear a pain courageously or not. He adds, that God has to have the right to allow the evils in question. He argues further that good free choices are not merely good in themselves, they provide opportunities for soul-growth. He claims that the reason for this is often that being allowed to suffer for the benefit of someone else is also often a benefit for the sufferer as well. He considers only briefly, whether the good that accrues to the person who suffers is a *greater good* than the evil that may occur, but he does allow that there is plausibility in the claim that "the expected benefit of God allowing the suffering to occur *outweighs* the evil. He illustrates this with a thought experiment involving a person who is viewed as choosing the pain of childbirth, which results in "good effects" eventually for others.

Some think that the logical problem of evil is diffusible if some defensive strategy works, such as some form of the free will defense, the soul-making defense, the greater-good defense or perhaps a combination of some sort. However many are persuaded that the problem of evil can't be dismissed so easily, and that the probabilistic challenge comprises the most formidable charge against the Christian faith.

IV. The Attributes of God

Philosophy of religion literature, especially recently, has been exploring various Christian doctrines, and the attributes of God in particular. The enormity and complexity of the issues are formidable if not daunting, especially if one considers that studies of the nature of *knowledge* without the omni-prefix continue to evade final formulation notwithstanding the careful scrutiny and creative efforts of those who have taken the task seriously.

Two of the attributes of God examined in this anthology are those which are central to the logical and probabilistic formulations of the problem of evil, *omnipotence* and *omniscience*. Another, God's *eternity* is included if only because of the interest it generates in the literature of the history of philosophy of religion.

In "Some Puzzles Concerning Omnipotence," George I. Mavrodes applies Thomas Aquinas's notion of *omnipotence* to the paradox of the stone, and attempts to resolve the difficulty. While he doesn't try to show that God is omnipotent, or offer a final sense of the attribute in question, he does try to show this one sense of the attribute doesn't face the charge of incoherence.

In his classic "Omnipotence and Almightiness," Peter Geach tries to show that four standard glosses on God's *omnipotence* fail, and so in its place, he offers the notion of *almightiness*, contending it does not present the problems facing the readings of the alternative concept. But he also issues a caveat that locutions such as, "God can do so-and-so," are not easy to unpack, and that the logic of such discourse is far from simple.

The article "Middle Knowledge," by William Hasker first examines the medieval doctrine offered in support of the idea that God has complete foreknowledge of everything that will happen, and then gives a critical account of Plantinga's *reinvention* of the idea in the context of his modal free will defense. He observes that the doctrine pivots on another doctrine, the compatibilist take on free will and divine foreknowledge. After considering objections to the doctrine in its more recent formulation, he takes up an idea central to the doctrine, that there are such things as *counterfactual conditionals of freedom* (see the glossary). He then asks, who, or what is it that brings about these propositions as true? He finally concludes in this brief excerpt, that the putative counterfactuals held to be true are not really counterfactuals at all. Hence middle knowledge is rejected.

In contrast to Hasker's tack, Linda Zagzebski in "The Molinist Solution," sketches Luis de Molina's attempted solution to *the dilemma of freedom and foreknowledge* (the title of her book on the subject). After a careful examination of the details of Molina's account, touching on Freddoso's take along the way, and responding to various objections, Zagzebski proffers a modest version of middle knowledge, but with an acknowledgement that there are not enough true counterfactuals of freedom known to be true to rescue foreknowledge.

The inclusion of the "Eternity" piece was judged a must, if any attribute of God were to be examined at all. And the now *classic contemporary* (if these can be affirmed together) account given attention is the one so carefully crafted by Eleonore Stump and Norman

Kretzmann. Their design is to give exposition to the doctrine of God's timeless eternity as Boethius conceived it, and to address problems and challenges that have been leveled against it in contemporary discourse. They conclude that Boethius's account is not as troublesome as it might prima facie appear, and they go on to show how this notion figures in other philosophy of religion issues.

Alan Padgett, in "God, Eternity, and the Nature of Time," argues that while the Boethian account of God's timeless eternity may not work, his own approach which sees God as the Lord of time does. Objections are critically examined, and the conclusion is drawn that his proposal allows God a certain limited sort of *timeless time* which we call eternity.

The selections provide a very limited account of the vast scope of the materials that address the nature of God, and a very brief glimpse of the divine attributes at best. But it is a starter to a very important direction the literature is presently taking, and justifiably so.

V. Miracles

One would think that paying attention to starting points, for example the assumption of an omnipotent Creator, would resolve all of the alleged difficulties facing the theist who holds that miracles occur. But such is not the case. Theists not only have the challenge of responding to the skeptic on the matter, they also face the task of specifying as clearly and precisely as possible the nature of miracles.

David Hume, in his "Of Miracles," formulates the classical statement of miracles as *violations of the laws of nature*. He goes on to try to show that the evidence in favor of such a view flies in the face of his principle that one should proportion one's belief to the evidence. And for him, the evidence for miracles requires greater credulity by far than their rejection.

Michael Martin's "The Argument from Miracles," considers the appeal to miracles as evidence for God's existence. While he admits that there is no a priori reason for rejecting miracles, there are substantial a posteriori grounds for calling their existence into question. Two accounts are offered, the direct and indirect, and for him even if there were good reasons to think that miracles existed in either sense, this does not of itself provide substantial grounds for thinking this provides inductive support for theism.

In "Miracles and the Laws of Nature," George I. Mavrodes construes miracles in the Humean sense as "violations" of the laws of nature. He goes on to state that a law of nature must specify some kind of possibility. If the theist were to read *laws of nature* as some sort of analogous sense of what is naturally possible, then there is no need to see them as being invalidated by a *rare* violation, and so the Humean sort of miracle remains an open possibility.

There are of course other definitions of miracles that should be examined if one is to provide a fair account of the issues and arguments. It is an area of inquiry that conveniently serves another more immediate purpose, that of affording an easy transition to our next topic which has as its main concern the proper relationship between the scientific and the religious.

VI. Religion and Science

Some think it is the majority opinion that there is no discipline so pitted against the religious as the scientific. Some, including theists, take these disciplines as having completely different and sovereign realms allowing no intersection whatsoever. Others such as Thomas Aquinas, contend that the two are complementary because "all truth is God's truth." The entries in this collection are some of the most recent and exciting in philosophy of science and religion.

William Lane Craig, in "What Place, Then, for a Creator?; Hawking on God and Creation," takes a serious look at Stephen Hawking's model of the universe in which God is absent. His first criticism centers on what he takes to be Hawking's failure to take account of significant philosophical assumptions which Craig takes to be unexamined, unjustified, and at worst false. Craig's conclusion is, "The postulate of metaphysical superspace, the metamorphosis of real to imaginary time, the conflation of time and space" are all taken as extravagant moves to avoid a *creation out of nothing* hypothesis. Craig's conclusion: "What price, then, for no Creator?"

In the article, "Toward a Theory of Religious Explanation," Philip Clayton urges a religious account of explanation that takes into account the religious beliefs held by the person or community in question. This leads him to examine the explanatory function of such beliefs. He rejects Paul Tillich's notion that any object of ultimate concern is a religious object for the individual, and defines *religious belief* as a *reciprocal relationship between an inherited institutionalized belief, practice and experience, and an individual's unique world*. Hence, he treats religious belief and religious experience as sustaining a *reciprocal relationship*. Now he can give account of *religious explanation*. The former, *religious belief*, is capable of propositional formulation. He judges that in virtually all traditions religious explanations are formulated in terms of such beliefs. They are the believer's attempt to forge a *nondissonant fit* between the person's *beliefs* and *attitudes*. He then examines the various levels of religious explanation and concludes that there is a *multilevel* account, one that involves making sense of one's *private concrete experience*, and another which gives account of the *whole of experience*. The latter, on his account, works with a sense of explanation quite different from his main sense, which comes closer to intersecting with the sense the term has in the sciences. On this level, understood as at the level of total experience, we leave behind any ascertainable sense, more probable than another. Here the believer moves from a *propositional analysis* approach to a more *aesthetically pleasing* sense of beauty wherein one finds a *mystic sense* of things fitting together.

In "Quantum Theory and Free Will," the physicist Stephen M. Barr examines three arguments for the thesis that quantum theory does not allow for the possibility of free will. The first is based on the difference between randomness and rational choice. The second is the argument of Roger Penrose that quantum indeterminacy is irrelevant to free will. And the third is that quantum indeterminacy is completely irrelevant to the brain's functioning. His counter to the three arguments is that the present very limited body of knowledge of the brain's function doesn't allow us to draw any hard and fast conclusions regarding the affect of quantum theory on the brain's function and freedom of choice. Whereas there was a time when the free will theorist had an uphill challenge all the way coming from the physical sciences, Barr now sees the scientist as having a less conclusive picture because of the huge gaps that exist in our present knowledge of the brain's function.

VII. Religion and Ethics

Three essays afford the reader a beginning account of some of the issues relating to religious beliefs about God and normative and metaethical issues and concerns.

The first, John Hare's "Kant on Recognizing Our Duties as God's Commands," deals with a controversial issue relating to the Kantian charge that one should recognize one's duties as God's commands and at the same time take heed to Kant's objection to theological heteronomy. How Kant brings the two together is the main task of his paper. Going against interpreters (such as Christian August Crusius) who claim that Kant was really disabused of the divine command theory, Hare argues contrariwise that the argument Kant supplies in his *Groundwork* against the theory doesn't really work, and moreover Kant knew this. This leads Hare to believe that Kant didn't thereby intend to reject the divine command theory. For his final point, he examines Kant's notion of autonomy and three conditions affecting it as outlined by Schneewind. The first is that humans coorporate with God in order to promote happiness. The second is that we see ourselves as the major instruments to this end. The third is that we see ourselves as cooperating with others to promote this end. Schneewind's point, "As God's supervision and activity lessen, man's responsibility increases," is challenged by Hare. He doubts whether this account is the way Kant and the theist want to go, but if contrariwise the theist wishes to go this way, then traditional theism is going to have to undergo significant revision.

Robert Merrihew Adams, in "Divine Commands and the Social Nature of Obligation," tries to show how facts about human relationships can fill some of the role that facts of obligation are supposed to play in moral motivation and guilt. He examines some of the problems that social accounts of obligation encounter, and then he argues that if God is introduced into the picture as a Primary Actor, then these problems can be dealt with more adequately.

In "Morality and God," Richard Swinburne argues that God issues commands to his creatures, and does so for four reasons: (1) to give us further motivation to do what we are under obligation to do by reason of divine requirement; (2) to give us further motivation to do what is beyond obligation, or supererogatorily good; (3) to contribute so as to coordinate with other good outcomes; (4) to give us a place in God's plan for the world.

VIII. Death and Immortality

Ever since humans have appeared on the scene, Job's question has been on the lips of all who reflect seriously about life, "If a person dies, shall they live again?"

Bertrand Russell's answer, in "The Finality of Death," is an emphatic *no*. How does he arrive at his conclusion? He commences with a radical materialism that disallows the existence of anything like the soul. For him, matter is all that matters. And in order for any sense to be made of an afterlife, the account must be rendered in materialistic terms. For Russell, if there *is* to be life after death, there have to be *purturbations* (movements) of the *body*. Since there are no movements of the body after death, then simply by a move of modus tollens, there is no life after death.

Bruce Reichenbach, in "Monism and Immortality," takes Russell's materialism seriously, rejecting a dualism that affirms the existence of souls or spirits and body on the grounds that such a view presents too many unmanageable difficulties. For example, if personal identity pivots on the soul's or spirit's continued existence after death, he thinks this leads to the denial of a person's really dying, since affirming the continuance of the soul or spirit after death leads to the denial of a person's really dying. Weaknesses in dualism inclines Reichenbach toward a materialistic monism he judges compatible with Christian theism. He wants to affirm the spiritual dimension, which he takes as reducible to statements about behavior to God's invitation to a relationship of faith and repentance. As for the hope of resurrection, Reichenbach entertains the doctrine of re-creation whereby God recreates another body similar in significant ways with the person's earlier body, but not continuous in any material way with it. There is no claim to the second body's being of the same *material elements*. Resolving the issue of identity in ways that are unproblematic he sees as perhaps ultimately unresolvable.

In "The Possibility of Resurrection," Peter van Inwagen, also working with a materialistic view of persons, offers a recreation view of persons that invokes a *simulacrum* notion. That is, there is conceivably a *material core* possibly maintained and preserved by God at death, and this sameness of matter allows him to preserve one's personal identity in a material mode in a re-creation at the Resurrection.

In contrast to both Russell, Reichenbach and van Inwagen, Richard Swinburne in "What Makes Me Me" argues that persons are constituted by mind or a non-physical soul and body; hence he lines himself up with metaphysical dualists like René Descartes and Charles Taliaferro. As for what constitutes the identity of a person, he first tackles the idea of physical continuity and then soulish continuity. It is in this latter metaphysical component that personal identity resides. Ultimately for him, each person has a *thisness*, a uniqueness which makes it the soul that it is; not dependent upon the mental properties it has (that is in the life it has led). At the same time one might hope for a new body, in which case the new body will be brought into a close intercausal interaction with the continuing self, the soul. Thus he affirms a Cartesian dualism, along with a strong notion (along with Charles Taliaferro) of interactionism, and a strong affirmation of soulish identity.

IX. Religious Pluralism

The existence of a plurality of religions generates all sorts of problems. One problem has to do with truth claims and religious beliefs. Is there one religion which is true in such a way as to rule out the possibility of any truth at all in the others? Or is it possible that truth can be found in many if not all? And what about salvific issues and questions? What about the path of salvation, assuming humanity has that option? Is salvation an exclusive thing, found in one religion only, or are there many salvific paths leading to God? Assuming that there is some sort of final felicity, how might one achieve that goal?

In "Religious Pluralism and Salvation," John Hick argues that the diverse truth claims of various religions of the world express their different perceptions through disparate cultural lenses while focusing on the one ultimate Reality. Though there are disparate historical memories, and different accounts of this one Reality, these disparities do not stand in the way of salvation being extended to all since true answers to these questions are not necessary for salvation. Thus he affirms a universalist thesis along with multi-paths that lead to the one *Reality*.

David Basinger, in "Planatinga, Pluralism and Justified Religious Belief," brings Plantinga's Reformed epistemology back center stage with concern now directed at the phenomenon of religious pluralism. Basinger draws our attention to a central feature of Plantinga's Reformed approach, that propositional evidence is not needed to support our formed beliefs or the reliability of our belief-forming mechanisms. The central point is, even when challenged with the claims of various religious alternatives to Christianity, the Christian need not worry about propositional evidence; moreover, the theist can continue to hold that the beliefs in question can be held as properly basic.

The final essay, "Pluralism," by Alvin Plantinga, looks as the phenomenon of pluralism as a possible defeater against theism. Pluralism is first reviewed as forming the basis for a probabilistic strategy, as suggested by J. L. Schellenberg. The idea at work is that consideration of pluralism should lead one to conclude that the probability of one's belief in the Trinity is relatively low. The view of rationality proposed by Schellenberg is an attempt to challenge Plantinga's basic contention that the *proper basicality* of a belief doesn't hinge on other beliefs. That's what makes such beliefs properly basic. But Plantinga's rejoinder is, To what does the probability apply? What is the body of evidence? And what about the charge against the theist of moral artibrariness? Isn't there something arbitrary about accepting the morality of Christianity in view of religious pluralism? Again, Plantinga's response is *no*. Once again the believer can affirm the proper basicality of the belief because its status is neither confirmed nor challenged by contrary moral points of view.

Conclusion

We have reviewed in brief albeit incomplete fashion interesting and thought-provoking articles falling under the nine central topics in philosophy of religion literature. And while final answers may not be forthcoming, maybe significant insight has been the good fortune for some. For others, perhaps the issues remain as problematic as ever, if not altogether intractable. Philosophy doesn't guarantee that our problems will eventually be resolved even if we use our best lights. But the discipline may often help us see the issues more clearly and sometimes point us in directions that we may wish to explore more fully.

As a high and lofty hope, perhaps there will be moments when philosophy's careful exercise will take us beyond clarifying some of the questions and issues. Maybe some of the authors will by their insights and incisiveness point the reader in the direction of truth. When and to whatever extent this may happen, perhaps then and in whatever measure there will hopefully be a corresponding sense of liberation as well, all of which may be salutary to the enjoyment of this fascinating and most engaging of disciplines, philosophy of religion. Perhaps the ultimate motive behind the fascination is not philosophical ataraxia, but the pressing inner need to discover what the human condition is all about, and how persons are to view their existence, as limited to this life, or open to another infinitely expansive life beyond the grave, a promise central to some of the main religious traditions, the Islamic, Jewish, and certainly the Christian which has been so central in our discussions, partly because that is where the bulk of the literature takes us.

Figure 1

Part I

Faith and Reason

KIERKEGAARD'S ARGUMENTS AGAINST OBJECTIVE REASONING IN RELIGION*

Robert Merrihew Adams

Robert Merrihew Adams examines three arguments offered by Kierkegaard supportive of his fideism, the approximation argument, postponement argument and passion argument, and judges the first is a bad argument, and the other two work with a notion of religiousness he does not accept.

It is sometimes held that there is something in the nature of religious faith itself that renders it useless or undesirable to reason objectively in support of such faith, even if the reasoning should happen to have considerable plausibility. Søren Kierkegaard's *Concluding Unscientific Postscript* is probably the document most commonly cited as representative of this view. In the present essay I shall discuss three arguments for the view. I call them the Approximation Argument, the Postponement Argument, and the Passion Argument; and I suggest they can all be found in the *Postscript*. I shall try to show that the Approximation Argument is a bad argument. The other two will not be so easily disposed of, however. I believe they show that Kierkegaard's conclusion, or something like it, does indeed follow from a certain conception of religiousness—a conception which has some appeal, although for reasons which I shall briefly suggest, I am not prepared to accept it.

Kierkegaard uses the word "objective" and its cognates in several senses, most of which need not concern us here. We are interested in the sense in which he uses it when he says, "it is precisely a misunderstanding to seek an objective assurance," and when he speaks of "an objective uncertainty held fast in the appropriation-process of the most passionate inwardness" (pp. 41, 182).[1] Let us say that a piece of reasoning, R, is *objective reasoning* just in case every (or almost every) intelligent, fair-minded, and sufficiently informed person would regard R as showing or tending to show (in the circumstances in which R is used, and to the extent claimed in R) that R's conclusion is true or probably true. Uses of "objective" and "objectively" in other contexts can be understood from their relation to this one; for example, an objective uncertainty is a proposition which cannot be shown by objective reasoning to be certainly true.

I. The Approximation Argument

"Is it possible to base an eternal happiness upon historical knowledge?" is one of the central questions in the *Postscript*, and in the *Philosophical Fragments* to which it is a "postscript." Part of Kierkegaard's answer to the question is that it is not possible to base an eternal happiness on objective reasoning about historical facts. For nothing is more readily evident than that the greatest attainable certainty with respect to anything historical is merely an approximation. And an approximation, when viewed as a basis for an eternal happiness, is wholly inadequate, since the incommensurability makes a result impossible. [p. 25]

---

* Reprinted from *The Monist*, vol. 60, no. 2 (1977), by permission of the author and The Hegeler Institute, La Salle, Ill. Footnotes edited.

[1] Søren Kierkegaard, *Concluding Unscientific Postscript*, translated by David F. Swenson; introduction, notes, and completion of translation by Walter Lowrie (Princeton: Princeton University Press, 1941). Page references in parentheses in the body of the present paper are to this work.

Kierkegaard maintains that it is possible, however, to base an eternal happiness on a belief in historical facts that is independent of objective evidence for them, and that that is what one must do in order to be a Christian. This is the Approximation Argument for the proposition that Christian faith cannot be based on objective reasoning. (It is assumed that some belief about historical facts is an essential part of Christian faith, so that if religious faith cannot be based on objective historical reasoning, then Christian faith cannot be based on objective reasoning at all.) Let us examine the argument in detail.

Its first premise is Kierkegaard's claim that the greatest attainable certainty with respect to anything historical is merely an approximation. I take him to mean that historical evidence, objectively considered, never completely excludes the possibility of error. "It goes without saying," he claims, "that it is impossible in the case of historical problems to reach an objective decision so certain that no doubt could disturb it" (p. 41). For Kierkegaard's purposes it does not matter how small the possibility of error is, so long as it is finitely small (that is, so long as it is not literally infinitesimal). He insists (p. 31) that his Approximation Argument makes no appeal to the supposition that the objective evidence for Christian historical beliefs is weaker than the objective evidence for any other historical belief. The argument turns on a claim about *all* historical evidence. The probability of error in our belief that there was an American Civil War in the nineteenth century, for instance, might be as small as 10(1/2,000,000); that would be a large enough chance of error for Kierkegaard's argument.

It might be disputed, but let us assume for the sake of argument that there is some such finitely small probability of error in the objective grounds for all historical beliefs, as Kierkegaard held. This need not keep us from saying that we "know," and it is "certain," that there was an American Civil War. For such an absurdly small possibility of error is as good as no possibility of error at all, "for all practical intents and purposes," as we might say. Such a possibility of error is too small to be worth worrying about.

But would it be too small to be worth worrying about if we had an infinite passionate interest in the question about the Civil War? If we have an infinite passionate interest in something, there is no limit to how important it is to us. (The nature of such an interest will be discussed more fully in section 3 below.) Kierkegaard maintains that in relation to an infinite passionate interest no possibility of error is too small to be worth worrying about. "In relation to an eternal happiness, and an infinite passionate interest in its behalf (in which latter alone the former can exist), an iota is of importance, of infinite importance . . ." (p. 28). This is the basis for the second premise of the Approximation Argument, which is Kierkegaard's claim that "an approximation, when viewed as a basis for an eternal happiness, is wholly inadequate" (p. 25). "An approximation is essentially incommensurable with an infinite personal interest in an eternal happiness" (p. 26).

At this point in the argument it is important to have some understanding of Kierkegaard's conception of faith, and the way in which he thinks faith excludes doubt. Faith must be decisive; in fact it seems to consist in a sort of decision-making. "The conclusion of belief is not so much a conclusion as a resolution, and it is for this reason that belief excludes doubt." The decision of faith is a decision to disregard the possibility of error—to act on what is believed, without hedging one's bets to take account of any possibility of error.

To disregard the possibility of error is not to be unaware of it, or fail to consider it, or lack anxiety about it. Kierkegaard insists that the believer must be keenly *aware* of the risk of error. "If I wish to preserve myself in faith I must constantly be intent upon holding fast the objective uncertainty, so as to remain out upon the deep, over seventy thousand fathoms of water, still preserving my faith" (p. 182).

For Kierkegaard, then, to ask whether faith in a historical fact can be based on objective reasoning is to ask whether objective reasoning can justify one in disregarding the possibility of error which (he thinks) historical evidence always leaves. Here another aspect of Kierkegaard's conception of faith plays its part in the argument. He thinks that in all genuine religious faith the believer is *infinitely* interested in the object of his faith. And he thinks it follows that objective reasoning cannot justify him in disregarding *any* possibility of error about the object of faith, and therefore cannot lead him all the way to religious faith where a historical fact is concerned. The farthest it could lead him is to the conclusion that *if* he had only a certain finite (though very great) interest in the matter, the possibility of error would be too small to be worth worrying about and he would be justified in disregarding it. But faith disregards a possibility of error that *is* worth worrying about, since an infinite interest is involved. Thus faith requires a "leap" beyond the evidence, a leap that cannot be justified by objective reasoning (cf. p. 90).

There is something right in what Kierkegaard is saying here, but his Approximation Argument is a bad argument. He is right in holding that grounds of doubt which may be insignificant for most practical purposes can be extremely troubling for the intensity of a religious concern, and that it may require great decisiveness, or something like courage, to overcome them religiously. But he is mistaken in holding that objective reasoning could not justify one in disregarding any possibility of error about something in which one is infinitely interested.

The mistake, I believe, lies in his overlooking the fact that there are at least two different reasons one might have for disregarding a possibility of error. The first is that the possibility is too small to be worth worrying about. The second is that the risk of not disregarding the possibility of error would be greater than the risk of disregarding it. Of these two reasons only the first is ruled out by the infinite passionate interest.

I will illustrate this point with two examples, one secular and one religious. A certain woman has a very great (though not infinite) interest in her husband's love for her. She rightly judges that the objective evidence available to her renders it 99.9 per cent probable that he loves her truly. The intensity of her interest is sufficient to cause her some anxiety over the remaining 1/1,000 chance that he loves her not; for her this chance is not too small to be worth worrying about. (Kierkegaard uses a similar example to support his Approximation Argument; see p. 511.) But she (very reasonably) wants to *disregard* the risk of error, in the sense of not hedging her bets, if he does love her. This desire is at least as strong as her desire not to be deceived if he does not love her. Objective reasoning should therefore suffice to bring her to the conclusion that she ought to disregard the risk of error, since by not disregarding it she would run 999 times as great risk of frustrating one of these desires.

Or suppose you are trying to base your eternal happiness on your relation to Jesus, and therefore have an infinite passionate interest in the question whether he declared Peter and his episcopal successors to be infallible in matters of religious doctrine. You want to be committed to whichever is the true belief on this question, disregarding any possibility of error in it. And suppose, just for the sake of argument, that objective historical evidence renders it 99 per cent probable that Jesus did declare Peter and his successors to be infallible—or 99 per cent probable that he did not—for our present discussion it does not matter which. The one per cent chance of error is enough to make you *anxious*, in view of your infinite interest. But objective reasoning leads to the conclusion that you ought to commit yourself to the more probable opinion, *disregarding* the risk of error, if your strongest desire in the matter is to be so committed to the true opinion. For the only other way to satisfy this desire would be to commit yourself to the less probable opinion, disregarding the risk of error in it. The first way will be successful if and only if the more probable opinion is true, and the second way if and only if the less probable opinion is true. Surely it is prudent to do what gives you a 99 per cent chance of satisfying your strong desire, in preference to what gives you only a one per cent chance of satisfying it.

In this argument your strong desire to be committed to the true opinion is presupposed. The reasonableness of this desire may depend on a belief for which no probability can be established by purely historical reasoning, such as the belief that Jesus is God. But any difficulties arising from this point are distinct from those urged in the Approximation Argument, which itself presupposes the infinite passionate interest in the historical question.

There is some resemblance between my arguments in these examples and Pascal's famous Wager argument. But whereas Pascal's argument turns on weighing an infinite interest against a finite one, mine turns on weighing a large chance of success against a small one. An argument closer to Pascal's will be discussed in section 4 below.

The reader may well have noticed in the foregoing discussion some unclarity about what sort of justification is being demanded and given for religious beliefs about historical facts. There are at least two different types of question about a proposition which I might try to settle by objective reasoning: (1) Is it probable that the proposition is true? (2) In view of the evidence which I have for and against the proposition, and my interest in the matter, is it prudent for me to have faith in the truth of the proposition, disregarding the possibility of error? Correspondingly, we may distinguish two ways in which a belief can be *based on* objective reasoning. The proposition believed may be the conclusion of a piece of objective reasoning, and accepted because it is that. We may say that such a belief is *objectively probable*. Or one might hold a belief or maintain a religious faith because of a piece of objective reasoning whose conclusion is that it would be prudent, morally right, or otherwise desirable for one to hold that belief or faith. In this latter case let us say that the belief is *objectively advantageous*. It is clear that historical beliefs can be objectively probable; and in the Approximation Argument, Kierkegaard does not deny Christian historical beliefs can be objectively probable. His thesis is, in effect, that in view of an infinite passionate interest in their subject matter, they cannot be objectively advantageous, and therefore cannot be fully justified objectively, even if they are objectively probable. It is this thesis that I have attempted to refute. I have not been discussing the question whether Christian historical beliefs are objectively probable.

II. The Postponement Argument

The trouble with objective historical reasoning, according to the Approximation Argument, is that it cannot yield complete certainty. But that is not Kierkegaard's only complaint against it as a basis for religious faith. He also objects that objective historical inquiry is never completely finished, so that one who seeks to base his faith on it postpones his religious commitment forever. In the process of historical research "new difficulties arise and are overcome, and new difficulties again arise. Each generation inherits from its predecessor the illusion that the method is quite impeccable, but the learned scholars have not yet succeeded…and so forth…. The infinite personal passionate interest of the subject…vanishes more and more, because the decision is postponed, and postponed as following directly upon the result of the learned inquiry" (p. 28). As soon as we take "an historical document" as "our standard for the determination of Christian truth," we are "involved in a parenthesis whose conclusion is everlastingly prospective" (p. 28)—that is, we are involved in a religious digression which keeps religious commitment forever in the future.

Kierkegaard has such fears about allowing religious faith to rest on *any* empirical reasoning. The danger of postponement of commitment arises not only from the uncertainties of historical scholarship, but also in connection with the design argument for God's existence. In the *Philosophical Fragments* Kierkegaard notes some objections to the attempt to prove God's existence from evidence of "the wisdom in nature, the goodness, the wisdom in the governance of the world," and then says, "even if I began I would never finish, and would in addition have to live constantly in suspense, lest something so terrible should suddenly happen that my bit of proof would be demolished." What we have before us is a quite general sort of objection to the treatment of religious beliefs as empirically testable. On this point many analytical philosophers seem to agree with Kierkegaard. Much discussion in recent analytical philosophy of religion has proceeded from the supposition that religious beliefs are not empirically testable. I think it is far from obvious that that supposition is correct; and it is interesting to consider arguments that may be advanced to support it.

Kierkegaard's statements suggest an argument that I call the Postponement Argument. Its first premise is that one cannot have an authentic religious faith without being totally committed to it. In order to be totally committed to a belief, in the relevant sense, one must be determined not to abandon the belief under any circumstances that one recognizes as epistemically possible.

The second premise is that one cannot yet be totally committed to any belief which one bases on an inquiry in which one recognizes any possibility of a future need to revise the results. Total commitment to any belief so based will necessarily be postponed. I believe that this premise, suitably interpreted, is true. Consider the position of someone who regards himself as committed to a belief on the basis of objective evidence, but who recognizes some possibility that future discoveries will destroy the objective justification of the belief. We must ask how he is disposed to react in the event, however unlikely, that the objective basis of his belief is overthrown. Is he prepared to abandon the belief in that event? If so, he is not totally committed to the belief in the relevant sense. But if he is determined to cling to his belief even if its objective justification is taken away, then he is not basing the belief on the objective justification—or at least he is not basing it solely on the justification.

The conclusion to be drawn from these two premises is that authentic religious faith cannot be based on an inquiry in which one recognizes any possibility of a future need to revise the results. We ought to note that this conclusion embodies two important restrictions on the scope of the argument.

In the first place, we are not given an argument that authentic religious faith cannot have an objective justification that is subject to possible future revision. What we are given is an argument that the authentic believer's holding of his religious belief cannot *depend* entirely on such a justification.

In the second place, this conclusion applies only to those who *recognize* some epistemic possibility that the objective results which appear to support their belief may be overturned. I think it would be unreasonable to require, as part of total commitment, a determination with regard to one's response to circumstances that one does not recognize as possible at all. It may be, however, that one does not recognize such a possibility when one ought to.

Kierkegaard needs one further premise in order to arrive at the conclusion that authentic religious faith cannot without error be based on any objective empirical reasoning. This third premise is that in every objective empirical inquiry there is always, objectively considered, some epistemic possibility that the results of the inquiry will need to be revised in view of new evidence or new reasoning. I believe Kierkegaard makes this assumption; he certainly makes it with regard to historical inquiry. From this premise it follows that one is in error if in any objective empirical inquiry one does not recognize any possibility of a future need to revise the results. But if one does recognize such a possibility, then according to the conclusion already reached in the Postponement Argument, one cannot base an authentic religious faith on the inquiry.

Some philosophers might attack the third premise of this argument; and certainly it is controversial. But I am more inclined to criticize the first premise. There is undoubtedly something plausible about the claim that authentic religious faith must involve a commitment so complete that the believer is resolved not to abandon his belief under any circumstances that he regards as epistemically possible. If you are willing to abandon your ostensibly religious beliefs for the sake of objective inquiry, mightn't we justly say that objective inquiry is your real religion, the thing to which you are most deeply committed?

There is also something plausible to be said on the other side, however. It has commonly been thought to be an important part of religious ethics that one ought to be humble, teachable, open to correction, new inspiration, and growth of insight, even (and perhaps especially) in important religious beliefs. That view would have to be discarded if we were to concede to Kierkegaard that the heart of commitment in religion is an unconditional determination not to change in one's important religious beliefs. In fact I think there is something radically wrong with this conception of religious commitment. Faith ought not to be thought of as unconditional devotion to a belief. For in the first place the object of religious devotion is not a belief or attitude of one's own but God. And in the second place it may be doubted that religious devotion to God can or should be completely unconditional. God's love for sinners is sometimes said to be completely unconditional not being based on any excellence or merit of theirs. But religious devotion to God is generally thought to be based on His goodness and love. It is the part of the strong, not the weak, to love unconditionally. And in relation to God we are weak.

III. The Passion Argument

In Kierkegaard's statements of the Approximation Argument and the Postponement Argument it is assumed that a system of religious beliefs might be objectively probable. It is only for the sake of argument, however, that Kierkegaard allows this assumption. He really holds that religious faith, by its very nature, needs objective *im*probability. "Anything that is almost probable, or probable, or extremely and emphatically probable, is something [one] can almost know, or as good as know, or extremely and emphatically almost *know*—but it is impossible to *believe*" (p. 189). Nor will Kierkegaard countenance the suggestion that religion ought to go beyond belief to some almost-knowledge based on probability. "Faith is the highest passion in a man. There are perhaps many in every generation who do not even reach it, but no one gets further." It would be a betrayal of religion to try to go beyond faith. The suggestion that faith might be replaced by "probabilities and guarantees" is for the believer "a temptation to be resisted with all his strength" (p. 15). The attempt to establish religious beliefs on a foundation of objective probability is therefore no service to religion, but inimical to religion's true interests. The approximation to certainty which might be afforded by objective probability is rejected, not only for the reasons given in the Approximation Argument and Postponement Argument, but also from a deeper motive, "since on the contrary it behooves us to get rid of introductory guarantees of security, proofs from consequences, and the whole mob of public pawnbrokers and guarantors, so as to permit the absurd to stand out in all its clarity—in order that the individual may believe if he wills it; I merely say that it must be strenuous in the highest degree so to believe" (p. 190).

As this last quotation indicates, Kierkegaard thinks that religious belief ought to be based on a strenuous exertion of the will—a passionate striving. His reasons for thinking that objective probability is religiously undesirable have to do with the place of passion in religion, and constitute what I call the Passion Argument. The first premise of the argument is that the most essential and the most valuable feature of religiousness is passion, indeed an infinite passion, a passion of the greatest possible intensity. The second premise is that an infinite passion requires objective improbability. And the conclusion therefore is that that which is most essential and most valuable in religiousness requires objective improbability.

My discussion of this argument will have three parts. (a) First I will try to clarify, very briefly, what it is that is supposed to be objectively improbable. (b) Then we will consider Kierkegaard's reasons for holding that infinite passion requires objective improbability. In so doing we will also gain a clearer understanding of what a Kierkegaardian infinite passion is. (c) Finally I will discuss the first premise of the argument—although issues will arise at that point which I do not pretend to be able to settle by argument.

(a) What are the beliefs whose improbability is needed by religious passion? Kierkegaard will hardly be satisfied with the improbability of just any one belief; it must surely be at least an important belief. On the other hand it would clearly be preposterous to suppose that every belief involved in Christianity must be objectively improbable. (Consider, for example, the belief that the man Jesus did indeed live.) I think that what is demanded in the Passion Argument is the objective improbability of at least one belief which must be true if the goal sought by the religious passion is to be attained.

(b) We can find in the *Postscript* suggestions of several reasons for thinking that an infinite passion needs objective improbability. The two that seem to me most interesting have to do with (i) the risks accepted and (ii) the costs paid in pursuance of a passionate interest.

(i) One reason that Kierkegaard has for valuing objective improbability is that it increases the *risk* attaching to the religious life, and risk is so essential for the expression of religious passion that "without risk there is no faith" (p. 182). About the nature of an eternal happiness, the goal of religious striving, Kierkegaard says "there is nothing to be said...except that it is the good which is attained by venturing everything absolutely" (p. 382).

> But what then does it mean to venture? A venture is the precise correlative of an uncertainty; when the certainty is there the venture becomes impossible.... If what I hope to gain by venturing is itself certain, I do not risk or venture, but make an exchange.... No, if I am in truth resolved to venture, in truth resolved to strive for the attainment of the highest good, the uncertainty must be there, and I must have room to move, so to speak. But the largest space I can obtain, where there is room for the most vehement gesture of the passion that embraces the infinite, is uncertainty of knowledge with respect to an eternal happiness, or the certain knowledge that the choice is in the finite sense a piece of madness: now there is room, now you can venture! [pp. 380-82]

How is it that objective improbability provides the largest space for the most vehement gesture of infinite passion? Consider two cases. (A) You plunge into a raging torrent to rescue from drowning someone you love, who is crying for help. (B) You plunge into a raging torrent in a desperate attempt to rescue someone you love, who appears to be unconscious and *may* already have drowned. In both cases you manifest a passionate interest in saving the person, risking your own life in order to do so. But I think Kierkegaard would say there is more passion in the second case than in the first. For in the second case you risk your life in what is, objectively considered, a smaller chance that you will be able to save your loved one. A greater passion is required for a more desperate attempt.

A similar assessment may be made of the following pair of cases. (A') You stake everything on your faith in the truth of Christianity, knowing that it is objectively 99 per cent probable that Christianity is true. (B') You stake everything on your faith in the truth of Christianity, knowing that the truth of Christianity is, objectively, possible but so improbable that its probability is, say, as small as $10(1/2,000,000)$. There is passion in both cases, but Kierkegaard will say that there is more passion in the second case than in the first. For to venture the same stake (namely, everything) on a much smaller chance of success shows greater passion.

Acceptance of risk can thus be seen as a *measure* of the intensity of passion. I believe this provides us with one way of understanding what Kierkegaard means when he calls religious passion "infinite." An *infinite* passionate interest in x is an interest so strong that it leads one to make the greatest possible sacrifices in order to obtain x, on the smallest possible chance of success. The infinity of the passion is shown in that there is no sacrifice so great one will not make it, and no chance of success so small one will not act on it. A passion which is infinite in this sense requires, by its very nature, a situation of maximum risk for its expression.

It will doubtless be objected that this argument involves a misunderstanding of what a passionate interest is. Such an interest is a disposition. In order to have a great passionate interest it is not necessary actually to make a great sacrifice with a small chance of success; all that is necessary is to have such an intense interest that one *would* do so if an appropriate occasion should arise. It is therefore a mistake to say that there *is* more passion in case (B) than in case (A), or in (B') than in (A'). More passion is *shown* in (B) than in (A), and in (B') than in (A'); but an equal passion may exist in cases in which there is no occasion to show it.

This objection may well be correct as regards what we normally mean by "passionate interest." But that is not decisive for the argument. The crucial question is what part dispositions, possibly unactualized, ought to play in religious devotion. And here we must have a digression about the position of the *Postscript* on this question—a position that is complex at best and is not obviously consistent.

In the first place I do not think that Kierkegaard would be prepared to think of passion, or a passionate interest, as primarily a disposition that might remain unactualized. He seems to conceive of passion chiefly as an intensity in which one actually does and feels. "Passion is momentary" (p. 178), although capable of continual repetition. And what is momentary in such a way that it must be repeated rather than protracted is presumably an occurrence rather than a disposition. It agrees with this conception of passion that Kierkegaard idealizes a life of "persistent striving," and says that the religious task is to "exercise" the God-relationship and to give "existential expression to the religious choice (pp. 110, 364, 367).

All of this supports the view that what Kierkegaard means by "an infinite passionate interest" is a pattern of actual decision-making, in which one continually exercises and expresses one's religiousness by making the greatest possible sacrifices on the smallest possible chance of success. In order to actualize such a pattern of life one needs chances of success that are as small as possible. That is the room that is required for "the most vehement gesture" of infinite passion.

But on the other hand Kierkegaard does allow a dispositional element in the religious life, and even precisely in the making of the greatest possible sacrifices. We might suppose that if we are to make the greatest possible sacrifices in our religious devotion, we must do so by abandoning all worldly interests and devoting all our time and attention to religion. That is what monasticism attempts to do, as Kierkegaard sees it; and (in the *Postscript*, at any rate) he rejects the attempt, contrary to what our argument to this point would have led us to expect of him. He holds that "resignation" (pp. 353, 367) or "renunciation" (pp. 362, 386) of *all* finite ends is precisely the first thing that religiousness requires; but he means a renunciation that is compatible with pursuing and enjoying finite ends (pp. 362-71). This renunciation is the practice of a sort of detachment; Kierkegaard uses the image of a dentist loosening the soft tissues around a tooth, while it is still in place, in preparation for pulling it (p. 367). It is partly a matter of not treating finite things with a desperate seriousness, but with a certain coolness or humor, even while one pursues them (pp. 368, 370).

This coolness is not just a disposition. But the renunciation also has a dispositional aspect. "Now if for any individual an eternal happiness is his highest good, this will mean that all finite satisfactions are volitionally relegated to the status of what may have to be renounced in favor of an eternal happiness" (p. 350). The volitional relegation is not a disposition but an act of choice. The object of this choice, however, appears to be a dispositional state—the state of being such that one *would* forgo any finite satisfaction *if* it were religiously necessary or advantageous to do so.

It seems clear that Kierkegaard, in the *Postscript*, is willing to admit a dispositional element at one point in the religious venture, but not at another. It is enough in most cases, he thinks, if one is *prepared* to cease for the sake of religion from pursuing some finite end; but it is not enough that one *would* hold to one's belief in the face of objective improbability. The belief must actually be improbable, although the pursuit of the finite need not actually cease. What is not clear is a reason for this disparity. The following hypothesis, admittedly somewhat speculative as interpretation of the text, is the best explanation I can offer.

The admission of a dispositional element in the religious renunciation of the finite is something to which Kierkegaard seems to be driven by the view that there is no alternative to it except idolatry. For suppose one actually ceases from all worldly pursuits and enters a monastery. In the monastery one would pursue a number of particular ends (such as getting up in the middle of the night to say the offices) which, although religious in a way ("churchy," one might say), are still finite. The absolute *telos* or end of religion is no more to be identified with them than with the ends pursued by an alderman (pp. 362-71). To pretend otherwise would be to make an idolatrous identification of the absolute end with some finite end. An existing person cannot have sacrificed everything by actually having ceased from pursuing *all* finite ends. For as long as he lives and acts he is pursuing some finite end. Therefore his renouncing *everything* finite must be at least partly dispositional.

Kierkegaard does not seem happy with this position. He regards it as of the utmost importance that the religious passion should come to expression. The problem of finding an adequate expression for a passion for an infinite end, in the face of the fact that in every concrete action one will be pursuing some finite end, is treated in the *Postscript* as the central problem of religion (see especially pp. 386-468). If the sacrifice of everything finite must remain largely dispositional, then perhaps it is all the more important to Kierkegaard that the smallness of the chance for which it is sacrificed should be fully actual, so that the infinity of the religious passion may be measured by an actuality in at least one aspect of the religious venture.

(ii) According to Kierkegaard, as I have argued, the intensity of a passion is measured in part by the smallness of the chances of success that one acts on. It can also be measured in part by its costliness—that is, by how much one gives up or suffers in acting on those chances. This second measure can also be made the basis of an argument for the claim that an infinite passion requires objective improbability. For the objective improbability of a religious belief, if recognized, increases the costliness of holding it. The risk involved in staking everything on an objectively improbable belief gives rise to an anxiety and mental suffering whose acceptance is itself a sacrifice. It seems to follow that if one is not staking everything on a belief one sees to be objectively improbable, one's passion is not infinite in Kierkegaard's sense, since one's sacrifice could be greater if one did adhere to an improbable belief.

Kierkegaard uses an argument similar to this. For God to give us objective knowledge of Himself, eliminating paradox from it, would be "to lower the price of the God-relationship."

> And even if God could be imagined willing, no man with passion in his heart could desire it. To a maiden genuinely in love it could never occur that she had bought her happiness too dear, but rather that she had not bought it dear enough. And just as the passion of the infinite was itself the truth, so in the case of the highest value it holds true that the price is the value, that a low price means a poor value.... [p. 207]

Kierkegaard here appears to hold, first, that an increase in the objective probability of religious belief would reduce its costliness, and second, that the value of a religious life is measured by its cost. I take it his reason for the second of these claims is that passion is the most valuable thing in a religious life and passion is measured by its cost. If we grant Kierkegaard the requisite conception of an infinite passion, we seem once again to have a plausible argument for the view that objective improbability is required for such a passion.

(c) We must therefore consider whether infinite passion, as Kierkegaard conceives of it, ought to be part of the religious ideal of life. Such a passion is a striving, or pattern of decision-making, in which, with the greatest possible intensity of feeling, one continually makes the greatest possible sacrifices on the smallest possible chance of success. This seems to me an impossible ideal. I doubt that any human being could have a passion of this sort, because I doubt that one could make a sacrifice so great that a greater could not be made, or have a (nonzero) chance of success so small that a smaller could not be had.

But even if Kierkegaard's ideal is impossible, one might want to try to approximate it. Intensity of passion might still be measured by the greatness of sacrifices made and the smallness of chances of success acted on, even if we cannot hope for a greatest possible or a smallest possible here. And it could be claimed that the most essential and valuable thing in religiousness is a passion that is very intense (though it cannot be infinite) by this standard—the more intense the better. This claim will not support an argument that objective improbability is absolutely required for religious passion. For a passion could presumably be very intense, involving great sacrifices and risks of some other sort, without an objectively improbable belief. But it could still be argued that objectively improbable religious beliefs enhance the value of the religious life by increasing its sacrifices and diminishing its chances of success, whereas objective probability detracts from the value of religious passion by diminishing its intensity.

The most crucial question about the Passion Argument, then, is whether maximization of sacrifice and risk are so valuable in religion as to make objective improbability a desirable characteristic of religious beliefs. Certainly much religious thought and feeling places a very high value on sacrifice and on passionate intensity. But the doctrine that it is desirable to increase without limit or to the highest possible degree (if there is one) the cost and risk of a religious life is less plausible (to say the least) than the view that *some* degree of cost and risk may add to the value of a religious life. The former doctrine would set the religious interest at enmity with all other interests, or at least with the best of them. Kierkegaard is surely right in thinking that it would be impossible to live without pursuing some finite ends. But even so it would be possible to exchange the pursuit of better finite ends for the pursuit of worse ones—for example, by exchanging the pursuit of truth, beauty, and satisfying personal relationships for the self-flagellating pursuit of pain. And a way of life would be the costlier for requiring such an exchange. Kierkegaard does not, in the *Postscript*, demand it. But the presuppositions of his

Passion Argument seem to imply that such a sacrifice would be religiously desirable. Such a conception of religion is demonic. In a tolerable religious ethics some way must be found to conceive of the religious interest as inclusive rather than exclusive of the best of other interests—including, I think, the interest in having well-grounded beliefs.

IV. Pascal's Wager and Kierkegaard's Leap

Ironically, Kierkegaard's views about religious passion suggest a way in which his religious beliefs could be based on objective reasoning—not on reasoning which would show them to be objectively probable, but on reasoning which shows them to be objectively advantageous. Consider the situation of a person whom Kierkegaard would regard as a genuine Christian believer. What would such a person want most of all? He would want above all else to attain the truth through Christianity. That is, he would desire both that Christianity be true and that he himself be related to it as a genuine believer. He would desire that state of affairs (which we may call S) so ardently that he would be willing to sacrifice everything else to obtain it, given only the smallest possible chance of success.

We can therefore construct the following argument, which has an obvious analogy to Pascal's Wager. Let us assume that there is, objectively, some chance, however small, that Christianity is true. This is an assumption which Kierkegaard accepts (p. 31), and I think it is plausible. There are two possibilities, then: either Christianity is true, or it is false. (Others might object to so stark a disjunction, but Kierkegaard will not.) If Christianity is false it is impossible for anyone to obtain S, since S includes the truth of Christianity. It is only if Christianity is true that anything one does will help one or hinder one in obtaining S. And if Christianity is true, one will obtain S just in case one becomes a genuine Christian believer. It seems obvious that one would increase one's chances of becoming a genuine Christian believer by becoming one now (if one can), even if the truth of Christian beliefs is now objectively uncertain or improbable. Hence it would seem to be advantageous for anyone who can to become a genuine Christian believer now, if he wants S so much that he would be willing to sacrifice everything else for the smallest possible chance of obtaining S. Indeed I believe that the argument I have given for this conclusion is a piece of objective reasoning, and that Christian belief is therefore *objectively* advantageous for anyone who wants S as much as a Kierkegaardian genuine Christian must want it.

Of course this argument does not tend at all to show that it is objectively probable that Christianity is true. It only gives a practical, prudential reason for believing, to someone who has a certain desire. Nor does the argument do anything to prove that such an absolutely overriding desire for S is reasonable. It does show, however, that just as Kierkegaard's position has more logical structure than one might at first think, it is more difficult than he probably realized for him to get away entirely from objective justification.

Question

1. Distinguish between the 3 different sorts of arguments Adams sees Kierkegaard as raising in support of Kierkegaard's fideism.

2. What was Adams's response to each?

3. What does Adams conclude regarding Kierkegaard's attitude toward the objective justification of faith?

4. What is your appraisal of Kierkegaard's fideism?

5. What do you think of Kierekegaard's contention that faith faces an Absolute Paradox in the Incarnation?

THE EXTENDED AQUINAS/CALVIN MODEL*

Alvin Plantinga

In this piece Plantinga's focus is upon Christian belief, which may have justification, internal and external rationality and warrant. Faith is a special kind of knowledge resulting from the operation of the Holy Spirit. When the Spirit thus works, the cognitive process functions properly. He discusses properly basic beliefs, *and in this connection the role of Scripture, which he says are* auto-pistic, *that is self-authenticating. In this mode the believer's source of knowing transcends ordinary perceptual faculties in a way that assures proper functioning.*

I. Faith

Now Faith is the substance of things hoped for, the evidence of things not seen.
Hebrews 11:1

So much for the initial account of the model; I turn now to a more detailed development of some of its aspects, beginning with *faith*. The first thing to note is that this term, like nearly any philosophically useful term, is used variously, in a number of different but analogically connected senses. According to Mark Twain, faith is "believing what you know ain't true": this only slightly exaggerates a common use of the term to denote a belief that lacks warrant and, indeed, is unlikely with respect to what does have warrant for the believer. A mother who believes, in the teeth of the evidence, that her son is in fact still alive will be said to have faith that he is still alive. It is rather like a leap in the dark. A second way the term is used is to denote a vague and generalized trust that has no specific object, a confidence that things will go right, a sort of Bultmannian sitting loose with respect to the future, trusting that one can deal with whatever happens. To have faith in this sense is to "accept the universe," as the nineteenth-century transcendentalist Margaret Fuller was said to have declared she did.[1]

In setting out the model, however, I am using the term in a different sense from any of those. My sense will be much closer to that which the Heidelberg Catechism (following John Calvin) ascribes to "true faith":

> True faith is not only a knowledge and conviction that everything God reveals in his word is true; it is also a deep-rooted assurance, created in me by the Holy Spirit through the gospel, that, out of sheer grace earned for us by Christ, not only others, but I too, have had my sins forgiven, have been made forever right with God, and have been granted salvation. (Q. 21)

We can think of this account as making more explicit the content of the definition of faith offered by Calvin in the *Institutes* (above, page 244). The first thing to see is that faith, so taken, is a cognitive activity; it also involves the will, both the affections and the executive function. (It is a knowledge *sealed upon our hearts*, as well as revealed to our minds.) Still, even if faith is *more* than cognitive, it is also and *at least* a cognitive activity. It is a matter of *believing* ("knowledge," Calvin says) something or other. Christians, on this account, don't merely find

---

* This article is reprinted by courtesy of the author and Oxford University Press. It is Chapter 8, "The Extended Aquinas/Calvin Model: Revealed to Our Minds," in Vol. III, *Warranted Christian Belief*, by Alvin Plantinga, 2000.
[1] To which Thomas Carlyle retorted, "Gad! She'd better!" Mark Twain, by contrast, claimed he hadn't heard it had been offered to her.

their identity in the Christian story, or live in it or out of it:[2] they *believe* it, take the story to be the sober truth.

Now what one believes are propositions. To have faith, therefore, is (at least) to believe some propositions. Which ones? Not for example, that the world is the sort of place in which human beings can flourish, or even or primarily that there is such a person as God. [3] Indeed, on this model it isn't really by *faith* that one knows that there is such a person as God. Faith is instead, says Calvin, "firm and certain knowledge of God's benevolence towards us"; that is, a firm and certain knowledge that "not only others, but I too have had my sins granted salvation"; that is, a firm and certain knowledge of God's plan whereby we fallen humans can attain shalom, flourishing, well-being, happiness, felicity, salvation, all of which are essentially a matter of being rightly related to God. [4] So the propositional object of faith is the whole magnificent scheme of salvation God has arranged. To have faith is to know that and how God has made it possible for us human beings to escape the ravages of sin and be restored to a right relationship with him; it is therefore a knowledge of the main lines of the Christian gospel.[5] The content of faith is just the central teachings of the gospel; [6] it is contained in the intersection of the great Christian creeds.

What is at issue, in faith, furthermore, is not just knowing that there *is* such a scheme (as we saw above, the devils believe that, and they shudder), but also and most important, that this scheme applies to and is available to *me*.[7] So what I know, in faith, is the main lines of specifically Christian teaching—together, we might say, with its universal instantiation with respect to me. Christ died for *my* sins, thus making it possible for *me* to be reconciled with God.

---

[2] In this way, the model (apparently) differs from the postmodern Yale theology of Hans Frei (*The Eclipse of Biblical Narrative* [1974] and *The Identity of Jesus Christ* [1975] and George Lindbeck (The *Nature of Doctrine: Religion and Theology in a Postliberal Age* [1984]), which emphasizes the role of the Bible in the Christian life but is a bit coy as to whether its apparent teachings—creation, sin, incarnation, atonement, Christ's resurrection—are to be taken as actually true. (See, for example, pp.143—45 of *The Identity of Jesus Christ*.) This standoffishness about truth is perhaps the 'postliberal' element in Yale theology; according to the present model, however, it is also unnecessary. The model is designed to show that straightforward, downright, out—and—out belief in the great things of the gospel can have the epistemic virtues we are considering.

[3] "In understanding faith," says Calvin, "it is not merely a question of knowing that God exists...but also—and this especially—of knowing what is his will toward us. For it is not so much our concern to know who he is in himself, as what he wills to be toward us" (549).

[4] I take it this is a definition or description of faith by way of presenting a *paradigm* of it: fully formed and well—developed faith will be like this. Thus a person who (for example) believes these things, but without the *firmness* sufficient for knowledge of them, can still be said to have faith.

[5] And hence not everything a typical Christian believes (as a Christian) will be, strictly speaking, part of faith. For example, she may believe that Jesus Christ performed miracles, or that God is omniscient, or that the Bible is a specially inspired word from the Lord, or that faith naturally issues in good works; none of these is, as such, part of the content of faith. (This is not in any way to downgrade the importance of these things, and certainly the content of faith may enter into her reasons for believing in them.) And in thus specifying the content of faith, I am not, of course, trying to specify those beliefs which are such that accepting them is necessary for being a real Christian.

[6] On the present model, therefore, faith is a bit narrower than in the account of true faith from the Heidelberg Catechism (above, p. 247), which includes a "conviction that everything God reveals in his word is true." God presumably reveals more, in his word, than the great truths of the gospel. For example, there is Jesus' turning water into wine, healing the demoniac, and raising Lazarus from the dead; these are not among the central truths of the gospel, although they are related to and illustrative of those truths.

[7] See Calvin, 111, ii, 16, p. 561: "Here, indeed, is the chief hinge on which faith turns: that we do not regard the promises of mercy that God offers as true only outside ourselves, but not at all in us; rather that we make them ours by inwardly embracing them." As we'll see in the next chapter, there is more that distinguishes what the devils know from what the person of faith knows: she but not they also knows the beauty, loveliness, splendor of this plan of salvation; still further, she loves it, gives it her hearty approval, is grateful for it, and commits herself to love and trust the Lord.

Faith is initially and fundamentally *practical*; it is knowledge of the good news and of its application to me, and of what I must do to receive the benefits it proclaims. Still, faith is a matter of belief rather than doing something.

II. How Does Faith Work?

The principal answer is that faith is a work—the main work, according to Calvin-of the Holy Spirit; it is produced in us by the Holy Spirit. The suggestion that belief in the "great things of the gospel" (Jonathan Edwards's phrase) is a result of some special work of the Holy Spirit is often thought of as especially the teaching of such Calvinist thinkers as Edwards and John Calvin himself. It is, indeed, central to their teaching, and here the model follows them. On this point as on so many others, however, Calvin, despite his pugnacious noise about the pestilential papists and their colossal offenses, may be seen as following out and developing a line of thought already to be found in Thomas Aquinas. "The believer," says Aquinas, "has sufficient motive for believing, for he is moved by the authority of divine teaching confirmed by miracles and, what is more, *by the inward instigation of the divine invitation.*"[8] Here we have (embryonically, at any rate) the same trio of processes: there is *belief,* there is the *divine teaching* (as given in Scripture) which is the object of that belief, and there is also special divine activity in the production of the belief ("the inward instigation of the divine invitation").[9]

What is really involved in a believer's coming to accept the great things of the gospel, therefore, are three things: Scripture (the divine teaching), the internal invitation or instigation of the Holy Spirit, and faith, the human belief that results. What sort of phenomenology is involved in this epistemic process: what does it seem like from the inside? In the model, the beliefs constituting faith are typically taken as basic; that is, they are not accepted by way of argument from other propositions or on the evidential basis of other propositions. Of course they *could* be accepted on the basis of other propositions, and perhaps in some cases are. A believer could reason as follows: I have strong historical and archaeological evidence for the reliability of the Bible (or the church, or my parents, or some other authority); the Bible teaches the great things of the gospel; so probably these things are true. A believer *could* reason in this way, and perhaps some believers do in fact reason this way. But in model it goes differently.

---

[8] *Summa Theologiae II-II,* q.2, a.9, reply ob. 3 (my emphasis). According to Aquinas, therefore, faith is produced in human beings by God's action: "for since in assenting to the things of faith a person is raised above his own nature, he has this assent from a supernatural source influencing him; this source is God. The assent of faith, which is its principal act, therefore, has as its cause God, moving us inwardly through grace" (*ST* II-II, q.6, a. *1, respondeo).*

[9] Calvin explicitly identifies the third person of the trinity as the divine actor in question, and Aquinas does not; this is not a difference of any moment. According to Aquinas, some of the items proposed by God for our belief can also be the objects of *scientia;* when they are, they are not accepted by faith, for it isn't possible, he thinks, to have both *scientia* and faith with respect to the same proposition. Because *scientia is* often translated as 'knowledge', this makes it look as if Calvin contradicts Aquinas when he says that faith is a sure and certain *knowledge of* God's benevolence toward us. Appearances are deceiving, however, and there is no contradiction here. *Scientia* for Aquinas is a very special relation between a person and a proposition; it is one that holds when the person sees that the proposition follows from first principles she sees to be true. Thus *'scientia'* is much narrower than our term 'knowledge'. It is also narrower than Calvin's term *'cognitio',* which is much closer to our contemporary use of 'knowledge'. When Calvin says that faith is a sure and certain knowledge of God's benevolence to us, he isn't ascribing to faith a status Aquinas denies it. On this topic, see Arivin Vos, *Aquinas, Calvin & Contemporary Protestant Thought* (Grand Rapids: W. B. Eerdmans, 1985), pp. 18-20.

We read Scripture, or something presenting scriptural teaching, or hear the gospel preached, or are told of it by parents, or encounter a scriptural teaching as the conclusion of an argument (or conceivably even as an object of ridicule), or in some other way encounter a proclamation of the Word. What is said simply seems right; it seems compelling; one finds oneself saying, "Yes, that's right, that's the truth of the matter; this is indeed the word of the Lord." I read, "God was in Christ, reconciling the world to himself"; I come to think: "Right; that's true; God really was in Christ, reconciling the world to himself!" And I may also think something a bit different, something *about* that proposition: that it is a divine teaching or revelation, that in Calvin's words it is "from God." What one hears or reads seems clearly and obviously true and (at any rate in paradigm cases) seems also to be something the Lord is intending to teach. (As Calvin says, "the Spirit...is the only fit corrector and approver of doctrine, who seals it on our hearts, so that we may certainly know that God speaks. For while faith ought to look to God, he alone can be a witness to himself, so as to convince our hearts that what our ears receive has come from him.") So faith may have the phenomenology that goes with suddenly seeing something to be true: "Right! Now I see that this is indeed true and what the Lord is teaching!" Or perhaps the conviction arises slowly, and only after long and hard study, thought, discussion, prayer. Or perhaps it is a matter of a belief's having been there all along (from childhood, perhaps), but now being transformed, renewed, intensified, made vivid and alive. This process can go on in a thousand ways; in each case there is presentation or proposal of central Christian teaching and, by way of response, the phenomenon of being convinced, coming to see, forming of a conviction. There is the reading or hearing, and then there is the belief or conviction that what one reads or hears is true and a teaching of the Lord.

According to the model, this conviction comes by way of the activity of the Holy Spirit. Calvin speaks here of the internal 'testimony' and (more often) 'witness' of the Holy Spirit; Aquinas, of the divine 'instigation' and 'invitation'. On the model, there is both Scripture and the divine activity leading to human belief. God himself (on the model) is the principal author of Scripture. Scripture is most importantly a message, a communication from God to humankind; Scripture is a word from the Lord.[10] But then this just is a special case of the pervasive process of testimony, by which, as a matter of fact, we learn most of what we know.[11] From this point of view, Scripture is as much a matter of testimony as is a letter you receive from a friend. What is proposed for our belief in Scripture, therefore, just *is* testimony —divine testimony. So the term 'testimony' is appropriate here. However, there is also the special work of the Holy Spirit in getting us to believe, in enabling us to see the truth of what is proposed. Here Aquinas's terms 'invitation' and 'instigation' are more appropriate. I shall therefore use the term 'inward instigation of the Holy Spirit' to denote this activity of the Holy Spirit, and (where no confusion threatens) the term 'faith' to denote both the whole tripartite process (Scripture, the inward instigation of the Holy Spirit, belief in the great things of the gospel) and the last member of that trio.

So Scripture is, indeed, testimony, even if it is testimony of a very special kind. First, the principal testifier is God. It also differs from ordinary testimony in that in this case,

---

[10] On this model *(pace* most twentieth century Christian theologians), it is not the case that revelation occurs just by way of *events,* which must then be properly interpreted. No doubt this does indeed happen, but much of Scripture is centrally a matter of God's speaking, of his telling us things we need to know, of his communicating *propositions* to us. See Nicholas Wolterstorff's *Divine Discourse* (Cambridge: Cambridge University Press, 1995) for a specific account of precisely how it could be that the Bible constitutes divine speech and a divine communication to us. For the sake of definiteness, in what follows I shall incorporate in the model the proposition that something like Wolterstorff's account is in fact correct. (Of course other accounts could also serve in the model.)

[11] See *Warrant and Proper Function* (hereafter *WPF*), pp. 77ff.

unlike most others, there is both a principal testifier and subordinate testifiers: the human authors.[12] There is still another difference: it is the instigation of the Holy Spirit, on this model, that gets us to see and believe that the propositions proposed for our beliefs in Scripture really *are* a word from the Lord. This case also differs from the usual run of testimony, then, in that the Holy Spirit not only writes the letter (appropriately inspires the human authors)[13] but also does something special to enable you to believe and appropriate its contents. So this testimony is not the usual run of testimony; it is testimony nonetheless. According to the model, therefore, faith is belief in the great things of the gospel that results from the internal instigation of the Holy Spirit.

III. Faith and Positive Epistemic Status

A. Justification

I'm proposing this model as a model of Christian belief's having the sorts of epistemic virtues or positive epistemic status with which we've been concerned: justification, rationality of both the internal and the external variety, and warrant. Justification needn't detain us for long. There should be little doubt that Christian belief can be and probably is (deontologically) *justified,* and justified even for one well acquainted with Enlightenment and postmodern demurrers. If your belief is a result of the inward instigation of the Holy Spirit, it may seem obviously true, even after reflection on the various sorts of objections that have been offered. Clearly, one is then violating no intellectual obligations in accepting it. No doubt there are intellectual obligations and duties in the neighborhood; when you note that others disagree with you, for example, perhaps there is a duty to pay attention to them and to their objections, a duty to think again, reflect more deeply, consult others, look for and consider other possible defeaters. If you have done these things and still find the belief utterly compelling, however, you are not violating duty or obligation—especially if it seems to you, after reflection, that the teaching in question comes from God himself.

Of course some writers charge that if you have faith (as on the model) and think your belief comes from God, then you are arrogant and hence unjustified). Among the more vivid is the theologian John Macquarrie:

> The Calvinist believes that he himself, as one of the elect, has been rescued from this sea of error and that his mind has been enlightened by the Holy Spirit. However much he may insist that this is God's doing and not his own, his claim is nevertheless one of the most arrogant that has ever been made. It is this kind of thing that has rightly earned for theology the contempt of serious men.[14]

A Calvinist's first impulse might be to retort by asking whom or what Macquarrie credits with furnishing *him* with the truth, when he finds himself disagreeing with the bulk of humankind on religious matters (as, of course, he does): his own cognitive prowess and native sagacity? his own self-developed penetration and perspicacity? And is that attribution less arrogant than to attribute enlightenment to the work of the Holy Spirit? Rather than pursue this unprofitable retort, however, let's think a bit more soberly about the charge. First, note that the

---

[12] *Most* others: it sometimes happens with human testimony that one person is deputized to speak for another, and in those cases there is the same principal—subordinate structure. See Wolterstorff, *Divine Discourse,* pp. 38ff.

[13] According to Acts *28:25,* Paul says, "The Holy Spirit spoke the truth to your forefathers when he said through Isaiah the prophet: "Go to this people and say. You will ever..." (Isaiah 6:9, 10).

[14] *Principles of Christian Theology* (New York: Charles Scribner, 1966, 1977), p. 50.

accusation initially seems to be brought, not necessarily against someone who actually *has* been enlightened by the Holy Spirit, but against someone who *believes* that she has. No doubt it was the Holy Spirit who was at work in the hearts of the faithful and faith-filled patriarchs and others mentioned in Hebrews 11; but presumably they didn't know about the Holy Spirit and didn't have any views to the effect that their beliefs were due to the activity of the Holy Spirit. So perhaps Macquarrie's idea is that it's all right to know something others don't, but it's not all right to *believe* that you do, attributing your knowledge to the Holy Spirit. His criticism is directed, not necessarily toward a person who accepts Christian teaching (even if in fact such a person has, as in the model, been enlightened by the Holy Spirit), but toward someone who accepts the bit of Reformed theology according to which the Holy Spirit illuminates only some of us, and thinks that she is one of those thus illuminated. And the criticism is that such a person has culpably come to think more highly of herself than she ought.

We'll look further into this charge of arrogance in chapter 13; for now, let me just ask this. Suppose you believe that you have been favored by the Lord in a way in which some others haven't been: does it really follow that you are arrogant? You recognize that in some respect you are better off than someone else: perhaps you have a happy marriage, or your children turn out well, or you are enjoying glowing good health while a good friend is succumbing to melanoma. And suppose you attribute at least part of the difference to God's activity. Are you then automatically arrogant? Isn't it rather that would be arrogant if, instead, you thought the difference wasn't attributable to God but was a manifestation, say, of personal strength or virtue, or wisdom on your part? Suppose you think you know something someone else doesn't—perhaps Macquarrie thinks that he, as opposed to his Calvinist friends, knows that the Calvinist view of faith is mistaken. Is he thereby arrogant? If not, is it that he fails to be arrogant because he does not attribute his good fortune to God, perhaps attributing it instead to his own native good sense? That hardly seems promising.

The fact is there isn't any arrogance involved as such in recognizing that God has given you something he hasn't (or hasn't yet) given everyone. Human beings are, indeed, tempted to arrogance, and often succumb; still, one isn't arrogant just by virtue of recognizing that God has given you a good thing he hasn't (yet, anyway) given everyone else. (You might be as puzzled as anyone else that it is *you* who are the recipient of the gift.) Arrogance would be involved, no doubt, if you thought of this gift as your *right*, so that God would be unjust if he didn't give it to you. But you're not culpable if you believe your faith is a gift from the Lord and note that not everyone has as yet received this gift. Indeed, the right attitude here, far from a crestfallen admission that you have been arrogant in thus believing, is gratitude and thanksgiving for this wonderfully great gift.[15] Hearing of Jesus Christ's resurrection, the apostle Thomas declared, "Unless I see the nail marks in his hands and put my finger where the nails were, and put my hand into his side, I will not believe it" (John 20:25). Later, Jesus shows himself to Thomas, inviting him to look at the nail marks, and put his hand into his side. Thomas then believes—upon which Jesus says to him, "Because you have seen me, you have believed; blessed are those who have not seen and yet have believed" (John 20:29). No doubt there is more than one point here; a central point, surely, is that those who have been given faith are indeed blessed. Their faith is a gift requiring joyful thanksgiving, not a moral lapse requiring shamefaced repentance. One who has faith, therefore, is (or may very well be) justified according to the model. And

---

[15] See my "*Ad de Vries*," *The Christian Scholar's Review* 19, no. 2 (1989), pp. 171-78.

even apart from the model: how could you fail to be justified, within your epistemic rights, in believing what seems to you, after reflection and investigation, to be no more than the truth?

B. Internal Rationality

Internal rationality (see above, pp. 110ff.) has a dual aspect: on the one hand, it requires proper function in the part of the cognitive system that lies "downstream from experience"; on the other, it requires more generally that you have done your best or anyway well enough with respect to the formation of the belief in question.[16] You have considered how it fits in with your other beliefs, engaged in the requisite seeking for defeaters, considered the objections that you have encountered, compared notes with the right people, and so on. Clearly, on the model (and even apart from the model), someone who accepts the Christian beliefs in question can easily meet these conditions. Suppose my experience is of the sort that goes with the testimony of the Holy Spirit (and in chapter 9 we'll see more of what that experience involves), so that the great things of the gospel seem powerfully plausible and compelling to me: then (given that I have no undefeated defeaters for these propositions) there will be nothing dysfunctional or contrary to proper function in accepting the beliefs in question. Indeed, given those experiences, it would be dysfunctional *not* to form them. And suppose I carefully consider the objections people raise, consult with others, ask how the beliefs in question match the rest of my beliefs, and all the rest. Then clearly I will have done my part with respect to the formation of these beliefs. On the testimonial model, therefore, Christian belief enjoys both justification and internal rationality.[17]

C. External Rationality and Warrant: Faith Is *Knowledge*

The part of Calvin's definition of faith that is especially striking contemporary ears is that on his account, faith is a really special sort *of knowledge* ("a sure and certain knowledge"; compare also with the account of true faith in the Heidelberg Catechism, above, p. 247). Faith is not to be *contrasted* with knowledge: faith (at least in paradigmatic instances) *is* knowledge, knowledge of a certain special kind. It is special in at least two ways. First, in its object: what is allegedly known is (if true) of stunning significance, certainly the most important thing a person could possibly know. But it is also unusual in the way in which that content is known; it is known by way of an extraordinary cognitive process or belief—producing mechanism. Christian belief is "revealed to our minds" by way of the Holy Spirit's inducing, in us, belief in the central message of Scripture. The belief-producing process is dual, involving both the divinely inspired Scripture (perhaps directly, or perhaps at the head of a testimonial chain) and the internal instigation of the Holy Spirit. Both involve the special activity of God.

---

[16] This requirement of internal rationality may seem to overlap with justification. It does, if in fact there are intellectual duties prescribing the behavior required by rationality. Even if there are no such duties, however, internal rationality still requires the behavior in question.

[17] But aren't there many different theories of (say) incarnation and atonement? Don't Christians disagree about this? So which of the many views of Incarnation and Atonement are in fact rational? The question is misplaced. There are many different theories as to how it is that people are able to think; it is still plain to many of us that some people do (sometimes) think. There are many theories about what numbers are; it is still plain that $7 + 5 = 12$. We can quite properly believe in the Atonement even if we don't see exactly how it is supposed to go and don't embrace any of the theories; it can also be that we are rational in believing in the Atonement but not in accepting some specific theory of it.

If faith is such an extraordinary way of holding belief, why call it 'knowledge' at all? What about it makes it a case of knowledge? Here we must look a bit more deeply into the model. The believer encounters the great truths of the gospel; by virtue of the activity of Holy Spirit, she comes to see that these things are indeed true. And the first thing to see is that, on this model, faith is a belief-producing *process* or activity, like perception or memory. It is a cognitive device, a means by which belief, and belief on a certain specific set of topics, is regularly produced in regular ways.[18] In this it resembles memory, perception, reason, sympathy, induction, and other more standard belief—producing processes. It differs from them in that it also involves the direct action of the Holy Spirit, so that the immediate cause of belief is not to be found just in her natural epistemic equipment. There is the special and supernatural activity of the Holy Spirit. Nevertheless, faith is a belief-producing process. Now as we saw in chapter 7, what is required for *knowledge* is that a belief be produced by cognitive faculties or processes that are working properly, in an appropriate epistemic environment (both maxi and mini) according to a design plan that is aimed at truth, and is furthermore *successfully* aimed at truth. But according to this model, what one believes by faith (the beliefs that constitute faith) meets these four conditions

First, when these beliefs are accepted by faith and result from the internal instigation of the Holy Spirit, they are produced by cognitive processes working properly;[19] they are not produced by way of some cognitive malfunction. Faith, the whole process that produces them, is specifically designed by God himself to produce this very effect— just as vision, say, is designed by God to produce a certain kind of perceptual beliefs. When it does produce this effect, therefore, it is working properly; thus the beliefs in question satisfy the external rationality condition, which is also the first condition of warrant. Second, according to the model, the maxienvironment in which we find ourselves, including the cognitive contamination produced by sin, is precisely the cognitive environment for which this process is designed. The typical minienvironment is also favorable. Third, the process is designed to produce *true* beliefs;[20] and fourth, the beliefs it produces—belief in the great things of the gospel—are in fact true; faith is a reliable belief-producing process, so that the process in question is *successfully* aimed at the production of true beliefs.

> Reliability, of course, demands more than just that these beliefs be true. A thermometer stuck on 72°F is not reliable even if it is somewhere—San Diego, say—where it is always 72°F. What it would do if things were relevantly different (what it would do in appropriately nearby possible worlds) is also relevant; a process or instrument is reliable only if it would produce a true output under different conditions. On the current model, this condition is also met. The Holy Spirit doesn't work just by accident or at random, and there are a thousand ways in which, even if things had been different, the Holy Spirit would have produced the results *actually* produced. Clearly, any circumstances in which it produces this output are circumstances in which this output is true; hence, under those circumstances, it would have produced a true

---

[18] Although this regularity is typical of cognitive processes, it isn't really necessary; see my reply to Lehrer in *Warrant in Contemporary Epistemology*, ed. J. Kvavig (New York: Rowman and Littlefield, 1996), pp. 332 ff.

[19] A *caveat:* as Andrew Dole points out in "Cognitive Processes, Cognitive Faculties, and the Holy Spirit in Plantinga's Warrant Series" (as yet unpublished), it is not obvious that one can directly transfer necessary and sufficient conditions for warrant from beliefs produced by *faculties* to beliefs produced by *processes*.

[20] Though this need not be the *only* purpose involved. Perhaps the beliefs produced have other virtues in addition to truth: perhaps they enable one to stand in a personal relationship with God, to face life's vicissitudes with equanimity, to enjoy the comfort that naturally results from the belief that constitutes faith, and so on.

output. Under what conditions would the Holy Spirit have *failed*, with respect to a given person, to do this work of enabling one to see the truth of the great things of the gospel? The model need take no stand on this issue, but it is part of much traditional Christian teaching to hold that a necessary condition of my receiving the gift of faith is my acquiescing, being willing to accept the gift, being prepared to receive it. There is a contribution to this process that I myself must make, a contribution that I can withhold. According to this model, faith as a belief—producing mechanism involves a supernatural element; it involves God's doing something specially and directly and quite out of the ordinary. Does that compromise the claim that the deliverances of faith constitute knowledge? I can't see how. There was no suggestion in the original account that cognitive mechanisms must all be *natural*, whatever precisely that comes to. Must the account be revised because faith doesn't go just by natural laws or regularities, working instead by way of the free cooperation of a person—God himself—whose speaking in Scripture is, of course, free, as is the action of the Holy Spirit in revealing and sealing the great truths of gospel? Again, I can't see why. The same goes for the mechanism Thomas Reid calls 'testimony', a mechanism whereby we learn from others; this mechanism too (often) works by way of free human agency. (When you ask me how old I am, I can [freely] tell you, or in a minor fit of pique, freely refuse.)

Why, then, does faith constitute knowledge? Because what one believes by faith satisfies the conditions that are jointly sufficient and severally necessary for warrant. If the degree of warrant (which, given the satisfaction of the above conditions, is determined by the firmness or strength of belief) is high enough, then the beliefs in question will constitute knowledge.[21]

IV. Proper Basicality and the Role of Scripture

According to the model, Christian belief in the typical case is not the conclusion of an argument (which is not to say arguments cannot play an important role in its acceptance),[22] or accepted on the evidential basis of other beliefs, or accepted just because it constitutes a good explanation of phenomena of one kind or another. Specific Christian beliefs may, indeed, constitute excellent explanations of one or another phenomenon (the Christian teaching of sin leaps to mind here), but they aren't accepted because they provide such an explanation. Nor are they accepted as the conclusion of an argument from *religious experience*. According to the model, experience of a certain sort is intimately associated with the formation of warranted Christian belief, but the belief doesn't get its warrant by way of an argument from the experience. It isn't that the believer notes that she or someone else has a certain sort of experience, and somehow concludes that Christian belief must be true. It is rather that (as in the case of perception) the experience is the occasion for the formation of the beliefs in question, and plays a causal role (a role governed by the design plan) in their genesis.

In the typical case, therefore, Christian belief is *immediate*; it is formed in the *basic* way. It doesn't proceed by way of an argument from, for example, the reliability of Scripture or the church. As Jonathan Edwards puts it, "This evidence, that they, that are spiritually enlightened, have of the truth of the things of religion, is a kind of intuitive and immediate evidence. They believe the doctrines of God's word to be divine, because they see divinity in them."[23] Christian belief is basic; furthermore, Christian belief is *properly* basic, where the

---

[21] On the account of knowledge given in WPF. I leave as homework the problem of showing how to modify the model in such a way as to accommodate the other main accounts of warrant.

[22] For example, in rebutting defeaters: see below, chapter 11.

[23] *A Treatise concerning Religious Affections*, ed. John E. Smith (New Haven: Yale University Press, 1959 [originally published 1746]), p. 298. Subsequent references to *Religious Affections* are to this edition.

propriety in question embraces all three of the epistemic virtues we are considering. On the model, the believer is *justified* in accepting these beliefs in the basic way and is *rational* (both internally and externally) in so doing; still further, the beliefs can have warrant, enough warrant for knowledge, when they are accepted in that basic way.[24] My Christian belief can have warrant, and warrant sufficient for knowledge, even if I don't know of and cannot make a good historical case for the reliability of the biblical writers or for what they teach. I don't *need* a good historical case for the truth of the central teachings of the gospel to be warranted in accepting them. I needn't be able to find a good argument, historical or otherwise, for the resurrection of Jesus Christ, or for his being the divine Son of God, or for the Christian claim that his suffering and death constitute an atoning sacrifice whereby we can be restored to the right relationship with God. On the model, the warrant for Christian belief doesn't require that I or anyone else have this kind of historical information; the warrant floats free of such questions. It doesn't require to be validated or proved by some source of belief *other* than faith, such as historical investigation.

Instead, Scripture (through the work of the Holy Spirit) carries its own evidence with it; as Calvin says, it is 'self-authenticating':

> Let this point therefore stand: that those whom the Holy Spirit has inwardly taught truly rest upon Scripture, and that Scripture deed is self-authenticated....

"Therefore," he says,

> illumined by his power, we believe neither by our own nor by anyone else's judgment that Scripture is from God; but above human judgment we affirm with utter certainty that it has flowed to us from the very mouth of God by the ministry of men. We seek no proofs, no marks of genuineness upon which our judgment may lean; but we subject our judgment and wit to it as to a thing far beyond any guess work! ... Such, then, is a conviction that requires no reason; such, a knowledge with which the best reason agrees—in which the mind truly reposes more securely and constantly than in any reasons. I speak of nothing other than what each believer experiences within himself—though my words fall far beneath a just explanation of the matter.[25]

Calvin speaks here of a certainty, a knowledge that Scripture "has flowed to us from the very mouth of God," even if it is "by the ministry of men." He does not mean to say, I think (at any rate this is how the model goes), that the Holy Spirit induces belief in the proposition *the Bible* (or the book of Job, or Paul's epistles, or the thirteenth chapter of First Corinthians) *comes to us from the very mouth of God.*[26] Rather, upon reading or hearing a given teaching —a given item from the great things of the gospel—the Holy Spirit teaches us, causes us to

---

[24] Of course that is not to say that a believer can properly reject proposed defeaters out of hand, without examination (see below, chapters 11-14); nor is she committed to refusing to think she could be wrong. No doubt she can be wrong: that is part of the human condition. If there were a demonstration or a powerful argument from other sources against Christian belief, an argument to which neither she nor the Christian community could see a satisfactory reply, then she might have a problem; this would be a genuine example of a clash between faith and reason. No such demonstration or argument, however, has so far reared its ugly head.

[25] I, vii, 5, pp. 80-81. Here Calvin speaks of "utter certainty" and of the mind "reposing securely" in these teachings. But this is only one side of the story: elsewhere he notes that even the best and most favored of its are subject to doubt and uncertainty: "For unbelief is so deeply rooted in our hearts, and we are so inclined to it, that not without hard struggle is each one able to persuade himself of what all confess with the mouth: namely, that God is faithful" (III, ii, 15); he also says that "unbelief, in all men, is always mixed with faith" (III, ii, 4, p. 547). (What he means, of course, is not that unbelievers always have a portion of faith, but that faith always contains a portion of unbelief.) It is only in the pure and paradigmatic instances of faith that there is that 'utter certainty'.

[26] As to what Calvin actually meant here, there has been considerable debate.

believe that *that* teaching is both true and comes from God. So the structure here is not: what is taught in Scripture is *this* (e.g., that in Christ, God was reconciling the world to himself) is taught in Scripture; therefore, this is true. It is rather that, on reading or hearing a certain teaching *t*, one forms the belief that *t*, that very teaching, is true and from God.

What is this 'self-authentication' of which Calvin speaks? Is he (or the model) claiming that the truths of the gospel are *self-evident* in something like the traditional sense in which 2 + 1 = 3 is said to be? Not at all. Self-evident propositions are necessarily true and, at least in the cases of maximal self-evidence, such that a properly functioning human being can't so much as grasp them without seeing that they couldn't be false.[27] But the great things of the gospel are not necessarily true (they are a result of God's free and gracious action), and it is entirely possible to grasp them without seeing that they are true (it is possible to understand them and reject them). So according the model (and Calvin), these truths are not self-evident. The propositions *Scripture is reliable* or *God is the author of the Bible* are not self-evident; neither are such teachings as that God was reconciling the world to himself in Christ, or that this reconciliation was accomplished by virtue of Christ's atoning suffering and death.[28]

Nor does Calvin mean to say (nor is it any part of the model to assert) that Scripture is self-authenticating in the sense that it offers evidence for *itself* or somehow *proves* itself to be accurate or reliable. Suppose a question is raised with respect to a given source of belief: is this source of belief really reliable? Suppose a question is raised with respect to a particular teaching of Scripture: is this particular teaching really true? Neither the source nor the particular teaching can, by itself, give an answer that (rationally) allays that doubt. Analogy: suppose I read Hume in an unduly receptive frame of mind and become doubtful that my cognitive faculties are, in fact, reliable. I can't rationally quell or quiet that doubt by offering myself an argument for their reliability. It is the reliability of those very faculties, that very source, that is at issue; and if I have a general doubt about their reliability, I should also have the same doubt about their reliability in this specific instance; I should have the same doubt about the premises of the argument I offer myself, and about my belief that the premises imply the conclusion. Similarly for Scripture: If I am doubt about its reliability, I can't sensibly quell or quiet that doubt by noting that, say, II Timothy 3:16 says all Scripture is God—breathed (even if I were convinced that what is taught here refers to just the books I take to be canonical). So Scripture isn't self-authenticating in *that* sense either.

What, then, could Calvin mean when he says that Scripture is self—authenticating? We can see what he means by noting a respect in which the gospel truths resemble self-evident propositions. According to the model, these truths, like self-evident truths, are indeed evident (do indeed have warrant); and, like self-evident truths, they have their evidence *immediately*—that is—not by way of propositional evidence. They do not get their evidence or warrant by way of being believed on the evidential basis of other propositions. So from that point of view, these truths too could be said to be self-evident—in a different and analogically extended sense of that term. They are evident, but don't get their evidence

---

[27] See *WPF*, 108-9.

[28] According to Richard Swinburne, "Very few parts of the Bible seem to claim either `self-evident' authority or indeed even to be the immediate `word of the Lord'... much of Scripture has not seemed self-evident to so many of its readers; argument is needed to show how it is to be understood and why it is to be believed. Those to whom Scripture seems `self-evident' are well advised to reflect on these facts before reaffirming their conviction that its truth needs no argument" (*Revelation* [Oxford: Clarendon Press, 1992], p. 118). Here two issues are conflated: (a) are these gospel truths self-evident? and (b) can they properly be believed without argument? According to the present model the answer to (b) is `yes' but to (a) is `no'. (There is also still a further issue: according to the model, the central truths of the gospel are self-authenticating in this way; the same does not (necessarily) go for the rest of what Bible teaches.)

from other propositions; they have their evidence in themselves (and not by way of inference from other propositions).[29] In this same extended sense, perceptual and memory beliefs too are self-evident. They too are 'evident in themselves', in that they don't get their warrant (or evidence) by way of warrant transfer from other propositions. To say that a proposition p is self-evident in this sense is just to say that p does, indeed, have warrant or evidence and does not get that warrant by way of warrant transfer (that is, by way of being believed on the basis of other propositions)—in a word (or two), p is properly basic.[30]

What Calvin means, then (and what the testimonial model endorses), is that we don't require argument from, for example, historically established premises about the authorship and reliability of the bit of Scripture in question to the conclusion that the bit in question is in fact true; that whole process gets short—circuited by way of the tripartite process producing faith. Scripture is self—authenticating in the sense that for belief in the great things of the gospel to be justified, rational, and warranted, no historical evidence and argument for the teaching in question, or for the veracity or reliability or divine character of Scripture (or the part of Scripture in which it is taught) are necessary. The process by which these beliefs have warrant for the believer swings free of those historical and other consideration these beliefs have warrant in the basic way.

But suppose someone *does* believe these things with a degree of firmness sufficient to constitute knowledge: isn't this attitude, however it is caused, irrational, contrary to reason? Suppose I read the gospels and come to believe, for example, that Jesus Christ is in fact the divine son of God and that by his passion, death, and resurrection we human beings, fallen and seriously flawed as we are, can be reconciled and have eternal life. Suppose I believe these things without any external evidence. Suppose, further, I pay little attention to Scripture scholarship and give no thought to the identity or credentials of the real or alleged authors of these documents. I pay little or no attention to such questions as when they were composed or redacted, by whom or how many, whether the redactor was trying to make a theological point in editing as he did, and so on.[31] Won't I be leaping to conclusions, forming belief too hastily? What am I really going on, in such a case? Where is my basis, my ground, my evidence? If I have neither propositional evidence nor the sort of ground afforded perception by perceptual experience, am I not just taking a blind leap? Isn't this leap of faith a leap in the dark? Am I not like someone whose house is on fire and blindly jumps from his third—story window, desperately hoping to catch hold of a branch of the tree he knows is somewhere outside the window? And isn't that irresponsible[32] and irrational?

Not at all. Faith, according to the model, is far indeed from being a blind leap; it isn't even remotely like a leap in the dark. Suppose you are descending a glacier at twelve thousand feet on Mount Rainier; there is a nasty whiteout and you can't see more than four feet before you. It's getting very late, the wind is rising and the temperature dropping, and you won't survive (you are wearing only jeans and a T-shirt) unless you get down before

---

[29] Compare Jonathan Edwards: "The gospel of the blessed God doesn't go abroad a begging for its evidence, so much as some think; it has its highest and most proper evidence in itself" (*Religious Affections*, p. 307).

[30] Faith resembles perception, memory, and rational intuition (whereby one grasps what is self—evident) in that in all three cases the beliefs in question are properly basic with respect to warrant. But faith differs from perception (though not from memory and rational intuition) in that it does not involve anything like the highly articulated and detailed sort of sensuous phenomenology that prompts perceptual belief.

[31] I don't mean for a moment to suggest that Scripture scholarship is unimportant or unimportant for the Christian life (see chapter 12); what I mean is only that knowledge of its results is not necessary for warranted Christian belief.

[32] As is argued by, e.g., James L. Muyskens, *The Sufficiency of Hope: The Conceptual Foundations of Religion* (Philadelphia: Temple University Press, 1979), p. 113; see also pp. 134-44.

nightfall. So you decide to try to leap the crevasse before you, even though you can't see its other side and haven't the faintest idea how far it is across it. *That's* a leap in the dark. In the case of faith, however, things are wholly different. You might as well claim that a memory belief, or the belief that 3 + 1 = 4 is a leap in the dark. What makes something a leap in the dark is that the leaper doesn't know and has no firm beliefs about what there is out there in the dark—you might succeed in jumping the crevasse and triumphantly continue your descent, but for all you know you might instead plummet two hundred feet into the icy depths of the glacier. You don't really *believe* that you can jump the crevasse (though you don't disbelieve it either); you *hope* you can, and act on what you *do* believe—namely, that if you don't jump it, you don't have a chance.

The case of faith, this sure and certain knowledge, is very different. For the person with faith (at least in the paradigmatic instances), the great things of the gospel seem clearly true, obvious, compelling. She finds herself convinced—just as she does in the case of clear memory beliefs or her belief in elementary truths of arithmetic:[33] Phenomenologically, therefore, from the inside, there is no similarity at all to a leap in the dark. Nor, of course, is there (on the model) any similarity from the outside. This is no leap in the dark, not merely because the person with faith is wholly convinced but also because, a matter of fact, the belief in question meets the conditions for rationality and warrant.

> Compare belief of this sort with the *a priori* and memory beliefs I spoke of above. In a certain sense, there isn't anything to go on in any of the three cases. You don't accept memory and obvious *a priori* beliefs on the basis of other beliefs; but you also lack the detailed phenomenological basis, the rich and highly articulated sensuous imagery that is involved in perception. What you do have in all three cases is another kind of phenomenal evidence, what I have been calling *doxastic* evidence. (In WPF I called it *impulsional* evidence.) There is a certain kind of phenomenology that distinguishes entertaining a proposition you believe from one you do not: the former simply seems right, correct, natural, approved—the experience isn't easy to describe (WPF, 190ff.). You have this doxastic evidence in all three sorts of cases (as, indeed, in any case of belief), and you have nothing else to go on. But you don't *need* anything else to go on: it is not as if things would be better, from an epistemic point of view, if you believed, say, 2 + 1 = 3 or that you had oatmeal for breakfast this morning on the evidential basis of other propositions, or on the basis of some kind of sensuous imagery more or less like that involved in perception. (I don't mean that you can't get more evidence, for something you believe by way of memory, but that you would not necessarily be better off, epistemically speaking, if you believed the proposition in question on the basis of other beliefs or on the basis of sensuous imagery.) The same goes (on the model) for the beliefs of faith: you don't have either sensuous imagery or evidence from other things you believe to go on; the beliefs are none the worse, epistemically speaking, for that. In fact (on the model) they are all the better for that; they have (or can have) much more firmness and stability than they could sensibly have if accepted on the basis of rational argument or, as in this case, historical investigation; they can also have much more warrant. These beliefs (on the model) are not accepted on the basis of other beliefs; in fact, other beliefs are accepted on the basis of *them*.
>
> You might think this model is a model of how, broadly speaking, Christian belief can have warrant by way of *religious experience*. That's not exactly right—or if it *is* right, then memory and *a priori* beliefs also get *their* warrant by way of experience. But suppose we think that (on the model) the beliefs of faith do get their warrant by way of experience—that is, by way *of doxastic* experience—and suppose we describe that experience as *religious* experience. What is crucially important to note is that we don't have here an *argument* from

---

[33] Again, in the paradigmatic cases; but of course the fact is the conviction and belief involved in faith come in all degrees of firmness. As Calvin puts it, "in the believing mind certainty is mixed with doubt" and "we are troubled on all sides by the agitation of unbelief'." In typical cases, therefore, as opposed to paradigmatic cases, degree of belief will be less than maximal. Furthermore, degree of belief, on the part of the person who has faith, typically varies from time to time, from circumstance to circumstance.

religious experience to the truth of these Christian beliefs. There *could* be something like that, a model according to which Christian belief got warrant by way of an argument from religious experience. This would be one in which you have religious experience (or note that others do), and then argue (perhaps by way of something roughly like the analogical argument for other minds) to the truth of these doctrines. Alternatively, it might be like the arguments some have offered from the facts of perceptual experience for the truth of perceptual beliefs. This model isn't like that. The experience in question is an *occasion* for the belief in question, not a phenomenon whose existence serves as a premise in an argument for that belief.

According to Hebrews 11, "Now faith is the substance of things hoped for and the evidence of things not seen" (King James translation). The key words 'substance' and 'evidence' are translated variously; for example, the more recent Revised Standard Version has "faith is the *assurance* of things hoped for, the *conviction of* things not seen" (my emphasis). Perhaps the former way is the better translation; in any event, it is the richer. For faith, according to Christian doctrine, is many things. It is the means or vehicle of salvation: "for it is by grace you have been saved, through faith" (Ephesians 1:8). It is also that by which we are *justified* (above, p. 87), as well as that by means of which we are *regenerated,* becoming new creatures in Christ. And it is also the foundation and substance (etymologically, that which 'stands under') of Christian hope.

But faith is also "the evidence of things not seen:" By faith—the whole process, involving the internal instigation of the Holy Spirit—something becomes *evident (i.e.,* acquires warrant, has what it takes to be knowledge). And what thus becomes evident or warranted is indeed not seen. This doesn't mean that it is indistinct, blurred, uncertain, or a matter of guesswork; what it means is that the belief in question isn't made evident by way of the workings of the ordinary cognitive faculties with which we were originally created. (The author refers, by way of synecdoche, to these faculties as vision.) Return to the account of Thomas's skepticism (above, pp. 254): Thomas would not believe until he saw the nail holes, put his finger where the nails were, thrust his hand into Christ's side. Jesus then says to him, "Because you have seen me, you have believed; blessed are those who have not seen and yet have believed" (John 20:29). From the present point of view, this is neither a general counsel commending credulity nor a rebuke addressed to such embryonic empiricists as Thomas. It is, instead, the observation that those who have faith have a source of knowledge that transcends our ordinary perceptual faculties and cognitive processes, a source of knowledge that is a divine gift; hence they are indeed blessed.[34]

---

[34] Compare Aquinas: "Accordingly, if anyone would reduce the foregoing words to the form of a definition, he may say that *faith is a habit of the mind, whereby eternal life is begun in us, making the intellect assent to what is non—apparent* (*ST* II—II, q.4, a.i. *respondeo*).

Questions

1. What does Plantinga mean by internalism when speaking of the work of the Holy Spirit?

2. What does Plantinga mean by a belief's being *properly basic*?

3. What do you make of the claim that the Scriptures are auto-pistic/self-authenticating?

4. In what way does Plantinga think that the believer's source of knowing is extraordinary?

5. Can the Christian's belief in the Trinity be a *properly basic belief* and if so, how?

ON FAITH*

St Thomas Aquinas

Aquinas examines the nature of faith, its corresponding gifts, knowledge and understanding. Faith gives assent to the truth of God, and its object is not a propostion, *but* the heavenly vision. *The light of faith directs the believer to things which are above. Two ways of knowing are distinguished, the way of* natural reason *which gives assent to first principles, and the mode of* faith, *by which one perceives the invisible things of God through Special Revelation, the Word of God The two are complementary, because God is the source of all truth.*

Question I. Of Faith. *(In Ten Articles.)*

Having to treat now of the theological virtues, we shall begin with Faith, secondly we shall speak of Hope, and thirdly, of Charity.

The treatise on Faith will be fourfold: (1) Of faith itself. (2) Of the corresponding gifts, knowledge and understanding: (3) Of the opposite vices: (4) Of the precepts pertaining to this virtue.

About faith itself we shall consider: (1) its object: (2) its act: (3) the habit of faith.

Under the first head there are ten points of inquiry: (1) Whether the object of faith is the First Truth? (2) Whether the object of faith is something complex or incomplex, i.e. whether it is a thing or a proposition? (3) Whether anything false can come under faith? (4) Whether the object of faith can be anything seen? (5) Whether it can be anything known? (6) Whether the things to be believed should be divided into a certain number of articles? (7) Whether the same articles are of faith for all times? (8) Of the number of articles. (9) Of the manner of embodying the articles in a symbol (10) Who has the right to propose a symbol of faith?

First Article. Whether the Object of Faith Is the First Truth?
We proceed thus to the First Article:—

Objection 1. It seems that the object of faith is not the First Truth. For it seems that the object of faith is that which is proposed to us to be believed. Now not only things pertaining to the Godhead, i.e. the First Truth, are proposed to us to be believed, but also things concerning Christ's human nature, and the sacraments of the Church, and the condition of creatures. Therefore the object of faith is not only the First Truth.

Obj. 2. Further, Faith and unbelief have the same object since they are opposed to one another. Now unbelief can be about all things contained in Holy Writ, for whichever one of them a man denies, he is considered an unbeliever. Therefore faith also is about all things contained in Holy Writ. But there are many things therein, concerning man and other creatures. Therefore the object of faith is not only the First Truth, but also created truth.

Obj. 3. Further, Faith is codivided with charity, as stated above (I.-II., Q. LXII., A. 3). Now by charity we love not only God, who is the sovereign Good, but also our neighbour. Therefore the object of Faith is not only the First Truth.

---

* This article is reprinted by courtesy of the publisher, R & T Washbourne, and it taken from Thomas Aquinas's *Summa Theologiae*, Part II, translated by the Fathers of English Dominican Province, London, 1917.

On the contrary, Dionysius says (*Div. Nom. vii.*) that *faith is about the simple and everlasting truth.* Now this is the First Truth. Therefore the object of faith is the First Truth.

I answer that, The object of every cognitive habit includes two things: first, that which is known materially, and is the material object, so to speak, and, secondly, that whereby it is known, which is the formal aspect of the object. Thus in the science of geometry, the conclusions are what is known materially, while the formal aspect of the science is the mean of demonstration, through which the conclusions are known.

Accordingly if we consider, in faith, the formal aspect of the object, it is nothing else than the First Truth. For the faith of which we are speaking, does not assent to anything, except because it is revealed by God. Hence the mean on which faith is based is the Divine Truth. If, however, we consider materially the things to which faith assents, they include not only God, but also many other things, which, nevertheless, do not come under the assent of faith, except as bearing some relation to God, in as much as, to wit, through certain effects of the Divine operation, man is helped on his journey towards the enjoyment of God. Consequently from this point of view also the object of faith is, in a way, the First Truth, in as much as nothing comes under faith except in relation to God, even as the object of the medical art is health, for it considers nothing save in relation to health.

Reply Obj. 1. Things concerning Christ's human nature, and the sacraments of the Church, or any creatures whatever, come under faith, in so far as by them we are directed to God, and in as much as we assent to them on account of the Divine Truth.

The same answer applies to the Second Objection, as regards all things contained in Holy Writ.

Reply Obj. 3. Charity also loves our neighbour on account of God, so that its object, properly speaking, is God, as we shall show further on (Q. XXV., A. I).

Second Article. Whether the Object of Faith is Something Complex, by Way of a Proposition?
We proceed thus to the Second Article:—

Objection 1. It seems that the object of faith is not something complex by way of a proposition. For the object of faith is the First Truth, as stated above (A. I). Now the First Truth is something simple. Therefore the object of faith is not something complex.

Obj. 2. Further, The exposition of faith is contained in the symbol. Now the symbol does not contain propositions, but things: for it is not stated therein that God is almighty, but: I *believe in God... almighty.* Therefore the object of faith is not a proposition but a thing.

Obj. 3. Further, Faith is succeeded by vision, according to I Cor. xiii. 12: *We see now through a glass in a dark manner: but then face to face. Now I know in part; but then I shall know even as I am known.* But the object of the heavenly vision is something simple, for it is the Divine Essence. Therefore the faith of the wayfarer is also.

On the contrary Faith is a mean between science and opinion. Now the mean is in the same genus as the extremes. Since, then, science and opinion are about propositions, it seems that faith is likewise about propositions; so that its object is something complex.

I answer that, The thing known is in the knower according to the mode of the knower. Now the mode proper to the human intellect is to know the truth by synthesis and analysis, as stated in the First Part (Q LXXXV., A. 5). Hence things that are simple in themselves, are known by the intellect with a certain amount of complexity, just as on the other hand, the Divine intellect knows, without any complexity, things that are complex in themselves.

Accordingly the object of faith may be considered in two ways. First, as regards the thing itself which is believed, and thus the object of faith is something simple, namely the thing itself about which we have faith. Secondly, on the part of the believer, and in this respect the object of faith is something complex by way of a proposition.

Hence in the past both opinions have been held with a certain amount of truth.

Reply Obj. 1. This argument considers the object of faith on the part of the thing believed.

Reply Obj. 2. The symbol mentions the things about which faith is, in so far as the act of the believer is terminated in them, as is evident from the manner of speaking about them. Now the act of the believer does not terminate in a proposition, but in a thing. For as in science we do not form propositions, except in order to have knowledge about things through their means, so is it in faith.

Reply Obj. 3. The object of the heavenly vision will be the First Truth seen in itself, according to 1 John iii. 2: *We know that when He shall appear, we shall be like to Him: because we shall see Him as He is:* hence that vision will not be by way of a proposition but by way of simple understanding. On the other hand, by faith, we do not apprehend the First Truth as it is in itself. Hence the comparison fails....

Fourth Article. Whether the Object of Faith Can Be Something Seen?
We proceed thus to the Fourth Article:—

Objection 1. It seems that the object of faith is something seen. For Our Lord said to Thomas (John xx. 29): *Because thou hast seen Me, Thomas, thou hast believed.* Therefore vision and faith regard the same object.

Obj. 2. Further, The Apostle, while speaking of the knowledge of faith, says (I Cor. xiii.12): *We see now through a glass in a dark manner.* Therefore what is believed is seen.

Obj. 3. Further, Faith is a spiritual light. Now something is seen under every light. Therefore faith is of things seen.

Obj. 4. Further, *Every sense is a kind of sight,* as Augustine states *(De Verb. Domini, Serm. xxxiii.).* But faith is of things heard, according to Rom. x. 17: *Faith ... cometh by hearing.* Therefore faith is of things seen.

On the contrary, The Apostle says (Heb. xi. I) that *faith is the evidence of things that appear not.*

I answer that, Faith implies assent of the intellect to that which is believed. Now the intellect assents to a thing in two ways. First, through being moved to assent by its very object, which is known either by itself (as in the case of first principles, which are held by the habit of understanding), or through something else already known (as in the case of conclusions which are held by the habit of science). Secondly the intellect assents to something, not through being sufficiently moved to this assent by its proper object, but through an act of choice, whereby it turns voluntarily to one side rather than to the other: and if this be accompanied by doubt and fear of the opposite side, there will be opinion, while, if there be certainty and no fear of the other side, there will be faith.

Now those things are said to be seen which, of themselves, move the intellect or the senses to knowledge of them. Wherefore it is evident that neither faith nor opinion can be of things seen either by the senses or by the intellect.

Reply Obj. 1. Thomas *saw one thing, and believed another.*[*] he saw the Man, and believing Him to be God, he made profession of his faith, saying: My *Lord and my God.*

---

[*] S. Gregory: *Hom.* xxvi. *in Evang.*

Reply Obj. 2. Those things which come under faith can be considered in two ways. First, in particular; and thus they cannot be seen and believed at the same time, as shown above. Secondly, in general, that is, under the common aspect of credibility; and in this way they are seen by the believer. For he would not believe unless, on the evidence of signs, or of something similar, he saw that they ought to be believed.

Reply Obj. 3. The light of faith makes us see what we believe. For just as, by the habits of the other virtues, man sees what is becoming to him in respect of that habit, so, by the habit of faith, the human mind is directed to assent to such things as are becoming to a right faith, and not to assent to others.

Reply Obj. 4. Hearing is of words signifying what is of faith, but not of the things themselves that are believed; hence it does not follow that these things are seen.

Fifth Article. Whether Those Things That Are of Faith Can Be an Object of Science?
We proceed thus to the Fifth Article:—

Objection 1. It seems that those things that are of faith can be an object of science. For where science is lacking there is ignorance, since ignorance is the opposite of science. Now we are not in ignorance of those things we have to believe, since ignorance of such things savours of unbelief, according to 1 Tim. i. 13: *I did it ignorantly in unbelief.* Therefore things that are of faith can be an object of science.

Obj. 2. Further, Science is acquired by reasons. Now sacred writers employ reasons to inculcate things that are of faith. Therefore such things can be an object of science.

Obj. 3. Further, Things which are demonstrated are an object of science, since a *demonstration is a syllogism that produces science.* Now certain matters of faith have been demonstrated by the philosophers, such as the Existence and Unity of God, and so forth. Therefore things that are of faith can be an object of science.

Obj. 4. Further, Opinion is further from science than faith is, since faith is said to stand between opinion and science. Now opinion and science can, in a way, be about the same object, as stated in *Poster.* i. Therefore faith and science can be about the same object also.

On the contrary, Gregory says *(Hom. xxi. in Ev.)* that *when a thing is manifest, it is the object, not of faith, but of perception.* Therefore things that are of faith are not the object of perception, whereas what is an object of science is the object of perception. Therefore there can be no faith about things which are an object of science.

I answer that, All science is derived from self-evident and therefore *seen* principles; wherefore all objects of science must needs be, in a fashion, seen.

Now as stated above (A. 4) it is impossible that one and the same thing should be believed and seen by the same person. Hence it is equally impossible for one and the same thing to be an object of science and of belief for the same person. It may happen, however, that a thing which is an object of vision or science for one, is believed by another: since we hope to see some day what we now believe about the Trinity, according to 1 Cor. xiii. 12: *We see now through a glass in a dark manner; but then face to face:* which vision the angels possess already; so that what we believe, they see. In like manner it may happen that what is an object of vision or scientific knowledge for one man, even in the state of a wayfarer, is, for another man, an object of faith, because he does not know it by demonstration.

Nevertheless that which is proposed to be believed equally by all, is equally unknown by all as an object of science: such are the things which are of faith simply. Consequently faith and science are not about the same things.

Reply Obj. 1. Unbelievers are in ignorance of things that are of faith, for neither do they see or know them in themselves, nor do they know them to be credible. The faithful, on the other hand, know them, not as by demonstration, but by the light of faith which makes them see that they ought to believe them, as stated above (A. 4, *ad* 2, 3).

Reply Obj. 2. The reasons employed by holy men to prove things that are of faith, are not demonstrations; they are either persuasive arguments showing that what is proposed to our faith is not impossible, or else they are proofs drawn from the principles of faith, i.e. from the authority of Holy Writ, as Dionysius declares (Div. *Nom. ii.*). Whatever is based on these principles is as well proved in the eyes of the faithful, as a conclusion drawn from self-evident principles is in the eyes of all. Hence again, theology is a science, as we stated at the outset of this work (P L, Q, L, A. 2).

Reply Obj. 3. Things which can be proved by demonstration are reckoned among the articles of faith, not because they are believed simply by all, but because they are a necessary presuppositions to matters of faith, so that those who do not know them by demonstration must know them first of all by faith.

Reply Obj. 4. *As* the Philosopher says (*loc. cit.*), *science and opinion about the same object can certainly be in different men,* as we have stated above about science and faith; yet it is possible for one and the same man to have science and faith about the same thing relatively, i.e. in relation to the object, but not in the same respect. For it is possible for the same person, about one and the same object, to know one thing and to think another: and, in like manner, one may know by demonstration the unity of the Godhead, and, by faith, the Trinity. On the other hand, in one and the same man, about the same object, and in the same respect, science is incompatible with either opinion or faith, yet for different reasons. Because science is incompatible with opinion about the same object simply, for the reason that science demands that its object should be deemed impossible to be otherwise, whereas it is essential to opinion, that its object should be deemed possible to be otherwise. Yet that which is the object of faith, on account of the certainty of faith, is also deemed impossible to be otherwise; and the reason why science and faith cannot be about the same object and in the same respect is because the object of science is some thing seen, whereas the object of faith is the unseen, as stated above....

Tenth Article. Whether It Belongs to the Sovereign Pontiff to Draw up a Symbol of Faith?
We proceed thus to the Tenth Article:—

Objection 1. It seems that it does not belong to the Sovereign Pontiff to draw up a symbol of faith. For a new edition of the symbol becomes necessary in order to explain the articles of faith, as stated above (A. 9). Now, in the Old Testament, the articles of faith were more and more explained as time went on, by reason of the truth of faith becoming clearer through greater nearness to Christ, as stated above (A. 7). Since then this reason ceased with the advent of the New Law, there is no need for the articles of faith to be more and more explicit. Therefore it does not seem to belong to the authority of the Sovereign Pontiff to draw up a new edition of the symbol.

Obj. 2. Further, No man has the power to do what is forbidden under pain of anathema by the universal Church. Now it was forbidden under pain of anathema by the universal Church, to make a new edition of the symbol. For it is stated in the acts of the first council of Ephesus (P ii., Act. 6) that *after the symbol of the Nicene council had been read through, the holy synod decreed that it was unlawful to utter, write or draw up any other creed, than that which was defined by the Fathers assembled at Nicaea together with the Holy Ghost,* and this under pain of anathema. The same was repeated in the acts of the council of Chalcedon (P ii., Act. 5). Therefore it seems that the Sovereign Pontiff has no authority to publish a new edition of the symbol.

Obj. 3. Further, Athanasius was not the Sovereign Pontiff, but patriarch of Alexandria, and yet he published a symbol which is sung in the Church. Therefore it does not seem to belong to the Sovereign Pontiff any more than to other bishops, to publish a new edition of the symbol.

On the contrary, The symbol was drawn up by a general council. Now such a council cannot be convoked otherwise than by the authority of the Sovereign Pontiff, as stated in the Decretals (Dist. xvii., Cap. 4, 5). Therefore an edition of the symbol belongs to the authority of the Sovereign Pontiff.

I answer that, As stated above *(Obj.* 1*),* a new edition of the symbol becomes necessary in order to set aside the errors that may arise. Consequently to publish a new edition of the symbol belongs to that authority which is empowered to decide matters of faith finally, so that they may be held by all with unshaken faith. Now this belongs to the authority of the Sovereign Pontiff, to whom the more important and more difficult questions that arise in the Church are referred, as stated in the Decretals (Extra, *De Baptismo,* Cap. *Majores).* Hence Our Lord said to Peter whom he made Sovereign Pontiff (Luke xxii. 32): *I have prayed for thee,* Peter, *that thy faith fail not, and thou, being once converted, confirm thy brethren.* The reason of this is that there should be but one faith of the whole Church, according to 1 Cor. i. 10: *That you all speak the same thing, and that there be no schisms among you:* and this could not be secured unless any question of faith that may arise be decided by him who presides over the whole Church, so that the whole Church may hold firmly to his decision. Consequently it belongs to the sole authority of the Sovereign Pontiff to publish a new edition of the symbol, as do all other matters which concern the whole Church, such as to convoke a general council and so forth.

Reply Obj. 1. The truth of faith is sufficiently explicit in the teaching of Christ and the apostles. But since, according to 2 Pet. iii. 16, some men are so evil-minded as to pervert the apostolic teaching and other doctrines and Scriptures to their own destruction, it was necessary as time went on to express the faith more explicitly against the errors which arose.

Reply Obj. 2. This prohibition and sentence of the council was intended for private individuals, who have no business to decide matters of faith: for this decision of the general council did not take away from a subsequent council the power of drawing up a new edition of the symbol, containing not indeed a new faith, but the same faith with greater explicitness. For every council has taken into account that a subsequent council would expound matters more fully than the preceding council, if this became necessary through some heresy arising. Consequently this belongs to the Sovereign Pontiff, by whose authority the council is convoked, and its decision confirmed.

Reply Obj. 3. Athanasius drew up a declaration of faith, not under the form of a symbol, but rather by way of an exposition of doctrine, as appears from his way of speaking. But since it contained briefly the whole truth of faith, it was accepted by the authority of the Sovereign Pontiff, so as to be considered as a rule of faith.

Question II. Of The Act Of Faith. (*In Ten Articles.*)

We must now consider the act of faith, and (1) the internal act, (2) the external act.

Under the first head there are ten points of inquiry: (1) What is *to believe,* which is the internal act of faith? (2) In how many ways is it expressed? (3) Whether it is necessary for salvation to believe in anything above natural reason? (4) Whether it is necessary to believe those things that are attainable by natural reason? (5) Whether it is necessary for salvation to believe certain things explicitly? (6) Whether all are equally bound to explicit faith? (7) Whether explicit faith in Christ is always necessary for salvation? (8) Whether it is necessary for salvation to believe in the Trinity explicitly? (9) Whether the act of faith is meritorious? (10) Whether human reason diminishes the merit of faith?

First Article. Whether to Believe Is to Think with Assent?
We proceed thus to the First Article:—

Objection 1. It seems that to believe is not to think with assent. Because the Latin word *cogitatio (thought)* implies a research; for *cogitare (to think)* seems to be equivalent *coagitare* i.e. *to discuss together.* Now Damascene says *(De Fide Orthod.* iv.) that faith is *an assent without research.* Therefore thinking has no place in the act of faith.

Obi. 2. Further, Faith resides in the reason, as we shall show further on (Q. IV., A. 2). Now to think is an act of the cogitative power, which belongs to the sensitive faculty as stated in the First Part (Q. LXXVIIL., A. 4). Therefore thought has nothing to do with faith.

Obj. 3. Further, To believe is an act of the intellect, since its object is truth. But assent seems to be an act not of the intellect, but of the will, even as consent is, as stated above (I.-II, ,Q. XV., A. 1, *ad* 3). Therefore to believe is not to think with assent.

On the contrary, This is how *to believe* is defined by Augustine *(De Praedest. Sanct.* ii.).

I answer that, To think can be taken in three ways. First, in a general way for any kind of actual consideration of the intellect, as Augustine observes *(De Trin.* xiv.): *By understanding I mean now the faculty whereby we understand when thinking.* Secondly, *to think* is more strictly taken for that consideration of the intellect, which is accompanied by some kind of inquiry, and which precedes the intellect's arrival at the stage of perfection that comes with the certitude of sight. In this sense Augustine says *(De Trin.* xv.) that *the Son of God is not called the Thought, but the Word of God. When our thought realizes what we know and takes form therefrom, it becomes our world. Hence the Word of God must be understood without any thinking on the part of God, for there is nothing there that can take form, or be unformed.* In this way thought is, properly speaking, the movement of the mind while yet deliberating, and not yet perfected by the clear sight of truth. Since, however, such a movement of the mind may be one of deliberation either about universal notions, which belongs to the intellectual faculty, or about particular matters, which belongs to the sensitive part, hence it is that *to think is* taken secondly for an act of the deliberating intellect, and thirdly for an act of the cogitative power.

Accordingly, if *to think* be understood broadly according to the first sense, then to *think with assent,* does not express completely what is meant by *to believe:* since, in this way, a man thinks with assent even when he considers what he knows by science, or understands. If, on the other hand, *to think* be understood in the second way, then this expresses completely the nature of the act of believing. For among the acts belonging to the intellect, some have a firm assent without any such kind of thinking, as when a man considers the things that he knows by science, or understands, for this consideration is already formed. But some acts of the intellect have unformed thought devoid of a firm assent, whether they incline to neither side, as in one who *doubts;* or incline to one side rather than the other, but on account of some slight motive, as in one who *suspects* or incline to one side yet with fear of the other, as in one who *opines.* But this act to *believe,* cleaves firmly to one side, in which respect belief has something in common with science and understanding; yet its knowledge does not attain the perfection of clear sight, wherein it agrees with doubt, suspicion and opinion. Hence it is proper to the believer to think with assent: so that the act of believing is distinguished from all the other acts of the intellect, which are about the true or the false.

Reply Obj. 1. Faith has not that research of natural reason which demonstrates what is believed, but a research into those things whereby a man is induced to believe, for instance that such things have been uttered by God and confirmed by miracles.

Reply Obj. 2. To think is not taken here for the act of the cogitative power, but for an act of the intellect, as explained above.

Reply Obj. 3. The intellect of the believer is determined to one object, not by the reason, but by the will, wherefore assent is taken here for an act of the intellect as determined to one object by the will. (Q.I, A. 1). One of these is the material object of faith, and in this way an act of faith is *to believe in a God;* because, as stated above *(ibid.)* nothing is proposed to our belief, except in as much as it is referred to God. The other is the formal aspect of the object, for it is the medium on account of which we assent to such and such a point of faith; and thus an act of faith is *to believe God,* since, as stated above *(ibid.)* the formal object of faith is the First Truth, to Which man gives his adhesion, so as to assent for Its sake to whatever he believes.

Thirdly, if the object of faith be considered in so far as the intellect is moved by the will, an act of faith is *to believe in God.* For the First Truth is referred to the will, through having the aspect of an end.

Reply Obj. 1. These three do not denote different acts of faith, but one and the same act having different relations to the object of faith.

This suffices for the *Reply* to the *Second Objection.*

Reply Obj. 3. Unbelievers cannot be said *to believe in a God* as we understand it in relation to the act of faith. For they do not believe that God exists under the conditions that faith determines; hence they do not truly believe in a God, since, as the Philosopher observes *(Met.* ix.) *to know simple things defectively is not to know them at all.*

Reply Obj. 4. As stated above (I.-II., Q. IX., A. 1) the will moves the intellect and the other powers of the soul to the end: and in this respect an act of faith is *to believe in God.*

Third Article. Whether It Is Necessary for Salvation to Believe Anything Above the Natural Reason?
We proceed thus to the Third Article:—

Objection 1. It seems unnecessary for salvation to believe anything above the natural reason. For the salvation and perfection of a thing seem to be sufficiently insured by its natural endowments. Now matters of faith, surpass man's natural reason, since they are things unseen as stated above (Q. I., A. 4). Therefore to believe seems unnecessary for salvation.

Obj. 2. Further, It is dangerous for man to assent to matters, wherein he cannot judge whether that which is proposed to him be true or false, according to Job xii. 11: *Doth not the ear discern words?* Now a man cannot form a judgment of this kind in matters of faith, since he cannot trace them back to first principles, by which all our judgments are guided. Therefore it is dangerous to believe in such matters. Therefore to believe is not necessary for salvation.

Obj. 3. Further, Man's salvation rests on God, according to Ps. xxxvi. *39: But the salvation of the just is from the Lord. Now the invisible things* of God *are clearly seen, being understood by the things that are made; His eternal power also and Divinity,* according to Rom. i. 20: and those things which are clearly seen by the understanding are not an object of belief. Therefore it is not necessary for man's salvation, that he should believe certain things.

On the contrary, It is written (Heb. xi. 6): *Without faith it is impossible to please God.*

I answer that, Wherever one nature is subordinate to another, we find that two things concur towards the perfection of the lower nature, one of which is in respect of that nature's proper movement, while the other is in respect of the movement of the higher nature. Thus water by its proper movement moves towards the centre (of the earth), while according to the movement of the moon, it moves round the centre by ebb and flow. In like manner the planets have their proper movements from west to east, while in accordance with the movement of the first heaven, they have a movement from east to west. Now the created rational nature alone is immediately subordinate to God, since other creatures do not attain to the universal, but only to something particular, while they partake of the Divine goodness either in *being* only, as inanimate things, or also in *living,* and in *knowing singulars,* as plants and animals; whereas the rational nature, in as much as it apprehends the universal notion of good and being, is immediately related to the universal principle of being.

Consequently the perfection of the rational creature consists not only in what belongs to it in respect of its nature, but also in that which it acquires through a supernatural participation of Divine goodness. Hence it was said above (I.-II., Q. III., A. 8) that man's ultimate happiness consists in a supernatural vision of God: to which vision man cannot attain unless he be taught by God, according to John vi. 45: *Every one that hath heard of the Father and hath learned cometh to Me.* Now man acquires a share of this learning, not indeed all at once, but by little and little, according to the mode of his nature: and every one who learns thus must needs believe, in order that he may acquire science in a perfect degree; thus also the Philosopher remarks *(Elench.* i.) that *it behoves a learner to believe.*

Hence, in order that a man arrive at the perfect vision of heavenly happiness, he must first of all believe God, as a disciple believes the master who is teaching him.

Reply Obj. 1. Since man's nature is dependent on a higher nature, natural knowledge does not suffice for its perfection, and some supernatural knowledge is necessary, as stated above.

Reply Obj. 2. Just as man assents to first principles, by the natural light of his intellect, so does a virtuous man, by the habit of virtue, judge aright of things concerning that virtue; and in this way, by the light of faith which God bestows on him, a man assents to matters of faith and not to those which are against faith. Consequently *there is no* danger or *condemnation to them that are in Christ Jesus,* and whom He has enlightened by faith.

Reply Obj. 3. In many respects faith perceives the invisible things of God in a higher way than natural reason does in proceeding to God from His creatures. Hence it is written (Ecclus. iii. 25): *Many things are shown to thee above the understanding of man....*

Eighth Article. Whether It Is Necessary for Salvation To Believe Explicitly in the Trinity?
We proceed thus to the Eighth Article:—

Objection 1. It seems that it was not necessary for salvation to believe explicitly in the Trinity. For the Apostle says (Heb, xi. 6): *He that cometh to God must believe that He is, and is a rewarder to them that seek Him.* Now one can believe this without believing in the Trinity. Therefore it was not necessary to believe explicitly in the Trinity.

Obj. 2. Further, Our Lord said (John xvii. 5, 6): *Father, . . . I have manifested Thy name to men,* which words Augustine expounds *(Tract* cvi.) as follows: *Not the name by which Thou art called God, but the name whereby Thou art called My Father,* and further on he adds: *In that He made this world, God is known to all nations; in that He is not to be worshipped together with false gods; 'God is known in Judea'; but, in that He is the Father of this Christ, through Whom He takes away the sin of the world, He now makes known to men this name of His, which hitherto they knew not.* Therefore before the coming of Christ it was not known that Paternity and Filiation were in the Godhead: and so the Trinity was not believed explicitly.

Obj. 3. Further, That which we are bound to believe explicitly of God is the object of heavenly happiness. Now the object of heavenly happiness is the sovereign good, which can be understood to be in God, without any distinction of Persons. Therefore it was not necessary to believe explicitly in the Trinity.

On the contrary, In the Old Testament the Trinity of Persons is expressed in many ways; thus at the very outset of Genesis it is written in manifestation of the Trinity: *Let Us make man to Our image and likeness* (Gen. i. 26). Therefore from the very beginning it was necessary for salvation to believe in the Trinity.

I answer that, It is impossible to believe explicitly in the mystery of Christ, without faith in the Trinity, since the mystery of Christ includes that the Son of God took flesh; that He renewed the world through the grace of the Holy Ghost; and again, that He was conceived by the Holy Ghost. Wherefore just as, before Christ, the mystery of Christ was believed explicitly by the learned, but implicitly and under a veil, so to speak, by the simple, so too was it with the mystery of the Trinity. And consequently, when once grace had been revealed, all were bound to explicit faith in the mystery of the Trinity: and all who are born again in Christ, have this bestowed on them by the invocation of the Trinity, according to Matth. xxviii. 19: *Going therefore teach ye all nations, baptizing them in the name of the Father, and of the Son, and of the Holy Ghost.*

Reply Obj. 1. Explicit faith in those two things was necessary at all times and for all people: but it was not sufficient at all times and for all people.

Reply Obj. 2. Before Christ's coming, faith in the Trinity lay hidden in the faith of the learned, but through Christ and the apostles it was shown to the world.

Reply Obj. 3. God's sovereign goodness as we understand it now through its effects, can be understood without the Trinity of Persons: but as understood in itself, and as seen by the Blessed, it cannot be understood without the Trinity of Persons. Moreover the mission of the Divine Persons brings us to heavenly happiness.

Ninth Article. Whether to Believe Is Meritorious?

We proceed thus to the Ninth Article:—

Objection 1. It seems that to believe is not meritorious. For the principle of all merit is charity, as stated above (I.-II., Q. CXIV., A. 4). Now faith, like nature, is a preamble to charity. Therefore, just as an act of nature is not meritorious, since we do not merit by our natural gifts, so neither is an act of faith.

Obj. 2. Further, Belief is a mean between opinion and scientific knowledge or the consideration of things scientifically known. Now the considerations of science are not meritorious, nor on the other hand is opinion. Therefore belief is not meritorious.

Obj. 3. Further, He who assents to a point of faith, either has a sufficient motive for believing, or he has not. If he has a sufficient motive for his belief, this does not seem to imply any merit on his part, since he is no longer free to believe or not to believe: whereas if he has not a sufficient motive for believing, this is a mark of levity, according to Ecclus. xix. 4: *He that is hasty to give credit, is light of heart,* so that, seemingly, he gains no merit thereby. Therefore to believe is by no means meritorious.

On the contrary, It is written (Heb. xi. 33) that the saints *by faith ... obtained promises,* which would not be the case if they did not merit by believing. Therefore to believe is meritorious.

I answer that, As stated above (L-IL., Q. CXIV, AA. 3, 4), our actions are meritorious in so far as they proceed from the free-will moved with grace by God. Therefore every human act proceeding from the free-will, if it be referred to God, can be meritorious. Now the act of believing is an act of the intellect assenting to the Divine truth at the command of the will moved by the grace of God, so that it is subject to the free-will in relation to God; and consequently the act of faith can be meritorious.

Reply Obj. 1. Nature is compared to charity which is the principle of merit, as matter to form: whereas faith is compared to charity as the disposition which precedes the ultimate form. Now it is evident that the subject or the matter cannot act save by virtue of the form, nor can a preceding disposition, before the advent of the form: but after the advent of the form, both the subject and the preceding disposition act by virtue of the form, which is the chief principle of action, even as the heat of fire acts by virtue of the substantial form of fire. Accordingly neither nature nor faith can, without charity, produce a meritorious act; but, when accompanied by charity, the act of faith is made meritorious thereby, even as an act of nature, and a natural act of the free-will.

Reply Obj. 2. Two things may be considered in science; namely, the scientist's assent to a scientific fact, and his consideration of that fact. Now the assent of science is not subject to free-will, because the scientist is obliged to assent by the force of the demonstration, wherefore scientific assent is not meritorious. But the actual consideration of what a man knows scientifically is subject to his free-will for it is in his power to consider or not to consider. Hence scientific consideration may be meritorious if it be referred to the end of charity, i.e. to the honour of God or the good of our neighbour. On the other hand, in the case of faith, both these things are subject to the free-will, so that in both respects the act of faith can be meritorious: whereas in the case of opinion, there is no firm assent, since it is weak and infirm, as the Philosopher observes (*Poster.* i.), so that it does not seem to proceed from a perfect act of the will: and for this reason, as regards the assent, it does not appear to be very meritorious, though it can be as regards the actual consideration.

Reply Obj. 3. The believer has sufficient motive for believing, for he is moved by the authority of Divine teaching confirmed by miracles, and, what is more, by the inward instinct of the Divine invitation: hence he does not believe lightly. He has not, however, sufficient reason for scientific knowledge, hence he does not lose the merit....

Third Article. Whether Charity Is the Form of Faith?
We proceed thus to the Third Article:—

Objection 1. It seems that charity is not the form of faith. For each thing derives its species from its form. When, therefore, two things are opposite members of a division, one cannot be the form of the other. Now faith and charity are stated to be opposite members of a division, as different species of virtue (I Cor. xiii. 13). Therefore charity is not the form of faith.

Obj. 2. Further, A form and the thing of which it is the form are in one subject, since together they form one simply. Now faith is in the intellect, while charity is in the will. Therefore charity is not the form of faith.

Obj. 3. Further, The form of a thing is a principle thereof. Now obedience, rather than charity, seems to be the principle of believing, on the part of the will, according to Rom. i. 5: *For obedience to the faith in all nations.* Therefore obedience rather than charity, is the form of faith.

On the contrary, Each thing works through its form. Now faith works through charity. Therefore the love of charity is the form of faith.

I answer that, As appears from what has been said above (I.-II., Q. I, A. 3: Q. XVIII., A. 6), voluntary acts take their species from their end which is the will's object. Now that which gives a thing its species, is after the manner of a form in natural things. Wherefore the form of any voluntary act is, in a manner, the end to which that act is directed, both because it takes its species therefrom, and because the mode of an action should correspond proportionately to the end. Now it is evident from what has been said (A. I), that the act of faith is directed to the object of the will, i.e. the good, as to its end: and this good which is the end of faith, viz. the Divine Good, is the proper object of charity. Therefore charity is called the form of faith, in so far as the act of faith is perfected and formed by charity.

Reply Obj. 1. Charity is called the form of faith because it quickens the act of faith. Now nothing hinders one act from being quickened by different habits, so as to be reduced to various species in a certain order, as stated above (I.-II., Q. XVIII., AA. 6, 7: Q. LXL., A. 2) when we were treating of human acts in general.

Reply Obj. 2. This objection is true of an intrinsic form. But it is not thus that charity is the form of faith, but in the sense that it *quickens the act of faith*, as explained above.

Reply Obj. 3. Even obedience, and hope likewise, and whatever other virtue might precede the act of faith, is quickened by charity, as we shall show further on (Q. XXIII., A. 8), and consequently charity is spoken of as the form of faith....

Fifth Article. Whether Faith Is a Virtue?
We proceed thus to the Fifth Article:—

Objection 1. It seems that faith is not a virtue. For virtue is directed to the good, since *it is virtue that makes its subject good,* as the Philosopher states *(Ethic.* ii.). But faith is directed to the true. Therefore faith is not a virtue.

Obj. 2. Further, Infused virtue is more perfect than acquired virtue. Now faith, on account of its imperfection, is not placed among the acquired intellectual virtues, as the Philosopher states *(Ethic.* vi.). Much less, therefore, can it be considered an infused virtue.

Obj. 3. Further, Living and lifeless faith are of the same species, as stated above (A. 4). Now lifeless faith is not a virtue, since it is not connected with the other virtues. Therefore neither is living faith a virtue.

Obj. 4. Further, The gratuitous graces and the fruits are distinct from the virtues. But faith is numbered among the gratuitous graces (I Cor. xii. 9) and likewise among the fruits (Gal. v. 23). Therefore faith is not a virtue.

On the contrary, Man is justified by the virtues, since *justice is all virtue* as the Philosopher states *(Ethic.* v.). Now man is justified by faith according to Rom. v. I: *Being justified therefore by faith let us have peace,* etc. Therefore faith is a virtue.

I answer that, As shown above, it is by human virtue that human acts are rendered good; hence, any habit that is always the principle of a good act, may be called a human virtue. Such a habit is living faith. For since to believe is an act of the intellect assenting to the truth at the command of the will, two things are required that this act may be perfect: one of which is that the intellect should infallibly tend to its object, which is the true; while the other is that the will should be infallibly directed to the last end, on account of which it assents to the true: and both of these are to be found in the act of living faith. For it belongs to the very essence of faith that the intellect should ever tend to the true, since nothing false can be the object of faith, as proved above (Q. I, A. 3): while the effect of charity, which is the form of faith, is that the soul ever has its will directed to a good end. Therefore living faith is a virtue.

On the other hand, lifeless faith is not a virtue, because, though the act of lifeless faith is duly perfect on the part of the intellect, it has not its due perfection as regards the will: just as if temperance be in the concupiscible, without prudence being in the rational part, temperance is not a virtue, as stated above (I.-II., Q. LXV., A. 1), because the act of temperance requires both an act of reason, and an act of the concupiscible faculty, even as the act of faith requires an act of the will, and an act of the intellect.

Reply Obj. 1. The truth is itself the good of the intellect, since it is its perfection: and consequently faith has a relation to some good in so far as it directs the intellect to the true. Furthermore, it has a relation to the good considered as the object of the will, inasmuch as it is formed by charity.

Reply Obj. 2. The faith of which the Philosopher speaks is based on human reasoning in a conclusion which does not follow, of necessity, from its premisses; and which is subject to be false: hence suchlike faith is not a virtue. On the other hand, the faith of which we are speaking is based on the Divine Truth, which is infallible, and consequently its object cannot be anything false; so that faith of this kind can be a virtue.

Reply Obj. 3. Living and lifeless faith do not differ specifically, as though they belonged to different species. But they differ as perfect and imperfect within the same species. Hence lifeless faith, being imperfect, does not satisfy the conditions of a perfect virtue, for virtue is a kind of perfection (Phys. vii.).

Reply Obj. 4. Some say that faith which is numbered among the gratuitous graces is lifeless faith. But this is said without reason, since the gratuitous graces, which are mentioned in that passage, are not common to all the members of the Church: where fore the Apostle says: *There are diversities of graces,* and again: *To one is given* this grace and *to another* that. Now lifeless faith is common to all the members of the Church, because its lifelessness is not part of its substance, if we consider it as a gratuitous gift. We must, therefore, say that in that passage, faith denotes a certain excellency of faith, for instance, *constancy in faith,* according to a gloss, or the *word of faith.*

Faith is numbered among the fruits, in so far as it gives a certain pleasure in its act by reason of its certainty, wherefore the gloss on the fifth chapter to the Galatians, where the fruits are enumerated, explains faith as being *certainty about the unseen....*

Second Article. Whether in the Demons There Is Faith?
We proceed thus to the Second Article:—

Objection 1. It seems that the demons have no faith. For Augustine says *(De Pradest. Sanct. v.)* that *faith depends on the believe's will.* and this is a good will, since by it man wishes to believe in God. Since then no deliberate will of the demons is good, as stated above (P. I, Q. LXIV., A. 2, *ad 5),* it seems that in the demons there is no faith.

Obj. 2. Further, Faith is a gift of Divine grace, according to Eph. ii. 8: *By grace you are saved through faith, . . . for it is the gift of God.* Now, according to a gloss on Osee iii. I, *They look to strange gods, and love the husks of the grapes,* the demons lost their gifts of grace by sinning. Therefore faith did not remain in the demons after they sinned.

Obj. 3. Further, Unbelief would seem to be graver than other sins, as Augustine observes *(Tract.* lxxxix.. *super Joan.)* on John xv. *22, If I had not come and spoken to them, they would not have sin: but now they have no excuse for their sin.* Now the sin of unbelief is in some men. Consequently, if the demons have faith, some men would be guilty of a sin graver than demons, which seems unreasonable. Therefore in the demons there is no faith.

On the contrary, It is written (James ii. 19): *The devils ... believe and tremble.*

I answer that, As stated above (Q. I, A. 4: Q. II, A. 1), the believer's intellect assents to that which he believes, not because he sees it either in itself, or by resolving it to first self-evident principles, but because his will commands his intellect to assent. Now, that the will moves the intellect to assent, may be due to two causes. First, through the will being directed to the good, and in this way, to believe is a praiseworthy action. Secondly, because the intellect is convinced that it ought to believe what is said, though that conviction is not based on objective evidence. Thus if a prophet, while preaching the word of God, were to foretell something, and were to give a sign, by raising a dead person to life, the intellect of a witness would be convinced so as to recognize clearly that God, Who lieth not, was speaking, although the thing itself foretold would not be evident in itself, and consequently the essence of faith would not be removed.

Accordingly we must say that faith is commended in the first sense in the faithful of Christ: and in this way faith is not in the demons, but only in the second way, for they see many evident signs, whereby they recognize that the teaching of the Church is from God, although they do not see the things themselves that the Church teaches, for instance that there are three Persons in God, and so forth.

Reply Obj. 1. The demons are, in a way, compelled to believe, by the evidence of signs, and so their will deserves no praise for their belief.

Reply Obj. 2. Faith, which is a gift of grace, inclines man to believe, by giving him a certain affection for the good, even when that faith is lifeless. Consequently the faith which the demons have, is not a gift of grace. Rather are they compelled to believe through their natural intellectual acumen.

Reply Obj. 3. The very fact that the signs of faith are so evident, that the demons are compelled to believe, is displeasing to them, so that their malice is by no means diminished by their belief.

Questions

1. What sort of knowledge does natural reason supply regarding God?

2. Why does Thomas Aquinas think that faith is a necessary supplement to reason?

3. What sort of relationship does Aquinas think holds between faith and reason? Which if either comes first?

4. If God is the source of all truth, does Aquinas think that science could ever be in conflict with the claims of religious faith?

5. What sort of formula is Thomas Aquinas finally offering for reason and faith?

JONATHAN EDWARDS AND THE HEART[*]

William J. Wainwright

Jonathan Edwards, the subject of this paper, is both an heir to the strong emphasis upon reason found in the Modern Period, but also to the Reformed Tradition which had such a strong distrust of humanity's natural capacities. The purpose of Wainwright is to "weave" the two elements together in a reason-and-the-heart way through an evidentialist/foundationalist approach, where belief must rest on the sufficiency of the evidence, and where evidence must be met with the passion of the heart.

Jonathan Edwards was strongly influenced by continental rationalists such as Malebranche, by some of the Cambridge Platonists (Henry More, for example), and by the empiricists (especially Locke). He was also excited by Newton and the new science. Although these traditions were diverse, they had an important feature in common—an almost uncritical confidence in reason's power and scope. Edwards's practice reflects this confidence. Philosophical arguments are deployed to demolish critics, justify the principal Christian doctrines, and erect a speculative metaphysics (a subjective idealism like Berkeley's). But Edwards was also a Calvinist who shared the Reformed tradition's distrust of humanity's natural capacities and its skepticism about natural theology.

The impact of these diverse strands is reflected in the apparent ambiguity of Edwards's remarks on reason. Thus, on the one hand, he can say that, "arguing for the being of a God according to the natural powers from everything we are conversant with is short, easy, and what we naturally fall into" (Misc. 268, T 78)[1] or claim that we can know that a just God governs the world by the "light of nature." Conscience that sees "the relation and agreement there is between that which is wrong or unjust and punishment" and finds unpunished wrongs "shocking" naturally leads us to conclude that God is "a just being" (Misc. 353, T 110-111). Yet he can also insist that, in thinking about God, reason is baffled by "mystery," "paradox,"

---

[*] This article is reprinted by courtesy of the author and Cornell University Press. It is from Chapter I (pp. 7-54) of *Reason and the Heart, A Prolegomena to a Critique of Passional Reason*, by William Wainwright, *Cornell Studies in Philosophy of Religion*, 1995.

[1] Jonathan Edwards's principal discussions of reason are located in the "Miscellanies" (a number of which can be found in *The Philosophy of Jonathan Edwards from His Private Notebooks*, ed. Harvey G. Townsend [Eugene, Ore.: University of Oregon Monographs, 1955], hereafter Misc. T; "A Divine and Supernatural Light" and "Miscellaneous Observations" (in *The Works of President Edwards* [New York: B. Franklin, 1968; reprint of the Leeds edition reissued with a two-volume supplement in Edinburgh, 1847], vol. VIII), hereafter DSL and Misc. Obs., respectively; "The Mind," "Subjects to Be Handled in the Treatise on the Mind," and "Of the Prejudices of Imagination" (in *Scientific and Philosophical Writings*, ed. Wallace E. Anderson [New Haven: Yale University Press, 1980], hereafter *Mind, Subjects, and Prejudices*, respectively; and *Original Sin* (Boston 1758; reprint, New Haven: Yale University Press, 1970), hereafter *OS*. Other relevant material can be found in *Religious Affections* (Boston 1746; reprint, New Haven: Yale University Press, 1959), hereafter *RA*; *The Nature of True Virtue* (Boston 1765; reprinted in *Ethical Writings*, ed. Paul Ramsey [New Haven: Yale University Press, 1989], hereafter *TV*; and *History of the Work of Redemption* (Edinburgh, 1774; reprint, New Haven: Yale University Press, 1989), hereafter *HR*. The "Miscellaneous Observations" must he used with caution. It was originally published in 1793 and consists of material from the "Miscellanies." The editor (John Erskine) "took great liberties with the text, disregarded all chronological order, patched together widely separated excerpts, and added whatever connections or conjunctions seemed appropriate to him" (Townsend, *Philosophy of Edwards*, p. xi, n. 14).

and "seeming inconsistence." (Examples are an omnipresence without extension, an immutability [which Edwards thinks implies duration] without succession, and the idea of a "perfect knowledge of all...things of external sense, without any sensation or any reception of ideas from without" [Misc. 1340, T 231].) Even though "the invisible things of God are indeed to be understood by the things that are made," uninstructed reason invariably errs (Misc. 986, T 212). It is "almost impossible [for example] for unassisted reason" to demonstrate "that the world, and all things contained therein, are effects, and had a beginning." A person who was "left to himself" "would be apt to reason" that because causes and effects must be "similar and conformable, matter must have a material cause" and "evil and irregularity...must be attributed to an evil and unwise cause." Indeed, without assistance, "the best reasoner in the world...might be led into the grossest errors and contradictions" (Misc. Obs., 185-86). If "God never speaks to or converses at all with mankind," we would most likely think "there is no being that made and governs the world" or that, if there is, it is not "properly an intelligent, volitive being" (Misc. 1298, T 218).

Even though Edwards thinks that reason *can* prove God's existence, determine the nature of many of His attributes, discern our obligations to Him, and establish the credibility of scripture, he believes that grace is needed both to help "the natural principles against those things that tend to stupefy it and to hinder its free exercise" (Misc. 626, T 111) and to "sanctify the reasoning faculty and assist it to see the clear evidence there is of the truth of religion in rational arguments" (Misc. 628, T 251).

In many respects, Edwards simply restates Puritan commonplaces. Although they conceded that "some of the things 'plainly proved' by scripture could also be detected by the 'light of natural reason,'" Puritans emphasized reason's powerlessness.[2] Robert Bolton, for instance, thought that if "a man looke upon Gods wayes onely with the eye of reason they are foolishnesse to him." Thomas Adams said, "there is no greater ods in the world than betweene our owne reason and God's wisdome." Peter Sterry maintained that "To seek out spiritual things by the scent and sagacity of reason were to plough with an Oxe and an Asse.... You cannot reach the things of reason by the hand of sense...You cannot understand spirituall things Rationally.... Some say, that all truths which come by revelation of the Spirit, may also be demonstrated by Reason. But if they be, they are then no more Divine, but humane truths; They lose their certainty, beauty, *efficacy*;...Spirituall truths discovered by demonstrations of Reason, are like the Mistresse in her Cook-maid's clothes." According to the great Puritan divine William Perkins, one "must reject his owne naturall reason, and stoppe up the eyes of his naturall minde, like a blinde man, and suffer himselfe wholly to be guided by God's spirit in the things of God." And the Puritan mystic Francis Rous commended those who "have ... quenched their owne naturall lamps, that they might get them kindled above by the Father of Lights."[3]

As John Morgan points out, Puritan strictures on reason reflect the Reformed (and ultimately Augustinian and Pauline) insistence on human corruption. Reason is not exempt from the consequences of the Fall. Although natural reason may discover some truths about God (along with many errors), it is incapable of grasping His saving actions on our behalf. Puritan

---

[2] John Morgan, *Godly Learning; Puritan Attitudes towards Reason, Learning and Education* (Cambridge: Cambridge University Press, 1986), p. 51.

[3] The quotations from Bolton, Adams, Perkins, and Rous are found in ibid.., pp. 51-53. The quotation from Sterry is found in Geoffrey F. Nuttall, *The Holy Spirit in Puritan Faith and Experience,* 2d ed. (Chicago: University of Chicago Press, 1992), p.37.

strictures also reflect their emphasis on an "experimental knowledge" of God's favor toward us. According to Arthur Dent, "the knowledge of the reprobate is like the knowledge which a mathematicall geographer hath of the earth and all the places in it, which is but a generall notion and a speculative comprehension of them. But the knowledge of the elect is like the knowledge of a traveller which can speake of experience and feeling, and hath beene there and seene and knowen the particulars."[4] Or, as William Baxter said;

> I do, therefore, neither despise evidence as unnecessary, nor trust to it alone as the sufficient total cause of my belief; for if God's grace do not open mine eyes, and come down in power upon my will, and insinuate into it a sweet acquaintance with the things unseen, and a taste of their goodness to delight my soul, no reasons will serve to stablish and comfort me, however undeniable soever; the way to have the firmest belief of the Christian faith, is to draw near and taste, and try it, and lay bare the heart to receive the impression of it, and then, by the sense of its admirable effects, we shall know that which bare speculation could not discover.[5]

Edwards shares these attitudes. What distinguishes him from other Puritan divines is not his learning or use of philosophical resources[6] but his philosophical acumen and the fact that the intellectual currents that most influenced him (continental rationalism and British empiricism) are those that have both shaped modern philosophy and underlie the dominant view of rationality.

The following sections explore Edwards's position in detail. The first discusses his remarks on mystery and paradox and defends the claim that Edwards believed in the possibility of natural theology. The second examines his discussion of the sense of the heart, and the third shows why Edwards thought that grace is needed to reason properly.

I. The Possibility of Natural Theology

Edwards's remarks about mystery, paradox, and the impossibility of discovering spiritual truths do not preclude natural theology. The inconsistencies Edwards alludes to, for instance, are only "*seeming* inconsistencies" and "*seeming* contradictions" (my emphases); they are not real ones. And the only sense in which theology is incomprehensible is that we lack "clear ideas of the things that are the subject of" its truths (Misc. 1100, T 234).[7] We know *that* God necessarily exists, for example, but not *how* this can be true. Or we know "that the Godhead was united to man so as to be properly looked upon [as] the same person" but not "how it was effected" (Misc. 1340, T 234).[7]

But the most important point is this. "Paradox" and "incomprehensibility" also characterize other disciplines whose credentials are beyond dispute. Mathematical truths concerning "surd quantities and fluxions" are incomprehensible in the same sense, and "the reasonings and conclusions of the best metaphysicians and mathematicians concerning infinities are attended with paradoxes and seeming inconsistencies" (Misc. 1100, T 213; Misc. 1340, T 230). Philosophy provides other examples. Reason cannot "comprehend, or explain, or show, or

---

[4] Quoted in Morgan, *Godly Learning*, p. 59.
[5] Quoted in Nuttall, *Holy Spirit*, p.47.
[6] In spite of their strictures on reason., Puritans insisted on a learned clergy, and Puritan divines commonly drew on the ancient philosophers, the schoolmen, Ramus, and so on.
[7] At one point, Edwards glosses "inconsistent" and incomprehensible" as (merely) "contrary to what would be expected" (Misc. 1340, T 232).

conceive of any way that" minds and bodies can interact although it is obvious that they do (Misc. 1340, T 222). And when we attempt to formulate idealism (which Edwards. believes to be both true and demonstrable), "we have got so far beyond those things for which language was chiefly contrived, that *unless we use extreme caution* we cannot speak...without literally contradicting ourselves" (*Mind* 355, my emphasis).

Paradoxes attend these disciplines because they deal with matters remote from "the common business and vulgar affairs of life, things obvious to sense and men's direct view" Their subject matters are not "the objects and affairs which earthly language was made to express," and the truths they discern "are not agreeable to such notions ... and ways of thinking that grow up with us and are connatural to us" (Misc. 1340, T 227-28). The difficulties that attend theology are no greater in kind (although greater in degree) than those attending other disciplines dealing with "high" and "abstract" matters. It would be as illegitimate to conclude that natural or revealed theology is impossible, then, as to conclude that mathematics or metaphysics are.

Edwards's remarks concerning the impossibility of knowing God apart from revelation should be treated with the same caution. The following is typical. If people are not "led by revelation and direct teaching into a right way of using their reason, in arguing from effects to causes, etc., they would remain forever in the most woeful doubt and uncertainty concerning the nature and the very being of God. This appears not only by the state of the heathen world ... but also by what appears among those who in these late ages have renounced divine revelation, even the wisest and greatest of 'em," such as Hobbes, Toland, Shaftesbury, and Hume (Misc. 1297, T 214).

I believe that Edwards wishes to make two points. The first is that "uninstructed" reason is powerless; no one is capable of erecting the fabric of *any* discipline on his or her own. The second is that we are powerless to *discover* theological truths although reason can *demonstrate* the truth of (many of) them *after* they have been revealed. Neither implies the impossibility of natural theology.

Miscellany 1297 is instructive. "The state of the heathen world" and "what appears among...the wisest and greatest of" the modern "deistical writers" shows that men and women who are not "led by revelation and direct teaching" fall into error. But the deists' errors are greater than those made by people "before the Gospel." For the heathen philosophers did not despise the revelation they had "by tradition from their ancestors, the ancient founders of nations, or from the Jews, which led 'em to embrace many truths contained in the Scripture." Nor did they reject everything beyond their comprehension. The ancients were willing to learn from tradition and to accept truths they did not fully understand, because they did not "proceed in" the deists' "exceeding haughtiness and dependence on their own mere singular understanding, disdaining all dependence on teaching." Nor did they "proceed with" the deists' "enmity against moral and divine truth having not been so irritated by it" (T 214, 217-18).

Sound reasoning is a social product. It presupposes instruction in an intellectual tradition and membership in a community that shares it. Intellectual traditions include beliefs about a subject matter, methods for resolving problems concerning it, and shared values that guide the process of inquiry. Traditions are not static. Beliefs are dropped and added. Sometimes the community is forced to modify its values or revise its methods of investigation.[8] Contributions to this process, however, are normally restricted to those who have been initiated into the community and have thus mastered its intellectual traditions, employ its methods of inquiry, and

---

[8] Consider, for example, the shift in interest from taxonomy and classification to developmental explanations that occurs between the eighteenth and nineteenth centuries or increasing refinements in sampling techniques.

share its values.⁹ As Edwards's remarks, "knowledge bears an exact proportion to instruction. Why [else] does the learned and well educated reason better than the mere citizen?...There is no fallacy more gross than to imagine reason, utterly untaught and undisciplined, capable of the same attainments in knowledge as reason well refined and instructed" (Misc. Obs. 186).

Contributions to science or philosophy, for example, are seldom made by outsiders. Isolated reason is impotent. If we stand aloof from the scientific or philosophical community and (relying only on our "own singular understandings") refuse to accept anything we have not worked out on our own or fully understood, we are not likely to contribute to science or philosophy, or even to understand them. If we are also hostile to them, we are still less likely to do so. Why should religion be different? Why suppose that those who cut themselves off from the religious community and its intellectual traditions,¹⁰ rely only on their own reasonings, refuse to accept anything they have not fully understood, and are indifferent to religion or hostile to it are likely to establish truths about God?

Viable religious traditions are unlike other intellectual traditions, however, in one important respect. They can only be inaugurated by God. "In ordinary articles of knowledge, our sense and experience furnish reason with ideas and principles to work on.... But in respect to God, it can have no right idea nor axiom to set out with, till he is pleased to reveal it" (Misc. Obs. 186). "That the ancient philosophers and wiser heathen had so good notions of God as they had seems to be much more owing to tradition, which originated from divine revelation, than from their own invention" (Misc. 1340, T 231-32). Revelation is needed because "the first principles of religion, being of a high and spiritual nature, are harder to be found out than those of any other science...the minds of men are gross and earthly, used to objects of sense; and all their depraved appetites and corrupt dispositions, which are by nature opposite to true religion, help to increase the natural weakness of their reason" (Misc. Obs. 193).

Nevertheless, "it is one thing" to "strike upon" a point, and quite another "to work out a demonstration of" it "once it is proposed" (Misc. Obs. 185). "It is very needful that God should declare unto mankind what manner of being he is," but reason "is sufficient to confirm such a declaration after it is given, and enable us to see its consistence, harmony, and rationality, in many respects" (Misc. Obs. 217). "After once suggested and delivered," God's declarations are seen to be "agreeable to reason" (Misc. 1340, T 232). That there is only one God, for example, "is what we, now the gospel has so taught us, can see to be truth by our own reason...it can easily be shown by reason to be demonstrably true" (*HR* 398-99).

What Edwards denies is that correct ideas of God would have occurred to us if humanity had been left to its own devices. Whether this is true or not¹¹ is irrelevant to the possibility of

---

⁹ See Basil Mitchell, *The Justification of Religious Belief* (London: Macmillan, 1973), chap. 7.

¹⁰ But *which* community? There is no agreement on paradigms. The situation in religion resembles the current state of the social sciences or the situation in the physical sciences in the sixteenth and early seventeenth centuries. (See Gary Gutting, "Paradigms and Hermeneutics: A Dialogue on Kuhn, Rorty, and the Social Sciences," *American Philosophical Quarterly* 21 [1984], 1-16.) Even in cases like these, however, a person is not likely to do good work if he or she stands aloof from *all* traditions or is hostile to *all* science. One should also consider the possibility (of which I am skeptical) that the world's religions are converging toward a single tradition or community that will incorporate earlier ones. (See John Hick and Wilfred Cantwell Smith on this point.) Edwards assumes that the Christian tradition is paradigmatic. If it is, the analogy is strengthened.

¹¹ Could not human beings *construct* the idea of God? Is it not probable that (as Hume, Feuerbach, and Freud argued) a weak, needy, and frightened humanity would invent ideas of supernatural beings? Edwards would undoubtedly agree with Calvin and Barth. Without supernatural assistance, the mind only manufactures idols—magnified images of itself, projections of its own hopes and fears. Edwards's criterion of idolatry would, of course, be the extent to which an idea of God conforms to Christian revelation. A nontheological (and possibly more

natural theology. For the process of discovery is *in general* nonrational. (There are no rational procedures for discovering illuminating new scientific hypotheses, for example, or perspicacious interpretations of literary texts.) Whatever their origins, reason has ideas of God. Having them, it can show that they are not fictions; the truths of natural religion (that God exists, that He is sovereign, righteous, and so on) are demonstrable.

Natural reason can also ascertain that scripture is God's revelation and, knowing this, it can learn truths it could not acquire in other ways.

"Divine testimony" cannot be opposed to reason, evidence, or argument because it is a *rule* of reason, a *kind* of evidence, and a *type* of argument like the "human testimony of credible eye-witnesses," "credible history," "memory," "present experience," "geometrical mensuration," "arithmetical calculation," and "strict metaphysical distinction and comparison" (Misc. Obs. 228).[12] The statement that "Scripture is reliable" resembles such rules as "The testimony of our senses may be depended on," "The agreed testimony of all we see and converse with continually is to be credited," and "The testimony of history and tradition is to be depended on, when attended with such and such credible circumstances" (Misc. 1340, T 221). Principles such as these can be established, or at least certified, by reason[13] and then used to establish other truths that cannot be established without their help ("Fire engines are red," for example, or "Christ atoned for our sins").

That reason can be appropriately used to assess the credentials of a rule of reasoning does not imply that opinions formed by a reason that does not employ the rule can be used to determine the truth or falsity of opinions established *by* its means. The naked eye, for example, "determines the goodness and sufficiency" of the optic glass, yet it would be absurd for a person to "credit no representation made by the glass, wherein the glass differs from his eye" and to refuse to believe, "that the blood consists partly of red particles and partly of limpid liquor because it all appears red to the naked eye" (Misc. Obs. 227). It would be equally absurd to reject truths that can be established by a reason that employs the rule "Memories are generally reliable" because what memory reports cannot be established by a reason that does not. It is just as unreasonable to discount what can be discovered by a reason that employs the rule that scripture is credible on the grounds that truths learned in this way cannot be established by a reason that rejects it.[14]

---

persuasive) version of his argument might be this: Religious ideas cannot be adequately explained without appealing to religious experiences that are sui generis (Otto's numinous feelings, for example, or mystical experiences), or, more strongly, they cannot be adequately explained without appealing to *veridical* religious experiences.

[12] Edwards does not clearly distinguish between evidence, argument, and rule of reason. The distinction is presumably this: Apparent memories are a type of evidence, justifying claims by appealing to memory is a type of argument, and the appropriate rule is "One's memories are normally reliable." Similarly, the contents of scripture are a type of evidence, justifying claims by appealing to scripture is a type of argument, and the appropriate rule is "Scripture is trustworthy."

[13] Edwards says, for example, that "general propositions" such as "Memory is dependable" "can be known only by reason" (Misc. 1340, T 220). Unfortunately, he does not explain *how* reason knows them. Are there arguments? Are the rules expressions of something like Hume's natural beliefs or Reid's inborn belief dispositions? Does the answer differ from case to case? One test of a rule's rationality is whether the results of applying it agree with the results of applying other rules. A check on the credibility of sense experience, for example, is "the agreement of the testimonies of the senses with other criteria of truth" (Misc. Obs. 230).

[14] Edwards does not discuss instances of apparent conflict—cases in which the results of appropriately applying a rule conflict with the results of appropriately applying others. For example, we sometimes discount memory when it conflicts with the testimony of others. Or testimony is rejected when it conflicts with our perceptual experience. We presumably use some (rough) hierarchy of rules to adjudicate conflicts of this kind. We also refine rules as a result of experience. We learn, for example, when memory is reliable and when it is not. Of special interest are cases in which

Although this passage does not explain *how* "Scripture is credible" can be established or certified, what Edwards has in mind is reasonably clear. The strongest evidence for scripture's divine authority is its spiritual beauty—a feature that natural reason cannot detect. Only those with converted hearts can perceive, taste, and relish the stamp of divine splendor on scripture and thus be *certain* of its teachings. (More on this shortly.) The unsanctified are nonetheless capable of acquiring a *probable* conviction of their truth. Scripture's authority is certified by miracles and fulfilled prophecy, the harmony between revealed and natural religion, scripture's beneficial effect on morality, and so on.[15] "None will doubt," says Edwards, "but that some natural men do yield a kind of assent...to the truths of the Christian religion, from the rational proofs or arguments that are offered to evince it" (*RA* 295). Probabilistic arguments for the truth of the gospel can be drawn from history, and "lately...these...have been set in a clear and convincing light" by the "learned" (*RA* 305). By exercising its natural faculties, reason can know that scripture is God's declaration and can therefore use "Scripture is reliable" as a rule to extend its knowledge.

Natural reason is thus capable of establishing the authority of scripture as well as the truths of natural religion. Why, then, does it so often find it difficult to do so? Not because the *evidence* is not obvious enough. Because these truths nearly concern us, God would not be good if He had not clearly declared them[16] (*OS* 155-57). We have sufficient "means of knowledge," therefore, as well as "a sufficient capacity" (*OS* 148). What is lacking is "a disposition to improve" the "light" God has given us (*OS* 149).

The following two sections examine the ways in which grace repairs our damaged dispositions. The role that moral and spiritual virtues play in sound reasoning about divine matters will become evident as we proceed.

II. The Sense of the Heart

Jonathan Edwards is well known for his insistence on a "practical," or "experimental," religion that engages the human heart. At its core is a sense of God's excellence and loveliness, or of the beauty and splendor of divine things.

The savingly converted enjoy "gracious discoveries" of "God, in some of his sweet and glorious attributes manifested in the gospel, and shining forth in the face of Christ"—for example, "the all-sufficiency of the mercy and grace of God" or "the infinite power of God, and his ability to save them.... In some, the truth and certainty of the Gospel in general is the first joyful discovery they have.... More frequently Christ is distinctly made the object of the mind, in his all-sufficiency and willingness to save sinners" (*FN* 171).[17] Recalling his own conversion, Edwards says:

---

scripture appears to conflict with the results of applying rules such as "The testimony of history and tradition is to be depended on" (the question of the historicity of *Daniel* or *Esther,* for example) or the results of employing "strict metaphysical distinction and comparison." Edwards thinks that conflicts like these are only apparent and undoubtedly believes that "Scripture is reliable" takes precedence over other rules. Nevertheless, one wishes that he had discussed the issue more thoroughly.

[15] These arguments were commonly employed in the eighteenth century. For one of the better examples, see Samuel Clarke's *A Discourse concerning the Unchangeable Obligations of Natural Religion and the Truth and Certainty of the Christian Revelation* (London, 1706), especially Propositions VII-XV.

[16] That the evidence is intrinsically clear is confirmed by the fact that it seems clear when the scales of *sin* are removed from our eyes.

[17] Edwards's discussions of the sense of the heart are located in *The Nature of True Virtue* and the "Miscellanies." For other relevant material, see *A Faithful Narrative of the Surprising Work of God, in the*

> The first instance that I remember of that sort of inward, sweet delight in God and divine things that I have lived much in since, was on reading those words, I Tim. i. 17. *Now unto the King eternal, immortal, invisible, the only wise God, be honor and glory for ever and ever, Amen.* As I read the words, there came into my soul, and was as it were diffused through it, a sense of the glory of the Divine Being; a new sense, quite different from any thing I ever experienced before. Never any words of scripture seemed to me as these words did. I thought with myself, how excellent a Being that was and how, happy I should be, if I might enjoy that God, and be rapt up to him in heaven, and be as it were swallowed up in him for ever! (*PN* 59).

Again, Edwards tells us, "I remember the thoughts I used then to have of holiness.... It appeared to me, that there, was nothing in it but what was ravishingly lovely; the highest beauty and amiableness...a *divine* beauty; far purer than anything here upon earth" (*PN* 63). "God," he says, "has appeared to me a glorious and lovely Being, chiefly on account of his holiness.... The doctrines of God's absolute sovereignty, and free grace, in showing mercy to whom he would show mercy; and man's absolute dependence on the operations of God's Holy Spirit, have very often appeared to me as sweet and glorious doctrines. These doctrines have been much my delight" (*PN* 67).

Some express their new experiences by the terms "sight or discovery," others by "a lively or feeling sense of heart" (*FN* 171-72). Both expressions refer to a new understanding of spiritual notions. Those who have these experiences find that phrases such as "a spiritual sight of Christ," "faith in Christ," "poverty of spirit," and so on, had not previously conveyed "those special and distinct ideas to their minds which they were intended to signify; in some respects no more than the names of colors are to convey the ideas to one that is blind from birth" (*FN* 174). But now "things of religion" seem "new to them...preaching is a new thing...the bible is a new book" (*FN* 181). Indeed, "the light and comfort which some of them enjoy...causes all things about 'em to appear as it were beautiful, sweet and pleasant to them: all things abroad, the sun, moon and stars, the clouds and sky, the heavens and earth, appear as it were with a cast of divine glory and sweetness upon them" (*FN* 183).

This section examines Edwards's attempt to make philosophical and theological sense of these experiences. It is divided into six parts. The first two discuss the nature of the idea of spiritual beauty and Edwards's reasons for thinking that our apprehension of beauty is a kind of sensation or perception. The third explores the implications of Edwards's theory for the epistemic status of religious belief, and the fourth and fifth examine his defense of the objectivity of the new "spiritual sense." The last part explores the bearing of Edwards's remarks on current discussions.

A. A New Simple Idea

The objects of a sense or feeling of the heart are (1) "actual [i.e., lively, clear, and distinct] ideas," (2) of things pertaining to the will or affections, (3) that involve a "feeling of sweetness

---

Conversion of Many Hundred Souls..., and *The Distinguishing Marks of a Work of the Spirit of God* (respectively, Boston, 1737; Boston 1741; both reprinted in *The Great Awakening,* ed. C. C. Goen [New Haven: Yale University Press, 1972]), hereafter *FN* and *DM,* respectively; "A Divine and Supernatural Light"; "The Mind"; and "Personal Narrative" *(Jonathan Edwards: Representative Selections,* ed. Clarence H. Faust and Thomas H. Johnson [New York: American Book Co., 1935]), hereafter *PN.*

or pleasure, or of bitterness or pains." They include (the ideas of)[18] (1) "beauty and deformity," "good or evil," as well as "excellency," "value," "importance" and their opposites, (2) delight and pleasure and pain and misery, (3) affective and conative attitudes, dispositions, and states ("desires and longings, esteem...hope, fear, contempt, choosing, refusing...loving, hating, anger," (4) "dignity," "terrible greatness, or awful majesty," "meanness or contemptibleness," and so on, and (5) the nonevaluative characteristics on which beauty and deformity, pleasure and pain, and attributes such as dignity or majesty depend.[19] The object of a sense or feeling of the heart is, in essence, good and evil, and what pertains to it. Natural good or evil is "good or evil which is agreeable or disagreeable to human nature as such." Spiritual good or evil is what is agreeable or disagreeable to people with "spiritual frames," that is, to those who, because the Spirit dwells within them, love being in general (i.e., God and the beings that derive from Him, are absolutely dependent on Him, and reflect Him) (Misc. 782, T 113-26).

The "immediate object of this spiritual sense" is "the beauty of holiness" (RA 260), "the spiritual excellency, beauty, or sweetness of divine things" (Misc. 782), "true moral or spiritual beauty" (TV 548), "the highest and primary beauty" (TV 561)—a "new simple idea" that cannot be produced by the "exalting, varying or compounding of that kind of perceptions or sensations which the mind had before" (RA 205).

What kind of idea is this? Or, put another way, what does Edwards mean by "(true) beauty?" His remarks are open to at least three interpretations: that (1) "beauty" refers to the delight or pleasure that holy things evoke in people with spiritual "frames" or "tempers," (2) "beauty" refers to a dispositional property, the tendency of holy things to produce this pleasure or delight in the converted, and (3) "beauty" designates a love of being in general, that is, the consent of being to being that holiness consists in.

There is some evidence that Edwards held the first or second view. He asserts, for example; that "That form or quality is called 'beautiful,'...the view or idea of which is immediately pleasant to the mind...this agreeableness or gratefulness of the idea is what is called beauty...we come by the idea or sensation of beauty...by immediate sensation of the gratefulness of the idea [thing] called 'beautiful'" (TV 619). In "The Mind" 1 (332) Edwards assimilates beauty and excellence and then says, "We would know, why proportion is more excellent than disproportion, that is, why proportion is pleasant to the mind and disproportion unpleasant." Passages such as these imply that beauty is some kind of pleasure or agreeableness,[20] or a tendency to produce it in appropriate circumstances.

We probably should not attribute the second (dispositional) view to Edwards. If "(true) beauty" referred to the tendency to produce a unique sort of delight in those with spiritual

---

[18] Edwards believes that the immediate objects of mental acts are ideas. Like Berkeley, he tends to conflate ideas and their contents (what the ideas are ideas *of*).

[19] Why regard these as objects of a sense or feeling of the heart? Presumably because (for example) a perception of beauty or importance involves a perception of the nonevaluative features on which beauty or importance depend, or because one cannot fully grasp or understand these nonevaluative properties without perceiving their beauty or importance, or both.

[20] Edwards clearly thinks that there are qualitative differences between pleasures. The pleasure that the natural man takes in secondary beauty (i.e., in "regularity, order, uniformity, symmetry, proportion, harmony, etc." [TV 561-62]) is qualitatively different from the spiritual person's delight in holiness.

frames, the idea of beauty would be a complex idea or "mixed mode."[21] This conflicts with the claim that spiritual beauty is a new simple idea (*RA* 205).[22]

There are also problems in attributing the first view to Edwards. The philosophers who most influenced Edwards (Locke and the Cartesians) explicitly denied that ideas of pleasure and pain tell us anything about the nature of the objects that produce them.[23] The idea of true beauty does. Edwards explicitly rejects the suggestion that "the idea we obtain by this spiritual sense could in no respect be said to be a knowledge or perception of anything besides what was in our own minds," or that it is "no representation of anything without." On the contrary, the idea of spiritual beauty is "the representation and image of the moral perfection and excellency of the Divine Being ... of which we could have no true idea without it" (*TV* 622-23).[24]

A more compelling reason for doubting that Edwards identified beauty with pleasure (or a tendency to produce it) is that he so often speaks as if it were an *objective* property of the things that have it. One of Edwards's central theses is that God's nature and activity are overwhelmingly beautiful, and that the spiritual and natural beauty of creatures is a reflection of, or participation in, God's own beauty The tenor of passages expressing these claims seems inconsistent with the suggestion that beauty is no more than a sensation which holy things produce in the suitably disposed (or a power to produce it). Edwards was strongly influenced by Locke and other empiricists. But he also belongs to a Puritan tradition that contains an important Platonic strand.[25] It may therefore be significant that Platonism thinks of beauty as an objective property.

Finally, a number of texts appear to identify beauty with the consent of being to being. This, too, seems inconsistent with the notion that beauty is some sort of pleasure or delight.

In "The Mind" 1, for example, Edwards assimilates beauty and excellency and then says, "excellency *consists in* the similarities of one being to another—not merely equality and proportion, but any kind of similarness....This is an universal *definition* of excellency: The consent of being to being, or being's consent to entity" (336, my emphasis). Edwards continues to speak this way in later works. He says, for example, that "the true beauty and loveliness of all intelligent beings does primarily and most essentially *consist in* their moral excellency or holiness," that is, in their benevolence or love of being in general. "Holiness *is*... the beauty of the divine nature" (*RA* 257, my emphasis; cf. 258-59). In *The Nature of True Virtue,* Edwards asserts that true benevolence "is the thing wherein true moral or spiritual beauty primarily *consists*. Yea, spiritual beauty *consists wholly in* this and in" what proceeds

---

[21] Locke's mixed modes are a species of complex ideas. Roughly, a mixed mode is an idea of a set of properties that cannot subsist by itself. (Ideas of substances, therefore, are not mixed modes.)

[22] This is not absolutely decisive. In Locke's view, "red" can be used to refer not only to a simple sensation but also to a power of producing this sensation that certain objects possess in virtue of their primary qualities; that is, "red" can be used to express a mixed mode as well as a simple idea. I will argue that Edwards's use of "beauty" exhibits a similar ambiguity. Nevertheless, it is reasonably clear that Locke believed that, in its primary sense, "red" denotes a simple idea and that Edwards thought the same of "beauty."

[23] See Locke, *Human Understanding* (hereafter *HU*) 2.8. See also Hutcheson who says that moral approbation (i.e., the disinterested delight in morally good actions and dispositions) "cannot be supposed an image of anything external, more than the pleasures of harmony, of taste, of smell" *(Illustrations on the Moral Sense* [Cambridge: Harvard University Press, 1971], p. 164, hereafter *Illustrations).*

[24] This point is inconclusive, however, because Edwards sometimes departs from Locke. For example, he asserts that beauty is a simple idea although Locke thought it was a mixed mode *(HU* 2.12.51).

[25] Edwards was influenced by Henry More (who self-consciously combined Platonism and Cartesianism). He was also familiar with Ralph Cudworth and John Smith and quotes both with approval.

from it (*TV* 648, my emphasis). "There is [also] another, inferior, secondary beauty, which is some image of this ... which *consists in* a mutual consent and agreement of different things, in form, manner, quantity, and visible end or design; called by the various names of regularity, order, uniformity, symmetry, proportion, harmony, etc." (*TV* 561, my emphasis). Passages of this kind imply that beauty just *is* (i.e., is identical with) some kind of agreement. Primary or spiritual beauty is one and the same thing as benevolence or the "consent or agreement, or union of being to being," and secondary beauty is identical with symmetry, harmony, or proportion, that is, "uniformity in the midst of variety" (*TV* 561-62).

But there are also serious objections to *this* interpretation. Edwards often speaks as if beauty were a property of holiness and hence not the *same* thing as holiness. In the *Religious Affections,* for example, he speaks of "the loveliness of the moral excellency of divine things...the beauty and sweetness of their moral excellency" (253 f.), "the beauty of their moral excellency," "the beauty of his holiness," "the beauty of his moral attributes" (256), "the loveliness of divine things...viz.,...the beauty of their moral perfection" (271), "the beauty of the moral perfection of Christ" (273), "the beauty of holiness, or true moral good" (274), and so on. Edwards also asserts that the unconverted can see everything that pertains to God's and the saints' moral attributes *except* their "beauty and amiableness" (RA 264), thus implying some sort of distinction between these attributes and their beauty. Finally, beauty is a *simple* idea. The consent of (conscious) being to being, however, is complex.[26]

In short, there is textual evidence for the claim that Edwards identified true beauty with a spiritual sensation or a tendency to produce it and also for the claim that he identified it with consent. Both views appear incompatible with some of Edwards's other positions. The first seems inconsistent with his belief that the apprehension of beauty is a "perception" of something existing "without" the mind, and the second is inconsistent with his conviction that beauty is a simple idea. Can a coherent position be constructed from Edwards's remarks? He may have been driving at this: Beauty is identical with benevolence or agreement in somewhat the same way in which water is identical with H_2O or in which (according to materialists) consciousness is identical with certain arrangements of matter. (This accommodates the fact that one can perceive benevolence or agreement without perceiving its beauty even though its beauty "consists in" benevolence or agreement.) But benevolence is also the "objective" or "physical" basis of a dispositional property (the tendency to produce a new simple idea in those with converted hearts). The new idea is a delight or pleasure in being's consent to being which somehow "represents" or is a "perception of" it.

On this interpretation, the idea of true beauty resembles Locke's ideas of primary and secondary qualities. Spiritual delight is, in Locke's words, a simple "sensation or perception in our understanding" like our ideas of color or solidity. (*HU* 2.8.8). The dispositional property is what Locke calls a "quality," a "power to produce those ideas in us" (ibid.). Benevolence is the objective configuration underlying this power and corresponds to the microstructure of bodies that underlie their tendency to excite ideas of primary and secondary qualities in minds like ours. Like simple ideas of primary and secondary qualities, the new spiritual sensation "represents" or is a "perception" of its object. Just as "extension" or "red" can refer to the idea, the power, or the physical configuration that is the base of the power, so "beauty" can refer to the sensation, to the

---

[26] Of course, Edwards *might* have believed that the relevant relational terms ("consents," "is equal to," "agrees with," "harmonizes with," etc.) stand for simple ideas, but he never says this, and although Locke thinks that the ideas of relations *"terminate* in simple ideas" (arise from the comparison of simple ideas), he does not seem to think that relations themselves are simple ideas (HUz.25.9-zo; z.a8.i8-zo).

relevant dispositional property, or to benevolence. (My interpretation thus accounts for the ambiguity of Edwards's remarks.)[27]

Edwards' account of spiritual perception is subject to some of the same difficulties as Locke's account of sense perception.[28] Is it, in any way, *less* satisfactory? It may be in one respect. If I am right, the idea of true beauty is a kind of delight or relish and *also* an apparent cognition. *Can* something be both? It is not sufficient to argue that perceptions of objectively real value properties can be inherently affective (and thus pleasurable or painful), for Edwards does not think of pleasure and pain in this way. Pleasures and pains are not qualities or affective dimensions of more complex experiences. They are discrete internal sensations. But if spiritual pleasure is a kind of internal delight or thrill, how can it *also* be a true representation of something existing without? Ordinary pleasures and pains differ from visual or auditory impressions in lacking what Berkeley called "outness"; they do not seem to point beyond themselves. Either spiritual pleasure is unlike ordinary pleasure in this respect, or it is not an apparent cognition.

In the next subsection we will see *why* Edwards calls the feeling of spiritual pleasure a "perception." Whether this resolves the difficulty, however, is doubtful.

B. Spiritual Sensing

Even though the spiritual sense is closely connected with a person's will or inclination,[29] it is a cognitive faculty—"a new foundation laid in the nature of the soul, for a new kind of exercises of the...faculty of understanding" (*RA* 206, my emphasis).[30] A sense of the heart involves a person's will or inclination because "when the mind is sensible" of spiritual beauty "that implies a sensibleness of sweetness and delight in the presence of the idea of it", "the mind...relishes and feels." But "there is [also] the nature of instruction in it"; it is a "kind of understanding" (*RA* 272).

Why does Edwards speak of this new cognition as a kind of perception or sensation? Partly because the idea of a spiritual sense was a Puritan commonplace. For example, John Owen said that God "gives...a spirituall sense, a Taste of the things themselves upon the mind, Heart and Conscience." According to Richard Sibbes, "It is knowledge with a taste...God giveth knowledge *per modum gustus*." Francis Rous said that "after we have tasted those heavenly things...from this taste there ariseth a new, but a true, lively, and experimental knowledge of the things so tasted.... For even in natural fruits there are certain relishes...which nothing but the taste it self can truly represent and shew unto us. The West-Indian Piney [pineapple] cannot be so expressed in words, even by him that hath tasted it, that he can deliver over the true shape and

---

[27] Does the idea of beauty not only "represent" but also "resemble" its object, as Locke's ideas of extension, figure and motion "resemble" the objective configurations that cause them? Edwards never explicitly says it does. (That the idea is a "perception" of "something without" only distinguishes it from ideas of tertiary qualities.) In calling it "knowledge," however, and in insisting that we can have no true idea of its object without it, Edwards implies that the idea *accurately* represents (some aspect of) its object. This suggests that the idea of beauty should be assimilated to Locke's ideas of primary qualities.

[28] It is not clear that the mind's immediate objects are ideas, how they represent or resemble their objects, and so on.

[29] At one point, Edwards asks, "concerning speculative understanding and sense of heart; whether any difference between the sense of the heart and the will or inclination" (Subjects 14).

[30] Cf. *RA* 275. It involves a new "sort of *understanding* or *knowledge*...[viz.] that *knowledge* of divine things from whence all truly gracious affections do proceed" (my emphasis).

character of that taste to another that hath not tasted it."[31] Edwards was indebted to his predecessors for the idea of a spiritual sensation. His development of that concept, however, is heavily influenced by empiricists such as Locke and (possibly) Hutcheson.[32]

The object of the spiritual sense is a new simple idea, and Edwards shared Locke's conviction that simple ideas come "from experience" (*HU* 2.1.2). As Francis Hutcheson said, "Reasoning or intellect seems to raise no new species of ideas but [only] to discover or discern the relation of" ideas "received by some immediate powers of perception internal or external which we may call sense" (*Illustrations* 135).

Spiritual understanding also involves a kind of relish or delight, and Edwards follows Locke and Hutcheson in thinking that being pleased or pained, like a feeling of tactual pressure or being appeared to redly, is a kind of sensation or perception. (All three believe that pleasure and pain are simple ideas.)

Then again, the new simple idea occurs involuntarily, and Edwards associates sensation with passivity (cf. Subjects 29). This too was a commonplace. For example, Hutcheson said that a sense is "a determination of the mind to receive any idea from the presence of an object... independent on our will" (*Inquiry*, Second Treatise, I, I).

Finally, the mind's apprehension of true or spiritual beauty is immediate (noninferential). As Edwards says, "this manner of being affected with the" beauty of a thing "depends not...on any reasonings...but on the frame of our minds whereby they are so made that" as soon as we perceive or cognize it, it "appears beautiful" (*TV* 619).[33] A comparison with Hutcheson is again instructive, for Hutcheson argued that the power of receiving the idea of beauty should be called a "sense" because "we are struck at the first with the beauty" (*Inquiry*, Second Treatise, I, XII).

It is thus clear *why* Edwards speaks of the new cognition as a perception or sensation. Whether he should have done so is another matter.

There is little force in the third and fourth considerations. Our sensations (and the beliefs directly based on them) appear involuntary and immediate, but so too does our recognition of the fact that $2 + 2 = 4$. Passivity and immediacy are not peculiar to ideas derived from (internal or external) sensation.

The first two considerations carry more weight. Locke and Hutcheson identify reason with reasoning. Reason is sharply distinguished from the will and its affections and from the senses. Its sole function is to manipulate ideas received from other sources. Edwards shares these views.[34] Reason does not have an affective dimension and is not the source of new

---

[31] The quotations are from Nuttall, *Holy Spirit*, pp. 39, 139.

[32] Locke was a major influence. Hutcheson's *Inquiry into the Original of our Ideas of Beauty and Virtue* (London: 1725; hereafter *Inquiry*) is referred to in Edwards's "Catalogue of Books" on p. 8 and p. 22. On p. 22, Edwards writes, "Hutcheson's Essay on the Passions cited in his Enquiry into the Original of our Ideas of Beauty and Virtue," which implies that he had read the *Inquiry* by that time. (Thomas H. Johnson ["Jonathan Edwards's Background of Reading," *Publications of the Colonial Society of Massachusetts* 28 (1930-33), 194-222] estimates that pages 15-43 date from 1746 to 1757.) Hutcheson is mentioned three times in *True Virtue*, and quotations from the *Inquiry* occur in *Original Sin* on pages 225 and 226. Hutcheson's *An Essay on the Nature and Conduct of the Passions and Affections* and, *Illustrations on the Moral Sense* (two essays) appeared in 1728 (three years after the first edition of the *Inquiry*). This work is entered in the "Catalogue" on pages 22 and 32. In the "Book of Controversies," the *Nature and Conduct of the Passions*" is quoted, and this passage is incorporated into *Original Sin* but credited to Turnbull" (Clyde A. Holbrook, "Introduction," *OS* 74-75). The implication is that Edwards was familiar with the two essays. Whether he was significantly influenced by Hutcheson, though, is unclear.

[33] Cf *Religious Affections*, 281-82, where Edwards speaks of the immediacy with which this new sense judges of the spiritual beauty of actions. See also *The Nature of True Virtue*, pp. 619-20.

[34] "If we take *reason* strictly—not for the faculty of mental perception in general [which would include sense perception], but for ratiocination...the perceiving of spiritual beauty and excellency no more belongs to reason,

simple ideas. The cognition of true beauty, on the other hand, *has* an affective dimension since it involves relish or delight. Furthermore, its object is a new simple idea. Spiritual cognition must therefore be some kind of sensation or perception.

This conclusion seems inconsistent with other aspects of Edwards's position. A number of Hutcheson's critics took exception to his moral sense theory because they believed that (1) at least some moral propositions are necessarily true, and (2) necessary truths are discerned by reason.[35] Hutcheson maintained that the moral sense grasps the goodness of benevolent actions and dispositions, that is, perceives that benevolence is (morally) good. His critics objected that "benevolence is good" is necessarily true and that necessary truths are apprehended by *reason*. It is therefore significant that Edwards, too, apparently believed that moral truths are necessary.[36] Nor is he likely to have thought that the connection between benevolent actions and dispositions and spiritual beauty is only contingent—that holiness or benevolence might not have been truly beautiful. But if "holiness is beautiful" *is* necessarily true, Edwards seems committed to the view that our knowledge of at least some necessary truths is derived from a sense, that is, that some necessary truths are perceived by a kind of sensation. And this is not plausible.

One *may* be able to apprehend the redness of a table without apprehending *that* the table is red. (Perhaps animals and infants do.) But *can* one apprehend the moral goodness of a benevolent action without apprehending *that* the action is morally good or apprehend its spiritual beauty without apprehending *that* it is truly beautiful? This seems doubtful. The idea of beauty derives from experience in the sense that one acquires it by encountering beautiful objects. But the idea of beauty does not seem to be a discrete feeling or sensation (like a feeling of sexual pleasure or a raw sensation of redness) that is *first* received from experience and *then* incorporated in a judgment. On the contrary, receiving the idea of beauty appears to *be* judging that what one is contemplating is beautiful. Edwards seems committed to claiming that this judgment is necessarily true. Does it make any sense, then, to speak of a person's apprehension of a thing's beauty as some kind of internal or external sensing?

If one were to interpret spiritual cognition as an "intellectual intuition" with affective overtones, one could avoid this problem as well as that raised at the end of the last subsection. Spiritual "perception" would then be something like our immediate recognition of the prima facie rightness of an instance of justice or kindness on a view like W. D. Ross's. Edwards was familiar with at least one account of this type, that of the Cambridge Platonist John Smith.

Like Edwards, Smith insisted on the inadequacy of a merely notional or intellectual understanding of spiritual things. He, too, thought that divine truths can only be understood by those who lead holy lives, and he, too, spoke of a "spiritual sensation." "The soul," said Smith, "itself hath its sense, as well as the body: and therefore David...calls not for speculation but sensation, Taste and see bow good the Lord is." But Smith's spiritual sensation is an act of "that reason that is within us...[the] eye of the soul...our intellectual faculty" This intellectual

---

than it belongs to the sense of feeling to perceive colors.... Reason's work is to perceive truth and not excellency" (DSL 18).

[35] See, for example, the correspondence between Hutcheson and Gilbert Burnet.

[36] Edwards clearly thinks that at least some moral truths are necessary. See *Freedom of the Will* (Boston, 1754: reprint, New Haven: Yale University Press, 1957), p. 153. Edwards's example is, "It is...fit and suitable, that men should do to others, as they would that they should do to them." It is worth observing that Locke, too, thinks that moral truths are necessary (*HU* 3.11.15-18; 4.3.18-20; and 4.4.7-10.).

intuition or perception of reason *incorporates* love or delight but is not identical with them.[37] (Smith does not find this problematic because he shares the Platonic view that reason itself has an affective dimension. Knowing the good involves loving it and delighting in it).[38]

A view such as Smith's sidesteps the two problems confronting Edwards—how a feeling of delight can also be an apparent cognition, and how a necessary truth can be grasped by a kind of sensation. Edwards's commitment to empiricism precluded this solution. Philosophers such as Locke identified reason with ratiocination and insisted that simple ideas originate in experience (internal or external sensation). Because Edwards accepted these theses, he could not construe spiritual cognitions as rational intuitions. Whether they are essential to his epistemology, however, is debatable.[39]

C. The Cognition of Spiritual Truths

Although the spiritual sense's direct object is true beauty or excellency, it also has an indirect object—spiritual facts or truths. There are two cases to consider.

In the first, the spiritual sense enables us to recognize the truth of propositions that are logically or epistemically related to the excellency of divine things. For example: Our apprehension of Christ's beauty and excellency produces a conviction of His sufficiency as a Mediator (Misc. 782, T 126; *RA* 273, 302). To grasp the appropriateness of God's end in creation, namely, the communication of His glory ad extra, one must perceive its beauty. An appreciation of the splendor of God's glory is also needed to comprehend the fitness of the means He employs to secure it and thus understand His wisdom (*RA* 274, 302). Nor can one discern "the amiableness of the duties...that are required of us" unless one perceives the excellency of divine things (*RA* 274). Or again, one must see the beauty of holiness to appreciate the "hatefulness of sin" (*RA* 274, 301) and thus be convinced of the justice of divine punishment and our inability to make satisfaction (*RA* 302). The spiritual sense, then, enables us to grasp the truth of a number of important doctrines.

But it also helps us grasp the truth of the gospel scheme as a whole (*RA* 291-92). A conviction of the gospel's truth is an inference from the beauty or excellency of what it depicts, namely, "God and Jesus Christ...the work of redemption, and the ways and works of God" (DSL 8). "There is a divine and superlative glory in these things" that distinguishes "them from all that is earthly and temporal" (DSL 8). A spiritual person "truly sees" this glory (*RA* 298); his perception of it is as immediate and direct as a perception of color or the sweetness of food (DSL 18). (This was not, of course, a new idea. Thus, Richard Sibbes said, "God...causeth him to see a divine majesty shining forth in the scriptures, so that there must be an infused establishing by the Spirit to settle the heart in this first principle...that the Scriptures are the word of God." Or again,

---

[37] The quotations are from Smith's "Of the True Way or Method of Attaining to Divine Knowledge," in *Select Discourses* (New York: Garland, 1978). (I have modernized the capitalization and spelling.) In his introduction to *Religious Affections*, John E. Smith denies that Smith's spiritual sensation is an intellectual intuition (*RA* 66). Quotations like the last, however, and the Platonic tenor of the discourse as a whole, seem to support my interpretation.

[38] "Intellectual life, as [the Platonists] phrase it" is a nondiscursive " knowledge...[that] is always pregnant with divine virtue, which ariseth out of an happy union of souls with God, and is nothing else but a living imitation of a Godlike perfection drawn out by a strong fervent love of it. This divine knowledge...makes us amorous of divine beauty...and this divine love and purity, reciprocally exalts divine knowledge" (Smith, *Select Discourses*, p. 20).

[39] For one thing (as John E. Smith and others have pointed out), the line between will and understanding is more flexible in Edwards than in Locke or Hutcheson.

"How do you know the word to be the word? It carrieth proof and evidence in itself: It is an evidence that the fire is hot to him that feeleth it, and that the sun shineth to him that looks on it; how much more doth the word.... I am sure I felt it, it warmed my heart, and converted me.")[40]

A conviction of the gospel's truth "is an effect and natural consequence of this perception" (DSL 8). The perception and conviction are nonetheless distinct. The mind infers the truth and reality of the things the gospel contains from its perception of their spiritual beauty. There is, however, no "long chain of arguments; the argument is but one, and the evidence direct; the mind ascends to the truth of the gospel but by one step, and that is its divine glory" (*RA* 298-99; cf. Misc. 782, T 126).[41] Because only one step is involved, we can truly say that the divinity, or reality, or truth of the gospel is "as it were" known intuitively, that "a soul may have a kind of intuitive knowledge of the divinity [or truth, or reality of the things exhibited in the gospel]" (*RA* 298).[42]

The mind's object differs in the two cases. In the first, it is a comparatively specific doctrinal proposition that is logically or epistemically connected with other propositions that affirm that some person or characteristic or activity or state of affairs is truly amiable or beautiful or excellent. Our spiritual sense enables us to *perceive* the truth of the latter and from this we *infer* the truth of the former. In the second, the mind's object is the content of the gospel as a whole—what Paul Ricoeur has called "the world of the text."[43] The central or controlling features of this world—God, Christ, and the scheme of salvation—are *perceived* to be truly beautiful. On the basis of this perception one immediately, concludes that the biblical world is not fictional like those depicted in *The Brothers Karamazov* or *Moby-Dick,* but *real.*

Edwards's view has some interesting implications. If my interpretation is correct, the new spiritual sense does not involve a direct or immediate or quasi-perceptual awareness of God Himself. Instead, God's reality is *inferred* from the excellency and beauty of the things depicted in scripture. As we have seen, however, the inference "is without any long chain of arguments; the argument is but one, and the evidence direct." Because of the inference's spontaneity and immediacy, a person can even be said to have "a kind of intuitive knowledge" of divinity (*RA*

---

[40] Quoted in Nuttall, *Holy Spirit*, pp. 23, 39.

[41] Presumably the argument is: (1) Gospel doctrines exhibit a divine excellency or beauty. Therefore, (2) Gospel doctrines are true. (2) follows from (1) *if* doctrines that exhibit this supernatural radiance or splendor have a supernatural author. (On this point, see DSL 10; Misc. 256, T 249; and Misc. 782, T 126.) How is this generalization related to the argument? If the inference involves only one step, it cannot be functioning as a premise. Perhaps, then, the generalization is an inference rule. Or perhaps Edwards thinks of it as a necessary truth. (If it is, then [1] entails [2].) Or perhaps it is simply an inductive generalization from a set of "natural inferences"—judgments that the redeemed find themselves spontaneously making in the presence of the gospel and that are trustworthy given that their new faculties are God-given. (If the third alternative is correct, the generalization plays *no* role in the argument. The second and third interpretations seem most likely.)

[42] A superficial reading of some passages might suggest that Edwards thinks that our knowledge of divine reality is immediate. Thus *Miscellanies* 201 (T 246-47) and 408 (T 249-50) assert that ideas that are clear and lively and cohere with each other and with other ideas are quite properly regarded as real or true. Those with converted hearts find the ideas of religion (scripture) clear, lively, internally coherent, and in harmony, with their other ideas. They, therefore, quite properly take them to be real or true. But this "appearing real...cannot be drawn out into formal arguments." It depends on "ten thousand little relations and mutual agreements that are ineffable" "and is a sort of seeing rather than reasoning the truth of religion." But Edwards is not clearly denying that the conviction of reality is inferential. (He may simply be insisting on its psychological immediacy and coerciveness and on the fact that it does not rest on *formal* argument.) In any case, his normal view is that presented in "Divine and Supernatural Light" and *Religious Affections,* namely, that the reality of divine things is inferred by one step from their spiritual beauty and excellency.

[43] Paul Ricoeur, "Philosophy and Religious Language," *Journal of Religion* 54 (1974), 71-85.

298). Edwards's interpretation of the redeemed's knowledge of God's reality thus resembles Descartes' and Locke's account of our knowledge of other minds and physical objects. These things are not directly perceived, but their reality or presence is spontaneously and immediately inferred from sensations or impressions that *are* directly apprehended. Edwards thinks our knowledge of God is similar. Although God is not *directly* perceived, His reality is no more remote or uncertain than other minds or physical objects are in Locke's view.

If I am right, Edwards's position differs from a basic beliefs approach. One's belief in God is not basic like our memory beliefs, or perceptual beliefs, or beliefs in simple necessary truths but is, instead, inferential. On the other hand, the inference on which one's belief is based does not involve a long or complicated chain of reasoning, and it is as spontaneous and compelling as our (alleged) inference to other minds or the reality of the physical world. The redeemed's belief in God is thus similar to some of Hume's natural beliefs—the belief in the continued existence of unperceived physical objects, for example, and (on some interpretations) the belief in a designer.[44] It differs in that the *basis* of the inference is a new simple idea that God bestows on the regenerate and because (in Edwards's opinion) the inference is *sound*.

D. The Objectivity of the Spiritual Sense

The final chapter of *The Nature of True Virtue* attempts to show that "the frame of mind, or inward sense...whereby the mind is disposed to" relish true virtue for its spiritual beauty, is not "given arbitrarily" but agrees "with the necessary nature of things" (*TV* 620). But the "frame of mind" that disposes a person to delight in true beauty (i.e., to be pleased with benevolence) is benevolence itself. Edwards concludes that it will be sufficient to show that *benevolence* agrees with the nature of things.

Edwards's strategy, in other words, is this. True benevolence is the mechanism underlying the new spiritual sense. If we can show that benevolence has a foundation in the nature of things, we can conclude that the spiritual sense, too, is aligned with reality. Edwards's task, then, is to prove that benevolence agrees with the "necessary nature of things." He has four arguments for this conclusion. The first two are unconvincing. The third and fourth are more persuasive.

Edwards's first argument is this:

1. A being with understanding and inclinations necessarily desires its own happiness (i.e., it desires what it wants or desires or finds agreeable).
2. Benevolence is the disposition to benefit being *in general*.
3. Therefore, a being with understanding and inclinations must approve of benevolence (for it benefits *him*). (From 1 and 2.).
4. Hence, if a being with understanding and inclinations approves if vice (i.e., of malevolence or indifference to being in general), then his attitudes are inconsistent, (From 3.).
5. Virtue (benevolence) can be approved without inconsistency.
6. If virtue (benevolence) can be approved without inconsistency and vice (malevolence or indifference) cannot, then virtue agrees with the nature of things and vice does not.
7. Therefore, virtue agrees with the nature of things and vice does not. (From 4, 5, and 6.) (*TV* 621-22).

---

[44] Cf., for example, Ronald J. Butler, "Natural Belief and the Enigma of Hume," *Archiv für Geschichte der Philosophie 42* (1960), 73-100, or John Hick, "A New Form of Theistic Argument," *Proceedings of the XIV. International Congress of Philosophy 5* (1970), 336-41. See also J. C. A. Gaskin, *Hume's Philosophy of Religion* (London Barnes and Noble,, 1978) chap. 8.

The argument, if sound, shows that virtue agrees with the nature of things in the sense that loving virtue is a more rational (i.e., coherent) response to reality than loving vice.

But the proof is not persuasive. A person is not inconsistent in approving and disapproving (or not approving) of the same thing if he or she approves and disapproves (or fails to approve) of it in different respects. And this is surely the case here. The wicked approve of benevolence when it benefits them but hate it, or are indifferent toward it, when it benefits others. They approve of (or are indifferent to) malevolence or indifference when directed toward others but not when directed toward themselves. These attitudes may be reprehensible but they are not inconsistent. Let us therefore turn to Edwards's second argument:

1. Benevolence is "agreement or consent of being to being."
2. Being or "general existence" is the nature of things.
3. Therefore, benevolence agrees with the nature of things (*TV* 620). The argument establishes its conclusion by identifying the nature of things with what is (viz., being in general) and identifying agreement with being's consent to being.

This too seems unconvincing. Edwards's argument only establishes a tautology—that consent to being (i.e., benevolence) is consent to (i.e., agreement with) being (i.e., the nature of things). What *needs* to be shown is that benevolence or consent to being is an *appropriate* response to the nature of things, and his argument does not do this.

But this criticism, although correct, is superficial. For it neglects the argument's theistic context. Edwards believes that being in general is *God* and the "particular beings" that depend on Him and manifest His glory. A consent to, or love of, being in *this* sense is surely an appropriate response to it. The theistic metaphysics becomes explicit in Edwards's third argument.

1. God "is in effect being in general." (All being either is God or unconditionally depends on Him.)
2. It is "necessary, that God should agree with himself, be united with himself, or love himself."
3. Therefore, God is necessarily benevolent. (From 1 and 2—in loving Himself, God loves "being in general" and is therefore benevolent.)
4. Consequently, benevolence agrees with the nature of God. (From 3.)
5. Now, whatever agrees with the nature of what "is in effect being in general" agrees with the nature of things.
6. Therefore, benevolence agrees with the nature of things. (From 1, 4, and 5.) (*TV* 621).

The third argument uses "agreement" in yet another sense. Edwards's point is roughly that the nature of things is divine benevolence. Human benevolence agrees with it because it is its image.

Edwards is an occasionalist like Malebroch, an idealist like Berkeley, and a mental phenomenalist like Hume. What are "vulgarly" called causal relations are mere constant conjunctions. *True* causes necessitate their effects. Because God's will alone meets this condition, God is the only true cause. He is also the only true substance. Physical objects are collections of "corporeal ideas" (ideas of color, for example, or solidity, resistance, and so on). Minds are series of "thoughts" or "perceptions." Any substance underlying perceptions, thoughts, and corporeal ideas would be something that "subsisted by itself, and stood underneath and kept up" physical and mental properties. But God alone subsists by Himself, stands underneath, and keeps up thoughts, perceptions, solidity, color, and other corporeal qualities (ideas). Hence, "the substance of bodies [and minds] at last becomes either nothing, or nothing but the Deity acting in that particular manner...where he thinks fit."[45] The only real cause and the only real substance are thus God Himself. God's essence, however, is love. The real nature of things, then, is an infinite and omnipotent benevolence.

Our benevolence "agrees with" this in the sense that it resembles it or is an image of it. The thrust of Edwards's argument is therefore this. Benevolence is appropriate because it mirrors reality. Nature's activity is really *God's* activity. (Because God is the only true substance and the only true cause, He is *natura naturans*.) Love is thus "natural" because it imitates the activity of "Nature" itself.

Edwards's theistic metaphysics is also implicit in his fourth argument.

1. Harmony among being is more agreeable to the nature of things than disharmony.
2. Benevolence (the consent of being to being) promotes (or is) harmony among beings.
3. Therefore, benevolence agrees with the nature of things. (*TV* 100-101)

Edwards assumes that whatever promotes harmony in a system accords or agrees with its nature. This is plausible when the system is organic or social. In Edwards's opinion, being in general is an organic or social system. The only things that exist without qualification are minds, and minds form a social system in which God is sovereign.[46]

Benevolence, then, has a "foundation in the nature of things." Because the spiritual sense is an *expression* of benevolence, Edwards concludes that it, too, is founded "in the nature of things." "The idea we obtain by this spiritual sense" is thus "a knowledge or perception" of something outside our minds, a true "representation" of something "without," namely, God's moral perfection and excellence and its created reflections (*TV* 622f).

Edwards's defense of the objectivity of the new spiritual sense has four steps. (1) Benevolence agrees with the nature of things. The world is an interconnected system of minds and ideas in which the only true substance and cause are an infinite and omnipotent love. Human benevolence, therefore, is an appropriate or fitting response to reality. (2) A delight in benevolence also agrees with reality. Benevolence is pleased by benevolence; it relishes it, or delights in it, for its own sake (*TV* 546-49). If benevolence is an appropriate response to reality, so, too, then, is benevolence's delight in benevolence. (3) Delight in benevolence is identified with a perception of its spiritual beauty. (4) The redeemed's spiritual perceptions are veridical. Spiritual sensations are a "representation" of something "without," that is, they are noetic or perceptionlike. In Berkeley's words, they have "outness." The second step established that our spiritual sense is in order, that its motions are appropriate to reality. If spiritual sensations were merely subjective feelings such as indignation and admiration or physical pleasure and pain, then the second step would only show that these feelings are appropriate affective responses to their objects. But the third step informs us that spiritual sensations *are not* mere feelings; they are apparent cognitions. Because the apparent cognitions are an appropriate response to reality, they are a "knowledge or perception" of something "without"; the representations are "true representations."

How successful is Edwards's defense? The first two steps are plausible. Although Edwards's occasionalism, idealism, and mental phenomenalism undoubtedly strengthened his belief in benevolence's agreement with the nature of things, similar conclusions follow from any

---

[45] Jonathan Edwards, "Of Atoms" (*Scientific and Philosophical Writings*, p. 215). The quotations are from an argument "proving" that God is the only substance underlying corporeal properties. Edwards clearly thinks, however, that similar considerations show that God is also the only substance underlying mental qualities.

[46] Edwards also thinks that God (who is "in effect being in general") is triune and thus inherently social.

theistic (or at least Christian) metaphysics. The second step is also plausible. An essential feature of an appropriate response is itself appropriate. And Edwards's fourth step follows from his second and third.

The problem is the third step. Because Edwards's identification of spiritual perception with a kind of pleasure is suspect (see the first two subsections), his defense is not fully successful. Nevertheless, Edwards's reflections provide a promising start. Benevolence may really *be* spiritual perception's underlying mechanism. The nature of this perception, though, and its relation to benevolence, need further clarification.

E. The Appeal to Theistic Metaphysics and the Problem of Circularity

The most instructive feature of Edwards's defense is the way it uses theistic metaphysics. I suspect that any persuasive justification of a spiritual sense's reliability will do the same. Is it therefore circular? It is not if theistic metaphysics can be established without appealing to spiritual perceptions. Does Edwards think it can? He believes that theistic metaphysics is supported by natural reason and sometimes suggests that the rational evidence is sufficient. On the other hand, he also talks as if it often will not *seem* sufficient to those with unconverted hearts.

If Edwards is right, justifications of spiritual perceptions are not circular in the sense that they employ premises that explicitly or implicitly assert that spiritual perceptions are reliable. Nor are they circular in the sense that they employ premises that *in principle* can only be known to be true by those who rely on their spiritual sense. As we shall see in the following section, however, there is a de facto psychological or causal connection between having spiritual perceptions and appreciating the force of the evidence for a theistic metaphysics and thereby appreciating the force of justifications of the spiritual sense's reliability. It seems, then, both that these justifications are not logically or epistemically circular *and* that those who lack spiritual perceptions, or distrust them, will normally find them unpersuasive.

An example may clarify my point. Suppose that someone sees the force of an inductive argument for the guilt of his brother only after he has been persuaded of his brother's guilt. (Perhaps his brother confessed.) Is the argument circular? Is it circular for him? Not clearly. The nature of his noetic equipment is not such that he cannot know the premises without knowing the conclusion. Indeed, he may have firmly believed that the premises are true. Nor is its nature such that he *cannot* see that the premises establish the conclusion. The fault is not with his noetic equipment but with his attachment to his brother, which blinded him to the force of the evidence and prevented him from using his noetic equipment properly. The relation between believing the conclusion and recognizing the force of the argument for it is thus extrinsic or accidental. His inability to appreciate the weight of the evidence prior to accepting the argument's conclusion is the result of a psychological or moral aberration, not a matter of logic or a consequence of the nature of his cognitive faculties.

Edwards's view is similar. The reliability of our spiritual sense can be justified by a theistic metaphysics that is itself adequately supported by evidence accessible to natural reason. But sin blinds us to the evidence's force. There is thus a causal connection between spiritual perception and rational persuasion. Appeals to spiritual perceptions play no role, however, in the justificatory process itself. If this is correct, it seems misleading to say that the reliability of the spiritual sense cannot be justified without circularity. But this is a difficult issue, and we will return to it in Chapter 4.

F. The Bearing of Edwards's Theory on Contemporary Discussions

Edwards's account of the sense of the heart goes some way toward filling an important gap in contemporary discussions—the failure adequately to explain *how* theistic belief-producing mechanisms operate. The issue is important for two reasons.

First, the nature of the mechanism has a bearing on its reliability. For example, Freud offers several accounts of the nature of the theistic belief-producing mechanism that, if true, cast doubt on its reliability. Theists can defuse criticisms of this sort by providing alternative and equally plausible accounts of the mechanism's operation that do not impugn its reliability.

The second reason is this. On reading the *Vedas,* an Advaitin may find himself spontaneously believing that they express the Nirguna Brahman. On reading the *Isa Upanishad* or having a monistic mystical experience, he may find himself spontaneously believing that all differences are unreal or that the impersonal Brahman is ultimate. On surveying the evidence, he may conclude that Advaita Vedanta has fewer difficulties than its rivals and is therefore more likely to be true. If these beliefs are true, theism is false. On the face of it, the theist's beliefs and the Advaitin's beliefs are formed in similar ways. The same sort of belief-producing mechanism seems involved in both cases. If it is, then if one is reliable, so presumably is the other. And yet they cannot *both* be reliable, for they produce conflicting beliefs. Hence, neither seems reliable.

What is needed is an explanation of the difference between theistic and (for example) Advaitin or Mahayanan belief-producing mechanisms, together with an indication of why the former are reliable and the latter are not.

Edwards may provide some assistance here for he has the beginnings of an account of how one theistic belief-producing mechanism operates. His account is also the *right* sort. If the mechanism is (a function of ?) benevolence rather than wish fulfillment or the working out of an oedipal complex, there may be less reason for thinking it untrustworthy. Again, if (1) the disposition to form true religious beliefs is a function of benevolence or love, (2) benevolence or love agrees with the nature of things, and (3) the love of being in general is either absent or less fully developed in Advaita or Mahayana, one has some indication of why the theist's religious belief-producing mechanism is more reliable than the latter's.[47]

My point, of course, is not that Edwards *has* provided a fully adequate account but that some account is needed to defuse certain sorts of criticism and that the kind of account Edwards presents is the *right* kind.

These brief remarks are not sufficient to allay the spectres of subjectivism and relativism; those issues will be addressed in Chapters 4 and 5. Our task now is to look at Edwards's account of religious reasoning more closely.

---

[47] It will be more difficult for a Christian to cast aspersions on (e.g.) a Vaisnava's religious belief-producing mechanism. Vaisnavism is a theistic grace religion that values love. To discriminate between the Christian's and the Vaisnava's intuitions, one must either (1) distinguish between the quality of the Christian's and the Vaisnava's benevolence, or (2) appeal to cultural or (less plausibly) psychological or moral factors that impede the proper operations of the Vaisnava's spiritual faculties. The Christian might, however, concede that some true beauty is perceived in the *Bhagavad-Gita* and the theistic Upanishads. For he or she may think that these texts, too, are revelations though not as perfect as the Christian revelation. Cf. Clement of Alexandria's claim that philosophy may have been "given to the Greeks directly; for it was a 'schoolmaster,' to bring Hellenism to Christ, as the Law was for the Hebrews" (Henry Bettenson, *The Early Christian Fathers* [London: Oxford University Press, 1963], p. 232).

III. Sanctified Reason

Edwards uses "reason" in two closely related senses. Sometimes the term refers to "ratiocination, or a power of inferring by arguments" (DSL 18). At others it refers to "the power...an intelligent being has to judge of the truth of propositions...immediately by only looking on the propositions" as well as to ratiocination (Misc. 1340, T 219).[48] The difference between these characterizations is not important; in either case, "reason's work is to perceive truth and not excellency" (DSL 18). Excellency and what pertains to it are perceived by the heart. Even though Edwards concedes that there is a more extended sense in which "reason" refers to "the faculty of mental perception in general" (DSL 18), he clearly prefers the stricter usage. His official view is that of other modern philosophers who deny that reason has an affective dimension (a love of the good, for example, or a delight in excellence).[49]

Grace affects reason as well as the heart. "Common grace" helps the faculties "to do that more fully which they do by nature," strengthening "the natural principles [e.g., conscience] against those things that tend to stupify [sic] it and to hinder its free exercise." "Special grace," on the other hand, "causes those things to be in the soul that are above nature; and causes them to be in the soul habitually" (Misc. 626, T 111). Special grace sanctifies by infusing benevolence or true virtue (viz., the love of being in general). Infused benevolence is the basis of a new epistemic principle; a sense of the heart that tastes, relishes, and perceives the beauty of holiness (i.e., benevolence). By its means, the sanctified acquire a new simple idea (the idea of "true beauty") that the unredeemed lack.[50] Because this idea is needed to understand divine matters properly, the "saints" are in a superior epistemic position. One cannot rightly understand God's moral attributes, for example, if one does not perceive their beauty. Nor can one adequately grasp truths that logically or epistemically depend on God's holiness and its splendor such as the infinite heinousness of sin or the appropriateness of God's aiming at His own glory. The saints also behold old data with new eyes. They perceive the stamp of divine splendor on the world's order and design, and on the events recorded in sacred history. They thereby acquire a more accurate sense of this evidence's force and impressiveness.

The perception of spiritual beauty was discussed in the preceding section. This section focuses on another epistemic effect of special grace. The new principle that God infuses "sanctifies the reasoning faculty and assists it to see the clear evidence there is of the truth of religion in rational arguments, and that in two ways, viz., as it removes prejudices and so lays the mind more open to the force of arguments, and also secondly, as it positively enlightens and assists it to see the force of rational arguments...by adding greater light, clearness and strength to the judgment" (Misc. 628, T 251).[51] There is nothing intrinsically supernatural about many of

---

[48] In *Freedom of the Will* Edwards asserts that propositions are self-evident when they express necessary truths or things present to (immediately perceived by) the mind. Examples are mathematical propositions, analytic truths, metaphysical principles, true moral statements, and reports of present ideas and sensations (see pp. 153, 181-82, and 259).

[49] Although Edwards's identification with this tradition is not entirely straightforward. Edwards's sense of the heart, for example, is a *cognitive* faculty whereas (e.g.) Hutcheson's is not. Furthermore, even though Edwards normally assigns the sense of the heart to the will (i.e., to our affective nature), he sometimes assigns it to the understanding. See, for example, *RA* 206.

[50] The saints are not wholly passive with respect to the reception of this new simple idea, for they can increase its clarity and intensity. They can do so, however, only "by the practice of virtue and holiness—for we cannot have the idea without the adapted disposition of mind" (Misc. 123, T 246).

[51] Insofar as special grace simply strengthens natural principles, its effects are the same as those of common grace.

these benefits. The cause of the mind's reasoning soundly is supernatural, but the effect (sound reasoning) need not be;[52] the spirit simply helps us use our natural epistemic faculties rightly.

What sorts of "prejudices" interfere with reason's "free exercise"? "Opinions arising from imagination" are one example. They "take us as soon as we are born, are beat into us by every act of sensation, and so grow up with us from our very births; and by that means grow into us so fast that it is almost impossible to root them out, being as it were so incorporated with our very minds that whatsoever is objected to them, contrary thereunto, is as if it were dissonant to the very constitution of them. Hence, men come to make what they can actually perceive by their senses, or immediate and outside reflection into their own souls, the standard of possibility and impossibility" (*Prejudices* 196). Biases arising from temperament, education, custom, and fashion furnish other examples (*Mind* 68 and *Subjects* 384 and 387).

Sin's essence is a failure to obey the love commandment. Those who do not love being in general love "private systems." Their loves are partial, extending to only some beings. They are also inordinate; lives are centered on the self or more extensive private systems rather than on God (who is "in effect" being in general) and the creatures who are absolutely dependent on Him and reflect His glory.[53]

Sin has noetic consequences. Edwards refers, for example, to "the great subjection of the soul in its fallen state to the external senses" (Misc. 782, T 122). (This subjection is presumably a consequence of the soul's inordinate love of temporal goods.)[54] Again, self-love blinds us to everything that does not bear on immediate self-interest (*OS* 145-57). In addition, "the mind of man is naturally full of enmity against the doctrines of the gospel" that cause "arguments that prove their truth...to lose their force upon the mind" (*RA* 307). (God crosses our self-love and love of temporal things, and this arouses hostility.)[55]

Our corrupt inclinations even affect our sense of what is and is not reasonable. "Common inclination or the common dictates of inclination, are often called common sense." A person who says that the doctrine of eternal damnation offends common sense is using the expression in this way. But the inclinations behind this judgment have been shaped by an insensibility to "the great evil of sin." They are therefore corrupt (Misc. Obs. 253).

William James has suggested that our judgments of credibility reflect what we have a use for, what vitally concerns us. "In...the sense in which we contrast reality with simple unreality, and in which one thing is said to have more reality than another, and to be more believed, reality means simply relation to our emotional and active life. This is the only sense that the word ever has in the mouths of practical men. In this sense whatever excites and stimulates our interests is real."[56] "The natural propensity of man is to believe that whatever has great value for life is thereby certified as true."[57] Our judgments of truth and reality, in other words, are (partly) functions of our emotional engagement. Edwards would agree. If our interests are badly misdirected, our judgments of what is and is not credible will be correspondingly distorted.

---

[52] The exceptions will become clear as we proceed.
[53] For a fuller treatment of these points, see my "Original Sin," in *Philosophy and the Christian Faith*, ed. Thomas V Morris (Notre Dame, Ind.: University of Notre Dame Press, 1988).
[54] Cf. Plato in *Phaedo* and elsewhere. As noted, there is an important Platonic strand in Puritanism.
[55] "Hostility" may be too strong. But we do have a natural tendency to *resist* demands that cross our self-love and love of temporal goods by diverting our attention to other things, for example, or by rationalizing.
[56] William James, *The Principles of Psychology*, vol. 2 (Cambridge: Harvard University Press, 1981), p. 924 (James's emphases).
[57] William James, *The Varieties of Religious Experience* (New York: Modern Library, c. 1902), p. 500, n.

Grace frees the mind from these "prejudices." An unprejudiced reason, however, is not dispassionate. For it is affected by *epistemically benign* feelings and inclinations. A love of wider systems alone checks self-interest. Nor is it sufficient to replace hostility toward religion with indifference or neutrality; the heart must be receptive to it. An unprejudiced reason is also affected by natural motions of the heart as well as by true benevolence (gratitude for one's being, for example, or a sense that it would be unfitting for the injustice that evades human tribunals to escape punishment).[58] And because our love of temporal goods is not subordinate to a love of eternity, it is inordinate, and the latter is needed to correct it.[59]

Another point is relevant as well. Natural reason reveals many truths about God and our relation to Him. Yet even at the level of nature these truths are not properly understood if the heart lacks a due sense of the natural good and evil in them[60] (a proper sense of the natural unfittingness of disobeying the world's sovereign, for example, a horror of the natural evils consequent on offenses against Him, or a proper sense of the natural benefits He has bestowed on us and of the obligations these gifts create).

I conclude, then, that *common* grace not only inhibits the action of passional factors corrupting reason; it also causes better natural affections to influence it (at least temporarily): *Sanctifying* grace replaces the effects of corrupt affections by the influences of true benevolence. A reason that is exercising itself "freely" and without "prejudice," therefore, is affected by passional factors.

But grace does more than remove the impediments ("prejudices") hindering reason's free exercise by restructuring our affections. It adds "greater light, clearness and strength to the judgment." Edwards refers us to Miscellany 408 for "one way" in which it does so.[61] That entry argues that ideas of spiritual things "appear more lively and with greater strength and impression" after conversion and that, consequently, "their circumstances and various relations and connections between themselves and with other ideas appear more" (Misc. 408, T 249-50).

How does the spirit accomplish this? By focusing the mind's attention on "actual ideas." Thought has a tendency to substitute signs for ideas, to use signs without having the "actual" (i.e., lively, clear, and distinct) ideas they signify. The signs may be words or (confused) ideas of "some sensible part, …effect, …or concomitant, or a few sensible circumstances" of what we are thinking about (Misc.782, T 116).[62] Our ability to make this substitution is advantageous because some actual ideas are not easy to elicit and because thought would be too slow without it; it serves us well for "many of the common purposes of thinking." Nevertheless, it is a disadvantage when "we are at a loss concerning a connection or consequence, or have a new inference to draw, or would see the force of some new argument," for the "use of signs…causes mankind to run into a multitude of errors" (Misc. 782, T 117-18). The tendency to make this substitution is strongest when the ideas terms signify are ideas of "kinds and sorts," or things "of a spiritual nature, or things that consist in the ideas, acts, and exercises of minds" (Misc. 782, T

---

[58] See Miscellany 3S3 (T 110-11) for an instance in which a natural sentiment legitimately affects the reasoning process. Our sense of justice (rightly) leads us to suppose that the world is governed by it.

[59] This need not involve an infusion of supernatural principles. A love of God for His holiness is saving and truly supernatural. A love of God based on disinterested admiration of His greatness and on gratitude for His temporal benefits is not.

[60] Natural goods and evils are those that can be appreciated without the help of infused supernatural principles (i.e., without a love of being in general and the sense of divine beauty that is rooted in it).

[61] There is no indication of what other "ways" Edwards had in mind—if any.

[62] Why must the parts, effects, and so on be sensible? Presumably, because sensible ideas are easier to excite and because sensible things are the kind "we are mainly concerned with" in ordinary life (T 177).

115). This tendency infects *all* (and not merely religious) thinking and can be remedied by attending to ideas instead of the signs that express them.[63]

Actual ideas and attention are closely connected. An idea will not become actual unless one "dwells" on it; "attentive reflection" is necessary. Indeed, "attention of the mind" itself consists "very much" in "exciting the actual idea and making it as lively and clear as we can" (Misc. 782, T 118). But attention is difficult. Even in temporal affairs, taking an "ideal view" (having actual ideas) often depends "not merely on the force of our thoughts but the circumstances we are in, or some special accidental situation and concurrence of things in the course of our thoughts and meditations, or some particular incident in providence that excites a sense of things" (ibid. 121-22). As for *eternal* matters, our attention is distracted by "the great subjection of the soul...to the external senses" and by "the direction of the inclinations...[away] from...things as they are" (ibid. 122). Grace remedies this defect, for one of its effects is to "engage the attention of the mind, with more fixedness and intenseness to that kind of objects; which causes it to have a clearer view of them" (DSL 9-10). Grace "makes even the speculative notions more lively" by assisting and engaging "the attention of the mind" (*RA* 307). Yet why should such extraordinary measures be necessary?

Actual ideas of kinds or sorts are clear and distinct ideas "of those things that are principally essential" in the idea, those things wherein it "most essentially consists" (Misc. 782, T 113, 114). Edwards is undoubtedly thinking of Locke's theory of ideas. Our ideas of God, human nature, and perplexity (Edwards's examples) are complex. The idea of God, for instance, is constructed from the ideas of "supremacy, of supreme power, of supreme government, of supreme knowledge, of will, etc;" (Ibid. 113). Actual ideas of complex ideas such as these involve actual ideas of the ("principally essential"?) simple ideas that compose them.

Actual ideas of things pertaining to good or evil present another difficulty. One cannot have them without being suitably affected, pleased or displeased as the case may be. Actual ideas of these things involve the heart.

Finally, actual ideas of "the ideas, acts, and exercises of minds" are "repetitions of those very things." One cannot have them without experiencing what they are ideas of (Misc. 238, T 247).[64] (Actual ideas of the will or inclination, or the affections, and of things pertaining to them, will thus also involve the heart. An idea of love, for example, is a repetition of it, and love's seat is the heart.)

Our failure to attend to actual ideas has two causes. Sometimes we substitute words and images for ideas we have. Sometimes we lack relevant simple ideas. Both can adversely affect religious reasoning. Those parts of the idea of God that everyone has (ideas of His power, knowledge, and justice, for instance) are not attended to or, when they are, do not affect us with a proper sense of the natural good or evil associated with them. Other parts are simply missing. Without the simple idea of true beauty, people cannot understand God's holiness and the facts that depend on it such as the infinite heinousness of sin or the infinite importance of holiness. Nor can the "carnal" understand genuine benevolence and other properties and qualifications which the elect share with God. Because the idea of true benevolence is a repetition of it, the

---

[63] Cf. Locke's chapters on the imperfection and abuse of words (HU 3.9-11). In 11.8-9, Locke tells us to avoid terms that do not stand for clear and distinct, or determinate, ideas.

[64] Although Edwards overstates his case, there is a measure of truth in it. The idea of an idea is not another instance of it but does include it. The ideas of fear and love are not fear and love, but an experience of these emotions may be needed to acquire them or to have the same ideas of fear and love that others do. Perhaps, too, ideas of this sort only become lively and vivid when we recall the relevant experiences, that is, when how they "feel" comes back to us.

truly benevolent alone have an actual idea of it. Those who are not benevolent only discern its circumstances, effects, and so on, "explaining" the idea of benevolence to themselves and others in "general terms" that do not adequately delimit it (Misc. 123, T 245f).[65]

It should by now be clear how sin affects reasoning. Our immersion in temporal concerns distracts us so that we do not attend to our ideas. Our subjection to the senses aggravates the tendency to substitute words and other sensible signs for ideas, and our disordered loves make it difficult for us to appreciate even natural goods and evils associated with religion. (For example, our blunted conscience blinds us to the natural fittingness of obeying God's commands, and our inordinate attachment to the present life leads us to neglect more important natural goods that extend beyond it.) A lack of true benevolence (which is sin's essence) makes it impossible to understand God's holiness (which consists in it) or to appreciate its beauty.

We are now also in a position to understand why rational arguments for religious truths are not always convincing. Miscellanies 201 (T 246-47) and 408 (T 249-50) imply that a conviction of reality is created by (1) an idea's clarity and liveliness, (2) its internal coherence and coherence with our other ideas, and (3) its agreement with "the nature and constitution of our minds themselves." Why, then, do religious ideas so often fail to carry conviction? Partly because the clarity and intensity of spiritual ideas is a function of "the practice of virtue and holiness'." (Misc. 123, T 246) and our own practice falls woefully short, and partly because the "tempers" or "frames" of the ungodly are not suited to them. (See William James's claim that what seems true and real to us is what we have use for.) It is possible that those without spiritual frames cannot even discern their coherence. Sang Hyun Lee argues that because beauty, on Edwards's view, consists in harmony or proportion, a perception of beauty is a perception of harmony.[66] If proportion and pleasing order are included in coherence, unaided reason may have difficulty grasping it; for it may miss the "sweet harmony" among the ideas of religion and between those ideas and other ideas. (Consider those who reject religion because it does not seem to "fit" or "hang together" with science, although they concede there is no formal inconsistency.)

Special or sanctifying grace remedies these defects by enabling us to attend more easily to the actual ideas the words of religion stand for and by disposing the heart to be suitably affected by the natural and supernatural good and evil associated with them. Common grace has similar effects, but (because it does not replace the love of private systems with true benevolence) it does not furnish the mind with actual ideas of true virtue and true beauty and only affects it with a sense of the relevant *natural* goods and evils.

The sense of divine beauty alone is intrinsically supernatural. A reason that has been freed from the bonds of imagination; prejudice, and narrow self-interest, attends to ideas of God's being, power, knowledge, justice, munificence, and other "natural" attributes and is suitably

---

[65] Although "apprehension" or "an ideal view or contemplation of the thing thought of" (i.e., having an actual idea of it) are closely connected with a sense of the heart, they are not identical with it. The former is contrasted with "mere cogitation," "which is a kind of mental reading wherein we don't look on the things themselves but only on those signs of them that are before our eyes." The latter is contrasted with "mere speculation or understanding of the head," which includes "all that understanding that is without any proper ideal apprehension or view" and all understanding that does not "consist in or imply some motion of the will," that is, that does not involve the heart (Misc. 782, T 118-19). These, distinctions cut across each other. A sense of the heart is not needed to "apprehend" (take "an ideal view" of) mathematical objects.

[66] Sang Hyun Lee, *The Philosophical Theology of Jonathan Edwards* (Princeton: Princeton University Press, 1988). Whether this interpretation is compatible with the simplicity of the idea of true beauty is a moot point. On my account (second section), the idea of true beauty is ontologically distinct from the order or harmony that underlies the disposition to excite it in suitably disposed subjects.

affected by the natural good and evil associated with them is not functioning above its nature.[67] A reason that has been strengthened in these ways is capable, however, of seeing the force of rational arguments for the truths of "natural religion" (i.e., for truths about God that depend neither logically nor epistemically on the ideas of holiness and true beauty). A suitably disposed natural reason is thus capable of establishing God's existence and general nature, and some of our obligations toward Him. Truths that depend on the ideas of holiness and true beauty can also be established by rational arguments, but the force of these can only be appreciated by people with spiritual frames.

IV. Edwards and Evidentialism

Edwards was the philosophical heir of rationalists and empiricists whose confidence in reason was comparatively unqualified. He was the theological heir of a Reformed tradition that distrusted humanity's natural capacities. Did he succeed in coherently weaving these apparently inconsistent strands together? The answer, I believe, is a qualified "Yes."

The key is a distinction between good rational arguments and the conditions necessary for their acceptance. I may have a good argument against smoking, for example, but my desire to smoke prevents me from appreciating its force. What is needed is not a better argument but a reorientation of my desires.

Edwards's position is roughly this. Although reason is capable of generating good rational arguments for God's existence, His providential government of human affairs, predestination, and many other theological and metaphysical doctrines, self-deception, prejudice, self-interest, and other passional factors make it difficult for us to see their force. These faults cannot be corrected by applying Descartes' rules for correct thinking, Locke's "measures…to regulate our assent and moderate our persuasion,"[68] or other methods of this sort. What is needed is a set of excellences that are themselves expressions of morally desirable character traits and rightly ordered affections. The defects distorting human reasoning are deeply rooted in human nature and can only be eliminated by the appropriate virtues.

Two features of Edwards's position are especially significant. First, the epistemic virtues are not merely negative; they involve more than the exclusion of the passions and selfish partialities that subvert reason. Nor are the epistemic virtues confined to noncontroversial excellences such as the love of truth. They include properly ordered natural affections such as gratitude and a love of being in general that God infuses into the hearts of His elect. These affections not only cast out others that adversely affect reasoning; they also affect it themselves. Under their influence, we reason differently and more accurately.

The other significant feature is this. Two views should be distinguished. One is that there are circumstances in which it is legitimate for people's passions and affections to make up deficiencies in the evidence. Although the (objective) evidence is not sufficient to warrant belief, one is entitled to let one's passional nature tip the balance. The other is that a person's passional

---

[67] Although, if I understand Edwards correctly, our bondage to the senses and self-interest can be fully eliminated only by God's infusing true virtue, that is, by His infusing a supernatural principle. Without a supernatural principle to govern them, our natural principles fall into disorder. "Man's nature, being left to itself, forsaken of the spirit of God…of itself became exceedingly corrupt" (*OS* 279). "The absence of positive good principles [holiness or true virtue]…leaving the common natural principles of self-love, natural appetite, etc. (which were in man in innocence)…will certainly be followed with corruption" (*OS* 381).

[68] *HU*, "Introduction," section 3.

nature is sometimes needed to evaluate the evidence properly (to assess its force accurately). The first view is often attributed to James. Edwards holds the second.

Edwards's position differs significantly from the more familiar views of James, Kierkegaard, and others who appeal to passional factors. Edwards is a foundationalist and an evidentialist. A proper, and therefore rational, belief must be self-evident or based on adequate evidence. A properly held belief *in God* rests on evidence (the beauty of scripture, the effects of the Holy Spirit in our souls, apparent design, and so on).[69] But unlike most evidentialists, Edwards believes that passional factors are needed to appreciate the evidence's force. Only those with properly disposed hearts can read the evidence rightly.

Edwards's view thus also differs from Locke's. Fully rational judgments are not only determined by one's evidence and evidential standards; they are also determined by feelings and attitudes that express theological virtues.

But are not the promptings of true benevolence *themselves* evidence of a sort? And if so, is not the difference between Edwards and Locke illusory? I suggest that it is not.

The promptings of true benevolence in this context just *are* the assessments of the force of a body of evidence, e, made by a truly benevolent heart.[70] Suppose that one treats this assessment as a new piece of evidence, e^1. If one does, one must now assess *its* force (or the force of one's other evidence plus e^1). But this new assessment also reflects the state of one's heart. It, too, therefore, must be treated as a new piece of evidence, e^2, whose force (or the combined force of $e + e^1 + e^2$) must in turn be assessed. Hence, if one's assessment of the force of a body of evidence is itself part of one's evidence, then either the force of some of one's evidence is not assessed or one's evidence includes an infinite number of items.

Treating true benevolence's assessment of the force of the evidence as a piece of evidence is as misguided as treating an intellectually honest, critical, and fair-minded historian's assessment of the strength of her argument as one of her premises. One's evidence must be distinguished from one's take on it.

It does not follow that true benevolence's take on the evidence is a "nonrational ground of belief" in Richard Swinburne's sense. A nonrational ground for belief that p is a reason for "believing it to be true other than that it [is] likely to be true." It might be good, for instance, to hold a certain belief although the evidence seems to count against it. (For example, respect for persons might entail a duty to think well of them in spite of appearances.) Or it might be prudentially worthwhile to hold a belief. But (Swinburne argues) even if you have a nonrational ground for believing p, you cannot believe p unless you believe that your evidence makes p probable. To get yourself to believe p, you must therefore get yourself to believe that your evidence supports p. Yet "to get yourself to believe that your evidence makes p probable" when it (now) seems to you that it does not involves "getting yourself to change your inductive standards by adopting standards which you now believe to be incorrect, or by getting yourself to forget about some of the unfavorable evidence, or by getting yourself to acquire new favorable evidence through looking only where favorable evidence is to be found and then forgetting the selective character of your investigation." It thus involves deliberately inducing beliefs that are irrational by your present standards.[71]

---

[69] One must remember, however, that the most compelling evidence is the divine beauty or splendor that the elect see in the Gospel, in Christ, in the saints, and so on. (The belief that these are truly beautiful is properly basic.)

[70] The assessments made by a truly benevolent heart must be distinguished from its perception of true beauty. The latter is a new piece of evidence.

71. Although they will not *seem* irrational once you have acquired them, and although (after you have acquired them) they will be rationally held in the sense that they follow from the evidence you will then have by the

True benevolence's assessment of the evidence is not a nonrational ground for belief in this sense. It does not lead the saints to construct new inductive or deductive standards, forget about some of the evidence, or engage in selective investigation. Nor does it provide them with a *reason* for doing so. True benevolence is not a nonrational ground for belief in Swinburne's sense because it is not a *ground* for belief at all, although its presence *does* partially explain why the saints hold the beliefs they do. In the same way, a good scientist's impartiality, intellectual honesty, and desire for the truth help explain why she holds the beliefs she does and not the views of some less scrupulous or more credulous colleague. But they are not *grounds* for her belief.

The position Edwards represents must be distinguished, then, from other more familiar views. Whether it can be defended against charges of subjectivism, circularity, and relativism will be discussed in Chapters 4 and 5.

Questions

1. In what way if any, do you think Edwards affirms rationality?

2. Do you think that Edwards gives a good account of the rational side, and the skeptical slant on nature's gifts taught by the Reformers?

3. What weaknesses if any do you see in an evidentialist approach?

4. What weakness if any do you see in a foundationalist approach?

5. What strengths do you find in Edwards estimation of evidence as it relates to faith?

---

inductive standards you will then hold. (For Swinburne's discussion, see *Faith and Reason* [Oxford: Clarendon, 1981], pp. 82-92.)

WHICH KINDS OF RELIGIOUS BELIEFS ARE WORTH HAVING?[*]

Richard Swinburne

Swinburne offers an internalist approach to the justification of religious belief. He contends that religious beliefs worth having are those which are epistemically justified because of their probability. Three senses of probability are examined. According to his Principle of Credulity, all basic propositions have a probability proportioned to the strength of our belief in them. He concludes most have a need for historical argument and evidence in order to have probably true beliefs.

In this paper I am concerned with which of rival theories of epistemic justification (which I equate with rationality) or warrant (in the sense of that quantity enough of which turns strong true belief into knowledge) have the consequence that rational religious belief or knowledge are attainable and worth having. I understand by theories of epistemic justification theories in which the point of having a justified belief is that justification is an indication of truth; a justified belief is one that is probably true. Most current theories, internalist and externalist, are of this kind (though they are sometimes not up-front about this.)[1] Since true belief is obviously worth having, and so often the nearest thing we can get to it is probably true belief, it is clearly a good thing to have probably true belief. Yet there are different ways in which beliefs are probably true; and before going further, we need to sort these out.

There are, in my view, three basic kinds of probability—physical, statistical and inductive. Physical probability is a measure of the extent to which nature has a propensity towards bringing forth events. The propensity may vary with time. A possible event has a probability of 1 if and when it is predetermined to happen and a probability of 0 if and when it is predetermined not to happen. Values intermediate between 1 and 0 of the probability of an event measure the extent of the bias in nature towards the occurrence of an event. I mention this kind of probability only to distinguish it from the other two kinds of probability which will be our main concern. Statistical probability is a measure of the proportion of events of one kind in some class of events. The probability of an American voting for George Bush in the 2000 election just is the proportion of

---

[*] This article is printed by courtesy of the author, Richard Swinburne.
[1] Plantinga has claimed that classical internalism (especially in the writings of Descartes and Locke) has a deontogical structure, being concerned with our epistemic duties—which beliefs we ought epistemically to adopt. See Alvin Plantinga, *Warrant: The Current Debate*, Oxford University Press, 1993, p. 4. But the concept of duty has application only to actions which we can choose to perform; and at a given time we cannot choose what to believe then and there. So any "epistemic duty" involved in synchronic justification has to be spelled out as it is by Chisholm, as a duty to believe something if—*per impossibile*—one could choose one's beliefs. (See R.M. Chisholm, *Theory of Knowledge*, Third edition. Prentice-Hall, 1989, pp. 58-60.) And for Chisholm that duty is a duty to believe what is probably true; and his theory of epistemic justification is a theory of probable truth. The notion of duty clearly has a place in a theory of diachronic justification (in the sense of having a belief which is not merely synchronically justified, that is the right response to the believer's situation at the time—which is what I am concerned with in this paper, but is also the result of adequate investigation), because adequately to investigate a belief is something we can choose to do or not to do. I think that quite a lot of earlier talk about epistemic duty was concerned with a duty to investigate rather than a duty to believe this or that in response to evidence. Locke certainly had a considerable concern with the former—in the very passage which Plantinga quotes from Locke to illustrate his thesis about him, Locke writes that he who "seeks sincerely to discover truth by those [God-given] helps and abilities he has, may have this satisfaction in doing his duty as a rational creature" (J. Locke, *An Essay Concerning Human Understanding* 4.17.24. Cited by Plantinga, op.cit. p.13.) But there are certainly other sentences in Locke which seem concerned with how one should respond to given evidence.

Americans who did so vote. The class may be an actual class (as in this example) or a hypothetical class—the proportion of heads in a series of tosses of this coin if we were to toss it a trillion times (and to have a clear notion, we need to specify the conditions under which the toss would be made). Finally there is inductive probability (which I shall equate with logical probability), which is a measure of the extent to which one proposition (which may be the content of a belief) makes another proposition likely to be true[2].

A theory of justification is internalist if the justification of a belief is a matter of something internal to the belief or to its relation to other mentally accessible phenomena—either introspectible mental states, or a priori truths. A theory is externalist if it is not internalist—if justification depends on phenomena of which the subject may be unaware. The normal form of externalist theory is a reliabilist theory, or one which has a central reliabilist element. The reliabilist's "probability" is statistical probability. A given belief is justified to the extent to which the statistical probability of a belief produced by a process of the type which produces it being true is high. It may be probability in the actual class of beliefs produced by that process, or probability in the class of beliefs produced by that process if we continued to repeat the productive process indefinitely often. The internalist's "probability" is logical probability. He is concerned with how far someone's mental states render a given belief logically probable. I shall assume—for the sake of simplicity of exposition—that the internalism is doxastic internalism, that is that the only relevant states are the subject's other beliefs or inclinations to believe. A subject starts with inclinations of different strengths to believe various propositions, in so far as he finds himself with them (because they seem to him forced on him by the world), and not in so far as (in his view) they are rendered probable by other of his beliefs. These are the subject's evidence. The strength of an inclination to believe a proposition is measured by the probability which the subject would ascribe to that proposition (if he had that conception the evidence merely of his having that inclination;) those propositions to which he ascribes a probability greater than half are his basic beliefs. For an internalist a belief is justified in so far as it is based upon and rendered logically probable by the subject's rightly (or properly) basic beliefs, these being those which do have the degree of probability which the subject ascribes to them in virtue of being believed.

So much for what the theories are. What is to be said in favor of each theory? To begin with, why does the reliabilist think it a good thing to have his beliefs produced by a process which has a high statistical probability of producing true beliefs? The answer is surely because he believes a version of what Lewis called the Principal Principle, that the fact that proportion n of A's are B make it logically probable to degree n that any named A will be B. The higher the statistical probability of some process producing beliefs, the greater the logical probability on the evidence that a particular belief was produced by that process is that that belief is true. The Principal Principle is without doubt a correct principle of logical probability. Hence, on the evidence of that statistical probability, the belief is probably true. And that, plausibly, is a reason for having a belief justified in the reliabilist sense. And why does the internalist think it a good thing to have beliefs rendered probable by his rightly basic proportions? By definition, in so far as the propositions are rightly basic, they are probably true in virtue of being believed. And in so

---

[2] For a fuller account of these kinds of probability see my *Epistemic Justification*, Clarendon Press, 2001, chapter 3. I distinguish there three kinds of inductive probability—logical probability as the probability of one proposition on another by correct criteria of inductive probability, epistemic probability as the measure of this which is attainable by a person of a certain logical competence, and subjective probability as the measure of this by a certain person using his own criteria of inductive probability. The latter two measures are person-relative. I ignore these two latter kinds of inductive probability and so the kinds of rationality to which they give rise, as less central to the issues of this paper.

far as what is probable makes something else probable, that something else has quite a degree of probability—not of course quite as much as the initial basic proposition, but so long as the logical probability is quite high, not too much less. So both theorists are interested in having beliefs rendered logically probable by their starting point.

However, the two theorists have considerable problems. And the first problem for both theorists is to justify their starting point. The reliabilist's problem here is "the generality problem." He needs to justify his assessing the probability of a token belief by one piece of evidence (misleadingly perhaps called "evidence" because the believer may have no access to it), when it will have quite a different probability on other evidence of the same kind (no more or less accessible than the evidence the reliabilist has privileged). For the token process which produced the believer's belief will belong to innumerable different types of belief production, and the statistical probabilities of beliefs produced by processes of these types may be very different from each other. For any token process of belief production involves many different factors; it therefore belongs to very many different types, delineated in terms of different combinations of those causal factors. I have the belief that I was in Greece in 1982. This belief was produced by apparent memory. Apparent memory in all humans is, let us say, 70% reliable. But I'm not just any human; I have all sorts of particular features which affect whether my memories of different kinds are true. I am an aged Professor and maybe the memories of aged Professors are a lot less accurate than are those of most other people. And my memory concerns an event twenty-two years ago and maybe we should measure the justification of my belief by the proportion of true beliefs among beliefs about events twenty-two years ago by aged Professors, and maybe that brings my justification down to the 55% level. Maybe too I've taken LSD recently, and maybe the proportion of true beliefs produced by apparent memory in LSD takers of a kind considered so far is low—say 30%. Once the statistical probability falls below 50%, the belief in question is no longer justified. We could take into account more and more causal factors, until we individuate the process of belief production so narrowly that the given belief is the only one actually produced by it. And then if we measure its justification by the proportion of true beliefs actually produced by that process, it will be 1 if the belief is true and 0 if the belief is false. Justification has collapsed into truth. An alternative is to measure justification by the proportion of true beliefs produced by this process if we repeated the exact same circumstances again and again. But the proportions would still be 1 or 0 in deterministic universes, and close thereto in many other universes. Clearly we have to refer the token process to a type of process described less narrowly—but there seems no principled way of choosing one such type rather than another and so for supposing that any one kind of reliabilist justification is worth having. I regard this problem as insuperable within a pure reliabilist theory.

The internalist starts from a clearly delimitable finite class of basic propositions (with given strengths). Justification is relative to the total available evidence. But perhaps not all basic propositions are rightly basic, and maybe they need to have ascribed to them probabilities other than the believer is initially inclined to ascribe. The internalist's problem is to justify an account of how to ascribe probabilities to rightly basic proportions. Sometimes we may have a posteriori grounds for trusting basic propositions of certain kinds and not others. But these grounds will be in the form of other basic propositions which make probable a theory which renders the former basic propositions improbable. Such considerations however do not affect the right basicality of these former propositions, only whether they get promoted to beliefs in the light of our overall evidence. In the main we operate with, and are purely right to operate with the Principle of Credulity, that *all* basic propositions have a logical probability proportional to the strength of our belief in them, merely on the (infallible) evidence that they are believed with this strength. But there is an issue of whether there are any a priori considerations which affect the probability of basic propositions considered individually, considerations which suggest that we should give them a higher or lower probability than the probability which reflects our initial degree of conviction of their truth. I think there is one major such consideration—scope. A very detailed basic belief (one that holds in fewer possible worlds) is as such less probable than a much less detailed one—I should trust my belief that I've seen a lot of people in the room more than my belief that I've seen exactly 67 people in the room. And in consequence those which hold in all logically possible worlds should have a probability of 1, and those which hold in no logically possible worlds should have a probability of 0. Since the consideration of scope suffices to deal with the probabilities of logically necessary and improbable propositions, the Principle of Credulity then becomes a principle for dealing with the apparent deliverances of experience, what we seem to see or remember. It says: they are probably true in so far as you are inclined to believe them. And it is surely generally correct in this. There is no a priori reason for confining the application of this principle to a certain kind of basic proposition (e.g. inclinations to belief produced by the five senses). For it cannot be an a priori truth that we have five senses. This latter is something to be discovered by inference from the whole collection of our basic propositions. So I claim that the Principle of Credulity, qualified as above and possibly subject to one or two minor further a priori qualifications[3], is one that seems to almost all of us in our non-philosophical moments to be evidently true. If you don't trust experience in the absence of counter-evidence, you will have to be massively skeptical about the external world, other minds etc. And since virtually none of us are thus skeptical, we must recognize the foundation of that lack of skepticism—the Principle of Credulity. The internalist appeals to a principle which we can all recognize. So the internalist has a vastly more secure starting point than the reliabilist.

The second problem for the internalist is—why use one set of criteria for extrapolating from his basic propositions rather than any other set. And my answer here is the same as my answer to the first problem—within rough limits, 99.999% of us all do use the same criteria about mundane observable matters, and these criteria seem to us obviously correct. Without these criteria there would not be the almost unanimous consensus of the human race about what will happen and how things will behave tomorrow in a whole class of respects. We believe that the sun will rise tomorrow, approximately 24 hours after it has risen today because this has happened innumerable times in the past without exception. For the same kind of reason we believe that the next stone I drop will fall to the ground, that houses will not vanish in the night and so on. The use of common criteria for extrapolation alone explains this consensus. And the consensus continues when the criteria are extrapolated into the more complicated areas of sophisticated science and historical investigation.

My account of these criteria is as follows.[4] We regard an explanatory hypothesis h on the

---

[3] I argue in *Epistemic Justification* (pp. 110-15) that all propositions have an intrinsic probability deriving from their scope and the simplicity of the possible worlds in which they are true. The apparent deliverancies of experience to have observed that some proposition is true then add to that intrinsic probability. I mention in the text the role of scope in affecting probability; it does this in virtue of the fact that propositions with large scope start from a lower intrinsic probability which someone's apparent observation that they are true will increase in virtue of the Principle of Credulity. But the greater its scope, the less the probability which an apparent observation of its truth of given strength will give to the proposition. Simplicity plays a similar role (in increasing probability). But I do not discuss this in the text because the simplicity of the possible worlds to which they belong is not going to create much difference between propositions reporting the deliverances of experience about what happened on some particular occasion (which is what most basic propositions concern). Simplicity does however make a great difference to the intrinsic probability of explanatory theories, and I comment on this later.

[4] The probability referred to in (1), (2) and (3) below is logical probability. The value of the probability in (1) is a deductive consequence of h in virtue of principles of "downward inference" such as the Principal Principle which I discuss in the text. Then if h is "all As are B", and "this an A" and e is "this is a B", the probability of e given h is 1. The value of the probability in (2) involves not only principles of "downward inference" but the prior probabilities

basis of evidence e and background knowledge k as probably true in so far as (1) h makes e probable (given k), (2) not -h makes e improbable (given k) and (3) h has high prior probability (given k). k maybe our knowledge of how things behave in other fields of inquiry, but where h a very wide-ranging hypothesis, there will be no contingent background knowledge. The prior probability of h is to be determined solely by a priori considerations—scope (the more detailed and wide-ranging the theory, the lower its probability, for this reason), and—much more importantly—simplicity (the simpler the theory, the greater its probability for this reason). Our evidence is provided by the content of our own rightly basic propositions and also those of other people who tell us what they have observed or believe to be generally accepted on the basis of observation by others—"what everybody knows". We use the evidence of others in virtue of a Principle of Testimony, that what others tell us about their own basic propositions is probably true. This principle may itself be a basic principle, as some have urged; or rendered probable (in the light of the above criteria) by the content of our own basic propositions. Either way, it is clearly a principle we all accept and think it right to accept.

On the basis of the above criteria, I believe, we infer to hypotheses about how things work—sophisticated scientific ones or simple hypotheses about the causal powers of observable things (such as "stones have an innate tendency to fall to the ground") and thence to predictions about the future. There is philosophical dispute about how these criteria, especially the criterion of simplicity, are to be spelled in detail; and also about how to apply them to areas such as metaphysics and religion. But the extent of agreement about how to apply these criteria to other areas is so great, and metaphysical and religious claims are claims differing only in their scope and ultimacy from narrower claims, that it should be possible to work out how to apply the criteria to them. In general we all agree about these criteria, and they seem to us obviously correct. The internalist can meet all objections to his theory.

Reliabilism however has a further problem beyond the—to my mind insuperable "generality problem"; and this is a problem that will also beset any other form of externalism. I have been discussing different theories of what constitutes the justified response by way of belief to the believer's circumstances at a particular moment. But believers will try to improve their beliefs, seek ones which are better justified (whether the same ones, or rival ones, or ones about new topics—a task which we all believe that we can set about). The internalist has a recipe for setting about this—look for more evidence. For beliefs on the given topic new evidence (in the form of new basic propositions) *may* either make your belief more probable than it was, or make its contradictory more probable than the original belief. Although new evidence may not have this effect, it is worth looking for it in the hope that it may. And there is a theorem of the probability calculus that it is *always* probable that new evidence will give you a belief more probably true.[5] And the believer can look for evidence on a new topic. And he can reflect on the correctness of his a priori criteria, and consider whether they yield intuitively correct judgments about various cases and correct his criteria and perhaps also those judgments by reflective equilibrium.

But how is the reliabilist to improve the quality of his beliefs? What makes his beliefs justified or not need not be in any way accessible to him—they may be produced by an unreliable process, but he may not be aware of this. If the justifying facts are accessible to him, reflect on how this will have come about. He may just have a basic belief that a certain type of process is reliable (unlikely), or (more likely) he may form a basic belief that he has observed, or

---

of theories rival to h, as determined by the principles described in the text. For a far fuller account of these criteria, see my *Epistemic Justification*, chapter 4.

[5] See *Epistemic Justification*, pp. 171-2.

(more likely still) he may have a basic belief that he has heard from others that this type of process has produced true beliefs on many past occasions. So he had good evidence that the process is reliable, because this is rendered logically probable by his basic beliefs using the Principles of Credulity and Testimony and the other inductive criteria which I have described. Hence he can have an internally justified belief about which processes of belief acquisition are reliable, and he can improve the quality of his belief about this, by getting and using more evidence of the same kind; and so be in a position to believe only beliefs produced by reliable processes. But if he is prepared to use internalist criteria in this way to get information about which processes are reliable, there can be no principled rationale for not using the same criteria and other basic propositions to add to or subtract from the probability that a given belief (produced by a reliable process) is true—for he may have other strong evidence that that belief is false. And there can be no principled rationale for not using the internalist criteria for the justification of beliefs in cases where the believer has no access to evidence about the reliability of belief-forming processes. And having acquired probably true beliefs in this way it would seem absurd to say that these beliefs were not in any important sense "rational" or "justified".

Yet if the reliabilist refuses the comfort of internalism to give him a justified belief about whether some belief was produced by a reliable process, there is nothing he can do to improve the quality of his beliefs. Looking for more evidence will not help, for he declines to rely on a priori criteria of what that evidence shows. And clearly any externalist other than a reliabilist who refuses to use internalist criteria faces the same insuperable difficulty—unless you can have internally justified evidence about which kinds of beliefs satisfy your externalist criteria, you can have no procedure for getting beliefs better justified on those externalist criteria.

I conclude that internalism appeals to considerations which we all recognize to be correct and without which we could not live in this world, and provides a recipe for improving the quality of our beliefs; whereas pure reliabilism cannot provide a principle for selecting the relevant type of belief forming process; and even if it could, neither it or any other form of pure externalism gives us any way of improving the quality of our beliefs, which is something which we all want to do and believe that we can do. Pure externalism surely has no future as a plausible account of rationality.

Interestingly most forms of externalism are not pure externalist theories, for many of them are of the form "A belief B is justified if it is produced by a reliable process [or satisfies some other externalist criterion] so long as the believer does not have a defeater", and "having" a defeater tends to mean having accessible evidence which renders the belief logically improbable! It's very difficult to be a pure externalist.

Externalist theories of warrant have just the same problems. Take Plantinga's theory (which is not a pure reliabilist theory). For Plantinga, you will recall [6], a belief has warrant (subject to defeaters) if and only if: (1) it is produced by cognitive faculties functioning properly, (2) in a cognitive environment sufficiently similar to that for which the faculties were designed, (3) according to a design plan aimed at the production of true beliefs, when (4) there is a high statistical probability of such beliefs being true.

Thus my belief that there is a table in front of me has warrant if in the first place, in producing it, my cognitive faculties were functioning properly, the way they were meant to function, by which Plantinga's understands "in the way their creator (whoever that was) meant them to function". If God made us, our faculties function properly if they function in the way God designed them to function; whereas if Evolution (uncaused by God) made us, (the main alternative which Plantinga considers), then our faculties function properly if they function in the

---

[6] Alvin Plantinga, *Warrant and Proper Function*, Oxford University Press, 1993, p. 194.

way that (in some sense) Evolution designed them to function.

God or Evolution designed us to function only in a particular environment (e.g. in a particular ecological niche, or in a society where people always tell the truth). Plausibly, whether God or Evolution made us, they meant most of our cognitive faculties to work in such a way that they yield true beliefs, e.g. so that when we look at a desk, we acquire the belief that there is a desk in front of us—in a typical Earth environment. However some of our cognitive faculties may be designed to produce beliefs having characteristics other than or additional to truth—e.g. comforting or inspiring beliefs; and warrant only arises when the cognitive faculty operating is the one designed to produce true beliefs. But some possible designers (e.g. lesser deities) may be bad designers, and so the faculty has to produce true beliefs most of the time, for a particular belief which it produces to have warrant. This final requirement is of course a reliabilist requirement, but it is not immediately open to the normal reliabilist problem of how the type is to be specified. For the type is that of "the design plan aimed at the production of true beliefs", that is the type by which the creator intended our true beliefs to be produced. So long as the creator has intentions, then the type is uniquely specified. God is an agent who has intentions, and so there is clear meaning to clause (1) given the way Plantinga understands "proper functioning"; and so to clauses (2), (3), and (4), given that God does design some faculties aimed at the production of true beliefs. The type of cognitive faculty is uniquely specified by God's plan about how we should acquire true beliefs of various kinds. But if God (or any other intentional agent) did not create us (and Plantinga is seeking an account of warrant which does not presuppose this), then there is a big problem about how (1) is to be understood. For evolution (or any other inanimate cause) is not an agent who has intentions (despite the incautious talk by some biologists about our organs having "design plans"). The only sense which I can give to Evolution "intending" anything is that it causes it. Cognitive faculties function properly if they function the way Evolution causes them to function; their design plan is "aimed" at the production of true beliefs only in so far as it does produce true beliefs in that environment; and an environment is "sufficiently similar" to that for which the faculties were "designed" only in so far as they produce true beliefs just as well in that new environment. And so the whole edifice collapses on to (4) which is simple reliabilism. If "Evolution" made us, then if the cognitive faculties which it produced produce largely true beliefs, then those beliefs are warranted. We've seen that a reliabilist theory of warrant has just the same problems as a reliabilist theory of justification. But even if there is a God, the "proper functioning" theory of warrant still suffers from the other major problem of externalist theories that they give us no access to whether our beliefs are warranted without help from an internalist theory of justification. In order to improve the quality of our beliefs we need first to discover whether or there is a God, for only with this knowledge can we be aware of what constitutes our cognitive faculties functioning properly. And then we need to discover how God intended our cognitive faculties to function (a harder task!) Externalism provides no means for us to discover these things. Internalism does provide such a means—but with internalist resources we can go straight to investigating whether or not there is a God; it is irrelevant how he intended our cognitive faculties to function. Plantinga's conclusion to his 500-page *Warranted Christian Belief* that "if Christian belief is true, it very likely does have warrant"[7], may well-given Plantinga's sense of "warrant"—be correct; and indeed be internally justified by the arguments of that book. But this conditional is of little use to anyone without some information about the truth of the antecedent; and on that, Plantinga explicitly acknowledges in his final paragraph, he cannot help us. He writes that "the really important question" is whether Christian belief is true, "and here we pass beyond the competence

---

[7] Alvin Plantinga, *Warranted Christian Belief*, Oxford University Press, 2000, p. 498.

of philosophy."

I conclude that any externalist theory of justification or warrant has at least one and normally two enormous deficiencies. We cannot give a principled reason for choosing the particular variant that we do; and we have no way of improving the quality (that is the epistemic justification) of our beliefs. It is however pretty obvious that we do have a way of improving the quality of our beliefs, and so internalism must be true—which is just as well because a theory which offers us rationality without a way of improving the rationality of our beliefs offers us a great deal less than one which does. This is not to say that everyone can articulate the correct internalist theory. That requires philosophical work. I've made suggestions earlier in this paper as to what the structure of a correct internalist theory should be.

What follows for religious belief? Basic beliefs vary with the believer. There is no doubt that some people have a very strong basic belief that there is a God, normally produced by an apparent awareness of his presence. Given my Principle of Credulity, they are right so to believe. If the belief is strong enough, then counter-evidence form evil or anything else will not weaken it very much. "There is a God" may indeed by a properly basic belief—for some people. Reformed epistemology Phase One (that is The Reformed Epistemology typified by Plantinga's contribution to *Faith and Rationality* [8] in contrast to the externalist epistemology of Phase Two, typified by *Warranted Christian Belief*) taught this, and taught in effect that this is an a priori truth. [9] It notoriously had difficulty in justifying the claim that "The Great Pumpkin returns every Halloween" could not also be—for some people—a properly basic belief. My principles suggest that it could be, though I do not think that it ever is; and anyway there is a lot of counter-evidence to this claim. Also, I do not think that very many people, either today or in earlier times, have been in the fortunate position of having "There is a God" as a strong properly basic belief [10]. Certainly many people have had experiences of the apparent presence of God which are not overwhelming experiences and so need backing up by argument. And many people including theists have had no such experiences. I may be mistaken about proportions here, but certainly there are theists in all these categories. And most theists as well of course as atheists, therefore need arguments, at least to back up the deliverancies of experience.

A class of argument which was, I suspect, very influential in the Middle Ages and has had some influence at all periods has been the argument from authority. Many a medieval villager believed that there was a God because his parents or the village priest or some visiting

---

[8] "Reason and Belief in God" in (ed.) Alvin Plantinga and Nicholas Wolterstorff, *Faith and Rationality*, University of Notre Dame Press, 1983.

[9] Plantinga claims there (pp. 74-82) that when we find ourselves forming the belief that there is a God under certain conditions (e.g. when reading the Bible and feeling guilty for what one has done), that belief is properly basic. We can be rational in believing that it is properly basic without having or having justified a theory of proper basicality. But the way to form and justify such a theory is, he claims, (p. 76) to "assemble examples of beliefs and conditions such that the former are obviously properly basic in the latter, and examples of beliefs and conditions such that the former are obviously *not* properly basic in the latter. We must then frame hypotheses as to the necessary and sufficient conditions of proper basicality and test these hypotheses by reference to those examples". Plantinga describes this method as "inductive"; but this seems a mistaken description for it is characteristic of an inductive argument that it only yields probable truth if its premises are contingent truths. But it is irrelevant to Plantinga's method whether the examples are examples of actually held beliefs and actual conditions; they are examples of basic beliefs which would be proper to hold under certain conditions if those conditions occurred, and that this is so is an a priori discovery of a necessary truth. The method is the method of "reflective equilibrium" by which we reach principles of morality by reflecting on what people ought and ought not to do in various specific circumstances—an a priori method. Since the kind of circumstances which he describes are ones to which we have access, we can know that "there is a God" without having any view about the process which caused us to have that belief.

[10] "I am sure there are many who never had a showing or vision, but only the normal teaching of Holy Church, and who love God better than I do"—Julian of Norwich, *Revelations of Divine Love* (transl.) E. Spearing, Penguin Books, 1998, p. 54.

friar told him that there is a God, because—they said—they had experienced God or it was well authenticated that miracles (which could be performed only by God) occurred, or simply that wise men had established that there is a God. In virtue of the Principle of Testimony, the villager was right so to believe (it was probably true)—in the absence of counter-evidence (which may be simply counter-testimony; other people telling our villager differently). One strong piece of evidence that others are telling you what they believe strongly and so believe to be very probable is that this belief manifestly makes a great difference to the way they live, that relying on this belief they have come to live in a way otherwise quite unnatural. Even if we do not have their experiences and cannot appreciate the arguments, the fact that people have come to live sacrificial lives in consequence of those experiences and arguments is evidence of their worth. But people differ in respect of whether they have much of this kind of evidence on authority, and whether it is nullified by the existence of people, apparently at least as learned, who tell them that there is no God.

Into this category comes the argument of popular medieval apologetic that "the conversion of the western world" without force of arms is strong evidence for Christianity. It is an argument of some worth, but inevitably not as strong for us who know that rival movements have also had considerable success in converting without force of arms—Buddhism, for example.

In an age of religious skepticism when there are good arguments against theism known to most people, and there are always authorative atheists as well as authorative theists, we need arguments for the existence of God which start from basic beliefs held very strongly by theist and atheist alike and proceed thence by criteria shared between theist and atheist. To produce such arguments is the aim of natural theology. It starts from the most general natural phenomena—the existence of the world, its conformity to natural laws, and such like and attempts to argue thence deductively or by criteria of inductive reasoning used in other areas of inquiry. And the historical truths of the Christian religion need to be backed up by inductive arguments beginning in part from historical data recognized by theist and atheist alike—I stress "in part" because the important events of the life, death and Resurrection of Jesus are events far more likely to occur if there is a God than if there is not, and hence the evidence of natural theology is also evidence relevant to these events. Detailed historical arguments have not normally been thought as part of "natural theology", but they clearly belong to the same genre of objective reasoning from public data, though to more specific conclusions.

Though more people need natural theology today than ever before, it has always been needed; and almost all Christian theologians of the first 1750 years of Christianity (as well as several of the biblical authors) have taught that there are cogent arguments of natural theology available for those who need them. It is sometimes not immediately obvious that some biblical or patristic argument is a piece of natural theology, because it takes the existence of a "god" of some sort for granted and argues to his goodness or his wisdom. But it is natural theology if it argues that the power in charge of the Universe is not just any "god", but God—omnipotent, omniscient, and perfectly good. Given that, there are various short passages of the Old and New Testaments which are pieces of natural theology,[11] as well as longer passages in *The Wisdom of Solomon*.[12] So many of the Christian fathers of the first millennium A.D. have their brief few

---

[11] On this see James Barr, *Biblical Faith and Natural Theology*, Clarendon Press, 1993.

[12] And St. Paul tells us that pagans have no excuse for not worshipping God because "what can be known about God is plain to them, because God has shown it to them. Ever since the creation of the world his eternal power and divine nature, invisible though they are, have been understood and seen through the things he has made". (*Epistle to the Romans*, 1. 19-20). St Paul does however seem to assume that pagans of ancient times looking at the natural world

paragraphs of natural theology, arguing especially that the regular behavior of the natural world points to an omnipotent and omniscient God as its creator. To cite but a few examples— Irenaeus, *Against Heresies*, II. 1-9; Gregory of Nyssa, *On the Soul and the Resurrection*, chapter 1; Augustine, *On Free Will*, 2.12.33; Maximus the Confessor, *Difficulties*, 10.35; and St. John of Damascus, *On the Orthodox Faith*, 1.3.

The brief paragraphs of the fathers of the first millennium became the long treatises of the medieval West; and Anselm, Bonaventure, Aquinas and Scotus, developed natural theology at great length. And the tradition continued with Leibniz and Clark, Butler and Paley. It was only as a result of what I can only regard as rather bad arguments by Hume, Kant, and followers of Darwin, that natural theology went out of favor for most of the nineteenth and twentieth centuries.

Similarly, it is hard to read the Gospels, Acts of the Apostles, and I Corinthians without seeing them as claiming that various historical events (above all, the Resurrection) occurred and that others can know these things on the testimony of the apostles to have seen them. St. Luke tells us that in writing his Gospel, he was one of many who were putting into writing what they had been told by those who, "from the beginning were eyewitnesses and servants of the Word", and he was doing so in order that the recipient of his Gospel, Theophilus, "may know the truth concerning the things about which you have been instructed".[13] The earliest writings of the next century appealed to the New Testament not as authoritative scripture, but as historical evidence. Clement tells us that the apostles' doubts were "set at rest by the Resurrection of Our Lord Jesus Christ from the dead".[14] Ignatius[15] and Justin[16] (or the author of *On the Resurrection* attributed to him) both emphasize that the disciples touched the risen Christ; and Justin writes that they were "by every kind of proof persuaded that it was [Jesus] Himself". Irenaeus appeals for the truth of his teaching to Polycarp who was instructed by apostles, and conversed with many who had seen Christ".[17]

With the third century different strains of apologetic become far more prevalent. The conversion of the Western world without force of arms and the apparent miracles associated therewith, were used as evidence of the truth of Christian doctrines. But this, I think, is only because as time went by, the chain of witnesses required to authenticate the historical events became longer and longer and so more and more open to the suspicion that there was at some stage misreporting. We however are in a much better position than the medieval world to detect (by comparing texts) where scribes have miscopied, and to trace common sources of events reported by more than one author. We have historical knowledge and expertise which puts us in a position as good as that of the second century to assess the detailed historical evidence (to be supported by the evidence of natural theology) for the historical claims of Christianity.

Most of us need natural theology and historical argument in order to have probably true religious beliefs, and Christian Tradition claims that these are available.

---

would inevitably see that there is a God (perhaps as a basic belief) and that there would be no need for complicated argument.

[13] Luke 1. 1-4.

[14] Clement's First Epistle to the Corinthians 42.

[15] *Epistle to the Smyrnaeans* 3.

[16] *On the Resurrection* 9. (*The Writings of the Fathers*, vol. 1. *Justin Martyr and Athenagoras*, transl. M. Dodds, G. Reith and B.P. Pratten, T. and T. Clark, 1868.)

[17] *Against Heresies* 3.3.4. (*The Writings of the Fathers*, vol. 5. *Irenaeus*, vol. I, transl. A. Roberts and W.H. Rambault, T. And T. Clark, 1868.)

Questions

1. What makes Swinburne's approach internalistic in contrast to Plantinga's externalism?

2. What for Swinburne makes a religious belief worth having?

3. Do you think that Swinburne is right about his claim regarding religious beliefs worth having?

4. What counts as a religious belief worth having for you?

5. What do you make of Swinburne's Principle of Credulity?

LECTURES ON RELIGIOUS BELIEFS*

Ludwig Wittgenstein

For Wittgenstein, appraisals of truth, meaning, and justification of religious beliefs must occur within the context of cultural-linguistic thought forms. Since all terms derive their meaning from contextual usage, attention must be given to the linguistic/cultural contextual frameworks if one is to follow sound principles in such matters as appraisal of truth claims, unpacking the meaning of terms, and the business of justifying religious beliefs.

I

An Austrian general said to someone: "I shall think of you after my death, if that should be possible." We can imagine one group who would find this ludicrous, another who wouldn't.

(During the war, Wittgenstein saw consecrated bread being carried in chromium steel. This struck him as ludicrous.)

Suppose that someone believed in the Last Judgment, and I don't, does this mean that I believe the opposite of him, just that there won't be such a thing? I would say "not at all, or not always."

Suppose I say that the body will rot, and another says "No. Particles will rejoin in a thousand years, and there will be a Resurrection of you."

If some said: "Wittgenstein, do you believe in this?" I'd say: "No." "Do you contradict the man?" I'd say: "No."

If you say this, the contradiction already lies in this.

Would you say: "I believe the opposite," or "There is no reason to suppose such a thing"? I'd say neither.

Suppose someone were a believer and said: "I believe in a Last Judgment," and 1 said: "Well, I'm not so sure. Possibly" You would say that there is an enormous gulf between us. If he said "There is a German aeroplane overhead," and I said "Possibly I'm not so sure," you'd say we were fairly near.

It isn't a question of my being anywhere near him, but on an entirely different plane, which you could express by saying: "You mean something altogether different, Wittgenstein."

The difference might not show up at all in any explanation of the meaning.

Why is it that in this case I seem to be missing the entire point?

Suppose somebody made this guidance for this life: believing in the Last Judgment. Whenever he does anything, this is before his mind. In a way, how are we to know whether to say he believes this will happen or not?

Asking him is not enough. He will probably say he has proof.

But he has what you might call an unshakeable belief. It will show, not by reasoning or by appeal to ordinary grounds for belief, but rather by regulating for in all his life.

This is a very much stronger fact—foregoing pleasures, always appealing to this picture. This is one sense must be called the firmest of all beliefs, because the man risks things on

---

* This article is reprinted by courtesy of the publisher. *Source:* Ludwig Wittgenstein, *Lectures and Conversations an Aesthetics, Psychology, and Religious Belief,* translated/edited by Cyril Barrett (Berkeley, CA.: University of California Press, 1996), pp. 53-66.

account of it which he would not do on things which are by far better established for him. Although he distinguishes between things well-established and not well-established.

Lewy: Surely, he would say it is extremely well-established.

First, he may use "well-established" or not use it at all. He will treat this belief as extremely well-established, and in another way as not well-established at all.

If we have a belief, in certain cases we appeal again and again to certain grounds, and at the same time we risk pretty little—if it came to risking our lives on the ground of this belief.

There are instances where you have a faith—where you say "I believe"—and on the other hand this belief does not rest on the fact on which our ordinary everyday beliefs normally do rest.

How should we compare beliefs with each other? What would it mean to compare them?

You might say: "We compare the states of mind."

How do we compare states of mind? This obviously won't do for all occasions. First, what you say won't be taken as the measure for the firmness of a belief? But, for instance, what risks you would take?

The strength of a belief is not comparable with the intensity of a pain.

An entirely different way of comparing beliefs is seeing what sorts of grounds he will give.

A belief isn't like a momentary state of mind. "At 5 o'clock he had very bad toothache."

Suppose you had two people, and one of them, when he had to decide which course to take, thought of retribution, and the other did not. One person might, for instance, be inclined to take everything that happened to him as a reward or punishment, and another person doesn't think of this at all.

If he is ill, he may think: "What have I done to deserve this?" This is one way of thinking of retribution. Another way is, he thinks in a general way whenever he is ashamed of himself "This will be punished."

Take two people, one of whom talks of his behavior and of what happens to him in terms of retribution, the other one does not. These people think entirely differently. Yet, so far, you can't say they believe different things.

Suppose someone is ill and he says: "This is a punishment," and I say: "If I'm ill, I don't think of punishment at all." If you say: "Do you believe the opposite?"—you can call it believing the opposite, but it is entirely different from what we would normally call believing the opposite.

I think differently, in a different way. I say different things to myself. I have different pictures.

It is this way: if someone said: "Wittgenstein, you don't take illness as punishment, so what do you believe?"—I'd say: "I don't have any thoughts of punishment."

There are, for instance, these entirely different ways of thinking first of all—which needn't be expressed by one person saying one thing, another person another thing.

What we call believing in a Judgment Day or not believing in a Judgment Day—The expression of belief may play an absolutely minor role.

If you ask me whether or not I believe in a Judgment Day, in the sense in which religious people have belief in it, I wouldn't say: "No. I don't believe there will be such a thing." It would seem to me utterly crazy to say this.

And then I give an explanation: "I don't believe in...,"but then the religious person never believes what I describe.

I can't say. I can't contradict that person.

In one sense, I understand all he says—the English words "God," "separate,"etc. I understand. I could say: "I don't believe in this," and this would be true, meaning I haven't got these thoughts or anything that hangs together with them. But not that I could contradict the thing.

You might say: "Well, if you can't contradict him, that means you don't understand him. If you did understand him, then you might." That again is Greek to me. My normal technique of language leaves me. I don't know whether to say they understand one another or not.

These controversies look quite different from any normal controversies. Reasons look entirely different from normal reasons.

They are, in a way, quite inconclusive.

The point is that if there were evidence, this would in fact destroy the whole business.

Anything that I normally call evidence wouldn't in the slightest influence me.

Suppose, for instance, we knew people who foresaw the future; make forecasts for years and years ahead; and they described some sort of a Judgment Day. Queerly enough, even if there were such a thing, and even if it were more convincing than I have described but, belief in this happening wouldn't be at all a religious belief.

Suppose that I would have to forego all pleasures because of such a forecast. If I do so and so, someone will put me in fires in a thousand years, etc. I wouldn't budge. The best scientific evidence is just nothing.

A religious belief might in fact fly in the face of such a forecast, and say "No. There it will break down."

As it were, the belief as formulated on the evidence can only be the last result—in which a number of ways of thinking and acting crystallize and come together.

A man would fight for his life not to be dragged into the fire. No induction. Terror. That is, as it were, part of the substance of the belief.

That is partly why you don't get in religious controversies, the form of controversy where one person is *sure* of the thing, and the other says: 'Well, possibly'.

You might be surprised that there hasn't been opposed to those who believe in Resurrection those who say "Well, possibly".

Here believing obviously plays much more this role: suppose we said that a certain picture might play the role of constantly admonishing me, or I always think of it. Here, an enormous difference would be between those people for whom the picture is constantly in the foreground, and the others who just didn't use it at all.

Those who said: "Well, possibly it may happen and possibly not" would be on an entirely different plane.

This is partly why one would be reluctant to say: "These people rigorously hold the opinion (or view) that there is a Last Judgment." "Opinion" sounds queer.

It is for this reason that different words are used: "dogma," "faith."

We don't talk about hypothesis, or about high probability. Nor about knowing.

In a religious discourse we use such expressions as: "I believe that so and so will happen," and use them differently to the way in which we use them in science.

Although, there is a great temptation to think we do. Because we do talk of evidence, and do talk of evidence by experience.

We could even talk of historic events.

It has been said that Christianity rests on an historic basis.

It has been said a thousand times by intelligent people that indubitability is not enough in this case. Even if there is as much evidence as for Napoleon. Because the indubitability wouldn't be enough to make me change my whole life.

It doesn't rest on an historic basis in the sense that the ordinary belief in historic facts could serve as a foundation.

Here we have a belief in historic facts different from a belief in ordinary historic facts. Even, they are not treated as historical, empirical, propositions.

Those people who had faith didn't apply the doubt which would ordinarily apply to *any* historical propositions. Especially propositions of a time long past, etc.

What is the criterion of reliability, dependability? Suppose you give a general description as to when you say a proposition has a reasonable weight of probability. When you call it reasonable, is this *only* to say that for it you have such and such evidence, and for others you haven't?

For instance, we don't trust the account given of an event by a drunk man.

Father O'Hara[1] is one of those people who make it a question of science.

Here we have people who treat this evidence in a different way. They base things on evidence which taken in one way would seem exceedingly flimsy. They base enormous things on this evidence. Am I to say they are unreasonable? I wouldn't call them unreasonable.

I would say, they are certainly not *reasonable,* that's obvious.

"Unreasonable" implies, with everyone, rebuke.

I want to say: they don't treat this as a matter of reasonability.

Anyone who reads the Epistles will find it said: not only that it is not reasonable, but that it is folly.

Not only is it not reasonable, but it doesn't pretend to be.

What seems to me ludicrous about O'Hara is his making it appear to be *reasonable*.

Why shouldn't one form of life culminate in an utterance of belief in a Last Judgment? But I couldn't either say "Yes" or "No" to the statement that there will be such a thing. Nor "Perhaps," nor "I'm not sure."

It is a statement which may not allow of any such answer.

If Mr. Lewy is religious and says he believes in a Judgment Day, I won't even know whether to say I understand him or not. I've read the same things as he's read. In a most important sense, I know what he means.

If an atheist says: "There won't be a Judgment Day, and another person says there will," do they mean the same?—Not clear what criterion of meaning the same is. They might describe the same things. You might say, this already shows that they mean the same.

We come to an island and we find beliefs there, and certain beliefs we are inclined to call religious. What I'm driving at is, that religious beliefs will not…They have sentences, and there are also religious statements.

These statements would not just differ in respect to what they are about. Entirely different connections would make them into religious beliefs, and there can easily be imagined transitions where we wouldn't know for our life whether to call them religious beliefs or scientific beliefs.

You may say they reason wrongly.

In certain cases you would say they reason wrongly, meaning they contradict us. In other cases you would say they don't reason at all, or "It is an entirely different kind of reasoning." The first, you would say in the case in which they reason in a similar way to us, and make something corresponding to our blunders.

Whether a thing is a blunder or not—it is a blunder in a particular system. Just as something is a blunder in a particular game and not in another.

---

[1] Contribution to a Symposium on *Science and Religion* (London: Gerald Howe, 1931, pp. 107-116).

You could also say that where we are reasonable, they are not reasonable—meaning they don't use *reason* here.

If they do something very like one of our blunders, I would say, I don't know. It depends on further surroundings of it.

It is difficult to see, in cases in which it has all the appearances of trying to be reasonable.

I would definitely call O'Hara unreasonable. I would say, if this is religious belief, then it's all superstition.

But I would ridicule it, not by saying it is based on insufficient evidence. I would say: here is a man who is cheating himself. You can say: this man is ridiculous because he believes, and bases it on weak reasons.

II

The word 'God' is amongst the earliest learnt—pictures and catechisms, etc. But not the same consequences as with pictures of aunts. I wasn't shown [that which the picture pictured].

The word is used like a word representing a person. God sees, rewards, etc.

"Being shown all these things, did you understand what this word meant?" I'd say: "Yes and no. I did learn what it didn't mean. I made myself understand. I could answer questions, understand questions when they were put in different ways—and in that sense could be said to understand."

If the question arises as to the existence of a god or God, it plays an entirely different role to that of the existence of any person or object I ever heard of. One said, had to say, that one *believed* in the existence, and if one did not believe, this was regarded as something bad. Normally if I did not believe in the existence of something no one would think there was anything wrong in this.

Also, there is this extraordinary use of the word 'believe.' One talks of believing and at the same time one doesn't use 'believe' as one does ordinarily. You might say (in the normal use): "You only believe—oh well…"Here it is used entirely differently; on the other hand it is not used as we generally use the word 'know'.

If I even vaguely remember what I was taught about God, I might say: "Whatever believing in God may be, it can't be believing in something we can test, or find means of testing." You might say: "This is nonsense, because people say they believe on *evidence* or say they believe on religious experiences." I would say: "The mere fact that someone says they believe on evidence doesn't tell me enough for me to be able to say now whether I can say of a sentence 'God exists' that your evidence is unsatisfactory or insufficient."

Suppose I know someone, Smith. I've heard that he has been killed in a battle in this war. One day you come to me and say: "Smith is in Cambridge." I inquire, and find you stood at Guild-hall and saw at the other end a man and said: "That was Smith." I'd say: "Listen. This isn't sufficient evidence." If we had a fair amount of evidence he was killed I would try to make you say that you're being credulous. Suppose he was never heard of again. Needless to say, it is quite impossible to make inquiries: "Who at 12.05 passed Market Place into Rose Crescent?" Suppose you say: "He was there." I would be extremely puzzled.

Suppose there is a feast on Mid-Summer Common. A lot of people stand in a ring. Suppose this is done every year and then everyone says he has seen one of his dead relatives on the other side of the ring. In this case, we could ask everyone in the ring. "Who did you hold by the hand?" Nevertheless, we'd all say that on that day we see our dead relatives. You could in this case say: "I had an extraordinary experience. I had the experience I can express by saying: 'I saw my dead cousin.'" Would we say you are saying this on insufficient evidence? Under certain circumstances I would say this, under other circumstances I wouldn't. Where what is said sounds a bit absurd I would say: "Yes, in this case insufficient evidence." If altogether absurd, then I wouldn't.

Suppose I went to somewhere like Lourdes in France. Suppose I went with a very credulous person. There we see blood coming out of something. He says: "There you are, Wittgenstein, how can you doubt?" I'd say: "Can it only be explained one way? Can't it be this or that?" I'd try to convince him that he'd seen nothing of any consequence. I wonder whether I would do that under all circumstances. I certainly know that I would under normal circumstances.

"Oughtn't one after all to consider this?" I'd say: "Come on. Come on." I would treat the phenomenon in this case just as I would treat an experiment in a laboratory which I thought badly executed.

"The balance moves when I will it to move." I point out it is not covered up, a draught can move it, etc.

I could imagine that someone showed an extremely passionate belief in such a phenomenon, and I couldn't approach his belief at all by saying: "This could just as well have been brought about by so and so" because he could think this blasphemy on my side. Or he might say: "It is possible that these priests cheat, but nevertheless in a different sense a miraculous phenomenon takes place there."

I have a statue which bleeds on such and such a day in the year. I have red ink, etc. "You are a cheat, but nevertheless the Deity uses you. Red ink in a sense, but not red ink in a sense."

Cf. Flowers at seance with label. People said: "Yes, flowers are materialized with label." What kind of circumstances must there be to make this kind of story not ridiculous?

I have a moderate education, as all of you have, and therefore know what is meant by insufficient evidence for a forecast. Suppose someone dreamt of the Last Judgment, and said he now knew what it would be like. Suppose someone said: "This is poor evidence." I'd say: "If you want to compare it with the evidence for it's raining tomorrow it is no evidence at all." He may make it sound as if by stretching the point you may call it evidence. But it may be more than ridiculous as evidence. But now, would I be prepared to say: "You are basing your belief on extremely slender evidence, to put it mildly." Why should I regard this dream as evidence—measuring its validity as though I were measuring the validity of the evidence for meteorological events?

If you compare it with anything in Science which we call evidence, you can't credit that anyone could soberly argue: "Well, I had this dream…therefore…Last Judgment." You might say: "For a blunder, that's too big." If you suddenly wrote numbers down on the blackboard, and then said: "Now, I'm going to add," and then said: "2 and 21 is 13," etc. I'd say: "This is no blunder."

There are cases where I'd say he's mad, or he's making fun. Then there might be cases where I look for an entirely different interpretation altogether. In order to see what the explanation is I should have to see the sum, to see in what way it is done, what he makes follow from it, what are the different circumstances under which he does it, etc.

I mean, if a man said to me after a dream that he believed in the Last Judgment, I'd try to find what sort of impression it gave him. One attitude: "It will be in about 2,000 years. It will be bad for so and so and so, etc." Or it may be one of terror. In the case where there is hope, terror, etc., would I say there is insufficient evidence if he says: "I believe…"? I can't treat these words as I normally treat 'I believe so and so.' It would be entirely beside the point, and also if he said his friend so and so and his grandfather had had the dream and believed, it would be entirely beside the point.

I would not say: "If a man said he dreamt it would happen tomorrow," would he take his coat? etc.

Case where Lewy has visions of his dead friend. Cases where you don't try to locate him. And case where you try to locate him in a business-like way. Another case where I'd say: "We can presuppose we have a broad basis on which we agree."

In general, if you say: "He is dead" and I say: "He is not dead" no one would say: "Do they mean the same thing by 'dead'? "In the case where a man has visions I wouldn't offhand say: "He means something different."

Cf. A person having persecution mania.

What is the criterion for meaning something different? Not only what he takes as evidence for it, but also how he reacts, that he is in terror, etc.

How am I to find out whether this proposition is to be regarded as an empirical proposition—'You'll see your dead friend again?' Would I say: "He is a bit superstitious?" Not a bit.

He might have been apologetic. (The man who stated it categorically was more intelligent than the man who was apologetic about it).

'Seeing a dead friend,' again means nothing much to me at all. I don't think in these terms. I don't say to myself "I shall see so and so again" ever.

He always says it, but he doesn't make any search. He puts on a queer smile. "His story had that dreamlike quality." My answer would be in this case "Yes," and a particular explanation.

Take "God created man." Pictures of Michelangelo showing the creation of the world. In general, there is nothing which explains the meanings of words as well as a picture, and I take it that Michelangelo was as good as anyone can be and did his best, and here is the picture of the Deity creating Adam.

If we ever saw this, we certainly wouldn't think this the Deity. The picture has to he used in an entirely different way if we are to call the man in that queer blanket 'God,' and so on. You could imagine that religion was taught by means of these pictures. "Of course, we can only express ourselves by means of picture." This is rather queer...I could show Moore the pictures of a tropical plant. There is a technique of comparison between picture and plant. If I showed him the picture of Michelangelo and said: "Of course, I can't show you the real thing, only the picture"... The absurdity is, I've never taught him the technique of using this picture.

It is quite clear that the role of pictures of Biblical subjects and role of the picture of God creating Adam are totally different ones. You might ask this question: "Did Michelangelo think that Noah in the ark looked like this, and that God creating Adam looked like this?" He wouldn't have said that God or Adam looked as they look in this picture.

It might seem as though, if we asked such a question as: "Does Lewy really mean what so and so means when he says so and so is alive?"—it might seem as though there were two sharply divided cases, one in which he would say he didn't mean it literally. I want to say this is not so. There will be cases where we will differ, and where it won't be a question at all of more or less knowledge, so that we can come together. Sometimes it will be a question of experience, so you can say: "Wait another 10 years." And I would say: "I would disencourage this kind of reasoning" arid Moore would say: "I wouldn't disencourage it." That is, one would *do* something. We would take sides, and that goes so far that there would really be great differences between us, which might come out in Mr. Lewy saying: "Wittgenstein is trying to undermine reason," and this wouldn't be false. This is actually where such questions rise.

III

Today I saw a poster saying: "'Dead' Undergraduate speaks."

The inverted commas mean: "He isn't really dead." "He isn't what people call dead. They call it 'dead' not quite correctly."

We don't speak of "door" in quotes.

It suddenly struck me: "If someone said 'He isn't really dead, although by the ordinary criteria he is dead'—couldn't I say "He is not only dead by the ordinary criteria; he is what we all call 'dead.'"

If you now call him "alive," you're using language in a queer way, because you're almost deliberately preparing misunderstandings. Why don't you use some other word, and let "dead" have the meaning it already has?

Suppose someone said: "It didn't always have this meaning. He's not dead according to the old meaning" or "He's not dead according to the old idea."

What is it, to have different ideas of death? Suppose you say: "I have the idea of myself being a chair after death" or "I have the idea of myself being a chair in half-an-hour"—you all know under what circumstances we say of something that it has become a chair.

C.f. (1) "This shadow will cease to exist."

(2) "This chair will cease to exist." You say that you know what this chair ceasing to exist is like. But you have to think. You may find that there isn't a use for this sentence. You think of the use.

I imagine myself on the death-bed. I imagine you all looking at the air above me. You say "You have an idea."

Are you clear when you'd say you had ceased to exist?

You have six different ideas [of 'ceasing to exist'] at different times.

If you say: "I can imagine myself being a disembodied spirit. Wittgenstein, can you imagine yourself as a disembodied spirit?"—I'd say: "I'm sorry. I [so far] connect nothing with these words."

I connect all sorts of complicated things with these words. I think of what people have said of sufferings after death, etc.

"I have two different ideas, one of ceasing to exist after death, the other of being a disembodied spirit."

What's it like to have two different ideas? What is the criterion for one man having one idea, another man having another idea?

You gave me two phrases, "ceasing to exist," "being a disembodied spirit." "When I say this, I think of myself having a certain set of experiences." What is it like to think of this?

If you think of your brother in America, how do you know that what you think is, that the thought inside you is, of your brother being in America? Is this an experiential business?

Cf. How do you know that what you want is an apple? [Russell].

How do you know that you believe that your brother is in America?

A pear might be what satisfied you. But you wouldn't say: "What I wanted was apple."

Suppose we say that the thought is some sort of process in his mind, or his saying something, etc.—then I could say: "All right, you call this a thought of your brother in America, well, what is the connection between this and your brother in America?"

Lewy: You might say that this is a question of convention.

Why is it that you don't doubt that it is a thought of your brother in America? One process [the thought] seems to be a shadow or a picture of something else. How do I know that a picture is a picture of Lewy?—Normally by its likeness to Lewy, or, under certain circumstances, a picture of Lewy may not be like him, but like Smith. If I give up the business of being like [as a criterion], I get into an awful mess, because anything may be his portrait, given a certain method of projection.

If you said that the thought was in some way a picture of his brother in America—Yes, but by what method of projection is it a picture of this? How queer it is that there should be no doubt what it's a picture of.

If you're asked: "How do you know it is a thought of such and such?" the thought that immediately comes to your mind is one of a shadow, a picture. You don't think of a causal relation. The kind of relation you think of is best expressed by "picture," "shadow," etc.

The word "picture" is even quite all right-in many cases it is even in the most ordinary sense, a picture. You might translate my very words into a picture.

But the point is this, suppose you drew this, how do I know it is my brother in America? Who says it is him—unless it is here ordinary similarity?

What is the connection between these words, or anything substitutable for them, with my brother in America?

The first idea [you have] is that you are looking at your own thought, and are absolutely sure that it is a thought that so and so. You are looking at some mental phenomenon, and you say to yourself "obviously this is a thought of my brother being in America." It seems to be a super-picture. It seems, with thought, that there is no doubt whatever. With a picture, it still depends on the method of projection, whereas here it seems that you get rid of the projecting relation, and are absolutely certain that this is thought of that.

Smythies's muddle is based on the idea of a super-picture.

We once talked about how the idea of certain superlatives came about in Logic. The idea of a super-necessity, etc.

"How do I know that this is the thought of my brother in America?"—that *what* is the thought?

Suppose my thought consists of my *saying* "My brother is in America"—how do I know that I *say* my brother is in America?

How is the connection made?—We imagine at first a connection like strings. *Lewy:* The connection is a convention. The word designates.

You must explain "designates" by examples. We have learnt a rule, a practice, etc.

Is thinking of something like painting or shooting at something?

It seems like a projection connection, which seems to make it indubitable, although there is not a projection relation at all.

If I said "My brother is in America"—I could imagine there being rays projecting from my words to my brother in America. But what if my brother isn't in America?—then the rays don't hit anything.

[If you say that the words refer to my brother by expressing the proposition that my brother is in America—the proposition being a middle link between the words and what they refer to]—What has the proposition, the mediate link, got to do with America?

The most important point is this-if you talk of painting, etc. your idea is that the connection exists now, so that it seem as though as long as I do this thinking, this connection exists.

Whereas, if we said it is a connection of convention, there would be no point in saying it exists while we think. There is a connection by convention—What do we mean?—This connection refers to events happening at various times. Most of all, it refers to a technique.

["Is thinking something going on at a particular time, or is it spread over the words?" "It comes in a flash." "Always?—it sometimes does come in a flash, although this may be all sorts of different things."]

If it does refer to a technique, then it can't be enough, in certain cases, to explain what you mean in a few words; because there is something which might be thought to be in conflict with the idea going on from 7 to 7.5, namely the practice of using it [the phrase].

When we talked of "So and so is an automaton," the strong hold of that view was [due to the idea] that you could say: "Well, I know what I mean"..., as though you were looking at something happening while you said the thing, entirely independent of what came before and after, the application [of the phrase]. It looked as though you could talk of understanding a word, without any reference to the technique of its usage. It looked as though Smythies said he could understand the sentence, and that we then had nothing to say.

What was it like to have different ideas of death?—What I meant was—Is having an idea of death something like having a certain picture, so that you can say "I have an idea of death from 5 to 5.1 etc."? "In whatever way anyone will use this word, I have now a certain idea"—if you call this "having an idea," then it is not what is commonly called "having an idea," because what is commonly called "having an idea," has a reference to the technique of the word, etc.

We are all here using the word "death," which is a public instrument, which has a whole technique [of usage]. Then someone says he has an idea of death. Something queer; because you might say "You are using the word 'death', which is an instrument functioning in a certain way."

If you treat this [your idea] as something private, with what right are you calling it an idea of death?—I say this, because we, also, have a right to say what is an idea of death.

He might say "I have my own private idea of death"—why call this an 'idea of death' unless it is something you connect with death. Although this [your 'idea'] might not interest us at all. [In this case,] it does not belong on the game played with 'death,' which we all know and understand.

If what he calls his "idea of death" is to become relevant, it must become part of our game.

'My idea of death is the separation of the soul from the body'—if we know what to do with these words. He can also say: "I connect with the word 'death' a certain picture—a woman lying in her bed"-that may or may not be of some interest.

If he connects

with death, and this was his idea, this might be interesting psychologically.

"The separation of soul from body"[only had a public interest]. This may act like black curtains or it may not act like black curtains. I'd have to find out what the consequences [of your saying it] are. I am not, at least, at present at all clear. [You say this]—"So what?"—I know these words, I have certain pictures. All sorts of things go along with these words.

If he says this, I won't know yet what consequences he will draw. I don't know, what he opposes this to.

Lewy: "You oppose it to being extinguished."

If you say to me—"Do you cease to exist?"—I should be bewildered, and would not know what exactly this is to mean. "If you don't cease to exist, you will suffer after death," there I begin to attach ideas, perhaps ethical ideas of responsibility. The point is, that although these are well-known words, and although I can go from one sentence to another sentence, or to pictures [I don't know what consequences you draw from this statement].

Suppose someone said: "What do you believe, Wittgenstein? Are you a skeptic? Do you know whether you will survive death?" I would really, this is a fact, and say "I can't say I don't know," because I haven't any clear idea what I'm saying when I'm saying "I don't cease to exist," etc.

Spiritualists make one kind of connection.

A Spiritualist says "Apparition" etc. Although he gives me a picture I don't like, I do get a clear idea. I know that much, that some people connect this phrase with a particular kind of verification. I know that some people don't—religious people e.g.—they don't refer to a verification, but have entirely different ideas.

A great writer said that, when he was a boy, his father set him a task, and he suddenly felt that nothing, not even death, could take away the responsibility [in doing this task]; this was his duty to do, and that even death couldn't stop it being his duty.
He said that this was, in a way, a proof of the immortality of the soul-because if this lives on [the responsibility won't die]. The idea is given by what we call the proof. Well, if this is the idea, [all right].

If a Spiritualist wishes to give me an idea of what he means or doesn't mean by "survival," he can say all sorts of things—.

[If I ask what idea he has, I may be given what the Spiritualists say or I may be given what the man I quoted said, etc., etc.]

I would at least [in the case of the Spiritualist] have an idea of what this sentence is connected up with, and get more and more of an idea as I see what he does with it.

As it is, I hardly connect anything with it at all.

Suppose someone, before going to China, when he might never see me again, said to me: "We might see one another after death"—would I necessarily say that I don't understand him? I might say [want to say] simply, "Yes. I *understand* him entirely."

Lewy "In this case, you might only mean that he expressed a certain attitude."

I would say "No, it isn't the same as saying 'I'm very fond of you'"—and it may not be the same as saying anything else. It says what it says. Why should you be able to substitute anything else?

Suppose I say: "The man used a picture.

"Perhaps now he sees he was wrong." What sort of remark is this?

"God's eye sees everything"—I want to say of this that it uses a picture.

I don't want to belittle him [the person who says it.]

Suppose I said to him "You've been using a picture," and he said "No, this is not all"—mightn't he have misunderstood me? What do I want to do [by saying this]? What would be the real sign of disagreement? What might be the real criterion of his disagreeing with me?

Lewy: "If he said: 'I've been making preparations [for death].''

Yes, this might be a disagreement—if he himself were to use the word in a way in which I did not expect, or were to draw conclusions I did not expect him to draw: I wanted only to draw attention to a particular technique of usage. We should disagree, if he was using a technique I didn't expect.

We associate a particular use with a picture.

Smythies: 'This isn't all he does—associate a use with a picture.'

Wittgenstein: Rubbish. I meant: what conclusions are you going to draw? etc. Are eyebrows going to be talked of, in connection with the Eye of God?

"He could just as well have said so and so"—this [remark] is foreshadowed by the word "attitude." He couldn't just as well have said something else.

If I say he used a picture, I don't want to say anything he himself wouldn't say. I want to say that he draws these conclusions.

Isn't it as important as anything else, what picture he does use?

Of certain pictures we say that they might just as well be replaced by another—e.g. we could, under certain circumstances, have one projection of an ellipse drawn instead of another.

[He *may* say]: "I would have been prepared to use another picture, it would have had the same effect...."

The whole *weight* may be in the picture.

We can say in chess that the exact shape of the chessmen plays no role. Suppose that the main pleasure was, to see people ride; then, playing it in writing wouldn't be playing the same game. Someone might say: "All he's done is change the shape of the head"—what more could he do?

When I say he's using a picture I'm merely making a *grammatical* remark: [What I say] can only be verified by the consequences he does or does not draw.

If Smythies disagrees, I don't take notice of this disagreement.

All I wished to characterize was the conventions he wished to draw. If I wished to say anything more I was merely being philosophically arrogant.

Normally, if you say "He is an automaton" you draw consequences, if you stab him, [he'll feel pain]. On the other hand, you may not wish to draw any such consequences, and this is all there is to it—except further muddles.

Questions

1. What do you think Wittgenstein means when he says that the meaning of a word is determined by its use?

2. What does Wittgenstein mean by *the linguistic/cultural contextual framework* as it relates to the use of words?

3. Do you think that Wittgenstein would settle on a final single meaning of a word? If not, why not, if yes, why yes?

4. Why do you suppose that Wittgenstein had very great difficulty with expressions used in the case of human behavior when talking about God?

5. What lessons might one draw from Wittgenstein regarding religious beliefs?

Figure 2

Part II

Arguments for God's Existence

THE ONTOLOGICAL ARGUMENT

St. Anselm of Canterbury

Anselm proceeds from a definition of the nature of the being of God as that being than which none greater can be conceived, and hypothesizes that the being in question be thought of as existing in the mind only. Offering an ad absurdum line, he then assumes that this greatest conceivable being exists in the mind only, but the entity thus described is not the greatest, for he can think of a greater, namely one that exists in the mind and in reality. Hence, the being than which no greater can be thought, must exist in reality.

Truly there is a God, although the fool has said in his heart, there is no God.

And so, Lord, do thou, who dost give understanding to faith, give me, so far as thou knowest it to be profitable, to understand that thou art as we believe; and that thou art that which we believe. And, indeed, we believe that thou art a being than which nothing greater can be conceived. Or is there no such nature, since the fool hath said in his heart, there is no God? (Psalms xiv.I). But, at any rate, this very fool, when he hears of this being of which I speak—a being than which nothing greater can be conceived—understands what he hears, and what he understands is in his understanding; although he does not understand it to exist.

For, it is one thing for an object to be in the understanding, and another to understand that the object exists. When a painter first conceives of what he will afterwards perform, he has it in his understanding, but he does not yet understand it to be, because he has not yet performed it. But after he has made the painting, he both has it in his understanding, and he understands that it exists, because he has made it.

Hence, even the fool is convinced that something exists in the understanding, at least, than which nothing greater can be conceived. For, when he hears of this, he understands it. And whatever is understood, exists in the understanding, And assuredly that, than which nothing greater can be conceived, cannot exist in the understanding alone. For, suppose it exists in the understanding alone: then it can be conceived to exist in reality; which is greater.

Therefore, if that, than which nothing greater can be conceived, exists in the understanding alone, the very being, than which nothing greater can be conceived, is one, than which a greater can be conceived. But obviously this is impossible. Hence, there is not doubt that there exists a being, than which nothing greater can be conceived, and it exists both in the understanding and in reality.

God cannot be conceived not to exist.—God is that, than which nothing greater can be conceived.—
That which can be conceived not to exist is not God.

And it assuredly exists so truly, that it cannot be conceived not to exist; and this is greater than one which can be conceived not to exist. Hence, if that, than which nothing greater can be conceived, can be conceived not to exists, it is not that, than which nothing greater can be conceived. But this is an irreconcilable contradiction. There is, then, so truly a being than which nothing greater can be conceived to exist, that is cannot even be conceived not to exist; and this being thou art, O Lord, our God.

---

* This article is reprinted by courtesy of the publisher. "The Ontological Argument," is from St. Anselm's *Proslogion*, trans. M. J. Charlesworth (Notre Dame: University of Notre Dame Press, 1979).

So truly, therefore, dost exist, O Lord, my God, that thou canst not be conceived not to exist; and rightly. For, if a mind could conceive of a being better than thee, the creature would rise above the Creator; and this is most absurd. And, indeed, whatever else there is, except thee alone, can be conceived not to exist. To thee alone, therefore, it belongs to exist more truly than all other beings, and hence in a higher degree than all others. For, whatever else exists does not exist so truly, and hence in a less degree it belongs to it to exist. Why, then has the fool said in his heart, there is no God (Psalms xiv.I), since it is so evident, to a rational mind, that thou dost exist in the highest degree of all? Why, except that he is dull and a fool?

How the fool has said in his heart what cannot be conceived.—A thing may be conceived in two ways: (1) when the word signifying it is conceived; (2) when the thing itself is understood. As far as the word goes, God can be conceived not to exist; in reality he cannot.

> But how has the fool said in his heart what he could not conceive; or how is it that he could not conceive what he said in his heart? Since it is the same to say in the heart, and to conceive.

But, if really, nay, since really, he both conceived, because he said in his heart; and did not say in his heart, because he could not conceive; there is more than one way in which a thing is said in the heart or conceived. For, in one sense, an object is conceived, when the word signifying it is conceived; and in another, when the very entity, which the object is, is understood.

In the former sense, then, God can be conceived not to exist; but in the latter, not at all. For no one who understands what fire and water are can conceive fire to be water, in accordance with the nature of the facts themselves, although this is possible according to the words, So, then, no one who understands what God is can conceive that God does not exist; although he says these words in his heart, either without any, or with some foreign signification. For, God is that than which a greater cannot be conceived. And he who thoroughly understands this, assuredly understands that this being so truly exists, that not even in concept can it be non-existent. Therefore, he who understands that God so exists, cannot conceive that he does not exist.

I thank thee, gracious Lord, I thank thee; because what I formerly believed by thy bounty, I now so understand by thine illumination, that if I were unwilling to believe that thou dost exist, I should not be able to understand this to be true.

Questions

1. What basic feature is there about Anselm's argument that makes it ontological?

2. What do you see as the most significant flaw, if any, in Anselm's manner of reasoning in the ontological argument?

3. Do you think that there is any promise in the sort of reasoning Anselm uses in his proof for God's existence in the *Proslogion?*

4. What is the basic difference between Anselm's pattern of reasoning and Thomas Aquinas' pattern of reasoning in their respective efforts to prove God exists?

5. Two versions of the ontological argument have been drawn from the *Proslogion* text. How does each one proceed?

THE COSMOLOGICAL ARGUMENT*

Bruce Reichenbach

Reichenbach gives a concise summary of the most recent formulations of the cosmological proofs, including the Kalām form of it, and he concludes that Swinburne's examination of this main pattern of reasoning leaves us with questions as to what counts as an adequate explanation of simplicity and of determining prior probabilities. The further problem of showing that the Necessary Being, the Unmoved Mover, the Uncaused Cause is the God of Christianity is discussed and suggestions are made as to how this problem might be resolved.

I. Historical Overview

Although in Western philosophy the earliest formation of a version of the cosmological argument is found in Plato's *Laws*, 893-6, the classical argument is firmly rooted in Aristotle's *Physics* (VIII, 4-6) and *Metaphysics* (XII, 1-6). Islamic philosophy enriches the tradition, developing two types of arguments. The Arabic philosophers (falasifa) developed the atemporal argument from contingency, which is taken up by Thomas Aquinas (1225-74) in his *Summa Theologica* (I,q.2,a.3) and his *Summa Contra Gentiles* (I, 13). The mutakallimūm, theologians who used reason and argumentation to support their revealed Islamic beliefs, developed the temporal version of the argument from the impossibility of an infinite regress, known as the *kalām* argument. For example, al-Ghāzāli (1058-1111) argued that everything that begins to exist requires a cause of its beginning. The world is composed of temporal phenomena preceded by other temporally ordered phenomena. Since such a series of temporal phenomena cannot continue to infinity, the world must have had a beginning and a cause of its existence, namely, God (Craig 1979, part 1). This version of the argument enters the Christian tradition through Bonaventure (1221-74) in his Sentences (II Sent. D.1,p.1,a.1,q.2).

During the Enlightenment, writers such as G.W.F. Leibniz and Samuel Clarke reaffirmed the cosmological argument. Leibniz (1646-1716) appealed to a strengthened principle of sufficient reason, according to which "no fact can be real or existing and no statement true without a sufficient reason for its being so and not otherwise" (*Monadology*, §32). Leibniz uses the principle to argue that the sufficient reason for the "series of things comprehended in the universe of creatures" (§36) must exist outside this series of contingencies and is found in a necessary being that we call God. The principle of sufficient reason is likewise employed by Samuel Clark in his cosmological argument (Rowe 1975, chap. 2).

Although the cosmological argument does not figure prominently in Asian philosophy, a very abbreviated version of it, proceeding from dependence, can be found in Uddiyāna's *Nyāyakusumāñjali* I,4. In general philosophers in the Nyāya tradition argue that since the universe has parts that come into existence at one occasion and not another, it must have a cause. We could admit an infinite regress of causes if we had evidence for such, but lacking such evidence, God must exist as the non-dependent cause. Many of the objections to the argument contend that God is an inappropriate cause because of God's nature. For example, since God is immobile and has no body, he cannot properly be said to cause anything. The Naiyāyikas reply

---

* This article is reprinted by courtesy of the author, Bruce Reichenbach and the editors of the *Stanford Encyclopedia of Philosophy*.

that God could assume a body at certain times, and in any case, God need not create in the same way humans do (Potter, 100-7).

The cosmological argument came under serious assault in the 18th century, first by David Hume and then by Immanuel Kant. Hume attacks both the view of causation presupposed in the argument (that causation is an objective, productive relation that holds between two things) and the Causal Principle—every contingent being has a cause of its being—that lies at the heart of the argument. Kant contends that the cosmological argument, in identifying the necessary being, relies on the ontological argument, which in turn is suspect. We will return to these criticisms below.

Both theists and non-theists in the last part of the 20th century generally have shown a healthy skepticism about the argument. Alvin Plantinga (1967, chap. 1) concludes "that this piece of natural theology is ineffective." Richard Gale contends, in Kantian fashion, that since the conclusion of all versions of the cosmological argument invokes an impossibility, no cosmological arguments can provide examples of sound reasoning (1991, ch. 7). Similarly, Michael Martin reasons that no current version of the cosmological argument is sound (1990, ch. 4), as do John Mackie (ch. 5) and Quentin Smith (Craig and Smith, 1993). Yet dissenting voices can be heard. William Lane Craig defends the kalām argument, and Richard Swinburne, though rejecting deductive versions of the cosmological argument, proposes an inductive argument which is part of a larger cumulative case for God's existence. "There is quite a chance that if there is a God he will make something of the finitude and complexity of a universe. It is very unlikely that a universe would exist uncaused, but rather more likely that God would exist uncaused. The existence of the universe...can be made comprehensible if we suppose that it is brought about by God" (1979, 131-2). Thus, contemporary philosophers continue to contribute detailed arguments on both sides of the debate.

II. Typology of Cosmological Arguments

Craig distinguishes three types of cosmological arguments. The first, advocated by Aquinas, is based on the impossiblity of an essentially ordered infinite regress. The second, which he terms the kalām argument, holds that an infinite temporal regress is impossible because an actual infinite is impossible. The third, espoused by Leibniz and Clarke, is founded on the Principle of Sufficient Reason (Craig 1980, 282). Another way of distinguishing between versions of the argument is in terms of the relevance of time. In the first and third versions, consideration of the essential ordering of the causes or sufficient reasons proceeds independent of temporal concerns. The relationship between cause and effect is treated as logical, not temporal. Put in more contemporary terms, one is after the best explanation for what exists. In the kalām version, however, the temporal ordering of the causal sequence in central. The distinction between these types of argument is important because the objections raised against one version might not be relevant to the other versions. So, for example, a critique of the principle of sufficient reason, which one finds developed in William Rowe or Richard Gale, might not be telling against the Thomistic or kalām versions of the argument.

III. Argument for a First Sustaining Cause

Thomas Aquinas held that among the things whose existence needs explanation are contingent beings, which depend for their existence upon other beings. Richard Taylor (1992, 99-108) and others argue that the universe (meaning everything that ever existed), as contingent, needs explanation. Arguing that the term "universe" refers to an abstract entity or set, William Rowe rephrases the issue, "Why does that set (the universe) have the members that it does rather than some other members or none at all?" (Rowe 1975, 136). That is, "Why is there something rather than nothing?" (Smart, in Haldane and Smart, 36). The response of the cosmological argument is that what is contingent exists because of a necessary being.

A. The Deductive Argument from Contingency

The cosmological argument begins with a fact about experience, namely, that something exists. We might sketch out the argument as follows.

1. A contingent being exists (a contingent being is such that if it exists, it can not-exist)
2. This contingent being has a cause or explanation[1] of its existence.
3. The cause or explanation of its existence is something other than the contingent being itself.
4. What causes or explains the existence of this contingent being must either be solely other contingent beings or include a non-contingent (necessary) being.
5. Contingent beings alone cannot cause or explain the existence of a contingent being.
6. Therefore, what causes or explains the existence of this contingent being must include a non-contingent (necessary) being.
7. Therefore, a necessary being (a being which, if it exists, cannot not exist) exists.

Over the centuries philosophers have suggested various instantiations for the contingent being noted in premise 1. In his *Summa Theologica* I, q. 2, a 3, Aquinas argued that we need a causal explanation for things in motion, things that are caused, and contingent beings. Others, such as Richard Taylor and Richard Swinburne (1979), propose that the contingent being referred to in premise 1 is the universe. The connection between the two is supplied by John Duns Scotus, who argued that even if the essentially ordered causes were infinite, "the whole series of effects would be dependent upon some prior cause" (Scotus, 46). Whereas the contingency of the former is generally undisputed, the contingency of the universe deserves some defense (see 3.2). Premise 2 invokes a version of the Principle of Causation or the Principle of Sufficient Reason; if something is contingent, there must be a cause of its existence or a reason why it exists rather than not exists. The point of 3 is simply that something cannot cause its own existence, for this would require it to already be (in a logical if not a temporal sense). Premise 4 is true by virtue of the Principle of Excluded Middle: what explains the existence of the contingent being is either other contingent beings or a non-contingent being. Conclusions 6 and 7 follow validly from the respective premises.

For many critics, premise 5 holds the key to the argument's success or failure. Whether 5 is true depends upon the requirements for an adequate explanation. According to the Principle of Sufficient Reason, what is required is a full explanation, that is, an explanation that includes a causal account in terms of sufficient conditions and the reason why the cause had the effect it did (Swinburne 1979, 24). If the contingent being in premise 1 is the universe, then a complete explanation would require something beyond the contingent factors that, as part of the universe, are to be explained. It requires the existence of a non-contingent or necessary being. That contingent or dependent things (e.g., a universe) have always existed does not provide an alternative explanation, for it fails to provide an explanation for why the universe exists rather than not.

---

[1] I include the disjunct "cause or explanation" because not all versions of the cosmological argument invoke the Principle of Sufficient Reason expressed in the Enlightenment sense. The Thomistic arguments emphasize a causal account. Since an explanation is usually (but not always) given in causal language, we will not exploit the difference.

Finally, it should be noted in 7 that if the contingent being identified in 1 is the universe, the necessary being cannot provide a natural explanation for it, for we know of no natural, non-contingent causes and laws or principles exist from which the existence of the universe follows. What is required is a personal explanation in terms of the intentional acts of some eternal supernatural being. Since the argument proceeds independent of temporal considerations, the argument does not propose a first cause in time, but rather a first or primary sustaining cause of the universe. As Aquinas noted, the philosophical arguments for God's existence are compatible with the eternity of the universe.

Critics have objected to most of these premises. Let us consider the most important objections and responses.

B. Objection 1: The Universe Just Is

Interpreting the contingent being in premise 1 as the universe, Bertrand Russell denies that the universe needs an explanation; it just is. Russell contends that since we derive the concept of cause from our observation of particular things, we cannot ask about the cause of something like the universe that we cannot experience. The universe is "just there, and that's all" (Russell, 175). But, the theist responds, if the components of the universe are contingent, isn't the universe itself contingent? Russell replies that the move from the contingency of the components of the universe to the contingency of the universe commits the Fallacy of Composition, which mistakenly concludes that since the parts have a certain property, the whole likewise has that property. Hence, whereas we can ask for the cause of particular things, we cannot ask for the cause of the universe or the set of all contingent beings.

Russell correctly notes that arguments of the part-whole type can commit the Fallacy of Composition. For example, the argument that since all the bricks in the wall are small, the wall is small, is fallacious. Yet sometimes the totality has the same quality as the parts because of the nature of the parts invoked—the wall is brick because it is built of bricks. The universe's contingency, theists argue, resembles the second case. If all the contingent things in the universe, including matter and energy, ceased to exist simultaneously, the universe itself, as the totality of these things, would cease to exist. But if the universe can cease to exist, it is contingent and requires an explanation for its existence.

Some reply that this argument for the contingency of the universe still is fallacious, for even if every contingent being were to fail to exist in some possible world, it may be the case that there is no possible world that lacks a contingent being. That is, though no being would exist in every possible world, every world would possess at least one contingent being. Rowe gives the example of a horse race. "We know that although no horse in a given horse race necessarily will be the winner, it is, nevertheless, necessary that some horse in the race will be the winner" (1975, 164).

Rowe's example, however, fails, for it is possible that all the horses break a leg and none finishes the race. That is, the necessity that some horse will win follows only if there is some reason to think that some horse must finish the race. Similarly, the objection to the universe's contingency will hold only if there is some reason to think that the existence of something is necessary. One argument given in defense of this thesis is that the existence of one contingent being may be necessary for the nonexistence of some other contingent being. But though the fact that something's existence is necessary for the existence of something else holds for certain properties (for example, the existence of children is necessary for someone to be a parent), it is doubtful that something's existence is necessary for something else's nonexistence *per se*, which is what is needed to support the argument that denies the contingency of the universe. Hence, given the contingency of everything in the universe, it remains that there is a possible world without any contingent beings. (This argument to a possible world without contingent beings, however, is not equivalent to Aquinas's fallacious argument in the Third Way from the contention that everything has the possibility of not being to the conclusion that at one time there *was nothing* (Kenny, 56-66).)

Rowe (1975, 166) develops a different argument to support the thesis that the universe must be contingent. He argues that it is necessary that if God exists, then it is possible that no dependent beings exist. Since it is possible that God exists, it is possible that it is possible that no dependent beings exist. (This conclusion is licensed by the following modal principle: If it is necessary that if p then q, then if it is possible that p, it is possible that q.) Hence, it is possible that there are no dependent beings; i.e., that the universe is contingent. Rowe takes the conditional as necessarily true in virtue of the classical concept of God, according to which God is free to decide whether or not to create dependent beings.

C. Objection 2: Explaining the Individual Constituents Is Sufficient

Whereas Russell argued that the universe just is, David Hume held that when the parts are explained the whole is explained.

> But the *whole*, you say, wants a cause. I answer that the uniting of these parts into a whole... is performed merely by an arbitrary act of the mind, and has no influence on the nature of things. Did I show you the particular causes of each individual in a collection of twenty particles of matter, I should think it very unreasonable should you afterwards ask me what was the cause of the whole twenty. This is sufficiently explained in explaining the parts. (Hume, part 9)

Sometimes it is true that the whole is sufficiently explained in explaining its parts, but not always. An explanation of the parts may provide a partial but incomplete explanation; what remains unexplained is why these parts exist rather than others, why they exist rather than not, or why the parts are arranged as they are. However, although this shows that Hume's principle that the whole is explained in explaining the parts is sometimes false, it does not show it is false in the case under consideration, namely, when the universe is treated as a set rather than as an aggregate. But suppose Hume is correct that the explanation of the parts explains the whole. In terms of what are the parts themselves explained? Each is explained either in terms of themselves or in terms of something else. The former would make them necessary, not contingent, beings. If they are explained in terms of something else, the entire collection still remains unaccounted for. For as Rowe notes:

> When the existence of each member of a collection is explained by reference to some other member *of that very same collection* then it does not follow that the collection itself has an explanation. For it is one thing for there to be an explanation of the existence of each dependent being and quite another thing for there to be an explanation of why there are dependent beings at all. (Rowe 1975, 264)

But what if the parts are themselves necessary beings? Will not that suffice to explain the whole? Suppose that in premise 1 the contingent beings to be accounted for are macro-objects. These objects are composed of matter and energy. But according to the Principle of Conservation of Mass-Energy, matter and energy are never lost but rather transmute into each other. That is, the components of the universe are contingent vis-à-vis their form, but not vis-à-vis their matter. On this reading, though the argument is sound, it does not require the existence of anything other than the universe or its components. Instead of one, there are many necessary beings.

Interestingly enough, this approach was anticipated by Aquinas in his third way in his *Summa Theologica* (I,q.2,a.3). Once Aquinas concludes that necessary beings exist, he then goes on to ask whether these beings have their existence from themselves or from another. If from another, then we have an unsatisfactory infinite regress of explanations. Hence, there must be something whose necessity is uncaused. As Kenny points out, Aquinas understands this necessity in terms of being unable to cease to exist (Kenny, 48). Although Aquinas understands the uncaused necessary being to be God, the modern critic might take this to be matter-energy itself.

Any reply to the critic will have to invoke empirical evidence, such as from the Big Bang Theory, to show the contingency of even the fundamental building blocks or constitutents of the universe. We will return to this debate in section 4 when we consider the kalām argument.

Finally, Richard Swinburne has asked how far must any explanation go? Whereas traditional cosmological arguments contend that we need to explain the existence of every relevant contingent causal condition in order to explain another's existence (Scotus's ordering of *per se* causes), Swinburne terms this requirement the *completist fallacy* (1979, 73). Swinburne notes that an explanation is complete when "any attempt to go beyond the factors which we have would result in no gain of explanatory power or prior probability" (1979, 86). But explaining why something exists rather than nothing and why it is as it is gives additional explanatory power in explaining why a universe exists at all. Gale (1991, 257-8) concludes from this that if we are to explain the parts of the universe and their particular concatenation, we must appeal to something other than those parts.

D. Objection 3: The Causal Principle is Suspect

Critics of the argument contend that the Causal Principle or, where applicable, the Principle of Sufficient Reason, that underlies versions of the argument is suspect. As Hume argued, there is no reason for thinking that the Causal Principle is true *a priori*, for we can conceive of effects without conceiving of their being caused (*Enquiry Concerning Human Understanding*, IV). Neither can an argument for the application of the Causal Principle to the universe be drawn from inductive experience. Even if the Causal Principle applies to events in the world, we cannot extrapolate from the way the world works to the world as a whole (Mackie, 85). To assume that the universe complies with our own preferences for causal order is not justified.

Defenders of the argument reply that the Principles are necessary to make the universe intelligible. Without such presuppositions, science itself would be undercut. But even then, critics reply, the principle has only methodological and not ontological justification. As Mackie argues, we have no right to assume that the universe complies with our intellectual preferences. We can simply work with brute facts.

Clearly, the soundness of the deductive version of the argument hinges on whether principles such as that of Causation or Sufficient Reason are more than methodologically true, and on the extent to which these principles can be applied.

E. Objection 4: The Conclusion is Contradictory

Immanuel Kant objected to the conclusion of the cosmological argument that a necessary being exists. Kant held that the cosmological argument, in concluding to the existence of a necessary being, argues for the existence of a being whose nonexistence is absolutely inconceivable. But the only being that meets this condition is the most real or maximally excellent being, the very concept of which lies at the heart of the ontological argument. Accordingly, the cosmological argument presupposes the cogency of the ontological argument. But since the ontological argument is defective, the cosmological argument that depends on it likewise must be defective (Kant, A606; Smart, in Haldane and Smart, 36-8).

However, the contention that the cosmological argument depends on the ontological argument is based on a confusion. The term *necessary being* can be understood in different ways. Kant, like some modern defenders of the ontological argument, understands "necessary being" as having to do with logically necessary existence, that is, with existence that is logically undeniable. But this is not the sense in which "necessary being" is understood in the cosmological causal argument. Necessity is understood in the sense of ontological or metaphysical necessity. A necessary being is one that if it exists, it cannot cease to exist, and correspondingly, if it does not exist, it cannot come into existence. Since such a concept is not self-contradictory, the existence of a necessary being is not intrinsically impossible (Reichenbach, chap. 6).

Mackie replies that if God has metaphysical necessity, God's existence is contingent, such that some reason is required for God's own existence (Mackie, 84). That is, if God necessarily exists in the sense that if he exists, he exists in all possible worlds, it remains logically possible that God does not exist in any (and all) possible world. Hence, God is a logically contingent being and so could have not-existed. Why, then, does God exist? The principles of Causation or Sufficient Reason can be applied to the necessary being.

The theist responds that the Principle of Sufficient Reason does not address logical contingency, but metaphysical contingency. For what is not metaphysically contingent one is not required to find a reason. It is not that the necessary being is self-explanatory; rather, a demand for explaining its existence is inappropriate. Hence, the theist concludes, Hawking's question, "Who created God?" (Hawking, 174), is out of place.

In short, defenders of the cosmological argument defend the Causal Principle (or alternatively Principle of Sufficient Reason), but limit its application to contingent beings, whereas critics of the argument either question these principles or want to apply them to the necessary being.

IV. The *Kalām* Cosmological Argument

A second type of cosmological argument, contending for a first or beginning cause of the universe, has a venerable history, especially in the Islamic tradition. Although it had numerous defenders through the centuries, it received new life in the recent writings of William Lane Craig. Craig formulates the *kalām* cosmological argument this way (in Craig and Smith 1993, chap. 1):

1. Everything that begins to exist has a cause of its existence.
2. The universe began to exist.
3. Therefore, the universe has a cause of its existence.
4. Since no scientific explanation (in terms of physical laws) can provide a causal account of the origin of the universe, the cause must be personal (explanation is given in terms of a personal agent).

This argument has been the subject of much recent debate, some of which we will summarize here.

A. The Causal Principle and Quantum Physics

The basis for the argument's first premise is the Causal Principle that undergirds all cosmological arguments. Craig holds that this premise is intuitively obvious; no one, he says, seriously denies it (Craig, in Craig and Smith 1993, 57). Although Craig suggests that one might treat the principle as an empirical generalization based on our ordinary and scientific experiences, ultimately, he argues, the truth of the causal principle rests "upon the metaphysical intuition that something cannot come out of nothing" (Craig, in Craig and Smith 1993, 147).

The Causal Principle has been the subject of extended criticism. We addressed objections to the Causal Principle from a philosophical perspective earlier in 3.4. Here we need to consider objections critics raise from quantum physics (Davies, 1984, 200). On the quantum level, the connection between cause and effect, if not entirely broken, is to some extent loosened. For example, it appears that electrons can pass out of existence at one point and come back into existence elsewhere. One can neither trace their intermediate existence nor determine what causes them to come into existence at one point rather than another. Neither can one precisely determine or predict where they will reappear; their subsequent location is only statistically probable given what we know about their antecedent states. Hence, "quantum-mechanical considerations show that the causal proposition is limited in its application, if applicable at all, and consequently that a probabilistic argument for a cause of the Big Bang cannot go through" (Smith, in Craig and Smith, 1993, 121-3, 182).

Craig responds that appeals to quantum phenomena do not affect the *kalām* argument. For one thing, quantum events are not completely devoid of causal conditions. Even if one grants that the causal conditions are not jointly sufficient to determine the event, at least some necessary conditions are involved in the quantum event. But when one considers the beginning of the universe, he notes, there are no prior necessary causal conditions; simply nothing exists (Craig, in Craig and Smith, 1993, 146).

For another, a difference exists between predictability and causality. It is true that, given Heisenberg's principle of uncertainty, we cannot precisely predict individual subatomic events. What is debated is whether this inability to predict is due to the absence of sufficient causal conditions, or whether it is merely a result of the fact that any attempt to precisely measure these events alters their status. The very introduction of the observer into the arena so affects what is observed that it gives the appearance that effects occur without sufficient or determinative causes. But we have no way of knowing what is happening without introducing observers into the situation and the changes they bring. In the above example, we simply are unable to discern the intermediate states of the electron's existence. When Heisenberg's indeterminacy is understood not as describing the events themselves but rather our knowledge of the events, the causal principle still holds and can still be applied to the initial singularity, although we cannot expect to achieve any kind of determinative predictability about what occurs given the cause.

At the same time, it should be recognized that showing that indeterminacy is a real feature of the world at the quantum level would have significant negative implications for the more general Causal Principle that underlies the deductive cosmological argument. The more this indeterminacy has ontological significance, the weaker is the causal principle. The more this indeterminacy has merely epistemic significance, the less it affects the causal principle. Quantum accounts allow for additional speculation regarding origins and structures of universes. In effect, whether Craig's response to the quantum objection succeeds depends upon deeper issues, in particular, the epistemic and ontological status of quantum indeterminacy and the nature of the Big Bang as a quantum phenomemon.

B. Impossibility of an Actual Infinite?

What can be said about premise 2? Craig develops both *a priori* and *a posteriori* arguments to defend the second premise. His primary *a priori* argument is

> 5. An actual infinite cannot exist.
> 6. A beginningless temporal series of events is an actual infinite.
> 7. Therefore, a beginningless temporal series of events cannot exist.

Since 7 follows validly, if 5 and 6 are true, the argument is sound. In defense of premise 5, Craig argues that if actual infinites that neither increase nor decrease in the number of members they contain were to exist, we would have rather absurd consequences. For example, imagine a library with an actually infinite number of books. Suppose that the library also contains an infinite number of red and an infinite number of black books, so that for every red book there is a black book, and vice versa. It follows that the library contains as many red books as the total books in its collection, and as many red books as red and black books combined. But this is absurd. Hence, it cannot exist in reality

Craig's point is this. Two sets A and B are the same size just in case they can be put into one-to-one correspondence, that is, if and only if every member of A can be correlated with exactly one member of B in such a way that no member of B is left out. It is well known that in the case of infinite sets, this notion of "same size" yields results like the following: the set of all natural numbers (let this be 'A') is the same size as the set of squares of natural numbers ('B'), since every member of A can be correlated with exactly one member of B in a way that leaves out no member of B (correlate $0\leftrightarrow 0$, $1\leftrightarrow 1$, $2\leftrightarrow 4$, $3\leftrightarrow 9$, $4\leftrightarrow 16$,...). So this is a case—recognized in fact as early as Galileo (*Dialogues Concerning Two New Sciences*)—where two infinite sets have the same size but, intuitively, one of them appears to be smaller than the other; one set consists of only some of the members of another, but you nonetheless never run out of either when you pair off their members.

Craig uses a similar, intuitive notion of "smaller than" in his argument concerning the library. It appears that the set B of red books in the library is smaller than the set A of all the books in the library, even though both have the same (infinite) size. Craig concludes that it is absurd to suppose that such a library is possible *in actuality*, since the set of red books would simultaneously have to be smaller than the set of all books and yet equal in size.

Critics fail to be convinced by these paradoxes of infinity. When the intuitive notion of "smaller than" is replaced by a precise definition, finite sets and infinite sets behave somewhat differently. Cantor, and all subsequent set theorists, define a set B to be smaller than set A (i.e., has fewer members) just in case B is the same size as a subset of A, but A is not the same size as any subset of B. The application of this definition to finite and infinite sets yields results that Craig finds counter-intuitive but which mathematicians and logicians see as our best understanding for comparing the size of sets. They see the fact that an infinite set can be put into one-to-one correspondence with one of its own proper subsets as one of the *defining characteristics* of an infinite set, not an absurdity. Say that set C is a *proper* subset of A just in case every element of C is an element of A while A has some element that is not an element of C. In finite sets, but not necessarily in infinite sets, when set B is a proper subset of A, B is smaller than A. But this doesn't hold for infinite sets — we've seen this above where B is the set of squares of natural numbers and A is the set of all natural numbers.

Cantorian mathematicians argue that these results apply to any infinite set, whether in pure mathematics, imaginary libraries, or the real world series of concrete events. Thus, Smith has argued that Craig has begged the question by wrongly presuming that an intuitive relationship that holds between finite sets and their proper subsets—that a set has more members than its proper subsets—must hold even in the case of infinite sets (Smith, in Craig and Smith 1993, 85). So while Craig thinks that Cantor's set theoretic definitions yield absurdities when applied to the world of concrete objects, set theorists see no problem so long as the definitions are maintained.

Why should one think premise 6 is true—that a beginningless series, such as the universe up to this point, is an actual rather than a potential infinite? For Craig, an actual infinite is a determinate totality or a completed unity, whereas the potential infinite is not. Since the past events of a beginningless series can be conceptually collected together and numbered, the series is a determinate totality. And since the past is beginningless, it has no starting point and is infinite. If the universe had a starting point, so that events were added to or subtracted from this point, we would have a potential infinite that increased through time by adding new members. The fact that the events do not occur simultaneously is irrelevant.

Craig is well aware of the fact that he is using actual and potential infinite in a way that differs from the traditional usage in Aristotle and Aquinas. For Aristotle all the elements in an actual finite exist simultaneously, whereas a potential infinite is realized over time by addition or division. Hence, the temporal series of events, as formed by successively adding new events, was a potential, not an actual, infinite (Aristotle, *Physics*, III, 6). For Craig, however, an actual infinite is a timeless totality that cannot be added to or reduced. "Since past events, as determinate parts of reality, are definite and distinct and can be numbered, they can be conceptually collected into a totality" (Craig, in Craig and Smith 1993, 25). Hence, a further critical issue in the *kalām* argument is whether, as Craig suggests, completeness (in terms of being a determinate totality) characterizes an actual infinite, or whether an infinite formed by successive synthesis is a potential infinite.

C. The Big Bang Theory of Cosmic Origins

Craig's a posteriori argument for premise 2 invokes recent cosmology and the Big Bang theory of cosmic origins. Since the universe is expanding as the galaxies recede from each other, if we reverse the direction of our view and look back in time, the farther we look, the smaller the universe becomes. If we push backwards far enough, we find that the universe reaches a state of compression where the density and gravitational force are infinite. This unique singularity constitutes the beginning of the universe—of matter, energy, space, time, and all physical laws. It is not that the universe arose out of some prior state, for there was no prior state. Since time too comes to be, one cannot ask what happened before the initial event. Neither should one think that the universe expanded from some initial 'point' into space. Since the Big Bang initiates the very laws of physics, one cannot expect any physical explanation of this singularity; physical laws used to explain the expansion of the universe no longer hold at any time before t>0.

One picture, then, is of the universe beginning in a singular, non-temporal event roughly 13-14 billion years ago. Something, perhaps a quantum vacuum, came into existence. Its tremendous energy caused it, in the first factions of a second, to expand and explode, creating the four-dimensional space-time universe that we experience today. How this all happened in the first 10^{-35} seconds and subsequently is a matter of serious debate; what advocates of premise 2 maintain is since that the universe began in the Big Bang, the universe is temporally finite.

D. The Big Bang Is Not An Event

The response to this argument is that, given the Grand Theory of Relativity, the Big Bang is not an event at all. An event takes place within a space-time context. But the Big Bang has no space-time context; there is neither time prior to the Big Bang nor a space in which the Big Bang occurs. Hence, the Big Bang cannot be considered as a physical event occurring at a moment of time. As Hawking notes, the finite universe has no space-time boundaries and hence lacks a singularity and a beginning (Hawking 116, 136). Time might be multi-dimensional or imaginary, in which case one asymptotically approaches a beginning singularity but never reaches it. And without a beginning the universe requires no cause. The best one can say is that the universe is finite with respect to the past, not that it had some beginning event.

Given this understanding of event, could we reconceive the *kalām* argument?

8. If something has a finite past, its existence has a cause.
9. The universe has a finite past.
10. Therefore, the universe has a cause of its existence.
11. Since space-time originated with the universe and therefore similarly has a finite past, the cause of the universe's existence must transcend space-time (must have existed aspatially and, when there was no universe, atemporally).
12. If the cause of the universe's existence transcends space-time, no scientific explanation (in terms of physical laws) can provide a causal account of the origin of the universe.
13. If no scientific explanation can provide a causal account of the origin of the universe, the cause must be personal (explanation is given in terms of a personal agent).

The problem with this formulation is with premise 8. Whereas behind premise 1 lays the ancient Parmenidean contention that out of nothing nothing comes, no principle directly connects finitude with causation. We have no reason to think that just because something is finite it must have a cause of its coming into existence. Grünbaum argues that events can only result from other events. "Since the Big Bang singularity is technically a non-event, and t=0 is not a *bona fide* time of its occurrence, the singularity cannot be the effect of any cause in the case of either event-causation or agent causation alike.... The singularity t=0 cannot have a cause" (Grünbaum 1994).

One response to this objection is to opt for broader notions of "event" and "cause." We might broaden the notion of "event" by removing the requirement that it must be relational, taking place in a space-time context. In the Big Bang the space-time universe commences and then continues to exist in time measurable subsequent to the initiating singularity (Silk 2001, 456). Thus, one might consider the Big Bang as either the event of the commencing of the universe or else a state in which "any two points in the observable universe were arbitrarily close together" (Silk 2001, 63). As such, one might inquire why there was this initial state of the universe in the finite past. Likewise, one need not require that causation embody the Humean condition of temporal priority, but may treat causation conditionally, or perhaps even, as traditionally, a relation of production. Any causal statement about the universe would have to be expressed atemporally, but for the theist this presents no problem provided that God is conceived atemporally and sense can be made of atemporal causation.

E. A Non-finite Universe

Some have suggested that since we cannot "exclude the possibility of a prior phase of existence" (Silk 2001, 63); it is possible that the universe has cycled through oscillations, perhaps infinitely, so that Big Bangs occurred not once but an infinite number of times in the past and will do so in the future. The current universe is a "reboot" of previous universes that have expanded and then contracted (Musser 2004).

The idea of an oscillating universe faces significant problems. For one, no set of physical laws accounts for a series of cyclical universe-collapses and re-explosions. That the universe once exploded into existence provides no evidence that the event could reoccur once, if not an infinite number of times, should the universe collapse. Even an oscillating universe seems to be finite (Smith, in Craig and Smith 1993, 113). Further, the cycle of collapses and expansions would not, as was pictured, be periodic (of even duration). Rather, entropy would rise from cycle to cycle, so that even were a series of universe-oscillations possible, they would become progressively longer (Davies 1992, 52). If the universe were without beginning, by now that cycle would be infinite in duration, without any hope of contraction. Third, though each recollapse would destroy the components of the universe, the radiation would remain, so that each successive cycle would add to the total. "The radiation ends up as blackbody radiation. Because we measure a specific amount of cosmic blackbody radiation in the background radiation, we infer that a closed (oscillating) universe can have undergone only a finite number of repeated bounces" or cycles, no more than 100 and certainly not the infinite number required for a beginningless series. "We reluctantly conclude that a future singularity is inevitable in a closed universe; hypothetical observers cannot pass through it, and so the universe probably cannot be cyclical" (Silk 2001, 380, 399).

The central thesis of the oscillating theory has been countered by recent discoveries that the expansion of the universe is actually speeding up. Observations of distant supernova show that they appear to be fainter than they should be were the universe expanding at a steady rate. "Relative dimness of the supernovae showed that they were 10% to 15% farther out than expected, ... indicating that the expansion has accelerated over billions of years" (Glanz, 2157). The hypothesis that these variations in intensity are caused by light being absorbed when passing through cosmic dust is no longer considered a viable explanation because the most distant supernova yet discovered is brighter than it should be if dust were the responsible factor (Sincell). Some force in the universe not only counteracts gravity but pushes the galaxies in the universe apart ever faster. This increased speed appears to be due to dark energy, a mysterious type of energy, characterized by a negative pressure, composing as much as 70% of the universe. Dark matter, it seems, is overmatched by dark energy.[2]

F. Personal Explanation

Finally, something needs to be said about statement 4, which asserts that the cause of the universe is personal. Defenders of the cosmological argument suggest two possible kinds of explanation. *Natural explanation* is provided in terms of precedent events, causal laws, or necessary conditions that invoke natural existents. *Personal explanation* is given "in terms of the intentional action of a rational agent" (Swinburne, 1979, 20). We have seen that one cannot provide a natural causal explanation for the initial event, for there are no precedent events or natural existents to which the laws of physics apply. The line of scientific explanation runs out at the initial singularity, and perhaps even before we arrive at the singularity (at 10^{-35} seconds). If no scientific explanation (in terms of physical laws) can provide a causal account of the origin of the universe, the explanation must be personal, i.e., in terms of the intentional action of a rational, supernatural agent. One might wonder how a supernatural agent brought about the

---

[2] An alternate explanation to dark energy is that, according to string theory, the universe has multiple dimensions and that gravity is lost as gravitons pass from one dimension to another. See George Dvali, "Out of Darkness," *Scientific American* (Feb. 2004): 68-75.

universe, but acceptance of the argument does not depend on an explanation of the manner of causation. When we explain that the girl raised her hand because she wanted to ask a question, we can accept that she was the cause of the raised hand without understanding how her wanting to ask a question brought about her raising it. As Swinburne notes, an event is "fully explained when we have cited the agent, his intention that the event occur, and his basic powers" that include his ability to bring about events of that sort (1979, 33). Similarly, theists argue, we may never know why and how creation took place. Nevertheless, we may accept it as an explanation in the sense that we can say that God created that initial event, that he had the intention to do so, and that such an event lies within the power of an omniscient and omnipotent being.

Paul Davies argues that one need not appeal to God to account for the Big Bang. Its cause, he suggests, is found within the cosmic system itself. Originally a vacuum lacking space-time dimensions, the universe "found itself in an excited vacuum state," a "ferment of quantum activity, teeming with virtual particles and full of complex interactions" (Davies 1984, 191-2), which, subject to a cosmic repulsive force, resulted in an immense increase in energy. Subsequent explosions from this collapsing vacuum released the energy in this vacuum, reinvigorating the cosmic inflation and setting the scenario for the subsequent expansion of the universe. But what is the origin of this increase in energy that eventually made the Big Bang possible? Davies's response is that the law of conservation of energy (that the total quantity of energy in the universe remains fixed despite transfer from one form to another), which now applies to our universe, did not apply to the initial expansion. Cosmic repulsion in the vacuum caused the energy to increase from zero to an enormous amount. This great explosion released energy, from which all matter emerged. Consequently, he contends, since the conclusion of the *kalām* argument is false, one of the premises of the argument—in all likelihood the first—is false.

Craig argues that several problems face this scenario. For one thing, how can empty space explode without there being matter or energy? Since space is a function of matter, if no matter existed, neither could space, let alone empty space, exist. Further, if the vacuum has energy, the question arises concerning the origin of the vacuum and its energy. In short, merely pushing the question of the beginning of the universe back to some primordial quantum vacuum does not escape the problem of what brought this vacuum laden with energy into existence. A quantum vacuum is not nothing (as in Newtonian physics) but "a sea of continually forming and dissolving particles which borrow energy from the vacuum for their brief existence" (Craig 1993, 143). Hence, he concludes, the appeal to a vacuum as the initial state is misleading. Defenders of the argument affirm that only a personal explanation can provide the sufficient reason for the existence of the universe.

The issues raised by the *kalām* argument concern not only the nature of explanation and when an explanation is necessary, but even whether an explanation of the universe is possible (given the above discussion). Whereas all agree that it makes no sense to ask about what occurs before the Big Bang (since there is no prior time), the dispute rests on whether there need be a cause of the first natural existent (whether the universe is caused or not, even if finite), and if so, what is the nature of that cause and its causal activity would be.

V. An Inductive Cosmological Argument

Richard Swinburne contends that the cosmological argument is not deductively valid; if it were so, "it would be incoherent to assert that a complex physical universe exists and that God does not" (1979, 119). Rather, he develops an inductive cosmological argument that appeals to the inference to the best explanation. Swinburne distinguishes between two varieties of inductive arguments: those that show that the conclusion is more probable than not (what he terms a correct P-inductive argument) and those that further increase the probability of the conclusion (what he terms a correct C-inductive argument). In *The Existence of God* he presents a cosmological argument that he claims falls in the category of C-inductive arguments. However, this argument is part of a larger, cumulative case for a P-inductive argument for God's existence.

Swinburne notes that if only scientific explanations are allowed, the universe would be a brute fact. If the universe is finite, the first moment would be a brute fact because no scientific causal account could be given for it. If the universe is infinite, each state would be a brute fact, for though each state would be explained by the causal conditions found in prior states plus the relevant physical laws, there is no reason why any particular state holds true rather than another, since the laws of physics are compatible with diverse states. That is, although the features F of the universe at time t are explained by F at time t_1 plus the relevant physical laws L, and F at t_1 is explained by F and L at t_2, given an infinite regress there is no reason why F or L at t_n might not have been different than they were. Since F and L at t_n are brute facts, the same holds for any F explained by F and L at t_n. Hence, regardless of whether the universe is infinite or finite, if only scientific evidence is allowed, the existence of the universe and its individual states is merely a brute fact, devoid of explanation.

The universe, however, is complex, whereas God is simple. But if something is to occur that is not explained, it is more likely that what occurs will be simple rather than complex. Hence, though the prior likelihood of neither God nor the universe is particularly high, the prior probability of a simple God exceeds that of a complex universe. Hence, if anything is to occur unexplained, it would be God, not the universe. On the other hand, it is reasonable to appeal to God as an explanation for the existence of a complex universe, since there are good reasons why God would make such a complex universe "as a theatre for finite agents to develop and make of it what they will" (Swinburne 1979, 131). Consequently, if we are to explain the universe, we must appeal to a personal explanation "in terms of a person who is not part of the universe acting from without. This can be done if we suppose that such a person (God) brings it about at each instant of time, that L operates" (Swinburne 1979, 126). Although for Swinburne this argument does not make the existence of God more probable than not (it is not a P-inductive argument), it does increase the probability of God's existence (is a C-inductive argument) because it provides a more reasonable explanation for the universe than merely attributing it to brute fact.

Swinburne's point is that to find the best explanation, one selects among the possible theories the theory that provides the best explanation. In light of the complexity of the universe, which of the overarching theories of materialism, humanism, or theism provides the best explanation? Swinburne notes four criteria to be used to determine the best explanation: a explanation is justified insofar as it provides predictability, is simple, fits with our background knowledge, and explains the phenomena better than any other theory (1996, 26). He suggests that fit with background knowledge does not apply in the case of the cause of the universe, for there are no "neighbouring fields of enquiry" where we investigate the cause of the universe. Indeed, he suggests, this criterion reduces to simplicity, which for him is the key to the inductive cosmological argument (1996, chap. 3). Appeals to God's intentions and actions, although not leading to specific predictions about what the world will look like, better explain specific phenomena than materialism, which leaves the universe as a brute fact. Swinburne concludes that "Theism does not make [certain phenomena] very probable; but nothing else makes their occurrence in the least probable, and they cry out for explanation. *A priori*, theism is perhaps very unlikely, but it is far more likely than any rival supposition. Hence our phenomena are substantial evidence for the truth of theism" (Swinburne 1976, 290).

Why does Swinburne hold that God provide the best or ultimate explanation of the universe? Part of the answer is that the Principle of Causation does not apply to God or a necessary being. On the one hand, there can be no scientific explanation of God's existence, for there are neither antecedent beings nor scientific principles from which God's existence follows. On the other hand, the Principle of Causation applies only to contingent and not to necessary beings. Explanation is required only of what is contingent. It is not that God's existence is logically necessary, but that if God exists, he cannot not exist. That God is eternal and not dependent on anything for his existence are not reasons for his existence but his properties. (See 3.5 above for Mackie's discussion of this argument.)

A second reason for Swinburne is that explanation can be reasonably thought to have achieved finality when one gives a personal explanation that appeals to the intentions of a conscious agent. One may attempt to provide a scientific account of why someone has particular intentions, but there is no requirement that such an account be supplied, let alone be possible. We may not achieve any better explanation by trying to explain physically why persons intended to act as they did. However, when we claim that something happened because persons intended it and acted on their intentions, we can achieve a complete explanation of why that thing happened.

Third, appeal to God as an intentional agent leads us to have certain expectations about the universe: that it manifests order, is comprehensible, and favors the existence of beings that can comprehend it. For Swinburne, who in his works often discusses this antecedent probability, this accords with his predictability criterion. Finally, Swinburne introduces a fourth feature, namely, the simplicity of God that, by its very nature, makes further explanation either impossible or makes theism the best explanation.[3] This consideration leads to discussion of God's properties and the nature of simplicity.

Still, Mackie notes, raising the probability of God's existence is not of geat assistance, for "the hypothesis of divine creation *is* very unlikely." (Mackie, 100). Indeed, it is very unlikely that a God possessing the traditional theistic properties exists. Hence, increasing the probability of something very unlikely initially leaves us with the unlikely. Swinburne's response is that although theism is perhaps very unlikely, it is far more likely than any supposition that things just happen to be. So we return to what constitutes the best explanation of the existence of the universe.

So Swinburne and his critics leave us with the difficulties of determining what counts as an adequate explanation, of defining simplicity, and of determining prior probabilities.

Finally, even if the Cosmological Argument is sound or cogent, the difficult task remains to show that the necessary being to which the cosmological argument concludes is the God of religion, and if so, of what religion. Rowe suggests that the cosmological argument has two parts, one to establish the existence of a first cause or necessary being, the other that this necessary being is God (1975, 6). It is not clear, however, that the second contention is an essential part of the cosmological argument. Although Aquinas was quick to make the identification between God and the first mover or first cause, such identification goes beyond the causal reasoning that informs the argument. Instead, to give any religious substance to the concept of a necessary being requires lengthy discussion of the supreme beings found in the diverse religions and careful correlation of the properties of a necessary being with those of a religious being, to discern compatibilities and incompatibilities (Attfield). Defenders of the cosmological argument point to the subsequent relevance of such a task; critics find themselves freed from such endeavors.

---

[3] At times it is unclear whether Swinburne is claiming the virtue of God's simplicity or that of theism. Swinburne entitles chapter 3 of *Is There a God?*, "The Simplicity of God." But a subheading is "The Simplicity of Theism."

Questions

1. What are the distinctive features of the *kalām* argument?

2. List the 3 cosmological arguments. What makes them a posteriori?

3. What sorts of objections do you see Thomas's proofs facing?

4. What sorts of strengths do you see in Thomas's proofs?

5. Of the five proofs, which one do you think is the strongest and why?

Bibliography

- Aquinas, Thomas, 13th c., *Summa Theologica* I, q. 2. [Available Online].
- Attfield, Robin, 1975, "The God of Religion and the God of Philosophy," *Religious Studies* 9: 1-9.
- Barrow, John and Frank Tipler, 1986, *The Anthropic Cosmological Principle,* Oxford: Clarendon Press.
- Brown, Patterson, 1966, "Infinite Causal Regression," *Philosophical Review* 75: 510-25.
- Craig, William Lane, 1980, *The Cosmological Argument from Plato to Leibniz, London*: The Macmillan Press.
- Craig, William Lane, 1979, The Kalām Cosmological Argument, London: The Macmillan Press.
- Craig, William Lane and Quentin Smith, 1993, *Theism, Atheism, and Big Bang Cosmology*, New York: Oxford University Press.
- Davies, Paul, 1992, *The Mind of God, New York*: Simon and Schuster.
- Davies, Paul, 1984, *Superforce,* New York: Simon and Schuster.
- Fakry, Majid, 1957, "The Classical Islamic Arguments for the Existence of God," *The Muslim World*: 133-145. [Available Online].
- Gale, Richard and Alexander R. Pruss, 1999, "A New Cosmological Argument," *Religious Studies* 35: 461-476.
- Gale, Richard, 1991, *On the Nature and Existence of God*, Cambridge: Cambridge University Press.
- Glanz, James, 1998, "Cosmic Motion Revealed," *Science* 282: 2157.
- Grübaum, Adolf, 1994, "Some Comments on William Craig's 'Creation and Big Bang Cosmology'", *Philosophia Naturalis*, 31/2, pp. 225-236. [Preprint available online.]
- Hawking, Stephen, 1988, *A Brief History of Time*, New York: Bantam Books.
- Hume, David, 1980, *Dialogues Concerning Natural Religion*, Indianapolis: Hackett. [Available Online].
- Kant, Immanuel, 1998, *Critique of Pure Reason*, Cambridge: Cambridge University Press.
- Kenny, Anthony, 1969, *The Five Ways*, New York: Schocken Books.
- Leslie, John, ed., 1990, *Physical Cosmology and Philosophy*, New York: Macmillan.
- Mackie, J. L., 1982, *The Miracle of Theism*, Oxford: Clarendon Press.
- Martin, Michael, 1990, *Atheism: A Philosophical Justification*, Philadelphia: Temple University Press.
- Martin, Michael, 1991, *The Case Against Christianity*, Philadelphia: Temple University Press.
- Miethe, Terry L., 1978, "The Cosmological Argument: A Research Bibliography," *New Scholasticism* 52: 285-305.
- Musser, George, 2004, "Four Keys to Cosmology", *Scientific American*, February, p. 43.
- Plantinga, Alvin, 1967, God and Other Minds, Ithaca: Cornell University Press.
- Potter, Karl H., ed., 1977, *Indian Metaphysics and Epistemology: The Tradition of Nyāya-Vaiśeṣika up to Gangeśa,* Princeton: Princeton University Press.
- Reichenbach, Bruce R., 1972, *The Cosmological Argument: A Reassessment*, Springfield: Charles Thomas.
- Rowe, William, 1975, *The Cosmological Argument*, Princeton: Princeton University Press.
- Rowe, William, 1962, "The Fallacy of Composition," *Mind* 71: 87-92.
- Russell, Bertrand, and Frederick Copleston, 1964, "Debate on the Existence of God," in John Hick, ed., *The Existence of God*, New York: Macmillan.

- Scotus, John Duns, 1962, *Philosophical Writings*, Indianapolis: Bobbs-Merrill Co.
- Silk, Joseph, 2001, *The Big Bang*, San Francisco: W.H. Freeman.
- Sincell, Marc, 2001, "Farthest Supernova Yet Bolsters Dark Energy," *Science* 292: 27.
- Smart, J.J.C. and J.J. Haldane, 1996, *Atheism and Theism*, Oxford: Blackwells.
- Srianand, R., P. Petitjean, C. Ledoux, 2000, "The Cosmic Microwave Background Radiation Temperature at a Redshift of 2.34," *Nature* 406: 931-35.
- Stafford, Betty L., and Bruce Cordell, 1987, "God and Modern Science: New Life for the Teleological Argument," *International Philosophical Quarterly* 27, no. 4: 409-35.
- Swinburne, Richard, 1977, *The Coherence of Theism*, Oxford: Clarendon Press.
- Swinburne, Richard, 1979, *The Existence of God*, Oxford: Clarendon Press.
- Swinburne, Richard, 1996, *Is There a God*? Oxford: Oxford University Press.
- Taylor, Richard, 1992, *Metaphysics*, Englewood Cliffs: Prentice-Hall.

AN EXAMINATION OF THE COSMOLOGICAL ARGUMENT*

William Rowe

Rowe begins by distinguishing between a priori and a posteriori arguments and setting the cosmological argument in historical perspective. Next, he divides the argument into two parts: that which seeks to prove the existence of a self-existent being and that which seeks to prove that this self-existent being is the God of theism. He introduces the principle of sufficient reason: "There must be an explanation (a) of the existence of any being, and (b) of any positive fact whatever" and shows its role in the cosmological argument. In the light of this principle, he examines the argument itself and four objections to it.

Stating the Argument

Arguments for the existence of God are commonly divided into *a posteriori* arguments and *a priori* arguments. An *a posteriori* argument depends on a principle or premise that can be known only by means of our experience of the world. An *a priori* argument, on the other hand, purports to rest on principles all of which can be known independently of our experience of the world, by just reflecting on and understanding them. Of the three major arguments for the existence of God—the Cosmological, the Teleological, and the Ontological—only the last of these is entirely *a priori*. In the Cosmological Argument one starts from some simple fact about the world, such as that it contains things which are caused to exist by other things. In the Teleological Argument a somewhat more complicated fact about the world serves as a starting point, the fact that the world exhibits order and design. In the Ontological Argument, however, one begins simply with a concept of God.

Before we state the Cosmological Argument itself, we shall consider some rather general points about the argument. Historically, it can be traced to the writings of the Greek philosophers, Plato and Aristotle, but the major developments in the argument took place in the thirteenth and in the eighteenth centuries. In the thirteenth century Aquinas put forth five distinct arguments for the existence of God, and of these, the first three are versions of the Cosmological Argument.[1] In the first of these he started from the fact that there are things in the world undergoing change and reasoned to the conclusion that there must be some ultimate cause of change that is itself unchanging. In the second he started from the fact that there are things in the world that clearly are caused to exist by other things and reasoned to the conclusion that there must be some ultimate cause of existence whose own existence is itself uncaused. And in the third argument he started from the fact that there are things in the world which need not have existed at all, things which do exist but which we can easily imagine might not, and reasoned to the conclusion that there must be some being that had to be, that exists and could not have failed to exist. Now it might be objected that even if Aquinas' arguments do prove beyond doubt the existence of an unchanging changer, an uncaused cause, and a being that could not have failed to exist, the arguments fail to prove the existence of the theistic God. For the theistic God, as we saw, is supremely good, omnipotent, omniscient, and creator of but separate from and independent of the world. How do we know, for example, that the unchanging changer isn't evil or slightly ignorant? The answer to this objection is that the Cosmological Argument has two parts. In the first part the effort is to prove the existence of a special sort of being, for example, a

---

* Reprinted from William Rowe, *Philosophy of Religion* (Wadsworth Publishing Co., 1978), by permission.
[1] See St. Thomas Aquinas, *Summa Theologica,* la. 2, 3.

being that could not have failed to exist, or a being that causes change in other things but is itself unchanging. In the second part of the argument the effort is to prove that the special sort of being whose existence has been established in the first part has, and must have, the features—perfect goodness, omnipotence, omniscience, and so on—which go together to make up the theistic idea of God. What this means, then, is that Aquinas' three arguments are different versions of only the first part of the Cosmological Argument. Indeed, in later sections of his *Summa Theologica* Aquinas undertakes to show that the unchanging changer, the uncaused cause of existence, and the being which had to exist are one and the same being and that this single being has all of the attributes of the theistic God.

We noted above that a second major development in the Cosmological Argument took place in the eighteenth century, a development reflected in the writings of the German philosopher, Gottfried Leibniz (1646-1716), and especially in the writings of the English theologian and philosopher, Samuel Clarke (1675-1729). In 1704 Clarke gave a series of lectures, later published under the title *A Demonstration of the Being and Attributes of God.* These lectures constitute, perhaps, the most complete, forceful, and cogent presentation of the Cosmological Argument we possess. The lectures were read by the major skeptical philosopher of the century, David Hume (1711-1776), and in his brilliant attack on the attempt to justify religion in the court of reason, his *Dialogues Concerning Natural Religion,* Hume advanced several penetrating criticisms of Clarke's arguments, criticisms which have persuaded many philosophers in the modern period to reject the Cosmological Argument. In our study of the argument we shall concentrate our attention largely on its eighteenth century form and try to assess its strengths and weaknesses in the light of the criticisms which Hume and others have advanced against it.

The first part of the eighteenth-century form of the Cosmological Argument seeks to establish the existence of a self-existent being. The second part of the argument attempts to prove that the self-existent being is the theistic God, that is, has the features which we have noted to be basic elements in the theistic idea of God. We shall consider mainly the first part of the argument, for it is against the first part that philosophers from Hume to Russell have advanced very important objections.

In stating the first part of the Cosmological Argument we shall make use of two important concepts, the concept of a *dependent being* and the concept of a *self-existent being.* By *a dependent being* we mean *a being whose existence is accounted for by the causal activity of other things.* Recalling Anselm's division into the three cases: "explained by another," "explained by nothing," and "explained by itself," it's clear that a dependent being is a being whose existence is explained by another. By *a self-existent being* we mean *a being whose existence is accounted for by its own nature.* This idea . . . is an essential element in the theistic concept of God. Again, in terms of Anselm's three cases, a self-existent being is a being whose existence is explained by itself. Armed with these two concepts, the concept of a dependent being and the concept of a self-existent being, we can now state the first part of the Cosmological Argument.

1. Every being (that exists or ever did exist) is either a dependent being or a self-existent being.
2. Not every being can be a dependent being.

Therefore,

3. There exists a self-existent being.

Deductive Validity

Before we look critically at each of the premises of this argument, we should note that this argument is, to use an expression from the logician's vocabulary, *deductively valid*. To find out whether an argument is deductively valid, we need only ask the question: If its premises were true, would its conclusion have to be true? If the answer is yes, the argument is deductively valid. If the answer is no, the argument is deductively invalid. Notice that the question of the validity of an argument is entirely different from the question of whether its premises are in fact true. The following argument is made up entirely of false statements, but it is deductively valid.

1. Babe Ruth is the President of the United States.
2. The President of the United States is from Indiana.

Therefore,

3. Babe Ruth is from Indiana.

The argument is deductively valid because even though its premises are false, if they were true its conclusion would have to be true. Even God, Aquinas would say, cannot bring it about that the premises of this argument are true and yet its conclusion is false, for God's power extends only to what is possible, and it is an absolute impossibility that Babe Ruth be the President, the President be from Indiana, and yet Babe Ruth not be from Indiana.

The Cosmological Argument (that is, its first part) is a deductively valid argument. If its premises are or were true, its conclusion would have to be true. It's clear from our example about Babe Ruth, however, that the fact that an argument is deductively valid is insufficient to establish the truth of its conclusion. What else is required? Clearly that we know or have rational grounds for believing that the premises are true. If we know that the Cosmological Argument is deductively valid, and can establish that its premises are true, we shall thereby have proved that its conclusion is true. Are, then, the premises of the Cosmological Argument true? To this more difficult question we must now turn.

PSR and the First Premise

At first glance the first premise might appear to be an obvious or even trivial truth. But it is neither obvious nor trivial. And if it appears to be obvious or trivial, we must be confusing the idea of a self-existent being with the idea of a being that is not a dependent being. Clearly, it is true that any being is either a dependent being (explained by other things) or it is not a dependent being (not explained by other things). But what our premise says is that any being is either a dependent being (explained by other things) or it is a self-existent being (explained by itself). Consider again Anselm's three cases.

a. explained by another
b. explained by nothing
c. explained by itself

What our first premise asserts is that each being that exists (or ever did exist) is either of sort *a* or of sort *c*. It denies that any being is of sort *b*. And it is this denial that makes the first premise both significant and controversial. The obvious truth we must not confuse it with is the truth that any being is either of sort *a* or not of sort *a*. While this is true it is neither very significant nor controversial.

Earlier we saw that Anselm accepted as a basic principle that whatever exists has an explanation of its existence. Since this basic principle denies that any thing of sort *b* exists or ever did exist, it's clear that Anselm would believe the first premise of our Cosmological Argument. The eighteenth-century proponents of the argument also were convinced of the truth of the basic principle we attributed to Anselm. And because they were convinced of its truth, they readily accepted the first premise of the Cosmological Argument. But by the eighteenth century, Anselm's basic principle had been more fully elaborated and had received a name, the *Principle of Sufficient Reason*. Since this principle (PSR, as we shall call it) plays such an important role in justifying the premises of the Cosmological Argument, it will help us to consider it for a moment before we continue our enquiry into the truth or falsity of the premises of the Cosmological Argument.

The Principle of Sufficient Reason, as it was expressed by both Leibniz and Samuel Clarke, is a very general principle and is best understood as having two parts. In its first part it is simply a restatement of Anselm's principle that there must be an explanation of the *existence* of any being whatever. Thus if we come upon a man in a room, PSR implies that there must be an explanation of the fact that that particular man exists. A moment's reflection, however, reveals that there are many facts about the man other than the mere fact that he exists. There is the fact that the man in question is in the room he's in, rather than somewhere else, the fact that he is in good health, and the fact that he is at the moment thinking of Paris, rather than, say, London. Now, the purpose of the second part of PSR is to require an explanation of these facts, as well. We may state PSR, therefore, as the principle that *there must be* an *explanation (a) of the existence of any being, and (b) of any positive fact whatever.* We are now in a position to study the role this very important principle plays in the Cosmological Argument.

Since the proponent of the Cosmological Argument accepts PSR in both its parts, it is clear that he will appeal to its first part, PSRa, as justification for the first premise of the Cosmological Argument. Of course, we can and should inquire into the deeper question of whether the proponent of the argument is rationally justified in accepting PSR itself. But we shall put this question aside for the moment. What we need to see first is whether he is correct in thinking that *if* PSR is true then both of the premises of the Cosmological Argument are true. And what we have just seen is that if only the first part of PSR, that is, PSRa, is true, the first premise of the Cosmological Argument will be true. But what of the second premise of the argument? For what reasons does the proponent think that it must be true?

The Second Premise

According to the second premise, not every being that exists can be a dependent being, that is, can have the explanation of its existence in some other being or beings. Presumably, the proponent of the argument thinks there is something fundamentally wrong with the idea that every being that exists is dependent, that each existing being was caused by some other being which in turn was caused by some other being, and so on. But just what does he think is wrong with it? To help us in understanding his thinking, let's simplify things by supposing that there exists only one thing now, A_1, a living thing perhaps, that was brought into existence by something else, A_2, which perished shortly after it brought A_1, into existence. Suppose further that A_2 was brought into existence in similar fashion some time ago by A_3, and A_3 by A_4, and so forth back into the past. Each of these beings is a *dependent* being, it owes its existence to the preceding thing in the series. Now if nothing else ever existed but these beings, then what the second premise says would not be true. For if every being that exists or ever did exist is an A and was produced by a preceding A, then every being that exists or ever did exist would be dependent and, accordingly, premise two of the Cosmological Argument would be false. If the proponent of the Cosmological Argument is correct there must, then, be something wrong with the idea that every being that exists or did exist is an A and that they form a causal series. A_1 caused by A_2, A_2 caused by A_3, A_3 caused by A_4,...A_n caused by A_{n+1}. How does the proponent of the Cosmological Argument propose to show us that there is something wrong with this view?

A popular but mistaken idea of how the proponent tries to show that something is wrong with the view, that every being might be dependent, is that he uses the following argument to reject it.

1. There must be a *first* being to start any causal series.

2. If every being were dependent there would be no *first* being to start the causal series.

Therefore,

3. Not every being can be a dependent being.

Although this argument is deductively valid, and its second premise is true, its first premise overlooks the distinct possibility that a causal series might be *infinite,* with no first member at all. Thus if we go back to our series of A beings, where each A is dependent, having been produced by the preceding A in the causal series, it's clear that if the series existed it would have no first member, for every A in the series there would be a preceding A which produced it, *ad infinitum.* The first premise of the argument just given assumes that a causal series must stop with a first member somewhere in the distant past. But there seems to be no good reason for making that assumption.

The eighteenth-century proponents of the Cosmological Argument recognized that the causal series of dependent beings could be infinite, without a first member to start the series. They rejected the idea that every being that is or ever was is dependent not because there would then be no first member to the series of dependent beings, but because there would then be no explanation for the fact that there are and have always been dependent beings. To see their reasoning let's return to our simplification of the supposition that the only things that exist or ever did exist are dependent beings. In our simplification of that supposition only one of the dependent beings exists at a time, each one perishing as it produces the next in the series. Perhaps the first thing to note about this supposition is that there is no individual A in the causal series of dependent beings whose existence is unexplained—A_1 is explained by A_2, A_2 by A_3, and A_n by A_{n+1}. So the first part of PSR, PSRa, appears to be satisfied. There is no particular being whose existence lacks an explanation. What, then, is it that lacks an explanation, if every particular A in the causal series of dependent beings has an explanation? If is the series itself that lacks an explanation. Or, as I've chosen to express it, *the fact that there are and have always been dependent beings.* For suppose we ask why it is that there are and have always been As in existence. It won't do to say that As have always been producing other As—we can't explain why there have always been As by saying there always have been As. Nor, on the supposition that only As have ever existed, can we explain the fact that there have always been As by appealing to something other than an A—for no such thing would have existed. Thus the supposition that the only things that exist or ever existed are dependent things leaves us with a fact for which there can be no explanation; namely, the fact that there are and have always been dependent beings.

Questioning the Justification of the Second Premise

Critics of the Cosmological Argument have raised several important objections against the claim that if every being is dependent the series or collection of those beings would have no explanation. Our understanding of the Cosmological Argument, as well as of its strengths and weaknesses, will be deepened by a careful consideration of these criticisms.

The first criticism is that the proponent of the Cosmological Argument makes the mistake of treating the collection or series of dependent beings as though it were itself a dependent being, and, therefore, requires an explanation of its existence. But, so the objection goes, the collection of dependent beings is not itself a dependent being any more than a collection of stamps is itself a stamp.

A second criticism is that the proponent makes the mistake of inferring that because each member of the collection of dependent beings has a cause, the collection itself must have a cause. But, as Bertrand Russell noted, such reasoning is as fallacious as to infer that the human race (that is, the collection of human beings) must have a mother because each member of the collection (each human being) has a mother.

A third criticism is that the proponent of the argument fails to realize that for there to be an explanation of a collection of things is nothing more than for there to be an explanation of each of the things making up the collection. Since in the infinite collection (or series) of dependent beings, each being in the collection does have an explanation—by virtue of having been caused by some preceding member of the collection—the explanation of the collection, so the criticism goes, has already been given. As David Hume remarked, "Did I show you the particular causes of each individual in a collection of twenty particles of matter, I should think it very unreasonable, should you afterwards ask me, what was the cause of the whole twenty. This is sufficiently explained in explaining the cause of the parts."[2]

Finally, even if the proponent of the Cosmological Argument can satisfactorily answer these objections, he must face one last objection to his ingenious attempt to justify premise two of the Cosmological Argument. For someone may agree that if nothing exists but an infinite collection of dependent beings, the infinite collection will have no explanation of its existence, and still refuse to conclude from this that there is something wrong with the idea that every being is a dependent being. Why, he might ask, should we think that everything has to have an explanation? What's wrong with admitting that the fact that there are and have always been dependent beings is a *brute* fact, a fact having no explanation whatever? Why does everything have to have an explanation anyway? We must now see what can be said in response to these several objections.

Responses to Criticism

It is certainly a mistake to think that a collection of stamps is itself a stamp, and very likely a mistake to think that the collection of dependent beings is itself a dependent being. But the mere fact that the proponent of the argument thinks that there must be an explanation not only for each member of the collection of dependent beings but for the collection itself is not sufficient

---

[2] David Hume, *Dialogues Concerning Natural Religion,* Part IX, ed. H. D. Aiken (New York: Hafner Publishing Company, 1948), pp. 59-60.

grounds for concluding that he must view the collection as itself a dependent being. The collection of human beings, for example, is certainly not itself a human being. Admitting this, however, we might still seek an explanation of why there is a collection of human beings, of why there are such things as human beings at all. So the mere fact that an explanation is demanded for the collection of dependent beings is no proof that the person who demands the explanation must be supposing that the collection itself is just another dependent being.

The second criticism attributes to the proponent of the Cosmological Argument the following bit of reasoning.

1. Every member of the collection of dependent beings has a cause or explanation.

Therefore,

2. The collection of dependent beings has a cause or explanation.

As we noted in setting forth this criticism, arguments of this sort are often unreliable. It would be a mistake to conclude that a collection of objects is light in weight simply because each object in the collection is light in weight, for if there were many objects in the collection it might be quite heavy. On the other hand, if we know that each marble weighs more than one ounce, we could infer validly that the collection of marbles weighs more than an ounce. Fortunately, however, we don't need to decide whether the inference from 1 to 2 is valid or invalid. We need not decide this question because the proponent of the Cosmological Argument need not use this inference to establish that there must be an explanation of the collection of dependent beings. He need not use this inference because he has in PSR a principle from which it follows immediately that the collection of dependent beings has a cause or explanation. For according to PSR, every positive fact must have an explanation. If it is a fact that there exists a collection of dependent beings then, according to PSR, that fact too must have an explanation. So it is PSR that the proponent of the Cosmological Argument appeals to in concluding that there must be an explanation of the collection of dependent beings, and not some dubious inference from the premise that each member of the collection has an explanation. It seems, then, that neither of the first two criticisms is strong enough to do any serious damage to the reasoning used to support the second premise of the Cosmological Argument.

The third objection contends that to explain the existence of a collection of things is the same thing as to explain the existence of each of its members. If we consider a collection of dependent beings where each being in the collection is explained by the preceding member which caused it, it's clear that no member of the collection will lack an explanation of its existence. But, so the criticism goes, if we've explained the existence of every member of a collection, we've explained the existence of the collection—there's nothing left over to be explained. This forceful criticism, originally advanced by David Hume, has gained considerable support in the modern period. But the criticism rests on an assumption that the proponent of the Cosmological Argument would not accept. The assumption is that to explain the existence of a collection of things it is *sufficient* to explain the existence of every member in the collection. To see what is wrong with this assumption is to understand the basic issue in the reasoning by which the proponent of the Cosmological Argument seeks to establish that not every being can be a dependent being.

In order for there to be an explanation of the existence of the collection of dependent beings, it's clear that the eighteenth-century proponents would require that the following two conditions be satisfied:

C1. There is an explanation of the existence of each of the members of the collection of dependent beings.

C2. There is an explanation of why there are any dependent beings.

According to the proponents of the Cosmological Argument, if every being that exists or ever did exist is a dependent being—that is, if the whole of reality consists of nothing more than a collection of dependent beings—C1 will be satisfied, but C2 will not be satisfied. And since C2 won't be satisfied, there will be no explanation of the collection of dependent beings. The third criticism, therefore, says in effect that if C1 is satisfied, C2 will be satisfied, and, since in a collection of dependent beings each member will have an explanation in whatever it was that produced it, C1 will be satisfied. So, therefore, C2 will be satisfied and the collection of dependent beings will have an explanation.

Although the issue is a complicated one, I think it is possible to see that the third criticism rests on a mistake: the mistake of thinking that if C1 is satisfied C2 must also be satisfied. The mistake is a natural one to make for it is easy to imagine circumstances in which if C1 is satisfied C2 also will be satisfied. Suppose, for example, that the whole of reality includes not just a collection of dependent beings but also a self-existent being. Suppose further that instead of each dependent being having been produced by some other dependent being, every dependent being was produced by the self-existent being. Finally, let us consider both the possibility that the collection of dependent beings is finite in time and has a first member, and the possibility that the collection of dependent beings is infinite in past time, having no first member. Using G for the self-existent being, the first possibility may be diagramed as follows:

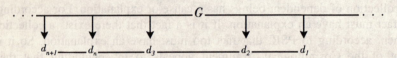

G, we shall say, has always existed and always will. We can think of d_1 as some presently existing dependent being, d_2, d_3, and so forth as dependent beings that existed at some time in the past, and d_n as the first dependent being to exist. The second possibility may be portrayed as follows:

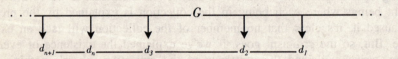

On this diagram there is no first member of the collection of dependent beings. Each member of the infinite collection, however, is explained by reference to the self-existent being G which produced it. Now the interesting point about both these cases is that the explanation that has been provided for the members of the collection of dependent beings carries with it, at least in part, an answer to the question of why there are any dependent beings at all. In both cases we may explain why there are dependent beings by pointing out that there exists a self-existent being that has been engaged in producing them. So once we have learned that the existence of each member of the collection of dependent beings has its existence explained by the fact that G produced it, we have already learned why there are dependent beings.

Someone might object that we haven't really learned why there are dependent beings until we also learn *why* G has been producing them. But, of course, we could also say that we haven't really explained the existence of a particular dependent being, say d_3, until we also learn not just that G produced it but *why* G produced it. The point we need to grasp, however, is that once we admit that every dependent being's existence is explained by G, we must admit that the fact that there are dependent beings has also been explained. So it is not unnatural that someone should think that to explain the existence of the collection of dependent beings is nothing more than to explain the existence of its members. For, as we've seen, to explain the collection's existence is to explain each member's existence and to explain why there are any dependent beings at all. And in the examples we've considered, in doing the one (explaining why each dependent being exists) we've already done the other (explained why there are any dependent beings at all). We must now see, however, that on the supposition that the whole of reality consists *only* of a collection of dependent beings, to give an explanation of each member's existence is not to provide an explanation of why there are dependent beings.

In the examples we've considered, we have gone *outside* of the collection of dependent beings in order to explain the members' existence. But if the only beings that exist or ever existed are dependent beings then each dependent being will be explained by some other dependent being, ad infinitum. This does not mean that there will be some particular dependent being whose existence is unaccounted for. Each dependent being has an explanation of its existence; namely, in the dependent being which preceded it and produced it. So C1 is satisfied: there is an explanation of the existence of each member of the collection of dependent beings. Turning to C2, however, we can see that it will not be satisfied. We cannot explain why there are (or have ever been) dependent beings by appealing to all the members of the infinite collection of dependent beings. For if the question to be answered is why there are (or have ever been) any dependent beings at all, we cannot answer that question by noting that there always have been dependent beings, each one accounting for the existence of some other dependent being. Thus on the supposition that every being is dependent, it seems there will be no explanation of why there are dependent beings. C2 will not be satisfied. Therefore, on the supposition that every being is dependent there will be no explanation of the existence of the collection of dependent beings.

The Truth of PSR

We come now to the final criticism of the reasoning supporting the second premise of the Cosmological Argument. According to this criticism, it is admitted that the supposition that every being is dependent implies that there will be a *brute fact* in the universe, a fact, that is, for which there can be no explanation whatever. For there will be no explanation of the fact that dependent beings exist and have always been in existence. It is this brute fact that the proponents of the argument were describing when they pointed out that if every being is dependent, the series or collection of dependent beings would lack an explanation of *its* existence. The final criticism asks what is wrong with admitting that the universe contains such a brute, unintelligible fact. In asking this question the critic challenges the fundamental principle, PSR, on which the Cosmological Argument rests. For, as we've seen, the first premise of the argument denies that there exists a being whose existence has no explanation. In support of this premise the proponent appeals to the first part of PSR. The second premise of the argument claims that not every being can be dependent. In support of this premise the proponent appeals to the second part of PSR, the part which states that there must be an explanation of any positive fact whatever.

The proponent reasons that if every being were a dependent being, then although the first part of PSR would be satisfied—every being would have an explanation—the second part would be violated; there would be no explanation for the positive fact that there are and have always been dependent beings. For first, since every being is supposed to be dependent, there would be nothing outside of the collection of dependent beings to explain the collection's existence. Second, the fact that each member of the collection has an explanation in some other dependent being is insufficient to explain why there are and have always been dependent beings. And, finally, there is nothing about the collection of dependent beings that would suggest that it is a self-existent collection. Consequently, if every being were dependent, the fact that there are and have always been dependent beings would have no explanation. But this violates the second part of PSR. So the second premise of the Cosmological Argument must be true: Not every being can be a dependent being. This conclusion, however, is no better than the principle, PSR, on which it rests. And it is the point of the final criticism to question the truth of PSR. Why, after all, should we accept the idea that every being and every positive fact must have an explanation? Why, in short, should we believe PSR? These are important questions, and any final judgment of the Cosmological Argument depends on how they are answered.

Most of the theologians and philosophers who accept PSR have tried to defend it in either of two ways. Some have held that PSR is (or can be) known *intuitively* to be true. By this they mean that if we fully understand and reflect on what is said by PSR we can see that it must be true. Now, undoubtedly, there are statements which are known intuitively to be true. "Every triangle has exactly three angles" or "No physical object can be in two different places in space at one and the same time" are examples of statements whose truth we can apprehend just by understanding and reflecting on them. The difficulty with the claim that PSR is intuitively true, however, is that a number of very able philosophers fail to apprehend its truth, and some even claim that the principle is false. It is doubtful, therefore, that many of us, if any, know intuitively that PSR is true.

The second way philosophers and theologians who accept PSR have sought to defend it is by claiming that although it is not known to be true, it is, nevertheless, a presupposition of reason, a basic assumption that rational people make, whether or not they reflect sufficiently to become aware of the assumption. It's probably true that there are some assumptions we all make about our world, assumptions which are so basic that most of us are unaware of them. And, I suppose, it might be true that PSR is such an assumption. What bearing would this view of PSR have on the Cosmological Argument? Perhaps the main point to note is that even if PSR is a presupposition we all share, the premises of the Cosmological Argument could still be false. For PSR itself could still be false. The fact, if it is a fact, that all of us *presuppose* that every existing being and every positive fact has an explanation does not imply that no being exists, and no positive fact obtains, without an explanation. Nature is not bound to satisfy our presuppositions. As the American philosopher William James once remarked in another connection, "In the great boarding house of nature, the cakes and the butter and the syrup seldom come out so even and leave the plates so clear."

Our study of the first part of the Cosmological Argument has led us to the fundamental principle on which its premises rest, the Principle of Sufficient Reason. Since we do not seem to know that PSR is true, we cannot reasonably claim to know that the premises of the Cosmological Argument are true. They might be true. But unless we do know them to be true they cannot *establish* for us the conclusion that there exists a being that has the explanation of its existence within its own nature. If it were shown, however, that even though we do not *know* that PSR is true we all, nevertheless, presuppose PSR to be true, then, whether PSR is true or not, to be consistent we should accept the Cosmological Argument. For, as we've seen, its premises imply its conclusion and its premises do seem to follow from PSR. But no one has succeeded in *showing* that PSR is an assumption that most or all of us share. So our final conclusion must be that although the Cosmological Argument might be a *sound* argument (valid with true premises), it does not provide us with good rational grounds for believing that among these beings that exist there is one whose existence is accounted for by its own nature. Having come to this conclusion, we may safely put aside the second part of the argument. For even if it succeeded in showing that a self-existent being would have the other attributes of the theistic God, the Cosmological Argument would still not provide us with good rational grounds for belief in God, having failed in its first part to provide us with good rational grounds for believing that there is a self-existent being.

Questions

1. For Rowe, what differences are there between *a priori* and *a posteriori* arguments for God's existence?

2. What is the Principle of Sufficient Reason (PSR)?

3. Did the eighteenth-century defenders of the cosmological argument think that the causal series could be infinite?

4. What is Rowe's verdict regarding PSR?

5. What is Rowe's opinion regarding the effectiveness of arguments for God's existence?

THE ARGUMENT TO GOD FROM LAWS OF NATURE[*]

Richard Swinburne

Swinburne focuses upon the confirmatory force of the argument for God's existence from the laws of nature. He comes to conclude that the degree to which the universe is governed by simple laws of nature and not by chaotic forces adds to the probability of theism.

I have campaigned for many years for the view that most of the traditional arguments for the existence of God can be construed as inductive arguments from phenomena to the hypothesis of theism (that there is a God) which best explains them.[1] Each of these phenomena gives some probability to the hypothesis, and together they make it more probable than not. The phenomena can be arranged in decreasing order of generality. The cosmological argument argues from the existence of the Universe; the argument from temporal order argues from its being governed by simple laws of nature; the argument from fine-tuning argues from the initial conditions and form and constants of the laws of nature being such as to lead (somewhere in the Universe) to the evolution of animal and human bodies. Then we have arguments from those humans being conscious, from various particular characteristics of humans and their environment (their free will, capacity for causing limited good and harm to each other and especially molding their own characters for good or ill), various historical events (including violations of natural laws), and finally the religious experiences of so many millions of humans.

I assess these arguments as arguments to the existence of 'God' in the traditional sense of a being essentially eternal, omnipotent, omniscient, perfectly free and perfectly good. I argue that his perfect goodness follows from the other four properties. This is because being omniscient God will see which actions are good. To recognize an action as 'good' involves having some motivation to do it. Being perfectly free, God will (unlike ourselves) be subject to no irrational inclinations deterring him from pursuing the good and so he will be perfectly good.[2] God's omnipotence is his ability to do anything logically possible. God's perfect goodness is to be understood as his doing only what is good and doing the best in so far as that is logically possible and in so far as he has the moral right to do so. So he will inevitably bring about a unique best-possible world (if there is one), or one of a disjunction of equal best-possible worlds (if there are such). But if for every good possible world, there is a better, all that God's perfect goodness can amount to is that he will bring about a good possible world.[3] So God will bring about any state of affairs which belongs to the best or all the equal best of all the good possible worlds. If there is some state of affairs which is such that any world is equally good for having it or not having it, then we can say that there is a probability of ½ that he will make it. God will exercise this choice among worlds (and so states of affairs) which it is logically possible for him to bring about and

---

[*] This article is printed by courtesy of Richard Swinburne and was originally published in *Reason, Faith, and History: Essays in Honor of Paul Helm*, ed. Martin Stone (Ashgate, 2005) and in *Debating Design*, W. A. Dembski and M. Ruse, editors, Cambridge University Press, 2004.
[1] See especially my *The Existence of God*, revised edition, 1993, and the simpler version of this in *Is there a God?*, Oxford University Press, 1996. (See chapter 8 of the former and chapter 4 of the latter for the argument from laws of nature.) The present paper is a revised version of a paper originally published in (ed.) Martin Stone *Reason, Faith and History*: Essays in Honour of Paul Helm, Ashgate, 2002.
[2] See, for example, my *The Coherence of Theism* revised edition, Clarendon Press, 1993, pp 149-52 and 207-9.
[3] For a fuller account of what God's goodness must amount to when there is no best or equal best possible world, see my *The Christian God*, Clarendon Press, 1994, pp 65-71 and 134-6.

which he has the moral right to bring about.

The grounds for believing any scientific, historical or super-scientific explanatory theory to be true are, first, that it makes probable the observed data (when otherwise they would not be as probable); and, secondly, since there will always be an infinite number of mutually incompatible theories satisfying the first requirement—that the theory is simple and has small-scope. By the latter I mean that it tells you about less in less detail—the less you say the more likely you are to be right. However, in order to make my paper of reasonable length I shall simply contrast theism with naturalism with the latter understood as the view that there is a large extended physical universe and nothing non-physical. (I thus ignore theories intermediate between theism and naturalism such as polytheism). Naturalism is thus a theory of equal scope to theism—an all-embracing world theory—and so we can ignore the criterion of scope. So whether evidence makes it probable that theism is true depends on the relative simplicity of theism and naturalism, which determines their relative intrinsic probabilities (i.e. a priori probabilities on zero contingent evidence); and how probable it is on the respective hypotheses that you would find the phenomena which I cited in the first paragraph. Note at this state that while almost everyone can be got to agree that a simpler theory is as such more probable than a complex theory, rational people disagree about how much greater is the probability of a simpler theory—whether a simple theory is more probable than any one complex theory; or whether a very simple theory is more probable than the disjunction of a very large number of complex theories. I will come back to this point of how much weight is to be given to the criterion of simplicity in due course.

I have argued elsewhere[4] that the hypothesis of theism is simpler than naturalism, and that the existence of a universe (entailed by naturalism) is fairly probable given theism. Thereafter, I claim each of the phenomena mentioned are improbable, given only naturalism and the phenomena mentioned in the previous argument. Thus the Universe being governed by simple laws of nature is improbable, given only naturalism; these laws being such as to lead to the evolution of animal and human bodies is improbable, given only naturalism and there being simple laws of nature—and so on. The argument then claims that if there is a God, these phenomena are much more to be expected than if there is no God; and hence they each increase (from its intrinsic probability) the probability that there is a God. By how much they increase it, and how probable in the end they make it depends on the relative intrinsic probabilities of theism and naturalism, and on how probable they make the various phenomena.

Having now set the framework of the discussion, I shall concern myself in this paper only with the confirmatory force of the argument from laws of nature, that is with how much the Universe being governed by simple laws rather than being chaotic adds to the probability of theism. The argument from the regular behavior of things—his way of putting an argument from simple laws of nature—constituted St Thomas Aquinas's 'fifth way' to prove the existence of God:

> "The fifth way is based on the guidedness of things. Some things lacking awareness seek a goal—which is apparent from the fact that always or most usually they behave in the same way which leads to the best result. From this it is evident that it is not by chance but by intention that they reach their goal. Nothing however that lacks awareness tends to a goal except under the direction of someone with awareness and understanding; the arrow for example requires an archer. Everything in nature, therefore, is directed to its goal by someone with understanding and this we call 'God'".[5]

---

[4] In Plantinga's terminology God can only weakly actualize such a world, not strongly actualize it. See Alvin Plantinga *The Nature of Necessity*, Clarendon Press, 1974, p. 173.

[5] For a full account of the criteria of simplicity and scope, see my *Epistemic Justification*, Clarendon Press, Chapter 4.

Aquinas seems to suppose that his 'ways' are good deductive arguments; and that, I think cannot be. It is more profitable to investigate whether they are good inductive, that is probabilistic arguments. To see whether such an argument as the 5th way is a good probabilistic argument we must ask, first, how probable is it if there is a God, that any Universe would be governed by simple laws.

God, being omnipotent, can bring about any state. He is essentially good; so it is probable that he will bring about a state of affairs in so far as it is good.[6] A major reason why God will bring about all the phenomena listed in my opening paragraph is that among the good worlds which a God has reason to make are ones in which there are creatures with a limited free choice between good and evil and limited powers to make deeply significant differences to themselves, each other, and their world by those choices (including the power to increase their powers and freedom of choice.) The goodness of significant free choice is, I hope, evident. We think it a good gift to give to our children that they choose their own path in life for good or ill, and influence the kinds of persons (with what kinds of character and powers) they and others are to be. But good though this is, there is the risk that the children will do evil and make themselves evil. Because of the evil they may do if God creates beings with the freedom to choose between good and evil, they must be finite, limited creatures. Even so, the risks are—as we know very well—considerable; and so, I suggest that God would not inevitably bring about such a world. So I suggest that any world which God could make containing such creatures would be no worse for not containing such creatures. But I suggest that the converse also holds: any world which God could make to which you add such creatures would be none the worse for such an addition. If that is correct if follows that there is a probability of ½ that he will make such a world. But my arguments do not depend on giving such a precise or such a high probability to God (if there is a God) making such a world. All that I am claiming is that there is a significant probability that a God would create such a world.

Let us call creatures with limited powers of the above kinds free rational creatures. If humans have (libertarian) free will (as is not implausible),[7] evidently our world is a world containing such creatures. We humans make deeply significant choices, affecting ourselves, each other, and our world; and our choices include choices to take steps to increase our powers and freedom, and form our characters for good or ill. But our powers in these respects are limited ones. Our world is thus a world of a kind which God can (with significant probability) be expected to make. Free rational creatures will have to begin life with a limited range of control, and the power to choose to extend that range or—alternatively—not to bother to do so. That limited range is their bodies. In order for them to be able to extend their range of control, there must be some procedure which they can utilize—This bodily movement will have this predictable extra-bodily effect; that one will have that effect. Hence the world must be subject to regularities, simple natural laws (either deterministic or probabilistic), which such creatures can choose to try to discover and then choose to utilize, to make differences to things distant in space and time. You can learn that if you plant seeds and water them, they will grow into edible plants which will enable you to keep alive yourself and others; or that if you pull the trigger of a gun loaded in a certain way and pointing in a certain direction, it will kill some distant person. And so on. We can choose whether to seek out such knowledge (of how to cure or kill) or not to bother; and we can choose whether to utilize this knowledge for good or ill. In a chaotic world,

---

[6] See *The Existence of God*, Chapter 5 and *Is There a God*, Chapter 3.

[7] For my arguments in favor of the view that we do have such free will, see my *The Evolution of the Soul*, Clarendon Press, revised edition, 1997, Chapter 13.

that would not be possible—for there would be no recipe for producing effects.

So given that there is a significant probability that a God would create free rational creatures, there is a significant probability that he will create this necessary condition for the existence of such creatures—a world regular in its conformity to simple natural laws by which a variety of different sorts of effects are produced. It is not sufficient that there be natural laws; they must be sufficiently simple to be discoverable by rational creatures. This involves their being instantiated frequently, and that the simplest extrapolation from their past instantiations will often yield correct predictions. There could be a world with a trillion unconnected laws of nature, each determining that an event of a certain kind would be followed by an event of a certain other kind, but where there were only one or two events of the former kind in the history of the Universe. No rational creature could discover such laws. Or there could be laws governing events of a type frequently instantiated, but of such enormous mathematical complexity that the simplest extrapolation from the past occurrences would never yield correct predictions. The laws must be sufficiently simple and frequently instantiated to be discoverable from a study of past history at least by a logically omniscient rational being (one who could entertain all possible scientific theories, recognize the simplest, and draw the logical consequences thereof). But the laws must also be such as to produce in different circumstances a variety of different sorts of effects, so that rational creatures have many different choices of which effects to produce in themselves, each other and the world.

Their utility to human beings is not, I should add the only reason why a God might make the physical world conform to natural laws. Conformity to such laws is often beautiful and a good in itself. The simple elegant motions of the stars and of all matter conforming to discoverable laws form a beautiful dance. Taking that into account, it is not, I suggest an exaggerated claim that we might well expect with the probability of the order of ½ that if there is a God the Universe will be governed by laws of nature.

I now seek to investigate further my claim that, given naturalism, even if there is a Universe, it is most unlikely that it would be governed by simple laws of nature. My argument in the past has been that if we are confined to scientific explanation, while we can explain lower level laws by higher level ones, there can be no explanation of the conformity of nature to the most fundamental laws. Yet this conformity consists simply in everything in the Universe behaving in exactly the same way. Such a vast coincidence of behavior, as a vast brute fact would be a priori extremely improbable. Hence, while simple laws of nature are quite probable if there is a God, they are very improbable otherwise. So their operation is good evidence for the existence of God.

I stand by my argument that, given naturalism, it is vastly improbable that the Universe (that is, the one in which we live) would be governed by (simple) laws of nature. But I had not given proper attention in previous writings to the different philosophical accounts of what laws of nature are and phrased the argument in terms of these. Nor had I appreciated previously that the argument should be phrased as an argument from simple laws of nature (and so ones discoverable in the sense defined earlier), which produce a variety of different sorts of effect. I seek to remedy these deficiencies in the present paper, and in the course of it to show the relevance to the argument of the Universe having a beginning (if it did have a beginning).

The argument is an argument from "the Universe" being governed by simple (i.e. discoverable) laws of nature. By "the Universe" I mean that system of physical bodies spatially related to (i.e. at some distance in some direction from) ourselves. I do not rule out the possibility of there being other universes, systems of physical bodies not so related, and we will need to consider that possibility in due course. It is a well-justified extrapolation from study of the spatio-temporal region accessible to our telescopes, a region vastly wider than the region in which we live, that the whole spatial Universe is governed over all time by the same fundamental laws. They may be the laws of General Relativity, Quantum Theory and a few other theories; or the laws of a Grand Unified Theory, or the laws of a theory of everything. These fundamental laws entail the operation of less fundamental laws in particular circumstances—for example that all bodies of small mass near the surface of the Earth fall to that surface. Humans can discover these less fundamental laws fairly easily and then use them to produce effects. But they can also choose whether to do science and try to discover more fundamental laws and thereby extend their power over nature.

But what is meant by the claim that the Universe is so governed; what is the truth-maker for there being laws of nature? One view, originating from Hume's views on causation, is, of course, the regularity view. "Laws of Nature" are simply the ways things behave— have behaved, are behaving, and will behave. "All copper expands when heated"[8] is a law of nature if and only if all bits of copper when heated always have expanded, now expand, and will expand. We need, however, a distinction between laws of nature, and accidental generalizations such as "all spheres of gold are less than one mile in diameter"; and we need to take account of probabilistic laws such as 'all atoms of C_{14} have a probability of decaying within 5,600 years, of ½".[9] Regularity theory has reached a developed form which takes account of these matters, in the work of David Lewis.

For Lewis, "regularities earn their lawhood not by themselves, but by the joint efforts of a system in which they figure either as axioms or theorems.[10] The best system is the one which has (relative to rivals) the best combination of strength and simplicity. Strength is a matter of how much it successfully predicts (that is, that it makes actual many events, past, present or future— whether observed or not—probable; and very few actual events improbable); simplicity is a matter of the laws fitting together, and, no doubt, each having internal simplicity in a way which Lewis does not, but presumably could, spell out. The true laws are the laws of the best system. So "all spheres of gold are less than one mile in diameter" is probably not a law, because it does not follow from the best system, as is evidenced by the fact that it certainly does not follow from our current best approximation to the ultimate best system, a conjunction of Relativity Theory and Quantum Theory. Laws may be probabilistic as well as universal; if "there is a 90%

---

[8] I have argued elsewhere (*The Existence of God*, pp. 141-2, and *Is There a God*, p. 43) that the hypothesis of the existence of one eternal, omnipotent, omniscient and perfectly free being is a far simpler hypothesis than any polytheistic hypothesis. But Mark Wynn has pointed out that there are very many different possible hypotheses, each postulating different numbers of gods with different powers, causing the existence and orderliness of the Universe; whereas there is only one hypothesis postulating one God of infinite power, causing the existence and orderliness of the Universe. Hence, he claims, although each of the former hypotheses might be less probable a priori than the hypothesis of theism, the disjunction of the former is plausibly more probable than the hypothesis of theism, as an explanation of the order of the Universe. (See his "Some Reflections on Richard Swinburne's Argument from Design", *Religious Studies* 29 (1993), 325-35.) But if the order of the Universe is to be explained by many gods, then some explanation is required for how and why they cooperate in producing exactly the same patterns of order throughout the Universe—something which would otherwise be a very considerable coincidence. This co-operation becomes a new datum requiring explanation for the same reason as the fact of order itself. The need for further explanation ends when we postulate one being who is the cause of the existence of all others, and the simplest conceivable such—I urge—is God.

[9] I also ignore the claims of John Leslie and Hugh Rice, considered seriously by Derek Parfit, that there is at work an inanimate principle producing states of affairs because they are good. For my reasons for ignoring this see my "Response to Derek Parfit" in (ed.) P. Van Inwagen and D. W. Zimmerman *Metaphysics: The Big Questions*, Blackwell, 1998.

[10] David Lewis *Philosophical Papers*, vol 2, Oxford University Press, "A Subjectivist's Guide to Objective Chance—Postscript", p. 122.

probability of an *A* being *B*" is a consequence of some theory, it will confer strength on that theory in so far as 90% actual *A*'s (past, present, and future) are *B*. Lewis's account of laws of nature is part of his campaign on behalf of "Humean Supervenience", that everything there is supervenes (logically) on "a vast mosaic of local matters of particular fact", which he interprets as a spatio-temporal arrangement of intrinsic properties, or "qualities".[11] Laws of nature and causation are for Lewis among the things thus supervenient.

Now there do seem to be overwhelming well-known objections to any Humean account, including Lewis's, if laws of nature are supposed to explain anything—and in particular to explain why one thing causes another, as Humeans suppose that they do. The reason why laws explain causation, according to Humeans, is because causality reduces to components which include laws of nature. Hume's famous regularity definition of a "cause" was as "an object precedent and contiguous to another, and where all the objects resembling the former are placed in a like relation of priority and contiguity to those objects that resemble the latter".[12] "Objects" for Humeans are events or states of affairs, and are constituted by instantiations of bundles of purely categorical properties (such as, perhaps, being 'square' or 'red') in contrast to dispositional properties whose nature it is to cause or to permit other objects to cause certain effects (such as is perhaps being 'soluble'). For a present day Humean such as Lewis, as I noted earlier, only certain kinds of regularities are laws and so function in an account of causation. Then the heating of a particular piece of copper causing its expansion is a matter of the former being followed by the latter, where there is a law that events like the former are followed by events like the latter. But since whether some lawlike statement constitutes a law depends, on this account, not merely on what has happened but on what will happen in the whole future history of the Universe, it follows that whether *A* causes *B* now depends on that future history. Yet, how can what is yet to happen (in maybe two billion years' time) make it the case that *A* now causes *B*, and thus explain why *B* happens? Whether *A* causes *B* is surely a matter of what happens now, and whether the world ends in two billion years time cannot make any difference to whether *A* now causes *B* and hence none of this can make any difference to what is the true explanation of why *B* occurs (viz, that A occurred and caused it)—though, of course, it might make a difference to what we justifiably believe to be the true explanation. (Put another way, that some proposed explanation is the simplest explanation of the data, past and future is evidence that it is the true explanation; but it does not constitute it being the true explanation).

Further it is because of their role in causation, that laws of nature are said to generate counterfactuals. Suppose that I don't heat the copper; it is all the same fairly evidently the case that "if the copper had been heated, it would have expanded". But if a law simply states what does (or did or will) happen, what grounds does it provide for asserting the counterfactual? It would only do that if there were some kind of necessity built into it.

These seem to me conclusive objections to the regularity account. If, however, despite them, we were to adopt this account, the conformity of all objects to laws of nature being just the fact that they do so conform, would have no further cause except from outside the system. If there were no God it would be a highly improbable coincidence if events in the world fell into kinds in such ways that the simplest extrapolation from the past normally yields correct predictions. There are innumerable logically possible ways in which objects could have behaved today, very few of them being in approximate conformity with a simple extrapolation from the past. If, on the other hand, God causes the behavior of physical things, then the coincidence is to be expected for reasons given earlier. We would, however, need to give some non-Humean

---

[11] *Philosophical Papers*, vol 2, pp ix-x.
[12] David Hume *A Treatise on Human Nature*, 1. 3. 14.

account of God's intentional causation—otherwise its universal efficacy would itself constitute a brute coincidence!

So, dismissing Humean accounts of laws for good reason, let us consider alternative accounts of laws of nature, that is accounts which represent talk of "laws" as talk about a feature of the world additional to the mere succession of events, a feature of physical necessity which is part of the world. This feature of physical necessity may be thought of either as separate from the objects which are governed by it, or as a constitutive aspect of those objects. The former approach leads to a picture of the world as consisting of events (constituted perhaps by substances with their properties) on the one hand, and laws of nature on the other hand; and this approach can be developed so as to allow for the possibility of there being universes in which there are no events, but merely laws of nature.[13] Laws of nature are thus in some sense ontologically concrete entities. The version of this account which has been much discussed recently is the version which claims that laws of nature are logically contingent relations between universals—either Aristotelian instantiated universals (Armstrong) or Platonist not-necessarily-instantiated universals (Tooley). For Armstrong there being a fundamental law of nature that all F's are G consists in there being a connection of physical necessity between the universal F and the universal G. It being a fundamental law of nature that "all photons travel at 300,000 km/sec relative to every inertial reference frame" consists in there being such a connection between the universal "being a photon" and the universal "travelling at 300,000 km/sec relative to every inertial reference frame". We can represent such a connection by $N(F, G)$. This relation between universals is itself a (logically) contingently existing universal. The instantiation of F thus inevitably brings with it the instantiation of G. One can perhaps begin to make sense of this suggestion if one thinks of the causing of states of affairs as making properties, which are universals, to be instantiated; and this involving the bringing of them down to Earth from an eternal Heaven, together with whatever is involved with those universal—viz, other universals of (physical) necessity connected thereto. But for Armstrong, there is no such eternal Heaven—"there is nothing to the law except what is instantiated. The law... has no existence except in the particular sequences."[14] But then—does the relation between universals exist before the law is instantiated for the first time, or not? If yes, there is an eternal Heaven in which it exists. If not, what causes it rather than some alternative to exist? Tooley thinks of the relations between universals as existing in an eternal Heaven prior to their instantiation in this world. This will meet the problem of why they are instantiated on the first occasion, and also allow from the plausible possibility of there being laws which are never instantiated:

> Imagine a world containing ten different types of fundamental particles. Suppose further that the behavior of particles in interactions depends upon the types of the interacting particles. Considering only interactions involving two particles, there are 55 possibilities with respect to the types of the two particles. Suppose that 54 of these possible interactions have been carefully studied, with the result that 54 laws have been discovered, one for each case, which are not interrelated in any way. Suppose finally that the world is sufficiently deterministic that, given the way particles of the types X and Y are currently distributed, it is impossible for them ever to interact at any time, past, present, or future. In such a situation it would seem very reasonable to believe that there is some *underived* law dealing with the interaction of particles of types X and Y.[15]

---

[13] Thus "I hold...that many empty [possible] universes exist. As I see it, there is a world devoid of all material objects and events in which the general principles of Newtonian mechanics are laws; there is another empty world in which the general principles of Aristotelian physics are laws"—John W. Carroll *Laws of Nature*, Cambridge University Press, 1994, p. 64 n 4.

[14] D. M. Armstrong *A World of States of Affairs*, Cambridge University Press, 1997, p. 227.

[15] Michael Tooley, "The Nature of Laws", *Canadian Journal of Philosophy* 7 (1977), 667-98. See p. 669.

If there is such a law, and it consists in a relation between universals, they can only be ones in a Platonist heaven.

But Platonist heavens are very mysterious. God, as an intentional agent, could exercise power over the Universe in the way in which we exercise it over our bodies.[16] If there is a God, his causal agency is of a familiar type. But how do universals act on the world? This is a very mysterious causal relation between the non-spatio-temporal world and our world for which we have no analogue.

If, despite this difficulty, we adopt a relation-between-universals theory, the question then is—if there is no God—why should there be any connections between universals at all, and why should there be universals instantiated frequently enough and the mathematical connections be sufficiently simple so as to yield a variety of discoverable regularities?[17]

I suggest that a universe without connections between universals would be simpler than one with connections, for such relations with their causal consequences are mysterious additions to the world; and one with simpler patterns of connection would be simpler than one with such complicated patterns of connections that rational beings would not be able to infer the future behavior of objects by means of the simplest extrapolation from their past behavior. I repeat that among theories of the universe as a whole (which will thus have equal scope), simplicity is the sole indicator of intrinsic probability. It then follows that if we give it very great weight, it would be very probable that there would be no connections between universals at all—that the universe would be chaotic. Alternatively we may suppose merely that a simpler theory is somewhat more probable than a somewhat more complicated theory, and so that it is only somewhat less probable that there would be connections of particular kinds than that there would be no connections. But in that case, since there are a very large number of complex ways in which universals could be associated, and we are only giving simplicity a moderate weight, then it would be far more probable that one of the complex associations between universals would be the true one as that one of the simple associations would be the true one—there being so many (infinitely many) of the former. Either way, it is going to be improbable that in a Godless universe there will be simple connections between universals and so simple laws of nature.

The alternative to thinking of the physical necessity involved in laws of nature as separate from the objects governed by it, is to think of it as a constitutive aspect of those objects. The way in which this is normally developed is what we may call the substances-powers-and-liabilities account of laws of nature. The "objects" which cause are individual substances—this planet, those molecules of water. They cause effects in virtue of their powers to do so and their liabilities (deterministic or probabilistic) to exercise those powers under certain conditions, often when caused to do so by other substances. Powers and liabilities are thus among the properties of substances. Laws of nature are then just (logically) contingent regularities—not of mere spatiotemporal succession (as with Hume), but of causal succession, regularities in the causal powers (manifested and unmanifested) of substances of various kinds. That heated copper expands is a law is just a matter of every piece of copper having the causal power to expand, and the liability to exercise that power when heated. As a matter of contingent fact substances fall

---

[16] Or rather, since we do this by exercising power over our brains, in the way in which we exercise power over our brains. In so doing, we normally think of the power over the brain only in terms of the effect which it causes. But clearly we could, and some people do, train themselves to produce brain states of a kind defined by their internal nature—e.g. to produce ⇒rhythms—and not in terms of the effects which they normally cause.

[17] op. cit. p. xii. A similar objection is raised in John Foster, "Regularities, Laws of Nature, and The Existence of God", *Proceedings of the Aristotelian Society* 101 (2000-1), pp 145-61—see pp. 154-6.

into kinds, such that all objects of the same kind have the same powers and liabilities. The powers and liabilities of large-scale things (lumps of copper) derive from the powers and liabilities of the small-scale things which compose them (atoms: and ultimately quarks, electrons etc.). And, given a satisfactory theory integrating all science, all ultimate particulars will have exactly the same powers and liabilities (e.g. the power to cause an effect proportional in a certain way to their mass, charge, spin etc.), and the liability to exercise that under conditions varying with the mass. charge, spin etc., of other objects. This account of the ultimate determinants of what happens as merely substances and their causal powers and liabilities does provide explanation of what happens, and in familiar terms. (We ourselves have causal powers which we, unlike inanimate objects, can choose to exercise). It was the way of explaining things familiar to the ancient and medieval world, before "laws of nature" began to play their role in the sixteenth century. It was revived by Rom Harré and E.H. Madden in *Causal Powers*.[18] On this account, causation is an essential component of laws rather than laws being an essential component of causation.[19] Laws are simply regularities, not in the actual behavior of substances (as with Hume), but in the causal powers and liabilities preserved by substances.

The question then becomes—why do all substances have similar powers and liabilities to each other, for example some exactly the same as each other (e.g. the power to attract each other in accord with a force proportional to mm/r^2, and the liability always to exercise that power), and some powers and liabilities a bit different so that substances fall into a small number of kinds (photons, protons etc.), making possible by means of different combinations the production of a whole variety of different sorts of effects? Unlike the other models which have no answer to the parallel question, this model has an answer to that question in terms of ancestry. A substance has the powers and liabilities it does because it was produced by another substance exercising (in virtue of some liability to do so) its power to produce a substance with just those powers and liabilities. If a proton is produced (together with an electron and a neutrino) by the decay of a neutron, then the proton's powers and liabilities are caused by the neutron, in virtue of its powers and liabilities. There are then different ways in which it could have come about that all substances fall into a small number of kinds in the way described, according to whether this process had a beginning and of what kind that beginning was.

Suppose, first, that the Universe did have a beginning, a 'Big Bang' of some sort. There are two different kinds of theories of a beginning. The first state might have been a spatially extended state, or a spatially pointlike state. In the first case, we would still have a lot of substances, but perhaps crammed into a very small space. In terms of the Big Bang model, there would not have been literally a singularity; it would just have been that as you approach the first instant in the temporally backward direction, you would find denser and denser states; but it really all started in a very but not infinitely dense state. If that state was to give rise to our present universe of very few kinds of substance, it must itself have consisted of a very large number of substances of very few kinds. The alternative first state would be a literally pointlike one. In the first instant on this theory, there was an unextended point, endowed with the power to

---

[18] Blackwell, 1975.
[19] This allows the logical possibility of singular causation, that is causation which does not exemplify a pattern captured in a law. I have argued elsewhere that human agency is such causation. When, to take a simple example, I try to lift a weight and succeed, this cannot be represented as an instance of a law like succession in virtue of exemplifying some regularity of my trying law likely causing my success. This is because to try to do x just is to exert causal influence in favor of x occurring. 'Trying' isn't something separate from 'causing'; if it is successful, it just is causing. There is no law at work here connecting independent states. Or so I have argued. See my "The Irreducibility of Causation", *Dialectica* 51(1997), 79-92.

decay into innumerable substances of very few kinds, and the liability to exercise that power at some time or other. Suppose now that the Universe has an infinite age. The properties (of powers and liabilities) of every substance are then caused by those of a preceding substance. So there can only be many substances with exactly the same such properties (including the power to produce substances of the existing kinds) if there always have been.

Study of the present data of physics and cosmology will allow us to say roughly how probable on those data are the three different theories—on the basis of how probable it is that we would find these data given each of the theories, and of how simple are the different theories.

The issue for us, however, is not what are the posterior probabilities on the physical data that the different theories are true, but how probable is it a priori if there is no God that the true theory will be such as to lead to substances of a very few kinds. This will depend solely on the simplicity of the three theories, and the probability on each of these theories that substances of very few kinds would result. Simplicity I reemphasize is the sole relevant a priori criterion.[20] There is no doubt that the theory that the Universe began at a point is simpler than any particular theory (or, in my view, any disjunction of theories) that it began with many substances or that it always consisted of many substances. But if it did begin from an unextended point, the simplest theory of such a beginning would seem to be that it would have no power to produce extended substances. If it did have such a power it would seem simpler to suppose that it would have the power to produce just one similar extended substance. The theory that it would have the power to produce extended substances falling into few kinds, themselves having the power to produce more such substances; all with the liability to exercise these powers from time to time seems just one of a number of equally simple theories, less simple than the theory that the unextended point had no power or only the power to reproduce itself. And there will be an infinite number of more complex theories of the liabilities possessed by the unextended point to produce particles which would not yield simple laws of nature. But any theory that at a beginning or always if there were many substances, they would all fall into kinds with identical powers and liabilities is a theory of very improbable coincidences. It cries out for explanation in terms of some single common source with the power to produce these coincidences. Just as we would seek to explain all the coins of the realm having an identical pattern in terms of their origin from a common mould, or all of many pictures having a common style in terms of their being pained by the same painter, so we should seek to explain all physical objects having the same powers in terms of their deriving them from a common source.

So again, if we give a lot of weight to simplicity, it will be very improbable that there will be the right sort of unextended point, let alone at the beginning or always many substances falling into kinds with identical powers and liabilities. But if we give rather less weight to simplicity, there are so many possible theories of an unextended point having the power to produce substances of innumerably different kinds, or theories of the universe beginning from or always having had such substances, that it remains very improbable that the universe would begin from the right kind of unextended point, or that there would be—uncaused by such a point—many substances falling into few kinds with identical powers and liabilities. Either way, on the substances—powers—and liabilities account of laws of nature, as on the universals account (and *a fortiori* on the Humean account) it is very improbable that there would be laws of nature sufficiently simple for rational beings to extrapolate from past to future with normal success.

---

[20] The other a priori criterion of choice between theories, scope, does not discriminate between these three theories. The scope of a theory is a matter of the more it tells you; and the greater the scope, the lower the prior probability. But each of the three theories are theories of equal scope—telling us all about the origin and nature of the universe.

Theism, however, leads us to expect that by one of these routes a universe will be produced in which substances of few kinds have all the same powers and liabilities, and will be conserved by God in this state. Either he will bring about an initial point of the right kind or a right arrangement of substances with the right powers and liabilities and conserve substances in subsequent existence with their resulting powers and liabilities; or he will always have kept in existence substances with the right powers and liabilities.

I have been assuming so far that there is only one Universe. But there may be many universes. If there were actually existing all possible universes, some of them (by a natural measure covering a small range) will be of exactly the kind one would expect God to produce. However it would be the height of irrationality to postulate innumerable universes just to explain the particular features of our universe, when we can do so by postulating just one additional entity—God. Science requires us to postulate the simplest explanation of the data, and one entity is simpler than a trillion. We would need to find new data in our universe best explained by postulating that there are also other universes. Our only grounds for believing that there are other universes would be if extrapolating back from the present state of our Universe in accord with the mathematically simplest supposition about what are its laws, leads us to a state at which there was a Universe split, a state in which those laws will have dictated that another Universe would "bud off" from our Universe. But in that case the other Universe would be governed by the same fundamental laws as govern our Universe, and so we can consider the two universes (or however many universes we learn about) as one multiverse, and the whole preceding structure of argument gives the same results as before. So it does not affect the issue of why things are law-governed if we suppose (on good evidence) there is more than one Universe. And I have argued that whether talk of "laws" is talk of regular successions of events, of connections between universals determining the behavior of substances, or of the powers and liabilities of substances, it is a priori improbable that a Godless Universe would be governed by simple laws but there is quite a significant probability that a God-created Universe would be governed by such laws. Hence the operation of laws of nature is evidence—one strand of a cumulative argument—for the existence of God.

Questions

1. What for Swinburne, adds to the probability of theism?

2. Exactly what is the Argument from the Laws of Nature?

3. What do you think of Swinburne's account of the Argument referred to in question (2)?

4. How does Swinburne detail the simple laws of nature?

5. Do you agree with Swinburne, that because of the evidence he sees in the simple laws of nature, that the Christian option is more probably true?

GOD, DESIGN, AND FINE-TUNING*

Robin Collins[1]

In this paper, Collins appeals to findings in recent science which he takes as strongly suggesting that the universe is finely tuned in a manner suited to human existence, and then he anticipates and responds to several objections.

I. Introduction

A. The Evidence of Fine-tuning

Suppose we went on a mission to Mars, and found a domed structure in which everything was set up just right for life to exist. The temperature, for example, was set around 70° F and the humidity was at 50%; moreover, there was an oxygen recycling system, an energy gathering system, and a whole system for the production of food. Put simply, the domed structure appeared to be a fully functioning biosphere. What conclusion would we draw from finding this structure? Would we draw the conclusion that it just happened to form by chance? Certainly not. Instead, we would unanimously conclude that it was designed by some intelligent being. Why would we draw this conclusion? Because an intelligent designer appears to be the only plausible explanation for the existence of the structure. That is, the only alternative explanation we can think of—that the structure was formed by some natural process—seems extremely unlikely. Of course, it is *possible* that, for example, through some volcanic eruption various metals and other compounds could have formed, and then separated out in just the right way to produce the "biosphere," but such a scenario strikes us as extraordinarily unlikely, thus making this alternative explanation unbelievable.

The universe is analogous to such a "biosphere," according to recent findings in physics. Almost everything about the basic structure of the universe—for example, the fundamental laws and parameters of physics and the initial distribution of matter and energy—is balanced on a razor's edge for life to occur. As eminent Princeton physicist Freeman Dyson notes, "There are many...lucky accidents in physics. Without such accidents, water could not exist as liquid, chains of carbon atoms could not form complex organic molecules, and hydrogen atoms could not form breakable bridges between molecules" (1979, p. 251)—in short, life as we know it would be impossible.

Scientists and others call this extraordinary balancing of the fundamental physical structure of the universe for life the "fine-tuning of the cosmos." It has been extensively discussed by philosophers, theologians, and scientists, especially since the early 1970s, with many articles and books written on the topic. Today, many consider it as providing the most persuasive current argument for the existence of God. For example, theoretical physicist and

---

* This article is printed by courtesy of Robin Collins.
[1] A full-scale treatment of the fine-tuning argument, and related design arguments, will be presented in a book I am currently working on entitled *The Well-Tempered Universe: God, Fine-tuning, and the Laws of Nature*. This paper is an adapted version of an earlier paper, "The Fine-tuning Design Argument," published in *Reason for the Hope Within*, Michael Murray (ed.), Grand Rapids, MI: Eerdmans, 1999. This earlier paper was made possible in part by a Discovery Institute grant for the fiscal year 1997-1998. Further work on this topic—which is incorporated in this version of the paper—was made possible by a year-long fellowship from the Pew Foundation, several grants from the Discovery Institute, and a grant from Messiah College.

popular science writer Paul Davies claims that with regard to basic structure of the universe, "the impression of design is overwhelming" (Davies, 1988, p. 203).

The fine-tuning for life falls into four distinct types, each of which we will briefly discuss below:

(i) The fine-tuning of the laws of physics.
(ii) The fine-tuning of the constants of physics.
(iii) The fine-tuning of the initial conditions of the universe.
(iv) The fine-tuning of certain higher-level features of the universe, such as various properties of the chemical elements.

To say that the laws are fine-tuned means that if we did not have just the right combination of laws, complex intelligent life would probably be impossible. For example, according to current physics, there are four forces in nature—gravity, the weak force, electromagnetism, and the strong nuclear force that binds protons and neutrons together in an atom. The existence of each of these forces is necessary for complex life. If gravity did not exist, masses would not clump together to form stars or planets, and hence the existence of complex, intelligent life would be seriously inhibited, if not rendered impossible; if the electromagnetic force didn't exist, there would be no chemistry; if the strong force didn't exist, protons and neutrons could not bind together and hence no atoms with atomic number greater than hydrogen would exist; and if the strong force were a long-range force (like gravity and electromagnetism) instead of a short range force that only acts between protons and neutrons in the nucleus, all matter would either almost instantaneously undergo nuclear fusion and explode or be sucked together forming a black hole.[2] It follows, therefore, that if any of these force laws did not exist, complex, intelligent life would be much less likely, if not impossible.

Similarly, other laws and principles are necessary for complex life: as physicist Freeman Dyson points out (1979, p. 251), if the Pauli-exclusion principle did not exist, which dictates that no two fermions can occupy the same quantum state, all electrons would occupy the lowest atomic orbit, eliminating complex chemistry; and if there were no quantization principle, which dictates that particles can only occupy certain discrete allowed quantum states, there would be no atomic orbits and hence no chemistry since all electrons would be sucked into the nucleus.

Another particularly important category of fine-tuning is that of the *constants* of physics.[3] The constants of physics are a set of fundamental numbers that, when plugged in to the laws of physics, determine the basic structure of the universe. An example of such a constant is the gravitational constant G that is part of Newton's law of gravity, $F = GM_1M_2/r^2$. G essentially determines the strength of gravity between two masses. If one were to double the value of G, for instance, then the force of gravity between any two masses would double. Each of the other forces in nature has its own coupling constant that determines its strength, in analogy to the gravitational constant G. Using one of the standard dimensionless measures of force strengths (Barrow and Tipler, 1986, pp. 293-295), gravity is the weakest of the forces, and the strong nuclear force is the strongest, being a factor of 10^{40}—or ten thousand billion, billion, billion, billion—times stronger than gravity.

Various calculations show that the strength of each of the forces of nature must fall into a relatively small region for intelligent life to exist. (See Collins, 2003). As one example, consider

---

[2] We are assuming throughout this discussion that life requires significant, self-reproducing complexity, especially life of comparable intelligence to ourselves.
[3] For an up-to-date analysis of the evidence for the fine-tuning of the constants, with a careful physical analysis of what I consider the six strongest cases, see Collins, 2003. More detailed treatments of the cases of fine-tuning of the constants cited below are presented in that paper, along with more detailed references to the literature.

gravity. If, for instance, we increased the strength of gravity on earth a billionfold the force of gravity would be so great that any land-based organism anywhere near the size of human beings would be crushed. (The strength of materials depends on the electromagnetic force via the fine-structure constant, which would not be affected by a change in gravity.) As astrophysicist Martin Rees notes, "In an imaginary strong gravity world, even insects would need thick legs to support them, and no animals could get much larger." (Rees, 2000, p. 30). Now, the above argument assumes that the size of the planet on which life formed would be an earth-sized planet. Could life forms of comparable intelligence to ourselves develop on a much smaller planet in such a strong-gravity world? The answer appears to be no. A planet with a gravitational pull of a thousand times that of earth—which would make the existence of organisms of our size very improbable—would have a diameter of about 40 feet or 12 meters, once again not large enough to sustain the sort of large-scale ecosystem necessary for organisms like us to evolve. Of course, a billion-fold increase in the strength of gravity is large in absolute terms, but compared to the total range of strengths of the forces in nature (which span a range of 10^{40} as we saw above), this still amounts to a fine-tuning of one part in 10^{31}. Indeed, other calculations show that stars with life-times of more than a billion years, as compared to our sun's life-time of ten billion years, could not exist if gravity were increased by more than a factor of three thousand.[4] This would have significant intelligent life-inhibiting consequences.

There are other cases of the fine-tuning of the constants of physics besides the strength of the forces, however. Probably the most widely discussed among physicists and cosmologists—and esoteric—is the fine-tuning of what is known as the *cosmological constant*.[5] The cosmological constant was a term that Einstein included in his central equation of his theory of gravity—that is, general relativity—which today is thought to correspond to the energy density of empty space. A positive cosmological constant acts as a sort of anti-gravity, a repulsive force causing space itself to expand. If the cosmological constant had a significant positive value, space would expand so rapidly that all matter would quickly disperse, and thus galaxies, stars, and even small aggregates of matter could never form. The conclusion is that it must fall exceedingly close to zero, relative to its natural range of values, for complex life to be possible in our universe.

Now, the fundamental theories of particle physics set a natural range of values for the cosmological constant. This natural range of values, however, is at least 10^{53}—that is, one followed by fifty three zeros—times the range of life-permitting values. That is, if 0 to L represent the range of life-permitting values, the theoretically possible range of values is at least 0 to 10^{53}L. To intuitively see what this means, consider a dartboard analogy: suppose that we had a dartboard that extended across the entire visible galaxy, with a target on the dartboard of less than an inch in diameter. The amount of fine-tuning of the cosmological constant could be compared to randomly throwing a dart at the board and landing exactly in the target!

Further examples of the fine-tuning of the fundamental constants of physics can also be given, such as that of mass difference between the neutron and the proton. If, for example, the mass of the neutron were slightly increased by about one part in seven hundred, stable hydrogen burning stars would cease to exist. (Leslie, 1989, pp. 39-40, Collins, 2003.)

The third type of fine-tuning is that of the initial conditions of the universe, which refers to the fact that the initial distribution of mass-energy must fall within an exceedingly narrow range for (intelligent) life to occur. One aspect of this fine-tuning is the exceedingly low entropy

---

[4] See Collins, 2003.
[5] The fine-tuning of the cosmological constant is widely discussed in the literature (e.g., see Davies, 1982, 105-109, Rees, pp. 95-102, 154-155.) For an accessible, current discussion, see Collins, 2003.

at the beginning of the universe, which requires an extraordinarily precise arrangement of mass and energy. As Roger Penrose, one of Britain's leading theoretical physicists, has commented, "In order to produce a universe resembling the one in which we live, the Creator would have to aim for an absurdly tiny volume of the phase space of possible universes" (Penrose, 1989, p. 343). How tiny is this volume? According to Penrose, if we let $x = 10^{123}$, the volume of phase space would be about $1/10^x$ of the entire phase space (p. 343). This precision is much, much greater than the precision that would be required to hit an individual proton given the entire visible universe were a dartboard! Finally, in his book *Nature's Destiny*, biochemist Michael Denton extensively discusses various higher-level features of the natural world, such as the many unique properties of carbon, oxygen, water, and the electromagnetic spectrum, that are conducive to the existence of complex biochemical systems. As one of many examples Denton presents, both the atmosphere and water are transparent to electromagnetic radiation in a thin band in the visible region, but nowhere else except radio waves. If instead either of them absorbed electromagnetic radiation in the visible region, the existence of terrestrial life would be seriously inhibited, if not rendered impossible. (pp. 56-57)

As the above examples indicate, the evidence for fine-tuning is extensive, involving four different types of fine-tuning: that of the laws of nature, the constants of physics, the initial conditions of the universe, and various higher-level features of the world. As philosopher John Leslie has pointed out, "clues heaped upon clues can constitute weighty evidence despite doubts about each element in the pile" (1988, p. 300). Imaginatively, one could think of each instance of fine-tuning mentioned above as a radio dial: unless all the dials are set exactly right, complex, intelligent life would be impossible. Or, one could think of the values of the initial conditions of the universe and the constants of physics as coordinates on a dart board that fills the whole galaxy, and the conditions necessary for life to exist as an extremely small target, say less than a trillionth of an inch: unless the dart hits the target, complex life would be impossible. The fact that the dials are perfectly set, or the dart has hit the target, strongly suggests that some intelligent being set the dials or aimed the dart, for it seems enormously improbable that such a coincidence could have happened by chance. Below we will develop this argument more rigorously instead of relying on these sorts of analogies.

B. A Preliminary Distinction

Many people take the evidence mentioned above, along with the dartboard analogy, as sufficient reason to infer to theism as the best explanation of the fine-tuning. In this paper, however, I will attempt to make the argument more rigorous. To rigorously develop the fine-tuning argument, we will find it useful to distinguish between what I shall call the *atheistic single-universe hypothesis* and the *many-universes hypothesis*.[6] According to the atheistic single universe hypothesis, there is only one universe, and it is ultimately an inexplicable, "brute" fact that the universe exists and is fine-tuned. Many atheists, however, advocate another hypothesis, what I call the many-universes hypothesis. According to the most popular version of this hypothesis, there exists some physical process that could be imaginatively thought of as a "universe generator" that produces a very large or infinite number of universes, with each universe having a randomly selected set of initial conditions and values for the constants of physics. Because this generator produces so many universes, just by chance it will eventually produce one that is fine-tuned for intelligent life to occur.

---

[6] In this paper, I take atheism as more than simply the denial of the God of traditional theism, but as also involving the denial of any overall intelligence that could be considered responsible for the existence or apparent design of the universe.

Given this distinction, we will next attempt to rigorously develop the argument from fine-tuning against the atheistic single universe hypothesis, and then consider four major objections to it. Finally, in section IV we will consider the many-universes hypothesis and some theistic responses to it.

II. Argument Against Atheistic Single-Universe Hypothesis

In this section, we will attempt to rigorously develop the argument for preferring theism over the atheistic single-universe hypothesis, an argument I refer to as the *core* version of the fine-tuning argument. It should be stressed, however, that the soundness of the inference to design based on the fine-tuning does not crucially depend on the ability to make this argument rigorous. We accept many inferences in science, even though philosophers have yet to produce a philosophically rigorous account of these inferences.[7] Of course, the skeptic might object that scientific theories are testable, whereas the theistic explanation of the fine-tuning is not. But why should testability be epistemically relevant? After all, testability is about being able to find evidence against a theory in the future. What matters for the likelihood of an hypothesis's truth (or empirical adequacy), however, is the current evidence in its favor, not whether it is possible to find evidence against it in the future.

In order to show inference to design based on the fine-tuning is flawed, skeptics must show that it is based on a manifestly problematic form of reasoning. Indeed, a typical atheist objection against the design argument, going back to the famous Scottish philosopher David Hume, is to cast it as an argument from analogy, and then to argue that arguments from analogy in this context are fatally flawed. As we will show below, however, the argument from fine-tuning can be cast into a form that is very different from the argument from analogy, a form that is difficult to refute. This should go a long way both toward making the argument rigorous and toward answering the criticism of some skeptics that the fine-tuning argument relies on a manifestly flawed form of reasoning.

Although the fine-tuning argument against the atheistic single-universe hypothesis can be cast in several different forms—such as inference to the best explanation—I believe the most rigorous way of formulating the argument is in terms of what I will call the *prime principle of confirmation* (PPC), and which Rudolph Carnap has called the *"increase in firmness"* principle, and others have simply called the *likelihood principle*.[8] The prime principle of confirmation is a general principle of reasoning which tells us when some observation counts as evidence in favor of one hypothesis over another. *Simply put, the principle says that whenever we are considering two competing hypotheses, an observation counts as evidence in favor of the hypothesis under which the observation has the highest probability (or is the least improbable)*. (Or, put slightly

---

[7] The closest philosophers have come to providing a systematic account of scientific inference is the Bayesian account. (See Howson and Urbach, 1989.) As leading philosopher of science John Earman notes, Bayesianism provides the "best hope for a comprehensive and unified treatment of induction, confirmation, and scientific inference." (Earman, 1992, p. xi.) Yet this account of scientific inference has several serious problems, and has thus not gained wide acceptance. One major problem is that taken as a complete account of scientific rationality it crucially relies on the subjectivist theory of probability. This ultimately makes one's belief in the truth or empirical adequacy of a scientific theory largely a matter of subjective opinion falling outside the constraints of rationality. According to many philosophers, therefore, a full acceptance of the Bayesian account largely ends up undermining the rationality of science.

[8] See Carnap (1962). For a basic, but somewhat dated, introduction to confirmation theory and the prime principle of confirmation, see Swinburne, (1973). For literature specifically discussing the likelihood principle, see Edwards (1992), and Elliot Sober (2002).

differently, the principle says that whenever we are considering two competing hypotheses, H_1 and H_2, an observation, O, counts as evidence in favor of H_1 over H_2 if O is more probable under H_1 than it is under H_2.)[9] Moreover, the degree to which the evidence counts in favor of one hypothesis over another is proportional to the degree to which the observation is more probable under the one hypothesis than the other.[10] For example, I will argue that the fine-tuning is much more probable under the theism than under the atheistic single-universe hypothesis, so it counts as strong evidence for theism over this atheistic hypothesis. In the next major subsection, we will present a more formal and elaborated rendition of the fine-tuning argument in terms of the prime principle. First, however, let's look at a couple of illustrations of the principle and then present some support for it.

For our first illustration, suppose that I went hiking in the mountains, and found underneath a certain cliff a group of rocks arranged in a formation that clearly formed the pattern "Welcome to the mountains Robin Collins." One hypothesis is that, by chance, the rocks just happened to be arranged in that pattern—ultimately, perhaps, because of certain initial conditions of the universe. Suppose the only viable alternative hypothesis is that my brother, who was in the mountains before me, arranged the rocks in this way. Most of us would immediately take the arrangements of rocks to be strong evidence in favor of the "brother" hypothesis over the "chance" hypothesis. Why? Because it strikes us as extremely *improbable* that the rocks would be arranged that way by chance, but *not improbable* at all that my brother would place them in that configuration. Thus, by the prime principle of confirmation we would conclude that the arrangement of rocks strongly supports the "brother" hypothesis over the chance hypothesis.

Or consider another case, that of finding the defendant's fingerprints on the murder weapon. Normally, we would take such a finding as strong evidence that the defendant was guilty. Why? Because we judge that it would be *unlikely* for these fingerprints to be on the murder weapon if the defendant was innocent, but *not unlikely* if the defendant was guilty. That is, we would go through the same sort of reasoning as in the above case.

Finally, several things can be said in favor of the prime principle of confirmation. First, many philosophers think that this principle can be derived from what is known as the *probability calculus*, the set of mathematical rules that are typically assumed to govern probability. Second, there does not appear to be any case of recognizably good reasoning that violates this principle. Finally, the principle appears to have a wide range of applicability, undergirding much of our reasoning in science and everyday life, as the examples above illustrate. Indeed, some have even claimed that a slightly more general version of this principle undergirds all scientific reasoning. (See Howson and Urbach, 1989 and Earman, 1992).

---

[9] To avoid certain potential counterexamples, one might need to restrict the principle to apply only to those cases in which H1 has some independent plausibility apart from evidence E, or was at least not merely constructed to account for E. This is certainly the case with theism since it was believed long before the evidence for fine-tuning was known. The likelihood principle, however, is typically not stated with this restriction. For a brief discussion of this issue, see Sober (2002) and Collins ("Who Designed God Objection," forthcoming).

[10] For those familiar with the probability calculus, a precise statement of the degree to which evidence counts in favor of one hypothesis over another can be given in terms of the odds form of Bayes's Theorem: that is, $P(H_1/E)/P(H_2/E) = [P(H_1)/P(H_2)] \times [P(E/H_1)/P(E/H_2)]$, where $P(\ /\ )$ represents the conditional epistemic probability of one proposition on another. The general version of the principle stated here, however, does not require the applicability or truth of Bayes's theorem.

A. Further Development of Argument

To further develop the core version of the fine-tuning argument, we will summarize the argument by explicitly listing its two premises and its conclusion:

> *Premise* 1. The existence of the fine-tuning is not improbable under theism.
>
> *Premise* 2. The existence of the fine-tuning is very improbable under the atheistic single-universe hypothesis.[11]
>
> *Conclusion*: From premises (1) and (2) and the prime principle of confirmation, it follows that the fine-tuning data provides strong evidence in favor of the design hypothesis over the atheistic single-universe hypothesis.

At this point, we should pause to note two features of this argument. First, the argument does not say that the fine-tuning evidence proves that the universe was designed, or even that it is likely that the universe was designed. Indeed, of itself it does not even show that we are epistemically warranted in believing in theism over the atheistic single-universe hypothesis. In order to justify these sorts of claims, we would have to look at the full range of evidence both for and against the design or theistic hypothesis, something we are not doing in this paper. Rather, the argument merely concludes that the fine-tuning strongly *supports* theism *over* the atheistic single-universe hypothesis.

In this way, the evidence of fine-tuning is much like fingerprints found on a gun: although they can provide strong evidence that the defendant committed the murder, one could not conclude merely from them alone that the defendant is guilty; one would also have to look at all the other evidence offered. Perhaps, for instance, ten reliable witnesses claimed to see the defendant at a party at the time of the shooting. In this case, the fingerprints would still count as significant evidence of guilt, but this evidence would be counterbalanced by the testimony of the witnesses. Similarly the evidence of fine-tuning strongly supports theism over the atheistic single-universe hypothesis, though it does not itself show that everything considered theism is the most plausible explanation of the world.

The second feature of the argument we should note is that, given the truth of *the prime principle of confirmation*, the conclusion of the argument follows from the premises. Specifically, if the premises of the argument are true, then we are guaranteed that the conclusion is true: that is, the argument is what philosophers call *valid*. Thus, insofar as we can show that the premises of the argument are true, we will have shown that the conclusion is true. Our next task, therefore, is to attempt to show that the premises are true, or at least that we have strong reasons to believe them.

B. Support for the Premises

Support for Premise (1).
The argument in support of premise (1) can be simply stated as follows: *since God is an all good being, and it is good for intelligent, conscious beings to exist, it not surprising or improbable*

---

[11] To be precise, the fine-tuning refers to the conjunction of the claim that the range of life-permitting values for the constants of physics is small compared to the "theoretically possible" range R for those values *with* the claim that the values actually fall in the life-permitting range. It is only this latter fact that we are arguing is highly improbable under the atheistic single-universe hypothesis.

that God would create a world that could support intelligent life. Thus, the fine-tuning is not improbable under theism, as premise (1) asserts.

Support for Premise (2).

Upon looking at the data, many people find it very obvious that the fine-tuning is highly improbable under the atheistic single-universe hypothesis. And it is easy to see why when we think of the fine-tuning in terms of the analogies offered earlier. In the dartboard analogy, for example, the initial conditions of the universe and the fundamental constants of physics are thought of as a dartboard that fills the whole galaxy, and the conditions necessary for life to exist as a small one-foot wide target. Accordingly, from this analogy it seems obvious that it would be highly improbable for the fine-tuning to occur under the atheistic single-universe hypothesis—that is, for the dart to hit the board by chance.

Often advocates of the fine-tuning argument are satisfied with resting the justification of premise (2), or something like it, on this sort of analogy. Many atheists and theists, however, question the legitimacy of this sort of analogy, and thus find the argument unconvincing. Although a full scale, rigorous justification of premise (2) is beyond the scope of this paper, we will briefly sketch how such a further justification could be given in section III below, under objection (5).

III. Some Objections to Core Version

As powerful as the fine-tuning argument for theism against the atheistic single-universe hypothesis is, several major objections have been raised to it by both atheists and theists. In this section, we will consider these objections in turn.

A. Objection 1: More Fundamental Law Objection

One criticism of the fine-tuning argument is that, as far as we know, there could be a more fundamental law under which the constants of physics *must* have the values they do. Thus, given such a law, it is not improbable that the known constants of physics fall within the life-permitting range.

Besides being entirely speculative, the problem with postulating such a law is that it simply moves the improbability of the fine-tuning up one level, to that of the postulated physical law itself. As astrophysicists Bernard Carr and Martin Rees note "even if all apparently anthropic coincidences could be explained [in terms of some grand unified theory], it would still be remarkable that the relationships dictated by physical theory happened also to be those propitious for life" (1979, p. 612).

A similar sort of response can be given to the claim that the fine-tuning is not improbable because it might be *logically necessary* for the constants of physics to have life-permitting values. That is, according to this claim, the constants of physics must have life-permitting values in the same way 2 + 2 must equal 4, or the interior angles of a triangle must add up to 180 degrees in Euclidian geometry. Like the "more fundamental law" proposal above, however, this postulate simply transfers the improbability up one level: of all the laws and constants of physics that conceivably could have been logically necessary, it seems highly improbable that it would be those that are life-permitting.[12]

---

[12] Those with some training in probability theory will want to note that the kind of probability invoked here is what philosophers call *epistemic probability*, which is a measure of the rational degree of belief we should have in a proposition. (See objection (5) below) Since our rational degree of belief in a necessary truth can be less than 1, we

B. Objection 2: Other Forms of Life Objection

Another objection people commonly raise against the fine-tuning argument is that as far as we know, other forms of life could exist even if the constants of physics were different. So, it is claimed, the fine-tuning argument ends up presupposing that all forms of intelligent life must be like us. One answer to this objection is that many cases of fine-tuning do not make this presupposition. Consider, for instance, the cosmological constant. If the cosmological constant were much larger than it is, matter would disperse so rapidly that no planets, and indeed no stars could exist. Without stars, however, there would exist no stable energy sources for complex material systems of any sort to evolve. So, all the fine-tuning argument presupposes in this case is that the evolution of life forms of comparable intelligence to ourselves requires some stable energy source. This is certainly a very reasonable assumption.

Of course, if the laws and constants of nature were changed enough, other forms of embodied intelligent life might be able to exist of which we cannot even conceive. But this is irrelevant to the fine-tuning argument since the judgment of improbability of fine-tuning under the atheistic single-universe hypothesis only requires that, given our current laws of nature, the life-permitting range for the values of the constants of physics (such as gravity) is small compared to the *surrounding* range of non-life-permitting values. A dartboard analogy might help illustrate the point. If we saw a dart hit a very small target surrounded by a much, much larger blank area, we would still count its hitting the target as evidence that the dart was aimed even if we did not know whether other areas of the dart board were covered with targets. Why? Because even if other parts of the dart board had targets on them, it would still be very surprising under the chance hypothesis, but not under the aiming hypothesis, for it to hit the target *instead of* somewhere else in the surrounding blank area.[13]

C. Objection 3. Anthropic Principle Objection:

According to the weak version of so-called *anthropic principle*, if the laws of nature were not fine-tuned, we would not be here to comment on the fact. Some have argued, therefore, that the fine-tuning is not really *improbable or surprising* at all under atheism, but simply follows from the fact that we exist. The response to this objection is simply to restate the argument in terms of our existence: our existence as embodied, intelligent beings is extremely unlikely under the atheistic single-universe hypothesis (since our existence requires fine-tuning), but not improbable under theism. Then, we simply apply the prime principle of confirmation to draw the conclusion that *our existence* strongly confirms theism over the atheistic single-universe hypothesis.

To further illustrate this response, consider the following "firing-squad" analogy. As John Leslie (1988, p. 304) points out, if fifty sharp shooters all miss me, the response "if they had not missed me I wouldn't be here to consider the fact" is not adequate. Instead, I would naturally conclude that there was some reason why they all missed, such as that they never really intended to kill me. Why would I conclude this? Because my continued existence would be very improbable under the hypothesis that they missed me by chance, but not improbable under the

---

can sensibly speak of it being improbable for a given law of nature to exist necessarily. For example, we can speak of an unproven mathematical hypotheses—such as Goldbach's conjecture that every even number greater than 6 is the sum of two odd primes—as being probably true or probably false given our current evidence, even though all mathematical hypotheses are either necessarily true or necessarily false.

[13] This objection is also addressed by John Leslie, who offers a similar sort of analogy. (1989, pp. 17-18).

hypothesis that there was some reason why they missed me. Thus, by the prime principle of confirmation, my continued existence strongly confirms the latter hypothesis.

D. Objection 4: The "Who Designed God?" Objection

Perhaps the most common objection that atheists raise to the argument from design, of which the fine-tuning argument is one instance, is that postulating the existence of God does not solve the problem of design, but merely transfers it up one level. Atheist George Smith, for example, claims that

> If the universe is wonderfully designed, surely God is even more wonderfully designed. He must, therefore, have had a designer even more wonderful than He is. If *God* did not require a designer, then there is no reason why such a relatively less wonderful thing as the universe needed one. (1980, p. 56.)

Or, as philosopher J. J. C. Smart states the objection:

> If we postulate God in addition to the created universe we increase the complexity of our hypothesis. We have all the complexity of the universe itself, and we have in addition the at least equal complexity of God. (The designer of an artifact must be at least as complex as the designed artifact).... *If the theist can show the atheist that postulating God actually reduces the complexity of one's total world view, then the atheist should be a theist.* (pp. 275-276; italics mine)

    The first response to the above atheist objection is to point out that the atheist claim that the designer of an artifact must be as complex as the artifact designed is certainly not obvious. But I do believe that their claim has some plausibility: for example, in the world we experience, organized complexity seems only to be produced by systems that already possess it, such as the human brain/mind, a factory, or an organisms' biological parent.

    The second, and better, response is to point out that, at most, the atheist objection only works against a version of the design argument that claims that all organized complexity needs an explanation, and that God is the best explanation of the organized complexity found in the world. The version of the argument I presented against the atheistic single-universe hypothesis, however, only required that the fine-tuning be more probable under theism than under the atheistic single-universe hypothesis. But this requirement is still met even if God exhibits tremendous internal complexity, far exceeding that of the universe. Thus, even if we were to grant the atheist assumption that the designer of an artifact must be as complex as the artifact, the fine-tuning would still give us strong reasons to prefer theism over the atheistic single-universe hypothesis.

    To illustrate, consider the example of the "biosphere" on Mars presented at the beginning of this paper. As mentioned, the existence of the biosphere would be much more probable under the hypothesis that intelligent life once visited Mars than under the chance hypothesis. Thus, by the prime principle of confirmation, the existence of such a "biosphere" would constitute strong evidence that intelligent, extraterrestrial life had once been on Mars, even though this alien life would most likely have to be much more complex than the "biosphere" itself.

    The final, and I believe the best, response theists can give to this objection is to show that a "supermind" such as God's would *not* require a high degree of unexplained organized complexity to create the universe. Although I have presented this response elsewhere (Collins, "Who Designed God Objection," forthcoming), presenting it here is beyond the scope of this paper. Here I simply note that, for reasons entirely independent of the argument from design,

God has been thought to have little, if any, internal complexity. Indeed, Medieval philosophers and theologians often went as far as advocating the doctrine of Divine Simplicity, according to which God is claimed to be absolutely simple, without any internal complexity. So, atheists who push this objection have a lot of arguing to do to make it stick.

E. Objection 5: No Probability Objection

Some philosophers object to claim that the fine-tuning is highly improbable under the atheistic single-universe hypothesis (that is, premise (2) above) by arguing that since we only have one universe, the notion of the fine-tuning of the universe being probable or improbable is meaningless. Further, they argue, even if it were meaningful, we would have no way of adequately justifying, besides appealing to intuition, that the fine-tuning is very improbable under the atheistic single-universe hypothesis. Typically, the claim behind the first part of this objection is that probability only makes sense in terms of relative frequency within some reference class. Thus, for instance, the assertion that the probability that a randomly selected male smoker will die of lung cancer is 30% means that the 30% of the members of the class of male smokers die of lung cancer. But, if there is only one universe, there is no reference class of universes to compare it to, and hence claims regarding the probability or improbability of fine-tuning in this context do not make sense.

The problem with this argument is that it completely ignores other prominent conceptions of probability. One of these is the epistemic notion of probability. *Epistemic probability* is a widely-recognized type of probability that applies to claims, statements, and hypotheses—that is, what philosophers call *propositions*.[14] Roughly, the epistemic probability of a proposition can be thought of as the degree of credence—that is, degree of confidence or belief—we rationally should have in the proposition. Put differently, epistemic probability is a measure of our rational degree of belief under a condition of ignorance concerning whether a proposition is true or false. For example, when one says that the universe is probably older than fifteen billion years, one is making a statement of epistemic probability. After all, the universe is actually either older than fifteen billion years or it is not. But, we do not know for sure which one it is, so we use the word "probably" to indicate that we should put more confidence in its being older than fifteen billion years than its being younger.

Besides epistemic probability simpliciter, philosophers also speak of what is known as the *conditional* epistemic probability of one proposition on another. (A proposition is any claim, assertion, statement, or hypothesis about the world). The conditional epistemic probability of a proposition R on another proposition S—written as $P(R/S)$—can be defined as the degree to which the proposition S *of itself* should rationally lead us to expect that R is true. Under the epistemic conception of probability, therefore, the statement that *the fine-tuning of the cosmos is very improbable under the atheistic single-universe hypothesis* makes sense: it is to be understood as making a statement about the degree to which the atheistic single-universe hypothesis would or should, *of itself*, rationally lead us to expect cosmic fine-tuning. The claim that a state of affairs is epistemically very improbable, therefore, can be thought of as equivalent to the claim that it is very unexpected or surprising. Thus, for instance, one could reword premise (2) of our main argument to say that the fine-tuning is very surprising under the atheistic single-universe hypothesis. Rewording premises (1) and (2), and the prime principle of

---

[14] For an in-depth discussion of epistemic probability, see Swinburne (1973), Hacking, (1975), and Plantinga (1993), chapters 8 and 9.

confirmation, in terms of degrees of surprise might be especially helpful for those trained in the sciences who associate probability primarily with some sort of relative frequency.

Now that we know what it means to say that the fine-tuning of the constants of physics is very unlikely under the atheistic single-universe hypothesis, it is time to briefly outline how such a statement could be justified. Here I think we need to apply what is known as the *principle of indifference*. Applied to the case at hand, the principle of indifference could be roughly stated as follows: *when we have no reason to prefer any one value of a parameter over any other, we should assign equal probabilities to equal ranges of the parameter, given that the parameter in question directly corresponds to a natural parameter.*[15] Specifically, if the "theoretically possible" range (that is, the range allowed by the relevant background theories) of such a parameter is R and the life-permitting range is r, then the probability is r/R. Suppose, for instance, that the "theoretically possible" range, R, of values for the strength of gravity is zero to the strength of the strong nuclear force—that is, 0 to $10^{40}G_0$, where G_0 represents the current value for the strength of gravity. As we saw above, the life-permitting range r for the strength of gravity is at most 0 to $10^9 G_0$. Now, *of itself* (specifically, apart from the knowledge that we exist), the atheistic single-universe hypothesis gives us *no* reason to think that the strength of gravity would fall into the life-permitting region instead of any other part of the theoretically possible region. Thus, assuming the strength of the forces constitute a natural variable, the principle of indifference would state that equal ranges of this force should be given equal epistemic probabilities, and hence the epistemic probability of the strength of gravity falling into the life-permitting region would be at most $r/R = 10^9 / 10^{40} = 1/10^{31}$.[16] In sum, we should find it very surprising under the atheistic single-universe hypothesis for the strength of gravity to have fallen into the life-permitting range given the enormous range of force strengths in nature.

One major problem with this rough version of the principle of indifference is the well-known Bertrand Paradoxes (e.g., see Weatherford, 1982, p. 56), in which there are two equally good but conflicting parameters that directly correspond to a physical quantity. A famous example of the Bertrand paradox is that of a factory that produces cubes whose sides vary from zero to two inches, which is equivalent to saying that it produces cubes whose volumes vary from zero to eight cubic inches. Given that this is all we know about the factory, the naive form of the principle of indifference implies that we should assign both equal probabilities to equal ranges of lengths *and* equal probabilities to equal ranges of volumes, since both lengths and volumes correspond to actual physical magnitudes. It is easy to see, however, that this leads to conflicting probability assignments—e.g., using lengths, we get a probability of 0.5 of a cube being between zero and one inch in length, whereas using volumes we get a probability of 0.125.

Although many philosophers have taken the Bertrand Paradoxes as constituting a fatal objection to the principle of indifference, one can easily avoid this objection either by restricting the applicability of the principle of indifference to those cases in which Bertrand Pardoxes do not arise or by claiming that the probability should not be assigned an exact value but rather a range

---

[15] A natural parameter is a parameter that directly corresponds to a physical magnitude. Alternatively, if one is an anti-realist about the physical theories in which a parameter occurs, a natural parameter can be defined as a parameter that occurs in the standard expressions of the relevant physical theories within the physics community. As an example, consider the mass m of an object versus another parameter "u" that designates that mass cubed ($u = m3$). Assuming the mass directly corresponds to a physical quantity, m should be considered a natural parameter. On the other hand, u should not be considered natural since it does not directly correspond to a physical magnitude nor is it part of the simplest expression of those theories that refer to mass.

[16] In general relativity, gravity is not thought of as a force but rather as curvature of space-time. To think of gravity as a force only makes sense in Newtonian mechanics or in a quantum view of gravity in which gravity involves an exchange of quanta (gravitons) in analogy to the other forces of nature.

of values. This range would be the range spanning the values given by the various conflicting parameters. The problem of conflicting parameters, however, does not seem to arise for most cases of fine-tuning.

Another problem is the total theoretically possible range R of values a constant of physics could have. This is a difficult issue beyond the scope of this paper to address. Here we simply note that often one can make plausible estimates of a lower bound for the theoretically possible range—e.g., since the actual range of forces in nature span a range of 10^{40}, the value of 10^{40} provides a natural lower bound for the theoretically possible range of force strengths.[17]

Finally, several powerful reasons can be offered for its soundness of the principle of indifference if it is restricted in the ways explained above. First, it has a wide range of applicability. As philosopher Roy Weatherford notes in his book, *Philosophical Foundations of Probability Theory*, "an astonishing number of extremely complex problems in probability theory have been solved, and usefully so, by calculations based entirely on the assumption of equiprobable alternatives [that is, the principle of indifference]"(p. 35). Second, at least for the discrete case, the principle can be given a significant theoretical grounding in information theory, being derivable from Shannon's important and well-known measure of *information*, or *negative entropy* (Sklar, p. 191; van Fraassen, p. 345). Third, in certain everyday cases the principle of indifference seems to be the only justification we have for assigning probability. To illustrate, suppose that in the last ten minutes a factory produced the first fifty-sided die ever produced. Further suppose that every side of the die is (macroscopically) perfectly symmetrical with every other side, except for there being different numbers printed on each side. (The die we are imagining is like a fair six-sided die except that it has fifty sides instead of six.) Now, we all immediately know that upon being rolled the probability of the die coming up on any given side is one in fifty. Yet, we do not know this directly from experience with fifty-sided dice, since by hypothesis no one has yet rolled even one fifty sided die to determine the relative frequency with which it comes up on each side. Rather, it seems our only justification for assigning this probability is the principle of indifference: that is, given that every side of the die is macroscopically symmetrical with every other side, we have no reason to believe that the die will land on one side over any other side, and thus we assign them all an equal probability of one in fifty.[18]

Although we have only had space to provide a brief account of how one could go about rigorously defending the claim that the fine-tuning is very improbable under the atheistic single-universe hypothesis, the above account does show, I believe, that there is an initially plausible method available of rigorously supporting our intuitive judgment of the improbability of fine-tuning under the atheistic single-universe hypothesis. Nonetheless, it should be stressed again that even if ultimately our method of support fails, this is not fatal to the fine-tuning argument. As with arguments in science, the fine-tuning argument has great initial intuitive plausibility. Accordingly, to defeat this initial plausibility, the burden is on the skeptic to show that the fine-tuning argument rests on a clearly faulty form of reasoning.

---

[17] Such plausible lower bounds are provided for each case of fine-tuning that I discuss in my paper "Evidence for Fine-tuning" (2003). This issue is also briefly discussed in my "The Fine-Tuning Design Argument" (1999, pp. 69-70) and will be discussed in much more depth in the book I am currently working on entitled *The Well-Tempered Universe: God, Fine-Tuning, and the Laws of Nature*.

[18] A full-scale defense of the principle of indifference is beyond the scope of this paper, but will be provided in the book on the fine-tuning design argument that I am currently working on. Also, see Schlesinger (1985, chapter 5) for a lengthy defense of the principle. A somewhat more in-depth treatment of the justification of premise (2) than offered here is presented in the appendix of Collins, 1999.

IV. The Many-Universes Hypothesis

A. The Many-Universes Hypothesis Explained

In response to this theistic or intelligent design explanation of the fine-tuning, many atheists have offered an alternative explanation, what I will call the *many-universes hypothesis,* but which in the literature goes under a variety of names, such as many-worlds hypothesis, the many-domains hypothesis, the world-ensemble hypothesis, the multi-universe hypothesis, and so on. According to this hypothesis, there are a very large—perhaps infinite—number of universes, with the constants of physics varying from universe to universe.[19] Of course, in the vast majority of these universes the constants of physics would *not* have life-permitting values. Nonetheless, in a small proportion of universes they would, and consequently it is no longer improbable that universes such as ours exist in which the constants of physics have just the right values for intelligent life.

Further, usually these universes are thought to be produced by some sort of physical mechanism, which I call a many-universes generator. The universe generator can be thought of as analogous to a lottery ticket generator: just as it would be no surprise that a winning number is eventually produced if enough tickets are generated, it would be no surprise that a universe fine-tuned for life would occur if enough universes are generated.[20]

B. The Inflationary Many-Universes Model

Most many-universes models are entirely speculative, having little basis in current physics. One many-universes model, however, does have a reasonable basis in current physics—namely, that based on inflationary cosmology. Inflationary cosmology is a currently widely discussed cosmological theory that attempts to explain the origin of the universe. Essentially, it claims that our universe was formed by a small area of pre-space being massively blown up by an

---

[19] I define a "universe" as any region of space-time that is disconnected from other regions in such a way that the constants of physics in that region could differ significantly from the other regions. A more thorough discussion of the many-universes hypothesis is presented in Collins, "The Argument from Design and the Many-Worlds Hypothesis" (2002).

[20] Some have proposed what could be called a *metaphysical* many-universes hypothesis, according to which universes are thought to exist on their own without being generated by any physical process. Typically, advocates of this view—such as the late Princeton University philosopher David Lewis (1986) and University of Pennsylvania astrophysicist Max Tegmark (1998)—claim that every possible world exists. According to Lewis, for instance, there exists a reality parallel to our own in which I am president of the United States and a reality in which objects can travel faster than the speed of light. Dream up a possible scenario, and it exists in some parallel reality, according to Lewis. Besides being completely speculative (and in many people's mind, outlandish), a major problem with this scenario is that the vast majority of possible universes are ones which are chaotic, just as the vast majority of possible arrangement of letters of a thousand characters would not spell a meaningful pattern. So, the only way that these metaphysical hypotheses can explain the regularity and predictability of our universe, and the fact that it seems to be describable by a few simple laws, is to invoke an "observer selection" effect. That is, Lewis and Tegmark must claim that only universes like ours in this respect could support intelligent life, and hence be observed. The problem with this explanation is that it is much more likely for there to exist local islands of the sort of order necessary for intelligent life than for the entire universe to have such an ordered arrangement. Thus, a randomly selected observer from among the many universes should expect to find herself in a universe with a local island of order surrounded by vast regions of disorder. Accordingly, Lewis and Tegmark's hypotheses do not appear to be able to explain why we, *qua* supposedly generic observers, live in a universe that is highly ordered throughout. (Among others, George Schlesinger (1984) has raised this objection against Lewis's hypothesis. This sort of objection was raised against a similar explanation of the high degree of order in our universe offered by the famous physicist Ludwig Boltzman, and has generally been considered fatal to Boltzman's explanation (Davies, 1974, p. 103).)

hypothesized *inflaton* field, in much the same way as a soup bubble would form in an ocean full of soap. In chaotic inflation models—widely considered the most plausible—various points of the pre-space are randomly blown up, forming innumerable bubble universes. Further, because of the inflaton field, the pre-space expands so rapidly that it becomes a never-ending source of bubble universes, much as a rapidly expanding ocean full of soap would become a never ending source of soap bubbles. Thus, inflationary cosmology can naturally give rise to many universes.[21]

In order to get the initial conditions and constants of physics to vary from universe to universe, as they must do if this scenario is going to explain the fine-tuning, there must be a further physical mechanism to cause the variation. Such a mechanism *might* be given by superstring theory, but it is too early to tell. Superstring theory is currently one of the most hotly discussed hypotheses about the fundamental structure of the physical universe (Greene, 1999, p. 214). According to superstring theory, the ultimate constituents of matter are strings of energy that undergo quantum vibrations in a 10 (or 11) dimensional space-time, six or seven dimensions of which are "compactified" to extremely small sizes and are hence unobservable. The shape of the compactified dimensions, however, determines the modes of vibration of the strings, and hence the types and masses of fundamental particles, along with many characteristics of the forces between them. Thus, universes in which compactified dimensions have different shapes will have different constants of physics and different lower-level laws governing the forces. It is presently controversial whether superstring theory allows for significant variation in the shape of the compactified dimensions, though the direction of current research indicates that it does. (See Susskind, forthcoming). If it does, however, it is then possible that an inflationary/superstring scenario could be constructed in which the shape of the compactified dimensions, and hence the constants of physics, underwent enough variation from universe to universe to explain the fine-tuning.[22]

Thus, it is in the realm of real physical plausibility that a viable inflationary/superstring many-universes scenario could be constructed that would account for the fine-tuning of the constants of physics. Nonetheless, it should be noted that despite the current popularity of both inflationary cosmology and superstring theory, both are highly speculative. For instance, as Michio Kaku states in his recent textbook on superstring theory, "Not a shred of experimental evidence has been found to confirm...superstrings" (1999, p. 17). The major attraction of string theory is its mathematical elegance and the fact that many physicists think that it currently offers the most plausible proposal for providing a truly unified physical theory that combines gravitation with quantum mechanics, the two cornerstones of modern physics (Greene, 1999, p. 214).

It should be stressed, however, that even if superstring theory or inflationary cosmology turn out to be false, they have opened the door to taking the many-universes explanation of the fine-tuning as a serious physical possibility since some other physical mechanisms could give rise to multiple universes with a sufficiently large number of variations in the constants of physics. The only way we could close this door is if we were to discover that the ultimate laws of physics do not allow either many universes or sufficient variation in the constants and laws of physics among universes.

---

[21] For a good, accessible overview of inflationary cosmology, see Guth, 1997.t
[22] I am indebted to Gerald Cleaver, a string theorist at Baylor University, for helpful discussions of this issue. The sort of inflationary/superstring many-universes explanations of the fine-tuning discussed above have been suggested by a number of authors, such as Linde, (1990, PP&IC, p. 306; 1990, IQC, p. 6) and Greene (1999, pp. 355-363). To date, however, no one has adequately verified or worked-out the physics of superstring theory or inflationary cosmology, let alone the combination of the two, so this scenario remains highly speculative.

C. Theistic Responses to Many-Universes Generator Scenario

One major theistic response to the many-universes generator scenario, whether of the inflationary variety or some other type, is that a "many-universes generator" would seem to need to be "well-designed" in order to produce life-sustaining universes. After all, even a mundane item like a bread machine, which only produces loaves of bread instead of universes, must be well designed to produce decent loaves of bread. If this is right, then invoking some sort of many-universes generator as an explanation of the fine-tuning only kicks the issue of design up one level, to the question of who designed the many-universes generator.

The inflationary scenario discussed above is a good test case of this line of reasoning. The inflationary/superstring many-universes generator can only produce life-sustaining universes because it has the following "components" or "mechanisms:"

i) *A mechanism to supply the energy needed for the bubble universes*: This mechanism is the hypothesized inflaton field. By imparting a constant energy density to empty space, as space expands the inflaton field can act "as a reservoir of unlimited energy" for the bubbles (Peacock, 1999, p. 26).

ii) *A mechanism to form the bubbles*: This mechanism is Einstein's equation of general relativity. Because of its peculiar form, Einstein's equation dictates that space expand at an enormous rate in the presence of a field, such as the inflaton field, that imparts a constant (and homogenous) energy density to empty space. This causes both the bubble universes to form and the rapid expansion of the pre-space (the "ocean") which keeps the bubbles from colliding.

iii) *A mechanism to convert the energy of the inflaton field to the normal mass-energy we find in our universe.* This mechanism is Einstein's relation of the equivalence of mass and energy (i.e., $E = mc^2$) combined with an hypothesized coupling between the inflaton field and normal mass-energy fields we find in our universe.

iv) *A mechanism that allows enough variation in the constants of physics among universes:* The most physically viable candidate for this mechanism is superstring theory. As explained above, superstring theory *might* allow enough variation in the variations in the constants of physics among bubble universes to make it reasonably likely that a fine-tuned universe would be produced. The other leading alternatives to string theory being explored by physicists, such as the currently proposed models for Grand Unified Field Theories (GUTS), do not appear to allow for enough variation. [23]

Without all these "components," the many-universes generator would almost certainly fail to produce a single life-sustaining universe. For example, Einstein's equation and the inflaton field harmoniously work together to enormously inflate small regions of space while at the same time both imparting to them the positive energy density necessary for a universe with significant mass-energy and causing the pre-space to expand rapidly enough to keep the bubble universes from colliding. Without either factor, there would neither be regions of space that inflate nor would those regions have the mass-energy necessary for a universe to exist. If, for example, the universe obeyed Newton's theory of gravity instead of Einstein's, the vacuum energy of the inflaton field would at best simply create a gravitational attraction causing space to contract, not to expand. Thus no universes would be formed.

In addition to the four factors listed above, the inflationary/superstring many-universes

---

[23] The simplest and most studied GUT, SU(5), allows for three differing sets of values for the fundamental constants of physics when the other non-SU(5) Higgs fields are neglected (Linde, PP&IC, p. 33). Including all the other Higgs fields, the number of variations increases to perhaps several dozen (Linde, IQC, p. 6). Merely to account for the fine-tuning of the cosmological constant, however, which is estimated to be fine-tuned to one part in 10^{53}, would require on the order of 10^{53} variations of the physical constants among universes.

generator can only produce life-sustaining universes because the right background laws are in place. For example, as mentioned earlier, without the principle of quantization, all electrons would be sucked into the atomic nuclei and hence atoms would be impossible; without the Pauli-exclusion principle, electrons would occupy the lowest atomic orbit and hence complex and varied atoms would be impossible; without a universally attractive force between all masses, such as gravity, matter would not be able to form sufficiently large material bodies (such as planets) for life to develop or for long-lived stable energy sources such as stars to exist. [24]

In sum, even if an inflationary/superstring many-universes generator exists, it along with the background laws and principles could be said to be an *irreducibly complex* system, to borrow a phrase from biochemist Michael Behe (1996), with just the right combination of laws and fields for the production of life-permitting universes: if one of the components were missing or different, such as Einstein's equation or the Pauli-exclusion principle, it is unlikely that any life-permitting universes could be produced. In the absence of alternative explanations, the existence of such a system suggests design since it seems very unlikely that such a system would have just the right components by chance. It does not seem, therefore, that one can escape the conclusion of design merely by hypothesizing some sort of many-universes generator.

Further, the many-universes generator hypothesis cannot explain other features of the universe that seem to exhibit apparent design, whereas theism can. For example, many physicists, such as Albert Einstein, have observed that the basic laws of physics exhibit an extraordinary degree of beauty, elegance, harmony, and ingenuity. Nobel Prize winning physicist Steven Weinberg, for instance, devotes a whole chapter of his book *Dreams of a Final Theory* (Chapter 6, "Beautiful Theories") explaining how the criteria of beauty and elegance are commonly used to guide physicists in formulating the right laws. Indeed, one of most prominent theoretical physicists of this century, Paul Dirac, went so far as to claim that "it is more important to have beauty in one's equations than to have them fit experiment." (1963, p. 47).

Now such beauty, elegance, and ingenuity make sense if the universe was designed by God. Under the atheistic many-universes hypothesis, however, there is no reason to expect the fundamental laws to be elegant or beautiful. As theoretical physicist Paul Davies writes, "If nature is so 'clever' as to exploit mechanisms that amaze us with their ingenuity, is that not persuasive evidence for the existence of intelligent design behind the universe? If the world's finest minds can unravel only with difficulty the deeper workings of nature, how could it be supposed that those workings are merely a mindless accident, a product of blind chance?"(1984, pp. 235-36.)[25]

Finally, I have argued elsewhere (Collins, "A Theistic Perspective on the Multiverse Hypothesis," forthcoming) that even if we obtained compelling scientific evidence for such a universe generator, this would pose no threat to theism. Given that God is infinite, and infinitely creative, it makes sense that God would create not only a universe that is vast in both space and time, but perhaps many such universes. Thus, one could argue, theists should welcome such an hypothesis as further illustrating the infinite nature of God.

---

[24] Although some of the laws of physics can vary from universe to universe in string theory, these background laws and principles are a result of the structure of string theory and therefore cannot be explained by the inflationary/superstring many-universes hypothesis since they must occur in all universes. Further, since the variation among universes would consist of variation of the masses and types of particles, and the form of the forces between them, complex structures would almost certainly be atom-like and stable energy sources would almost certainly require aggregates of matter. Thus, the above background laws seem necessary for there to be life in any of the many-universes generated in this scenario, not merely a universe with our specific types of particles and forces.

[25] For more on the case for design from the simplicity and beauty of the laws of nature, see part II of my "The Argument from Design and the Many-Worlds Hypothesis" (2002).

V. Conclusion

In this paper, I have argued that the fine-tuning of the cosmos for life provides strong evidence for preferring theism over the atheistic single-universe hypothesis. I then argued that although one can partially explain the fine-tuning of the constants of physics by invoking some sort of many-universes generator, we have good reasons to believe that the many-universes generator itself would need to be well designed, and hence that hypothesizing some sort of many-universes generator only pushes the case for design up one level. The arguments I have offered do not prove the truth of theism, or even show that theism is epistemically warranted or the most plausible position to adopt. To show this would require examining all the evidence both for and against theism, along with looking at all the alternatives to theism. Rather, the arguments in this paper were only intended to show that the fine-tuning of the cosmos offers us significant reasons for preferring theism over atheism, where atheism is understood as not simply the denial of theism, but as also including the denial of any sort of intelligence behind the existence or structure of the universe.

For more information, and updates on the argument from design from physics and cosmology, see my fine-tuning webpage at www.robincollins.org.

Questions

1. In what ways does Collins see the universe as finely tuned?

2. How do you respond to Collins claim?

3. What shortcomings, if any, do you see in Collins argument?

4. Do you find this argument cogent, and if so, why?

5. Of all the arguments for God's existence, how do you rank this one in terms of its effectiveness, and why?

Bibliography:

- Barrow, John and Tipler, Frank. *The Anthropic Cosmological Principle*. Oxford: Oxford University Press, 1986.
- Behe, Michael. *Darwin's Black Box: The Biochemical Challenge to Evolution*. New York: The Free Press, 1996.
- Carnap, Rudolph. (1962) *The Logical Foundations of Probability*. Chicago: University of Chicago Press, 1962).
- Carr, B. J., and Rees, M. J. (April, 1979). "The Anthropic Cosmological Principle and the Structure of the PhysicalWorld." *Nature*, Vol. 278, 12 April 1979, pp. 605-612.
- Collins, Robin. (1999) "The Fine-Tuning Design Argument" in *Reason for the Hope Within*, Michael Murray (ed.), Grand Rapids, MI: Eerdman's Publishing Company.
- Collins, Robin. (2002). "The Argument from Design and the Many-Worlds Hypothesis," in *Philosophy of Religion: a Reader and Guide*, William Lane Craig, editor, New Brunswick, NJ: Rutgers University Press, 2002.
- Collins, Robin. (2003). "The Evidence for Fine-tuning," in *God and Design: The Teleological Argument and Modern Science*, Neil Manson (ed.), Routledge.
- Collins, Robin (Forthcoming) "Answering the Who Designed God Objection?", in James Sennett and Douglas Groothius, editors, *In Defense of Natural Theology: A Post-Humean Reassessment*, Downers Grove, IL: Intervarsity Press.
- Collins, Robin (Forthcoming). "A Theistic Perspective on the Multiverse Hypothesis," in Bernard Carr, editor, *Universe or Multiverse?* Cambridge University Press.
- Davies, Paul. (1974). *The Physics of Time Asymmetry*. Berkeley, CA: University of California Press.
- Davies, Paul. *The Accidental Universe*. Cambridge: Cambridge University Press, 1982.
- _____. *Superforce: The Search for a Grand Unified Theory of Nature*. New York: Simon and Schuster, 1984.
- _____. *The Cosmic Blueprint: New Discoveries in Nature's Creative Ability to Order the Universe*. New York, Simon and Schuster, 1988.
- Denton, Michael. (1998). *Nature's Destiny: How the Laws of Biology Reveal Purpose in the Universe*, New York, NY: The Free Press.
- Dirac, P. A. M. "The evolution of the physicist's picture of nature." *Scientific American*, May 1963.
- Dyson, Freeman. (1979). *Disturbing the Universe*. New York: Harper and Row.
- Greene, Brian. *The Elegant Universe: Superstrings, Hidden Dimensions, and the Quest for the Ultimate Theory*. New York: W. W. Norton and Company, 1999.
- Earman, John. (1992) *Bayes or Bust? A Critical Examination of Bayesian Confirmation Theory*. Cambridge, MA: The MIT Press.
- Edwards, A. W. F. (1972) *Likelihood*. Baltimore: Johns Hopkins University Press, 1992.
- Guth, Alan. *The Inflationary Universe: The Quest for a New Theory of Cosmic Origins*. New York, Helix Books, 1997.
- Hacking, Ian. *The Emergence of Probability: A Philosophical Study of Early Ideas About Probability, Induction and Statistical Inference*. Cambridge: Cambridge University Press, 1975.
- Howson, Colin, and Urbach, Peter. (1989). *Scientific Reasoning: The Bayesian Approach*, La Salle, IL: Open Court, 1989.
- Kaku, Michio. *Introduction to Superstrings and M-Theory*, Second Edition. New York, Springer-Verlag, 1999.
- Leslie, John. "How to Draw Conclusions From a Fine-Tuned Cosmos." In Robert Russell, et. al., eds., *Physics, Philosophy and Theology: A Common Quest for Understanding*. Vatican City State: Vatican Observatory Press, pp. 297-312, 1988.
- _____. *Universes*. New York: Routledge, 1989.
- Lewis, David. *On the Plurality of Worlds*, New York, Basil Blackwell, 1986.
- Linde, Andrei. *Particle Physics and Inflationary Cosmology*. Translated by Marc Damashek. Longhorne, Pennsylvania: Harwood Academic Publishers, 1990.
- Linde, Andrei. *Inflation and Quantum Cosmology*. New York: Academic Press, Inc., 1990.
- Oberhummer, H., Csoto, A. and Schlattl, H. (2000a). "Fine-Tuning of Carbon Based Life in the Universe by Triple-Alpha Process in Red Giants," *Science*, Vol. 289, No. 5476, 7 July 2000, pp. 88-90.

- Peacock, John. (1999). *Cosmological Physics*. Cambridge: Cambridge University Press, 1999.
- Penrose, Roger. (1989). *The Emperor's New Mind: Concerning Computers, Minds, and the Laws of Physics*, Roger Penrose New York : Oxford University Press.
- Plantinga, Alvin. *Warrant and Proper Function*. Oxford: Oxford University Press, 1993.
- Rees, Martin. *Just Six Numbers: The Deep Forces that Shape the Universe*, New York, NY: Basic Books, 2000.
- Schlesinger, George (1984), "Possible Worlds and the Mystery of Existence" *Ratio*, 26, pp. 1-18.
- Schlesinger, George. (1985). *The Intelligibility of Nature*. Aberdeen, Scottland: Aberdeen University Press.
- Sklar, Lawrence. *Physics and Chance: Philosophical Issues in the Foundation of Statistical Mechanics*. Cambridge: Cambridge University Press, 1993.
- Sober, Eliot. (2002). "Bayesianism—Its Scope and Limits" in *Bayes's Theorem,* Richard Swinburne (ed), Oxford: Oxford University Press, 2002, pp. 21-38
- Smart, J. J. C. "Laws of Nature and Cosmic Coincidence", *The Philosophical Quarterly*, Vol. 35, No. 140.
- Smith, George. "Atheism: The Case Against God." Reprinted in *An Anthology of Atheism and Rationalism,* edited by Gordon Stein, Prometheus Press, 1980.
- Susskind, Leonard. "The Anthropic Landscape of String Theory," in Bernard Carr, editor, *Universe or Multiverse?* Cambridge University Press.
- Swinburne, Richard. *An Introduction to Confirmation Theory*. London: Methuen and Co. Ltd, 1973.
- Tegmark, Max. "Is 'the theory of everything' merely the ultimate ensemble theory?" *Annals of Physics*, 270, (1998), pp. 1-51.
- Van Fraassen, Bas. *Laws and Symmetry*. Oxford: Oxford University Press, 1989.
- Weatherford, Roy. *Foundations of Probability Theory*. Boston, MA: Routledge and Kegan Paul, 1982.
- Weinberg, Steven. *Dreams of a Final Theory*. New York: Vintage Books, 1992.

RELIGIOUS EXPERIENCE AS SELF-TRANSCENDENCE AND SELF-DECEPTION*

Merold Westphal

Religious experience can be defined as self-transcendence. Models of this decentering of the self are not found in the transcendence of intentionality or in either contemplative or ecstatic self-forgetfulness, since all these leave the self as center. While they play important roles in authentic religion, experience that does not get beyond them is self-deceived and ultimately idolatrous. Only in the ethical claim that places limits on my will to be the center do I encounter the truly other. Even here the form of true religion may assist self-deception about the presence of its substance.

Perhaps you've heard those lemonade ads that refer to the good old days when we listened to baseball games on the radio. That part reminds me of my own conversion—to lifetime membership in the Diehard Cubs Fan Club. Every summer afternoon, as I sat in front of my grandmother's floor model radio, Bert Wilson would preach the good news, "We don't care who wins, as long as it's the Cubs." And in spite of the fact that in good years they only managed to beat out the Pirates for seventh place, I became a true believer. But when the lemonade ad suggests that it's "sorta cheatin' " to watch baseball on television, I am reminded of something quite different. It was my sophomore year in college and one of the most gifted students I have ever known, whose specialty was the oral interpretation of literature, was giving his senior speech recital. Like an ancient Greek rhapsode, and all in a little under an hour, he gave us *Doctor Zhivago*. For all its visual splendor, like televised baseball, the movie version that I was to see later did not surpass this old-fashioned oral version in dramatic power. The concluding line, taken from one of Pasternak's poems, was utterly shattering and unforgettable. "To live life to the end is no childish task."

Kierkegaard expresses this same conviction that life is the task of a lifetime by satirizing those for whom most of life is supposed to consist in living happily ever after. For such, "when they have arrived at a certain point in their search for truth, life takes on a change. They marry, and they acquire a certain position, in consequence of which they feel that they must in all honor have something finished, that they must have result.... And so they come to think of themselves as really finished.... Living in this manner, one is relieved of the necessity of becoming executively aware of the strenuous difficulties which the simplest of propositions about existing *qua* human-being involves" (1941: 78-79; cf. 1980: 55-56).

By arguing that such persons are strangers to religion, no matter how orthodox or pious, Kierkegaard suggests that this enduring adult task has religious import. But what is this task, which is the *sine qua non* of religion, and from which, apparently, only death can release us? The Augustinian tradition, to which Kierkegaard belongs, is united in its answer: self-transcendence. This is why Augustine speaks of the incarnation as the means by which Jesus "might detach from themselves those who were to be subdued and bring them over to Himself, healing the swelling of their pride and fostering their love so that instead of going further in their own self-confidence, they should put on weakness...should cast themselves down upon that divinity which, rising would bear them up aloft" (1963: 155). From this perspective follows the Augustinian beatitude: "Blessed is the man who loves you, who loves his friend in you, and his enemy because of you" (79).

---

* *Faith and Philosophy*, Vol. 9 No. 2 April 1992. All rights reserved.

Thomas Merton gives the same answer when he writes, "We do not detach ourselves from things in order to attach ourselves to God, but rather we become detached *from ourselves* in order to see and use all things in and for God" (1972: 21).

Gabriel Marcel puts the point on the horizontal plane in describing the nature and difficulty of admiration, "whose enormous spiritual and even metaphysical significance is still not recognized. The verb *lift* forcefully and accurately denotes the kind of effect admiration evokes in us, or rather realizes in us as a function of the object which evokes it.... It is clear that the function of admiration is to tear us away from ourselves and from the thoughts we have of ourselves.... Not so long ago a dramatist affirmed during an interview that admiration was for him a humiliating state which he resisted with all his force.... An analysis similar to the one Scheler has given of resentment should disclose that there is a burning preoccupation with self at the bottom of this suspicion [of anything superior], a 'but what about me, what becomes of me in that case?'...To affirm: admiration is a humiliating state, is the same as to treat the subject as a power existing for itself and taking itself as a center. To proclaim on the other hand, that it is an exalted state is to start from the inverse notion that the proper function of the subject is to emerge from itself and realize itself primarily in the gift of oneself" (1964: 47-49).

Finally, as if to exhibit the agreement between Protestant and Catholic Augustinians on this point, we can return to Kierkegaard himself. His definitions of the self and of faith spell out his understanding of self-transcendence as the lifelong task of life. The self is "a relation that relates itself to itself and in relating itself to itself relates itself to another" (1980: 13-14). This latter relation is faith when "in relating itself to itself and in willing to be itself, the self rests transparently in the power that established it" (49; cf. 14, 30, 82, 131).

Augustine and Merton introduce the basic notion of becoming detached from ourselves. Marcel makes it clear that this involves the transition from a self preoccupied with itself and its position as the center to a self capable of giving itself in admiration and creative fidelity to another. From the point of view of the point of departure, this is a humiliating tearing away from that to which I cling with all my might. From the point of view of the destination, this is a liberating elevation above the narrow horizons defined by the question, But what about me? In short, self-transcendence is the journey from the false self to the true self, with all of its agony and its ecstasy.

In spite of its austere from, Kierkegaard's formula for faith recapitulates these themes and introduces another. First, with Augustine and Merton he is explicit that we are to be detached from ourselves in order to be attached to God. 'Freedom from' is in the service of 'freedom for.' Here we encounter the wonderful ambiguity of the term 'transcendence.' It can mean that which is beyond, the transcendent. Or it can mean going beyond, transcending. For the Augustinian tradition the two are united, and transcending is toward the transcendent. What is beyond my false self is not simply my true self, but the not-myself in proper relation to which it first becomes possible for me to be my true self. Only by losing myself, in the sense of going beyond myself toward the not-myself, do I ever truly find myself.

Second, with Marcel, Kierkegaard is explicit that the relation to the other is a humble, decentering relation. (This is why it is experienced by pride as humiliation.) Self-transcendence means willing to be myself while at the same time willing to let God be God, that is, willing to be myself without insisting on being God. It is the exact opposite of Nietzsche's Zarathustra, who says, "*if* there were gods, how could I endure not to be a god! *Hence* there are no gods" (1966b: 86, "Upon the Blessed Isles"). It means learning to pray:

Hallowed be Thy name

> Thy kingdom come
> Thy will be done

without surreptitiously co-opting the name and the kingdom so that *my* will may be done on earth and in heaven.

Finally, for all of its emphasis on the role of the transcendent in self-transcendence, Kierkegaard's account explicitly links relation-to-an-other to self-relation. Only as self-relating selfhood does the self transcend itself toward its true self in relation to the transcendent. Given the historical linkage of the Augustinian *dubito* to the Cartesian *cogito*, this introduction of inwardness should not take us by surprise. Among its most important implications is that the metaphor of organic development can never be more than a metaphor, and a rather poor one at that, for self-transcendence. The latter presupposes too much in the way of self-awareness and self-involvement (Evans, 1963).

On the other hand, by making self-presence itself a task rather than an achievement, Kierkegaard excludes that total self-presence by virtue of which the self could claim to be the center. This expresses the great gulf fixed between his Augustinianism and its modern, secular counterpart, the Cartesian-Humean (Husserlian-positivist) tradition. In its self-relation the self is not posited as the ground of certainty, the criterion of truth, the self-sufficient and absolute mode of being, in short, the center. If I may be permitted to express the point oxymoronically, to counter Cartesian modernity's arrogant Augustinianism, Kierkegaard develops the inwardness of a decentered Cartesianism. The I of the Augustinian "I think" is always a problem, never a possession nor an Archimedean *pou sto*.

Having given this somewhat extended Augustinian definition of self-transcendence, I now want to suggest that we use it as at least a working definition of religious experience. Religious experience $=_{df}$ self-transcendence, the self-aware, self-involving, self-transforming relation to the ultimately transcendent. While I believe this definition has advantages at the descriptive level for the phenomenological and historical study of religion, the present essay will focus on its prescriptive employment as a norm for distinguishing authentically religious experience from its look alikes. Not all the beliefs, practices, and feelings that are easily recognized as religious are acts of self-transcendence. Prayer, for example, can easily be "a burning preoccupation with self," a solemn repetition of the question, "But what about me, what becomes of me in that case?"

Alterity is a big topic among philosophers these days, and a number of contemporary conversations have reminded us how difficult it is for the human spirit to be "at home [*bei sich*] with itself in its otherness *as such*" (Hegel, 1949: 790, my italics; cf. Taylor, 1987). This formula of Hegel's is strikingly similar to Kierkegaard's designation of faith as a self-relating that is simultaneously an other-relating. Its "as such" is meant as a reminder that the other is meant to remain other. But for all his emphasis on dialectic as the path of otherness, opposition, negation, contradiction, and so forth, Hegel himself stands accused of taking away with dialectical reconciliation what he first gives in the form of dialectical difference. Dialectic turns out to be a monological self-mediation rather than a dialogical other-mediation (Habermas, 1987 and Desmond, 1987).

In a similar vein, Derridean deconstruction, flying significantly under the banner of *différance*, is a sustained polemic against the metaphysics of presence precisely as the reduction of the different to the same. The debate with Gadamer, for example, can perhaps best be summarized as the reciprocal claims, I am more open to otherness than you are (Michelfelder and Palmer, 1989; cf. Caputo, 1987).

These discussions provide an important context for any contemporary discussion of religious experience as self-transcendence. What is more, reflection on specifically religious experience can make an important contribution to the wider discussion of otherness in general. For, in the first place, the holy, the ultimately transcendent, has appropriately been designated, not merely as other but as "wholly other." It is quintessentially transcendent. Secondly, self-transcendence may be more than casually linked to the transcendent; it may well be the condition and measure of the transcendent. This would mean, not that there is the transcendent only to the degree that we are able to transcend ourselves, but that we experience the transcendent as such, as truly other, only to the degree that we are able to transcend ourselves. Conversely, to the degree that self-transcendence fails, transcendence is only apparent, that is, idolatrous.

In order to explore this hypothesis and to clarify the normative significance of the concept of religious experience as self-transcendence, I want to look at a variety of other modes of experience in order to highlight the tenuousness of transcendence in them. The claim that knowledge is self-transcendence is a good point of departure both because religion is so often identified with religious beliefs and because philosophers so often speak of knowledge as transcendence. For example, Fichte says that "the I forgets itself in the object of its activity.... *Intuition* is the name of this action, a silent, unconscious contemplation, which loses itself in its object" (Breazeale, 1988: 260). Kojève expands on this idea. "Now, the analysis of 'thought,' 'reason,' 'understanding,' and so on—in general, of the cognitive, contemplative, passive behavior of a being or a 'knowing subject'—never reveals the why or the how of the birth of the word 'I'... The man who contemplates is 'absorbed' by what he contemplates; the 'knowing subject' 'loses' himself in the object that is known. Contemplation reveals the object, not the subject.... The man who is 'absorbed' by the object that he is contemplating can be 'brought back to himself' only by a Desire" (1969: 3). In other words, in desire we are related to the other, for example, something we want to eat, only as the mode in which we are preoccupied with ourselves and satisfying our needs; but in cognition real transcendence occurs as we lose ourselves and become absorbed in the object.

Since Husserl treats intentionality primarily as cognitive, his claim that intentionality is transcendence can help us make this claim more precise. In the first place there is the transcendence of the physical object to perception. It is transcendent by virtue of exceeding whatever it is able to give of itself "in person," whatever is directly present to perception. It can present its front side, but not its other sides. It can only present itself in adumbrations (*abschattungen*) which it always infinitely exceeds (1983: par. 41-42). In this way the object transcends the perception of it.

Other objects, such as mental processes (*Erlebnisse*) are not given in this way. "*Ein Erlebnis shattet sich niche ab.*" For this reason there is a sharp distinction to be drawn between a mental process and a physical thing (*Ding*), namely that the former "can be perceived in an immanental perception," while the latter is always transcendent (par. 42).

There are also non-spatial objects that have their own mode of transcendence. In reflection my intentional object is a cogitatio, one of my own, and we might label this "internal perception." But Husserl prefers the language of immanence and transcendence to that of internal and external. So he says that "by *intentive mental processes related to something immanent*, we understand those to which it is *essential that their intentional objects, if they exist at all, belong to the same stream of mental processes to which they themselves belong....* Intentive mental processes of which that is not the case are directed to something transcendent" (par. 38, his italics). This means that my cognition is transcendent whenever it is directed to an "object" that is not a *cogitatio* or *Erlebnis* of my own. Among such objects are not only spatial objects but essences, other egos, and their *Erlebnisse*.

This seems to be very close to the realism of G. E. Moore, grounded in the distinction between the act and the object of consciousness (1953: ch. XVI and 1959: ch. I-II). Given the way in which both Moore and Husserl distinguish the intentional object (*noema*) from the act that intends it (*noesis*), it is not clear why we shouldn't say that every intentional act involves transcendence. Whether or not that is what they intend us to conclude, we can distinguish three theses about intentionality and transcendence:

1) We encounter transcendence in every intentional object (since the act and the object can always be distinguished).
2) We encounter transcendence in those intentional objects which are not themselves our own *cogitationes* or *Erlebnisse* (since they do not belong to the stream of mental acts that includes the acts that intend them).
3) We encounter transcendence in those intentional objects that are physical, i.e., spatial (since there can only give themselves partially, perspectivally, *abschattungsweise*).

No doubt each of these theses embodies a legitimate and useful concept of transcendence. But none of them gives us the self-transcendence we are looking for, that detachment from self that moves us beyond preoccupation with what Kant calls "the dear self."

The first reason for this is clear if we return briefly to Kojève. The separation of cognition from desire that he attributes to the knowing subject is by no means typical of cognition. Hume, the father of positivism, says, "Reason is, and ought only to be the slave of the passions, and can never pretend to any other office than to serve and obey them" (1888: 41S). Nietzsche, the father of post modernism, agrees: "but reason is merely an instrument, and Descartes is superficial" (1966a: 104). If we think of positivism and post modernism as diseases to be eliminated like polio and smallpox, the best we can hope to do is show that Hume and Nietzsche are not right all of the time. We would surely be kidding ourselves to deny that they are right at least most of the time. And whether instrumental reason is to be seen as the glory or the curse of modernity, it is nothing if not preoccupation with the self (personal and collective) and its desires.

But, it may well be objected, did not Fatuity and Kojève speak explicitly about contemplation, making it clear they have disinterested cognition in mind? The Greeks and their modern followers often speak of philosophy as *theoria* in this sense, but at least since the eighteenth century the notion of disinterested contemplation has primarily been developed in relation to aesthetic experience. A tradition that extends from Shaftesbury, Hutcheson, Burke, and Alison through Kant and Schopenhauer to Croce and Edward Bullough has sought to make the transcendence of self-interest the key to aesthetic appreciation (see Westphal, 1984: 131-35). The anti-instrumental, anti-utilitarian theme of this tradition is succinctly expressed by C. S. Lewis, "the many *use* art and the few *receive* it" (1961: 19), and by Oscar Wilde, "All art is quite useless" (1981: xxiv).

The examples Shaftesbury gives of disinterested contemplation make it clear that breaking the link between intentionality and desire is the heart of the matter. It is the absence of the desire to command, the desire to own, the desire to eat, and the desire to touch sexually that makes the perception of beauty disinterested, and Shaftesbury understandably speaks of this as the transcendence of "selfishness," "self-interest," and "self-love" (1964: II, 12628, I, 78, 274-75, 317).

There can be little doubt that in theoretical and aesthetic contemplation we have the self-forgetfulness Fichte and Kojève have in mind, in which the subject sinks from sight, playing at most the role of background or horizon while the object becomes foreground and theme. If we remember that Shaftesbury's primary interest in disinterestedness was not aesthetics but ethics and religion, we may think that we have found what we are looking for (cf. O'Connor, 1972: 151-52). But this model is also too weak.

Contemplative self-forgetfulness takes us beyond instrumental reason, to be sure. Hume and Nietzsche might deny that it ever exists, and we would do well to take their suspicions seriously. But let us retain the hypothesis that it sometimes does occur, at least to a significant degree. The problem begins with Aristotle, whose *Metaphysics* begins with the words, "All men by nature desire to know." It looks as if the link between knowledge and desire has not been cut after all. Of course, the desire to know is not a selfish desire, as if knowledge were a zero sum game. But it is, even when it has no instrumental significance, the desire to satisfy and fulfill the self. To use a Rawlsian distinction (1971: 127-29), it is a desire both of the self (my desire) and in the self (for my satisfaction). For this reason, Aristotle's ethics, including his theory of contemplation as an intellectual virtue, is properly identified as a self-realization theory.

Shaftesbury points us in the same direction. "For though the habit of selfishness and the multiplicity of interested views are of little improvement to real merit or virtue, yet there is a necessity for the preservation of virtue, that it should be thought to have no quarrel with true interest and self-enjoyment" (1964: 274). The point is not that self-realization and self-enjoyment are evil. It is simply that contemplative experience, theoretical or aesthetic, that is properly interpreted in these terms can hardly be a convincing model for religious experience conceived as detachment from self. Disinterestedness may delimit but it does not displace the supremacy of the self, which remains the horizon for contemplative self-forgetfulness. Conversely, if religious experience is to be conceived as self-transcendence, any piety that does not get beyond both instrumental self-seeking and contemplative self-enjoyment is not genuine religious experience.

C. S. Lewis fails to see this point in an otherwise illuminating discussion of heaven in *The Problem of Pain*. People are nervous about "pie in the sky" escapism, he notes. But if there is no "pie in the sky" then Christianity is false, and if there is, then we must deal with it. He writes, "we are afraid that heaven is a bribe, and that if we make it our goal we shall no longer be disinterested. It is not so. Heaven offers nothing that a mercenary soul can desire. It is safe to tell the pure in heart that they shall see God, for only the pure in heart want to." With the right kind of glosses on these claims Lewis could take us beyond disinterestedness to genuine transcendence. But instead of doing so he remains within the dichotomy of disinterested and mercenary. "There are rewards that do not sully motives. A man's love for a woman is not mercenary because he wants to marry her, nor his love for poetry mercenary because he wants to read it, nor his love of exercise less disinterested because he wants to run and leap and walk. Love, by definition, seeks to enjoy its object" (1962: 144-45). By being satisfied as long as enjoyment is not mercenary, Lewis, like Shaftesbury, fails to notice the limitations of enjoyment with reference to transcendence.

The mercenary is one who does what is not enjoyable for the sake of what is. Mercenary behavior is instrumental, means-end behavior. Mercenary love is false love, as when a man loves a woman for her money or a woman loves a man for the security he provides. Disinterested behavior does not have this means-end structure, and disinterested love does not arise from ulterior motives. When the Psalmist prays, "For God alone my soul in silence wait" (62.1), this can be a mercenary prayer meaning, "Only God can get me out of this mess," or it can be a disinterested prayer meaning, "Not even the benefits of divine grace, but only God in person can satisfy me." There is a huge difference between these two prayers, but in both cases the self is concerned with its own satisfaction, and the love that seeks to enjoy its object is caught up in its own enjoyment.

It is Levinas who sees more clearly than anyone that the other enjoyed is not necessarily transcendent, and, consequently, that enjoyment is not necessarily self-transcendence. Echoing the Hegelian formula we noted earlier, Levinas finds us not content merely to be at home with ourselves in familial surroundings (his *chez soi* = Hegel's *bei sich*) but disposed to reach out "toward an alien outside-of-oneself, toward a yonder." He calls this desire for genuine otherness metaphysical desire. But the other thus desired "is not 'other' like the bread I eat, the land in which I dwell, the landscape I contemplate...] can 'feed' on these realities and to a very great extent satisfy myself, as though I had simply been lacking them. Their *alterity* is thereby reabsorbed into my own identity as a thinker or a possessor. The metaphysical desire tends toward *something else entirely*, toward the *absolutely other*" (1969: 33).

As this passage indicates, eating is the paradigm of enjoyment and the source of the appearance of transcendence therein. Against all forms of idealism, which interpret knowledge as the primacy of subject over object, the reduction of the latter's otherness to the sameness of the former, alimentation reminds me that I am a body within the world and not just a mind for whom the world is a spectacle. Food overflows its meaning as an object of representation and becomes a condition for the very acts by which such meaning is constituted (127-30). In my dependence on the elements of life I seem to encounter something quite other than myself.

Levinas makes three points about enjoyment so construed that are relevant to our project. First, as Shaftesbury and Lewis have noted, in enjoyment we are beyond self-interest conceived in instrumental or mercenary terms. "Here lies the permanent truth of hedonist moralities: to not seek, behind the satisfaction of need, an order relative to which alone satisfaction would require a value; to take satisfaction, which is the very meaning of pleasure, as a term. The need for food does not have existence as its goal, but food. Biology teaches the prolongation of nourishment into existence; need is naïve" (134).

Second, enjoyment is pure egoism, not self-transcendence. "In enjoyment am absolutely for myself. Egoist without reference to the Other, I am alone without solitude, innocently egoist and alone. Not against the Others, not 'as for me...'—but entirely deaf to the Other, outside of all communication and all refusal to communicate—without ears, like a hungry stomach" (134; his ellipsis). I may be dependent on the elements from which I draw my nourishment, but "in the satisfaction of need the alienness of the world that founds me loses its alterity.... Through labor and possession the alterity of nutriments enters into the same" (129).

Finally, as the phrase 'like a hungry stomach' suggests, eating is but a model of many different modes of enjoyment. As "an ultimate relation with the substantial plenitude of being," enjoyment "embraces all relations with things" (133). I take this to mean not that there is nothing but enjoyment, but that there is no relation that cannot be elevated to/reduced to enjoyment. In spite of the initial distinction between knowledge and enjoyment, Levinas is explicit that cognitive relations can have this structure, especially when they have a contemplative character. Thus, "I but open my eyes and already enjoy the spectacle" (130). And we have already seen him assimilate "the landscape I contemplate" to "the bread I eat." The psalmist who thirsts for the face of God as a deer for streams of water (42:1-2) has surely made spiritual progress over those whose only appetites are for "wine, women, and song." But the journey toward genuine religious experience may not be over.

There is still another mode of self-forgetfulness that turns out to be something less than the self-transcendence we are seeking to clarify. Like contemplation it takes us beyond the mercenary, and it often turns up in religious contexts. We can call it ecstatic self-forgetfulness, as distinct from contemplative. The two are not totally different, for there surely is a contemplative ecstasy, for example, in Yoga.

We can consider play, as interpreted by Gadamer, as something of a transition experience. Since he relates play to the religious festival and claims that "The player experiences the game as a reality that surpasses him" (110, 97-98), there is obvious reference to our own question about religious experience. Even the spectator is able "to forget one's own purposes.... To be present...has a character of being outside oneself." This "ecstasy of being outside oneself [*Ecstatic des Aussersichseins*]" is "the positive possibility of being wholly with something else. This kind of being present is a self-forgetfulness, and it is the nature of the spectator to give himself in self-forgetfulness to what he is watching" (110-11; cf. 113-14).

More sharply distinct from contemplative self-forgetfulness than Gadamerian play is the Dionysian, as described by Nietzsche. It is not only a self-forgetfulness by contrast with Apollonian self-knowledge; it also dwells among the "wilder emotions" from which Apollonian calm is free (1967: 45, 35). Far from being any kind of spectator sport, it is a realm of *Rausch* (intoxication, delirium, frenzy, transport, ecstasy, rapture) and *Verzückung* (ecstasy, rapture, transport, trance, convulsion). In the "dancers of St. John and St. Vitus," in the Bacchic choruses of the Greeks," and "as far back as Babylon and the orgiastic Sacaea," we find the Dionysian experience in which "everything subjective vanishes into complete self-forgetfulness" (33-37).

There is clearly a dimension of self-transcendence here, even of detachment from self. But ecstatic self-forgetfulness is no more what we are looking for than was contemplative self-forgetfulness. Gadamer tells us as much himself when he writes, "Thus to the ecstatic self-forgetfulness of the spectator there corresponds his continuity with himself. Precisely that in which he loses himself as a spectator requires his own continuity...the absolute moment in which a spectator stands is at once self-forgetfulness and reconciliation with self. That which detaches him from everything also gives him back the whole of his being" (1975: 113-14).

This sounds so much like the words of Jesus (Mark 8:35) that we might easily think we have found the definition of religious self-transcendence if Gadamer had not also said, in the middle of the passage just quoted, "It is the truth of [the spectator's] own world, the religious and moral world in which he lives, which presents itself to him and in which he recognizes himself." William James is said to have complained that for Josiah Royce "the world is real but not so very damn real." We might say here that the ecstatic self encounters something other than itself, but not so very damn other. In other words, though the elements on which the self feeds here are spiritual rather than physical, we have not gotten beyond the realm of nutrition. Like its contemplative counterpart, ecstatic self-forgetfulness is a species of enjoyment.

That this is also true for Nietzsche's wilder version is perhaps clearest in his linkage of the Dionysian with sexual ecstasy (1967: 36; 1968: sec. 798-801). I do not mean simply that sex is fun. What I have in mind is best expressed in the comment one of my students made to me years ago. After living together for a while, she and her boyfriend had broken up and separated. Though she had no apparent scruples about having lived together, she was obviously not comfortable about the fact that they still secretly got together to have sex. Her explanation/excuse: "the only time I can ever forget myself is when I'm having sex." Her ex-boyfriend was "other but not so very damn other" because he was but an element through which her need was satisfied. That her need was primarily for oblivion rather than for pleasure or intimacy does not take her experience, or Nietzsche's Dionysian of which it is a model, beyond the framework of enjoyment. Self-forgetfulness continues to be a mode of being preoccupied with oneself, in this case with killing for oneself the pain of being oneself.

Although we have not yet found the model that will clarify for us what is essential about the peculiar combination of transcendence and self-transcendence which the Augustinian tradition offers as a normative concept of religious experience, the time has come to introduce our second major theme, self-deception. For it will throw light on our negative results to this point. Our point of departure can be the suspicion Nietzsche directs toward religious experience, even that of religious founders. "One sort of honesty has been alien to all founders of religions and their kind: They have never made their experiences a matter of conscience for knowledge. 'What did I really experience?'…None of them has asked such questions, nor do any of our dear religious people ask them even now" (1974: 253).

Paul Ricoeur translates this kind of question into the language of the biblical prophets on the warpath against idolatry as he introduces his own hermeneutics of suspicion. "In our time we have not finished doing away with idols and we have barely begun to listen to symbols. It may be that this situation, in its apparent distress, is instructive: it may be that extreme iconoclasm belongs to the restoration of meaning" (1970: 27). To listen to religious symbols is to open oneself to a claim from what purports to be ultimately transcendent and to entertain the possibility of transcending oneself in that direction. To do away with idols is to take seriously the suspicion that what purports to be listening to religious symbols is actually something quite different, an acoustic illusion in which my own voice is mistaken for the divine voice. When this occurs, religion becomes a disguised form of self-centering or preoccupation with oneself. For corresponding to false-consciousness are false gods, and the deities who are the means or the elements for self-centering are wish-fulfilling projections whose fictitious character does not keep them from being rivals to whatever may be truly sacred (see Westphal, 1987).

Ricoeur's suggestion is that the pursuit of any possibly genuine self-transcendence must include a negative, iconoclastic moment. He calls us to renew the question that Jonathan Edwards put so sharply with reference to the "holy affections" in which "true religion, in great part, consists" (1959: 95)—how can we distinguish the truly holy affections from their counterfeit counterparts? Precisely our failure, to this point, to find an adequate model for the self-transcendence that constitutes genuine religious experience puts us in a good position to see why Nietzsche and Ricoeur and Edwards (like Amos and Jesus) refuse to take everything that offers itself as religious experience at face value. For that failure contains the transcendental deduction, so to speak, of three idols.

To begin with, any religious experience that contents itself with what we have called intentional transcendence can be shown to be idolatrous. Religion that consists of nothing more than doctrinal knowledge of a transcendent creator and savior, for example, no matter how correct and orthodox such doctrine may be, reduces God to one of my clear and distinct ideas. Having already reduced the wholly other to the propositionally possessed, it will complete itself as the instrumental religion in which the truth serves as a security blanket or a weapon against one's opponents and thus as an escape from the call to a decentered selfhood (see Westphal, 1980).

Similarly, insofar as religious experience can be adequately described in terms of either contemplative or ecstatic self-forgetfulness, its gods will be but vehicles of enjoyment, nutritional elements lacking the kind of transcendence in themselves that would make them wholly and genuinely other or enable them to inspire any detachment from self.

To call the gods of such religions idols is to recognize them as convenient fictions masked as transcendent realities. But the iconoclasm that labels them as such should not be misunderstood to be the claim that there is no place in true religion for doctrinal affirmation or for either contemplative or ecstatic self-forgetfulness. On the contrary, I want to insist that there is an important place for each of these in true religion. The point is that by themselves these moments do not make up the true religion we seek. Something is missing, something so essential that without it these important moments of true religion become the embodiment of false. What is it?

There is an important clue in Gadamer's analysis of contemplative and ecstatic self-forgetfulness. Much as Lewis distinguishes the few who receive art from the many who use it, Gadamer emphasizes the "important difference between a spectator who gives himself entirely to the play of art, and someone who merely gapes at something out of curiosity." For the former "the play of art does not simply exhaust itself in the ecstatic emotion of the moment, but has a claim to permanence and the permanence of a claim" (1975: 111-12).

We might take this talk about a claim in purely aesthetic terms, as if the work of art lays claim to be recognized as a classic. But Gadamer seems to have in mind something more nearly like the experience Rilke expresses in his scant, "Archaic Torso of Apollo."

> Never will we know his fabulous head
> where the eyes apples slowly ripened. Yet
> his torso glows: a candelabrum set
> before his gaze which is pushed back and hid,
> > restrained and shining. Else the curving breast
> > could not thus blind you nor through the soft turn
> > of the loins could this smile easily have passed
> > into the bright groins where the genitals burned.
>
> Else stood this stone a fragment and defaced,
> with lucent body from the shoulders falling,
> too short, not gleaming like a lion's fell;
> > nor would this star have shaken the shackles off,
> > bursting with light, until there is no place
> > that does not see you. You must change your life.

(MacIntyre, 1957: 92-93)

We are not prepared for these last five words, 'You must change your life.' Like the words, 'To live life to the end is no childish task' at the conclusion of *Doctor Zhivago*, their claim upon us shatters the calm of contemplation and calls us beyond the realm of aesthetic enjoyment to ethical, even religious responsibility. For this reason Gadamer explicates his notion of the claim in terms of Kierkegaard's challenge to contemporaneity with Christ and to hearing the proclamation of the gospel in a sermon, as understood by dialectical theology (1975: 112-13). His earlier notion that "the player experiences the game as a reality that surpasses him" (98), now becomes the notion that in the claim we encounter the "truth" of the "moral and religious world" in which we live (113).

There is an ambiguity here. As a moral and religious claim, this truth seems to have the categorical character that would render it truly other. But, as Kant and Freud insist with the greatest clarity and persuasiveness, the voice of categorical claims may very well be our very own voice. And Gadamer himself qualifies the alterity of the claim by saying, with reference to the spectator, "It is the truth *of his own world*, the religious and moral world *in which he lives*, which presents itself to him and *in which he recognizes himself* (113, my italics). If the truth that claims me is simply the tradition that has already shaped me, the spiritual world in and from which I live, and move, and have my being, its voice is other but not so very damn other. If Gadamer wants us to take seriously his appeal to Kierkegaard and to dialectical theology he must identify a claim that evokes fear and trembling not only from me as an existing individual but from my established order as well (Kierkegaard, 1944: 89; Barth, 1968: 27-54). His lack of enthusiasm for such a task is notorious.

For an unambiguous development of the clue we have found in Gadamer, the idea that it is in the form of a claim upon us that we encounter the otherness of the other, we can return to Levinas' account of metaphysical desire as directed toward "something else entirely, toward the absolutely other" (1969: 33). His analysis of enjoyment as involving self-centering rather than self-transcendence is one of several foils against which he develops the thesis that "the absolutely other is the Other" (39).

Who is this Other? In the first instance it is the one whom I encounter face to face in conversation (39, 71). In other words, the Other is another human being. Because our encounter takes place in language, it can be no animal other, and because it takes place face to face it can be no divine other. Rather, "it is only man who could be absolutely foreign to me" (73; cf. 71-79).

Secondly, the Other is the one whose face and speech I first encounter, beyond all knowing, all using, and all enjoying (38), as a claim, the unconditional constraint upon my freedom that leaves me fully free to accept or reject it and that is expressed in the words, "You shall not commit murder" (199, 216, 262, 303). Only in the realm of ethics, only in "the ethical impossibility of killing [the Other]" (87), do I encounter otherness as truly other.

This claim has a radically decentering intent. "To welcome the Other is to put in question my freedom (85; cf. 51, 43). It reminds me that I am not the center to which all else is peripheral, the end to which all else is the means. In the claims of the Other I am suddenly beyond all objects to be known, all tools to be used, and all elements on which to feed either body or soul.

What is worse, from the perspective of the "dear self," the relation is asymmetrical. It is not a prudent, contractual arrangement among equals in which I offer to spare your life (and liberty) if you agree to spare mine. On the one hand is the asymmetry of loftiness. The unconditional character of the Other's claim can only be expressed in images of height and authority. For this reason, although the Other is human and not divine, Levinas speaks of the Other as "Most-High" (34) and "Master" (72, 75, 86). On the other hand there is the asymmetry of indigence. This is why Levinas also refers to the Other as the stranger, the widow, the orphan, and the poor (77-78). The Other has nothing to offer in exchange for my welcoming, least of all a bribe. With such indigent loftiness it is impossible to negotiate or to strike a deal.

Finally, the face of the Other "*expresses itself*," it manifests itself "*kath' auto*" (51). We are familiar with this Greek phrase through its Latin equivalent, *per se*. The face of the other expresses itself, and it does so through itself and not through another. This does not consist in its being disclosed, "its being exposed to the gaze that would take it as a theme for interpretation, and would command an absolute position dominating the object. Manifestation *kath' auto* consists in a being telling itself to us independently of every position we would have taken in its regard, *expressing itself*" (65; cf. 67, 74, 77).

The concept of disclosure that Levinas here contrasts with expression *kath' auto* or 'revelation' has Husserlian-Heideggerian connotations. "To recognize truth to be disclosure is to refer it to the horizon of him who discloses.... The disclosed being is relative to us and not *kath' auto*" (64). By contrast, the notion of the face as self-revelatory "brings us to a notion of meaning prior to my *Sinngebung* and thus independent of my initiative and my power" (51). Even more important, it is independent of the horizons of meaning we bring with us, the tacit dimensions of our awareness that confer meaning without our noticing it (28).

Levinas knows exactly what he is doing here. He is claiming immediacy for the Other's self-expression. "The immediate is the face to face (52). In spite of all attacks on the "myth of the given," he is claiming that the face is a theory free datum. In willful disregard for the alleged inescapability of the hermeneutical circle, he finds us pointed toward "the possibility of signification without a context" (23). And in spite of all attacks on the metaphysics of presence and the transcendental signifier (Derrida, 1976: 49-50, 69-71; 1981: 19-20, 29, 44), he insists that "the signification of the face is due to an essential coinciding of the existent and the signifier. Signification is not added to the existent. To signify is not equivalent to presenting oneself as a sign, but to expressing oneself, that is, presenting oneself in person" (262).

Such claims are bold heresy in the present philosophical climate. But in spite of the avalanche of criticism they are bound to evoke, Levinas will want to stick by them, for they are the key to his project. Without self-expression *kath' auto*, I could not welcome the Other as such. The Other would be permitted to encounter me only as a meaning relative to my own (present) acts of *Sinngebung* or to the sedimented (past) acts of myself and of others that I bring with me as horizon, context, pre-understanding, *a priori*, tacit dimension, prejudice. Since as thematizing and as operative intentionality would be the condition of the possibility of her appearance, she would clearly be merely phenomenal. No *per se*, no *an sich*. Such an Other is not so very damn other. But as the claim that challenges my centrality in its own term and not in my own, the Other is very other indeed.

This is not the immediacy that ends up as pure indeterminacy (Hegel, 1969 82; cf. 1959: Par. 86). It is concerned with presence, to be sure, but not with sheer presence beyond difference. It is Derrida, pursuing his own agenda of *différance*, who points this out. By virtue of the lofty majesty attributed by Levinas to the Other, the encounter with the Other "does not take the form of an intuitive contact since the Other is present "not as a total presence but as a *trace*" (Derrida, 1978: 95). What we have here is "absolute proximity and absolute distance.... A community of nonpresence, and therefore of non-phenomenality.... Only the other, the totally other, can be manifested...within a certain non manifestation and *a certain absence*.... It can be said only of the other that its phenomenon is a certain non phenomenon, *a certain absence*" (90-91, my italics).

This is why Levinas sometimes speaks of the Other simply as "the Stranger who disturbs the being at home with oneself" (1969: 39). Without the additional appellations of widow, orphan, and poor, such a reference evokes Camus rather than the Law and the Prophets and serves to make it clear that the Other, when encountered as truly other, is an intangible intrusion and not an intuitive intelligibility. It is for the same reason that Levinas emphasizes the nudity of the face. This is not to deny that the face may be the bearer of cultural codes, as when an expensive coiffure, a matted beard, or the unmistakable signs of Downs syndrome enable me to assign faces to their place in the social hierarchy. It is simply to deny that the meaning and validity of the Other's claim, "You shall not commit murder," is in any way dependent on these cultural codes. The ethical immediacy of the Other as face has nothing to do with pre-predicative indeterminacy; it is rather a matter of expressing a claim unmediated by the cultural codes that normally censor all claims.

The face as the presence of the Other as absolutely other "is produced concretely as a temptation to total negation, and as the infinite resistance to murder...in the hard resistance of these eyes without protection—what is softest and most uncovered (262). If Camus' *The Stranger* renders uncomfortably concrete this "temptation to total negation," the death of the black man, Christmas, in Faulkner's *Light in August* reveals "the infinite resistance to murder...in...these eyes without protection." A white lynch mob is determined to kill him, in spite of the testimony of the preacher, Hightower, that, "He was here that night. He was with me the night of the murder, I swear to God—" Grimm, their leader, finally corners Christmas, fires five shots into him, and, as he lies dying, castrates him. The others catch up. "But the man on the floor had not moved. He just lay there, with his eyes open and empty of everything save consciousness...For a long moment he looked up at them with peaceful and unfathomable and unbearable eyes. Then his face, body, all, seemed to collapse, to fall in upon itself, and from out of the slashed garments about his hips and loins the pent black blood seemed to rush like a released breath...upon that black blast the man seemed to rise soaring into their memories forever and ever. They are not to lose it, in whatever peaceful valleys, beside whatever placid and reassuring streams of old age, in the mirroring faces of whatever children they will contemplate old disasters and newer hopes. It will be there, musing, quiet, steadfast, not fading and not particularly threatful, but of itself alone serene, of itself alone triumphant" (1950: 406-407).

From out of the gaze of that black face the whole body of Christmas becomes face, so much so that the black blood that gushes from between his legs is transformed into a breath exuding from that face. According to the cultural codes that are the horizon for white perceptions of that black face, it is possible to interpret this killing, in spite of the victim's humanity, as equivalent to slaughtering a hog, and simultaneously, in spite of the victim's innocence, as a just punishment. If that were the whole story, it would be possible to forget the deed. But those who were there cannot do so, because the face of Christmas, against all the operative cultural codes, expresses unambiguously and unforgettably a claim that they could reject but not refute, "You shall not commit murder."

They can kill him, but they cannot reify him. They cannot reduce his otherness to an object of their knowledge, a tool for their use, or nourishment for their enjoyment. Helpless and humiliated, defeated and dying, he embodies a transcendence unlike any they have ever encountered in church. For the gods they worship are idols, but Christmas is "wholly other."

Here we have the model we have been seeking to help us clarify the Augustinian notion of self-transcendence. This is an Other whose transcendence consists in an unconditional claim that removes me from the center of the universe both ethically by constraining my will and epistemologically by refusing to be constrained by the cultural codes of the world in which I recognize myself.

This is the double decentering that constitutes Augustine's double conversion in Books VII and VIII of the *Confessions*. That independence of cultural codes precludes any account of knowledge as recollection is not only the argument of Augustine's critique of Platonism in Book VII, but also, and in greater detail, of Kierkegaard's *Fear and Trembling and Philosophical Fragments*, taken jointly. Levinas reprises this argument by sharply distinguishing the ethical, in which I encounter the Other as truly other, from the political, in which I do not, and by repudiating recollection repeatedly as the vehicle of the ethical (1969: 21-24, 43, 51, 61, 171, 180, 204). According to Derrida's apt summary, Levinas sees western philosophy as "dominated since Socrates by a Reason which receives only what it gives itself, a Reason which does nothing but recall itself to itself." In this way "it has always *neutralized* the other, in every sense of the word" (Derrida, 1978: 96; cf. n. 27).

What here separates ethics from politics is what joins it to religion. Thus Kierkegaard's tight linkage in the *Postscript* of ethics and religion as the life-world of subjectivity, totally different from that of aesthetic-speculative objectivity, finds its echo in Levinas's claim that true religion presupposes ethics (77-78). We cannot truly love God while hating our sister and brother (I John 4:40). If Marcel and Merton are the great Catholic Augustinians of our time, and Kierkegaard the great Protestant Augustinian, Levinas is the great Jewish Augustinian.

The Other whose transcendence Levinas has helped us to specify provides us with the opportunity for a unique self-transcendence. To welcome an Other so unwelcome to the pride that the Augustinian tradition finds to be the heart of our darkness and the darkness of our heart is to become a new person indeed. We are, of course, still in the realm of ethics and not yet talking about religious experience. For this Other is human and not divine. But all we have to do is replace the human with the divine Other to have the normative concept of religious experience we are looking for. Genuine religious experience is the self-transcendence in relation to a divine transcendence that radically decenters us as will, and, correspondingly, as belief and affection. Perhaps this link between the ethical and the religious is the truth behind Kant's claims that "morality does not need religion at all," that "morality leads inevitably to religion," and that "Religion is (subjectively regarded) the recognition of all duties as divine commands" (1960: 3, 7n., 142).

It is now possible to specify just where a couple of earlier formulations that looked so promising came up short. Gadamer's account of ecstatic self forgetfulness in play, art, and religious ritual culminates in these words—"That which detaches him from everything also gives him back the whole of his being" (1975: 113-14). These words evoked for us the claim of Jesus that only those who lose their life will find it. But what Jesus says is this—"whoever loses his life *for my sake and the gospel's* will save it" (Mark 8:35, my italics).

Who is this Jesus, and what is this "gospel of Jesus Christ" (Mark 1:1)? Jesus is the one who has just responded to Peter's "You are the Messiah" with the announcement, to be repeated on two subsequent occasions (9:30-32, 10:32-34, cf. 45), that far from being the Davidic warrior who has come to slay the pharisaical-scribal Goliath of the Galilean synagogue, or the priestly Goliath of the Jerusalem temple, or the imperial Goliath of Rome, he is the Human One who must suffer and die at the hands of these Goliaths. And the good news about him centers in the call to a discipleship of self-denial and joining him on the way of the cross (8:34). By leaving out the crucial words, "for my sake and the gospel's," Gadamer leaves out precisely that decentering of the self as will (to power, cf. 10:35-45) that distinguishes the Markan account of self-transcendence as losing and finding oneself.

Similarly, we can now identify what C. S. Lewis failed to say when he wrote, "Heaven offers nothing that a mercenary soul can desire. It is safe to tell the pure in heart that they shall see God, for only the pure in heart want to" (1962: 144-45). His glosses on this claim, you will recall, were in terms of love as enjoyment of the object of desire. In order to get beyond the self-referential character of enjoyment, we need to specify that the pure in heart are precisely those who have learned to welcome Mark's Jesus as their center. It is safe to tell them of the "pie in the sky" that consists in seeing God not simply because they want to see God. For the God some want to see is an idol, the cosmic legitimizer and guarantor of their own will to power (Peter in Mark 8—"Get behind me, Satan," James and John in Mark 10, the crowd on Palm Sunday). Rather, it is safe to tell them that they shall see God because their purity of heart consists in willing the one thing they cannot will from the center—

Hallowed be *Thy* name
Thy kingdom come
Thy will be done

The enjoyment of God known to such pure hearts is authentic self-transcendence, and the God enjoyed is genuinely transcendent. Transcendence is an ethical category relating to the will, not an ontological category relating to being.

A normative concept of religious experience defined in terms of welcoming Mark's Jesus and learning to pray the prayer of his kingdom may seem too specific, even sectarian, to define religious as distinct from Christian experience. But the generic character of the concept is not compromised by the concreteness of the tradition through which it has been introduced. It is, for example, not difficult to show that the Brahman of the Hindu tradition and the Nirvana of the Buddhist tradition are wholly other in the sense we have now identified, for they confront me as an ethical claim that in both its ascetic and altruistic dimensions defines the false self as the will to be the center.

It would seem, then, that the concept of self-transcendence is useful beyond the biblical framework used here to render it concrete. It focuses attention on the ubiquitous challenge of religion to autonomous selfhood. It is not the task of this essay to spell out in detail the differences and similarities that emerge as the concept is employed across the spectrum of religious phenomena.

Rather the question is whether this generic concept of genuine religious self-transcendence takes us beyond the dangers of religious self-deception? Will it no longer be necessary to ask Nietzsche's question, "What did I really experience?"

Let us make the question even more concrete, returning to the tradition we know best. Suppose I am Thomas à Kempis, and that I offer the following prayer in all sincerity. "O Lord, Thou knowest what is the better way, let this or that be done, as Thou shalt please. Give what Thou wilt, and how much Thou wilt, and when Thou wilt. Deal with me as Thou knowest, and as best pleaseth Thee, and is most for Thy honour. Set me where Thou wilt, and deal, with me in all things just as Thou wilt. I am in Thy hand: turn me round, and turn me back again, even as a wheel. Behold, I am Thy servant, prepared for all things; for I desire not to live unto myself, but unto Thee; and O that I could do it worthily and perfectly" (1900: 127). Can we be confident that this prayer is offered to a truly transcendent God, rather than an idol, and that this prayer belongs to an experience of genuine self-transcendence?

Unfortunately not. We have already stipulated that these words are sincere. We can further stipulate that their sincerity is attested by the appropriate deeds. Our Thomas lives, let us say, an exemplary life of poverty, chastity and obedience. Still, we will be reminded, "However painstaking our work, so long as we omit to surrender ourselves to God while performing it…our efforts build up within us not so much a true spirit of grace but the spirit of a Pharisee" (Chariton, 1966: 137). But how could such words and deeds fail to express a decentering surrender of oneself to God?

The answer is simple. Sincerity is no guarantee against self-deception. Corresponding to the three idols whose transcendental deduction we noted earlier are three modes of religious experience which do not even have the form of true godliness, decentering self-transcendence. This piety, by contrast, has that form so conspicuously that it could be used as its paradigm. But that form may still be but appearance not supported by the reality it professes. Our Thomas may unconsciously be a hypocrite.

To see how this is possible let us recall *The Total Woman*. Perhaps like me you feel you have read this book even though you haven't. It suggests that the way to happiness for a woman is to subordinate herself entirely to the happiness of her lord and master. No, not God, but her husband. The combination of the theological claim that a radically hierarchical relation should exist between husband and wife with an emphasis on the wife's responsibility to keep the husband both sexually stimulated and satisfied, led Martin Marty to summarize his review in four words: fundies in their undies. Some years ago a student of mine wrote a review of this book which revealed the manipulative character of this conspicuous subordination. Again and again the book said, in so many words, Treat your husband as your lord and master and he'll be yours. You'll have no trouble keeping him for yourself or getting him to do what you want. You'll be in control.

The life of the total woman has the form of decentering self-transcendence, but not the substance. She may sincerely hold the beliefs and feel the emotions that her idea calls for, and she may perform a lifetime of sacrificial service for her husband. But this does not keep her from being self-deceived about what she has experienced, nor does it keep her devotion from being manipulative. What appears to her as subordination and service is in fact a complex web of strategic action in the service of her will to power. Secretly, and she keeps this secret even from herself, she is the center of her world.

Exactly the same may be true of our saintly Thomas à Kempis. The form of his piety is that of a decentering self-transcendence. Its inner content may or may not correspond. The form is visible, to others and to him. The content may be hidden from both. If it does not correspond and if he has managed not to notice this, he is self-deceived and the god he serves, so far from being genuinely transcendent, is not only constituted by his intentionality but also constructed by his (hidden) intentions. Such a god, so far from being "wholly other," is not so very damn other at all.

Given the multiple possibilities for self-deception, perhaps we can now see why self-transcendence is the task of a lifetime and why genuine transcendence is so elusive. And perhaps the current preoccupation with alterity among some philosophers is more the expression of hunger than of curiosity.

I want to suggest two conclusions for the philosophy of religion that seem to me to follow from these reflections. If this essay were addressed primarily to pastors or spiritual directors, I would address a very practical issue at this point. While the foregoing has shown, I hope, the need for suspicion and self-examination (since suspicion reduced to a tool for unmasking others becomes thereby a tool for sustaining our own self-deceptions), it has not mentioned the dangers this entails, dangers of morbidity, masochism, and cynicism. Since I do not want to draw too sharp a line between the pastoral and the philosophical, the therapeutic and the theoretical, I pause at least long enough to mention these issues.

But the two conclusions with which I want to conclude concern philosophy as theory. It may seem as if our phenomenological reflections have ignored one of the most intensely debated philosophical questions relating to religious experience, namely whether it can provide good reasons to support religious beliefs. But this is not so. Instead, the account of religious experience we have developed together would seem to place a major obstacle in the way of any positive answer to this question we might seek to develop. Our normative concept suggests that the intentional object of religious experience that lacks either the form or the substance of true godliness will be an idol of one sort or another. Such experience can hardly provide rational support for beliefs that purport to express the genuine transcendence of the truly divine. For religious experience to have any evidential value, it will first have to be shown to be authentic.

There are perhaps two reasons why this task has been conspicuously absent from most discussions. One is its obvious difficulty. The other is the principle of charity, the tendency to consider religious experience innocent until proven guilty. But neither of these is a good reason. An essential task becomes less essential because of its difficulty only in the presence of self-deceptive laziness. And no matter how wonderfully American it may sound, the innocent-until-proven-guilty principle simply ignores 1.) the biblical claim that "the heart is deceitful above all things, and desperately corrupt" (Jer. 17:9), 2.) the powerful theoretical analyses, only briefly developed in this essay, of self-deception whenever self-transcendence is at issue, and 3.) our own "thou art the man" experience in the presence of such analyses.

One way to put this point would be to say that religious experience cannot provide any evidence for truth as objectivity until it has passed the test of truth as subjectivity. This link between the hermeneutics of suspicion and questions of inwardness and authenticity leads to a second conclusion. It puts in question the wisdom of doing business as usual within the religious epistemology industry. No doubt reflection is and ought to be *ancilla vitae*. But when the philosophy of religion, on this issue or any other, so focuses on objectivity as to let issues of subjectivity get forgotten or rendered peripheral, it shows itself to be ancillary to the life of some objectivist culture, Hegelian, positivist, technocratic, or whatever, that is systematically prejudiced against religious experience in general and the life of Christian faith in particular. This fact, if it is indeed a fact, is deserving of more attention than it usually gets among Christians in philosophy.

Fordham University

Questions

1. Westphal sees Kierkegaard as adding an element to faith not found in either Augustine or Merton. What is it?

2. How does Husserl's treatment of intentionality "primarily as cognitive" help Westphal in giving account of "self-transcendence?"

3. How does the realism of G. E. Moore figure in Westphal's account of "intentional acts?"

4. Westphal thinks that C. S. Lewis fails to see something important with regard to transcendence. What is it? What do you make of Westphal's point?

5. How might the theist benefit from Westphal's understanding of the notion of self-transcendence?

Bibliography:

- Augustine (1963). *The Confessions of St. Augustine*. Trans. Rex Warner. New York: New American Library.
- Barth, Karl (1968). *The Epistle to the Romans*. Trans. Edwyn C. Hoskyns. New York: Oxford University Press.
- Breazeale, Daniel, trans. and ed. (1988). *Fichte: Early Philosophical Writings*. Ithaca, NY: Cornell University Press.
- Caputo, John D. (1987). *Radical Hermeneutics*. Bloomington, IN: Indiana University Press.
- Chariton of Valamo, Igumen, ed. (1966). *The Art of Prayer: An Orthodox Anthology*. Trans. E. Kadloubovsky and E. M. Palmer. London: Faber and Faber.
- Derrida, Jacques (1976). *Of Grammatology*. Trans. Gayatri Chakravorty Spivak. Baltimore, MD: Johns Hopkins University Press.
- Derrida, Jacques (1978). *Writing and Difference*. Trans. Alan Bass. Chicago: University of Chicago Press.
- Derrida, Jacques (1981). *Positions*. Trans. Alan Bass. Chicago: University of Chicago Press.
- Desmond, William (1987). *Desire, Dialectic, and Otherness*. New Haven, CT: Yale University Press.
- Edwards, Jonathan (1959). *A Treatise Concerning Religious Affections*. New Haven, CT: Yale University Press.
- Evans, Donald (1963). *The Logic of Self-Involvement*. London: SCM Press.
- Faulkner, William (1950). *Light in August*. New York: Random House.
- Gadamer, Hans-Georg (1975). *Truth and Method*. Trans. Garrett Barden and John Cumming. New York: Seabury Press.
- Habermas, Jurgen (1987). *The Philosophical Discourse of Modernity*. Trans. Frederick Lawrence. Cambridge, MA: The MIT Press.

- Hegel, G. W. F. (1949). *The Phenomenology of Mind*. Trans. J. B. Baillie. London: George Allen & Unwin.
- Hegel, G. W. F. (1959). *The Logic of Hegel*. Trans. William Wallace. Oxford: Oxford University Press. Reprinted from the second, revised edition, 1892.
- Hegel, G. W. F. (1969). *Hegel's Science of Logic*. Trans. A. V. Miller. London: George Allen & Unwin.
- Hume, David (1888). *A Treatise of Human Nature*. Oxford: Clarendon Press.
- Husserl, Edmund (1983). *Ideas Pertaining to a Pure Phenomenology and to a Phenomenological Philosophy*, First Book. Trans. F. Kersten. The Hague: Martinus Nijhoff.
- Kant, Immanuel (1960). *Religion Within the Limits of Reason Alone*. Trans. Theodore M. Greene and Hoyt H. Hudson. New York: Harper and Brothers.
- Kempis, Thomas à (1900). *Of the Imitation of Christ*. London: Oxford University Press.
- Kierkegaard, Søren (1941). *Concluding Unscientific Postscript*. Trans. David Swenson and Walter Lowrie. Princeton, NJ: Princeton University Press.
- Kierkegaard, Søren (1944). *Training in Christianity*. Trans. Walter Lowrie. Princeton, NJ: Princeton University Press.
- Kierkegaard, Søren (1980). *The Sickness Unto Death*. Trans. Howard V. Hong and Edna H. Hong. Princeton, NJ: Princeton University Press.
- Kojève, Alexandre (1969). *Introduction to the Reading of Hegel*. Trans. James H. Nichols, Jr. New York: Basic Books.
- Levinas, Emmanuel (1969). *Totality and Infinity*. Trans. Alfonso Lingis. Pittsburgh: Duquesne University Press.
- Lewis, C. S. (1961). *An Experiment in Criticism*. Cambridge: Cambridge University Press.
- Lewis, C. S. (1962). *The Problem of Pain*. New York: Macmillan.
- MacIntyre, C. F., trans. (1957). *Rainer Maria Rilke, Selected Poems*. Berkeley, CA: University of California Press.
- Marcel, Gabriel (1964). *Creative Fidelity*. Trans. Robert Rosthal. New York Farrar, Strauss and Company.
- Merton, Thomas (1972). *New Seeds of Contemplation*. New York: New Directions Books.
- Michelfelder, Diane P., and Palmer, Richard E. eds. (1989). *Dialogue and Deconstruction: The Gadamer-Derrida Encounter*. Albany, NY: State University of New York Press.
- Moore, G. E. (1953). *Some Main Problems of Philosophy*. London: George Allen and Unwin.
- Moore, G. E. (1959). *Philosophical Studies*. Patterson, NJ: Littlefield, Adams & Co.
- Nietzsche, Friedrich (1966a). *Beyond Good and Evil*. Trans. Waite Kaufmann. New York: Random House.
- Nietzsche, Friedrich (1966b). *Thus Spoke Zarathustra*. Trans. Waite Kaufmann. New York: Viking Press.
- Nietzsche, Friedrich (1967). *The Birth of Tragedy and The Case of Wagner*. Trans. Walter Kaufmann. New York: Random House.
- Nietzsche, Friedrich (1968). *The Will to Power*. Trans. Walter Kaufmann and R. J. Hollingdale. New York: Random House.

RELIGIOUS EXPERIENCE AND RELIGIOUS BELIEF

William P. Alston

In this essay Alston argues that religious experience can offer grounds for religious belief. When compared with the epistemology of sense experience, the epistemology of religious experience has the same epistemic status, notwithstanding justifiable differences. Valid experiences of the former include the criteria of verifiability and predictability, but the fact that God is wholly other stands in the way of these criteria applying to religious experience. He concludes the CP [Christian Epistemic Practice] has basically the same epistemic status as PP [Perceptual Practice] and that no one who subscribes to the latter is in any position to cavil at the former.

I

Can religious experience provide any ground or basis for religious belief? Can it serve to justify religious belief, or make it rational? This paper will differ from many others in the literature by virtue of looking at this question in the light of basic epistemological issues. Throughout we will be comparing the epistemology of religious experience with the epistemology of sense experience.

We must distinguish between experience directly, and indirectly, justifying a belief. It indirectly justifies belief B_1 when it justifies some other beliefs, which in turn justify B_1. Thus I have learned indirectly from experience that Beaujolais wine is fruity, because I have learned from experience that this, that, and the other bottle of Beaujolais is fruity, and these propositions support the generalization. Experience will directly justify a belief when the justification does not go through other beliefs in this way. Thus, if I am justified, just by virtue of having the visual experiences I am now having, in taking what I am experiencing to be a typewriter situated directly in front of me, then the belief that there is a typewriter directly in front of me is directly justified by that experience.

We find claims to both direct and indirect justification of religious beliefs by religious experience. Where someone believes that her new way of relating herself to the world after her conversion is to be explained by the Holy Spirit imparting supernatural graces to her, she supposes her belief *that the Holy Spirit imparts graces to her* to be indirectly justified by her experience. What she directly learns from experience is that she sees and reacts to things differently; this is then taken as a reason for supposing that the Holy Spirit is imparting graces to her. When, on the other hand, someone takes himself to be experiencing the presence of God, he thinks that his experience justifies him in supposing that God is *what* he is experiencing. Thus, he supposes himself to be directly justified by his experience in believing God to be present to him.

In this paper I will confine myself to the question of whether religious experience can provide direct justification for religious belief. This has implications for the class of experiences we shall be considering. In the widest sense 'religious experience' ranges over any experiences one has in connection with one's religious life, including any joys, fears, or longings one has in a religious context. But here I am concerned with experiences that could be taken to *directly* justify religious beliefs, i.e. experiences that give rise to a religious belief and that the subject takes to involve a direct awareness of what the religious belief is about. To further focus the discussion,

---

* Reprinted by permission of the author and of the editor of *Noûs*, Vol. 16 (1982): 3-12. Footnotes deleted.

let's confine ourselves to beliefs to the effect that God, as conceived in theistic religions, is doing something that is directed to the subject of the experience—that God is speaking to him, strengthening him, enlightening him, giving him courage, guiding him, sustaining him in being, or just being present to him. Call these "*M*-beliefs" ('*M*' for 'manifestation').

Note that our question concerns what might be termed a general "epistemic practice", the accepting of *M*-beliefs on the basis of experience, rather than some particular belief of that sort. I hold that practices, or habits, of belief formation are the primary subject of justification and that particular beliefs are justified only by issuing from a practice (or the activation of a habit) that is justified. The following discussion of concepts of justification will provide grounds for that judgment.

Whether *M*-beliefs can be directly justified by experience depends, *inter alia*, on what it is to be justified in a belief. So let us take a look at that.

First, the justification about which we are asking is an "epistemic" rather than a "moral" or "prudential" justification. Suppose one should hold that the practice in question is justified because it makes us feel good. Even if this is true in a sense, it has no bearing on epistemic justification. But why not? What makes a justification *epistemic*? Epistemic justification, as the name implies, has something to do with knowledge, or, more broadly, with the aim at attaining truth and avoiding falsity. At a first approximation, I am justified in believing that p when, from the point of view of that aim, there is something O.K., all right, to be approved, about that fact that I believe that p. But when we come to spell this out further, we find that a fundamental distinction must be drawn between two different ways of being in an epistemically commendable position.

On the one hand there is what we may call a "normative" concept of epistemic justification (J_n), "normative" because it has to do with how we stand *vis-à-vis* norms that specify our intellectual obligations, obligations that attach to one *qua* cognitive subject, *qua* truth-seeker. Stated most generally, J_n consists in one's not having violated one's intellectual obligations. We have to say "not having violated" rather than "having fulfilled" because in all normative spheres, being *justified* is a negative status; it amounts to ones behavior not being in violation of the norms. If belief is under direct voluntary control, we may think of intellectual obligations as attaching directly to believing. Thus one might be obliged to refrain from believing in the absence of adequate evidence. But if, as it seems to me, belief is not, in general, under voluntary control, obligations cannot attach directly to believing. However, I do have voluntary control over moves that can influence a particular belief formation, e.g., looking for more evidence, and moves that can affect my general belief forming habits or tendencies e.g., training myself to be more critical of testimony. If we think of intellectual obligations as attaching to activities that are designed to influence belief formation, we may say that a certain epistemic practice is normatively justified provided it is not the case that the practitioner would not have engaged in it had he satisfied intellectual obligations to engage in activities designed to inhibit it. In other words, the practice is justified if and only if the practitioner did not fail to satisfy an obligation to inhibit it.

However epistemologists also frequently use the term 'justified' in such a way that it has to do not with how the subject stands *vis-à-vis* obligations, but rather with the strength of her epistemic position in believing that p, with how likely it is that a belief of that sort acquired or held in that way is true. To say that a practice is justified in this, as I shall say, "evaluative" sense, (J_e) is to say that beliefs acquired in accordance with that practice, in the sorts of circumstances in which human beings typically find themselves, are generally true. Thus we might say that a practice is J_e if and only if it is reliable.

One further complication in the notion of Jt remains to be canvassed. What is our highest reasonable aspiration for being J_n in accepting a belief on the basis of experience? Being J_n no matter what else is the case? A brief consideration of sense perception would suggest a negative answer. I may be justified in believing that there is a tree in front of me by virtue of the fact that I am currently having a certain kind of sense experience, but this will be true only in "favorable circumstances." If I am confronted with a complicated arrangement of mirrors, I may not be: justified in believing that there is an oak tree in front of me, even though it looks for all the world as if there is. Again, it may look for all the world as if water is running uphill, but the general improbability of this greatly diminishes the justification the corresponding belief receives from that experience.

What this shows is that the justification provided by one's experience is only defeasibly so. It is inherently liable to be overridden, diminished, or cancelled by stronger considerations to the contrary. Thus the justification of beliefs about the physical environment that is provided by sense experience is a defeasible or, as we might say, *prima facie* justification. By virtue of having the experience, the subject is in a position such that she will be adequately justified in the belief *unless* there are strong enough reasons to the contrary.

It would seem that direct experiential justification for *M*-beliefs, is also, at most, *prima facie*. Beliefs about the nature and ways of God are often used to override *M*-beliefs, particularly beliefs concerning communications from God. If I report that God told me to kill all phenomenologists, fellow Christians will, no doubt, dismiss the report on the grounds that God would not give me any such injunction as that. I shall take it that both sensory experience and religious experience provide, at most, *prima facie* justification.

One implication of this stand is that a particular experiential epistemic practice will have to include some way of identifying defeaters. Different theistic religions, even different branches of the same religion, will differ in this regard, e.g., with respect to what sacred books, what traditions, what doctrines are taken to provide defeaters. We also find difference of this kind in perceptual practice. For example, with the progress of science new defeaters are added to the repertoire. Epistemic practices can, of course, be individuated with varying degrees of detail. To fix our thoughts with regard to the central problem of this paper let's think of a "Christian epistemic practice" *(CP)* that takes its defeaters from the Bible, the classic creeds, and certain elements of tradition. There will be differences between sub-segments of the community of practitioners so defined, but there will be enough commonality to make it a useful construct. My foil to *CP*, the practice of forming beliefs about the physical environment on the basis of sense-experience, I shall call "perceptual practice" *(PP)*.

Actually it will prove most convenient to think of each of our practices as involving not only the formation of beliefs on the basis of experience, but also the retention of these beliefs in memory, the formation of rationally self-evident beliefs, and various kinds of reasoning on the basis of all this. *CP* will be the richer complex, since it will include the formation of perceptual beliefs in the usual way, while *PP* will not be thought of as including the distinctive experiential practice of *CP*.

One final preliminary note. J_n is relative to a particular person's situation. If practice P_1 is quite unreliable, I may still be J_n in engaging in it either because I have no way of realizing its unreliability or because I am unable to disengage myself: while you, suffering from neither of these disabilities, are not J_n. When we ask whether a given practice is J_n, we shall be thinking about some normal, reasonably well informed contemporary member of our society.

II

Let's make use of all this in tackling the question as to whether one can be justified in *CP* and in *PP*. Beginning with J_n, we will first have to determine more precisely what one's intellectual obligations are *vis-à-vis* epistemic practices. Since our basic cognitive aim is to come into possession of as much truth as possible and to avoid false beliefs, it would seem that one's basic intellectual obligation *vis-à-vis* practices of belief formation would be to do what one can (or, at least, do as much as could reasonably be expected of one) to see to it that these practices are as *reliable* as possible. But this still leaves us with an option between a stronger and a weaker view as to this obligation. According to the stronger demand one is obliged to refrain (or try to refrain) from engaging in a practice unless one has adequate reasons for supposing it to be reliable. In the absence of sufficient reasons for considering the practice reliable, it is not justified. Practices are guilty until proved innocent. While on the more latitudinarian view one is justified in engaging in a practice provided one does not have sufficient reasons for regarding it to be unreliable. Practices are innocent until proved guilty. Let's take J_{ns} as an abbreviation for 'justified in the normative sense on the stronger requirement,' and 'J_{nw}' as an abbreviation for 'justified in the normative sense on the weaker requirement.'

Now consider whether Mr. Everyman is J_{nw} in engaging in *PP*. It would seem so. Except for those who, like Parmenides and Bradley, have argued that there are ineradicable inconsistencies in the conceptual scheme involved in *PP*, philosophers have not supposed that we can show that sense perception is not a reliable guide to our immediate surroundings. Skeptics about *PP* have generally confined themselves to arguing that we can't show that perception is reliable; i.e., they have argued that *PP* is not J_{ns}. I shall assume without further ado that *PP* is J_{nw}.

J_{ns} and J_e can be considered together. Although a practice may actually be reliable without my having adequate reasons for supposing so, and *vice versa*, still in considering whether a given practice is reliable, we will be seeking to determine whether there are adequate reasons for supposing it reliable, that is whether Everyman *could* be possessed of such reasons. And if we hold, as we shall, that there are no such reasons, the question of whether they are possessed by one or another subject does not arise.

I believe that there are no adequate noncircular reasons for the reliability of *PP* but I will not be able to argue that point here. If I had a general argument I would unveil it, but, so far as I can see, this thesis is susceptible only of inductive support, by unmasking each pretender in turn. And since this issue has been in the forefront of the Western philosophical consciousness for several centuries, there have been many pretenders. I do not have time even for criticism of a few representative samples. Instead I will simply assume that *PP* is not J_{ns}, and then consider what bearing this widely shared view has on the epistemic status of *CP*.

If J_{nw} is the most we can have for perceptual practice, then if *CP* is also J_{nw} it will be in at least as strong an epistemic position as the former. (I shall assume without argument that *CP* can no more be noncircularly shown to be reliable than can *PP*.) And *CP will* be J_{nw} for S, provided S has no significant reasons for regarding it as unreliable. Are there any such reasons? What might they be? Well, for one thing, the practice might yield a system that is ineradicably internally inconsistent. (I am not speaking of isolated and remediable inconsistencies that continually pop up in every area of thought and experience.) For another, it might yield results that come into ineradicable conflict with the results of other practices to which we are more firmly committed. Perhaps some fundamentalist Christians are engaged in an epistemic practice that can be ruled out on such grounds as these. But I shall take it as obvious that one *can* objectify certain stretches of one's experience, or indeed the whole of one's experience, in Christian terms without running into such difficulties.

III

One may grant everything I have said up to this point and still feel reluctant to allow that *CP is J_{nw}*. *CP* does differ from *PP* in important ways, and it may be thought that some of these differences will affect their relative epistemic status. The following features of *PP*, which it does not share with *CP*, have been thought to have this kind of bearing.

1. Within *PP* there are standard ways of checking the accuracy of any particular perceptual belief.

2. By engaging in *PP* we can discover regularities in the behavior of the objects putatively observed, and on this basis we can, to a certain extent, effectively predict the course of events.

3. Capacity for *PP*, and practice of it, is found universally among normal adult human beings.

4. All normal adult human beings, whatever their culture, use basically the same conceptual scheme in objectifying their sense experience.

If *CP* includes *PP* as a proper part, as I ruled on above, how can it lack these features? What I mean is that there is no analogue of these features for that distinctive part of *CP* by virtue of which it goes beyond *PP*. The extra element of *CP* does not enable us to discover extra regularities, e.g., in the behavior of God, or increase our predictive powers. *M*-beliefs are not subject to interpersonal check in the same way as perceptual beliefs. The practice of forming *M*-beliefs on the basis of experience is not engaged in by all normal adults. And so on.

Before coming to grips with the alleged epistemic bearing of these differences, I want to make two preliminary points. (1.) We have to engage in *PP* to determine that this practice has features 1.-4., and that *CP* lacks them. Apart from observation, we have no way of knowing that, e.g., while all cultures agree in their way of cognizing the physical environment they differ in their ways of cognizing the divine, or that *PP* puts us in a position to predict while *CP* doesn't. It might be thought that this is loading the dice in favor of my opponent. If we are to use *PP*, rather than some neutral source, to determine what features it has, shouldn't the same courtesy of self-assessment be accorded *CP?* Why should *it* be judged on the basis of what we learn about it from another practice, while that other practice is allowed to grade itself? To be sure, this is a serious issue only if answers to these questions *are* forthcoming from *CP* that differ from those we arrive at by engaging in *PP*. Fortunately, I can avoid getting involved in these issues by ruling that what I am interested in here is how *CP* looks from the standpoint of *PP*. The person I am primarily concerned to address is one who, like all the rest of us, engages in *PP*, and who, like all of us except for a few outlandish philosophers, regards it as justified. My aim is to show this person that, on his own grounds, *CP* enjoys basically the same epistemic status as *PP*. Hence it is consonant with my purposes to allow *PP* to determine the facts of the matter with respect to both practices. (2.) I could quibble over whether the contrast is as sharp as is alleged. Questions can be raised about both sides of the putative divide. On the *PP* side, is it really true that all cultures have objectified sense experience in the same way? Many anthropologists have thought not. And what about the idea that all *normal* adult human beings engage in the same perceptual practice? Aren't we loading the dice by taking participation in what we regard as standard perceptual practice as our basic criterion for normality? On the *CP* side, is it really the case that this practice reveals no regularities to us, or only that they are very different from regularities in the physical world? What about the Point that God is faithful to His promises? Or that the pure in heart will see God? However, I believe that when all legitimate quibbles have been duly registered there will still be very significant differences between the two practices in these respects. So rather than contesting the factual allegations, I will concentrate on the *de jure* issue as to what bearing these differences have on epistemic status.

How could the lack of 1.-4. prevent *CP* from being J_{nw}? Only by providing an adequate ground in a judgment of unreliability. And why suppose that? Of course, the lack of these features implies that we lack certain reasons we might conceivably have had for regarding *CP* as reliable. If we could ascertain that *PP* has those features, without using *PP* to do so, that would provide us with strong reasons for judging *PP* to be reliable. And the parallel possibility is lacking for *CP*. This shows that we cannot have *certain* reasons for taking *CP* to be reliable, but it doesn't follow that we have reasons for unreliability. That would follow only if we could also premise that a practice is reliable *only if* (as well as *if*) it has 1.-4. And why suppose that?

My position is that it is a kind of parochialism that makes the lack of 1.-4. appear to betoken untrustworthiness. The reality *CP* claims to put us in touch with is conceived to be vastly different from the physical environment. Why should the sorts of procedures required to put us in effective cognitive touch with this reality not be equally different? Why suppose that the distinctive features of *PP* set an appropriate standard for the cognitive approach to God? I shall sketch out a possible state of affairs in which *CP* is quite trustworthy while lacking 1.-4., and then suggest that we have no reason to suppose that this state of affairs does not obtain.

Suppose, then, that

(A) God is too different from created beings, too "wholly other," for us to be able to grasp any regularities in His behavior.

Suppose further that

(B) for the same reason we can only attain the faintest, sketchiest, and most insecure grasp of what God is like.

Finally, suppose that

(C) God has decreed that a human being will be aware of His presence in any clear and unmistakable fashion only when certain special and difficult conditions are satisfied.

If all this is the case, then it is the reverse of surprising that *CP* should lack 1.-4. even if it does involve a genuine experience of God. It would lack 1.-2. because of (A). It is quite understandable that it should lack 4. because of (B). If our cognitive powers are not fitted to frame an adequate conception of God, it is not at all surprising that there should be wide variation in attempts to do so. This is what typically happens in science when investigators are grappling with a phenomenon no one really understands. A variety of models, analogues, metaphors, hypotheses, hunches are propounded, and it is impossible to secure universal agreement. 3. is missing because of (C). If very difficult conditions are set it is not surprising that few are chosen. Now it is compatible with (A)-(C) that

(D) religious experience should, in general, constitute a genuine awareness of the divine

and that

(E) although any particular articulation of such an experience might be mistaken to a greater or lesser extent, indeed even though all such articulations might miss the mark to some extent, still such judgments will, for the most part, contain some measure of truth; they, or many of them, will constitute a useful approximation of the truth;

and that

(F) God's designs contain provision for correction and refinement, for increasing the accuracy of the beliefs derived from religious experience. Perhaps as one grows in the spiritual life ones spiritual sight becomes more accurate and more discriminating; perhaps some special revelation is vouchsafed under certain conditions; and there are many other conceivable possibilities.

If something like all this were the case then CP would be trustworthy even though it lacks features 1.-4. This is a conceivable way in which CP would constitute a road to the truth, while differing from PP in respects 1.-4. Therefore unless we have adequate reason for supposing that no such combination of circumstances obtains, we are not warranted in taking the lack of 1.-4. to be an adequate reason for a judgment of untrustworthiness.

Moreover it is not just that A.-C. constitute a bare possibility. In the practice of CP we seem to learn that this is the way things are. As for (A) and (B) it is the common teaching of all the higher religions that God is of a radically different order of being from finite substances and, therefore, that we cannot expect to attain the grasp of His nature and His doings that we have of worldly objects. As for (C), it is a basic theme in Christianity, and in other religions as well, that one finds God within one's experience, to any considerable degree, only as one progresses in the spiritual life. God is not available for *voyeurs*. Awareness of God, and understanding of His nature and His will for us, is not a purely cognitive achievement; it requires the involvement of the whole person; it takes a practical commitment and a practice of the life of the spirit, as well as the exercise of cognitive faculties.

Of course these results that we are using to defend CP are derived from that same practice. But in view of the fact that the favorable features of PP, 1.-4., are themselves ascertained by engaging in PP, our opponent is hardly in a position to fault us on this score. However I have not forgotten that I announced it as my aim to show that even one who engaged only in PP should recognize that CP is J_{nw}. For this purpose, I ignore what we learn in CP and revert to the point that my opponent has no basis for ruling out the conjoint state of affairs A.-F., hence has no basis for taking the lack of 1.-4. to show CP to be untrustworthy, and hence has no reason for denying that CP is J_{nw}.

I conclude that CP has basically the same epistemic status as PP and that no one who subscribes to the latter is in any position to cavil at the former.

Questions

1. Why does William Alston think that the epistemology of sense experience shares the same epistemic status with the epistemology of religious experience? Do you agree? If so why? If not, why not?

2. What does Alston mean by the claim that God is wholly other?

3. What is the "normative" concept of epistemic justification?

4. How does Alston characterize defeaters?

5. In what ways do you think Alston's discussion is helpful to the theist's cause?

Figure 3

Part III

Problems of Evil and Defensive Strategies

EVIL AND OMNIPOTENCE*

J. L. Mackie

In this essay Mackie argues that theists face a logical problem regarding their core of beliefs because the God of Christianity would not allow evil to exist. Since evil exists, God must not.

The traditional arguments for the existence of God have been fairly thoroughly criticized by philosophers. But the theologian can, if he wishes, accept this criticism. He can admit that no rational proof of God's existence is possible. And he can still retain all that is essential to his position, by holding that God's existence is known in some other, non-rational way. I think, however, that a more telling criticism can be made by way of the traditional problem of evil. Here it can be shown, not that religious beliefs lack rational support, but that they are positively irrational, that the several parts of the essential theological doctrine are inconsistent with one another, so that the theologian can maintain his position as a whole only by a much more extreme rejection of reason than in the former case. He must now be prepared to believe, not merely what cannot be proved, but what can be *disproved* from other beliefs that he also holds.

The problem of evil, in the sense in which I shall be using the phrase, is a problem only for someone who believes that there is a God who is both omnipotent and wholly good. And it is a logical problem, the problem of clarifying and reconciling a number of beliefs: it is not a scientific problem that might be solved by further observations, or a practical problem that might be solved by a decision or an action. These points are obvious; I mention them only because they are sometimes ignored by theologians, who sometimes parry a statement of the problem with such remarks as "Well, can you solve the problem yourself?" or "This is a mystery which may be revealed to us later" or "Evil is something to be faced and overcome, not to be merely discussed."

In its simplest form the problem is this: God is omnipotent; God is wholly good; and yet evil exists. There seems to be some contradiction between these three propositions, so that if any two of them were true the third would be false. But at the same time all three are essential parts of most theological positions: the theologian, it seems, at once *must* adhere and *cannot consistently* adhere to all three. (The problem does not arise only for theists, but I shall discuss it in the form in which it presents itself for ordinary theism.)

However, the contradiction does not arise immediately; to show it we need some additional premises, or perhaps some quasi-logical rules connecting the terms 'good,' 'evil,' and 'omnipotent.' These additional principles are that good is opposed to evil, in such a way that a good thing always eliminates evil as far as it can, and that there are no limits to what an omnipotent thing can do. From these it follows that a good omnipotent thing eliminates evil completely, and then the propositions that a good omnipotent thing exists, and that evil exists, are incompatible.

I. Adequate Solutions

Now once the problem is fully stated it is clear that it can be solved, in the sense that the problem will not arise if one gives up at least one of the propositions that constitute it. If you are prepared

---

* From *Mind*, Vol. LXIV, No. 254 (1955). Reprinted by permission of Oxford University Press.

to say that God is not wholly good, or not quite omnipotent, or that evil does not exist, or that good is not opposed to the kind of evil that exists, or that there are limits to what an omnipotent thing can do, then the problem of evil will not arise for you.

There are, then, quite a number of adequate solutions of the problem of evil, and some of these have been adopted, or almost adopted, by various thinkers. For example, a few have been prepared to deny God's omnipotence, and rather more have been prepared to keep the term 'omnipotence' but severely to restrict its meaning, recording quite a number of things that an omnipotent being cannot do. Some have said that evil is an illusion, perhaps because they held that the whole world of temporal, changing things is an illusion, and that what we call evil belongs only to this world, or perhaps because they held that although temporal things *are* much as we see them, those that we call evil are not really evil. Some have said that what we call evil is merely the privation of good, that evil in a positive sense, evil that would really be opposed to good, does not exist. Many have agreed with Pope that disorder is harmony not understood, and that partial evil is universal good. Whether any of these views is *true* is, of course, another question. But each of them gives an adequate solution of the problem of evil in the sense that if you accept it this problem does not arise for you, though you may, of course, have *other* problems to face.

But often enough these adequate solutions are only *almost* adopted. The thinkers who restrict God's power, but keep the term 'omnipotence' may reasonably be suspected of thinking, in other contexts, that his power is really unlimited. Those who say that evil is an illusion may also be thinking, inconsistently, that this illusion is itself an evil. Those who say that "evil" is merely privation of good may also be thinking, inconsistently, that privation of good is an evil. (The fallacy here is akin to some forms of the "naturalistic fallacy in ethics, where some think, for example, that "good" is just what contributes to evolutionary progress, and that evolutionary progress is itself good.) If Pope meant what he said in the first line of his couplet, that "disorder" is only harmony not understood, the "partial evil" of the second line must, for consistency, mean "that which, taken in isolation, falsely appears to be evil," but it would more naturally mean "that which, in isolation, really is evil." The second line, in fact, hesitates between two views, that "partial evil" isn't really evil, since only the universal quality is real, and that "partial evil" is really an evil, but only a little one.

In addition, therefore, to adequate solutions, we must recognize unsatisfactory inconsistent solutions, in which there is only a half-hearted or temporary rejection of one of the propositions which together constitute the problem. In these, one of the constituent propositions is explicitly rejected, but it is covertly re-asserted or assumed elsewhere in the system.

II. Fallacious Solutions

Besides these half-hearted solutions, which explicitly reject but implicitly assert one of the constituent propositions, there are definitely fallacious solutions which explicitly maintain all the constituent propositions, but implicitly reject at least one of them in the course of the argument that explains away the problem of evil.

There are, in fact, many so-called solutions which purport to remove the contradiction without abandoning any of its constituent propositions. These must be fallacious as we can see from the very statement of the problem, but it is not so easy to see in each case precisely where the fallacy lies. I suggest that in all cases the fallacy has the general form suggested above: in order to solve the problem one (or perhaps more) of its constituent propositions is given up, but in such a way that it appears to have been retained, and can therefore be asserted without qualification in other contexts. Sometimes there is a further complication: the supposed solution moves to and fro between, say, two of the constituent propositions, at one point asserting the first of these but covertly abandoning the second, at another point asserting the second but covertly abandoning the first. These fallacious solutions often turn upon some equivocation with the words 'good' and 'evil,' or upon some vagueness about the way in which good and evil are opposed to one another, or about how much is meant by 'omnipotence.' I propose to examine some of these so-called solutions, and to exhibit their fallacies in detail. Incidentally, I shall also be considering whether an adequate solution could be reached by a minor modification of one or more of the constituent propositions, which would, however, still satisfy all the essential requirements of ordinary theism.

(1) "Good cannot exist without evil" or "Evil is necessary as a counterpart to good."

It is sometimes suggested that evil is necessary as a counterpart to good, that if there were no evil there could be no good either, and that this solves the problem of evil. It is true that it points to an answer to the question "Why should there be evil?" But it does so only by qualifying some of the propositions that constitute the problem.

First, it sets a limit to what God can do, saying that God *cannot* create good without simultaneously creating evil, and this means either that God is not omnipotent or that there are *some* limits to what an omnipotent thing can do. It may be replied that these limits are always presupposed, that omnipotence has never meant the power to do what is logically impossible, and on the present view the existence of good without evil would be a logical impossibility. This interpretation of omnipotence may, indeed, be accepted as a modification of our original account which does not reject anything that is essential to theism, and I shall in general assume it in the subsequent discussion. It is, perhaps, the most common theistic view, but I think that some theists at least have maintained that God can do what is logically impossible. Many theists, at any rate, have held that logic itself is created or laid down by God, that logic is the way in which God arbitrarily chooses to think. (This is, of course, parallel to the ethical view that morally right actions are those which God arbitrarily chooses to command, and the two views encounter similar difficulties.) And *this* account of logic is clearly inconsistent with the view that God is bound by logical necessities—unless it is possible for an omnipotent being to bind himself, an issue which we shall consider later, when we come to the Paradox of Omnipotence. This solution of the problem of evil cannot, therefore, be consistently adopted along with the view that logic is itself created by God.

But, secondly, this solution denies that evil is opposed to good in our original sense. If good and evil are counterparts, a good thing will not "eliminate evil as far as it can." Indeed, this view suggests that good and evil are not strictly qualities of things at all. Perhaps the suggestion is that good and evil are related in much the same way as great and small. Certainly, when the term 'great' is used relatively as a condensation of 'greater than so-and-so,' and 'small' is used correspondingly, greatness and smallness are counterparts and cannot exist without each other. But in this sense greatness is not a quality, not an intrinsic feature of anything; and it would be absurd to think of a movement in favour of greatness and against smallness in this sense. Such a movement would be self-defeating, since relative greatness can be promoted only by a simultaneous promotion of relative smallness. I feel sure that no theists would be content to regard God's goodness as analogous to this—as if what he supports were not the *good* but the *better*, and if he had the paradoxical aim that all things should be better than other things.

This point is obscured by the fact that 'great' and 'small' seem to have an absolute as well as a relative sense. I cannot discuss here whether there is absolute magnitude or not, but if there is, there could be an absolute sense for 'great,' it could mean of at least a certain size, and it would make sense to speak of all things getting bigger, of a universe that was expanding all over, and therefore it would make sense to speak of promoting greatness. But in *this* sense great and small are not logically necessary counterparts: either quality could exist without the other. There would be no logical impossibility in everything's being small or in everything's being great.

Neither in the absolute nor in the relative sense, then, of 'great' and 'small' do these terms provide an analogy of the sort that would be needed to support this solution of the problem of evil. In neither case are greatness and smallness *both* necessary counterparts *and* mutually opposed forces or possible objects for support and attack.

It may be replied that good and evil are necessary counterparts in the same way as any quality and its logical opposite: redness can occur, it is suggested, only if non-redness also occurs. But unless evil is merely the privation of good, they are not logical opposites, and some further argument would be needed to show that they are counterparts in the same way as genuine logical opposites. Let us assume that this could be given. There is still doubt of the correctness of the metaphysical principle that a quality must have a real opposite: I suggest that it is not really impossible that everything should be, say, red, that the truth is merely that if everything were red we should not notice redness, and so we should have no word 'red'; we observe and give names to qualities only if they have real opposites. If so, the principle that a term must have an opposite would belong only to our language or to our thought, and would not be an ontological principle, and, correspondingly, the rule that good cannot exist without evil would not state a logical necessity of a sort that God would just have to put up with. God might have made everything good, though we should not have noticed it if he had.

But, finally, even if we concede that this is an ontological principle, it will provide a solution for the problem of evil only if one is prepared to say, "Evil exists, but only just enough evil to serve as the counterpart of good." I doubt whether any theist will accept this. After all, the *ontological* requirement that non-redness should occur would be satisfied even if all the universe, except for a minute speck, were red, and, if there were a corresponding requirement for evil as a counterpart to good, a minute dose of evil would presumably do. But theists are not usually willing to say, in all contexts, that all the evil that occurs is a minute and necessary dose.

(2) "Evil is necessary as a means to good."

It is sometimes suggested that evil is necessary for a good not as a counterpart but as a means. In its simple form this has little plausibility as a solution of the problem of evil, since it obviously implies a severe restriction of God's power. It would be a causal law that you cannot have a certain end without a certain means, so that if God has to introduce evil as a means to good, he must be subject to at least some causal laws. This certainly conflicts with what a theist normally means by omnipotence. This view of God as limited by *causal* laws also conflicts with the view that causal laws are themselves made by God, which is more widely held than the corresponding view about the laws of logic. This conflict would, indeed, be resolved if it were possible for an omnipotent being to bind himself, and this possibility has still to be considered. Unless a favorable answer can be given to this question, the suggestion that evil is necessary as a means to good solves the problem of evil only by denying one of its constituent propositions, either that God is omnipotent or that 'omnipotent' means what it says.

(3) "The universe is better with some evil in it than it could be if there were no evil."

Much more important is a solution which at first seems to be a mere variant of the previous one, that evil may contribute to the goodness of a whole in which it is found, so that the universe as a whole is better as it is, with some evil in it, than it would be if there were no evil. This solution may be developed in either of two ways. It may be supported by an aesthetic analogy, by the fact that contrasts heighten beauty, that in a musical work, for example, there may occur discords which somehow add to the beauty of the work as a whole. Alternatively, it may be worked out in connection with the notion of progress, that the best possible organization of the universe will not be static, but progressive, that the gradual overcoming of evil by good is really a finer thing than would be the eternal unchallenged supremacy of good. In either case, this solution usually starts from the assumption that the evil whose existence gives rise to the problem of evil is primarily what is called physical evil, that is to say, pain. In Hume's rather half-hearted presentation of the problem of evil, the evils that he stresses are pain and disease, and those who reply to him argue that the existence of pain and disease makes possible the existence of sympathy, benevolence, heroism, and the gradually successful struggle of doctors and reformers to overcome these evils. In fact, theists often seize the opportunity to accuse those who stress the problem of evil of taking a low, materialistic view of good and evil, equating these with pleasure and pain, and of ignoring the more spiritual goods which can arise in the struggle against evils. But let us see exactly what is being done here. Let us call pain and misery 'first order evil' or 'evil (1).' What contrasts with this, namely, pleasure and happiness, will be called 'first order good' or 'good (1).' Distinct from this is 'second order good' or 'good (2)' which somehow emerges in a complex situation in which evil (1) is a necessary component—logically not merely causally, necessary. (Exactly *how* it emerges does not matter: in the crudest version of this solution good [2] is simply the heightening of happiness by the contrast with misery, in other versions it includes sympathy with suffering, heroism in facing danger, and the gradual decrease of first order evil and increase of first order good.) It is also being assumed that second order good is more important than first order good or evil, in particular that it more than outweighs the first order evil it involves. Now this is a particularly subtle attempt to solve the problem of evil. It defends God's goodness and omnipotence on the ground that (on a sufficiently long view) this is the best of all logically possible worlds, because it includes the important second order goods, and yet it admits that real evils, namely first order evils, exist. But does it still hold that good and evil are opposed? Not, clearly, in the sense that we set out originally: good does not tend to eliminate evil in general. Instead, we have a modified, a more complex pattern. First order good (e.g. happiness) *contrasts with* first order evil (e.g. misery): these two are opposed in a fairly mechanical way; some second order goods (e.g. benevolence) try to maximize first order good and minimize first order evil; but God's goodness is not this, it is rather the will to maximize second order good. We might, therefore, call God's goodness an example of a third order goodness, or good (3). While this account is different from our original one, it might well be held to be an improvement on it, to give a more accurate description of the way in which good is opposed to evil, and to be consistent with the essential theist position. There might, however, be several objections to this solution.

First, some might argue that such qualities as benevolence—and *a fortiori* the third order goodness which promotes benevolence—have a merely derivative value, that they are not higher sorts of good, but merely means to good (1), that is, to happiness, so that it would be absurd for God to keep misery in existence in order to make possible the virtues of benevolence, heroism, etc. The theist who adopts the present solution must, of course, deny this, but he can do so with some plausibility, so I should not press this objection.

Secondly, it follows from this solution that God is not in our sense benevolent or sympathetic: he is not concerned to minimize evil (1), but only to promote good (2); and this might be a disturbing conclusion for some theists.

But, thirdly, the fatal objection is this. Our analysis shows clearly the possibility of the existence of a *second* order evil, an evil (2) contrasting with good (2) as evil (1) contrasts with good (1). This would include malevolence, cruelty, callousness, cowardice, and states in which good (1) is decreasing and evil (1) increasing. And just as good (2) is held to be the important kind of good, the kind that God is concerned to promote, so evil (2) will, by analogy, be the important kind of evil, the kind which God, if he were wholly good and omnipotent, would eliminate. And yet evil (2) plainly exists, and indeed most theists (in other contexts) stress its existence more than that of evil (1). We should, therefore, state the problem of evil in terms of second order evil, and against this form of the problem the present solution is useless.

An attempt might be made to use this solution again, at a higher level, to explain the occurrence of evil (2); indeed the next main solution that we shall examine does just this, with the help of some new notions. Without any fresh notions, such a solution would have little plausibility: for example, we could hardly say that the really important good was a good (3), such as the increase of benevolence in proportion to cruelty, which logically required for its occurrence the occurrence of some second order evil. But even if evil (2) could be explained in this way, it is fairly clear that there would be third order evils contrasting with this third order good: and we should be well on the way to an infinite regress, where the solution of a problem of evil, stated in terms of evil (n), indicated the existence of an evil ($n + 1$), and a further problem to be solved.

(4) "Evil is due to human freewill."

Perhaps the most important proposed solution of the problem of evil is that evil is not to be ascribed to God at all, but to the independent actions of human beings, supposed to have been endowed by God with freedom of the will. This solution may be combined with the preceding one: first order evil (e.g. pain) may be justified as a logically necessary component in second order good (e.g. sympathy) while second order evil (e.g. cruelty) is not *justified*, but is so ascribed to human beings that God cannot be held responsible for it. This combination evades my third criticism of the preceding solution.

The freewill solution also involves the preceding solution at a higher level. To explain why a wholly good God gave men freewill although it would lead to some important evils, it must be argued that it is better on the whole that men should act freely, and sometimes err, than that they should be innocent automata, acting rightly in a wholly determined way. Freedom that is to say, is now treated as a third order good, and as being more valuable than second order goods (such as sympathy and heroism) would be if they were deterministically produced, and it is being assumed that second order evils, such as cruelty, are logically necessary accompaniments of freedom, just as pain is a logically necessary precondition of sympathy.

I think that this solution is unsatisfactory primarily because of the incoherence of the notion of freedom of the will: but I cannot discuss this topic adequately here, although some of my criticisms will touch upon it.

First I should query the assumption that second order evils are logically necessary accompaniments of freedom. I should ask this: if God has made men such that in their free choices they sometimes prefer what is good and sometimes what is evil, why could he not have made men such that they always freely choose the good? If there is no logical impossibility in a man's freely choosing the good on one, or on several, occasions, there cannot be a logical impossibility in his freely choosing the good on every occasion. God was not, then, faced with a choice between making innocent automata and making beings who, in acting freely, would sometimes go wrong: there was open to him the obviously better possibility of making beings who would act freely but always go right. Clearly, his failure to avail himself of this possibility is inconsistent with his being both omnipotent and wholly good.

If it is replied that this objection is absurd, that the making of some wrong choices is logically necessary for freedom, it would seem that 'freedom' must here mean complete randomness or indeterminacy, including randomness with regard to the alternatives good and evil, in other words that men's choices and consequent actions can be "free" only if they are not determined by their characters. Only on this assumption can God escape the responsibility for men's actions; for if he made them as they are, but did not determine their wrong choices, this can only be because the wrong choices are not determined by men as they are. But then if freedom is randomness, how can it be a characteristic of *will*? And, still more, how can it be the most important good? What value or merit would there be in free choices if these were random actions which were not determined by the nature of the agent?

I conclude that to make this solution plausible two different senses of 'freedom' must be confused, one sense which will justify the view that freedom is a third order good, more valuable than other goods would be without it, and another sense, sheer randomness, to prevent us from ascribing to God a decision to make men such that they sometimes go wrong when he might have made them such that they would always freely go right.

This criticism is sufficient to dispose of this solution. But besides this there is a fundamental difficulty in the notion of an omnipotent God creating men with free will, for if men's wills are really free this must mean that even God cannot control them, that is, that God is no longer omnipotent. It may be objected that God's gift of freedom to men does not mean that he *cannot* control their wills, but that he always *refrains* from controlling their wills. But why, we may ask, should God refrain from controlling evil wills? Why should he not leave men free to will rightly, but intervene when he sees them beginning to will wrongly? If God could do this, but does not, and if he is wholly good, the only explanation could be that even a wrong free act of will is not really evil, that its freedom is a value which outweighs its wrongness, so that there would be a loss of value if God took away the wrongness and the freedom together. But this is utterly opposed to what theists say about sin in other contexts. The present solution of the problem of evil, then, can be maintained only in the form that God has made men so free that he *cannot* control their wills.

This leads us to what I call the Paradox of Omnipotence: can an omnipotent being make things which he cannot subsequently control? Or, what is practically equivalent to this, can an omnipotent being make rules which then bind himself? (These are practically equivalent because any such rules could be regarded as setting certain things beyond his control, and *vice versa*.) The second of these formulations is relevant to the suggestions that we have already met, that an omnipotent God creates the rules of logic or causal laws, and is then bound by them.

It is clear that this is a paradox: the questions cannot be answered satisfactorily either in the affirmative or in the negative. If we answer "Yes," it follows that if God actually makes things which he cannot control, or makes rules which bind himself, he is not omnipotent once he has made them: there are *then* things which he cannot do. But if we answer "No,' we are immediately asserting that there are things which he cannot do, that is to say that he is already not omnipotent.

It cannot be replied that the question which sets this paradox is not a proper question. It would make perfectly good sense to say that a human mechanic has made a machine which he cannot control: if there is any difficulty about the question it lies in the notion of omnipotence itself.

This, incidentally, shows that although we have approached this paradox from the free will theory, it is equally a problem for a theological determinist. No one thinks that machines have free will, yet they may well be beyond the control of their makers. The determinist might reply that anyone who makes anything determines its ways of acting, and so determines its subsequent behavior: even the human mechanic does this by his *choice* of materials and structure for his machine, though he does not know all about either of these: the mechanic thus determines, though he may not foresee, his machine's actions. And since God is omniscient, and since his creation of things is total, he both determines and foresees the ways in which his creatures will act. We may grant this, but it is beside the point. The question is not whether God *originally* determined the future actions of his creatures, but whether he can *subsequently* control their actions, or whether he was able in his original creation to put things beyond his subsequent control. Even on determinist principles the answers "Yes" and "No" are equally irreconcilable with God's omnipotence.

Before suggesting a solution of this paradox, I would point out that there is a parallel Paradox of Sovereignty. Can a legal sovereign make a law restricting its own future legislative power? For example, could the British parliament make a law forbidding any future parliament to socialize banking, and also forbidding the future repeal of this law itself? Or could the British parliament, which was legally sovereign in Australia in, say, 1899, pass a valid law, or series of laws, which made it no longer sovereign in 1933? Again, neither the affirmative nor the negative answer is really satisfactory. If we were to answer "Yes," we should be admitting the validity of a law which, if it were actually made, would mean that parliament was no longer sovereign. If we were to answer "No," we should be admitting that there is a law, not logically absurd, which parliament cannot validly make, that is, that parliament is not now a legal sovereign. This paradox can be solved in the following way. We should distinguish between first order laws, that is laws governing the actions of individuals and bodies other than the legislature, and second order laws, that is laws about laws, laws governing the actions of the legislature itself. Correspondingly, we should distinguish two orders of sovereignty, first order sovereignty (sovereignty (1)) which is unlimited authority to make first order laws, and second order sovereignty (sovereignty (2)) which is unlimited authority to make second order laws. If we say that parliament is sovereign we might mean that any parliament at any time has sovereignty (1), or we might mean that parliament has both sovereignty (1) and sovereignty (2) at present, but we cannot without contradiction mean both that the present parliament has sovereignty (2) and that every parliament at every time has sovereignty (1), for if the present parliament has sovereignty (2) it may use it to take away the sovereignty (1) of later parliaments. What the paradox shows is that we cannot ascribe to any continuing institution legal sovereignty in an inclusive sense.

The analogy between omnipotence and sovereignty shows that the paradox of omnipotence can be solved in a similar way. We must distinguish between first order omnipotence (omnipotence (1)), that is unlimited power to act, and second order omnipotence (omnipotence (2)), that is unlimited power to determine what powers to act things shall have. Then we could consistently say that God all the time has omnipotence (1), but if so no beings at any time have powers to act independently of God. Or we could say that God at one time had omnipotence (2), and used it to assign independent powers to act to certain things, so that God thereafter did not have omnipotence (1). But what the paradox shows is that we cannot consistently ascribe to any continuing being omnipotence in an inclusive sense.

An alternative solution of this paradox would be simply to deny that God is a continuing being that any times can be assigned to his actions at all. But on this assumption which also has difficulties of its own no meaning can be given to the assertion that God made men with wills so free that he could not control them. The paradox of omnipotence can be avoided by putting God outside time but the freewill solution of the problem of evil cannot be saved in this way and equally it remains impossible to hold that an omnipotent God binds himself by causal or logical laws.

Conclusion

Of the proposed solutions of the problem of evil which we have examined none has stood up to criticism. There may be other solutions which require examination but this study strongly suggests that there is no valid solution of the problem which does not modify at least one of the constituent propositions in a way which would seriously affect the essential core of the theistic position.

Quite apart from the problem of evil the paradox of omnipotence has shown that God's omnipotence must in any case be restricted in one way or another that unqualified omnipotence cannot be ascribed to any being that continues through time. And if God and his actions are not in time can omnipotence or power of any sort be meaningfully ascribed to him?

Questions

1. J.L.Mackie thinks that the theist faces a logical problem. What is it?
2. How does Mackie view giving up one of the beliefs held as a way out of the alleged difficulty for the theist?
3. What do you think of the revision–of–belief proposal?
4. What does Mackie think of the free will defense?
5. What do you think of Mackie's challenge to theism? What follows if the theist cannot answer Mackie's challenge in any helpful way?

CAN THE THEIST REFUSE TO ANSWER THE PROBLEM OF EVIL?*

Robin Le Poidevin

Le Poidevin examines several alternative ways of responding to the problem of evil for the believer, first, the approach which offers a full defense for the believer to the challenge based on evil, and the second which avoids this task altogether. He opines that the latter leaves the apologetic cupboard bare and leaves the Christian with a set of religious option that is unintelligible.

We have asked the question, 'Can suffering be justified on the theist picture?' I now want to ask, '*Should* it be justified?' Some theists believe that attempted justifications of suffering are, in a sense, complacent: they trivialize, or at best underplay, the degree of suffering in the world. The horrors of religious persecution under the Spanish Inquisition or in the reign of Mary I, the genocide of Hitler's regime, Stalin's treatment of the kulaks—these are simply too horrible to be explained away as the necessary, though regrettable, side-effects of the attainment of some greater good. Such theists take the view that it is a mistake to attempt to justify such suffering. We should, rather, trust to God that there is a reason for it which we simply cannot grasp. If belief in God is a matter of simple faith, not rational argument, then so too is the belief that God intends the best for us. The fact that we are beset by paradoxes when we try to reason about God is only evidence of our limited capacities, not of the fundamentally flawed nature of theism.

Before we ask whether this position is coherent, we should briefly explore a middle position between offering a full justification of suffering and avoiding the problem of evil altogether. We can distinguish between merely *explaining* suffering and *justifying* it. The theist can attempt to explain suffering by attributing it to the effects of free human action. This does not, however, justify it. To justify suffering, the theist needs to fit it into a view of God's purposes. The distinction, however, leaves open the possibility that explanation outruns justification. The theist who appeals to free will need not justify the worst excesses of human cruelty, in terms of the place it has in God's scheme of things, in order to explain why, in a world created by a loving God, there is such cruelty. The position the theist adopts will be that God is not responsible for these excesses, but any attempt by God to prevent them would be an infringement of human freedom. The discussion of the previous section, however, suggested that this middle position is not tenable. If we are compatibilists, then we will believe that our freedom is *not* infringed by God's determination of our action, so if God does not prevent suffering there must be some justification for it. If, on the other hand, we are incompatibilists, then the moral agent is completely independent of God—a view which is not at all congenial to theism. The theist, therefore, must believe that there is a justification of suffering, even if we have no access to that justification.

We should concede at the outset that the believer is not required to be a philosopher. It is no criticism of someone's faith that they cannot produce a watertight intellectual defense of their belief. Even in the absence of such rational support, their faith may be of the purest and most sincere kind. As we noted in the Introduction, it is an important issue, and one to which we shall return, whether rational justification is at all appropriate in a religious context. But, at

---

* This article is reprinted by courtesy of the author and publisher. It is from *Arguing for Atheism, An Introduction to the Philosophy of Religion,* by Robin Le Poidevin, Routledge, 1996.

the moment, we are engaged with a specific kind of believer, the putatively rational theist, whose faith is in part an attempt to answer intellectual problems of the 'why does anything exist?' kind, and also in part an attempt to account for objective moral values. Such a theist will understand the challenge of the problem of evil, and a refusal to answer the problem is not to be construed as the expression of a simple faith which does not look for rational justification, but a rational defense of what is taken to be a rational belief. If we can locate any inconsistency, or tension, within this defense, then we will have shown that this particular kind of theist is irrational.

There does, at least at first sight, appear to be an inconsistency in this approach to (or rather, retreat from) the problem of evil. On the one hand it is maintained that any attempted justification belittles suffering. This would seem to imply that, since suffering must be taken seriously, it has no justification. But, on the other hand, it is also maintained that suffering is not gratuitous: if we understood God's purposes, we would understand why there is—has to be —so much suffering in the world. Now this seems to imply that suffering *does* have a justification. So suffering both is, and is not, justified.

To get rid of the inconsistency, the theist's position may be further clarified as follows: the attempt to make suffering intelligible to limited, human intelligence inevitably belittles suffering. Nevertheless, were we to look at the matter from God's perspective (which we cannot do, even in principle), we would see that suffering *was* justified. We know this, because a loving God would not, without good reason, permit atrocious and gratuitous suffering.

This certainly removes the inconsistency, but at a high cost. As with certain approaches to human freedom, discussed in the previous section, a discrepancy has been introduced between the human perspective on things, and the divine perspective. Surely the whole point of the theistic outlook is the attempt to see things from God's point of view, and to free ourselves from the illusory perspective we are forced to adopt while immersed in the ephemera of human affairs. If it is impossible to adopt the divine perspective, then theism has nothing to tell us about the world and our place in it. But perhaps the most serious objection to this approach to the problem of evil is that it involves an admission that theism is irrational. Since this is a serious charge, I need to say something about what is involved in irrational belief.

The word 'rational' can be used in two quite different senses, an *external* sense and an *internal* sense. We sometimes say that belief in, say, astrology, is irrational. What we mean by this is that astrology conflicts with a 'scientific' picture of human personality. Now, if someone ignorant, or skeptical, of this scientific account persists in accepting astrological explanations, then the description of them as 'irrational' would be using the word in the external sense, meaning that their belief conflicts with some public, external, standard of acceptable thought. We might suggest that the alchemists were irrational, without wanting to imply that their standards of rational thought were the same as ours and that, by their own lights, they failed to match up to those standards. When someone is described as irrational in the internal sense, however, what is meant is that something has gone wrong in the way in which they have processed some information. For example, imagine someone learning of some personal catastrophe. Because the contemplation of the event is so awful, he persuades himself, perhaps unconsciously, that the event did not really happen, and so is guilty of self-deception. No one thinks that self-deception is the way to acquire true beliefs, but some people nevertheless manage to deceive themselves. Such people fail to live up to their own standards of rationality: they are irrational by their own lights. If it turned out that the alchemists held beliefs which should not have survived their own standards of rationality, then we would be justified in describing them as irrational in the internal sense. A charge of internal irrationality is more serious than a charge of external rationality, because there is less excuse, if we can put it that way, for failing to apply one's own standards than for failing to apply someone else's.

Theists are often accused of irrationality by atheists. Now, if the accusation is that theists are irrational in the external sense, then theists have a comeback: they may question the standards of rationality adopted by the atheist, or the application of those standards to theistic belief. Much more serious is the accusation of *internal* irrationality, because this would be a problem intrinsic to theism. What I want to suggest is that theists who refuse to answer the problem of evil are guilty of internal irrationality, at least if they hold the following beliefs:

1. Belief in a loving creator is intellectually defensible.
2. We cannot solve the problem of evil; that is, we cannot explain how the existence and nature of suffering can be consistent with the existence of a loving creator.

Now, if, from the human perspective, belief in a loving creator cannot be squared with the presence of suffering, then it is simply not rational to continue to hold on to that belief. It is simply irrelevant that we can imagine *another* perspective in which there is no inconsistency between suffering and a loving creator. After all, we can imagine another perspective in which alchemy, or astrology, does not conflict with standards of rational thought: astrologers (presumably) are not irrational from their own perspectives. But, unless we are relativists, that is a reason for us to reject those perspectives as mistaken. Similarly, if, from our perspective, there is no justification for suffering, then that is a reason to reject, as mistaken, any perspective (including God's) in which there is a justification for suffering. If it turned out that, from God's perspective, any amount of human suffering is perfectly acceptable, that would be a horrible discovery to make. We simply could not go on believing that God was genuinely benevolent, at least as we conceive of benevolence. So, if we believe that theism can only be entertained if it is rational, and we believe that we cannot produce a satisfactory justification of suffering in terms of God's purposes, then we must reject theism. If the theist admits to (2), then (1) must be given up.

We shall end the chapter by citing an instance of the tension between beliefs (1) and (2), as it arises in the context of the teleological argument. The theist who believes the doctrine to be intellectually defensible may advance the teleological argument, if not as a foolproof argument against atheism, at least as a consideration which makes theism highly attractive. The argument might be put in terms of a challenge to the atheist: what explanation can you offer of the order in the world which is as simple and satisfying as an explanation in terms of a benevolent deity? The universe is indeed ordered, the atheist might reply, but it also contains evil, and if you are looking for the best explanation of the universe you must take into account the presence of evil no less than the presence of order. This makes it far harder to infer the existence of a benevolent deity. A refusal to answer the problem of evil, then, considerably weakens the force of the challenge posed by the teleological argument. This was noted, and expressed with characteristic vividness, by Hume in the *Dialogues Concerning Natural Religion,* through the mouth of his character Philo:

> I will allow that pain or misery in man is compatible with infinite power and goodness in the Deity...what are you advanced by all these concessions? A mere possible compatibility is not sufficient. You must prove these pure, unmixt, and uncontrollable attributes from the present mixed and confused phenomena, and from these alone. A hopeful undertaking! Were the phenomena ever so pure and unmixed, yet, being finite, they would be insufficient for that purpose. How much more, where they are also so jarring and discordant!
>
> (Hume 1779, Part X)

Summary

The problem discussed in this chapter was the problem of reconciling the existence of a benevolent deity with the presence of evil in the world. If God intends us to suffer, then it seems he cannot be benevolent. On the other hand, if he does not intend us to suffer, then he is ineffective. Two strategies in dealing with this problem were examined: (a) the theist can try to distance God from direct responsibility for suffering by treating it as a consequence of the acts of free human agents; alternatively, (b) the theist can simply refuse to answer the problem on the ground that, although it must in God's eyes be justified, any attempted justification which we could produce simply trivializes suffering.

At first sight, (a) seems a promising strategy because it is plausible to suppose both that God wishes to create objects for his benevolence, and that he wishes such creatures to be genuinely free and not just automata. However, to understand (a) we need to be provided with an account of human freedom and its relation to determinism, the view that every state of the universe is fixed by some antecedent state. Two positions on this issue were defined: *compatibilism,* which holds that freedom is reconcilable with determinism, and *incompatibilism,* which holds that freedom cannot be reconciled with determinism. Here, however, we faced a dilemma. If we adopt compatibilism, then we admit that God could have created free agents while still determining our every action. But the question would then arise why God did not so determine things that we would avoid those acts which lead to unnecessary suffering. If, on the other hand, we adopt incompatibilism, then God could only create free agents by creating agents whose actions are uncaused. Apart from the obscurity of this idea, which involves the paradox of God's causing it to be the case that some things are uncaused, it is in tension with the theistic belief that we can only do certain things through God's help.

The trouble with strategy (b) is that it threatens to make theism irrational. On the one hand, it is admitted that we cannot solve the problem of suffering, and that we are therefore unable to reconcile the obvious fact of suffering with belief in a benevolent God, and yet, on the other hand, we are supposed to hold on to belief in a benevolent God on the grounds that there is a justification for suffering which nevertheless is inaccessible to us. The question is whether we can be justified in assuming that there is such a justification. But we can only be justified in making this assumption if we are justified in our belief that there does exist a benevolent deity. But this is precisely what the problem of suffering casts into doubt. If theism is supposed to be a rationally defensible belief, this position is simply unintelligible.

Further Reading

There are numerous discussions of the problem of evil. For a guide to the problem and a selection of essays on the topic, see Marilyn McCord Adams and Robert Merrihew Adams (eds), *The Problem of Evil,* Oxford: Oxford University Press, 1990.

Hume's striking presentation of the problem can be found in Part X of his *Dialogues Concerning Natural Religion*, ed. J.C.A. Gaskin, Oxford: Oxford University Press, 1993.

Examples of the attempt to reconcile suffering with the benevolence of God in terms of human freedom can be found in Basil Mitchell's *The Justification of Religious Belief*, London: Macmillan, 1973, and Richard Swinburne's *The Existence of God*, Oxford: Clarendon Press, 1979. Swinburne's account is criticized in Richard Gale's *On the Nature and Existence of God*, New York: Cambridge University Press, 1991.

For a helpful introduction to the issue of freedom and determinism, see Gary Watson (ed.), *Free Will*, Oxford: Oxford University Press, 1982.

Questions

1. Do you think that the Christian theist has to respond in a clear and decisive way to the problem of evil as Le Poidevin formulates it?

2. What sort of justification for evil do you think holds promise? Why?

3. Do you think that someone who holds to a fideist point of view would be concerned to respond to Le Poidevin?

4. Why do you suppose that Le Poidevin gives any consideration to the option that the theist not respond to the problem of evil challenge?

5. What do you think is Le Poidevin's most serious charge against the theist based on evil, and why?

THE GREATER GOOD DEFENSE

Keith E. Yandell

Keith Yandell attempts to establish three theses: (1) that the orthodox theist is committed to some version of the greater good defense; (2) that the defense cannot be limited to polemic contexts; (3) that acceptance of the defense is not unreasonable.

I hope to establish three theses in the argument that follows: first, that the orthodox theist is committed to the truth of some version of a greater good defense; second, that the theist's use of the greater good defense cannot consistently be limited to polemic contexts in which the defense is viewed as merely a logically consistent set of propositions; third, that acceptance of the greater good defense is not unreasonable. The second thesis is an obvious consequence of the first, and my reason for noting it separately will appear shortly.

I

The orthodox theist is committed to the truth of at least these claims:

(1) God exists, and is an all-knowing, all-powerful, all-good Creator and Providence;
(2) There is evil in the world.

As I understand the theistic tradition, (1) is to be understood along the following lines. *God is all-powerful* entails, and is entailed by, *For any proposition P, if P is consistent, and 'God makes P true' is consistent, then God can in fact make P true. God is all-knowing* entails, and is entailed by, *For any proposition P, if it is logically possible that P be known, and that God know that P, then God does in fact know that P. God is all-good* entails (among other things) that *God wills that each man attain his greatest good. God is Creator* entails (and *perhaps* is entailed by) *Everything else depends for its existence on God, but not conversely* and *God is providential* entails (among other things) *God controls the course of history so that each man has maximal opportunity to attain his greatest good.*

As I understand the theistic tradition, (2)—that there is evil in the world—is what gives point to talk of repentance and forgiveness, judgement and mercy, damnation and redemption, and hell and heaven. Central, then, if not exhaustive among the evils with which this tradition is concerned are those which seem to frustrate, or actually do frustrate, man's attaining the greatest good available to him, for it is after all the forgiveness, redemption, and attainment of heaven by men which is most in view in theistic thinking and preaching. That man is created in the image of God and that his good is gained through (or compromised by) his imitation of God are basic themes in this context. It seems, then, a relevant (if perhaps partial) theistic characterization of evil to say that anything which frustrates (either prevents or diminishes) a man's attainment of his greatest good is evil. To the degree a man's own free actions and choices frustrate his self-attainment, he is evil. If God brings about, or allows, something to occur which frustrates such development, except insofar as permitting men to frustrate their own development is required for the existence of moral agency, or insofar as such frustration is just punishment, He is not all-good.

---

* *Sophia*, October 1974, Essay III.

I include this very incomplete analysis of a theistic view of the nature of evil for two reasons. For one thing, it serves as a reminder that theism *has* a doctrine of good and evil—one which is relevant to the meaning of *God is all-good* and to the *problem* of evil. For another, this analysis indicates the necessity of, and provides content for, the greater good defense.

Of course it has at times been denied that theism has any ethic, or at any rate any ethic which provides positive meaning to *God is all-good*. Notoriously, negative theology (remarkably tenacious in both Eastern and Western philosophic and religious thought) has made this denial, contending that no proposition of the form *God is* ϕ (where ϕ is any "positive" property at all) is intelligible. For this viewpoint, that God is all-knowing entails that He is not impotent, but not (say) that He can move a mountain. But in a context where *God is not impotent* does not entail *God is potent*, the meaningfulness of *both* propositions is surely open to question. A consequence of this is that (say) *God is just* is not any longer true (or false either). Whatever one thinks of the motivations, philosophical or otherwise, of this view, one thing is clear: if "just" means (at least substantially) the same thing with respect to both Creator and creature, that God is just will involve (what after all Biblical authors affirm) that God is not partial to some, rendering judgment differently in relevantly similar cases, but is fair to all, and so on. That God is just does not involve these things for the negative theologian. What happens to "good" and "just" on this view happens to *all* moral (and non-moral predicates, and so the resultant view is that while God has no vices He has (so far as we can say) no virtues either. Imitation of God is hence impossible. Why worship, or even respect, toward God should remain becomes altogether puzzling, for God the Creator and Providence and Husband of Israel and Father of Jesus Christ becomes the Cosmic Unknown; and it is hard to know how to behave toward cosmic unknowns.

Returning to the main course of the argument, we have seen that the theist accepts (1) and (2). How is this related to the greater good defense? Given (1) and (2), it seems clear that for a theist whatever evil God creates or permits will be justified in the sense that God has a morally sufficient reason for creating or allowing it. Indeed, I take it that *God is good* entails *Insofar as He can God creates or allows no evil which He has no morally sufficient reason for creating or allowing*. But given God's existence and properties, everything that exists—and so everything that is evil—is quite under His control, being created or permitted by an omnicompetent God. So: (3) *Every evil is such that God has a morally sufficient reason for creating or allowing it*. And anyone who holds that (4) *Some evil exists for which there is no morally sufficient reason*, will, if consistent, deny (1), for:

(2) There is evil in the world.

Not—(3) Not every evil is such that God has a morally sufficient reason for creating or allowing it.

So: not—(1) God does not exist or is not an all-knowing, all-powerful, all-good Creator and Providence

is a valid argument. The theist, as indicated, accepts (1) and (2). He thus accepts (3), since (1) and (2) entail (3). So he rejects not—(3). The critic accepts (2), but also thinks that not—(3) is true. So he rejects (1).

The theist, then accepts:

(3) *Every evil is such that God has a morally sufficient reason for creating or allowing it.*

This not yet the greater good defense. That defense consists of a single though complex proposition. So we must state that proposition and see how it may be derived from (3).

Some evils are related to certain goods, by logical necessity. Thus *Andrew is courageous* entails *Andrew has conquered fear.* If fear is an evil, and courage a virtue (and so a good), then necessarily this virtue exists only if evil exists. It is, of course, only *some fear or other*, not any particular fear, that is entailed. The grounds for regarding fear as an evil are, I take it, that if someone could prevent or eliminate fear on the part of another, and does not, having no morally sufficient reason, then he is morally culpable. The same holds for *producing* fear. A man might escape moral culpability for producing, not preventing, or not eliminating an evil due to ignorance or impotence, or because he knew the evil would produce a justifying good. Only this last escape from culpability is available to an omnicompetent being.

An evil which is related to a good by logical necessity is not therefore justified by that good in the sense that a being who could prevent the evil and did not is not culpable. For the good might be of insufficient value—it might neither counterbalance nor overbalance the evil. So an evil E open to greater-good treatment is such that: (a) there is a good G such that G *exists* entails that E *exists,* and (b) G at least counterbalances E. A good G counterbalances an evil E if and only if G *exists* entails E *exists* and if an agent who creates or permits E for the sake of G performs a morally neutral action (is neither praiseworthy nor blameworthy). A good G overbalances an evil E if and only if G *exists* entails E *exists* and an agent who creates or permits G for the sake of E is thereby morally praiseworthy. That God is all-good presumably entails that He is praiseworthy, and that He is providential presumably entails that He acts in a praiseworthy or morally good manner with respect to men. So the greater good defense can be expressed thusly:

(4) Every evil is logically necessary to some good which either counterbalances or overbalances it, and some evil is overbalanced by the good to which it is logically necessary.

Alternatively, since E overbalances G if and only if G entails E and an agent who created or permitted E for the sake of G is thereby morally blameworthy, the greater good defense may be expressed via:

(4') Every evil is logically necessary to some good, some evil is overbalanced by some good to which it is logically necessary, and *no* evil overbalances the good to which it is logically necessary.

But I will stick to the formulation embodied in (4). How, then, do we get from (3) to (4), and what exactly does (4)—the greater good defense—amount to?

Unless we make explicit appeal to the (admittedly rather general) characterizations of *God is all-good* and *God is providential* offered above, the trip from (3) to (4) is tautologically short. For (3) says that for whatever evil He allows God has a morally sufficient reason. Ringing the changes on "morally sufficient reason", we may rephrase (3) as:

(3a) Every evil God allows is such that He is morally praiseworthy or morally neither praiseworthy nor blameworthy for so doing, and there is some evil such that He is morally praiseworthy for allowing it.

Or. (3b) No evil God allows is such that He is morally blameworthy for allowing it, and there is some evil such that He is morally praiseworthy for allowing it.

But the difference between (3a) and (4), or between (3b) and (4'), is (so far as I can see) the same as that between (3), (3a) and (3b), or between (4) and (4'); that is, the difference is purely verbal. If so, the move from (3) to (4) is trivial.

But if we make explicit appeal to the meaning of *God is all-good and providential,* (4) is not simply (3) recycled. For then (4) says what is more explicitly put as:

(5) Every evil that God allows is logically necessary to some at least counterbalancing good state of affairs, and some evil is overbalanced by the good to which it is logically necessary, where one applicable criterion for a state of affairs being good is that it furthers the growth to moral maturity of some moral agent, and where the evils occurring to each agent are so arranged as to provide him maximal opportunity for moral maturity.

And the inference from (3) to (4), where (4) is taken to be identical to (5), will require this (or some similar) pattern of thought:

1. (3) Every evil is such that God has a morally sufficient reason for creating or allowing it. (from (1) and (2)).
2. God wills that each man attain his greatest good. (entailed by *God is all-good*).
3. Man's greatest good is his realization of his capacities as one made in the *imago dei* and one who is to act always in *imitatio dei*. (Part One of an outline interpretation of theistic ethics.)
4. God controls the course of history so that each man has maximal opportunity to attain his greatest good. (entailed by *God is providential*).
5. Logically necessary conditions of attaining moral maturity are: (a) free moral agency, where an agent *A* is free with respect to a choice *x or not-x* if and only if *A* can in fact choose *x* or choose *not-x;* (b) the existence of states of affairs which are evil (in the sense that it would be blameworthy to allow them without morally sufficient reason) and which are logically necessary to states of affairs which are both good (in the sense of being virtues which comprise, or are logically necessary to, mature moral character) and at least counterbalancing. (Part Two of an outline interpretation of theistic ethics.)
6. Some good overbalances the evil to which it is logically necessary. (entailed by the theistic claim that God's creation of men is a good state of affairs).

So: 7. (5) Every evil that God allows is logically necessary to some at least counterbalancing state of affairs, and some evil is overbalanced by the good to which it is logically necessary, where one applicable criterion for a state of affairs being good is that it furthers the growth to moral maturity of some moral agent, and where the evils occurring to each agent are so arranged as to provide him maximal opportunity for moral maturity.

Now plainly (1-7) is roughly hewn; there are plenty of loose ends, uninvestigated consequences, and undefended assumptions. While I cannot pretend here to tie everything neatly together, I think it worthwhile to serially note several points relevant to that large and difficult task:

(a) While of course a theist might object to the outline reading of theistic ethics offered above, *some* interpretation of "good" is requisite if (4) (or (3)) is maintained. It is indeed logically possible for someone to know a proposition of the form *x is ϕ* is true without knowing what ϕ means (e.g., I might know, on the basis of being told by an expert, that some particles have negative energy without knowing what "negative energy" means). So it is possible that one know that God is good without knowing what "good" means. Or one can know that "good" means, say "of positive moral value" without knowing what *is* of positive moral value. But the theist is, I think, not in a position to stay at this aloof level. Theistic theology and life style, its thinking and preaching, is chock full of moral content, the source of which it takes to be the nature and will of God. The theist may confess that the *means* God chooses are mysterious in the sense that he cannot tell how they will lead to ends God (*ex hypothesi*) takes to be good. The same may be said for a novice watching a surgeon whom he trusts. But he cannot consistently pretend total ignorance concerning the *ends* the divine surgeon pursues. The commitment and trust required by worship (in contrast to sheer abasement) require at least a general sense of the ends God has in view. In sum, a theist who accepts *God is all-good and providential* accepts thereby a particular concept of goodness and providence—not necessarily the one sketched above, but if not that, then some other. And hence he accepts *some* version of what I have called "the greater good defense" ("defense" because it is in part by appeal to his concept of goodness and providence that the theist endeavours to rebut the charge that evil provides counter-theistic evidence).

(b) It is easy to draw subtly mistaken inferences from *God is all-good* and its theistic kin. Although Aquinas long ago suggested (as a necessary truth I suppose) the claim that *for any world God creates, He can create a better one*, it has often been mistakenly supposed that *necessarily, an all-good God would create the best possible world*. Again, in accord with the principle of treating all men as ends and never only as means, it would seem that if God allows an evil E to occur to an agent A, A must in justice reap an at least counterbalancing good G to which E is necessary, and this would require further amendment to (5). But it seems to me not clear whether such amendment is justified, for it is (so far as I can see) logically possible that enduring evil for the sake of others is itself of moral worth (or perhaps in that case that very worth is the at least counterbalancing good). In general, it seems clear that exactly what follows from such propositions as (3), (4) or (5) will depend on the particular context of moral theory in which they are embedded.

(c) As has often been noted, a good when added to an evil state of affairs may make the result worse, and the addition of an evil to a good state of affairs may make the result better. This, too, will affect the final statement of (5)-like propositions.[1]

(d) The remarks to this point (and in what follows) assume that some moral propositions are true. But some theists have denied this, though retaining something analogous to theistic ethics. One possibility along these lines concerns non-moral values. Another (not incompatible) line is to try to do more than is usually thought possible with emotivist ethics.[2] But, being an ethical cognitivist, I do not pursue these lines here.

(e) The questions of a theistic view of human nature and a theistic account of morality, and to what degree these are compatible with (and can draw upon) scientific data about human biology and psychology (normal and abnormal, psycho-analytic and social), and the like, are in fact central to what, in the long run, can or cannot be said about the various phases of the problem of evil. Indeed, I think nothing very definitive *can* be said without investigation of these further questions. And plainly any view of man and morality requires attention to the sort of world in which we live, involving answers to the sort of metaphysical questions positivists officially eschewed and covertly answered.

(f) Finally, as I have construed the greater good defense, the free will defense falls under its rubric. For any wrong and free choice God permits an agent A to make, it is (*ex hypothesi*) better that God allow moral agency to be misused than that it be temporarily withdrawn, the good of even misused agency (in its cosmic context) being a good that at least counterbalances the

---

[1] Cf. John Wisdom, "God and Evil", *Mind* (1935).
[2] See Charles Kielkopf's provocative "Emotivism As A Solution to the Problem of Evil", *Sophia* (July, 1970).

evilness of a wrong choice (and perhaps its consequences, or perhaps the consequences of the choice are also related to other justificatory goods).

II

Whereas I have presented (3) as an entailment of orthodox theism, it is often brought into the discussion of God and evil by a less direct route. If one wishes to show that two propositions, *A* and *B*, are consistent, one technique is to discover some third proposition *C* such that the conjunct *A and C* is plainly consistent with *B*. It then takes no logical genius to see that if *A and C* is consistent with *B*, *A* by itself is consistent with *B*. This is so, whether or not *C* is true. The truth value of *C* is quite irrelevant to the appropriateness of its use in this perfectly legitimate technique.[3]

If one wishes to show that *God exists* is not incompatible with *There is evil*, he can note that the conjunct comprised of God *exists* and *Every evil that exists is such that God has a morally sufficient reason for creating or permitting it* is compatible with *There is evil*. In this way, (3) appears as one proposition useful for showing that two other propositions are compatible. For that purpose, as we noted, (3) need not be true. Further, other propositions will be available for the same purpose. One could, for example, appeal to (5), or to (3') *Every evil that exists is such that its non-existence is logically impossible*. The conjunct of this last proposition with *God exists* is itself consistent, and is compatible with *There is evil*. So if one simply wants to argue that *God exists* and *There is evil* are compatible, and in so doing to utilize the technique we have described, use of (3') will be quite as appropriate as use of (3). The fact that (3') is patently false is, in this context, not to the point. If (3) is patently false, that too is irrelevant so far as its use in arguing the point of consistency is concerned.

Nonetheless, as we noted, (1) entails (3) but not (3'). That (3') is false says nothing about (1). But if (3) is false, (1) is also false. Put differently (3) is entailed by orthodox theism, while (3') is certainly not. Thus while use of (3) in showing that (1) and (2) are logically compatible is perfectly legitimate, the theist is committed to (3) in a stronger sense than that in which (3) is one of various propositions he may adopt for legitimate logical maneuvers, and I think this is worth emphasizing.

III

Having endeavored to show in what sense and for what reasons the theist is committed to the truth of the greater good defense, and having noted a polemic use of that defense, I turn from exposition to appraisal. Is it reasonable to accept the greater good defense?

Several things seem evident from the outset of reflection on this matter. First, for any specific good *G* and evil *E* which are proffered as an example of greater-good-requiring-evil complexes, the example may be questioned. Does the good at least counter-balance the evil? Is the evil logically necessary to the good? Is there no good *G'* which could replace the state of affairs *G and E* with net moral gain? Is the good in question valuable for its own sake, or simply (so to say) the best alternative available given its corresponding evil? These are matters of moral philosophy. They are also matters on which reasonable men notoriously differ. The theist is, if the above argument is correct, committed to a greater good thesis concerning evils. He is not committed to any particular examples of greater-good-requiring-evils (except, perhaps, at a very

---

[3] Alvin Plantinga, *God and Other Minds* (Ithaca, 1967), Ch. 5 and 6. George Mavrodes, *Belief in God: A Study in the Epistemology of Religion*, (New York, 1970), Ch. 4, make superb use of this technique.

general level). But he is committed to there being *some* examples of such complexes, and of course if *no* examples seem forthcoming this casts doubt on whether there are any such cases. But I think there are relevant examples, and have suggested above what I take some of them to be.

Second, there will almost surely be evils for which the theist finds no plausible greater good he can name. But surely this is not surprising. Even if *God exists and has a providential plan* were shown to be a necessary truth, or as well-confirmed a contingent truth as *There is a Pacific Ocean*, it would still be the case that there are evils the theist cannot place with any confidence in any justificatory basket he can name. But this is not evidence that there are evils which fit no such basket whatever.[4]

Third, basic to a theistic treatment of evil is a theistic view of man as *imago dei* and ethics as *imitatio dei*. For at least one central theistic tradition, this places an enormous value on human freedom and moral maturity.[5] One who occupies the perspective of B. F. Skinner's *Beyond Freedom and Dignity* will reject altogether such a view of man, and the theist will view Skinner's view as beneath freedom and dignity. I suspect that the fundamental issue which disturbs believer and non-believer alike with regard to "the problem of evil" is the suspicion that there is no adequate moral theory on which (in conjunction with a correct account of human nature) actual evils could possibly be justified. Unfortunately, systematic and philosophically articulate formulations of theistic ethics are rare, making it hard to confirm or alleviate this suspicion in any definitive way. The following remarks are intended as prolegomena to such alleviation.

Suppose that *if* Andrew's fears result in Andrew becoming courageous, and that *if* Alice's pains result in Alice becoming fortudinous, then these fears and pains are evils related as logically necessary conditions (though not *simpliciter*) to over-balancing goods.[6] One (I think not implausible) way of understanding these remarks will run thusly:

(A) Andrew's fears and Alice's pains are, considered by themselves, evil—at least in the sense that if an agent who could prevent or remove them did not, and had no morally sufficient reason, he would thereby be morally blameworthy.

(B) Andrew's free response to his fears, and Alice's to her pains, was morally creative (virtuous) in such a manner that fears-plus-responses and pains-plus-responses were good states of affairs to which evils were necessary (though not *simpliciter*) but which overbalanced their respective evils (which are hence justified).

As we have seen, other fears or pains might have served as well, and other equally lamentable stimuli might have produced other equally valuable virtues, quite compatibly with the truth of (A) or (B).

But suppose Andrew succumbs to his fears and becomes a coward, and Alice curses her pain and becomes a shrew. Then the fears and pains do not exactly shout their moral necessity, and there is something insipid about the reply that Andrew's fears at any rate give him the opportunity to develop courage. The missed chance seems neither worth the price nor proper in a God-made world.

---

[4] For reasons detailed in my "A Premature Farewell to Theism", *Religious Studies* (Dec., 1969).
[5] Cf. John Hick, *Evil and the God of Love* (New York, 1966).
[6] On various senses of "justified evil", see my "Ethics, Evils and Theism", *Sophia*, (July, 1969), or *Basic Issues in the Philosophy of Religion* (Boston, 1971), Ch. 2.

Nonetheless, I think there is considerable force to the reply which is feebly mis-stated along the lines just suggested. From the viewpoint of theistic morality, Andrew's fears and Alice's pains are occasions for free moral growth. As is so for any such occasion, there may be moral failure. But if Andrew becomes a coward, the status of his moral failure should be described (from the indicated perspective) in such terms as:

(C) It is better that Andrew be given opportunity to respond freely (and so creatively or destructively) to his fears than that he not have this opportunity—there is justificatory value in even the wrong exercise of moral agency.

If Andrew would have done no better given any other occasion of free and morally relevant choice, then not even God could both leave him a free agent and provide him with a better shot at goodness. The alternatives to cowardly Andrew will then be an unfree Andrew or not Andrew at all. Either way, Andrew is no moral agent (at least on the view presently being considered). And the same goes *mutatis mutandis*, for Alice, and for us all.

This view of moral agency, of course, assumes (what seems to me true) that moral agents are necessarily free agents, and that free agents are necessarily not determined. Alternatively, one could hold that (a) in one sense of "free" (say, free$_1$) libertarianism and determinism cannot both be true with respect to any particular choice or action (b) in another sense of "free" (say, free$_2$) libertarianism and determinism can be co-true, (c) correspondingly, there are two possible sorts of moral agents, those who are free$_1$, and those who are free$_2$, with respect to the choices for which they are morally responsible, and (d) it is vastly more valuable that there be free$_1$ agents than that there be free$_2$ agents. I suspect that disagreements concerning the relative worth of different sorts of freedom is as important for the dispute concerning evil as is the hoary controversy as to whether a choice or action may be both free and determined.

Perhaps a theist who argues along the lines of (A) through (C) is committed to such claims as:

(D) For every moral agent A, A is given those circumstances of moral choice which maximise his opportunity to act in a morally creative way (though he may miserably bungle things anyway).

(E) There is no set S' of moral agents whose members, had they been created, would have chosen better than the members of the set S of actual persons have chosen.

(F) For any actual agent A, whatever the actual choices he makes, it is better that A exist (have been created) than otherwise.

Concerning (F), it will perhaps suffice to note that (a) (F) seems plausible with respect to a being *ex hypothesi* created in the *imago dei* and (b) it is compatible with (F) that there be a (possible but not actual) choice C such that an agent who made C would be such that his non-existence was better than his existence.

I think (though I am not sure) that (D), or something like it, is entailed by *God is providential* (and so by (1)). It seems worth noting that in orthodox Christianity, salvation is "by grace, not works"—including the 'work' of a good moral character, so that if theism does entail something like (D), this entailment will have to be understood in terms of a theologically-informed theistic ethic. In spite of some popular versions of heaven, nothing in orthodox theism entails that man-in-heaven is "frozen" at some level of moral development (even the highest).

Indeed, being (in *that* sense) "confirmed in righteousness" may be incompatible with being a *person* at all. If these remarks are sound, they too must be considered when unpacking (D).

In sum, then, even cowardly Andrew and shrewish Alice are not so, simply because they were given a test which God (*ex hypothesi*) knew they would fail. Rather, they were granted moral agency (were created as moral agents) even though God (*ex hypothesi*) knew they, in important ways, would misuse it. More carefully, they were created as moral agents even though God (*ex hypothesi*) knew they would not become very good people. (Or perhaps only worse vices than cowardice or shrewhood would justify this harsh a judgment—but then there *are* worse vices.)

Turning briefly to (E)—the claim that no other set *S'* of moral agents would have produced better choices than the actual set *S* has—I offer three comments: (a) from the fact that *S'* is conceivable, it does not follow that *S'* is creatable;[7] (b) any evidence we have, then, concerning what possible agents might do must be derived from what actual agents have done. The performance of actual persons is our only sample class for the projection of how possible persons, were they created, would use their moral agency. (c) Plainly, it would be fallacious to infer that the members of the reference class (all actual and possible persons) contains some subset of possible persons who would (collectively or distributively) fare morally better (or worse) than have the members of the sample class (all actual persons). This would be analogous to arguing from the fact that all known elephants (the sample class) fear mice to the conclusion that the reference class (all elephants) contains some subset (of unobserved elephants) which delight in the company of their tiny brethren. So either the performance of merely possible persons, were they created, would be of familiar caliber, or we've no idea what they would do. The former alternative substantiates (E) and the latter does it no damage.

Still, it may be felt, even if (A) through (F) are granted, accepting the greater good defense remains unreasonable. For what of the painful death of an infant? And what of the growth to fine moral maturity of a saint who then decays into senility and becomes but the pale shadow of a fully-functioning adult? The road to moral maturity is not only strewn with wrecks; some entrants deceased before they left the driveway and others traverse the road fully only to crash at the end.

I grant the psychological forcefulness of appeal to infant mortality and geriatric disability. Perhaps it is just that forcefulness which not only often prevents us from looking at such matters clearly but makes any such attempt seem crass. It might indeed be crass (and that is charitable) to offer philosophical reflection to a bereaved parent or a grieving child when their need is so clearly for simple kindness. But no good is done by confusing appraisal of putative evidence with counsel to the griefstricken, and each has its proper place. What, then, of the proffered evidence that acceptance of the greater good defense is irrational? While I cannot pretend to deal with all the relevant issues, I offer four comments. First, either the infant is possessed of personal worth or not. If not, only the suffering of the parent is relevant, and (A) through (F) suggest how such suffering may be dealt with along "greater good" lines. If so (and presumably this is the correct alternative), then perhaps the point is that a person has been obliterated before he had a chance to develop—perhaps the idea is that cessation of existence of a potentially mature person is an evil. One question is whether this high value of personal worth can be sustained in a non-theistic perspective, but that issue is too large to broach here. Another question is whether cessation of existence has in fact occurred. At least orthodox Christian theism asserts that it is not, and this is no *ad hoc* assumption made to deal with critical points. Rather, it is intimately intertwined with

---

[7] As Plantinga, *op. cit.,* notes, while it is logically possible that a world not created by God exists, it is not therefore (or at all) possible that God created a world not created by God.

the themes of mercy and judgment, heaven and hell, and the like which we mentioned above. The thrust of the problem of infant mortality is altogether different for one who accepts either immortality of the soul or resurrection of the body than for one who does not. For the death of an infant (or of anyone) to by itself count as evidence against theism, we must (not merely not have good reason to believe but) have good reason to disbelieve all doctrines of personal survival. I do not myself know of such reasons. Hence I do not take death (infant or other) to constitute evidence against theism.

Second, the case of the senile saint is, it may be suggested, relevantly different. Perhaps the infant is not really a person (a natural extension of some pro-abortion arguments leads to this view). Perhaps the infant does survive to exercise moral agency in (so to say) another context. But the person who attains moral maturity, and then suffers disintegration of his mind as well as his body, raises another matter altogether. A man who really prizes artistic masterpieces does not allow them to go to ruin, even if he can restore them as good as new. If God really prizes moral maturity, why does He then allow even very good men to become senile, or even go mad? Well, I do not know, and I notice that the question does not seem to come up much in the literature. Perhaps no one else knows either, and I should think that it is appeal to such tragic reversals that provides one of the most cogent platforms of criticism of theism. But is this case really any different from that of other evils for which no point or justification can be specified? Perhaps *if* any such case were cogent counter-evidence, then the evil of demised sainthood is that case. But I have argued that such cases are not counter-evidence, and I do not see that identifying the sort of case that would be counter-evidence if any case were provides any counter to that argument.

As a (for the present) final move, we may imagine the critic arguing that the theist, in making the reply just rehearsed, covertly gives up the greater good defense. For the greater good defense is acceptable only if, as a necessary but not sufficient condition, "good" is not equivocal with respect to God and man. But the above defense allows that a good God can do things no good man can do without forfeiting his goodness. So if good at all, God is good in some sense other than that in which man is. Hence farewell to the greater good defense.

Putting the criticism formally, we get this argument:

(A1)   If under circumstance c, ϕ applies to all values of x but to no value of y, ϕ means one thing when applied to the values of x and another thing when applied to the values of y.

(A2)   Under the circumstance of permitting an infant to die when he can prevent the death (or permitting a saint to become senile or mad when he can prevent it), "good" applies to God but not to man.

So: (A3)   "Good" means one thing when applied to God and another thing when applied to man.

In fact, since (A3) entails that "good" is equivocal with respect to God and man, unless some new and relevant sense for "good" as applied to God is provided, "God is good" will be meaningless. But given just (A3), the greater good defense is unacceptable. Does, then, this argument succeed?

It does not. For while (A1) and (A2) *seem* to entail (A3), (A1) is either false (in which case (A1) and (A2) fruitlessly entail (A3)) or true (in which case (A1) and (A2) do not entail (A3)). To see this, consider under what specification of "circumstance" narrowly, allowing for example only those descriptions of states of affairs which include no reference to the motives, intentions, etc. of the agent and no consideration of what effect difference in knowledge and power has on the question of moral appraisal, (A1) will be false. For on (A1), so read, "good" may be applied to a surgeon who operates under emergency conditions rather than running for help, but not to me if under the same circumstances I run for help rather than operate. We may share intent (that the man live) and differ in ways relevant to moral appraisal (medical knowledge and prowess), but this is ruled out of consideration by the present restrictions on "circumstances" in (A1). (A1) will entail that, if the surgeon and I are (in the context of action on the described occasion) good at all, we are good in different senses. Yet this is false. We are both (given all the relevant features of the context) good, though we act differently, for we act for the same good end, each tailoring our actions to both that shared end and our respective talents. Narrowly construed, then, (A1) plus (A2) entails (A3), but this is polemically useless since (A1)—so restricted—is false.

Suppose, then, we do the reasonable thing and allow "circumstances" in (A1) to be widely read so as to include descriptions of the motives, intentions, etc. of agents and (insofar as relevant) differences in their knowledge and power. *Ex hypothesi*, that a man attain moral maturity is an important good. So a good God, and a good man, will allow each man maximal chance to attain this maturity. No man can achieve this end by permitting the death of another, for once dead a man is beyond all influence of his peers. But he is not beyond God's influence. So God sharing the same good end, may act differently, relative to His knowledge and prowess, than any man can act who shares the same end.

Widely read, (A1) is true. But it does not apply in the relevant case, for then "good" applies to God and man in the same circumstances—those in which God and man differ in capacity but coincide in valuation (just as did the surgeon and I in the previous example). Or, if one prefers, when (A1) is widely read, (A2) is false. In any case, (A3) is not, so far as I can see, entailed by any version of this argument (or any other) which is both sound and valid.

The last shred of plausibility is, I think, removed from the criticism under review when we note a further similarity between "God is good" and "Socrates is good." "God" may do duty as a description (then meaning "a being who is omnipotent, omniscient, onmibenevolent, etc.") or a proper name (then functioning as does "Jehovah"). We may designate these uses, respectively, as "$God(_1)$" and "$God(_2)$". Then *x is $God(_1)$* entails *x is all-good,* or (alternatively) *Necessarily, if x is $God(_1)$, x is good* is true. But *x is Jehovah* does not entail *x is all-good*, or (alternatively) *Necessarily, if x is $God(_2)$, x is good* is false. So *$God(_2)$ is all-good* is contingent, as is *Socrates is good*. Further, I take it that *being a saint* entails *being good*. *X is a saint* entails *x is good,* or (alternatively) *Necessarily, if x is a saint then x is good*. Hence *Saint Socrates is good* is a necessary truth. Socrates, *qua* saint, is *necessarily good*, just as Jehovah, *qua* God, is *necessarily all-good*. Socrates, *qua* Socrates, is (at most) *contingently good*, just as Jehovah, *qua* Jehovah, is *contingently good*. And just as Socrates is praised for a goodness he might not have possessed, and so may be credited for possessing, so perhaps Jehovah (or $God(_2)$) is praised for a goodness He might not have possessed, and so may be credited for possessing. At least, I see nothing philosophically or theologically objectionable in such a view.[8] But even if I am wrong about this, it is clear that the attempt to show that "good" is equivocal with respect to God and man fails. So far as I can see, so do the other attempts, noted above, to prove that it is unreasonable to accept the greater good defense.

---

[8] Cf. Dewey Hoitenga, "Logic and the Problem of Evil", *American Philosophical Quarterly* (April, 1967) for critique of this line of reasoning. For a reply to Hoitenga's critique, see my "Logic and the Problem of Evil: A Reply to Hoitenga" in Keith Yandell, ed. *God, Man and Religion* (New York, 1972), in which Hoitenga's essay is included.

Questions

1. Keith Yandell outlines the greater good defense. In terms that you can understand, how would you express it?
2. Why does Yandell think that the theist is committed to some version of the greater good defense? Do you agree?
3. What are the chief divine attributes that figure in the greater good defense?
4. According to Yandell, what sort of connection must there be between a good and the evil it is viewed as justifying?
5. What problems do you see with the greater good defense?

THE FREE WILL DEFENSE*

Alvin Plantinga

Plantinga argues that Mackie, and other atheists are wrong to think that the inconsistency strategy works. He develops a free will defense in two stages that incorporates a possible-worlds ontology and a notion of transworld depravity designed to diffuse the charge of inconsistency based on evil.

I. On the Alleged Contradiction in Theism

In a widely discussed piece entitled "Evil and Omnipotence" John Mackie makes this claim:

> I think, however, that a more telling criticism can be made by way of the traditional problem of evil. Here it can be shown, not that religious beliefs lack rational support, but that they are positively irrational, that the several parts of the essential theological doctrine are *inconsistent* with one another....[1]

Is Mackie right? Does the theist contradict himself? But we must ask a prior question: just what is being claimed here? That theistic belief contains an inconsistency or contradiction, of course. But what, exactly, is an inconsistency or contradiction? There are several kinds. An *explicit* Contradiction is a *proposition* of a certain sort—a conjunctive proposition, one conjunct of which is the denial or negation of the other conjunct. For example:

> Paul is a good tennis player, and it's false that Paul is a good tennis player.

(People seldom assert explicit contradictions). Is Mackie charging the theist with accepting such a contradiction? Presumably not; what he says is:

> In its simplest form the problem is this: God is omnipotent; God is wholly good; yet evil exists. There seems to be some contradiction between these three propositions, so that if any two of them were true the third would be false. But at the same time all three are essential parts of most theological positions; the theologian, it seems, at once *must* adhere and *cannot consistently* adhere to all three.

According to Mackie, then, the theist accepts a group or set of three propositions; this set is inconsistent. Its members, of course, are

(1) God is omnipotent
(2) God is wholly good

and

(3) Evil exists.

Call this set *A*; the claim is that *A* is an inconsistent set. But what is it for a *set* to be inconsistent or contradictory? Following our definition of an explicit contradiction, we might say that a set of propositions is explicitly contradictory if one of the members is the denial or

---

* From *God, Freedom, and Evil* by Alvin Plantinga (Harper & Row, 1974). Reprinted by permission of the author. Footnotes edited. The numbering of the sections has been changed because the first section in the book was omitted which deals with Hume's account of the theist's problem of evil.
[1] John Mackie, "Evil and Omnipotence," in *The Philosophy of Religion*, ed. Basil Mitchell (London: Oxford University Press, 1971), p. 92. [See previous reading.]

negation of another member. But then, of course, it is evident that the set we are discussing is not explicitly contradictory; the denials of (1), (2), and (3), respectively, are

(1') God is not omnipotent (or it's false that God is omnipotent)
(2') God is not wholly good

and

(3') There is no evil

none of which is in set A.

Of course many sets are pretty clearly contradictory, in an important way, but not *explicitly* contradictory. For example, set B:

(4) If all men are mortal, then Socrates is mortal
(5) All men are mortal
(6) Socrates is not mortal.

This set is not explicitly contradictory; yet surely *some* significant sense of that term applies to it. What is important here is that by using only the rules of ordinary logic—the laws of propositional logic and quantification theory found in any introductory text on the subject—we can deduce an explicit contradiction from the set. Or to put it differently, we can use the laws of logic to deduce a proposition from the set, which proposition, when added to the set, yields a new set that is explicitly contradictory. For by using the law *modus ponens* (if p, then q; p; therefore q) we can deduce

(7) Socrates is mortal

from (4) and (5). The result of adding (7) to B is the set $\{(4), (5), (6), (7)\}$. This set, of course, is explicitly contradictory in that (6) is the denial of (7). We might say that any set which shares this characteristic with set B is *formally* contradictory. So a formally contradictory set is one from whose members an explicit contradiction can be deduced by the laws of logic. Is Mackie claiming that set A is formally contradictory?

If he is, he's wrong. No laws of logic permit us to deduce the denial of one of the propositions in A from the other members. Set A isn't formally contradictory either.

But there is still another way in which a set of propositions can be contradictory or inconsistent. Consider set C, whose members are

(8) George is older than Paul
(9) Paul is older than Nick

and

(10) George is not older than Nick.

This set is neither explicitly nor formally contradictory; we can't, just by using the laws of logic, deduce the denial of any of these propositions from the others. And yet there is a good sense in which it is consistent or contradictory. For clearly it is *not possible* that its three members all be true. It is *necessarily true* that

(11)   If George is older than Paul, and Paul is older than Nick, then George is older than Nick.

And if we add (11) to set *C*, we get a set that is formally contradictory; (8), (9), and (11) yield, by the laws of ordinary logic, the denial of (10).

I said that (11) is *necessarily true*; but what does *that* mean? Of course we might say that a proposition is necessarily true if it is impossible that it be false, or if its negation is not possibly true. This would be to explain necessity in terms of possibility. Chances are, however, that anyone who does not know what necessity is, will be equally at a loss about possibility; the explanation is not likely to be very successful. Perhaps all we can do by way of explanation is to give some examples and hope for the best. In the first place many propositions can be established by the laws of logic alone—for example,

(12) If all men are mortal and Socrates is a man, then Socrates is mortal.

Such propositions are truths of logic; and all of them are necessary in the sense of question. But truths of arithmetic and mathematics generally are also necessarily true. Still further, there is a host of propositions that are neither truths of logic nor truths of mathematics but are nonetheless necessarily true; (11) would be an example, as well as

(13) Nobody is taller than himself
(14) Red is a color
(15) No numbers are persons
(16) No prime number is a prime minister

and

(17) Bachelors are unmarried.

So here we have an important kind of necessity—let's call it "broadly logical necessity." Of course there is a correlative kind of *possibility:* a proposition *p* is possibly true (in the broadly logical sense) just in case its negation or denial is not necessarily true (in that same broadly logical sense). This sense of necessity and possibility must be distinguished from another that we may call *causal* or *natural* necessity and possibility. Consider

(18) Henry Kissinger has swum the Atlantic.

Although this proposition has an implausible ring, it is not necessarily false in the broadly logical sense (and its denial is not necessarily true in that sense). But there is a good sense in which it is impossible: it is *causally* or *naturally* impossible. Human beings, unlike dolphins, just don't have the physical equipment demanded for this feat. Unlike Superman, furthermore, the rest of us are incapable of leaping tall buildings at a single bound or (without auxiliary power of some kind) traveling faster than a speeding bullet. These things are *impossible* for us—but not *logically* impossible, even in the broad sense.

So there are several senses of necessity and possibility here. There are a number of propositions, furthermore, of which it's difficult to say whether they are or aren't possible in the broadly logical sense; some of these are subjects of philosophical controversy. Is it possible, for example, for a person never to be conscious during his entire existence? Is it possible for a (human) person to exist *disembodied*? If that's possible, is it possible that there be a person who at *no time at all* during his entire existence has a body? Is it possible to see without eyes? These are propositions about whose possibility in that broadly logical sense there is disagreement and dispute.

Now return to set C.... What is characteristic of it is the fact that the conjunction of its member—the proposition expressed by the result of putting "and's" between (8), (9), and (10)—is necessarily false. Or we might put it like this: what characterizes set C is the fact that we can get a formally contradictory set by adding a necessarily true proposition—namely (11). Suppose we say that a set is *implicitly contradictory* if it resembles C in this respect. That is, a set S of propositions is implicitly contradictory if there is a necessary proposition p such that the result of adding p to S is a formally contradictory set. Another way to put it: S is implicitly contradictory if there is some necessarily true proposition p such that by using just the laws of ordinary logic, we can deduce an explicit contradiction from p together with the members of S. And when Mackie says that set A is contradictory, we may properly take him, I think, as holding that it is implicitly contradictory in the explained sense. As he puts it:

> However, the contradiction does not arise immediately; to show it we need some additional premises, or perhaps some quasi-logical rules connecting the terms "good" and "evil" and "omnipotent." These additional principles are that good is opposed to evil, in such a way that a good thing always eliminates evil as far as it can, and that there are no limits to what an omnipotent thing can do. From these it follows that a good omnipotent thing eliminates evil completely, and then the propositions that a good omnipotent thing exists, and that evil exists, are incompatible.[2]

Here Mackie refers to "additional premises"; he also calls them "additional principles" and "quasi-logical rules"; he says we need them to show the contradiction. What he means, I think, is that to get a formally contradictory set we must add some more propositions to set A; and if we aim to show that set A is implicitly contradictory, these propositions must be necessary truths—"quasi-logical rules" as Mackie calls them. The two additional principles he suggests are

(19) A good thing always eliminates evil as far as it can

and

(20) There are no limits to what an omnipotent being can do.

And, of course, if Mackie means to show that set A is implicitly contradictory, then he must hold that (19) and (20) are not merely *true* but *necessarily true*.

But, are they? What about (20) first? What does it mean to say that a being is omnipotent? That he is *all-powerful*, or *almighty*, presumably. But are there no limits at all to the power of such a being? Could he create square circles, for example, or married bachelors? Most theologians and theistic philosophers who hold that God is omnipotent, do not hold that He can create round squares or bring it about that He both exists and does not exist. These theologians and philosophers may hold that there are no *nonlogical* limits to what an omnipotent being can do, but they concede that not even an omnipotent being can bring about logically impossible states of affairs or cause necessarily false propositions to be true. Some theists, on the other hand—Martin Luther and Descartes, perhaps—have apparently thought that God's power is unlimited even by the laws of logic. For these theists the question whether set A is contradictory will not be of much interest. As theists they believe (1) and (2), and they also, presumably, believe (3). But they remain undisturbed by the claim that (1), (2), and (3) are jointly inconsistent—because, as they say, God can do what is logically impossible. Hence He can bring it about that the members of set A are all true, even if that set is contradictory (concentrating very intensely upon this suggestion is likely to make you dizzy). So the theist who thinks that the power of God isn't limited *at all*, not even by the laws of logic, will be unimpressed by Mackie's

---

[2] Ibid., p. 93. [*Philosophy of Religion: Selected Readings*, Second Edition, p. 224.]

argument and won't find any difficulty in the contradiction set *A* is alleged to contain. This view is not very popular, however, and for good reason; it is quite incoherent. What the theist typically means when he says that God is omnipotent is not that there are *no* limits to God's power, but at most that there are no nonlogical limits to what He can do; and given this qualification, it is perhaps initially plausible to suppose that (20) is necessarily true.

But what about (19), the proposition that every good thing eliminates every evil state of affairs that it can eliminate? Is that necessarily true? Is it true at all? Suppose, first of all, that your friend Paul unwisely goes for a drive on a wintry day and runs out of gas on a deserted road. The temperature dips to ⁻10°, and a miserably cold wind comes up. You are sitting comfortably at home (twenty-five miles from Paul) roasting chestnuts in a roaring blaze. Your car is in the garage; in the trunk there is the full five-gallon can of gasoline you always keep for emergencies. Paul's discomfort and danger are certainly an evil, and one which you could eliminate. You don't do so. But presumably you don't thereby forfeit your claim to being a "good thing"—you simply didn't know of Paul's plight. And so (19) does not appear to be necessary. It says that every good thing has a certain property—the property of eliminating every evil that it can. And if the case I described is possible—a good person's failing through ignorance to eliminate a certain evil he can eliminate—then (19) is by no means necessarily true.

But perhaps Mackie could sensibly claim that if you *didn't know* about Paul's plight, then in fact you were *not*, at the time in question, able to eliminate the evil in question; and perhaps he'd be right. In any event he could revise (19) to take into account the kind of case I mentioned:

(19a) Every good thing always eliminates every evil that *it knows about* and can eliminate.

{(1), (2), (3), (20), (19a)}, you'll notice is not a formally contradictory set—to get a formal contradiction we must add a proposition specifying that God *knows about* every evil state of affairs. But most theists do believe that God is omniscient or all-knowing; so if this new set—the set that results when we add to set *A* the proposition that God is omniscient—is implicitly contradictory then Mackie should be satisfied and the theist confounded. (And, henceforth, set *A* will be the old set *A* together with the proposition that God is omniscient.)

But is (19a) necessary? Hardly. Suppose you know that Paul is marooned as in the previous example, and you also know another friend is similarly marooned fifty miles in the opposite direction. Suppose, furthermore, that while you can rescue one or the other, you simply can't rescue both. Then each of the two evils is such that it is within your power to eliminate it; and you know about them both. But you can't eliminate both; and you don't forfeit your claim to being a good person by eliminating only one—it wasn't within your power to do more. So the fact that you don't doesn't mean that you are not a good person. Therefore (19a) is false; it is not a necessary truth or even a truth that every good thing eliminates every evil it knows about and can eliminate.

We can see the same thing another way. You've been rock climbing. Still something of a novice, you've acquired a few cuts and bruises by inelegantly using your knees rather than your feet. One of these bruises is fairly painful. You mention it to a physician friend, who predicts the pain will leave of its own accord in a day or two. Meanwhile, he says, there's nothing he can do, short of amputating your leg above the knee, to remove the pain. Now the pain in your knee is an evil state of affairs. All else being equal, it would be better if you had no such pain. And it is within the power of your friend to eliminate this evil state of affairs. Does his failure to do so mean that he is not a good person? Of course not; for he could eliminate this evil state of affairs only by bringing about another, much worse evil. And so it is once again evident that (19a) is false. It is entirely possible that a good person fail to eliminate an evil state of affairs that he knows about and can eliminate. This would take place, if, as in the present example, he couldn't eliminate the evil without bringing about a *greater* evil.

A slightly different kind of case shows the same thing. A really impressive good state of affairs G will *outweigh* a trivial E—that is, the conjunctive state of affairs G *and* E is itself a good state of affairs. And surely a good person would not be obligated to eliminate a given evil if he could do so only by eliminating a good that outweighed it. Therefore (19a) is not necessarily true; it can't be used to show that set A is implicitly contradictory.

These difficulties might suggest another revision of (19); we might try

(19b) A good being eliminates every evil E that it knows about and that it can eliminate without either bringing about a greater evil or eliminating a good state of affairs that outweighs E.

Is this necessarily true? It takes care of the second of the two difficulties afflicting (19a) but leaves the first untouched. We can see this as follows. First, suppose we say that a being *properly eliminates* an evil state of affairs if it eliminates that evil without either eliminating an outweighing good or bringing about a greater evil. It is then obviously possible that a person find himself in a situation where he could properly eliminate an evil E and could also properly eliminate another evil E', but couldn't properly eliminate them *both*. You're rock climbing again, this time on the dreaded north face of the Grand Teton. You and your party come upon Curt and Bob, two mountaineers stranded 125 feet apart on the face. They untied to reach their cigarettes and then carelessly dropped the rope while lighting up. A violent, dangerous thunderstorm is approaching. You have time to rescue one of the stranded climbers and retreat before the storm hits; if you rescue both, however, you and your party and the two climbers will be caught on the face during the thunderstorm, which will very likely destroy your entire party. In this case you can eliminate one evil (Curt's being stranded on the face) without causing more evil or eliminating a greater good; and you are also able to properly eliminate the other evil (Bob's being thus stranded). But you can't properly eliminate them *both*. And so the fact that you don't rescue Curt, say, even though you could have, doesn't show that you aren't a good person. Here, then, each of the evils is such that you can properly eliminate it; but you can't properly eliminate them both, and hence can't be blamed for failing to eliminate one of them.

So neither (19a) nor (19b) is necessarily true. You may be tempted to reply that the sort of counterexamples offered—examples where someone is able to eliminate an evil A and also able to eliminate a different evil B, but unable to eliminate them both—are irrelevant to the case of a being who, like God, is both omnipotent and omniscient. That is, you may think that if an omnipotent and omniscient being is able to eliminate each of two evils, it follows that he can eliminate them *both*. Perhaps this is so; but it is not strictly to the point. The fact is the counterexamples show that (19a) and (19b) are not necessarily true and hence can't be used to show that set A is implicitly inconsistent. What the reply does suggest is that perhaps the atheologian will have more success if he works the properties of omniscience and omnipotence into (19). Perhaps he could say something like

(19c) An omnipotent and omniscient good being eliminates every evil that it can properly eliminate.

And suppose, for purposes of argument, we concede the necessary truth of (19c). Will it serve Mackie's purposes? Not obviously. For we don't get a set that is formally contradictory by adding (20) and (19c) to set A. This set (call it A') contains the following six members:

(1) God is omnipotent
(2) God is wholly good
(2') God is omniscient
(3) Evil exists
(19c) An omnipotent and omniscient good being eliminates every evil that it can properly eliminate

and

(20) There are no nonlogical limits to what an omnipotent being can do.

Now if A' were formally contradictory, then from any five of its members we could deduce the denial of the sixth by the laws of ordinary logic. That is, any five would *formally entail* the denial of the sixth. So if A' were formally inconsistent, the denial of (3) would be formally entailed by the remaining five. That is, (1), (2), (2'), (19c), and (20) would formally entail

(3') There is no evil.

But they don't; what they formally entail is not that there is no evil *at all* but only that

(3'') There is no evil that God can properly eliminate.

So (19c) doesn't really help either—not because it is not necessarily true but because its addition [with (20)] to set A does not yield a formally contradictory set. Obviously, what the atheologian must add to get a formally contradictory set is

(21) If God is omniscient and omnipotent, then he can properly eliminate every evil state of affairs.

Suppose we agree that the set consisting in A plus (19c), (20), and (21) is formally contradictory. So if (19c), (20), and (21) are all necessarily true, then set A is implicitly contradictory. We've already conceded that (19c) and (20) are indeed necessary. So we must take a look at (21). Is this proposition necessarily true?

No. To see this let us ask the following question. Under what conditions would an omnipotent being be unable to eliminate a certain evil E without eliminating an outweighing good? Well, suppose that E is *included in* some good state of affairs that outweighs it. That is, suppose there is some good state of affairs G so related to E that it is impossible that G obtain or be actual and E fail to obtain. (Another way to put this: a state of affairs S includes S' if the conjunctive state of affairs S *but not* S' is impossible, or if it is necessary that S' obtains if S does.) Now suppose that some good state of affairs G includes an evil state of affairs E that it outweighs. Then not even an omnipotent being could eliminate E without eliminating G. But *are* there any cases where a good state of affairs includes, in this sense, an evil that it outweighs?[3] Indeed there are such states of affairs. To take an artificial example, let's suppose that E is Paul's suffering from a minor abrasion and G is your being deliriously happy. The conjunctive state of affairs, G and E—the state of affairs that obtains if and only if both G and E obtain—is then a good state of affairs: it is better, all else being equal, that you be intensely happy and Paul suffer a mildly annoying abrasion than that this state of affairs not obtain. So G and E is a good state of affairs. And clearly G and E includes E: obviously it is necessarily true that if you are deliriously happy and Paul is suffering from an abrasion, then Paul is suffering from an abrasion.

---

[3] More simply, the question is really just whether any good state of affairs includes an evil; a little reflection reveals that no good state of affairs can include an evil that it does *not* outweigh.

But perhaps you think this example trivial, tricky, slippery, and irrelevant. If so, take heart; other examples abound. Certain kinds of values, certain familiar kinds of good states of affairs, can't exist apart from evil of some sort. For example, there are people who display a sort of creative moral heroism in the face of suffering and adversity—a heroism that inspires others and creates a good situation out of a bad one. In a situation like this the evil, of course, remains evil; but the total state of affairs—someone's bearing pain magnificently, for example—may be good. If it is, then the good present must outweigh the evil; otherwise the total situation would not be *good*. But, of course, it is not possible that such a good state of affairs obtain unless some evil also obtain. It is a necessary truth that if someone bears pain magnificently, then someone is in pain.

The conclusion to be drawn, therefore, is that (21) is not necessarily true. And our discussion thus far shows at the very least that it is no easy matter to find necessarily true propositions that yield a formally contradictory set when added to set A.[4] One wonders, therefore, why the many atheologians who confidently assert that this set is contradictory make no attempt whatever to *show* that it is. For the most part they are content just to *assert* that there is a contradiction here. Even Mackie, who sees that some "additional premises" or "quasi-logical rules" are needed, makes scarcely a beginning towards finding some additional premises that are necessarily true and that together with the members of set A formally entail an explicit contradiction.

II. Can We Show That There Is No Inconsistency Here?

To summarize our conclusions so far: although many atheologians claim that the theist is involved in contradiction when he asserts the members of set A, this set, obviously, is neither *explicitly* nor *formally* contradictory; the claim, presumably, must be that it is *implicitly* contradictory. To make good this claim the atheologian must find some necessarily true proposition p (it could be a conjunction of several propositions) such that the addition of p to set A yields a set that is formally contradictory. No atheologian has produced even a plausible candidate for this role, and it certainly is not easy to see what such a proposition might be. Now we might think we should simply declare set A implicitly consistent on the principle that a proposition (or set) is to be presumed consistent or possible until proven otherwise. This course, however, leads to trouble. The same principle would impel us to declare the atheologian's claim—that set A is *in*consistent—possible or consistent. But the claim that a given set of propositions is implicitly contradictory, is itself either necessarily true or necessarily false; so if such a claim is *possible*, it is not necessarily false and is, therefore, true (in fact, necessarily true). If we followed the suggested principle, therefore, we should be obliged to declare set A implicitly consistent (since it hasn't been shown to be otherwise), but we should have to say the same thing about the atheologian's claim, since we haven't shown *that* claim to be inconsistent or impossible. The atheologian's claim, furthermore, is necessarily true if it is possible. Accordingly, if we accept the above principle, we shall have to declare set A both implicitly consistent and implicitly inconsistent. So all we can say at this point is that set A has not been shown to be implicitly inconsistent.

Can we go any further? One way to go on would be to try to *show* that set A is implicitly consistent or possible in the broadly logical sense. But what is involved in showing such a thing? Although there are various ways to approach this matter, they all resemble one another in an

---

[4] In Plantinga, *God and Other Minds* (Ithaca, N.Y.: Cornell University Press, 1967), chap. 5, I explore further the project of finding such propositions.

important respect. They all amount to this: to show that a set S is consistent you think of a *possible state of affairs* (it needn't *actually obtain*) which is such that if it were actual, then all of the members of S would be true. This procedure is sometimes called *giving a model of S*. For example, you might construct an axiom set and then show that it is consistent by giving a model of it; this is how it was shown that the denial of Euclid's parallel postulate is formally consistent with the rest of his postulates.

There are various special cases of this procedure to fit special circumstances. Suppose, for example, you have a pair of propositions p and q and wish to show them consistent. And suppose we say that a proposition p_1 *entails* a proposition p_2 if it is impossible that p_1 be true and p_2 false—if the conjunctive proposition p_1 and not p_2 is necessarily false. Then one way to show that p is consistent with q is to find some proposition r whose conjunction with p is both possible, in the broadly logical sense, and entails q. A rude and unlettered behaviorist, for example, might hold that thinking is really nothing but movements of the larynx; he might go on to hold that

    P   Jones did not move his larynx after April 30

is inconsistent (in the broadly logical sense) with

    Q   Jones did some thinking during May.

By way of rebuttal, we might point out that P appears to be consistent with

    R   While convalescing from an April 30 laryngotomy, Jones whiled away the idle hours by writing (in May) a splendid paper on Kant's *Critique of Pure Reason*.

So the conjunction of P and R appears to be consistent; but obviously it also entails Q (you can't write even a passable paper on Kant's *Critique of Pure Reason* without doing some thinking); so P and Q are consistent.

We can see that this is a special case of the procedure I mentioned above as follows. This proposition R is consistent with P; so the proposition P and R is possible, describes a possible state of affairs. But P and R entails Q; hence if P *and R* were true, Q would also be true, and hence both P and Q would be true. So this is really a case of producing a possible state of affairs such that, if it were actual, all the members of the set in question (in this case the pair set of P and Q) would be true.

How does this apply to the case before us? As follows, let us conjoin propositions (1), (2), and (2') and henceforth call the result (1):

    (1) God is omniscient, omnipotent, and wholly good.

The problem, then, is to show that (1) and (3) (evil exists) are consistent. This could be done, as we've seen, by finding a proposition r that is consistent with (1) and such that (1) and (r) together entail (3). One proposition that might do the trick is

    (22) God creates a world containing evil and has a good reason for doing so.

If (22) is consistent with (1), then it follows that (1) and (3) (and hence set *A*) are consistent. Accordingly, one thing some theists have tried is to show that (22) and (1) are consistent.

One can attempt this in at least two ways. On the one hand, we could try to apply the same method again. Conceive of a possible state of affairs such that, if it obtained, an omnipotent, omniscient, and wholly good God would have a good reason for permitting evil. On the other, someone might try to specify *what God's reason is* for permitting evil and try to show, if it is not obvious, that it is a good reason. St. Augustine, for example, one of the greatest and most influential philosopher-theologians of the Christian Church, writes as follows:

> ...some people see with perfect truth that a creature is better if, while possessing free will, it remains always fixed upon God and never sins; then, reflecting on men's sins, they are grieved, not because they continue to sin, but because they were created. They say: He should have made us such that we never willed to sin, but always to enjoy the unchangeable truth.
>
> They should not lament or be angry. God has not compelled men to sin just because He created them and gave them the power to choose between sinning and not sinning. There are angels who have never sinned and never will sin.
>
> Such is the generosity of God's goodness that He has not refrained from creating even that creature which He foreknew would not only sin, but remain in the will to sin. As a runaway horse is better than a stone which does not run away because it lacks self-movement and sense perception, so the creature is more excellent which sins by free will than that which does not sin only because it has no free will.[5]

In broadest terms Augustine claims that God could create a better, more perfect universe by permitting evil than He could by refusing to do so:

> Neither the sins nor the misery are necessary to the perfection of the universe, but souls as such are necessary, which have the power to sin if they so will, and become miserable if they sin. If misery persisted after their sins had been abolished, or if there were misery before there were sins, then it might be right to say that the order and government of the universe were at fault. Again, if there were sins but no consequent misery, that order is equally dishonored by lack of equity.[6]

Augustine tries to tell us *what God's reason is* for permitting evil. At bottom, he says, it's that God can create a more perfect universe by permitting evil. A really top-notch universe requires the existence of free, rational, and moral agents; and some of the free creatures He created went wrong. But the universe with the free creatures it contains and the evil they commit is better than it would have been had it contained neither the free creatures nor this evil. Such an attempt to specify God's reason for permitting evil is what I earlier called a *theodicy*; in the words of John Milton it is an attempt to "justify the ways of God to man," to show that God is just in permitting evil. Augustine's kind of theodicy might be called a Free Will Theodicy, since the idea of rational creatures with free will plays such a prominent role in it.

A theodicist, then, attempts to tell us why God permits evil. Quite distinct from a Free Will Theodicy is what I shall call a Free Will Defense. Here the aim is not to say what God's reason *is*, but at most what God's reason *might possibly be*. We could put the difference like this. The Free Will Theodicist and Free Will Defender are both trying to show that (1) is consistent with (22), and of course if so, then set A is consistent. The Free Will Theodicist tries to do this by finding some proposition *r* which in conjunction with (1) entails (22); he claims, furthermore, that this proposition is *true*, not just consistent with (1). He tries to tell us what God's reason for permitting evil *really is*. The Free Will Defender, on the other hand, though he also tries to find a proposition *r* that is consistent with (1) and in conjunction with it entails (22), does *not* claim to know or even believe that *r* is true. And here, of course, he is perfectly within his rights. His aim

---

[5] *The Problem of Free Choice*, Vol. 22 of *Ancient Christian Writers* (Westminster, Md.: The Newman Press, 1955), bk. 2, pp. 14-15.
[6] Ibid., bk. 3, p. 9.

is to show that (1) is consistent with (22); all he need do then is find an *r* that is consistent with (1) and such that (1) and (*r*) entail (22); whether *r* is *true* is quite beside the point.

So there is a significant difference between a Free Will Theodicy and a Free Will Defense. The latter is sufficient (if successful) to show that set *A* is consistent; in a way a Free Will Theodicy goes beyond what is required. On the other hand, a theodicy would be much more satisfying, if possible to achieve. No doubt the theist would rather know what God's reason *is* for permitting evil than simply that it's possible that He has a good one. But in the present context (that of investigating the consistency of set *A*), the latter is all that's needed. Neither a defense or a theodicy, of course, gives any hint to what God's reason for some *specific* evil—the death or suffering of someone close to you, for example—might be. And there is still another function—a sort of pastoral function[7]—in the neighborhood that neither serves. Confronted with evil in his own life or suddenly coming to realize more clearly than before the *extent* and *magnitude* of evil, a believer in God may undergo a crisis of faith. He may be tempted to follow the advice of Job's "friends"; he may be tempted to "curse God and die." Neither a Free Will Defense nor a Free Will Theodicy is designed to be of much help or comfort to one suffering from such a storm in the soul (although in a specific case, of course, one or the other could prove useful). Neither is to be thought of first of all as a means of pastoral counseling. Probably neither will enable someone to find peace with himself and with God in the face of the evil the world contains. But then, of course, neither is intended for that purpose.

III. The Free Will Defense

In what follows I shall focus attention upon the Free Will Defense. I shall examine it more closely, state it more exactly, and consider objections to it; and I shall argue that in the end it is successful. Earlier we saw that among good states of affairs there are some that not even God can bring about without bringing about evil: those goods, namely, that *entail* or *include* evil states of affairs. The Free Will Defense can be looked upon as an effort to show that there may be a very different kind of good that God can't bring about without permitting evil. These are good states of affairs that don't include evil; they do not entail the existence of any evil whatever; nonetheless God Himself can't bring them about without permitting evil.

So how does the Free Will Defense work? And what does the Free Will Defender mean when he says that people are or may be free? What is relevant to the Free Will Defense is the idea of *being free with respect to an action*. If a person is free with respect to a given action, then he is free to perform that action and free to refrain from performing it; no antecedent conditions and/or causal laws determine that he will perform the action, or that he won't. It is within his power, at the time in question, to take or perform the action and within his power to refrain from it. Freedom so conceived is not to be confused with unpredictability. You might be able to predict what you will do in a given situation even if you are free, in that situation, to do something else. If I know you well, I may be able to predict what action you will take in response to a certain set of conditions; it does not follow that you are not free with respect to that action. Secondly, I shall say that an action is *morally significant*, for a given person, if it would be wrong for him to perform the action but right to refrain or *vice versa*. Keeping a promise, for example, would ordinarily be morally significant for a person, as would refusing induction into the army. On the other hand, having Cheerios for breakfast (instead of Wheaties) would not normally be morally significant. Further, suppose we say that a person is *significantly free*, on a given

---

[7] I am indebted to Henry Schuurman (in conversation) for helpful discussion of the difference between this pastoral function and those served by a theodicy or a defense.

occasion, if he is then free with respect to a morally significant action. And finally we must distinguish between *moral evil* and *natural evil*. The former is evil that results from free human activity; natural evil is any other kind of evil.[8]

Given these definitions and distinctions, we can make a preliminary statement of the Free Will Defense as follows. A world containing creatures who are significantly free (and freely perform more good than evil actions) is more valuable, all else being equal, than a world containing no free creatures at all. Now God can create free creatures, but He can't *cause* or *determine* them to do only what is right. For if He does so, then they aren't significantly free after all; they do not do what is right *freely*. To create creatures capable of *moral good*, therefore, He must create creatures capable of moral evil; and He can't give these creatures the freedom to perform evil and at the same time prevent them from doing so. As it turned out, sadly enough, some of the free creatures God created went wrong in the exercise of their freedom; this is the source of moral evil. The fact that free creatures sometimes go wrong, however, counts neither against God's omnipotence nor against His goodness; for He could have forestalled the occurrence of moral evil only by removing the possibility of moral good.

I said earlier that the Free Will Defender tries to find a proposition that is consistent with

(1) God is omniscient, omnipotent, and wholly good

and together with (1) entails that there is evil. According to the Free Will Defense, we must find this proposition somewhere in the above story. The heart of the Free Will Defense is the claim that it is *possible* that God could not have created a universe containing moral good (or as much moral good as this world contains) without creating one that also contained moral evil. And if so, then it is possible that God has a good reason for creating a world containing evil.

Now this defense has met with several kinds of objections. For example, some philosophers say that *causal determinism* and *freedom*, contrary to what we might have thought, are not really incompatible.[9] But if so, then God could have created free creatures who were free, and free to do what is wrong, but nevertheless were causally determined to do only what is right. Thus He could have created creatures who were free to do what was wrong, while nevertheless preventing them from ever performing any wrong actions—simply seeing to it that they were causally determined to do only what is right. Of course this contradicts the Free Will Defense, according to which there is inconsistency in supposing that God determines free creatures to do only what is right. But is it really possible that all of a person's actions are causally determined while some of them are free? How could that be so? According to one version of the doctrine in question, to say that George acts freely on a given occasion is to say only this: *if George had chosen to do otherwise, he would have done otherwise*. Now George's action *A* is causally determined if some event *E*—some event beyond his control—has already occurred, where the state of affairs consisting in *E*'s occurrence conjoined with George's *refraining* from performing *A*, is a causally impossible state of affairs. Then one can consistently hold both that all of a man's actions are causally determined and that some of them are free in the above sense. For suppose that all of a man's actions are causally determined and that he *couldn't*, on any occasion, have made any choice or performed any action different from the ones he did make and perform. It could still be true that if he *had* chosen to do otherwise, he would have done otherwise. Granted,

---

[8] This distinction is not very precise (how, exactly, are we to construe "results from"?), but perhaps it will serve our present purposes.

[9] See, for example, A. Flew, "Divine Omnipotence and Human Freedom," in *New Essays in Philosophical Theology*, eds. A. Flew and A. MacIntyre (London: SCM, 1955), pp. 150-53.

he couldn't have chosen to do otherwise; but this is consistent with saying that *if* he had, things would have gone differently.

This objection to the Free Will Defense seems utterly implausible. One might as well claim that being in jail doesn't really limit one's freedom on the grounds that if one were *not* in jail, he'd be free to come and go as he pleased. So I shall say no more about this objection here.[10]

A second objection is more formidable. In essence it goes like this. Surely it is possible to do only what is right, even if one is free to do wrong. It is *possible*, in that broadly logical sense, that there would be a world containing free creatures who always do what is right. There is certainly no *contradiction* or *inconsistency* in this idea. But God is omnipotent; his power has no nonlogical limitations. So if it's possible that there be a world containing creatures who are free to do what is wrong but never in fact do so, then it follows that an omnipotent God could create such a world. If so, however, the Free Will Defense must be mistaken in its insistence upon the possibility that God is omnipotent but unable to create a world containing moral good without permitting moral evil. J. L. Mackie...states this objection:

> If God has made men such that in their free choices they sometimes prefer what is good and sometimes what is evil, why could he not have made men such that they always freely choose the good? If there is no logical impossibility in a man's freely choosing the good on one, or on several occasions, there cannot be a logical impossibility in his freely choosing the good on every occasion. God was not, then, faced with a choice between making innocent automata and making beings who, in acting freely, would sometimes go wrong; there was open to him the obviously better possibility of making beings who would act freely but always go right. Clearly, his failure to avail himself of this possibility is inconsistent with his being both omnipotent and wholly good.[11]

Now what, exactly, is Mackie's point here? This. According to the Free Will Defense, it is possible both that God is omnipotent and that He was unable to create a world containing moral good without creating one containing moral evil. But, replies Mackie, this limitation on His power to create is inconsistent with God's omnipotence. For surely it's *possible* that there be a world containing perfectly virtuous persons—persons who are significantly free but always do what is right. Surely there are *possible worlds* that contain moral good but no moral evil. But God, if He is omnipotent, can create any possible world He chooses. So it is *not* possible, contrary to the Free Will Defense, both that God is omnipotent and that He could create a world containing moral good only by creating one containing moral evil. If He is omnipotent, the only limitations of His power are *logical* limitations; in which case there are no possible worlds He could not have created.

This is a subtle and important point. According to the great German philosopher G. W. Leibniz, *this* world, the actual world, must be the best of all possible worlds. His reasoning goes as follows. Before God created anything at all, He was confronted with an enormous range of choices; He could create or bring into actuality any of the myriads of different possible worlds. Being perfectly good, He must have chosen to create the best world He could; being omnipotent, He was able to create any possible world He pleased. He must, therefore, have chosen the best of all possible worlds; and hence *this* world, the one He did create, must be the best possible. Now Mackie, of course, agrees with Leibniz that God, if omnipotent, could have created any world He pleased and would have created the best world he could. But while Leibniz draws the conclusion that this world, despite appearances, must be the best possible, Mackie concludes instead that

---

[10] For further discussion of it see Plantinga, *God and Other Minds*, pp. 132-35.
[11] Mackie, in *The Philosophy of Religion*, pp. 100-101.

there is no omnipotent, wholly good God. For, he says, it is obvious enough that this present world is not the best of all possible worlds.

The Free Will Defender disagrees with both Leibniz and Mackie. In the first place, he might say, what is the reason for supposing that there *is* such a thing as the best of all possible worlds? No matter how marvelous a world is—containing no matter how many persons enjoying unalloyed bliss—isn't it possible that there be an even better world containing even more persons enjoying even more unalloyed bliss? But what is really characteristic and central to the Free Will Defense is the claim that God, though omnipotent, could not have actualized just any possible world He pleased.

IV. Was It Within God's Power to Create Any Possible World He Pleased?

This is indeed the crucial question for the Free Will Defense. If we wish to discuss it with insight and authority, we shall have to look into the idea of *possible worlds.* And a sensible first question is this: what sort of thing is a possible world? The basic idea is that a possible world is a *way things could have been*; it is a *state of affairs* of some kind. Earlier we spoke of states of affairs, in particular of good and evil states of affairs. Suppose we look at this idea in more detail. What sort of thing is a state of affairs? The following would be examples:

> Nixon's having won the 1972 election
> 7 + 5's being equal to 12
> All men's being mortal

and

> Gary, Indiana's, having a really nasty pollution problem.

These are *actual* states of affairs: states of affairs that do in fact *obtain*. And corresponding to each such actual state of affairs there is a true proposition—in the above cases, the corresponding propositions would be *Nixon won the 1972 presidential election, 7 + 5 is equal to 12, all men are mortal,* and *Gary, Indiana, has a really nasty pollution problem.* A proposition *p corresponds* to a state of affairs *s*, in this sense, if it is impossible that *p* be true and *s* fail to obtain and impossible that *s* obtain and *p* fail to be true.

But just as there are false propositions, so there are states of affairs that do *not* obtain or are *not* actual. *Kissinger's having swum the Atlantic* and *Hubert Horatio Humphrey's having run a mile in four minutes* would be examples. Some states of affairs that do not obtain are *impossible*: e.g. *Hubert's having drawn a square circle, 7 + 5's being equal to 75,* and *Agnew's having a brother who was an only child.* The propositions corresponding to these states of affairs, of course, are necessarily false. So there are states of affairs that *obtain* or *are actual* and also states of affairs that don't obtain. Among the latter some are *impossible* and others are possible. And a possible world is a possible state of affairs. Of course not every possible state of affairs is a possible world; *Hubert's having run a mile in four minutes* is a possible state of affairs but not a possible world. No doubt it is an *element* of many possible worlds, but it isn't itself inclusive enough to be one. To be a possible world, a state of affairs must be very large — so large as to be *complete* or *maximal.*

To get at this idea of completeness we need a couple of definitions. As we have already seen…a state of affairs *A includes* a state of affairs *B* if it is not possible that *A* obtain and *B* not obtain or if the conjunctive state of affairs *A but not B*—the state of affairs that obtains if and only if *A* obtains and *B* does not—is not possible. For example, *Jim Whittaker's being the first American to climb Mt. Everest* includes *Jim Whittaker's being an American*. It also includes *Mt. Everest's being climbed, something's being climbed, no American's having climbed Everest before Whittaker did*, and the like. *Inclusion* among states of affairs is like *entailment* among propositions; and where a state of affairs *A* includes a state of affairs *B*, the proposition corresponding to *A* entails the one corresponding to *B*. Accordingly, *Jim Whittaker is the first American to climb Everest* entails *Mt. Everest has been climbed, something has been climbed*, and *no American climbed Everest before Whittaker did*. Now suppose we say further that a state of affairs *A* precludes a state of affairs *B* if it is not possible that both obtain, or if the conjunctive state of affairs *A and B* is impossible. Thus *Whittaker's being the first American to climb Mt. Everest* precludes *Luther Jerstad's being the first American to climb Everest*, as well as *Whittaker's never having climbed any mountains*. If *A* precludes *B*, then *A*'s corresponding proposition entails the denial of the one corresponding to *B*. Still further, let's say that the *complement* of a state of affairs is the state of affairs that obtains just in case *A* does not obtain. [Or we might say that the complement (call it -*A*) of *A* is the state of affairs corresponding to the *denial* or *negation* of the proposition corresponding to *A*.] Given these definitions, we can say what it is for a state of affairs to be *complete*: *A* is a complete state of affairs if and only if for every state of affairs *B*, either *A includes B or A precludes B*. (We could express the same thing by saying that if *A* is a complete state of affairs, then for every state of affairs *B*, either *A* includes *B* or *A* includes -*B*, the complement of *B*.) And now we are able to say what a possible world is: a possible world is any possible state of affairs that is complete. If *A* is a possible world, then it says something about everything; every state of affairs *S* is either included in or precluded by it.

Corresponding to each possible world *W*, furthermore, there is a set of propositions that I'll call *the book on W*. A proposition is in the book on *W* just in case the state of affairs to which it corresponds is included in *W*. Or we might express it like this. Suppose we say that a proposition *P is true in a world W* if and only if *P would have been true if W had been actual*—if and only if, that is, it is not possible that *W* be actual and *P* be false. Then the book on *W* is the set of propositions true in *W*. Like possible worlds, books are complete; if *B* is a book, then for any proposition *P*, either *P* or the denial of *P* will be a member of *B*. A book is a *maximal consistent set* of propositions; it is so large that the addition of another proposition to it always yields an explicitly inconsistent set.

Of course, for each possible world there is exactly one book corresponding to it (that is, for a given world *W* there is just one book *B* such that each member of *B* is true in *W*); and for each book there is just one world to which it corresponds. So every world has its book.

It should be obvious that exactly one possible world is actual. At *least* one must be, since the set of true propositions is a maximal consistent set and hence a book. But then it corresponds to a possible world, and the possible world corresponding to this set of propositions (since it's the set of *true* propositions) will be actual. On the other hand there is at *most* one actual world. For suppose there were two: *W* and *W'*. These worlds cannot include all the very same states of affairs; if they did, they would be the very same world. So there must be at least one state of affairs *S* such that *W* includes *S* and *W'* does not. But a possible world is maximal; *W'*, therefore, includes the complement *S* of *S*. So if both *W* and *W'* were actual, as we have supposed, then both *S* and -*S* would be actual—which is impossible. So there can't be more than one possible world that is actual.

Leibniz pointed out that a proposition *p* is necessary if it is true in every possible world. We may add that *p* is possible if it is true in one world and impossible if true in none.

Furthermore, *p entails q* if there is no possible world in which *p* is true and *q* is false, and *p is consistent with q* if there is at least one world in which both *p* and *q* are true.

A further feature of possible worlds is that people (and other things) *exist* in them. Each of us exists in the actual world, obviously; but a person also exists in many worlds distinct from the actual world. It would be a mistake, of course, to think of all of these worlds as somehow "going on" at the same time, with the same person reduplicated through these worlds and actually existing in a lot of different ways. This is not what is meant by saying that the same person exists in different possible worlds. What is meant, instead, is this: a person Paul exists in each of those possible worlds *W* which is such that, if *W had been actual*, Paul would have existed—actually existed. Suppose Paul had been an inch taller than he is, or a better tennis player. Then the world that does in fact obtain would not have been actual; some other world—*W'*, let's say—would have obtained instead. If *W'* had been actual, Paul would have existed; so Paul exists in *W'*. (Of course there are still other possible worlds in which Paul does not exist—worlds, for example, in which there are no people at all.) Accordingly, when we say that Paul exists in a world *W*, what we mean is that Paul *would have* existed had *W* been actual. Or we could put it like this: Paul exists in each world *W* that includes the state of affairs consisting in Paul's existence. We can put this still more simply by saying that Paul exists in those worlds whose books contain the proposition Paul exists.

But isn't there a problem here? *Many* people are named "Paul": Paul the apostle, Paul J. Zwier, John Paul Jones, and many other famous Pauls. So who goes with "Paul exists"? Which Paul? The answer has to do with the fact that books contain *propositions*—not sentences. They contain the sort of thing sentences are used to express and assert. And the same sentence— "Aristotle is wise," for example—can be used to express many different propositions. When Plato used it, he asserted a proposition predicating wisdom of his famous pupil; when Jackie Onassis uses it, she asserts a proposition predicating wisdom of her wealthy husband. These are distinct propositions (we might even think they differ in truth value); but they are expressed by the same sentence. Normally (but not always) we don't have much trouble determining which of the several propositions expressed by a given sentence is relevant in the context at hand. So in this case a given person, Paul, exists in a world *W* if and only if *W*'s book contains the proposition that says that *he*—that particular person—exists. The fact that the sentence we use to express this proposition can also be used to express *other* propositions is not relevant.

After this excursion into the nature of books and worlds we can return to our question. Could God have created just any world He chose? Before addressing the question, however, we must note that God does not, strictly speaking, *create* any possible worlds or states of affairs at all. What He creates are the heavens and the earth and all that they contain. But He has not created states of affairs. There are, for example, the state of affairs consisting in God's existence and the state of affairs consisting in His nonexistence. That is, there is such a thing as the state of affairs consisting in the existence of God, and there is also such a thing as the state of affairs consisting in the nonexistence of God, just as there are the two propositions *God exists* and *God does not exist*. The theist believes that the first state of affairs is actual and the first proposition true, the atheist believes that the second state of affairs is actual and the second proposition true. But, of course, both propositions *exist*, even though just one is true. Similarly, there are two states of affairs here, just one of which is actual. So both states of affairs *exist*, but only one *obtains*. And God has not created either one of them since there never was a time at which either did not exist. Nor has He created the state of affairs consisting in the earth's existence; there was a time when *the earth* did not exist, but none when the state of affairs consisting in the earth's existence didn't exist. Indeed, God did not bring into existence any states of *affairs* at all. What

He did was to perform actions of a certain sort—creating the heavens and the earth, for example—which resulted in the *actuality* of certain states of affairs. God *actualizes* states of affairs. He actualizes the possible world that does in fact obtain; He does not create it. And while He has created Socrates, He did not create the state of affairs consisting in Socrates' existence.[12]

Bearing this in mind, let's finally return to our question. Is the atheologian right in holding that if God is omnipotent, then he could have actualized or created any possible world He pleased? Not obviously. First, we must ask ourselves whether God is a *necessary* or a *contingent* being. A *necessary* being is one that exists in every possible world—one that would have existed no matter which possible world had been actual; a contingent being exists only in some possible worlds. Now if God is not a necessary being (and many, perhaps most, theists think that He is not), then clearly enough there will be many possible worlds He could not have actualized—all those, for example, in which He does not exist. Clearly, God could not have created a world in which He doesn't even exist.

So, if God is a contingent being then there are many possible worlds beyond His power to create. But this is really irrelevant to our present concerns. For perhaps the atheologian can maintain his case if he revises his claim to avoid this difficulty; perhaps he will say something like this: if God is omnipotent, then He could have actualized any of those possible worlds *in which He exists*. So if He exists and is omnipotent, He could have actualized (contrary to the Free Will Defense) any of those possible worlds in which He exists and in which there exist free creatures who do no wrong. He could have actualized worlds containing moral good but no moral evil. Is this correct?

Let's begin with a trivial example. You and Paul have just returned from an Australian hunting expedition: your quarry was the elusive double-wattled cassowary. Paul captured an aardvark, mistaking it for a cassowary. The creature's disarming ways have won it a place in Paul's heart; he is deeply attached to it. Upon your return to the States you offer Paul $500 for his aardvark, only to be rudely turned down. Later you ask yourself, "What would he have done if I'd offered him $700?" Now what is it, exactly, that you are asking? What you're really asking in a way is whether, under a *specific set of conditions*, Paul would have sold it. These conditions include your having offered him $700 rather than $500 for the aardvark, everything else being as much as possible like the conditions that did in fact obtain. Let *S'* be this set of conditions or state of affairs. *S'* includes the state of affairs consisting in your offering Paul $700 (instead of the $500 you did offer him); of course it does not include his *accepting* your offer, and it does not include his *rejecting* it; for the rest, the conditions it includes are just like the ones that did obtain in the actual world. So, for example, *S'* includes Paul's being free to accept the offer and free to refrain; and if in fact the going rate for an aardvark was $650, then *S'* includes the state of affairs consisting in the going rate's being $650. So we might put your question by asking which of the following conditionals is true:

(23) If the state of affairs *S'* had obtained, Paul would have accepted the offer

(24) If the state of affairs *S'* had obtained, Paul would not have accepted the offer.

It seems clear that at least one of these conditionals is true, but naturally they can't both be; so exactly one is.

---

[12] Strict accuracy demands, therefore, that we speak of God as *actualizing* rather than creating possible worlds. I shall continue to use both locutions, thus sacrificing accuracy to familiarity. For more about possible worlds see my book *The Nature of Necessity* (Oxford: The Clarendon Press, 1974), chaps. 4-8.

Now since *S'* includes neither Paul's accepting the offer not his rejecting it, the antecedent of (23) and (24) does not entail the consequent of either. That is,

(25) *S'* obtains

does not entail either

(26) Paul accepts the offer

or

(27) Paul does not accept the offer.

So there are possible worlds in which both (25) and (26) are true, and other possible worlds in which both (25) and (27) are true.

We are now in a position to grasp an important fact. Either (23) or (24) is in fact true; and either way there are possible worlds God could not have actualized. Suppose, first of all, that (23) is true. Then it was beyond the power of God to create a world in which (1) Paul is free to sell his aardvark and free to refrain, and in which the other states of affairs included in *S'* obtain, and (2) Paul does not sell. That is, it was beyond His power to create a world in which (25) and (27) are both true. There is at least one possible world like this, but God, despite His omnipotence, could not have brought about its actuality. For let *W* be such a world. To actualize *W*, God must bring it about that Paul is free with respect to this action, and that the other states of affairs included in *S'* obtain. But (23), as we are supposing, is true; so if God had actualized *S'* and left Paul *free* with respect to this action, he would have sold: in which case *W* would not have been actual. If, on the other hand, God had *brought it about* that Paul didn't sell or had *caused him* to refrain from selling, then Paul would not have been free with respect to this action; then *S'* would not have been actual (since *S'* includes Paul's being free with respect to it), and *W* would not have been actual since *W* includes *S'*.

Of course if it is (24) rather than (23) that is true, then another class of worlds was beyond God's power to actualize—those, namely, in which *S'* obtains and Paul *sells* his aardvark. These are the worlds in which both (25) and (26) are true. But either (23) or (24) is true. Therefore, there are possible worlds God could not have actualized. If we consider whether or not God could have created a world in which, let's say, both (25) and (26) are true, we see that the answer depends upon a peculiar kind of fact; it depends upon what Paul would have freely chosen to do in a certain situation. So there are any number of possible worlds such that it is partly up to Paul whether God can create them.[13]

That was a past tense example. Perhaps it would be useful to consider a future tense case, since this might seem to correspond more closely to God's situation in choosing a possible world to actualize. At some time *t* in the near future Maurice will be free with respect to some insignificant action—having freeze-dried oatmeal for breakfast, let's say. That is, at time *t* Maurice will be free to have oatmeal but also free to take something else—shredded wheat, perhaps. Next, suppose we consider *S'*, a state of affairs that is included in the actual world and includes Maurice's being free with respect to taking oatmeal at time *t*. That is, *S'* includes Maurice's being free at time *t* to take oatmeal and free to reject it. *S'* does not include Maurice's taking oatmeal, however; nor does it include his rejecting it. For the rest *S'* is as much as possible like the actual world. In particular there are many conditions that do in fact hold at time *t* and are *relevant* to his choice—such conditions, for example, as the fact that he hasn't had oatmeal

---

[13] For a fuller statement of this argument see Plantinga, *The Nature of Necessity*, chap. 9, secs. 4-6.

lately, that his wife will be annoyed if he rejects it, and the like; and *S'* includes each of these conditions. Now God no doubt knows what Maurice will do at time *t*, if *S* obtains; He knows which action Maurice would freely perform if *S* were to be actual. That is, God knows that one of the following conditionals is true:

(28) If *S'* were to obtain, Maurice will freely take the oatmeal

or

(29) If *S'* were to obtain, Maurice will freely reject it.

We may not know which of these is true, and Maurice himself may not know; but presumably God does.

So either God knows that (28) is true, or else He knows that (29) is. Let's suppose it is (28). Then there is a possible world that God, though omnipotent, cannot create. For consider a possible world *W'* that shares *S'* with the actual world (which for ease of reference I'll name "Kronos") and in which Maurice does *not* take oatmeal. (We know there is such a world, since *S'* does not include Maurice's taking the oatmeal.) *S'* obtains in *W'* just as it does in Kronos. Indeed, everything in *W'* is just as it is in Kronos up to time *t*. But whereas in Kronos Maurice takes oatmeal at time *t*, in *W'* he does not. Now *W'* is a perfectly possible world; but it is not within God's power to create it or bring about its actuality. For to do so He must actualize *S'*. But (28) is in fact true. So if God actualizes *S'* (as He must to create *W'*) and leaves Maurice free with respect to the action in question, then he will take the oatmeal; and then, of course, *W'* will not be actual. If, on the other hand, God causes Maurice to *refrain* from taking the oatmeal, then he is not *free* to take it. That means, once again, that *W'* is not actual; for in *W'* Maurice is free to take the oatmeal (even if he doesn't do so). So if (28) is true, then this world *W'* is one that God can't actualize, it is not within His power to actualize it even though He is omnipotent and it is a possible world.

Of course, if it is (29) that is true, we get a similar result; then too there are possible worlds that God can't actualize. These would be worlds which share *S'* with Kronos and in which Maurice does take oatmeal. But either (28) or (29) is true; so either way there is a possible world that God can't create. If we consider a world in which *S'* obtains and in which Maurice freely chooses oatmeal at time *t*, we see that whether or not it is within God's power to actualize it depends upon what Maurice would do if he were free in a certain situation. Accordingly, there are any number of possible worlds such that it is partly up to Maurice whether or not God can actualize them. It is, of course, up to God whether or not to create Maurice and also up to God whether or not to make him free with respect to the action of taking oatmeal at time *t*. (God could, if He chose, cause him to succumb to the dreaded *equine obsession*, a condition shared by some people and most horses, whose victims find it *psychologically impossible* to refuse oats or oat products.) But if He creates Maurice and creates him free with respect to this action, then whether or not he actually performs the action is up to Maurice—not God.[14]

Now we can return to the Free Will Defense and the problem of evil. The Free Will Defender, you recall, insists on the possibility that it is not within God's power to create a world containing moral good without creating one containing moral evil. His atheological opponent—Mackie, for example—agrees with Leibniz in insisting that *if* (as the theist holds) God is

---

[14] For a more complete and more exact statement of this argument see Plantinga, *The Nature of Necessity*, chap. 9, secs. 4-6.

omnipotent, then it *follows* that He could have created any possible world He pleased. We now see that this contention—call it "Leibniz' Lapse"—is a mistake. The atheologian is right in holding that there are many possible worlds containing moral good but no moral evil; his mistake lies in endorsing Leibniz' Lapse. So one of his premises—that God, if omnipotent, could have actualized just any world He pleased—is false.

IV. Could God Have Created a World Containing Moral Good but No Moral Evil?

Now suppose we recapitulate the logic of the situation. The Free Will Defender claims that the following is possible:

> (30) God is omnipotent, and it was not within His power to create a world containing moral good but no moral evil.

By way of retort the atheologian insists that there are possible worlds containing moral good but no moral evil. He adds that an omnipotent being could have actualized any possible world he chose. So if God is omnipotent, it follows that He could have actualized a world containing moral good but no moral evil, hence (30), contrary to the Free Will Defender's claim, is not possible. What we have seen so far is that his second premise—Leibniz' Lapse—is false.

Of course, this does not settle the issue in the Free Will Defender's favor. Leibniz' Lapse (appropriately enough for a lapse) is false; but this doesn't show that (30) is possible. To show this latter we must demonstrate the possibility that among the worlds God could not have actualized are all the worlds containing moral good but no moral evil. How can we approach this question?

Instead of choosing oatmeal for breakfast or selling an aardvark, suppose we think about a morally significant action such as taking a bribe. Curley Smith, the mayor of Boston, is opposed to the proposed freeway route; it would require destruction of the Old North Church along with some other antiquated and structurally unsound buildings. L. B. Smedes, the director of highways, asks him whether he'd drop his opposition for $1 million. "Of course," he replies. "Would you do it for $2?" asks Smedes. "What do you take me for?" comes the indignant reply. "That's already established," smirks Smedes; "all that remains is to nail down your price." Smedes then offers him a bribe of $35,000; unwilling to break with the fine old traditions of Bay State politics, Curley accepts. Smedes then spends a sleepless night wondering whether he could have bought Curley for $20,000.

Now suppose we assume that Curley was free with respect to the action of taking the bribe—free to take it and free to refuse. And suppose, furthermore, that he would have taken it. That is, let us suppose that

> (31) If Smedes had offered Curley a bribe of $20,000, he would have accepted it.

If (31) is true, then there is a state of affairs S' that (1) includes Curley's being offered a bribe of $20,000; (2) does not include either his accepting the bribe or his rejecting it; and (3) is otherwise as much as possible like the actual world. Just to make sure S' includes every relevant circumstance, let us suppose that it is a *maximal world segment*. That is, add to S' any state of affairs compatible with but not included in it, and the result will be an entire possible world. We could think of it roughly like this: S' is included in at least one world W in which Curley takes the bribe and in at least one world W' in which he rejects it. If S' is a maximal world segment, then *S'* is what remains of *W* when *Curley's taking the bribe* is deleted; it is also what remains of *W'* when *Curley's rejecting the bribe* is detected. More exactly, if *S'* is a maximal world segment, then every possible state of affairs that includes *S'*, but isn't included by *S'*, is a possible world. So if (31) is true, then there is a maximal world segment *S'* that (1) includes Curley's being offered a bribe of 520,000; (2) does not include either his accepting the bribe or his rejecting it; (3) is otherwise as much as possible like the actual world—in particular, it includes Curley's being free with respect to the bribe, and (4) is such that if it were actual then Curley would have taken the bribe. That is,

(32) if *S'* were actual, Curley would have accepted the bribe is true.

Now, of course, there is at least one possible world *W'* in which *S'* is actual and Curley does not take the bribe. But God could not have created *W'*; to do so, He would have been obliged to actualize *S'*, leaving Curley free with respect to the action of taking the bribe. But under these conditions Curley, as (32) assures us, would have accepted the bribe, so that the world thus created would not have been *S'*.

Curley, as we see, is not above a bit of Watergating. But there may be worse to come. Of course, there are possible worlds in which he is significantly free (i.e., free with respect to a morally significant action) and never does what is wrong. But the sad truth about Curley may be this. Consider *W'*, any of these worlds: in *W'* Curley is significantly free, so in *W'* there are some actions that are morally significant for him and with respect to which he is free. But at least one of these actions—call it *A*—has the following peculiar property. There is a maximal world segment *S'* that obtains in *W'* and is such that (1) *S'* includes Curley's being free *re A* but neither his performing *A* nor his refraining from *A*; (2) *S'* is otherwise as much as possible like *W'*; and (3) if *S'* had been actual, Curley would have gone wrong with respect to *A*.[15] (Notice that this third condition holds in fact, in the actual world; it does not hold in that world *W'*.)

This means, of course, that God could not have actualized *W'*. For to do so He'd have been obliged to bring it about that *S'* is actual; but then Curley would go wrong with respect to *A*. Since in *W'* he always does what is right, the world thus actualized would not be *W'*. On the other hand, if God causes Curley to go right with respect to *A* or *brings it about that* he does so, then Curley isn't free with respect to *A*; and so once more it isn't *W'* that is actual. Accordingly God cannot create *W'*. But *W'* was just any of the worlds in which Curley is significantly free but always does only what is right. It therefore follows that it was not within God's power to create a world in which Curley produces moral good but no moral evil. Every world God can actualize is such that if Curley is significantly free in it, he takes at least one wrong action.

Obviously Curley is in serious trouble. I shall call the malady from which he suffers transworld depravity. (I leave as homework the problem of comparing transworld depravity with what Calvinists call "total depravity.") By way of explicit definition:

(33) A person *P suffers from transworld depravity* if and only if the following holds: for every world *W* such that *P* is significantly free in *W* and *P* does only what is right in *W*, there is an action *A* and a maximal world segment *S'* such that

(1) *S'* includes *A*'s being morally significant for *P*
(2) *S'* includes *P*'s being free with respect to *A*

---

[15] A person goes wrong with respect to an action if he either wrongfully performs it or wrongfully fails to perform it.

(3) S' is included in W and includes neither P's performing A nor P's refraining from performing A

and

(4) If S' were actual, P would go wrong with respect to A.

(In thinking about this definition, remember that (4) is to be true in fact, in the actual world—not in that world W.)

What is important about the idea of transworld depravity is that if a person suffers from it, then it wasn't within God's power to actualize any world in which that person is significantly free but does no wrong—that is, a world in which he produces moral good but no moral evil. We have been here considering a crucial contention of the Free Will Defender: the contention, namely, that

(34) God is omnipotent, and it was not within His power to create a world containing moral good but no moral evil.

How is transworld depravity relevant to this? As follows. Obviously it is possible that there be persons who suffer from transworld depravity. More generally, it is possible that everybody suffers from it. And if this possibility were actual, then God, though omnipotent, could not have created any of the possible worlds containing just the persons who do in fact exist, and containing moral good but no moral evil. For to do so He'd have to create persons who were significantly free (otherwise there would be no moral good) but suffered from transworld depravity. Such persons go wrong with respect to at least one action in any world God could have actualized and in which they are free with respect to morally significant actions; so the price for creating a world in which they produce moral good is creating one in which they also produce moral evil.

Questions

1. What is the alleged contradiction challenge that Alvin Plantinga addresses?

2. What are the two stages to Plantinga's free will defense?

3. According to Plantinga, why is it not within God's power to create "any possible world he pleases?"

4. What do you make of Plantinga's notion of "transworld identity?"

5. In what ways is Plantinga's notion of "transworld depravity" different from John Calvin's notion of "total depravity?" What problems, if any, do you see for the theist who wants to work with the notion of "transworld depravity?

EVIL AND SOUL-MAKING[*]

John Hick

Hick develops both a free will defense and a soul-making defense in response to the charge that Christian belief is inconsistent because an omniscient, omnipotent, omnibenevolent deity would not allow evil. Evil comes into existence as a result of the misuse of free will, but not through an historic fall. Following Irenaeus, humans have a nature that is in the image of God, but God desires that they grow into his likeness, and this occurs through a process of soul-growth in a world that serves as a "vale of soul-making." It is an Irenaean rather than Augustinian type theodicy.

Fortunately there is another and better way. As well as the "majority report" of the Augustinian tradition, which has dominated Western Christendom, both Catholic and Protestant, since the time of Augustine himself, there is the "minority report" of the Irenaean tradition. This latter is both older and newer than the other, for it goes back to St. Irenaeus and others of the early Hellenistic Fathers of the Church in the two centuries prior to St. Augustine, and it has flourished again in more developed forms during the last hundred years.

Instead of regarding man as having been created by God in a finished state, as a finitely perfect being fulfilling the divine intention for our human level of existence, and then falling disastrously away from this, the minority report sees man as still in process of creation. Irenaeus himself expressed the point in terms of the (exegetically dubious) distinction between the "image" and the "likeness" of God referred to in Genesis 1.26: "Then God said, Let us make man in our image, after our likeness." His view was that man as a personal and moral being already exists in the image, but has not yet been formed into the finite likeness of God. By this "likeness" Irenaeus means something more than personal existence as such; he means a certain valuable quality of personal life which reflects finitely the divine life. This represents the perfecting of man, the fulfillment of God's purpose for humanity, the "bringing of many sons to glory," the creating of "children of God" who are "fellow heirs with Christ" of his glory.

And so man, created as a personal being in the image of God, is only the raw material for a further and more difficult stage of God's creative work. This is the leading of men as relatively free and autonomous persons, through their own dealings with life in the world in which He has placed them, towards that quality of personal existence that is the finite likeness of God. The features of this likeness are revealed in the person of Christ, and the process of man's creation into it is the work of the Holy Spirit. In St. Paul's words, "And we all, with unveiled faces, beholding the glory of the Lord, are being changed into his likeness (eikovn) from one degree of glory to another; for this comes from the Lord who is the Spirit";[1] or again, "For God knew his own before ever they were, and also ordained that they should be shaped to the likeness (eikovn) of his Son."[2] In Johannine terms, the movement from the image to the likeness is a transition from one level of existence, that of animal life (*Bios*), to another and higher level, that of eternal life (*Zoe*), which includes but transcends the first. And the fall of man was seen by Irenaeus as a failure within the second phase of this creative process, a failure that has multiplied the perils and complicated the route of the journey in which God is seeking to lead mankind.

---

[*] Pp. 253-261 from *Evil and the God of Love*, revised edition, by John Hick. Copyright © 1966, 1977 by John Hick. Reprinted by permission of Harper & Row, Publishers, Inc. Footnotes edited.

[1] II Corinthians 3:18.

[2] Romans 8:29. Other New Testament passages expressing a view of man as undergoing a process of spiritual growth within God's purpose are: Ephesians 2:21; 3:16; Colossians 2:19; I John 3:2; II Corinthians 4:16.

In the light of modern anthropological knowledge some form of two-stage conception of the creation of man has become an almost unavoidable Christian tenet. At the very least we must acknowledge as two distinguishable stages the fashioning of *homo sapiens* as a product of the long evolutionary process, and his sudden or gradual spiritualization as a child of God. But we may well extend the first stage to include the development of man as a rational and responsible person capable of personal relationship with the personal Infinite who has created him. This first stage of the creative process was, to our anthropomorphic imaginations, easy for divine omnipotence. By an exercise of creative power God caused the physical universe to exist, and in the course of countless ages to bring forth within it organic life, and finally to produce out of organic life personal life; and when man had thus emerged out of the evolution of the forms of organic life, a creature had been made who has the possibility of existing in conscious fellowship with God. But the second stage of the creative process is of a different kind altogether. It cannot be performed by omnipotent power as such. For personal life is essentially free and self-directing. It cannot be perfected by divine fiat, but only through the uncompelled responses and willing co-operation of human individuals in their actions and reactions in the world in which God has placed them. Men may eventually become the perfected persons whom the New Testament calls "children of God," but they cannot be created ready-made as this.

The value-judgment that is implicitly being invoked here is that one who has attained to goodness by meeting and eventually mastering temptations, and thus by rightly making responsible choices in concrete situations, is good in a richer and more valuable sense than would be one created *ab initio* in a state either of innocence or of virtue. In the former case, which is that of the actual moral achievements of mankind, the individual's goodness has within it the strength of temptations overcome, a stability based upon an accumulation of right choices, and a positive and responsible character that comes from the investment of costly personal effort. I suggest, then, that it is an ethically reasonable judgment, even though in the nature of the case not one that is capable of demonstrative proof, that human goodness slowly built up through personal histories of moral effort has a value in the eyes of the Creator which justifies even the long travail of the soulmaking process.

The picture with which we are working is thus developmental and teleological. Man is in process of becoming the perfected being whom God is seeking to create. However, this is not taking place—it is important to add—by a natural and inevitable evolution, but through a hazardous adventure in individual freedom. Because this is a pilgrimage within the life of each individual, rather than a racial evolution, the progressive fulfillment of God's purpose does not entail any corresponding progressive improvement in the moral state of the world. There is no doubt a development in man's ethical situation from generation to generation through the building of individual choices into public institutions, but this involves an accumulation of evil as well as of good. It is thus probable that human life was lived on much the same moral plane two thousand years ago or four thousand years ago as it is today. But nevertheless during this period uncounted millions of souls have been through the experience of earthly life, and God's purpose has gradually moved towards its fulfillment within each one of them, rather than within a human aggregate composed of different units in different generations.

If, then, God's aim in making the world is "the bringing of many sons to glory," that aim will naturally determine the kind of world that He has created. Antitheistic writers almost invariably assume a conception of the divine purpose which is contrary to the Christian conception. They assume that the purpose of a loving God must be to create a hedonistic paradise; and therefore to the extent that the world is other than this, it proves to them that God is either not loving enough or not powerful enough to create such a world. They think of God's relation to the earth on the model of a human being building a cage for a pet animal to dwell in. If he is humane he will naturally make his pet's quarters as pleasant and healthful as he can. Any respect in which the cage falls short of the veterinarian's ideal, and contains possibilities of accident or disease, is evidence of either limited benevolence or limited means, or both. Those who use the problem of evil as an argument against belief in God almost invariably think of the world in this kind of way. David Hume, for example, speaks of an architect who is trying to plan a house that is to be as comfortable and convenient as possible. If we find that "the windows, doors, fires, passages, stairs, and the whole economy of the building were the source of noise, confusion, fatigue, darkness, and the extremes of heat and cold" we should have no hesitation in blaming the architect. It would be in vain for him to prove that if this or that defect were corrected greater ills would result: "still you would assert in general, that, if the architect had had skill and good intentions, he might have formed such a plan of the whole, and might have adjusted the parts in such a manner, as would have remedied all or most of these inconveniences.[3]

But if we are right in supposing that God's purpose for man is to lead him from human *Bios*, or the biological life of man, to that quality of *Zoe*, or the personal life of eternal worth, which we seen in Christ, then the question that we have to ask is not, Is this the kind of world that an all-powerful and infinitely loving being would create as an environment for his human pets? or, Is the architecture of the world the most pleasant and convenient possible? The question that we have to ask is rather, Is this the kind of world that God might make as an environment in which moral beings may be fashioned, through their own free insights and responses, into "children of God"?

Such critics as Hume are confusing what heaven ought to be, as an environment for perfected finite beings, with what this world ought to be, as an environment for beings who are in process of becoming perfected. For if our general conception of God's purpose is correct the world is not intended to be a paradise, but rather the scene of a history in which human personality may be formed towards the pattern of Christ. Men are not to be thought of on the analogy of animal pets, whose life is to be made as agreeable as possible, but rather on the analogy of human children, who are to grow to adulthood in an environment whose primary and overriding purpose is not immediate pleasure but the realizing of the most valuable potentialities of human personality.

Needless to say, this characterization of God as the heavenly Father is not a merely random illustration but an analogy that lies at the heart of the Christian faith. Jesus treated the likeness between the attitude of God to man, and the attitude of human parents at their best towards their children, as providing the most adequate way for us to think about God. And so it is altogether relevant to a Christian understanding of this world to ask, How does the best parental love express itself in its influence upon the environment in which children are to grow up? I think it is clear that a parent who loves his children, and wants them to become the best human beings that they are capable of becoming, does not treat pleasure as the sole and supreme value. Certainly we seek pleasure for our children, and take great delight in obtaining it for them; but we do not desire for them unalloyed pleasure at the expense of their growth in such even greater values as moral integrity, unselfishness, compassion, courage, humor, reverence for the truth, and perhaps above all the capacity for love. We do not act on the premise that pleasure is the supreme end of life; and if the development of these other values sometimes clashes with the provision of pleasure, then we are willing to have our children miss a certain amount of this, rather than fail to

---

[3] *Dialogues Concerning Natural Religion*, pt. xi. Kemp-Smith's ed. (Oxford: Clarendon Press, 1935), p. 251.

come to possess and to be possessed by the finer and more precious qualities that are possible to the human personality. A child brought up on the principle that the only or the supreme value is pleasure would not be likely to become an ethically mature adult or an attractive or happy personality. And to most parents it seems more important to try to foster quality and strength of character in their children than to fill their lives at all times with the utmost possible degree of pleasure. If, then, there is any true analogy between God's purpose for his human creatures, and the purpose of loving and wise parents for their children, we have to recognize that the presence of pleasure and the absence of pain cannot be the supreme and overriding end for which the world exists. Rather, this world must be a place of soulmaking. And its value is to be judged, not primarily by the quantity of pleasure and pain occurring in it at any particular moment, but by its fitness for its primary purpose, the purpose of soul-making.

In all this we have been speaking about the nature of the world considered simply as the God-given environment of man's life. For it is mainly in this connection that the world has been regarded in Irenaean and in Protestant thought. But such a way of thinking involves a danger of anthropocentrism from which the Augustinian and Catholic tradition has generally been protected by its sense of the relative insignificance of man within the totality of the created universe. Man was dwarfed within the medieval world-view by the innumerable hosts of angels and archangels above him—unfallen rational natures which rejoice in the immediate presence of God, reflecting His glory in the untarnished mirror of their worship. However, this higher creation has in our modern world lost its hold upon the imagination. Its place has been taken, as the minimizer of men, by the immensities of outer space and by the material universe's unlimited complexity transcending our present knowledge. As the spiritual environment envisaged by Western man has shrunk, his physical horizons have correspondingly expanded. Where the human creature was formerly seen as an insignificant appendage to the angelic world, he is now seen as an equally insignificant organic excrescence, enjoying a fleeting moment of consciousness on the surface of one of the planets of a minor star. Thus the truth that was symbolized for former ages by the existence of the angelic hosts is today impressed upon us by the vastness of the physical universe, countering the egoism of our species by making us feel that this immense prodigality of existence can hardly all exist for the sake of man—though, on the other hand, the very realization that it is not all for the sake of man may itself be salutary and beneficial to man!

However, instead of opposing man and nature as rival objects of God's interest, we should perhaps rather stress man's solidarity as an embodied being with the whole natural order in which he is embedded. For man is organic to the world; all his acts and thoughts and imaginations are conditioned by space and time; and in abstraction from nature he would cease to be human. We may, then, say that the beauties and sublimities and powers, the microscopic intricacies and macroscopic vastnesses, the wonders and the terrors of the natural world and of the life that pulses through it, are willed and valued by their Maker in a creative act that embraces man together with nature. By means of matter and living flesh God both builds a path and weaves a veil between Himself and the creature made in His image. Nature thus has permanent significance; for God has set man in a creaturely environment, and the final fulfillment of our nature in relation to God will accordingly take the form of an embodied life within "a new heaven and a new earth." And as in the present age man moves slowly towards that fulfillment through the pilgrimage of his earthly life, so also "the whole creation" is "groaning in travail," waiting for the time when it will be "set free from its bondage to decay."

And yet however fully we thus acknowledge the permanent significance and value of the natural order, we must still insist upon man's special character as a personal creature made in the image of God; and our theodicy must still centre upon the soul-making process that we believe to be taking place within human life.

This, then, is the starting-point from which we propose to try to relate the realities of sin and suffering to the perfect love of an omnipotent Creator. And as will become increasingly apparent, a theodicy that starts in this way must be eschatological in its ultimate bearings. That is to say, instead of looking to the past for its clue to the mystery of evil, it looks to the future, and indeed to that ultimate future to which only faith can look. Given the conception of a divine intention working in and through human time towards a fulfillment that lies in its completeness beyond human time, our theodicy must find the meaning of evil in the part that it is made to play in the eventual outworking of that purpose; and must find the justification of the whole process in the magnitude of the good to which it leads. The good that outshines all ill is not a paradise long since lost but a kingdom which is yet to come in its full glory and permanence.

Questions

1. How might one subsume John Hick's soul-making theodicy under the greater good heading?
2. Hick's theodicy is Irenaean rather than Augustinian. What are the key elements that incline him to the former rather than the latter?
3. What do you make of the soul-making theodicy?
4. On Hick's view, what is the difference between "image" and "likeness?"
5. How might one relate the soul-making theodicy of Hick to the free will defense?

O FELIX CULPA, REDEMPTION, AND THE GREATER-GOOD DEFENSE[*]

Melville Y. Stewart

Stewart contends that the Redemption Specification (R-Specification), is a specification of the greater-good defense that he outlines in his book bearing that title, which is a reworking of Keith Yandell's original work on the topic. Stewart contends that without a Fall of some sort, God's love revealed in Redemption would be without meaning, furthermore this manifestation of his love shows a dimension of it that would otherwise not be known by humanity. This route taken by God is justified even though it is a means-to-an-end course of action, since the end could not (logically could not) have been achieved without a Fall of some sort.

Common to Alvin Plantinga's Free Will Defense, John Hick's Soul-Growth Theodicy, and Keith Yandell's Growth-to-Moral-Maturity Specification of his Greater-Good Defense, is a concept that almost gets lost in laberynthian discussions of possible-worlds ontology, epistemic distance, and justification patterns. The concept is redemption, and in the following I argue that the concept in question should be given a more central role in the formulation of a Christian theistic response to the problem of evil than the above defenses might be thought to suggest. An effort is made to furnish a preliminary account of how this concept might be used to formulate a specification of the Greater-Good Defense. The defense runs roughly as follows.[1]

> GGD: For every evil that God permits, there is a good state of affairs which counterbalances and which logically requires the evil in question (or some other evil of at least equal negative value), and some evil is overbalanced by a good state of affairs (or good states of affairs) which logically require the evil in question (or some other evil of at least equal negative value).[2]

In order to meet the above criterion, a specification must be of a good or kind of goods which, when separately considered, logically require an evil of some sort, and the good or kind of goods when separately considered, must either counterbalance or overbalance the evils they require. But the GGD does not require that a specification be comprehensive—that it cover all the goods thus justified because it is a specification. It only requires that a GGD specification meet the conditions of both conjuncts. If a proposal satisfies only one of the conjuncts, then the proposal counts as a 'partial' GGD specification. If the good in question only counterbalances some evil or other that it requires, then it falls within the scope of goods which are contemplated in the first conjunct; but if the good overbalances some evil or other that it requires, then it falls within the scope of those goods which are contemplated in the second conjunct.

The specification of the GGD I wish to propose meets the conditions of both conjuncts. Simply stated, the good which logically requires the *existence* of evil is *redemption*. And the sort of evil that must exist in order for there to be redemption in any meaningful way is moral evil—evil that is brought about by moral agents who abuse their freedom of choice. Pre-lapsarian humanity does not need redemption, but post-lapsarian humanity does. It is precisely this point

---

[*] This article is reprinted by courtesy of the author and publisher. It is Chapter 7 of *The Greater-Good Defence, An Essay on the Rationality of Faith*, Macmillan of London and St. Martin's of New York, in Macmillan's Library of Philosophy and Religion, John Hick, General Editor, 1993.
[1] Cf. p. 56 of Chapter 3.
[2] In the discussion that follows there will be no need to observe the distinction made in the second conjunct between *a good state of affairs* and *good states of affairs* which logically require some evil, cf. p. 69 of Chapter 3. I am not going to discuss different greater-good defenses either; hence I shall simply refer to the greater-good defense as GGD.

that led some of the early church fathers to view the fall as a 'happy' event. Influence of this early perception can be detected in the mainstream of theodicy literature down to the present. According to Hick, some form of the 'happy fall' concept is thematic to both the Augustinian and Irenaean theodicies.[3]

The notion in early thought was part of the fuller paradoxical locution, "'*O certe necessarium Adae peccatum, quod Christi morte deletum est! O felix culpa, quae tatem ac tantum meruit habere redemporem!* (O fortunate crime (or, happy fault), which merited [to have] such and so great a redeemer!).'"[4] Known down through the centuries as the *'felix culpa'* principle, the above utterance occurs in the Roman Missal as part of the *'Exultet,'* a hymn of praise offered to God, after the paschal candle is lit and placed on its stand,[5] which is celebrated on Holy Saturday—the Saturday before Easter. The utterance became part of the Easter liturgy perhaps as early as the fifth, but no later than the seventh century.[6]

As to the author of the 'felix culpa' utterance, Arthur Lovejoy lists several possible candidates. St. Ambrose of the fourth century A.D. is mentioned because of his remark that Adam's sin brought 'more benefit than harm.'[7] Another has suggested St. Ennodius of Pavia (d. 521).[8] Most noteworthy among them is Augustine. Lovejoy conjectures that this is because of a reference which Augustine made to his having written a hymn in his discussion of the 'fall of the sons of God.' But as Lovejoy correctly points out, the context shows clearly that the hymn is not the *'O felix culpa.'*[9]

The authorship question aside, Lovejoy and Walker make two points important to the proposed specification of the GGD. In the Latin locution the fall of the human race is reckoned as a 'happy fault' *(felix culpa)* and as 'certainly necessary' *(certe necessarium)*.[10] The 'fault' or 'fall' is happy because it provides occasion for something good to take place, viz., redemption. At the same time the reality of the fault confronts us when we see its intrinsic negative value—inherently it (the fall) is an evil thing. Its positive value is instrumental only. Moreover, this 'happy fault' is 'certainly necessary' not because it follows necessarily from some flaw residing in the moral agents who precipitate it. It is a necessity that attaches to the evil in question because without it or something like it, redemption would be gratuitous. Redemption is meaningful and possible only against the backdrop of some sort of fall. As Lovejoy says, 'Adam's sin

---

[3] John Hick, *Evil and the God of Love*, rev. ed., p. 239.

[4] Ibid., p. 244, n. 1. See S.T., pt. III, Q. i, article 3, where Aquinas cites the same locution as part of the liturgy of the Pascal candle. Cf. Anthony O'Hear, *Experience, Explanation and Faith* (London: Routledge & Kegan Paul Ltd., 1984), p. 220. (The same statement appears in Aquinas' S.T., pt. III, Q. i, article 3.) Gottfried Leibniz makes a direct reference to the *Felix Culpa* locution in his *Theodicy*, p. 129, Austin Farrer (ed.), E. M. Huggard (Trans.), (London: Routledge and Kegan Paul Ltd., 1952).

[5] According to Lovejoy, in the early church it was the practice of the deacon to write his own hymn of praise to the Easter candle, a custom which is traceable back to Augustine, p. 286, n. 23, *Essays in the History of Ideas* (Baltimore: The Johns Hopkins Press, 1948).

[6] Arthur Lovejoy, *Essays in the History of Ideas*, p. 286, n. 23.

[7] Ibid., p. 286, n. 23.

[8] Ibid., p. 286, Cf., *Augustine's City of God*, 15, 22, p. 416, *Great Books of the Western World*, Vol. 18 (ed. Raymond Hutchins) (Chicago: Encyclopedia Britannica, Inc., 1952). Dennis R. Danielson in *Milton's Good God* (Cambridge: Cambridge University Press, 1982), p. 209, translates a passage from Francis Roberts' *Mysterium et Medulla Bibliorum (The Mysterie and the Marrow of the Bible*, London, 1657) that in the original contains the *'O felix culpa'* locution. According to Danielson, Roberts attributes the passage to Augustine: "'August. in meditat. lib. cap. 6. Tom. 9,'" p. 264, n. 20, but Danielson admits that it was probably not written by Augustine, p. 264, n. 20.

[9] Ibid., pp. 285-286. Cf., Charlton Walker, *'Exultet,'* p.731.

[10] Ibid., p.286

was...necessary to the very possibility of the redemptive act, which, it may be supposed, was by the author of the hymn, conceived as itself a necessary, and the central event in the divine plan of the terrestrial history.'[11]

John Hick sees in the *'felix culpa'* principle a whole theodicy ready to be unpacked, and he unpacks it with an emphasis on soul-making. He does so not along Augustinian lines, in which humans, the chief actors, are regarded as having been created by God in a 'finished state' of 'finite perfection,' but along Irenaean lines, in which humans are 'in process of creation.'[12] It is a process through which God desires to bring many persons to glory.[13] In this process persons are 'drawn by God' from a lower life of biological existence to a higher-quality life involving personal fellowship with God through Christ as redeemer.[14]

The 'starting-point' for Hick is the fact that humans are created in the image of God *and* that they are called to a soul-making process whereby they reach out to become *like* God.[15] Redemption has a place in the overall theodicy, since the only way whereby a fallen humanity can be rescued from its self-centered alienation from God is by a divinely initiated redemptive act.[16]

Working with some of Hick's ideas, I want to argue on an Augustinian base (because it appears to have fewer liabilities, a point which I hope to make shortly) that some sort of fall is necessary to the meaningfulness of redemption as a *theological concept,* and to the possibility of redemption as a *restorative act.*[17] On the conceptual side, some sort of the evil-of-the-fall notion is built into the concept of *redemption.* On the *restorative act* side, on a priori grounds, an act such as redemption is gratuitous unless some sort of fall has occurred. If the preceding point is basically correct, then it looks as if we have a good which in order to exist requires a prior existence of evil. We have not yet looked at the question, Does the good of redemption overbalance or even counterbalance the evil it requires? Let us assume for the moment a point that is argued later, viz., that the way divine love can be manifest in a fall-redemption world has a special merit or value that a world without a fall of some sort cannot have because it cannot provide the conditions needed for a disclosure of love in this special way. On this assumption we might have a specification where the good which logically requires an evil counterbalances, perhaps even overbalances, the evil required. Assuming that the good in question overbalances the evil it logically requires, let us call this the 'R-specification.' The task now before us is to look more closely at some of the ideas and issues important to the suggestion, in order to obtain a fuller picture of the R-specification. Then we shall take up the matter of whether the good specified might be viewed legitimately as overbalancing the evil it requires.

---

[11] John Hick, *Evil and the God of Love*, rev. ed., p.254.
[12] Ibid., p. 254.
[13] Ibid., p. 257.
[14] Ibid., p. 259.
[15] Ibid., p. 287.
[16] Here, in agreement with Augustine, I am assuming that the human family began in a state of innocence. An Irenaean account might not require a fall, since it is allowed that the human family might not have been untainted by sin from the very beginning. I should also note that by the term *fall* here, all is meant is some sort of lapse from innocence or goodness, that is, some sin or other is necessary. If the Augustinian account is taken, then some sort of fall is necessary, and if the Irenaean picture is assumed, then some sort of sin is necessary. Fall is not taken thus as equivalent in meaning to sin, though there might be a sense of the former that is coterminous with a standard sense of sin, viz., some sort of violation of God's law by an actual transgression or neglect.

It might be helpful to sketch something of a theological prolegomena to serve as a handy reference point for the proposal. Let us look first at the concepts of *redemption* and *necessity*, principally as they figure in the belief-system of traditional Christianity as conceived, for example, by Augustine, Anselm, and Aquinas. In a rough and ready way, the source or cause of redemption according to the aforementioned medieval thinkers is the love of God. In very general terms the concept of redemption involves the idea that God's purpose and plan for post-lapsarian humanity is salvation, which includes forgiveness and a new life extending forever into the future, vouchsafed by Christ's atonement, but conditioned on a repentance/faith response on the part of the creature.

The term *necessity* has come to have a very important role in distinctions made relating to the doctrine of the atonement, a kindred notion to the notion of redemption. Two central views regarding the necessity of the atonement have been distinguished in theological discourse: hypothetical necessity and consequent absolute necessity. The former view, held by Augustine and Aquinas,[18] is the idea that God could have forgiven sin and brought about salvation without an atonement, but the atonement is the route whereby the greatest number of blessings can be made available, and by this means God's grace is most gloriously demonstrated. So on this account, given the circumstances of post-lapsarian humanity, atonement is the way God redeems, but there is nothing in his nature that requires he take this route. Strictly speaking, there is no necessity to the atonement, but it is merely the most *fitting way* for God to provide redemption. *Consequent absolute necessity*, on the other hand, is the view that, 'Necessarily, if God redeems, he does so through an atonement.' While God was not bound to save, since salvation was his purpose, 'it was necessary to secure this salvation through a satisfaction that could be rendered only through substitutionary sacrifice and blood-bought redemption.'[19] The consequent-absolute-necessity view, where something in the nature of God requires that he redeem, is especially compatible with supralapsarianism—the doctrine that God creates the universe in order to redeem it. Furthermore, a doctrinal synthesis of this sort would strongly support the '*felix culpa*' principle. And presumably, on such a view, the good of redemption would likely count at least as a counterbalancing good, since the good of redemption is something required for some reason or other by God's nature. Just how plausible and desirable the synthesis is remains to be seen.

I should like to make three points regarding evil as actual. First, the evil putatively justified, is not merely possible evil (some possible evil or other) or the 'possibility of evil' (an occasion or environment which allows evil to occur). An evil necessary to the good of redemption has to be real—it has to exist in the world with which we are familiar. Second, the evil paired with the good that justifies it also has to be real in the sense that it is genuinely antithetic to God's goodness and what we know to be goodness. Thus, if the evil in question were not a means to some good, it would have no positive value, and so agents who did not (try to) eliminate or avoid it (God included) would be blameworthy for failing to do so if they could

---

[18] Augustine, *On the Trinity*, Bk. XIII, Chapter 10, and Thomas Aquinas, *Summa Theologica*, Part III, Q. 46, Arts, 2,3.

[19] John Murray, *Redemption Accomplished and Applied* (Grand Rapids: William B. Eerdmans Publishing Company, 1955), p. 16. Murray refrains from expatiating on just what there is in the nature of God that requires satisfaction for sin in just this way, but only draws attention to the fact that some things are necessary for God. In this case, there is, according to his view, a clear Biblical teaching that 'without the shedding of blood, there is no remission,' but he resists going any further on the grounds that the Scriptures do not say 'what is *de jure* indispensable for God,' p. 16.

(eliminate it or avoid it).[20] Third, a fall of some sort or other is logically necessary to redemption, but no one particular moral evil as opposed to some other is necessary.[21] According to one interpretation of the Biblical narrative of the fall, the prohibition that was issued in the Garden required that Adam and Eve not eat of the fruit of a certain tree. Here two points are in order. The doctrine of the fall need not be tied to such a literal reading of the Biblical data. Second, a fall could have come about any one of a number of ways and any one of the moral failures would have given meaning to the redemptive act.

On the creaturely side, in some way or other, the agents who precipitate the fall are blameworthy for having done so. On the basis of some sort of libertarian thesis the agents would be thought to enjoy some measure of freedom of choice, and thus to be responsible for their actions.

In the above, I argue that in order for redemption to be meaningful, some sort of fall or moral failure is necessary. In our discussion the doctrine of the necessity of the atonement came into view. Little if anything was said as to the nature of the atonement. The following is in small measure designed to take care of that hiatus.

More generally construed, atonement may be viewed as including at least two components: repentance and reparation or payment.[22] Repentance involves first an acknowledgement on the part of the person who did the wrong that he is responsible for the offense. In addition, there needs to be some change of mind regarding the act. There must be evidence of a desire to turn away from the wrong, or avoid similar sorts of behavior in the future. By contrast, reparation or payment involves an attempt if possible to make things right, to make payment or restore what was taken away, or what was rightfully the possession of another person. In the following, I will argue that repentance is not constitutive of the divine Atonement, but is rather a condition to accepting God's gift of atonement, and that Christ's atonement is mainly reparation, or as some would say, ransom in the sense of 'payment.'

Given the Christian understanding that the human condition suffers from the consequences of sin, there is strong indication that help for rescue must come from outside—from God. How has the Church viewed that rescue effort? As a matter of fact, there is little in the way of a definitive statement of the nature of the Atonement, when compared with the clear and definitive formulation of the doctrine of the Trinity in the credal statement of the Council of Nycea and the doctrine of the Incarnation in the pronouncement of the Council of Chalcedon. The only thing that the literature strongly indicates is that theologians have been at odds as to how the Atonement is to be understood. Views range from the 'example' theory of Socinus, to Augustine's and Origen's 'ransom' view. There is Biblical evidence for taking God's redemptive act as a ransom, since that is stated as a central purpose of the Atonement in both Matthew's and Mark's gospels.[23] The idea of ransom appears to be indicated by these passages, but there is

---

[20] In drawing attention to the point that the Redemption Specification of the Greater-Good Defense works with and justifies actual evil—evil associated with some sort of fall, I should hasten to add that the possibility of evil might still (in part or whole) be justified by the Free Will Defense.

[21] Actually a fall is not necessary to redemption, but some sort of state other than innocence in respect to sin is necessary. As I have already observed, if an Irenaean line is taken, then a fall isn't necessary, since humanity is already in some way spoiled by sin, and so is in need of redemption. A fall isn't necessary then, but something roughly akin to what is involved in the lapsarian condition is necessary, i.e., some sort of transgression of some divine prohibition or requirement is necessary.

[22] Richard Swinburne lists four, repentance, apology, penance and reparation, but I think that apology may be subsumed under repentance, and penance and reparation could be lumped together under payment or ransom. See p. 81, of Swinburne's, *Responsibility and Atonement* (Oxford: Clarendon Press, 1989).

[23] Matthew 20:28 and Mark 10:45 use the same term, $\lambda\acute{u}\tau\rho o\nu$ which translates as, 'ransom,' or 'price of release.'

controversy as to how central the notion of ransom is, since those who hold a satisfaction view of the atonement reject the atonement as ransom. But even if a ransom view is held, theologians have puzzled over the agent to whom payment is made. Origen held that ransom is paid by Christ to Satan. But why should one think Satan needed payment? If one argues that Christ 'made payment' to God, the suggestion might be thought reducible to, 'God makes payment to God,' if one takes seriously the claim that Christ is God. If payment is made by Christ to the Father, then that might be taken to suggest that somehow the Father is offended by sin, but Christ the Son is not, since the former requires payment, whereas the Son does not. There is yet another way to go with the ransom view. The theist could contend that on a Chalcedonian view, the human nature—Jesus of Nazareth—made payment to God. The ransom view aside, there is a satisfaction or reparation view offered by Swinburne. He suggests that Christ's offering on the cross could be construed as a gift such that, those seeing that they need redemption could freely choose to accept God's offer in faith. He comments, 'On this model Christ's death has no efficacy until men choose to plead it in atonement for their sins.'[24] It is thus taken as an offering of payment for sin available to the sinner, and the sinner can take this gift and present it to God in faith. Payment then is something that God offers so that the sinner can make payment to God. Until he perceives this gift and offers it in faith, it does not count as 'penance and reparation.' Acceptance of this gift involves an act of faith, which may be taken as the positive side of a believer's turning to God for help. Swinburne includes apology and repentance as part of the atonement notion. Strictly speaking, those of the Augustinian and Calvinian tradition might disagree, since repentance and apology have been construed as human actions. If the atonement is something that God alone does, in order for it to be a matter of grace, then repentance and apology cannot be constitutive of atonement.[25] Moreover, if salvation is to be a matter of grace, theologians of the Reformed tradition have argued, among others, that repentance and faith itself must somehow issue from grace. Whatever the case, the Atonement can be viewed then as satisfaction in the sense that payment is made for sin by the sinner by accepting God's free gift.

God is also an actor in the whole drama, because he is the one who decrees redemption and who assumes the role of redeemer. During the Reformation era, two positions regarding his decrees[26] were distinguished, supralapsarianism and infralapsarianism.[27] L. Berkhof comments that supralapsarianism 'proceeds on the assumption that in planning the rational mind passes from the end to the means in a retrograde movement, so that what is first in design is last in accomplishment.'[28] The order of the decrees according to this view is:

(a) The decree of God to glorify Himself, and particularly to magnify His grace and justice in the salvation of some of the perdition of other rational creatures, which exist in the divine mind as yet only as possibilities.
(b) The decree to create those who were thus elected and probated.

---

[24] Richard Swinburne, *Responsibility and Atonement*, p. 153.
[25] John Murray, in *Redemption Accomplished and Applied*, for example, sees repentance as part of the order of the application of redemption (the *ordo salutis*). See pp. 140-143. For a discussion of the nature of the atonement, see pp. 25-56. Moreover, if salvation is to be a matter of grace, theologians of the Reformed tradition, among others, have argued that repentance and faith itself must somehow issue from grace. Whatever the case, the Atonement is clearly a ransom in the sense that payment is made for sin by the sinner by accepting God's free gift.
[26] Some theologians prefer to speak of the decree rather than decrees of God.
[27] Those representative of the Counter Reformation strongly objected to the Reformed doctrine of predestination. Predestination unto reprobation was explicitly anathematized in the Council of Trent's 'Canons of Justification,' see John Clarkson, John Edwards, William Kelly, John Welch, *The Church Teaches* (St. Louis: B. Herder Book Co., 1955), p. 244.
[28] L. Berkhof, *Systematic Theology* (Grand Rapids: Wm. B. Eerdmans Publishing Company, 1959), p. 119.

(c) The decree to permit them to fall.
(d) The decree to justify the elect and to condemn the nonelect.[29]

The order of the decrees according to the infralapsarian position reflects a 'more historical' arrangement:

(a) The decree to create man in holiness and blessedness.
(b) The decree to permit man to fall by the self-determination of his own will.
(c) The decree to save a certain number out of this guilty aggregate.
(d) The decree to leave the remainder in their self-determination in sin, and to subject them to the righteous punishment which their sin deserves. [30]

Historically, Augustine, Anselm, and Aquinas held views which are fairly well in line with the infralapsarian position, and those in the mainstream of orthodox theism who were not part of the Counter Reformation have tended to support infralapsarianism rather than supralapsarianism. Supralapsarianism was introduced by a 'certain class of Augustinians'[31] and was affirmed later by John Calvin in his early theological career, and reaffirmed by Beza, Calvin's successor in Geneva.[32] One of the more weighty objections to the supralapsarian view has been the contention that given this scheme of things, it might be a greater good for God not to create. Whether one opts for the view that God creates in order to redeem (supralapsarianism) or whether one holds the doctrine that God first decrees to create, then to allow the fall, and then to effect redemption (infralapsarianism) may depend on how strong a reading one gives to the *'felix culpa'* principle. For example, the theist who sees redemption rather than creation as the principal value might on this account be more comfortable with supralapsarianism than infralapsarianism. Of course, if the theist argues that God created in order to redeem, then if redemption is something God wills, and in order to bring it about, He has to allow the fall, then the theist might face at least two major difficulties. First, such a view might attribute to God an ethical stance that is both deontological and teleological if the prohibition has a deontological base, and the allowance to sin is teleological. On this account the fall is blameworthy (on deontological grounds), and praiseworthy (on teleological grounds). If the theist allows that the fall is justified, as in the account I have given of Adam's fall, then the fall though still an evil is not so bad after all, since on the teleological scheme, the ends are all that count (there are intrinsically evil ends, but not intrinsically evil acts). Is there any way out of either or both difficulties? One possible route might be to affirm that God desired to create, and that created free moral agents are obligated to God according to some sort of deontological ethic. Such an account is not incompatible with his allowing some sort of fall and his making good use of that fall. On such a view, the free moral agent's fall would be an evil, but it is something God can use to a good end. The proposed construction is consonant with infralapsarianism but incompatible with supralapsarianism as it is generally conceived, since the latter view holds that God created in order to redeem. According to the proposal, God created the world not in order to bring about redemption, but ultimately to manifest His love. The choice of the free moral agent to disobey God is wrong, but God can

---

[29] Ibid., pp. 119-120
[30] Ibid., p. 120.
[31] Charles Hodge, *Systematic Theology* (Grand Rapids: Wm. B. Eerdmans Publishing Company, 1952), Vol. II, p. 316.
[32] L. Berkhof, *Systematic Theology*, p.118.

make good use of it in providing redemption. Thus for God, the fall in question becomes a means to a good end, but His ethical modus operandi was and continues to be deontological.[33]

As to whether the fall is likely or even possible, Hick has drawn attention to what may be a major flaw in the Augustinian description of pre-lapsarian humanity. Pre-lapsarian humans, according to Augustine, have unspoiled wills; and, as Hick argues, the prospect of Adam and Eve's turning away from the good purpose of God and choosing a 'lesser reality' is a 'glaring improbability.'

I should like to propose the following resolution to the difficulty (of accounting for the likelihood of the fall). Suppose that pre-lapsarian Adam and Eve, on the basis of information given to them by God, know that a violation of a certain prohibition regarding the fruit of a certain tree—the tree of the knowledge of good and evil—would bring about disastrous consequences. Suppose further that they come by another piece of information (either as a result of some rational process or other that is reliable, or because God discloses it to them), such that they know that if they fall, a counterbalancing, perhaps even overbalancing good would result. We have then the following scenario. Adam and Eve are both morally obligated to refrain from taking the forbidden fruit. But they also know that the evil of taking the fruit will become a means to some counterbalancing, perhaps even overbalancing good.[34] They might even know that the good would be redemption. They would thus be obligated to refrain from an evil that they know to be justified, i.e., God is just in allowing it. We have before us an instance of an evil which is both justified and someone has an obligation to try to remove it.

In the above, that which is right, viz., *refraining from eating the forbidden fruit*, arguably might not result in the greater amount of good over evil when compared with the result of *eating the fruit*, because the latter act brings about circumstances which make redemption meaningful and possible, which result might be at least as great a good as the good resulting from obedience. Most theists perhaps would hold that innocence and perfect obedience is the greater good, since redemption's role involves restoring a fallen humanity to a state of 'innocence' by means of justification. That is, the person who believes is constituted and declared righteous by reason of the imputed righteousness of Christ. But a theist might argue that redemption is at least as great a good (envisioned as an end motivationally by Adam and Eve), on the grounds that it (redemption) not only involves a restoration to righteousness, but redemption allows God to demonstrate his love in a way that otherwise he could not. There is a hint in this direction in the words of Peter, when he wrote about the redemptive sufferings of Christ in the context of a brief discourse about anticipatory revelations given to the prophets of old, 'It was revealed to them [the prophets] that they were serving not themselves but you, in the things which have not been announced to you by those who preached the good news to you through the Holy Spirit sent from heaven, things into which angels long to look.'[35] The language suggests that angels who had not fallen were curious to inquire into redemptive revelation, presumably because there was something there about which they were ignorant. The next verse, directs the reader's attention to another revelation, viz., Jesus Christ, and to the grace that was to 'be brought' to believers. Then, interestingly, there is an exhortation to holiness. The fuller picture is that redemption brings about a restoration to holiness, so that the fall/redemption motif, includes a *restoration* to what

---

[33] See Chapter 3 for a fuller discussion of God as operating with both frameworks, the deontological and teleological.
[34] Here I should note that from the point of view of Augustine, Anselm, and Aquinas that Adam's having been confirmed in uprightness prior to the fall—had he not sinned—would have been a greater good than his redemption, involving as it does the perdition of many of his descendents.
[35] I Peter 1:12, Revised Standard Version.

was lost in the fall, and beyond that, an unfolding of God's love in a special way. Thus redemption includes the good things that obtained before the fall, with the added values of grace and love that come through the unique channel of God's redemptive revelation, Jesus Christ. I do not wish to contend here that a fall/redemption universe clearly brings about a greater good than a universe where no fall occurs, but only want to argue that there is some plausibility in the suggestion that the former might bring about as much good as one where no fall occurs, and possibly more.

A number of objections to the 'fortunate fall motif' have been raised by Bruce Reichenbach.[36] The first objection is, this sort of justification has weight only if it is reasonable to take the fall as historical. This, Reichenbach avers, is not a viable option since modern science has shown that there was 'no earlier golden era of ideal moral life,' and so he claims that the view that there was a fall is mythological. He cites Hick to back up his claim. The reference to Hick involves a passage, where Hick himself fails to provide a detailed account of why a fall cannot be taken seriously. All one has to do is go over the 'biological, anthropological, geological, and paleontological work of the past century and half,'[37] and one would conclude the position is untenable. It is not my purpose here to show how Hick's claim is mistaken, but rather to call it into question on the ground that it rests on insufficient evidence. However, a theist who might wish to defend an historical fall, admittedly has precious little evidence to go on, except perhaps the Biblical data. There are able Biblical scholars who take an historical reading of the early chapters of Genesis seriously, who also have awareness of the findings of contemporary science.[38] Surely a pre-fallen state is conceivable. That there is little if any evidence for such a state, if there ever was one, should come as no surprise since its time of existence is so far removed from our own. That contemporary scientists have difficulty imagining such a state and its implications for nature, might be evidence of imagination's impoverishment, rather than evidence that such a world never existed.

The second objection is, if this justificatory pattern works, it justifies only moral evil not natural evil. First, this study was not designed to be a theodicy, though the discussion has at times taken on the appearance of a theodicy. Not a lot of attention has been given to natural evil. But a fall/redemption motif could be expanded to handle at least some natural evils. One such strategy is the soul-growth line of Hick and Yandell. That is, if there are to be certain virtues, given the fall, then natural evils are required. Since this has been discussed at some length earlier, I will not expand on it further here.

A number of variables would have to be considered and appraised before any judgment can be made as to which option—obedience or disobedience—holds the greater positive value, if such a judgment can be made at all. Some of those variables are roughly expressed in the following. What is good for God? What is good for humankind? What is good for creation, humankind aside? What is good for some species that might be of greater worth to God than the human family (allowing that there might be such a species)? The rather complex and difficult issue of which option—obedience or disobedience—is a greater good aside, if we assume that redemption, which requires the moral evil of a fall, *is* a greater good than the evil it requires, and further that this good is at least as great a good as (or a greater good than) the positive result accompanying obedience to the original prohibition, can God be moral and require of Adam and

---

[36] Bruce Reichenbach, 'Evil and a Reformed View of God,' *International Journal for Philosophy of Religion*, Vol. 24 (1988), 67-85.
[37] John Hick, *Evil and the God of Love*, p. 175.
[38] The list includes Meredith Kline and the late Edward J. Young. The former takes a framework hypothesis reading of Genesis 1, but holds to a pristine state before a fall, and the latter takes the fall as historical.

Eve obedience? How one answers the question might depend on what sort of ethical principles are entertained, or might be thought 'authorized' or 'warranted' by some sort of theistic ethic (thus far, much of the discussion of the greater-good defense has been in teleological ethical categories, since the focus has been largely on consequences). Working with a deontological approach, one might argue that obedience to God is right no matter what the circumstances. Or one might reach a similar conclusion working with the utilitarian line that obedience to God in general results in the greatest amount of good over evil. (It is only this one act of disobedience [to the prohibition of the probation] that allows a greater good to become a reality, viz., redemption.)[39]

The preceding account is only one possible way to draw the distinction between *right* and *duty*. At best it is only a preliminary and tentative theological and ethical conceptual-scheme for the R-specification. No doubt it raises more questions than it answers. But, then, any more elaborate attempt would take us beyond the limits and concerns of this chapter.

With the basic R-specification in place, I should like to consider two further, perhaps more weighty objections against it. The first is a variation on an objection raised by G. Stanley Kane against Yandell's concept of mature moral character (hereafter, MMC). Kane sees Yandell as holding that forgiveness is logically necessary to MMC. He contends that this means that if there is to be forgiveness, then sin must exist. So the possession of MMC requires the existence of sin. The objection to the view is that the MMC of one person is 'parasitic' on the fall of another. In a somewhat similar fashion the atheist might argue against the R-specification that God's redemption—including his forgiveness, which comes through his redemptive decree and act—is parasitic on the fall of humanity. God cannot be forgiving—i.e., he cannot be disposed to forgive—without the occurrence of the episodic property of man's fall. Another way of putting the difficulty runs as follows: traditionally at least, theologians have argued that the fall provides an opportunity for God to show the redemptive side of his nature. But what sense does it make to speak of the redemptive side of his nature if the 'side' or disposition in question cannot exist apart from the occurrence of an episodic property—the fall?

One possible way of answering the objection involves drawing a distinction between an eternal disposition, on the one hand, and a disposition toward the creature, on the other. The theist could speak of the eternal loving disposition of the divine nature (assuming God has a nature) as not depending on the occurrence of episodic properties for its existence. Then redemption (mercy/grace/forgiveness/salvation) might be viewed as a manifestation of this loving disposition to the creature. The manifestation of the latter, in contrast to the former, is conditioned by the occurrence of episodic properties. On this view redemption is a particularization and concretization of love in behalf of the creature. But God does not need the creature or the occurrence of episodic properties relative to the creature in order for him to love, since according to traditional theism at least, love is extant among the persons of the Trinity.

---

[39] The view that Adam and Eve's fall provided opportunity for a greater good than if they had remained innocent has never characterized the mainstream of Christianity. According to Arthur Lovejoy in 'Milton and the Paradox of the Fortunate Fall,' the number of theological writers and religious poets who gave clear expression to the *'felix culpa'* principle itself has never been very large, p. 279. But it is noteworthy that some who endorsed the principle also held that the fall provided an opportunity for God to bring about a greater good than if Adam and Eve had not fallen. John Milton (17th c.), for example, held that three greater goods spring from the fall: (1) greater glory to God; (2) greater benefits to man from God; (3) manifestation of God's grace as predominant over his wrath, ibid., p. 285 (Cf. the passage taken from Milton's *Paradise Lost, p.* 329). The list of those who agreed with Milton that a greater good results from the fall includes: St. Ambrose (4th c.), Pope Leo I (5th c.), Gregory the Great (6th c.), Thomas Aquinas (13 c.), John Wyclif (14th c.), Du Bartas (17th c.), Francis de Sales (17th c.). Jonathon Edwards espoused such a view in *Freedom of the Will,* pp. 410, 411, Yale University Press, 1957.

A variant of the objection, with a slightly different twist, occurs in the Biblical writings of Paul when he asks the Romans, 'What shall we say then? Are we to continue in sin that grace may abound?'[40] This question reflects somewhat the thought of an earlier one he raises—one that might come closer in substance to the issue presently being discussed: 'And why not do evil that good may come.'[41] One of his responses to the issue occurs in the context that includes the earlier of the two questions, and it (the response) may be constructed as an argument as follows:

1) If Christians are to live as though they were 'dead' to sin, then they ought not still live in sin.
2) Christians are to live as though they were 'dead' to sin, therefore,
3) They ought not still live in sin.[42]

Several points are in order here. First, Paul does not offer a carefully couched argument to counter the inference, but a question instead. If the Christian is 'dead' to sin, then, how shall such a person 'live in it [sin]?' Just as death and life cannot be predicated of a person, the believer cannot live in sin if she is supposed to be dead to it. Second, there is a counter in Paul's rejoinder that comes to the reader indirectly. That is, since the believer is to be 'dead' to sin, she is to be 'alive' to righteousness. More precisely, the believer's first and highest obligation is unqualified obedience to God. This is 'living' in righteousness. Doing evil that good may come, clearly, on Paul's account, does not involve compliance with that highest obligation, but rather, in fact, goes counter to it. Paul answers the mistaken inference, indirectly, but decisively. The question more to the point at hand is, Does God's redemptive act not depend on some sort of fall or transgression? Paul's response to this question—a response only roughly sketched below—might be taken as also suggesting support for the R-specification. He does say in the fifth chapter of the same epistle that sin, or moral evil, entered by Adam (by the fall) and that the remedy for this moral failure is the 'one righteous act' (redemption) of the 'Second Adam' (Christ).[43] Thus a very plausible reading of Paul's reasoning here is that the fall, precipitated by the sin of the first Adam, provides an occasion (the occurrence of an appropriate episodic property) and a context for the meaningfulness and possibility of the second Adam's redemptive act.[44]

Whatever one's verdict regarding the Biblical data cited and their relevance to the question before us, there does not appear to be any good reason for not answering the question originally posed (Does God's redemptive act require the fall?) in the affirmative. Doing so need not carry the implication that God's omnipotence is thereby diminished. Redemption is not logically possible without some sort of fall (if our earlier reasoning is correct); hence not even God can redeem without a fall. The justification contemplated then is of God allowing persons freely to choose evil, because this makes possible (not necessary) God's freely redeeming those who have fallen.

If in order for an agent to possess MMC he must possess the dispositional property of forgiveness, and if in order to possess the property in question the agent must endure or pass through episodic properties relevant to the dispositional property in question (such episodic properties as being offended or injured in some way by another), then obviously the agent cannot be said to possess MMC without certain episodic properties or something like them. But the

---

[40] Romans 6:1.
[41] Romans 3:8.
[42] Romans 6:2, my own paraphrase.
[43] Romans 5.
[44] Romans 5:21, 'So that, as sin reigned in death, grace also might reign through righteousness to eternal life through Jesus Christ our Lord,' (RSV) might be viewed as suggesting that the fall provides an occasion for redemption.

condition obtains only in a world where created moral agents offend each other or God, say world W*. By contrast in world W, where no evil occurs, forgiveness would be unnecessary, and persons could be said to have MMC without forgiveness. Forgiveness is thus only hypothetically necessary to MMC. Similarly, God cannot be forgiving or redemptive without a fall or move away from innocence (assuming with Augustine that created moral agents were initially innocent) on the part of the creature. For this reason a redemptive act on his part would be parasitic on humanity's fall or move away from innocence. But then the fall or something like it is logically necessary to redemption's being meaningful for the creature—that the one (the dispositional property) is parasitic on the other (some episodic property of the sort in question)—does not detract from divinity. As with the creature, so also for God, forgiveness is only hypothetically necessary to MMC. That is, forgiveness is necessary to MMC just in case there is a need for forgiveness. So God does not need a fall, and he does not need to be forgiving, unless there is something to be forgiven.

The second objection can be expressed as a question: Could God not have created a world, say W, containing moral worth, without redemption, and so without the evil necessary to redemption? Such a world was a possibility for God, but the free will defense points out that God could not, in creating, guarantee that he get such a world. The R-specification theorist might argue by way of response, that perhaps God has brought about numerous universes, which make up the world or all that is the case. Perhaps there is a universe, say U_1, where there is no evil, and so no redemption. Clearly there is a universe where evil has occurred. Perhaps the latter universe, call it U_2, has as much positive value as U_1, because U_2 is a universe where some sort of fall occurs or where free moral agents are morally flawed, and so God can offer redemption, and hence the mercy-grace side of God can be disclosed to the creature with greater depth and to a greater degree than in U_1. The viability of this claim, viz., that U_Z might have at least as much positive worth as U_1, might turn on whether the theist can *show* that redemption is a positive value, *not* independent of its being a remedy for the fall, and that this positive value arises from the consideration that a fall-redemption universe perhaps provides a better context or environment for the manifestation of certain dispositional proper-ties of divinity than its rival. Here, I should only like to suggest that this might be so. The theist might want to argue that love is or can be more fully manifest to the creature in fall-redemption sort of universe U_Z than in U_1. Numerous theologians have held that it is through the act of redemption that God manifests his love more clearly and fully to the creature. The Biblical parable of the prodigal son helps illustrate the point.[45] As the story goes, the father had two sons, one who was obedient to the father's directives, the other took his inheritance and left home, and followed a life of moral bankruptcy. When he ran out of money, he came to have a change of mind, and returned home. The father is pictured as seeing the son from a great distance, and when the two met, he forgave, accepted and embraced the son. Here is a story of a father's love, and so a heavenly Father's love. As an embellishment to the story, we might say that the obedient son knows the special favor of the father through a closeness that comes because of obedience, and from being with the father daily. But there is a special insight into the father's love on the occasion of the return of the profligate son. There is another dimension of love unknown by the obedient son, because there was no occasion for its manifestation in a meaningful way. Moreover, we should not be surprised that the father loved the obedient son. But love comes in a special way to the profligate son. The theist might then contend, similarly, the door of heaven is ajar, and the universe is shown heavenly love in a tender and compassionate way through redemption. Love comes

---

[45] Luke 15:11-32.

through this event with clarity and distinctness. Through forgiving mercy, there is no mistaking God's intent to reach down to the creature. One might be hard pressed if asked to rank the loves or weigh them. Arguably, love for the profligate is as profound a manifestation of love as love for the obedient son. Similarly, God's love for fallen humanity evidences divine love as uniquely and profoundly as love for prelapsarian agents.

If the R-specification can be formulated to handle the really significant objections, as our preliminary exploration is intended to show, and if furthermore it satisfies the conditions discussed earlier in connection with the GGD, the theist may be on his way toward providing substance to his claim that faith in a loving God exercised in a world which contains evil is rational.

Maybe the theist can develop other specifications which do not answer the GGD description, but which justify evils, given the fall. This suggestion might require more complex and involved greater-good notions than the GGD. Such revised notions would have to allow that there might be goods, which, on the condition that the fall occurred, might justify certain evils. Here, we have goods which require evils, but the logical necessity is conditional on there being a fall.

In conclusion, the theist might be a long way from providing anything in the way of a complete justification for the different sorts of evil that there are in the world. The preliminary and tentative account of the R-specification we have considered does not justify those natural evils which are so prolific and so (apparently) unmitigated. And then there is the question, Might it not be a greater good had God not created at all, rather than bring about a world where in order for redemption to meaningfully occur, a fall must take place, which will inevitably result in everlasting condemnation for part of humanity and part of the angelic host? One way whereby the theist might be able to affirm that creation is the greater good, might involve some sort of 'second-chance' thesis, which might lead to some sort of universalism. The mainstream of theism has tended to reject such a proposal. As incomplete as the defense is, the theist is not left with the plight of having no pattern of justification at all. We have considered only one possible specification of the GGD in a positive light, viz., the R-specification. No doubt it stands in need of further clarification and development than can be given in this preliminary study.

If the theist utterly fails to supply a plausible specification of the GGD, then there might be good reason to doubt whether the GGD pattern for which certain specifications are sought and explored is very useful as a defense. Furthermore, if the theist is not able to come up with a pattern which proves itself useful in this way, then when confronted with the reality of evil in the world he might rightly question the rationality of his belief that God is good. In this chapter and the two preceding it which focused on other justification patterns, I have tried to show that the theist's cupboard is not all that bare—that there is a pattern that is worth exploring, viz. the GGD pattern, or some variant of it, and that there are specifications (the free will defense, the soul-making defense, and the R-specification) that might be places where the theodicist (in the non-technical sense of that term) can begin to stake off the terrain of rationality.

In chapters 5, 6, and 7, three different specifications of the greater-good defense have been examined. The first two, the free will defense and the soul-growth defense, Peterson extends so as to allow for and cover $surd_2$ evils. Each specification, including the expanded versions, assumes some sort of ends-justifies-the-means principle. Notwithstanding the differences of the respective specifications, there is a sense in which they bear a 'family resemblance,' because they operate with a common pattern of reasoning, viz. evils in some way or other are justified by some greater good. Perhaps it is in order to say that the greater-good defense is in some way 'parent' to its specificational 'offspring,' even though theorists rarely, if ever, piece together some particular specification after having first consciously thought out a general greater-good defensive scheme.

Genealogically, the GGD pattern has itself a 'parent,' viz. the EJM Principle. The latter is more general yet than the GGD pattern. The former says that some state of affairs is a means to some other state of affairs, and that the former justifies in some way or other the latter. There is no claim that the justifying state of affairs *outweighs* the other state of affairs, as in the case of the greater-good defense. Moreover, the greater-good defense, at least the GGD_1 version, explicitly states that *every* evil is thus justified.

If there is a certain priority of the EJM Principle over the GGD because the former is more logically primitive, and in turn the GGD also has a priority over its 'offspring insofar as they count as offspring,' what sort of connections are there, or might there be with regard to the 'offspring' themselves? For starters, perhaps the theist might see it to his advantage to work with some sort of redemption specification in tandem with a version of the free will defense. We have seen that Plantinga's version of the modal free will defense answers Mackie's challenge (if our analysis is correct), that God could not guarantee that a world that he creates populated with morally free creatures be a world without moral evil. But conceivably, the free will defense would be strengthened, if the theist were to add the redemption specification, since if the possible world God brings about ends up being the one populated with morally free agents who are transworld depraved, then though the good of freedom of choice is preserved, and though moral goods are possible in the world in question, if the creatures inflicted with this depravity end up forever lost because of it, that would likely make bringing about such a world clearly objectionable because the negative consequences might be viewed as outweighing the above mentioned goods. But if the moral free agents turn out to be transworld depraved, then the moral failure or 'fall' of these agents makes something like a divine redemptive act meaningful, and further, God can perhaps thereby show his love in a special way that would not otherwise be possible. The free will defense completes the apologetic story, since there can be no genuine fall unless persons are genuinely free. So there is a sense in which the redemption specification needs the free will defense, and the latter needs the redemption specification. Regarding the order of the two defenses, there is obviously a priority of free will defense over the redemption specification, since in order to have redemption as a meaningful act, there must be some sort of fall, and there cannot be a genuine moral fall unless persons have a freedom to choose between good and evil.

Finally, according to most traditional theists, the good of redemption is necessary if persons are to experience soul growth (given, that some sort of fall has occurred). Hence there might be a priority of the redemption specification over the soul-growth specification (given a fall of some sort). If there is a priority, it is conditional, since it obtains only if some sort of fall has taken place. Conceivably, then if there is no fall, soul growth is possible without redemption, since redemption would be unnecessary. This is compatible with regard to the incarnate Son and the property of TWH. That is, the Son may be spoken of as experiencing soul growth without redemption, since at every stage of his life, conceivably there was perfect obedience to the revelation he had at that stage, as well as the moral requirements laid upon him. The Scriptures speak of his having learned obedience. But this learning need not have involved anything in the way of failure. Rather, at each stage, as revelation came, he exhibited obedience—full complicity with the Father's will. Hence he was not in need of redemption himself, since his every act and motive was in conformity to divine righteousness and holiness. Thus on this account, the Son may be properly spoken of as experiencing soul growth, without his having experienced a fall or moral failure, and without his having need in any way of redemption.

In this study of the GGD, we have not been so bold as to think or suggest that the GGD and its 'offspring' comprise a comprehensive justification for all the evils that there are. This would be to assume a theodicy posture. The theist might wish to argue that there are $surd_2$ evils, so long as he can subsume them under one of the specifications outlined. Even if only one of the justification patterns works, the inconsistency strategy is defused. I have argued that the redemption specification works, and that the parent GGD does as well. Further, it has been contended that Plantinga's free will defense also works and is compatible with the redemption specification. The theist could also incorporate the soul-growth defense into a larger apologetic complex, since they are not only compatible, but they complement each other in significant ways. All defenses together, weaken the probabilistic argument, since if these defensive schemes work, they reduce the kinds of evil unaccounted for, thereby diminishing the probability that God does not exist.

It has been contended that the GGD and its 'offspring' can be formulated as viable defenses. If this effort does not represent ill-gotten apologetic gains, then in the final round of this study of the rationality of theism the theist has secured a place to stand. In doing so, the defender has not staked off a wholly new terrain of rationality in respect to the issue of evil. He clearly falls within the tradition of Augustine, who said, "God judged it better to bring good out of evil than not to permit any evil to exist," [46] and of Aquinas, who similarly remarked, "God allows evils to happen in order to bring a greater good therefrom,"[47] both of which comments arise in conjunction with the *'felix culpa'* principle, and the third and final specification of the GGD.

More apt concluding lines perhaps cannot be found than those in John Milton's *Paradise Lost*. After being given a glimpse of the Incarnation, Redemption, and Second Coming by the angel Michael, Adam expresses both the paradoxical *'felix culpa'* principle *and* a greater-good notion:

> O goodness infinite, goodness immense!
> That all this good of evil shall produce,
> And evil turn to good; more wonderful
> Than that which by creation first brought forth
> Light out of darkness! Full of doubt I stand
> Whether I should repent me now of sin
> By me done and occasioned, or rejoice
> Much more, that much more good thereof shall spring,
> To God more glory, more good will to men
> From God, and over wrath grace shall abound [48]

---

[46] John Hick, *Evil and the God of Love*, rev. ed., p. 239, taken from Ench. viii. 27.
[47] Ibid., p. 239, taken from S. T., pt. III, Q.i, art. 3.
[48] Dennis Richard Danielson, *Milton's Good God, p.* 204, taken from *Paradise Lost,* [12.469-78].

Questions

1. Doesn't Stewart's defense suggest that God allows humans to fall so that he can come to their rescue?

2. How does Stewart get around the objection suggested in question number (1)?

3. Do you think that Stewart's response works? If so, why, and if not, why not?

4. Do you agree that a qualified ends-justifies-the-means principle works with the qualifier Stewart introduces?

5. On Stewart's account, is a redemption of some sort necessary for God?

RESOURCES TO THE RESCUE[*]

Marilyn McCord Adams

Adams contends that there are evils in the world that are horrendous, and that the most efficient and worthwhile route to take to handle them in terms of offering some sort of justification, is to access the Biblical data, which means going beyond the route of natural theology. This approach, on her account, better accounts for the terrible evils that are an existential part of the real world.

I. Making Good on the Horrors

My central thesis in this book is that horrendous evils require defeat by nothing less than the goodness of God. My strategy for showing how this can be done is to identify ways that created participation in horrors can be integrated into the participants' relation to God, where God is understood to be the incommensurate Good, and the relation to God is one that is overall incommensurately good *for the participant*. Our surveys in Part 2—of alternative models of Divine power and agency on the one hand, and neglected values on the other—are strewn with hints and suggestions. I want now to gather up these resources and join them with others to focus a variety of proposals for solving the logical problem of horrendous evil. A few methodological preliminaries will position us for this task.

1.1 Revisiting the Criteria

Let me first review the conditions laid down in earlier chapters for a successful solution. My suggestion (in Chapter 3) has been that to show God to be logically compossible with horrendous evils, it is not necessary to produce a logically possible morally sufficient reason why God does not prevent them. Indeed, I concluded the attempt is doubly misguided: first, because how bad horrors are finds its epistemic measure in our inability to think of plausible candidates for sufficient reasons why; second, because the pressure to provide such rationales anyway drives us to advance credible *partial* reasons why as *total* explanations, thereby exacerbating the problem of evil by attributing perverse motives to God. At the same time, I conceded that God as person would act for reasons why, that possible partial reasons why are accessible to us, and that because we are persons it may be more satisfying to or some partial reasons why rather than saying nothing at all.

In place of the futile search for sufficient reasons why, my strategy substitutes an effort to show how it is logically possible for God to *be good to* participants in horrors nonetheless. On my account (in Chapters 2 and 4), for God to be *good* to a created person, God must guarantee him/her a life that is a great good *to him/her* on the whole and one in which any participation in horrors is defeated within the context of his/her own life. Moreover, I have distinguished (in Chapter 4) between objective versus recognized and appropriated meanings, and insisted that for a person's life to be, a great good to, him/her on the whole, it is not enough that his/her life be objectively full of positive meaning or that these meanings be appreciated by others; s/he must recognize and appropriate meanings sufficient to render it worth living.

---

[*] This article is reprinted by courtesy of the author and publisher, It is Chapter 8 from *Horrendous Evils and the Goodness of God*, by Marilyn McCord Adams, Cornell University Press, 1999.

1.2. Symbolic versus Concrete Values?

The exploration (in Chapter 6) of the category of symbolic value prompts yet another distinction—between *balancing off (or defeat) by symbolic valuables versus balancing off (or defeat) by concrete valuables*. Unsurprisingly, these dimensions can break apart. It is plausible, for example, to suppose that since God is a good incommensurate with any creature, any relation of honoring or being honored by God confers incommensurate symbolic value on a creature—symbolic worth sufficient to balance off any and all its concrete or symbolic evils, even participation in horrors. Thus, Christians with a high doctrine of Eucharistic presence tell how God immeasurably honors communicants, whether by "coming under their roofs" bodily under forms of bread and wine (as Roman Catholics and some Anglicans hold; cf. Matt. 8:8; Luke 7:6) or by raising faithful hearts to spiritual communion in heaven (as Calvinists say). Stoics attribute to us humans the remarkable capacity to endow concrete ruin with great positive significance by humbly submitting ourselves to the natural order and praising its Maker and ours.[1] Similarly, religious martyrs transform their tortured deaths from degrading occasions of victimization into acts of worship by offering the selves in sacrifice to God.

1.3. Contentious Standards?

My own estimate of what it would take to defend Divine *goodness to* created persons packs two further controversial assumptions into its baggage.

1.3.1. The Scope of Redemption. First, my criterion universalist in insisting that God be good to each created person. Given the ruinous power of horrors, I think (contrary to Hartshorne and Griffin) that it would be cruel for God to create (allow to evolve) human beings with such radical vulnerability to horrors, unless Divine power stood able, and Divine love willing, to redeem. Given my estimate of the size gap between Divine and created agency, and my sense that much of what God does in relation to us is agency-enabling and thus could not count as coercion (Chapters 3 and 5), I do not share the worries of free will defenders about how God can make sure to win human cooperation without violating our freedom. I agree with them—since it is in any event empirically obvious—that created agency has been allowed to "do its thing" to the point of producing one horrendous mess after another. For that reason, I flatter the Creator with enormous resourcefulness to enable human agency to work (Chapter 4), not only to "grow it up" in the first place, but to rehabilitate it with new environments and therapeutic exercises (for example, through the indwelling of Holy Spirit; see Chapter 5) sufficient to enable it to recognize and appropriate positive meanings sufficient to defeat its own participation in horrors. If this should mean God's causally determining some things to prevent everlasting ruin, I see this as no more an insult to our dignity than a mother's changing a baby's diaper is to the baby.

1.3.2 Concrete Satisfaction? Spiritual writers disagree about the role of concrete well-being in Divine goodness to individuals. The stoically inclined and stout of heart might hold that God honors us simply by including us in creation and that this is objective, symbolic balancing off sufficient for Divine goodness to each created person. Other Stoics maintain that Divine goodness to creatures is vouched safe by the additional gift of the above-mentioned capacity for

---

[1] For an account of Stoic psychotherapy, in its ancient and modern classical forms, see Derk Pereboom, "Stoic Psychotherapy in Descartes and Spinoza," *Faith and Philosophy II* (1994): 592-625.

self-transcendence. Those who exercise it, recognize and appropriate this meaning, even add to it by repaying the honor. Some appear to hold that such Divine-human exchange of honors is sufficient for symbolic defeat.[2]

In my judgment, such Stoic positions are deep and should be savored, to let the value of reciprocal honor sink in (see Chapter 6). My own contrary reading of the Christian tradition does not depend on the notion that God owes participants in horrors more than this. On the contrary, my estimate of the size gap between Divine and human personal agency drives me to deny that God has any obligations to creatures at all. I have, however, denied that God can honor human persons by assigning them vocations that permanently crush them. Moreover, Stoic therapy is elitist, insofar as it requires a Stoic education to develop virtues strong enough to weather participation in horrors. The Nazi death camps show how, in our world, horrors are not selective, visiting only the morally well prepared. My principal reason for thinking Divine goodness to created persons includes an eventual and permanent over balance of concrete well-being, however, is that this is what the Bible seems to promise—the land of milk and honey (Deut. 31:20), the Messianic banquet (Luke 5:33-34; 14:8, 15-24; 22:14-15; Rev. 19:1-9), rejoicing in God's presence (Exod. 24:9-11; Rev. 21:1-4) in the realms of light (Rev. 21:23-24).

While it is only fair for me to lay these cards on the table so that the reader will know what I am looking for, I hope in what follows to be fair another way: by including in my review scenarios with different estimates of what is sufficient for evils to be overcome.

1.4 Theoretical Economy versus Explanatory Power

Mackie's original target was theism, what Rowe later came to specify as "restricted standard theism," the unadorned assertion of (1) the existence of an omnipotent, omniscient, and perfectly good God (Chapter 1, section 1).[3] Splendid analytic philosopher that he was, Mackie doubtless prized economy, assumed that showing theism to be "positively irrational" would thereby eviscerate" expanded" theisms—Christianity, Judaism, and Islam—in the bargain. In response, I have argued (in Chapters 1 and 2) that Mackie's strategy gets caught in the snares of equivocation. It is now time to add that where theories stand in competition, even genuine economies must be weighed in the balance against explanatory power. All of the proposals I am about to review marshall troops of philosophical and theological assumptions by way of showing how God might overcome horrendous ruin. To the extent that they tell a coherent story, these expanded theisms arguably trump Mackie's false economy by exhibiting their explanatory resourcefulness.

2. Divine Suffering and Symbolic Defeat

Rolt and Hartshorne find it easy, at one level of abstraction, to explain *why* suffering occurs: namely, it is metaphysically inevitable, something God lacks power to prevent. Neither can consistently maintain that God will be *good to* created persons by guaranteeing each a life in which suffering is balanced off by concrete well-being. At the same time, each identifies several ways in which God confers positive meaning on the lives of suffering personal creatures.

---

[2] For a discussion of these Stoic approaches, see Diogenes Allen, "Natural Evil and the Love of God," *Religious Studies* 16 (1980): 439-56; reprinted in *The Problem of Evil*, ed. Marilyn McCord Adams and Robert Merrihew Adams (Oxford: Oxford University Press, 1990), 189-208.

[3] William L. Rowe, "Evil and the Theistic Hypothesis: A Response to Wykstra," *International Journal for Philosophy of Religion* 16 (1984): 95-100.

For Rolt, exemplar goodness is suffering love, love which finds self-fulfillment through suffering. Because God suffers, created suffering has positive symbolic value as a dimension of Godlikeness. Because Divine suffering is paradigm, God functions as exemplar cause drawing creatures away from self-assertion to cooperation, in the case of personal creatures, to self-sacrifice. Insofar as this evolution occurs, created persons increase in dignity as they acquire a higher degree of Godlikeness. They win the honor of sharing God's work of suffering for the world's redemption by bringing an end to their own non-cooperative self-assertion and by serving as created loci where suffering is defeated by absorption rather than coercion. Clearly, Rolt believes that those thus strengthened for imitative self-sacrifice will (ironically) find self-fulfillment through it, just as God does. Translating into my terminology, he would hold that imitative collaboration with God would constitute *objective, sometimes recognized and appropriated, symbolic defeat* of their suffering within the context of their individual lives. Unfortunately, this benefit is not universally available: for if Rolt's God suffers without losing integrity, what makes participation in horrors so bad is precisely that it is integrity destroying. And, once more, it is empirically obvious that many participants in horrors do not find a way to avail themselves of the Divine paradigm's strengthening presence.

Hartshorne's God is responsible for horrendous suffering to the degree that Divine ideas for cosmic integration reflect an allegedly justified preference for complexity over triviality. By way of compensation, Hartshorne's God awards creatures double honors. First, Hartshorne insists, because Divine perfection includes maximal empathetic capacity, God pays creatures the respect of *com*passion: God literally suffers with creatures by feeling everything they feel. Second, God pays creatures the respect of eternal appreciation that accurately estimates the value of each and continually seeks to give it new positive meanings by organizing it as a constitutive part of ever more valuable global wholes. For Hartshorne, this means that God loves and understands every creature. Translated into my terminology, he probably believes that the honor of such Divine attention is sufficient to constitute not only the objective, symbolic *balancing off,* but also the objective, symbolic *defeat* of created suffering, which—to the extent that it is recognized and appropriated—motivates created cooperation with Divine persuasion.

If both Rolt and Hartshorne resign themselves to the Stoic conclusion that God cannot guarantee the concrete well-being of each created person, both are determined to distance themselves from the Stoic ideal of personal impassibility and detachment. Rolt and Hartshorne would find morally obtuse objections that because suffering is intrinsically bad, the morally mature would not wish it on those who love them, that compassion could have at most instrumental value, while in the case at hand, Divine suffering would only multiply the misery without doing any good.[4] Rolt deems Divine suffering intrinsically valuable because he identifies it with paradigm goodness; it is also instrumentally valuable insofar as it redeems the world—that is, insofar as it draws creatures away from self-assertion towards cooperation by absorbing blows without striking back. Psychological commonplaces get at the intuitions behind Rolt's absorption theory. Most of us know from experience how emotions (anger, fear, pain) can seem overpowering, as if—were we consciously to expose ourselves to their full force—our subjective worlds would come apart. We also know that such feelings are easier to face in contexts of personal intimacy, where the burden is somehow shared. Switching roles, we sometimes experience how by just being in the same room with someone who is hostile or anxious, we also come to feel hostile or anxious—as if one way (not the only way) perceive the feeling is to have

---

[4] Richard Creel repeatedly voices such objections and promotes the Stoic idea in chapter 8 of his book *Divine Impassibility: An Essay in Philosophical Theology* (Cambridge: Cambridge University Press, 1986), 140-58, esp. 155-58.

or share the feeling. Notice that for a friend or therapist to have the feeling, it is not necessarily for them to *be* angry fearful or anxious; it is a matter of there being a sympathetic vibration in the feeling core of friend or therapist, that enables them to perceive other person's emotions.[5] Such experiences of shared feelings, of bear one another's burdens, of having one's own load lightened, suggest that sympathetic presence cures by absorbing energy from the emotional storm so that it doesn't have to be contained, converted, or redirected. Given the additional hypotheses that this process can operate at the unconscious level and that God is omnipresent with defenses down ready to empathize, Rolt's picture of God's gradually weaning humans away from hostile self-assertion and toward cooperation becomes clearer; so does his notion that God's empathetic love might strengthen us to suffer: for insofar as God absorbs the destructive energy of our own anger, fear, and anxiety so that we don't have to manage them, we are freed to spend our resources suffering the emotions of others.

Both Rolt and Hartshorne recognize Divine suffering as a move in a personal relationship, as an expression of solidarity, of cost sharing in the expensive project of cosmic ordering, as a manifestation of Divine love. Because of God's privileged metaphysical position, it is only "meet and right" that God should take the initiative in sharing the pains and agonies of the world. Without going so far as to claim that love for the suffering *requires* the lover to suffer, my sympathies are with them in recognizing *com*passion as a powerful and appropriate way to express love, in my judgment, one not out of character for the Bible's God.

3. Suffering as a Vision into the Inner Life of God

An alternative suggestion for integrating horrendous suffering into the participant's relationship with God, is indifferent on the question of Divine passibility (perhaps also on the issue of Divine personality). It arises out of reflection on religious (indeed, mystical) experience, and consists of the hypothesis that suffering itself is a vision of God. To grasp the intuitive appeal of this idea, reach back to Chapter 5 for Rudolf Otto's notion that a paradigm religious experience of God triggers characteristic feeling accompaniments—fear, dread, radical dependence, terror, stupefying confusion, uncleanness, shame, fascination, and attraction. Otto himself recognizes that such feelings can be triggered by circumstances other than paradigm visions of God and that they can be had separately. Given Divine omnipresence and the size gap between God and creatures, would it be so implausible to propose that these feelings are themselves ways that human being perceives God? Simone Weil thought not when she compared *affliction*—a condition associated with long-term physical pain, which crushes the afflicted by destroying social relations and filling them with self-loathing, shame, and defilement almost in proportion to their innocence—to the painfully tight grip of a beloved's embrace (in this case God's). Nor is it surprising if many (perhaps all but the last) of these feelings should be brought on both by Divine presence and by horrendous suffering. For both are disproportioned to the human psyche and, as such, "mind-blowing," anxiety producing, incapacitating, and humiliating.

Were this hypothesis—that horrendous suffering itself is a vision into the inner life of God—true, it would follow that, alongside its horrendous aspect, horrendous suffering has a good aspect insofar as it is cognitive contact with the Divine. Simone Weil, recognizing (as she thought) the true character of affliction as Divine embrace, found experience of it to confer positive meaning, even in the absence of any hope of her affliction's being eventually balanced

---

[5] Richard Creel usefully makes a distinction like this in *Divine Impassibility,* 130-31. See also sections 6.2-3 below.

off by concrete well-being. Not only does she regard Divine embrace as an honor that would symbolically *balance off* the negative concrete and symbolic aspects of affliction, she also suggests that by virtue of this good aspect, affliction can be integrated into a relationship with God, the whole of which is sufficient for the objective, symbolic *defeat* of its horrendous aspect. Weil commends the subjective appropriation of this assessment as an occasion of self-transcendence in which the afflicted are in a position to love God for God's own sake, despite (perhaps in part because of) their own sense of degradation and even in the face of permanent *concrete* ruin.[6]

Alternatively, and in my view preferably, the notion that horrendous suffering has an objective good-making aspect (cognitive contact with the Divine) could also be combined with the assumptions that God preserves created persons alive after their death in wholesome environments, that their relationships with God resolve into beatific intimacy so that the "sufferings of this present life" are concretely balanced off. We could thereby arrive at the view that everyone will eventually be enabled to recognize any antemortem participation in horrors as other moments of intimacy with God and so, integrate them into the relationship that floods their lives with objective and (by then) recognized and appropriated positive meaning. Participation in horrors would still be defeated via its organic relation to the participant's relationship with God; the good-making aspect of horrors (cognitive contact with the Divine) would be significant, not as itself sufficient for defeat, but as the objective feature that constitutes the experience as part of the participant's relationship with God.

4. Divine Gratitude, Heavenly Bliss

If Simone Weil seeks meaning for affliction in our antemortem experiences, Julian of Norwich envisions a postmortem happy ending that could be a textbook case of Chisholmian defeat. As she sees it, God will usher us into heaven with the greeting, "Thank you for your suffering, the suffering of your youth!"[7] Because she reckons sin as the worst scourge a soul can endure,[8] she imagines that God will publicly compensate us for what we have undergone and that such Divine rewards will bring everlasting honor and unending joy.

Surely, God's expressed gratitude to us and eagerness to compensate us for our participation in horrors would integrate such participation into our relationships with God. Moreover, if God is the incommensurate good and beatific relationship with God is incommensurately good for human beings, then such Divine gestures constitute objective, symbolic defeat of horrendous evils within the context of the participant's life. Julian makes clear that many dimensions of this symbolic defeat are recognized and appropriated, not only by the participant, but also by the assembled heavenly multitude, including fellow human beings.[9] Finally, she is unequivocal that heaven is utopic in that not only symbolic but concrete well-being is eternally guaranteed.[10]

Julian's account combines a vivid appreciation of the size gap between God and creatures with an emphasis on God's delightful determination to pay human beings honors that they can't metaphysically deserve. There is, however, one honor that she omits: Julian's God does not pay

---

[6] Diogenes Allen discusses Weil's position in "Natural Evil and the Love of God," 198-204.
[7] Julian of Norwich, *Revelations of Divine Love*, trans. Clifton Wolters (London: Penguin Books, 1966), chap. 14, p. 85.
[8] *Revelations of Divine Love*, chap. 39, p. 120; chap. 40, p. 122; chap. 63, p. 175; chap. 77, p. 199.
[9] *Revelations of Divine Love*, chap. 14, pp. 85-86.
[10] *Revelations of Divine Love*, chap. 21, p. 96; chap. 39, pp. 120-21.

created persons the respect of revealing any partial or total reasons why horrendous evils were allowed, the courtesy of disclosing what purpose they serve in the Divine plan. When Julian presses God about the problems of sin and reprobation, she receives twin assurances: that sin is necessary and that God will do a deed on the last day that will make everything all right.[11] Perhaps she believes that—because of the size gap—even in heaven, human nature at its postmortem best will lack the cognitive and emotional maturity necessary to grasp any of God's many reasons. No doubt, her religious experiences give her confidence that in heaven our incomprehension will not matter because the intimate presence of Divine Goodness will be so convincing, the overcoming of evil too evident. At another level, however, she may find one partial answer too obvious—namely, that God wanted to rejoice in human children, while vulnerability to participation in horrors is part of leading a merely human life (see Chapter 2).

While I myself want to harvest fruits from each of the above three stratagems, it is important to note that none of them is exclusively Christian. For example, versions of each would constitute satisfactory responses within Judaism as well. With the last two proposals, however, I seize the offensive against Mackie, to show how, when it comes to defeating horrendous evils, the central doctrines of Christian theology—Christology and the Trinity—have considerable explanatory power.

5. Chalcedonian Christology—A Christian Solution to the Problem of Horrors

Within the circle of Christian theology, my own Christological approach makes certain distinctive choices. (1) Over the centuries, there have been many philosophical accounts of the claim "God was in Christ reconciling the world to Himself." Insofar as contemporary Protestant theology has been dominated by German thinkers, its formulations tend to be shaped by Hegel and other post-Kantian idealists. The other main influence is, of course, process philosophy. Relative to these, my own position reaches back to that other period of analytic philosophy and might be counted neoscholastic insofar as it embraces medieval philosophical interpretations of the so-called Chalcedonian definition. Recall, the problem for the Fathers at Chalcedon in 451 C.E. was to define the relation of Divine and human natures in Christ.[12] On the one hand, they claimed that each nature was in Christ *complete* and *without confusion.* In particular, they maintained, the human nature of Christ includes not only a human body but a fully human soul with a finite consciousness: as the Sixth Ecumenical Council at Constantinople (680-81) was later to make explicit, a finite will distinct from the Divine.[13] On the other hand, the Fathers insisted that these two natures were united in one person, where the term 'person' is not understood in the contemporary ordinary sense as an individual center of thought and volition, but in a technical sense as an individual suppposit of a rational substance nature. Thus, their claim was not—contrary to Apollinarius—that there was but one center of consciousness in Christ. Rather, where other substance individuals (such as Socrates) supposit (instantiate) only one natural kind (for example, human nature), the Divine Word, the Second Person of the Trinity (in the technical sense), supposits the Divine nature eternally and necessarily and also a particular human nature tempo-rally and contingently. (2) For present purposes, I am interested in that part of the work of Christ that sheds light on Divine defeat of horrendous evils in the lives of all

---

[11] *Revelations of Divine Love,* chap. 32, p. 110.
[12] H. H. Denzinger, "Conc. Chalcedonense 451: Oecumenicum IV (contra Monophysitas)," in *Enchiridion Symbolorum et Definitionum* (Freiberg-in-Brisgaw: B. Herder, 1911), 65-67.
[13] H. H. Denzinger,"Conc. Constantinopolitanum III 680-681: Oecumenicum VI (contra Monotheletas)," in *Enchiridion Symbolorum et Definitionum,* 129.

participants (victims as well as perpetrators). In this connection, Anselm's satisfaction theory will be less helpful than Julian of Norwich's themes of at-one-ment and identification (see Chapter 6).

5.1. Partial Reasons Why: Divine Commitment to Material Creation

Returning to our question—how can God be seen to love human nature, to be good to each individual human person He creates, when He has set us in a world like ours?—the first part of my answer is that God *loves* material creation, and this love finds its focus in human nature three ways. First, like any good parent with its offspring, God wants as far as possible, for creatures to be like God and yet still possess their own integrity And so God creates physico-chemical processes, with energy and dynamic power to interact, produce new things within a framework of order and stability. Beyond that, God wants creation not only to move and change, but to live. And so God makes plants and animals with a capacity for self-replication and self-sustenance. Moreover, God endows life with perception, so that it can take and interact with the world from its own point of view. Finally, God endows animal nature with personality, with self-consciousness, with the capacity for relationship, with the ability to give and receive love. Thus, human nature is the culmination and crown of God's efforts to make material creation—while yet material—more and more like God.

Second, love seeks union with its object. Classical theology insists God and creatures are united by a real relation of dependence of the creature on God. Divine love drives beyond such metaphysical necessities for more. But God and material creation make an unmatched pair: for God is infinite, creation, finite; hence they are ontologically incommensurate (see Chapter 4). God is Spirit, matter, something of a fundamentally different kind (see Chapter 5). So, much as a pet owner domesticating its animal, God seeks to cross the gap between God and God's beloved, by lifting the material up into the spiritual, first by animating it, endowing it with perception and appetite, then by personalizing it. Human nature thus stands at the frontier of material creation, the point at which God can enter into loving intimacy with it. God specially prizes human nature, because here the material creation takes an independent point of view on what God has made. It interests God to learn what we will think of it and how we will value it.

Yet, God was not content to join Godself to material creation in relations of loving intimacy with created persons. God's desire for it was so great, that God decided to enter it Godself, to unite a particular human nature to the Divine person as God's very own nature, to become a human being. Incarnation is the culmination of a series of things Divine love does to unite itself with material creation. (Note: strictly speaking, the result would not have to be precisely Chalcedonian. If the Divine essence, or another of the Divine persons, or each of them could assume human nature, those would constitute alternative ways for God to unite material creation to Godself.)[14]

---

[14] Ockham speculated that it was logically possible for the Divine essence or each of Divine persons to assume a human nature; cf. my article "Relations, Subsistence, and Inherence, or Was Ockham a Nestorian in Christology?" *Nous* 16 (1982): 62-75; and my other article "The Metaphysics of the Incarnation in Some Fourteenth-Century Franciscans," in *Essays Honoring Allan B. Wolter*, ed. Girard Etzkorn (St. Bonaventure, N.Y: Franciscan Institute Publications, 1985), 21-57.

5.2 Identification: The "How" of Horrors Defeated

According to the account I am proposing, Divine love chooses to identify with material creation by assuming a particular human nature, by becoming a particular human being, because it is in human nature that the cost of joining spirit to matter, personality to animaliry is most keenly (because most self-consciously) felt, most prominently in human vulnerability to horrors. God Incarnate led a merely human life, saw the world from a finite human consciousness that did not have access to Divine omniscience. God Incarnate learned obedience through suffering (Heb. 5:7-8), working God's way through our developmental struggles. In God's merely human personality, God gave Godself to persons of unstable loyalties who deserted and betrayed Him. In the crucifixion, God identified with all human beings who, participate in actual horrors—not only with the victims (of which He was one), but also with the perpetrators. For although Christ never performed any blasphemous acts in His human nature, nevertheless, His death by crucifixion made Him ritually cursed (Deut. 21:23; Gal. 3:13), and so symbolically a blasphemer. Thus, God in Christ crucified is God casting His lot with the cursed and blaspheming (and hence the perpetrators of horrors) as well.

God in Christ crucified cancels the curse of human vulnerability to horrors. For the very horrors, participation in which threatened to undo the positive value of created personality, now become secure points of identification with the crucified God. To paraphrase St. Paul, neither the very worst humans can suffer, nor the most abominable things we can do can separate us from the love of God in Christ Jesus (Rom. 8:31-39). Once again, I do not say that participation in horrors thereby loses its horrendous aspect: on the contrary, they remain by definition prima facie ruinous to the participant's life. Nevertheless, I do claim that because our eventual postmortem beatific intimacy with God is an incommensurate good for human persons, Divine identification with human participation in horrors confers a positive aspect on such experiences by integrating them into the participant's relationship with God (see section 3 above). Retrospectively, I believe, from the vantage point of heavenly beatitude, human victims of horrors will recognize those experiences as points of identification with the crucified God, and not wish them away from their life histories. God's becoming a blasphemy and a curse for us will enable human perpetrators of horrors to accept and forgive themselves. For they will see, first of all, that these acts did not separate them from the love of the God who thus identified with them on the cross (see Chapter 5). They will also be reassured by the knowledge that God has compensated their victims (once again through Divine identification and beatific relationship). Finally, they will be amazed and comforted by Divine resourcefulness, not only to engulf and defeat, but to force horrors to make positive contributions to God's redemptive plan. (As noted in Chapter 7, the prototype for such Divine reversals is, of course, the synoptic Passion narratives, in which everything Jesus' enemies do to demonstrate that He cannot be Messiah, including bringing Him to a ritually cursed death, actually plays into His hands and enables Him to fulfill that vocation.) Hence, God's identification with human participation in horrors, enables God to defeat their evil aspect within the course of the individual participant's life.

Note, my view does not make participation in horrors necessary for the individual's incommensurate good. A horror-free life that ended in beatific intimacy with God would also be one in which the individual enjoyed incommensurate good. My contention is rather that by virtue of endowing horrors with a good aspect, Divine identification makes the victim's experience of horrors so meaningful that one would not retrospectively wish it away, enables the perpetrator to accept his/her participation in horrors as part of a good and worthwhile life. Nor is participation in horrors merely instrumentally related to the beatific end, as God's necessary or chosen means for educating one into beatitude. As a point of identification with God it *is partially constitutive* of the relationship that makes one's life overwhelmingly worth living and, so, is meaningful apart from any putative causal or educational consequences. Moreover, unlike Hick's soul-making theodicy, which allows individual participation in horrors to contribute to the mysterious aspect of the world, but delays individual participation in the good to some later point when the educational process has taken better hold (see Chapter 3), my approach makes present participation in horrors *already* meaningful because they are partially constitutive of the most meaningful relationship of all. My claim is that the Incarnation *already* endows participation in horrors with a good aspect that makes way for their objective, symbolic defeat, even if participants do not yet recognize or appropriate this dimension of meaning (say, because they are non-Christians or atheists). If postmortem, the individual is ushered into a relation of beatific intimacy with God and comes to recognize how past participation in horrors is thus defeated, and if his/her concrete well-being is guaranteed forever afterward so that concrete ills are balanced off, then God will have been good to that individual despite participation in horrors. Theologically, my concern is obvious: to insure that each person's earthly antemortem career has deep positive significance for her/him.

Once again, let me emphasize how Chalcedonian Christology (or its metaphysically near relatives) is key here. If what does the soteriological job of meaning-making is God's identification with human beings and God's participation in horrors, this value cannot be obtained by sending someone else, however exalted. It is *God's* becoming a human being, experiencing the human condition from the inside, from the viewpoint of a finite consciousness, that integrates the experience into an incommensurately valuable relationship.

6. Passibility in the Divine Nature?

Of the proposals reviewed thus far, only the first and fourth appeal to Divine suffering as an instrument of the defeat of horrendous evil, and they do so in different ways. Rolt and Hartshorne locate the suffering preeminently in the Divine nature, indeed make it not only metaphysically necessary but self-fulfilling for God as a loving and omniscient being. As developed so far, my Christological approach shifts metaphysical frameworks and posits Divine participation in horrors by virtue of God's assumed human nature. Thus, like the second and third strategies, marshalling the resources of Chalcedon preserves neutrality where the impassibility of the Divine nature is concerned. Put otherwise, because each of the second through fourth proposals is logically independent of the impassibility of the Divine nature, each could consistently be combined either with this thesis or with its denial.

6. 1. Diametric Oppositions

The time is ripe to pause briefly over the problems and advantages of this idea. The doctrine of Divine impassibility takes its inspiration from the *political* model of the self-sufficient patron able not only to flourish but to wield unobstructable power from behind the walls of his impregnable fortress (see Chapter 6). On its metaphysical interpretation, this picture spawned what I have called the classical explanatory model, with its corollary that the ultimate explainer must be pure actuality and so lack any capacity to be causally acted upon or affected by any alien power. Stoics took this portrait to signify an *ethical* ideal of self-sufficient peace of mind so detached from externals as to be incapable of emotional disturbance. Classical theology took the first to imply the second (at least where Divine happiness is concerned), because it understood the having of emotions (*passiones*) to involve genuine causal passivity (being acted upon by something else). Hence, Anselm, Maimonides, and Aquinas offer reductive analyses of Biblical talk of Divine emotions: God does not literally feel mercy (etymologically, *misericordia* means 'have a miserable heart') or anger, but only produces effects of the sort that merciful or angry human rulers would produce.[15] Coming from the other side, Rolt also grants that God's suffering love involves His being causally affected, while Hartshorne seems to agree that empathetic omniscience involves the same. Philosophical theologians of various stripes have begged to differ, rejecting any "causal theory of perception" where Divine cognitive psychology is concerned.[16] Berkeley's God was supposed to perceive any and all ideas—presumably pains and feelings as much as colors and flavors—without being causally affected by anything else. In any event, I have already sketched (in Chapter 4) how the classical explanatory model might be modified to permit the Divine essence to be causally affected by creatures without giving passive power such prominence as Rolt and Hartshorne do.

So far as the Stoic ethical ideal is concerned, Rolt and Hartshorne simply counterchallenge with another one diametrically opposed to it. They maintain that if benevolence might, love cannot be reduced to simply willing good for another. Rather, the capacity for love includes the capacity for understanding and empathy. Rolt goes further virtually to exclude the possibility that actual love escapes suffering. It follows for him that because love is God's nature, suffering love is paradigm goodness and thus intrinsically valuable. It is also instrumentally valuable insofar as it drains off hostility and strengthens creatures to cooperate with one another, even embrace their sacrificial vocations to suffer with God. Likewise, without buying into their metaphysical pictures, Julian of Norwich views Christ's desire to suffer for human creatures positively, as an extravagant gesture in God's romance with the human race. It is the currency of honor insofar as Christ undertakes crucifixion as the most difficult deed of knightly valor conceivable in His suit to win the soul's love. It shouts out solidarity, when "fairest Lord Jesus" submits to caricature by crucifixion to maintain the family resemblance, to make sure God and humans are still images of one another even after Adam's bruising fall (see Chapter 6). Again, compassion affects the character of collaborative enterprise, especially if (as I suggest in section 5) God's project of "wedding heaven to earth and earth to heaven" requires us to play a central and costly role. There is a relationship difference between the general who stays back at headquarters or who watches the battle from a hilltop high above and the commander who gets down in the trenches to take the fire with his soldiers.

Nevertheless, talk of God's suffering with us can be fast and loose, some think, even sentimental.[17] And, leaving classical explanatory models and Stoic ethics to one side, issues of intelligibility still remain. For Hartshorne not only declares that Divine omniscience feels all our feelings; he tries to comfort us with the notion that "God suffers what we suffer." Moreover, he appears to treat these two claims as equivalent. Two recent commentators have begged to differ.

---

[15] Anselm, *Proslogion*, chaps. 7-8, in *Opera Omnia*, ed. E S. Schmitt (Edinburgh: Thomas Nelson & Sons, 1938-61) 1.105.9-106.14 (vol. 1, p. 105, line 9, through p. 106, line i4). Maimonides, *The Guide for the Perplexed*, trans. M. Friedlander (New York: Dover, 1956), chaps. 50-58, 67-83: Aquinas, *Summa Theologica* 1.25.3 (part 1, quest. 25, art. 3), ad 2um.

[16] Cf. Marilyn McCord Adams, *William Ockham* (Notre Dame, Ind.: University of Notre Dame Press, 1987), 1115-50, esp. 1117-30.

[17] Rowan Williams seems to lodge this criticism against me in "Reply: Redeeming Sorrows," in *Religion and Morality*, ed. D. Z. Phillips (New York: St. Martin's Press), 132-48.

6.2. Divine Will, How Thwartable?

Paul Fiddes warns that feeling what we feel will not guarantee Divine suffering, because suffering requires that the inner feeling is relevantly against one's will or appetite and so involves a measure of causal constraint.[18] Berkeley's God, Who feels all our feelings without being causally affected in any way, would not—on Fiddes's analysis—suffer thereby. Divine suffering is a possibility only on the assumption of other agencies operating independently enough of the Divine will as to be able to oppose it. Fiddes believes only free creatures fill this bill, and so opts for the process picture according to which all creatures are "free" in the sense of being self-determined to a degree. He reasons that what happens by natural necessity would not qualify where God freely and wittingly created things of that nature.[19]

Granting Fiddes's intuitive contention that suffering has to be relevantly against the sufferer's will or appetite, classical medieval metaphysics would contest his further inference that only free creatures could oppose God in the requisite degree. Classical medieval metaphysics was virtually unanimous that the constitution of created natures (what it is to be fire or horse or human), as opposed to their real or thought *existence,* was metaphysically necessary and independent of anyone's will, human or Divine. Not even omnipotence included the power to make fire a natural coolant.[20] More importantly for present purposes, not even God could place human beings in a world like this without their being radically vulnerable to horrors. It seems to me that the metaphysically necessary constitution of created natures is something God has to work with and around in deciding whether and which sorts of things to produce in what circumstances. And this sort of independence of God's will constrains Divine plans in a sense robust enough to occasion frustration and grief.

6.3. Suffering What We Suffer?

Richard Creel raises the different objection that even if God feels all of our feelings, it will not follow that God *has the same emotions* as we have.[21] Consider a child who is terrified of having her teeth filled. In an effort to comfort and reassure, the parent schedules back-to-back appointments, so that the child can watch her mother safely undergo the ordeal before getting in the chair herself. Even if we grant for the sake of argument that the mother's sensory feelings are the same as the child's, their emotions will differ. When the dentist looms over the child with huge hypodermic in hand, panic may take over, driving the mother's example out of mind or making it appear a clever ruse. So far as the child is concerned, the needle's bite, the skull-vibrating drill may be meek preludes to unknown and gruesome tortures, stretching out for eternity or ending in death. By contrast, the adult has power to halt the procedure and knowledge to place the episode in a wider benevolent context, both of which enable the mother to submit with reasonable equanimity, at most wincing at a few twinges. Were this not so, watching the mother would not fortify but only frighten the child further. The mother must react to the same sensations with different emotions if she is to teach her daughter that dentistry is not really dangerous to one's health!

---

[18] Paul Fiddes, *The Creative Suffering of God* (Oxford: Clarendon Press, 1988), 48-76.
[19] Ibid., 207-57.
[20] Adams, *William Ockham,* 1065-83; and Adams, "Ockham on Truth," *Medioevo* 16 1990: 143-72.
[21] Creel, *Divine Impassibility,* 130-31.

So, too, and all the more so, where God and human participants in horrendous evils are concerned. (i) Because there is a limit to how much finite minds can hold, it is possible for pain, dread, terror, anxiety, shame, or rage to crowd everything else out of our awareness. By contrast, even if God feels our negative feelings, Divine consciousness would contain so much else—such as joy and delight in Divine perfections, in the love of one Divine person for another, in cosmic goodness—that our feelings would represent less than "a drop in the bucket" of Divine awareness. Even Hartshorne admits the affective tone of the Divine mind could not reasonably be dominated by our feelings. Finite imagination has limited capacity to manage complexity with simplicity, even keep its subjective bearings. The problem of horrendous evils gets its purchase from the fact that our meaning-making capacities are limited, indeed characteristically stumped by our participation in horrendous evils. Even on passibilist conceptions, however, it pertains to Divine perfection that the Divine mind cannot be "blown"; however silent, God cannot be the subject of dumbfounded confusion; in the Divine nature, God cannot lose cognitive grip.

Many meaning-threatening emotions involve beliefs and judgments that omniscient omnipotence could not share. Fear and dread, terror and anxiety often depend upon uncertainties and our inability to see developments in a wider context. Anger, fear, and anxiety respond to situations that damage our prospects for survival and flourishing beyond our powers to repair. Even for Rolt and Hartshorne, God's existence is metaphysically necessary; no matter how much suffering there is in creation, it belongs to God's nature to be able to respond to it in a creative and loving way. Thus, even if God feels whatever we feel, and has a comprehensive awareness of our beliefs, God cannot experience the Ottonian emotions that I have suggested might characterize participation in horrors (see Chapter 5, and section 3 of this chapter).

If the size gap makes it metaphysically impossible for God to have our emotions simply by virtue of feeling our feelings, Creel and Fiddes both press the point that we should not really want God to have all the same emotions.[22] If—like the child in the dentist's office—we want God to be present in our suffering in such a way as to cancel our sense of abandonment, we also need God to keep Divine composure in order to help us make good on the evils we experience. But in that case, it might seem, God's feeling our feelings would serve little purpose. For the surface appeal of Divine sympathy rests on analogies with human relationships, on the human cognitive limitation (see Chapter 2) that, for example, we can't fully know what it is like to lose a beloved child in a senseless accident if we haven't experienced it ourselves. People who have been through the same thing can sometimes comfort us with their understanding, as well as with the testimony of their very lives that this too can be humanly survived. If the size gap prevents Divine being from playing this role, how could possibility in the Divine nature make possible the relationship moves that allegedly deepen love and solidarity? If the hypothesis is both otherwise troublesome and useless for the purpose appointed (that is, for solving the problem of horrendous evils), should it not be dropped?

6.4. God-Sized Suffering?

In my judgment, such reasoning would move too fast. For it omits consideration of the idea that God—like the parent—might have His own (higher) way of responding to our plight. The father who signs the consent form for his son's open heart surgery may be angry at the necessity and grieved by the child's suffering, even though he understands what ills can be avoided and what

---

[22] Ibid., 117-21, 155-56; Fiddes, *The Creative Suffering of God,* 32, 100-104, 107-9, 144-46.

greater goods can come from it. A mother may experience frustration, anger, grief at sibling conflicts, even when she knows that the fights will be short-lived and the relationships resolve into lasting friendships. Parents who watch their offspring make serious mistakes feel torn as the son or daughter is taken off to answer the consequences even when the young person is defiant and unrepentant. So too, with God, since even omnipotence is stuck with metaphysical necessities about the constitution of created natures and their (mis-)fits with one another. Even though God created personal animals on purpose with eyes open to their consequent vulnerability to horrors, even though God knows how to defeat participation in horrors by weaving it into many good and creative plots, He may be grieved, angry, and frustrated for us and with us while we participate in them. Even though horrors are metaphysically inevitable where humans are left to function without major miraculous interventions in a world like this, God may still wish with the force of Divine passion that we didn't have to pay that price. Despite Divine knowledge, power, and future plans, God could feel torn with anger and grief at the way we treat each other, perpetrate horror upon horror, amplifying through the social fabric, multiplying so that the sins of the fathers and mothers descend to third and fourth generation. No matter that Divine omniscience would recognize the size gap, that Divine wisdom would consider the source, God might also feel exasperated at our individual and collective inability to discern the benevolence of Divine intentions. Classical theology to the contrary notwithstanding, the Bible—on its most straightforward reading—tells us so.

6.5 Dividing the Labor

Unattracted as I am to Stoic ethical ideals (in no small part because they are elitist and beyond the reach of most participants in horrors) but drawn to the Franciscan thought that in soteriology God does not always follow Ockham's razor,[23] I prefer a version of my Christological hypothesis according to which God the Son suffers in *both* natures—in the Divine nature (not only feeling our feelings but also "God-sized" distress of the sorts just mentioned in section 6.4) and in the human nature (participation in horrors within the framework of a finite consciousness; cf. section 5.2 above). Divine consciousness is comprehensive and so is able to feel the feelings of all participants in horrors at every place and every time. Divine consciousness is knowledgeable enough and wise enough to respond to each appropriately, with perfect attention to nuance and detail. At the same time, the Divine mind is at once too vast and too stable to experience our participation in horrors in anything like the way we do. Here Christ's human nature compensates, enabling God the Son to experience this world, its joys and horrors, from a finite point of view. Divine and human natures in Christ thus make complementary contributions to God's solidarity with created suffering, with human participation in horrors here below. Let me add the Biblical footnote that such dual solidarity explains why it is "the Lamb that was slain" Who is worthy to open the meaning of history (Rev. 5:6-10).

Particularity is required for God the Son to "know from the inside" what it is like to be tied down to place and time and culture. For present purposes, its scandal remains that no single finite consciousness can experience each and every type of horror, and yet—among humans—no suffering can be adequately known and appreciated by those who have not undergone it themselves (see Chapter 2). Here I am inclined to be satisfied with what seems within reach: namely, that Christ, in His human nature, participates in a representative sample of horrors

---

[23] William Ockham, *Ordinatio*, bk. 1, dist. 14, quest. 2, in vol. 3 of *Opera Theologica*, ed. Girard J. Etzkorn (St. Bonaventure, N.Y: St. Bonaventure University, 1977), 430, 432. Cf. Adams, *William Ockham*, 156-61.

sufficient to guarantee His appreciation of the depth of their ruinous potential. Alternatively, one could envision multiple incarnations to fill out God's experience of just how bad horrendous sufferings can be. Jürgen Moltmann takes reflections about how much God suffers with us further still, with particular attention to a kind of suffering that has been relatively left out.

7. Jürgen Moltmann: Crucified God, Trinitarian Solidarity

For Mackie, evil challenges the *existence* of God. For medievals, who take Divine existence and goodness to be logically secure or at least theoretically entrenched, the focus is on soteriology, the doctrine of how God redeems humans from evils. For Moltmann, working as he does with Biblical categories, suffering and injustice raise the question of the *righteousness* of God. Somebody may be "out there," but is it God or the devil?[24] Coming out of his experience, first as a young German prisoner and then as a citizen of Cold War Europe, Moltmann is particularly sensitive to how unjust social and political systems impoverish, oppress, and terrorize (4, 24, 62-63; cf. 11). With Auschwitz vividly in mind, he writes, "the question about God for me has been identical with the cry of victims for justice and the hunger of perpetrators for a way back from the path of death" (ix).

Moltmann is convinced that evil's challenge to Divine righteousness has to be met by God's suffering with us. He agrees with Rolt and Hartshorne against classical theology, that because love involves (the capacity for) compassion, Divine being would be impoverished by the inability to suffer and even by the inability to die (215-17, 227-28). Unlike Hartshorne, however, Moltmann's focus is Christological in that he centers Divine solidarity with the human condition in the Incarnation but, preeminently, in the cross of Christ: "God's passion...reveals itself in Christ's passion" (x, 49-50, 275).

Like Hick, Moltmann is clear that the scope of God's redemptive activity is universal. To testify against the injustice and oppression of exclusive human social arrangements, Christ identifies with the poor and oppressed—condemned as a blasphemer by the religious establishment and executed as a political criminal by Rome (130-34, I36, 140, I44-45). More difficult, God means to save perpetrators as well as victims, to rehabilitate not only oppressed but oppressors into functional citizens in the Realm of God (xi, *25,* 178). By contrast with the script of apocalyptic theology where haves and have-nots simply change places, Moltmann's God aims neither at distributive justice nor just deserts (174; see also Chapter 7 above). Rather God can save everyone because (to take a page from Luther) Divine justice "makes just" or justifies (177).

So far, Moltmann travels the road of my Christological approach, in effect, insisting that universal defeat of horrors within the context of the participants' lives requires Divine solidarity with the worst that humans can suffer, be; or do. His distinctive move reaches beyond Christology to claim, that only a Trinitarian (at least, multipersonal) God could adequately identify with created misery. Humans not only suffer natural evils (pain, disease, bodily harm, death) and ills imposed by human society, but also *abandonment by God* (cf. 55, 276). Surely most participants in horrors experience their predicament that way, whether as atheists who are not conscious of any undergirding Divine presence, or as believers who cry to God in their troubles but find the heavens closed. Indeed, this silence of God—such apparent failure of the

---

[24] Jürgen Moltmann, *The Crucified God: The Cross of Christ as the Foundation and Criticism of Christian Theology* (Minneapolis: Fortress Press, 1993), 60, 174-75. Parenthetical page citations throughout the rest of this chapter refer to this work.

Divine to vindicate and rescue—seemed to many Jews in Auschwitz to belie God's covenant faithfulness, to falsify everything they had proclaimed God to be. Moltmann believes that for many this sense of abandonment breaks many backs that could otherwise bear up under the load. He concludes that Divine solidarity with our human predicament must include God's sharing our experience of abandonment by God (252).

Fixing, with Luther, on Jesus' dying words—his quoting of Psalm 22:1, "My God, my God, why have you forsaken me?" (Mark 15:34)—Moltmann makes it axiomatic that in His last gasp, Christ crucified took Himself to have been deserted by God (146-47, 149). And he expends further exegetical efforts to promote the conclusion that God was in Christ crucified in such a way as to make it true that on the cross *God* was abandoned by God (190-92). Moltmann rejects any maneuvers by classical theology to accommodate the latter claim by appealing to the two natures of Christ, in order to quarantine the sense of abandonment to Christ's human nature while leaving Christ's Divine consciousness as omniscient as ever.[25] Rather, he concludes, if God is to be abandoned by God, there must be some distinction within the Godhead itself between the Father who delivers the Son up to be crucified and the Son who feels abandoned (151-53, 243-44). Both Father and Son suffer, but differently: the Son suffers the pains of crucifixion and death; the Father does not suffer crucifixion but "suffers the death of the Son" by grieving in love (243). Moltmann's provocative conclusion is that crucifixion is first and foremost a disruptive event within the relationship of Father to Son! Nevertheless, if the actual event of crucifixion brings a subjective sense of alienation, the earthly career and passion of the Son is a matter of agreed policy among the Divine persons: the Father sends the Son, but the Son actively chooses to suffer in order to identify with the poor and oppressed, with those who feel abandoned by God (51, 244).

For Moltmann, the crucified God does not merely swell the ranks of the world's miserable, but rather functions as a symbol of transformation. Because God identifies with participants in horror, they are not abandoned after all. The initiative of Divine love to identify with what is other, confers value and includes the outcaste within the society of the Trinity (25, 27-28, 51). Moreover, because their history is taken up into the life of the Trinity, it is incorporated into "the future of God" and opened up to the new positive meanings that the Trinity will make for Itself. Once again, the scope of this project is universal—God's future actions will make good on horrors, not only for participants who survive to see the day, but for those who have long since been murdered and gassed (163, 175-76, 246, 255).

If such Trinitarian identification and future meaning-making are—in my terminology—the stuff of objective, symbolic defeat, what about the participants' *subjective* recognition and appropriation of positive significance? Moltmann finds Rolt instructive where human agency and capacity to believe in God have not been utterly disabled by life's experiences. The miserable who "feel [Christ's] solidarity with them," may be thus empowered to return the compliment—to give their misery positive meaning by turning it into an act of solidarity with Christ.(51) The socially privileged, who are thus complicit in the horrors of others, can identify themselves with Divine solidarity with what is alien by casting their lot with the poor and oppressed and by working for a new social order (253-54, 277). Recognizing that these spiritual exercises are not available to everybody, Moltmann reminds readers that the resurrection of Jesus was not a purely private affair, but a downpayment on the general resurrection, when this benefit will be shared with everyone, when the plot will resolve for each individually and for all collectively, into a

---

[25] Ibid., 227, 231-35, 245-46. Thus, Moltmann does not seem to understand the Chalcedonian definition in a neoscholastic fashion, as I do in section 6 above. When I asked him (in October 1997) what his alternative metaphysics of Christology is, he replied simply, "Every German is a Hegelian and a Lutheran!"

universal solidarity among humans, between the Trinity and humankind (162, 171, 178). Speaking as he does of "eternal salvation, infinite joy, indestructible election and divine life," Moltmann apparently envisions a situation, not only of (in my terminology) *subjective appropriation of dimensions of symbolic defeat of horrors,* but also of *eternally secured concrete well-being.*

8. Presumptions and Possibilities: A Methodological Correction

Nothing is free in philosophy. In presenting the above five scenarios as solutions to the logical problem of horrendous evils, am I trying to get something for nothing? It could be charged that I am. My advertised strategy was to quarry the particulars of Biblical religions for ways God is thought to make good on horrendous evil and to present them as logically possible methods of Divine defeat. (In section 5, I factored into the bargain some logically possible *partial* reasons why.) My focus on the special resources of expanded theisms has been overdetermined by my desire to avoid the snares of equivocation, by my conviction that only religious value-theories are rich enough to defeat horrendous evils, and by my desire to proceed aporetically and consider Mackie's argument as a puzzle that forces one to burrow more deeply into the theoretical resources of the belief system in order to better understand how it works. If Mackie wanted to shift attention from evidential to logical problems of evil in order to nail theism into its coffin for good, many defenders stuck with the logical problem in the hope of winning epistemic advantage for themselves. Just as a professor can readily think of many logically possible reasons a responsible student might have for turning in a late paper without knowing which if any were the actual reasons, so too the actual mind of the Lord is hard to know even though logically possible reasons why seem to be within epistemic reach. In concentrating on the logical problem of horrendous evil, I have also been attempting to exploit the explanatory power of expanded theisms without assuming the obligation to convince atheologians of their truth.

Yet, to repeat, nothing is free in philosophy. Even within the supposed parameters of religion-neutral value theory, this strategy proved problematic. Recall how in mounting his best-of-all-possible-worlds defense, Pike ran up against the problem that 'the best of all possible worlds contains evils' seems not to be a contingent proposition but rather the sort of proposition that is necessary if true and otherwise incoherent or impossible. In such cases, the epistemic gap between granting logical possibility and conceding truth closes, so that one cannot expect to persuade the open-eyed to assent the former when they are unwilling to accept the latter.

Pike is unusually candid in facing up to the complication this forces in his argument (see Chapter 2): for all Pike knows, he has not succeeded in presenting a logically possible morally sufficient reason; but for all Mackie knows, Pike has! In fact, all of the approaches we have surveyed are loaded with philosophical assumptions of comparable status. Plantinga, Swinburne, Stump, Walls, Hartshorne, and Griffin all appeal to the metaphysically controversial notion of incompatibilist freedom; for Plantinga, this includes even more contested views about counterfactuals of freedom.[26] Hick, Swinburne, Stump, and Walls presuppose that postmortem survival is metaphysically possible for humans, while Hartshorne seems to deny it. Against classical theology, Rolt and process theologians hold the existence of the material world to be metaphysically necessary and the Divine nature to be passible. My Christological approach appeals to substance-ontology, while process thinkers advance a metaphysics of events or

---

[26] David Lewis (in "Evil for Freedom's Sake," *Philosophical Papers* 22, no. 3 [1993]: 149-72, esp. 152, 156) gives ironic coverage to Plantinga's suggestion that defenses involve less theoretical controversy than theodicy, given the way Plantinga helps himself to such metaphysically loaded assumptions.

occasions. Whether they seek for logically possible reasons why or logically possible explanations how, the writers I have discussed (myself included) don't seem to be able to tell a story that is rich enough to commend the logical compossibility of (1) and (2) (see Chapter 1, section 1) without deploying equally controversial metaphysical and value-theory assumptions—claims that would be necessary if true and otherwise incoherent or impossible. The result is that no one is in a position—*pace* Plantinga—to mount a demonstrative defense. The proposed solutions are thus *parochial*, at best strategies that might make sense within a given framework of philosophical assumptions—free-will approaches, for example, would be available to adherents of incompatibilist freedom, best-of-all-possible-worlds approaches to compatibilists and consequentialists.

One obvious way to limit the effects of parochialism is to economize by trimming such philosophical assumptions to a minimum, thereby making one's approach available within a wider range of philosophical positions. (This desire to secure wide acceptance was part of what drove defenders to agree to conduct the debate on religion-neutral value turf in the first place.) I cannot follow their lead because I am interested in an aporetic approach and because in the end I find "minimalist" proposals inadequate in the face of horrendous evils.

My alternative way of overcoming parochialism has been to consider a variety of contrasting positions and to probe the resources of each for showing how an omnipotent, omniscient, and perfectly good God could defeat horrors within the context of the participants' lives. Without being an exhaustive survey, the five proposals discussed above do run the gamut from classical to process to nineteenth and twentieth-century German philosophies. My strategy thus bears an analogy to that adopted by Alston in answering evidential arguments from evil.[27] Just as multiplication of reasons God might have had for permitting a given evil undercuts the presumption that the evil in question is pointless, so—I suggest—showing how a variety of philosophical frameworks would afford God the means for defeating horrors erodes any presumption that no philosophically co theory including both God and horrendous evil can be found. Modally speaking, my claim to "solve" the logical problem of horrendous evil can thus be no stronger than Pike's at the end of his article. Happily fits well enough with my general posture as a *skeptical realist* about philosophical theories. I am a *realist* about philosophical/theological theories that I believe there are facts of the matter, independently of what we believe, or conceive of in our theories. I am a *skeptic*, however, because I believe that the defense of any well-formulated philosophical position will eventually involve premisses which are fundamentally controversial and so unable to command the assent of all reasonable persons. Given this outlook, I conceive of the task of philosophy as that of mapping the problems by formulating the alternative positions as fully as possible. This task will involve conceptual analysis and argumentation to clarify the interrelations among, the various claims and the costs and benefits of alternative approaches. Each philosopher will have a certain set of intuitions that draw him/her in the direction of one premiss set or another, and s/he will have a particular commitment to develop that particular theoretical outlook so thoroughly and rigorously as to exhibit it as a viable competitor in the theoretical marketplace, where alternative frameworks will be assessed for clarity, coherence. simplicity, fruitfulness, and explanatory power. But demonstrative proofs and disproofs—for example, that idealism or incompatibilist freedom is true, that materialism or consequentialism are false—will not be in the offing.

---

[27] William P Alston, "The Inductive Argument from Evil and the Human Cognitive Condition," *Philosophical Perspectives 5, Philosophy of Religion* (1991): 26-67. Cf. Daniel Howard-Snyder, ed., *The Evidential Argument from Evil* (Bloomington: Indiana University Press, 1996).

Since the nature of reality and value is something we struggle towards via successive approximations, most humanly contrived theories can be expected to score better on some parameters than others. In this book, I have been arguing that allegedly more economical approaches to evil, those with supposedly less controversial assumptions (for example, Pike's best-of-all-possible-worlds and Plantinga's free will defense) pay compensating prices in explanatory power; while more expanded theisms are better able to explain how God can defeat horrors, precisely because of their richer assumptions. Once again, nothing is free in philosophy!

Questions

1. What are horrendous evils? What makes them horrendous?

2. What do you think of Adams opening the door to additional revelation in order to respond to the challenge of horrendous evils?

3. Do you think that Adams's strategy works?

4. What shortcoming(s) does Adams think diminishes the force of defenses like Plantinga's and Hick's?

5. Which sort of strategy works better for you, Plantinga's or Adams's? Why?

THE INDUCTIVE ARGUMENT FROM EVIL AND THE HUMAN COGNITIVE CONDITION*

William P. Alston

In this paper William Alston contributes to a criticism of the inductive argument from evil, based on a low estimate of human cognitive capacities in a certain application.

I

The recent outpouring of literature on the problem of evil has materially advanced the subject in several ways. In particular, a clear distinction has been made between the "logical" *argument against the existence of God*" ("atheological argument") from evil, which attempts to show that evil is logically incompatible with the existence of God, and the "inductive" ("empirical", "probabilistic") argument, which contents itself with the claim that evil constitutes (sufficient) empirical evidence against the existence of God. It is now acknowledged on (almost) all sides that the logical argument is bankrupt, but the inductive argument is still very much alive and kicking.

In this paper I will be concerned with the inductive argument. More specifically, I shall be contributing to a certain criticism of that argument, one based on a low estimate of human cognitive capacities in a certain application. To indicate the point at which this criticism engages the argument, I shall use one of the most careful and perspicuous formulations of the argument in a recent essay by William Rowe (1979).

1. There exist instances of intense suffering which an omnipotent, omniscient being could have prevented without thereby losing some greater good or permitting some evil actually bad or worse.
2. An omniscient, wholly good being would prevent the occurrence of any intense suffering it could, unless it could not do so without thereby losing some greater good or permitting some evil equally bad or worse
3. There does not exist an omnipotent, omniscient, wholly good being (p. 336).

Let's use the term 'gratuitous suffering' for any case of intense suffering, E, that satisfies premise 1, that is, which is such that an omnipotent, omniscient being could have prevented it without thereby losing some greater good or permitting some evil equally bad or worse.[1] 2 takes what we might call the "content" of 1 (losing a greater good or permitting some worse or equally bad evil) as a necessary condition for God to have a sufficient reason for permitting E. E's being gratuitous, then, is the contradictory of the possibility of God's having a sufficient reason to permit it, and equivalent to the impossibility of God's having a sufficient reason for permitting it. I will oscillate freely between speaking of a particular case of suffering, E, being gratuitous, and speaking of the impossibility of God's having a sufficient reason for permitting E. I shall call a proponent of an inductive argument from evil the "critic".

---

* This article is reprinted by courtesy of the author and publisher, and appeared in *Philosophical Perspectives*, 5, *Philosophy of Religion*, 1991, edited by James Tomberlin, Ridgeview Publishing Co.
[1] The term 'gratuitous' is used in different ways in the literature. Lately it has sprouted variations. My use of the term is strictly tied to Rowe's 1.

The criticism I shall be supporting attacks the claim that we are rationally justified in accepting 1, and it does so on the grounds that our epistemic situation is such that we are unable to make a sufficiently well grounded determination that 1 is the case. I will call this, faute de mieux, the *agnostic* thesis, or simply *agnosticism*. The criticism claims that the magnitude or complexity of the question is such that our powers, access to data, and so on are radically insufficient to provide sufficient warrant for accepting 1. And if that is so, the inductive argument collapses.[2]

How might one be justified in accepting 1? The obvious way to support an existential statement is to establish one or more instantiations and then use existential generalization. This is Rowe's tack, and I don't see any real alternative. Thus Rowe considers one or another case of suffering and argues, in the case of each, that it instantiates 1. I will follow him in this approach. Thus to argue that we cannot be justified in asserting 1, I shall argue that we cannot be justified in asserting any of its instantiations, each of which is of the form

> 1A. E is such that an omnipotent, omniscient being could have prevented it without thereby losing some greater good or permitting some evil equally bad or worse.

In the sequel when I speak of being or not being justified in accepting 1, it must be remembered that this is taken to hang on whether one is, or can be justified, in accepting propositions of the form 1A.

Does the agnostic thesis, in my version, also claim that we are unable to justifiably assert the denial of 1, as we would have to do to develop a successful theodicy? It is no part of my task in this paper to address this question, but I will make a couple of remarks. First, my position is that we could justifiably believe, or even know, the denial of 1, and that in one of two ways. We might have sufficient grounds for believing in the existence of God—whether from arguments of natural theology, religious experience or whatever—including sufficient grounds for taking God to be omnipotent, omniscient, and perfectly good, and that could put us in a position to warrantedly deny 1. Or God might reveal to us that 1 is false, and we might be justified in accepting the message as coming from God. Indeed, revelation might not only provide justification for denying 1, but also justification for beliefs about what God's reasons are for permitting this or that case of suffering or type of suffering, thereby putting us in a position to construct a theodicy of a rather ambitious sort.[3] If, however, we leave aside the putative sources just mentioned and restrict ourselves to what we can do by way of tracing out the interconnections of goods and evils in the world by the use of our natural powers, what are we to say? Well, the matter is a bit complicated. Note that 1 is an existential statement, which says that

---

[2] In (1979) Rowe considers this criticism. He says of it: "I suppose some theists would be content with this rather modest response...But given the validity of the basic argument and the theist's likely acceptance of (2), he is thereby committed to the view that (l) is false, not just that we have no good reasons for accepting (1) as true" (338). No doubt, the theist is committed to regarding (1) as false, at least on the assumption that it embodies necessary conditions for God's having sufficient reason for permitting suffering (on which see F in the next section). But Rowe does not explain why he thinks that showing that we are not justified in asserting 1 does not constitute a decisive reason for rejecting his argument.

[3] There is considerable confusion in the literature over what it takes to have a theodicy, or, otherwise put, what a reasonable level of aspiration is for theodicy. Even if we were vouchsafed an abundance of divine revelations I cannot conceive of our being able to specify God's reason for permitting each individual evil. The most that could sensibly be aimed at would be an account of the sorts of reasons God has for various sorts of evil. And a more modest, but still significant, ambition would be to make suggestions as to what God's reasons might be, reasons that are plausible in the light of what we know and believe about God, His nature, purposes, and activities. See Stump, 1990.

there are instances of intense suffering of which a certain negative claim is true. To deny 1 would be to say that this negative claim is false for *every* case of intense suffering. And even if we could establish the non-gratuitousness of certain cases by tracing out interconnections—and I don't see that this is necessarily beyond our powers—that would not be sufficient to yield the denial of 1. To sum up: I think that examining the interconnections of good and evil in the world by our natural powers cannot suffice to establish either 1 or its negation.[4] For particular cases of suffering we might conceivably be able to establish non-gratuitousness in this way, but what I shall argue in this paper is that no one can justifiably assert gratuitousness for any case.

II

Before setting out the agnostic thesis in more detail and adding my bit to the case for it, let me make some further comments about the argument against which the criticism is directed and variants thereof.

A. The argument is stated in terms of intense suffering, but it could just as well have appealed to anything else that can plausibly be claimed to be undesirable in itself. Rowe focuses on intense suffering because he thinks that it presents the greatest difficulty for anyone who tries to deny a premise like 1. I shall follow him in this, though for concision I shall often simply say 'suffering' with the 'intense' tacitly understood.

B. Rowe doesn't claim that all suffering is gratuitous, but only that some is. He takes it that even one case of gratuitous suffering is incompatible with theism. I go along with this assumption (though in E, I question whether Rowe has succeeded in specifying necessary and sufficient conditions for gratuitousness, and for God's having a sufficient reason for permitting suffering). As already noted, Rowe does not argue for 1 by staying on its level of unspecificity; rather he takes particular examples of suffering and argues in the case of each that it is gratuitous; from there it is a short step of existential generalization to 1. In (1979) and subsequent papers Rowe focuses on the case of a fawn trapped in a forest fire and undergoing several days of terrible agony before dying (hereinafter 'Bambi'). In (1988) he adds to this a (real life) case introduced by Bruce Russell (1989), a case of the rape, beating, and murder by strangulation of a 5-year old girl ('Sue') by her mother's boyfriend. Since I am specifically interested in criticizing Rowe's argument I will argue that we are not justified, and cannot be justified, in judging these evils to be gratuitous. It will turn out that some of my discussion pertains not to Rowe's cases but to others. I will signal the reader as to how to understand the dummy designator, 'E', in each part of the paper.

---

[4] In arguing for 1 in (1979) Rowe proceeds as if he supposed that the only alternatives are (a) its being reasonable to believe 1 and (b) its being reasonable to believe not-1. "Consider again the case of the fawn's suffering. Is it reasonable to believe that there is some greater good so intimately connected to that suffering that even an omnipotent, omniscient being could not have obtained that good without permitting that suffering or some evil at least as bad? It certainly does not appear reasonable to believe this. Nor does it seem reasonable to believe that there is some evil at least as bad as the fawn's suffering such that an omnipotent being simply could not have prevented it without permitting the fawn's suffering. But even if it should somehow be reasonable to believe either of these things of the fawn's suffering, we must then ask whether it is reasonable to believe either of these things of *all* the instances of seemingly pointless human and animal suffering that occur daily in our world. And surely the answer to this more general question must be no...It seems then that although we cannot *prove* that (1) is true, it is nevertheless, altogether *reasonable* to believe that (1) is true, that (1) is a *rational* belief" (337-38). The form of this argument is: "It is not rational to believe that p. Therefore it is rational to believe that not-*p*." But this is patently lacking in force. There are many issues on which it is rational to believe neither *p* nor not-*p*. Take *p* to be, e.g, the proposition that it was raining on this spot exactly 45,000 years ago.

C. The argument deals with a classical conception of God as omnipotent, omniscient and perfectly good; it is designed to yield the conclusion that no being with those characteristics exists. I shall also be thinking of the matter in this way. When I use 'God' it will be to refer to a being with these characteristics.

D. There are obvious advantages to thinking of the inductive argument from evil as directed against the belief in the existence of God as God is thought of in some full blown theistic religion, rather than as directed against what we may call "generic theism". The main advantage is that the total system of beliefs in a religion gives us much more to go on in considering what reasons God might possibly have for permitting E. In other terms, it provides much more of a basis for distinguishing between plausible and implausible theodicies. I shall construe the argument as directed against the traditional Christian belief in God.[5] I choose Christianity for this purpose because (a) I am more familiar with it than other alternatives, as most of my readers will be, and (b) most of the philosophical discussions of the problem of evil, both historically and currently, have grown out of Christian thought.

E. Rowe does not claim to know or to be able to prove that 1 is true. With respect to his fawn example he acknowledges that "Perhaps, for all we know, there is some familiar good outweighing the fawn's suffering to which that suffering is connected in a way we do not see" (1979, p. 337). He only claims that we have sufficient rational grounds for believing that the fawn's suffering is gratuitous, and still stronger rational grounds for holding that at least some of the many cases of suffering that, so far as we can see, instantiate 1 actually do so.[6] Not all of Rowe's fellow atheologians are so modest, but I will concentrate my fire on his weaker and less vulnerable version.

F. A final comment will occupy us longer. Rowe obviously supposes, as premise 2 makes explicit, that cases of "gratuitous" evil count decisively against the existence of God. That is, he takes it that an omnipotent, omniscient, and perfectly good God would not permit any gratuitous evil; perhaps he regards this as conceptually or metaphysically necessary. Thus he holds that God could have no other reason for permitting suffering except that preventing it would involve losing some greater good or permitting some equally bad or worse evil.[7] But this is highly controversial. It looks as if there are possible divine reasons for permitting evil that would be ruled out by (2). (i) Suppose that God could bring about a greater good only by permitting any one of several equally bad cases of suffering. Then no one is such that by preventing it He would lose that greater good. And if we stipulate that God has a free choice as to whether to permit any of these disjuncts, it is not the case that to prevent it would be to permit something equally bad or worse; that might or might not ensue, depending on God's choice. But if we are to allow that

---

[5] The qualifier 'traditional' adheres to the restrictions laid down in D and excludes variants like process theology. Admittedly, "traditional Christianity" contains a number of in-house variants, but in this paper I will appeal only to what is common to all forms of what could reasonably be called "traditional Christianity".

[6] Rowe does not often use the term 'justified belief', but instead usually speaks of its being *rational* to hold a belief. I shall ignore any minor differences there may be between these epistemic concepts.

[7] The point at issue here is whether being non-gratuitous in this sense is necessary for divine permission. But there is also a question as to whether it is sufficient. Would any outweighing good for which a particular bit of suffering is necessary, however trivial and insignificant that good, justify that suffering? Suppose that some minor suffering on my part is necessary for my enjoying my dinner to the extent I did, and that the enjoyment outweighs the suffering? Would that give God a reason for permitting the suffering? I doubt it. Again, suppose that it is necessary for some greater good, but that the universe as whole would be better without E and the greater good than with them? Would God be justified in permitting E? (Note that in (1986) Rowe's substitute for 1 is in terms of the world as a whole: "There exists evils that O [God] could have prevented, and had O prevented them the world as a whole would have been better") (228). However I am not concerned here with what is sufficient for God to have a reason for permitting evil, only with what is necessary for this.

being necessary for a greater good can justify permission of evil, it looks as if we will have to allow this case as well. (ii) More importantly, human free will complicates God's strategies for carrying out His purposes. As we will be noting later in the paper, if God has a policy of respecting human free will, He cannot guarantee human responses to His initiatives where those responses would be freely made if at all.[8] Hence if God visits suffering on us in an attempt to turn us from our sinful ways, and a particular recipient doesn't make the desired response, God could have prevented that suffering without losing any greater good (no such good was forthcoming), even though we might reasonably take God to be justified in permitting the suffering, provided that was His best strategy in the situation, the one most likely to get the desired result. (iii) Look at "general policy" theodicies.[9] Consider the idea that God's general policy of, e.g., usually letting nature take its course and not interfering, even when much suffering will ensue, is justified by the overall benefits of the policy. Now consider a particular case of divine non-intervention to prevent intense suffering. Clearly, God could have intervened in this case without subverting the general policy and losing its benefits. To prevent this particular suffering would not be to lose some greater good or permit something worse or equally bad. And yet it seems that general policy considerations of the sort mentioned could justify God in refraining from intervening in this case. For if it couldn't, it could not justify His non-intervention in any case, and so He would be inhibited from carrying out the general policy.[10]

Since my central aim in this paper is not to refine principles like 2 in microscopic detail, I will take a shortcut in dealing with these difficulties. (i) can be handled by complicating the formula to allow the permission of any member of a disjunction, some member of which is necessary for a greater good. Consider it done. (ii) and (iii) can be accommodated by widening the sphere of goods for which the evil is necessary. For cases of the (ii) sort, take the greater good to be having as great a chance as possible to attain salvation, and let's say that this good is attained whatever the response. As for (iii), we can say that E is permitted in order to realize the good of maintaining a beneficial general policy except where there are overriding reasons to make an exception, and the reasons in this case are not overriding. With these modifications we can take Rowe to have provided a plausible formulation of necessary conditions for divine sufficient reasons for permitting E. But if you don't think I have successfully defended my revision of *Rowe,* then you may think in terms of an unspecific substitute for I like "There are instances of suffering such that there is no sufficient reason for God to allow them". That will still enable me to argue that no one is in a position to justifiably assert that God could have no sufficient reason for allowing E.

III

Clearly the case for 1 depends on an inference from "So far as I can tell, p" to "p" or "Probably, p". And, equally clearly, such inferences are sometimes warranted and sometimes not. Having

---

[8] This presupposes that God does not enjoy "middle knowledge". For if He did, He could see to it that suffering would be imposed on people only where they will in fact make the desired response. I owe this point to William Hasker.

[9] Such a theodicy will be discussed in section ix.

[10] There are also more radical objections to Rowe's 2. I think particularly of those who question or deny the principle that God would, by virtue of His nature, create the best possible universe or, in case there can be no uniquely best possible universe, would create a universe that comes up to some minimal evaluative level. See, e.g., R. Adams (1987). On these views an argument like Rowe's never gets out of the starting gate. Though I have some sympathy with such views I will not take that line in this paper.

carefully examined my desk I can infer 'Jones' letter is not on my desk 'from' So far as I can tell, Jones 'letter is not on my desk'. But being ignorant of quantum mechanics I cannot infer 'This treatise on quantum mechanics is well done' from 'So far as I can tell, this treatise on quantum mechanics is well done'. I shall be contending that our position vis-à-vis 1 is like the latter rather than like the former.

I am by no means the first to suggest that the atheological argument from evil is vitiated by an unwarranted confidence in our ability to determine that God could have no sufficient reason for permitting some of the evils we find in the world. A number of recent writers have developed the theme.[11] I endorse many of the reasons they give for their pessimism. Wykstra points out that our cognitive capacities are much more inferior to God's than is a small child's to his parents; and in the latter case the small child is often unable to understand the parents' reasons for inflicting punishment or for requiring him to perform tasks that are distasteful to him. (88). Ahern points out that our knowledge of the goods and evils in the world (51-5) and of the interconnections between things (57, 72-3) are very limited. Fitzpatrick adduces the deficiencies in our grasp of the divine nature (25-28). This is all well taken and, I believe, does provide support for the agnostic thesis. But then why am I taking pen in hand to add to this ever swelling stream of literature? For several reasons. First, I will not be proceeding on the basis of any general skepticism about our cognitive powers either across the board or generally with respect to God. I will, rather, be focusing on the peculiar difficulties we encounter in attempting to provide adequate support for a certain very ambitious negative existential claim, viz., that there is (can be) no sufficient divine reason for permitting a certain case of suffering, E.[12] I will be appealing to the difficulties of defending a claim of this particular kind, rather than to more generalized human cognitive weaknesses. Second, much of the literature just alluded to has centered around Wykstra's claim that to be justified in asserting 1 it would have to be the case that if 1 were false that would be indicated to one in some way.[13] By contrast I will not be proceeding on the basis of any such unrestrictedly general epistemological principle. Third, I will lay out in much more detail than my predecessors the range of conceivable divine reasons we would have to be able to exclude in order to be justified in asserting 1. Fourth, I can respond to some of the defenses the likes of Rowe have deployed against the agnostic criticism.

VI

Now, at last, I am ready to turn to my central project of arguing that we cannot be justified in accepting 1A. As already noted, I will be emphasizing the fact that this is a negative existential claim. It will be my contention that to be justified in such a claim one must be justified in excluding all the live possibilities for what the claim denies to exist. What 1A denies is that there is any reason God could have for permitting it. I will argue that we are not, and cannot, be justified in asserting that none of these possibilities are realized. I will draw on various theodicies to compile a (partial) list of the reasons God might conceivably have for permitting E. That will provide me with a partial list of the suggestions we must have sufficient reason to reject in order

---

[11] See, e.g., Ahern (1971), Fitzpatrick (1981), Reichenbach (1982), Wykstra (1984).

[12] To be sure, 1 is in the form of a positive existential statement. However when we consider an instantiation of it with respect to a particular case of suffering, E, as Rowe does in arguing for it, it turns out to be a negative existential statement about E, that *there is no sufficient divine reason for permitting E*. It is statements of this form that, so I claim, no one can be justified in making.

[13] Wykstra labors under the additional burden of having to defend a thesis as to the conditions under which one is justified in making an assertion of the form "It appears that *p*", and much of the considerable literature spawned by his article is taken up with this side-issue.

to rationally accept 1. Note that it is no part of my purpose here to develop or defend a theodicy. I am using theodicies only as a source of *possibilities* for divine reasons for evil, possibilities the realization of which the atheologian will have to show to be highly implausible if his project is to succeed.

Since I am criticizing Rowe's argument I am concerned to argue that we are not justified in asserting 1A for the particular kinds of suffering on which Rowe focuses. And we should not suppose that God would have the same reason for permitting every case of suffering.[14] Hence it is to be expected that the reasons suggested by a given theodicy will be live possibilities for some cases of evil and not others. I am, naturally, most interested in suggestions that constitute live possibilities for divine reasons for permitting Bambi's and Sue's suffering. And many familiar theodicies do not pass this test. (This is, no doubt, why these cases were chosen by Rowe and Russell.) Bambi's suffering, and presumably Sue's as well, could hardly be put down to punishment for sin, and neither case could seriously be supposed to be allowed by God for the sake of character building. Nevertheless, I shall not confine the discussion to live possibilities for these two cases. There are two reasons for this. First, a discussion of other theodicies will help to nail down the general point that we are typically unable to exclude live possibilities for divine reasons in a particular case. Second, these discussions will provide ammunition against atheological arguments based on other kinds of suffering.

Thus I shall first consider theodical suggestions that seem clearly not to apply to Bambi or Sue. Here I shall be thinking instead of an adult sufferer from a painful and lengthy disease (fill in the details as you like) whom I shall call 'Sam'. Having argued that we are not in a position to exclude the possibility that God has reasons of these sorts for permitting Sam's suffering, I shall pass on to other suggestions that do constitute genuine possibilities for Bambi and/or Sue.

V

I begin with a traditional theme, that human suffering is God's punishment for sin. Though it hardly applies to Bambi or Sue, it may be a live possibility in other cases, and so I will consider it. The punishment motif has tended to drop out of theodicies in our "soft-on-criminals" and "depravity-is-a-disease" climate, but it has bulked large in the Christian tradition.[15] It often draws the criticism that, so far as we can see, degree or extent of suffering is not nicely proportioned to degree of guilt. Are the people of Vietnam, whose country was ravaged by war in this century, markedly more sinful than the people of Switzerland, whose country was not? But, remembering the warnings of the last section, that does not show that this is never God's reason for permitting suffering, and here we're concerned with a particular case, Sam. Let's say that it seems clear, so far as we can tell, that Sam's suffering is not in proportion to his sinfulness. Sam doesn't seem to have been a bad sort at all, and he has suffered horribly. Can we go from that to "Sam's suffering

---

[14] Hence the very common procedure of knocking down theodical suggestions, one by one, by pointing out, in the case of each, that there are evils it does not cover, will not suffice to make the critic's case. For it may be that even though no one divine reason covers all cases each case is covered by some divine reason.

[15] It is often dismissed nowadays on the grounds that it presupposes a morally unacceptable theory of punishment, viz., a retributive conception. But it need not make any such presupposition; whatever the rationale of punishment, the suggestion is that (in some cases) God has that rationale for permitting suffering. Though it must be admitted that the "retributive" principle that *it is intrinsically good that persons should suffer for wrongdoing* makes it easier to claim that suffering constitutes justifiable punishment than a reformatory theory does, where a necessary condition for the justification of punishment is the significant chance of an improvement of the punishee. For purposes of this discussion I will not choose between different theories of punishment.

was not a punishment for sin", or even to "It is reasonable to suppose that Sam's suffering was not a punishment for sin". I suggest that we cannot.

First, we are often in a poor position to assess the degree and kind of a certain person's sinfulness, or to compare people in this regard. Since I am thinking of the inductive argument from evil as directed against Christian belief in God, it will be appropriate to understand the punishment-for-sin suggestion in those terms. Two points about sin are particularly relevant here. (I) Inward sins—one's intentions, motives, attitudes—are more serious than failings in outward behavior.[16] (2) The greatest sin is a self-centered refusal or failure to make God the center of one's life. (2) is sharply at variance with standard secular bases for moral judgment and evaluation. Hence the fact that X does not seem, from that standpoint, more wicked than Y, or doesn't seem wicked at all, does nothing to show that God, or a Christian understanding of God, would make the same judgment. Because of (1) overt behavior is not always a good indication of a person's condition, sin-wise. This is not to say that we could not make a sound judgment of a person's inner state if we had a complete record of what is publicly observable concerning the person. Perhaps in some instances we could, and perhaps in others we could not. But in any event, we rarely or never have such a record. Hence, for both these reasons our judgments as to the relation between S's suffering and S's sinfulness are usually of questionable value.

Second, according to Christianity, one's life on earth is only a tiny proportion of one's total life span. This means that, knowing nothing about the immeasurably greater proportion of Sam's life, we are in no position that deny that the suffering qua punishment has not had a reformative effect, even if we can see no such effect in his earthly life.[17]

I might be accused of begging the question by dragging in Christian convictions to support my case. But that would be a misunderstanding. I am not seeking to prove, or give grounds for, theism or Christianity. I am countering a certain argument against Christian theism. I introduce these Christian doctrines only to spell out crucial features of what is being argued against. The Christian understanding of sin, human life, God's purposes, and so on, go into the determination of what the critic must be justified in denying if she is to be justified in the conclusion that Sam's suffering would not have been permitted by God.

VI

I have led off my survey of theodical suggestions with the punishment motif, despite the fact that it is highly controversial and the reverse of popular. Nor would I want to put heavy emphasis on it were I constructing a theodicy. I have put my worst foot forward in order to show that even here the critic is in no position to show that Sam's suffering is not permitted by God for this reason. If the critic can't manage even this, he will presumably be much worse off with more plausible suggestions for divine reasons, to some of which I now turn.

---

[16] I don't mean to suggest that a person's inner sinfulness or saintliness cannot be expected to manifest itself in behavior. Still less do I mean to suggest that one could be fully or ideally living the life of the spirit, whatever her outward behavior.

[17] Rowe writes: "Perhaps the good for which *some* intense suffering is permitted cannot be realized until the end of the world, but it certainly seems likely that much of this good could be realized in the lifetime of the sufferer...In the absence of any reason to think that O [God] would need to postpone these good experiences, we have reason to expect that many of these goods would occur in the world we know" (1986, 244-45). But why suppose that we are entitled to judge that justifying goods, if any, would be realized during the sufferer's earthly life, unless we have specific reasons to the contrary? Why this initial presumption? Why is the burden of proof on the suggestion of the realization of the goods in an after-life? Rowe doesn't say, nor do I see what he could say.

One of the most prominent theodical suggestions is that God allows suffering because He is interested in a "vale of soul making". He takes it that by confronting difficulties, hardships, frustrations, perils, and even suffering and only by doing this, we have a chance to develop such qualities of character as patience, courage, and compassion, qualities we would otherwise have no opportunity to develop. This line has been set forth most forcefully in our time by John Hick in *Evil and the God of Love* revised edition, (1978), a book that has evoked much discussion. To put the point most generally, God's purpose is to make it possible for us to grow into the kind of person that is capable of an eternal life of loving communion with Himself. To be that kind of person one will have to possess traits of character like those just mentioned, traits that one cannot develop without meeting and reacting to difficulties and hardships, including suffering. To show that *E* would not be permitted by God, the critic has to show that it does not serve the "soul-making" function.

To get to the points I am concerned to make I must first respond to some standard objections to this theodicy. (1) God could surely just create us with the kind of character needed for fellowship with Himself, thereby rendering the hardships and suffering unnecessary. Hick's answer is that what God aims at is not fellowship with a suitably programmed robot, but fellowship with creatures who freely choose to work for what is needed and to take advantage of the opportunity thus engendered. God sees the realization of this aim for some free creatures[18], even at the cost of suffering and hardship for all, as being of much greater value than any alternative, including a world with no free creatures and a world in which the likes of human beings come off the assembly line pre-sanctified. As usual, I am not concerned to defend the claim that this is the way things are, but only to claim that we are in no position to deny that God is correct in this judgment. (For a discussion of difficulties in carrying out comparative evaluation of total universes, see the end of section ix.)

(2) "If God is using suffering to achieve this goal, He is not doing very well. In spite of all the suffering we undergo, most of us don't get very far in developing courage, compassion, etc." There are two answers to this. First, we are in no position to make that last judgment. We don't know nearly enough about the inner springs of peoples' motivation, attitudes, and character, even in this life. And we know nothing about any further development in an after-life. Second, the theism under discussion takes God to respect the free will of human beings. No strategy consistent with that can guarantee that all, or perhaps any, creatures will respond in the way intended. Whether they do is ultimately up to them. Hence we cannot argue from the fact that such tactics often don't succeed to the conclusion that God wouldn't employ them. When dealing with free creatures God must, because of self-imposed limitations, use means that have some considerable likelihood of success, not means that cannot fail. It is amazing that so many critics reject theodicies like Hick's on the grounds of a poor success rate. I don't say that a poor success rate could not, under any circumstances, justify us in denying that God would permit E for the sake of soul making. If we really did know enough to be reasonably sure that the success rate is very poor *and* that other devices open to God would be seen by omniscience to have a significantly greater chance of success, *then* we could conclude that Hick's line does not get at what God is up to. But we are a very long way indeed from being able to justifiably assert this.

We cannot take the kind of reason stressed by Hick to be a live possibility for the Bambi and Sue cases. The former is much more obvious than the latter, but even in the latter case Sue has no chance to respond to the suffering in the desired way, except in an after life, and it strains

---

[18] Actually, Hick is a universalist and believes that all free creatures will attain this consummation; but I do not take this thesis as necessary for the soul making theodicy.

credulity to suppose that God would subject a 5-year old to *that* for the sake of character building in the life to come. Hence once more, and until further notice, we will stick with Sam.

Let's stipulate that Sam's suffering does not appear, on close examination, to be theistically explainable as aimed by God at "soulmaking". He seems already to have more of the qualities of character in question than most of us, or the amount of suffering seems to be too much for the purpose, or to be so great as to overwhelm him and make character development highly unlikely. And so our best judgment is that God wouldn't be permitting his suffering for that reason. But that judgment is made in ignorance of much relevant information. Perhaps a more penetrating picture of Sam's spiritual condition would reveal that he is much more in need of further development than is apparent to us from our usual superficial perspective on such matters. Since we don't see his career after death, we are in a poor position to determine how, over the long run, he reacts to the suffering; perhaps if we had that information we would see that this suffering is very important for his full development. Moreover, we are in a poor position, or no position, to determine what is the most effective strategy for God to use in His pursuit of Sam. We don't know what alternatives are open to God, while respecting Sam's freedom, or what the chances are, on one or another alternative, of inducing the desired responses. We are in a poor position to say that this was too much suffering for the purpose, or to say how much would be just right. And we will continue to be in that position until our access to relevant information is radically improved.

Thus we cannot be justified in holding that Sam's suffering is not permitted by God in order to further His project of soul-making. There is an allied, but significantly different theodical suggestion by Eleonore Stump concerning which I would make the same points. Briefly, and oversimply, Stump's central suggestion is that the function of natural evil in God's scheme is to bring us to salvation, or, as she likes to put it, to contribute to the project of "fixing our wills", which have been damaged by original sin. Natural evil tends to prod us to turn to God, thereby giving Him a chance to fix our wills.

> Natural evil—the pain of disease, the intermittent and unpredictable destruction of natural disasters, the decay of old age, the imminence of death—takes away a person's satisfaction with himself. It tends to humble him, show him his frailty, make him reflect on the transience of temporal goods, and turn his affections towards other-worldly things, away from the things of this world. No amount of moral or natural evil, of course, can *guarantee* that a man will seek God's help. If it could, the willing it produced would not be free. But evil of this sort is the best hope, I think, and maybe the only effective means, for bringing men to such a state (Stump, 1985, p. 409).

Objections will be raised somewhat similar to those that have been made to Hick. A perfectly good God wouldn't have let us get in this situation in the first place. God would employ a more effective technique.[19] There's too much suffering for the purpose. It is not distributed properly. And so on. These will answered in the same way as the analogous objections to Hick. As for Sam, if we cannot see how his suffering was permitted by God for the reason Stump suggests, I will do a rerun of the parallel points concerning Hick's soul making suggestion.

Closely related suggestions have been made by Marilyn McCord Adams in her essay, "Redemptive Suffering: A Christian Solution to the Problem of Evil" (1986). She takes martyrdom as her model for redemptive suffering, though she by no means wishes to limit her discussion to martyrdom strictly so called. "...the redemptive potential of many other cases that, strictly speaking, are not martyrdoms can be seen by extrapolation" (p. 261). In other words her suggestion is that the benefits for the martyr and others that can flow from martyrdom in the

---

[19] Stump gives her answer to this one in the passage quoted.

strict sense, can also flow from suffering that does not involve undergoing persecution for the faith. Her bold suggestion is that "martyrdom is an expression of God's righteous love toward the onlooker, the persecutor, and even the martyr himself" (257). Here I want to focus on her account of the benefits to the martyr. "...the threat of martyrdom is a time of testing and judgment. It makes urgent the previously abstract dilemma of whether he loves God more than the temporal goods that are being extracted as a price...the martyr will have had to face a deeper truth about himself and his relations to God and temporal goods than ever he could in fair weather...the time of trial is also an opportunity for building a relationship of trust between the martyr and that to which he testifies. Whether because we are fallen or by the nature of the case, trusting relationships have to be built up by a history of interactions. If the martyr's loyalty to God is tested, but after a struggle he holds onto his allegiance to God and God delivers him (in his own time and way), the relationship is strengthened and deepened" (259). Adams is modest in her claims. She does not assert that all cases of suffering are analogous to martyrdom in these respects. "Some are too witless to have relationships that can profit and mature through such tests of loyalty. Some people are killed or severely harmed too quickly for such moral struggles to take place. At other times the victim is an unbeliever who has no explicit relationship with God to wrestle with."[20] However none of these disqualifications apply to her boldest suggestion, that given the Christian doctrine of the suffering of God incarnate on the cross, "temporal suffering itself is a vision into the inner life of God" (264), a theme that she takes from Christian mysticism. That value of suffering, if such it be, can be enjoyed by any sufferer, whatever the circumstances. To be sure, one might not realize at the time that the suffering has that significance. But if one reaches the final term of Christian development, "he might be led to reason that the good aspect of an experience of deep suffering [the aspect just pointed to] is great enough that, from the standpoint of the beatific vision, the victim would not wish the experience away from his life history, but would, on the contrary, count it as an extremely valuable part of his life" (265). It should also be noted that Adams does not suggest that God's reasons for permitting suffering in any particular case are restricted to one of the considerations she has been presenting, or indeed to all of the points she makes.

If we were to try to decide whether Sam's suffering is permitted by God for any of these reasons, we would be in a poor position to make a negative judgment for reasons parallel to those brought out in the discussion of Hick. Given the limits of our access to the secrets of the human heart and the course of the after life, if any, we are, in many instances, in no position to assert with any confidence that this suffering does not have such consequences, and hence that God does not permit it (at least in part) for the sake of just those consequences.

VII

Thus far I have been restricting myself to conceivable divine reasons for suffering that involve the use of that suffering to bring about good for the *sufferer*. This is obvious except for the punishment reason. As for that one, this claim is equally obvious if we are thinking of punishment in terms of reformation of the punishee,[21] but what about a "retributive" theory, according to which the rationale of punishment is simply that the sinner *deserves* to suffer for his sin, that justice demands this, or that a proportionate suffering for wickedness is intrinsically

---

[20] All these disclaimers may well apply to Sue.

[21] Here, of course, as in the other cases in which God's action is designed to evoke a free response from the patient, there is no guarantee that the reformation will be effected. But it still remains true that the good aimed at is a good for the sufferer.

good? Well, though one might balk at describing this as a *good* for the sufferer, it remains that such good as is aimed at and effected by the punishment, on this conception, terminates with the sufferer and does not extend to the welfare of others.

Where divine reasons are restricted this narrowly, the critic is operating on the most favorable possible terrain. If he has any hope of making his case it will be here, where the field of possibilities that must be excluded is relatively narrow. What we have seen is that wherever the reasons we have canvassed are live possibilities, even this is too much for his (our) powers. Our ignorance of relevant facts is so extensive, and the deficiencies in our powers of discernment are so fundamental, as to leave us without any sufficient basis for saying, with respect to a particular case of suffering, that God does not permit it for reasons such as these.

To be sure, this is cold comfort for the critic of Rowe's argument since, as noted earlier, the possibilities we have been canvassing do not seem to be live possibilities for Bambi or Sue. The only real chance for an exception is Adams' suggestion that the experience of suffering constitutes a vision of the inner life of God. Since this is not confined to those who identify it as such, it could apply to Sue, and perhaps to Bambi as well, though presumably only Sue would have a chance to recognize it and rejoice in it, retrospectively, in the light of the beatific vision. However, I don't want to insist on this exception. Let us say that a consideration of the theodicies thus far canvassed does nothing to show that we can't be justified in affirming an instantiation of 1 for Bambi or Sue.

Nevertheless, that does *not* show that we can be justified in excluding the possibility that God has no patient-centered reason for permitting Bambi's or Sue's suffering. It doesn't show this because we are not warranted in supposing that the possible reasons we have been extracting from theodicies exhaust the possibilities for patient-centered reasons God might have for permitting Bambi's or Sue's suffering. Perhaps, unbeknownst to us, one or the other of these bits of suffering is necessary, in ways we cannot grasp, for some outweighing good of a sort with which we are familiar, e.g., supreme fulfillment of one's deepest nature. Or perhaps it is necessary for the realization of a good of which we as yet have no conception. And these possibility are by no means remote ones. "There are more things in heaven and earth, Horatio, than are dreamt of in your philosophy." Truer words were never spoken. They point to the fact that our cognitions of the world, obtained by filtering raw data through such conceptual screens as we have available for the nonce, acquaint us with only some indeterminable fraction of what is there to be known. The progress of human knowledge makes this evident. No one explicitly realized the distinction between concrete and abstract entities, the distinction between efficient and final causes, the distinction between knowledge and opinion, until great creative thinkers adumbrated these distinctions and disseminated them to their fellows. The development of physical science has made us aware of a myriad of things hitherto undreamed of, and developed the concepts with which to grasp them—gravitation, electricity, electromagnetic fields, space-time curvature, irrational numbers, and so on. It is an irresistible induction from this that we have not reached the final term of this process, and that more realities, aspects, properties, structures remain to be discerned and conceptualized. And why should values, and the conditions of their realization, be any exception to this generalization? A history of the apprehension of values could undoubtedly be written, parallel to the history just adumbrated, though the archeology would be a more difficult and delicate task.

Moreover, remember that our topic is not the possibilities for future human apprehensions, but rather what an omniscient being can grasp of modes of value and the conditions of their realization. Surely it is eminently possible that there are real possibilities for the latter that exceed anything we can anticipate, or even conceptualize. It would be exceedingly strange if an omniscient being did not immeasurably exceed our grasp of such matters. Thus there is an unquestionably live possibility that God's reasons for allowing human suffering may have to do, in part, with the appropriate connection of those sufferings with goods in ways that have never been dreamed of in our theodicies. Once we bring this into the picture, the critic is seen to be on shaky ground in denying, of Bambi's or Sue's suffering, that God could have any patient-centered reason for permitting it, even if we are unable to suggest what such a reason might be.[22]

This would be an appropriate place to consider Rowe's argument that we can be justified in excluding the possibility that God permits one or another case of suffering in order to obtain goods of which we have no conception. In his latest article on the subject (1988) Rowe claims that the variant of 1 there put forward:

> Q. No good state of affairs is such that an omnipotent, omniscient being's obtaining it would morally justify that being in permitting $E1$ or $E2$ (p. 120).[23]

can be derived probabilistically from:

> P. No good state of affairs we know of is such that an omnipotent, omniscient being's obtaining it would morally justify that being's permitting $E1$ or $E2$ (p. 121).

I have been arguing, and will continue to argue, that Rowe is not justified in asserting P, since he is not justified in supposing that none of the particular goods we have been discussing provide God with sufficient reason for permitting the suffering of Bambi and Sue. But even if Rowe were justified in asserting P, what I have just been contending is that the argument from P to Q does not go through. In defending the argument Rowe says the following.

> My answer is that we are justified in making this inference in the same way we are justified in making the many inferences we constantly make from the known to the unknown. All of us are constantly inferring from the A's we know of to the A's we don't know of. If we observe many A's and all of them are B's we are justified in believing that the A's we haven't observed are also B's. If I encounter a fair number of pit bulls and all of them are vicious, I have reason to believe that all pit bulls are vicious (1988, pp.123-24).

But it is just not true that Rowe's inference from known goods to all goods is parallel to inductive inferences we "constantly make". Typically when we generalize from observed instances, at least when we are warranted in doing so, we know quite a lot about what makes a sample of things like that a good base for general attributions of the properties in question. We know that temperamental traits like viciousness or affectionateness are often breed-specific in dogs, and so when a number of individuals of a breed are observed to exhibit such a trait it is a good guess that it is characteristic of that breed. If, on the other hand, the characteristic found throughout the sample were a certain precise height or a certain sex, our knowledge indicates that

---

[22] There is, to be sure, a question as to why, if things are as I have just suggested they may be, God doesn't fill us in on His reasons for permitting suffering. Wouldn't a perfectly benevolent creator see to it that we realize why we are called upon to suffer? I acknowledge this difficulty, in fact it is just another form taken by the problem of evil. And I will respond to it in the same way. Even if we can't see why God would keep us in the dark in this matter, we cannot be justified in supposing that God does not have sufficient reason for doing so.

[23] $E1$ is Bambi's suffering and $E2$ is Sue's suffering. There are, of course, various differences between Q and 1. For one thing, Q, unlike 1 makes reference to God's being morally justified. For another, Q has to do with God's *obtaining* particular goods, apparently leaving out of account the cases in which cooperation from human free choice is required. However these differences are not germane to the present point.

an inference that all members of that breed are of that height or of that sex would be foolhardy indeed. But, as I have been arguing, an inference from known goods lacking J to all goods (including those we have never experienced and even those of which we have no conception) is unlike both the sorts just mentioned in the way they resemble one another, viz., our possession of knowledge indicating which characteristics can be expected to be (fairly) constant in the larger population. We have no background knowledge that tells us the chances of J's being a "goods-specific" characteristic, one that can reasonably be expected to be present in all or most goods if it is found in a considerable sample. Hence we cannot appeal to clearly warranted generalizations in support of this one. Rowe's generalization is more like inferring from the fact that no one has yet produced a physical theory that will unify relativity and quantum mechanics, to the prediction that no one will ever do so, or inferring, in 1850, from the fact no one has yet voyaged to the moon that no one will ever do so. We have no way of drawing boundaries around the total class of goods; we are unable to anticipate what may lie in its so-far-unknown sub-class, just as we are unable to anticipate future scientific developments and future artistic innovations. This is not an area in which induction by simple enumeration yields justified belief.[24]

VIII

It is now time to move beyond the restriction on divine reasons to benefits to the sufferer. The theodical suggestions we will be discussing from here on do not observe this restriction. Since I am moving onto territory less favorable to my opponent, I must give some indication of what might justify dropping the restriction. For my central purposes in this paper I do not need to show that the restriction is unjustified. I take myself to have already shown that the critic is not entitled to his "no sufficient divine reasons" thesis even with the restriction. But I do believe that the restriction is unwarranted, and I want to consider how the land lies with respect to conceivable divine reasons of other sorts. As a prelude to that I will point out the main reasons for and against the restriction to benefits to the sufferer.

On the pro side by far the main consideration is one of justice and fairness. Why should suffering be laid on me for the sake of some good in which I will not participate, or in which my participation is not sufficient to justify my suffering? Wouldn't God be sacrificing me to His own ends and/or to the ends of others if that were His modus operandi, and in that case how could He be considered perfectly good?

> Undeserved suffering which is uncompensated seems clearly unjust; but so does suffering compensated only by benefits to someone other than the sufferer...other things being equal, it seems morally permissible to allow someone to suffer involuntarily only in case doing so is a necessary means or the best possible means in the circumstances to keep the sufferer from incurring even greater harm.[25]

I agree with this to the extent of conceding that a perfectly good God would not wholly sacrifice the welfare of one of His intelligent creatures simply in order to achieve a good for others, or for Himself. This would be incompatible with His concern for the welfare of each of His creatures. Any plan that God would implement will include provision for each of us having a

---

[24] Cf. the criticism of Rowe's move from P to Q in *Christlieb* (forthcoming). Note too that Rowe restricts his consideration of the unknown to "good states of affairs" we do not know of. But, as is recognized in my discussion, it is an equally relevant and equally live possibility that we do not grasp ways in which good states of affairs we know of are connected with cases of suffering so to as to provide God with a reason for permitting the latter. Both types of unknown factors, if realized, would yield divine reasons for permitting suffering of which we are not cognizant.
[25] Stump (1990), p. 66. Many other thinkers, both theistic and atheistic, concur in this judgment.

life that is, on balance, a good thing, and one in which the person reaches the point of being able to see that his life as a whole is a good for him. Or at least, where free creaturely responses have a significant bearing on the overall quality of the person's life, any possible divine plan will have to provide for each of us to have the chance (or perhaps many chances) for such an outcome, if our free responses are of the right sort. Nevertheless, this is compatible with God having as part of his reason for permitting a given case of suffering that it contributes to results that extend beyond the sufferer.[26] So long as the sufferer is amply taken care of, I can't see that this violates any demands of divine justice, compassion, or love. After all, parents regularly impose sacrifices on some of their children for the overall welfare of the family. Of course, in doing so they are acting out of a scarcity of resources, and God's situation is enormously different in this respect. Nevertheless, assuming that Sue's suffering is necessary even for God to be able to achieve a certain good state of affairs, then, provided that Sue is taken care of in such a way that she will eventually come to recognize the value and justifiability of the proceeding and to joyfully endorse it (or at least has ample opportunities to get herself into this position), I cannot see that God could be faulted for setting things up this way.[27]

From now on I will be considering possible divine reasons that extend beyond benefit to the sufferer. Though in line with the previous paragraph I will not suppose that any of these (so far as they exclusively concern persons other than the sufferer) could be God's whole reason for permitting a bit of suffering, I will take it as a live possibility that they could contribute to a sufficient divine reason. The theodicies to be considered now will give us more specific suggestions for Bambi and Sue.

I will begin with the familiar free will theodicy, according to which God is justified in permitting creaturely wickedness and its consequences because he has to do so if he is bestow on some of his creatures the incommensurable privilege of being responsible agents who have, in many areas, the capacity to choose between alternatives as they will, without God, or anyone or anything else (other than themselves), determining which alternative they choose. The suggestion of this theodicy is that it is conceptually impossible for God to create free agents and also determine how they are to choose, within those areas in which they are free. If He were so to determine their choices they would, ipso facto, not be free. But this being the case, when God decided to endow some of His creatures, including us, with free choice, He thereby took the chance, ran the risk, of our sometimes or often making the wrong choice, a possibility that has been richly realized. It is conceptually impossible for God to create free agents and not subject Himself to such a risk. Not to do the latter would be not to do the former. But that being the case, He, and we, are stuck with whatever consequences ensue. And this is why God permits such horrors as the rape, beating, and murder of Sue. He does it not because that particular wicked choice is itself necessary for the realization of some great good, but because the permission of such horrors is bound up with the decision to give human beings free choice in many areas, and

---

[26] Note that we are assuming (what seems to be obvious) that God might have a number of reasons for permitting a particular case of suffering, no one of which reasons is sufficient by itself though the whole complex is. This obvious possibility is often ignored when critics seek to knock down theodical suggestions one by one.

[27] In "Victimization and the Problem of Evil" [forthcoming], Thomas F. Tracy persuasively argues that although "God must not actualize a world that contains persons whose lives, through no fault of their own, are on balance an evil (i.e., an intrinsic disvalue) for them rather than a good" (20), nevertheless, we cannot also claim that "God must not actualize a world in which a person suffers some evil E if the elimination of E by God would result in a better balance *for this individual* of the goods God intends for persons and the evils God permits" (23).

that (the capacity to freely choose) is a great good, such a great good as to be worth all the suffering and others evils that it makes possible.[28]

This theodicy has been repeatedly subjected to radical criticisms that, if sound, would imply that the value of creaturely free will is not even a possible reason for God's allowing Sue's attacker to do his thing. For one thing, it has been urged that it is within God's power to create free agents so that they always choose what is right. For another, it has been denied or doubted that free will is of such value as to be worth all the sin and suffering it has brought into the world. In accord with my general policy in this paper, I will not attempt to argue that this theodicy does succeed in identifying God's reasons for permitting wrongdoing and its results, but only that the possibility of this cannot be excluded. Hence I can confine myself to arguing that these criticisms do not dispose of that possibility. Though lack of space prevents a proper discussion, I will just indicate what I would say in such a discussion. On the first point, if we set aside middle knowledge as I am doing in this paper, it is logically impossible for God to create beings with genuine freedom of choice and also guarantee that they will always choose the right. And even granting middle knowledge Plantinga (1974) has established the *possibility* that God could not actualize a world containing free creatures that always do the right thing. As for the second point, though it may be beyond our powers to show that free will has sufficient value to carry the theodical load, it is surely equally beyond our powers to show that it does not.[29]

Thus we may take it to be a live possibility that the maintenance of creaturely free will is at least part of God's reason for permitting wrongdoing and its consequences. But then the main reason one could have for denying that this is at least part of why God would allow the attack on Sue is that God could, miraculously or otherwise, prevent any one incipient free human action without losing the value of human free will. Clearly a divine interference in normal human operations in this one instance is not going to prevent even Sue's attacker from being a free moral agent in general, with all that that involves. This point is supported by the consideration that, for all we know, God does sometimes intervene to prevent human agents from doing wicked things they would otherwise have done, and, so the free will theodicist will claim, even if that is the case we do enjoy the incommensurable value of free choice. We can also think of it this way. It is perfectly obvious that the scope of our free choice is not unlimited. We have no effective voluntary control over, e.g., our genetic constitution, our digestive and other biological processes, and much of our cognitive operations. Thus whatever value the human capacity for free choice possesses, that value is compatible with free choice being confined within fairly narrow limits. But then presumably a tiny additional constriction such as would be involved in God's preventing Sue's attacker from committing that atrocity would not render things radically different, free-will-wise, from what they would have been without that. So God could have prevented this without losing the good emphasized by this theodicy. Hence we can be sure that this does not constitute a sufficient reason for His not preventing it.

To be sure, if God were to act on this principle in every case of incipient wrongdoing, the situation would be materially changed. Human agents would no longer have a real choice between good and evil, and the surpassing worth that attaches to having such a choice would be lost. Hence, if God is to promote the values emphasized by the free will theodicy, He can intervene in this way in only a small proportion of cases. And how are these to be selected? I

---

[28] The reader may well wonder why it is only now that I have introduced the free will theodicy, since it has such an obvious application to Sue's case. The reason is that I wanted at first to focus on those suggestions that confined the rationale of suffering to benefit to the sufferer.

[29] On this point, see the discussion in the next section of our inability to make evaluative comparisons on the scale required here.

doubt that we are in a position to give a confident answer to this question, but let's assume that the critic proposes that the exceptions are to be picked in such a way as to maximize welfare, and let's go along with that. Rowe's claim would then have to be that Sue's murder was so horrible that it would qualify for the class of exceptions. But that is precisely where the critic's claims far outrun his justification. How can we tell that Sue falls within the most damaging $n\%$ of what would be cases of human wrongdoing apart from divine intervention. To be in a position to make such a judgment we would have to survey the full range of such cases and make reliable assessments of the deleterious consequences of each. Both tasks are far beyond our powers. We don't even know what free creaturely agents there are beyond human beings, and with respect to humans the range of wickedness, past, present, and future, is largely beyond our ken. And even with respect to the cases of which we are aware we have only a limited ability to assess the total consequences. Hence, by the nature of the case, we are simply not in a position to make a warranted judgment that Sue's case is among the $n\%$ worst cases of wrongdoing in the history of the universe. No doubt,--it strikes us as incomparably horrible on hearing about it, but so would innumerable others. Therefore, the critic is not in a position to set aside the value of free will as at least part of God's reason for permitting Sue's murder.

IX

Next I turn to theodicies that stress benefit to human beings other than the sufferer or to humanity generally.[30] And first let's return to Marilyn Adams 'discussion of martyrdom in (1986). In addition to her account, already noted, of martyrdom as a vehicle of God's goodness to the martyr, she discusses "Martyrdom as a vehicle of God's goodness to the onlooker". "For onlookers, the event of martyrdom may function as a prophetic story, the more powerful for being brought to life. The martyr who perseveres to the end presents an inspiring example. Onlookers are invited to see in the martyr the person they ought to be and to be brought to a deeper level of commitment. Alternatively, onlookers may see themselves in the persecutor and be moved to repentance. If the onlooker has ears to hear the martyr's testimony, he may receive God's redemption through it" (p. 257). She also suggests that martyrdom may be redemptive for the persecutor. "First of all, the martyr's sacrifice can be used as an instrument of divine judgment, because it draws the persecutor an external picture of what he is really like—the more innocent the victim, the clearer the focus…In attempting to bring reconciliation out of judgment, God may find no more promising vehicle than martyrdom for dealing with the hard-hearted" (p. 258). (Again, in making these suggestions for a theodicy of suffering, Adams is not restricting their scope to martyrdom strictly so called.) To be sure, sometimes there is no persecutor, but often there is, as in child and wife abuse. And there is always the possibility, and usually the actuality, of onlookers.[31]

Can the critic be justified in holding that Sue's suffering, e.g., would not be permitted by God at least in part for reasons of these sorts? Once more, even if we cannot see that Sue's suffering brings these kinds of benefits to her attacker or to onlookers, our massive ignorance of the recesses of the human heart and of the total outcomes, perhaps through eternity, for all such people, renders us poor judges of whether such benefits are indeed forthcoming. And, finally, even if no goods of these sorts eventuate, there is once more the insoluble problem of whether

---

[30] Or to other creatures. Most discussions of the problem of evil are markedly anthropocentric, in a way that would not survive serious theological scrutiny.

[31] These suggestions will draw many of the objections we have already seen to be leveled against Hick's, Stump's, and Adams' sufferer-centered points. See section vi for a discussion of these objections.

God could be expected to use a different strategy, given His respect for human free will. Perhaps that was (a part of) the strategy that held out the best chance of evoking the optimal response from these particularly hard-hearted subjects.

Next I want to consider a quite different theodicy that also sees God's reasons for permitting suffering in terms of benefits that are generally distributed, viz., the appeal to the benefits of a lawlike natural order, and the claim that suffering will be an inevitable byproduct of any such order. I choose the exposition of this theodicy in Bruce Reichenbach in *Evil and a Good God* (1982).

> ...creation, in order to make possible the existence of moral agents...had to be ordered according to some set of natural laws (p. 101).

The argument for this is that if things do not happen in a lawlike fashion, at least usually, agents will be unable to anticipate the consequences of their volitions, and hence will not be able to effectively make significant choices between good and evil actions. Reichenbach continues:

> Consequently, the possibility arises that sentient creatures like ourselves can be negatively affected by the outworkings of these laws in nature, such that we experience pain, suffering, disability, disutility, and at times the frustration of our good desires. Since a world with free persons making choices between moral good and evil and choosing a significant amount of moral good is better than a world without free persons and moral good and evil, God in creating had to create a world which operated according to natural laws to achieve this higher good. Thus, his action of creation of a natural world and a natural order, along with the resulting pain and pleasure which we experience, is justified. The natural evils which afflict us—diseases, sickness, disasters, birth defects—are all the outworking of the natural system of which we are a part. They are the byproducts made possible by that which is necessary for the greater good (100-01).

This is a theodicy for natural evil, not for the suffering that results from human wickedness. Hence it has possible application to Bambi, but not to Sue, and possible application to any other suffering that results from natural processes that are independent of human intentional action.

Let's agree that significant moral agency requires a natural lawful order. But that doesn't show that it is even possible that God had a sufficient reason to allow Bambi's suffering. There are two difficulties that must be surmounted to arrive at that point.

First, a natural order can be regular enough to provide the degree of predictability required for morally significant choice even if there are exceptions to the regularities. Therefore, God could set aside the usual consequences of natural forces in this instance, so as to prevent Bambi's suffering, without thereby interfering with human agents' reasonable anticipations of the consequences of their actions. So long as God doesn't do this too often, we will still have ample basis for suppositions as to what we can reasonably expect to follow what. But note that by the same line of reasoning God cannot do this too often, or the desired predictability will not be forthcoming. Hence, though any one naturally caused suffering could have been miraculously prevented, God certainly has a strong prima facie reason in each case to refrain from doing this; for if He didn't He would have no reason for letting nature usually take its course. And so He has a possible reason for allowing nature to take its course in the Bambi case, a reason that would have to be overridden by stronger contrary considerations.

This means that in order to be justified in supposing that God would not have a sufficient reason to refrain from intervening in this case, we would have to be justified in supposing that God would have a sufficient reason to make, in this case, an exception to the general policy. And how could we be justified in supposing that? We would need an adequate grasp of the full range of cases from which God would have to choose whatever exceptions He is going to make, if any, to the general policy of letting nature take its course. Without that we would not be in a position to judge that Bambi is among the *n%* of the cases most worthy of being miraculously prevented.[32] And it is abundantly clear that we have and can have no such grasp of this territory as a whole. We are quite unable, by our natural powers, of determining just what cases, or even what kinds of cases, of suffering there would be throughout the history of the universe if nature took its course. We just don't know enough about the constituents of the universe even at present, much less throughout the past and future, to make any such catalogue. And we could not make good that deficiency without an enormous enlargement of our cognitive capacities. Hence we are in no position to judge that God does not have sufficient reason (of the Reichenbach sort) for refraining from interfering in the Bambi case.[33]

But all this has to do with whether God would have interfered with the natural order, as it actually exists, to prevent Bambi's suffering. And it will be suggested, secondly, that God could have instituted a quite different natural order, one that would not involve human and animal suffering, or at least much less of it. Why couldn't there be a natural order in which there are no viruses and bacteria the natural operation of which results in human and animal disease, a natural order in which rainfall is evenly distributed, in which earthquakes do not occur, in which forests are not subject to massive fires? To be sure, even God could not bring into being just the creatures we presently have while subjecting their behavior to different laws. For the fact that a tiger's natural operations and tendencies are what they are is an essential part of what makes it the kind of thing it is.[34] But why couldn't God have created a world with different constituents so as to avoid subjecting any sentient creatures to disease and natural disasters? Let's agree that this is possible for God. But then the critic must also show that at least one of the ways in which God could have done this would have produced a world that is better on the whole than the actual world. For even if God could have instituted a natural order without disease and natural disasters, that by itself doesn't show that He would have done so if He existed. For if that world had other undesirable features and/or lacked desirable features in such a way as to be worse, or at least no better than, the actual world, it still doesn't follow that God would have chosen the former over the latter. It all depends on the overall comparative worth of the two systems. Once again I am not concerned to argue for Reichenbach's theodicy, which would, on the rules by which we are playing, require arguing that no possible natural order is overall better than the one we have. Instead I merely want to show that the critic is not justified in supposing that some alternative natural order open to God that does not involve suffering (to the extent that we have it) is better on the whole.

There are two points I want to make about this, points that have not cropped up earlier in the paper. First, it is by no means clear what possibilities are open to God. Here it is important to remember that we are concerned with metaphysical possibilities (necessities...), not merely with conceptual or logical possibilities in a narrow sense of 'logical'. The critic typically points out that we can consistently and intelligibly conceive a world in which there are no diseases, no

---

[32] There are also questions as to whether we are capable of making a reasonable judgment as to which cases from a given field have the strongest claim to being prevented. Our capacity to do this is especially questionable where incommensurable factors are involved, e.g., the worth of the subject and the magnitude of the suffering. But let this pass.

[33] The reader will, no doubt, be struck by the similarity between this problem and the one that came up with respect to the free will theodicy. There too it was agreed that God can occasionally, but only occasionally, interfere with human free choice and its implementation without sacrificing the value of human free will. And so there too we were faced with the question of whether we could be assured that a particular case would be a sufficiently strong candidate for such interference that God would have sufficient reason to intervene.

[34] Reichenbach, 110-11.

earthquakes, floods, or tornadoes, no predators in the animal kingdom, while all or most of the goods we actually enjoy are still present. He takes this to show that it is possible for God to bring about such a world. But, as many thinkers have recently argued,[35] consistent conceivability (conceptual possibility) is by no means sufficient for metaphysical possibility, for what is possible given the metaphysical structure of reality. To use a well worn example, it may be metaphysically necessary that the chemical composition of water is H_2O since that is what water essentially is, even though, given the ordinary concept of water, we can without contradiction or unintelligibility, think of water as made of up of carbon and chlorine. Roughly speaking, what is conceptually or logically (in a narrow sense of 'logical') possible depends on the composition of the concepts, or the meanings of the terms, we use to cognize reality, while metaphysical possibility depends on what things are like in themselves, their essential natures, regardless of how they are represented in our thought and language.

It is much more difficult to determine what is metaphysically possible or necessary than to determine what is conceptually possible or necessary. The latter requires only careful reflection on our concepts. The former requires—well, it's not clear what will do the trick, but it's not something we can bring off just by reflecting on what we mean by what we say, or on what we are committing ourselves to by applying a certain concept. To know what is metaphysically possible in the way of alternative systems of natural order, we would have to have as firm a grasp of this subject matter as we have of the chemical constitution of familiar substances like water and salt. It is clear that we have no such grasp. We don't have a clue as to what essential natures are within God's creative repertoire, and still less do we have a clue as to which combinations of these into total lawful systems are doable. We know that you can't have water without hydrogen and oxygen and that you can't have salt without sodium and chlorine. But can there be life without hydrocarbons? Who knows? Can there be conscious, intelligent organisms with free will that are not susceptible to pain? That is, just what is metaphysically required for a creature to have the essential nature of a conscious, intelligent, free agent? Who can say? Since we don't have even the beginnings of a canvass of the possibilities here, we are in no position to make a sufficiently informed judgment as to what God could or could not create by way of a natural order that contains the goods of this one (or equal goods of other sorts) without its disadvantages.

One particular aspect of this disability is our inability to determine what consequences would ensue, with metaphysical necessity, on a certain alteration in the natural order. Suppose that predators were turned into vegetarians. Or rather, if predatory tendencies are part of the essential natures of lions, tigers, and the like, suppose that they were replaced with vegetarians as much like them as possible. How much like them is that? What other features are linked to predatory tendencies by metaphysical necessity? We may know something of what is linked to predation by natural necessity, e.g., by the structure and dispositional properties of genes. But to what extent does metaphysical possibility go beyond natural possibility here? To what extent could God institute a different system of heredity such that what is inseparable from predation in the actual genetic code is separable from it instead? Who can say? To take another example, suppose we think of the constitution of the earth altered so that the subterranean tensions and collisions involved in earthquakes are ruled out. What would also have to be ruled out, by metaphysical necessity? (Again, we know something of what goes along with this by natural necessity, but that's not the question.) Could the earth still contain soil suitable for edible crops? Would there still be mountains? A system of flowing streams? We are, if anything, still more at a loss when we think of eradicating all the major sources of suffering from the natural order. What

---

[35] See, e.g., Kripke (1972), Plantinga (1974).

metaphysical possibilities are there for what we could be left with? It boggles the (human) mind to contemplate the question.[36]

The second main point is this. Even if we could, at least in outline, determine what alternative systems of natural order are open to God, we would still be faced with the staggering job of comparative evaluation. How can we hold together in our minds the salient features of two such total systems sufficiently to make a considered judgment of their relative merits? *Perhaps* we are capable of making a considered evaluation of each feature of the systems (or many of them), and even capable of judicious comparisons of features two-by-two. For example, we might be justified in holding that the reduction in the possibilities of disease is worth more than the greater variety of forms of life that goes along with susceptibility to disease. But it is another matter altogether to get the kind of overall grasp of each system to the extent required to provide a comprehensive ranking of those systems. We find it difficult enough, if not impossible, to arrive at a definitive comparative evaluation of cultures, social systems, or educational policies. It is far from clear that even if I devoted my life to the study of two primitive cultures, I would thereby be in a position to make an authoritative pronouncement as to which is better on the whole. How much less are we capable of making a comparative evaluation of two alternative natural orders, with all the indefinitely complex ramification of the differences between the two.[37]

Before leaving this topic I want to emphasize the point that, unlike the theodicies discussed earlier the natural law theodicy bears on the question of animal as well as human suffering. If the value of a lawful universe justifies the suffering that results from the operation of those laws, that would apply to suffering at all levels of the great chain of being.

X

I have been gleaning suggestions from a variety of theodicies as to what reasons God might have for permitting suffering. I believe that each of these suggestions embody one or more sorts of reasons that God might conceivably have for some of the suffering in the world. And I believe that I have shown that none of us are in a position to warrantedly assert, with respect to any of those reasons, that God would not permit some cases of suffering for that reason. Even if I am mistaken in supposing that we cannot rule out some particular reason, e.g. that the suffering is a punishment for sin, I make bold to claim that it is extremely unlikely that I am mistaken about all those suggestions. Moreover, I have argued, successfully I believe, that some of these reasons are at least part of possible divine reasons for Rowe's cases, Bambi and Sue, and that hence we are

---

[36] I hope it is unnecessary to point out that I am not suggesting that we are incapable of making any reasonable judgments of metaphysical modality. Here, as elsewhere, my point is that the judgments required by the inductive argument from evil are of a very special and enormously ambitious type and that our cognitive capacities that serve us well in more limited tasks are not equal to this one. (For more on this general feature of the argument see the final section.) Indeed, just now I contrasted the problem of determining what total systems of nature are metaphysically possible with the problem of the chemical composition of various substances, where we are in a much better position to make judgments of metaphysical modality.

[37] This point cuts more than one way. For example, theodicists often confidently assert, as something obvious on the face of it, that a world with free creatures, even free creatures who often misuse their freedom, is better than a world with no free creatures. But it seems to me that it is fearsomely difficult to make this comparison and that we should not be so airily confident that we can do so. Again, to establish a natural law theodicy along Reichenbach's lines one would have to show that the actual natural order is at least as beneficial as any possible alternative; and the considerations I have been adducing cast doubt on our inability to do this. Again, please note that in this paper I am not concerned to defend any particular theodicy.

unable to justifiably assert that God does not have reasons of these sorts for permitting Rowe-like cases.

However that does not suffice to dispose of Rowe's specific argument, concerned as it is with the Bambi and Sue cases in particular. For I earlier conceded, for the sake of argument, that (1) none of the sufferer-centered reasons I considered could be any part of God's reasons for permitting the Bambi and Sue cases, and (2) that nonsufferer-centered reasons could not be the whole of God's reasons for allowing any case of suffering. This left me without any specific suggestions as to what might be a fully sufficient reason for God to permit those cases. And hence showing that no one can be justified in supposing that reasons of the sort considered are not at least part of God's reasons for one or another case of suffering does not suffice to show that no one can be justified in supposing that God could have no sufficient reason for permitting the Bambi and Sue cases. And hence it does not suffice to show that Rowe cannot be justified in asserting 1.

This lacuna in the argument is remedied by the point that we cannot be justified in supposing that there are no other reasons, thus far unenvisaged, that would fully justify God in permitting Rowe's cases. That point was made at the end of section vii for sufferer-centered reasons, and it can now be made more generally. Even if we were fully entitled to dismiss all the alleged reasons for permitting suffering that have been suggested, we would still have to consider whether there are further possibilities that are undreamt of in our theodicies. Why should we suppose that the theodicies thus far excogitated, however brilliant and learned their authors, exhaust the field. The points made in the earlier discussion about the impossibility of anticipating future developments in human thought can be applied here. Just as we can never repose confidence in any alleged limits of future human theoretical and conceptual developments in science, so it is here, even more so if possible. It is surely reasonable to suppose that God, if such there be, has more tricks up His sleeve than we can envisage. Since it is in principle impossible for us to be justified in supposing that God does not have sufficient reasons for permitting E that are unknown to us, and perhaps unknowable by us, no one call be justified in holding that God could have no reasons for permitting the Bambi and Sue cases, or any other particular cases of suffering.[38]

This last point, that we are not warranted in supposing that God does not have sufficient reasons unknown to us for permitting E, is not only an essential part of the total argument against the justifiability of 1. It would be sufficient by itself. Even if all my argumentation prior to that point were in vain and my opponent could definitively rule out all the specific suggestions I have put forward, she would still face the insurmountable task of showing herself to be justified in supposing that there are no further possibilities for sufficient divine reasons. That point by itself would be decisive.

XI

In the case of each of the theodical suggestions considered I have drawn on various limits to our cognitive powers, opportunities, and achievements in arguing that we are not in a position to deny that God could have that kind of reason for various cases of suffering. In conclusion it may be useful to list the cognitive limits that have formed the backbone of my argument.

---

[38] For Rowe's objection to this invocation of the possibility of humanly unenvisaged divine reasons for permitting suffering, and my answer thereto, see the end of section vii.

1. *Lack of data.* This includes, inter alia, the secrets of the human heart, the detailed constitution and structure of the universe, and the remote past and future, including the afterlife if any.

2. *Complexity greater than we can handle.* Most notably there is the difficulty of holding enormous complexes of fact—different possible worlds or different systems of natural law—together in the mind sufficiently for comparative evaluation.

3. *Difficulty of determining what is metaphysically possible or necessary.* Once we move beyond conceptual or semantic modalities (and even that is no piece of cake) it is notoriously difficult to find any sufficient basis for claims as to what is metaphysically possible, given the essential natures of things, the exact character of which is often obscure to us and virtually always controversial. This difficulty is many times multiplied when we are dealing with tota possible worlds or total systems of natural order.

4. *Ignorance of the full range of possibilities.* This is always crippling when we are trying to establish negative conclusions. If we don't know whether or not there are possibilities beyond the ones we have thought of, we are in a very bad position to show that there can be no divine reasons for permitting evil.

5. *Ignorance of the full range of values.* When it's a question of whether some good is related to E in such a way as to justify God in permitting E, we are, for the reason mentioned in 4., in a very poor position to answer the question if we don't know the extent to which there are modes of value beyond those of which we are aware. For in that case, so far as we can know, E may be justified by virtue of its relation to one of those unknown goods.

6. *Limits to our capacity to make well considered value judgments.* The chief example of this we have noted is the difficulty in making comparative evaluations of large complex wholes.

It may seem to the reader that I have been making things too difficult for the critic, holding him to unwarrantedly exaggerated standards for epistemic justification. "If we were to apply your standards across the board", he may complain, "it would turn out that we are justified in believing little or nothing. That would land us in a total skepticism. And doesn't that indicate that your standards are absurdly inflated?" I agree that it would indicate that if the application of my standards did have that result, but I don't agree that this is the case. The point is that the critic is engaged in attempting to support a particularly difficult claim, a claim that there isn't something in a certain territory, while having a very sketchy idea of what is in that territory, and having no sufficient basis for an estimate of how much of the territory falls outside his knowledge. This is very different from our more usual situation in which we are forming judgments and drawing conclusions about matters concerning which we antecedently know quite a lot, and the boundaries and parameters of which we have pretty well settled. Thus the attempt to show that God could have no sufficient reason for permitting Bambi's or Sue's suffering is quite atypical of our usual cognitive situation; no conclusion can be drawn from our poor performance in the former to an equally poor performance in the latter.[39]

I want to underline the point that my argument in this paper does not rely on a general skepticism about our cognitive powers, about our capacity to achieve knowledge and justified belief. On the contrary, I have been working with what I take to be our usual nonskeptical standards for these matters, standards that I take to be satisfied by the great mass of our beliefs in many areas. My claim has been that when these standards are applied to the kind of claim exemplified by Rowe's 1, it turns out this claim is not justified and that the prospects for any of us being justified in making it are poor at best. This is because of the specific character of that

---

[39] See the end of section vii for a similar point.

claim, its being a negative existential claim concerning a territory about the extent, contents, and parameters of which we know little. My position no more implies, presupposes, or reflects a general skepticism than does the claim that we don't know that there is no life elsewhere in the universe.

This completes my case for the "agnostic thesis", the claim that we are simply not in a position to justifiably assert, with respect to Bambi or Sue or other cases of suffering, that God, if He exists, would have no sufficient reason for permitting it. And if that is right, the inductive argument from evil is in no better shape that its late lamented deductive cousin.

Questions

1. What does William Alston mean by "gratuitous suffering?"

2. What are the six points Alston makes by way of setting the stage for further discussion of William Rowe's inductive argument from evil?

3. Alston takes a stand on the matter of the "punishment motif." What is it?

4. What objections does Alston respond to in connection with Hick's "vale of soul making" theme?

5. What do you think of Alston's contention that a perfectly good God would not "wholly sacrifice the welfare of one of His intelligent creatures simply in order to achieve a good for others or for Himself?"

Bibliography:

- Adams, Marilyn McCord, "Redemptive Suffering: A Christian Approach to the Problem of Evil", in *Rationality, Religious Belief, and Moral Commitment*, ed. R. Audi & W.J. Wainwright (Ithaca, NY: Cornell U. Press, 1986).
- Adams, Robert M.,"Must God Create the Best?", in *The Virtue of Faith and Other Essays in Philosophical Theology* (New York: Oxford University Press, 1987).
- Ahern, M.B., *The Problem of Evil* (London: Routledge & Kegan Paul, 1971).
- Christlieb, Terry, "Which Theism's Face an Evidential Problem of Evil?", *Faith and Philosophy*, forthcoming.
- Fitzpatrick, F.J., "The Onus of Proof in Arguments about the Problem of Evil", *Religious Studies*, 17 (1981).
- Hasker, William, "The Necessity of Gratuitous Evil", *Faith and Philosophy*.
- Hick, John, *Evil and the God of Love*, rev. ed. (New York: Harper & Row, 1978).
- Keller, James, "The Problem of Evil and the Attributes of God", Int. *Journ. Philos. Relig.*, 26 (1989).
- Kripke, Saul A., "Naming and Necessity", in *Semantics of Natural Language*, ed. Donald Davidson & Gilbert Harman (Dordrecht: D. Reidel Pub. Co., 1972).
- Plantinga, Alvin, *The Nature of Necessity* (Oxford: Clarendon Press, 1974).
- Reichenbach, Bruce, *Evil and a Good God* (New York: Fordham U. Press, 1982).
- Rowe, William L., "Evil and Theodicy", *Philosophical Topics*, 16, no. 2 (Fall, 1988).
- Russell, Bruce, "The Persistant Problem of Evil", *Faith and Philosophy*, 6, no. 2. (April, 1989).
- Stump, Eleonore, "Providence and Evil", in *Christian Philosophy*, ed. Thomas P. Flint (Notre Dame, IN: U. of Notre Dame Press, 1990).
- Wykstra, Stephen, "The Humean Obstacle to Evidential Arguments from Suffering: On Avoiding the Evils of 'Appearance'", Int. *Journ. Philos. Relig.*, 16 (1984).

THE PROBLEM OF EVIL*

Richard Swinburne

In this piece Swinburne tries to show that God can be viewed as allowing evil for certain goods which could not happen in any other way. He argues further that good free choices are not mere goods in themselves, but provide opportunity for soul-growth. And soul growth is not confined to the individuals who experience the suffering, but to others who by virtue of good choices also experience growth themselves. He takes up but does not resolve the issue of whether goods are greater in value than the evils they require.

The God of traditional theism (as worshipped by Christians, Jews and Muslims) is by definition omnipotent, omniscient, perfectly free, and perfectly good. God being omnipotent is his being able to do anything logically possible (that is, anything the description of which does not involve a self-contradiction). God being omniscient, I shall understand likewise, as his knowing everything that it is logically possible to know. If, as some have argued, it is not logically possible for anyone to know our future free choices, then God's omniscience will not include such knowledge. But of course it will only be by God's choice that we have any free choices, and so that there is such a limit to his knowledge.

The evils of the world—the things intrinsically bad, such as pain and suffering and wrongdoing—seem to be such that such a God would not allow them to occur. For fairly obviously, being omnipotent, he could prevent the evils of the world if he chose. And if there is a God, then it seems evident to many, in virtue of his perfect goodness he would seek to prevent those evils. So it seems to many, that the existence of evils provides conclusive evidence against the existence of God. However a human is none the less good for allowing someone to suffer so long as that suffering is the only way in which he can promote some greater good, so long as he does promote that good and has the right to allow the suffering (i.e. it is morally permissible for him to do so). For example a human parent may take a child to the dentist and allow him to suffer a tooth being filled, for the sake of his subsequent dental health so long as that is the only way in which he can promote this good state, and as a parent, he does have the right to do this for the child. The latter clause is important. It is often the case that bringing about some evil, e.g. giving an unjust punishment to someone accused of a crime he did not commit, will promote a great good (e.g. deter others from committing a similar crime). But that does not justify bringing about the evil. Now we humans cannot always give a child dental health without the child having to suffer, but God could. So extrapolating from the case of suffering to the case of evils generally, and from that case to the case of God who can do anything logically possible, I suggest that God can allow an evil e to occur, compatibly with his perfect goodness, so long as four conditions are satisfied.

First, it must be logically impossible for God to bring about some good g in any other morally permissible way than by allowing e (or an evil equally bad) to occur. For example, it is logically impossible for God to give us libertarian free will to choose between good and bad (i.e. free will to choose between these despite all the causal influences to which we are subject); and yet also cause us to choose the good. It is logically impossible for God to bring about the good of us having such a free choice without allowing the evil of a bad choice to occur (if that is what we choose). Secondly, God does bring about g. Thus if he brings about pain in order to give us the

---

* This article is printed by courtesy of Richard Swinburne.

opportunity of freely choosing whether to bear it courageously or not, he has also to have given us free will. Thirdly, he has to have the right to allow e to occur (that is, it is morally permissible for him to allow *e* to occur). And finally, some sort of comparative condition must be satisfied. It cannot be as strong as the condition that *g* be a good better than *e* is a bad. For obviously we are often justified, in order to ensure the occurrence of a substantial good in risking the occurrence of a greater evil. A plausible formal way of capturing this condition, is to say that the expected value of allowing *e* to occur, given that God does bring about *g*, must be positive. I shall summarize the claim, with respect to some evil e that if there is a God, he could, compatibly with his perfect goodness, allow it to occur, in order to promote a good g; as the claim that *e* serves a greater good.

It follows that if the only good states were sensory pleasures, God would not be justified in allowing any of the world's evils to occur; for the four conditions would be satisfied with respect to none of them. God could eliminate all the sensory pains, and all the grief and mental distress and whatever else is wrong with the world, and give sentient creatures ((including ourselves) endless blissful sensory states of the sort caused by heroin. Hence the existence of the world's evils would count conclusively against the existence of God. So what a theist must maintain is that there are many other good states than sensory pleasures which God cannot (logically) bring about without allowing evils to occur, and that all the evils in the world serve such a greater good.

Now it is not plausible to suppose that we know what are all the possible good states which evils could promote; and so it might seem that there is no irrationality in a theist claiming that all the world's evils serve greater goods, although he cannot for the most part say what they are. For if there is a God, these evils must serve a greater good. (Otherwise God would not have allowed them to occur.) And if you have very strong reason to suppose that there is a God, you have very strong reason to suppose that they do serve a greater good. The trouble is that seems to many people at first sight fairly obvious that many of the world's evils could not be such as to serve any greater good. To many people it seems that incurable pain, cruelty to children, the Holocaust, animal suffering etc. could serve no greater goods, not because they claim to know what all the possible goods are, but because they claim to know enough about them to know that at least one of the conditions could not be satisfied with respect to some of the evils, e.g. that a God would not have the right to allow them to occur for the sake of any greater good, or that the only goods which some of these evils could promote are ones which do not in fact occur (although, given the evils, God could have brought them about). Almost all people, including in my view most religious believers, who do not have overwhelmingly strong belief that there is a God, are inclined to think at first sight that many of the world's evils do not promote greater goods, and so that the existence of evil seems to constitute a strong argument against the existence of God. It is to such people that theodicy is addressed. Theodicy is the enterprise of showing that appearances are misleading, and that (probably) all the world's evils do promote greater good, and so their existence does not provide evidence against the existence of God. I believe that the task of theodicy is an achievable one; and I have argued this at a little length in my book, *Providence and The Problem of Evil*. In a short lecture I can only give you a flavor of the general line of argument, and also try to make plausible a more limited thesis, which makes its contribution towards my total theodicy. This is the thesis that for those evils for which conditions (1) and (2) are satisfied, condition (3) is also satisfied (or can be satisfied, if God so chooses).

There are plausibly various ways in which if God allows the world's evils to occur (sometimes by bringing them about himself), thereby he brings about a logically necessary condition of a good state which could not be brought about in any other morally permissible way; and that he does in consequence bring about that good. I have already alluded to the traditional free will defense which points out that a free choice between good and evil (logically) can only be brought about by allowing the agent to bring about evil. It is good that the free choices of humans should include *genuine* responsibility for other humans, and that involves the opportunity to benefit or harm them. God has the power to benefit or harm humans. If other agents are to be given a share in his creative work, it is good that they have that power too (although perhaps to a lesser degree). A world in which agents can benefit each other but cannot do each other harm is one where they have only very limited responsibility for each other. If my responsibility for you is limited to whether or not to give you a camcorder, but I cannot cause you pain, stunt your growth, or limit your education, then I do not have a great deal of responsibility for you. A God who gave agents only such limited responsibilities for their fellows would not have given much. God would have reserved for himself the all-important choice of the kind of world it was to be, while simply allowing humans the minor choice of filling in the details. He would be like a father asking his elder son to look after the younger son, and adding that he would be watching the elder son's every move and would intervene the moment the elder son did a thing wrong. The elder son might justly retort that, while he would be happy to share his father's work, he could really do so only if he were left to make his own judgments as to what to do within a significant range of the options available to the father. A good God, like a good father, will delegate responsibility. But in order to allow creatures a share in creation, God has to allow them the choice of hurting and maiming, of frustrating the divine plan. So by allowing such hurting and maiming God makes possible the greater good of humans freely choosing to benefit each other and thus co-operate in God's plan.

But human good free choices are not merely good in themselves and in virtue of their immediate consequences. All human choices are character forming, each good choice makes it easier to make the next choice a good one, agents can form their own characters. Aristotle famously remarked: "we become just by doing just acts, prudent by doing prudent acts, brave by doing brave acts." That is, by doing a just act when it is difficult, when it goes against our natural inclinations (which is what I understand by desires), we make it easier to do a just act next time. We can gradually change our desires, so that, for example, doing just acts becomes natural. Thereby we can free ourselves from the power of the less good desires to which we are subject. But again the great good of us having the free choice of character formation (choosing the sort of people we are to be) can (logically) only be had if there is the danger that we will allow ourselves to corrupt our characters (to become bad people). Then what is known as the "higher-order goods" defense points out that certain kinds of especially valuable free choice are only possible as responses to evil. I can (logically) only show courage in bearing my suffering if I am suffering (an evil state). It is good that we should have the opportunity (occasionally) to do such actions which involve resisting great temptations, because thereby we manifest our total commitment to the good. (A commitment which we do not make when the temptation to do otherwise is not strong is not a total commitment.) It is good too that among the good actions which we should have the (occasional) opportunity to do is to help others who are suffering and deprived by showing sympathy to them and helping them to cope. Help is most significant when it is most needed, and it is most needed when its recipient is suffering and deprived. But I can (logically) only help others who are suffering if there is the evil of their suffering. In these cases, if there is a God, he makes possible the good of free choices of particular kinds, between good and evil, which, logically, he could not give us without allowing the evils (or evils equally bad) to occur. Or rather, it is the only morally permissible way in which he could give us this freedom. He could, it is true, give us the choice between trying to help them or refusing to do so (a choice which plausibly would give just as much opportunity for manifesting our commitments to good or evil) without the possibility of any actual suffering. For God could make a basically deceptive world in which other people appeared to be in great pain when really they were not. But first we would not have the real responsibility for others which is a great good. And secondly it would not be morally permissible—in my view, for God to make a world where people are moved to help others at great cost when the others don't really need help at all. God, if he is not to deceive us and yet give us a real free choice between helping and not helping others, must make a world where others really do suffer. Plausibly too in these cases when free will, and especially free will of certain kinds, is the great good, for which God allowing evil to occur is a necessary condition, we do have the free will which makes such choice a good thing, at any rate so it seems to most of us who choose, and so I will assume for present purposes. The other evils of the world, I would also claim, are such that God allowing them to occur brings about a logically necessary condition of some great good, which he could not bring about in any other morally permissible way.

Consider a natural evil such as disease. It is good that among the choices available to humans should be the choice of whether to make their fellow humans healthy or allow them to be sick. But they can only have that choice if there are natural processes (bacteria, viruses etc.) which bring about disease; and which they can then study (or not bother to study) to know the causes of diseases. Disease is a natural evil initially unpreventable by humans, but they can have the great good of studying it and so learning how to prevent it. But they can only do that if there are regular processes producing the diseases and they can only learn what these are by studying many populations, and studying under which circumstances the disease is transmitted and under which it is not. So for the great good of this choice of investigating (or alternatively, not bothering to investigate), there is required the necessary evil of the actual disease. If humans are to have the great opportunity of devoting their lives to scientific research for human benefit or not bothering to do so—rather than God just providing knowledge on a plate—there have to be sufferers from disease to make this possible. But suppose there are goods and evils for which conditions (1) and (2) are justified, what about condition (3)? It is on that that I wish to focus for the rest of this lecture. Does God have the right to cause or allow evil to occur to humans (and animals) for the sake of some greater good? The trouble may seem more acute in that in many cases, including some mentioned above, good for one individual is promoted by evil endured by a different individual. Does God have the right to make you suffer for my benefit?

To allow someone to suffer for his own good or the good of someone else one has to stand in some kind of parental relationship towards him. I do not have the right to let some stranger, Joe Bloggs, suffer for his own good or that of Bill Snoggs, but I do have the some right if this kind in respect of my own children. I may let my son suffer somewhat for his own good, or for the good of his elder brother, as when I entrust the younger to the temporary care of the elder with the risk that the elder may hurt the younger. Or I may send my daughter to a neighborhood school which she may not enjoy very much but which will benefit others of the neighborhood. I have such a right in respect of a child of mine, because in small part I am responsible for his or her life and so many of the good things which it involves. It is because the parent is the source of much good for the child that he is entitled to take some of it (or its equivalent) back if necessary (e.g. in the form of the life having bad aspects). If the child could understand, he would understand that the parent gives life, nourishment, and education, subject to possible retraction of some of the gift. If this is correct, then a fortiori, a God who is, ex hypothesi, so much more the source of our being than are our parents, has so many more rights in this respect. For we depend on him totally from moment to moment, and the ability of parents and others to benefit us depends on him. But it must remain the case that God's rights are limited by the condition that he must not over time take back more than he gives. He must be on balance a benefactor.

But there do so often look to be lives in which bad outweighs good. I urge however that this is a wrong assessment of many lives because it does not take into account a good which I have so far not mentioned, the good of being of use to others. It is an enormous good for anyone to be of use, whether by what they do by free choice, or by what they do involuntarily or by what happens to them, including what they suffer. Helping someone freely is clearly a great good for the helper. We often help prisoners, not by giving them more comfortable quarters, but by letting them help the handicapped; and pity rather than envy the "poor little rich girl" who has everything and does nothing for anyone else. And one phenomenon prevalent in contemporary Western Europe in recent years draws this good especially to our attention—the evil of unemployment. Because of our systems of Social Security the unemployed on the whole have enough money to live without too much discomfort; certainly they are a lot better off than are many employed in Africa or Asia or Victorian Britain. What is evil about unemployment is not so much any resulting poverty but the uselessness of the unemployed. They often report feeling unvalued by society, of no use, "on the scrap heap". They rightly think it would be a good for them to contribute; but they can't.

It is not only intentional actions freely chosen, but also ones performed involuntarily, which have good consequences for others which constitute a good for those who do them. If the unemployed were compelled to work for some useful purpose, they would surely be right to regard that as a good for them in comparison with being useless. And it is not only intentional actions but experiences undergone involuntarily (or involuntary curtailment of good experiences, as by death) which have good consequences which constitute a good for him who has them (even if a lesser good than that of a free intentional action causing those consequences). Consider the conscript killed in a just and ultimately successful war in defense of his country against a tyrannous aggressor. Almost all peoples, apart from those of the Western world in our generation, have recognized that dying for one's country is a great good for the one who dies, even if he was conscripted. Consider too someone hurt or killed in an accident, where the accident leads to some reform which prevents the occurrence of similar accidents in the future (e.g. someone killed in a rail crash which leads to the installation of a new system of railway signaling which prevents similar accidents in the future). The victim and his relatives often comment in such a situation that at any rate he did not suffer or die in vain. Although they still normally regard the suffering or death as on balance an evil, they would have regarded it as a greater misfortune for the victim (quite apart from the consequences for others) if his suffering or death served no useful purpose. It is a good for us if our experiences are not wasted but are used for the good of others, if they are the means of a benefit, which would not have come to others without them.

Someone may object that the good for the victim is not (e.g.) dying in a railway crash when that leads to improved safety measures, but dying in a railway crash when you know that improved safety measures will result; and, more generally, that the good is the experience (the "feel good") of being of use, not merely being of use. But that cannot be right. For what one is glad about when one learns that one's suffering (or whatever) has had a good effect, is not that one learns it, but that it has in fact had a good effect. If one did not think that, whether one knows about it or not, it would be good that the suffering should have some effect, one would not be glad about it when one learnt that it did. To take an analogy, it is only because I think it a good thing that you pass your exams even if I don't know about it, that I am glad when I come to know about it. And so generally. It is of course a further good that one has a true belief that one's suffering has had a good effect; but that can only be because it's a good in itself that it has had that effect. And if one thing which is good when one learns about it is that not merely have others benefited in some way, but that by one's own suffering one has been of use in causing that effect, then that is good even if one does not learn about it.

It follows from being-of-use being a great good that whenever God allows some evil to occur to B (e.g. causes B to suffer) in order to provide some good for A (e.g. the free choice of how to react to this suffering) that B is benefited as well, his life is not wasted, he is of use (either by enduring some evil or by his availability to do so). He is of use to A, but also of use to God; he plays a role in God's plan for A. And to be of use to the good source of being in the redemption of his creation is an enormous good. The starving are of use to the wealthy on whose doorstep they appear, because, but for them, the wealthy would have no opportunity to be of use. They are the vehicle whereby alone the wealthy can be saved from self-indulgence and learn generosity. And thereby they are of use to God himself.

When one takes into account that those whose evil state is the means of great good to others (and of course also often to themselves) thereby also receive this enormous benefit, it becomes plausible to suppose that God has the right to cause the evil. For, however you weigh the one against the other, the evil carries with it the great good of being-of-use, which contributes towards making the lives of the victims on balance good lives, and so ones in which God has the right to include some evil. But, I must add, if any life on Earth is still on balance bad, God has a duty to compensate for the bad in the after-life so that the total life of such an individual will be on balance good. That, in his omnipotence, he can do. The great value for us of being of use (by our action or suffering) to others is, I believe something very near the surface of the New Testament. An obvious text is the words of Christ as cited by St Paul in his farewell sermon to the Church at Ephesus when he urged them "to remember the words of the Lord Jesus, how he himself said, It is more blessed to give than to receive." (1) Or again recall these words of Jesus: "Ye know that they which are accounted to rule over the Gentiles lord it over them; and their great ones exercise authority over them. But it is not so among you: but whoever would be first among you shall be servant of all. For verily the Son of Man came not to be ministered unto, but to minister, and to give his life a ransom for many." (2) The passage classically connects greatness with service, and it is most plausibly read as saying that greatness consists in service. Then there are passages, which tell us that those who suffer in consequence of their choice to confess the name of Christ are fortunate to be allowed to have such a significant role in the proclamation of the Gospel. The apostles beaten for preaching the Gospel rejoiced "that they were counted worthy to suffer for the name." (3) St Paul's reward for preaching the Gospel is to preach the Gospel, without being paid for it. (4) Conversely, the "sentence" on those that did not believe "on the name of the only begotten son of God", is, according to Jesus as St John reports him, "that the light is come into the world, and men loved the darkness rather than the light; for their works were evil."(5) Good and evil actions are their own reward and punishment. Of course the Gospel also has another message which is bound to get mixed up with this one: that God is only too anxious to give further rewards to those who do good, and give other punishments to those who do bad. But, as biblical critics now appreciate, the Gospel has both a "realized escatology" and yet-to-be-realized escatology.

I have not discussed the fourth-comparative-condition. But when one begins to take into account the benefits to the sufferer of being privileged thereby to help others and of having a free choice of how to cope with his suffering and form a holy character, there begins, I believe, to be considerable plausibility in the claim that the expected benefit of God allowing the suffering to occur outweighs the evil of the suffering. Let me help you to see this by a small thought experiment. Suppose that you exist in another world before your birth in this one, and are given a choice as to the sort of life you are to have in this one. You are told that you are to have only a short life, maybe of a few minutes, although it will be an adult life in the sense that you will have the richness of sensation and belief characteristic of adults. You have a choice as to the sort of life you will have. You can have either a few minutes of very considerable pleasure, of the kind produced by some drug such as heroin, which you will experience by yourself and which will have no effects at all in the world (for example, no one else will know about it); or you can have a few minutes of considerable pain, such as the pain of childbirth, which will have (unknown to you at the time of pain) considerable good effects on others over a few years. You are told that, if you do not make the second choice, those others will never exist, and so you are under no moral obligation to make the second choice. (Moral obligations are obligations to someone, and you can only have moral obligations to those who exist at some time, past, present, or future.) But you seek to make the choice, which will make *your* own life the best life for *you* to have led. How will you choose? The choice is, I hope, obvious. You should choose the second alternative.

Of course God would be mad to allow endless suffering to give endless such opportunities for painful service; but God does not give any of us (except through our own choice) endless suffering. He gives suffering at most for the short period of our earthly life in order that in that life we may help others and form ourselves, and we would be poorer without those opportunities.

Questions

1. Why does Swinburne contend that God must have the *right* to allow sin?

2. Do you agree with Swinburne on the claim that God must have the right to allow sin, and if so why, and if not, why not.

3. What does Swinburne mean when he says that God allows suffering to provide opportunities for soul growth?

4. Does Swinburne allow that maybe God brings about a greater good out of an evil?

5. How does Swinburne see the suffering of one bringing about some good as a result in the lives of others?

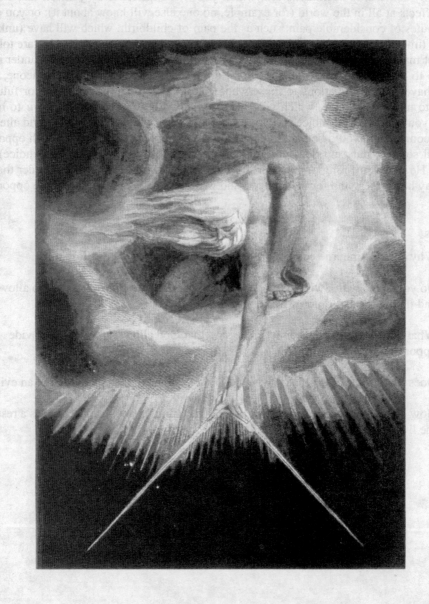

Figure 4

Part IV

The Attributes of God

SOME PUZZLES CONCERNING OMNIPOTENCE*

George Mavrodes

In this essay Mavrodes applies the Thomistic conception of divine omnipotence to the paradox of the stone, and argues that there is no problem because the task contemplated in the paradox involves self-contradictory descriptions.

The doctrine of God's omnipotence appears to claim that God can do anything. Consequently, there have been attempts to refute the doctrine by giving examples of things which God cannot do; for example, He cannot draw a square circle.

Responding to objections of this type, St. Thomas pointed out that "anything" should be here construed to refer only to objects, actions, or states of affairs whose descriptions are not self-contradictory.[1] For it is only such things whose nonexistence might plausibly be attributed to a lack of power in some agent. My failure to draw a circle on the exam may indicate my lack of geometrical skill, but my failure to draw a square circle does not indicate any such lack. Therefore, the fact that it false (or perhaps meaningless) to say that God could draw one does no damage to the doctrine of His omnipotence.

A more involved problem, however, is posed by this type of question: can God create a stone too heavy for Him to lift? This appears to be stronger than the first problem, for it poses a dilemma. If we say that God can create a stone, then it seems that there might be such a stone. And if there might be a stone too heavy for Him to lift, then He is evidently not omnipotent. But if we deny that God can create such a stone, we seem to have given up His omnipotence already. Both answers lead us to the same conclusion.

Further, this problem does not seem obviously open to St. Thomas' solution. The form "x is able to draw a square circle" seems plainly to involve a contradiction, while "x is able to make a thing too heavy for x to lift" does not. For it may easily be true that I am able to make a boat too heavy for me to lift. So why should it not be possible for God to make a stone too heavy for Him to lift?

Despite this apparent difference, this second puzzle *is* open to essentially the same answer as the first. The dilemma fails because it consists of asking whether God can do a self-contradictory thing. And the reply that He cannot does no damage to the doctrine of omnipotence.

The specious nature of the problem may be seen in this away. God is either omnipotent or not.[2] Let us assume first that He is not. In that case the phrase 'a stone too heavy for God to lift" may not be self-contradictory. And then, of course, if we assert either that God is able or that He is not able to create such a stone, we may conclude that He is not omnipotent. But this is no more than the assumption with which we began, meeting us again after our roundabout journey. If this were all that the dilemma could establish it would be trivial. To be significant it must derive this same conclusion *from the assumption that God is omnipotent;* that is, it must show that the assumption of the omnipotence of God leads to a *reductio*. But does it?

---

* This article is reprinted by courtesy of the author and publisher. It appears in *The Philosophical Review*, 73 (1964).
[1] St. Thomas Aquinas, *Summa Theologiae*, Ia, q. 25, a. 3.
[2] I assume, of course, the existence of God, since that is not being brought in question here.

On the assumption that God is omnipotent, the phrase "a stone too heavy for God to lift" becomes self-contradictory. For it becomes "a stone which cannot be lifted by Him whose power is sufficient for lifting anything." But the "thing" described by a self-contradictory phrase is absolutely impossible and hence has nothing to do with the doctrine of omnipotence. Not being an object of power at all, its failure to exist cannot be the result of some lack in the power of God. And, interestingly, it is the very omnipotence of God which makes the existence of such a stone absolutely impossible, while it is the fact that I am finite in power which makes it possible for me to make a boat too heavy for me to lift.

But suppose that some die-hard objector takes the bit in his teeth and denies that the phrase "a stone too heavy for God to lift" is self-contradictory, even on the assumption that God is omnipotent. In other words, he contends that the description "a stone too heavy for an omnipotent God to lift" is self-coherent and therefore describes an absolutely possible object. Must I then attempt to prove the contradictory which I assume above as intuitively obvious? Not necessarily. Let me reply simply that if the objector is right in this contention, then the answer to the original question is "Yes, God can create such a stone." It may seem that this reply will force us into the original dilemma. But it does not. For now the objector can draw no damaging conclusion from this answer. And the reason is that he has just now contended that such a stone is compatible with the omnipotence of God. Therefore, from the possibility of God's creating such a stone it cannot be concluded that God is not omnipotent. The objector cannot have it both ways. The conclusion which he himself wishes to draw from an affirmative answer to the original question is itself the required proof that the descriptive phrase which appears there is self-contradictory. And "it is more appropriate to say that such things cannot be done, than that God cannot do them."[3]

The specious nature of this problem may also be seen in a somewhat different way.[4] Suppose that some theologian is convinced by this dilemma that he must give up the doctrine of omnipotence. But he resolves to give up as little as possible, just enough to meet the argument. One way he can do so is by retaining the infinite power of God with regard to lifting, while placing a restriction on the sort of stone He is able to create. The only restriction required here, however, is that God must not be able to create a stone too heavy for Him to lift. Beyond that the dilemma has not even suggested any necessary restriction. Our theologian has, in effect, answered the original question in the negative, and he now regretfully supposes that this has required him to give up the full doctrine of omnipotence. He is now retaining what he supposes to be the more modest remnants which he has salvaged from that doctrine.

We must ask, however, what it is which he has in fact given up. Is it the unlimited power of God to create stones? No doubt. But what stone is it which God is now precluded from creating? The stone too heavy for Him to lift, of course. But we must remember that nothing in the argument required the theologian to admit any limit on God's power with regard to the lifting of stones. He still holds that to be unlimited. And if God's power to lift is infinite, then His power to create may run to infinity also without outstripping that first power. The supposed limitation turns out to be no limitation at all, since it is specified only by reference to another power which is itself infinite. Our theologian need have no regrets, for he has given up nothing. The doctrine of the power of God remains just what it was before.

Nothing I have said above, of course, goes to prove that God is, in fact, omnipotent. All I have intended to show is that certain arguments intended to prove that He is not omnipotent fail. They fail because they propose, as tests of Gods' power, putative tasks whose descriptions are

---

[3] St. Thomas, *loc. cit.*

[4] But this method rests finally on the same logical relations as the preceding one.

self-contradictory. Such pseudo-tasks, not falling within the realm of possibility, are not objects of power at all. Hence the fact that they cannot be performed implies no limit on the power of God, and hence no defect in the doctrine of omnipotence.

Questions

1. How does Thomas Aquinas unpack the notion of "anything" in connection with defining "omnipotence?"
2. Mavrodes judges that the second puzzle is open to the same answer as the first. What is it?
3. Why does Mavrodes think that the problem regarding God's omnipotence and the paradox of the stone is not open to Thomas Aquinas' solution?
4. What does Mavrodes think he has achieved in the discussion?
5. Do you think Mavrodes has succeeded in his task?

OMNIPOTENCE AND ALMIGHTINESS*

Peter Geach

Peter Geach was professor of philosophy at Leeds University. In this essay he draws a distinction between the notion of omnipotence and almightiness, and argues that the latter is a Biblical concept but the former isn't. He considers four accounts of omnipotence and finds each involving significant problems.

It is fortunate for my purposes that English has the two words "almighty" and "omnipotent," and that apart from any stipulation by me the words have rather different associations and suggestions. "Almighty" is the familiar word that comes in the creeds of the Church; "omnipotent" is at home rather in formal theological discussions and controversies, e.g. about miracles and about the problem of evil. "Almighty" derives by way of Latin "omnipotens" from the Greek word "*pantokrator*"; and both this Greek word, like the more classical "*pankrates*," and "almighty" itself suggest God's having power over all things. On the other hand the English word "omnipotent" would ordinarily be taken to imply ability to do everything; the Latin word "omnipotens" also predominantly has this meaning in Scholastic writers, even though in origin it is a Latinization of "*pantocrator*." So there already is a tendency to distinguish the two words; and in this paper I shall make the distinction a strict one. I shall use the world "almighty" to express God's power over all things, and I shall take "omnipotence" to mean ability to do everything.

I think we can in a measure understand what God's almightiness implies, and I shall argue that almightiness so understood must be ascribed to God if we are to retain anything like traditional Christian belief in God. The position as regards omnipotence, or as regards the statement "God can do everything," seems to me to be very different. Of course even "God can do everything" may be understood simply as a way of magnifying God by contrast with the impotence of man. McTaggart described it as "a piece of theological etiquette" to call God omnipotent: Thomas Hobbes, out of reverence for his Maker, would rather say that "omnipotent" is an attribute of honor. But McTaggart and Hobbes would agree that "God is omnipotent" or "God can do everything" is not to be treated as a proposition that can figure as premise or conclusion in a serious theological argument. And I too wish to say this. I have no objection to such ways of speaking if they merely express a desire to give the best honor we can to God our Maker, whose Name only is excellent and whose praise is above heaven and earth. But theologians have tried to prove that God can do everything, or to derive conclusions from this thesis as a premise. I think such attempts have been wholly unsuccessful. When people have tried to read into "God can do everything" a signification not of Pious Intention but of Philosophical Truth, they have only landed themselves in intractable problems and hopeless confusions; no graspable sense has ever been given to this sentence that did not lead to self-contradiction or at least to conclusions manifestly untenable from a Christian point of view.

I shall return to this; but I must first develop what I have to say about God's almightiness, or power over all things. God is not just more powerful than any creature; no creature can compete with God in power, even unsuccessfully. For God is also the source of all power; any

---

* Reprinted from *Philosophy* 48 (1973) by permission of Cambridge University Press. Copyright © The Royal Institute of Philosophy 1973.

power a creature has comes from God and is maintained only for such time as God wills. Nebuchadnezzar submitted to praise and adore the God of heaven because he was forced by experience to realize that only by God's favor did his wits hold together from one end of a blasphemous sentence to the other end. Nobody can deceive God or circumvent him or frustrate him; and there is no question of God's trying to do anything and failing. In Heaven and on Earth, God does whatever he will. We shall see that some propositions of the form "God cannot do so-and-so" have to be accepted as true; but what God cannot be said to be able to do he likewise cannot will to do; we cannot drive a logical wedge between his power and his will, which are, as the Scholastics said, really identical, and there is no application to God of the concept of trying but failing.

I shall not spend time on citations of Scripture and tradition to show that this doctrine of God's almightiness is authentically Christian; nor shall I here develop rational grounds for believing it is a true doctrine. But it is quite easy to show that this doctrine is indispensable for Christianity, not a bit of old metaphysical luggage that can be abandoned with relief. For Christianity requires an absolute faith in the promises of God: specifically, faith in the promise that some day the whole human race will be delivered and blessed by the establishment of the Kingdom of God. If God were not almighty, he might will and not do; sincerely promise, but find fulfillment beyond his power. Men might prove untamable and incorrigible, and might kill themselves through war or pollution before God's salvific plan for them could come into force. It is useless to say that after the end of this earthly life men would live again; for as I have argued elsewhere, only the promise of God can give us any confidence that there will be an afterlife for men; and if God were not almighty, this promise too might fail. If God is true and just and unchangeable and almighty, we can have absolute confidence in his promises: otherwise we cannot—and there would be an end of Christianity.

A Christian must therefore believe that God is almighty; but he need not believe that God can do everything. Indeed, the very argument I have just used shows that a Christian must not believe that God can do everything: for he may not believe that God could possibly break his own word. Nor can a Christian even believe that God can do everything that is logically possible; for breaking one's word is certainly a logically possible feat.

It seems to me, therefore, that the tangles in which people have enmeshed themselves when trying to give the expression "God can do everything" an intelligible and acceptable content are tangles that a Christian believer has no need to enmesh himself in; the spectacle of others enmeshed may sadden him, but need not cause him to stumble in the way of faith. The denial that God is omnipotent, or able to do everything, may seem dishonoring to God; but when we see where the contrary affirmation, in its various forms, has led, we may well cry out with Hobbes: "Can any man think God is served with such absurdities? As if it were an acknowledgment of the Divine Power, to say, that which is, is not; or that which has been, has not been."

I shall consider four main theories of omnipotence. The first holds that God can do everything absolutely; everything that can be expressed in a string of words that makes sense; even if that sense can be shown to be self-contradictory, God is not bound in action, as we are in thought, by the laws of logic. I shall speak of this as the doctrine that God is absolutely omnipotent.

The second doctrine is that a proposition..."God can do so-and-so" is true when and only when "so-and-so" represents a logically consistent description.

The third doctrine is that "God can do so-and-so" is true just if "God does so-and-so" is logically consistent. This is a weaker doctrine than the second; for "God is doing so-and-so" is logically consistent only when -so-and-so represents a logically consistent description, but on the other hand there may be consistently describable feats which it would involve contradiction to suppose done *by God*.

The last and weakest view is that the realm of what can be done or brought about includes all future possibilities, and that whenever "God will bring so-and-so about is logically possible, "*God can* bring so-and-so about" is true.

The first sense of "omnipotent" in which people have believed God to be omnipotent implies precisely: ability to do absolutely everything describable. You mention it, and God can do it. McTaggart insisted on using "omnipotent" in this sense only; from an historical point of view we may of course say that he imposed on the word a sense which it, and the corresponding Latin word, have not always borne. But Broad seems to me clearly unjust to McTaggart when he implies that in demolishing this doctrine of omnipotence McTaggart was just knocking down a man of straw. As Broad must surely have known, at least one great philosopher, Descartes, deliberately adopted and defended this doctrine of omnipotence: what I shall call the doctrine of absolute omnipotence.

As Descartes himself remarked, nothing is too absurd for some philosopher to have said it some time; I once read an article about an Indian school of philosophers who were alleged to maintain that it is only a delusion, which the wise can overcome, that anything exists at all—so perhaps it would not matter all that much that a philosopher is found to defend absolute omnipotence. Perhaps it would not matter all that much that the philosopher in question was a very great one; for very great philosophers have maintained the most preposterous theses. What does make the denial of absolute omnipotence important is not that we are thereby denying what a philosopher, a very great philosopher, thought he must assert, but that this doctrine has a live influence on people's religious thought–I should of course say, a pernicious influence. Some naive Christians would explicitly assert the doctrine; and moreover, I think McTaggart was right in believing that in popular religious thought a covert appeal to the doctrine is sometimes made even by people who would deny it if it were explicitly stated to them and its manifest consequences pointed out.

McTaggart may well have come into contact with naive Protestant defenders of absolute omnipotence when he was defending his atheist faith at his public school. The opinion is certainly not dead, as I can testify from personal experience. For many years I used to teach the philosophy of Descartes in a special course for undergraduates reading French; year by year, there were always two or three of them who embraced Descartes' defense of absolute omnipotence *con amore* and protested indignantly when I described the doctrine as incoherent. It would of course have been no good to say I was following Doctors of the Church in rejecting the doctrine; I did in the end find a way of producing silence, though not, I fear, conviction, and going on to other topics of discussion; I cited the passages of the Epistle to the Hebrews which say explicitly that God cannot swear by anything greater than himself (vi.13) or break his word (vi.18). Fortunately none of them ever thought of resorting to the ultimate weapon which, as I believe George Mavrodes remarked, is available to the defender of absolute omnipotence; namely, he can always say: "Well, you've stated a difficulty, but of course being omnipotent God can overcome that difficulty, though I don't see how." But what I may call, borrowing from C. S. Lewis's story, victory by the Deplorable Word is a barren one; as barren as a victory by an incessant demand that your adversary should prove his premises or define his terms.

Let us leave these naive defenders in their entrenched position and return for a moment to Descartes. Descartes held that the truths of logic and arithmetic are freely made to be true by God's will. To be sure we clearly and distinctly see that these truths are necessary; they are necessary in our world, and in giving us our mental endowments God gave us the right sort of clear and distinct ideas to see the necessity. But though they are necessary, they are not necessarily necessary; God could have freely chosen to make a different sort of world, in which other things would have been necessary truths. The possibility of such another world is something we cannot comprehend, but only dimly apprehend; Descartes uses the simile that we may girdle a tree-trunk with our arms but not a mountain—but we can touch the mountain. Proper understanding of the possibility would be possessed by God, or, no doubt, by creatures in the alternative world, who would be endowed by God with clear and distinct ideas corresponding to the necessities of their world.

In recent years, unsound philosophies have been defended by what I may call shyster logicians: some of the more dubious recent developments of modal logic could certainly be used to defend Descartes. A system in which "possibly p" were a theorem—in which everything is possible—has indeed never been taken seriously; but modal logicians have taken seriously systems in which "possibly possibly p," or again "it is not necessary that necessarily p," would be a theorem for arbitrary interpretation of "p." What is more, some modern modal logicians notoriously take possible worlds very seriously indeed; some of them even go to the length of saying that what you and I vulgarly call the actual world is simply the world we happen to live in. People who take both things seriously—the axiom "possibly possibly p" and the ontology of possible worlds—would say: You mention any impossibility, and there's a possible world in which that isn't impossible but possible. And this is even further away out than Descartes would wish to go; for he would certainly not wish to say that "It is possible that God should not exist" is even *possibly* true. So *a fortiori* a shyster logician could fadge up a case for Descartes. But to my mind all that this shows is that modal logic is currently a rather disreputable discipline: not that I think modal notions are inadmissible—on the contrary, I think they are indispensable—but that current professional standards in the discipline are low, and technical ingenuity is mistaken for rigour. On that showing, astrology would be rigorous.

Descartes' motive for believing in absolute omnipotence was not contemptible: it seemed to him that otherwise God would be *subject to* the inexorable laws of logic as Jove was to the decrees of the Fates. The nature of logical truth is a very difficult problem, which I cannot discuss here. The easy conventionalist line, that it is our arbitrary way of using words that makes logical truth, seems to me untenable, for reasons that Quine among others has clearly spelled out. If I could follow Quine further in regarding logical laws as natural laws of very great generality—revisable in principle, though most unlikely to be revised, in a major theoretical reconstruction—then perhaps after all some rehabilitation of Descartes on this topic might be possible. But in the end I have to say that as we cannot say how a non-logical world would look, we cannot say how a supra-logical God would act or how he could communicate anything to us by way of revelation. So I end as I began: a Christian need not and cannot believe in absolute omnipotence.

It is important that Christians should clearly realize this, because otherwise a half-belief in absolute omnipotence may work in their minds subterraneously. As I said, I think McTaggart was absolutely right in drawing attention to this danger. One and the same man may deny the doctrine of absolute omnipotence when the doctrine is clearly put to him, and yet reassure himself that God can certainly do so-and-so by using merely the premise of God's omnipotence. And McTaggart is saying this is indefensible. At the very least this "so-and-so" must represent a logically consistent description of a feat; and proofs of logical consistency are notoriously not always easy. Nor, as we shall see, are our troubles at an end if we assume that God can do anything whose description is logically consistent.

Logical consistency in the description of the feat is certainly a necessary condition for the truth of "God can do so-and-so": if "so-and-so" represents an inconsistent description of a feat, then "God can do so-and-so" is certainly a false and impossible proposition, since it entails "It could be the case that so-and-so came about"; so, by contraposition, if "God can do so-and-so" is to be true, or even logically possible, then "so-and-so" must represent a logically consistent description of a feat. And whereas only a minority of Christians have explicitly believed in absolute omnipotence, many have believed that a proposition of the form "God can do so-and-so" is true whenever "so-and-so" represents a description of a logically possible feat. This is our second doctrine of omnipotence. One classic statement of this comes in the *Summa Theologica* 1a q. xxv art. 3. Aquinas rightly says that we cannot explain "God can do everything" in terms of what is within the power of some agent; for "God can do everything any created agent can do," though true, is not a comprehensive enough account of God's power, which exceeds that of any created agent; and "God can do everything God can do" runs uselessly in a circle. So he puts forward the view that if the description "so-and-so" is in itself possible through the relation of the terms involved—if it does not involve contradictories' being true together—then "God can do so-and-so" is true. Many Christian writers have followed Aquinas in saying this; but it is not a position consistently maintainable. As we shall see, Aquinas did not manage to stick to the position himself.

Before I raise the difficulties against this thesis, I wish to expose a common confusion that often leads people to accept it: the confusion between self-contradiction and gibberish. C. S. Lewis in *The Problem of Pain* says that meaningless combinations of words do not suddenly acquire meaning simply because we prefix to them the two other words "God can," and Antony Flew has quoted this with just approval. But if we take Lewis's words strictly, his point is utterly trivial, and nothing to our purpose. For gibberish, syntactically incoherent combination of words, is quite different from self-contradictory sentences or descriptions; the latter certainly have an intelligible place in our language.

It is a common move in logic to argue that a set of premises *A*, *B*, *C* together yield a contradiction, and that therefore *A* and *B* as premises yield as conclusion the contradictory of *C*; some logicians have puritanical objections to this manoeuvre, but I cannot stop to consider them; I am confident, too, that neither Aquinas nor Lewis would share these objections to *reductio ad absurdum*. If, however, a contradictory formula were gibberish, *reductio ad absurdum* certainly would be an illegitimate procedure—indeed it would be a nonsensical one. So we have to say that when "so-and-so" represents a self-contradictory description of a feat, "God can do so-and-so" is likewise self-contradictory, but that being self-contradictory it is not gibberish, but merely false.

I am afraid the view of omnipotence presently under consideration owes part of its attractiveness to the idea that then "God can do so-and-so" would never turn out false, so that there would be no genuine counterexamples to "God can do everything." Aquinas says, in the passage I just now cited: "What implies contradiction cannot be a word, for no understanding can conceive it." Aquinas, writing seven centuries ago, is excusable for not being clear about the difference between self-contradiction and gibberish; we are not excusable if we are not. It is not gibberish to say "a God can bring it about that in Alcala there lives a barber who shaves all those and only those living in Alcala who do not shave themselves"; this is a perfectly well-formed sentence, and not on the face of it self-contradictory; all the same, the supposed feat notoriously is self-contradictory, so this statement of what God can do is not nonsense but false.

One instance of a description of a feat that is really but not overtly self-contradictory has some slight importance in the history of conceptions of omnipotence. It appeared obvious to

Spinoza that *God can bring about everything that God can bring about*, and that to deny this would be flatly incompatible with God's omnipotence (Ethics 1.17, scholium). Well, the italicized sentence is syntactically ambiguous. "Everything that God can bring about God can bring about" is one possible reading of the sentence, and this is an obvious, indeed trivial predication about God, which must be true if there is a God at all. But the other way of taking the sentence relates to a supposed feat of *bringing about everything that God can bring about—all* of these bringable-about things together—and it says that God is capable of this feat. This is clearly the way Spinoza wishes us to take the sentence. But taken this way, it is not obvious at all; quite the contrary, it's obviously false. For among the things that are severally possible for God to bring about, there are going to be some pairs that are not *com*possible, pairs which it is logically impossible should both come about; and then it is beyond God's power to bring about such a pair together—let alone, to bring about all the things together which he can bring about severally.

This does not give us a description of a *logically possible* feat which God cannot accomplish. However, there is nothing easier than to mention feats which are logically possible but which God cannot do, if Christianity is true. Lying and promise-breaking are logically possible feats: but Christian faith, as I have said, collapses unless we are assured that God cannot lie and cannot break his promises.

This argument is an *ad hominem* argument addressed to Christians; but there are well-known logical arguments to show that on any view there must be some logically possible feats that are beyond God's power. One good example suffices: making a thing which its maker cannot afterwards destroy. This is certainly a possible feat, a feat that some human beings have performed. Can God perform the feat or not? If he cannot there is already some logically possible feat which God cannot perform. If God can perform the feat, then let us suppose that he does: *ponatur in esse*, as medieval logicians say. Then we are supposing God to have brought about a situation in which he *has* made something he cannot destroy; and in that situation destroying this thing is a *logically* possible feat that God cannot accomplish, for we surely cannot admit the idea of a creature whose destruction is logically *im*possible.

There have been various attempts to meet this argument. The most interesting one is that the proposition "God cannot make a thing that he cannot destroy" can be turned round to "Any thing that God can make he can destroy"—which does not even look like an objection to God's being able to do everything logically possible. But this reply involves the very same bracketing fallacy that I exposed a moment ago in Spinoza. There, you will remember, we had to distinguish two ways of taking "God can bring about everything that God can bring about":

A. Everything that God can bring about, God can bring about.
B. God can bring about the following feat: to bring about everything that God can bring about.

And we saw that A is trivially true, given that there *is* a God, and B certainly false. Here, similarly, we have to distinguish two senses of "God cannot make a thing that its maker cannot destroy":

A. Anything that its maker cannot destroy, God cannot make.
B. God cannot bring about the following feat: to make something that its maker cannot destroy.

And here A does contrapose, as the objectors would have it, to "Anything that God can make, its maker can destroy," which on the face of it says nothing against God's power to do anything logically possible. But just as in the Spinoza example, the B reading purports to describe a single feat, *bringing about everything that God can bring about* (this feat, I argued, is impossible for God, because logically impossible): so in our present case, the B reading purports to describe a single feat, making something that its maker cannot destroy. This, as I said, is a logically possible feat, a feat that men sometimes do perform; so we may press the question whether this is a feat God can accomplish or not; and either way there will be some logically possible feat God cannot accomplish. So this notion of omnipotence, like the Cartesian idea of absolute omnipotence, turns out to be obviously incompatible with Christian faith, and moreover logically untenable.

Let us see, then, if we fare any better with the third theory: the theory that the only condition for the truth of "God can do so-and-so" is that "God does so-and-so" or "God is doing so-and-so" must be logically possible. As I said, this imposes a more restrictive condition than the second theory: for there are many feats that we can consistently suppose to be performed but cannot consistently suppose to be performed by God. This theory might thus get us out of the logical trouble that arose with the second theory about the feat: *making a thing that its maker cannot destroy*. For though this is a logically possible feat, a feat some creatures do perform, it might well be argued that "God has made a thing that its maker cannot destroy" is a proposition with a buried inconsistency in it; and if so, then on the present account of omnipotence we need not say "God can make a thing that its maker cannot destroy."

This suggestion also, however, can easily be refuted by an example of great philosophical importance that I borrow from Aquinas. "It comes about that Miss X never loses her virginity" is plainly a logically possible proposition: and so also is "God brings it about that Miss X never loses her virginity." All the same, if it so happens that Miss X already has lost her virginity, "God can bring it about that Miss X never loses her virginity" is false (1a q. xxv art. 4 ad 3 um). Before Miss X had lost her virginity, it would have been true to say this very thing; so what we can truly say about what God can do will be different at different times. This appears to imply a change in God, but Aquinas would certainly say, and I think rightly, that it doesn't really do so. It is just like the case of Socrates coming to be shorter than Theaetetus because Theaetetus grows up; here, the change is on the side of Theaetetus not of Socrates. So in our case, the change is really in Miss X not in God; something about her passes from the realm of possibility to the realm of *fait accompli*, and thus no longer comes under the concept of the accomplishable— *deficit a ratione possibilium* (Aquinas, loc. cit., ad 2 um). I think Aquinas's position here is strongly defensible; but if he does defend it, he has abandoned the position that God can do everything that it is not a priori impossible *for God to do*, let alone the position that God can bring about everything describable in a logically consistent way.

Is it a priori impossible for God to do something wicked? And if not, *could* God do something wicked? There have been expressed serious doubts about this: I came across them in that favorite of modern moral philosophers, Richard Price. We must distinguish, he argues, between God's natural and his moral attributes: if God is a free moral being, even as we are, it must not be absolutely impossible for God to do something wicked. There must be just a chance that God should do something wicked: no doubt it will be a really infinitesimal chance—after all, God has persevered in ways of virtue on a vast scale for inconceivably long—but the chance must be there, or God isn't free and isn't therefore laudable for his goodness. The way this reverend gentleman commends his Maker's morals is so startling that you may suspect me of misrepresentation; I can only ask any skeptic to check in Daiches Raphael's edition of Price's work! Further comment on my part is I hope needless.

A much more restrained version of the same sort of thing is to be found in the Scholastic distinction between God's *potentia absoluta* and *potentia ordinata*. The former is God's power considered in abstraction from his wisdom and goodness, the latter is God's power considered as controlled in its exercise by his wisdom and goodness. Well, as regards a man it makes good sense to say: "He has the bodily and mental power to do so-and-so, but he certainly will not, it would be pointlessly silly and wicked." But does anything remotely like this make sense to say about Almighty God? If not, the Scholastic distinction I have cited is wholly frivolous.

Let us then consider our fourth try. Could it be said that the "everything" in "God can do everything" refers precisely to things that are not in the realm of *fait accompli* but of futurity? This will not do either. If God can promulgate promises to men, then as regards any promises that are not yet fulfilled we know that they certainly will be fulfilled: and in that case God clearly has not a *potentia ad utrumque*—a two-way power of either actualizing the event that will fulfill the promise or not actualizing it. God can then only do what will fulfill his promise. And if we try to evade this by denying that God can make promises known to men, then we have once more denied something essential to Christian faith, and we are still left with something that God cannot do.

I must here remove the appearance of a fallacy. God cannot but fulfill his promises, I argued; so he has not a two-way power, *potentia ad utrumque*, as regards these particular future events. This argument may have seemed to involve the fallacy made notorious in medieval logical treatises, of confusing the necessity by which something follows—*necessitas consequentiae*—with the necessity of that very thing which follows—*necessitas conseguentis*. If it is impossible for God to promise and not perform, then if we know God has promised something we may infer with certainty that he will perform it. Surely, it may be urged, this is enough for Christian faith and hope; we need not go on to say that God *cannot not* bring about the future event in question. If we do that, are we not precisely committing the hoary modal fallacy I have just described?

I answer that there are various senses of "necessary." The future occurrence of such-and-such, when God has promised that such-and-such shall be, is of course not logically necessary; but it may be necessary in the sense of being, as Arthur Prior puts it, now unpreventable. If God has promised that Israel shall be saved, then there is nothing that anybody, even God, can do about that; this past state of affairs is now unpreventable. But it is also necessary in the same way that if God has promised then he will perform; God cannot do anything about that either—cannot make himself liable to break his word. So we have as premises "Necessarily p" and "Necessarily if p then q," in the same sense of "necessarily"; and from these premises it not merely necessarily follows that q—the conclusion in the necessitated form, "Necessarily q" with the same sense of "necessarily," follows from the premises. So if God has promised that Israel shall be saved, the future salvation of Israel is not only certain but inevitable; God must save Israel, because he cannot not save Israel without breaking his word given in the past and he can neither alter the past nor break his word.

Again, in regard to this and other arguments, some people may have felt discomfort at my not drawing in relation to God the sort of distinction between various applications of "can" that are made in human affairs: the "can" of knowing how to, the "can" of physical power to, the "can" of opportunity, the "can" of what fits in with one's plans. But of course the way we make these distinct applications of "he can" to a human agent will not be open if we are talking about God. There is no question of God's knowing how but lacking the strength, or being physically able to but not knowing how; moreover (to make a distinction that comes in a logical example of Aristotle's) though there is a right time when God may bring something about, it is inept to speak of his then having the opportunity to do it. (To develop this distinction: if "x" stands for a finite agent and "so-and-so" for an act directly in x's power, there is little difference between "At time *t* it is suitable for x to bring so-and-so about" and "It is suitable for *x* to bring so-and-so about at time *t*"; but if "*x*" means God, the temporal qualification "at time *r* can attach only to what is brought about; God does not live through successive times and find one more suitable than another.)

These distinct applications of "can" are distinct only for finite and changeable agents, not for a God whose action is universal and whose mind and character and design are unchangeable. There is thus no ground for fear that in talking about God we may illicitly slip from one sort of "can" to another. What we say God can do is always in respect of his changeless supreme power.

All the same, we have to assert different propositions at different times in order to say truly what God can do. What is past, as I said, ceases to be alterable even by God; and thus the truth-value of a proposition like "God can bring it about that Miss *X* never loses her virginity" alters once she has lost it. Similarly, God's promise makes a difference to what we can thereafter truly say God can do; it is less obvious in this case that the real change involved is a change in creatures, not in God, than it was as regards Miss *X*'s virginity, but a little thought should show that the promulgation or making known of God's intention, which is involved in a promise, is precisely a change in the creatures to whom the promise is made.

Thus all the four theories of omnipotence that I have considered break down. Only the first overtly flouts logic; but the other three all involve logical contradictions, or so it seems; and moreover, all these theories have consequences fatal to the truth of Christian faith. The last point really ought not to surprise us; for the absolute confidence a Christian must have in God's revelation and promises involves, as I said at the outset, both a belief that God is almighty, in the sense I explained, and a belief that there are certain describable things that God cannot do and therefore will not do.

If I were to end the discussion at this point, I should leave an impression of Aquinas's thought that would be seriously unfair to him; for although in the passage I cited Aquinas appears verbally committed to our second theory of omnipotence, it seems clear that this does not adequately represent his mind. Indeed, it was from Aquinas himself and from the *Summa Theologica* that I borrowed an example which refutes even the weaker third theory, let alone the second one. Moreover, in the other *Summa* (Book II, c. xxv) there is an instructive list of things that *Deus omnipotens* is rightly said not to be able to do. But the mere occurrence of this list makes me doubt whether Aquinas can be said to believe, in any reasonable interpretation, the thesis that God can do everything. That God is almighty in my sense Aquinas obviously did believe; I am suggesting that here his "omnipotens" means "almighty" rather than "omnipotent." Aquinas does not say or even imply that he has given an *exhaustive* list of kinds of case in which "God can do so-and-so" or "God can make so-and-so" turns out false; so what he says here does not commit him to "God can do everything" even in the highly unnatural sense "God can do everything that is not excluded under one or other of the following heads."

I shall not explore Aquinas's list item by item, because I have made open or tacit use of his considerations at several points in the foregoing and do not wish to repeat myself. But one batch of items raises a specially serious problem. My attention was drawn to the problem by a contribution that the late Mr. Michael Foster made orally during a discussion at the Socratic Club in Oxford. Aquinas tells us that if "doing so-and-so" implies what he calls passive potentiality, then "God can do so-and-so" is false. On this ground he excluded all of the following:

- God can be a body or something of the sort.
- God can be tired or oblivious.
- God can be angry or sorrowful.

- God can suffer violence or be overcome.
- God can undergo corruption.

Foster pointed out that as a Christian Aquinas was committed to asserting the contradictory of all these theses. *Contra factum non valet ratio*; it's no good arguing that God cannot do what God has done, and in the Incarnation God did do all these things Aquinas said God cannot do. The Word that was God was made flesh (and the literal meaning of the Polish for this is: The Word became a body!); God the Son was tired and did sink into the oblivion of sleep; he was angry and sorrowful; he was bound like a thief, beaten, and crucified; and though we believe his Body did not decay, it suffered corruption in the sense of becoming a corpse instead of a living body—Christ in the Apocalypse uses of himself the startling words "I became a corpse," "*egenomen nekros*," and the Church has always held that the dead Body of Christ during the *triduum mortis* was adorable with Divine worship for its union to the Divine Nature.

Foster's objection to Aquinas is the opposite kind of objection to the ones I have been raising against the various theories of omnipotence I have discussed. I have been saying that these theories say by implication that God can do certain things which Christian belief requires one to say God *cannot* do; Foster is objecting that Aquinas's account says God *cannot* do some things which according to Christian faith God *can* do and has in fact done.

It would take me too far to consider how Aquinas might have answered this objection. It would not of course be outside his intellectual milieu; it is the very sort of objection that a Jew or Moor might have used, accepting Aquinas's account of what God cannot do, in order to argue against the Incarnation. I shall simply mention one feature that Aquinas's reply would have had: it would have to make essential use of the particle "as," or in Latin "*secundum quod*." God did become man, so God can become man and have a human body; but God as God cannot be man or have a body.

The logic of these propositions with "as" in them, reduplicative propositions as they are traditionally called, is a still unsolved problem, although as a matter of history it was a problem raised by Aristotle in the *Prior Analytics*. We must not forget that such propositions occur frequently in ordinary discourse; we use them there with an ill-founded confidence that we know our way around. Jones, we say, is Director of the Gnome Works and Mayor of Middletown; he gets a salary as Director and an expense allowance as Mayor; he signs one letter as Director, another as Mayor. We say all this, but how far do we understand the logical relations of what we say? Very little, I fear. One might have expected some light and leading from medieval logicians; the theological importance of reduplicative propositions did in fact lead to their figuring as a topic in medieval logical treatises. But I have not found much that is helpful in such treatments as I have read.

I hope to return to this topic later. Meanwhile, even though it has nothing directly to do with almightiness or omnipotence, I shall mention one important logical point that is already to be found in Aristotle. A superficial grammatical illusion may make us think that "A as P is Q" attaches the predicate "Q" to a complex subject "A as P." But Aristotle insists, to my mind rightly, on the analysis: "A" subject, "is as P, Q" predicate—so that we have not a complex subject-term, but a complex predicate-term; clearly, this predicate entails the simple conjunctive predicate "is both P and Q" but not conversely. This niggling point of logic has in fact some theological importance. When theologians are talking about Christ as God and Christ as Man, they may take the two phrases to be two logical subjects of predication, if they have failed to see the Aristotelian point; and then they are likely to think or half think that Christ as God is one entity or *Gegenstand* and Christ as Man is another. I am sure some theologians have yielded to this temptation, which puts them on a straight road to the Nestorian heresy.

What Aquinas would have done, I repeat, to meet Foster's objection in the mouth of a Jew or Moor is to distinguish between what we say God can do, *simpliciter*, and what we say God as God can do, using the reduplicative form of proposition. Now if we do make such a distinction, we are faced with considerable logical complications, particularly if we accept the Aristotelian point about the reduplicative construction. Let us go back to our friend Jones: there is a logical difference between:

1. Jones as Mayor can attend this committee meeting.
2. Jones can as Mayor attend this committee meeting.

as we may see if we spell the two out a little:

1. Jones as Mayor has the opportunity of attending the committee meeting.
2. Jones has the opportunity of (attending this committee meeting as Mayor).

We can easily see now that 1 and 2 are logically distinct: for one thing, if Jones is not yet Mayor but has an opportunity of becoming Mayor and *then* attending the committee meeting, 2 would be true and 1 false. And if we want to talk about what Jones as Mayor *cannot* do, the complexities pile up; for then we have to consider how the negation can be inserted at one or other position in a proposition of one of these forms, and how all the results are logically related.

All this is logical work to be done if we are to be clear about the implications of saying that God can or cannot do so-and-so, or again that God *as God* can or cannot do so-and-so. It is obvious, without my developing the matter further, that the logic of all this will not be simple. It's a far cry from the simple method of bringing our question "Can God do so-and-so?" under a reassuring principle "God can do *everything*." But I hope I have made it clear that any reassurance we get that way is entirely spurious.

Questions

1. What is the difference, for Peter Geach, between "omnipotence" and "almightiness?"
2. Geach discusses four views of omnipotence. What are they?
3. How does Rene Descartes' view of the truths of logic and arithmetic figure in the discussion?
4. According to Richard Price, why is God praiseworthy for his acts of goodness?
5. What are the senses of "necessary" Geach discusses?

MIDDLE KNOWLEDGE*

William Hasker

This selection is an adaptation, with minor changes, of chapter 2 of God, Time, and Knowledge, *where he considers the doctrine of middle knowledge as it emerged in the sixteenth-century controversy and mentions some of the arguments pro and con that were put forward. Then he considers the doctrine as it has been reinvented by Plantinga. Finally, he considers objections to the theory, one of which he thinks is decisive.*

I. Introduction

The theory of divine middle knowledge offers a particular way of understanding the traditional view that God has complete foreknowledge of everything that will ever happen. Middle knowledge assumes, first of all, that human beings possess free will in the libertarian sense—that they are capable, on occasion, of performing actions that are not predetermined by anything whatever, either by natural causes or by the will and decrees of God. But it goes on to ascribe to God a very special kind of knowledge concerning these free actions. It holds that God knows in advance all of the free choices and free actions that will ever be performed by his creatures. But beyond that, it holds that God knows what choices *would* have been made by any of these creatures, in any situation of libertarian free choice that they *might* have found themselves in, even if the situations in question never arose and the choices were never made. Indeed, it holds that God has this knowledge, not only concerning his *actual* free creatures, but concerning all the *possible* free creatures which he might have created but in fact has not created.

The theory of middle knowledge seems to offer some important advantages for theology, but it also raises major difficulties which have made it a center of controversy. It is the purpose of this selection to explore these issues. In the first section, we take an overview of the "classical theory" of middle knowledge, as it was first introduced by the Jesuit theologian Luis de Molina in the sixteenth century. Then, we turn to the version of the theory that has become prominent—originally through the influence of Alvin Plantinga—in recent analytical philosophy of religion. The third section explores certain objections which cast doubt on the viability of the theory, and the final section develops a particular argument which, if successful, shows conclusively that the theory of middle knowledge cannot be true.

The selection is an adaptation, with very minor changes, of chapter 2 of my book, *God, Time, and Knowledge* (Ithaca: Cornell University Press, 1989). There are references in the notes to some of the other chapters of the book, but the material presented here is self-contained on all of the main points. The text contains numerous references to previous discussions, but the reader might also wish to consult some more recent writings on the topic. Thomas Flint, "Hasker's *God, Time, and Knowledge*" *(Philosophical Studies* 60 (1990): 103-15), provides a general critique of the approach taken in this selection, especially the argument in section 4. My "Response to Thomas Flint" *(Philosophical Studies* 60 (1990): 117-26), replies to Flint's concerns. Robert M.

---

* This article reprinted by courtesy of the author and publisher. It appears in *God, Time and Knowledge*, Chapter 2, Cornell University Press, 1989.

Adams' "An Anti-Molinist Argument" (*Philosophical Perspectives* 5 (1991): 343-53) develops an argument parallel to the one given in section 4, arriving at the same conclusion by a somewhat different route. Rod Bertolet's "Hasker on Middle Knowledge" (*Faith and Philosophy* 10 (1993): 3-17) discusses the objections to middle knowledge given in section 3. My own most recent contribution is "Middle Knowledge: A Refutation Revisited," in *Faith and Philosophy*.

II. Middle Knowledge

The theory of divine middle knowledge depends on the truth of theological compatibilism, the view that comprehensive divine foreknowledge and human free will are logically consistent with each other. But it also serves to strengthen theological compatibilism in at least two ways. For one thing, it offers an account of *how* God is able to know future free actions, and the account of this given by middle knowledge is free of some of the difficulties—for instance, retroactive causation—that plague other accounts of the matter. More important, middle knowledge provides the key to a uniquely powerful conception of the operation of divine providence, almost certainly the strongest view of providence that is possible short of complete theological determinism. In contrast with this, it can be argued that foreknowledge *without* middle knowledge—"simple foreknowledge"—does *not* offer the benefits for the doctrine of providence that its adherents have sought to derive from it. In view of this, it could be argued that a good many theists who are not explicit adherents of middle knowledge nevertheless hold to a conception of divine providence that implicitly commits them to this theory.[1] And if this is so, a refutation of middle knowledge substantially weakens the doctrine of foreknowledge by removing one of its principal motivations.

Our procedure in this chapter will be as follows: First, we shall consider the doctrine as it emerged in the sixteenth-century controversy and mention briefly some of the arguments pro and con that were put forward at that time. Then, we shall turn to the modern form of the doctrine as it has been revived—or rather, reinvented[2]—by Alvin Plantinga. Finally, a series of objections to this theory will be considered, leading up to one that I consider decisive.

A. The Classical Theory

The theory of middle knowledge holds that, for each possible free creature that might exist, and for each possible situation in which such a creature might make a free choice, there is a truth, known to God prior to and independent of any decision on God's part, concerning what definite choice that creature would freely make if placed in that situation. In effect, middle knowledge extends the doctrine of divine foreknowledge to include knowledge of the outcome of choices that *might have been* made but in fact were not.

On casual consideration, middle knowledge may appear to be simply an obvious implication of divine omniscience: If God knows everything, how could he fail to know *this*? And by the same token, it may seem relatively innocuous. Both impressions, however, are mistaken. Middle knowledge is not a straightforward implication of omniscience, because it is

---

[1] This point, and also the uselessness of simple foreknowledge for the doctrine of providence, are argued in David Basinger, "Middle Knowledge and Classical Christian Thought," *Religious Studies* 22 (1986): 407-22. And see ch. 3 below.

[2] Plantinga developed his view independently; it was Anthony Kenny who pointed out to him the similarity between this view and the classical theory of middle knowledge. See Plantinga, "Self-Profile," in James E. Tomberlin and Peter van Inwagen, eds., *Alvin Plantinga, Profiles* vol. 5 (Dordrecht: D. Riedel, 1985), p. 50.

not evident that the truths postulated by this theory exist to be known. In ordinary foreknowledge, it may be argued, what God knows is the agent's *actual decision* to do one thing or another. But with regard to a situation that never in fact arises, no decision is ever made, and none exists for God to know. And if the decision in question is supposed to be a *free* decision, then all of the circumstances of the case (including the agent's character and prior inclinations) are consistent with any of the possible choices that might be made. Lacking the agent's *actual* making of the choice, then, there is nothing that disambiguates the situation and makes it true that some one of the options is the one that *would be* selected. This line of argument indicates the single most important objection that the proponent of middle knowledge must seek to answer.

But the very same feature that makes middle knowledge problematic (viz., that God can know the outcome of choices that are never actually made) also makes it extraordinarily useful for theological purposes. Consider the following counterfactual: "If *A* were in circumstances *C*, she would do *X*." According to middle knowledge, God knows the truth of this *whether or not A* ever actually *is* placed in circumstances *C*; indeed, God knows this whether or not *A* even exists, so that his knowledge about this is entirely independent of any of *God's own decisions* about creation and providence. But this, of course, makes such knowledge ideal for God to use in *deciding* whether or not to create *A*, and, if he does create her, whether or not to place her in circumstances *C*. As Molina says:

> God in his eternity knew by natural knowledge all the things that he could do: that he could create this world and infinitely many other worlds...[and] given his complete comprehension and penetrating insight concerning all things and causes, he saw what would be the case if he chose to produce this order or a different order; how each person, left to his own free will, would make use of his liberty with such and such an amount of divine assistance, given such and such opportunities, temptations and other circumstances, and what he would freely do, retaining all the time the ability to do the opposite in the same opportunities temptations and other circumstances.[3]

Another way to look at the matter is this: It is evident that, if God had created a thoroughly deterministic world, his creative plan would have involved no risks whatsoever; all of the causal antecedents of such a world would be set up to produce exactly the results God intended. But it seems extremely plausible that in a world involving libertarian free choice, some risks are inevitable: God in creating such a world makes it possible for us to freely bring about great good, but also great evil—and which we in fact choose is up to us, not to God. Thus, the frequently heard statement that God "limits his power" by choosing to create free creatures. But according to the theory of middle knowledge, this is not quite correct. To be sure, it is still the creatures, not God, who determine their own free responses to various situations. But God, in choosing to create them and place them in those situations, knew exactly what their responses would be; he views the future, not as a risk taker seeking to optimize probable outcomes, but as a planner who knowingly accepts and incorporates into his plan exactly those outcomes that in fact *occur*—though, to be sure, some of them may not be the outcomes he would most prefer. The element of risk is entirely eliminated.

As we have already seen, the chief difficulty that the proponent of middle knowledge must confront is the contention that the truths God is alleged to know, commonly called "counterfactuals of freedom," do not exist to be known. Most of the arguments for counterfactuals of freedom seem to depend on general considerations of philosophical plausibility, but in the medieval controversy there were also arguments based on Scripture. A favorite text for this purpose is found in I Samuel 23, which recounts an incident in the troubled

---

[3] Molina, "De Scientia Dei," quoted by Anthony Kenny, *The God of the Philosophers* (Oxford: Oxford University Press, 1979), pp. 62-63.

relationship of David with King Saul.[4] David, currently in occupation of the city of Keilah, consults Yahweh by means of the ephod about the rumors that Saul intends to attack the city:

> "Will Saul come down, as thy servant has heard? O LORD, the God of Israel, I beseech thee, tell thy servant. "And the LORD said, "He will come down." Then said David, "Will the men of Keilah surrender me and my men into the hand of Saul?" And the LORD said, "They will surrender you." (I Samuel 23:11-12, RSV)

The advocates of middle knowledge took this passage as evidence that God knew the following two propositions to be true:

(1) If David stayed in Keilah, Saul would besiege the city.
(2) If David stayed in Keilah and Saul besieged the city, the men of Keilah would surrender David to Saul.

But (given the assumption that Saul and the men of Keilah would act freely in performing the specified actions), these two propositions are counterfactuals of freedom, and the incident as a whole is a dramatic demonstration of the existence and practical efficacy of middle knowledge.

But this argument is hardly compelling. As Anthony Kenny points out, the ephod seems to have been a yes-no device hardly possessing the subtlety required to distinguish between various possible conditionals that might have been asserted in answer to David's questions. Kenny, indeed, suggests that we may understand material conditionals here,[5] but that seems hardly likely, since on that construal both conditionals would be true simply in virtue of the fact that their antecedents are false. Much more plausible candidates are given by Robert Adams:

(3) If David stayed in Keilah, Saul would *probably* besiege the city.
(4) If David stayed in Keilah and Saul besieged the city, the men of Keilah would *probably* surrender David to Saul.

As Adams points out, "(3) and (4) are enough for David to act on, if he is prudent, but they will not satisfy the partisans of middle knowledge."[6] The prospects for a scriptural proof of middle knowledge, therefore, do not seem promising.

But of course, the argument just given shows only that the responses to David's questions *need not* be taken as asserting counterfactuals of freedom, not that they *cannot* be so understood. And there are not lacking situations in everyday life in which it seems plausible that we are taking counterfactuals of freedom to be true. Plantinga, for example, says he believes that "If Bob Adams were to offer to take me climbing at Tahquitz Rock the next time I come to California, I would gladly (and freely) accept."[7] And Adams notes that "there does not normally seem to be any uncertainty at all about what a butcher, for example, would have done if I had asked him to sell me a pound of ground beef, although we suppose he would have had free will in the matter."[8]

So the discussion of examples seems to end in a stand-off. Still, the proponent of middle knowledge needs to address the question mentioned earlier: How is it possible for counterfactuals of freedom to be *true*? What is the truth maker for these propositions? At this

---

[4] For my discussion of this passage I rely chiefly on R. M. Adams, "Middle Knowledge and the Problem of Evil," *American Philosophical Quarterly* 14 (1977): 109-117. See also Kenny, *The God of the Philosophers*, pp. 63-64.
[5] Kenny, *The God of the Philosophers*, p. 64.
[6] Adams, *"Middle Knowledge,"* p. 111.
[7] "Reply to Robert M. Adams," in Tomberlin and van Inwagen, eds., *Alvin Plantinga*, p. 373.
[8] Adams, "Middle Knowledge," p. 115.

point the advocate of middle knowledge is presented with an attractive opportunity, but one that it is imperative for her to resist. The opportunity is simply to claim that counterfactuals of freedom are true in virtue of the *character and psychological tendencies* of the agents named in them. The attractiveness of this is evident in that in nearly all of the cases where we are disposed to accept such counterfactuals as true, the epistemic grounds for our acceptance would be found precisely in our knowledge of such psychological facts—Saul besieging Keilah, Adams's compliant butcher, and Plantinga climbing Tahquitz Rock are all cases in point. But the weakness of the suggestion becomes apparent when the following question is asked: Are the psychological facts about the agent, together with a description of the situation, plus relevant psychological laws, supposed to *entail* that the agent would respond as indicated? If the answer is yes, then the counterfactual may be *true* but it is not a counterfactual of *freedom;* the agent is not then free in the relevant (libertarian) sense.[9] If on the other hand the answer is no, then how can those psychological facts provide good grounds for the assertion that the agent *definitely would* (as opposed, say, to *very probably would*) respond in that way?

Probably the best line for the proponent of middle knowledge to take here is the one suggested by Suarez: When a counterfactual of freedom is true, it is simply an ultimate fact about the free agent in question that, if placed in the indicated circumstances, she would act as the counterfactual states; this fact requires no analysis or metaphysical grounding in terms of further, noncounterfactual states of affairs. (Or, if the agent in question does not actually exist, it is a fact about a particular *essence* that, if it were instantiated and its instantiation were placed in such circumstances, the instantiation would act as stated.) Adams, commenting on this, says, "I do not think I have any conception . . . of the sort of . . . property that Suarez ascribes to possible agents with respect to their acts under possible conditions. Nor do I think that I have any other primitive understanding of what it would be for the relevant subjunctive conditionals to be true." Nevertheless, he admits that Suarez's view on this is of the "least clearly unsatisfactory type," because "It is very difficult to refute someone who claims to have a primitive understanding which I seem not to have."[10]

B. The Modern Theory

The modern theory of middle knowledge[11] differs from the classical version in virtue of the application to the counterfactuals of freedom of the powerful possible-worlds semantics for counterfactuals developed by Robert Stalnaker, David Lewis, and John L. Pollock.[12] The central

---

[9] There are complexities in our use of such expressions as "acting freely" that are not always sufficiently taken note of. For example, it may happen that an action is "psychologically inevitable" for a person, based on that person's character and dispositions, yet we say that the person acts "freely" *if the character and dispositions are thought to be the result of previous freely chosen actions of the person.* Thus, it is said of the redeemed in heaven both that they freely serve and worship God, and that they are not able to sin; this happy inability is the result of their own free choices and is not typically seen as a diminution of freedom. But acts of this sort are *not* free in the very strict sense required by libertarianism. If we are exacting in our *definition* of "free" but lax in *applying* the term, trouble is inevitable.

[10] Adams, "*Middle Knowledge*," p. 112.

[11] The basic source for the modern theory of middle knowledge is Alvin Plantinga, *The Nature of Necessity* (Oxford: Oxford University Press, 1974), chap. 9.

[12] See Robert Stalnaker, "A Theory of Conditionals," in N. Rescher, ed., *Studies in Logical Theory* (Oxford: Blackwell, 1968); David Lewis, *Counterfactuals* (Cambridge: Harvard University Press, 1973); and John L. Pollock, *Subjunctive Reasoning* (Dordrecht: D. Riedel, 1976). It should be noted, however that some contemporary adherents of middle knowledge have reservations about this semantics. Alfred J. Freddoso, for example, writes: "I

idea of this semantics is that a counterfactual is true if some possible world in which the antecedent and the consequent are both true is more similar to the actual world than any in which the antecedent is true and the consequent false.[13] Thus (1) above is correctly analyzed as

(5) The actual world is more similar to some possible world in which David stays in Keilah and Saul besieges the city than to any possible world in which David stays in Keilah and Saul does not besiege the city.[14]

At this point it will be well to get a bit clearer about the exact positions both of the advocate and of the opponent of middle knowledge. First of all, it may be noted that the term "counterfactual," though customary and convenient, is not strictly accurate as a designation of the propositions in question. In some cases (namely, those whose antecedents God decides to actualize) both the antecedent and the consequent of the conditionals will be true, and so not counterfactual at all. A better term, therefore, would be, as Adams suggests, "deliberative conditionals." Having said that, however, we shall continue to refer to them as "counterfactuals of freedom."

But just what kind of conditionals are these? Both Lewis and Pollock distinguish "would" conditionals from "might" conditionals; the "might" conditional corresponding to (1) would be

(1m) If David stayed in Keilah, Saul *might* besiege the city.

But Pollock goes further and distinguishes three different kinds of "would" conditionals; these distinctions are not explicitly made by Lewis.[15] There are "simple subjunctives"; these are the conditionals most frequently, and most naturally, expressed by English sentences of the form "If it were the case that P, it would be the case that Q." Second, there are "even if" conditionals, of the form "Even if it were the case that P, it would (still) be the case that Q." These are the conditionals Nelson Goodman calls "semi-factuals"; they are asserted when their consequents are believed to be true, whereas their antecedents may or may not be true, and their force is to deny that the truth of the antecedent would bring about the falsity of the consequent. Finally, there are "necessitation conditionals"; according to Pollock, "the notion of necessitation that I am trying to analyze here is that of the truth of one statement 'bringing it about' that another statement is true,"[16] so an appropriate formula might be "Its being the case that P would bring it about that Q."

Now, into which of these categories do we place the counterfactuals of freedom? Evidently they cannot be "might" conditionals. "Even if" conditionals are true only in (some of) those possible worlds in which their consequents are true, but the truth of the counterfactuals of freedom must be known to God quite independently of whether or not their consequents are true

---

repudiate the claim that the standard semantics applies to [counterfactuals of freedom] or to any other 'simple' conditionals that involve causal indeterminism" (personal communication).

[13] Pollock argues that the relevant notion is not that of comparative similarity but rather that of a possible world "minimally changed" from the actual world so as to make the antecedent of the counterfactual true. (See *Subjunctive Reasoning*, pp. 17-23.) Pollock's argument seems to be correct, but the difference between the two formulations is not significant for present purposes, so we shall continue to employ the more familiar terminology.

[14] Adams, "*Middle Knowledge*," p. 112.

[15] See Pollock, *Subjunctive Reasoning*, chap. 2, "Four Kinds of Conditionals."

[16] Ibid., pp. 35-36. Pollock says, "Perhaps the term 'necessitation' is inappropriate for the notion I have in mind here, but I have been unable to find a better term" (p. 36). Pollock does not identify any single English locution that is customarily used in stating necessitation conditionals, though he thinks the force of such conditionals may be captured by the formula "If it were true that P, it would be true that Q *since* it was true that P" (p. 27).

in the actual world. Pollock shows that a simple subjunctive is equivalent to the disjunction of a necessitation conditional and an "even if" conditional. If, then, we were to equate counterfactuals of freedom with simple subjunctives, it would follow that in those cases where the necessitation conditional is false the counterfactual of freedom would be equivalent to an "even if" conditional, which we have seen to be impossible. So if the counterfactuals of freedom are to be found among the varieties discussed by Pollock, they must be necessitation conditionals. As he says, "All counterfactual conditionals express necessitation."[17]

Now that we have clarified the nature of the counterfactuals of freedom, how exactly shall we characterize the view taken of such counterfactuals by the opponents of middle knowledge? There seem to be three alternatives: One may deny that such propositions exist at all; one may concede their existence but deny that they possess truth-values; or one may hold that all such propositions are false. The denial that there are such propositions as counterfactuals of freedom does not seem to have much to recommend it; as Plantinga says, he may conceivably be *wrong* in believing that if Adams were to invite him to climb Tahquitz Rock he would accept, but it would be passing strange to deny that *there is* such a proposition as the one he claims to believe. I think, in fact, that this view may best be understood as arising from an exigency; if one thinks (as the second view holds) that there is no way to assign truth-values to counterfactuals of freedom, and if one is also convinced that every proposition must be either true or false, then one is virtually forced to deny that there are such propositions—that is, one is forced to deny that the relevant sentences express any propositions at all.

The second view, according to which counterfactuals of freedom lack truth-values, probably arises from the reflection that there is no way to assign the truth-values because (where the consequent expresses a free choice to be made in hypothetical circumstances) there is in principle no way of knowing whether the consequent would be true if the antecedent were true. This, however, overlooks the possibility that we might be able to know whether the counterfactual is true *without* knowing this.

But how is this possible? The general relationship between counterfactuals and libertarian free will is something that still needs to be worked out. (Indeed, it is really the central theme of the present discussion.) But an extremely plausible view to take is the following: A situation in which an agent makes a libertarian free choice with respect to doing or not doing something is a situation in which the agent *might* do that thing but also might refrain from doing it. Suppose that A, if she found herself in circumstances C, would freely decide whether or not to do X. Then both of the following counterfactuals will be true:

(6) If A were in C, she might do X.
(7) If A were in C, she might refrain from doing X.

But if this is so, then there is no true counterfactual of freedom with respect to A's doing X in C. For (6) is inconsistent with

(8) If A were in C, she would refrain from doing X.

Likewise, (7) is inconsistent with

(9) If A were in C, she would do X.

---

[17] Ibid., p. 34.

If propositions like (6) and (7) properly characterize a situation of libertarian free choice, then all counterfactuals of freedom are false. In the ensuing discussion, this is the position which we shall assume the opponent of middle knowledge to be asserting and defending.

C. Objections to Middle Knowledge

Now that the opposition between proponents and opponents of middle knowledge has been delineated, how can we make progress on resolving the issue? As noted, proponents seem willing to rest their case on general considerations of plausibility, perhaps buttressed by allusions to the alleged theological necessity of the doctrine. Opponents can do the same, of course, and many do, but if the discussion is to be advanced, more substantial arguments are needed. And, in fact, such arguments are available. In this section three brief arguments against the theory will be spelled out, and in the next a somewhat more detailed argument will be developed.

The first objection to be considered is one we have already alluded to: What, if anything, is the *ground* of the truth of the counterfactuals of freedom? It is important to see that the question here is metaphysical, not epistemological. The question is not, How can we *know* that a counterfactual of freedom is true? It may be that we cannot know this, except perhaps in a very few cases, and although it is claimed that *God* knows them, it is not clear that the friend of counterfactuals (or any other theist, for that matter) is required to explain *how* it is that God knows what he knows. The question, rather, is What *makes* the counterfactuals true—what is the *ground* of their truth? As Adams says, "I do not understand what it would be for [counterfactuals of freedom] to be true."[18]

In replying to this Plantinga finds this notion of a requirement that there be something that "grounds" the truth of a proposition to be obscure. But insofar as the requirement does hold, he thinks the counterfactuals of freedom are no worse off with respect to it than are other propositions whose credentials are unimpeachable.

> Suppose, then, that yesterday I freely performed some action A. What was or is it that grounded or founded my doing so? I wasn't *caused* to do by anything else; nothing relevant *entails* that I did so. So what grounds the truth of the proposition in question? Perhaps you will say that what grounds its truth is just that in fact I did A. But this isn't much of an answer; and at any rate the same kind of answer is available in the case of Curley. For what grounds the truth of the counterfactual, we may say, is just that in fact Curley is such that if he had been offered a $35,000 bribe, he would have freely taken it.[19]

This answer of Plantinga's appears to be an endorsement of the view already attributed to Suarez: When a counterfactual of freedom is true, it is simply an ultimate fact about the free agent in question that, if placed in the indicated circumstances, she would act as the counterfactual states; this fact requires no analysis or "grounding" in terms of further, noncounterfactual states of affairs.[20] It seems to me, however, that there is something seriously wrong about this answer. In order to bring this out, I want to try and formulate a certain intuition—an intuition that, I believe, underlies Adams's objection even though Adams does not explicitly formulate it. The intuition is this: In order for a (contingent) conditional state of affairs to obtain, its obtaining must be grounded in some categorical state of affairs. More colloquially, truths about "what *would be the case... if*" must be grounded in truths about what *is in fact* the

---

[18] Adams, *"Middle Knowledge,"* p. 110.
[19] Reply to Robert M. Adams," p. 374. Plantinga here alludes to an example found in *The Nature of Necessity*, pp. 173-74.
[20] That this is Plantinga's view is clearly implied by the argument given on pp. 177-79 of *The Nature of Necessity*.

case. This requirement seems clearly to be satisfied for the more familiar types of conditionals. The truth of a material conditional is grounded either in the truth of its consequent, or the falsity of its antecedent, or both.[21] More interestingly, the truth of causal conditionals, and of their associated counterfactuals, are grounded in the natures, causal powers, inherent tendencies, and the like, of the natural entities described in them.[22] The lack of anything like this as a basis for the counterfactuals of freedom seems to me to be a serious problem for the theory.[23]

Perhaps it is worthwhile to repeat here that the grounding *cannot* be found in the character, psychological tendencies, and the like of the agent. This point is, in effect, conceded by the defenders of middle knowledge; they recognize that such psychological facts are insufficient as a basis for the counterfactuals. And yet there is the following point: *In virtually every case where we seem to have plausible examples of true counterfactuals of freedom, the plausibility is grounded precisely in such psychological facts as these.* (Again we recall Saul besieging Keilah, Plantinga climbing Tahquitz Rock, and Adams's butcher selling him a pound of hamburger.) And this, I think, ought to make us very suspicious of those examples. If the basis for the plausibility of the examples is in all cases found in something that has no tendency to show that the examples are correct—no tendency, that is, to show that the propositions in question really *are* true counterfactuals of freedom[24]—then the examples lose all force as support for the theory. And without the examples, there is very little in sight that even looks like supporting evidence.[25]

The second difficulty to be considered—one, so far as I know, not noticed in the literature to date—concerns the *modal status of* counterfactuals of freedom. To do the job required of them, these counterfactuals must be logically contingent—but I shall argue that, based on the assumptions of the theory of counterfactual logic, certain crucial counterfactuals should be regarded rather as necessary truths, if indeed they are true at all.[26]

The examples of counterfactuals considered so far (e.g., "If David stayed in Keilah, Saul would besiege the city") are in a certain way notoriously incomplete. The antecedent specifies a

---

[21] Some would deny that these are genuinely *conditionals,* in the interesting sense of that term.

[22] I am assuming that whereas these natures, causal powers, etc., may, because of our limitations, have to be *described* in terms of conditional statements, the *truth* of these conditionals is itself grounded in occurrent states of affairs—for example, in the microstructures of physical materials. It is noteworthy that Humeans, who deny the existence of causal powers, natures, etc., have great difficulty in dealing with counterfactuals generally.

[23] Freddoso points out that middle knowledge "cuts against the spirit, if not the letter, of the standard possible worlds semantics for subjunctive conditionals. For it is usually assumed that the similarities among possible worlds invoked in such semantics are conceptually prior to the acquisition of truth-values by the subjunctive conditionals themselves.... On the Molinist view the dependence runs in just the opposite direction when the conditionals in question are conditional future contingents.... If the standard possible worlds semantics for subjunctive conditionals presupposes otherwise, then Molinists will have to modify it or propose an alternative capable of sustaining realism with respect to conditional future contingents" (Introduction to Luis de Molina, *On Divine Foreknowledge (Part IV of the Concordia),* trans. Alfred J. Freddoso [Ithaca, N.Y.: Cornell University Press, 1988, sec. 5.6).

[24] Note, however, that such psychological facts might very well provide grounding for conditionals such as (3) and (4), asserting that under given conditions the agents would *probably* act in a certain way.

[25] Plantinga says, "Surely there are many actions and many creatures such that God knows what he would have done if one of the latter had taken one of the former. There seem to be true counterfactuals of freedom about God; but what would ground the truth of such a counterfactual of freedom?" ("Reply to Robert M. Adams," p. 375). The answer to this, however, is obvious: The truth of such a counterfactual about God's action is grounded in God's *conditional intention* to act in a certain way. But humans, for the most part, have no such conditional intentions about choices they might be called upon to make—or, when they do have them, the intentions at best ground "*would probably*" counterfactuals.

[26] Jonathan Kvanvig actually holds that the counterfactuals of freedom are contained in the *essence* of the free creature, (see Jonathan L. Kvanvig, *The Possibility of an All-Knowing God* [New York: St. Martin's, 1986], pp. 124-25). But this is fatal to the theory: No individual chooses, or is responsible for, what is contained in that individual's essence.

single crucial fact but leaves unstated many other facts about the situation which would undoubtedly be relevant to Saul's decision—facts about Saul's character and state of mind, but also facts about the strength and readiness of Saul's own military forces, about other threats to the kingdom, and so on. Now, it cannot seriously be supposed that the counterfactuals God considers in deciding about his own activity in creation and providence are incomplete in this way. Surely, the antecedents of the conditionals *he* considers must include *everything* that might conceivably be relevant to Saul's deciding one way or the other. In order to have some grasp on this sort of counterfactual, I suggest that we think in terms of *initial-segment counterfactuals*, in which the antecedent specifies a *complete initial segment of a possible world*[27] up to a given point in time, and the consequent an event that may or not take place at that time. (Of course, the antecedent will include any relevant causal laws that have held up until that time in that possible world.) If now we symbolize such counterfactuals using a capital letter followed by an asterisk to stand for the antecedent, then the initial-segment counterfactual corresponding to (1) would be:

(10) $A^* \rightarrow$ Saul besieges Keilah,

where 'A^*' represents a proposition specifying the entire initial segment of the possible world envisaged by God as the one in which Saul makes his decision. The contrary counterfactual then would be

(11) $A^* \rightarrow$ Saul does not besiege Keilah.

If, as we have been assuming all along, (1) is true, then (10) also will be true, and (11) false. The interesting question, however, is whether (10) is a contingent or a *necessary* truth. Clearly, the theory of middle knowledge requires that it be contingent; if on the contrary it is necessary, then Saul's decision is *entailed* by a complete statement of antecedent conditions and his action is not free. (10), in fact, is to be evaluated in the same way as any other counterfactual proposition: To assert (10) is in effect to assert that some world in which "A^*" is true and Saul besieges Keilah is more similar to the actual world than any in which "A^*" is true and Saul does not do this. But, we may ask, if (10) is contingent, then under what possible circumstances would it be false? The answer is that (10) might be false if the actual world were different than it is; what is crucial is the similarity of envisaged possible worlds to the actual world, and so if the actual world were a different world (in ways we need not attempt to specify) than the one which is in fact actual, it might turn out that the world specified in (11) would be more similar to *that* world than is the world specified in (10), in which case (11) would be true and (10) false.

But this, I want to say, violates the fundamental idea that underlies the possible-worlds semantics for counterfactuals. For why exactly is it that counterfactuals are to be evaluated in terms of comparative similarity of possible worlds to the actual world? The answer to this is crucially related to the incompleteness, noted above, which attaches to the antecedents of the counterfactuals we use in everyday discourse. We simply do not have the resources to specify in the antecedents of our counterfactuals everything that might be relevant to the occurrence of the consequent, and even when we are clear in our own minds what the circumstances should be, we often do not take the trouble to state them. The notion of similarity to the actual world, then, removes what would otherwise be the ambiguity of our counterfactuals by specifying how the unstated conditions are to be understood: We are to think of the actual world as being modified

---

[27] In order fully to explicate the notion of an "initial segment" of a possible world, we need the distinction between hard facts and soft facts about the past; for this distinction see chapter 5.

as little as possible so as to accommodate the counterfactual antecedent. Thus, David Lewis states that the point of his "system of spheres representing comparative similarity of worlds" is "to rule out of consideration many of the various ways the antecedent could hold, especially the more bizarre ways."[28] He also says

> A counterfactual $\phi \not\square\!\!\!\rightarrow \psi$ is true at world i if and only if ψ holds at certain ϕ-worlds; but certainly not all ϕ-worlds matter. "*If kangaroos had no tails, they would topple over*" is true (or false, as the case may be) at our world, quite without regard to those possible worlds where kangaroos walk around on crutches, and stay upright that way. Those worlds are too far away from ours. What is meant by the counterfactual is that, things being pretty much as they are—the scarcity of crutches for kangaroos being pretty much as it actually is, the kangaroos' inability to use crutches being pretty much as it actually is, and so on—if kangaroos had no tails they would topple over.[29]

So the point of the notion of comparative similarity between possible worlds is to place limits on the worlds that are relevant for the evaluation of a given counterfactual. But of course, (10) is already maximally limited in this way; it already includes *everything* about the envisaged world up until the time when Saul makes his decision. With regard to initial-segment counterfactuals, then, comparative similarity has no work left to do. Ask yourself this question: In evaluating (10), *why* should it make a difference whether the actual world is as it is, or is a world different in various ways from this one? After all, if A^* *were* actual, then *neither* "our" actual world nor that other one would *be* actual—so why should the truth of (10) depend in any way on which of those worlds is actual as things now stand? This contrasts sharply with the situation as regards Lewis's kangaroos: If, for instance, we lived in a world in which a large and active Animal Friendship League was assiduously providing prosthetic devices for "handicapped" animals, then we would "fill in" these conditions as we evaluate his counterfactual and would very likely judge it to be false. But with initial-segment counterfactuals there is just no room for this to happen; there are no spaces left to *be* filled in.

The situation, then, is as follows: The theory of middle knowledge is obliged to hold that some initial-segment counterfactuals are logically contingent. But in order to do this, the theory must apply to these counterfactuals the notion of comparative similarity to the actual world, and I have argued that this notion has no legitimate application here—which is to say, the notion is misapplied. The correct conclusion to be drawn from counterfactual logic, then, is that if initial-segment counterfactuals are true at all, they are true in *all* worlds and thus are *necessarily* true. But this conclusion is fatal to middle knowledge.

There is another, closely related point, one that connects this second argument with the first one given. Plantinga admits that "We can't look to similarity, among possible worlds, as *explaining* counterfactuality, or as *founding* or *grounding* it. (Indeed, any founding or grounding in the neighborhood goes in the opposite direction.)"[30] This means that (in some cases at least) of two worlds W and W', one is more similar to the actual world *precisely because it shares counterfactuals* with the actual world—it is *not* the case that, because one of those worlds is more similar to the actual world *in other respects,* certain counterfactuals are true. But this, as I have argued above, violates the reason for introducing the comparative-similarity notion in the first place—that reason being, as explained by Lewis, to secure that counterfactuals are evaluated in worlds sufficiently similar to the actual world *in noncounterfactual respects*. How can

---

[28] Lewis, *Counterfactuals*, p. 66.
[29] Ibid., pp. 8-9.
[30] "Reply to Robert M. Adams," p. 378.

Plantinga justify relying on the principles of counterfactual logic when at the same time he undercuts the rationale for accepting those same principles?

The third (and final) objection of this group is one that was discovered independently by Robert Adams and Anthony Kenny.[31] This difficulty arises as we bring together the account given of the truth-conditions for counterfactuals and the use God is said to make of them. As Kenny says, "If it is to be possible for God to know which world he is actualizing, then his middle knowledge must be logically prior to his decision to actualize; whereas if middle knowledge is to have an object, the actualization must already have taken place."[32]

Let's spell this out a bit more. We will suppose, contrary to the argument in the preceding section, that some initial-segment counterfactuals (namely, those whose consequents involve freely chosen actions) are contingently true. Their truth, according to the theory, depends on the similarity of various possible worlds to the actual world, and thus it depends on which world *is* the actual world. But, which world is actual depends, in part at least, on God's decision about what to create: It is only by deciding to create that God settles which world is actual, and therefore which counterfactuals are true. So rather than the counterfactuals providing *guidance* for God's decision about what to create, the fact is that their truth is determined only as a consequence of that very decision!

Plantinga's answer to this is spelled out in his reply to Adams. In order for the truth of the counterfactuals to be "available" to God as he makes his creative decisions, it need not be already settled *in every respect* which world is the actual world. What needs to be settled, in order for the truth of a given counterfactual to be determinate and knowable, is only that the actual world is a member of the *set of worlds* in which that particular counterfactual is true. Now, why shouldn't this be the case, even prior to God's decision about which particular world to actualize? Why shouldn't it be the case, in other words, that *the same counterfactuals of freedom are true in all the worlds God could actualize?*[33] Why shouldn't the truth of the counterfactuals of freedom be "*counterfactually independent* of the various courses of action God could have

---

[31] See Adams, "Middle Knowledge," pp. 113-14; Kenny, *The God of the Philosophers*, pp. 70-71.

[32] *The God of the Philosophers*, p. 71.

[33] Plantinga seems to say that an even weaker requirement than this will suffice to enable the theory to work. He says:

> It isn't at all clear that if (8) ["If God created Adam and Eve, there would be more moral good than moral evil in the history of the world"] could be God's reason for creating Adam and Eve, then there was nothing he could do to make it the case that (8) is false. For suppose (8) would have been false if God had created no free creatures. We can still imagine God reasoning as follows: "If I were to create no free creatures there would not, of course, be more moral good than moral evil; and it would be better to have more moral good than moral evil. But if I were to create free creatures, (8) would be true, in which case if I were to create Adam and Eve, there would be more moral good than moral evil. So I shall create Adam and Eve." Thus even if God could bring it about that (8) was false, (8) could perfectly well serve as his reason, or part of his reason, for creating Adam and Eve. ("Reply to Robert M. Adams," p. 377)

I believe this suggestion to be incoherent. For consider the following supposition, which on Plantinga's principles ought to be possible: Suppose, as Plantinga hypothesizes, (8) would be true if God created free creatures but false if he did not create free creatures. Suppose, furthermore, that God decided not to create free creatures. (Possibly he is more repelled by the prospect of moral evil than attracted by the prospect of moral good.) Then God, looking back on his decision to create a world that lacks free creatures, can truthfully say, "I'm glad I decided not to create Adam and Eve, for if I had created them there would have been more moral evil than moral good." But this contradicts the supposition of the example, which is that if God were to create free creatures, (8) would have been true. So the example is incoherent, and the correct requirement for the theory of middle knowledge is the one slated in the text: the same counterfactuals of freedom must be true in all the worlds God can actualize.

taken"?[34] If this is so, then the truth of the counterfactuals is settled prior to God's decision about which world to actualize, and the Adams-Kenny objection collapses.[35]

It must be acknowledged that this reply suffices as a formal answer to the objection, but I think it leaves us with a further, major problem. *How are we to explain* the alleged fact that the same counterfactuals of freedom are true in all the worlds God could actualize? These counterfactuals, according to the theory, are not necessary truths. Their truth, furthermore, is not due to *God's* decision; on the contrary, they constitute an *absolute limit* on which worlds God is able to actualize. For example: There are possible worlds, plenty of them, in which it is true that, if God had created Adam and placed him in Eden just as he did in the actual world, Adam would freely have refrained from sinning. (We will symbolize this initial-segment counterfactual as "$E^* \to$ Adam refrains from sinning.") Now, why didn't God actualize one of *those* worlds in preference to this one? The answer is, that *in fact* the true counterfactual, the one true in all the worlds God could actualize, *is* "$F^* \to$ Adam sins." But *why* is this counterfactual true? Not because of God's decision, and not because of any noncounterfactual truths about the creatures God has created. We will see in the next section that a very few of these counterfactuals are said to be true in virtue of the free choices made by created beings, but even if this answer proves tenable, it can account only for a tiny proportion of the whole. So we are confronted with this vast array of counterfactuals—probably, thousands or even millions for each actual or possible free creature—almost all of which simply *are true* without any explanation whatever of this fact being given. Is this not a deeply puzzling, even baffling state of affairs?

The three objections in this section have been developed independently, yet on close inspection they reveal a common theme. The first objection complained about the lack of a *ground* for the truth of counterfactuals in nonhypothetical, noncounterfactual reality. The reply is, that no such ground is needed. The second objection points out that if this is so, then the rationale is cut from under the principles of counterfactual logic on which the theory relies, thus making such reliance dubious at best. In the third objection, the groundlessness of counterfactuals reappears at a higher level, not concerned this time merely with individual counterfactuals but rather with the whole vast array of them, all allegedly true in all the worlds God could have actualized, and true without there being any ground for this either in the nature and actions of God, or in the natures of created beings, or (except for a tiny fraction) in the choices of created free agents. Without doubt, we are here confronted with something deeply mysterious—but is this the mystery of God's creation, or simply the mysteriousness of a misguided philosophical theory?[36]

---

[34] Ibid. p. 376.

[35] It should be pointed out that Adams anticipated the possibility of a reply along these lines but rejected it because it seemed implausible to him that (for example) a world in which there are no free creatures at all would be "more like a world in which most free creaturely decisions are good ones than like a world in which most free creaturely decisions are bad ones" ("Middle Knowledge," p. 114). Plantinga, however, is unmoved by this—as we have already noted, he sees no reason why the similarities between worlds that are relevant for the truth of counterfactuals must have anything to do with similarities in noncounterfactual characteristics of those worlds.

[36] It is evident that many (though not all) of these difficulties result from the applications to counterfactuals of freedom of the possible-worlds semantics. Thus, the proponent of middle knowledge may be tempted to dispense with the semantics, perhaps agreeing with Freddoso that "we might wonder why it wasn't perfectly obvious from the start that comparative similarity wouldn't help us if the conditionals in question involve genuine causal indeterminism" (personal communication). It is true that getting rid of the semantics makes the theory somewhat harder to attack, but it also eliminates a good deal of the theory's philosophical substance. Those philosophers (their name is legion) who are disposed in any case to be suspicious of counterfactuals can only have their suspicions confirmed if we are deprived of any systematic account of their semantics.

D. A Refutation of Middle Knowledge

We turn now to a final, and slightly more complex, argument.[37] In this argument we shall not, as previously, argue directly against the counterfactuals of freedom. Instead, we shall concede, provisionally, that there are true counterfactuals of freedom and ask about them the question suggested in the last section: Who or what is it (if anything) that *brings it about*[38] that these propositions are true?

In order to give the discussion a touch of concreteness, imagine the following situation: Elizabeth, a doctoral student in anthropology, is in the concluding phase of her course work and is beginning to make plans for her dissertation field research. Her advisor has been asked to make a recommendation for a foundation grant to be awarded for observation of a recently discovered tribe in New Guinea. This assignment offers exciting prospects for new discoveries but would also involve considerable hardship and personal risk. The advisor asks himself whether Elizabeth would choose to undertake this study, or whether she would prefer to continue with her present plans to study a relatively placid group of South Sea islanders. He wonders, in other words, which of the following two counterfactuals of freedom is true:

(12) If Elizabeth were offered the grant, she would accept it (in symbols, $O \rightarrow A$).
(13) If Elizabeth were offered the grant, she would not accept it ($O \rightarrow \sim A$).

Now, Elizabeth's advisor may find himself unable to decide which counterfactual is true, or he may reach the wrong conclusion about this. But according to the theory of middle knowledge, one of the two counterfactuals is true, and God, if no one else, knows which one. For the sake of our discussion, we will assume it is (12) that is true rather than (13); we shall assume, moreover, that Elizabeth is in fact offered the grant and she accepts it. All this, however, is merely preparatory to raising the question already suggested: Who or what is it that *brings it about* that this proposition is true?

In the previous section we have considered the reasons why it cannot be *God* who brings it about that counterfactuals of freedom are true; we shall not rehearse those reasons here. The answer to this question that is in fact given by the friends of middle knowledge is that it is the *agent named in the counterfactual* who brings it about that the counterfactual is true. More precisely, it is the agent who brings this about *in those possible worlds in which the antecedent is true*.[39] It is this claim, then, that will be the principal subject of discussion throughout this section.

How might it be possible for the agent to bring it about that a given counterfactual of freedom is true? It would seem that the only possible way for the agent to do this is to perform the action specified in the consequent of the counterfactual under the conditions stated in the antecedent. That is to say: In the case of a genuinely free action, the only way to insure the action's being done is to do it. I believe the proponents of middle knowledge accept this, which

---

[37] See William Hasker, "A Refutation of Middle Knowledge," *Noûs* 20 (1986): 545-57.

[38] The concept of *bringing about* employed here and elsewhere throughout the book will be discussed in detail in chapter 6. For the present, suffice it to say that the concept is of an asymmetrical relation of dependence of what is brought about on the action or event that brings it about; the dependence in question may be, but is not necessarily, causal.

[39] This is a view I have heard stated in discussion by Plantinga; I know of no written source. In any case, the attribution is not crucial, since we shall also be discussing the consequences for middle knowledge if this claim is *not* made.

is why they claim that the agent brings about the truth of the counterfactual *only in those possible worlds in which the antecedent is true*. It is in other words an accepted principle that

(14)   It is in an agent's power to bring it about that a given counterfactual of freedom is true, only if its truth would be brought about by the agent's performing the action specified in the consequent of the conditional under the conditions specified in the antecedent.

But is it possible for the agent to bring about the truth of a counterfactual of freedom in this way? What is required if it is to be the case that a particular event brings it about that a proposition is true? It seems initially plausible that

(15)   If E brings it about that "Q" is true, then "Q" would be true if E occurred and would be false if E did not occur ((E occurs) $\to Q$ and ~ (E occurs) $\to$ ~Q).[40]

But this cannot be quite right, as is shown by the following examples: I knock on your door at ten o'clock, Sam knocks on your door at eleven o'clock, and no one else knocks on your door all day. It seems clear that my knocking on your door brings it about that "Someone knocks on your door today" is true, in spite of the fact that this would still be true even if I did not knock on your door. Or suppose we are bowling against each other, and you need a count of 5 or better on your last ball to win the game. If you roll a 9, your doing so brings about that you win the game, even though it need not be true that if you had not rolled a 9 you would not have won. (It may be that if you had not rolled a 9 you would have rolled a 7 or an 8.) In each case the problem arises because the event in question is a token of a type of event such that the occurrence of any event of that type (someone's knocking on the door, your rolling a 5 or better on your last ball) would bring about the truth of the proposition in question. With this in mind, we revise (15) as follows:

(16)   If E brings it about that "Q" is true, then E is a token of an event-type T such that (some token of T occurs) $\to Q$ and ~(some token of T occurs) $\to$ ~Q, and E is the first token of T which occurs.

If then we add the simplifying assumption that if E were not to occur, no other token of T would occur, we get (15) as a special case. When, on the other hand, we have an event and a proposition such that the conditions specified in (15) and (16) are not satisfied, we will say that the truth of the proposition is independent of the event in question.

Applying this to our example, what we need to know is whether Elizabeth brings about the truth of the counterfactual of freedom "$O \to A$" by accepting the grant, or whether its truth is independent of her action, in the sense just specified. In order to determine this, we need to know whether the following propositions are true:

(17)   If Elizabeth were to accept the grant, it would be true that $O \to A$ (i.e., $A \to (O \to A)$).

(18)   If Elizabeth were not to accept the grant, it would be true that $O \to A$ (i.e., ~ $A \to (O \to A)$).

There can be no question about the truth of (17); if both "O" and "A" are true in the actual world, the counterfactual will be true. It might seem equally obvious that (18) is false: If Elizabeth does

---

[40] I speak both of an *event* as bringing about the truth of a proposition, and of a *person* as doing so. Thomas Flint ("Hasker's 'Refutation' of Middle Knowledge," unpublished, n. 12) correctly points out that there is a need for a principle to connect these two uses. The required principle is as follows: A person brings it about that a proposition is true just in case that person's performance of some action brings it about.

not accept the grant, how can it be true that, if offered it, she would accept it? This, however, is a mistake. If (18) seems to us to be obviously false, we are probably misreading (18) as

(19) If Elizabeth were to reject the grant, it would be true that $O \rightarrow A$ (i.e., $(O \,\&\, {\sim}A) \rightarrow (O \rightarrow A)$).

This is indeed obviously false, but it is not the same as (18); the antecedent of (18) says, not that Elizabeth rejects the offer, but merely that she does not accept it. It is consistent both with her rejecting the offer, and with the offer's never having been made. If she rejects it, then "$O \rightarrow A$" must be false, but if no offer is made, "$O \rightarrow A$" will still be true. So now we have to evaluate the counterfactuals

(20) If Elizabeth does not accept the offer it will be because she rejected it (i.e., ${\sim}A \rightarrow (O \,\&\, {\sim}A)$).[41]

(21) If Elizabeth does not accept the offer, it will be because the offer was not made (i.e., ${\sim}A \rightarrow ({\sim}O \,\&\, {\sim}A)$).

If (20) is true, (18) will be false, but if (21) is true, so is (18).

How shall we decide this question? According to our semantics for counterfactuals, the question about (20) and (21) comes down to this: Is a world in which Elizabeth received the offer and rejected it more or less similar to the actual world (in which the offer was accepted) than a world in which the offer was neither made nor accepted?

One's first thought might be that the world specified in (20), which differs from the actual world with respect to Elizabeth's acceptance of the offer, is more similar to the actual world than the world specified in (21), which differs with respect both to the making of the offer and to its acceptance. If so, however, then one's first thought (as is so often the case in matters counterfactual) would have overlooked important considerations. To see why, consider the following example: I have been hard at work making a poster announcing an upcoming event, and just as the poster is nearly completed I knock over my ink bottle, spilling ink on the poster and forcing me to start all over again. As I do this, I pause from cursing my clumsiness long enough to wonder what it would have been like not to have had my poster ruined in this way. Two possibilities occur to me: I might have refrained from knocking over the ink bottle in the first place, or, I might have knocked it over just as I did in the actual world, but instead of spilling any ink, the bottle spontaneously righted itself and come to rest again in its original position. I then wonder which of these scenarios would have occurred if I had not gotten the ink spilled on my poster. I am wondering, in other words, which of the following counterfactuals is true:

(22) If no ink had been spilled on my poster, it would have been because I did not knock over my ink bottle (${\sim}S \rightarrow ({\sim}K \,\&\, {\sim}S)$).

(23) If no ink had been spilled on my poster, it would have been because I knocked over my ink bottle but no ink spilled (${\sim}S \rightarrow (K \,\&\, {\sim}S)$).

---

[41] The verbal formulations in (20) through (23) represent my attempts to express in natural-sounding ways some propositions that under normal circumstances we would seldom if ever have any occasion to state. No special emphasis is to be laid on the "because" language; the logically relevant content of the propositions is what is contained in the symbolic formulations.

I puzzle over this for a few moments, but my question is quickly answered along the same lines already suggested for (20) and (21). The (22)-world would have differed from the actual world with respect both to the bottle's being knocked over and the ink's spilling, whereas the (23)-world differs from it only in the latter respect. So the (23)-world is more similar to the actual world than the (22)-world; it is (23) that is true and not (22), and I realize that if my poster had not been ruined, the reason for this would have been, not that I was careful about my ink bottle, but that after I knocked over the bottle it miraculously righted itself without spilling any ink. And that makes me feel a little better about my clumsiness.

Of course this is absurd, but why is it absurd? What exactly is wrong with the reasoning that led me to conclude that (23) is true rather than (22)? The answer seems to be this: In the actual world certain counterfactuals are true, among them

(24)   If I were to knock my ink-bottle in such-and-such a way, the bottle would fall over and spill ink on my poster.

This counterfactual is true in the actual world (as events have shown), and it is also true in the (22)-world, but not in the (23)-world. And in weighing the comparative similarity to the actual world of the (22)-world and the (23)-world, the truth in the (22)-world of the counterfactual (24) counts far more heavily than the slightly greater similarity of the (23)-world with respect to factual content. So as we thought all along, it is (22) that is true rather than (23).

But of course exactly similar considerations apply in the case of (20) and (21). In the actual world, it is true that

(12)   If Elizabeth were offered the grant, she would accept it.

This counterfactual is true in the actual world, and also in the (21)-world, but not in the (20)-world. And in a comparison of the latter two worlds, the truth of the counterfactual (12) outweighs the slight difference with respect to similarity in factual content, so that the (21)-world is indeed more similar to the actual world than the (20)-world, and it is (21) that is true rather than (20).

It might be suggested that the reason (24) is decisive with respect to the decision between (22) and (23) is that (24) is backed by laws of nature; counterfactuals of freedom such as (12) do not have such backing and are therefore not decisive with regard to the choice (for example) between (20) and (21). But this really will not do. For one thing, Plantinga himself is pretty clearly committed to the view that, in deciding the comparative similarity of possible worlds, counterfactuals outweigh differences in matters of fact *whether or not* they are backed by laws of nature.[42] And there are reasons that make it very difficult to justify weighting counterfactuals of freedom less heavily than laws of nature. First, there is the contention, noted in the last section, that the same counterfactuals of freedom are true in all the worlds God can actualize and constitute *absolute limitations* on God's power to bring about states of affairs. (Laws of nature, clearly, do *not* limit God's power in this way; he could have created a world in which different laws obtained.)

The proponent of middle knowledge, however, may object to this piece of reasoning. He may point out that, although *God* cannot control which counterfactuals of freedom are true, the *human beings* in question—the agents named in the counterfactuals—*do* have control over this, since it is they who, by making the choices that they do, bring about that those counterfactuals

---

[42] I take this to be the upshot of the argument given in *The Nature of Necessity*, pp. 177-78.

are true. Now, of course, whether or not the agent brings about the truth of the counterfactual is the very point at issue in the present discussion. In view of this, one might tend to consider it question-begging to introduce this point on *either* side at this stage of the argument.[43] But the proponent of middle knowledge may feel this is unfair to him. The claim that the agent brings about the truth of counterfactuals of freedom is, he points out, an integral part of his position, one that he should be permitted to appeal to until and unless it is refuted by his opponent.[44] Suppose we concede this point and agree to evaluate the immediate point in question—the question, that is, whether it is (20) or (21) that is true—in the light of the claim that the agent decides which of the counterfactuals about her actions are true. How will this affect the outcome of the discussion?

A natural view to take would seem to be that this point made by the proponent of middle knowledge tends to balance off, and thus to neutralize, the last point made in the previous paragraph. There it was pointed out that God has control over which laws of nature obtain, but not over which counterfactuals of freedom are true. The rejoinder is that human beings have control over some counterfactuals of freedom, but not over natural laws. If, as would seem to be the case, these considerations weight about equally on either side of the argument, the upshot would seem to be that we cannot decide, on the basis of these considerations alone, whether counterfactuals of freedom are more fundamental than laws of nature, or vice versa. If anything, what seems to be suggested is that the two are roughly at a parity. If we wish for a more definitive answer to our question, we must look further.

Now, what is at issue is whether it is counterfactuals backed by laws of nature or counterfactuals of freedom that have counterexamples in possible worlds "closer" to the actual world. It is relevant in this connection that we now know with virtual certainty that the fundamental laws of nature are probabilistic rather than strictly deterministic; thus, the counterfactuals backed by the laws of nature (such as [24]) are in fact *would-probably conditionals* rather than true necessitation conditionals. Surely, however, necessitation conditionals (such as the counterfactuals of freedom are supposed to be) have to be weighted *more* heavily than "would-probably" conditionals in determining the relative closeness of possible worlds. There is also the important point that God, according to Christian belief, can and does work miracles. If this is so, then some counterfactuals backed by laws of nature have counterexamples *in the actual world itself,* and therefore also in possible worlds as close to the actual world as you please. In view of all this, the counterfactuals of freedom seem to be considerably more fundamental, with respect to explaining why things are as they are, than the laws of nature; *a fortiori,* they are more fundamental than particular facts such as that Elizabeth is offered the grant.[45]

---

[43] Flint accuses me of begging the question (in my "Refutation of Middle Knowledge") by assuming that "since *God* has no control over which counterfactuals of creaturely freedom are true, neither do *we* ("Hasker's 'Refutation' of Middle Knowledge," p. 20). But this is just false. I do not *assume* this; I *argue* for it, and the reader will search in vain to find this proposition, or anything equivalent to it, among the premises of my argument. What is true, however, is that I fail to consider this point (viz., the proponent's claim that agents control the truth of the counterfactuals of freedom) in my discussion of whether counterfactuals of freedom outweigh laws of nature, or vice versa.

[44] The position then would be similar to the one that obtains in discussions of the problem of evil, where the burden of proof is assumed by the nontheist and the theist is entitled to invoke all of her theistic beliefs unless and until the nontheist has refuted them.

[45] Freddoso, commenting on the version of this argument given in the article "A Refutation of Middle Knowledge," claims that the argument is "seriously flawed" because of my claim that "the proponents of middle knowledge hold, or should hold, that the truth of a counterfactual of freedom is as fixed in the worlds closest to the actual world as is the truth of a law of nature" (*Introduction to Molina, On Divine Foreknowledge,* sec. 5.7 and n. 96).

But if (21) is true, then so is (18), and (since [17] is also true) it follows that the truth of the counterfactual "$O \to A$" is independent of whether or not Elizabeth actually accepts the grant. (It is not true if she *rejects* the grant, but that is another matter.) And it also follows (by [16]) that Elizabeth's acceptance of the offer does *not* bring it about that the counterfactual "$O \to A$" is true. And in general, it is not true that the truth of a counterfactual of freedom is brought about by the agent.[46]

Does the conclusion we have reached constitute a serious problem for middle knowledge? Perhaps not. David Basinger has recently argued that the proponent of middle knowledge need not and should not hold that the truth of the counterfactual of freedom is brought about by the agent.[47] To be sure, the view that the truth of these counterfactuals is brought about by God must also be excluded, for the reasons already discussed. Rather, these counterfactuals simply *are true* without their truth having been brought about either by God or by anyone else. "Who is responsible for the truth of [the counterfactuals of freedom] in the actual world? The answer is that no one is responsible."[48]

Now, since I do not think any counterfactuals of freedom are true *at all*, I have no views of my own concerning *when* they are true; I must therefore rely on inferences from principles that are or should be accepted by the proponents of middle knowledge. If the particular conclusion criticized by Freddoso turned out to be stronger than warranted, this would not create serious difficulties for my overall argument. What is required for my argument is only the much weaker claim that, in determining the relative similarity of possible worlds, counterfactuals of freedom outweigh particular facts such as that Elizabeth is offered the grant. Plantinga's argument cited in note 42 above seems to commit him to holding that they do, and in view of this the difficulty here does not seem especially serious.

But I am by no means convinced that the conclusion I have drawn is too strong. I believe that the arguments given in the text provide cogent reason for holding that, if there are true counterfactuals of freedom, they outweigh laws of nature in determining the relative similarity of possible worlds. If the friends of counterfactuals disagree with this, they are invited to present (at least) equally cogent arguments for the contrary conclusion.

[46] I am indebted to Alvin Plantinga for an extremely interesting objection to this argument. He suggests that the argument cannot be general in its force, because it will not work if we change the original supposition slightly. Suppose that in the actual world it is true that (14) $O \to \sim A$, rather than that (13) $O \to A$, and suppose furthermore that Elizabeth is offered the grant, and she rejects it. We then ask what it would have been like had she *accepted* the grant. And here, it may seem, the only reasonable answer is that, if she had accepted the grant, it would have been true that $O \to A$, and from this it is but a short step to say that she would *bring about* the truth of "$O \to A$" by accepting the grant. If we do not say that, what can we say? Surely not, that she accepted the grant because she was not offered it!

No, we can't say *that!* Rather, we proceed as follows: Starting with the assumption that "$O \to \sim A$" is true, and she in fact rejects the grant, we ask ourselves this question: What is the minimal change that would be needed in the actual world, such that if things were different in that way, Elizabeth would accept the grant? It may not be obvious what the answer is, but surely there must *be* an answer. Possibly the minimal change would be that all her other opportunities for field research have fallen through, so that if she does not accept the grant, her research, and the granting of her degree, will be postponed indefinitely. (If we represent the proposition saying that she is offered the grant under those modified circumstances as '$O\#$', then it follows from what has been said that "$O\# \to A$" is true even though "$O \to A$" is false.) Supposing this to be the case, we then ask, If Elizabeth were to accept the grant, would it be because "$O\#$" was true rather than "O," or because "$O \to A$" was true? And for the reasons already discussed, the correct answer will be that if she were to accept it this would be because the circumstances were different than they are in the actual world (in which she rejects it), and not because the counterfactual "$O \to A$" would be true. So it still is not true that Elizabeth brings about the truth of a counterfactual of freedom. The beauty of Plantinga's objection is that it brings out the generality of the argument in a way in which the original example does not.

[47] "Divine Omniscience and Human Freedom: A Middle Knowledge Perspective," *Faith and Philosophy* I (1984): 291-302.

[48] Ibid., p. 300.

This proposal, however, creates serious difficulties for middle knowledge. On the proposed view, Elizabeth is not responsible for the fact that, if she were offered the grant, she would accept it (i.e., for the truth of the counterfactual "$O \rightarrow A$"). Nor, we may assume, is she responsible for the truth of the antecedent—that is, for the fact that she is offered the grant. But if she is responsible for neither of these things, it is difficult to see how she can be responsible for accepting the grant—a conclusion that is entirely unwelcome to the proponents of middle knowledge.

But there is another, even more fundamental, difficulty. We have learned that Elizabeth does not bring it about that the counterfactual "$O \rightarrow A$" is true. What effect, if any, does this have on the question of what is in her power when the grant offer is made? In order to investigate this, we need what I call *power entailment principles,* principles that state that an agent's possessing the power to perform a certain kind of action entails that the agent also possesses the power to perform another kind of action. More will be said about power entailment principles in chapter 6, but a principle that will suffice for our present purposes is

(PEP) If it is in A's power to bring it about that P, and "P" entails "Q" and "Q" is false, then it is in A's power to bring it about that Q.

A little thought will show this principle to be correct. If "P" entails "Q", it cannot be the case that P unless it is also the case that Q. If "Q" is already true, then the entailment presents no obstacle to A's being able to bring it about that P. (Since the sun is in fact rising, it is in your power to bring it about that you see the sunrise, even though you completely lack the power to bring about the sunrise itself.) But if "Q" is not true, it is not possible for you to bring it about that P unless it is also possible for you to bring it about that Q. (I approach your house with the intention of ringing your doorbell, only to discover that you do not have a doorbell. Unless it is in my power to bring it about that you have a doorbell—e.g., by installing one myself or having one installed—it is not in my power to ring your doorbell.)[49]

How does this principle apply to the matter in hand? In order to proceed we will make the assumption, which is sanctioned by the theory of middle knowledge, that of any pair of counterfactuals such as (12) and (13) one or the other is true; this implies that the disjunction of the two is necessarily true, true in all possible worlds. Given this assumption, we have the following as necessary truths:

(25) If Elizabeth is offered the grant and accepts it, it is true that $O \rightarrow A$ ((O & A) $\Rightarrow (O \rightarrow A)$).

(26) If Elizabeth is offered the grant and rejects it, it is true that $O \rightarrow \sim A$ ((O & $\sim A$) $\Rightarrow (O \rightarrow \sim A)$)

That is to say, Elizabeth's acceptance or rejection of the grant *entails* the truth of the corresponding counterfactual of freedom.[50]

---

[49] Freddoso (*Introduction to Molina, On Divine Foreknowledge,* sec. 5.7) rejects this principle, and with it the conclusion of the present argument. For his objection to (PEP), see chapter 6.

[50] If the inference-rule

(A) P & Q; therefore, $P \rightarrow Q$

is accepted as valid, (25) and (26) can be derived without recourse to the assumption made in the text. But (A) may occasion some discomfort. Lewis admits that "it would seem very odd to pick two completely unrelated truths ϕ and ψ and, on the strength of their truth...to assert the counterfactual

Now we are ready to consider what is in Elizabeth's power when the offer is made. First of all, is it in her power to accept the grant? One would suppose that it is, since in fact she actually does so. And (PEP) places no obstacle in the way of this conclusion. Her accepting the offer entails the truth of the counterfactual "$O \to A$," but that counterfactual is in fact true, and so the question of whether it is in her power to *bring about* its truth does not arise.

But now let us ask, does she have it in her power to *reject* the grant? Her rejecting the grant entails that the counterfactual "$O \to {\sim}A$" be true, but this counterfactual is in fact false. So—according to (PEP)—she can have the power to reject the grant only if it is in her power to bring it about that this counterfactual is true. If she does not have this power, then she lacks power to reject the grant.

And now the situation becomes serious. We have seen that it would be in Elizabeth's power to bring it about that the counterfactual "$O \to {\sim}A$" is true only if the truth of this counterfactual would be brought about by her rejecting the offer. But we have also seen that the truth of a counterfactual of freedom is *not* brought about in this way. It follows that Elizabeth does *not* have it in her power to bring it about that $O \to {\sim}A$, and lacking this, she also—by (PEP)—lacks the power to reject the offer.

It is time to summarize. In this section we are investigating the question, Who or what brings it about that the counterfactuals of freedom are true? We first considered the possibility that it is the agent named in the counterfactual who does this—in terms of our example, that Elizabeth by accepting the grant offer brings it about that $O \to A$. It turns out, however, that this counterfactual is true independently of whether or not she accepts the offer: It would be true if she were to accept the offer, and it would also be true were she not to accept the offer. To be sure, it would not be true if she were to *reject* the offer, but this turns out not to be relevant; if she did not accept the offer, this would be because the offer was never made and not because it was made and she rejected it. But since the counterfactual is true independently of whether or not she accepts the offer, it cannot be the case that she *brings about* the truth of the counterfactual by her acceptance of the grant.

We then went on to consider what Elizabeth has it in her power to do when the grant is offered to her. Clearly, she has it in her power to accept the grant, and she demonstrates this by doing so. But does she also have the power to reject the grant? Of particular importance here is the fact that (given the truth of the theory of middle knowledge) her rejection of the grant entails the truth of the counterfactual "$O \to {\sim}A$." But this counterfactual is not true, so it can be in her power to reject the grant only if it is also in her power to bring about the truth of this counterfactual. But we have already seen that this is impossible. She could have the power to bring about the truth of the counterfactual "$O \to {\sim}A$" only if its truth could be brought about by her rejection of the offer, but we have seen that the agent *cannot* in this way bring about the truth of a counterfactual of freedom. So it is not in her power to reject the grant.

The conclusion to be drawn from this is that the concession made earlier—that some counterfactuals of freedom are true—was unwarranted. It turns out from our consideration of the case of Elizabeth that insofar as such counterfactuals are *true*, they are not counterfactuals of

---

$\phi_{TM} \to \psi$" (*Counterfactuals*, p. 28). Lewis suggests a semantics on which (A) would not hold, but in his own, "official" theory (A) is accepted.

I believe the right solution here is to be found in the distinctions made by Pollock between various kinds of subjunctive conditionals. (A) is valid for simple subjunctives, and also for "even if" conditionals. But as we have seen, the counterfactuals of freedom are necessitation conditionals, and for these conditionals (A) is invalid. (See Pollock, *Subjunctive Reasoning*, chap. 2.) (A), then, is not valid for the counterfactuals of freedom.

freedom: If the counterfactual "$O \to A$" is true, it is not in Elizabeth's power to reject the offer, and she is not free in the required sense. And, on the other hand, insofar as an agent is genuinely free, there *are* no true counterfactuals stating what the agent would definitely do under various possible circumstances. And so the theory of middle knowledge is seen to be untenable: *There are no true counterfactuals of freedom.*

Questions

1. What is middle knowledge?
2. How is middle knowledge to be differentiated from foreknowledge?
3. What are the chief characteristics of the Classical Theory?
4. What are the main objections to Middle Knowledge?
5. What is a counterfactual conditional of freedom. Give an example of one. Why does Hasker think that God does not know them?

THE MOLINIST SOLUTION*

Linda Zagzebski

Zagzebski gives account of the Medieval philosopher/theologian, Luis de Molina's way of handling the dilemma of freedom and foreknowledge, and that is by means of a compatibilism thesis regarding both. Zagzebski proposes her own solution in terms of a modest version of middle knowledge, to which she attaches an acknowledgement that there are not enough true counterfactual conditionals of freedom that are known by God if he is going to have foreknowledge.

I. Introduction

A. What Middle Knowledge Is

Perhaps the most ingenious solution to the dilemma of foreknowledge and freedom was devised by the sixteenth-century Jesuit philosopher, Luis de Molina, in his theory of *scientia media,* or middle knowledge. This theory has lately attracted some attention and now has a number of adherents.[1] As we will see, if the theory is true, it has the advantage of solving at least two and perhaps three important theological problems simultaneously. In this chapter I will examine the theory as a solution to the foreknowledge dilemma and only incidentally will consider its other virtues.

Middle knowledge is said to be the knowledge of what any possible free creature would freely choose in any possible circumstance. Molina called it "middle" knowledge because it stands midway between God's natural knowledge, or his knowledge of what is necessary and possible, and God's free knowledge, or his knowledge of what is actual. Middle knowledge is like free knowledge and unlike natural knowledge in that its objects are metaphysically contingent propositions. All of God's natural knowledge, in contrast, is of metaphysically necessary propositions. So if God knows that *A is necessary*, the proposition *A is necessary* is itself necessary; if God knows that B is possible, the proposition *B is possible is* itself necessary, and so on. But if by middle knowledge God knows the proposition *In circumstance C Peter would do S,* that proposition is contingent and, hence, in a distinct category from the objects of natural knowledge. On the other hand, middle knowledge is like natural knowledge and unlike free knowledge in that it is

---

* This article is reprinted by courtesy of the author and the publisher. It is Chapter Chapter 5 in *The Dilemma of Freedom and Foreknowledge*, by Linda Zagzebski, Oxford University Press, 1991.

[1] Some of the recent defenders of middle knowledge include Alvin Plantinga, *The Nature of Necessity* (Oxford: Oxford University Press, 1974), Chap. 9, and "Reply to Robert Adams," in Tomberline and van Inwagen (eds.), *Alvin Plantinga, Profiles*, Vol. 5 (Dordrecht: D. Reidel, 1985): Alfred Freddoso, introduction to *On Divine Foreknowledge: Part IV* of the *Concordia* by Luis de Molina (Ithaca, N.Y.: Cornell University Press, 1988); Jonathan Kvanvig, *The Possibility of an All-Knowing God* (Grand Rapids: Baker Publishing House, 1987); Edward Wierenga, *The Nature of God* (Ithaca, Ny.Y.: Cornell University Press, 1989), Chapat. 5; David Basinger, "Divine Omniscience and Human Freedom: A Middle Knowledge Perspective," *Faith and Philosophy*, 1 (1984), pp. 291-302. Vocal opponents include Robert Adams "Middle Knowledge and the Problem of Evil," *American Philosophical Quarterly*, 14 (April 1977), pp. 109-117, and "Plantinga on the Problem of Evil," Tomberlin and van Inwagen (eds.), *Alvin Plantinga*; and William Hasker *God, Time, and Knowledge* (Ithaca, N.Y.: Cornell University Press, 1989), Chap. 2.

prevolitional. It is logically or explanatorily prior to God's will to bring about what he does in the creation. All other contingent propositions except those expressing God's will itself are postvolitional. That is, they depend for their truth on the fact that God has willed what he has willed. So the objects of God's middle knowledge are both contingent and prevolitional.

This means that God's foreknowledge of contingent states of affairs is logically or explanatorily subsequent to his middle knowledge. Freddoso explains how middle knowledge gives rise to foreknowledge as follows:

> On Molina's view, then, the source of God's foreknowledge of absolute future contingents is threefold: (i) His prevolitional natural knowledge of metaphysically necessary states of affairs, (ii) His prevolitional middle knowledge of conditional future contingents, and (iii) His free knowledge of the total causal contribution He Himself wills to make to the created world. By (i) He knows which spatio-temporal arrangements of secondary causes are possible and which contingent effects might emanate from any such arrangement. By (ii) He knows which contingent effects *would in fact* emanate from any possible spatiotemporal arrangements of secondary causes. By (iii) He knows which secondary causes He wills to create and conserve and how He wills to cooperate with them via His intrinsically neutral general concurrence. So given His natural knowledge, His middle knowledge and His free knowledge of His own causal contribution to the created world, He has free knowledge of all absolute future contingents.[2]

So on Molina's theory, God's free knowledge, or his knowledge of the actual, can be fully explained by his natural knowledge, His middle knowledge, and his knowledge of his own will. Since all foreknowledge is contained in free knowledge, this theory explains foreknowledge.

For the theory of middle knowledge to be a successful solution to the foreknowledge dilemma it is not actually required that God know what every *possible* free creature would freely choose in each possible circumstance, but only what every *actual* free creature would so choose. So the well-known difficulties with individuating possible but nonactual beings, while a problem for the full theory, are not a problem for that part of it relevant to foreknowledge.

The objects of middle knowledge are supposed to include propositions such as the following:

(1) If Peter were asked if he knows Christ (at a certain place and time), he would (freely) deny it.

(2) If Elizabeth were offered a (certain) grant, she would (freely) accept it.[3]

In modern parlance, conditionals such as (1) and (2) are called *counterfactuals of freedom*. So this theory explains God's foreknowledge of the consequents of (1) and (2) by the combination of his knowledge of (1) and (2) and his knowledge of the antecedents of (1) and (2).

Middle knowledge would solve the foreknowledge dilemma provided that for every actual contingent event expressed by a proposition ϕ, including every human choice, there is some true subjunctive conditional $\psi > \phi$ that has the following features: (a) $\psi > \phi$ is

---

[2] Alfred Freddoso, Introduction to Molina's *On Divine Foreknowledge*: *Part IV of the Concordia* (Ithaca, N.Y.: Cornell University Press, 1988), pp. 23-234.

[3] (1) was discussed by Molina, while (2) is an example of Hasker.

knowable by God logically prior to his knowledge of his own creative will, and (b) ψ is knowable by God independently of anything but his prevolitional knowledge and his knowledge of his own will.

How can God know the antecedents of (1) and (2) by using only his natural knowledge, his knowledge of counterfactuals of freedom, and his knowledge of his own will? Call the proposition expressing what God originally wills to create $\psi 1$. Suppose that $\psi 1$ includes the creation of Adam and Eve. If God also knows counterfactuals of freedom about Adam and Eve, his knowledge of other contingent states of affairs $\psi 2$ can be explained. By knowing other counterfactuals of freedom about the actions of creatures in circumstances expressed by $\psi 2$, as well as anything God chooses to directly bring about in $\psi 2$, he would know further contingent states of affairs, $\psi 3$, and so on. God's knowledge that Peter exists and finds himself in certain circumstances can then be explained simply by his knowledge of $\psi 1$, his knowledge of counterfactuals of freedom, and his knowledge of his own will.[4]

Molina was embroiled in a vicious controversy with Banez over the status of the objects of middle knowledge. As Freddoso describes this dispute, both Molinists and Banezians accepted the fact of middle knowledge, but the Banezians denied that any metaphysically contingent state of affairs could be logically prior to God's decreeing that it obtain.[5] They therefore denied clause (a) (two paragraphs preceding) and claimed instead that counterfactuals of freedom are true because God has willed them to be true. In my opinion, this position is highly unappealing. If God brings about the truth of a counterfactual of freedom by willing it to be so, God is responsible for the fact that if I were in a certain circumstance I would freely bring about evil. But even if this is possible, it is surely distasteful. I therefore take the Molinist view of middle knowledge to be the most compelling version of the theory, and it is this version that I will investigate in this chapter. For those readers who prefer the Banezian version, the discussion of whether the theory satisfies clause (a) is, of course, irrelevant.

The theory of middle knowledge is remarkably powerful. If it succeeded, it would go a long way toward producing a positive solution to the foreknowledge dilemma. This is because it aims at much more than a simple demonstration of the logical consistency of foreknowledge arid freedom that, as we have seen, is only the weakest form of compatibilism. By giving a theory of *how* God knows the future, it aims at showing that divine foreknowledge and human free will are coplausible, not just copossible. Furthermore, middle knowledge can easily be combined with the Thomistic theory of divine knowing, either with or without the doctrine of timelessness, and it attempts to answer the mystery of how God can know what *I* freely do by knowing his own essence. As Molina himself expresses it:

> Finally, the third type is *middle* knowledge, by which, in virtue of the most profound and inscrutable comprehension of each free will, He saw in His own essence what each such will would do with its

---

[4] It might be thought that since transitivity fails for the counterfactual, $\psi 1 >$ Peter denies Christ is false. But transivity does not fail for subjunctive conditionals with true antecedents and true consequents, the kind we are considering. Also, even if transivity does fail, this theory still explains how God could know *Peter denies Christ* by knowing nothing but $\psi 1$ counterfactuals of freedom, and his own will

[5] Freddoso, introduction to Molina, pp. 23-24.

innate freedom were it to be placed in this or that or, indeed, in infinitely many orders of things—even though it would really be able, if it so willed, to do the opposite....[6] (Emphasis mine.)

Middle knowledge has other advantages. Recall that in Chapter 1, I argued that the dilemma of a divine and infallible foreknower has special problems not encountered by the dilemma of a nondivine but infallible foreknower, a point stressed by Freddoso.[7] Any acceptable solution to the dilemma must at least be compatible with the doctrine of divine providence. The theory of middle knowledge is not only compatible with that doctrine, it helps to explain it in a way that seems to preserve both God's sovereignty and human free will. This advantage of the theory is enthusiastically expressed by Craig.

> Since God knows what any free creature would do in any situation, he can, by creating the appropriate situations, bring it about that creatures will achieve his ends and purposes and that they will do so *freely*. When one considers that these situations are themselves the results of earlier free decisions by creatures, free decisions which God had to bring about, one begins to see that providence over a world of free creatures could only be the work of omniscience. Only an infinite Mind could calculate the unimaginably complex and numerous factors that would need to be combined in order to bring about through the free decisions of creatures a single human event such as, say, the enactment of the lend-lease policy prior to America's entry into the Second World War. Think then of God's planning the entire course of world history so as to achieve his purposes! Given middle knowledge, the apparent contradiction between God's sovereignty, which seems to crush human freedom, and human freedom, which seems to break God's sovereignty, is resolved. In his infinite intelligence, God is able to plan a world in which his designs are achieved by creatures acting freely. Praise be to God![8]

In addition, the theory of middle knowledge was reinvented by Plantinga as a solution to the problem of evil. In much of his discussion, Plantinga uses the possible worlds interpretation of counterfactuals discussed in Chapter 4.[9] On that interpretation, a counterfactual conditional $A > B$ is (nonvacuously) true just in case there is a world in which A and B are both true that is closer to the actual world than any world in which A is true and B is false. Of course, some of the propositions that are the objects of middle knowledge are not *counter*factuals, since the antecedent is true, and it is these that allow middle knowledge to give rise to foreknowledge on Molina's theory. But it is usually thought that the analysis of counterfactuals applies to these conditionals, also. So if both A and B are true in the actual world, there is obviously a world in which both are true that is more similar to the actual world than any world in which A is true and B false, namely, the actual world itself.

Plantinga argues that God's middle knowledge can be used to show that it is possible that a certain set of counterfactuals of freedom are true that are such that if they are true, God cannot actualize certain possible worlds. Such worlds are *unrealizable,* to use Robert Adams's terminology. So even if there are worlds that contain a better balance of good over evil than ours, and even if some of those worlds contain free creatures, it might be that God cannot bring them into existence. The theory deserves a more lengthy discussion than I can give for the purposes of

---

[6] Molina, *On Divine Foreknowledge: Part IV of the Concordia*, trans. By Alfred J. Freddoso, disputation 52, para. 9, p. 168
[7] Freddoso, pp. 2-7.
[8] William Lane Craig, *The Only Wise God*, op. cit., p. 135.
[9] Plantinga, *The Nature of Necessity*, Chap. 9. Plantinga's free will defense does not depend on the doctrine of middle knowledge, although it is somewhat more interesting if that doctrine is true. For his version of the defense without middle knowledge , see *The Nature of Necessity*, op. cit., pp. 182-184, and "Reply to Robert M. Adams," *Alvin Plantinga, Profiles*, pp. 379-380.

this chapter but, since it is well known, I will simply present my own simplified version of it in what follows.

There are good reasons for holding that God does not create a complete possible world, but only the foundations of a world. We might say he creates a world-germ. A world-germ probably contains certain substances and laws and the results of any direct action by God on these substances. We need not settle just how far God's direct action goes in the creation, since the point is that whatever God does, he does not bring about a complete world. His creative activity is compatible with a great number of possible worlds, probably an infinite number of them. What makes the actual world this particular world rather than some other one compatible with what God has created is determined by both God's direct action in the world subsequent to the creation and by the free action of the creatures God has made.

So for each world-germ God might have created, there is a set of possible worlds compatible with that world-germ. Let us call each such set of worlds a galaxy. So galaxy 1 is the set of worlds compatible with world-germ 1, galaxy 2 is the set of worlds compatible with world-germ 2, and so forth. This can be represented diagrammatically as follows.[10]

world-germ 1	world-germ 2...	world-germ n...
↓	↓	↓
world w1.1	w2.1	wn.1
world w1.2	w2.2	wn.2
world w1.3	w2.3	wn.3
w1. ...	w2. ...	wn. ...
GALAXY1	GALAXY 2 ...	GALAXY N

Now suppose that there are possible worlds that contain free creatures who always choose good. Why doesn't God just create those worlds? The short answer is that it is *possible* that there are true propositions such as the following:

(i)   If God created world-germ 1, world w1.2 would be actual,

---

[10] Plantinga calls those states of affairs God directly brings about in the world, both in the creation and as a response to human acts, states of affairs strongly acutualized by God. Those states of affairs brought about by human free choices but permitted by God are states of affairs weakly actualized by God. I hav enot used this distinction in my version of the theory, since the states of affairs brought about in the creations, together with the counterfacutals of freedom, should be suffiecent on this tehory to determine that the actual world be what it is. That is because those things which God strongly actualizes other than the original creation—responses to prayer and the like—are presumably explainable by counterfactuals of freedom about God's choices. If the amaendement to the theory is unsatisfactory, my presentation can be easily read in Plantinga's way. What I call world-germ 1 would be identified with what God strongly actualizes in galaxy 1,. world-germ 2 would be identified with what God strongly actualizes in galaxy 2, etc.

(ii) If God created world-germ 2, world w2.4 would be actual,
(iii) If God created world-germ 3, world w3.1 would be actual,

where *in each case* the world that would have resulted given God's creative activity would have been one containing evil—perhaps very great evil.

So even if, say, worlds w1.1, w2.3, and w3.2 have no evil in them, they would not result even if God did *his part* in bringing them about. It is not God's fault, then, that there is evil, even if there are possible worlds with free creatures and no evil. Such worlds are unrealizable.

This way out of the problem of evil requires that God have middle knowledge, for God could not know which world would result given any one of his own creative options unless he knew in particular each event that would actually occur given any creative choice of his own. And it assumes that God himself does not choose to make counterfactuals such as (i) to (iii) true. Even if God wills them in the sense of permits them to be true, their truth is logically or explanatorily prior to God's willing them to be so. Plantinga's theory, then, requires a Molinist rather than a Banezian version of middle knowledge.

The theory of middle knowledge therefore has many advantages. If successful, not only can it account for the compatibility of divine foreknowledge and human freedom, it can also account for the compatibility of divine providence and human freedom, and it can be used in the formulation of an interesting solution to the problem of evil. Furthermore, it blends well with traditional theories about the nature of God and his knowing, particularly the views of Aquinas. The theory's conceptual importance, then, makes it deserving of a sympathetic hearing.

B. The Middle Knowledge Solution

In this book we have looked at a number of responses to two arguments that divine foreknowledge would make our future acts unfree. How does the Molinist theory of middle knowledge respond to these arguments? Freddoso discusses Molina's answer to a version of the argument from accidental necessity in more detail than Molina gives it himself.[11] According to Freddoso, Molina explicitly rejects three common responses to this argument: the Aristotelian move of denying that future contingents have a truth value, the Thomistic move of denying that God knows anything *as future,* and the Ockhamist move of denying that God's past beliefs are really or strictly past. Freddoso says:

> At this point it might seem that Molina has closed off every viable avenue of escape. And, indeed, I can attest from personal experience that at first glance his response to the argument is apt to strike one as rather astonishing. In a word, he rejects...the thesis that accidental necessity is closed under entailment.[12]

Freddoso's rendition of the argument from accidental necessity is similar to the version of my argument that uses the weaker TNP.

Transfer of Accidental Necessity Principle 1

If *A is* accidentally necessary and *A* entails *B*, then *B* is accidentally necessary*.

---

[11] Freddoso, pp. 53-62.
[12] Freddoso, pp. 57-58.

In my second version of the argument, I use an even more plausible principle on line 2.

Transfer of *Accidental Necessity Principle 2*

> If A is accidentally necessary and *A is* strictly equivalent to *B,* then *B is* accidentally necessary*.

Molina's move is to accept the position that God's past beliefs are necessary in whatever sense other states of affairs in the past are necessary but to deny TNP 1.

> ... even if (i) the conditional is necessary (because...these two things cannot both obtain, viz., that God foreknows something to be future and that the thing does not turn out that way), and even if (ii) the antecedent is necessary in the sense in question (because it is past-tense and because no shadow of alteration can befall God), nonetheless the consequent can be purely contingent. [13]

There is no indication that Molina considered my second version of the argument from accidental necessity, but it looks as if his only way out of that argument would be to deny TNP 2 as well as TNP 1. Even though this may seem like a hopelessly implausible move, I will present an argument in Chapter 6, Section 2.2, that shows, I think, that even the denial of TNP 2 is reasonable. I will do this in the context of one of my own solutions to the foreknowledge dilemma rather than the middle knowledge solution. In both Molina's solution and my own, the way out of the dilemma is to present a model for understanding the relation between God's knowledge and human acts that makes it plausible to deny the TNPs. How does the middle knowledge solution accomplish this?

As Freddoso explains it, Molina allows no power of any sort over the past, so Peter cannot cause it to have been true that God never foreknew that he would sin at *t*. Nor, presumably, can Peter cause it to have been true that God did not know the counterfactual of freedom that explains God's knowledge that Peter sins at *t*. But since Peter's sin at *t* will be free, it is true at some time prior to *t* that Peter has the power to contribute causally to its being false that he sins at *t*.

> So even though Peter cannot now cause it to be true that God never believed that he would sin at *t*, he nonetheless can now cause something, viz., his not sinning at *t*, such that had it been true from eternity that he would cause it if placed in the relevant circumstances, God would never have believed that he would sin at *t*. And, significantly, the theory of middle knowledge provides an intuitively accessible model on which both parts of this claim come out true. [14]

It is not perfectly clear to me from Freddoso's account just how middle knowledge is connected with the denial of the TNPs, but I can think of ways the former might make the latter more plausible. Molina's position seems to be that before *t* Peter cannot cause it to be true that God never believed he would sin at *t*, yet he has the power to cause it to be true that he does not sin at *t*, and this clearly involves denying TNP. The theory of middle knowledge makes the claim plausible provided that Peter's power before *t* not to sin at *t* does not entail the power to make it false that in circumstances *C* Peter sins at *t*. Presumably, Peter has no power over the truth of the

---

[13] Disputation 52, paragraph 34; discussed by Freddoso, introduction, p. 58.
[14] Freddoso, p. 60.

counterfactual of freedom or God's knowledge of it. That is, Peter cannot cause it to be true that in circumstances C he does not sin at t, nor can he cause it to be true that God never believed that in circumstances C, he would sin at t. But as long as power not to sin does not involve power over a counterfactual of freedom, the fact that God knows the truth of the counterfactual of freedom and Peter has no power over its truth explains God's knowledge of Peter's future sin *and is* compatible with Peter's power not to sin at t.

So Molina's theory of middle knowledge can give a way out of both the accidental necessity and causal necessity versions of the foreknowledge dilemma, but it does so at the cost of denying the intuitively plausible TNP, and the plausibility of this in turn requires denying that power over the truth of S involves power over the truth of $C > S$. The price may be worth paying but, as far as I know, little attention has been paid to it in discussions of middle knowledge.

II. Conditional Excluded Middle and the Asymmetry of Time

In Chapter 4 we examined the logical peculiarity of backward-looking subjunctive conditions. We related the fact that such conditionals are not true as standardly interpreted to the asymmetry of time. We noted, in fact, that Lewis claims that the best, if not the only, way to express temporal asymmetry is to say that there is an asymmetry of counterfactual dependency. Later times counterfactually depend on earlier times, but earlier times do not counterfactually depend on later times.

In my view, the connection between temporal asymmetry and the problems with backward-looking counterfactuals can help us to understand ordinary forward-looking counterfactuals. The reason backward counterfactuals are so strange is that the relation between the antecedent and consequent states of affairs in a counterfactual conditional is like the relation between the present and the future. In some cases, states of affairs in the present are sufficient to determine that something obtain in the future, and in those cases it is true that $A_{present} > B_{future}$, but the openness of the future means that the totality of states of affairs in the past and present is not sufficient to determine that the future be what it is going to be. So *The totality of present and past > actual future* is false. That is, it is false that if the past and present were just as it is, the actual future would follow. Alternative futures *might* follow instead.

To take a particular example, consider the following subjunctive conditional, where the antecedent is about the actual present, and past and the consequent is about the future:

(4) If I lived my life the way I have up to now (May 1988), I would be living in Chicago in 1999.

It seems to me that (4) is false. Defining the might; counterfactual in terms of the would-counterfactual, as Lewis and Pollock do, (4) is equivalent to the following.

(5) ~ (If I lived my life the way I have up to now (May 1988), I might *not* be living in Chicago in 1999).

But (5) is surely false, and it seems false because it seems true instead that the following:

(6) If I lived my life the way I have up to now (May 1988), I might be living in Chicago in 1999.
(7) If I lived my life the way I have up to now (May 1988), I might *not* be living in Chicago in 1999).

I have not proposed an account of counterfactuals in this book, but it is clear to me that there is a large class of paradigm cases of the might-counterfactual in which the antecedent is about the actual past or present and the consequent about the future. In these cases we think that both $A > \textit{might } B$ and $A > \textit{might not } B$ are true. This means that the principle of Conditional Excluded Middle (CEM), $(A > B)$ or $(A > \sim B)$, is false when A is about the actual past and present and B is about either the actual or possible future. CEM fails in these cases because one mark of the difference between the future and the past is just that the future is such that there is more than one alternative that might be the future, whereas there is only one alternative that (now) might be the past. The ordinary notion of time explained in Chapter 1, then, supports the rejection of CEM for propositions in this category.

In a similar fashion, it seems to me that we use counterfactual conditionals when we want to treat the past as if it were still future. Suppose I say the following:

(8) If I had taught a course on Aristotle last semester I might have assigned the Categories.

or

(9) If I had taught a course on Aristotle last semester I might *not* have assigned the Categories.

I suggest that to understand these propositions we consider the time immediately prior to the time at which the antecedent would have obtained. The future, relative to that time, was still open. There were many ways things could have turned out in the course I would have been planning. Each possible future can be represented by branching paths on some of which I assign the Categories and on some of which I do not assign the Categories. So I might have assigned the Categories but, then again, I might not have. Of course, some of those branching paths represent futures farther removed from the way the actual world turned out than others. But it still seems likely that some world in which I assign the Categories is just as similar to the actual world as one in which I do not.[15] And even if the interpretation of (8) and (9) in terms of similarity of worlds is not accurate, I am more sure of the truth of (8) and (9) than I am of the semantics for counterfactuals currently in use.[16]

The truth of (8) and (9) is contained, then, in the intuition of the openness of the future, the idea that there are many possible futures, but only one possible past. And if (8) and (9) are true, given the interdefinability of might- and would-counterfactuals, the following propositions are both false:

(10) If I had taught a course on Aristotle last semester I would have assigned the Categories.
(11) If I had taught a course on Aristotle last semester I would *not* have assigned the Categories.

As pointed out by Robert Adams, it is compatible with the falsity of both (10) and (I1) that the following is true:

(12) If I had taught a course on Aristotle last semester I would *probably* have assigned the Categories.

---

[15] For the possible worlds interpretation of a counterfactual conditional $A > B$ to work, it must make similarity of worlds to the actual world before the event expressed by A much more important than similarity afterward. In fact, there are cases in which similarity afterward does not seem to matter at all (If the nuclear button had been pushed, ...). I think the possible worlds interpretation of counterfactuals can be used in a way that is compatible with the intuitions I am discussing in this chapter, but it need not be. Since my objections to middle knowledge do not require the use of the current semantics, I prefer not to discuss the problems with it here.

[16] Note that this argument is the exact parallel of Plantinga's argument that he is more sure of the truth of certain counterfactuals of freedom than he is of the possible worlds semantics for counterfactuals.

And it is compatible with the falsity of (10) and (11) that the following is true:

(13) If I had taught a course on Aristotle last semester *I probably* would *not* have assigned the Categories.

So even though (12) is incompatible with (13), each is compatible with the negations of (10) and (11).[17]

So both (10) and (11) are false, and this means that principle CEM is false for counterfactuals as well as for subjunctive conditionals with true antecedents about the present. I have not argued, however, that there are *no* true would-counterfactuals with an antecedent such as (10) and (11). In fact, I am reasonably confident that there are some, and some no doubt express propositions about my free choices. So there are true counterfactuals of freedom. For example, I would claim the truth of the following:

(14) If I had taught a course on Aristotle last semester, I would not have primarily assigned readings from Hegel.

The truth of (14), means, I think, that certain well-known objections to middle knowledge are misplaced. We will look at some of these in the next section. My point here is simply that even though there are pairs of states of affairs, one earlier, one later, in which the obtaining of the earlier one is sufficient to determine that the later one *would* obtain, and even if some of the latter are freely brought about by human beings, we should not expect that given any state of affairs, it is either true that it would obtain, given its past, or it is true that it would not obtain, given its past.

We have considered subjunctive conditionals with true antecedents about the present and consequents about the future and subjunctive conditionals with false antecedents about the past and have seen that CEM fails in both cases. Subjunctive conditionals with true antecedents and where both antecedent and consequent are about the past form a special category. These propositions are peculiar, and I think there is more than one way to understand them. Suppose that I did, in fact, teach Aristotle last semester and that I did, in fact, assign the Categories. To assert (10) would certainly be misleading, since the form of (10) suggests that the antecedent is false. However, I might assert a structurally similar proposition about someone else if I did not know whether or not the antecedent is true.

(15) If David Blake had taught a course on Aristotle last semester, he would have assigned the Categories.

One way to understand propositions such as (15) is to see them as no different than the first category we have considered. We imagine a time prior to the time Blake teaches the Aristotle course and, since the future was open and Blake might or might not have assigned the Categories at that time, (15) is false, even though both antecedent and consequent are true. So on this way of interpreting (15), CEM fails for this group of subjunctive conditionals as well. We might call this the forward-looking interpretation of counterfactuals about the actual past. They are forward looking because we imagine a time in the past when the consequent of the conditional was still future. My preferred way to handle propositions in this class is to interpret them all as forward looking, but my argument in this section does not depend on it.

---

[17] Robert Adams, "Middle Knowledge and the Problem of Evil," op. cit

There is, however, another way to interpret (15). We can examine it from the viewpoint of the present. When doing so, we are looking backward on the states of affairs expressed in (15). In this case (15) seems true, unlike (6), which seems to me to be false even if both antecedent and consequent are true. Why is there this difference between (15) and (6)?

Our inclination to treat the two cases differently, I submit, can again be explained by the asymmetry of time. We treat the counterfactual past as like the present or future, with an open future laying ahead of it, but we treat the factual past as fixed. That is, it seems fixed when we look backward on it from the vantage point of the present. If the antecedent is not about the actual past, it does not come under the necessity of the past, and so its counterfactual implications are open, just as they are for the future. If antecedent and consequent *are* about states of affairs in the actual past, the negation of the consequent is now precluded, although it is instructive that we usually do not use subjunctive conditionals at all in such cases. So at best, CEM holds for propositions about the actual past, but only because of the necessity of the past. I suggest that this is the reason there is a tendency to put *counter*factual conditionals in a separate category from the rare *factual* subjunctive conditionals in the past tense, and why *deliberative* future subjunctives are put in the same category with the counterfactuals, whether or not they are contrary to fact.

If I am right that counterfactual conditionals are a way of speaking about the past as if it were future, we can see what is wrong with a certain common argument in favor of the principle of CEM. There must be *something* I would assign if I taught Aristotle, the objector says, and of any option I would have, either I would choose it or I would not. A good way to *tell* what I would choose, although not a foolproof method, is actually to teach the course. For each pair of choices, whichever one I *do* choose is the one I *would* choose.

But if I am right about the connection between counterfactuals and the asymmetry of time, this objection misses the point. If CEM holds, there are no true might-counterfactuals except those entailed by would-counterfactuals. There are no pairs of true propositions of the form $A > \text{might } B$ and $A > \text{might not } B$. But surely the *point* of might-counterfactuals is to indicate more than one branching path of possibilities compatible with the antecedent. And in the case of either the future, or any moment of time considered *as if* it were either present or future, there are branching paths ahead. To bring about the antecedent in order to find out if the consequent obtains is irrelevant, since then the imagined future becomes past.

CEM might get some of its plausibility from a confusion between the counterfactual "would" and the use of "would" to express the simple future relative to some past time. If ϕ is a nonconditional (absolute) future contingent,

> It was true that it would be the case that ϕ

just means

> The proposition *It will be the case that ϕ was* true.

So

(18) It was true in 1900 that Reagan would be elected president in 1984

is interpreted as

> (19) The proposition *Reagan will be elected president in 1984* was true in 1900.

But this use of "would" is not the same as the use of "would" in the consequent of a counterfactual. So the truth of (18) and (19) should not lead us to think it is also true that

> (20) If ϕ occurred in 1900, Reagan would be elected president in 1984.

The use of "would" in the consequent of a subjunctive conditional indicates a certain relation with the antecedent, a relation I have argued indicates the lack of branching paths from the state of affairs described in the antecedent to any state of affairs precluded by the consequent. So as long as it was the case in 1900 that Reagan might not be elected in 1984, (20) is false, even if (18) is true. At best, (20) is true only in those cases in which ϕ is something that *did* happen in 1900. And even then, it is true only when interpreted in the backward-looking rather than in the for-ward-looking manner.

Counterexamples to CEM have already appeared in the literature.[18] Some of the more well-known ones are unfortunate choices, however, and the defenders of middle knowledge are right to point out that these examples prove nothing.[19] For instance, Lewis offers the following as a counterexample:

> (21) If Verdi and Bizet were compatriots, Bizet would be Italian.
>
> (22) If Verdi and Bizet were compatriots, Bizet would not be Italian.

On Lewis's reasoning, there are worlds in which Verdi and Bizet are both French that are equally close to the actual world as worlds in which they ire both Italian. Hence (21) and (22) are false and CEM fails.

Kvanvig and Wierenga have pointed out that propositions such as (21) and (22) both seem false largely because of our substantial ignorance about the intentions, inclinations, and opportunities of Verdi's and Bizet's respective parents. Furthermore, they claim, even if neither (21) nor (22) is true, this does not necessarily threaten middle knowledge, since the version of CEM required for middle knowledge does not require the truth of either (21) or (22).[20]

To see this point, consider the fact that on counterfactual logic, even if neither $A > B$ nor $A > \sim B$ is true, one of them may be true if the antecedent is strengthened. In other words, the fact that CEM fails for certain propositions A and B does not demonstrate that CEM fails if A is conjoined with some suitable proposition. The criteria for a successful theory given at the beginning of this chapter require only that for each set of possible circumstances A and possible choice B, there is some proposition ϕ that, when added to A, is such that either (*A and ϕ*) $> B$ or (*A and ϕ*) $> \sim B$ is true and that is knowable by God independently of anything but his prevolitional knowledge.

However, the argument I have given against CEM holds against this version as well. Assuming we have eliminated the possibility that (*A and ϕ*) $> B$ is backward looking, ϕ can

---

[18] David Lewis, *Counterfactuals* (Oxford: Oxford University Press, 1973), p. 79f; John Pollock, "Four kinds of Conditionals," *American Philosophical Quarterly*, 12 (1975), p. 53.

[19] Jonathan Kvanvig, *The Possibility of an All-Knowing God* (New York: St. Martin's Press, 1986); Edward Wierenga, *The Nature of God: An Inquiry into Divine Attributes* (Ithica, N.Y.; Cornell University Press, 1989).

[20] Kvanvig, pp. 147-148; Wierenga, Chap. 5, pp. 134-139.

include only states of affairs present or prior to the imagined states of affairs expressed by A. But, if so, no matter how much A is strengthened, no ϕ will be strong enough to eliminate the openness of the future relative to that time. Except for certain cases of true counterfactuals of freedom already noted, there will always be branching paths indicating the ways the future might turn out, and these branches are not eliminated even if we pack *all* of the past into the antecedent. So even though Kvanvig and Wierenga are quite right that middle knowledge does not require the truth of certain forms of CEM, my objection based on the asymmetry of time would hold against any version, including that required for middle knowledge.

Sometimes upholders of middle knowledge say that they are more sure that there are true counterfactuals of freedom than they are of the possible worlds interpretation of counterfactuals. So when they are confronted with an objection based on that semantics, they can always reject the semantics rather than the truth of their favorite examples of counterfactuals of freedom. Since I do not deny that there are true counterfactuals of freedom, this move is not directed against my position. But I think it fair to point out that the same argument can be made against the principle of CEM. I find that I am more sure of the truth of both (8) and (9) and the falsehood of both (10) and (11) than I am of the principle of CEM.

Defenders of middle knowledge often concentrate on arguing for the truth of particular counterfactuals of freedom. I have not denied that there are some and, for all I know, (1) and (2) might be examples, although I doubt it. In Chapter 4 I argued that there may even be strict implications of freedom, a claim I have not heard even from defenders of middle knowledge. However, I see no reason to believe that the principle of CEM holds for counterfactuals. In fact, I think there are strong intuitive reasons against it, at least as strong as the intuitions supporting the truth of anyone's favorite example of a counterfactual of freedom. Furthermore, these intuitions hold equally against the version of CEM required for middle knowledge.

In this section I have argued that the relation between the antecedent and the consequent of a counterfactual conditional is like the relation between the present and the future. Given that the present is what it is, there are many ways the future might be. It might include the election of one president or it might include the election of another; it might include my moving to one city or to another, or I might stay where I am. Each way the future might be can be represented by a branching path extending from the single path representing the actual past up to the present. There are also some ways the future *would* be, given that the past is what it is, so every branching path may include the same event. Some of these events are logical or causal consequences of the past, but not all are. As we saw in Chapter 4, the failure to reduce the causal relation to any common counterfactual shows that the counterfactual relation includes more than the relation of causal or logical necessity. So some ways the future would be, given the past, are not logical or causal consequences of the past, and some of these may even be determined to be so by human free choice.

So there are counterfactuals of freedom, but CEM is false. If it were true, this would in effect be to say that given the present as it is, there is only one future that would follow and no other future that might follow. But this is to think of the future as no different than the past. If I am right that the antecedent of a counterfactual conditional is considered like the present and the consequent like the future, CEM must be false far counterfactuals. This means it is not the case that for each contingent state of affairs, including each human choice, ϕ, there is a true proposition $\psi > \phi$, where ψ is knowable by God without knowing any contingent proposition except his own will, and where $\psi > \phi$ is knowable by God independently of everything except his prevolitional knowledge. This theory therefore cannot explain how God knows ϕ.

III. Objections to Middle Knowledge

A number of intriguing objections to middle knowledge have appeared in the literature, particularly those of Robert Adams and, more recently, William Hasker. In my opinion, some of these objections are overstated, and this weakens the position of those opposed to the theory. It seems to me to be fairly clear that the proponents of middle knowledge are right that certain counterfactuals of freedom are true. I suggested (12) as an example. Plantinga has claimed the truth of the following:

> (23) If Adams were to ask me to go climbing at Tahquiz Rock the next time I come to California, I would gladly (and freely) accept.[21]

Weirenga has suggested that:

> (24) If my daughter asked me for bread, I would not give her a stone.

I have no objections to the truth of (23) or (24), and it seems to me to obfuscate the problems with middle knowledge to insist that these propositions are false.[22] But the defense of the truth of certain carefully selected examples of counterfactuals of freedom is nowhere near sufficient to show the truth of the theory of middle knowledge, or even its plausibility. In Section 2, I argued that many free choices are not counterfactually implied by even the totality of the past up to the time of the choice, so God cannot know these choices by knowing counterfactuals and his own will. In this section I will consider some of the more important objections to middle knowledge already in the literature. I am sympathetic with some of these objections, but not others.

A. The No-grounds Objections

Adams has said that he does not know "what it would be" for counterfactuals of freedom to be true. Hasker has expressed his agreement with this objection and has, in addition, proposed a variation of it. There is no one, he says, who could coherently be said to "bring about" the truth of a counterfactual of freedom. Both Adams and Hasker say they are looking for the grounds of truth for such counterfactuals, and both argue that there aren't any. Both of them conclude that all such counterfactuals are false, although Adams had earlier taken the more cautious position that none are true.

Consider first Hasker's query about who or what could bring about a counterfactual of freedom. Hasker argues that a counterfactual of freedom must be contingent if it is to be applicable to middle knowledge, and apparently he thinks that all contingent propositions need somebody or something to bring about their truth.[23] We must be careful, however, of talk about *bringing about* the truth of any proposition. Such terminology suggests a causal relation that is, at best, misleading. I have no objections, though, to saying that the ground of truth of some proposition is my concrete act. So the truth of the proposition *Linda Zagzebski is*

---

[21] Alvin Plantinga, Profiles, p. 373.
[22] Hasker says in his new book, *God, Time, and Knowledge* (Ithaca, N.Y.; Cornell University Press, 1989), that he assumes that the position of the opponent of middle knowledge is that all counterfactuals of freedom are false (p. 28).
[23] Hasker, pp 35-39.

looking at her computer screen is grounded in my actual act of looking at the screen. The same relationship holds between modalized propositions and my acts in other possible worlds. For example, the proposition *It is possible that Linda Zagzebski visit Antarctica is* true in that there is some possible world, no doubt not the actual one, in which I visit Antarctica. We might take this to mean that my act in some *other* world grounds the truth of a proposition in *this* world. But there is nothing mysterious about this unless possible worlds semantics is itself mysterious, and it certainly does not suggest that my act in one world causes the truth of a proposition in another:

Now consider the proposition If *Linda Zagzebski hadn't read so many novels this year, she would have finished her book sooner.* On the possible worlds interpretation of this proposition, it is to be understood as saying that in some other world I read fewer novels and finish my book sooner than I do in the actual world, and that such a world is closer to the actual world than any world in which I read fewer novels and do not finish my book sooner. But what is so mysterious about that? To say I bring about the truth of this proposition in one world by my act in another world is only unacceptable if that relation is thought to be causal: But since the relation between acts and truth is probably not causal anyway, there is no worry that this interpretation of counterfactuals of freedom implies that my act in one world causes something in another. The possible worlds interpretation of counterfactuals gives us a way of understanding what those propositions say, and what they say is that certain things go on in some other possible worlds. But any modalized proposition does that much. If it is not bothersome in the case of *It is possible that Linda Zagzebski visit Antarctica,* it should not be bothersome in the case of counterfactuals of freedom either.

Adams's version of the objection is not primarily ontological. He says he cannot "see how" a counterfactual of freedom can be true. First, he considers and rejects the possibility that the antecedent of such a conditional necessitates the consequent, either logically or causally. I believe he is right to reject that possibility. Next he considers the possibility that the antecedent provides nonnecessitating grounds for the consequent in the agent's intentions, desires, and character. He argues that these characteristics would ground the truth of a "would probably" counterfactual, but not a "would" counterfactual. Apparently, he thinks that whatever the connection is between antecedent and consequent in a true "would" counterfactual, it prevents the consequent from being contingent in the senses needed for free will.

Adams's argument here is more convincing than it should be because he is probably right about his example. Although I have said there are true counterfactuals of freedom, I am very doubtful about the truth of

(25) If David remained in Keilah, Saul would besiege the city,

which is Adams's main example. However, I deny that we should reject the truth of (25) because the connection between antecedent and consequent in a true counterfactual precludes the consequent from having the contingency needed for free will. The best way to see this, I think, is to consider the failure of the current attempt to define the causal relation in terms of any commonly used subjunctive conditional. As we saw in Chapter 4, this failure demonstrates that the relation between the antecedent and consequent in a counterfactual is weaker than that between a proposition and its logical or causal consequence. An act can therefore be both logically and causally contingent and related to some circumstance as the consequent is related to the antecedent in a "would" counterfactual. I have not, of course, said here *what the relation is* that holds between antecedent and consequent in a counterfactual, but only that whatever it is, it is weaker than the relation of logical or causal necessity. Adams need not worry, then, that the freedom of an act expressed as the consequent of a true counterfactual is precluded by lack of logical or causal contingency.

As a third possibility for the ground of truth of a counterfactual of freedom, Adams considers Suarez's view that the property of being an agent who would in circumstance S freely do *a is* a primitive property that some being *c* has, "although there is nothing either internal or external to *c*, except the property itself, which would make or determine *c* to have one of these properties rather than the other." But in response to this Adams says:

> I do not think I have any conception, primitive or otherwise, of the sort of *habitudo* or property that Suarez ascribes to possible agents with respect to their acts under possible conditions. Nor do I think that I have any other primitive understanding of what it would be for the relevant subjunctive conditionals to be true.[24]

I am sympathetic with Adams's worry here, but I find it difficult to express the worry very clearly. Part of the problem may be an intuition that the property of being such that he would freely do a in circumstance S cannot be a primitive property because of the grammatical form in which the property is expressed. A similar form is used to express dispositional or supervenient properties—properties that are parasitic on more primitive properties, so it is natural to think this one also must be parasitic on more primitive properties of the agent. Whatever the underlying properties are, they must be dependent on the agent's will. Otherwise, it is hard to see how the agent can be responsible for the property of being such that he would freely do *a* in *S*. If I understand Adams correctly, he cannot bring himself to understand a counterfactual-of-freedom property as primitive and, at the same time, he is not hopeful that an account of such a property in terms of more primitive properties can be given. I also cannot bring myself to take Suarez's view that such a property is primitive. I know of no argument to that effect. On the other hand, I am more hopeful than Adams is that it can be understood as supervenient or in some other way derivative from other properties. As I have argued in Section 2, however, I find it impossible to believe that for *every* act-option and possible circumstance, I possess the property of what I would do in that circumstance. I have already defended this claim by examples and by the intuition of the asymmetry of time.

B. The Circularity Objection

There is another interesting objection to middle knowledge in the literature, and this one, I think, successfully refutes the Molinist version of the theory. This is an objection proposed by Adams and by Kenny. The objection is formulated in a way that assumes the similarity-of-worlds interpretation of counterfactuals, but I do not think the heart of the objection relies on the standard semantics. The objection does not deny that there are true counterfactuals of freedom or that God knows them. What it denies is that God can know them independently of his knowledge of anything but his natural knowledge. So clause (a) of the criteria for a successful theory given in Section 1.1 is violated. This means that even if there is such

---

[24] Adams, p. 112.

knowledge, it is not useful to God either in the creation or as a basis for foreknowledge. Wierenga has called this the "Not true soon enough" objection.
Adams expresses the objection as follows:

> Consider a deliberative conditional,
>
> [(26)] If I did x, y would happen.
>
> Is [(26)] true? According to the possible worlds explanation, that depends on whether the actual world is more similar to some world in which I do x and y happens than to any world in which I do x and y does not happen. That in turn seems to depend on which world is the actual world. And which world is the actual world? That depends in part on whether I do x. Thus the truth of [(26)] seems to depend on the truth or falsity of its antecedent.[25]

Kenny expresses what I take to be the same objection this way:

> Prior to God's decision to actualize a particular world those counterfactuals cannot yet be known: for their truth-value depends...on which world is the actual world. It is not simply that God's knowledge of these counterfactuals cannot be based on a decision which has to be taken subsequent to knowledge of them.... The problem is that what makes the counterfactuals true is not yet there at any stage at which it is undecided which world is the actual world.... The difficulty is simply that if it is to be possible for God to know which world he is actualizing, then his middle knowledge must be logically prior to his decision to actualize; whereas, if middle knowledge is to have an object, the actualization must already have taken place. As long as it is undetermined which action an individual human being will take it is undetermined which possible world is the actual world—undetermined not just epistemologically, but metaphysically.[26]

Plantinga dismisses the objection of Adams by pointing out that the "depends on" relation is not transitive. He says:

> This argument, I fear, does not warrant the trust Adams apparently reposes in it. It is true that
>
> [(27)] the truth of [(26)] depends upon which world is actual
>
> in the sense that [(26)] is true in some worlds and false in others; it is also true that
>
> [(28)] which world is actual depends on whether the antecedent of [(26)] is true
>
> again, in the sense that the antecedent of [(26)] is true in some worlds and false in others. It doesn't follow, however, that the truth of [(26)] depends on the truth of its antecedent. Consider the following analogue:
>
> [(27*)] the truth of The Allies won the Second World War depends on which world is actual;
>
> [(28*)] which world is actual depends on whether I mow my lawn this afternoon;
>
> therefore,
>
> [(29*)] the truth of The Allies won the Second World War depends on whether I mow my lawn this afternoon.

---

[25] Adams, p. 113-114
[26] Anthony Kenny, *The God of the Philosophers* (Oxford: Oxford University Press, 1979), pp. 68-71.

Clearly, the relation expressed by the relevant sense of "depends on" isn't transitive.[27]

Plantinga's rejoinder is quoted approvingly by Wierenga in his discussion of middle knowledge.[28]

I cannot see, though, that Adams's and Kenny's point depends on the transitivity of the "depends on" relation. Their argument calls attention to a certain feature of the Molinist version of middle knowledge, the position that the truth of counterfactuals of freedom and God's knowledge of them is logically or explanatorily prior to God's volitional and postvolitional knowledge, or his knowledge of the actual. We might call this the Molinist constraint to distinguish this version of the theory of middle knowledge from the Banezian version. According to Banez, counterfactuals of freedom are true *because* God wills them to be true; they are part of God's volitional knowledge. But given the Molinist constraint, the truths about the actual world are graded in a logical or explanatory order. Metaphysically necessary truths come first and are the objects of God's natural knowledge. Counterfactuals of freedom come next. They are contingent, yet prevolitional. Next come the truths about God's own will. God decides to bring about certain states of affairs directly and knows what these are. Finally, there are all other contingent truths, and these constitute the objects of God's postvolitional knowledge. The point of the theory of middle knowledge, of course, is that the truths in the final category can be fully explained by the truths in the other categories. That is, all God needs to know in order to have postvolitional knowledge is his natural knowledge, his knowledge of counterfactuals of freedom, and his knowledge of his own will.

If I understand Adams's and Kenny's argument, the possible worlds understanding of counterfactuals of freedom violates the Molinist constraint. The point is not that there are no true counterfactuals of freedom or that God knows them. The point is that their truth cannot be logically or explanatorily prior to the truth of all the contingent truths that are in the category of God's volitional and postvolitional knowledge. The argument does not require the transitivity of "depends on." It requires only that it be asymmetrical, as it surely is in this context. So the argument does not proceed from (27) and (28) to the conclusion of Adams and Kenny. Instead, the argument goes as follows.

(27) The truth of (26) depends on which world is actual.

That is, by the possible worlds interpretation of (26) the fact that a particular world is actual is logically prior to the fact that (26) is true. However,

(28**) Which world is actual depends on the truth of (26).

That is, by the Molinist constraint, the fact that (26) is true is logically prior to the fact that a particular world is actual. But (27) and (28**) are inconsistent.

Plantinga's response to this objection, I believe, would be to deny (27) in the sense of "depends on" intended in (27). Let us use the expression "the actual world" to refer attributively to whichever world is the actual world. So in *w1* "the actual world" refers to *w1*, in *w2* "the actual world" refers to *w2*, and so on. Plantinga points out that the truth of a counterfactual in the actual world is determined by the truth values of antecedent and consequent in worlds similar to the

---

[27] Alvin Plantinga, Profiles, p. 376.
[28] Wierenga, p. 150.

actual world, and that, of course, depends on which world is the actual world. But he seems to deny this in the sense of "depends on" that indicates logical or explanatory order. This is because one thing that helps determine similarity between worlds is the degree to which they share their counterfactuals. Plautinga says:

> Of course this means we can't look to similarity, among possible worlds, as explaining counterfactuality, or as founding or grounding it. (Indeed, any founding or grounding in the neighborhood goes in the opposite direction.) We can't say that the truth of $A \rightarrow C$ is explained by the relevant statement about possible worlds, or that the relevant similarity relation is what makes it true. But it doesn't follow that the possible worlds account of counterfactuals is viciously circular or of no use. In the same way we can't sensibly explain necessity as truth in all possible worlds; nor can we say that p's being true in all possible worlds is what makes p necessary. It may still be extremely useful to note the equivalence of *p is necessary* and *p* is *true in all possible* worlds: it is useful in the way diagrams and definitions are in mathematics; it enables us to see connections, entertain propositions and resolve questions that could otherwise be seen, entertained and resolved only with the greatest difficulty if at all.[29]

I interpret this passage from Plantinga as giving the following answer to the circularity objection. (27) is false because the determination of which world is actual is not logically or explanatorily prior to the determination of the truth value of a counterfactual. The truth value of a counterfactual $A > B$ in the actual world obviously depends on which world is the actual world in one sense of "depends on:" But this is not to say that the determination of the actual world as one world rather than another is logically prior to the determination of the truth value of $A > B$.

This response is a reasonable one to one version of Adams's objection, but I do not think it avoids the fundamental difficulty. As I see it, the main problem can be expressed without reference to the current manner of assigning a truth value to counterfactuals on the basis of similarity of worlds. On the Molinist theory of middle knowledge adapted by Plantinga, there are true propositions such as (i) to (iii) of Section 1.1, and God knows them. Both Molina and Plantinga would say these propositions are contingent. They are, after all, just big counterfactuals of freedom. To say they are necessary conflicts with the standard semantics, but worse than that, it does not make sense. If there is any doubt about this, consider:

(i) If God created world-germ 1, world w1.2 would be actual.

(i) is, of course, true in world w1,2. But if (i) is a necessary truth, it would also be true in w1.1 and w1.3. But that is absurd. So (i) must be contingent. It is true in some worlds and not others. One of the worlds in which it is true is w1.2. It may also be true in some worlds in other galaxies. Whether the standard interpretation of counterfactuals in terms of world similarity can be used to determine its truth value in worlds in other galaxies is not the question. Perhaps it can and perhaps it cannot. In any case, (i) is true in w1.2 and in no other world in galaxy 1. In wl.1 (i) is false, and it is true instead that

(iv) If God created world-germ 1, world wl.1 would be actual.

And in w1.3 both (i) and (iv) would be false, and it would be true instead that

---

[29.] Alvin Plantinga, *Profiles*, p. 378.

(v) If God created world-germ 1, world w1.3 would be actual,

and so on.

But there is a problem here. Suppose that the actual world is w1.2. On the Molinist theory, God's knowledge that

(vi) The actual world is w1.2

is explained by his knowledge of (i). So his knowledge of (i) is logically prior to his knowledge of (vi). But how can God know (i) logically prior to his knowledge of (vi)? How can he know that (i) is true and (iv) and (v) are false rather than that, say, (iv) is true and (i) and (v) are false without knowing (vi)? It would seem that the only explanation of his knowledge of (i) is his knowledge of (vi), but then, of course, the explanation is circular.

I understand the Adams and Kenny objections as different versions of this same point. The theory of middle knowledge seems backward. There is no reason or explanation for the truth of (i) other than the fact that the actual world is w1.2. But the theory of middle knowledge was supposed to explain the knowledge that the actual world is w1.2 by the knowledge of (i).

The only way out of this problem for the middle knowledge proponent, as far as I can see, is to admit that there is no explanation for God's knowledge of (i). Since the actual world is w1.2, (i) is true, and since it is true and God is omniscient, God knows (i). And that is all there is to say. But if this is the position, the function of the theory of middle knowledge in solving the foreknowledge problem has been completely abandoned. Why not just say instead that since w1.2 is the actual world (vi) is true, and since (vi) is true and God is omniscient, God knows (vi)? But this is, of course, totally unsatisfactory to those who feel the grip of the fore-knowledge dilemma. There is a problem of seeing how God can know certain truths. But that problem is as severe for the knowledge of (i) as it is for (vi). I cannot see, then, that a theory that explains God's knowledge of (vi) by his knowledge of (i) can succeed. I conclude that either the Plantinga position has the order of explanation of the truth of future contingents and counterfactuals of freedom backward, in which case the theory of middle knowledge cannot explain how God knows the absolute contingent future through this knowledge of counterfactuals of freedom, or the truth of conditional future contingents is just as logically primitive as the truth of absolute future contingents, in which case again knowledge of the former cannot explain knowledge of the latter. Either way, middle knowledge cannot explain foreknowledge.

This problem with middle knowledge also affects its ability to solve the problem of evil and the creation in the way outlined by Plantinga. Suppose God wants to see that world w1.2 is actualized. Can he do so by creating world-germ 1 and knowing (i)? It would seem not if he cannot know (i) logically prior to his knowledge that w1.2 is actual. Furthermore, there are problems even with his knowledge of very general counterfactuals, such as:

(vii) If God created world-germ 1, more good than evil would result

which, presumably, could be true in many worlds in galaxy 1. Could it be true in all of them? I do not see how it could if galaxy 1 includes the creation of free creatures, but let us see what would happen if (vii) *is* true in all worlds in galaxy 1. Even then, (vii) is not true in all worlds, since it is contingent. Let us say that it is not true in any of the worlds in galaxy 2. In that galaxy let us suppose it is true instead that:

(viii) If God created world-germ 2, more good than evil would result.

So in galaxy 1 (vii) is true and (viii) is false; in galaxy -2 (viii) is true and (vii) is false. But then how can God use his knowledge of the truth values of these propositions as part of a plan of creation? Plantinga defends the fact that God could use a proposition such as (vii) as a reason for creating what he created.[30] He could reason that if he were to create world-germ 1, (vii) would be true. Since he wants there to be more good than evil, he can use the creation of world-germ 1 as a means to that end since the creation of world-germ 1 also makes (vii) true.

I do not deny that God could reason that way. But I deny that that gives God a reason to create world-germ 1 rather than world-germ 2. If he did the latter, (viii) would be true and (vii) false. And, of course, there are an infinite number of other such alternatives. So even if a proposition such as (vii) is true in all worlds of some galaxy, an assumption I deny, this account would make God's choice of a world-germ to create arbitrary.

This objection to middle knowledge shows that Plantinga's solution to the problem of evil by way of middle knowledge is unsuccessful. My objection is not a general objection to the free will defense, however. In fact, as Plantinga has argued, if God does not have middle knowledge, the problem of evil is less difficult to answer, and Adams has shown that this is so on his position.[31] Furthermore, although my objection shows that middle knowledge cannot explain foreknowledge, it should be noted that even though Plantinga is a proponent of middle knowledge, he does not himself believe that foreknowledge proceeds by way of middle knowledge.[32]

IV. Objections to My View on Middle Knowledge

My theory on middle knowledge is a moderate one. I have not denied that there are true counterfactuals of freedom or that God knows the ones there are, as other opponents of middle knowledge have done. What I have argued is that there are not enough of them to do the job of explaining foreknowledge. And I have argued that even if there were enough of them, God's knowledge of them could not be logically prior to his knowledge of the simple future contingents they are supposed to explain.

But some proponents of middle knowledge and even one vocal opponent have argued that foreknowledge without middle knowledge is useless.[33] Apparently what it is useless for is divine providence. Now it seems to me that foreknowledge is not valuable only as a means to the exercise of divine providence. Divine foreknowledge is important because foreknowledge is required by omniscience, and omniscience is essential to deity. But even so, it is important that my view on middle knowledge be consistent with the doctrine of divine providence. In this section I will argue that it is.

David Basinger has discussed a case in which a woman is trying to decide which of two men to marry. Middle knowledge is critical to God's ability to help her, he argues.

---

[30] *Profiles*, p. 377.
[31] Adams, p. 117.
[32] Plantinga has told me this in conversation.
[33] The proponents who have so argued include Craig and Basinger. The opponent is Hasker.

> For example, in the case of Sue's marriage proposals, a God with MK is not limited to knowing only what might or will in fact happen. He knows before he gives guidance to Sue exactly what would happen if she marries Tom, exactly what would happen if she marries Fred, and exactly what would happen if she marries neither. He knows, for instance, if Tom would still love her thirty years after their marriage or if Sue would meet someone better if she refused both proposals. Accordingly, Sue can be assured she is getting infallible, long-term advice. To the extent to which she believes she has correctly discerned God's guidance on this issue, and has acted in accordance with it, she need never wonder whether she has made a mistake—i.e., whether things would have been better if she had acted differently. No matter what problems develop, she can steadfastly believe that she is pursuing the best "life-plan" available to her.[34]

There is something appealing about the work of God in Sue's life as described in this passage. Nonetheless, I find myself unable to believe that this is the way it works, even on the assumption that God is inclined to give Sue direct advice. God certainly knows and could advise Sue about the truth of counterfactuals based on natural necessity, and he could also advise her that certain counterfactuals of freedom about Tom and Fred are true; for example, if she married Fred, he would never intentionally bring serious harm to any of their children. But she probably knows most of the important ones in this category already. I do not see that God could tell her that if she married Tom she would be happy in 30 years, or that she would be happier with Tom than with Fred. Presumably, he would tell her that she might be happy with Tom and she might not be. To the extent to which happiness is the result of human choice, it is up to her and Tom, as well as perhaps other persons who would significantly affect their lives, such as their children. To the extent to which happiness is the result of circumstances that occur by natural necessity, God could inform her of those circumstances. So he could tell her that if she married Fred this summer he would develop multiple sclerosis within 3 years. This means that at best he could tell her that she would *probably* be happier with Tom than with Fred, and I would think that that is all the advice she would be looking for.

Of course, whether or not we can expect to be given certain divine guidance is not the deeper issue. Whatever view we have of God's knowledge, it is important to Christian belief that God never lose control of his creation and that he always be able to bring it to the end he has in mind. This includes bringing good out of evil, and probably many other, more particular ends. How can God do this without the full range of middle knowledge?

On the view I have defended in this chapter, God knows that if he creates world-germ N, any one of the worlds in galaxy N might result, but there isn't any particular one that *would* result. God does not intend that, say, world w2.3 be actual and so creates world-germ 2 as a means to that end. He cannot do this because it is not true that if he created world-germ 2, w2.3 would be actual, and it is not true even if w2.3 is in fact the actual world. The Plantinga picture is attractive because it describes God as acting in order to see that a particular chain of events, down to every particular, becomes actualized. And it is attractive because God need not fear that some world other than the one he wants becomes actualized instead. Presumably, some of those worlds in galaxy 2 are well worth fearing.

But rather than glorify God's omnipotence, as this picture is intended to do, it seems to me actually to detract from it. Recall that each world in galaxy 2 includes not only all the actions of free creatures, but God's responses to those actions as well. To think it necessary that God be assured that w2.3 result rather than, say, w2.4, is to say that God would somehow be defeated in w2.4. Things would get to such a point in that world that he would be at a loss as to how to

---

[34] David Basinger, "Middle Knowledge and Classical Christian Thought," *Religious Studies*, 22 (1986), pp. 412-413.

respond, so it is much safer if he always knows that a particular chain of events would result from any one of his own creative choices and can count on the actual world being w2.3 rather than w2.4 or something else even worse.

But surely God does not have such worries. Why couldn't an omnipotent and omniscient being have a providential plan for *each* world that might result from his creative choice?[35] If he can do it for one world, he can do it for an infinite number of them. Isn't it likely that God is able to respond to *whatever* free creatures bring about in a way that he can lead to his own ends? To deny this is to deny his omnipotence. And if God is able to do this, middle knowledge would not be necessary for providence. It seems to me that this is, in fact, the way it is.

Questions

1. How does Molina handle the dilemma of freedom and foreknowledge?

2. What does Zagzebski mean when she says that she holds to a modest middle knowledge thesis?

3. Why does she think that her account of middle knowledge fails to allow God can have foreknowledge?

4. What are counterfactual conditionals of freedom?

5. If God were not to have middle knowledge, how would this affect his omniscience?

---

[35] Since a possible world includes God's own action in that world, I should not say that God could have a providential plan for each complete world. Rather I mean to say that he could have such a plan for each world minus that part of it that consists in his carrying out such a plan.

# ETERNITY*

Eleonore Stump & Norman Kretzmann

In this paper Stump and Kretzmann expound the concept defended by Boethius of God's atemporal eternity, analyze implications of the concept, examine reasons for considering it incoherent, and sample the results of bringing it to bear on issues in the philosophy of religion.

The concept of eternity makes a significant difference in the consideration of a variety of issues in the philosophy of religion, including, for instance, the apparent incompatibility of divine omniscience with human freedom, of divine immutability with the efficacy of petitionary prayer, and of divine omniscience with divine immutability; but, because it has been misunderstood or cursorily dismissed as incoherent, it has not received the attention it deserves from contemporary philosophers of religion.[1] In this paper we expound the concept as it is presented by Boethius (whose definition of eternity was the locus classicus for medieval discussions of the concept), analyse implications of the concept, examine reasons for considering it incoherent, and sample the results of bringing it to bear on issues in the philosophy of religion.

Eternality—the condition of having eternity as one's mode of existence—is misunderstood most often in either of two ways. Sometimes it is confused with limitless duration in time—sempiternality—and sometimes it is construed simply as atemporality, eternity being understood in that case as roughly analogous to an isolated, static instance. The second misunderstanding of eternality is not so far off the mark as the first; but a consideration of the views of the philosophers who contributed most to the development of the concept shows that atemporality alone does not exhaust eternity as they conceived of it, and that the picture of eternity as a frozen instant is a radical distortion of the classic concept.

I. Boethius's Definition

Boethius discusses eternity in two places: *The Consolation of Philosophy*, book 5, prose 6, and *De Trinitate*, chapter 4.[2] The immediately relevant passages are these:

CP:

---

* From *The Journal of Philosophy*, Vol LXXVIII, 8 (August 1981), pp. 429-53. Reprinted by permission of the authors and *The Journal of Philosophy*.

[1] At least one contemporary philosopher of religion has recently turned his attention to the concept of divine eternality in order to reject it as incompatible with biblical theology and, in particular, with the doctrine of divine redemption. 'God the Redeemer cannot be a God eternal. This is so because God the Redeemer is a God who changes' (Nicholas Wolterstorff, 'God Everlasting', in Clifton J. Orlebeke and Lewis B. Smedes (eds.), *God and the Good* (Grand Rapids, Mich., 1975), pp. 181-203, p. 182). (We are grateful to Kenneth Konyndyk for having supplied us with copies of this article, which is obviously highly relevant to our purposes in this paper. The work we are presenting here was substantially complete by the time we had access to Professor Wolterstorff's work.) Although it is no part of our purposes here to discuss Wolterstorff's arguments, it will become clear that we think he is mistaken in his assessment of the logical relationship between the doctrine of divine eternality and other doctrines of orthodox Christianity, including the doctrine of redemption, even in their Biblical formulations. Passages that have been or might be offered in evidence of a Biblical conception of divine eternality include Malachi 3:6; John 8:58; James 1:17.

[2] Ed. E. K. Rand, in H. E. Stewart, E. K. Rand, and S. J. Tester, *Boethius: The Theological Tractates and The Consolation of Philosophy* (London and Cambridge, Mass., 1973).

> That God is eternal, then, is the common judgment of all who live by reason. Let us therefore consider what eternity is, for this makes plain to us both the divine nature and knowledge. Eternity, then, is the complete possession all at once of illimitable life. This becomes clearer by comparison with temporal things. For whatever lives in time proceeds as something present from the past into the future, and there is nothing placed in time that can embrace the whole extent of its life equally. Indeed, on the contrary, it does not yet grasp tomorrow but yesterday it has already lost; and even in the life of today you live no more fully than in a mobile, transitory moment.... Therefore, whatever includes and possesses the whole fullness of illimitable life at once and is such that nothing future is absent from it and nothing past has flowed away, this is rightly judged to be eternal, and of this it is necessary both that being in full possession of itself it be always present to itself and that it have the infinity of mobile time present [to it]. (*CP*, 422.5-424.31)

> *DT*:
> What is said of God, [namely, that] he is always, indeed signifies a unity, as if he had been in all the past, is in all the present—however that might be—[and] will be in all the future. That can be said, according to the philosophers, of the heaven and of the imperishable bodies; but it cannot be said of God in the same way. For he is always in that for him *always* has to do with present time. And there is this great difference between the present of our affairs, which is *now*, and that of the divine: our now makes time and sempiternity, as if it were running along; but the divine now, remaining, and not moving, and standing still, makes eternity. If you add '*semper*' to 'eternity', you get sempiternity, the perpetual running resulting from the flowing, tireless now. (*DT*, 20.64-22.77)[3]

The definition Boethius presents and explains in *CP* and elucidates in the earlier *DT* is not original with him,[4] nor does he argue for it in those passages.[5] Similarly, we mean to do no more in this section of our paper than to present and explain a concept that has been important in Christian and pre-Christian theology and metaphysics. We will not argue here, for instance, that there is an eternal entity, or even that God must be eternal if he exists. It is a matter of fact that many ancient and medieval philosophers and theologians were committed to the doctrine of God's eternality in the form in which Boethius presents it, and our purpose in this section of the paper is simply to elucidate the doctrine they held.

Boethius's definition is this: *Eternity is the complete possession all at once of illimitable life.*[6]

---

[3] There are at least two misleading features of this passage. In the first place, Boethius says that God's eternality *always* has to do with present *time*. In the second place, Boethius's etymology of 'sempiternity' is mistaken. '*Sempiternitas*' is an abstract noun constructed directly on '*semper*,' somewhat as we might construct 'alwaysness'. His etymology is not only false but misleading, associating 'sempiternity' with 'eternity' in a context in which he has been distinguishing between sempiternity and eternity.

[4] Its elements stem from Parmenides via Plato, and Plotinus had already framed a definition of eternity on which Boethius's seems to have been based. See note 6 below. Cf. Romano Amerio, 'Probabile fonte della nozione boeziana di eternità', *Filosofia* 1 (1950), pp. 365-73.

[5] The argument that is concluded in the last sentence of passage *CP* is based on premisses about God's eternality and omniscience, and is not an argument in support of the definition.

[6] *Aeternitas igitur est interminabilis vitae tota simul et perfecta possesio'*, *De Trinitate*, p. 422.9-11. This definition closely parallels the definition developed by Plotinus in *Enneads* iii 7: 'The life, then, which belongs to that which exists and is in being, all together and full, completely without-extension-or-interval, is what we are looking for, eternity' (A. H. Armstrong (ed.), *Plotinus* (London and Cambridge, Mass., 1967), vol. 3, p. 304.37-39). The way in which Boethius introduces eternity suggests that he considers himself to be presenting a familiar philosophical concept associated with a recognized definition. The parallel between the Plotinian and Boethian definitions is closest in their middle elements: '*zoe homou pasa kai pleres'/'vitae tota simul et perfecta'*. Plotinus describes the possessor of this life, and Boethius does not; but, in view of the fact that Boethius is talking about God, he, too, would surely describe the possessor of eternity as 'that which exists and is in being'. The most interesting difference between the two definitions is that the Plotinian has 'completely without-extension-or-interval' and the Boethian has 'illimitable', which suggests that Boethius takes eternity to include duration but Plotinus does not. In the rest of *Enneads* iii 7, however, Plotinus goes on to derive duration from his definition and to stress its importance

We want to call attention to four ingredients in this definition. It is clear, first of all, that anything that is eternal has life. In this sense of 'eternal', then, it will not do to say that a number, a truth, or the world is eternal, although one might want to say of the first two that they are atemporal and of the third that it is sempiternal—that it has beginningless, endless temporal existence.[7]

The second and equally explicit element in the definition is illimitability: the life of an eternal being cannot be limited; it is impossible that there be a beginning or an end to it. The natural understanding of such a claim is that the existence in question is infinite duration, unlimited in either 'direction'. But there is another interpretation that must be considered in this context despite its apparent unnaturalness. Conceivably, the existence of an eternal entity is said to be illimitable in the way in which a point or an instant may be said to be illimitable: what cannot be extended cannot be limited in its extent. There are passages that can be read as suggesting that this second interpretation is what Boethius intends. In *CP* eternal existence is expressly contrasted with temporal existence described as extending from the past through the present into the future, and what is eternal is described contrastingly as possessing its entire life *at once*. Boethius's insistence in *DT* that the eternal now is unlike the temporal now in being fixed and unchanging strengthens that hint with the suggestion that the eternal present is to be understood in terms of the present instant 'standing still'. Nevertheless, there are good reasons, in these passages themselves and in the history of the concept of eternity before and after Boethius, for rejecting this less natural interpretation. In the first place, some of the terminology Boethius uses would be inappropriate to eternity if eternity were to be conceived as illimitable in virtue of being unextended. He speaks in *CP* more than once of the *fullness* of eternal life. In *DT*, and in *The Consolation of Philosophy* immediately following our passage *CP*, he speaks of the eternal present or an eternal entity as *remaining* and *enduring*.[8] And he claims in *DT* that it is correct to say of God that he is *always*, explaining the use of 'always' in reference to God in such a way that he can scarcely have had in mind a life illimitable in virtue of being essentially durationless. The more natural reading of 'illimitable', then, also provides the more natural reading of these texts. In the second place, the weight of tradition both before and after Boethius strongly favours interpreting illimitable life as involving infinite duration, beginningless as well as endless. Boethius throughout the *Consolation*, and especially in passage *CP*, is plainly working in the Platonic tradition, and both Plato and Plotinus understand eternal existence in that sense.[9] Medieval philosophers after Boethius, who depend on him for their conception of eternity, also clearly understand 'illimitable' in this way.[10] So, for both these sets of reasons, we understand this part of Boethius's definition to mean that the life of an eternal entity is characterized by beginningless, endless, infinite duration.

---

in the concept. For an excellent presentation and discussion of Plotinus on eternity and time, see Werner Beierwaltes, *Plotin über Ewigkeit und Zeit* (*Enneade* iii 7) (Frankfurt am Main, 1967).

[7] The many medieval discussions of the possibility that the world is 'eternal' really concern the possibility that it is sempiternal, and most often their concern is only with the possibility that the world had no beginning in time. Thomas Aquinas provides an important summary and critique of such discussions in *Summa Contra Gentiles*, bk. ii, chs. 32-8.

[8] See, e.g., p. 424.51-56.

[9] See Plato, *Timaeus* 37D-38C; Plotinus, *Enneads* iii 7 (and cf. note 6 above).

[10] See, e.g., Thomas Aquinas, *Summa Theologiae*, pt. i, q. 10. Augustine, who is an earlier and in general an even more important source for medieval philosophy and theology than Boethius and who is even more clearly in the Platonist tradition, understands and uses this classic concept of eternity (see, e.g., *Confessions*, bk. xi, ch. 11; *The City of God*, bk. xi, ch. 21); but his influence on the medieval discussion of eternity seems not to have been so direct or important as Boethius's.

The concept of duration that emerges in the interpretation of 'illimitable life' is the third ingredient we mean to call attention to. Illimitable life entails duration of a special sort, as we have just seen, but it would be reasonable to think that any mode of existence that could be called a life must involve duration, and so there may seem to be no point in explicitly listing duration as an ingredient in Boethius's concept of eternality. We call attention to it here, however, because of its importance as part of the background against which the fourth ingredient must be viewed. The fourth ingredient is presented in the only phrase of the definition still to be considered: 'The complete possession all at once'. As Boethius's explanation of the definition in *CP* makes clear, he conceives of an eternal entity as atemporal, and he thinks of its atemporality as conveyed by just that phrase in the definition. What he says shows that something like the following line of thought leads to his use of those words. A living temporal entity may be said to possess a life, but, since the events constituting the life of any temporal entity occur sequentially, some later than others, it cannot be said to possess all its life *at once*. And since everything in the life of a temporal entity that is not present is either past and so no longer in its possession or future and so not yet in its possession, it cannot be said to have the *complete* possession of its life.[11] So whatever has the complete possession of all its life at once cannot be temporal. The life that is the mode of an eternal entity's existence is thus characterized not only by duration but also by atemporality.

With the possible exception of Parmenides, none of the ancients or medievals who accepted eternity as a real, atemporal mode of existence meant thereby to deny the reality of time or to suggest that all temporal experiences are illusory. In introducing the concept of eternity, such philosophers, and Boethius in particular, were proposing two separate modes of real existence. Eternity is a mode of existence that is, on Boethius's view, neither reducible to time nor incompatible with the reality of time.

In the next two sections of this paper, we will investigate the apparent incoherence of this concept of eternity. We will begin with a consideration of the meaning of atemporality in this connection, including an examination of the relationship between eternity and time; and we will go on to consider the apparent incoherence generated by combining atemporality with duration and with life.

II. The Atemporality of an Eternal Entity: Presentness and Simultaneity

Because an eternal entity is atemporal, there is no past or future, no earlier or later, *within* its life; that is, the events constituting its life cannot be ordered sequentially from the standpoint of eternity. But, in addition, no temporal entity or event can be earlier or later than or past or future with respect to the whole life of an eternal entity, because otherwise such an eternal life or entity would itself be part of a temporal series. Here it should be evident that, although the stipulation that an eternal entity completely possesses its life all at once entails that it is not part of any sequence, it does not rule out the attribution of presentness or simultaneity to the life and relationships of such an entity, nor should it. In so far as an entity is, or *has* life, completely or otherwise, it is appropriate to say that it has present existence in some sense of 'present'; and unless its life consists in only one event or it is impossible to relate an event in its life to any temporal entity or event, we need to be able to consider an eternal entity or event as one of the *relata* in a simultaneity relationship. We will consider briefly the applicability of presentness to something eternal and then consider in some detail the applicability of simultaneity.

---

[11] Notice that these characteristics of a temporal entity's possession of its life apply not just to finite temporal lives but even to a temporal life of beginningless, endless duration—a sempiternal life.

If anything exists eternally, it exists. But the existing of an eternal entity is a duration without succession, and, because eternity excludes succession, no eternal entity has existed or will exist; it *only* exists. It is in this sense that an eternal entity is said to have present existence. But since that present is not flanked by past and future, it is obviously not the temporal present. And, furthermore, the eternal, pastless, futureless present is not instantaneous but extended, because eternity entails duration. The temporal present is a durationless instant, a present that cannot be extended conceptually without falling apart entirely into past and future intervals. The eternal present, on the other hand, is by definition an infinitely extended, pastless, futureless duration.

Simultaneity is of course generally and unreflectively taken to mean existence or occurrence at one and the same time. But to attribute to an eternal entity or event simultaneity with anything we need a coherent characterization of simultaneity that does not make it altogether temporal. It is easy to provide a coherent characterization of a simultaneity relationship that is not temporal in case both the *relata* are eternal entities or events. Suppose we designate the ordinary understanding of temporal simultaneity *T-simultaneity*:

(T) T-simultaneity = existence or occurrence at one and the same time.

Then we can easily enough construct a second species of simultaneity, a relationship obtaining between two eternal entities or events:

(E) E-simultaneity = existence or occurrence at one and the same eternal present.

What really interests us among species of simultaneity, however, and what we need for our present purposes, is not E-simultaneity so much as a simultaneity relationship between two *relata* of which one is eternal and the other temporal. We have to be able to characterize such a relationship coherently if we are to be able to claim that there is any connection between an eternal and a temporal entity or event. An eternal entity or event cannot be earlier or later than, or past or future with respect to, any temporal entity or event. If there is to be any relationship between what is eternal and what is temporal, then, it must be some species of simultaneity.

Now in forming the species T-simultaneity and E-simultaneity, we have in effect been taking the genus of those species to be something like this:

(G) Simultaneity = existence or occurrence at once (i.e., together).

And we have formed those two species by giving specific content to the broad expression 'at once'. In each case, we have spelled out 'at once' as meaning at one and the same *something*—time, in the case of T-simultaneity; eternal present, in the case of E-simultaneity. In other words, the *relata* for T-simultaneity occur together at the same time, and the *relata* for E-simultaneity occur together at the same eternal present. What we want now is a species of simultaneity—call it *ET-simultaneity* (for eternal-temporal simultaneity) that can obtain between what is eternal and what is temporal. It is only natural to try to construct a definition for ET-simultaneity as we did for the two preceding species of simultaneity, by making the broad 'at once' in (G) more precise. Doing so requires starting with the phrase 'at one and the same _____' and filling in the blank appropriately. To fill in that blank appropriately, however, would be to specify a single mode of existence in which the two *relata* exist or occur together, as the *relata* for T-simultaneity coexist (or co-occur) in time and the *relata* for E-simultaneity coexist (or co-occur) in eternity.[12] But, on the view we are explaining and defending, it is theoretically impossible to specify a single mode of existence for two *relata* of which one is eternal and the other temporal. To do so would be to reduce what is temporal to what is eternal (thus making time illusory), or what is eternal to what is temporal (thus making eternity illusory), or both what is temporal and what is eternal to some *third* mode of existence; and all three of these alternatives are ruled out. The medieval adherents of the concept of eternity held that both time and eternity are real and that there is no mode of existence besides those two.[13]

Against this background, then, it is not conceptually possible to construct a definition for ET-simultaneity analogous to the definitions for the other two species of simultaneity, by spelling out 'at once' as 'at one and the same _____' and filling in the blank appropriately. What is temporal and what is eternal can coexist, on the view we are adopting and defending, but not within the same mode of existence; and there is no single mode of existence that can be referred to in filling in the blank in such a definition of ET-simultaneity.

The significance of this difficulty and its implications for a working definition of ET-simultaneity can be better appreciated by returning to the definition of T-simultaneity for a closer look. Philosophers of physics, explaining the special theory of relativity, have taught us to be cautious even about the notion of temporal simultaneity; in fact, the claim that temporal simultaneity is relative rather than absolute is fundamental to the special theory of relativity.

For all ordinary practical purposes, and also for our theoretical purposes in this paper, time can be thought of as absolute, along Newtonian lines. But, simply in order to set the stage for our characterization of ET-simultaneity, it will be helpful to look at a standard philosophical presentation of temporal simultaneity along Einsteinian lines.[14] Imagine a train traveling *very* fast, at six-tenths the speed of light. One observer (the 'ground observer') is stationed on the embankment beside the track; another observer (the 'train observer') is stationed on the train. Suppose that two lightning bolts strike the train, one at each end, and suppose that the ground observer sees those two lightning bolts simultaneously. The train observer also sees the two lightning bolts, but, since he is traveling toward the light ray emanating from the bolt that strikes the front of the train and away from the bolt that strikes the rear of the train, he will see the lightning bolt strike the front of the train before he sees the other strike the rear of the train. 'This, then, is the fundamental result events occurring at different places which are simultaneous in one frame of reference will not be simultaneous in another frame of reference which is moving with respect to the first. This is known as *the relativity of simultaneity*'.[15]

We want to leave to one side the philosophical issues raised by this example and simply accept it for our present purposes as a standard example illustrating Einstein's notion of the relativity of temporal simultaneity. According to this example, the very same two lightning flashes are simultaneous (with respect to the reference frame of the ground observer) and not simultaneous (with respect to the reference frame of the train observer). If we interpret 'simultaneous' here in accordance with our definition of T-simultaneity, we will have to say that the same two lightning flashes occur at the same time and do not occur at the same time; that is, it will be both true and false that these two lightning flashes occur at the same time. The

---

[12] In the interest of simplicity and brevity, we will for the most part speak only of coexistence in what follows, taking it as covering co-occurrence too.

[13] The medieval concept of the *aevum* or of *aeviternitas* seems to us to be not the concept of a third mode of existence, on a par with time and eternity. See, e.g., Thomas Aquinas, *Summa Theologiae*, pt. i, q. 10, arts. 5 and 6.

[14] Our adaptation of this example is a simplified version of Wesley C. Salmon's presentation of it in his *Space, Time, and Motion* (Encino, Cal., 1975), pp. 73-81. We mean to do little more here than cite the example. An understanding of its significance for relativity theory requires a consideration of a presentation as full (and clear) as Salmon's.

[15] Salmon, *Space, Time, and Motion*, p. 76.

incoherence of this result is generated by filling in the blank for the definition of T-simultaneity with a reference to one and the same time, where time is understood as one single uniform mode of existence. The special theory of relativity takes time itself to be relative and so calls for a more complicated definition of temporal simultaneity than the common, unreflective definition given in (T), such as this relativized version of temporal simultaneity:

(RT) RT-simultaneity = existence or occurrence at the same time within the reference frame of a given observer.

This relativizing of time to the reference frame of a given observer resolves the apparent incoherence in saying that the same two lightning flashes occur and do not occur at one and the same time. They occur at the same time in the reference frame of one observer and do not occur at the same time in the reference frame of a different observer.[16]

Once this is understood, we can see that, if we persist in asking whether or not the two lightning bolts are *really* simultaneous, we are asking an incoherent question, one that cannot be answered. The question is asked about what is assumed to be a feature of reality, although in fact there is no such feature of reality; such a question is on a par with 'Is Uris Library *really* to the left of Morrill Hall?' There is no absolute state of being temporally simultaneous with, any more than there is an absolute state of being to the left of. We determine the obtaining of the one relationship as we determine the obtaining of the other, by reference to an observer and the observer's point of view. The two lightning flashes, then, are RT-simultaneous in virtue of occurring at the same time within the reference frame of the ground observer and not RT-simultaneous in virtue of occurring at different times within the reference frame of the train observer. And, Einstein's theory argues, there is no privileged observer (or reference frame) such that with respect to it we can determine whether the two events are *really* simultaneous; simultaneity is irreducibly relative to observers and their reference frames, and so is time itself. Consequently, it would be a mistake to think that there is one single uniform mode of existence that can be referred to in specifying 'at once' in (G) in order to derive a definition of temporal simultaneity.

These difficulties in spelling out even a very crude acceptable definition for temporal simultaneity in the light of relativity theory foreshadow and are analogous to the difficulties in spelling out an acceptable definition of ET-simultaneity. More significantly, they demonstrate that the difficulties defenders of the concept of eternity encounter in formulating such a definition are by no means unique to their undertaking, and cannot be assumed to be difficulties in the concepts of ET-simultaneity or of eternity themselves. Finally, and most importantly, the way in which we cope with such difficulties in working out a definition for RT-simultaneity suggests the sort of definition needed for ET-simultaneity. Because one of the *relata* for ET-simultaneity is eternal, the definition for this relationship, like that for E-simultaneity, must refer to one and the same present rather than to one and the same time. And because in ET-simultaneity we are dealing with two equally real modes of existence, neither of which is reducible to any other mode of existence, the definition must be constructed in terms of *two* reference frames and *two* observers. So we can characterize ET-simultaneity in this way. Let 'x' and 'y' range over entities and events. Then:

---

[16] It is important to understand that by 'observer' we mean only that thing, animate or inanimate, with respect to which the reference frame is picked out and with respect to which the simultaneity of events within the reference frame is determined. In the train example we have two human observers, but the example could have been set up just as well if the observers had been nothing more than devices, primitive or sophisticated, for recording flashes of light.

(ET) for every x and for every y, x and y are ET-simultaneous iff

(i) either x is eternal and y is temporal, or vice versa; and

(ii) for some observer, A, in the unique eternal reference frame, x and y are both present—i.e., either x is eternally present and y is observed as temporally present, or vice versa; and

(iii) for some observer, B, in one of the infinitely many temporal reference frames, x and y are both present—i.e., either x is observed as eternally present and y is temporally present, or vice versa.

Given the concept of eternity, condition (ii) provides that a temporal entity or event observed as temporally present by some eternal observer A is ET-simultaneous with every eternal entity or event and condition (iii) provides that an eternal entity or event observed as eternally present (or simply as eternal) by some temporal observer B is ET-simultaneous with every temporal entity or event.

On our definition, if x and y are ET-simultaneous, then x is neither earlier nor later than, neither past nor future with respect to, y—a feature essential to any relationship that can be considered a species of simultaneity Further, if x and y are ET-simultaneous, x and y are not temporally simultaneous; since either x or y must be eternal, it cannot be the case that x and y both exist at one and the same time within a given observer's reference frame. ET-simultaneity is symmetric, of course; but, since no temporal or eternal entity or event is ET-simultaneous with itself, the relationship is not reflexive; and the fact that there are different domains for its *relata* means that it is not transitive. The propositions

(1) x is ET-simultaneous with y.

and

(2) y is ET-simultaneous with z.

do not entail

(3) x is ET-simultaneous with z.

And even if we conjoin with (1) and (2)

(4) x and z are temporal.

(1), (2), and (4) together do not entail

(5) x and z are temporally simultaneous.

(RT) and the Einsteinian conception of time as relative have served the only purpose we have for them in this paper, now that they have provided an introductory analogue for our characterization of ET-simultaneity, and we can now revert to a Newtonian conception of time, which will simplify the discussion without involving any relevant loss of precision. In the first place, at least one of the theological issues we are going to be discussing—the problem of omniscience and immutability—depends on the concept of an absolute present, a concept that is often thought to be dependent on a Newtonian conception of absolute time. But the concept of an absolute present which is essential to our discussion is not discredited by relativity theory.[17] Every conscious temporal observer has an undeniable, indispensable sense of the absolute present, *now*, and that thoroughly pervasive feature of temporal consciousness is all we need. We do not need and we will not try to provide a philosophical justification for the concept of an absolute present; we will simply assume it for our present purposes. And if it must be said that the absolute present is absolute only within a given observer's reference frame, that will not affect our use of the concept here. In the second place, in ordinary human circumstances, all human observers may be said—*should* be said—to share one and the same reference frame, and distinguishing individual reference frames for our discussion of time in the rest of this paper would be as inappropriate as taking an Einsteinian view of time in a discussion of historical chronology.

III. Implications of Et-Simultaneity

If x and z are temporal entities, they coexist if and only if there is some time during which both x and z exist. But if anything exists eternally, its existence, although infinitely extended, is fully realized, all present at once. Thus the entire life of any eternal entity is coexistent with any temporal entity at any time at which that temporal entity exists.[18] From a temporal standpoint, the present is ET-simultaneous with the whole infinite extent of an eternal entity's life. From the standpoint of eternity, every time is present, co-occurrent with the whole of infinite atemporal duration.[19]

---

[17] On this issue see William Godfrey Smith, 'Special Relativity and the Present', *Philosophical Studies*, 36(3) (Oct. 1979), pp. 233-44.

[18] Since no eternal entity or event can itself be an element in a temporal series, no temporal entity or event can be earlier or later than the whole life or than any part of the life of an eternal entity. It is not clear that it makes sense to think in terms of parts of atemporal duration (cf. Aquinas, *Summa Theologiae*, pt. i, q. 10, art. 1, ad. 3); but even if it does, it cannot make sense to think of any such part as earlier or later than anything temporal. If the Battle of Waterloo were earlier than some part of atemporal duration, it would be uniquely simultaneous with one other part of atemporal duration, in which case one part of atemporal duration would be earlier than another, which is impossible.

[19] In the development of the classic concept of eternity, geometric models were sometimes introduced in an attempt to clarify the relationship we are calling ET-simultaneity. There is a passage in Boethius, for instance (*Consolation*, bk. iv, prose 6; *De trinitate*, pp. 364.78-366.82), which suggests that he took the relationship between time and eternity to be analogous to that between the circumference and the centre of a circle. Aquinas developed this sort of analogy in connection with an account of an eternal entity's apprehension of temporal events: 'Furthermore, God's understanding, just like his being, does not have succession; it is, therefore, always enduring all at once, which belongs to the nature of eternity. The duration of time, on the other hand, is extended in the succession of before and after. Thus the relationship of eternity to the whole duration of time is like the relationship of an indivisible to a continuum—not indeed of an indivisible that is a limit of the continuum, which is not present to each part of the continuum (an instant of time bears a likeness to that), but of the indivisible that is outside the continuum and nevertheless coexists with each part of the continuum or with a designated point in the continuum. For, since time does not extend beyond change, eternity, which is entirely beyond change, is nothing belonging to time; on the other hand, since the being of what is eternal is never lacking, eternity in its presentness is present to each time or instant of time. A sort of example of this can be seen in a circle. For a designated point on the circumference, although it is an indivisible, does not coexist together with another point as regards position since it is the order of position that produces the continuity of the circumference. But the centre, which is outside the circumference, is directly opposite any designated point on the circumference. In this way, whatever is in any part of time coexists with what is eternal as being present to it even though past or future with respect to another part of time. But nothing can coexist with what is eternal in its presentness except as a whole, for it does not have the duration of succession. And so in its eternity the divine understanding perceives as present whatever takes place during the whole course of time. It is not the case, however, that what takes place in a certain part of time has been existent always. It remains, therefore, that God has knowledge of those things that, as regards the course of time, are not yet' (*Summa Contra Gentiles*, bk. i, ch. 66).

We can show the implications of this account of ET-simultaneity by considering the relationship between an eternal entity and a future contingent event. Suppose that Richard Nixon will die at noon on 9 August 1990, precisely sixteen years after he resigned the Presidency. Nixon's death some years from now *will be* present to those who will be at his death-bed, but it *is* present to an eternal entity. It cannot be that an eternal entity has a vision of Nixon's death before it occurs; in that case an eternal event would be earlier than a temporal event. Instead, the actual occasion of Nixon's dying is present to an eternal entity. It is not that the future pre-exists somehow, so that it can be inspected by an entity that is outside time, but rather that an eternal entity that is wholly ET-simultaneous with 9 August 1974, and with today, is wholly ET-simultaneous with 9 August 1990, as well. It is *now* true to say 'The whole of eternity is ET-simultaneous with the present'; and of course it was true to say just the same at noon of 9 August 1974, and it will be true to say it at noon of 9 August 1990. But since it is one and the same eternal present that is ET-simultaneous with each of those times, there is a sense in which it is now true to say that Nixon at the hour of his death is present to an eternal entity; and in that same sense it is now true to say that Nixon's resigning of the Presidency is present to an eternal entity. If we are considering an eternal entity that is omniscient, it is true to say that that entity is *at once* aware of Nixon resigning the Presidency and of Nixon on his death-bed (although of course an omniscient entity understands that those events occur sequentially and knows the sequence and the dating of them); and it is true to say also that for such an entity both those events are present at once.[20]

Such an account of ET-simultaneity suggests at least a radical epistemological or even metaphysical relativism, and perhaps plain incoherence. We *know* that Nixon is now alive. An omniscient eternal entity *knows* that Nixon is now dead. Still worse, an omniscient eternal entity also *knows* that Nixon is now alive, and so Nixon is apparently both alive and dead at once in the eternal present.

These absurdities appear to be entailed partly because the full implications of the concept of eternity have not been taken into account. We have said enough to induce caution regarding 'present' and 'simultaneous', but it is not difficult to overlook the concomitant ambiguity in such expressions as 'now' and 'at once'. To say that we know that Nixon is now alive although an eternal entity knows that Nixon is now dead does not mean that an eternal entity knows the opposite of what we know. What we know is that:

(6) Nixon is alive in the temporal present.

What an eternal entity knows is that

(7) Nixon is dead in the eternal present.

and (6) is not incompatible with (7). Still, this simple observation does nothing to dispel the appearance of incompatibility between (7) and

(8) Nixon is alive in the eternal present.

---

[20] In *The Consolation of Philosophy* Boethius introduces and develops the concept of eternity primarily in order to argue that divine omniscience is compatible with human freedom, and he does so by demonstrating that omniscience on the part of an eternal entity need not, cannot, involve *fore*knowledge. See also section VI below.

and, on the basis of what has been said so far, both (7) and (8) are true. But Nixon is temporal, not eternal, and so are his life and death. The conjunction of (7) and (8), then, cannot be taken to mean that the temporal entity Nixon exists in eternity, where he is simultaneously alive and dead, but rather something more nearly like this. One and the same eternal present is ET-simultaneous with Nixon's being alive and is also ET-simultaneous with Nixon's dying; so Nixon's life is ET-simultaneous with and hence present to an eternal entity, and Nixon's death is ET-simultaneous with and hence present to an eternal entity, although Nixon's life and Nixon's death are themselves neither eternal nor simultaneous.

These considerations also explain the appearance of metaphysical relativism inherent in the claim that Nixon's death is really future for us and really present for an eternal entity. It is not that there are two objective realities, in one of which Nixon's death is really future and in the other of which Nixon's death and life are really present; that *would* be incoherent. What the concept of eternity implies instead is that there is one objective reality that contains two modes of real existence in which two different sorts of duration are measured by two irreducibly different sorts of measure: time and eternity. Given the relations between time and eternity spelled out in section II of this paper, Nixon's death is really future or not depending on which sort of entity, temporal or eternal, it is being related to. An eternal entity's mode of existence is such that its whole life is ET-simultaneous with each and every temporal entity or event, and so Nixon's death, like every other event involving Nixon, is really ET-simultaneous with the life of an eternal entity. But when Nixon's death is being related to *us*, today, then, given our location in the temporal continuum, Nixon's death is not simultaneous (temporally or in any other way) with respect to us, but really future.[21]

IV. Atemporal Duration and Atemporal Life

With this understanding of the atemporality of an eternal entity's existence, we want to consider now the apparent incoherence generated by combining atemporality with duration and with life in the definition of eternity.

The notion of atemporal duration is the heart of the concept of eternity and, in our view, the original motivation for its development. The most efficient way in which to dispel the apparent incoherence of the notion of atemporal duration is to consider, even if only very briefly, the development of the concept of eternity. The concept can be found in Parmenides, we think,[22] but it finds its first detailed formulation in Plato, who makes use of it in working out the distinction between the realms of being and becoming; and it receives its fullest exposition in pagan antiquity in the work of Plotinus.[23] The thought that originally stimulated this Greek development of the concept of eternity was apparently something like this. Our *experience* of temporal duration gives us an impression of permanence and persistence which an analysis of

---

[21] The claim that Nixon's death is really future rests on the assumption around which we all organize our lives, the view that the temporal present is absolute, that the expressions 'the present', 'the past', and 'the future' are uniquely (and differently) referring expressions on each occasion of their use, that 'now' is an essential indexical. On the notion of an essential indexical see John Perry, 'The Problem of the Essential Indexical', *Noûs* 13(1) (March 1979), pp. 3-21. We are grateful to Marilyn Adams for letting us see some of her unpublished work which brings out the importance of the notion of the absolute present in discussions of this sort particularly in the discussion we will take up in section VI below, and for calling our attention to Perry's article.

[22] Most clearly in fr. 8, as we read it. For excellent examples of both sides of the controversy over the presence of the concept of eternity in Parmenides, see G. E. L. Owen, 'Plato and Parmenides on the Timeless Present', *Monist* L (3) (July 1966), pp. 317-340; and Malcolm Schofield, 'Did Parmenides Discover Eternity?. *Archiv für Geschichte der Philosophie* 52 (1970), pp. 113-35.

[23] See notes 6 and 9 above.

time convinces us is an illusion or at least a distortion. Reflection shows us that, contrary to our familiar but superficial impression, temporal duration is only apparent duration, just what one would expect to find in the realm of becoming. The existence of a typical existent temporal entity, such as a human being, is spread over years of the past, through the present, and into years of the future; but the past is not, the future is not, and the present must be understood as no time at all, a durationless instant, a mere point at which the past is continuous with the future.[24] Such radically evanescent existence cannot be the foundation of existence. Being, the persistent, permanent, utterly immutable actuality that seems required as the bedrock underlying the evanescence of becoming, must be characterized by genuine duration, of which temporal duration is only the flickering image. Genuine duration is fully realized duration—not only extended existence (even *that* is theoretically impossible in time) but also existence *none* of which is already gone and *none* of which is yet to come—and such fully realized duration must be atemporal duration. Whatever has atemporal duration as its mode of existence is 'such that nothing future is absent from it and nothing past has flowed away', whereas of everything that has temporal duration it may be said that from it *everything* future is absent and *everything* past has flowed away. What has temporal duration 'does not yet grasp tomorrow but yesterday it has already lost'; even today it exists only 'in a mobile, transitory moment', the present instant. To say of something that it is future is to say that it is not (yet), and to say of something that it is past is to say that it is not (any longer). Atemporal duration is duration none of which is not—none of which is absent (and hence future) or flowed away (and hence past). Eternity, not time, is the mode of existence that admits of fully realized duration.

The ancient Greek philosophers who developed the concept of eternity were using the word '*aion*', which corresponds in its original sense to our word 'duration', in a way that departed from ordinary usage in order to introduce a notion which, however counter-intuitive it may be, can reasonably be said to preserve and even to enhance the original sense of the word. It would not be out of keeping with the tradition that runs through Parmenides, Plato, and Plotinus into Augustine, Boethius, and Aquinas to claim that it is only the discovery of eternity that enables us to make genuinely literal use of words for duration, words such as 'permanence' and 'persistence', which in their ordinary, temporal application turn out to have been unintended metaphors. 'Atemporal duration', like the ancient technical use of '*aion*' itself, violates established usage; but an attempt to convey a new philosophical or scientific concept by adapting familiar expressions is not to be rejected on the basis of its violation of ordinary usage. The apparent incoherence in the concept is primarily a consequence of continuing to think of duration only as 'persistence *through time*'.

Since a life is a kind of duration, some of the apparent incoherence in the notion of an atemporal life may be dispelled in rendering the notion of atemporal duration less readily dismissible. But life is in addition ordinarily associated with processes of various sorts, and processes are essentially temporal, and so the notion of an atemporal entity that has life seems incoherent.[25] Now what Aquinas, for example, is thinking of when he attributes life to eternal

---

[24] For some discussion of this analysis of time in Aristotle and Augustine, see Fred Miller, 'Aristotle on the Reality of Time', *Archiv für Geschichte der Philosophie* 61 (1974), pp. 132-55; and Norman Kretzmann, 'Time Exists—But Hardly, or Obscurely (*Physics* iv, 10; 217b29-218a33)', *Aristotelian Society Supplementary Volume* I (1976), pp. 91-114.

[25] William Kneale has taken this notion to be genuinely incoherent and among the most important reasons for rejecting the classic concept of eternity. See his 'Time and Eternity in Theology', *Proceedings of the Aristotelian Society* 61 (1960), pp. 87-108; also his article 'Eternity' in Paul Edwards (ed.), *The Encyclopedia of Philosophy* (New York, 1967), vol 3, pp. 63-6. Cf. Martha Kneal, 'Eternity and Sempiternity', *Proceedings of the Aristotelian Society*, 69 (1968-9), pp. 223-38.

God is the doctrine that God is a mind. (Obviously what is atemporal cannot consist of physical matter; we assume for the sake of the argument that there is nothing incoherent in the notion of a wholly immaterial, independently existent mind.) Since God is atemporal, the mind that is God must be different in important ways from a temporal, human mind. Considered as an atemporal mind, God cannot deliberate, anticipate, remember, or plan ahead, for instance; all these mental activities essentially involve time, either in taking time to be performed (like deliberation) or in requiring a temporal viewpoint as a prerequisite to performance (like remembering). But it is clear that there are other mental activities that do not require a temporal interval or viewpoint. Knowing seems to be the paradigm case; learning, reasoning, inferring take time, as knowing does not. In reply to the question 'What have you been doing for the past two hours?' it makes sense to say 'Studying logic' or 'Proving theorems', but not 'Knowing logic'. Similarly, it makes sense to say 'I'm learning logic', but not 'I'm knowing logic'. And knowing is not the only mental activity requiring neither a temporal interval nor a temporal viewpoint. Willing, for example, unlike wishing or desiring seems to be another. Perceiving is impossible in any literal sense for a mind that is disembodied, but nothing in the nature of incorporeality or atemporality seems to rule out the possibility of awareness. And though *feeling* angry is impossible for an atemporal entity—if feelings of anger are essentially associated, as they seem to be, with bodily states—we do not see that anything prevents such an entity from *being* angry, a state the components of which might be, for instance, being aware of an injustice, disapproving of it, and willing its punishment. It seems, then, that the notion of an atemporal mind is not incoherent, but that, on the contrary, it is possible that such a mind might have a variety of faculties or activities. Our informal, incomplete consideration of that possibility is not even the beginning of an argument for such a conclusion, but it is enough for our purposes here to suggest the line along which such an argument might develop. The notion of an atemporal mind is not *prima facie* absurd, and so neither is the notion of an atemporal life absurd; for any entity that has or is a mind must be considered to be *ipso facto* alive, whatever characteristics of other living beings it may lack.

V. The Notion of an Eternal Entity's Acting In Time

The difficulties we have considered so far are difficulties in the concept of eternity itself. We have by no means dealt explicitly with all the objections to the concept which have been raised in contemporary discussions; but many of those objections involve difficulties over simultaneity, and such objections can, we think, be dealt with adequately in the light of our previous discussion of ET-simultaneity. We hope, for instance, to have revealed the misunderstanding underlying such attempted reductions of the concept to absurdity as this one:

> But, on St Thomas' view, my typing of this paper is simultaneous with the whole of eternity. Again, on his view, the great fire of Rome is simultaneous with the whole of eternity. Therefore, while I type these very words, Nero fiddles heartlessly on.[26]

We want now to turn to fundamental difficulties in theological applications of the concept, particularly those which arise in considering the possibility of interaction between eternal and temporal entities.

---

[26] Anthony Kenny, 'Divine Foreknowledge and Human Freedom', in Kenny (ed.), *Aquinas: A Collection of Critical Essays* (Garden City, NY, 1969), pp. 255-70, 264.

There are several reasons for thinking that an eternal entity, as we have characterized it, could not affect or respond to temporal entities, events, or state of affairs. Just as an eternal entity cannot exist in time, so, we might suppose, (I) an eternal entity cannot act in time. It might seem, furthermore, that (II) the nature of a temporal action is such that the agent itself must be temporal. Nelson Pike provides the following case in point:

Let us suppose that yesterday a mountain, 17,000 feet high, came into existence on the flatlands of Illinois. One of the local theists explains this occurrence by reference to divine creative action. He claims that God produced (created, brought about) the mountain. Of course, if God is timeless,

> He could not have produced the mountain *yesterday*. This would require that God's creative-activity and thus the individual whose activity it is have position in time. The theist's claim is that God *timelessly* brought it about that yesterday, a 17,000 feet high mountain came into existence on the flatlands of Illinois.... [But] The claim that God *timelessly* produced a temporal object (such as the mountain) is absurd.[27]

On this basis Pike denies that God, considered as atemporal, could produce or create anything; whatever is produced or created begins to exist and so has a position in time. And it might be argued along similar lines that (III) an atemporal entity could not preserve anything temporal in existence because to do so would require temporal duration on the part of the preserver.

If God is taken to be eternal, considerations I, II, and III are incompatible with some doctrines central to most versions of theism, such as the divine creation and preservation of the world, and divine response to petitionary prayer. More specifically, they militate against the central doctrine of Christianity, since the Incarnation of Christ entails that the second person of the Trinity has a temporal nature and performs temporal actions during a certain period of time.

We think all three of these considerations are confused. In connection with consideration I, a distinction must be drawn between (*a*) acting in such a way that the action itself can be located in time and (*b*) acting in such a way that the effect of the action can be located in time. For temporal agents the distinction between (*a*) and (*b*) is generally nugatory; for an atemporal entity, however, (*a*) is impossible. An agent's action is an event in the agent's life, and there can be no temporal event in the atemporal life of God. But such an observation does not tell against (*b*). If an eternal God is also omnipotent, he can do anything it is not logically impossible for him to do. Even though his actions cannot be located in time, he can bring about effects in time unless doing so is logically impossible for him.

Considerations II and III may be construed as providing reasons for thinking that it is indeed logically impossible for an atemporal entity to produce temporal effects. Pike's version of consideration II, however, involves a confusion like the confusion just sorted out for consideration I. He says:

(9) '[I]f God is timeless, He could not have produced the mountain *yesterday*.'

(10) 'The claim that God *timelessly* produced a temporal object (such as the mountain) is absurd.'

Both these propositions are ambiguous because of the possibility of assigning different scopes to 'yesterday' and to 'timelessly' (or 'atemporally'), and the ambiguities can be sorted out in this way:

---

[27] Nelson Pike, *God and Timelessness* (London, 1970), pp. 104-5.

(9)(a) If God is atemporal, he cannot yesterday have brought it about that a temporal object came into existence.

(9)(b) If God is atemporal, he cannot (atemporally) bring it about that a temporal object came into existence yesterday.

(10)(a) It is absurd to claim that God atemporally brings it about that a temporal object came into existence.

(10)(b) It is absurd to claim that God brings it about that a temporal object came into existence atemporally.[28]

Apparently without taking account of the ambiguity of propositions (9) and (10), Pike understands them as (9)(a) and (10)(b) respectively. Propositions (9)(a) and (10)(b) are indeed true, but they do not support Pike's inference that an atemporal God cannot produce a temporal object. In drawing that inference, Pike seems to be relying on an assumption about a temporal relationship that must hold between an action and its effect. The assumption is not entirely clear; in some passages of his *God and Timelessness* it looks as if Pike thinks that an action and its effect must be simultaneous, an assumption that is plainly false in general regarding actions and their effects as ordinarily conceived of. But if we do adopt co-occurrence as a theoretically justifiable condition on causal connection between an action and its effect, we can point out that any and every action of an eternal entity is ET-simultaneous with any temporal effect ascribed to it. And, since it would simply beg the question to insist that only *temporal* simultaneity between an action and its effect can satisfy this necessary condition of causal connection, we see no reason for denying of an eternal, omnipotent entity that its atemporal act of willing could bring it about that a mountain came into existence on [yesterday's date]. Consequently, we can see no reason for thinking it absurd to claim that a divine action resulting in the existence of a temporal entity is an atemporal action. In other words, we think that propositions (9)(b) and (10)(a) are false, although they are legitimate senses of the ambiguous propositions (9) and (10). And so we reject consideration II as well as I.

Our reasons for rejecting these first two considerations apply as well, *mutatis mutandis*, to consideration III. If it is not impossible for an omnipotent, eternal entity to act in eternity (by atemporally willing) in such a way as to bring it about that a temporal entity begins to exist at a particular time, it is not impossible for an omnipotent, eternal entity to act in eternity (by atemporally willing) in such a way that that temporal entity continues to exist during a particular temporal interval.

A different sort of difficulty arises in connection with answering prayers or punishing injustice, for instance, since in such cases it seems necessary that the eternal action occur later than the temporal action; and so our reasons for rejecting considerations I, II, and III, based on the ET-simultaneity of eternal actions with temporal events, seem inapplicable. The problem of answering prayers is typical of difficulties of this sort. An answer to a prayer must be later than the prayer, it seems, just because

(11) Something constitutes an answer to a prayer only if it is done because of the prayer.

and

---

[28] These ambiguities, like the two interpretations provided for consideration I above, are of the sort extensively investigated by medieval logicians under their distinction between the compounded and divided senses of propositions. Thus (9)(a) and (10)(a) present the compounded senses of propositions (9) and (10), whereas (9)(b) and (10)(b) present their divided senses.

(12) Something is done because of a prayer only if it is done later than the praying of the prayer.

We think that (11) is true; (12), on the other hand, seems doubtful even as applied to temporal entities. If at 3 o'clock a mother prepares a snack for her little boy because she believes that when he gets home at 3.30 he will ask for one, it does not seem unreasonable to describe her as preparing the food because of the child's request, even though in this case the response is earlier than the request. Whatever may be true regarding temporal entities, however, if (12) is true, it obviously rules out the possibility of an eternal entity's responding to prayers. But consider the case of Hannah's praying on a certain day to have a child and her conceiving several days afterward.[29] Both the day of her prayer and the day of her conceiving are ET-simultaneous with the life of an eternal entity. If such an entity atemporally wills that Hannah conceive on a certain day after the day of her prayer, then such an entity's bringing it about that Hannah conceives on that day is clearly a response to her prayer, even though the willing is ET-simultaneous with the prayer rather than later than it. If ET-simultaneity is a sufficient condition for the possibility of a causal connection in the case of God's bringing about the existence of temporal entity, it is likewise sufficient for the possibility of his acting because of a prayer prayed at a particular time.[30]

The principal difficulty in the doctrine of the Incarnation seems intractable to considerations of the sort with which we have been trying to alleviate difficulties associated with an eternal entity's willing to bring about a temporal event, because according to the doctrine of the Incarnation an eternal entity itself entered time. If we take the essence of the doctrine to be expressed in

(13) 'When the fulness of the time was come, God sent forth his Son, born of a woman' (Galatians 4:4).

it is not difficult to see, in the light of our discussion so far, how to provide an interpretation that shows that, as regards God's sending his Son, the doctrine is compatible with God's eternality:

(13') God atemporally wills that his Son be born of a woman at the appointed time.

But the possibility of making sense of an eternal action with a temporal effect does not settle this issue, because the principal difficulty here does not lie in the nature of the relationship between an eternal agent and a temporal effect. The difficulty here is rather that an eternal entity is also a *component* of the temporal effect—an effect which is, to put it simplistically, an eternal entity's having become temporal without having ceased (*per impossibile*) to exist eternally. Formulating the difficulty in the doctrine of the Incarnation simplistically, however, simply exacerbates it. And whereas this formulation of it may present an insuperable difficulty for one or more of the heresies of the Patristic period that took the person of Christ to be only divine or only human, it is ineffective against the orthodox doctrines of the Trinity and the dual nature of Christ. A full treatment of those philosophically intricate doctrines lies outside the scope of this paper, but we will consider them very briefly on the basis of our limited understanding of them in order to suggest some reasons for supposing that the doctrine of the Incarnation is not incompatible with the doctrine of God's eternality.

---

[29] 1 Samuel 1:9-20.

[30] For a discussion of other philosophical problems associated with petitionary prayer see Eleonore Stump, 'Petitionary Prayer', *American Philosophical Quarterly*, 16(1) (Jan. 1979), pp. 81-91.

The doctrine of the Trinity maintains that God, although one substance, consists in three persons, the second of which is God the Son. The doctrine of the dual nature maintains that the second person of the Trinity has not merely one essence or nature, like every other person divine or human, but two: one the divine nature common to all the persons of the Trinity, the other the human nature of the Incarnation. One of the explicitly intended consequences of the doctrine of the dual nature is that any statement predicating something of Christ is ambiguous unless it contains a phrase specifying one or the other or both of his two natures. That is, the proposition

(14) Christ died.

is ambiguous among these three readings:

(14)(a) Christ with respect to his divine nature (or *qua* God) died.

(14)(b) Christ with respect to his human nature (or *qua* man) died.

(14)(c) Christ with respect to his divine and human natures (or *qua* both God and man) died.

From the standpoint of orthodox Christianity (14)(a) and (14)(c) are false, and (14)(b) is true. (14)(b) is not to be interpreted as denying that God died, however—such a denial forms the basis of at least one Christian heresy—but to deny that God, the second person of the Trinity, died with respect to his divine nature. Such an account is loaded with at least apparent paradox, and it is not part of our purpose here even to sketch an analysis of it; but, whatever its internal difficulties may be, the doctrine of the dual nature provides *prima facie* grounds for denying the incompatibility of God's eternality and God's becoming man.

A Boethian account of the compatibility of divine eternality and the Incarnation might be developed along these lines, we think.[31] The divine nature of the second person of the Trinity, like the divine nature of either of the other persons of the Trinity, cannot become temporal; nor could the second person at some time acquire a human nature he does not eternally have. Instead, the second person eternally has two natures; and at some temporal instants, all of which are ET-simultaneous with both these natures in their entirety, the human nature of the second person has been temporally actual. At those times and only in that nature the second person directly participates in temporal events. We need no theologian to tell us how rudimentary this outline is, and no other philosopher to tell us how paradoxical it looks; but we are not now willing or able or required by our main purpose in this paper to undertake an analysis or defence of the role of the doctrine of the dual nature in establishing the compatibility of divine eternality and the Incarnation. We hope simply to have pointed out that the doctrine of the Incarnation cannot be reduced to the belief that God became temporal and that, if it is understood as including the doctrine of the dual nature, it can be seen to have been constructed in just such a way as to avoid being reduced to that simple belief. And those observations are all we need for now in order to allay the suspicion that eternality must be incompatible with the central doctrine of orthodox Christianity.

---

[31] Although Boethius treats of the Incarnation and the dual nature of Christ in his theological tractates, especially in his *Contra Eutychen et Nestorium* (in Stewart, Rand, and Testor, 1973), he does not apply his concept of eternity in those discussions as we think it ought to be applied.

It seems to us, then, that the concept of eternity is coherent and that there is no logical impossibility in the notion of an eternal being's acting in time, provided that acting in time is understood as we have explained it here.

Questions

1. How does Eleonore Stump and Norman Kretzmann characterize Boethius' notion of God's "atemporal eternity?"

2. How do the notions of "presentness" and "simultaneity" come to be defined?

3. What is "E-simultaneity?" What is "T-simultaneity?" What is "RT-simultaneity?" What is ET-simultaneity?"

4. How does the Einsteinian conception of time figure in Stump and Kretzmann's discussion of ET-simultaneity?

5. How do Stump and Kretzmann develop the atemporal notion of eternity in giving account of the Trinity?

GOD, ETERNITY, AND THE NATURE OF TIME*

Alan Padgett

(Chapter 6: A New Doctrine of Eternity)

In this chapter of his book, Alan Padgett defends the notion that God is relatively timeless, considers objections to this view, and defends the idea that God is the Lord of time.

In this essay I wish to defend the intuition that God transcends time, of which he is the Creator. To do this, I will develop a new understanding of the term 'timeless eternity' as it applies to God. This assumes the inadequacy of the traditional notion of divine eternity, as it is found in Boethius, Anselm and Aquinas. Very briefly, the reasons for this inadequacy are as follows. God sustains the universe, which means in part that he is responsible for the fundamental ontological status of things. Because the universe is an ever-changing reality, things do change in their fundamental ontological status at different time—a change we must ascribe to God, and cannot ascribe to the objects themselves, since this has to do with their very existence. God himself, therefore, does different things at different times. This implies change in God. Whenever a change occurs, a duration occurs. Therefore, God is in time. But I do not think it is proper to say that God is in our time. God transcends time, and he is the Creator of our space-time. It is theologically more proper to say that we are in God's time, and I will adopt this language here.[1]

Time is notoriously difficult to define. Augustine's well-known lament is usually cited: 'What, then, is time? if no one asks me, I know: but if I wish to explain it to no one who asks, I know not.'[2] Richard Gale may well be correct, that it cannot adequately be defined.[3] In a very general way, one can think of time as a series of durations. A duration, in turn, is a series of related moments. I leave the notion of a 'moment' undefined, understood as some small part of a duration. Two things are clearly in the same time, then, if moments of their life are related (i.e. simultaneous, before, or after each other). 'Our time' will thus be any set of moments related to our 'now'. Of course these moves do not define time so much as plot out the interrelationships between the different words used concerning it.

With respect to eternity, there are a variety of ways in which this term cannot be unrelated in this way to our time, if God sustains our universe. For sustaining is a causal relation. If both cause and effect are temporal, a cause must be either before or simultaneous with its effect (those who believe in retrocausation may add 'after'; it does not affect the argument). Since both God and the world are temporal, and since God effects the world, the world must be in the same time as God. We are in God's time.

God is in himself temporal in some ways, because his relationship with the world. Further, because of this causal relationship, human beings are in God's time, and God is in the same time as humans. Does this mean, then, that God cannot be timeless? This depends upon what one

---

* A version of this paper was presented to the XVIIIth World Congress of Philosophy, Brighton, 24 August 1988. The author wishes to express his gratitude to the Society of Christian Philosophers, and especially to Professor Konyndyk, for this opportunity.

[1] This paragraph is a brief presentation of conclusions argued for at length in my Oxford thesis, "Divine Eternity and the Nature of Time."

[2] *Confessions*, 11.14.

[3] *The Language of Time* (London: Routledge & Kegan Paul, 1968), p.5

means by 'timeless'. God cannot, to be sure, be absolutely timeless. But one would still think that, as the infinite Creator of all things, including time itself, God would in some way transcend time. I will argue that this is in fact the case. God is relatively timeless, and eternal in a revised sense of the term.

God experiences real change in relationship with the world. Therefore, God must in some way be temporal. For whenever a change occurs the subject of the change goes through some interval of time. Therefore, God is not absolutely timeless, and the traditional doctrine of eternity must be abandoned.

Yet this answer does not fully satisfied us at some deeper theological level. As the infinite Creator of all things, including time itself, God should in some way transcend time. Transcendence, of course, is a metaphor like so much of our talk about God. In this chapter I will unpack the idea of God "transcending" time more fully. I hope to show three aspects of this transcendence: God's life is the ground of time; God is the Lord of time, who is unchanged by time and lives forever and ever; and God is relatively timeless.

God as the Ground of Time

A timeless world is not an impossible world. This much, at least, has been argued well and at length by defenders of the traditional doctrine of divine eternity. Duns Scotus and his modern followers have shown us the ways in which something could be "alive" in an absolutely timeless world. Since an absolutely timeless world is possible, and God could live in such a world, it follows that the actual world could have been timeless. This means, further, that God has chosen eternally to live the kind of life he does and has chosen eternally to have a temporal universe in which to live. This choice is an eternal one, in that it must have always been made. There is not time before which this choice was made.

God's choice, then, to live a certain kind of life—to be dynamic, active, changing—is the ground of the temporality of the universe. I have suggested that we understand time to be the dimension of the possibility of change. This dimension, like space, is a creation of God's. The world could have been different. God's choice (eternally) to live a certain kind of life, a temporal and changing life, is the ground of time. Time need not have been in God's creation. This is one way in which God transcends time.

God is the Lord of Time

To speak of God as the "Lord" of time is just another sort of metaphor, of course. What are the implications of this metaphor? First of all, it signifies that God has a design or plan which he is enacting in history. God is the Lord of heaven and earth, of time and eternity. Any changes that happen on earth do so because of the will and power of God, which sustain all changing things in their being. Even free and random events take place within the parameters established by God, and the things which undergo these random or free changes exist only because God causes their continued existence. Thus nothing happens outside the will of God, even though God does not will every event which takes place to happen in exactly the way it does. God sets the parameters within which all events take place, even those free events whose exact outcomes are not willed by God (i.e. are undetermined).

To say that God is the Lord of time would include the fact that he is not limited by any amount of time, either in the actions he can perform or the length of his life. While humans can fear the passage of time, because it brings them closer to the end of their life, God is everliving. He cannot die, and has nothing to fear from the future. Moreover, for God time does not press.

Because of his infinite wisdom and power God is not limited in the amount of things he can accomplish, or problems he can work through, in a limited period of time. Nothing happens outside of his will, knowledge and power. In this way God's relationship to time is radically different from our human experience of time as a limitation upon us. John Lucas wrote in this regard (*Treaties on Time and Space*, 306):

> To understand eternity therefore we should not think of it as timeless or changeless, but as free from all those imperfections that make the passage of time for us a matter of regret. God is the master of events, not their prisoner; time passes, but does not press.

For the Lord of time and eternity, time is a servant and not a master.

Related to the idea that God is Lord of time is the fact that he is a necessary being, unchanged by time, who lives forever and ever. In traditional language, God is *a se*, necessary and immutable. God cannot die, and does not change in his fundamental nature. The aseity of God, as I understand it, means that God does not owe his existence to any other being(s) or states of affairs outside himself. God's existence does not have a causal explanation outside of himself, nor does it depend upon anything or anyone else.[4]

As well as being *a se*, I understand God to be "metaphysically necessary." By this I mean that he is the cause or he is a cause of every logically contingent "fact," or state of affairs, at any time and at any place (cf. Penelhum, "Divine Necessity"). If any state of affairs obtains, then God must exist either at that time, or earlier, in order to cause it. Finally, I understand God to be immutable, in that he cannot change in his nature, character, or perfections.

The fact that something was not changed by time, for Aristotle, was an important part of its being "timeless." The understanding of divine eternity developed in this book implies the falsity of the old, absolute notion of the immutability of God which has always been associated with his eternity. But this does not mean that God is not immutable, when the latter doctrine is properly understood. God is immutable in his character, nature and perfections. Such is the way that I. A. Dorner understood the doctrine of immutability, in what is arguably the single most important discussion of this doctrine in modern times.[5] We are fortunate that such excellent work on the doctrine of immutability has gone before us, and further that this modern understanding of immutability dovetails well the doctrine of eternity I am developing here.

On this view, God changes, indeed, but only in relationship to a changing reality of which he is the creator and Lord. God does not change in his basic nature, in his character, or in his perfections. The necessary existence of God, on the one hand, is immutable and eternal, since it is not affected or effected by anything else. But with respect to his power, for example, God's activity changes in relation to the changing world he sustains: but the fact that God is omnipotent does not change. God is immutable, therefore, but he is not absolutely immutable in the Augustinian-Thomistic sense. Paul Helm (*Eternal God*, 86) helpfully distinguishes between accidental and necessary immutability, and between immutability of all predicates and immutability of a particular set of predicates. In my view, then, God is necessarily or essentially immutable with respect to a limited set of predicates, which are his character and perfections.

From the properties of aseity, metaphysical necessity and immutability, it follows that God exists forever. As Lord of time, God cannot cease to exist, since he is immutable and his being is

---

[4] I exclude from this, of course, "states of affairs" which are themselves entailed by "God exists" (see Swinburne, *Coherence*, 250, 266).

[5] Dorner, "*Unveränderlichkeit Gottes.*" Ware, "Evangelical Reexamination of the Doctrine of the Immutability of God" is a significant thesis which develops Dorner's view in dialogue with process theology. My understanding of immutability is in debt to Dorner and Ware.

not caused by any other beings or states of affairs. Since God exists, he can never fail to exist, being immutable and *a se*. Thus God will always exist, and always has existed. This is a further aspect of his being the Lord of time.

The fact that God is the Lord of time I have understood to mean that he has a plan or design for human history, and nothing takes place outside of his will; that he is not limited or changed in any fundamental way by the passage of time; and that he is a necessary being (*a se* and metaphysically necessary) who lives forever and ever. These are further aspects of his transcendence of time.

God as Relatively Timeless

Is the "Lord of time" in time? Is he timeless or not? These are questions that need careful attention. Is some duration in God's life ever simultaneous, before or after some duration of our time? If so, it will follow that God is in our time, since we have defined a time as the sum of related moments.

Now it is hard to see how two temporal things, even if they are in different spaces, can lack temporal relations if they are causally connected. Consider the following logical necessity:

(33) When both cause and effect are temporal, a cause must be temporally related to its effect.

Consider the case where V causes W, and both are both in time. V will normally (or always) be before W in time. Perhaps, if one holds to simultaneous causation, V and W may be simultaneous. If one holds to retrocausation, then W may be before V. These different positions exhaust the logical possibilities. The gravamen is the same in any case: if V causes W, and both are temporal, then some temporal relation must (logically must) hold between V and W. If, as I have argued is the case with God, no duration occurs between direct divine act and immediate effect, then the divine cause will be Zero Time Related to the created effect. Since God is temporal in himself, and he sustains the world which is a causal relationship, there must be some temporal relationship between eternity and time.[6]

I have spoken previously of God being in our time. Yet the gravamen of this chapter will be to argue that, in fact, God transcends our time. Since this is the case, it is far more appropriate to say that we are in God's time, than that God is in our time. Since God is the ground of time, this is another reason to speak of us being in God's time, rather than God being in our time. The latter expression, though philosophically acceptable, is theologically backwards. It is not the Creator that is bound by and included in the creation; rather, the creation is bounded by the Creator. It is the Infinite that bounds the finite, not *vice versa*. Therefore it is best to speak of creation being "in" God's time or eternity.

God is in himself temporal in some ways: does this mean he cannot be timeless? This depends upon what one means by "timeless." Aristotle thought that something was timeless if (*i*)

---

[6] This consideration answers the problem raised by H. J. Nelson, "Time(s), Eternity, and Duration," 9. He argues that "God's time" cannot contain a trans-universal present which contains in one "now" the quite different presents of two different universes which by definition do not have the temporal relations of simultaneity, before or after. But since God must create both universes in order for them to exist at all, and since creating and sustaining are causal processes, from God's perspective at least there will be temporal relations between the two universes, given principle (33) above. Either God will create one and then the other after that one; or else the histories of the two will overlap and some instants will be simultaneous with some instant in God's time. Since simultaneity is a transitive relation, the two worlds will either sometimes be simultaneous, or one will be wholly before the other. In both cases temporal relations will exist between the two worlds. Therefore, Nelson was wrong in the beginning to stipulate that two universes, both created by God, cannot have any temporal relations between them.

it was not measured by time, and (ii) it was not affected by time or "contained" by time. In a similar way, I have suggested that God is in fact both temporal and "relatively" timeless.

This revised doctrine of eternity is fully in harmony with the biblical witness about God and his eternity, as well as some of the early Greek philosophers. In fact, Scripture declares that "a thousand years in Your eyes are like yesterday when it passes, or a watch in the night" (Ps. 90:4); and "with the Lord one day is like a thousand years, and a thousand years like one day" (2 Pet. 3:8). Does this not appear to be something like our notion of God's relative timelessness? Some traditional foundation, then, can be given to the revised doctrine of eternity I am developing.

It is my purpose to argue, then, that God is "timeless" in the sense that his time is immeasurable, meaning that he is not in any Measured Time. Measured Time Words, therefore, would not truly apply in eternity. It could be possible, of course, for God to simply decree that a certain Measured Time would apply to his eternity. Perhaps he might do this to ease communication with his creatures. But this would be a wholly arbitrary convention, and would apply to the whole of eternity only because of the power of the divine decree, and not by anything in the nature of God's time.

The laws of nature, or better the law-like regularities of nature, are essential to the measurement of time. It is the laws of nature, among other things, that allow for the periodic processes that underlie isochronic clocks. Is God in any Measured Time? If not, does our Measured Time measure the eternity of God? I will argue that God is not in any Measured Time, and is not measured by our time, based on two considerations: (i) God is not subject to the laws of nature, as anything in Measured Time must be; and (ii) any Measured Time is relative to a particular frame of reference, which need not apply to God's time.

God is not subject to any of the law-like regularities of the natural order. As the Creator of all things including the natural order itself, God is of course not subject to any laws of nature. While the actions of God are not arbitrary, and thus not "random" in one sense, from the point of view of a Measured Time God's acts are "random." He does not conform to any order of nature that would cause him to repeat the same process over and over again in a uniform manner, as an isochronic clock is supposed to do. Further, any laws of nature that may obtain are contingent, and can be altered by God. How, then, can God be limited or contained by them, or by any measured Time dependent upon them? Since any Measured Time must depend upon the natural order, of which God is creator and Lord, God is not in any of himself in any Measured Time. There is nothing in eternity that could act as a kind of "intrinsic metric" for the time of God.[7] It would seem, then, that God is not in any Measured Time.

In and of himself, God cannot be subject to the laws of nature, as anything in Measured Time must be. Therefore he is not in any Measured Time. I also rejected, earlier, the notion of a Newtonian, "absolute time" against which God's life might be measured. There is no absolute "flow" of temporal measure which would act as an absolute guide by which any time, including God's, would correctly be measured.

But, an objector might urge, cannot the cosmic time of our universe itself act as a kind of "clock" in order to measure the duration of God's time?[8] After all, clocks can measure things that are fairly random and chaotic in themselves. It would thus seem that even if God is not subject to the order of nature, the universe might act as a kind of clock to measure some duration in eternity.

---

[7] I argue this in my article, "Can History Measure Eternity?" which is a reply to William Lane Craig, "God and Real Time."

[8] This is the main point of W. L. Craig, "God and Real Time," a reply to an earlier article of mine, "God and Time."

To develop this objection, suppose that God sustains two episodes of some object, $E1$ and $E2$. Say further that there is exactly one "Stund" between $E1$ and $E2$, a stund being a measure of cosmic time based upon the flow of fundamental particles. God changes in his power-to-act at moments of eternity Zero Time Related to the times of $E1$ and $E2$. Doesn't this mean that the term "one Stund" has meaning for God as he is in himself? The fact that God acts in our time, and his life is sometimes simultaneous with our time, the objection will go, means that the universe itself could act as a sort of clock to measure the duration of God's being. Since God must exist in order for $E1$ and $E2$ to exist, and since they are one Stund apart, doesn't it follow that God lived for one Stund? But if this is so, then God cannot be timeless, even in a relative sense.

The problem with this argument is, assumptions are made about how God is in himself based upon how God seems from a limited temporal perspective (i.e. a particular frame of reference). For while the temporal measure between $E1$ and $E2$ in the cosmic time of our universe is one Stund, it does not follow that $E1$-to-$E2$ is one Stund in some absolute sense which would apply outside our universe and its Measured Time system. $E1$-to-$E2$ does not have to be one Stund in God's time. In fact I would argue that the word "one Stund" does not have any meaning in a language which refers to things outside our universe, such as God, or angels, or some other universe God may have created. From the fact that $E1$ is before $E2$ we can only infer that the act which sustained $E1$ came before the act which sustained $E2$, in God's time. But it does not follow that $E1$-to-$E2$ is one Stund in God's time.

In fact, it does not even follow for some other created observers, moving non-linearly with us at velocities near the speed of light relative to their basic frames, that $E1$-to-$E2$ is one Stund long. The fact that $E1$ is one Stund before $E2$ is a contingent fact. Indeed, even cosmic time is a contingent matter, which holds for any actual, but not every possible, proper frame of reference. We know that $E1$ is in the light cone of $E2$: since they are episodes of the same object, there is a causal link between them which established a conical order. But because of the well known fact of time dilation, an observer moving at a velocity near c relative to her basic frame *will not* measure the duration between $E1$ and $E2$ as one Stund. If, then, for different observers in our own space-time the difference between $E1$ and $E2$ is not always one Stund, how can we insist (as the argument above does) that the duration between $E1$ and $E2$ will be one Stund *in God's time*? Such a conclusion absolutizes our cosmos, as though God could not create a thousand such universes, all with different times. A "cosmic time" is not the same thing as an absolute, Newtonian time. Cosmic time is contingent, and applies to our universe alone, and to a limited and particular frame of reference. We cannot conclude that it applies to anything beyond or outside our universe, unless some method of synchronization is set up (as it might be between different spaces in the same Measured Time). Since God is not of himself limited by any law-like regularity of nature (there is no intrinsic metric in eternity), no synchronization can be established. Thus the argument above fails, and we can conclude that, indeed, God transcends any Measured Time, and is thus relatively timeless.

If God is indeed relatively timeless, does this mean that any language about God using Measured Time Words is false or meaningless? Not at all. Dates, for example, are our way of pointing to certain moments. So the sentence "God created the world in 4004 BC" is true if God created the world during the time picked out by our dating system as 4004 BC. Likewise, "God has been sustaining the world for one hour" is true if God has been sustaining the world for the duration picked out by our Measured Time as one hour. We must insist, however, that such a convention is simply our human way of thinking and it does not mean that hours, seconds and minutes have any application to eternity apart from this convention. It is also true to say that God has always existed in eternity. But what we cannot give is a definite measure to how long that is. For that would be to give a measure to the divine Being, which is immeasurable and infinite. Thus God is not in any Measured Time, and therefore not in the same Measured Time as we are. In this sense, God is timeless.

In arguing that God is relatively timeless, I have stressed that fact that he is "outside" of our universe. Let's explore this idea further. What does it mean to say that God is "outside" our universe? Doesn't he act all the time "in" our history, and "on" our world? While God does act in our history and in our universe, he is not contained within it. God is spaceless, that is, he does not have any spatial location or extension. This is what I understand by God being "outside" our space-time universe. He is free, in himself, to ground our universe, without entering into it as a member of it.

Granted that God does transcend space and time, must God, of logical necessity, transcend both space and time? Another way to ask this is, couldn't God have a body? A body gives an agent some particular spatial and temporal location. A body is a limited mode of action and knowledge acquisition, through a particular lump of matter. Agents normally regularly act and know through their body, if they have one. Couldn't God have a "body" in this sense? Here I think we must trade on our fundamental intuitions about God. Would such a limited being really be God? We must ask ourselves the question, is the being we call God essentially (*de re*) omniscient and omnipotent? Are these properties incompatible with having a body? I frankly find nothing logically impossible in the person we call God having a body, being measured by our time, and having a particular spatial location as opposed to some other. I do not find this incompatible with the properties of omnipotence or omniscience. However, as Swinburne has persuasively argued, the universe as a whole does not function as God's body. And I do not think that, as a matter of fact, in the actual world God does have a body in this technical sense. The Christian doctrine of incarnation, to be sure, does not teach that God as a whole is fully embodied. So God does in fact transcend time and space—but he does not have to. Further discussion of this point would take us beyond the scope of our present topic.[9]

God, then, can enter into our space or Measured Time at will, but is not contained within it of necessity. And this is as one might expect, since God is the Creator of space and time. It is he that calls the universe into existence, and thus he cannot be limited by that which is wholly dependent upon him. God transcends both time and space. I have argued that he transcends time in that his life is the ground of time, he is the Lord of time, and he is relatively timeless.

Objections Considered

Having developed a new concept of eternity, it seems right to consider objections to it, since they will not doubt be raised in any case! It might be objected, first of all, that this revised understanding of eternity is not really a doctrine of time-*less* eternity, since it allows that God is in our time. If God is in some way temporal, how can we then assert that he is "timeless?" Against this objection, consider what the word "time" means in ordinary language. Expressions like "what time is it?" or "a long time ago" or "how time flies!" are examples of ordinary usage of the word in English. Some reflection upon the use of "time" in normal everyday discourse indicates that in normal usage "time" refers to Measured Time, to our history, and to physical processes. In the loose and popular sense, "time" does not mean an ontological category but the specifically human time of our history and our universe: the time of seconds, days, and centuries;

---

[9] For further discussion, see Grace M. Jantzen, *God's World, God's Body,* and T. F. Tracy, *God, Action and Embodiment.* Cf. R. G. Swinburne, *The Coherence of Theism,* 99-125.

the time of our space-time. When "time" is used in this popular sense, then, *God is timeless*. Although we are in God's time (and thus God is in our time, too) God transcends our time. I have tried to capture these insights by saying that God is (relatively) timeless. It is only when "time" is used in a very strict and narrow sense—when it refers to any sort of temporality—that the revised doctrine of eternity affirms that God is temporal.

Our basic question concerns divine eternity, not immutability, simplicity and perfection. But our partners in dialogue make some discussion of these last three divine attributes necessary. Thus each objection will be considered in turn, briefly looking at these three attributes as well. This will help to flesh out the revised doctrine of eternity which we are advocating. But a full and complete discussion of all these divine attributes would take us too far from our main subject.

I have already discussed the divine immutability. I understand God to be immuable, in the sense that his fundamental attributes, perfections and character—those attributes which he has eternally—cannot change or pass away. This, of course, is different from the traditional view of immutability, which states that God does not change in any way whatsoever. While acknowledging this difference, I deny that the traditional view is the only proper one.

The second objection arising from traditional theology concerns the divine perfection. If we allow that in eternity, God lives his life in stages, then God cannot be a perfect being as traditionally understood. As Aquinas wrote,

> anything in change acquires something through its change, attaining something previously not attained. Now God, being limitless and embracing within himself the whole fullness of perfection of all existence, cannot acquire anything, nor can he move out towards something previously not attained. So one cannot in any way associate him with change (ST, Ia, q.9, a.1).

According to the revised doctrine of eternity, God does change. It would thus seem that he cannot be perfect. If anything changes, it either diminishes in perfection or it grows in perfection, "attaining something previously not attained." Since God changes, one of these two options must be true. But if God diminishes, then he is no longer a perfect being. On the other hand, if God grows in perfection, he was not a perfect being in the past. Either way, God is not essentially perfect.

Granted that this is a valid argument, is it a sound one? Just because something changes, it need not diminish or grow in perfection. This is the point in the above argument that we can and should call into question. A thing can change in response to a variety of changing circumstances, without itself growing better or worse. And changes in God, remember, are a result of his decision to create a changing world and to be really related to it. Therefore God can change in some ways, and still be immutable and perfect. An example can clarify this point.

Say that "Milton" is the name of an essentially perfect poet. After writing a perfect poem on the beauty of nature, Milton then writes another poem on the pathos of human life. It too is a perfect poem. Let us stipulate that in writing these poems, the character of Milton does not change. He is the same in writing each poem, in this sense. Yet clearly Milton has changed in one sense, in writing the two poems. He changed from writing about and considering beauty, to writing about and considering human fate, suffering and death. And surely this is a real change in Milton—but it is not a change for the better or the worse. In both cases, Milton is still the perfect poet, and his poems are the perfect poems about their subjects. But the subjects of the poems are different. Now this example (which is not about historical Milton!) is coherent. And since it is coherent, something can change without either growing or diminishing in perfection. Thus it follows that the argument above is valid, but the conclusion is false: God can be perfect, and yet change in some ways. God can change in what he does, without changing who he is. God can be a perfect, immutable and timeless being, as I define these terms, even though he changes in relation to a changing world.

Traditional theologians will ague that God, as the source of all movement in other things, is himself unmoved. Nothing can affect, move or change God, since in order to affect God it would have to be stronger than God: which is impossible. What such an argument fails to consider is the idea that God might want to change himself, in order to be in relationship with a changing world (see further Ware, "Reexamination.") Now it was a principle of Aristotelian philosophy that nothing can move or change itself: but I see no reason to accept this principle, especially in the case of an omnipotent being. The ultimate explanation for why God changes can be found in himself alone, and in his will to be in relationship with his creatures. This fact is not true of created things. The answer to the third objection lies in this difference.

Traditional theologians will argue that a changing God cannot be the explanation of the world. For a changing thing requires an explanation of why it changes; the inference is, only an unchanging thing can be the ultimate explanation of all changes. Now on our understanding of his aseity and immutability, God is the ultimate explanation of change, including changes in himself. God is the ultimate origin of all changes, including changes that he himself undergoes in order to be really related to the world. The will of God, therefore, is the ultimate explanation of all change, including changes in God. Thus God does not require any explanation outside of himself, and this is certainly not true of changing things as we know of them in our world. The aseity of God means that he owes his existence to no other thing. Because of his aseity, God is not in the class of things that owe their existence or changes, ultimately, to things outside of themselves.

One might agree that things in the class of objects that owe their existence and changes to something outside of themselves, do as a class need some explanation. Let us agree, for the sake of the argument, that an infinite regress of causes in this class is inadequate as a complete explanation of the reality of the class as a whole. But this will only mean that God is not an element of the class of every changing thing which owes its changes to something outside of itself. It does not follow that God cannot change in some ways, namely in relation to a changing world. Further, since God is not a member of this class, he can be the ultimate explanation for the existence of the elements of this class, and the changes they undergo, without violating the insights of the traditionalist regarding the problems of an infinite regress of causes. Even given the point about an infinite causal regress being impossible (which could be questioned) God's will could still be the ultimate explanation for every event.

Anselm (*Monologion*, ch. 22) objected further to the idea that God changed himself, since a cause must precede its effect. This would mean that, if God changes, there was some aspect of the life of God that precedes another aspect; and further, that the prior aspect no longer exists, since it is replaced by the next stage in the life of God. Now on the doctrine of eternity we are developing it does follow that there will be stages in the life of God. Thus some stages in the life of God have ceased to exist in eternity. But Anselm objected to the idea that some stage in the life of God no longer exists, since this undermines the divine simplicity. So we now turn to this objection.

Traditionally, the divine simplicity has been defined as God being identical to all of his properties. This was made clear in my analysis of Aquinas, for example. None of God's actions can cease to exist, since the actions of God are identical with the essence of God, which necessarily exists. As Stump and Kretzmann put this Thomistic point, "the one thing that is God and is atemporally actual has a variety of effects in time…[These effects] are to be understood as various temporal effects of the single eternal act indentical [*sic*] with God" ("Absolute

Simplicity," 356. If we follow the revised doctrine of divine timelessness, and the doctrine of immutability in the tradition of Dorner which it implies, this conception of divine simplicity must be abandoned. But this doctrine seems more at home in a Neoplatonic theology, such a Plotinus's, than in the Biblical theology of a dynamic God passionately involved in history.

I have responded to the four arguments which arise from traditional theology, with its emphasis on God as the ultimate origin of things, and on his simplicity, immutability and perfection. One other traditional attribute of God is usually linked to his eternity, and that is his foreknowledge. We owe the emphasis on this link to Boethius. But space does not permit further discussion of this divine attribute, since it is so involved with a number of other philosophical and theological difficulties. The doctrine of divine timelessness is theologically distinct from the discussion of divine foreknowledge. One may first examine the problem of what eternity is, and then turn to the problems associated with foreknowledge. This, at least, is the order I have followed.

Having dealt with problems arising from traditional theology, other possible objections to the revised doctrine of eternity come from two recent books: David Braine, *The Reality of Time and the Existence of God* and Paul Helm, *Eternal God*. Braine's stimulating and interesting work takes up the task of proving the existence of God from the reality of temporal order. Most of what Braine discuses will not concern us here. But Braine's concept of God as "incomposite" is at odds with the revised doctrine of eternity. And like the present work, Braine bases his conclusions about God on the fact that God sustains the world of changing things. Thus some response is in order, if only because of the similarity of topics.

With Braine I agree that God is "intrinsically underivative," or as I have expressed it, God has the properties of metaphysical necessity and aseity. God is not the effect of anything or anyone else. But Braine also insists that God is "incomposite," by which he means to contrast temporal things, which are "composite." Braine explains the term "composite":

> Temporal things, and anything whose existence is caused or contingent, are (we may say) 'composite,' defining compositeness in these rather abstract terms: a thing (or, we shall equivalently say, a thing's existence) is composite if and only if the distinction between a thing and its existence is positively pertinent to the efficient causal explanation of the thing's existence (p. 148).

What this seems to mean is, that every "substance" in an Aristotelian sense has a "nature" and an "existence." The "nature" of a thing,

> as a quasi-abstract object in the case of what has a cause is part of the formal specification of the causal background to the thing *qua* external or prior ground of its possibility, and in this way has its quasi-abstract existence prior to the actual existence of the thing (p. 166).

Thus the "nature" of an effected substance is the set of properties of a substance which it must have in virtue of those causes which bring it into being. God on the other hand, is "incomposite," in that he has no prior "nature" which is in any way different from his active existence. Since anything which is temporal must be composite, argues Braine, God is timeless.

Braine explains that "if the central indispensable realization of God's life and existence is not successive, then despite the tensedness of our statements about God, it will be false to describe the reality or nature they indicate as in itself temporal" (p. 132). Here we have to disagree with Braine. God may not change on his account, and may not have any succession. But this does not affect the judgment that God is in our time (or as I prefer to say, we are in God's time). As long as God's life can be measured by our Measured Time, or is temporally related to our time, then God is in our time. And Braine explicitly rejects the idea that God is "in eternity" and only God's effects are "in time."

> [I]t is vital to maintain the dependence of the tensing of existential statements about substances on the tensing of predications of their actions—and vital that the time of God's actions is the time of its 'effects' (p. 131).

It seems then, from this quotation, that Braine ought to think that God himself is in our time, since his effects are in our time. Now the principle just cited, upon which Braine makes this conclusion, is wrong in our view. God can be in eternity, and his effects can indeed be in our time, without God himself being in our time. But if one accepts Braine's point, then one ought to maintain that God is everlasting in our time, and not timeless. On our own understanding of what it means to be in Measured Time, Braine's view of God ought to be that he is in our Measured Time, and not timeless even in a relative sense. This ought to be, since for him God's "substance" is certainly datable by the date of its effects, and thus God should be in Measured Time.

One further point should be made. While I am willing to grant that God is not "composite" in Braine's sense I cannot conclude from this fact alone that God is simple in the Thomistic sense, as Braine does (e.g. pp. 161, 223). In fact, Braine sets up a false dichotomy between temporal, mundane things as "composite," and God as the "incomposite" as he interprets it (viz. simple in the Thomistic sense). In his own terminology, I question the timelessness of the composite. In fact, I have demonstrated above that if God does sustain the world of time, then he must change in some ways, and cannot be incomposite as Braine has it.

In his recent book, *Eternal God*, Paul Helm objects to arguments for God's temporality, on the ground that, *mutatis mutandis*, such arguments lead to the conclusion that God must be located in space (ch. 3). Since I affirm both that God is not necessarily embodied, and that he is not absolutely timeless, Helm's indirect proof could have force against the position I am developing. So consider in brief the following argument for God's being temporal.

(34) God directly causes different effects at different times.
(35) Agents can only directly cause different effects at different times if they change their action.
(36) God changes his action.
(37) Anything that undergoes real change is temporal.
(38) Changing one's action is a real change.
(39) God is temporal.

If Helm's criticism is correct, then the above argument should lead to the conclusion that God must be in space, if terms for time are replaced by terms for space. These changes yield the following revised argument:

(34') God directly causes different effects at different places.
(35') Agents can only directly cause different effects at different places if they change their action.
(36) God changes his action.
(37') Anything that undergoes real change is spatial.
(38) Changing one's action is a real change.
(39') God is spatial.

While the first argument is sound, the second Helmian modified argument is not. (37) in the first argument is true, for example, while (37') is not. The difference between time and space ensures the absurdity of the second argument. God can spacelessly act directly upon two different places simultaneously, because two different places can coexist at the same time. But God cannot timelessly act directly upon things at two different *instants*, because two different instants cannot coexist (that is, cannot be simultaneous) at the same place. So Helm's criticism fails, and one can coherently hold that God is both not essentially embodied and not absolutely timeless.

I have considered objections to the revised doctrine of divine eternity, and found none of them convincing. Further criticisms may be forthcoming, but for now we can conclude that the concept is internally coherent, and congruent with other Christian doctrines (which the traditional view is not). In its essence, the revised doctrine of eternity rests upon the basic intuition that God transcends time, as its infinite Creator. God, then, exists in a "timeless time" which we call eternity.

Questions

1. What does Alan Padgett mean by the phrase, "God is the Lord of time?"
2. Padgett speaks of God as "relatively timeless." What does he mean?
3. For Padgett, could God have a body?
4. What is "measured time?"
5. In what sorts of ways is Padgett's view of God's eternity different from Stump's and Kretzmann's?

Bibliography:

- Anselm, St. 1903. *Proslogium Monologuum, An Appendix on Behalf of the Fool of Gaunilon, and Cur Deus Homo*. Trans. S.N. Dean. Chicago: Open Court.
- Aquinas, Thomas. 1964-1981. *Summa Theologiae*. 61 vols. Eds. T. Bilby, *et al*. London: Eyre and Spottiswoode.
- Augustine, St. 1961. *Confessions*. Trans. R. S. Pine-coffin. Harmondsworth: Penguin.
- Braine, David, 1988. *The Reality of Time and the Existence of God*. Oxford: Oxford University Press.
- Craig, William Lane. 1978. "God and Real Time." *Religious Studies*. 26: 335-347.
- Dorner, I.A. 2883. "Uber die richtige Fassung des dogmatischen Unveränderlichkeit Gottes." *Gessamelte Schriften*, pp. 188-377. Berlin: W. Hertz.
- Gale, Richard. 1968. *The Language of Time*. London: Routledge
- Helm, Paul. 1988. *Eternal God: A Study of God Without Time*. Oxford: Oxford University Press.
- Jantzen, Grace. 1984. *God's World, God's Body*. London: Darton, Longman and Todd.
- Lucas, J.R. 1973. *A Treatise on Time and Space*. London: Methuen.
- Nelson, Herbert J. 1987. "Time(s), Eternity, and Duration." *International Journal for Philosophy of Religion* 22: 3-19.
- Padgett, Alan G. 1991. "Can History Measure Eternity? A Reply to William Craig." *Religious Studies* 27: 333-335.
- Penelhum, Terrence. 1960. "Divine Necessity." *Mind*. 69: 175-186.
- Pike, Nelson. 1970. *God and Timelessness*. London: Routledge.
- Stump, Eleanore and Norman Kretzmann. 1985. "Absolute Simplicity." *Faith and Philosophy* 2: 353-382.
- Swinburne, Richard. 1977. *The Coherence of Theism*. Oxford: Oxford University Press.
- Tracy, T.F. 1984. *God, Action and Embodiment*. Grand Rapids: Eerdmans.
- Ware, Bruce. 1984. "An Evangelical Reexamination of the Doctrine of the Immutability of God." Ph.D. thesis. Fuller Theological Seminary. Partial published in the following essays:
- _____. 1985. "An Exposition and Critique of the Process Doctrines of Divine Mutability and Immutability." *Westminster Theological Journal* 47: 175-196.
- _____. 1986. "an Evangelical Reformulation of the Doctrine of the Immutability of God." *Journal of the Evangelical Theological Society*. 29: 431-446.

Figure 5

Part V

Miracles

OF MIRACLES*

David Hume

Hume provides the locus classicus *definition of a miracle as a "violation of the laws of nature." He goes on to show that belief in them requires greater credulity than their rejection, and if one really proportions one's belief to the evidence, one will not believe in miracles.*

I

There is, in Dr. Tillotsan's[1] writings, an argument against the *real presence* which is as concise and elegant and strong as any argument can possibly be supposed against a doctrine so little worthy of a serious refutation. It is acknowledged on all hands, says that learned prelate, that the authority either of the Scripture or of tradition is founded merely on the testimony of the Apostles, who were eyewitnesses to those miracles of our Saviour by which he proved his divine mission. Our evidence, then, for the truth of the *Christian* religion is less than the evidence for the truth of our senses, because, even in the first authors of our religion, it was no greater; and it is evident it must diminish in passing from them to their disciples, nor can anyone rest such confidence in their testimony as in the immediate object of his senses. But a weaker evidence can never destroy a stronger; and therefore, were the doctrine of the real presence ever so clearly revealed in Scripture, it were directly contrary to the rules of just reasoning to give our assent to it. It contradicts sense, though both the Scripture and tradition, on which it is supposed to be built, carry not such evidence with them as sense when they are considered merely as external evidences, and are not brought home to everyone's breast by the immediate operation of the Holy Spirit.

Nothing is so convenient as a decisive argument of this kind, which must at least *silence* the most arrogant bigotry and superstition and free us from their impertinent solicitations. I flatter myself, that I have discovered an argument of a like nature, which, if just, will, with the wise and learned, be an everlasting check to all kinds of superstitious delusion, and consequently, will be useful as long as the world endures. For so long, I presume, will the accounts of miracles and prodigies be found in all history, sacred and profane.

Though experience be our only guide in reasoning concerning matters of fact; it must be acknowledged, that this guide is not altogether infallible, but in some cases is apt to lead us into errors. One, who in our climate, should expect better weather in any week of June than in one of December, would reason justly, and conformably to experience; but it is certain, that he may happen, in the event, to find himself mistaken. However, we may observe, that, in such a case, he would have no cause to complain of experience; because it commonly informs us beforehand of the uncertainty, by that contrariety of events, which we may learn from a diligent observation. All effects follow not with like certainty from their supposed causes. Some events are found, in all countries and all ages, to have been constantly conjoined together: Others are found to have been more variable, and sometimes to disappoint our expectations; so that, in our reasonings

---

* This article is reprinted by courtesy of the publisher, is in *An Inquiry Concerning Human Understanding*, Oxford University Press, 1990.

[1] John Tillotson (1630-1694) was an influential Presbyterian theologian. He submitted to the Act of Uniformity (1662) and in 1691 became Arch-bishop of Canterbury. In later years, his sermons emphasized the practical side rather than the theological aspects of Christianity.-Ed.

concerning matter of fact, there are all imaginable degrees of assurance, from the highest certainty to the lowest species of moral evidence.

A wise man, therefore, proportions his belief to the evidence. In such conclusions as are founded on an infallible experience, he expects the event with the last degree of assurance, and regards his past experience as a full *proof* of the future existence of that event. In other cases, he proceeds with more caution: He weighs the opposite experiments: He considers which side is supported by the greater number of experiments: to that side he inclines, with doubt and hesitation; and when at last he fixes his judgment, the evidence exceeds not what we properly call *probability*. All probability, then, supposes an opposition of experiments and observations, where the one side is found to overbalance the other, and to produce a degree of evidence, proportioned to the superiority. A hundred instances or experiments on one side, and fifty on another, afford a doubtful expectation of any event; though a hundred uniform experiments, with only one that is contradictory, reasonably beget a pretty strong degree of assurance. In all cases, we must balance the opposite experiments, where they are opposite, and deduct the smaller number from the greater, in order to know the exact force of the superior evidence.

To apply these principles to a particular instance; we may observe, that there is no species of reasoning more common, more useful, and even necessary to human life, than that which is derived from the testimony of men, and the reports of eye-witnesses and spectators. This species of reasoning, perhaps, one may deny to be founded on the relation of cause and effect. I shall not dispute about a word. It will be sufficient to observe that our assurance in any argument of this kind is derived from no other principle than our observation of the veracity of human testimony, and of the usual conformity of facts to the reports of witnesses. It being a general maxim, that no objects have any discoverable connexion together, and that all the inferences, which we can draw from one to another, are founded merely on our experience of their constant and regular conjunction; it is evident, that we ought not to make an exception to this maxim in favour of human testimony, whose connexion with any event seems, in itself, as little necessary as any other.

Were not the memory tenacious to a certain degree; had not men commonly an inclination to truth and a principle of probity; were they not sensible to shame, when detected in a falsehood: Were not these, I say, discovered by *experience* to be qualities, inherent in human nature, we should never repose the least confidence in human testimony. A man delirious or noted for falsehood and villainy has no manner of authority with us.

And as the evidence derived from witnesses and human testimony is founded on past experience, so it varies with the experience and is regarded either as a *proof* or a *probability,* according as the conjunction between any particular kind of report and any kind of object has been found to be constant or variable. There are a number of circumstances to be taken into consideration in all judgments of this kind; and the ultimate standard by which we determine all disputes that may arise concerning them is always derived from experience and observation. Where this experience is not entirely uniform on any side, it is attended with an unavoidable contrariety in our judgments and with the same opposition and mutual destruction of argument as in every other kind of evidence. We frequently hesitate concerning the reports of others. We balance the opposite circumstances which cause any doubt or uncertainty; and when we discover a superiority on any side, we incline to it, but still with a diminution of assurance, in proportion to the force of its antagonist.

This contrariety of evidence, in the present case, may be derived from several different causes: from the opposition of contrary testimony, from the character or number of the witnesses, from the manner of their delivering their testimony, or from the union of all these circumstances. We entertain a suspicion concerning any matter of fact when the witnesses contradict each other, when they are but few or of a doubtful character, when they have an interest in what they affirm, when they deliver their testimony with hesitation or, on the contrary, with too violent asseverations. There are many other particulars of the same kind which may diminish or destroy the force of any argument derived from human testimony.

Suppose, for instance, that the fact which the testimony endeavors to establish partakes of the extraordinary and the marvelous—in that case the evidence resulting from the testimony admits of a diminution, greater or less in proportion as the fact is more or less unusual. The reason why we place any credit in witnesses and historians is not derived from any *connection* which we perceive *a priori* between testimony and reality, but because we are accustomed to find a conformity between them. But when the fact attested is such a one as has seldom fallen under our observation, here is a contest of two opposite experiences, of which the one destroys the other as far as its force goes, and the superior can only operate on the mind by the force which remains. The very same principle of experience which gives us a certain degree of assurance in the testimony of witnesses gives us also, in this case, another degree of assurance against the fact which they endeavor to establish; from which contradiction there necessarily arises a counterpoise and mutual destruction of belief and authority.

"I should not believe such a story were it told me by Cato"[2] was a proverbial saying in Rome, even during the lifetime of that philosophical patriot.[3] The incredibility of a fact, it was allowed, might invalidate so great an authority.

The Indian prince who refused to believe the first relations concerning the effects of frost reasoned justly, and it naturally required very strong testimony to engage his assent to facts that arose from a state of nature with which he was unacquainted, and which bore so little analogy to those events of which he had had constant and uniform experience. Though they were not contrary to his experience, they were not conformable to it.[4]

But in order to increase the probability against the testimony of witnesses, let us suppose that the fact which they affirm, instead of being only marvelous, is really miraculous; and suppose also that the testimony, considered apart and in itself, amounts to an entire

---

[2] [Reference is to Marcus Porcius Cato (234-149 B.C.), also known as Cato the Elder or the Censor. Of a stern character, he strongly favored Roman simplicity and opposed the influence of Hellenistic culture-Ed.]

[3] Plutarch in *Vita Catonis*. [This paragraph and the reference to Plutarch were added in Edition M]

[4] [This paragraph and the following note were added in Edition L.] No Indian, it is evident, could have experience that water did not freeze in cold climates. This is placing nature in a situation quite unknown to him; and it is impossible for him to tell *a priori* what will result from it. It is making a new experiment, the consequence of which is always uncertain. One may sometimes conjecture from analogy what will follow, but still this is but conjecture. And it must be confessed that, in the present case of freezing, the event follows contrary to the rules of analogy and is such as a rational Indian would not look for. The operations of cold upon water are not gradual, according to the degrees of cold; but whenever it comes to the freezing point, the water passes in a moment from the utmost liquidity to perfect hardness. Such an event, therefore, may be denominated "extraordinary" and requires a pretty strong testimony to render it credible to people in a warm climate; but still it is not *miraculous*, nor contrary to uniform experience of the course of nature in cases where all the circumstances are the same. The inhabitants of Sumatra have always seen water fluid in their own climate, and the freezing of their rivers ought to be deemed a prodigy, but they never saw water in Muscovy during the winter, and therefore they cannot reasonably be positive what would there be the consequence.

proof—in that case there is proof against proof, of which the strongest must prevail, but still with a diminution of its force, in proportion to that of its antagonist.

A miracle is a violation of the laws of nature; and as a firm and unalterable experience has established these laws, the proof against a miracle, from the very nature of the fact, is as entire as any argument from experience can possibly be imagined. Why is it more than probable that all men must die, that lead cannot of itself remain suspended in the air, that fire consumes wood and is extinguished by water, unless it be that these events are found agreeable to the laws of nature, and there is required a violation of these laws, or, in other words, a miracle to prevent them? Nothing is esteemed a miracle if it ever happens in the common course of nature. It is no miracle that a man, seemingly in good health, should die on a sudden, because such a kind of death, though more unusual than any other, has yet been frequently observed to happen. But it is a miracle that a dead man should come to life, because that has never been observed in any age or country. There must, therefore, be a uniform experience against every miraculous event, otherwise the event would not merit that appellation. And as a uniform experience amounts to a proof, there is here a direct and full *proof*, from the nature of the fact, against the existence of any miracle, nor can such a proof be destroyed or the miracle rendered credible but by an opposite proof which is superior.[5]

The plain consequence is (and it is a general maxim worthy of our attention) that no testimony is sufficient to establish a miracle unless the testimony be of such a kind that its falsehood would be more miraculous than the fact which it endeavors to establish. And even in that case there is a mutual destruction of arguments, and the superior only gives us an assurance suitable to that degree of force which remains after deducting the inferior. When anyone tells me that he saw a dead man restored to life, I immediately consider with myself whether it be more probable that this person should either deceive or be deceived, or that the fact which he relates should really have happened. I weigh the one miracle against the other, and according to the superiority which I discover I pronounce my decision, and always reject the greater miracle. If the falsehood of his testimony would be more miraculous than the event which he relates, then, and not till then, can he pretend to command my belief or opinion.

II

In the foregoing reasoning we have supposed that the testimony upon which a miracle is founded may possibly amount to entire proof, and that the falsehood of that testimony would be a real prodigy. But it is easy to show that we have been a great deal too liberal in our concession, and that there never was a miraculous event established[6] on so full an evidence.

---

[5] Sometimes an event may not, *in itself, seem* to be contrary to the laws of nature, and yet, if it were real, it might, by reason of same circumstances, be denominated a miracle; because, in *fact*, it is contrary to these laws. Thus if a person claiming a divine authority should command a sick person to be well, a healthful man to fall down dead, the clouds to pour rain, the winds to blow—in short, should order many natural events, which immediately follow upon his command—these might justly be esteemed miracles, because they are really, in this case, contrary to the laws of nature. For if any suspicion remain that the event and command concurred by accident, there is no miracle and no transgression of the laws of nature. If this suspicion be removed, there is evidently a miracle, and a transgression of these laws; because nothing can be more contrary to nature than that the voice or command of a man should have such an influence. A miracle may be accurately defined, a *transgression of a law of nature by a particular volition of the Deity, or by the interposition* of *some invisible agent.* A miracle may either be discovered by men or not. This alters not its nature and essence. The raising of a house or ship into the air is a visible miracle. The raising of a feather, when the wind wants ever so little of a force requisite for that purpose, is as real a miracle, though not so sensible with regard to us.

[6] [Editions K and L: "in any history."]

For, *first*, there is not to be found, in all history; any miracle attested by a sufficient number of men of such unquestioned good sense, education, and learning as to secure us against all delusion in themselves; of such undoubted integrity as to place them beyond all suspicion of any design to deceive others; of such credit and reputation in the eyes of mankind as to have a great deal to lose in case of their being detected in any falsehood, and at the same time attesting facts performed in such a public manner and in so celebrated a part of the world as to render the detection unavoidable—all which circumstances are requisite to give us a full assurance in the testimony of men.

Secondly, we may observe in human nature a principle which, if strictly examined, will be found to diminish extremely the assurance which we might, from human testimony, have in any kind of prodigy. The maxim by which we commonly conduct ourselves in our reasonings is that the objects of which we have no experience resemble those of which we have; that what we have found to be most usual is always most probable; and that where there is an opposition of arguments, we ought to give the preference to such as are founded on the greatest number of past observations. But though, in proceeding by this rule, we readily reject any fact which is unusual and incredible in an ordinary degree, yet in advancing further, the mind observes not always the same rule; but when anything is affirmed utterly absurd and miraculous, it rather the more readily admits of such a fact upon account of that very circumstance which ought to destroy all its authority. The passion of *surprise* and *wonder,* arising from miracles, being an agreeable emotion, gives a sensible tendency toward the belief of those events from which it is derived. And this goes so far that even those who cannot enjoy this pleasure immediately, nor can believe those miraculous events of which they are informed, yet love to partake the satisfaction at second hand, or by rebound, and place a pride and delight in exciting the admiration of others.

With what greediness are the miraculous accounts of travelers received, their descriptions of sea and land monsters, their relations of wonderful adventures, strange men and uncouth manners? But if the spirit of religion join itself to the love of wonder, there is an end of common sense, and human testimony in these circumstances loses all pretensions to authority. A religionist may be an enthusiast and imagine he sees what has no reality; he may know his narrative to be false, and yet persevere in it with the best intentions in the world, for the sake of promoting so holy a cause. Or even where this delusion has not place, vanity, excited by so strong a temptation, operates on him more powerfully than on the rest of mankind in any other circumstances; and self-interest, with equal force. His auditors may not have, and commonly have not, sufficient judgment to canvass his evidence; what judgment they have, they renounce by principle, in these sublime and mysterious subjects. Or if they were ever so willing to employ it, passion and a heated imagination disturb the regularity of its operations. Their credulity increases his impudence, and his impudence overpowers their credulity.

Eloquence, when at its highest pitch, leaves little room for reason or reflection, but addressing itself entirely to the fancy or the affections, captivates the willing hearers, and subdues their understanding. Happily, this pitch it seldom attains. But what a Tully [Cicero] or a Demosthenes could scarcely effect over a Roman or Athenian audience, every Capuchin, every itinerant or stationary teacher can perform over the generality of mankind, and in a higher degree, by touching such gross and vulgar passions.

The many instances of forged miracles and prophecies and supernatural events, which, in all ages, have either been detected by contrary evidence or which detect themselves by their absurdity, prove sufficiently the strong propensity of mankind to the extraordinary and marvelous, and ought reasonably to beget a suspicion against all relations of this kind. This is our natural way of thinking, even with regard to the most common and most credible events. For instance, there is no kind of report which arises so easily and spreads so quickly, especially in country places and provincial towns, as those concerning marriages, insomuch that two young persons of equal condition never see each other twice, but the whole neighborhood immediately join them together. The pleasure of telling a piece of news so interesting, of propagating it, and of being the first reporters of it spreads the intelligence; and this is so well known that no man of sense gives attention to these reports till he find them confirmed by some greater evidence. Do not the same passions, and others still stronger, incline the generality of mankind to believe and report with the greatest vehemence and assurance all religious miracles?[7]

Thirdly, it forms a strong presumption against all super-natural and miraculous relations that they are observed chiefly to abound among ignorant and, barbarous nations; or if a civilized people has ever given admission to any of them, that people will be found to have received them from ignorant and barbarous ancestors, who transmitted them with that inviolable sanction and authority which always attend received opinions. When we peruse the first histories of all nations, we are apt to imagine ourselves transported into some new world where the whole frame of nature is disjointed, and every element performs its operations in a different manner from what it does at present. Battles, revolutions, pestilence, famine, and death are never the effect of those natural causes which we experience. Prodigies, omens, oracles, judgments quite obscure the few natural events that are intermingled with them. But as the former grow thinner every page, in proportion as we advance nearer the enlightened ages, we soon learn that there is nothing mysterious or supernatural in the case, but that all proceeds from the usual propensity of mankind toward the marvelous, and that, though this inclination may at intervals receive a check from sense and learning, it can never be thoroughly extirpated from human nature.

"It is strange," a judicious reader is apt to say, upon the perusal of these wonderful historians, "that such prodigious events never happen in our days!" But it is nothing strange, I hope, that men should lie in all ages. You must surely have seen instances enough of that frailty. You have yourself heard many such marvelous relations started which, being treated with scorn by all the wise and judicious, have at last been abandoned even by the vulgar. Be assured that those renowned lies which have spread and flourished to such a monstrous height arose from like beginnings, but being sown in a more proper soil shot up at last into prodigies almost equal to those which they relate.

It was a wise policy in that false prophet[8] Alexander, who, though now forgotten, was once so famous, to lay the first scene of his impostures in Paphlagonia, where, as Lucian tells us, the people were extremely ignorant and stupid, and ready to swallow even the grossest delusion.[9]

---

[7] [This paragraph was published as a note in Editions K to N]

[8] [Editions K to N: "cunning impostor."]

[9] [The story of Alexander, the false prophet, as related by Lucian, is, in short, the following: Alexander, who lived in the 2nd century A.D., was the leader of a cult. Being desirous of building up a lucrative oracle, he manufactured a miracle before the eyes of the people of Paphlagonia. He made god Asclepius appear in the form of a serpent with a human head. To that end he hid a newborn snake in a blown goose egg on the temple grounds, and kept a fully grown tame snake hidden in his room. On the first day, he "discovered" the egg and had Asclepius born. A few days later, he invited the townspeople to his house, where it a dimly lighted room he displayed the full-grown snake, claiming this to be the snake god which a few days earlier "appeared to the city." This in itself seemed miraculous and gave credence to the major hoax, i.e., presenting the snake with a head which appeared human, The snake's head was kept under cover and was replaced by a head made of linen and painted to look human: its mouth could be opened and closed by means of horsehairs.

Lucian tells us that the scheme was successful. The miracle was repeated several times and seemed to have been generally accepted by the people of Paphlagonia, and found credence in other parts of the Roman empire. It should, however, be noted that Lucian is the sole source for this fantastic story.—Ed.]

People at a distance, who are weak enough to think the matter at all worthy inquiry, have no opportunity of receiving better information. The stories come magnified to them by a hundred circumstances. Fools are industrious in propagating the imposture, while the wise and learned are contented, in general, to deride its absurdity, without informing themselves of the particular facts by which it may he distinctly refuted. And thus the impostor above mentioned was enabled to proceed from his ignorant Paphlagonians to the enlisting of votaries, even among the Grecian philosophers and men of the most eminent rank and distinction in Rome; nay, could engage the attention of that sage emperor Marcus Aurelius so far as to make him trust the success of a military expedition to his delusive prophecies.

The advantages are so great of starting an imposture among an ignorant people that, even though the delusion should be too gross to impose on the generality of them (*which, though seldom, is sometimes the case*), it has a much better chance for succeeding in remote countries than if the first scene had been laid in a city renowned for arts and knowledge. The most ignorant and barbarous of these barbarians carry the report abroad. None, of their countrymen have a large correspondence or sufficient credit and authority to contradict and beat down the delusion. Men's inclination to the marvelous has full opportunity to display itself. And thus a story which universally exploded in the place where it was first started shall pass far certain at a thousand miles distance. But had Alexander fixed his residence at Athens, the philosophers at that renowned mart of learning had immediately spread throughout the whole Roman empire their sense of the matter, which, being supported by so great authority and displayed by all the force of reason and eloquence, had entirely opened the eyes of mankind. It is true, Lucian, passing by chance through Paphlagonia, had an opportunity of performing this good office. But, though much to be wished, it does not always happen that every Alexander meets with a Lucian, ready to expose and detect his impostures.[10]

I may add, as a *fourth* reason which diminishes the authority of prodigies, that there is no testimony for any, even those which have not been expressly detected, that is not opposed by any infinite number of witnesses, so that not only the miracle destroys the credit of testimony, but the testimony destroys itself. To make this the better understood, let us consider that in matters of religion whatever is different is contrary, and that it is impossible the religions of ancient Rome, of Turkey, of Siam, and of China should all of them be established on any solid foundation. Every miracle, therefore, pretended to have been wrought in any of these religions (and all of them abound in miracles), as its direct scope is to establish the particular system to which it is attributed, so has it the same force, though more indirectly, to overthrow every other system. In destroying a rival system, it likewise destroys the credit of those miracles on which that system was established, so that all the prodigies of different religions are to be regarded as contrary facts, and the evidences of these prodigies, whether weak or strong, as opposite to each other. According to this method of reasoning, when we believe any miracle of Mahomet or his successors, we have for our warrant the testimony of a few barbarous Arabians. And, on the other hand, we are to regard

---

[10] It may perhaps be objected that I proceed rashly and form my notions of Alexander merely from the account given of him by Lucian, a professed enemy. It were indeed to be wished that some of the accounts published by his followers and accomplices had remained. The opposition and contrast betwixt the character and conduct of the same man as drawn by a friend or an enemy is as strong, even in common life, much more in these religious matters, as that betwixt any two men in the world; betwixt Alexander and St. Paul, for instance. See a *Letter to Gilbert West*, Esq., on the *Conversion and Apostleship of St. Paul*. [Note in the Editions prior to O.]

the authority of Titus Livius, Plutarch, Tacitus, and, in short, of all the authors and witnesses, Grecian, Chinese, and Roman Catholic, who have related any miracle in their particular religion—I say we are to regard their testimony in the same light as if they had mentioned the Mahometan miracle and had in express terms contradicted it with the same certainty as they have for the miracle they relate. This argument may appear oversubtile and refined, but is not in reality different from the reasoning of a judge who supposes that the credit of two witnesses maintaining a crime against anyone is destroyed by the testimony of two others who affirm him to have been two hundred leagues distant at the same instant when the crime is said to have been committed.

One of the best-attested miracles in all profane history is that which Tacitus reports of Vespasian, who cured a blind man in Alexandria by means of his spittle, and a lame man by the mere touch of his foot, in obedience to a vision of the god Serapis, who had enjoined them to have recourse to the emperor for these miraculous cures. The story may be seen in that fine historian,[11] where every circumstance seems to add weight to the testimony, and might be displayed at large with all the force of argument and eloquence, if anyone were now concerned to enforce the evidence of that exploded and idolatrous superstition: The gravity, solidity, age, and probity of so great an emperor, who, through the whole course of his life, conversed in a familiar manner with his friends and courtiers, and never affected those extraordinary airs of divinity assumed by Alexander and Demetrius; the historian, a contemporary writer noted for candor and veracity, and withal the greatest and most penetrating genius perhaps of all antiquity, and so free from any tendency to credulity that he even lies under the contrary imputation of atheism and profaneness; the persons from whose authority he related the miracle, of established character for judgment and veracity, as we may well presume; eyewitnesses of the fact, and confirming their testimony after the Flavian family was despoiled of the empire and could no longer give any reward as the price of a lie. *Utrumaque, qui inteafuere, nunc quoque memorant, postquam nullum mendacio pretium.*[12] To which, if we add the public nature of the facts, as related, it will appear that no evidence can well be supposed stronger for so gross and so palpable a falsehood.

There is also a memorable story related by Cardinal De Retz, which may well deserve our consideration. When that intriguing politician fled into Spain to avoid the persecution of his enemies, he passed through Saragossa, the capital of Aragon, where he was shown, in the cathedral, a man who had served seven[13] years as a doorkeeper and was well known to everybody in town that had ever paid his devotions at that church. He had been seen for so long a time wanting a leg; but recovered that limb by the rubbing of holy oil upon the stump; and the Cardinal assures us that he saw him with two legs. This miracle was vouched by all the canons of the church; and the whole company in town were appealed to for a confirmation of the fact, whom the Cardinal found, by their zealous devotion, to be thorough believers of the miracle. Here the relater was also contemporary to the supposed prodigy, of an incredulous and libertine character as well as of great genius; the miracle of so *singular* a nature as could scarcely admit of a counterfeit, and the witnesses very numerous, and all of them, in a manner, spectators of the fact to which they gave their testimony. And what adds mightily to the force of the evidence, and may double our surprise on this occasion, is that the Cardinal himself, who relates the story, seems not to give any credit to it and, consequently, cannot be suspected of any concurrence in the holy fraud. He considered justly that it was not requisite, in order to reject a fact of this nature, to be able accurately to disprove the testimony and to trace its falsehood through all the

---

[11] Hist. lib. V. cap. 8. Suetonius gives nearly the same account in *Vita Vesp*. [Added in Edition L.]

[12] ("Those who were present mention both incidents even now, when there is no longer any reward for telling a lie."- Ed.]

[13] [Editions prior to N read "twenty."]

circumstances of knavery and credulity which produced it. He knew that, as this was commonly altogether impossible at any small distance of time and place, so was it extremely difficult, even where one was immediately present, by reason of the bigotry, ignorance, cunning, and roguery of a great part of mankind. He therefore concluded, like a just reasoner, that such an evidence carried falsehood upon the very face of it, and that a miracle, supported by any human testimony, was more properly a subject of derision than of argument.

There surely never was a greater number of miracles ascribed to one person than those which were lately said to have been wrought in France upon the tomb of Abbé Paris, the famous Jansenist, with whose sanctity the people were so long deluded. The curing of the sick, giving hearing to the deaf and sight to the blind, were everywhere talked of as the usual effects of that holy sepulcher. But what is more extraordinary, many of the miracles were immediately proved upon the spot, before judges of unquestioned integrity, attested by witnesses of credit and distinction, in a learned age, and at the most eminent theater that is now in the world. Nor is this all: a relation of them was published and dispersed everywhere, nor were the Jesuits, though a learned body supported by the civil magistrate, and determined enemies to those opinions in whose favor the miracles were said to have been wrought, ever able distinctly to refute or detect them.[14] Where shall we find such a number of circumstances agreeing to the corroboration of one

---

[14] This book was written by Mons. Montgeron, counselor or judge of the parliament of Paris, a man of figure and character who was also a martyr to the cause, and is now said to be somewhere in a dungeon on account of his book.

There is another book in three volumes (called *Recueil des Miracles de l'Abbé Paris*) giving an account of many of these miracles, and accompanied with prefatory discourses, which are very well written. There runs, however, through the whole of these a ridiculous comparison between the miracles of our Saviour and those of the Abbé, wherein it is asserted that the evidence for the latter is equal to that for the former, as if the testimony of men could ever be put in the balance with that of God himself, who conducted the pen of the inspired writers. If these writers indeed were to be considered merely as human testimony, the French author is very moderate in his comparison, since he might, with some appearance of reason, pretend that the Jansenist miracles much surpass the other in evidence and authority. The following circumstances are drawn from authentic papers, inserted in the above-mentioned book.

Many of the miracles of Abbé Paris were proved immediately by witnesses before the officiality, or bishop's court, at Paris, under the eye of Cardinal Noailles, whose character for integrity and capacity was never contested, even by his enemies.

His successor in the archbishopric was an enemy to the Jansenists, and for that reason promoted to the See by the Court. Yet twenty-two rectors or *curés* of Paris, with infinite earnestness, press him to examine those miracles which they assert to be known to the whole world, and indisputably certain. But he wisely forbore.

The Molinist party had tried to discredit these miracles in one instance, that of Mademoiselle la Franc. But besides that their proceedings were in many respects the most irregular in the world, particularly in citing only a few of the Jansenist witnesses whom they tampered with—besides this, I say, they soon found themselves overwhelmed by a cloud of new witnesses, one hundred and twenty in number, most of them persons of credit and substance in Paris, who gave oath for the miracle. This was accompanied with a solemn and earnest appeal to the parliament. But the parliament were forbidden, by authority, to meddle in the affair. It was at last observed that where men are heated by zeal and enthusiasm, there is no degree of human testimony so strong as may not be procured for the greatest absurdity. And those who will be so silly as to examine the affair by that medium and seek particular flaws in the testimony are almost sure to be confounded. It must be a miserable imposture, indeed, that does not prevail in that contest.

All who have been to France about that time have heard about the reputation of Mons. Herault, the *Lieutenant de Police*, whose vigilance, penetration, activity, and extensive intelligence have been much talked of. This magistrate, who by the nature of his office is almost absolute, was invested with full powers on purpose to suppress or discredit these miracles, and he frequently seized immediately and examined the witnesses and subjects of them, but never could reach anything satisfactory against them.

In the case of Mademoiselle Thibaut, he sent the famous De Sylva to examine her, whose evidence is very curious. The physician declares that it was impossible she could have been so ill as was proved by witnesses, because it was impossible she could, in so short a time, have recovered so perfectly as he found her. He reasoned, like a man of sense, from natural causes, but the opposite party told him that the whole was a miracle, and that his evidence was the very best proof of it.

fact? And what have we to oppose to such a cloud of witnesses but the absolute impossibility or miraculous nature of the events which they relate? And this, surely, in the eyes of all reasonable people, will alone be regarded as a sufficient refutation.

Is the consequence just because some human testimony has the utmost force and authority in some cases, when it relates the battles of Philippi or Pharsalia, for instance, that therefore all kinds of testimony must in all cases have equal force and authority? Suppose that the Caesarean or Pompeian factions had, each of them, claimed the victory in these battles, and that the historians of each party had uniformly ascribed the advantage to their own side, how could mankind, at this distance, have been able to determine between them? The contrariety is equally strong between the miracles related by Herodotus or Plutarch, and those delivered by Mariana, Bede, or any monkish historian.

The wise lend a very academic faith to every report which favors the passion of the reported, whether it magnifies his country, his family, or. himself, or in any other way strikes in with his natural inclinations and propensities. But what greater temptation than to appear a missionary, a prophet, an ambassador from heaven? Who would not encounter many dangers and difficulties in order to attain, so sublime a character? Or if, by the help of vanity and a heated imagination, a man has first made a convert of himself and entered seriously into the

---

The Molinists were in a sad dilemma. They durst not assert the absolute insufficiency of human evidence to prove a miracle. They were obliged to say that these miracles were wrought by witchcraft and the devil. But they were told that this was the resource of the Jews of old.

No Jansenist was ever embarrassed to account for the cessation of the miracles when the churchyard was shut up by the king's edict. It was the touch of the tomb which produced these extraordinary effects; and when no one could approach the tomb, no effects could he expected. God, indeed, could have thrown down the walls in a moment, but he is master of his own graces and works, and it belongs not to us to account for them. He did not throw down the walls of every city, like those of Jericho, on the sounding of the rams' horns, nor break up the prison of every apostle, like that of St. Paul.

No less a man than the Duc de Chatlilon, a duke and peer of France, of the highest rank and family, gives evidence of a miraculous cure, performed upon a servant of his who had lived several years in his house with a visible and palpable infirmity.

I shall conclude with observing that no clergy are more celebrated for strictness of life and manner than the secular clergy of France, particularly the rectors or curés of Paris who bear testimony to these impostures.
The learning, genius, and probity of the gentlemen, and the austerity of the nuns of Port Royal, have been much celebrated all over Europe. Yet they all give evidence for a miracle wrought on the niece of the famous Pascal, whose sanctity of life, as well as extraordinary capacity, is well known. The famous Racine gives an account of this miracle in his famous history of Port Royal, and fortifies it with all tile proofs which a multitude of nuns, priests, physicians, and men of the world, all of them of undoubted credit, could bestow upon it. Several men of letters, particularly the bishop of Tournay, thought this miracle so certain as to employ it in the refutation of atheists and freethinkers. The queen-regent of France, who was extremely prejudiced against the Port Royal, sent her own physician to examine the miracle, who returned an absolute convert. In short, the supernatural cure was so incontestable that it saved, for a time, that famous monastery from the rain with which it was threatened by the Jesuits, Had it been a cheat, it had certainly been detected by such sagacious and powerful antagonists, and must have hastened the ruin of the contrivers. Our divines, who can build up a formidable castle upon such despicable materials—what a prodigious fabric could they have reared from these and many other circumstances which I have not mentioned! How often would the great names of Pascal, Ratcne, Arnaud, Nicole have resounded in our ears? But if they be wise, they had better adopt the miracle as being more worth a thousand times than all the rest of their collection. Besides, it may serve very much to their purpose. For that miracle was really performed by the touch of an authentic holy prickle of the holy thorn which composed the holy crown, which, etc. [*This note first occurs in Edition L, and the conclusion regarding the Port Royal miracle, beginning "The famous Racine," in Edition N.*]

° Edition L, adds here: "Though he also was a believer in that and many other miracles which he had less opportunity of being informed of. See his Life."

delusion, who ever scruples to make use of pious frauds in support of so holy and meritorious a cause?

The smallest spark may here kindle into the greatest flame, because the materials are always prepared for it. The *avidum genus auricularum*,[15] the gazing populace, receive greedily, without examination, whatever soothes superstition and promotes wonder.

How many stories of this nature have, in all ages, been detected and exploded in their infancy? How many more have been celebrated for a time, and have afterwards sink into neglect and oblivion? Where such reports, therefore, fly about, the solution of the phenomenon is obvious, and we judge in conformity to regular experience and observation when we account for it by the known and natural principles of credulity and delusion. And shall we, rather than have recourse to so natural a solution, allow of a miraculous violation of the most established laws of nature?

I need not mention the difficulty of detecting a falsehood in any private or even public history at the place where it is said to happen, much more when tile scene is removed to ever so small a distance. Even a court of judicature, with all the authority, accuracy, and judgment which they can employ, find themselves often at a loss to distinguish between truth and falsehood in the most recent actions, But the matter never comes to any issue if trusted to the common method of altercation and debate and flying rumors, especially when men's passions have taken part on either side.

In the infancy of new religions, the wise and learned commonly esteem the matter too inconsiderable to deserve their attention or regard. And when afterwards they would willingly detect the cheat, in order to undeceive the deluded multitude, the season is now past and the records and witnesses which might clear up the matter have perished beyond recovery.

No means of detection remain but those which must be drawn from the very testimony itself of the reporters; and these, though always sufficient with the judicious and knowing, are commonly too fine to fall under the comprehension of the vulgar.

Upon the whole, then, it appears that no testimony for any kind of miracle has ever amounted[16] to a probability, much less to a proof; and that, even supposing it amounted to a proof, it would be opposed by another proof derived from the very nature of the fact which it would endeavor to establish. It is experience only which gives authority to human testimony, and it is the same experience which assures us of the laws of nature. When, therefore, these two kinds of experience are contrary, we have nothing to do but to subtract the one from the other and embrace an opinion either on one side or the other with that assurance which arises from the remainder. But according to the principle here explained, this subtraction with regard to all popular religions amounts to an entire annihilation; and therefore we may establish it as a maxim that no human testimony can have such force as to prove a miracle and make it a just foundation for any such system of religion.

I beg the limitations here made may be remarked, when I say that a miracle can never be proved so as to be the foundation of a system of religion. For I own that otherwise there may possibly be miracles or violations of the usual course of nature, of such kind as to admit of proof from human testimony, though perhaps it will be impossible to find any such in all the records of history. Thus suppose all authors, in all languages, agree that from the first of

---

[15] Lucretius. [IV. 594. This reference was added in Edition L.]
[16] [Editions K and L: "can ever possibly amount."]

January, 1600, there was a total darkness over the whole earth for eight days; suppose that the tradition of this extraordinary event is still strong and lively among the people; that all travelers who reason. Our most holy religion is founded on *faith,* not on reason; and it is a sure method of exposing it to put it to such a trial as it is by no means fitted to endure. To make this more evident, let us examine those miracles related in Scripture, and, not to lose ourselves in too wide a field, let us confine ourselves to such as we find in the Pentateuch, which we shall examine according to the principles of these pretended Christians, not as the word or testimony of God himself, but as the production of a mere human writer and historian. Here, then, we are first to consider a book presented to us by a barbarous and ignorant people, written in an age when they were still more barbarous, and, in all probability, long after the facts which it relates, corroborated by no concurring testimony, and resembling those fabulous accounts which every nation gives of its origin. Upon reading this book we find it full of prodigies and miracles. It gives an account of a state of the world and of human nature entirely different from the present: Of our fall from that state; of the age of man extended to near a thousand years; of the destruction of the world by a deluge; of the arbitrary choice of one people as the favorites of heaven, and that people the countrymen of the author; of their deliverance from bondage by prodigies the most astonishing imaginable—I desire anyone to lay his hand upon his heart arid, after a serious consideration, declare whether he thinks that the falsehood of such a book, supported by such a testimony, would be more extraordinary and miraculous than all the miracles it relates; which is, however, necessary to make it be received according to the measures of probability above established.

What we have said of miracles may be applied without any variation to prophecies; and, indeed, all prophecies are real miracles and as such only can be admitted as proofs of any revelation. If it did not exceed the capacity of human nature to foretell future events, it would be absurd to employ any prophecy as an argument for a divine mission or authority from heaven. So that, upon the whole, we may conclude that the Christian religion not only was at first attended with miracles, but even at this day cannot be believed by any reasonable person without one. Mere reason is insufficient to convince us of its veracity. And whoever is move by *faith* to assent to it is conscious of a continued miracle in his own person which subverts all the principles of his understanding and gives him a determination to believe what is most contrary to custom and experience.

Questions

1. What does Hume mean when he says that a miracle involves a *violation of a law of nature*?

2. Can you think of a better definition of a miracle?

3. What do you think of Hume's contention that one should proportion one's belief to the evidence?

4. Do you think that the theist would have to abandone faith if he/she were to follow Hume's evidentialist requirement?

5. Do you think that the occurance of miracles count as evidence for God's existence? In what way(s)

THE ARGUMENT FROM MIRACLES*

Michael Martin

In Atheism: A Philosophical Justification, *chapter 7, Martin considers the argument from miracles for the existence of God. He acknowledges that there is no a priori reason for there not to be miracles, but there are difficult a posteriori obstacles to surmount before one can claim that miracles have occurred in either a direct or indirect sense. Furthermore, even if there were good reasons to suppose that miracles existed in either sense, this would not necessarily mean that the existence of miracles provides inductive support for theism.*

The Argument in General

The literature of religious traditions is filled with stories of strange and mysterious events. Christian literature is abundantly supplied with such stories. According to the Bible, Jesus was born of a virgin, turned water to wine, walked on water, healed the sick, raised the dead, and was resurrected.[1] Moreover, within the Christian tradition, accounts of these sorts of events have continued down through the centuries. There have been stories of wondrous cures, of bleeding religious statues, of stigmata, and of visitations of the Virgin Mary.[2] For example, in Zeitoun, Egypt, from 1968 to 1970, thousands of people observed what seemed to be a luminous figure of the Virgin Mary walking on the central dome of the Coptic church known as St. Mary's Church of Zeitoun and occasionally hovering above it.[3] In Lourdes, France, many unexplained cures have been reported. After having been investigated by the Catholic Church, some of them have been declared to be miraculous. Strange and mysterious events have also been reported in the context of other religious traditions, such as the levitation of Hindu yogis.[4]

It seems that these reports, if accepted as accurate, cannot be explained in either commonsense or scientific terms. For example, there appears to be no ordinary way of explaining how Jesus raised the dead or turned water into wine, no scientific explanation of the luminous figure on the dome of St. Mary's Church of Zeitoun or of the cures at Lourdes, no known ordinary way to account for the levitation of yogis.

An argument for the existence of God that is based on evidence of such unexplained events proceeds as follows. Since these events cannot be explained in ordinary terms, they are miracles. Miracles by definition can only be explained in terms of some supernatural power. The most plausible supernatural explanation of miracles is that God caused them to occur. Hence it is probable that God exists.

Some form of the argument from miracles has been used by philosophers and theologians down through the ages either to prove the existence of God or more commonly to support the truth of some particular religion. For example, both Augustine and Aquinas[5] in the Christian tradition, Philo Judaeus[6] in the Jewish tradition, and Avicenna[7] in the Islamic tradition appealed

---

* Chapter 7 of Michael Martin, *Atheism: A Philosophical Justification*. Philadelphia: Temple University Press, 1990.
[1] See Alan Richardson, *The Miracle-Stories of the Gospels* (New York: Harper & Brothers, 1941).
[2] See D. Scott Rogo, *Miracles* (New York: Dial Press, 1982).
[3] *Ibid.*, pp. 250-257.
[4] *Ibid.*, pp. 33-34.
[5] As we saw in Chapter 4, Aquinas appealed to miracles occurring within the Christian tradition to justify the reliance on Christian revelations.
[6] See Harry A. Wolfson, "Philo Judaeus," *The Encyclopedia of Philosophy*, ed. Paul Edwards (New York and London: Macmillan and Free Press, 1967), vol. 6, p. 152.

to miracles. Indeed, the belief that the truth of the Christian religion can be proved on the basis of miracles has been a dogma of the Catholic Church since the third session of the First Vatican Council in 1870.[8] Although belief in the existence of miracles has been deemphasized in recent years by sophisticated Christian theologians,[9] even today most Christian theologians have not given up the belief that Jesus was miraculously resurrected.[10] Further, there are still philosophers of religion who believe that the argument provides some support for theism. Thus Richard Swinburne in *The Existence of God*[11] maintains that it provides support for the hypothesis that God exists, and Richard Purtill in *Thinking About Religion: A Philosophical Introduction to Religion* argues for a limited use of the argument.[12]

The Concept of Miracles

Before we attempt to evaluate the argument from miracles, it is important to be clear on what a miracle is and what it is not. A miracle is not simply an unusual event. There are many unusual events that are not considered miracles; for example, snow flurries in July in Boston and a newborn baby weighing more than 11 pounds. Nor is a miracle just an event that cannot be explained by currently known scientific laws. After all, among the many such events that are not considered miracles are the occurrences of cancer and birth defects.

What then is a miracle? Traditionally it is defined as a violation of a law of nature.[13] However, this traditional account has a serious problem that precludes its being adopted here. Consider a possible world where a god brings about some event, such as a cure of someone's cancer, that cannot be explained by any law yet known to science. However, suppose that in this world the god's action is governed by a law that governs the powers of gods. We could say that in this world a miracle had occurred but there was no violation of any law in that the god's actions are themselves governed by laws.

It is for this reason that I provisionally define a miracle as an event brought about by the exercise of a supernatural power.[14] This definition is compatible with a miracle violating no law. But what is a supernatural power? It is one that is markedly superior to those powers possessed by humans. Supernatural powers are possessed by supernatural beings: gods, angels, Superman,

---

[7] Fazlur Rahman, "Islamic Philosophy," *Encyclopedia of Philosophy,* vol. 4, p. 222.
[8] The canon runs as follows: "If anyone shall say that miracles cannot happen...or that the divine origin of the Christian religion cannot properly be proved by them: let them be anathema." See H. Denzinger, *Enchiridion Symbolorum,* 29th rev. ed. (Freiburg im Breisgau: Herder, 1953), sec. 1813. Quoted in Antony Flew, *God: A Critical Enquiry,* 2d ed. (La Salle, Ind.: Open Court, 1984), p. 136.
[9] For an analysis of some recent views on miracles, see Ernst and Marie-Luise Keller, *Miracles in Dispute* (Philadelphia: Fortress Press, 1969).
[10] Flew, *God: A Critical Enquiry,* p. 136.
[11] Richard Swinburne, *The Existence of God* (Oxford: Clarendon Press, 1979), chap. 12.
[12] Richard S. Purtill, *Thinking About Religion: A Philosophical Introduction to Religion* (Englewood Cliffs, N.J.: Prentice Hall, 1978), pp. 124-134. Reprinted in Louis P. Pojman, *Philosophy of Religion* (Belmont, Calif.: Wadsworth, 1987), pp. 287-289.
[13] See, for example, Antony Flew, "Miracles," *Encyclopedia of Philosophy,* vol. 5, p. 346.
[14] I am indebted here to Paul Fitzgerald, "Miracles," *Philosophical Forum,* 18, 1985, pp. 48-64. The definition adopted here is compatible with the view that every event is brought about by some supernatural power. It is also compatible with the view that the world would not exist without the conserving power of some supernatural being. See Alvin Plantinga, "Is Theism Really a Miracle?" *Faith and Philosophy,* 3, 1986, p. 111. Our definition should be compared with Richard Swinburne's in *The Concept of Miracle* (London: Macmillan, 1970), p. 1. Swinburne gives a general definition of a miracle as an event of an extraordinary kind brought about by a god and of religious significance. However, he argues that the word is sometimes used in a narrower or wider sense.

devils.[15] If supernatural beings exist, the powers they possess need not be in violation of the laws of nature. Indeed, one could imagine these abilities being governed by causal laws. As philosophers of science have commonly understood such laws, they are true universal statements that support counterfactual inferences and perhaps meet other technical requirements such as substitutivity. There is no reason why there could not be true generalities about supernatural beings and their powers that fulfill these conditions.

One can think of the situation in this way.[16] Nature in its broadest sense, $nature_b$, includes all entities (supernatural and natural) and their activities (determined by natural and supernatural powers). Thus $nature_b$ comprises the sum total of entities and their causal interactions. The only things not included in $nature_b$ are entities that are incapable of any causal interaction, such as numbers or sets. All entities and their causal interactions in $nature_b$ are governed by causal laws.

Nature in a narrow sense, $nature_n$, consists of the realm of human and subhuman entities and their powers. $Nature_n$ is part of $nature_b$ and, if there are no supernatural entities or powers, is identical with it. Miracles, on this view, do not go beyond $nature_b$; they go beyond $nature_n$. Or, to put it in a different way, miracles cannot be explained by laws governing $nature_n$; they might be explained by laws governing $nature_b$. If there are laws governing $nature_b$ that go beyond $nature_n$, these laws are not investigated by science.

Now, it may be objected that if supernatural beings such as a theistic God exist, their powers are not governed by causal laws. If this were so, our definition would not be affected. We could still say that it is not part of the *meaning* of "miracle," that it is a violation of a law of nature. After all, there could be supernatural beings who perform miracles whose actions are governed by causal laws. If God's actions are not governed by laws, then miracles would violate laws of $nature_n$, and $nature_b$ would not be governed by causal laws. But this would not mean that by definition miracles were violations of natural laws.

On the traditional view, miracles are nonrepeatable as well as being violations of natural law,[17] but I reject this characterization too. On my definition there is no *a priori* reason why a miracle cannot be repeated numerous times.[18] For example, it is not logically impossible for a miracle worker to being many people back to life. Indeed, so-called faith healers such as W. V. Grant and Oral Roberts have allegedly brought about numerous miracles of the same type. One might question the truth of these claims,[19] but there is nothing incoherent in the stories. One cannot say that the stories are false simply because the "miracles" was repeated. But if nonrepeatability is part of the definition of a miracle, one could.

The Probability that God Exists, Given the Existence of Miracles

We are now ready to begin an evaluation of the argument from miracles. The first thing to be considered is whether the existence of miracles would in fact support the hypothesis that God exists. Let us suppose that miracles in the sense defined above—that is, events brought about by the exercise of a supernatural power—do occur. Would this be good evidence for the existence of

---

[15] Is it logically possible for a human being to have supernatural powers? It may be argued that it is logically possible for humans to have powers of ESP and psychokinesis. These are often called paranormal powers, but the difference between a paranormal and supernatural power is not completely clear. See Fitzgerald, "Miracles," pp. 5051; see also Stephen E. Braude, *ESP and Psychokinesis* (Philadelphia: Temple University Press, 1979), pp. 242-263.
[16] Fitzgerald, "Miracles" pp. 58-62.
[17] See, for example, Swinburne, *Existence of God*, pp. 228-230; see also Swinburne, *Concept of Miracle*, pp. 26-27.
[18] For a similar argument, see Andrew Rein, "Repeatable Miracles?" *Analysis*, 46, 1986, pp. 109-112.
[19] See the special issue of *Free Inquiry*, 6, Spring 1986, on faith healing.

God? To state my answer briefly, it would not be, since miracles might be the result of the actions of other supernatural beings besides God.

The question must be considered more carefully, however. By "evidence for the existence of God" is meant inductive evidence in the sense that was characterized earlier. Let us consider whether H_1 (= God exists) is inductively supported by E (= Miracles have occurred). Following Swinburne,[20] let us distinguish two types of inductive arguments for miracles: C-inductive arguments and P-inductive arguments. In a good C-inductive argument,

(1) $P(H_1/E\&K) > P(H_1/K)$

where K is the background knowledge and $P(p/q)$ means that p is probable relative to q. In a good P-inductive argument,

(2) $P(H_1/E\&K) > P(\sim H_1/E\&K)$.

Now, (1) is true if and only if

(3) $P(E/H\&K) > P(E/K)$

so long as $P(H/K) \neq 0$. In turn, (3) is equivalent to

(4) $P(E/H_1\&K) > P(E/\sim H_1\&K)$.

One can immediately see a problem with (4). It is completely unclear why one should suppose that (4) is true. After all, $\sim H_1$ can be interpreted as a disjunction of hypotheses consisting of H_1's rivals. Included in this disjunction would be hypotheses that postulate finite but very powerful beings that have as their basic motive the desire to work miracles. The probability of E relative to these hypotheses about finite miracle workers would be one. The probability of E relative to other members of this disjunction would vary from zero to near one. There's no *a priori* reason to suppose that the probability of E relative to the entire disjunction would be less than the probability of E relative to H_1. It is important to see that:

$P(E/H_1\&K) \neq 1$.

That is, the hypothesis of theism does not entail the existence of miracles. Swinburne, for example, maintains only that miracles are probable given God's existence—how probable is unclear. The crucial question is whether miracles are more probable if theism is false. In his analysis Swinburne wrongly seems to suppose that the only rival to theism is naturalism. But there are numerous rival supernatural hypotheses that would explain the existence of miracles.[21]

Furthermore, some of the miracles that are reported in the Christian tradition seem to be better explained by non-Christian supernatural hypotheses. Some of the miracles performed by Christ, such as driving the demons into the Gadarene swine and cursing the fig tree, seem difficult to reconcile with belief in a kind and merciful God.[22] Moreover, a miracle by definition cannot be explained by any law governing nature$_n$. As such, the existence of miracles cannot be

---

[20] Swinburne, *Existence of God*, chap. 1.
[21] See Swinburne, *Concept of Miracle*, chap. 6.
[22] Criticisms similar to this were raised by eighteenth-century deists Thomas Woolston and Thomas Chubb. See R. M. Burns, *The Great Debate on Miracles* (Lewisburg, Penna.: Bucknell University Press, 1981), pp. 77-79.

explained by science and indeed is an impediment to a scientific understanding of the world. Furthermore, there are great difficulties and controversies in identifying miracles. Thus whatever good effects miracles might have, they also impede, mislead, and confuse. A benevolent and all-powerful God would seemingly be able to achieve His purposes in ways that do not have these unfortunate effects. Moreover, some miracles seem to happen capriciously (for example, some people are cured and some are not), while other miracles seem trivial and unimportant (for example, bleeding statues and stigmata). They are not what one would have antecedently expected from a completely just and all-powerful being.[23]

So even if the existence of miracles is taken for granted, a good C-inductive argument for H_1 remains uncertain.[24] Thus even if one assumes that miracles exist, it is unclear whether this would support the hypothesis that God exists more than its negation.

Naturalism Versus Supernaturalism and the Existence of Miracles

Is there any reason to suppose that miracles do exist? And can we answer this question without a prior commitment to a general metaphysical position? C.S. Lewis, a well known Christian writer, maintains in *Miracles* that in order to assess whether miracles exist, it is first necessary to decide between naturalism and supernaturalism. He argues:

> It by no means follows from Supernaturalism that Miracles of any sort do in fact occur. God (the primary thing) may never in fact interfere with the natural system He has created.... If we decide that Nature is not the only thing there is, then we cannot say in advance whether she is safe from miracles or not.... But if Naturalism is true, then we know in advance that miracles are impossible: nothing can come into Nature from the outside because there is nothing outside to come in, Nature being everything.... Our first choice, therefore, must be between Naturalism and Supernaturalism.[25]

His argument can perhaps be constructed as follows. Appeal to neither historical evidence nor personal experience will prove that miracles exist if we have already decided that miracles are *a priori* impossible or unlikely. One can decide that they are *a priori* impossible or unlikely only if one has decided that naturalism is correct. On the other hand, if one maintains that miracles are *a priori* possible or at least not *a priori* improbable, one has accepted supernaturalism.

If Lewis is correct, then the evidence of miracles could not provide any independent support for supernaturalism, since in order to establish the existence of miracles one would already have to assume supernaturalism. Lewis's position, if accepted, would perhaps do more to undermine the argument from miracles than any naturalistic critique of this argument. But should it be accepted?

Lewis is certainly right to suppose that in considering the question of whether miracles exist there is a danger that one will appeal to *a priori* arguments and assumptions. But the solution to this problem is not to decide on naturalism or supernaturalism beforehand. Rather, one must attempt to reject the *a priori* arguments and instead base one's position on inductive

---

[23] This argument from miracles against the existence of God has obvious similarities to the argument from evil against the existence of God, which I consider in Part II. See Christine Overall, "Miracles as Evidence Against the Existence of God," *Southern Journal of Philosophy,* 13, 1985, pp. 347-353.

[24] C. S. Lewis, *Miracles* (New York: Macmillian, 1978), chaps. 12-16. Lewis argues at some length that belief in the Christian God is compatible with miracles. This does not seem very controversial. The crucial question is whether the existence of miracles gives more support to theism than to other supernatural theories. Lewis does not address this question.

[25] *Ibid.,* pp. 10-11.

considerations. Lewis has not shown that this is impossible. Thus he has not shown that one must choose between naturalism and supernaturalism before investigating the possibility of miracles.

Moreover, when Lewis attempts to provide reasons for choosing supernaturalism over naturalism (N) he fails miserably. He defines N as the view that all events occurring in space and time are caused by earlier events, and this causal process is "going on, *of its own accord*";[26] that is, there is nothing outside this causal system or whole that intervenes or interrupts the causal process.[27] N is incompatible with both rational reasoning[28] and ethical ideals and judgments, he maintains.[29] If N is true, no one could argue for its truth and no naturalist has any business advocating ethical principles. Thus N is self-refuting, and naturalists are inconsistent.

However, Lewis's arguments for these remarkable theses are either very weak or non-existent. His argument for the first claim can be reconstructed in this way:[30]

(1) If N is true, all our thinking must be explicated in terms of cause and effect.
(2) If all our thinking must be explicated in terms of cause and effect, then N can give no account of rational inference.
(3) If N can give no account of rational inference, then a naturalist cannot know that N is true.
(4) If a naturalist cannot know that N is true, there can be no justification for believing N.

(5) Therefore, if N is true, there can be no justification for believing N.

The crucial premise is (1), and it is difficult to understand why Lewis holds it. For some reason Lewis seems to suppose that naturalists must distinguish different kinds of thinking (for example, rational and irrational) in *completely* causal terms. But they do. There is no reason why naturalists cannot use terms such as truth, validity, and probability to explicate rational thinking. Indeed, this is precisely what recent naturalists have done.[31]

The argument for the second claim follows similar lines and is really a special case of the first argument.

(1') If N is true, then all moral judgments are unjustified.
(2') If all moral judgments are unjustified, good and evil are illusions.
(3') If good and evil are illusions, then naturalists are inconsistent when they advocate the good of humanity as an ethical idea.

(4') Therefore, if N is true, then naturalists are inconsistent when they advocate the good of humanity as an ethical ideal.

Here again the problem is premise (1'), for there is no reason to suppose that it is true. It seems to rest either on the first argument that N cannot give an account of reason (hence naturalists can give no account of moral reasoning) and/or on a mistaken view of what ethical naturalists hold. Most ethical naturalists simply do not believe the view that there is no such

---

[26] *Ibid.*, p. 6.
[27] It seems clear that Lewis is referring to what above we call nature.
[28] Lewis, *Miracles,* chap. 2.
[29] *Ibid.*, chap. 5.
[30] *Ibid.*, p. 18.
[31] See, for example, D. M. Armstrong, *Belief, Truth, and Knowledge* (London: Cambridge University Press, 1974), chap. 6.

thing as right or wrong, as Lewis seems to claim.[32] It is significant that Lewis does not cite *one* naturalist who holds the view he attributes to N.

I conclude that it is not necessary to choose between naturalism and supernaturalism prior to answering the question as to whether miracles exist. Moreover, supposing it is necessary, Lewis's arguments for rejecting naturalism are unsound.

The Difficulty of Showing the Existence of Miracles

Having considered the question of whether God's existence is inductively supported by the existence of miracles, I remain skeptical. Furthermore, Lewis's argument that one must decide between supernaturalism and naturalism before one can decide whether miracles exist is not compelling. The question remains, however, whether there is any reason to suppose that miracles do in fact exist.

David Hume gave a general argument against the existence of miracles in "Of Miracles."[33] According to one standard interpretation, Hume does not attempt to show that miracles are *a priori* impossible but rather that it is *a priori* impossible to have strong evidence for their existence. What does Hume mean by a miracle? On his view a miracle is a violation of a law of nature. Consequently, someone who argues that event E is a miracle has two burdens that are impossible to meet simultaneously:[34] to show that E has taken place *and* that E violates a law of nature. Consider the assumed law of nature L*:

(L*) No person has been brought back to life.

(L*) has been confirmed by the deaths of billions of people; the evidence is overwhelming. Now consider the hypothesis (H*):

(H*) Some people have been brought back to life.

If we had good evidence for (H*), this would disconfirm (L*). But we cannot have such evidence. The evidence that could support (H*) is based on human testimony, but even at its best it is subject to error. Thus there is no uniform relation in our experience between human testimony that something is so and its being so. However, our evidence for (L*) must be stronger than this. Since (L*) is a law of nature, there is a uniform relation in our experience between a person's dying and this person's not returning to life. Consequently, in terms of our experience the probability of (L*) must be greater than the probability of (H*). The low probability of (H*) relative to (L*) may be argued for in another way. On some interpretations of Hume, this violation is by definition nonrepeatable.[35] If miracles are nonrepeatable, there could at most be one confirmatory instance of (H*). However, there are billions of confirmatory instances of (L*). Again, the probability of (L*) must be higher than the probability of (H*).

---

[32] Lewis, *Miracles*, p. 36. For example, see Richard Brandt, *Ethical Theory* (Englewood Cliffs, N.J.: Prentice Hall, 1959), chap. 7.
[33] See David Hume, *An Inquiry Concerning Human Understanding* (New York: Liberal Arts Press, 1955), sec. 10. Reprinted under the title "Against Miracles," in Pojman, *Philosophy of Religion*, pp. 264-273.
[34] Cf. J. L. Mackie, *The Miracle of Theism* (Oxford: Clarendon Press, 1982), pp. 26-29, and Fitzgerald, "Miracles," p. 56.
[35] For example, Fitzgerald in "Miracles" clearly interprets Hume in this way. Whether Richard Swinburne ("Miracles," *Philosophical Quarterly*, 18, 1986; reprinted under the title "For the Possibility of Miracles," in Pojman, *Philosophy of Religion*, pp. 273-279) so interprets Hume is less clear. Whether Hume actually held that miracles by definition are nonrepeatable is uncertain.

There is much that is wrong with this argument. It assumes that our evidence for the laws of nature is based not on testimony but on personal experience. But it is not. For example, our knowledge of the truth of (L*) rests in large part on the testimony of others. Indeed, most of us have little direct experience of dead people. Our limited direct experience is supplemented and expanded by fallible human testimony. However, if we understand experience to include not just an individual's direct experience of no dead person's coming back to life but the combined experience of civilization that is based in part on testimony, then the argument seems to beg the question against (H*). After all, there have been a few reports of people coming back to life. How can we know *a priori* that their probability is low?

Moreover, if Hume's argument assumes the nonrepeatability of miracles, then the argument is further weakened. There is no reason why (H*) could not be confirmed by many instances. However, there is no reason why (H*) must be confirmed by many instances for (H*) to be probable. One confirmatory instance is enough. Suppose there were reports of Gandhi's being brought back to life (E). If the evidence for E was extremely good, there would be excellent grounds for thinking that (H*) was true and (L*) was false. For example, if the witnesses to E were extremely numerous, independent, and reliable, if there was excellent physical evidence of Gandhi's being brought back to life—video pictures, EEG records that brain death had actually occurred, and so on—this might be enough to reject (L*) as a law of nature.[36]

This Humean argument fails to show that there is any *a priori* reason to suppose that it is impossible to have strong evidence for the existence of miracles. But there are excellent *a posteriori* reasons, suggested by Hume and others,[37] to suppose that the evidence is not good.[38] Indeed, anyone who would argue for the existence of miracles must overcome at least three *a posteriori* obstacles.

The believer in miracles must give reasons to suppose that the event E, the alleged miracle, will probably not be explained by any unknown scientific laws that govern nature$_n$. Since presumably not all the laws that govern nature$_n$ have been discovered, this seems difficult to do. The advocates of the miracle hypothesis must argue the probability that E will not be explained by future science, utilizing heretofore undiscovered laws that govern nature$_n$. Given the scientific progress of the last two centuries, such a prediction seems rash and unjustified.[39] In medicine, for example, diseases that were considered mysterious are now understood without appeal to supernatural powers. Further progress seems extremely likely; indeed, many so-called miracle cures of the past may one day be understood, as some have already been, in terms of psychosomatic medicine. Whether other mysterious phenomena will be explained by future

---

[36] Cf. Gary Colwell, "On Defining Away Miracles," *Philosophy*, 57, 1982, pp. 327-336. Notice, however, that this evidence would not be enough to suppose that E was not governed by a law of nature. Consequently, it would not be enough to suppose that E was a miracle.

[37] As Burns has shown, Hume was not the first to propose the sort of *a posteriori* arguments found in "Of Miracles" against the existence of miracles. See Burns, *Great Debate on Miracles*, chaps. 3 and 4.

[38] See Mackie, *Miracle of Theism*, pp. 14-16, for a lucid exposition of these arguments.

[39] John B. Gill, "Miracles with Method," *Sophia*, 16, 1977, pp. 19-26. Gill has argued that miracle claims are compatible with scientific progress, since such claims may be only tentatively held and are compatible with reconsidering the claims in the light of new evidence. Although it may well be true that such openmindedness is logically compatible with miracle claims, one wonders if it in fact works this way. Historically it seems clear that belief in miracles has been detrimental to scientific progress; and given the psychology of typical believers, it is likely to remain so. Moreover, even if such claims are put forth tentatively, the question is whether they are justified in the light of the rapid increases in knowledge in such fields as medical science. As we show later, in discussing the cures at Lourdes, as medical knowledge has increased the number of inexplicable cures has decreased. This evidence suggests that miracle claims in the area of medical science, even if tentatively held, may be unjustified in terms of the progress of medicine.

scientific investigation is less certain, but the possibility cannot be ruled out. The luminous figure on the dome of St. Mary's Church of Zeitoun may be explained in the future by parapsychology. For example, Dr. Scott Rogo has suggested that the luminous figure can be explained in terms of the psychic energy generated by the Zeitounians' expectation of the visitation of the Virgin Mary.[40] At the present time Rogo's theory is pure speculation, and there are no known laws connected with the manifestations of psychic energy. But the believer in miracles must suppose that probably no laws about psychic energy *or any other laws* of nature will be discovered that could explain the luminous figure.

Believers in miracles may argue that some events not only are unexplained in terms of laws governing $nature_n$ but are in conflict with them. Someone who walks on water has done something that not only is not explained by the laws governing $nature_n$ but is in conflict with those laws. But then, in order to explain the event, it is necessary to appeal to the laws governing $nature_b$. The ability to walk on water indicates the causal influences of a supernatural power that goes beyond the working of $nature_n$.

The difficulty here is to know whether the conflict is genuine or is merely apparent. This is the second great obstacle for believers in miracles. They must argue that the conflict is more probably genuine than apparent, but this is difficult to argue, for there are many ways that appearances can mislead and deceive in cases of this sort.

One way in which an apparent conflict can arise is by means of deception, fraud, or trickery. The difficulties of ruling out hoax, fraud, or deception are legend. We have excellent reason today to believe that some contemporary faith healers use fraud and deceit to make it seem that they have paranormal powers and are getting miracle cures.[41] These men have little trouble in duping a public that is surely no less sophisticated than that of biblical times. Even in modern parapsychology, where laboratory controls are used, there is great difficulty in ruling out explanations of the results in terms of fraud. By various tricks, trained experimenters in ESP research have been deceived into thinking that genuine paranormal events have occurred.[42] Parapsychologists themselves have resorted to fraud—so-called experimenter fraud—to manufacture evidence favorable to the reality of ESP. It takes the most stringent controls, the use of experts such as magicians trained in detecting fakery, and inconsistence on independent investigators in order to have confidence that the positive results in ESP research are not based upon deceit. Thus when eyewitnesses report that they have seen yogis levitating, even when these reports are accompanied by photographs, they must be treated with skepticism unless there is excellent reason to rule out the possibility of fraud and hoax on the part of the yogi as well as of the witness to the event.

If it takes control and precaution today in scientific laboratories in order to eliminate fraud and deceit, what credence should we give to reports of miracles made in biblical times by less than educated and less sophisticated people without systematic controls against fraud?[43] The

---

[40] Rogo, *Miracles*, p. 256. Oddly enough, Rogo does not even consider the possibility that the luminous figure may have been the result of fraud and deception. The technical capacity to create such a luminous figure certainly existed in the late 1960s, yet Rogo provides no evidence of any attempt to rule out fraud.

[41] See James Randi, "'Be Healed in the Name of God!' An Exposé of the Reverend W. V. Grant," *Free Inquiry*, 6, 1986, pp. 8-19. See also James Randi, *The Faith Healers* (Buffalo, N.Y.: Prometheus Books, 1987).

[42] See James Randi, "The Project Alpha Experiment: Part I, The First Two Years," *Skeptical Inquirer*, 7, Summer 1983, pp. 24-33; "Part 2, Beyond the Laboratory," *Skeptical Inquirer*, 8, Fall 1983, pp. 36-45.

[43] Cf. Gary Colwell, "Miracles and History," *Sophia*, 22, 1983, pp. 9-14. Colwell argues that in the Bible in Lk. 24:1-11 and Jn. 20:24-29 one finds examples of skeptical humanity among Jesus' followers who were forced to accept his miracles from love of truth. But it is unclear why Colwell accepts these biblical stories as true, since there are many inconsistencies in the story of the resurrection, where the examples of skeptical humanity are supposed to be found.

plausible reply would be: "Very little." One surely must ask: Did Jesus really walk on water or only appear to because he was walking on rocks below the surface?[44] Did Jesus turn the water into wine, or did he only appear to because he had substituted wine for water by some clever trick? The hypothesis that Jesus was a magician has been seriously considered by some biblical scholars.[45] The success of some contemporary faith healers and psychic wonders in convincing the public by the use of deception and fraud indicates that it was possible for Jesus, if he was a magician, to do the same.

Further, alleged miracles may not be due to some trick or fraud but to a misperception based on religious bias. People full of religious zeal may see what they want to see, not what is really there. We know from empirical studies that people's beliefs and prejudices influence what they see and report.[46] It would not then be surprising that religious people who report seeing a miraculous event have projected their biases onto the actual event. Did Jesus still the storm (Matt. 8.23-27), or did the storm by coincidence happen to stop when "he rose and rebuked the wind and the sea"? And did witnesses in their religious zeal "see" him stilling the storm?

In addition, religious attitudes often foster uncritical belief and acceptance. Indeed, in a religious context uncritical belief is often thought to be a value, doubt and skepticism a vice. Thus a belief arising in a religious context and held at first with only modest conviction may tend to reinforce itself and develop into an unshakable conviction. It would hardly be surprising, then, if in this context some ordinary natural event were seen as a miracle.

For another thing, an event that is not a miracle may appear like one if the observer has incomplete knowledge of the law governing nature$_n$ that appears to be violated. A scientific law holds only in a known range of conditions, not in all conditions. Thus Boyle's law holds only for gases in a specific temperature range; Newton's laws only correctly predict the mass of a body at accelerations not close to the speed of light. Often the range of application of a law becomes known with precision only years after the law itself is first formulated. Thus consider some physiological and psychological laws governing sight that seem to conflict with the apparent miracle of a faith healer's restoring someone's sight. This law may hold only in a fixed range of applications, and in special circumstances other laws governing nature$_n$ that explain the restoration of sight may hold. Both sorts of laws may be derivable from a comprehensive, but as yet unknown, theory. The advocates of miracles must maintain that an explanation of the event in terms of such a theory is less likely than an explanation by some supernatural power.

However, even if one shows it is more likely than not that some event is in conflict with deterministic scientific laws governing nature$_n$, this would not mean it is more likely than not

---

Furthermore, Colwell ignores the independent evidence we have from contemporary faith healers, indicating the difficulty of being skeptical when one is deeply involved in a religious movement. See Paul Kurtz, *The Transcendental Temptation* (Buffalo, N.Y.: Prometheus Books, 1986), pp. 153-160, for an analysis of these inconsistencies; and see Randi, *Faith Healers,* for the lack of skepticism in the context of faith healing.

[44] Carl Friedrich Bahrdt, a German theologian of the Enlightenment, suggested that Jesus walked on floating pieces of timber. For a discussion of Bahrdt's views see Ernst and Marie-Luise Keller, *Miracles in Dispute,* pp. 69-70. The Kellers raise two objections to Bahrdt's explanation. They argue that according to Scripture the boat was not near the shore, and that in any case Jesus' disciples would have noticed the timber. However, it is uncertain whether Scripture is correct about the location of the boat. In any case, if we substitute rocks for timber, the location of the boat according to Scripture can be accepted. Rocks below the surface of the water may extend for many furlongs out to sea. The Kellers mention Bahrdt's not-implausible explanation of the failure of the disciples to notice. "They were 'held prisoner' by the prejudices of their own miracle-believing age—with constantly inflamed imaginations—always saw more in the phenomena than was there in reality" (p. 71).

[45] See Morton Smith, *Jesus the Magician* (New York: Harper & Row, 1978).

[46] See, for example, A. Daniel Yarmey, *The Psychology of Eyewitness Testimony* (New York: Free Press, 1979).

that the event is a miracle. In other words, it would not show that the event could only be explained by the laws governing nature$_b$.

This brings us to the third great obstacle: What we thought were strictly deterministic laws may in fact be statistical laws. Since statistical laws are compatible with rare occurrences of uncaused events, the events designated as miracles may be wrongly designated since they may be uncaused—that is, they may be neither naturally nor supernaturally determined. Advocates of the miracle hypothesis, then, must show that the existence of miracles is more probable than the existence of uncaused events.

In sum, the advocates of the hypothesis that event E is a miracle (H_m) must show that H_m is more probable than the following:

(H_s)   Event E will be explained by future scientific progress when more laws governing nature$_n$ are discovered.
(H_g)   Event E seems compatible with laws that govern nature$_n$ but it is not.
(H_u)   Event E is uncaused.

There is no easy way to assess the comparative probabilities that are involved. However, as we have already seen, the progress of science, the history of deception and fraud connected with miracles and the paranormal, and the history of gullibility and misperception all strongly suggest that (H_s) and (H_g) are better supported than (H_m).

It is less clear what one should say about the comparative probability of (H_m) and (H_u). Both seem unlikely in the light of the evidence. But it is certainly not clear that (H_u) is less likely than (H_m). Both seem unlikely in the light of the evidence. But it is certainly not clear that (H_u) is less likely than (H_m). On the one hand, science already allows indeterminacy on the micro level—for example, in quantum theory. On the other hand, macro indeterminacy, the sort of indeterminacy that would be relevant to explaining miracles, is not less incompatible with the present scientific world view than it is with (H_m). At the very least one can say that there is no reason to prefer (H_m) over (H_n) on probabilistic grounds.

Evidence of Miracles in One Religion as Evidence Against Contrary Religions

In a well-known passage in the *Inquiry*, David Hume says:

> Let us consider, that, in matters of religion, whatever is different is contrary; and that it is impossible the religions of ancient Rome, of Turkey, of Siam, and of China should, all of them, be established on any solid foundation. Every miracle, therefore, pretended to have been wrought in any of these religions (and all of them abound in miracles), as its direct scope is to establish the particular system to which it is attributed, so has it the same force, though more indirectly, to overthrow every other system. In destroying a rival system, it likewise destroys the credit of those miracles, on which that system is established; so that all the prodigies of different religions are to be regarded as contrary facts, and the evidence of these prodigies, whether strong or weak, as opposite to each other.[47]

Hume has been interpreted as claiming in this argument that every alleged miracle whose occurrence would be evidence in favor of a given religion is such that its occurrence would be evidence against any religion contrary to the first. He has also been interpreted as arguing that the evidence in favor of the existence of a miracle (which would constitute evidence for one religion)

---

[47] Hume, *Inquiry Concerning Human Understanding*, pp. 129-130.

would be evidence against the occurrence of any miracle (which would constitute evidence in favor of a contrary religion).

Put more formally, it has been argued that Hume is maintaining the validity of two arguments.[48] The first argument is as follows:

(1) E_1 increases the probability of H_1 more than H_2.
(2) H_1 and H_2 are contraries.

(3) Therefore, E_1 decreases the probability of H_2.

The second argument is as follows:

(1') E_1 is evidence for H_1 and against H_2.
(2') E_2 is evidence for H_2 and against H_1.
(3') H_1 and H_2 are contraries.

(4') Therefore, E_1 is evidence against E_2 and conversely.

However, both of these arguments are invalid.

Consider the following counterexample to the first argument form. Suppose that the fact that a .45 caliber gun was used to murder Smith (E) is evidence that Evans is the murderer (H_1). (We suppose Evans is suspect and always uses a .45 caliber gun.) Suppose further that H_2 (Jones is the murderer) is a contrary to H_1. Evidence E may still support H_2 although not as strongly. (We know that Jones uses a .45 caliber only 80 percent of the time.)

Consider the following counterexample to the second argument form. Let H_1 and H_2 represent what they did in the preceding example. Evans's fingerprints on the gun are evidence for H_2 and against H_1. Jones's footprints at the scene of the crime are evidence for H_2 and against H_1. But the one piece of evidence is not evidence against the other piece of evidence.

In the religious context, Jesus' walking on water (E_1) may be evidence for the truth of Christianity (H_1) but also for the truth of Hinduism (H_2), since Hindus might consider Jesus a manifestation of the absolute, not an incarnation of a personal God. A Baal priest curing a blind man (E_2), itself evidence for the hypothesis (H_3) that Baal is the supreme god, may support the fact that a priest of Zeus could cure a blind man, since we now have evidence that priests sometimes cure blind men. This in turn would be indirect evidence that the report that a priest of Zeus cured a blind man was true (E_3), which in turn would be evidence that Zeus was the supreme god (H_4).

When it is interpreted in the above way, Hume's two-part argument is invalid, but according to a different interpretation at least the first part of the argument is valid.[49] In the passage cited above, Hume's words suggest not just that the miracles of one religion make that religion more probable than it was before the occurrence of the miracles, but that the miracles make the religion more probable than not. Recall that he says it is impossible that rival religions should be "established on any solid foundation" by the evidence from miracles. Construed in this way, his argument becomes:

---

[48] See Bruce Langtry, "Hume on Miracles and Contrary Religions," *Sophia*, 14, 1975, pp. 29-34.
[49] Cf. David A. Conway, "Miracles, Evidence and Contrary Religion," *Sophia*, 22, 1983, pp. 3-14; Bruce Langtry, "Miracles and Rival Systems of Religion," *Sophia*, 24, 1985, pp. 21-31.

(1) Miracles $M_1, M_2, \ldots M_n$ occurring in the context of religion R_1 provide evidence that R_1 is more probable than not. $[P(R_1, M_1, M_2, \ldots M_n)] > 0.5]$

(2) Religion R_1 and religion R_2 are contraries

---

(3) Therefore, R_2 is less probable than not. $[P(R_2, M_1, M_2, \ldots M_n) < 0.5]$

However, a similar argument could be used to show that R_1 is less probable than not by citing other miracles that occur within the context of R_2. Hume was therefore correct to suppose that the miracles of one system can "destroy" rival systems. Of course, one could escape from Hume's argument by maintaining that the evidence of the miracles of one religion does not make it more probable than not but only more probable than it was without this evidence. However, Hume was no doubt correct to suppose that at least in his day the existence of the miracles of one religion was often supposed to make that religion more probable than not—that is, to use his words, to establish that religion on a solid foundation. What advocates of this way of arguing overlooked was that it could also be used to establish rival systems and thus indirectly "destroy" their own system.

What about the second part of Hume's argument: that the evidence of the miracles of one religion destroys the credibility of the evidence of miracles in another religion? Here Hume was clearly wrong, and I know no way of revising Hume's argument that is in keeping with its spirit. This is not to say that one cannot argue from the problematic nature of miracles in the context of one religion to the problematic nature in another. But what Hume was apparently trying to do was to argue thus: If evidence E_1 in religion R_1 allows us to show that R_1 is more probable than not, and if evidence E_1 in religion R_2 allows us to show that R_2 is more probable than not, then E_1 makes E_2 improbable and E_2 makes E_1 improbable. This inference is wrong. But it would not be wrong to argue that since the evidence of alleged miracles associated with, say, the Christian religion is weak, then probably the evidence for miracles in other religions is also weak. This would be a straightforward inductive argument, and its strength would be a function of the representative nature of evidence for Christian miracles. If such evidence is not atypical of miracles in other religions and the evidence is weak, then one is justified in making such an inference. Unfortunately, in the above-quoted passage Hume does not seem to be giving this completely sound argument.

Miracles at Lourdes

So far we have considered in a general way the difficulty in determining whether an event is a miracle. It would be useful now to relate the problems just outlined to a concrete case. In modern times the most famous occurrences of alleged miracles have been at Lourdes in France. These are probably the best documented and most carefully considered in history. If these alleged miracles are suspect, we would have good ground for maintaining that other claims of miracles—in more distant times, when superstition prevailed and objective documentation was either nonexistent or at least much less in evidence—should not be taken seriously.

It all began in February 1858, when a 14-year-old uneducated girl named Bernadette Soubirous, while collecting wood near the grotto of Massabielle in Lourdes, allegedly saw a beautiful lady wearing a white dress with a blue sash, with a yellow rose on each foot and a yellow rosary. Bernadette allegedly saw the Lady of the Grotto 18 times. Speaking the local patois, the Lady told Bernadette to pray for sinners and to tell the priest to have a chapel built. She also said that she wished people to come to the grotto in procession. It was claimed by those in attendance that during one session with the Lady of the Grotto, spring water miraculously came from the ground when Bernadette touched it. In another incident Bernadette knelt before the Lady of the Grotto with her hand cupped around the flame of a candle. Those in attendance claimed that the candle slipped out of place, "causing the flames to dance between Bernadette's fingers for a good ten minutes."[50] Bernadette never flinched, it was said, and the fire did not burn her. On another occasion Bernadette claimed that the Lady said, "I am the Immaculate Conception."

Naturally, Bernadette's claims caused a great stir at the time. She was denounced by skeptics as a fraud, yet many people flocked to the grotto to see her transfixed by her own vision. After a four-year inquiry the Roman Catholic Church declared that Bernadette's vision was the Virgin Mary. Pilgrims, mostly from the surrounding area, began to visit the shrine that had been built there eight years after Bernadette's vision. By 1947 more than a million people were coming from all parts of France. In 1979, the centennial year of Bernadette's death, about 4.5 million people visited Lourdes—only one-third of them from France. Although the Lady of the Grotto never said to Bernadette that people would be cured at Lourdes, several cures were reported at the very beginning of the pilgrimages to Lourdes: A stone mason with one blind eye applied earth moistened from the spring to his eye, and his sight was restored a few days later; a mother dipped her paralyzed son into the spring and he was instantly cured.

Lourdes is unique among Catholic shrines where miracles are supposed to occur, for only at Lourdes is there a definite procedure for investigating and recognizing miracles. The procedure is this:[51]

(1) A person whose health is dramatically altered by a trip to Lourdes may come before the medical bureau at Lourdes. The bureau has one full-time physician, who is joined in examining and interrogating the pilgrims by other doctors who happen to be visiting Lourdes at the time.

(2) If a dossier (an official medical file) is to be started, the person alleged to be cured must have a "complete" medical record confirming the nature of the illness and dates of recent treatments. In order to rule out the possibility that the alleged cure was brought about by ordinary medical treatment the pilgrim has undergone, the effectiveness of the treatment must be known.

(3) Special criteria of recovery must be met. The illness must be life-threatening and must be a distinct organic disorder. The recovery must be sudden and unforeseen, and it must occur "without convalescence." There must be "objective evidence"—X-rays, blood tests, biopsies—that the pilgrim had the disease before becoming cured. No disease for which there is effective treatment is considered as a possible miracle. Further, the pilgrim must stay cured and is therefore required to return several times for reexamination.

(4) Cures that meet all these tests are submitted to an international medical committee, appointed by the bishop of the adjacent towns of Tarbes and Lourdes, that meets annually in Paris. The committee votes on one issue: Is the cure medically inexplicable?

(5) If the majority of the committee decides that the cure is inexplicable, the patient's dossier is given to the canonical commission headed by the bishop of the diocese in which the allegedly cured person lives. Only the church can make the final decision as to whether the event is a miracle—that is, whether God has intervened in the natural course of events.

Before we consider the application of this procedure in actual practice, a few points should be noted in the light of previous discussion. First, it is difficult to see how the international committee that meets annually in Paris has the competence to decide if a cure is scientifically inexplicable in any absolute way—that is, in terms of nature$_n$. At best this committee would only

---

[50] Ellen Bernstein, "Lourdes," *Encyclopedia Britannica,* Medical and Health Annual, 1982, p.130.
[51] *Ibid.,* pp. 131-133.

have the competence to decide if the cure is scientifically explicable in terms of current knowledge of nature$_n$. This committee does not know what the future development of medical science will be; thus any judgment it makes about the absolute inexplicability of a cure in terms of nature$_n$ can and should have no particular authority.

In order to judge whether the cure is a miracle, one must be justified in believing that it will never and can never be explained in scientific terms—that is, in terms of nature$_n$. But would the committee have the competence to predict that, in the light of the evidence, probably no cure will ever be found? Given the rapid advances in medical knowledge, it is difficult to see that they would. Thus this committee's judgments exceed its scientific competence; indeed, a judgment of a committee *must* exceed its competence in order for it to be relevant to assessing whether a particular cure is a miracle.

Second, even if the international committee's judgment were justified that a particular cure was scientifically inexplicable in some absolute sense, the church seems to have no rational basis for making the final judgment that (a) the cure was a miracle and (b) the miracle was caused by God. As we have already seen, the cure could be uncaused. If so, it would be inexplicable in principle but not a miracle. Further, even if it was caused by some supernatural force or forces, this need not be the Christian God. Church officials who make the final decision about whether a cure is a miracle and, if so, is caused by God apparently ignore these alternatives. As a result, the final decision that the cure is a miracle explained by God's intervention is more like a leap of faith than a rational decision.

So far we have argued that although the doctors on the international committee do not have the competence to decide that a cure is inexplicable in terms of the law of nature$_n$ in some absolute way, they do have the competence to decide if a cure is inexplicable in terms of present scientific knowledge of nature$_n$. However, although they have this competence *in principle*, things may in fact be quite different. The doctors of the international committee may not have adequately applied the procedures specified.

One case in point is that of Serge Perrin, a French accountant, who in 1970 while at Lourdes experienced a sudden recovery from a long illness. After investigation the international committee said that Perrin was suffering from "a case of recurring organic hemiplegia [paralysis of one side of the body] with ocular lesions, due to cerebral circulatory defects."[52] They attempted to substantiate their findings in a 39-page document complete with a medical history of Perrin and his family, a review of the events leading up to his recovery, a detailed discussion of the symptoms of his illness, and supporting evidence including visual field diagrams and X-ray pictures. On the basis of its diagnosis and report, the international committee declared his recovery scientifically inexplicable; the church finally declared Perrin's cure to be a miracle, the 64th and latest official miracle in the history of Lourdes.

But was Perrin's cure inexplicable in terms of current scientific knowledge, let alone inexplicable in some absolute sense? In light of recent evidence this seems dubious. A small sample of specialists in the United States who independently examined the document produced by the international committee of doctors found the cure of Perrin very suspicious, the data in the document highly problematic, the document obscure and filled with technical verbiage. For example, Donald H. Harter, professor and chairman of the department of neurology at Northwestern University Medical School in Chicago, found "an absence of *objective* neurological abnormalities." Drummond Rennie, associate professor of medicine at Harvard Medical School, maintained that the document presented by the international committee of

---

[52] *Ibid.*, p. 134.

doctors "was unscientific and totally unconvincing." Robert A. Levine, assistant clinical professor of ophthalmology at the University of Illinois, argued that the visual field diagrams presented in the documented are mislabeled and inconsistent with the text of the document. He called the description as a whole "a lot of mumbo jumbo."[53]

The doctors who reviewed the document found a variety of problems. For example, although crucial laboratory tests such as a spinal tap and radioactive brain scan were standard in most hospitals for diagnosing the illness Perrin was said to have, they were not performed. The reviewers also considered the diagnosis of hemiplegia implausible; because he had right leg weakness *and* left visual and motor symptoms, more than one side of Perrin's brain had to be involved. In addition, symptoms of generalized constriction of his visual field and various sensorimotor disturbances suggested hysteria rather than an organic illness. Moreover, the American specialists who reviewed the document maintained that if there was an organic illness at all, multiple sclerosis was the most likely explanation of Perrin's symptoms. However, it is well known that multiple sclerosis has fleeting symptoms with periodic severe flare-ups followed by remissions that are sometimes complete.

There are also problems accepting the 63rd and penultimate official miracle in the history of Lourdes.[54] In this 1963 case, while at Lourdes a 22-year-old Italian, Vittorio Micheli, experienced a sudden recovery from a sarcoma type of tumor on his hip that had destroyed part of the pelvis, iliac, and surrounding muscles. The Lourdes medical bureau said X-rays confirmed that a bone reconstruction had taken place that was unknown in the annals of medicine. In 1976 the church official recognized Micheli's recovery as a miracle.

However, as James Randi has pointed out in his investigation of this case, spontaneous regression of malignant tumors of the hip are not unknown in the annals of medicine.[55] To be sure, if Micheli's hip had been completely regenerated, this would indeed be unprecedented. But in order to verify that complete regeneration of the bone had taken place, exploratory surgery would have been necessary. X-rays cannot distinguish between a genuine regeneration and a regrowth known as a pseudoarthrosis, which is not unknown in the annals of medicine. But there is no record of any surgical procedure being done to validate Micheli's complete regeneration. Indeed, Randi notes that a case virtually identical to Micheli's was reported in 1978 in the *Acta Orthopaedica Scandivanica*.[56] In both instances no medical treatment was reported, the recovery took place in the same way, and the results were the same. However, in this latter case no claim was made that a miracle had occurred.

Medical authorities to whom Randi submitted Micheli's dossier for examination were incredulous at the medical treatment Micheli is reported to have received. For example, according to the dossier the hospital waited 36 days before it took an X-ray and 43 days before it performed a biopsy. Moreover, according to the dossier Micheli lived in a military hospital for ten months before he went to Lourdes, during which time he received no medical treatment of any kind except painkillers, tranquilizers, and vitamins. On the other hand, there are hints in the dossier that he did receive drugs and radiation. All this is extremely puzzling and surely casts doubt on the accuracy of the dossier.

The problems with the 1963 Micheli case and the 1970 Perrin case suggest that there is something badly amiss in the application of the procedures used by the Catholic Church for officially declaring something a miracle cure at Lourdes. An apparently questionable diagnosis of

---

[53] *Ibid*
[54] See Patrick Marnharm, *Lourdes: A Modern Pilgrimage* (New York: Coward, McCann and Geoghegan, 1981).
[55] Randi, *Faith Healers,* pp. 27-29.
[56] *Acta Orthopaedica Scandinavica,* 49, 1978, pp. 49-53. Cited in Randi, *Faith Healers,* pp. 28-29.

Perrin and an unsubstantiated judgment about Micheli's cure were accepted by the Lourdes medical bureau and the international committee.

Furthermore, there is a general problem connected with the procedures at Lourdes that I have not yet mentioned: the expertise of the doctors who first examine a pilgrim at Lourdes who claims to have recovered from an illness. The only qualification needed for a person to join the full-time medical bureau doctor in examining an allegedly cured pilgrim is the person be a doctor and be visiting the shrine. But one might well question the objectivity of doctors who accompany the sick to Lourdes or who visit Lourdes for other reasons. For one thing, doctors who visit Lourdes may well get caught up in the awe and the excitement of the pilgrimage. For another, doctors who want to visit Lourdes may be initially disposed to accept miracle cures.

Every doctor has of course seen cures and remissions of diseases for which there is no explanation. Some of these diseases are self-limiting; others, like multiple sclerosis, have periods of flare-ups and remissions; still others have hysterical origins. It is difficult to separate hysterical symptoms from organic ones. The problem is made more difficult by the fact that hysterical symptoms may follow and take the place of organic ones. Moreover, in some illnesses, among them multiple sclerosis, physical and hysterical symptoms can exist at the same time. As we have seen, doctors in the United States who reviewed the report of the international committee suggested that Perrin suffered from hysteria or multiple sclerosis; it is conceivable that he had both types of symptoms.

If the alleged miracle cures at Lourdes are merely remissions or are cures based on natural processes that are not understood by the examining physicians at Lourdes then one would expect that the number of inexplicable cures accepted by the Lourdes medical bureau would decline over the years as medical knowledge and sophistication increased. Indeed, this is precisely what has happened. From 1883 to 1947 nearly 5,000 cures were accepted as inexplicable by the physicians at the Lourdes medical bureau. This is approximately 78 per year. But from 1947 to 1980 only 28 cures were accepted as inexplicable, less than one per year.[57] And we may well expect that there will be further decreases in the "inexplicable" cures as medical knowledge increases. Such evidence surely casts doubt on the 64 official declared miracles at Lourdes, especially the earlier ones. If the doctors at the Lourdes medical bureau had had the expertise of contemporary doctors, it is doubtful that many of the alleged miracles that occurred before 1947 would have made it through the first screening.

Since the cures at Lourdes are perhaps the best documented of all the so-called miracle cures, and their evidential value seems dubious, one may well have grave doubts about other claims of miracle cures that are less well documented.

Indirect Miracles

Earlier in this chapter, I provisionally defined a miracle as an event brought about by the exercise of a supernatural power. However, there is a modern view of miracles that is not captured by this definition,[58] namely that God set up the world in such a way that an unusual event would occur to serve as a sign or message to human beings. Suppose, for example, that God set up the world so that at a certain time in history the Red Sea would part. The parting would be governed by the laws of nature$_n$—for instance, a freak wind might part the sea. Given the circumstances surrounding the event, this parting would convey a message to religious believers. Although no direct intervention of God would be involved, God would be behind the scenes, setting up the

---

[57] Bernstein, "Lourdes," p. 139.
[58] See Fitzgerald, "Miracles," p. 61.

particular working of nature$_n$ so that the Red Sea parted at the exact time needed to save his chosen people.

This view of miracles has become popular in modern philosophy, although it can be traced back at least to Maimonides. To accommodate this sort of case, my provisional definition is revised in the following way: A miracle is an event brought about by the direct or not necessarily direct exercise of a supernatural power to serve as a sign or communicate a message.[59] The second disjunct of the definition is necessary to account for miracles on the modern view (*indirect miracles* let us call them), and the first disjunct accounts for ones on the traditional view (let us call them *direct miracles*).

The difficulties with indirect miracles are apparent. Why believe that an event is a miracle in this indirect sense? Why not suppose that it is merely a coincidence? Moreover, even if one has good reason to suppose that something is an indirect miracle, there is no good reason to believe that God, rather than some other supernatural force, indirectly brought it about.

There is an additional problem. One wonders how much free will is left to humans on this view of miracles. Consider the parting of the Red Sea. If the event had occurred an hour earlier, it would have been of no help; if the event had occurred an hour later, it would have been too late to help the Israelites. This seems to entail that the Israelites, in order to be at the right place at the right time, could not have chosen any differently than they did. For example, if they had decided to rest a little longer along the way, God's plan would have been upset; the sea would have parted before they arrived.

This seems to conflict with the commonly held religious belief that humans have free will and that even God cannot know what they will decide, in that, given the notion of an indirect miracle, it is essential to know what human beings will decide so that the miracle will occur at the right time.[60]

Conclusion

I must conclude that there is no *a priori* reason for there not to be miracles—no reason even for there not to be good evidence for miracles. However, there are difficult *a posteriori* obstacles to surmount before one can claim that miracles have occurred in either the direct or the indirect sense. Furthermore, even if there were good reasons to suppose that miracles existed in either sense, this would not necessarily mean that the existence of miracles provides inductive support for theism. As we have seen, the existence of miracles provides inductive support for theism only in the existence of a miracle is more probable relative to theism and background information than it is relative to the negation of theism and background information. But it is not at all clear that it is. Thus the argument from miracles fails.

---

[59] Ibid.
[60] As we shall see in Chapter 15 on the free will defense, some philosophers have argued that free will in the contracausal sense, in which human decisions are uncaused, is compatible with God's knowing how human beings will decide and how they would decide under certain hypothetical circumstances. However, as I argue, this view is difficult to make sense of.

Questions

1. What are the essentials of a miracle on Michael Martin's account?
2. Why does Martin think that there is no *a priori* reason why a miracle could not be repeated many times?
3. Why does Martin conclude that one does not have to choose between naturalism and supernaturalism prior to answering the question whether miracles have occurred?
4. What is the difficulty in "showing the existence of miracles?"
5. What is Martin's final verdict on miracles?

Questions:

1. What are the essentials of a miracle on Michael Martin's account?
2. Why does Martin think that there is no a priori reason why a miracle could not be repeated many times?
3. Why does Martin conclude that one does not have to choose between naturalism and supernaturalism prior to answering the question whether miracles have occurred?
4. What is the difficulty in "showing the existence of miracles"?
5. What is Martin's final verdict on miracles?

MIRACLES AND THE LAWS OF NATURE*

George I. Mavrodes

Construing miracles as "violations," I argue that a law of nature must specify some kind of possibility. But we must have here a sense of possibility for which the ancient rule of logic—ab esse ad posse valet consequentia—does not hold. We already have one example associated with the concept of statute law, a law which specifies what is legally possible but which is not destroyed by a violation. If laws of nature are construed as specifying some analogous sense of what is naturally possible, then they need not be invalidated by a (rare) violation, and Humean miracles remain a genuine possibility.

Some people, as you know, claim that miracles have actually occurred, they are a real part of the history of the world, just like the more ordinary wars, marriages, and inventions which figure in our history books. Christians, for example, characteristically claim that Jesus was a real historical man, and that he actually did some miracles. These claims generate a considerable range of philosophical questions and puzzles.

On one hand, there are the questions which are primarily *epistemological*. For example, what would be a satisfactory sort of evidence that a miracle had actually occurred? What sort of evidence do we have in fact for the reality of miracles? And, going in the other epistemological direction, what would a miracle be evidence *for*? What sort of religious position or doctrine could be established or supported by reference to a miracle? And so on. For the most part I will ignore questions of this epistemological variety in this paper.

There are also questions, however, which call directly for an analysis or clarification of the concept of a miracle. Just what are Christians claiming, for example, when they say that Jesus performed miracles? Were all of his acts miracles? If not, how are the allegedly miraculous acts supposed to differ from the others? And what must the world be like if an act or event of that sort is to be possible? These questions appear to combine a metaphysical concern with a desire for a better understanding of a suggestive and problematic concept. In this paper I try to follow out one such line of questioning.

More specifically, I want to explore to some degree the ways in which the concepts of the *miraculous* and of a *law of nature* react on one another. And I will also be speculating about what sorts of laws of nature the world must have if miracles are to be a genuine possibility in it.

Our inquiry can begin with David Hume's famous discussion which has generated so many responses and continuations. In that discussion Hume put forward what is probably the most influential philosophical definition of "miracle" ever given:

> A miracle may be accurately defined, a transgression of a law of nature by a particular volition of the Deity, or by the interposition of some invisible agent.[1]

This definition has two parts. On the one hand, it specifies the relation of the miraculous act or event to the laws of nature. On the other hand, it specifies the relation of that event to a divine or supernatural agent. It seems to me that both of these elements reflect aspects of the pre-philosophical way in which miracles are construed, at least in Christian contexts.

One of these pre-philosophical elements is that the miracle is something which would not have happened—indeed, which *could not* have happened—in the ordinary course of events. It

---

* *Faith and Philosophy*, Vol. 2 No. 4 October 1985. All rights reserved.
[1] David Hume, *Enquiry Concerning Human Understanding*, Sec. x, Part i.

strikes the observer, the observer who recognizes it as a miracle, as being somehow a break in the structure of the world. It need not, of course, be an unwelcome break. It may well be recognized, as C.S. Lewis suggests, as a break which is *fitting,* appropriate to the situation in which it occurs.[2] But it is seen as something which does not "naturally" belong to that situation.

In one of the Gospels, for example, it is said that Jesus was a guest at a wedding party in which the supply of wine was unexpectedly exhausted. He asked the servants to fill several jugs with water, and then immediately had them serve a sample of this drink to the master of the feast. That worthy gentleman found it to be wine of a better quality than had been originally provided.[3] Apparently the water had been converted, more or less instantaneously, into wine. Regardless of whether we believe this story to be true most of us, I think, will recognize it as belonging to a different genre than a story about someone who sends a servant out to buy some more wine from the local supplier.

One way of trying to formulate this difference—but it is only an initial approximation—is to say that this act, like the healings, the raising of Lazarus from the dead, and so on, is *hard*. Not everyone could do it. There is, as it were, a resistance in things against events of this sort, and it requires a special power to accomplish them. No doubt this power is sometimes construed simply as a force which coerces things into a course which they would not otherwise follow. But sometimes in the Gospels there seems to me to be a different suggestion, a construal of the requisite power not as a force but as an authority. This distinction, however, is not one we can follow out here.

That the miraculous act is hard to do is, of course, not exactly the right thing to say. It apparently is not hard in just the same way in which it is hard to run a mile in four minutes, and it does not require special powers in the same way as breaking an Olympic record requires unusual strength, endurance, and skill. We are tempted to say that it is even harder than that. But of course that is not quite right either. Maybe Hume's way of putting it, in terms of laws of nature, is more illuminating. At any rate, once we have the concept of a law of nature—once it seems to us that we can say something penetrating and revealing about the world by using that notion—then it also seems natural to try to explain the special character of the miraculous in those terms. That is the project which I want to explore in this paper.

Whether we can illuminate the idea of the miraculous, however, by means of the concept of the laws of nature will presumably depend on what the content of that latter concept is. It may be that the idea of a law of nature was first introduced in the West by thinkers operating more or less within a Christian framework of thought. But for several hundred years now that idea has been developed and applied in a largely secular way, without much concern for its religious connections. Does it still connect usefully with the religious concept of the miraculous?

Before we get into that, however, let us return to the pre-philosophical context for a moment to notice that the second element in it, that of the miracle's being the act of a special agent, is closely connected there with the first. We may try to get across a sense of the special character of the miraculous act by saying, as I did above, that not everyone could do it—it must take a very special sort of person to convert water into wine, to calm a storm by speaking to it, to call the dead from the grave, and so on. But of course we might also try to convey a sense of the special character of the person by reference (in part) to the miraculous acts which he did. Jesus, that is, must be a very special sort of man because he could, and did, raise the dead, etc. At the

---

[2] C. S. Lewis, *Miracles: A Preliminary Study* (London: Geoffrey Bles—The Centenary Press, 1947. 220 pp.), pp. 115-20 (ch. xii).
[3] John, ch. 2, vs. 1-11.

pre-philosophical stage, then, the two elements which appear in Hume's analysis are closely inter-twined. Perhaps we wish (is it for the sake of clarity?) that they could be separated.

In Hume's analysis itself, it seems to me, they *are* separated. Hume conjoins these elements, of course. Nothing will count as a Humean miracle unless it is *both* a violation of a law of nature and the action of a divine agent. But, so far as I can see, Hume leaves this conjunction as possibly purely external. He suggests no internal connection between these concepts. If we take his analysis seriously, therefore, we can ask whether it is possible that there is an event which satisfies one-half of the analysis but not the other. Could there be, for example, an event which was a violation of a law of nature, but which was not (in any special way, at least) an act of God? Such an event would not, of course, be a Humean miracle. But could such an event occur? Do such events occur? Do we have a special name for them? And on the other hand, could there be an act of God—in a sense, that is, in which not everything is an act of God—which was not a violation of a law of nature?

Though I mention these questions here, I will have only a little to say about them in this paper. Like most of the discussions growing out of Hume's analysis—indeed, like Hume's own discussion—mine here will focus mainly on the first element in his definition, the relation of the miraculous to the laws of nature. And I begin with what seems to me to be a powerful objection to the reality of Humean miracles.

The objection of which I am thinking is put by Alastair McKinnon, for example, in this way:

> The idea of a suspension of natural law is self-contradictory. This follows from the meaning of the term...[Natural laws] are simply highly generalized shorthand descriptions of how things do in fact happen.... Hence there can be no suspensions of natural law rightly understood.... Once we understand natural law in this proper sense we see that such a law, as distinct from our conception of it, is inherently inviolable. Hence anything which happens, even an apparent miracle, happens according to law.... This contradiction may stand out more clearly if for *natural law* we substitute the expression *the actual course of events*. *Miracle* would then be defined as "an event involving the suspension of the actual course of events." And someone who insisted upon describing an event as a miracle would be in the rather odd position of claiming that its occurrence was contrary to the actual course of events.[4]

McKinnon, as we see, holds that it is not logically possible that an event satisfy the first part of Hume's analysis—i.e., it is not logically possible that there be an event which is a violation of a law of nature. And why would miracles be logically impossible? It is because a law of nature does not allow—that is, it *logically* does not allow—of any violations.

I said earlier that miracles may be thought of as being hard to do, and as requiring special powers. The objection we are now considering does not proceed, however, by construing the laws of nature themselves as being so resistant as to surpass any counter-vailing power. McKinnon, in fact, says explicitly that laws of nature "exert no opposition or resistance to anything, not even to the odd or exceptional."[5] No, it is simply that the laws of nature are being construed either as invariant regularities in the natural world or else as the statements which express, or assert the occurrence of, such regularities. As McKinnon puts it, they are just generalized descriptions of the actual course of events, no matter what those events happen to be.

If we construe a law of nature in this way, then the proposition which corresponds to a law of nature will have the form of a universal generalization. The alleged violation, on the other

---

[4] Alastair McKinnon, " 'Miracle' and 'Paradox,' " *American Philosophical Quarterly*, Vol. 4, No. 4 (Oct. 1967) p. 309.
[5] *Ibid.*

hand, will presumably be a particular event—something like the conversion of the water into wine or the raising of Lazarus from the dead. The corresponding proposition will be either a singular proposition or an existential generalization. And now what is the logical relation of this proposition to the universal generalization which corresponds to the law of nature?

Well, if these two propositions are logically compatible then evidently the particular event is compatible with the invariant regularity. But in that case it is not a violation of that regularity, and hence it is not a Humean miracle. If, on the other hand, the two propositions are logically incompatible, then it is not logically possible that they should both be true. If it is the proposition asserting the occurrence of the particular event which is false, then that event did not occur. There has therefore been (so far, at least) no miracle. If, on the other hand, it is the universal generalization which is false, then the world does not in fact contain the corresponding invariant regularity. But (on this view) that amounts to saying that the world does not contain that law of nature after all. It was at best merely an *apparent* law of nature, what was *thought* to be a law of nature, or some such thing. But since the regularity was not in fact invariant it did not constitute a genuine law. Hence there has been no violation of a genuine law, and so again there has been no genuine Humean miracle.

Every possibility, therefore, seems to lead to the same result. No Humean miracle has occurred. And therefore, it would seem, no such miracle is possible. Put somewhat picturesquely, this view of things claims that either the alleged event can co-exist peacefully with the regularity or else it must kill the regularity, showing it to be a sham. In neither case is there a genuine violation of a genuine regularity, and therefore in neither case is there a genuine miracle.

As I said, this seems to me to involve a powerful and significant objection, but in the way in which it has been put here it invites an easy reply. We can begin by observing that the conclusion which we have attributed to the objector need not be greatly disturbing to any religious person or any "friend of miracles." Nothing that the objector has said tends to show at all, or to make it in any way probable, that Jesus did not turn water into wine, that he did not calm a storm with a word or raise Lazarus from the dead, and so on. Nor does it tend to show that these events did not have a profound religious significance. It does not even tend to show that these things, if they happened, were not miracles. At most (for better or worse) it tends to show that they are not *Humean* miracles. That is, if the objector is right in this argument, then the friend of miracles cannot use Hume's analysis to elucidate the concept of a miracle. Either he must leave that concept in its somewhat inchoate pre-philosophical condition, or he must find some illuminating alternative to Hume's suggestion. The concept of natural law which is adopted by McKinnon, then, is not helpful to the friend of miracles, but neither is it damaging to him. It simply turns out to be pretty much irrelevant to the topic of miracles.

We need not, it seems to me, think that it must be a great tragedy if the concept of natural law turns out not to be very useful in explaining the concept of a miracle. After all, we have lots of concepts which are not closely connected with the miraculous. And we might well be able to find some other useful way of analyzing and explaining what a miracle is. In this paper, however, I am continuing to explore what we can do with laws of nature in this connection.

As I say, we can observe that McKinnon's claim here need not be disturbing to the friend of miracles. Perhaps more fruitful, however, would be the observation that this objection itself relies on an unsatisfactory conception of a law of nature, or at least one which is widely thought to be unsatisfactory. If a law of nature is simply an invariant regularity then we do not provide for a distinction in this connection between those regularities which are *accidental* and those which are somehow more deeply rooted in the nature of things. Put in the more formal mode of speech, it is often pointed out that some universal generalizations seem to entail a corresponding set of counter-factual hypotheticals, while other generalizations do not. It may be true, for example, that everyone here today is a U.S. citizen. But even if this is true it does not seem to imply that if Margaret Thatcher were here today then she would be a U.S. citizen. If it is true, however, that all masses attract each other according to Newton's formula, then that *would* seem to imply that if I were wearing a massive helmet right now then it would be attracted by the earth. Generalizations of the latter sort are often called *nomological* or *law-like,* and the other sort are the accidentals. And it is rather commonly held that it is only the nomological generalizations which represent, or correspond to, laws of nature. And if that is correct, then McKinnon's account here is defective.

We may note in passing, however, that ignoring this distinction, as McKinnon appears to do, makes much more plausible something else that McKinnon holds. He says that scientists "assume that all events are law-like (whatever that really means) or, at least, that they must be treated as such. They assume that every event can be shown to be an instance of some generalization, whether simple or statistical. This is why the scientist holds that there are no suspensions of natural law."[6]

Now, it is a fact that if we place no restriction on the type of generalization which is allowable, then every event, no matter how bizarre and anomalous it may be, will be subsumable under some generalization. This is like the fact that no matter how randomly a set of points may be distributed on a graph, there is some line which can be drawn through them. Given, then, what appears to be McKinnon's version of a law of nature, what is here ascribed to the scientist as an "assumption" turns out to be a necessary truth.

If, however, we restrict the relevant generalizations to those which are nomological, and perhaps also (as Richard Swinburne does) to those which are relatively simple, then it is not at all clear that all events are subsumable in this way.[7] And if some scientists do *assume* that this is the case, as McKinnon says, then we might well ask them what has led them to this curious assumption.

Returning now to our main line of inquiry, I will proceed on the supposition that the nomological/accidental distinction is an important one for our concept of a law of nature. The notion of a nomological is, of course, not perfectly clear itself. I don't have much that is illuminating to say about it right here, though I will have one further suggestion later on. For the time being let me just observe that I find a suggestion of R. F. Holland attractive in this connection. Objecting to the view that a law of nature is just a description, Holland says that "the law tells us, defines for us, what is and is not *possible...*"[8] And he goes on to say that a law of nature, like a legal law, "stipulates" something. And this suggests that the formal representation of such a law will be a universal generalization with the modality of necessity.

Adopting this suggestion however, as I propose to do, seems to re-instate McKinnon's objection, perhaps now in a less vulnerable form. For the singular statement, "This A is not B" seems to be incompatible with "Necessarily, every A is B" just as it is with the unmodalized "Every A is B." And so must it not again be the case that every actual event which apparently violates a law of nature really only shows that this was not a genuine law after all, since the modalized generalization is shown to be false by the counter-example to it?

Holland's own solution to this difficulty is to propose that we reject "that time-honored logical principle," *ab esse ad possee valet consequentia.*[9] And this is equivalent to rejecting a stock theorem of modal logic to the effect that *Necessary p* entails *p.*

---

[6] *Ibid.*
[7] Richard Swinburne, *The Concept of Miracle* (London: Macmillan and Co., 1970. 76pp.), pp. 23ff.
[8] R. F. Holland, "The Miraculous," *American Philosophical Quarterly, Vol.* 2, No. I (Jan. 1965), p, 46.
[9] *Ibid.,* p. 49.

That proposal does seem to solve the difficulty. If "Necessarily, every A is B" does not entail "Every A is B," then "this A is not B" does not seem to be incompatible with the modalized statement. And consequently, it would seem, both the law-like "Necessarily, every A is B" and the anomalous singular statement "This A is not B" may be true together. And so, if we can swallow Holland's proposal, we need not take the violation to invalidate the putative law.

What, however, becomes of the idea of violation here? If the singular statement is not incompatible with the law-like, modalized, generalization, then how does the singular statement represent a *violation* of the corresponding law? I think that we can answer this question. We can introduce the expression, "the *formal content* of P," where P is a modalized proposition, to refer to whatever proposition follows the (first) modal operator in P. Thus, the formal content of "Necessarily, every A is B" will be simply "Every A is B." The "time-honored principle" which Holland proposes to reject says that every necessary proposition entails its own formal content. But even if we follow Holland in rejecting this entailment, we can still recognize that the formal content of a necessary proposition bears a special and intimate relation to that proposition. We can therefore say that, where L represents a law of nature and P represents an event, then P represents a *violation* of L IFF P is logically incompatible with the formal content of L.

Well, this would seem to give us a usable notion of a violation of a law of nature, but perhaps the price seems too high. If we must reject a standard theorem of modal logic in order to retain the idea of a violation would it not be better to give up on that idea, give up on Hume's definition, and look for some other way of explaining what a miracle is? After all, if "necessarily, p" does not entail "p," then what will be left of modal logic at all?

Well, I think that there is something to this reaction, alright, but it need not be conclusive. We do need to recognize, I think, that Holland's way of putting the thing is unnecessarily paradoxical. He speaks of rejecting the time-honored principle. (Curiously, he also speaks of accepting "a contradiction in our experience."[10] But the effect of rejecting the time-honored principle is precisely to prevent the miracle from being contradictory to the law.) But nothing in the situation requires us to reject that principle in general. The most that we need along this line is to find *some* sort of necessity for which the principle does not hold. If we could ascribe that sort of necessity to the laws of nature, then we would be in a position to recognize violations of those laws. But we would not need to deny that the time-honored principle of logic still held for other sorts of necessity, for example for logical necessity.

Now, it is a curious and significant fact that we seem *already* to have at hand, and in common use, a sense of necessity which has just this feature. It is a sort of necessity for which the time-honored principle does *not* hold, one in which the fact that something is necessary does not entail that the thing actually happens. And where do we find this sort of necessity? Well, one place is in the law—not a law of nature now, but the sort of law that legislatures enact and which courts enforce, what I will call *legal* law. In that sort of law there is a necessity for which "necessarily, p" does not entail "p."

One common way to express a legal law is simply as a universal generalization, something like "Every resident having an annual income over $1,000 shall file a return by April 15...." etc. Of course, there must be something in the context that indicates that the generalization is to be taken as a law. The fact that the generalization was adopted by a state legislature, for example, would perform that function. Given that context, however, the universal generalization expresses a legal law.

---

[10] *Ibid.*, p. 51.

Now, this legal law seems to invite just the sort of observations which Holland makes about the laws of nature. The legal law is not simply a description of actual regularities in human behavior. Rather, it defines or stipulates a certain sort of possibility—it tells us what is *legally* possible and impossible. And, of course, the law admits of violations. That is, it provides a context or background against which the idea of a violation makes sense and furthermore, the actuality of a violation does not invalidate the law. Though the violation is a *violation* precisely in virtue of its contrariety to the law, nevertheless both the law and its violation can co-exist.

We can, of course, imagine someone's making the analogue of McKinnon's objection. Observing that someone has not filed a return, he would point out that this fact is logically incompatible with the truth of the universal generalization. The generalization must therefore be false. And how, he may ask, could a false generalization express a true and valid law?

In the case of the legal law, however, we recognize this objection to be misdirected. A person who makes such an objection to the propriety of the alleged law betrays his misunderstanding of what a legal law amounts to.

Though legal laws are often expressed simply as categorical generalizations sometimes the modal element in them is made more explicit by the inclusion in them of some modal expression. "All residents *must* file a return...." Here the necessity seems to be open, on the surface of the expression. But it is a necessity for which the time-honored principle does not hold. A McKinnon-type objection to the validity of this law would again be misdirected.

Perhaps this point should be made more carefully. We can begin by observing that there is a sense in which expressions like

(1) Mr. N, a resident, etc., did not file a return.

can be taken as representing or reporting a fact about the world, an actual event, etc. And there is a sense in which

(2) All residents, etc., will file a return.

can be understood as a generalization which is logically incompatible with (1). (2), for example, might be a prediction made by a fortune teller or a political scientist. In that case, (1), if true, would show (2) to be false.

If legislature, however, were to adopt a sentence identical with the one which appears in (2) (doing so in the prescribed way, etc.) then it would not be asserting the proposition asserted in (2). The legislature would not be committing itself to something which was logically incompatible with (1). We could say that the legislature was adopting a *nomic* generalization.

(2N) All residents, etc., will file a return.

And this nomic generalization, though it uses the same sentence as (2), is not logically incompatible with (1). That is why a McKinnon-type objection fails. It confuses (2N) with (2).

In a similar way we need to distinguish

(3) Necessarily, all residents will file...

from its nomic analogue, (3N), which might be expressed using the same sentence or a similar one. There are some sorts of necessity—logical necessity, for example,—for which (3) entails (2), and for which, therefore, (3) is logically incompatible with (1). In order to understand the law we do not need to deny that there are such types of necessity, nor need we entertain any doubt about that entailment. (3N), however, does not involve that sort of necessity. Perhaps (3N) entails (2N) (though I suspect that they are identical), but it does not entail (2). And therefore it is not logically incompatible with (1).

Earlier, I defined the expression, "the formal content of P," where P was a modalized expression. We should now revise this definition. The formal content of (3N) should not be taken to be (2N). It is, rather, simply (2). I.e., the formal content of a modalized proposition is the *non-nomic* analogue of the proposition which follows the (first) modal operator. We can then explain the notion of a violation just as before. Since (1) is logically incompatible with (2), the formal content of (3N), it is a violation of (3N).

Legal laws are not logically incompatible with their violations, and are not invalidated by their violations. It does not follow, of course, that legal laws have no bearing on human behavior. In some societies at least, the fact that something was legally necessary would be a good reason for expecting the thing to happen, and the fact that an alleged event was legally impossible would be a good reason for suspecting that the event did not really happen. And we could also go in the other direction. If we could not discover the legal laws of that society "directly," e.g., by reading the law books, then we might attempt to determine them inductively, by generalizing from observed behavior. If we noticed a lot of people rushing to the post office to file tax returns on April 15, for example, we might form the hypothesis that this date was specified by a law. We might go on to test this hypothesis further, coming to think, perhaps, that it was not exactly accurate, refining it to include a provision for automatic extension, and so on, until we came to some formulation as our best guess, subject, of course, to future correction, of one of the laws underlying the behavior of that society.

Well, we have had a long excursion into the law, the legal law, that is. Can we return to the laws of nature? I know that it is often said that the laws of nature are not at all like legal laws, that it is an anthropomorphic fallacy to think that they are similar, and so on. This is repeated so often, it seems to me, that perhaps we should take it to be the currently received doctrine on the subject. Must we therefore also take it to be *true*? I guess that I am not now ready to do so. For one thing, despite this alleged complete dissimilarity it has apparently been natural for hundreds of years, right down to the present, to use the very same word, "law," for both of these cases. That strikes me as significant, suggesting that there has been a long and persistent recognition of important structural similarities. Nor need we be completely vague about what those similarities are. We have just been noticing some of them, at least, in the last few minutes. I suspect that our long practice in the West of using the same terminology for legal laws and laws of nature has a substantial foundation in the nature of the phenomena which are being discussed.

At any rate, we do not seem to be at a loss for a sense of necessity, already in hand, which allows for violations. If we were to construe the laws of nature as having that sort of necessity, or some similar sort, then it would seem possible for there to be events which satisfy the first part of Hume's definition. That concept of a law of nature seems to promise some utility in explaining what a miracle is.

Well, I suppose that we can have one concept or another. Is that all there is to it? One feels like saying that there must be more. What idea of the laws of nature actually fits the world? What sort of laws are there, "out there"? I don't know that I can say much that is illuminating about this. Let me close, however, with one observation. Much contemporary discussion of this sort of topic by contemporary philosophers of science leaves us, I think, in an unsatisfactory position. I mentioned, early on in this paper, the distinction between accidental and nomological generalizations. Well and good; there does seem to be such a distinction. Some of these propositions support the corresponding counter-factuals and others do not. But why is that? It doesn't seem as though it could be due to a difference in the surface grammar of these statements, since at that level they are the same, simply universal generalizations. Maybe, however, it can be said that these propositions are to be understood in different ways. One of them is to be taken "simply" as a generalization, entailing only those instantiations which fall under it in the actual world. The other, however, is intended to be taken as a *law*. I.e., it is intended to be understood as entailing not only its actual instantiations but also the counter-factuals. So it covers not only the actual world but also a range of possible worlds. And I, at least, suppose that some account like this is probably true.

What happens, however, if we insist on understanding the so-called accidental as if it were a nomological? I.e., we understand it to entail the corresponding counterfactuals, or at least to support them. Well, presumably what happens in that case is that it just turns out to be false. Understood as nomological, the statement "Everyone here is a citizen of the U.S." is just false. There is simply no such law of nature. But what is it that makes this proposition, interpreted nomically, false? Well, perhaps it is the fact that it entails a proposition such as "If Margaret Thatcher were here today she would be a U.S. citizen." And that counter-factual proposition is false.

Well, perhaps that is why the generalization, interpreted nomically, is false. But that, of course, invites us to ask why this counter-factual is false, while the counter-factual which asserts that if I were wearing a helmet it would be attracted by the earth it true. One is tempted to say that one of these is true and the other is false because there is a law of nature which governs the attraction of the helmet and the earth, while there is no law of nature connecting presence in this hall with U.S. citizenship. That, no doubt, is true. But we began this series of questions by trying to understand the difference between the propositions which express laws of nature and those which express universal, but accidental, generalizations. If the present claim, therefore, that there is a law of nature concerning the attraction of the helmet to the earth is to be illuminating in this connection the reference here to a law of nature can't be understood to be simply a reference to some proposition. It must rather be taken as a reference to some element of the actual world. We must be asserting that some propositions, understood nomically, actually connect with some feature or aspect of reality, while others, if they are taken in the nomic sense, do not. That is what makes some of them true and others false. The laws of nature, then, will be actual features of the real world. We cannot generate or produce a law of nature simply by formulating the corresponding proposition, nor by understanding it in the nomological way. For if we do understand, for example, the proposition about U.S. citizenship in this way, then we do not make it into a law of nature. We simply convert it into a falsehood.

Now, we may of course still be somewhat puzzled to know exactly what sort of features of the world a law of nature is. It does not appear to be a physical object. Perhaps it is more like a relation. But it is apparently not a spatial relation, not a temporal relation, and so on. Nor can it be the relation (if any) which is expressed by an ordinary universal generalization. For if it were then every such true generalization would express a law of nature. At least one striking oddity about it is that if it is a relation, then it relates non-existent things just as well as existent things. In order to generate the counterfactuals it has to govern the non-existent helmet which I might be wearing but am not, just as well as it governs the existing shoes which I am actually wearing.

Now, some of the things which David Hume says in connection with the idea of causality might be interpreted as maintaining that this alleged relation is not a perceptual object.[11] We have no sense impression of it. Consequently, the alleged concept of this relation does not refer to any

---

[11] David Hume, *A Treatise of Human Nature*, Book 1: Part i, Sec. i, and Part iii, Sec. ii.

such impression or to the residue of any impression. Consequently, there is no genuine idea there. The words which we use in this connection are *merely* words—empty sounds. We cannot, therefore, have any genuine assertions or denials involving it. If we do interpret Hume in this way then either the common distinction between accidental and nomological generalizations is vacuous, or else Humean theory itself is mistaken. And if it is mistaken, then either we do have an impression of this relation after all, or else it is possible to have a genuine concept without having the corresponding impression. I am strongly inclined to think that the accidental/nomological distinction is valid and important, and consequently I think that the theory which I have tentatively attributed to Hume is mistaken. But I do not right now have any strong leaning toward locating the mistake in one rather than the other of its two possible locations.

We might still feel, of course, that we don't yet have a full idea of just what relation this is. I don't know that I can now go much further with this. I'm inclined to try one further step, using the ideas of a "power." I'm not fully confident of it. You can try it yourself and see whether you come up with something better. I'm somewhat attracted by the idea that the laws of nature reflect powers which are somehow embedded in reality, powers which run along certain lines, we might say, and not along others. There is perhaps a power which "seizes," so to speak, upon objects which are close to one another, and which then, impels them toward one another. If there is such a power, then it would be what the law of gravity amounts to. There is, on the other hand, no deep power in nature which seizes upon people who enter this hall, and impels them into U.S. citizenship. The absence of such a power, then, would explain why the fact that everyone here is a U.S. citizen, if it is a fact, is an accidental rather than a nomological fact.

Well, whatever the fate of this idea of powers may be, it seems as though if we take up a realistic notion of the laws of nature as being features of reality, features which tend to produce certain effects, then we can also think of something which may over-ride such a feature or negate its effect. It appears, then, that a realistic construal of the laws of nature provides both a distinction which is apparently important to the understanding of science and also an attractive way of explaining at least part of the concept of the miraculous.

Questions

1. What two conditions are necessary for a Humean miracle?
2. Alastair McKinnon thinks that one of the conditions in the answer to question (1) cannot be satisfied. Which one is it and why?
3. What are "nomological generalizations?"
4. Mavrodes finds a sense of "necessity" required for a "law of nature" in what area?
5. What sort of "feature (or features) of the world" is a law of nature?

Figure 6

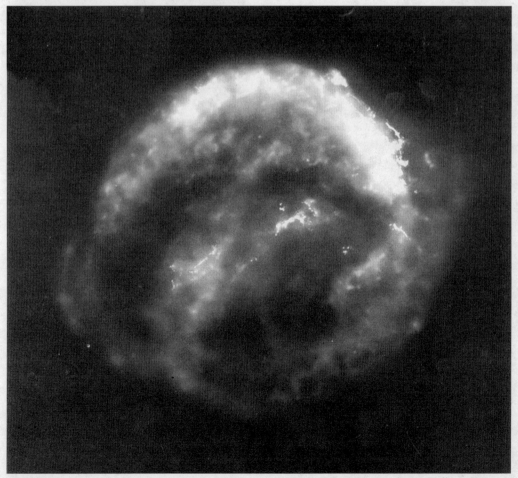

Figure 7

Part VI

Religion and Science

'WHAT PLACE, THEN FOR A CREATOR?': HAWKING ON GOD AND CREATION[*]

William Lane Craig

Craig first observes that Hawking begins with a universe where God is absent. And his first point by way of critical response is to point out that Hawking has not really taken into account assumptions that underlie his line of argument. Craig holds that Hawking leaves these assumptions largely unexamined, unjustified, and he further charges that they are at worst false. He charges that Hawking postulates metaphysical superspace, the metamorphosis of real to imaginary time, and the conflation of time and space, all of which are appraised as a very high price to pay for a "no Creator" thesis.

I. Introduction

Scientists working in the field of cosmology seem to be irresistibly drawn by the lure of philosophy. Now Stephen Hawking has followed lead of Fred Hoyle, Carl Sagan, Robert Jastrow, and P. C. W. Davies in speculating on what philosophical implications current mological models have for the existence of God. Although his recent best-seller A *Brief History of Time is* refreshingly free of the acrimony that characterized the works of some of his predecessors, one still might come away with the impression that Hawking is no more sympathetic to theism than they were. A recent article on Hawking's book in the German tabloid *Stern*, for example, headlined in 'Kein Platz für den lieben Gott', and concluded, 'In his system of thought there is no room for a Creator God. Not that God is dead: God never existed.'[1] This impression is no doubt abetted by the fact that the book carries an introduction by Sagan, in which he writes,

> This also a book about God...or perhaps about the absence of God. The word God fills these pages. Hawking embarks on a quest to answer Einstein's famous question about whether God had any choice in creating universe. Hawking is attempting, as he explicitly states, to understand the mind of God. And this makes all the more unexpected the conclusion of the effort, at least so far: a universe with no edge in space, no beginning nor end in time, and nothing for a Creator to do.[2]

II. God as Sufficient Reason

But such a characterization of Hawking's position is quite misleading. In point of fact, it is false that there is no place for God in Hawking's system or that God is absent. For while it is true that he rejects God's role as Creator of the universe in the sense of an efficient cause producing an absolutely first temporal effect, nevertheless Hawking appears to retain God's role as the Sufficient Reason for the existence of the universe, the final answer to the question, Why is there something rather than nothing? He distinguishes between the questions *what* the universe is and *why* the universe is, asserting that scientists have been too occupied with the former question to

---

[*] This article is reprinted here by courtesy of the author and publisher. It was first published in the *British Journal of Philosophical Science*, 41 (1990), 473-91.

[1] *Stern* (undated photocopy), 209. 'In seinem Gedankengebäude ist für einen schöpferischen Gott kein Raum. Gott ist nicht einmal tot, Gott hat nie existiert.'

[2] Carl Sagan, in S. W. Hawking, A *Brief History of Time: from the Big Bang to Black Holes,* intro. (New York: Bantam Books, 1988), p. x.

be able to ask the latter, whereas philosophers whose job it is to ask why-questions, have been unable to keep with the technical scientific theories concerning the origin of the universe and so have shunned metaphysical questions in favour of linguistic analysis. But Hawking himself is clear that having (to his satisfaction at least) answered the question what the universe is, he is still left with the unanswered why-question:

> The usual approach of science of constructing a mathematical model cannot answer the questions of why there should be a universe for the model to describe. Why does the universe go to all the bother of existing? Is the unified theory so compelling that it brings about its own existence? Or does it need a creator, and, if so, does he have any other effect on the universe? And who created him?[3]

Pursuing the question why we and the universe exist is a quest that, in Hawking's view, should occupy people in every walk of life. 'If we find the answer to that, it would be the ultimate triumph of human reason—for then we should know the mind of God.'[4]

At face value, then, God for Hawking serves as the Sufficent Reason for the existence of the universe. Of course, 'the mind of God' might well be a mere *façon de parler,* signifying something like 'the meaning of existence';[5] but, as Sagan noted, Hawking seems very much in earnest about determining the proper role of God as traditionally conceived in the scheme of things. And it is interesting to note that when a reader of an earlier summary draft of Hawking's book in *American Scientist*[6] complained that Hawking seemed afraid to admit the existence of a Supreme Being, Hawking countered that 'I thought I had left the question of the existence of a Supreme Being completely open.... It would be perfectly consistent with all we know to say that there was a Being who was responsible for the laws of physics.'[7]

Now it might seem at first somewhat baffling that Hawking senses the need to explain why the universe exists, since, as we shall see, he proposes a model of the universe according to which the universe is 'completely self-contained and not affected by anything outside itself', is 'neither created nor destroyed', but just is.[8] On his analysis, the universe is eternal (in the sense that it has neither beginning nor end and exists tenselessly) and therefore has no temporally antecedent cause. But if the cosmos is eternal and uncaused, what sense does it make to ask why it exists?

Leibniz, however, saw the sense of such a question.[9] He held that it is intelligible to ask why it is that an eternal being exists, since the existence of such a being is still logically contingent. Since it is possible that nothing exists, why is it that an eternal cosmos exists rather than nothing? There must still be a Sufficient Reason why there exists something—even an eternal something—rather than nothing. Leibniz concluded that this Sufficient Reason can only be found in a metaphysically necessary being, that is, a being whose nature is such that if it exists, it exists in all possible worlds. Hawking would be interested to learn that analytic

---

[3] Hawking, *A Brief History of Time,* 174.
[4] Ibid. 175
[5] Cf. the remark by Pagels: 'Physicists, regardless of their belief, may invoke God when they feel issues of principle are at stake because the God of the physicists is cosmic order.' (Heinz Pagels, *The Cosmic Code* [London: Michael Joseph, 1982.], 83).
[6] S. W. Hawking, 'The Edge of Spacetime', *American Scientist,* 72 (1984), 355-9.
[7] S. W. Hawking, 'Letters to the Editor: Time and the Universe', *American Scientist,* 73 (1985), 12.
[8] Hawking, *A Brief History of Time,* 136
[9] See G. W. Leibniz, 'On the Radical Origination of Things', 'The Principles of Nature and Grace, Based on Reason', and 'The Monadology', in *Philosophical Papers and Letters,* ed. L. E. Loemker, 2nd edn. (Dordrecht: D. Reidel, 1969), 486-91, 636-53.

philosophy in the past two decades has burst the skins of linguistic analysis and that certain analytic philosophers doing metaphysics have defended Leibniz's conception of God as a metaphysically necessary being.[10] Given the existence of such a being, Hawking need not trouble himself about who created God, since God, being metaphysically necessary and ultimate, can have no cause or ground of being.[11] Thus, it seems to me that far from banishing God from reality, Hawking invites us to make Him the basis of reality. Indeed, I think Hawking's book may rightly be read as a discussion of two forms of the cosmological argument: the so-called *kalām* cosmological argument for a temporally First Cause of the universe, which he rejects, and the Leibnizian cosmological argument for a Sufficient Reason of the universe, which he prefers.[12] In this essay, I am not concerned to evaluate the Leibnizian cosmological argument. Like Hawking, I feel the force of Leibniz's reasoning and am inclined to accept it; but unlike Hawking, it seems to me that the *kalām* argument is plausible as well. Accordingly, we need to ask, has Hawking eliminated the need for a Creator?

III. God as Metaphysically First Cause

Now at one level, the answer to that question is an immediate 'No.' For Hawking has a theologically deficient understanding of creation. Traditionally creation was thought to involve two aspects: *creatio originans* and *creatio continuans*. The first concerned God's bringing finite reality into being at a point in time before which no such reality existed, whereas the second involved (among other things) God's preservation of finite reality in being moment by moment. Only the first notion involves the idea of a beginning. *Creatio continuans* could involve a universe existing from everlasting to everlasting, that is to say, a universe temporally infinite in both the past and the future at any point of time. Thus, for example, Thomas Aquinas, confronted on the one hand with Aristotelian and Neoplatonic arguments for the eternity of the world, and, on the other hand, with Arabic *kalām*-style arguments for the finitude of, the past, concluded after a lengthy consideration of arguments both *pro* and *contra* that it can be proved neither that the universe had a beginning nor that it did not, but that the question of the temporal origin of the universe must be decided on the basis of divine revelation, that is, the teaching of the Scriptures.[13] Given this position, it appears at first paradoxical that Aquinas also held that the doctrine of divine *creatio ex nihilo* can be proved.[14] But once we understand that creation in the sense of *creatio continuans* involves no notion of a temporal beginning the paradox disappears. To affirm that God creates the world out of nothing is to affirm that God is the immediate cause of the world's existence, that there is no metaphysical intermediary between God and the universe.

---

[10] See e.g. Robert M. Adams, 'Has it Been Proved that All Real Existence Is Contingent?' *American Philosophical Quarterly*, 8 (1971), 284-91; Alvin Plantinga, *The Nature of Necessity*, Clarendon Library of Logic and Philosophy (Oxford: Clarendon Press, 1974), 197-221; William L. Rowe, *The Cosmological Argument* (Princeton, NJ: Princeton University Press, 1975), 202-21.

[11] On God as the ground of being for other metaphysically necessary entities, Thomas V. Morris and Christopher Menzel, 'Absolute Creation', *American Philosophical Quarterly*, 23 (1986), 353-62; Christopher Menzel, 'Theism, Platonism, and the Metaphysics of Mathematics', *Faith and Philosophy*, 4 (1987), 365-82. These bold essays should convince Hawking that the great tradition of metaphysics has been fully restored in analytic philosophy!

[12] On these arguments, as well as the Thomist argument, see William Lane Craig, *The Cosmological Argument from Plato to Leibniz*, Library of Philosophy and Religion (London: Macmillan, 1980).

[13] Thomas Aquinas, *Summa contra Gentiles*, 2.32-8; cf. Thomas Aquinas, *De Aeternitate Mundi contra Murmurantes*.

[14] Aquinas, *Summa contra Gentiles*, 2.16.

Actually, what Hawking has done is fail to distinguish from the *kalām* argument yet a third form of the cosmological argument, which we may call the Thomist cosmological argument, that comes to expression in Thomas's Third Way[15] and his *De Ente et Essentia*, 3. According to Aquinas, all finite beings, even those like the heavenly spheres or prime matter which have absolutely no potential for generation or corruption and are therefore by nature everlasting, are nevertheless metaphysically contingent in that they are composed of essence and existence, that is to say, their essential properties do not entail that such beings exist. If these essences are to be exemplified, therefore, there must be a being in whom essence and existence are not distinct and which therefore is uncaused, and it is this being which is the Creator of all finite beings, which he produces by instantiating their essences. Hence, *creatio ex nihilo* does not, in Aquinas's view, entail a temporal beginning of the universe.

Even if we maintain that a full-blooded doctrine of creation does entail a temporal beginning of the universe, the point remains that this doctrine also entails much more than that, so that even if God did not bring the universe into being at a point of time as in Hawking's model, it is still the case that there is much for Him to do, for without His active and continual bestowal of existence to the universe, the whole of finite reality would be instantly annihilated and lapse into non-being. Thus, any claim that Hawking has eliminated the Creator is seen to be theologically frivolous.

IV. God as Temporally First Cause

But has Hawking succeeded even in obviating the role of the Creator as temporally First Cause? This seems to me highly dubious, for Hawking's model is founded on philosophical assumptions that are at best unexamined and unjustified and at worst false. To see this, let us recall the fundamental form of the *kalām* cosmological argument, so that the salient points of Hawking's refutation will emerge. Proponents of that argument have presented a simple syllogism:

(1) Whatever begins to exist has a cause.
(2) The universe began to exist.
(3) Therefore, the universe has a cause.

Analysis of the cause of the universe established in (3) further discloses it to be uncaused, changeless, timeless, immaterial, and personal.

A. Hawking's Critique

Hawking is vaguely aware of the tradition of this argument in Christian, Muslim, and Jewish thought and presents a somewhat muddled version of it in chapter 1.[16] But it is interesting that, unlike Davies, Hawking does not attack premiss (I); on the contrary, he implicitly assents to it. Hawking repeatedly states that on the classical General Theory of Relativity (GTR) Big Bang model of the universe an initial spacetime singularity is unavoidable, and he does not dispute that the origin of the universe must therefore require a supernatural cause. He points out that one could identify the Big Bang as the instant at which God created the universe.[17] He thinks that a number of attempts to avoid the Big Bang were probably motivated by the feeling that a

---

[15] Aquinas, *Summa Theologiae*, 1a.2.3.
[16] Hawking, *A Brief History of Time*, 7.
[17] Ibid. 9.

beginning of time 'smacks of divine intervention'.[18] It is not clear what part such a motivation plays in Hawking's own proposal, but he touts his model as preferable because 'There would be no singularities at which the laws of science broke down and no edge of space-time at which one w have to appeal to God or some new law to set the boundary conditions for space-time.'[19] On Hawking's view, then, given the classical Big Bang model, the inference to a Creator or temporally First Cause seems natural and unobjectionable.

Hawking's strategy is rather to dispute premiss (2). Typically, proponents of *kalām* supported (2) by arguing against the possibility of an infinite temporal regress of events. This tradition eventually became enshrined in the thesis of Kant's First Antinomy concerning time.[20] Hawking's response to this line of argument is very ingenious. He claims that the argument of the thesis and antithesis 'are both based on his unspoken assumption that time continues back forever, whether or not the universe had existed forever', but that this assumption is false because 'the concept of time has no meaning before the beginning of the universe'[21] This brief retort is somewhat muddled, but I think the sense of it is the following: In the antithesis Kant assumes that 'Since the beginning is an existence which is preceded by a time in which the thing is not, there must have been a preceding time in which the world was not, i.e. an empty time.'[22] But on some version of a relational view of time, time does not exist apart from change; therefore, the first event marked the inception of time. Thus, there was no empty time prior to the beginning of the universe. In the thesis, on the other hand, Kant states, 'If we assume that the world has no beginning in time, then up to every given moment an eternity has elapsed and there has passed away in the world an infinite series of successive states of things.'[23] To my knowledge, scarcely anyone has ever thought to call into question this apparently innocuous assumption, but it is precisely here that Hawking launches his attack. Unlike other detractors of Kant's argument, Hawking does not dispute the impossibility of forming an actual infinite by successive addition; rather he challenges the more fundamental assumption that a beginningless universe entails an infinite past. The central thrust of Hawking's book and of his proposed cosmological model is to show that a beginningless universe may be temporally finite. Hence, *kalām*-style arguments aimed at proving the finitude of the past need not be disputed, for such arguments do not succeed in establishing (2), that the universe began to exist. Therefore, the universe need not have a cause, and God's role as Creator is circumscribed to that envisioned in the Thomist and Leibnizian versions of the cosmological argument.

This is a highly original, if not unique, line of attack on the *kalām* cosmological argument, and it will be interesting to see how Hawking essays to put it through.[24] It is Hawking's belief that the introduction of quantum mechanics into the GTR-based Big Bang

---

[18] Ibid. 46
[19] Ibid. 136
[20] For discussion, see William Lane Craig, 'Kant's First Antinomy and the Beginning of the Universe', *Zeitschrift für philosophische Forschung*, 33 (1979), 553-67.
[21] Hawking, *A Brief History of Time*, 8.
[22] Immanuel Kant, *Critique of Pure Reason*, trans. Norman Kemp-Smith (London: Macmillan, 1929), 397 (A427-8/B455-6).
[23] Ibid.
[24] One feels a bit diffident about criticizing someone's views as they are expressed in a popular exposition of his thought rather than in his technical papers. But the fact is that it is only in his popular exposition that Hawking feels free to reflect philosophically on the metaphysical implications of his model. For example, imaginary time, which plays so critical a role in his thought, is scarcely even mentioned in his relevant technical paper (J. Hartle and S. Hawking, 'Wave Function of the Universe', *Physical Review*, D28 (1983), 2960-75). In any case, I have in no instance based my criticism on the infelicities inherent in popular exposition of technical subjects.

model will be the key to success. Noting that at the Big Bang the density of the universe and the curvature of spacetime become infinite, Hawking explains that 'there must have been a time in the very early universe when the universe was so small, that one could no longer ignore the small scale effects of...quantum mechanics' and that the initial singularity predicted by the GTR 'can disappear once quantum effects are taken into account'.[25] What is needed here is a quantum theory of gravity, and although Hawking admits that no such theory exists, still he insists that we do have a good idea of what some of its central features will be.[26] First, it will incorporate Feynman's sum-over-histories approach to quantum mechanics. According to this approach to quantum theory, an elementary particle does not follow a single path between two spacetime points (that is, have a single history), but it is rather conceived as taking all possible paths connecting those points. In order to calculate the probability of a particle's passing through any given spacetime point, one sums the waves associated with every, possible history that passes through that point, histories represented by waves having equal amplitude and opposite phase mutually cancelling so that only the most probable histories remain. But in order to do this without generating intractable infinities, Haw explains, one must use imaginary numbers for the values of time coordinate. When this is done, it 'has an interesting effect on space-time: the distinction between time and space disappears completely'.[27] The resulting spacetime is Euclidean.

The second feature which any theory of quantum gravity must possess is that the gravitational field is represented by curved spacetime. When this feature of the theory is combined with the first, the analogue of the history of a particle now becomes a complete curved spacetime that represents the history of the whole universe. Moreover, 'To avoid the technical difficulties in actually performing the sum over histories, these curved space-times must be taken to be Euclidean. That is, time is imaginary and is indistinguishable from directions in space.[28] On the basis of these two features, Hawking proposes a model in which spacetime is the four-dimensional analogue to the surface of a sphere. It is finite, but boundless, and so possesses no initial or terminal singularities. Hawking writes,

> In the classical theory of gravity, which is based on real space-time, there are only two possible ways the universe can behave: either it has existed for an infinite time, or else it had a beginning at a singularity at some finite time in the past. In the quantum theory of gravity, on the other hand, a third possibility arises. Because one is using Euclidean space-times, in which the time direction is on the same footing as directions in space, it is possible for space-time to be finite in extent and yet to have no singularities that formed a boundary or edge.... There would be no singularities at which the laws of science broke down and no edge of space-time at which one would have to appeal to God or some new law to set the boundary conditions for space-time.... The universe would be completely self-contained and not affected by anything outside itself. It would be neither created nor destroyed. It would just BE.[29]

Hawking emphasizes that his model is merely a proposal, and so far as he describes it, it makes no unique successful predictions, which would be necessary to transform it from a metaphysical theory to a plausible scientific theory. Still Hawking believes that

---

[25] Hawking, *A Brief History of Time*, 50-1.
[26] Ibid. 133.
[27] Ibid 134.
[28] Ibid. 135
[29] Ibid. 135-6.

> The idea that space and time may form a closed surface without boundary ... has profound implications for the role of God in the affairs of the universe.... So long as the universe had a beginning, we could suppose it had a creator. But if the universe is really completely self-contained, having no boundary or edge, it would have neither beginning nor end. What place, then, for a creator?[30]

B. Assessment

Unfortunately, Hawking's model is rife with controversial philosophical assumptions, to which he gives no attention. Since Hawking is trying to explain how the universe could exist without the necessity of God's bringing it into being at a point of time, it is evident that he construes his theory to be, not merely an engaging mathematical model, but a realistic description of the universe. On a non-realist interpretation of science, there would be no contradiction between his model and temporal *creatio ex nihilo*. Hence, the central question that needs to be addressed in assessing his model as an alternative to divine creation is whether it represents a realistic picture of the world.

Now to me at least it seems painfully obvious that Hawking faces severe difficulties here. Both quantum theory and relativity theory inspire acute philosophical questions concerning the extent to which they picture reality. To begin with quantum theory, most philosophers and reflective physicists would not disagree with the remarks of Hawking's erstwhile collaborator Roger Penrose:

> I should begin by expressing my general attitude to present-day quantum theory, by which I mean standard, non-relativistic quantum mechanics. The theory has, indeed, two powerful bodies of fact in its favour, and only one thing against it. First, in its favour are all the marvellous agreements that the theory has had with every experimental result to date. Second, and to me almost as important, it is a theory of astonishing and profound mathematical beauty. The one thing that can be said against it is that it makes absolutely no sense![31]

Does Hawking believe, for example, that Feynman's sum-over-histories approach describes what really happens, that an elementary particle really does follow all possible spacetime paths until its wave function is collapsed by measurement? I think most people would find this fantastic. If he does interpret this approach realistically, then what justification is there for such an interpretation? Why not a Copenhagen Interpretation which eschews realism altogether with regard to the quantum world? Or an alternative version of the Copenhagen Interpretation which holds that no quantum reality exists until it is measured? Why not hold that the uncollapsed wave function is, in Bohr's words, 'only an abstract quantum mechanical description' rather than a description of how nature is? A disavowal of realism on the quantum level does not imply a rejection of a critical realism on the macroscopic level. Or why not interpret quantum mechanics as a statistical theory about ensembles of particles rather than about the behaviour of any individual particle? On this interpretation, the wave function describes the collective behaviour of particles in identical systems, and we could quit worrying about the measurement problem. Or again, what about a neo-realist interpretation along the lines of the de Broglie-Bohm pilot wave? A non-local hidden variables theory, in which a particle follows a definite spacetime trajectory, is compatible with all the experiment and evidence for quantum theory, is mathematically rigorous and complete, and yet avoids the philosophical difficulties occasioned by the typical wave

---

[30] Ibid. 140-1.
[31] Roger Penrose, 'Gravity and State Vector Reduction', in Roger Penrose and C. J. Isham (eds.), *Quantum Concepts in Space and Time* (Oxford: Clarendon Press, 1986), 129.

functional analysis. Obviously, it is not my intention to endorse any one of these views, but merely to point out that a realistic interpretation of Feynman's sum-over-histories approach on Hawking's part would be gratuitous.

In general, I think we should do well to reflect on de Broglie's attitude to the mathematical formalism of quantum theory. As Georges Lochak notes, 'He does not consider that mathematical models have any ontological value, especially geometrical representations in abstract spaces; he sees them as practical mathematical instruments among others and only uses them as such.'[32] The principle of the superposition of wave functions is a case in point. Simply because a mathematical model is operationally successful, we are not entitled to construe its representations physically. Feynman himself gave this sharp advice: 'I think it is safe to say that no one understands quantum mechanics. Do not keep saying to yourself, if you possibly can avoid it, "But how can it be like that?" because you will go "down the drain" into a blind alley from which nobody has yet escaped. Nobody can know how it can be like that.'[33] One can use the equations without taking them as literal representations of reality.

Now it might be said that Hawking's use of Feynman's sum-over-histories approach may be merely instrumental and that no commitment to a physical description is implied. But it is not evident that such a response will work for Hawking. For his model, based on the application of quantum theory to classical geometrodynamics, must posit the existence of a superspace which is ontologically prior to the approximations of classical spacetime that are slices of this superspace. This superspace is no *ens fictum*, but the primary reality. The various 3-geometries surrounding the classical spacetime slice in superspace are fluctuations of the classical slice. By 'summing the histories' of these 3-geometries one can construct a leaf of history in superspace which can be mapped on to a spacetime manifold. Since, as we have seen, Hawking takes the wave function of a particle to be the analogue of a physical spacetime that represents the history of the universe, an instrumentalist interpretation of the sum-over-histories approach leads to an equally instrumentalist, non-realist view of spacetime, which betrays Hawking's whole intent.

In short, Hawking's wave functional analysis of the universe requires the Many Worlds Interpretation of quantum physics, and in another place Hawking admits as much.[34] But why should we adopt this interpretation of quantum physics with its bloated ontology and miraculous splitting of the universe? John Barrow has recently remarked that the Many Worlds Interpretation is 'essential' to quantum cosmology because without it one is left, on the standard Copenhagen Interpretation, with the question, Who or what collapses the wave function of the universe?—some Ultimate Observer outside of space and time?[35] This answer has obvious theistic implications. Indeed, although 'the theologians have not been very eager to ascribe to God the role of Ultimate Observer who brings the entire quantum Universe into being', still Barrow admits that 'such a picture is logically consistent with the mathematics. To escape this step cosmologists have been forced to invoke Everett's "Many Worlds" interpretation of quantum theory in order to make any sense of quantum cosmology.'[36] 'It is no coincidence', he says, 'that

---

[32] Georges Lochak, 'The Evolution of the Ideas of Louis de Broglie on the Interpretation of Wave Mechanics', in A. O. Barut, A. V. D. Merwe, and J.P. Vigier (eds.), *Quantum, Space, and Time*, Cambridge Monographs on Physics (Cambridge: Cambridge University Press, 1984), 20.
[33] Cited in N. Herbert, *Quantum Reality: Beyond the New Physics* (Garden City, NY: Doubleday Anchor Books, 1985), p. xiii.
[34] S. W. Hawking, 'Quantum Cosmology', repr. in L. Z. Fang and R. Ruffmi (eds.), *Quantum Cosmology, Advanced Series in Astrophysics and Cosmology, iii* (Singapore: World Scientific, 1987), 192-3.
[35] John Barrow, *The World within the World* (Oxford: Clarendon Press, 1988), 156.
[36] Ibid. 232

all the main supporters of the Many Worlds interpretation of quantum reality are involved in quantum cosmology.'[37] But if we, like most physicists, find the Many Worlds interpretation outlandish, then quantum cosmology, far from obviating the place of a Creator, might be seen to create for Him a dramatic new role. Again, my intention is not to endorse this view, but simply to underscore the fact that a realist construal of Hawking's account involves extravagant and dubious metaphysical commitments, such that his model can hardly be said to have eliminated the place of a Creator.

The impression that Hawking's model is thoroughly non-realist is heightened by his use of imaginary time in summing the waves for particle histories and, hence, in his final model of spacetime. But does anyone seriously believe that one has thereby done anything more than perform a mathematical operation on paper, that one has thereby altered the nature of time itself? Hawking asserts, 'Imaginary time may sound like science fiction but it is in fact a well-defined mathematical concept.'[38] But that is not the issue; the question is whether that mathematical concept has any counterpart in physical reality. Already in 1920, Eddington suggested that his readers who found it difficult to think in terms of the unfamiliar non-Euclidean geometry of relativistic spacetime might evade that difficulty by means of the 'dodge' of using imaginary numbers for the time coordinate, but he thought it 'not very profitable' to speculate on the implications of this, for 'it can scarcely be regarded as more than an analytical device'.[39] Imaginary time was merely an illustrative tool which 'certainly do[es] not correspond to any physical reality'.[40] Even Hawking himself maintains, 'In any case, as far as everyday quantum mechanics is concerned, we may regard our use of imaginary time and Euclidean spacetime as merely a mathematical device (or trick) to calculate answers about real space-time.'[41] But now in his model this imaginary time and Euclidean spacetime are suddenly supposed to be, not merely conceptual devices, but actual representations (however unimaginable) of physical reality in the very early history of the universe. This 'ontologizing' of mathematical operations is not only neither explained nor justified, but is, to my mind, metaphysically absurd. For what possible physical meaning can we give to imaginary time? Having the opposite sign of ordinary 'real' time, would imaginary time be a sort of negative time? But what intelligible sense can be given, for example, to a physical object's enduring for, say, two negative moments, or an event's having occurred two negative moments ago or going to occur in two negative moments? If we are A-theorists and take temporal becoming as objective and real, what does it mean to speak of the lapse of imaginary time or the becoming of events in imaginary time? Since imaginary time is on Hawking's view merely another spatial dimension, he admits that there is no direction to time, even though the ordinary time with which we are acquainted is asymmetric.[42] Could anything be more obvious than that imaginary time is a mathematical fiction?[43]

Hawking recognizes that the history of the universe in real (=ordinary) time would look very different than its history in imaginary time. In real time, the universe expands from a

---

[37] Ibid. 156.
[38] Hawking, *A Brief History of Time*, 134.
[39] Arthur Eddington, *Space, Time and Gravitation*, Cambridge Science (first pub. 1920; repr. Cambridge: Cambridge University Press, 1987), 48.
[40] Ibid. 181.
[41] Hawking, *A Brief History of Time*, 134-5.
[42] Ibid. 144.
[43] As Mary Cleugh nicely puts it, 'What is the wildest absurdity of dreams is merely altering the sign to the physicist.' (*Mary Cleugh, Time and its Importance in Modern Thought* (London: Methuen, 1937), 46.)

singularity and collapses back again into a singularity. 'Only if we could picture the universe in terms of imaginary time would there be no singularities.... When one goes back to the real time in which we live, however, there will still appear to be singularities.'[44] This might lead one to conclude that Hawking's model is a mere mathematical construct without ontological import. Instead, Hawking draws the astounding conclusion,

> This might suggest that the so-called imaginary time is really the real time, and that what we call real time is just a figment of our imaginations. In real time, the universe has a beginning and an end at singularities that form a boundary to space-time and at which the laws of science break down. But in imaginary time, there are no singularities or boundaries. So maybe what we call imaginary time is really more basic, and what we call real is just an idea that we invent to help us describe what we think the universe is like.[45]

I can think of no more egregious example of self-deception than this. One employs mathematical devices (tricks) such as sum-over-histories and changing the sign of the time coordinate in order to construct a model spacetime, a model which is physically unintelligible, and then one invests that model with reality and declares that the time in which we live is in fact unreal.

Hawking defends his position by arguing that 'a scientific theory is just a mathematical model we make to describe our observations: it exists only in our minds. So it is meaningless to ask: Which is real, "real" or "imaginary" time? It is simply a matter of which is the more useful description.'[46] But this reasoning is fallacious and relapses into an instrumentalist view of science which contradicts Hawking's realist expressions and intentions. One may adopt a sort of nominalist view of the ontological status of theories themselves, but this says absolutely nothing about whether those theories are meant to describe, in approximate limits, physical reality or are merely pragmatic instruments for making new discoveries and advancing technology. I should like to know on what theory of meaning Hawking dismisses the question concerning physical time as meaningless. We seem to see here the vestige of a defunct positivism, which surfaces elsewhere in Hawking's book.[47] But a verificationist theory of meaning is today widely recognized as being simply indefensible.[48] The question Hawking brushes aside is not only obviously meaningful, but crucial for the purposes of his book, for only if he can prove that imaginary time is ontologically real and real time fictitious has he succeeded in obviating the need for a Creator. Which brings us again to his scientific realism: it seems clear that for Hawking the ontological status of time is not just a matter of the more useful description. He believes that 'The eventual goal of science is to provide a single theory that describes as the whole universe' and that this goal should be pursued even though the theory 'may not even affect

---

[44] Hawking, *A Brief History of Time*, 138-9.
[45] Ibid. 139.
[46] Ibid.
[47] Ibid. 55, 126.
[48] Healey describes the contemporary attitude toward positivism: 'Positivists attempted to impose restrictions on the content of scientific theories in order to ensure that they were empirically meaningful. An effect of these restrictions was to limit both the claims to truth of theoretical sentences only distantly related to observation, and the claims to existence of unobservable theoretical entities. More recently positivism has come under such sustained attack that opposition to it has become almost orthodoxy in the philosophy of science.' (Richard Healey (ed.), *Reduction, Time and Reality* (Cambridge: Cambridge University Press, 1981), p. vii.) For a disinterested and devastating critique of positivism, see Frederick Suppe, 'The Search for Philosophic Understanding of Scientific Theories,' in F. Suppe (ed.), *The Structure of Scientific Theories*, 2nd edn. (Urbana, Ill.: University of Illinois Press, 1977), 62-118.

our lifestyle.'[49] Hawking yearns to understand 'the underlying order of the world'.[50] Knowing the mind of God is for him not just a matter of pragmatic utility. Thus, he both needs and believes in scientific realism.

To address as meaningful the question posed above, then, it is evident that imaginary time is not ontological time. This is apparent not only from its physically unintelligible nature, but also from the fact that it transforms time into a spatial dimension, thus confounding the distinction between space and time. According to Hawking, the use of imaginary numbers 'has an interesting effect on space-time: the distinction between time and space disappears completely...there is no difference between the time direction and directions in space...time is imaginary and is indistinguishable from directions in space'.[51] This decisively disqualifies Hawking's model as a representation of reality, since in fact time is not ontologically a spatial dimension. Contemporary expositors of the Special Theory of Relativity (STR) have been exercised to dissociate themselves from the frequent statements of early proponents of the theory to the effect that Einstein's theory had made time the fourth dimension of space.[52] B-theorists of time have been especially sensitive to the allegation by A-theorists that they have been guilty of 'spatializing' time and have pointed to the opposite sign of the time coordinate as evidence that the temporal dimension is in fact not a mere fourth dimension of space. By changing the sign, Hawking conflates the temporal dimension with the spatial ones. Hawking apparently feels justified in this move because he, like certain early interpreters of STR, believes that STR itself treats time as a spatial dimension. He writes, 'In relativity, there is no real distinction between the space and time coordinates, just as there is no real difference between any two space coordinates.'[53] He justifies this statement by pointing out that one could construct a new time coordinate by combining the old time coordinate with one of the spatial coordinates.

In spatializing time, Hawking implicitly rejects an A-theory and identifies himself as a B-theorist. His statement concerning the universe as he models it that 'It would just BE' is an expression of the tenseless character of its existence. Unfortunately, he provides no justification whatsoever for adopting a B-theory of time. Perhaps he thinks that STR entails a B-theory; but A-theorists have argued repeatedly that the Special Theory is neutral with regard to the issue of temporal becoming, and the most sophisticated B-theorists do not appeal to it as proof of their view.[54] The debate between the A-theory and the B-theory is controversial. But in the absence of

---

[49] Hawking, *A Brief History of Time*, 10, 13; cf. his remarks in S. W. Hawking, 'The Boundary Conditions of the Universe', in H. A. Bruck, G. V. Coyne, and M. S. Longair (eds.), *Astrophysical Cosmology, Pontificiae Academiae Scientiarum Scripta Varia*, xlviii (Vatican City: Pontificia Academia Scientiarum, 1982), 563.

[50] Hawking, *A Brief History of Time*, 13.

[51] Ibid. 134-5.

[52] See the interesting citations in E. Meyerson, 'On Various Interpretations of Relativistic Time', repr. in M. Capek (ed.), *The Concepts of Space and Time*, Boston Studies in the Philosophy of Science, ii (Dordrecht: D. Reidel, 1976), 354-5. In his comments on Meyerson's book, Einstein repudiated the 'extravagances of the popularizers and even many scientists' who construed STR to teach that time is a spatial dimension: 'Time and space are fused into one and the same continuum, but this continuum is not isotropic. The element of spatial distance and the element of duration remain distinct in nature...' (A. Einstein, 'Comment on Meyerson's "La Deduction relativiste"', repr. in ibid. 367.)

[53] Hawking, *A Brief History of Time*, 24.

[54] For A-theoretic approaches to STR, see M. Capek, 'Time in Relativity Theory: Arguments for a Philosophy of Becoming', in J. T. Fraser (ed.), *Voices of Time* (New York: Braziller, 1966), 434-54; H. Stein, 'On Einstein-Minkowski Space-Time', *Journal of Philosophy*, 65 (1968), 5-23; K. Denbigh, 'Past, Present, and Future', in J. T. Fraser (ed.), *The Study of Time*, iii (Berlin: Springer Verlag, 1978), 301-29; G. J. Whitrow, *The Natural Philosophy of Time*, 2nd ed. (Oxford: Clarendon Press, 1980), 283-307, 371; and D. Dieks, 'Special Relativity and the Flow of Time', *Philosophy of Science*, 55 (1988), 456-60. A Grunbaum, 'The Status of Temporal Becoming', in R. M. Gale (ed.), *The Philosophy of Time* (London: Macmillan, 1968), 322-54, makes no appeal to STR to defend a B-theory.

some overwhelming proof of the B-theory, I see no reason to abandon our experience of temporal becoming as objective. D. H. Mellor, himself a B-theorist, agrees, commenting, 'Tense is so striking an aspect of reality that only the most compelling argument justifies denying it: namely, that the tensed view of time is self-contradictory and so cannot be true.'[55] Mellor accordingly tries to rehabilitate McTaggart's proof against the objectivity of the A-series, but, to my thinking, to no avail.[56] Moreover, it seems to me (although space does not permit me to argue it here) that no B-theorist has successfully defended that theory against the incoherence that if external becoming is mind-dependent, still the subjective experience of becoming is objective, that is, there is an objective succession of contents of consciousness, so that becoming in the mental realm is real. If an A-theory of time is correct, then Hawking's model is clearly a mere mathematical abstraction.

Whether the opposite sign of the time coordinate in the relativity equations is sufficient to establish a 'real difference' between time and space dimensions in the Special Theory need not be adjudicated here. If it is not sufficient, that only goes to show that the mathematical formalism of the theory is insufficient to capture the ontology of time and space, but is a useful mathematical abstraction from reality.[57] That time and space are ontologically distinct is evident from the fact that a series of mental events alone is sufficient to set up a temporal series of events even in the absence of spatial events.[58] Imagine, for example, that God led up to creation by counting, '1, 2, 3,...*fiat lux!*' In that case, time begins with the first mental event of counting, though the physical universe does not appear until later.[59] Clearly, then, time and space are ontologically distinct.

But what, then, of the oft-repeated claim of Minkowski that, 'Henceforth, space by itself, and time by itself, are doomed to fade away into mere shadows, and only a kind of union of the two will preserve an independent reality'?[60] This claim is based on one of the most widespread and persistent errors concerning the interpretation of the Special Theory that exists, namely, the failure to distinguish between what we may call measured or empirical time and ontological or real time. According to Hawking, 'the theory of relativity put an end to the idea of absolute time.... The theory of relativity does force us to change fundamentally our ideas of space and time. We must accept that time is not completely separate from and independent of space, but is

---

[55] D. H. Mellor, *Real Time* (Cambridge: Cambridge University Press, 1981), 5.

[56] See the relevant chapters in my *God, Time, and Eternity* (forthcoming). Mc-Taggart's fundamental error was his mistaken assumption that the A-theory combines a B-theoretical ontology with temporal becoming. Mellor makes the same assumption, but also errs decisively in making sentence tokens rather than propositions his truth-bearers, which leads to his misconceived token-reflexive truth conditions of tensed sentences.

[57] See helpful discussions in Cleugh, *Time and its Importance in Modern Thought*, 46-9, and Peter Kroes, *Time: Its Structure and Role in Physical Theories*, Synthese Library, clxxix (Dordrecht: D. Reidel, 1985), 60-96.

[58] On Minkowski spacetime, Wenzl cautions, 'From the standpoint of the physicist, this is a thoroughly consistent solution. But the physicist will [doubtless] understand the objection, raised by philosophy, that time is by no means merely a physical matter. Time is, as Kant put it, the form not merely of our outer but also of our inner sense.... Should our experiences of successiveness and of memory be mere illusion...?' (A. Wenzl, 'Einstein's Theory of Relativity, Viewed from the Standpoint of Critical Realism, and its Significance for Philosophy', in P. A. Schilpp (ed.), *Albert Einstein: Philosopher-Scientist*, Library of Living Philosophers, vii [La Salle, Ill.: Open Court, 1949], 587-8).

[59] For more on God's relationship to time see William Lane Craig, 'God and Real Time', *Religious Studies*, 26 (1990), 335-47; William Lane Craig, 'Theories of Divine Eternity and the Special Theory of Relativity', *Faith and Philosophy*, II (1994).

[60] H. Minkowski, 'Space and Time', repr. in *The Principle of Relativity*, trans. W. Perrett and G. B. Jeffery (New York: Dover, 1952), 75.

combined with it to form an object called space-time.'[61] Nothing could be farther from the truth. Einstein did not eliminate absolute simultaneity: he merely redefined simultaneity. In the absence of a detectable ether, Einstein, under the influence of Ernst Mach's positivism,[62] believed that it was quite literally meaningless to speak of events' occurring absolutely simultaneously because there was no empirical means of determining that simultaneity. By proposing to redefine simultaneity in terms of the light signal method of synchronization, Einstein was able to give meaning to the notion of simultaneity, only now the simultaneity was relative due to the invariant velocity of light and the absence of the ether frame. In so doing, Einstein established a sort of empirical time, which would be subject to dilation and in which the occurrence of identical events could be variously measured. But it is evident that he did nothing to 'put an end' to absolute time or absolute simultaneity.[63] To say that those notions are meaningless is to revert to the dead dogmas of positivism and the verificationist theory of meaning. J. S. Bell asserts that apart from matters of style, it is primarily this philosophical positivism which serves to differentiate the received interpretation from the Lorentz-Larmor interpretation, which distinguishes between empirical, local time and ontological, real time. Bell writes,

> The difference of philosophy is this. Since it is experimentally impossible to say which of two uniformly moving systems *is really* at rest, Einstein declares the notions 'really resting' and 'really moving' as meaningless. For him, only the relative motion of two or more uniformly moving objects is real. Lorentz, on the other hand, preferred the view that there is indeed a state of *real* rest, defined by the 'aether,' even though the laws of physics conspire to prevent us identifying it experimentally. The facts of physics do not oblige us to accept one philosophy rather than the other.[64]

Since verificationism is hopelessly flawed as a theory of meaning, it is idle to talk about STR's 'forcing' us to change our fundamental ideas of space and time. Lawrence Sklar concludes, 'One thing is certain. Acceptance of relativity cannot force one into the acceptance or rejection of any of the traditional metaphysical views about the reality of past and future.'[65]

Of course, Hawking might retort that ontological time is scientifically useless and may therefore be left to the metaphysician. Granted, but then the point is surely this: *Hawking is doing metaphysics.* When he begins to speculate about the nature of space and time and to claim

---

[61] Hawking, *A Brief History of Time*, 21, 23.

[62] The positivistic foundations of Einstein's STR are widely recognized by historians of science, but are surprisingly rarely discussed by philosophers exploring the philosophical foundations of that theory. For discussion, see G. Holton, 'Mach, Einstein, and the Search for Reality', in Ernst Mach: *Physicist and Philosopher, Boston Studies in the Philosophy of Science*, vi (Dordrecht: D. Reidel, 1970), 165-99; P. Frank, 'Einstein, Mach, and Logical Positivism', 271-86, H. Reichenbach, 'The Philosophical Significance of the Theory of Relativity', 289-311, P. Bridgman, 'Einstein's Theories and the Operational Point of View', 335-54, and V. Lenzen, 'Einstein's Theory of Knowledge', 357-84, all in Schilpp (ed.), *Albert Einstein*. According to Sklar, 'Certainly the original arguments in favor of the relativistic viewpoint are rife with verificationist presuppositions about meaning, etc. And despite Einstein's later disavowal of the verificationist point of view, no one to my knowledge has provided an adequate account of the foundations of relativity which isn't verificationist in essence.' (L. Sklar, 'Time, Reality, and Relativity', in Healey (ed.), *Reduction, Time, and Reality*, 141.) 'I can see no way of rejecting the old aether-compensatory theories...without invoking a verificationist critique of some kind or other.' (Ibid. 132.)

[63] Cleugh hits the essential point: 'It cannot be too often emphasized that physics is concerned with the measurement of time, rather than with the essentially metaphysical question as to its nature'; 'however useful "t" may be for physics, its complete identification with Time is fallacious.' (Cleugh, *Time and its Importance in Modern Thought*, 51, 30.)

[64] John S. Bell, 'How to Teach Special Relativity', in *Speakable and Unspeakable in Quantum Mechanics* (Cambridge: Cambridge University Press, 1987), 77.

[65] Sklar, 'Time, Reality, and Relativity', 140.

that he has eliminated the need for a Creator, then he has, as I said, entered the realm of the philosopher, and here he must be prepared to do battle with philosophical weapons on a broader conceptual field or else retreat within the walls of a limited scientific domain.

What is ironic is that even within that restricted domain there may now be empirical evidence for rejecting the received interpretation of STR. For the experimental results of the Aspect experiments on the inequalities predicted by Bell's Theorem have apparently established that widely separated elementary particles are in some way correlated such that measurements on one result instantly in the collapse of the wave function of the other, so that locality is violated. Even a hidden variables interpretation of the fabled EPR experiment must be a non-local theory. Nor is the violation of locality dependent upon the validity of quantum theory; it can be demonstrated on the macro-level, so that even if quantum theory should be superseded, any new theory will apparently have to include non-locality. But these data contradict the received interpretation of STR, not because non-locality posits superluminal signals, but rather because it goes to establish empirically relations of absolute simultaneity. Hence, disclaimers that STR is not violated because no signal or information is sent from one particle to another are beside the point. Rather the salient point is that the collapse of the wave function in both correlated particles occurs *simultaneously,* wholly apart from considerations of synchronization by light signals. Karl Popper thus regards the Aspect experiments as the first crucial test between Lorentz's and Einstein's interpretation of STR, commenting,

> The reason for this assertion is that the mere existence of an infinite velocity entails that of an absolute simultaneity and thereby of an absolute space. Whether or not an infinite velocity can be attained *in the transmission of signals is* irrelevant for this argument: the one inertial system for which Einsteinian simultaneity coincides with absolute simultaneity...would be the system at absolute rest—whether or not this system at absolute rest—can be experimentally identified.[66]

The establishment of non-local correlations in spacetime could thus vindicate even within the scientific domain the validity of Lorentz's distinction between local time and true time in opposition to the positivistic conflation of the two in the received view.

What this lengthy excursus goes to show is that it is metaphysically misguided to identify ontological time as a dimension of space. Since Hawking reduces empirical time in the very early history of the universe to a spatial dimension and conflates empirical time with ontological time, his model requires a tenselessly existing spacetime which he wishes to pass off as reality. Add to these errors the fact that the time involved is imaginary in its early stages, and the metaphysical absurdity of Hawking's vision of the world seems starkly apparent.

V. Conclusion

There are many other things which one should like to say about Hawking's view (for example, his misuse of the Anthropic Principle), but I think enough has been said to answer his fundamental question, 'What place, then, for a Creator?' We have seen that contrary to popular impression, God plays for Hawking an important role as a sort of Leibnizian Sufficient Reason for the universe. With regard to God's role as Creator, we saw that Hawking failed to distinguish between *creatio originans* and *creatio continuans,* so that even if God failed to play the former role, He may still carry out the latter as a sort of Thomistic ground of being. But finally we have

---

[66] Karl Popper, 'A Critical Note on the Greatest Days of Quantum Theory', in Barut et al., *Quantum, Space, and Time,* 54.

seen that Hawking's critique of God's assuming the office of temporally First Cause as demonstrated by the *kalām* cosmological argument is rife with unexamined and unjustified philosophical assumptions, assumptions that, when examined, degenerate to metaphysical absurdity. The success of Hawking's model appears to depend on a realist application of Feynman's sum-over-histories approach to the derivation of spacetime from an ontologically prior superspace, a construal which is implausible and in any case unjustified. Essential to Hawking's scheme is the identification of imaginary time with physical time in the early history of the universe, a construal which is again never justified and is in any case physically unintelligible. Hawking's model depends, moreover, on certain questionable philosophical assumptions about relativity theory as well, for example, the identification of time as a dimension of space, a move which is extremely dubious, since time can exist without space. Hawking's appeal to the Special Theory to justify this move rests on an interpretation of that theory which fails to distinguish empirical time from ontological time, an interpretation essentially dependent on a defunct positivistic theory of meaning and now perhaps called into question by empirical facts as well. Any attempt to interpret the temporal dimension as a tenselessly existing spatial dimension betrays the true nature of time.

The postulate of metaphysical superspace, the metamorphosis of real to imaginary time, the conflation of time and space: all these seem extravagant lengths to which to go in order to avoid classical theism's doctrine of *creatio ex nihilo*—which forces us and Hawking to confront squarely a different question: What price, then, for no Creator?

Questions

1. What basic flaw does Craig see in Hawking's argument?

2. Do you agree with Craig, that Hawking is basically mistaken for the reason that he fails to take into account the meaning and force of his assumptions?

3. Do you think that Hawking has a good answer for Craig? What might it be?

4. Has Craig offered proof for there being a Creator?

5. Which one has the stronger argument, Hawking or Craig? Why?

TOWARD A THEORY OF RELIGIOUS EXPLANATION*

Philip Clayton

Clayton examines religious beliefs as held by individuals and communities. He looks at the function of such beliefs and concludes that they are to be viewed as in a reciprocal relationship between an inherited institutionalized belief, practice or experience and an individual's real, existential world. Hence he treats religious beliefs and religious experience as sustaining a reciprocal relationship. Now he can give account of religious explanation. Religious belief is capable of being expressed in propositional form. All religious explanation is in terms of such beliefs. They are the believer's attempt to work out a good fit between one's beliefs and attitudes. A multilevel model is then proposed, by which one makes sense of one's private experience, and another which gives account of the whole of experience. The latter, he thinks, works with a very different sense of explanation, certainly not the main sense. It is the more ordinary sense that we find in the sciences. The personal is an effort to see things in their totality. The scientific slant falls in line with the propositional analytic approach, whereas the latter is more of an aesthetically pleasing sense of things "fitting together."

We have considered in sufficient detail the semantic level on which religious beliefs occur and the general nature of the meaning question that motivates them. What now is the relation between the project of making sense of one's total experience and the specific details of individual religious experience and belief? What role, if any, does the notion of explanation play in this process? Obviously, the locus of explanations in religion will be the set of beliefs held by persons or communities. In many cases the explanans (the explanatory account) or its warrants may include nonreligious beliefs: that the universe actually did begin at a particular moment in time; that I indeed recovered after the rite was performed; that a necessary being explains the existence of contingent beings. But most religious explanations are couched in terms of distinctively religious beliefs. Let us turn then to examine the explanatory function of religious beliefs.

Religious Belief as Explanation

Religious belief originates in an initial encounter with the divine. Natural theologians speak of revelation through Nature, Durkheim of an encounter with the sacred, van der Leeuw of an attitude of awe, Otto of the sense of the holy.[1] The response of the persons involved is characterized by intense respect (worship) and great attraction (Otto's *mysterium tremendum et fuscinans);* by a sense of contingency, finiteness, or sinfulness; and by a reorientation of values and priorities. Often associated with this encounter are extraordinary or charismatic phenomena. Weber has analyzed these phenomena in the

---

* This article is reprinted by courtesy of the author and publisher. It appears in Chapter 5, pp. 124-145, of *Explanations from Physics to Theology*, by Philip Clayton, Yale University Press, 1989.

[1] One might also say: an encounter with what is believed to be the divine. Recall that a phenomenology of religious belief does not yet make commitments to the truth of these beliefs. Also, a long discussion would be needed to justify my use of the term *divine*, a term which I believe still to be acceptable but which may be somewhat prejudicial in favor of the Western tradition. There are also difficulties with the other terms; Louis Dupré has, for example, questioned the contemporary usefulness of the notion of the sacred, defending *transcendence* as a more useful category. See his *Transcendent Selfhood* (1976), chap 2, esp. 22-26.

context of the founding of religious traditions and their prophetic renewal, using the ideal-type of the charismatic leader. He defines charisma as "a certain quality of an individual personality by virtue of which he is set apart from ordinary men and treated as endowed with supernatural, superhuman, or at least specifically exceptional powers or qualities."[2] Whether directly or mediated by the chosen or enlightened leader (Moses, the Buddha), the followers then sense the possibility of closeness to the transcendent, the potential for their own private religious experience, and the obligation of holiness that stems from encounter with the Holy.

Out of this initial encounter with or self-revelation of the divine, lasting possibly over a long period of time, the transition takes place to a more stable period, which Weber labels the institutionalization of charisma. In "normal religion" (to paraphrase Kuhn) relatively stable patterns of belief, feeling, and worship emerge: a set of stories, a scripture, a cultus with rites and rituals, a priestly caste, organizational structures for education, reinforcement, and control. Now it might be thought that individuals inheriting a tradition that has been institutionally transmitted in this way would also inherit, ready-made, a pregiven complex of meaning, and hence that the stress I have placed on the individual semantic project in religion is inappropriate for believers at a historical distance from their tradition's founding. In a sense this is true: a given sacred cosmogony, for instance, makes sense of the world in a distinctive manner; a specific rite such as the Roman Catholic Mass predisposes to (and possibly determines) the sort of religious experiences that may accompany it.

Nonetheless, a given moment of the religious experience, a given religious interpretation or practice, always remains the experience of an individual, similar to "my seeing this vision" or "my feeling this joy." It may be simultaneously a communal rite or ritual, yet it is experienced by a given person. Each individual's experience of his religious tradition is idiosyncratic and reflects a unique constellation of feelings, attitudes, and life-experiences. In this sense each individual reappropriates his tradition in his religious experience and understanding, making it his own. Admittedly, the amount of individual synthetic creativity in this process varies greatly between individuals (the prophet or great teacher as opposed to the uncreative "man in the pew") and between traditional and nontraditional cultures (the limited belief options of the tribesperson as opposed to the smorgasbord of alternatives facing the North American believer). Yet if, as we claimed above, each individual world is a unique synthesis of particular experiences and perceptions, then the appropriation of a given religious tradition and its symbols, the manner in which it makes sense of one's personal world, will also vary between individuals. Hence, it is true that "religious experience of individuals and their reflection upon it has been not only the origin of religious beliefs and practices but also a source of their continuation from age to age and of the transformations they have undergone in every religious community."[3] It is precisely the importance the semantic dimension in religion that confirms the frequent stress on religious *experience* in the philosophy and phenomenology of religion.

---

[2] Max Weber, *The Theory of Social and Economic Organization* (1947), 358f. It is intriguing to compare the founding of a new religious tradition with the process of a scientific revolution as described by Kuhn in *The Structure of Scientific Revolutions*, a comparison encouraged by Kuhn's talk of "conversation" to a new paradigm. Likewise, Weber's notion of the "institutionalization of charisma" in the next paragraph is reminiscent of Kuhn's description of the transition to "normal science," although there is no evidence that Kuhn has been influenced by Weber's work.

[3] George Thomas, *Philosophy and Religious Belief* (1970), 62.

For the purposes of relating religious beliefs and explanation, then, we can most profitably define religious belief as a reciprocal relationship between *an inherited tradition* of institutionalized belief, practice, and experience on the one hand, and *an individual's unique world,* personal appropriation or reinterpretation of the tradition, and individual religious experiences on the other. In suggesting this definition, I disagree by implication with Tillich's view that *any* object of "ultimate concern" is a religious object for the individual.[4] Some reference to a religious tradition is necessary, if only as that which the individual rejects in formulating his own complex of belief. Conversely, I also question purely sociological treatments of religious meaning that dwell on the details of the story told to exclusion of the horizon of appropriation.[5]

Though neither of the two poles can be treated in abstraction, the locus of the individual is a helpful means for incorporating both the traditionally given component *and* that modification or creative appropriation that is vital if a religious tradition is to avoid becoming old and dry, a "dead" tradition. It is the necessity of meaningful personal appropriation that has been underscored, for example, by Luther in his insistence on the *pro nobis* of personal faith. Likewise, the same emphasis stands at the heart of Schleiermacher's critique of natural religion in the *Speeches:* "Single perceptions and feelings are, as you know, the elements of religion, and it can never lead to the character of any one religion to regard them as a mere heap, tossed together without regard to number, kind or purpose."[6] Whatever other standards can in the end be applied to religious explanations, they at least depend upon the personal disclosure value of the beliefs in which they are expressed.[7]

It should be clear that I am treating religious beliefs and (personal or communal) religious experience as standing in a reciprocal relationship. That is, a system of beliefs suggests a type of experience while, conversely, certain experiences tend to give rise to particular types of belief. The experience of power in the natural or social realm may find expression in a belief-system of animism or monotheism (the creator god); that of personal concern or nurture may lead to a personalistic theism; that of unity with nature, to some form of pantheism or panentheism; that of God's love, to a highly-developed doctrine of divine providence. It has often been pointed out how well the experience of pointless suffering is described by the karmic notion of the cycle of death and rebirth. In fact, instead of the reciprocal relationship that I am defending, some students of religion prefer to speak of the synthesis of religious belief and experience in a (or the) "religious attitude."[8] However, even those who wish to analyze the religious life from a synthetic perspective such as that of the religious attitude would presumably be willing to distinguish between the cognitive content and the experiential or affective elements in the religious phenomenon. That it is sometimes difficult to isolate experience and belief in practice does not imply that it is impossible for a phenomenology of religion to describe the characteristics of each. Even when one views them as facets of a deeper reality, the descriptions of religious belief and experience may vary: they evidence different "logics."

---

[4] Perhaps this is to disagree with a caricature of Tillich's view. In *Dynamics of Faith* (1957), chap. 3, he does distinguish the "true ultimate" from "idolatrous" types of ultimate concern. But if a caricature, it is an influential one.
[5] In its insistence on the fusion (*Verschmelzung*) of the horizons of traditon and interpreter in understanding. Hans-Georg Gadamer, *Truth and Method* (1975), offers a helpful corrective to such positions.
[6] F. Schleiermacher, *On Religion: Speeches to Its Cultured Despisers* (1958), 219.
[7] The use of "personal disclosure value" as a criterion has been advocated by Arthur Holmes in *Christian Philosopher in the Twentieth Century* (1969), ix-x, and *Faith Seeks Understanding* (1971), 5ff.
[8] As the subtitle, "A Search for the Meaning of Religious Attitudes, " suggests, this is the guiding project of Louis Dupré's *Other Dimension*.

Given that we can in fact discuss the content of religious beliefs despite their imbeddedness in a personal or communal project of meaning-construction, it is now possible to gather the threads of this discussion into a theory of religious explanation. I have presented religious beliefs as that portion of the religious phenomenon that can be propositionally formulated, described, and in some cases critically evaluated. In virtually all traditions religious explanations are formulated in terms of such beliefs. Such explanations are the theoretical outworking of the quest for coherence or overall meaningfulness on the part of the religious believer. They are the reasoned attempt to achieve a nondissonant fit, a relationship of mutual implication, between one's beliefs and attitudes.

In explaining, the believer enters into a form of theoretical discourse, however tentatively and however strong his continuing commitment to the attitudinal aspects of his faith. As in other forms of theoretical discourse, here also various why-questions are formulated—why do I exist? why did this experience occur? why is the world the way it is?—which a religious tradition attempts to answer by means of its belief-structure. Question and answer do not necessarily represent a chronological progression, of course, but rather a logical relationship. It may well be that specific religious explanations give rise, after the fact, to their own particular set of why questions. Still, as the striving for systematic consistency from the Christian church fathers to Advaita Vedanta Hinduism, from the elaboration of tribal creation myths to creation science shows, the same quest for a far-reaching coherence is manifested on the religious-theoretical level as has been pursued on the level of individual religious meaning-sketches.

Taken together, I suggest, the individual beliefs accepted by the believer provide a coherent explanation of the world known to him. As noted, the religious tradition in which he has been socialized plays no small role in telling him what questions ought to be asked and what sorts of answers are likely to be accepted as explanatorily adequate. The explanation may not rise out of disinterested speculation and the evidence for the explanans may not be purely objective. Religious explanations are not paradigm-dependent. Nonetheless, the ruling religious tradition must offer answers to the queries that preoccupy the individual if it is to integrate his various experiences into a meaningful whole.

The penalty for explanatory failure is cognitive dissonance, a sense of tension between one's nonreligious intellectual (moral, affective) experience and the religious account of it. Such explanatory inadequacy *may* not lead to an immediate rejection of a religious tradition, since participation in a religious community serves other functions in addition to making sense of one's experienced world. It will, however, limit the ability of the individual to appropriate the tradition in question, as well as threaten the attempt of that tradition to perform its integrative semantic role ("making sense of total experience"). This failure may occur whether or not the tradition explicitly grants a place for formulating and questioning its basic explanatory accounts.[9]

Levels of Explanation in Religion

Forms and functions of religious explanations are as numerous as types of religious belief. They vary from the extremely personal function of explaining a given religious experience undergone by an individual, to justifying social mores or a societal structure of authority, to explaining "why there is something rather than nothing." We will turn to the question of evaluating religious

---

[9] An excellent example of such a failure is contained in Chinua Achebe's novel, *Things Fall Apart* (1959). The book chronicles the growing explanatory inadequacy of a religious tradition, drawn from the context of an African tribal religion

explanations in the following section. First, however, is important to clarify the relationship between religious explanation and understanding as it varies according to the various levels of religious experience.

We might distinguish between a narrow and a broad conception of religious experience—and, correspondingly, of religious belief[10]—as long as these are taken as expressing not a dichotomy but opposite ends of a continuum. According to the narrow conception, specific experiences are tied to specific beliefs about the world and God. The divine, understood as having a particular form and content that at is (at least partially) knowable, is encountered in individual experiences and moments of the believer's life. Certain times and places (Passover, the Temple), and certain of his actions (prayer), are interpreted as more spiritual than others. Beyond this, either in pure form or as a tendency within the narrow conception, the broad conception of religious experience sees all of life as falling under the control of the divine, everything as making it present, every action as a response to it. Religion in this broad sense is the clearest expression of that inherent movement to the broadest context that emerged in our discussion of meaning above. Yet even in the narrower conception the divine being or sacred truth that is manifested is one whose significance is understood to be universal.

These two conceptions of religious experience shed light on different tendencies in the religious impulse. The narrow conception has the specificity required for religious belief and practice: it allows for a creed or story and ethical maxims to live by, for a community of like-believing persons as a socialization and support network, and for a cultus to express the shared belief. Such needs have spawned and maintained the so-called positive religions as the major loci of religious experience and belief in all cultures. Nonetheless, in tension with this component, the broader religious impulse resists any ultimate compartmentalization. "Your God is too small!" claims one popular religious author; "you can't put God in a box," cries another. Visible in its purest form in mystical experience and negative theology, the synthetic tendency transcends creeds and the boundaries of positive religion, necessary as they may be in day-to-day practice, moving into an ultimately united realm where all distinctions fall away.[11]

I believe that the distinction between these two conceptions of religious experience requires a certain limitation of scope for all theories of religious belief and explanation. In the social sciences we found some tension between the broad explanatory power of higher-level theories and the explanatory detail of lower-level theories; the same tension returns with a vengence in religion. In virtually all religions the divine is perceived in or through particular objects or events, while transcending all limiting words and contexts. Jewish and Christian theologies stress God's salvation-history as the particular locus of his self-manifestation, for example, without wishing to give up the notion that God is Lord also of universal-history.[12]

I suggest that this phenomenon necessitates a multilevel account of religious explanations, one that distinguishes the project of making sense at more concrete levels of experience from making sense at the level of the whole of experience. At the narrowest level, the believer will take a particular complex of experience and belief to constitute an explanation for some particular event or events: Yahweh caused the Flood to punish the people's sinfulness; God allowed the flat tire to teach me patience. A religious explanation of the events in question will include reference to the activity of the divine in or behind the event. For the believer the

---

[10] Cf. Thomas, *Philosophy and Religious Belief*, 63-64, from whose work I here extrapolate. The terms *narrow* and *broad* are of course used in a nonevaluative sense.

[11] For a summary of this tendency in the various mystical traditions see Dupré, "The Mystical Vision," *The Other Dimension*, chap. 9.

[12] See W. Pannenberg et al., *Revelation as History* (1969).

explanation will be true if the divine actually acted in the way claimed. Such assertions, which appear to contain empirical claims, may not be immediately testable. However, internal contradictions within the believer's account, empirical predictions that are falsified, and tensions with, say, naturalistic explanations of the same event may in some cases count against his explanation.[13]

Even at a somewhat broader level, why-questions can still be formulated: Why did God create the world? Why is the circle of death and rebirth perpetuated? Here also doctrinal answers are given, usually by higher-order theological statements referring to the creation of the world or "God's plan in history." The reference is now to history as a whole. Truth is claimed for the belief that God exists or that *samara* will end when amassed karma no longer causes another cycle, although there may be no particular event in the present that could falsify these truth-claims. They function to explain for believers why their life is as it is, yet they do so by providing an overarching interpretation of experience that seems more to describe the whole than to explain any particular part of it.

Here we begin to see a shading over from explanations of experience to attitudes toward experience. One might claim that explanatory accounts still have empirical entailments at this level, but they will be of only the most attenuated sort. Perhaps there should not be suffering in the world if an omnipotent, omniscient, omnibenevolent being exists, or at least not a balance of evil over good—at least not in the long run. Definitive falsifications seem rather unlikely, insofar as these explanations extend over large periods of human (or divine) history; more appropriate is an appeal to "eschatological verification" or falsification (cf. n. 8 above). Nonetheless, broader religious accounts still evidence what we might call *explanatory coherence:* they attempt to explain human experience in the most general terms at which an explanation can still be formulated. As a result, certain types of incoherence might still provide a basis for intersubjective criticism at this level.

At the *broadest* level of religious experience, however, one can speak of explanation, if at all, only in a rather different sense from its meaning elsewhere in this book. Indeed, recalling our overall attempt to pursue the theory of explanation from physics to theology, here we face perhaps the greatest hiatus of all. Any explanation at this level is so different from scientific explanations that equivocation threatens any attempt at comparison. The existence of this level in religion underscores the element of truth in the appeal to "total interpretation" by thinkers like John Hick and W. Cantwell Smith. (That it is only one aspect of the religious life represents the element of truth in their opponents' positions.)

Understood at the level of total experience, faith is "an uncompelled mode of 'experiencing as'...No *way* of accounting for the data can be said to be, in any objectively ascertainable sense, more probable than another."[14] When concerned with the meaningfulness of the whole, basic intuitions are more at home than arguments; one speaks symbolically, if at all; and religious experience becomes undifferentiated, in the sense that meaning is ascribed directly to the whole and only by derivation to each of its parts. No wonder thinkers like Nygren, who wish to defend philosophy of religion as a process of linguistic analysis and clarification, rope in their theories of meaning short of this point by considering the religious

---

[13] See, for example. Raeburne Heimbeck, *Theology and Meaning* (1969), who argues that such claims often have entailments which are testable. A similar argument has recently been presented by Edward Schoen in his *Religious Explanations* (1985); see esp. chap. 5, "The Plausibility of Religious Explanations."

[14] Hick, *Faith and Knowledge*, 151, 154. Hick is wrong, as we shall see, in treating all religious faith, for example the dispute between theism and atheism, as falling on this level.

context only to the extent that it can be accounted for in purely propositional and epistemic terms.

At this level the believer's fundamental religious intuition makes sense of his experience as a whole more in the manner of an immediate aesthetic sense of beauty than in the manner of propositional analysis. The believer or mystic senses ("sees") that things fit together, that there is an underlying coherence, that "All shall be well, and / All manner of thing shall be well."[15] Here at the borders of propositionality scant analogy remains with explanatory projects elsewhere. Intuitive understanding is no longer a precondition for explanation but seems to supersede it. The best the student of religion can offer is the semantic line from limited to broadest contexts of meaning that has structured this chapter up to now; and even this line is more posited than observed. That is, we could say that this highest level, the making sense of total experience, is the limiting case for efforts to explain at other levels. Here the believer or mystic claims to have a final coherence, an ultimate, comprehensive fit. Here he may speak of harmony, or unity, or the acceptance of all that is. But the elements that typified explanations in our earlier discussions are now absent: no problem-situation can be specified, no field delimited, since the explanation encompasses everything; no why-question can be formulated; no distinction between general law and specific instances remains. The reference (if subject and object, intuition and reference, can be separated any longer) is not an item in the world but the world as a whole, its relationship to the transcendent as totally other. In an important sense, the entire explanatory effort has been left behind or transcended; understanding supersedes explanation.

Interestingly, this limiting case of religious explanation works its way back into the more concrete explanations that one finds within religious belief systems. I have already defended the interconnection of the broad and narrow conceptions of religion in most actual religious systems. A corollary of this reciprocity is that one finds a holistic component even in those religious explanations that are more limited in scope. Even in those traditions that are willing to speak in univocal or analogous terms about their god or cosmic principles, one often finds some reference to a transcendent or wholly other standing outside all language. The tacit presence of this final horizon, in which all distinctions are absolved, circles back to cast a preliminary or tentative pall onto the realm where distinctions are drawn, rendering their status finite and provisional, perhaps even hypothetical.

For all of these reasons, we can never reduce religion to a matter of the mere formulation and evaluation of explanations. Religious statements are never completely free of their telos in the whole or beyond; their explanatory role is consequently only part of their religious use. As we saw, the semantic or interpretive element is not so constrained. Since explanation fades over into understanding at the highest reaches of religious belief and experience, this process can by anticipation be said to be already at work, albeit in a less obvious way, in more limited religious contexts. It is unjustified to overlook the explanatory or epistemic element in religion because of its concern with meaning. It is equally unjustified to countenance only explanatory considerations.

---

[15] T.S. Eliot, "Little Gidding," *The Four Quartets*, in *The Complete Poems and Plays* (1971), 138f.

Questions

1. What sort of contrast does Clayton draw in his description of the multilevel model of explanation?

2. For the theist who works with an explanation which gives account of the whole, what shortcomings does Clayton see?

3. Do you think that Clayton is right or wrong? State why.

4. Do you agree with Clayton's appraisal of the holistic way of looking?

5. Do you agree with Clayton's contention that the Christian theistic sorts of explanations as wholistic pictures are different from scientific explanations in the way Clayton charges?

QUANTUM THEORY AND FREE WILL*

Stephen M. Barr

Barr examines contemporary quantum theory, which he feels has been viewed by the scientific community as in strong opposition to the possibility of human having free will. Barr counters three arguments with the main contention that there is not enough information available yet regarding the brain's functioning, and so the door should be left open on the matter of whether or not persons are free. While he hasn't established a freedom thesis from science, he calls into question current arguments based upon arguments against it.

Not surprisingly, a number of physicists, biologists, and philosophers have made the suggestion that quantum indeterminacy has something to do with human freedom.[1] One version of this idea is that quantum indeterminacy actually explains free will. The idea is that the "freedom" of the will is simply the fact that human behavior is unpredictable, and that this unpredictability is a con-sequence of the random character of "quantum processes" happening in the brain. However, this version of the idea is very dubious.

In the first place, if the human mind were significantly affected by really random processes happening at the atomic level, then our behavior would be erratic and undependable. This does not correspond to what we observe in normal people, and it certainly would not have been conducive to the survival of our species. Imagine that one of our primitive forebears, in the course of sneaking up on his dinner, was suddenly impelled by a random process in his brain to jump up and down making wild cries. He probably would not have lived long enough to be a forebear.

To be subject to random mental disturbance is not freedom but a kind of slavery or even madness. Merely introducing an element of randomness into the operation of the brain, therefore, is not the way to explain free will. Furthermore, if one's only goal is to introduce unpredictability or apparent randomness into behavior, quantum indeterminacy is not required. Even a classical system that behaves in a completely deterministic way can be highly unpredictable in practice. (As I noted earlier, this is one of the characteristics of "chaotic systems:") Things that are not really random can act, for all practical purposes, as if they were random. In other words, randomness can be simulated.

For example, suppose I needed for the purpose of some game of chance a sequence of one thousand "random" digits. One thing I could do is look up in a mathematical table the first one thousand digits of the number π. The number π begins 3.141592653. These digits are not truly random, of course, since there is a precise mathematical procedure that determines what each number in the sequence is. But to a person who did not know where these digits came from they would give every appearance of being random. In fact, they would pass all the usual statistical tests for randomness. Such a sequence of digits is called "pseudo-random" by mathematicians. The upshot is that to introduce an element of mere "randomness" into the behavior of a physical system

---

* This article is reprinted by courtesy of the author and publisher. It appears in *Modern Physics and Ancient Faith*, by Stephen M. Barr, The University of Notre Dame Press, 2003.

[1] John R. Lucas, *The Freedom of the Will* (Oxford: Oxford University Press, 1970); Eccles and Popper, *The Self and Its Brain*; David Hodgson, *The Mind Matters: Consciousness and Choice in a Quantum World* (Oxford: Oxford University Press, 1988); Michael Lockwood, *Mind, Brain, and Quantum: The Compound 'I'*, (Oxford: Blackwell, 1989); Euan Squires, *Conscious Mind in the Physical World* (London: Adam Hilger, IOP Publishing, Ltd., 1990); H.P. Stapp, *Mind, Matter and Quantum Mechanics* (New York: Springer-Verlag, 1993).

such as the brain it is not really necessary to have the true randomness of a quantum process; one can use the pseudo-randomness that is found in many deterministic non-quantum processes.

For all these reasons it does not seem that quantum theory will succeed in explaining free will. But that is not what the religious person would expect anyway. If quantum physics could explain free will, it would mean that free will was essentially nothing but a physical phenomenon. That would contradict the notion that free will is something that pertains to the "spiritual" and is therefore not completely "reducible to the merely material."

Most of those who suggest that quantum indeterminacy may have something to do with free will are saying something quite different. They do not say that quantum indeterminacy explains free will, but rather that it provides an opening for free will. Free will is conceived of as a faculty arising, at least in part, from something that is non-physical. However, in order for the non-physical to have room to operate, matter—in particular the human brain—must not be completely under the rigid control of physical cause and effect. To put it another way, true freedom implies that one actually has a choice. The alternatives one is choosing among must be real alternatives that are permitted by the laws of nature. The laws of physics, therefore, must be flexible enough that more than one outcome is possible in a particular situation: for free will to be possible, the laws of physics must have indeterminacy built into them. The key point is that quantum indeterminacy allows free will, it does not produce it.

However, some scientists and philosophers have argued that quantum theory does not even create an opening for free will. There are at least three arguments that they make:

Argument 1.

The first argument is based on the difference, emphasized earlier, between randomness and rational choice. It is claimed that quantum theory asserts that all events, to the extent that they are not determined, are governed only by chance. And if they are governed only by chance, then obviously they cannot be governed by something else, like a rational will. This argument is made, for example, by the philosopher David Chalmers in his book *The Conscious Mind:* "[T]he theory [that quantum indeterminacy allows free will] contradicts the quantum-mechanical postulate that these microscopic `decisions' are entirely random...."[2]

To understand better what Chalmers is saying, let us imagine that some decision of the human will is able to have an effect on the physical world by influencing the outcome of some "quantum process" in the brain. In particular, suppose that this quantum process is one that has two possible outcomes, and that quantum theory predicts that these outcomes have equal probability. What Chalmers is arguing is that the human "will" cannot select one of these outcomes, or even affect the odds, because that would change the probabilities from what quantum theory says they ought to be. Any influence of the will would therefore violate quantum theory.

I believe this argument to be subtly flawed and to be based on an unwarranted assumption. Specifically, Chalmers is interpreting the statements made by quantum theory in a way that is unnecessarily restrictive. If quantum theory says that two outcomes are equally probable, that can be interpreted simply as meaning that there is nothing in the physical situation itself that prefers one outcome to the other. That does not logically preclude the possibility that in certain cases something outside the physical situation may prefer one of the outcomes. If the only causes operating on the system in question are physical, and there

---

[2] Chamlers, *The Conscious Mind*, 157

is nothing in the physical situation that prefers one of the outcomes, then the odds will indeed be 50-50. If, however, some non-physical cause intervenes, then the odds could be different.

An analogy might be useful. If I flip a "fair" coin there is an equal chance that heads and tails will come up. That statement of probabilities is based on the fact that there is nothing about the coin itself, such as its shape or weighting, that would bias it toward one of the outcomes. But if instead of flipping the coin I deliberately place it on the table with heads up, that estimate of probabilities no longer applies, because something—my will—has influenced the situation.

Chalmers goes on to argue that if free will were to intrude itself into the physical realm it would lead to "detectable patterns" of results rather than the randomness predicted by quantum theory. This does not seem to me to be much of an argument against free will, for in practice that is just exactly what we do see when we study human behavior. There are detectable patterns in the way a human being acts, even when he is acting freely, but these patterns are neither so rigid that they can be reduced to a mechanical law, nor so erratic that they appear purely random.

Implicitly, what Chalmers is suggesting is an experimental test, which he believes would prove that free will does not affect outcomes in the physical world. To perform such a test one would have to present the same person with the same choice a large number of times. The choices would have to be the same even to the point that the person's brain, body, and environment—or at least the relevant parts of them—were known to be in exactly the same physical state prior to each choice. Using the principles of quantum theory one could then, in principle, calculate the relative probabilities for the various outcomes and compare them to the actual relative frequencies of the choices the person made. Needless to say, this is all hopelessly impossible in practice. Even supposing that some non-invasive way could be found to acquire all the relevant information about the state of a person's brain—and the human brain contains a few times 10^{25} atoms—one could never reproduce that state exactly, as required by the experiment. There is simply no way to control all the relevant variables. And even if one had all the necessary information, it would be impossible in practice to carry out the quantum-theoretical calculation of probabilities. Finally, even if all these things were possible, it is enough to point out that no such experiment has in fact ever been done, and there is no way of saying in advance what the results of it would be.

One might wonder why quantum processes are needed to produce an "opening" for free will. Could not classical, deterministic physics be interpreted in a similarly permissive way? That is, couldn't one say just as well that the precise behaviors predicted by the equations of classical physics are only to be thought of as the behaviors that would occur if no non-physical causes intervened? The answer is yes. In fact, that would be a way of allowing for free will even in a universe that had no quantum indeterminacy. However, there is a significant difference between the two cases. In the classical case, a deviation from the behaviors predicted by the physical laws due to a non-physical influence would show up as a *violation* of those laws. The laws would say that an atom should move a certain way, and it would move in a different way. For reasons that I have already indicated, it will never be possible to know if such violations of the laws of physics go on in the human brain. But the idea that they do is, to many people, rather ugly and philosophically unsatisfying.

On the other hand, in a quantum process, several alternative outcomes are truly allowed to happen by the laws of physics, and so a choice can be made without a "violation" of physical law. For example, let us suppose hypothetically that a person's brain is in a state where quantum theory says that there are only two things that he can do, *A* and *B*, and that they have an equal probability of occurring. Obviously, since the laws of physics say that he must do *A* or *B*, and give no preference to *A* or *B*, it cannot be a *violation* of those laws for him to make either choice. His freedom of choice in such a case would be unconstrained by the requirement of satisfying the laws of physics.

(There is an interesting objection that can be raised to this line of argument. Suppose that exactly the situation that we have just described is repeated one hundred times. If the person making the choices is truly free, he should be able to make the same choice—say A—all one hundred times. But the chance of this happening according to the quantum probability laws is only $(½)^{100}$, or about one chance in a thousand billion billion billion. While this is not strictly a zero probability, it is prohibitively low. So it appears that the more often the same choice is presented to a person, the more his "free decisions" have to fall in line with the statistical expectations given by the quantum probability laws. It would seem, then, that quantum indeterminacy does not really provide an opening for freedom as freedom is usually understood.

One can see that this objection is really a version of the Chalmers argument that we discussed earlier. And one answer we gave there applies here too. In practice, it is not possible for a person to face exactly the same choice one hundred times, or even twice. As Heraclitus pointed out thousands of years ago, one cannot step into the same stream twice, for the stream constantly changes. If I am deciding between going to the movies tonight and staying home, it is not precisely the same as when I decided last week between going to the movies and staying home. For one thing, I am not exactly the same person physically and mentally that I was one week ago. I have different thoughts and emotions and have undergone various experiences in the meantime. The atoms in my body and brain have undergone countless changes. Moreover, I am making the choice in an altered context. Therefore, the quantum calculations that would yield the probabilities in the two situations would be very different.)

Argument 2.

A related argument that quantum indeterminacy is irrelevant to free will has been made by the mathematician and physicist Roger Penrose. In *Shadows of the Mind,* he writes, "If the `will' could somehow influence Nature's choice of alternative that occurs [in quantum processes], then why is an experimenter not able, by the action of `will power,' to influence the result of a quantum experiment? If this were possible, then violations of the quantum probabilities would surely be rife!"[3]

The trouble with this argument is that it is directed against a position that nobody holds. No one is suggesting that there is some general ability of the human mind to control the way all quantum processes turn out. (Such a suggestion would even have problems of self-consistency, since different people could will contradictory outcomes for the same process.) The Penrose objection might be answered simply by saying that a person's will can control only certain quantum processes that go on in that person's brain. Clearly, to say that some unpredictable events are subject to human will is not to say that all of them must be. I can believe, for example, that it is within my power to control some part of my brain so that it will lift my arm and wave it about, without believing that I can also by willpower affect the movements of the Sun, Moon, and stars.

---

[3] Penrose, *Shadows of the Mind,* 350.

Argument 3.

The third argument is to the effect that quantum indeterminacy is not relevant to the functioning of the brain at all. This claim is based on the assertion that those structures in the brain, specifically neurons, that are involved in mental activity are simply too large for quantum indeterminacy to play a role in them. In other words, they are large enough that the "classical limit" of quantum theory applies. This is the prevailing view of brain researchers. However, it has been challenged. Interestingly, one of the scientists who has challenged it is Roger Penrose. Penrose has argued, on the basis of certain human intellectual capacities, that quantum processes are likely to be important in understanding the brain. And he points to very small structures, called "microtubules," in the "cytoskeletons" of the brain's neurons as sites where quantum effects could potentially play an important role.[4] Sir John Eccles, a renowned neurophysiologist, has made the alternative suggestion of a certain structure called the "presynaptic vesicular grid" as a possible site for quantum effects.'

Whether the particular suggestions of Penrose or Eccles have any merit or not, it is certainly quite rash for anyone to assert, given the present crude state of human knowledge about the brain, that quantum processes cannot be important in explaining its behavior. In the first place, precisely because quantum effects are generally most noticeable in systems of very small size, the relevant parts of the brain are likely to be somewhat inconspicuous. Moreover, as there is no detailed theory of how the will influences the brain, brain researchers have little to guide them in their search. It is difficult to see how they would recognize the relevant structures even if they found them. It is not even clear that there would be recognizable structures.

Some humility should be induced by the fact that there are many aspects of the human mind that are not yet understood in terms of the structure of the brain. Consciousness itself is one of them. In any event, the entire history of science counsels against the overweening confidence that one finds in so much writing on this subject. Whenever hitherto inaccessible realms of phenomena are opened up to detailed investigation, dramatic discoveries follow that often baffle and surprise the scientific community. Quantum theory itself is a prime example. Absolutely no one expected, when atomic spectroscopy began in the nineteenth century, that it would lead to the strange new world of quantum physics. When the study of very low temperatures began, no one foresaw that such remarkable effects as superfluidity and superconductivity would be found. Similarly, every new tool that astrophysicists and astronomers have brought to bear in studying the universe has led to dramatic surprises, such as the existence of pulsars, quasars, galactic jets, ultrahigh-energy cosmic rays, and gamma ray bursts. Every scientist ill testify to the remarkable richness and unpredictability of nature.

In the human brain one is dealing with what is agreed by all to be by far the most complex and remarkable system in nature. If there is anything that can be predicted with confidence, it is that the investigation of the brain will produce revolutionary surprises.

How free will fits into the structure of nature remains a deep and difficult questions. However, it can be said that there is nothing in the laws of nature or the character of physics as they exist today which is logically incompatible with free will. After all is said and done, the fact remains that the determinism which reigned in physical science for almost three centuries, and which seemed to leave no place for freedom, has been overthrown. It may come back, but there is not sign yet that it will. The great mathematician and scientist Hermann Weyl,

---

[4] Ibid., 348-49, 367-69.

reflecting upon the implications of quantum theory in 1931, made the following observations, which remain valid today:

> We may say that there exists a world, causally closed and determined by precise laws, but...the new insight which modern [quantum] physics affords...opens several ways of reconciling personal freedom with natural law. It would be premature, however, to propose a definite and complete solution of the problem. One of the great differences between the scientist and the impatient philosopher is that the scientist bides his time. We must await the future development of science, perhaps for centuries, perhaps for thousands of years, before we can design a true and detailed picture of the interwoven texture of Matter, Life, and Soul. But the old classical determinism of Hobbes and Laplace need not oppress us longer.[5]

This was a tremendous reversal of fortunes. The religious believer of a century ago was forced to maintain in the teeth of all physical theory of that day that determinism was false. But as it stands now, at least, it is his expectations that have been vindicated.

Questions

1. What are the three arguments Barr outlines as being offered against the thesis that humans are free?

2. Do you think that Barr is right on the matter concerning the lack of information regarding the operations of the human brain?

3. Do you think that the unknowns that Barr cites are relevant to the claim that humans might be free?

4. What flaws do you see in Barr's main argument?

5. Do you think that the evidence goes contrary to Barr's contention? If so why?

---

[5] F. Beck and J.C. Eccles, "Quantum aspects of consciousness and the role of consciousness," *Proceedings of the National Academy of Sciences* 89 (1992): 11357-61; J.C. Eccles, *How the Self Controls Its Brain* (Berlin: Springer-Verlag, 1994).

Figure 8

Figure 5

Part VII

Religion and Ethics

KANT ON RECOGNIZING OUR DUTIES AS GOD'S COMMANDS[*]

John E. Hare

Hare deals incisively with a controversial issue relating to Kant's charge that one must see one's duties as God's commands, while at the same time see Kant as opposing a theological version of hereronomy. How Kant is viewed as working with both is the main argument of the paper. He argues contrary to many interpreters of Kant, that Kant doesn't really reject the divine command theory, because Kant knowingly offers an argument against it in the Groundwork *that doesn't really work. He finally rejects the thesis that God's lessening of his supervisory role in history cashes out in greater human autonomy, contending that the theist who opts for this line, will have to significantly alter the Christian set of beliefs.*

Kant both says that we should recognize our duties as God's commands, and objects to the theological version of heteronomy, 'which derives morality from a divine and supremely perfect will'. In this paper I discuss how these two views fit together, and in the process I develop a notion of autonomous submission to divine moral authority. I oppose the 'constitutive' view of autonomy proposed by J. B. Schneewind and Christine Korsgaard. I locate Kant's objection to theological heteronomy against the background of Crusius's divine command theory, and I compare Kant's views about divine authority and human political authority.

I. Kant on Religion and Morality

I am going to focus on Kant's view that we should recognize our duties as God's commands, and on how this fits with his more familiar objection in the *Groundwork* to the theological version of heteronomy, 'which derives morality from a divine and supremely perfect will'. But before we get to that, I want to make a general point about Kant's view of the relation between morality and the Christian faith. We have tended to secularize Kant in a way that distorts the meaning of the texts. There has been a tendency to see modern philosophy as teleological, headed towards the death of God and the death of metaphysics heralded by Nietzsche at the end of the nineteenth century. The modern classics have accordingly been trimmed to fit this model by their twentieth century admirers. What we need to do is to recapture what I call 'the vertical dimension' of their thought. In the case of Kant, he is, in his own phrase, a 'pure rationalist'.[1] A pure rationalist is someone who 'recognizes revelation, but asserts that to know and accept it as real is not a necessary requisite to religion.' Implicit in this description is a distinction between two kinds of religion. In his second preface to *Religion within the Limits of Reason Alone* Kant suggests we think of revelation as two concentric circles. Historical revelation (for example, Scripture), which is given to particular people at particular times, belongs in the outer circle. Kant's project is to see if he can translate the items in this outer circle into the language of the inner circle, which is the revelation to reason, and is the same to all people at all times. Being a pure rationalist means that the items in the outer circle are not rejected, but they are held not to be necessary for all

---

[*] This article is reprinted by courtesy of the author and *Faith and Philosophy*, October 2000, pp. 459-478.
[1] Allen Wood denies that Kant is a pure rationalist, ('Kant's Deism', in *Kant's Philosophy of Religion Reconsidered, op. cit. 11.*) For arguments against Wood, see John Hare, *The Moral Gap,* Oxford: Clarendon Press, 1996, 42-45.

rational beings to come to saving faith. They are, Kant says, *vehicles* of the religion within the limits of reason alone. He himself and his European contemporaries have been introduced to God's requirements by this historical revelation, and Kant thinks it important that biblical preaching should continue and be kept under discipline, so that this vehicle can be maintained. He is not, then, rejecting special revelation in favor of morality. But Kant wants to use morality to translate as much as he can of special revelation into the language of reason. The translation exercise is going to show, if it is successful, that the two circles are indeed concentric, which is at least to say that they are consistent with each other. More than this, a life centered in one will also be centered in the other.[2]

On my reading of Kant's project, he finds that there are some items in the outer circle which he cannot translate, but which he needs to continue to believe in order to have morality make rational sense. Conspicuous among these items is the belief in divine grace. Kant believes in a strong version of the doctrine of original sin, that we are born under the dominion of the 'evil maxim', which makes us subordinate our duty to our own happiness. Kant also believes that we cannot by our own devices overcome this dominion, because it already underlies all our choices. We therefore require assistance from outside ourselves to accomplish what he calls 'the revolution of the will', by which the ranking of happiness over duty is reversed. Kant's candidate for this outside assistance is what he calls 'a divine supplement', and he holds that we have to believe that this is available if we are to hold ourselves accountable to the moral law. Twentieth century exegetes have tried to rescue Kant from these views by what I call 'cushion hermeneutics'. This is the strategy of suggesting that he did not really mean some of the things he says, but was saying them merely to cushion his disagreement with the authorities.[3] But this kind of interpretation should be adopted only as a last resort, if there is no straight-forward interpretation which fits the text. Especially this is true of Kant, who placed such a high value on sincerity.[4] We should not use cushion hermeneutics except as a last resort, if it is the only possible way to make sense of the text.

II. The 'Constitutive' View of Autonomy

Contemporary secular Kantians have interpreted Kant's views about autonomy as a form of creative anti-realism. I will interpret him, rather, as what I will call a 'transcendent realist', namely someone who *believes* that there is something beyond the limitations of our understanding.[5] In particular there is a God who is head of the kingdom of which we are merely members. When we recognize something as our duty we are in some way recapitulating the will of this head of the kingdom just as when we believe something true about the world we are in some way recapitulating the way things are in themselves. This is a traditional

---

[2] *Religion VI*, 13. I will be making references to Kant by using the page numbers of the relevant volume of the Academy edition.

[3] Allen Wood, 'Kant's Deism', in *Kant's Philosophy of Religion Reconsidered,* ed. Philip J. Rossi and Michael Wreen, Bloomington: Indiana University Press, 1991, 1-21, 14. See also the phrase in E. Troeltsch, 'utterances of prudence', quoted in Michel Despland, *Kant on History and Religion,* Montreal: McGill-Queen's University Press, 1973, 105, and the phrase 'cover' techniques in Yirmiahu Yovel, *Kant and the Philosophy of History,* Princeton: Princeton University Press, 1980, 114 and 215. Another similar strategy is to appeal to clumsy editing.

[4] e.g. *Conflict of the Faculties* VII, 10, and *KrV* III and IV, A748-50=B776-8.

[5] See Heinz Heimsoeth, 'Metaphysical Motives in the Development of Critical Idealism', in *Kant: Disputed Questions,* ed. M. S. Gram, Chicago: Quadrangle Books, 1967. I have been influenced by a paper by Robert M. Adams, 'Things in Themselves', *Philosophy and Phenomenological Research,* 57 (Dec. 1997), 801-25.

picture of Kant as an empirical realist, a transcendental idealist, and a transcendent realist. But interpreting Kant's view of autonomy as a form of creative anti-realism has been typical of Rawlsians such as Christine Korsgaard and J.B. Schneewind, and this interpretation has become very influential.[6]

Christine Korsgaard takes the view that our reflective endorsement of a prescription makes that prescription normative; it is the source of obligation, or even of all value.[7] Thus if a Mafioso can endorse reflectively the judgment that he should go out and kill, then he *should*. If human beings decided that human life was worthless, then it *would be* worthless. She says, 'The point is just this: if one holds the view, as I do, that obligations exist in the first-person perspective, then in one sense the obligatory is like the visible: it depends on how much of the light of reflection is on.' I hasten to add that Korsgaard goes on to say that the Mafioso has a *deeper* obligation to give up his immoral role. But she feels that she has to concede initially that the Mafioso has the obligation to do the hideous thing, because of her position that 'it is the endorsement that does the work' (that is, the normative work).

J.B. Schneewind's magisterial history of modern ethics leading up to Kant lays out, in Kant's name, what Schneewind calls a 'constitutive' method of ethics. Here is a statement of this view from an earlier article, 'Reflecting on one's motives one finds oneself giving them a unique kind of approval or disapproval; in any particular situation one is to act from the approved motive or set of motives, and the act so motivated is the appropriate action. There is no other source of rightness or wrongness in actions.'[8] Schneewind thinks this endorsement is the *source of the rightness* of the action. That is what makes his method 'constitutive', or a kind of constructivism or creative anti-realism. Schneewind goes on to use the language of creation, saying that our possession of a constitutive method of ethics 'shows that we *create* the moral order in which we live, and supply our own motives for compliance.'[9] The view is that if any other will, or anything external to us, or even our own non-rational appetites are the source of the normativity, then we are not free but slaves.

I have doubts about this kind of creative anti-realism in ethics, both in itself and as an interpretation of Kant. The best place to see why it does not fit Kant is those passages where Kant, throughout his writings, describes God as the head of the kingdom of which we are mere members, and where he says we should recognize our duties as God's commands to us. In these passages Kant denies that God is the author or creator of the moral demand, because Kant thinks this demand does not have an *author* at all. But if it does not have an author, then

---

[6] I am going to mention Christine Korsgaard again at the end; but for an extended review, see *Faith and Philosophy*, volume 17, 3, (July 2000) 371-83.

[7] Christine Korsgaard, *The Sources of Normativity*, Cambridge: Cambridge University Press, 1996, 91; and *Creating the Kingdom of Ends*, Cambridge: Cambridge University Press, 1996, 240-1.

[8] J. B. Schneewind, 'Natural Law, Skepticism, and the Methods of Ethics', *Journal of the History of Ideas*, 52 (1991) 298. Curiously, the actual treatment of Kant at the end of *The Invention of Autonomy* (Cambridge: Cambridge University Press, 1998) is brief, almost perfunctory. Schneewind has, however, given a fuller treatment of Kant's views on autonomy in a succession of articles, and I have made use especially of 'The Divine Corporation and the History of Ethics', in *Philosophy and History*, ed. Richard Rorty, J. B. Schneewind and Quentin Skinnner, Cambridge: Cambridge University Press, 1984, 173-92, 'Natural Law, Skepticism, and Methods of Ethics' *op, cit.*, and 'Autonomy, Obligation and Virtue: An Overview of Kant's Ethics', in *The Cambridge Companion to Kant*, ed. Paul Guyer, Cambridge: Cambridge University Press, 1992, 309-41.

[9] *Ibid. 302*, emphasis added. In *The Invention of Autonomy*, Schneewind does not emphasize the language of creation, but he does say that Kant agrees with his predecessors who hold that moral approval is 'like the Pufendorfian divine will that creates moral entities', so that 'our approval is what makes same motives good, others bad,', *op. cit.* 524.

we cannot be either its author or its creator. One passage is from the report of his lectures on ethics from 1775-80, 'No one, not even God, can be the author of the laws of morality, since they have no origin in will, but instead a practical necessity. But the moral laws can nevertheless be subject to a lawgiver *(unter einem Gesetzgeber stehen)*. There can exist a being which has the power and authority to execute these laws, to declare that they are in accordance with his will, and to impose upon every one the obligation of acting in accordance with them. This being is therefore the lawgiver, though not the author of the laws.'[10]

Kant revises this position in the *Groundwork* (1785), but what looks like a radical revision is not. He says, it is true, that we are authors of the law. But this is because he has made a distinction not present in the earlier discussion between two kinds of author. There is the author of the law and there is the author of the obligation in accordance with the law. Put carefully, it turns out that God and we can be seen as jointly authors in the one sense, namely authors of the obligation of the law, and neither God nor we can be seen as authors in the other sense, namely authors of the law directly.[11] I think this is Kant's view at the time of the *Groundwork* and throughout his ethical writing thereafter. Moreover, saying that God and we are jointly authors of the obligation of the law does not mean that we are on an equal footing with God as authors in this sense. It does not mean that our contributions are symmetrical. Even in the *Groundwork* Kant makes this clear. He distinguishes between the king of the kingdom of ends and the rest of the membership of this kingdom, 'A rational being belongs to the kingdom of ends as a *member,* when, although he makes its universal laws, he is also himself subject to these laws. He belongs to it as its *head,* when as the maker of laws he is himself subject to the will of no other'.[12] Kant goes on to say that a rational being can maintain the position of head of the kingdom only if he is a completely *independent* being, without needs and with an unlimited power adequate to his will. There is no doubt that Kant is talking about God here, as head or king of the kingdom, and without a king there cannot be a kingdom. There is the following asymmetry between the king and his subjects: We ordinary moral agents have to see our role as recapitulating in our own wills the declaration in God's will of our duties. This is how we are lawgivers; we declare a correspondence of our wills with the law (which we do not create). For me to will the law autonomously is to make it my law. Kant has similar language in the Second Critique about

---

[10] Kant, *Lectures on Ethics,* trans. Louis Infield, p. 51-2.
[11] Kant says that practical reason (the will) should be allowed to 'simply manifest its own sovereign authority as the supreme maker of law', and earlier he glosses this notion of the will *making the law* in terms of the will being its *author, Gl* IV, 441 and 431. Patrick Kain has traced with great elegance the emergence of the new way of making the distinction, in the fifth chapter of his dissertation from the University of Notre Dame (1999). For example, in the fragment of lecture notes referred to as 'Moral Mrongovius II', Kant is reported to have said to his students in 1785 (while he was writing the *Groundwork*), 'The lawgiver is not the author of the law, rather he is the author of the obligation of the law (*Autor der obligation des Gezetzes*)', XXIX 633-4. The new way of stating the distinction becomes standard for him, as in the following passage from the *Metaphysics of Morals* (1797), 'A (morally practical) *law* is a proposition that contains a categorical imperative (a command). One who commands (*imperans*) through a law is the lawgiver (*legislator*). He is the author (*autor, sic*) of the obligation in accordance with the law (*Urheber (autor) der Verbindlichkeit nach dem Gesetz),* but not always the author of the law. In the latter case the law would be a positive (contingent) and chosen law. A law that binds us a priori and unconditionally by our own reason can also be expressed as proceeding from the will of a supreme lawgiver, that is, one who has only rights and no duties (hence from the divine will); but this signifies only the Idea of a moral being whose will is a law for everyone, without his being thought as the author of the law.' Here we have essentially the same distinction between lawgiver and author, but now expressed in terms of two kinds of authorship (*MM* VI, 227).
[12] *Gl* IV, 433-4.

willing that there is a God, which sounds at first hearing like blasphemy.[13] But Kant means that we make God our God. He does not mean 'create' in either case, either that we create the law or that we create God. Neither God nor the law can do the job Kant needs them to do if we do create them. Autonomy on this reading is more nearly a kind of submission than a kind of creation. In what follows, I will use autonomy with this understanding, though I do not want to deny that the term has been used by others, especially by followers and interpreters of Kant, in a creative anti-realist way.[14]

The constructivist account of Kant has fallen into the trap of a false dichotomy. It is easy, but a mistake, to assume that if values are not entirely independent of or external to the will, they must be entirely dependent on it or internal to it. One way to think of this false dichotomy is to suppose that if values are not like armadillos, things we discover in the world outside us, they must be like armchairs, things we put into the world or create, our artifacts. What lies behind the appeal of this dichotomy is what John Austin called 'the descriptive fallacy', appealing to Kant as the philosopher who first uncovered it.[15] One way to be guilty of the descriptivist fallacy is to assume that to know the meaning of a normative word like 'good' is just like knowing the meaning of 'red', namely to know what things we may or may not apply it to.[16] But the assumption is a mistake, the mistake of thinking that language always works in the same kind of way. This is the mistake of those who think they have to move from a rejection of substantive moral realism, where the normativity is entirely external to the will, to a *creative* anti-realism, where the normativity is created by the will. I am encouraged here by Karl Ameriks's response to Schneewind, rejecting what he calls 'the false trichotomy: either imposed by us, or imposed by another, or simply "perceived" as a natural feature'.[17] Kant's theory is, I believe, an example of a theory which resists such a dichotomy or trichotomy.

III. Christian August Crusius

An important figure for us to consider here is Christian August Crusius.[18] Kant needs to be understood against the background of the discussion of divine command theory in the pietist circles he was familiar with. Schneewind's history of modern ethics, together with his earlier articles, gives Crusius a key place in the development that led to Kant's views on autonomy. Crusius' views were influential in Konigsberg at the time Kant was writing, and provided a pietist alternative within philosophy to the rationalist doctrine of Christian Wolff. Kant's teacher, Martin Knutzen, undertook the project of reconciling the two. Crusius is presented

---

[13] *KpV* V,143.
[14] See Don Cupitt, *Taking Leave of God*, (London: SCM Press, 1980, 9), 'A modern person must not any more surrender the apex of his self-consciousness to a god. It must remain his own.'
[15] John Austin, *How to do Things with Words,* Oxford: Oxford University Press, 1965, 3
[16] See R. M. Hare, *Moral Thinking*, Oxford: Clarendon Press, 1981, 67.
[17] Karl Ameriks, 'On Schneewind and Kant's Method in Ethics', *Ideas y Valores*, no. 102 Dec. 1996, 48.
[18] Paton already remarked on this importance, see Immanuel Kant, *Groundwork of the Metaphysic of Morals*, trans. and analysed by H. J. Paton, Harper, New York: 1964, p.141. For Crusius's views, see the selection from 'Guide to Rational Living', in *Moral Philosophy from Montaigne to Kant*, vol II, ed. J. B. Schneewind, Cambridge: Cambridge University Press, 1990, 568-585 (henceforth *GRL*). See also Giorgio Tonelli, 'La Question des bornes de l'entendement humain au XVIIIe siecle', *Revue de metaphysique et de morale* (1959), 396-427. In the Second Critique (*KpV* V, 40), Kant mentions Crusius as the source of the view which locates the practical material determining ground of morality externally in the will of God. See also *Moralphilosophie Collins*, KGS 262-3, 'Crusius believes that all obligation is related to the will of another (*die Willkur eines andern*)'.

by Schneewind as making two central points against Wolff's moral philosophy. First, he introduced what Schneewind calls 'a quite novel distinction' between two kinds of things we ought to do; there are actions that we ought to do as *means* to some end of ours and others we ought to do *regardless* of any ends we have, even the end of our own perfection. It is only this second kind of obligation that Crusius is willing to call 'moral obligation'. Here, says Schneewind, is the origin of Kant's notion of the categorical imperative. Second, Crusius tied this distinction to the notion of freedom. He said that the will is free only because it can choose in accordance with this second kind of obligation. That is to say that even if we perceive something clearly as required for an increase in perfection, we can choose either for it or against it. This is contrary to Wolff because Wolff taught that by nature the availability of increased perfection necessarily moves us, and we are always obligated to pursue it. We are always drawn to act so as to bring about what we believe is the greatest amount of perfection, and Wolff says we are bound or necessitated so to act.[19]

Now it may seem churlish to say of a 600 page history that it has not given us enough of the historical context, but I think in this case it is true. Schneewind is wrong to say that it is 'a quite novel distinction' to distinguish being drawn to some end of ours *as ours* and being drawn *regardless* of any ends we have, even the end of our own perfection. Both this distinction and the distinctive tying of this distinction to freedom come from Duns Scotus, and before Scotus from Anselm. Duns Scotus holds that there are two affections of the will, the affection for advantage, directed to one's own happiness or perfection, and the affection for justice, which is directed to what is good in itself regardless of one's ends. For Scotus we are only free because we have the affection for justice. This distinction between the affections is to be found in both Lutheran and Reformed theology.[20] Scotism was a widely accessible option in the intellectual milieu in which the Reformers lived. Luther makes the point repeatedly that one who does the good in order to promote his own blessedness is still not devoted to the good itself; rather, he is using it as a means for 'climbing up to the Divine majesty.'[21] Perhaps Crusius came to the distinction by reflecting on Luther.

In Scotus and in the Reformers and in Crusius, this distinction is tied into a version of divine command theory. Scotus thinks that God necessarily loves God, and then wills to have co-lovers (though God does not will this necessarily). Moreover God necessarily orders these creatures towards union with God, their primary good. From this come the first group of the ten commandments. But the *route* to this end is not necessary, and is within God's prescriptive discretion. Here we have the second group of the ten commandments specifying our duty to the

---

[19] J. B. Schneewind, 'Autonomy, Obligation, and Virtue', op. cit., 312-3.

[20] For Luther, the route is through Ockham. The nominalist tradition or *via moderna* was adopted by Gregory of Rimini, who was General of the Hermits of St. Augustine, which was Luther's order a century and a half later. Gabriel Biel, at Tubingen, wrote an influential exposition of Ockham's system, which was taught at Erfurt (by two of Luther's professors, Jaadokus Trutfetter and Bartholomaeus Arnoldi) and at Wittenberg (where Luther did most of his teaching). See especially Heiko Oberman, *Luther: A Man Between God and the Devil*, Eileen Walliser-Schwarzenbart, trans., New York: Doubleday, 1989, 118-19. For Calvin, the influence through John Major and the College de Montaigu was stated by Francois Wendel, *Calvin*, trans. Philip Mairet, New York: Harper and Row, 1950, and fully worked out by Karl Reuter, in *Das Grundverstaendnis der Theologie Calvins*, Neukirchen-Vluyn: Neukirchener-Verlag, 1963. An enthusiastic advocate is Thomas Torrance, in *The Hermeneutics of John Calvin*, Edinburgh: Scottish Academic Press, 1988, and also Alexander Broadie, *The Shadow of Scotus*, Edinburgh: T & T Clark, 1995. A more sceptical reading of the evidence can be found in A. Ganoczy, 'Le jeune Calvin: Genese et evolution de sa vocation reformatrice', Wiesbaden, 1966, and A. N. S. Lane, 'Calvin's Use of the Fathers and the Medievals', *Calvin Theological Journal* 16 (1981) 149-205.

[21] *WA* 2, 493,12ff.

neighbour, and these are binding upon us because God has chosen them; though they are not arbitrary, because they lead to our final end. Now Schneewind, like Socrates in the *Euthyphro,* presents us with a choice: 'whether morally right acts are right simply because God commands us to do them, or whether, by contrast, God commands us to do them because they are, in themselves, right'.[22] But the Scotist form of divine command theory does not fit this dichotomy. Our duties to the neighbour are right both because God chooses that route and because it is a route to our final good. In Crusius there is the same kind of structure as in Scotus. God has an essential tendency to self-affirmation and when God creates us (which is not necessary) God *must* desire that our strivings should be directed in accordance with our highest objec-tive end, which is union with God. But this means, Crusius says, that our highest formal end is compliance with God's will and command.[23]

Crusius does not merely recapitulate Scotus, however; he adds to him. I want to emphasize one such addition, and I want to claim that this addition is the focus of Kant's famous objection in the *Groundwork* to the theological version of heteronomy. The addition is most clearly seen in the way Crusius divides up the basic human desires. Scotus was concerned to deny eudaimonism, the view that all our motivation is directed towards happiness. He therefore divided up the affection for advantage and the affection for justice. Crusius is likewise opposed to eudaimonism. But for him there are not two but three basic categories of desire. The first is the drive to increase *our own* appropriate perfection, and from this come the desires for truth, clarity, good reasoning, the arts, bodily improvement, freedom, friendship, and honour. Second comes the *disinterested* or impartial drive for perfection, and from this comes a general desire to help others. But third, and distinct and incommensurable with these first two, is what Crusius calls 'the drive of conscience' which is 'the natural drive to recognize *a divine moral law'*. His idea is that we have within us this separate capacity to recognize divine command and to be drawn towards it out of a sense of dependence on the God who prescribes the command to us, and will punish us if we disobey (GRL 132). It is a good thing, Crusius thinks, that we do have this drive of conscience. For there is no way that most of us could most of the time reason out what we ought to do. God therefore gives us a 'shorter path' to knowledge of the divine law, and this makes God's will evident in such a way that it can come to everyone's knowledge (GRL 135). In this way, no one is excused from accountability.

What Crusius is doing is to propose a capacity humans have for receiving divine command as such, and he separates this from the mere disinterested desire for perfection (or what Scotus would call the affection for justice). He is giving a particular reading of Romans I and II in which the law is written 'on our hearts' and even those who 'suppress the truth' are 'without excuse'. This drive of conscience is supposed to be a sense which humans quite generally have of being dependent on some higher being and therefore of having obligation to do what that higher being tells them to do. But recognizing the commands of this being and being moved to obey is supposed to be a different drive from recognizing intrinsic good and being moved to pursue it.

Schneewind puts the distinction between Kant and Crusius this way. He thinks *Kant* is trying to show how we as moral agents can be independent of divine legislation, and how morality can be a human creation. Schneewind takes *Crusius,* on the other hand, to be arguing

---

[22] Schneewind, 'The Divine Corporation and the History of Ethics', *op, cit.,* 176.
[23] *GRL* 176 and 216.

that we are *dependent* on God. Here is Schneewind's dichotomy: Either there is *independence* of morality from God or there is a *Crusian dependence*. I am going to suggest that Kant's actual view is neither of these, and that we should follow Kant in this respect.

IV. Kant's Argument about Divine Commands in the Groundwork

What I want to do next is to return to the brief (and famous) argument in the *Groundwork* which is often taken to be an argument against divine command theory. Since Kant's argument is brief, I will quote it in full. Kant rejects 'the theological concept which derives morality from a divine and supremely perfect will; not merely because we cannot intuit God's perfection and can only derive it from our own concepts, among which that of morality is the most eminent; but because, if we do not do this (and to do so would be to give a crudely circular explanation), the concept of God's will still remaining to us--one drawn from such characteristics as lust for glory and domination and bound up with frightful ideas of power and vengefulness--would inevitably form the basis for a moral system which would be in direct opposition to morality.[24]

This argument has been taken, together with a brief and impenetrable passage in Plato's *Euthyphro,* as a decisive rejection of the whole idea of divine command theory.[25] But I think the argument sounds quite different, and is a better argument, if we construe it as an attack, not on divine command theory in general, but on Crusius's particular form of it. I think the heart of Kant's objection is to the separation of the 'drive of conscience' as a separate capacity.[26]

The typical reading of this argument in twentieth century analytic philosophy takes it as a refutation of the divine command theory of ethical obligation in general. Here, to give just one example, is R. M. Hare's verdict, 'Ever since Kant, it has been *possible* for people to insist on the autonomy of morals--its independence of human or divine authority. Indeed, it has been *necessary,* if they were to think morally, in the sense in which that word is now generally understood.'[27] The claim here is that Kant has made it possible for us to think of morality as independent of divine or human authority, and that we now have to think of it that way if we want to use the moral words in the way most people understand them.[28] R. M. Hare talks also of a 'God, whom Kant would have liked to believe in.'[29] Similarly Lewis White Beck

---

[24] *Groundwork of the Metaphysic of Morals* (henceforth, Gl) 443.
[25] For a statement of the problem with understanding the passage in the *Euthyphro* 10a1-11b5, see John E. Hare, *Plato's Euthyphro,* Bryn Mawr Commentaries, 1985, 21-25.
[26] Crusius also took the extreme position on the authority of Scripture that no rational criticism of the Bible was permitted, and that its meaning could be penetrated only by a kind of empathy or inner light. Kant objects to this claim as well, but not in the same argument.
[27] R. M. Hare in 'The Simple Believer', reprinted in *Essays on Religion and Education,* Oxford: Clarendon Press, 1992, 30. This argument in the Groundwork has had the same kind of status in Ethics as the treatment of the Ontological Argument in the First Critique has had in Metaphysics.
[28] It is a dubious empirical claim that the usage of most people in the world divorces morality from divine command. Perhaps this is true of most professional philosophers? Other examples of the kind of interpretation I am objecting to are A. C. Ewing, *Value and Reality,* London: Allen and Unwin, 1973, 183-187, and James Rachels, 'God and Human Attitudes', reprinted in *Divine Commands and Morality,* ed. Paul Helm, Oxford: Oxford University Press, 34-48, especially 44f. One vivid example is Iris Murdoch, *The Sovereignty of Good,* New York: Schocken Books, 1971, 80, 'Kant's man had already nearly a century earlier received a glorious incarnation in the work of Milton: his proper name is Lucifer.' The argument itself, without explicit attachment to Kant, is pervasive. One nice statement of it is in P. H. Nowell-Smith's *Ethics,* Harmondsworth: Penguin Books, 1954, 192-3.
[29] *Sorting Out Ethics,* Oxford: Clarendon Press, 1997, 27.

takes Kant to be arguing that moral duties do not owe their authority in any way to being divine commands. After conceding that Kant talks *as if* he were a divine command theorist (in this sense), Beck says on Kant's behalf, 'It is not that (duties) *are* divine commands, or that they owe their authority over us to their being decrees of a divine lawgiver who also created us; for in that event, we should have to know about God before we could know what our duty is, and we do not know God, while even the most unphilosophical person knows his duty. Moreover, such a theory would be incompatible with moral self-government, or autonomy.'[30] So Beck interprets Kant as saying that we should regard the moral law *as if* it were a divine command, and the people under this law *as if* it were 'a people united by common allegiance to a *supposed* author of these commands, namely God'. But the 'as if' in these contexts is stressed in such a way as to deny that we should believe in the actual existence of such divine commands or their legislator. God's existence is not, however, for Kant, 'as if.'[31] Kant is not an agnostic, except that he does not 'know' in his own very restricted sense of 'knowing', according to which we can only know what we could possibly experience with the senses or what is apodictically certain. We do not in this sense know that God exists. But Kant holds that we are required to *believe* that God exists. In just the same sense, he holds that we are required to believe that God is (with us) the legislator of moral law, and (unlike us) the rewarder and punisher of our lives as a whole in relation to this law. We have to deny knowledge in order to make room for faith.[32]

If, like most contemporary exegetes, one reads Kant's argument as an attack on divine command theory in general, it will naturally be construed as presenting the following two-horned dilemma. We have two choices on the divine command theory: Either we derive the notion of God's perfection from our moral concepts or we do not. If we do (the first horn), then the derivation which the divine command theory proposes is crudely circular. It says we have moral obligations because God commands them, and we should obey God's commands because they are morally right. But if we separate (on the second horn) our notion of God's will from the moral concepts, then the explanation of our obligation will depend merely on our ability to please God and God's ability (if we do not) to hurt us. The relationship between us, when stripped of right, will reduce to one of power. But then morality will be based on self-interest, and will not be what (on Kant's view) morality in fact is. So neither choice is available to us, and so the divine command theory should be rejected.[33]

---

[30] Lewis White Beck, *Six Secular Philosophers*, New York: Harper, 1960, 72-4. But it is not in general true for Kant that a prescription has authority only if we know about its source. As I shall argue, Kant thinks that the prescriptions of a legitimate political ruler have authority and have their source in his will; but we do not have knowledge about this will.

[31] Kant does use the 'as if' locution counterfactually, but to express what our moral lives would be like *without* God, 'each must, on the contrary, so conduct himself as if everything depended on him.'(*Rel.* VI, 101, where the point is that everything does *not* depend on the agent). At *Rel.* VI, 154 Kant makes the point that no assertoric knowledge is required in religion so far as *theoretical* cognition and profession of faith are concerned, since all that is required is a problematic assumption; but with respect to the object towards which our *morally* legislative moon bide us work, what is presupposed is an *assertoric* faith. He goes on (it is true) to say that this faith needs only *the idea of God*. But this again is an epistemological limitation, not a point about what we should *believe* exists.

[32] *KrV* III (second ed.), xxx.

[33] There are problems with the argument on this second horn. What needs to be attended to is the *different* ways in which we can separate God's will from the moral concepts. On God's side we can distinguish the claim that the divine will is inconsistent with what is morally right from the claim that this willing, though consistent, does not go through the moral concepts. On our side we can distinguish the claim that we have to obey even if God's will is

This is an important argument, and I will come back to it at the end. But it cannot be, if Kant is consistent, Kant's argument. For Kant accepts the view throughout his life that we should recognize our duties as God's commands. For example, there is the passage in *Lectures on Ethics,* 'Our bearing towards God must be characterized by reverence, love and fear-- reverence for Him as a holy lawgiver, love for His beneficent rule, and fear of Him as a just judge' (which is different, Kant says, from merely being afraid of God when we have transgressed). 'We show our reverence by regarding His law as holy and righteous, by due respect for it, and by seeking to fulfill it in our disposition.'[34] I have already mentioned the passage in the *Groundwork* about God as the head of the kingdom of ends, and there are passages in the Second Critique and *Religion within the Limits of Reason Alone* about recognizing our duties as God's commands.[35] Because this is a sustained theme in Kant, we are better off regarding his attack in the *Groundwork* as directed at some more specific target. The theory of Crusius is an excellent candidate.

Kant objects to Crusius's theory on three grounds. He starts the argument by saying that we cannot intuit God's perfection. This starting point makes sense if it is Crusius he has in mind. Crusius had proposed that we have a separate access to divine perfection through 'the drive of conscience', separate from the general moral love or the disinterested drive for perfection (GRL 132). Kant's position is, rather, that we cannot intuit God's perfection, because human intuition is limited within space and time. This is his first objection. Our access is, therefore, through concepts. Either these will be the moral concepts, or some other. This presents a Crusius-type divine command theory with a dilemma.

Suppose we take the first option, and reply that we *can* know what God wills, since he wills what the moral law prescribes. Here is the second objection. This would be, Kant says, *crudely* circular. He may be objecting to just such a crude circle in the passage from Crusius I quoted earlier, 'Finally, the third of the basic human drives is the natural drive to recognize a divine *moral* law' (GRL 132, emphasis added).[36] Crusius adds in the word 'moral' at a key point in his definition without showing how he can simultaneously insist on the separation of the three basic drives.[37] It is a crude circle to prove that A is B by adding B to the definition of A. What is needed is a 'third term' C, which can be connected first with A and then with B.[38] In Kant's own account the third term is provided by our member-ship with God in the kingdom of ends. But Crusius just gives us the crude circle without such mediation.

---

inconsistent with what is morally right from the claim that we must obey even in cases where we cannot determine whether it is consistent with what is morally right or not.

[34] Kant, *Lectures on Ethics,* trans. Louis Infield, Indianapolis: Hackett, 1963, 97.

[35] *KpV* V, 130. *Rel.* VI, 154.

[36] See Lewis White Beck, A *Commentary on Kant's Critique of Practical Reason,* Chicago: Chicago University Press, 1960, 107, 'Either Crusius surreptitiously introduces ethical predicates into the concept of divine perfection' (and Beck refers to this passage of Crusius), 'with the result that theological perfection no longer grounds the moral principle but presupposes it; or a hedonistic motivation is postulated as the ground of obedience to God.' But Kant is not exactly accusing Crusius of this second error, as I will argue in the following paragraph.

[37] 'It is thus not specially necessary to show that the drive of conscience is distinct from the previously distinguished basic drives, as its object is so very different from those of the other drives.' *(GRL* 134)

[38] An instructive comparison is Kant's fear in the third section of *Groundwork* that he may have argued in a circle about morality and freedom *(Gl* IV, 450). Kant thinks he has extricated himself from the viciousness of this circle when he later points out that 'when we think of ourselves as free, we transfer ourselves into the intelligible world as members' *(Gl* IV, 453). He gives us here a third term which mediates between morality and freedom, namely our membership in the intelligible world.

Finally, there is a third point Kant makes against Crusius. If we think we can understand what God is telling us to do *without* using the moral concepts, we will be left without morality at all. Kant must have in mind as his target a form of the divine command theory which forbids us to justify obedience on the grounds that God cares for the well-being of the whole creation. In other words, we are forbidden by this form of the theory to appeal to God's practical love. A Crusius-type divine command theory insists that we should obey God's will *just* because it is God's will, *whatever* our direct intuition tells us that will is.[39] This makes a nonsense of morality. The point of morality is to further one's own perfection and the happiness of others.[40] The kingdom of ends is the place where these two goals coincide. A morality which ignored one's own perfection and the happiness of others would be unintelligible. But this is just the kind of morality Crusius seems to be asking us to adopt as our own. It is not that Crusius is here making the gross claim that what should move us to obedience is hope of reward or fear of punishment. Indeed, I started from his insistence, which he holds in common with Scotus, that we have sources of motivation other than our happiness or perfection. It is notable that Kant also, in his reply, does not say that his opponent bases morality on hope of reward or fear of punishment, but rather 'that the concept of God's will remaining to us will be drawn from such characteristics as lust for glory and domination and bound up with frightful ideas of power and vengefulness'. What Kant is interested in is what our idea of God will be like if we separate out the drive of conscience from the distinterested desire to help other people, as Crusius suggests. And we find that Crusius does emphasize that it is a God who will punish us if we do not obey, even though this is not to be our motivation for obedience.[41] It would have been easy for Kant, if he were making a general attack on divine command theory, to make the point about not basing morality on fear or hope of reward, and I suspect that is the way his argument is in fact usually taught. I used to teach it that way myself. But it is not what Kant says. So all three steps of the argument are specifically tailored to attack Crusius.

Is Kant taking us back in this argument to a pre-Crusian Scotist form of divine command theory? In some ways, yes. Kant shares with Scotus the view that there are the two basic affections of the will, and that we start with the wrongful ranking of them. He shares the view that our freedom is tied to the good will. Two major differences are that in Kant there is no distinction in terms of necessity and contingency between the first and second tables of the law. And he describes our final end not as being co-lovers with God, but as a perfect combination of virtue and happiness. But there are two similarities I want to stress. In both Scotus and Kant, we share our final end with God, in the sense that both we and God aim at

---

[39] See Robert M. Adams, 'Autonomy and Theological Ethics', in *The Virtue of Faith*, Oxford University Press: 1987, 123-7. Adams approves of Tillich's notion of theonomous ethics, 'The theonomous agent acts morally because he loves God, but also because he loves what God loves.' Kant on my reading, but not Crusius, has a theonomous ethics. I will return to Adams at the end of this paper. Crusius himself would not be worried by this objection. See Tonelli, *op. cit.* 410 (my translation), 'Crusius underlines the importance of *mysteries of reason,* mainly theological doctrines which have to be admitted, even though we do not understand how certain things can be joined together or separated in such a way.'

[40] This is to put the point in terms of the *matter* of morality, rather than its form (which is more usual in the *Groundwork*). See the *Metaphysics of Morals* VI, 398.

[41] 'The motive of conscience', he says, 'is therefore merely a motive to recognize certain indebtednesses, that is, such universal obligations as one must observe *even if one does not wish to consider the advantages and disadvantages deriving from them,* whose transgression God *will punish* and, if his law is not to be in vain, *must punish.*' (*GRL* 133, emphasis added).

our own perfection. And in both Scotus and Kant God's willing is constrained by necessity, despite the Scotist emphasis on God's choosing the second table. I will return to these points at the end.[42]

V. Autonomous Relations to Political Authority

We can see that Kant is not making submission incompatible with autonomy if we compare what he says our relation is to *political* authority. Autonomy is being both legislator and subject to the law. One source of this idea is the tradition from Aristotle and the scholastics of seeing the good citizen as possessing 'the knowledge and capacity requisite both for ruling and for being ruled. The excellence of a citizen may be defined as consisting in a practical knowledge of the governance of free men from both points of view'.[43] Kant believes that the autonomy of a good citizen is not only consistent with submission to political authority, but requires this submission. He argues that coercion by the state is necessary in order to prevent coercion by individuals, which would be an obstacle to the external exercise of autonomy. External compulsion by the state is thus 'a hindering of the hindrances to freedom'.[44] To quote Mary Gregor's introduction to the *Metaphysics of Morals,* 'It is only within a civil condition, where there is a legislator to enact laws, an executive to enforce them, and a judiciary to settle disputes about rights by reference to such public laws, that human beings can do what it can be known a priori they must be able to do in accordance with moral principles'.[45] The justification of the state then rests for Kant on moral grounds, on the freedom of each individual person and our obligation to respect this in each other. A citizen is in this way morally justified in adopting into her own will the will of her ruler. The analogy with God's rule is systematic. Kant gives God executive and judicial as well as legislative functions within the kingdom, and God has to exercise those functions in order for the subjects in this kingdom 'to do what it can be known a priori they must be able to do in accordance with moral principles.' The analogy in fact goes beyond this, though I will not spell this out. Just as in God's kingdom, so in an earthly kingdom there are three kinds of mistake a citizen might make in claiming justification for her obedience. They are the same three kinds of mistake Crusius makes in analyzing our relation to God. The point I want to make here, though, is that Kant cannot mean to construct an argument from autonomy against all forms of external authority. The opposite is true. He thinks that autonomy requires submission to at least one kind of external authority, namely the authority of the state.

---

[42] In the *Lectures on Ethics (op. cit.* 22) Kant distinguishes between positive (or contingent) obligation and natural obligation, which arises from the nature of the action itself; and then complains, 'Crusius believer that all obligation is related to the will of another. So in his view all obligatIm would be a necessitation *per arbitrium alterius.* It may indeed seem that in an obligation we are necessitated *per arbitrium alterius;* but in fact I am necessitated by an *arbitrium internum,* not *externum,* and thus by the necessary condition of universal will.' What Kant is objecting to here, on my view, is not in itself the appeal to a superior will, but to making this will merely external, or separate from the universal will. In Kant's own way of recognizing our duties as God's commands, this can be and should be consistent with seeing them as permitted by the moral law, and thus the universal will. To put this more simply, what Kant wants in our autonomous submission is both our will and God's together, neither of them being sufficient without the other.

[43] Aristotle *Politics* III, 2,1277b14-16.

[44] *MM* VI, 396. See also *MM* VI, 231, '(Whatever) counteracts the hindrance of an effect promotes that effect and is consistent with it.'

[45] Mary Gregor, translator's introduction to *The Metaphysics of Morals,* Cambridge: Cambridge University Press, 1991,10.

The analogy with political authority is helpful in understanding the role of sanctions in our relation to God. As we have already seen, this is not supposed to be the ground of our obedience. But it is essentially tied to the way in which God can be the author of the obligation to obey the law in a way that we are not. Christine Korsgaard says, 'Why then are sanctions needed? The answer is that they are necessary to establish the authority of the legislator.... The legislator is necessary to make obligation possible, that is, to make morality normative.'[46] She gives the example of a student who takes a logic course because it is required by his department. It might seem that he acts more autonomously if he takes it because he independently sees its merit. But he acts autonomously out of his practical identity *as a student* only if he places the right to make and enforce some of the decisions about what he will study in the hands of his teachers. Similarly, a good citizen *as a citizen* does not pay her taxes because she thinks the government needs the money. She can *vote* for taxes for that reason. But once the vote is over, she must pay her taxes because it is the law. To extend this analysis to the context of divine command theory, we could say that an agent acts autonomously out of her practical identity as a citizen of God's kingdom only if she acts out of obedience to God. In none of these three cases (the student, the citizen of an earthly kingdom and the citizen of God's kingdom) is there any inconsistency with the agent sharing the ends of her superior. But in all three cases there is a true duty 'which must be represented as *at the same time* that (superior's) command.' (*Rel.* VI, 99). The role of the sanctions is to make the kingdom possible, and the ground of obedience is not fear of the sanctions but membership in the kingdom.

It is worth spelling out why the kingdom of ends has to be a *kingdom* and not, for example, a republic. Kant's view is that the only earthly constitution that accords with right is that of a pure republic.[47] The difference between republic and kingdom matters to him. It is therefore misleading to gloss the kingdom of ends as 'the republic of all rational beings', and to call a friendship 'a kingdom of two'.[48] Between friends there is no king. J. L. Mackie is more accurate here. He says, 'But for the need to give God a special place in it, (the kingdom of ends) would have been better called a commonwealth of ends.'[49] In Kant's theory God has combined in one person the legislative, executive and judicial functions which Kant thinks should be separated in well-run earthly republic. In brief, 'We must conceive a Supreme Being whose laws are holy, whose government is benevolent and whose rewards and punishments are just.'[50]

The *legislative* function we have already met. But there is a key difference from the legislation of an earthly state. Ethical legislation concerns the heart, and not merely the behavior of the citizenry. Kant accordingly says that the ruler of the ethical realm 'must be one

---

[46] Christine Korsgaard, *The Sources of Normativity, op. cit.*, 25f and 105-7. She goes on to argue against Hobbes and Pufendorf that our moral obligations have authority because of the *internal* sanction of a painful conscience. But Kant, I am arguing, preserves the need for an external imposition of sanctions, though they are not arbitrary sanctions (*KpV* V, 130). The fact that we feel badly if we break the law is not, for him, enough. The presence of these sanctions does not by itself lead to heteronomy, unless the *ground* for obedience is the fear of hell or hope of heaven.

[47] See *MM* VI, 340-42. It is significant also that Kant denies that the *church* should have a monarchical constitution, *Rel.* VI, 102.

[48] See Korsgaard, *The Sources of Normativity, op. cit.*, 99 and 127. Note also R. M. Hare, *Sorting Out Ethics, op. cit.*, 26, 'The Kingdom of Ends is not really a kingdom, but a democracy with equality before the law.'

[49] J. L. Mackie, *Ethics,* Harmondsworth, Middlesex: Penguin, 1977, 45.

[50] *Lectures on Ethics, op. cit.* 79-80. See also *Rel.* VI, 139.

who knows the heart, in order to penetrate to the most intimate parts of the disposition of each and everyone and, as must be in every community, give to each according to the worth of his actions.' God's promulgating the moral law to the heart is what Kant describes in the preface to the second edition of *Religion* as the revelation to reason. There is an additional point here. God, as legislator, will not ask us to do what is impossible for us, though God may ask us to do what is impossible for us on our own. The point is that God offers us the so-to-speak executive assistance to do what God as legislator calls us to do.

God's *executive* function can be divided into various parts. One part is the execution of the rewards and punishments which God declares in the judicial function. There is also, however, the 'maintenance' of the law *(Lectures* p. 81). We have to believe that a system is in place and is being maintained in which the ends of the other members of the kingdom are consistent with each other and with ours. This is what we might call a coordination problem. The world might be the kind of place in which I can only be happy if other people are not, or in which some of the people I affect by my actions can only be happy if other people I affect are not. Kant says that I am, as a creature of need, bound to desire my own happiness in everything else I desire, (though my happiness is not the only source of my motivation).[51] And I am required to pursue the happiness of others as much as my own, since we ought to share each other's ends as far as the moral law allows.[52] But we can only do all this if there is a system in place in which others' ends are first consistent with each other and, second, consistent with our own happiness.[53] Since we do not know the contents either of our own happiness or that of others, we cannot see by inspection whether these consistencies obtain.[54] We need to presuppose, Kant says, the idea of a higher moral being 'through whose universal organization the forces of single individuals, insufficient on their own, are united for a common effect.' *(Rel.* VI, 98) The common effect Kant has in mind here is the highest good, in which all are virtuous and all are happy. This is his translation of the psalmist's idea of righteousness and peace embracing each other *(Psalm* 85: 10). Kant's point is that we have to believe in God's executive functions in order to have the faith that such a good is possible. In fact, with this belief we can have not merely moral faith but moral hope, because God as Lord of history is bringing the kingdom to fruition.[55]

Finally, there is the *judicial* function. This is already implicit in what I have said. We have to suppose that God can see our hearts and can justly separate the sheep and the goats. It is not merely that God applies justly the standards, but that the standards God applies are just. I will sum up by quoting from the Second Critique, in which Kant stresses that moral rightness is an end common to us and to God, but that God's role is different and non-symmetrical with ours and is nonetheless essential to our moral life. 'Religion', Kant says, 'is the recognition of all duties as divine commands, not as sanctions, i.e. arbitrary and contingent ordinances of a

---

[51] *KpV* V, 25. There is an apparent difficulty here about whether Kant's argument is consistent. I have tried to lay out the argument in *The Moral Gap, op. cit.,* 69-96. Kant wants to say both that we inevitably desire our own happiness and that this desire should be subordinated to duty, which has (as in Crusius) a separate spring of motivation.

[52] This is one of the two ingredients in the *matter* of morality described in the *Metaphysics of Morals* (VI, 385-6).

[53] If one holds, like Thomas Reid, that there are many self-evident but logically independent moral axioms, then God is required to ensure *their* consistency.

[54] *KpV* V, 36.

[55] Kant says that the kingdom of heaven is represented 'not only as being brought ever nearer in an approach delayed at certain times yet never wholly interrupted, but also as arriving', *Rel.* VI, 134.

foreign will, but as essential laws of any free will as such. *Even as such,* they must be regarded as commands of the Supreme Being, because we can hope for the highest good (to strive for which is our duty under moral law) only from a morally perfect (holy and beneficent) and omnipotent will; and, therefore, we can hope to attain it only through harmony with this will' (*KpV* V,130, emphasis added).

VI. Conclusion

I have tried to show that Kant does not intend a general argument against divine command theory. I want to end by showing that the general argument usually but wrongly read into the *Groundwork* does not work. We can see this if we hold onto Kant's and Scotus's view that we and God are jointly but non-symmetrically engaged in our moral life, and that we share our final end with God. Autonomous submission, I want to say, is recapitulating in our wills what God has willed for our willing. This kind of mutuality is present in the idea of a covenant, because a covenant is between people who share commitment to the kind of life the covenant sets up as normative. This allows us to endorse a divine command theory which is what Robert Adams calls 'theonomous'.[56] He says, 'Let us say that a person is *theonomous* to the extent that the following is true of him: He regards his moral principles as given him by God, and adheres to them partly out of love or loyalty to God, but he also prizes them for their own sakes, so that they are the principles he *would* give himself if he were giving himself a moral law. The theonomous agent, in so far as he is right, acts morally because he loves God, but also because he loves what God loves.'[57]

I want to connect this idea of theonomy with the Scotist distinction between our final end of union with God and our route to that end. It needs a different paper to describe and evaluate the details of Scotus's account. But the key idea is that the second table of the law, the specification of our duties to the neighbor, is binding on us because God has selected it. Contrary to some versions of natural law theory, this part of the law is not deducible from our human nature. God could have chosen a different route for beings with our nature to reach our final end. I am not attributing this view to Kant. But I am suggesting that if Scotus is right about this, then autonomy can be reconciled with a version of divine command theory. If we try to mount the argument from autonomy that is usually (but wrongly) associated with Kant, we will fail. This is because there is nothing heteronomous about willing to obey a superior's prescription because the superior has prescribed it, as long as the final end is shared between us. The dichotomy which the usual version of the argument relies upon is false. The dichotomy is the one I mentioned before in connection with Schneewind's view of Kant: Kantian

---

[56] Adams takes the term 'theonomy' from Tillich in the article already referred to. There are also two important papers, 'A Modified Divine Command Theory of Ethical Wrongness' and 'Divine Command Metaethics Modified Again', both of which are reprinted (the second only in part) in Helm, *op. cit.* See also Adams, *Finite and Infinite Goods,* Oxford: Oxford University Press, 1999. Other contemporary philosophers have defended versions of divine command theory. Baruch A. Brody's views can be found in 'Morality and Religion Reconsidered'. *Readings in the Philosophy of Religion,* ed. Baruch A. Brody, Englewood Cliffs: Prentice Hall, 1974, 592-603. Philip Quinn's views can be found in *Divine Commands and Moral Requirements,* Oxford: Clarendon Press, 1978. See also Paul Rooney, *Divine Command Morality,* Aldershot: Avebury, 1996, and Richard L. Mouw, *The God Who Commands,* Notre Dame: Notre Dame University Press, 1990. For a version of the present paper in the context of a discussion of Duns Scotus and twentieth century moral theory, see John E. Hare, *God's Call,* Grand Rapids: Eerdmans, 2000.

[57] Adams, *op. cit.* Autonomous submission to political authority has the same structure.

independence or Crusian dependence; either our own wills entirely or entirely the will of another. What human moral life is actually like on the Scotist picture is a complex and rich mixture.

The notion of recapitulating God's will in ours is, however, vague in various ways. There is a range of cases here. Willing is always under a description, and the descriptions under which two people share an end may vary.[58] Take the following example, which I owe to Robert C. Roberts. A teenager's mother wills that her son not sleep with his girlfriend, and in willing this she wills that her son live a fully chaste life by Christian standards for the spiritual union properly surrounding sexual intercourse. Suppose her son does not share her Christian understanding. There is a range of possible ways in which the son might nonetheless repeat his mother's will. Perhaps he does not want to lose his inheritance. This would be crude form of heteronomy. Perhaps he respects his mother, though not her view. He does not want to hurt her, and he is grateful to her. This is neither heteronomy nor autonomous submission, but somewhere in between. Or perhaps he does accept the Christian teaching about sexuality, but barely understands it. He abstains because he wants to be a good Christian, but the proscription makes no sense to him. Here the mother and the son may even share a description under which something is willed, but it is not equally resonant for the two. Finally the son may share his mother's understanding as well as her prescription. But on Christian doctrine this kind of shared understanding is one we can *never* have completely with God, even in heaven. It is possible, then, to share ends with another person, or with God, with many different degrees of clarity and fullness.

Suppose the son shares an end with his mother, but does not understand it very well, certainly less well than she does. Is his response autonomous or heteronomous? For Schneewind, the answer is a matter of degree, as in the story I have just told, but will tend towards heteronomy. He constructs a picture of what he calls 'the Divine Corporation'.[59] He imagines a large corporation, the sort of corporation in which Dilbert is employed. The ordinary employees understand very little about each other's jobs or the purposes of the whole corporation, there is a strong back-up system so that failures by others will be remedied and ordinary employees do not have to feel responsible for the remedy themselves, and the supervisor has made it clear that they are paid for carrying out their duties strictly, 'looking neither to left nor to right'. This, he says, is the traditional Christian picture of the kingdom of God, with God as the head of the firm. Schneewind thinks progress towards autonomy occurs in the history of ethics as each of these three conditions weakens. First, we come to see the purpose of the 'corporation' as promoting human happiness. Second we see ourselves as the major instruments in producing this end or failing to produce it. Third we see ourselves as cooperating with each other in producing this end, and as responsible for repairing each other's omissions. In summary, 'As God's supervision and activity lessen, man's responsibility increases.' I do not want to deny that this movement of thought has occurred within academic philosophy in the last two hundred years. But as far as I can see, there is no way to determine whether this movement is progress towards a desirable kind of autonomy without settling first whether there is a God who has created us and rules the world providentially in the way the traditional picture and Kant himself suggest. If there is, and we decline to relate ourselves to God as God's subjects, this is not a desirable form of autonomy but it is like the graduate student in Korsgaard's example refusing on the grounds of autonomy to

---

[58] Scotus says, *nihil volitum quin praecognitum,* (nothing is willed but what is pre-cognized), *opus oxon.* II, d. 25, q. u. n. 19.

[59] Schneewind, 'The Divine Corporation and the History of Ethics', *op. cit.*

take the required courses for the degree. My main point has been that this is not Kant's notion of autonomy; and that if we want to say it is nonetheless a desirable notion of autonomy, we will have to do some prior dismantling of traditional theism.

Yale University

Questions

1. Do you think that Hare's argument works in defense of his contention that Kant works with a divine command theory?

2. What exactly is the tension Hare sees between Kant's holding to a sense of duty spelled out in terms of divine commands, and Kant's argument against the view?

3. Do you think that Hare is right that the theist who accepts a limitation of God's supervision is going to have to revise basic ideas integral to traditional theology?

4. Do you think that Hare has made a good case against those who contend that the less control God has, the better it is for human autonomy?

5. What weaknesses do you see in the divine command theory?

DIVINE COMMANDS AND THE SOCIAL NATURE OF OBLIGATION*

Robert Merrihew Adams

Divine command metaethics is one of those theories according to which the nature of obligation is grounded in personal or social relationships. In this paper I first try to show how facts about human relationships can fill some of the role that facts of obligation are supposed to play, specifically with regard to moral motivation and guilt. Then I note certain problems that arise for social theories of the nature of obligation, and argue that they can be dealt with more adequately by an expansion of our vision of the social dimension of ethics to include God as the most important participant in our system of personal relationships.

Divine command metaethics is a type of social theory of the nature of obligation. This statement makes two important points. (1) Divine command metaethics is not about the nature of all ethical properties and facts but only about the nature of those that we may call "the obligation family" of ethical properties and facts, those expressed by such terms as 'right', 'wrong', 'ought', and 'duty'. Other sorts of ethical properties and facts are not less important to Christian ethics, and theological theories may be offered about their nature too; but such theories may be expected to involve other features of God rather than his commands. For instance, we might theorize that the objectively disgusting is what disgusts God. The present paper is exclusively about divine command theories, however; and ethical properties not belonging to the obligation family will be mentioned without any inquiry being made into their nature.

(2) Divine command metaethics is one of those theories according to which the nature of obligation is social (in a broad sense of 'social' that encompasses intimate personal relationships as well as "impersonal," institutional relationships with larger groups). The central idea in divine command metaethics is the expansion of our vision of the social dimension of ethics to include God as the most important participant in our system of personal relationships. In this paper I will first try to show how facts about human relationships can fill some of the role that facts of obligation are supposed to play, specifically with regard to moral motivation (in section 1) and guilt (in section 2). Then (in section 3) I will note certain problems that arise for social theories of obligation, and argue that they can be dealt with more adequately by a divine command theory.

This paper presupposes a view, for which I have argued elsewhere, about the relation between conceptual analysis and theories of the nature of moral properties. On this view, what analysis of the concept of wrongness can tell us "is not sufficient to determine what wrongness is. What it can tell us… is that wrongness will be the property of actions (if there is one) that best fills" a certain role. Moreover the identity of that property with wrongness will be necessary, though not discoverable by conceptual analysis. I have little to add here to my defense of this conception of the relation of metaethical theories to conceptual analysis. What I hope to illuminate is rather the roles that wrongness, and other members of the obligation family of ethical properties, are supposed to fill, and the reasons for thinking (as I do) that those roles are best filled by properties involving a relation to the commands of a loving God.

---

* This article is reprinted by courtesy of the author and the publisher.

I. How Social Requirements Motivate

It is essential to the point of any conception of obligation that obligations motivate—that having an obligation to do *x* is generally regarded as a reason for doing *x*. One problem about the nature of obligation is to understand this motivation.

This will not be much of a problem if we assume that one is obliged only to do things that one expects to have good results. Then the goodness of the results provides a reason, and one's desires for such good consequences a motive, for doing what one is obliged to do. Unfortunately, those who (like me) are not utilitarians cannot assume that obligations will always be so happily attuned to the value of expected results. We think we are sometimes obliged to tell the truth and to keep promises, for example, when we do not expect the consequences to be good. What would motivate us to do such a thing?

Even non-utilitarian moralists may not be satisfied with the reply that the conscientious agent has good enough reason for her action simply in the fact that it is right. This seems too abstract. John Rawls (certainly no utilitarian) writes,

> The doctrine of the purely conscientious act is irrational. This doctrine holds...that the highest moral motive is the desire to do what is right and just simply because it is right and just, no other description being appropriate.... But on this interpretation the sense of right lacks any apparent reason; it resembles a preference for tea rather than coffee.

If we are to see the fact of having an obligation as itself a reason for action, we need a richer, less abstract understanding of the nature of obligation, in which we might find something to motivate us.

According to social theories of the nature of obligation, having an obligation to do something consists in being required (in a certain way, under certain circumstances), by another person or a group of persons, to do it. This opens more than one possibility for understanding obligations as reasons for action. One reason or motive for complying with a social requirement, of course, is that we fear punishment or retaliation for non-compliance. This is undoubtedly a real factor, which helps to keep morality (and other benign, and not so benign, social institutions) afloat. But here we are primarily interested in what *other* motives there may be for compliance.

The alternative explanation that I wish to pursue in this section is that *valuing one's social bonds* gives one, under certain conditions, a reason to do what is required of one by one's associates or one's community (and thus to fulfill obligations, understood as social requirements). This hypothesis is not to be understood in a teleological sense. No doubt the desire to obtain or maintain a certain kind of relationship does often contribute to the motivation for complying with social requirements, but that is not all there is to social bonds as a motive. The pattern of motivation to which I wish to call attention is one in which I value the relationship which I see myself as actually having, and my complying is an *expression* of my valuing and respecting the relationship. It is one in which I act primarily *out of* a valuing of the relationship, rather than with the obtaining or maintaining of the relationship as an *end*.

There are at least four aspects of the relational situation that matter motivationally with regard to compliance with social requirements. (1) It matters that the demand is actually made. It is a question here of what other people do in fact (reasonably or rightly) require of me, not just of what they could reasonably require. The demand need not take the form of an explicit command or legislation; it may be an expectation more subtly communicated; but the demand must actually be made.

It is much more fashionable in ethical theory to treat moral motivation as depending on judgments about what an ideal community or authority *would* demand under certain counterfactual conditions. However, I am very skeptical of all these conditional accounts, for two reasons. First (the metaphysical reason), I doubt that the relevant counterfactuals are true, partly because they seem to be about free responses that are never actually made. In the second place (the more distinctively moral or motivational reason), I do not think I care very much about whether these counterfactual conditionals are true. This is not to deny that I care about some things that are closely connected with them; it is just to say that the counterfactuals themselves are motivationally weak.

By contrast, actual demands made on us in relationships that we value are undeniably real and motivationally strong. Most actual conscientiousness rests at least partly on people's sense of such demands. Our awareness of this source of moral motivation is reflected in appeals to "be a good citizen"—or, when in a foreign country, to "remember that you are a guest."

The actual making of the demand is important, not only to the strength, but also to the character, of the motive. Not every good reason for doing something makes it intelligible that I should feel that I *have* to do it. This is one of the ways in which having even the best of reasons for doing something does not as such amount to having an obligation to do it. But the perception that something is demanded of me by other people, in a relationship that I value, does help to make it intelligible that I should feel that I have to do it.

(2) It also matters motivationally how the individual who is subject to the demand is related, and feels related, to those persons who are making the demand. Let us assume, for purposes of this discussion, that the demand is made by a community. The individual may be a member of the community, or a guest in the community; but it is essential that there be some relation, and indeed some favorably valued relation. The relation may arise through the individual's action—commonly through a history of acts of loyalty and caring within the relationship; occasionally through the action, beloved of social contract theorists, of voluntarily joining the community or consenting explicitly to its institutions and principles. But the commununity's attitude toward the individual is at least as important. Does the community value the individual? Is its attitude toward her supportive and respectful? It is well known that these questions have in fact a great influence on moral motivation. An individual who feels neglected, despised, abused by the community will be alienated, and will be much less inclined to comply conscientiously with society's demands. I do not mean to say that the alienated person should be exempt from blame for immoral or "anti-social" behavior, but that often such behavior should be seen, not mainly as a falling away from impersonal standards of right action, but as part of a conflict with society in which society was the first offender.

Where community prevails, rather than alienation, the sense of belonging is not to be sharply distinguished from the inclination to comply with the reasonable requirements of the community. A "community" is a group of people who live their lives to some extent—possibly a very limited extent—in common. To see myself as "belonging" to a community is to see the institution or other members of the group as "having something to say about" how I live and act—perhaps not about every department of my life, and only to a reasonable extent about any department of it, but it is part of the terms of the relationship that their demands on certain subjects are expected to have some weight with me. And valuing such a relationship—loving it or respecting it—implies some willingness to submit to reasonable demands of the community. One is willing to comply, not as a means of satisfying a desire *to* belong, but as an expression of one's sense that one *does* belong, and one's endorsement of that relationship.

(3) It also matters what are the attributes of the demander. To put it crudely and simply, one will have more reason to comply with demands made by an individual or group that one admires than by one that one holds a mean opinion of. If the demander is particularly impressive or admirable in any way—if she seems particularly wise and knowledgeable, for instance—one

will see more reason to comply than if the demander seems ill-informed, foolish, or in some other way contemptible.

(4) Finally, it matters motivationally how the demandee evaluates the demand itself. It must be possible to perform such an evaluation without relying on fully developed obligation concepts, if the character of the evaluation is to shed light, without circularity, as I hope, on the nature of obligation. This requirement can be satisfied, at least in part. You can start evaluating things simply on the basis of how you value them. Is the demand one which appeals to you, or one which disgusts or revolts you? Is it one which seems to be conducive to the things that you prize most, admire most, and so forth? You could ask that about your particular compliance, or you could ask it about general compliance, if that is what is being demanded. And what is the wider social significance of the demand? Is it an expression of a project or social movement that seems good or bad to you? No obligation concepts at all are employed in these questions; yet the answers to them both will and should affect the extent to which a social requirement gives you a reason for action. More serious problems for a social theory of the nature of obligation may indeed arise from reflection on such evaluation; but consideration of them is reserved for section 3.

II. Guilt and Relationship

The nature of obligations cannot be understood apart from the reactions that people have and are expected to have to the breach of an obligation; and central to these reactions is the notion of guilt. This is one of the main differences between obligations and other sorts of reasons for action. If I fail to do what I had the most reason to do, I am not necessarily guilty, and there is apt to be nothing offensive about my reacting quite light-heartedly to the lapse. But if I fail to do what have an obligation to do, then (other things being equal) I am guilty, and a light-hearted reaction would normally be offensive.

The word 'guilt' is not properly the name of a feeling, but of an objective moral condition which may rightly be recognized by others even if it is not recognized by the guilty person. However, feelings of guilt, and other reactions to guilt, may reasonably be taken as a source of understanding of the objective fact of guilt to which they point. We do not have the concept of guilt merely to signify in a general way the state of having done something wrong. Such an abstract conception of guilt fails to make intelligible, for example, the fact that guilt can be expiated, discharged, or forgiven. It also results in a rather tight and empty circle in understanding, inasmuch as a major part of what distinguishes wrongness (as a member of the obligation family of properties) from other sorts of badness is precisely its connection with guilt.

It is true that one is not guilty, however unfortunate the outcome, for anything that was not in some way wrong. But there are two other aspects of guilt that are responsible for much of its human significance. One is the harm one has caused to other people by one's (wrong) action. It is wrong to drive carelessly, for example, and no less wrong when one is lucky than when an accident results. But the burden of guilt one incurs is surely heavier when one's carelessness causes the death of another person than when no damage is done. Many moralists are uncomfortable with this fact; but even if we were to define 'guilt' one-sidedly as meaning only the state of having done something wrong, the other, more complicated fact of having caused great harm through one's wrongdoing remains, and is a fact that we care about in a special way which is reflected in our actual, intuitive use of the word 'guilt'.

Harm caused to other people is not a feature of all guilt, however. One can be guilty for a violation of other people's rights that in fact harmed no one. And even if harm has been caused, it is not a serious aggravation of guilt if it does not fall heavily on some individual person or on some important project. If one is responsible for a traffic accident, for example, it would be bizarre to feel seriously guilty about a three-minute delay caused thereby to each passing motorist, even if the number of people inconvenienced is large enough for the aggregate delay to amount to a considerable cost by the standards appropriate to a traffic engineer.

A more pervasive feature of guilt is alienation from other people, or (at a minimum) a strain on one's relations with others. If I am guilty, I am out of harmony with other people. Typically there is someone who is, or might well be, understandably angry at me. This feature is central to the role of guilt in human life. It is connected with such practices as punishing and apologizing. And it makes intelligible the fact that guilt can be (at least largely) removed by forgiveness.

Suppose I have done something that has offended a friend, resulting in estrangement. I think I was wrong to do it; I feel guilty. But if there is a reconciliation and my friend forgives me, I will feel released from the guilt. Indeed, I will *be* released from the guilt. The view that in such a case the guilt consists largely in an alienation produced by the wrong act is supported by the fact that the ending of the alienation ends the guilt.

This point is confirmed by reflection on an alternative scenario. Suppose I am not reconciled with my friend, but come to believe that the estrangement, though painful to him, has on the whole been good for him. Will this release me from the guilt? It will ease the burden, but not entirely remove it. In fact, I think it will not release me from guilt as completely as my friend's forgiveness (even combined with the belief that the estrangement has been bad for him) would. This suggests that alienation is not only a constituent, but a more important constituent of guilt, in this type of case, than the harm caused to the other person.

This should not surprise us if we reflect on the way in which we acquired the concept, and the sense, of guilt. In our first experience of guilt its principal significance was an action or attitude of ours that ruptured or strained our relationship with a parent. There did not have to be a failure of benevolence or a violation of a rule; perhaps we were even too young to understand rules. It was enough that something we did or expressed offended the parent, and seemed to threaten the relationship. This is the original context in which the obligation family of moral concepts and sentiments arise. We do not begin with a set of moral principles but with a relationship, actual in part and in part desired, which is immensely valued for its own sake. Everything that attacks or opposes that relationship seems to us bad.

Of course this starkly simple mentality is pre-moral. We do not really have obligation concepts until we can make some sort of distinction, among the things we do that strain relationships, between those in which we are at fault or wrong and those in which we are innocent or right (not to mention those in which we are partly wrong and partly right). We begin to grasp such a distinction as we learn such facts as the following: Not evey demand or expectation laid on us by other people constitutes an obligation, but only demands made in certain ways in certain kinds of relationship (for instance, commands of one's parents and teachers), and expectations that arise in certain ways (for instance, from promises). An unexpressed wish is not a command. One is not guilty for anything one has not really done. The fact that somebody is angry does not necessarily imply that an obligation has been violated.

This development is compatible, however, with regarding obligations as a species of social requirement, and guilt as consisting largely in alienation from those who have required of us what we did not do. I believe it is not childish, but perceptive and correct, to persist in this way of thinking about obligation and guilt. This is a controversial position. It is generally agreed that learning about guilt begins in the way that I have indicated, and that the value we place on good relationships, not only with parents but also with peers, is crucial to moral development. But many moralists hold that in the highest stages of the moral life (perhaps not reached by many adults) the center of moral motivation is transplanted from the messy soil of concrete relationships to the pure realm of moral principles; and a corresponding development is envisaged for the sense of guilt. Thus John Rawls traces the development of the sense of justice from a "morality of authority" through a "morality of association" to a "morality of principles"; corresponding to these three stages, he speaks of "feelings of (authority) guilt," "feelings of (association) guilt," and "feelings of (principle) guilt"—only the last of these counting as "feelings of guilt in the strict sense."

It is certainly possible to come to value—even to love—an ethical principle for its own sake, and this provides a motive for conforming to it. I doubt that this is ever the most powerful of ethical motives; but what I would emphasize here is that this way of relating to ethical principles has more to do with ideals than with obligations. To love truthfulness is one thing; to feel that one *has* to tell the truth is something else. Similarly, it seems to me that there is something wrong-headed about the idea of "principle guilt."

To be sure, there are *feelings* of guilt for the violation of a rule, where no person is seen as offended. But these are typically remnants of a morality of authority, and most plausibly understood as rooted in an internalization of childhood perceptions of requirements imposed by parents or other authority figures. They are part of a heternonomous, not an autonomous, reaction. The fact that the rule is seen as imposed on me, as something that I *have to* obey, is the ghost of my conception of it as sponsored by a person or persons who will be (understandably) offended if it is violated.

Feelings of "principle guilt," as Rawls conceives of them, are not like that. They are autonomous and based on one's valuing the rules, seeing them as expressing one's nature as a rational agent in a society of free and equal members. It is this non-compulsive, rational reaction to the breach of a personally valued principle that seems to me not to be a recognition of guilt, but of something different.

Suppose I have done something that is simply contrary to some principle that I believe in. It is not that I have done significant harm to anyone, or alienated myself from anyone. The situation does not call for apologies or reactions to anticipated or possible or appropriate anger, because there is no one (let's suppose not even God) who might be understandably angry with me about it. It does not seem either natural or appropriate for me to feel *guilty* in such a situation. Maybe someone is entitled to think less of me for the deed. Perhaps I will see less value in my own life on account of it. I may in this way be alienated from myself, though not from anyone else. But these are reasons for feeling ashamed or degraded, rather than for feeling guilty. Guilt is not necessarily worse than degradation, but they are different. And I think a main point of difference between them is that, in typical cases, guilt involves alienation from someone else who required or expected of us what we were obligated to do and have not done.

III. The Supreme Demander

Much can be understood about the nature of obligation in terms of human social relationships, as I have been trying to show. We even have a use for a notion of "an obligation" that can be understood purely sociologically, and therefore "naturalistically," in terms of a description of social practices such as commanding, promising, punishing, and apologizing, without any attempt to evaluate these practices as good or bad. This is a pre-moral notion in at least two ways.

(1) It is not the notion of an obligation that is "overriding" in the way that fully moral obligation is. An obligation, in this sense, must give most participants in the social system *some reason* to do what it obliges them to do; but it need not override other considerations. So no

understanding is presupposed here of the nature of such an overriding.

(2) More fundamentally, the purely sociological notion is not the notion of a morallly valid or binding obligation. It is just the notion of *an* obligation or duty, in the sense in which we can agree that Adolf Eichmann had *a* duty to arrange for the transportation of Jews to extermination camps. Certainly this was not a morally valid or binding duty at all, but it was in some sense *a* duty. It played a part in a system of social relationships such that there were superiors who, understandably (though immorally), would be angry if he did not do it, and in relation to whom he would feel uncomfortable if he did not do it, even if they did not know of this omission. Obligations in this pre-moral sense can be good or bad; they can even be morally repugnant, as Eichmann's was.

The nature of obligation in the pre-moral sense does not need a divine command theory to explain it. That is a good thing, because divine command metaethics itself presupposes a pre-moral, sociological conception of obligation. It is the very core of a divine command theory to think of the divine/ human relationship on the model of a social relationship in which authority, commands, obedience, loyalty, and belonging play a part. But we cannot really have these things without both the reality and the concept of an obligation, in some sense. A command imposes an obligation, or is the sort of thing that could impose an obligation. And one who obeys a command sees herself as fulfilling an obligation arising out of the command. There must therefore be some sort of obligation whose nature cannot without circularity be explained in terms of anyone's commands. What divine command metaethics is meant to explain is the nature of obligation, not in the minimal, pre-moral sense, but in a stronger, fully moral sense.

The earlier sections of this paper were meant to show something of the importance of interpersonal or social relationships for the nature of obligation in even a fully moral sense. The idea of trying to understand all obligation, including moral obligation, as constituted by some sort of social requirement has its attractions. As the Eichmann case makes clear, however, any acceptable account of the nature of moral obligation in terms of social requirements must incorporate some way of *evaluating* the requirements; and it may be doubted whether a descriptive sociological theory has the resources for the evaluation that is needed. In section 1 I described some ways in which, without appealing to any criterion of obligation as such, an individual can evaluate, and would naturally be expected to evaluate, demands made on her by other people, or by her community. That sort of evaluation is subjective, however. Its subjectivity does not keep it from being important to the motivational significance of obligation. But a definition of moral obligation in terms of social requirements that "pass" that kind of evaluation would not ascribe to moral obligation the objectivity or interpersonal validity that it is supposed to have.

The need for a standard by which to evaluate them is not the only disadvantage of human social requirements as a basis for understanding the nature of moral obligation. They also fail to cover the whole territory of moral obligation. We find that there are situations in which we would say, at least retrospectively, that none of the existing human communities demanded as much as they should have, or that there was something that really ought to have been required that was not demanded by any community, or perhaps even by any human individual, in the situation.

Moral obligation seems therefore to need a source or standard that is superior to human social requirements. Can it be found? And can it have (at least a lot of) the significance of obligations that are rooted in social requirements? In particular, how much can it have of the motivational significance of social requirements (as discussed in section 1 above)? And will it enable us to see moral guilt as something more robust than "principle guilt," and as removed by forgiveness (as discussed in section 2)? These advantages are not possessed by all the supreme sources of obligation that have been proposed in metaethical theories. I have already argued, for example, that the hypothetical deliverances of an "ideal observer" lack the motivational force of actual social demands.

Where could we find a supreme source or standard of moral obligation which has these advantages? The attempt has certainly been made to find it, after all, in a human society, in some way both actual and ideal, to which we can be seen as belonging. Emile Durkheim's lectures on *Moral Education* present a great sociologist's fascinating development of this idea. But it seems pretty clear that no actual human society is going to come close to filling this bill. To put it crudely and simply, no actual human society is good enough for that.

Where else would we look for an ideal source of moral obligation? My proposal is that we look to the set of ideas on which Durkheim quite openly and frankly modeled his secular, sociological account of morality—that is, to theistic ideas. Durkheim, following in the steps of Comte, was turning theistic ethics inside out, as it were, to get his conception of society as the source of moral obligation. I suggest that we turn the idea right side out again, and think of God as the source. More precisely, my view is that commands or requirements actually issued or imposed by a loving God are the supreme standard of moral obligation. I will argue that they have much of the significance of social requirements as a source of obligation.

The pivotal role of God's forgiveness in the ethical life of theists underlines the advantages of divine command metaethics for the understanding of *guilt*. If the supreme standard of ethical obligation is what is required by God, then a violation of it is an offense against a person and not just against a principle, and results in something that has the full relational significance of guilt, and not just of disgrace or degradation. This relational significance enriches the possibilities for dealing with guilt—most notably by helping us to understand ethical guilt as something that can be removed by forgiveness.

Moreover, divine commands have the *motivational* significance of actual social requirements. I will point out four motivational features of divine command metaethics and of the divine commander corresponding (but in a different order) to the four motivational features of human social requirements discussed in section 1 above.

(1) One thing that matters to the motivational force of divine commands is how God is related to us. It matters that he is our creator. It matters that he loves us. It matters that God has entered into covenant with us; it matters that there is a history of relationship between God and the individual and between God and the religious community—and that the divine commands play a significant role in this history, and are related to divine purposes that we see being worked out in this history and having a certain importance for our lives. It matters that all of these things about the relationship are such that, seeing them, we have reason to value the relationship, rather than to be alienated from it.

(2) It matters what God's attributes are. God is supremely knowledgeable and wise—he is omniscient, after all; and that is very important motivationally. It makes a difference if you think of commands as coming from someone who completely understands both us and our situation.

It matters not only that God is loving but also that he is just. 'Just' is to be understood here in a sense that is quite naturalistic and largely procedural. We are applying to God a concept that has its original home in courts of law. Without any appeal to a standard of fully moral obligation we can recognize certain truths about justice: A just judge punishes people, if at all, only for things that they have actually done. Merit and demerit have some relevance to the way it is just to treat people. The just judge is interested in getting out, and acting in accordance with, the truth.

Another important attribute of God is that he is beautiful or wonderful. This is a point at which Durkheim understood religious ethics rather well, and tried to exploit it for his purposes.

"The good," he wrote, "is society...insofar as it is a reality richer than our own, to which we cannot attach ourselves without a resulting enrichment of our nature." The religious root of this idea is obvious and requires no further comment, except to say that Durkheim is quite right in thinking that the richness, for us, of the being from which requirements proceed is a powerful motivating factor.

(3) It matters, for the motivational strength of divine command metaethics, what it is that is demanded of us. And it matters how what is demanded relates to our valuings. It matters motivationally, for example, that we do not believe that God demands cruelty for its own sake. Here again in thinking of our valuings we do not have to presuppose a full panoply of obligation concepts. It is enough if in some sense we love kindness and feel revolted or disgusted at cruelty. God's requirements function as an objective standard of obligation; but our subjective valuings are important to the way in which the divine requirements fulfill this function.

It is undoubtedly important that in theistic ethics the divine legislation is generally seen as upholding the binding character of a large proportion of the "obligations" defined by human institutions and practices. The divine/human relationship is not simply a superior alternative to human society as a source of obligation. Rather, God is seen as the chief member of a more comprehensive social system or "family," which is reflected, though imperfectly, in actual human relationships. Thus the motivational significance of divine and human requirements is to a large extent integrated.

(4) Finally, it matters that the requirements are actually imposed by God. Critics have argued that this does not really matter in divine command metaethics as I have expounded it. They suggest that all the work is being done by the stipulation that it is the demands of a *loving* God that bind—that really nothing would be lost if we just said that our overriding, fully moral obligation is constituted by what *would* be commanded by a loving God, whether there is one or not. I want to say why I think that that is not an adequate substitute.

My reasons on this point parallel my reasons for not being satisfied with an ideal, non-actual human authority as a source of moral obligation. First of all, I do not believe in the counterfactuals. I do not believe that there is a unique set of commands that would be issued by any loving God. There are some things that a loving God might command and might not command. In particular, among the things that I believe actually to be valid moral demands, there are some that I think might have been arranged differently by a God who would still be loving, and who would still satisfy the additional requirements of the metaethical theory. For example, a loving God could have commanded different principles regarding euthanasia from those that I believe are actually in force.

In the second place, even aside from any doubts about whether these counterfactuals about loving Gods are true, it seems to me that they are motivationally weak. They do not have anything like the motivational or reason-generating power of the belief that something actually is demanded of me by my loving creator and heavenly father. The latter belief is therefore one that metaethics cannot easily afford to exchange for the belief that such and such *would* have been demanded of me by a loving God.

Can the nature of moral obligation be adequately understood in terms of social requirements? Yes, if our system of social relationships includes God.

Questions

1. Outline as clearly as you can Adams' account of the divine command theory.

2. What fault(s) do you see with such a view?

3. Do you think that the theist must hold to some version of the theory? State why?

4. Why do you think Adams thinks it important to bring God into the picture regarding notions of obligation?

5. Do you think that Adams defense of the divine command theory works?

MORALITY AND GOD

Richard Swinburne[1]

Swinbure argues that God's issues commands to his creatures, and does so for four reasons: (1) to give us further motivation to do what we are under obligation to do by reason of divine requirement; (2) to give us further motivation to do what is beyond obligation or supererogatarily good; (3) to contribute to coordinate with other good outcomes; (4) to give us a place in God's plan for the world.

My topic is—what follows from the nature or will of God for the moral goodness or badness of different human actions? (i.e. what difference does it make if there is a God). I assume a standard Western account of the nature of God as omnipotent, omniscient, perfectly good, creator and sustainer (from moment to moment) of the Universe and all that it contains.

I

Actions may be morally good, bad, or indifferent. Among good actions are those which are obligatory, and ones which go beyond obligation and which we call "supererogatory". I am obliged to pay my debts, but not to give my life to save that of a comrade—supremely, supererogatorily, good though it is that I should do so. The obligatory are those which we are blameworthy for not doing[2], the supererogatory are those which we are praiseworthy for doing[3]. Likewise among bad actions, there are those which it is obligatory not to do—these are wrong actions; and there are bad actions which are not wrong. But what are we saying when we say that an action is *morally* good etc., as opposed to good etc. in other ways (prudentially good, legally obligatory, wrong from the point of view of etiquette etc.)? I suggest that we are picking a kind of goodness which has two crucial features.

If an action is morally good, it matters that it be done more than if it is just prudentially good. If it is morally obligatory, it has an obligatory character which overrides the merely legally obligatory. It may be legally obligatory for me to fight for my country in a certain war, but if the war is unjust, it is more important not to fight; it is morally obligatory not to fight. But this feature of "moral" goodness that it matters and overrides, is not enough to give the notion a sense in language. For in what sense does it "matter" or "override"? Mere definition by other words is never enough to give a word a sense in language; those other words, or words by which they are defined, have to be cashed by examples of things to which (at any rate probably) they apply. We need examples of actions which are morally good in order to get a grip on what it means for moral goodness to be overall goodness. One could have no idea of what it is for some action to

---

* This article is printed by courtesy of Richard Swinburne and *Revue Internationale De Philosophie* where it appeared in 3/2003.

[1] This paper is the latest version of my views on this topic. Earlier versions (which do not differ in general approach, but are in various ways less precise or less full) are to be found in my *The Coherence of Theism*, Clarendon Press, revised edition, 1993, ch.11; *Responsibility and Atonement*, Clarendon Press, 1989, chaps. 1 and 8; and—most recently—"God and morality" in (ed.) M.M. Olivetti *Philosophie de la Religion entre éthique et ontologie*, Cedam, 1996. Early paragraphs of the present article come from the latter.

[2] Given that we know about the obligation, and have no known conflicting obligations.

[3] Given that we know about the goodness of the action, and there are no known other actions which it is overall bette that we should do instead.

be morally obligatory unless one had some idea of which actions were morally obligatory.

Now, there is, of course, in the world a wide diversity in beliefs about the overall goodness of actions. Some believe euthanasia on balance good, others believe it bad. People disagree about the overall goodness of capital punishment, corporal punishment, abortion, strict parental discipline, marital fidelity in all circumstances, etc., etc. But such disagreement conceals much underlying agreement.

First, there is the fact that many who disagree about one such issue will often agree about others. And there will normally be a chain between any groups of persons who are diametrically opposed on many such issues, of groups who agree with one extreme group on most issues, groups who agree with the semi-extreme group on most issues, and so on until we come to the group at the other extreme. Between the extreme liberal and the extreme conservative there are so many who share many views with each other and with one or other extreme. Secondly, when two people disagree about the overall goodness or badness of some action, often both of them think that its overall goodness or badness arises from its possession of various properties, each of which is in itself good or bad as the case may be; they often agree which properties make for its goodness and which make for its badness, but disagree only as to which group of properties outweighs the other group. Each disputant agrees that the considerations adduced by his opponent have some force; that is, would show the action, for example, to be overall good but for the considerations which he adduces on the other side. Thus the opponent of the euthanasia involved in helping a depressed man to commit suicide argues that such an act is overall bad because of the sanctity and value of human life, the possibility of helping a depressed man to recover from his depression, the value of his actively co-operating in overcoming that depression, and so on. The advocate of euthanasia argues that helping a depressed man to commit suicide is helping him to do what he clearly and firmly wants to do and what hurts no one else in any way; the fact that the act has this character has the consequence that it is an overall good act, despite its other features. Both disputants appeal to considerations which the other will naturally admit to have some weight, although each holds that the considerations which he adduces outweigh those which the opponent adduces. There is a very wide *agreement* between different groups as to the moral relevance of various considerations, even if not as to the weight to be given to each.

Let us call all those properties which many humans consider to contribute to the overall goodness or badness of actions, such as (paradigmatically) causing pleasure or pain, "standard moral-making properties." Those among them which are supposed to make for an action's overall goodness (e.g. its causing pleasure) I will call positive properties, and those which are supposed to make for its overall badness (e.g. its causing pain) negative properties. By no means everyone thinks all the standard moral-making properties to be relevant to assessing overall goodness, and certainly they do not attribute the same importance to each; but there is, I have been emphasizing, a continuity between the kinds of property thought relevant by different people to assessing overall goodness. My proposed criterion for the goodness of an action being moral goodness is now that it have overall goodness arising from properties belonging to the set of standard moral-making properties, the positive ones counting for and the negative ones counting against its overall goodness; a claim that an action is morally good is a claim of this kind[4]. It is a claim that doing the action matters in the way that making people happy, or keeping

---

[4] Sometimes the notions of 'moral' goodness and obligation are understood in more restricted ways e.g. as the goodness or obligatory quality which acts possess is so far as they promote or exemplify human pleasure or pain. With a more restricted understanding of morality, one can then intelligibly claim that other things (e.g. the worship of God) are more important than being moral; a claim which is not coherent on my understanding of morality.

promises, or telling the truth etc., etc. (or at any rate most of these actions) matter. Conversely, the badness of an action being moral badness is a matter of it having overall badness arising from a balance of negative properties over positive properties, a claim that it is morally bad is a claim that its badness is of this kind. Claims that some action (among the good actions) is obligatory; or that some action (among the bad actions) is wrong is a claim that its obligation or wrongness arises in the same way as does the obligation or wrongness of (at any rate most of) a large number of paradigm examples. If someone cannot recognize most of the members of the set of positive moral-making properties as having something in common which counts for an overall goodness, and most of the members of the set of negative moral properties as having something in common which counts against an overall goodness, I see no reason to suppose that they have concepts of moral goodness and badness. And, analogously, if they do not recognize many of the factors which most of us recognize as counting for and against the existence of an obligation, and many of the factors which most of us recognize as counting for and against an action being wrong, I see no reason to suppose that they have the concepts of moral obligation and wrongness.

Now that I have clarified what is meant by attributing moral properties to actions, that is making moral judgments, we can, I suggest, see two further things about such judgments. The first is that certain of them are true, and others of them are false (i.e. that some judgments about which positive properties override which negative properties are true and others false). As a result of experience and reflection, it is evident to us Westerners at the end of the twentieth century that genocide is morally wrong, and so is suttee and so is slavery; and it is morally obligatory to keep your promises at any rate when it causes you little trouble, barring quite extraordinary counter-considerations. And so on, and so on. And if those of some other culture think otherwise, they are obviously mistaken—just as obviously mistaken as are solipsists and flat-Earthers. In morals, as in everything else, we must believe that things are as, overwhelmingly, they appear to be. And it more obvious to almost all of us that the genocide conducted by Hitler was morally wrong than that we are not now dreaming, or that the Earth is many millions of years old.

The second thing is that the moral properties (i.e. moral goodness, badness etc.) of particular actions (picked out in terms of who did them where and when) are supervenient on their moral-making properties, which latter are themselves non-moral properties. What Hitler did on such and such occasions in 1942 and 1943 was morally wrong because it was an act of genocide. What you did yesterday was good because it was an act of feeding the starving etc. No action can be just morally good or bad; it is good or bad because it has certain other non-moral properties—those of the kinds which I illustrated earlier. And any other action which had just those non-moral properties would have the same moral properties. The conjunction of non-moral properties which gives rise to the moral property may be a long one or a short one. It may be that all acts of telling lies are bad, or it may be that all acts of telling lies in such and such circumstances (the description of which is a long one) are bad. But it must be that if there is a world W in which a certain action a having various non-moral properties (e.g. being an act of killing someone to whom the killer had a certain kind of relation), was bad, there could not be another world W^* which was exactly the same as W in all non-moral respects, but in which a was not bad. A difference in moral properties has to arise from a difference in non-moral properties. If a certain sort of killing is not bad in one world, but bad in another world, there must be some difference between the two worlds (e.g. in social organization or the prevalence of crime) which

---

However such narrow senses can easily be separated off from the sense with which I am concerned, by the means used in the text of delineating the latter.

makes for the moral difference. Moral properties, to use the jargon, are supervenient on non-moral properties. And the supervenience must be logical supervenience. Our concept of the moral is such that it makes no *sense* to suppose both that there is a world W in which a is wrong and a world W^* exactly the same as W except that in W^* a is good. It follows that there are logically necessary truths of the form "If an action has non-moral properties A, B and C, it is morally good", "If an action has non-moral properties C and D, it is morally wrong" and so on. If there are moral truths, there are necessary moral truths—general principles of morality. I re-emphasize that, for all I have said so far, these may often be very complicated principles—e.g. "All actions of promise breaking in circumstances C, D, E, F, and G are wrong", rather than just "All actions of promise breaking are wrong". All moral truths are either necessary (of the above kind) or contingent. Contingent moral truths—e.g. that what you did yesterday was good—derive their truth from some contingent non-moral truth (e.g. that what you did yesterday was to feed the starving) and some necessary moral truth (e.g. that all acts of feeding the starving are good).

II

Can the will of God in any way determine what is good or bad? That will depend on what the necessary moral truths are. On one kind of theory, for which I will use the now traditional name "divine command theory" (although, as we shall see, the notion of a "command" only plays a crucial role in one variant of such a theory), the will of God determines the whole of morality. Given my account of morality in terms of necessary truths, this kind of theory must be expressed as claiming that the only necessary truths of morality are ones connecting the will of God and the morally good or bad. There are however different possible variants of such a theory. The connection may be between the will of God and the moral; or between the command of God and the moral.[5] There is a difference because the will of God may not be expressed by a command (which must be a humanly accessible phenomenon—e.g. announced to humans in their religious consciousness, or by some prophet or in some book). Although the unexpressed will of God might make things supererogatorily good (or bad but not wrong), presumably a command must create an obligation. The public expression of will which makes something supererogatorily good (or bad but not wrong) will be something like a commendation. (God lets us know that he would welcome us doing some action). On the reasonable assumption that, although God may not always express his will, what he commands is always what he wills, a theory which connects the moral with divine command and commendation will be a narrower form of a more general theory connecting the moral with the divine will. In future, for simplicity's sake, I shall consider divine command theory, and modifications thereto, only in its narrower form. It will be apparent how to apply what I shall write to other variants of divine command theory.

So then, what characterizes divine command theory thus understood, will be (given the results of my section I) that it holds that the only necessary moral truths are of the forms "Whatever and only whatever God commands is obligatory", "Whatever and only whatever God commends is good", "Whatever and only whatever God forbids is wrong", "Whatever and only whatever God commends us not to do is bad". Any such theory seems to me implausible—since it entails that if there were no God, there would be no moral good and bad. But surely torturing children just for fun is wrong whether or not there is a God. A slightly modified version of this

---

[5] For a full discussion of different variants of the divine command theory of obligation, see Mark C. Murphy, "Divine Command, Divine Will, and Moral Obligation", *Faith and Philosophy* 15 (1988), pp. 1-27. He regards the two most important variants as those considered above—connecting moral obligation with divine command, or with divine will.

theory says that if there is a God, his commands and commendations (and only these) determine what is morally good and bad; but if there is no God, other considerations determine these. [6] That however also seems to me implausible. Whatever God has commanded—even if he has not commanded us to torture children just for fun, torturing children just for fun is still wrong for another reason which has nothing to do with God. And no command of God could change that.

At the other extreme there is the view, held by Kant,[7] that God's commands (or commendations) make no difference to the content of morality: that, for example, there are no necessary truths of the form "If God commands an action of kind x, that action is obligatory". That view too I find implausible. The status of certain individuals and institutions (parents, teachers, careers, the State) surely gives them the right (within limits) to issue commands and makes conformity to those commands obligatory for certain other individuals. In particular parents who are not just biological parents but are educating and nurturing their children have certain rights over their children while they are still young to tell them to do certain things—e.g. to do the family shopping—and the command creates an obligation which would not otherwise exist. The parental right to command arises in virtue of a moral principle that beneficiaries have certain obligations to please benefactors. The first and obvious way to please benefactors is to obey their commands. It follows—given that there is a God—that if children have limited duties to obey parents, humans have obligations far less limited in extent to obey God. For God is so much more the source of our being than are parents. God keeps us in existence from moment to moment, gives us knowledge and power and friends; and all the help that other benefactors give us arises from God sustaining in them the power to do so. There are however limits to the rights of parents over children—parents do not have the right to command children to serve them day and night; and so, beyond a certain point, parental commands would impose no obligation. Likewise (though the main argument of this paper in no way depends on this view) my own view is that God's rights over us are also limited, even more narrowly than by the fact that he cannot command us to do what we are obliged (in virtue of some other necessary moral truth) not to do—e.g. torture children just for fun. God has the right to demand a lot from us by way of service to others and worship—but if he chooses to create free rational beings, I suggest, thereby he limits his right to control their lives. If there are such limits, it will then follow that in virtue of his perfect goodness, God will not command us to do actions beyond those limits—for to command what you have no right to command is wrong.

What God does not command, he may commend. And since (perhaps up to a limit) it is supererogatorily good to please benefactors more than you are obliged to, God's commendation can make an action supererogatorily good, when it does not make it obligatory. And God, like human parents, may command us to do what is obligatory anyway (e.g. keeping our promises to other humans), and commend us to do what is good anyway. And his command and commendation can add to the obligation or goodness of the act. Also of course, because he sees

---

[6] One or other of these positions is to be attributed to William of Ockham. See the exposition of Ockham's views on the status of morality in F. Copleston, *A History of Philosophy*, iii, Burnes and Oates, 1953, pp. 103-10. See too the Ockhamist Gabriel Biel—"The reason why the divine will accepts things as thus or thus, is not a goodness found independently in objects by God but the reason lies only in the divine will, which accepts things as having such and such a degree of goodness; that is why they are good to that degree, and not vice versa:— *Canonis missae expositio*, 23E.

[7] See e.g. his *Religion Within the Limits of Reason Alone,* trans. T. M. Greene and H.H. Hudson, Harper and Row, 1960, p.142—"There are no special duties to God in a universal religion"; and his *Lectures on Philosophical Theology*, trans. A.W. Wood and G.M. Clark, Cornell University Press, 1978, p.159—"The knowledge of God...must not determine whether something is morally good or a duty for me. This I have to judge from the nature of things."

what is good and obligatory for reasons other than his command and commendation, and we do not always, he can inform of such goodness and obligation. But, if what I have written earlier is correct, there are limits to what God can *make* to be good or obligatory (whether by command or unexpressed will).

That whatever God commands (within such and such limits) is obligatory will itself be a necessary truth—following no doubt from a more general truth of an obligation to obey benefactors (within such and such limits) in virtue of the *nature* of God as our creator. If then God has commanded us to do a certain action, it then becomes a contingent moral truth that we ought to do it. This depends on the expressed *will* of God. Similarly for what God commends. But there are other necessary truths of morality which relate the obligatory or the supererogatory good to features of human situations not connected with divine command or commendation.

In Plato's dialogue *Euthyphro*, Socrates asked the famous question: "Is that which is holy loved by the gods because it is holy, or is it holy because it is loved by the gods?"[8] Put in Christian terms (and phrased simply in terms of command and obligation), the Euthyphro dilemma becomes: does God command what is obligatory for other reasons, or is what is obligatory obligatory because God commands it? The view which I am putting forward takes the first horn for some obligations. We ought not to torture children just for fun, whether or not there is a God; here God can only command us to do what is our duty anyway. But I take the second horn for other obligations—but for a divine command there would be no obligation to worship on Sundays rather than on Tuesdays. That there are very general principles of morality, including not only the principle of the obligation to please benefactors but other principles as well, was recognized by both Aquinas and Scotus. Aquinas held that "the first principles of natural law are altogether unalterable"[9]. He does not tell us much in the *Summa Theologiae* about which these are, but he does write that they are principles too general to be mentioned in the ten commandments, such as that no one ought to do evil to anyone, which he says are "inscribed in natural reason as self-evident"[10]. Scotus tells us that the only moral obligations from which God could not dispense us are the duties to love and reverence God himself; which he sees as constituted by the first three of the Ten Commandments.[11] So both writers hold—and if my arguments are correct, must hold—that there are necessary moral truths independent of the will of God.

III

But does not recognizing that there are some moral truths which exist independently of the will of God and which God cannot alter have the consequence that God is not omnipotent? The view that God is omnipotent has normally been construed—since Aquinas[12], and put in more modern terminology—as the view that God can do anything logically possible. God is not supposed to be able to do anything logically impossible. So if there are, as I have claimed, moral truths which are logically necessary, God's inability to make them otherwise does not threaten his omnipotence. But the view that there is a realm of logical (including moral) truths independent of God might still seem to reduce his sovereignty over the Universe—the definition of omnipotence

---

[8] *Euthyphro* 9e.
[9] *Summa Theologiae* 1a. 2a. 94.
[10] *Summa Theologiae* 1a. 2a. 100.3
[11] *Ordinatio* III, suppl. dist. 37, text and translation on pp. 268-87 and commentary on pp. 60-4 of Allan B. Wolter (ed.) *Duns Scotus on the Will and Morality*, Catholic University of America Press, 1986.
[12] See *Summa Contra Gentiles* 2.25, entitled 'How the Omnipotent God is said to be incapable of certain things', and its long list of such things and the differing reasons of why God is said to be incapable of them.

might seem too limited.

That will seem to be so if you take a Platonist view of logical truth. For the Platonist it is timeless propositions, not human sentences, which are logically necessary, possible or impossible. These propositions exist in an eternal world and constrain what can happen in the contingent world; human sentences merely put these propositions into human words. On that view of logical truths, they do indeed limit God's powers of action. The alternative is nominalism. The nominalist holds that there are no such timeless propositions. There are no grounds for postulating them since all truths about logical modality can be expressed as truths about human sentences. There are not really such things as propositions, although sometimes it is convenient to talk as if there were, as if there were things which sentences express. I side with the nominalist[13]—logical modality belongs fundamentally to the sentences of human languages. A proposition is logically possible (necessary, etc.) if any declarative sentence which expresses it is logically possible (necessary, etc.). A declarative sentence is logically impossible if it has no ultimate sense; a sentence is logically necessary if its negation has no ultimate sense.

A declarative sentence, all of whose words have meaning and which is grammatically well formed has *prima facie* sense. But a sentence which has *prima facie* sense may fail to make an intelligible claim about the world; or may entail a sentence which fails to make an intelligible claim about the world. A sentence fails to make an intelligible claim (i.e. it is incoherent) if the rules for the use of the words of our language rule out the sentence from ever being there. Such a sentence, I shall say, has no ultimate sense. The paradigm example of such a sentence is a self-contradictory sentence.

God is nonetheless omnipotent for not being able to make "squooges fudgify", for the simple reason that the words I have used have no meaning, and so nothing is being described. And it is for the same reason that God cannot bring about a state of affairs purportedly described by a sentence where the words taken separately all have meaning, and they are put together grammatically, but they cancel each other out so that they rule out the sentence from ever being true. That is why God cannot bring about what is purportedly described by "there are more than ten people in my room and at the same time less than five people." The sentence fails to describe anything, because the rules for the use of English words ensure that there is nothing which would count as its being true.

Of course it sometimes requires much argument to show that some sentence is logically impossible, lacks ultimate sense. It looks to the schoolchild as if "there is a triangle conforming to all Euclid's axioms, whose interior angles add up to more than 180û" describes a state of affairs; but by drawing out what follows from the sentence by the rules for the use of English words and mathematical terms, we can show that what is purportedly described has no ultimate sense. And in that case the fact that God cannot bring about what some such sentence purports to describe, is not due to a weakness in God but to a weakness in the sentence—it does not describe anything which it makes any sense to suppose to hold. And likewise, given that general principles of morality are logically necessary truths, the reason why God cannot make them otherwise, is that it makes no sense to suppose that they be otherwise. Negations of the sentences which state such principles have no ultimate sense. There is no ultimate sense in "it is not wrong to torture children just for fun."

The major source of any reluctance to admit this will, I believe, arise from a belief that if the logical impossibility of some sentence amounts to lack of ultimate sense (e.g. entailing a self-contradiction), it will be provable to be such by substitution of synonyms and the rules of logic. Thus in the Euclid example, by substituting synonyms and following recognized logical rules,

---

[13] For a full defense of nominalism about logical truth, see my *The Christian God*, Clarendon Press, 1994, ch.5.

you can show there to be a self-contradiction entailed by supposing that there is a Euclidean triangle whose angles sum to more than 180E. But, says the objector, you cannot in that way derive an inconsistency from "it is not wrong to torture children just for fun" or from any other proffered example of an alleged moral falsehood.

I am certainly committed to the view that there is an incoherence in the cited sentence or in some sentence which it entails, although incoherence need not take the form of a straightforward self-contradiction ("p and-not-p"). But we recognize incoherences (and self-contradictions as a particular case thereof) before ever we build a system of logical rules. A major test of any proposed system is whether it always rules out the incoherent. If it sometimes allows the incoherent, then it is a bad system. Our recognition of the logically impossible, necessary etc. precedes our construction of logical systems. This can be seen by the fact that there are some very obvious logically necessary truths which no present logical system can show to be such (with the aid of substitution of synonyms)—e.g. "if it is red, it is colored", or "no surface can be both red and green all over at the same time." And logicians are all the time seeking to construct systems of tense logic, modal logic etc. which capture pre-existing logical necessities and entailments. The fact (if it is a fact) that the cited sentence does not entail an incoherence by following recognized logical rules shows only that we have not yet developed an adequate moral logic. If the arguments of section I are correct, there is such a logic waiting to be developed.

The method of discovering the necessary truths of morality is that of reflective equilibrium.[14] You begin with both particular moral judgments (contingent claims) made in particular non-moral circumstances; and also with apparently plausible general moral principles (apparent necessary truths). If these conflict at any point (i.e. it follows from the apparent necessary truth that for the non-moral circumstances, a particular moral judgment is false), you try to amend particular judgments and principles so as to remove the conflict. You amend particular judgments in the light of suggested principles if it seems more obvious that the latter are correct than that the former are correct; and amend suggested principles in the light of particular judgments if it seems more obvious that the latter rather than the former are correct. Individual moralists will do their best, but they will hope by co-operating with others in this activity to reach a system which will command widespread acceptance. But clearly it will take much time and much effort to reach such agreement. And not merely time and effort; but because adopting new moral views may have unwelcome consequences for our lives, we often have an inbuilt bias against recognizing new moral truths. Because of such bias humans may never reach agreement about moral truth. But if these are ever particular moral truths (and some examples are very obvious) and moral truths are logically supervenient on non-moral truths, there is a system of necessary moral truth waiting to be discovered, even if many humans will never recrecognize. One such truth, I have suggested, is that—if there is a God—it is obligatory for humans to do what he commands, and good for them to do what he commends.

IV

But why should a perfectly good God issue commands, and thereby lay moral burdens on his human children. For four reasons, I suggest. First, to give us further motivation to do what is obligatory anyway. As I noted earlier, parents often tell their children to do what they ought to do anyway—sometimes no doubt because children may not realize what they ought to do anyway; but on other occasions, when children do realize this, to reinforce the obligation.

---

[14] See of course John Rawls, *A Theory of Justice*, Oxford University Press, 1972, p.20.

Parents care that their children do what they ought to do. So, if there is a God, does God. Secondly, to give us further motivation to do what—but for God's command—would be merely supererogatarily good. Parents want their children to get into the habit of doing what is good beyond obligation. When the children are young, they command them to do it. Commands often have more effect than good advice but once children get into the habit of doing supererogatory good, the need for command diminishes. God rightly wants humans to be holy, and so he has reason to help the process of our sanctification by imposing obligations on us (by way of commands) for some or all of our earthly life. That still of course leaves us with the freedom not to conform to these obligations.

A third reason why God might command us to do certain actions is for purposes of coordination.[15] Often we have a choice of doing one of a number of equally good actions, of which we can only do one, but each of which it is important that someone should do. One human (in the days before telecommunications) could only preach the Gospel to one town at a time, yet many towns needed to hear the Gospel. If God told Jonah to preach to Nineveh, and someone else to preach to Babylon, this would ensure that the Gospel is preached in both towns. Otherwise both missionaries might journey to Babylon, and Nineveh might not hear the Gospel. And the fourth reason why God might issue commands is in order to give to each of us a special place in God's providential plan for the world. For a commander to tell a particular person to perform a particular task makes and shows that person important to the commander. God deals with us on an individual basis, and he wants us so much to play a particular role in his plan and it is so good for us that we should, that he may command us to do so.

Questions

1. Of the four reasons Swinburne says God issues divine commands, which one do you think is the most important, and why?

2. Is there any one of the reasons you think is problematic, and if so why?

3. Do you see Swinburne's case as convincing, and if so, why, and if not, why not?

4. What does Swinburne mean by a supererogatory good?

5. What does Swinburne mean by God's plan for the world?

---

[15] I owe this point to my doctoral supervisee, Joseph Shaw. I am most grateful to him for useful discussions of the issues of section IV.

Figure 9

Part IIX

Death and Immortality

THE FINALITY OF DEATH*

Bertrand Russell

Russell contends that life after death is not possible because it requires certain bodily states that are absent at death. He argues that it is not reasonable therefore to believe in life after death, and that the inclination to such belief is generated by emotional factors.

Before we can profitably discuss whether we shall continue to exist after death, it is well to be clear as to the sense in which a man is the same person as he was yesterday. Philosophers used to think that there were definite substances, the soul and the body, that each lasted on from day to day, that a soul, once created, continued to exist throughout all future time, whereas a body ceased temporarily from death till the resurrection of the body.

The part of this doctrine which concerns the present life is pretty certainly false. The matter of the body is continually changing by processes of nutriment and wastage. Even if it were not, atoms in physics are no longer supposed to have continuous existence; there is no sense in saying: this is the same atom as the one that existed a few minutes ago. The continuity of a human body is a matter of appearance and behavior, not of substance.

The same thing applies to the mind. We think and feel and act, but there is not, in addition to thoughts and feelings and actions, a bare entity, the mind or the soul, which does or suffers these occurrences. The mental continuity of a person is a continuity of habit and memory: there was yesterday one person whose feelings I can remember, and that person I regard as myself of yesterday; but, in fact, myself of yesterday was only certain mental occurrences which are now remembered and are regarded as part of the person who now recollects them. All that constitutes a person is a series of experiences connected by memory and by certain similarities of the sort we call habit.

If, therefore, we are to believe that a person survives death, we must believe that the memories and habits which constitute the person will continue to be exhibited in a new set of occurrences.

No one can prove that this will not happen. But it is easy to see that it is very unlikely. Our memories and habits are bound up with the structure of the brain, in much the same way in which a river is connected with the riverbed. The water in the river is always changing, but it keeps to the same course because previous rains have worn a channel. In like manner, previous events have worn a channel in the brain, and our thoughts flow along this channel. This is the cause of memory and mental habits. But the brain, as a structure, is dissolved at death, and memory therefore may be expected to be also dissolved. There is no more reason to think otherwise than to expect a river to persist in its old course after an earthquake has raised a mountain where a valley used to be.

All memory, and therefore (one may say) all minds, depend upon a property which is very noticeable in certain kinds of material structures but exists little if at all in other kinds. This is the property of forming habits as a result of frequent similar occurrences. For example: a bright light makes the pupils of the eyes contract; and if you repeatedly flash a light in a man's eyes and beat a gong at the same time, the gong alone will, in the end, cause his pupils to contract. This is a fact about the brain and nervous system—that is to say, about a certain material structure. It will

---

* From Bertrand Russell, *Why I Am Not a Christian* (London: George Allen & Unwin, 1957), pp. 88-93. Copyright © 1957 by George Allen & Unwin. Reprinted by permission of Simon & Schuster, Inc.

be found that exactly similar facts explain our response to language and our use of it, our memories and the emotions they arouse, our moral or immoral habits of behavior, and indeed everything that constitutes our mental personality, except the part determined by heredity. The part determined by heredity is handed on to our posterity but cannot, in the individual, survive the disintegration of the body. Thus both the hereditary and the acquired parts of a personality are, so far as our experience goes, bound up with the characteristics of certain bodily structures. We all know that memory may be obliterated by an injury to the brain, that a virtuous person may be rendered vicious by encephalitis lethargica, and, that a clever child can be turned into an idiot by lack of iodine. In view of such familiar facts, it seems scarcely probable that the mind survives the total destruction of brain structure which occurs at death.

It is not rational arguments but emotions that cause belief in a future life.

The most important of these emotions is fear of death, which is instinctive and biologically useful. If we genuinely and wholeheartedly believed in the future life, we should cease completely to fear death. The effects would be curious, and probably such as most of us would deplore. But our human and subhuman ancestors have fought and exterminated their enemies throughout many geological ages and have profited by courage; it is therefore an advantage to the victors in the struggle for life to be able, on occasion, to overcome the natural fear of death. Among animals and savages, instinctive pugnacity suffices for this purpose; but at a certain stage of development, as the Mohammedans first proved, belief in Paradise has considerable military value as reinforcing natural pugnacity. We should therefore admit that militarists are wise in encouraging the belief in immortality, always supposing that this belief does not become so profound as to produce indifference to the affairs of the world.

Another emotion which encourages the belief in survival is admiration of the excellence of man. As the Bishop of Birmingham says, "His mind is a far finer instrument than anything that had appeared earlier—he knows right and wrong. He can build Westminster Abbey. He can make an airplane. He can calculate the distance of the sun.... Shall, then, man at death perish utterly? Does that incomparable instrument, his mind, vanish when life ceases?"

The Bishop proceeds to argue that "the universe has been shaped and is governed by an intelligent purpose," and that it would have been unintelligent, having made man, to let him perish.

To this argument there are many answers. In the first place, it has been found, in the scientific investigation of nature, that the intrusion of moral or aesthetic values has always been an obstacle to discovery. It used to be thought that the heavenly bodies must move in circles because the circle is the most perfect curve, that species must be immutable because God would only create what was perfect and what therefore stood in no need of improvement, that it was useless to combat epidemics except by repentance because they were sent as a punishment for sin, and so on. It has been found, however, that, so far as we can discover, nature is indifferent to our values and can only be understood by ignoring our notions of good and bad. The Universe may have a purpose, but nothing that we know suggests that, if so, this purpose has any similarity to ours.

Nor is there in this anything surprising. Dr. Barnes tells us that man "knows right and wrong." But, in fact, as anthropology shows, men's views of right and wrong have varied to such an extent that no single item has been permanent. We cannot say, therefore, that man knows right and wrong, but only that some men do. Which men? Nietzsche argued in favor of an ethic profoundly different from Christ's, and some powerful governments have accepted his teaching. If knowledge of right and wrong is to be an argument for immortality, we must first settle whether to believe Christ or Nietzsche, and then argue that Christians are immortal, but Hitler and Mussolini are not, or vice versa. The decision will obviously be made on the battlefield, not in the study. Those who have the best poison gas will have the ethic of the future and will therefore be the immortal ones.

Our feelings and beliefs on the subject of good and evil are, like everything else about us, natural facts, developed in the struggle for existence and not having any divine or supernatural origin. In one of Aesop's fables, a lion is shown pictures of huntsmen catching lions and remarks that, if he had painted them, they would have shown lions catching huntsmen. Man, says Dr. Barnes, is a fine fellow because he can make airplanes. A little while ago there was a popular song about the cleverness of flies in walking upside down on the ceiling, with the chorus: "Could Lloyd George do it? Could Mr. Baldwin do it? Could Ramsay Mac do it? Why, NO." On this basis a very telling argument could be constructed by a theologically-minded fly, which no doubt the other flies would find most convincing.

Moreover, it is only when we think abstractly that we have such a high opinion of man. Of men in the concrete, most of us think the vast majority very bad. Civilized states spend more than half their revenue on killing each other's citizens. Consider the long history of the activities inspired by moral fervor: human sacrifices, persecutions of heretics, witch-hunts, pogroms leading up to wholesale extermination by poison gases, which one at least of Dr. Barnes's episcopal colleagues must be supposed to favor, since he holds pacifism to be un-Christian. Are these abominations, and the ethical doctrines by which they are prompted, really evidence of an intelligent Creator? And can we really wish that the men who practiced them should live forever? The world in which we live can be understood as a result of muddle and accident; but if it is the outcome of deliberate purpose, the purpose must have been that of a fiend. For my part, I find accident a less painful and more plausible hypothesis.

Questions

1. What does Russell say is needed if a person is to survive death?

2. Do you agree If so why if not why not?

3. Why does Russell think that experiences after death are unlikely?

4. What is the most important of the emotions that cause belief in the afterlife according to Russell?

5. What possible counter might one offer Russell's contention that persons are only matter?

MONISM AND IMMORTALITY

Bruce Reichenbach

This is a revision of chapter five of his book, Is Man the Phoenix? A Study of Immortality, *In this revision, he offers and analysis of dualism and concludes that there are no compelling arguments for dualism, and opts for monism, and acknowledges that though survival is not possible at death, life after death is possible through a recreation of the person.*

History is replete with human attempts to promote life after death. Chinese nobility were carefully and ritually interred, often in sumptuous tombs buried deep beneath earthen mounds. The ancient Egyptians mummified their pharaohs and nobility, placing them in rock-hewn tombs or stone pyramids, in rooms that contained the food and valuables that would ease their transition to the next life. Practitioners of traditional Chinese and African religions still remember and appease their ancestors with special ceremonies at home altars, on their graves, or at sacred sites. Hindus and Buddhists continue to speak of karma and its influence on reincarnation. The *Koran*, Islam's holy book, uses the term "hereafter" (*al-àkhira*) 113 times. Life after death is a fundamental feature of Christianity, which affirms not only that Jesus rose from the dead but that his resurrection guarantees our own life after death. In fact, the belief in life after death is so central to religion that one author contends that this belief is more fundamental than the belief in God, so that if God did not exist, God would have to be created to "function as the benevolent purveyor of man's immortality."[1]

"Immortality" may be understood in many ways. Some understand it to indicate a form of remembrance, whereby the deceased individual continues to exist in and through the memories of others. Famous people record their existence through memorable events, while artists and writers sign their creations so that they will be remembered. Others treat immortality as reunion with the One (e.g., Brahman or Tao). Here individuality, which is the bane of our existence, disappears in realizing our ultimate unity with everything. In what follows our interest is in another understanding that might be termed "personal immortality." We will view personal immortality as the actual existence of individual human persons for an indefinite period subsequent to their death, with that which makes for their personal identity and the awareness of this identity essentially intact.

The problem of human immortality really encompasses two problems. First, what must human beings be like so that they can live subsequent to their death, and second, what good reasons can be given believing in life after death? This piece will not address the second question; rather, it addresses the issue whether life after death is *possible*, for if life after death is impossible, arguments regarding its actuality are moot. Since the issue of possibility usually hinges on the nature of human beings, we need to explore various views of human nature. One might group these views under two classifications, anthropological dualism (or pluralism), in which the individual is composed of different kinds of elements, generally including an immaterial part called the mind or soul, and anthropological monism, where the individual is treated as a psycho-physical unity.

Dualists have an easier time establishing the possibility of immortality, for they accord humans an element (soul) that, as non-physical, is capable of surviving death. When the

---

[1] Corliss Lamont, *The Illusion of Immortality* (New York: Philosophical Library, 1959), 7.

individual "dies," the physical body dies, but since the true person (the soul) is nonphysical, it is not subject to death and decay and hence can continue to exist. However, many, though not all,[2] contemporary philosophers reject anthropological dualism on the grounds that it faces serious difficulties. Not only does its denial of the death of the real person contradict our ordinary way of speaking about human death, but more importantly it seriously conflicts with the conclusions of science that the physical body is a necessary condition for the existence and functioning of mental processes. Dualists give stories about how the mind (soul) and body interact, but none are very persuasive.

But if we abandon a qualitatively pluralistic analysis of humans and instead understand human beings as psychophysical unities, what does it mean to say that humans are such unities? How does this view account for and interpret human mental processes? And more to our point, is immortality possible if one adopts this view? The answer to these questions, especially the first and third, will occupy our attention in what follows.

Monistic Theories of the Human Person

The view of humans that stands opposed to anthropological dualism or pluralism is often termed anthropological monism. Monists reject the existence of a spiritual soul or mind that, though functioning within a body structured and operated according to natural laws, cannot be described in terms employed by physical scientists. For them, humans are physical organisms, all of whose functions and operations are ultimately physically based events.

Although anthropological monism has appeared in a number of guises throughout the course of Western thought, it became more prominent in the 20th century when Behaviorism dominated the scene. As a psychological method, Behaviorism rejected arm-chair, introspective procedures that characterized much of psychology. The phenomena reported by these procedures could not be observed and confirmed by independent observers, as was the case with phenomena studied by the natural sciences. The lack of objective checking procedures resulted in a great diversity of introspective accounts and interpretations of human mental processes. To be a science, all subjectivity had to be rigorously excluded. Since Behaviorism desired to develop a scientific account, it replaced introspective methods with allegedly objective accounts of human and animal behavior. Behaviorism, however, went beyond mere methodological concerns to proffer a view of humans. It claimed that mental concepts such as "mind," "thinking," and "consciousness" had no place in an objective, scientific account. Mental concepts were to be redefined or analyzed in terms of objectively observable behavior. What was once considered to be distinctively mental was now reduced to or seen to be nothing but behavioral responses of the organism as it interacted with the environment.

Subsequent versions sought to improve the Behaviorist model by appealing to dispositions to account for mental states. Mental processes are to be analyzed either in terms of behavioral acts of the organism or else in terms of dispositions of the individual to behave in a certain way should particular circumstances obtain. However, "dispositional statements are neither reports of observed or observable states of affairs, nor yet reports of unobserved or unobservable states of affairs. They narrate no incidents."[3] "To possess a dispositional property is not to be in a particular state, or to undergo a particular change; it is to be found or liable to be in

---

[2] Richard Swinburne, *Evolution of the Soul* (Oxford: Oxford University Press, 1986); Charles Taliaferro, *Consciousness and the Mind of God* (Cambridge: Cambridge University Press, 1994); William Hasker, *The Emergent Self* (Ithaca, N.Y.: Cornell University Press, 1999); Timothy O'Connor, *Persons and Causes* (New York: Oxford University Press, 2000); J.P. Moreland and Scott B. Rae, *Body and Soul* (Downers Grove, Ill.: InterVarsity Press, 2000).
[3] Gilbert Ryle, *The Concept of Mind* (New York: Barnes and Noble, 1949), 125.

a particular state, or to undergo a particular change, when a particular condition is realized."[4] Dispositional properties are logical constructions out of behavior. Thus, the Behaviorist thesis is maintained: "When we describe people as exercising qualities of mind, we are not referring to occult episodes of which their overt acts and utterances are effects; we are referring to those overt acts and utterances themselves."[5]

Many philosophers felt that more is needed to fully explain human conscious processes. For one thing, it is not enough to leave the analysis of mental processes simply on the level of behavior or dispositions, for one can suggest an explanation of this behavior or of these dispositional properties. Just as one might explain the dispositional property of brittleness in the glass vase by noting its molecular composition and the strength of the bond between the particles (by noting its physical properties), so too one might explain the behavior or disposition to behave by appeal to certain physical properties. The disposition to behave in a particular way can be explained by a physical state of the organism causally connected to the behavioral manifestation of the disposition. As such, an analysis of humans in terms of behavior and dispositions to behave does not go far enough.

Second, the mental appears to have a genuinely causal explanatory role. We might say that Robert acted the way he did at the party *because* he was envious. But an analysis in terms of dispositions eliminates this apparently causally explanatory aspect of the mental, for if envy as a disposition is merely a logical construct out of envy-behavior, we cannot rightly say that it caused an action.

Third, the reports of mental processes going on inside me, of which I am immediately aware, appear to be *genuine* reports of *real* processes. My behavior is not identical with my thought, as Behaviorism claims, but is rather the expression of my thought.

Some philosophers, rejecting Behaviorism as inadequate, developed what is termed the Identity Theory of the mind. The Identity Theory holds that insofar as a statement about a mental state or sensation is a report of something, that something is in fact a brain process, brain state, or a process within the central nervous system.[6] Identity theorists do not claim that "thought" means the same as "brain process of a certain sort." Statements about thoughts and sensations can neither be translated into nor are synonymous with statements about brain processes. Neither do they reduce or analyze statements about sensations and thought into statements about states of the brain. Theirs is not a theory about the meaning of mental terms or concepts, but rather about a logical identification that, if true, ultimately can be verified empirically.

Identity theorists do not deny the existence or reality of mental or psychical states such as perceiving, conceiving, and remembering; mental states are as real as those physical processes that can be objectively observed. However, the event that the mental language reports is ultimately the same as or identical with the event that would be reported by the neurologist. What they deny is that states of consciousness are irreducibly psychical. An event such as thinking is physical—an electro-chemical transference in the brain—though the perspectives from which the event is reported (as a mental state or as a process of the central nervous system) and the language used to report these perspectives (language about minds, thinking, and concepts, on the one hand, and language about brain waves, synapses and electro-chemical transfers on the other) are two. Both languages used are legitimate; but both refer to one and only one physical event, for thinking is a brain process.

---

[4] Ibid., 43.
[5] Ibid., 25.
[6] J.J.C. Smart, "Sensation and Brain Processes," *The Philosophical Review* LXVIII (1959); reprinted in C.V. Borst, *The Mind-Brain Identity Theory* (New York: St. Martin's Press, 1970).

The Identity Theory likewise faces problems, most notably that of cross-category identity. If the mental and brain states are strictly identical, then, according the Leibniz's principle of the identity of indiscernibles, every property of the one is likewise a property of the other. But the properties of mental states and brain states differ. For example, the one is private and nonspatial, the other public and spatial.

Toward the end of the 20th century, eliminative materialism came to dominate the scene.[7] On this view, since mental phenomena can be reduced to the neurophysical, neuroscience provides the correct account of human mental capacities. The self is "an active, self-updating collection of structures organized to 'mirror' the world as it evolves."[8] These high level structures are composed of lower-level active patterns, and these of still lower patterns, until we reach the lowest level, which consists of nothing more than neural firings. Taken individually, these neural firings are random and meaningless, but statistical regularity reveals patterns that encode the information necessary for the organism to respond interactively to other patterns of symbols in its environment. When the patterns of firings are interpreted at the highest level, we give them meaning, and these meaning-assigned patterns become alternative ways of explaining who we are.

Critics have argued that "it is hard to see how any set of presuppositions about behavior, functional organization, physiological makeup, environmental circumstances, or anything else that might feature in the chosen reductive analysis, could suffice to specify *how it feels to the subject* to be in pain, or to be having a certain type of sensory experience."[9] If reductionism is true, one should be able to know what hearing is like through knowing the physics of sound and the physiology of the auditory system, but if one is deaf, this cannot be the case.

Because a reductionist view of the person has difficulty accounting for top-down causation—for the fact that mental events seem to be genuine causes of events happening at the physiological or neurological levels, other monists have developed emergentist monisms. Robert Searle argues that mental phenomena are properties that emerge from physiological micro-elements and hence are as real as any other properties. Emergent mental properties are a kind of physical property, namely, a biological property that can bring about effects through "intentional causation," where the "cause both represents and brings about the effect."[10] Other models proposing a physical view of humans, such as supervenience accounts that hold that mental properties supervene on physical properties,[11] or a constitution view that holds that persons are constituted by but not identical with their bodies,[12] are currently debated.

A plethora of recent advances in neurophysiology and molecular biology provide good reasons for opting for a monist view of humans. Consonance with the results of science makes anthropological monism philosophically attractive. However, our interest lies not in spelling out and assessing the many monistic theories of the human person but rather in exploring the implications of these materialistic or physicalist views of the person for the possibility of life after death.

---

[7] Patricia Smith Churchland, *Neurophilosophy : Toward A Unified Science Of The Mind-Brain* (Cambridge, Mass.: MIT Press, 1986); Patricia Smith Churchland, *Brain-wise: Studies in Neurophilosophy* (Cambridge, Mass. : MIT Press, 2002).
[8] Douglas R. Hofstadter and Daniel C. Dennett, *The Mind's I* (New York: Basic Books, 1981), 192.
[9] John Foster, "A Brief Defense of the Cartesian View," in Kevin Corcoran, ed., *Soul, Body, and Survival*, (Ithaca, N.Y.: Cornell University Press, 2002), 21.
[10] John Searle, *Minds, Brains and Science* (Cambridge: Harvard University Press, 1984), 61.
[11] Jaegwon Kim, *Supervenience and Mind: Selected Philosophical Essays* (Cambridge: Cambridge University Press, 1986).
[12] Lynne Rudder Baker, *Persons and Bodies: A Constitution View* (Cambridge: Cambridge University Press, 2000).

The Possibility of Immortality

Traditionally, monists have held that life after death is not possible. Human beings are not mere assemblages of components but physical beings whose components have a particular causal history. Humans do not merely persist, but persist in ways where personal identity is established by relevant causal continuity between what exists before and what exists after. Hence, if personal identity between this and some subsequent life is to be possible, some sort of causal, material continuity must hold between our present material composition and our future composition. Thus, if we are to experience life after death, something physical, identified with our self, must causally continue. Disruption of the causal chain that connects our past components with any future components would terminate a person. Since it appears that nothing comparable to a self continues after the body dies, the prospects for life after death on a materialist position appear dim. Put another way, causally relevant spatial-temporal continuity is necessary for personal identity. Since humans as physical organisms cease to exist when their body ceases to function, nothing remains in or of the person that would allow persons to witness their own funeral.

Despite the formidable problem posed by a causally relevant spatial-temporal continuity, some theistic materialists have developed scenarios intended to show that life after death is possible. Some of these grant that spatial-temporal continuity is a condition of personal identity. On this view, life after death is possible if, at the moment of death, God preserves the essential matter that is the human person, which God then uses later to re-form that person.

The difficult task is to identify this critical, causally relevant matter. Peter van Inwagen, for example, vaguely refers to it as the "naked kernel," the seed that continues to exist until God "clothes it in a festal garment of new flesh."[13] Elsewhere he refers to it as "the 'core person'—the brain and central nervous system—or even some special part of it."[14] But if this material kernel or core part of the brain or central nervous system is physical, how can it be preserved through death and its accompanying decay or cremation? Van Inwagen responds that it is possible that we only *seem* to die, e.g., to decay or be burned. At the last moment before death God snatches away and preserves our core matter, substituting something that looks like it. To pull off this switch, God must act out of character and deceive, since no physician or embalmer has yet caught on about the true status of the deceased's remains.

The materialist Kevin Corcoran modifies this scenario. He suggests that God causes the simple elements that compose the body, at the very last instant of an earthly life, to fission (split) into spatially segregated sets of causally-related simple elements. One set becomes the corpse, while the other continues to exist in some other sphere.[15]

But which set is the real person: the corpse (so that the person really did die) or the fission-produced person living in another space (so that, as on the above view, the person really did not die)? How would one decide that one of these rather than the other is the person who had previously existed, since the respective composition of the two is the same. And if there is little reason to choose one rather than the other, how can persons conclude that they have survived their death rather than died? Perhaps neither is the person, for on the traditional view of identity, if both the deceased and the continuer can be the person, neither are.

---

[13] Peter van Inwagen, "Dualism and Materialism: Athens and Jerusalem?" *Faith and Philosophy* 12 (Oct. 1995): 486.

[14] Peter van Inwagen, "The Possibility of Resurrection," in Paul Edwards, ed., *Immortality* (New York: Macmillan, 1992), 246.

[15] Kevin Corcoran, "Physical Person and Postmortem Survival without Temporal Gaps," in *Soul, Body, and Survival*, 210-17.

Corcoran's response is that the person is the *closest continuer*. Since the deceased did not continue, there is only one continuer, the fissioned person living in another space. But then the continuer is contingently but not necessarily the same person, for it is possible that the corpse really survived after the fission for a period of time before dying. We would then have the problem of two identical persons occupying two different spaces, so that neither would be the same as the dying person. Corcoran responds that having what becomes the corpse live for a time after the fission and then die would not be a possible scenario, for God is a loving being who cannot let people suffer demise. Since God as omnipotent cannot do the impossible or what is contrary to God's nature, it is impossible for the deceased to have been that person.

But this theological reply restricts God's freedom with respect to the annihilation of persons. On the traditional view, God is free (though perhaps morally constrained) to dispose of his creation as he wills.[16] More seriously, this view assumes that annihilation is incompatible with God's love. But many hold that annihilation (rather than, e.g., consignment to hell) is compatible with God's love. Even more problematic would be giving an account of the fissioning, which sounds like but could not really be a natural process.

Re-creation

A different approach is suggested by anthropological materialists who contend that spatial-temporal continuity is not necessary for personal identity. Life after death is possible because, first, it is not self-contradictory that an individual can be physically re-created or reconstituted to possess all of the physical characteristics of the deceased, such that the re-created person would be physically identical to the person who died. And since consciousness is a physical process or an emergent property of brains and other physical processes, our brain could be re-created and programmed to have neural components and structures identical to those we had when we died. We would have the same memories, ideas, perspectives, and personality traits as we had before our death. In effect, as physiological organisms that at base are composed of coded matter, we could be re-created and re-programmed with all the physical and psychical characteristics we possessed before we died.

Second, such a scenario depends upon the existence and activity of a God. If God exists and is omnipotent, God can perform any action that does not entail a self-contradiction. Since the re-creation of the same individual is not self-contradictory, such a re-creation, where the individual begins to live at a future time and place of God's own choosing, is possible.

Thus, life after death is possible even where humans are viewed in a monistic fashion. This is possible even on a radically reductionist view of persons. If we are only programs that are to some extent independent of specific hardware, an omnipotent and omniscient being could re-create us simply by programming our unique software into hardware of some relevant sort. The precise nature of the hardware may be insignificant, so long as it can boot up, run, and carry out the functions and commands of the relevant programs. In this re-creative fashion, those who died can live again by the creative power of an omnipotent God. Humans would be gap-inclusive, existing, ceasing to exist at death, and again existing at the time of re-creation.

Objections to Re-creation

Philosophers raise several objections, of varying degrees of seriousness, against the view that persons can be gap-inclusive. First, some object that on this scenario the deceased will be in a state of unconsciousness for a time between death and re-creation. But this is not the case at all.

---

[16] Stephen T. Davis, "Physicalism and Resurrection," in *Soul, Body, and Survival*, 238.

In order for an individual to be unconscious, a person must exist who can be unconscious. But after death and prior to re-creation no such person exists. Thus, the individual who dies will not be unconscious for an intervening period of time (or to put it in more theological terms, soul-sleep cannot occur without a sleeper). The next moment of consciousness for the deceased will be at the time of that person's re-creation and re-programming.

But would not the deceased be aware of a time lapse between death and re-creation? Here again, the answer must be no. As in the case of non-dreaming sleep, where we are not conscious of time passing, so here too, without consciousness during the interval between death and re-creation, there is no awareness of a time lapse. To the re-created person, re-creation will appear to take place at the next moment after death, though speaking in terms of objective time, the re-creation may occur any number of years or eons later.

This point rests on a distinction we frequently make between subjective and objective time. Suppose you are sitting in your idling car in a "No Parking or Standing" zone, waiting for your daughter to come out of the post office after mailing a package. You sweat a little, maintain constant vigilance for prowling police cars, and glance anxiously at the post office door. It seems like she is taking forever to mail the package. When she finally emerges and gets into the car, you inquire, "What took you so long?" Puzzled, she turns and says, "What do you mean? I was only in there three minutes." The point of contrast is between two kinds of time: objective time as measured by reference to certain celestial movements, and subjective time as measured by an individual's subjective experience.

Applying this to the time of re-creation, measured in terms of objective time, the temporal interval between an individual's death and his re-creation might be thousands, even millions, of years. However, measured in terms of subjective time, that is, in terms of the individual's own experience, the re-creation will seem to occur at the very next moment after death. The reason is that the deceased has no experiences between those of dying and experiences immediately following re-creation. The latter seem to follow immediately upon the former. Thus, in speaking about the time of re-creation, one should make clear whether one is referring to objective time or to subjective time.

Finally, and undoubtedly the most significant objection, how can the individual who is re-created be the same person as the individual who died? Re-created persons will possess entirely different physical elements and will begin again to exist at a time significantly later than their death. Because the individual has a different composition and lacks causally-relevant, spatial-temporal continuity (is gap inclusive), is it not nonsense to suppose that the re-created person could be identical with the deceased? To answer this objection, we must consider whether these two features–composition from the same elements and spatial-temporally continuity—are necessary conditions for all cases of personal identity.

Personal Identity and Spatial-Temporal Continuity

One thing we apparently do not mean by "same person" is that individuals are composed of the same material elements now as they were previously. For example, between cooking my supper last evening and frying my eggs this morning, my wife has undergone significant material change. It is not that she looks different, but her body has produced millions of new cells while old cells were washed away by her morning shower or eliminated through bodily waste. Indeed, if I say that she is the same person as the person I married forty years ago, more than likely her entire organic cell structure has changed. One might respond that, in any case, during that forty years a significant number of elements were carried over from one moment to the next. But this simply shows that any plausibility that this purported criterion of same substance might initially have really derives from applying the criterion of causally-relevant, spatial-temporal continuity. Thus, continuity, not sameness of composition, is important.

A more likely interpretation of "same person" is in terms of causally-relevant, spatial-temporal continuous physical existence. My wife now is the same person I married because it is in principle possible to trace her continuous physical existence from that wedding day until this present moment. But is bodily continuity a necessary condition for personal identity? If this criterion holds in all cases of personal identity, the re-creationist's position is untenable; the presence of a space-time gap precludes such identification.

What grounds can be adduced for the truth of the claim that bodily continuity is a necessary condition for, is part of the meaning of, personal identity? On the one hand, it does not follow analytically from the concept of personal identity. Indeed, merely to stipulate this as a condition for personal identity would only beg the question at issue. Further, it might be contended that re-creation presents a relevant counter-example providing reason why this condition should not be incorporated into the definition of "personal identity."

On the other hand, ground for the necessity of this condition might be sought in experience. But if experience be the ground, the requisite universality is absent. This is particularly the case with respect to the re-creationist's thesis, for we have had no (or relatively little) experience with re-created individuals and therefore possess no experiential grounds from which to argue that the re-created person, although spatial-temporally discontinuous with the deceased, is not the same person. It remains possible that the re-created person provides a unique (and despoiling) case where the condition of spatial-temporal continuity does not apply.

But we need to do more than rest our case simply on an appeal to ignorance. Our position will be strengthened if we can supply cases where we know the criterion in question to be absent, and yet continue (or would continue) to identify the person as identical with the previously encountered person. If we are successful in this, we will have shown that experience likewise fails to establish this as a criterion covering all cases of personal identity.

Since anthropological materialists consider humans as physical beings, we might consider first the identity of other physical things. Consider, for example, a deck of cards. Generally speaking, we might agree that to predicate of a deck of cards that it is identical with a deck existing at a prior time requires that it have been spatial-temporally continuous between those times. However, suppose we consider the deck in the context of a *genuine* act of magic. The magician places the deck of cards into a hat, waves his magic wand, and then tilts it to the viewers, showing that the cards have disappeared. Another wave of the wand and, presto! they have returned. Note that we do not say that the deck of cards now in his hat is a new deck; rather, it is the same deck that disappeared and was magically returned to the hat. In saying that the deck of cards *disappeared* and was magically *restored*, we indicate that neither we nor the magician nor anyone else can trace its spatial-temporal existence between the first wave of the wand and the second. It simply disappeared. If we believe that we or he could trace its existence, or if we believe that the deck now in the hat is a different deck from the first, he would not be a real magician but an illusionist, someone skilled in slight of hand. Indeed, in this case the fact of their actual disappearance distinguishes genuine magic from slight of hand. In short, for this to be an instance of real magic, the restored deck must be the same deck as the original; hence, spatial-temporal continuity is not a necessary condition for all cases of identity.

Two objections might be raised against this example. First, it might be argued that this is a case involving merely an object and therefore not relevant to personal identity. However, since we are considering a physicalist view of persons, we could substitute George W. Bush for the deck of cards in the above example, with identical results. The second objection is more serious: such a case is not possible because there is no real magic, only sleight of hand. And the evidence that real magic is impossible is the necessity of spatial-temporal continuity, which real magic would violate.

We might consider other instances of physical objects that do not rely on appeals to magic. Consider the following case.

> Suppose a certain monastery claims to have in its possession a manuscript written in St. Augustine's own hand. And suppose the monks of this monastery further claim that this manuscript was burned by Arians in the year 457. It would immediately occur to me to ask how *this* manuscript, the one I can touch, could be the very manuscript that was burned in 457. Suppose their answer to this question is that God miraculously recreated Augustine's manuscript in 458. I should respond to this answer (that) the deed it describes seems quite impossible.[17]

It is impossible, van Inwagen says, because "it would never have known the impress of Augustine's hand," and hence could not have been written by him. But the argument contains an ambiguity. The manuscript is an *Augustine manuscript* if and only if it was penned by Augustine. That is, if we consider the identity of the manuscript to be found in its physical origin, then being actually penned by Augustine is a necessary condition of its being an *Augustine manuscript*. Were it destroyed by fire and recopied, though the content would be identical in that the precise sequence of words is the same or even the shape of the characters traced were identical, the document would not be an *Augustine manuscript,* for it is not penned by him. Spatial-temporal continuity is essential to the manuscript's identity as a genuine hand-written document by Augustine.

But spatial-temporal continuity is not necessary for the manuscript to have its identity as a particular copy of *De Trinitate*. If one considers the manuscript insofar as it is "*De Trinitate*" (where the makeup of the manuscript rather than its origins is relevant to its identity), one would look to the properties of the work to determine that it is a particular copy of *De Trinitate*.[18] What makes it this particular copy of the work is that it possesses certain features that make it this particular copy. We identify the book by its features, its unique set of essential characteristics, regardless of its origins.

Van Inwagen disagrees, contending that "the atoms of which I am composed occupy at each instant the positions they do because of the operations of certain processes within me."[19] They are part of a causal chain that, if broken, would sever the identity. But again, though normally we consider that causal chain as relevant, it is not necessary to require this chain in order to establish identity. Identity can be constitutional in terms of features, not causal or genetic. And if constitutional, God can be the origin of the re-created, and the re-created will still be the same as the deceased.

We might see this analogically at work in other contexts. Consider the way persons *as characters* function in theatrical productions. The character Hamlet maintains his identity through the various acts of a play; we experience no logical difficulty considering him in the play as a gap-inclusive person whose existence is punctuated by intermissions between acts. (Of course, the actor has spatial-temporal continuity between scenes or acts, but one clearly can distinguish between the actor portraying Hamlet and Hamlet.) It might be objected that the content of the play contains references to experiences off-stage, which requires we assume that the character has a life between acts. But one could write a play in which the character expressly

---

[17] Van Inwagen, "The Possibility of Resurrection," 242.

[18] There is general agreement that we do not require continuity for abstract objects, such as literary works, wars, plays, pieces of music, or even this chapter that, if erased on disk and then identically recopied, would be the same chapter. However, we are not referring to *De Trinitate* as a literary work (abstract object).

[19] Van Inwagen, "The Possibility of Resurrection," 244.

has no experiences between the acts. In short, just as persons in the context of plays have identity despite being gap-inclusive, so people in real life may be gap inclusive, with the re-creating assistance of God. And as the characters in Act One may not know that they are gap-inclusive, so we too may not know in this life that we are gap-inclusive persons.

In sum, the absence of spatial-temporal continuity does not constitute a falsifying condition of personal identity. Of course, we have not established nor are we trying to establish that in no conceivable situation would bodily continuity be necessary. All we assert is that "at least one case can be consistently constructed in which bodily identity fails."[20] Thus, the re-creationist's claim that individuals can be gap-inclusive is far from nonsense.

The Problem of Multiple Replicas

Re-creation faces another major objection, based on the contention that if God can create one person who looks identical, makes identical memory claims, or has an identical personality to the deceased, God can create more than one person like this. On this multiple replica scenario, where we have two claimants, Charles and Robert, both affirming to be re-creations of Guy Fawkes, it is argued that we have no grounds for deciding which is really Guy.[21] If we have no grounds for deciding, then since according to the principle of identity both persons cannot be Guy, neither person can be Guy. The fact that someone looks identical to Guy and makes memory claims about performing Guy's actions at a previous time does not compel us to assert that that person really is Guy and did the actions we ascribe to him.

One reply to this objection is that God can do only what is logically possible. But since it is logically impossible that two or more numerically distinct individuals be identical to each other and to the person who died, God cannot re-create two individuals identical to the deceased. But that he cannot make two persons identical to the deceased does not mean that he cannot re-create one such person. Hence, the multiple replica objection fails: though we might not be able to discern whether it was Charles or Robert who is identical with the deceased Guy, God cannot make both identical with him. One of the two would be at best similar to him.

But, the objector might respond, how would someone know which person was merely similar to and which was identical with the deceased? One response is that while it is true that we cannot deduce identity from memories, a person cannot have *true* memories about experiences undergone by a particular person and still not be that person. Identity is deducible from true memories. Hence, although an external observer may not be able to discern whether Charles or Robert is identical with the deceased Guy, both cannot be identical with him, given that only one can make true memory claims.

The introduction of internal states of consciousness, and in particular memory, provides the basis for two other objections to the re-creationist's thesis. The first objection seeks to return to bodily continuity as a necessary condition for personal identity by contending that the appeal to memory claims presupposes this very condition, whereas the second goes further to claim that neither bodily continuity, physical similarity, nor internal states of consciousness is sufficient to establish personal identity. The decision to call someone identical with rather than merely similar to another is a convention. Let me consider these in turn.

Regarding the first, it is argued that one cannot affirm memory but deny bodily continuity as a necessary condition for personal identity. Since memory claims are fallible, we need some way of distinguishing between mere claims to remember past performances and the actual remembering of these performances (which is infallible). But verification of memory claims

---

[20] B.A.O. Williams, "Personal Identity and Individuation," *Proceedings of the Aristotelian Society* 57 (1956-7): 229.
[21] Ibid., 239.

presupposes (1) previous physical (embodied) existence, and (2) continuous contemporary physical existence. Only if the person now exists physically continuous for a time can we test whether that person can correctly use the term "remember," that is, whether the person understands memory language. And only if the person existed for a length of time embodied can we check out claims to remember. But if this is the case, the objection proceeds, memory is not an independent standard of personal identity; it presupposes and is dependent upon bodily continuity.[22]

That the appeal to memory is dependent upon *previous*[23] continued bodily existence is indisputable. To use an illustration from B.A.O. Williams, suppose that a man went to a crowded party, where he sees a girl who is like all the other girls at the party except that she has red hair. This girl sings various songs and quarrels with the band; she is easily identified on each occasion by the color of her hair. The man later meets a platinum blonde who recalls singing songs at a party and quarreling with the band. He can identify her as the red-haired girl at the party, even though she has changed the color of her hair in the meantime.... [However] if the girl had remarkably changed the color of her hair between songs and before the quarrel, identifying her at the various stages of the party would have been more difficult, but not impossible; but if [she] had changed bodies frequently, identification would become not just difficult but impossible.[24]

In such a case, the recollection by the platinum blonde encountered later of being the singer at the party would be difficult or impossible to verify, because there was no continuously existent, embodied singer to be identified with.

That some sort of bodily continuity during the event remembered is required by the criterion of memory (to enable witnesses to identify the person who performed such and such a token act) does not entail that there *always* had to be bodily continuity. That is, it does not entail that the platinum blonde necessarily had continuous existence between the party and the later encounter. She might have ceased to exist immediately after the party and was re-created prior to the second encounter. In such a case it would be (theoretically) possible both to check out her memory claims about the past and also to test now whether she can correctly use "remember." Thus, though memory as a criterion for personal identity presupposes that at some time or other (that is, during the events which are purportedly remembered) there was or is bodily continuity on the part of the individual, this does not entail the stronger thesis that memory is dependent upon unbroken bodily continuity.

The second objection is that merely to have memory claims about being the person who performed such and such actions at a previous time does not *compel* us to assert the identity of the individual who makes the memory claims with the individual whose actions are purportedly recalled. The reason for this is that "it is not logically impossible that two different persons should *claim* to remember being this man, and this is the most we can get."[25]

Again, consider Charles and Robert, who come into existence or undergo changes and who both claim to remember performing actions that Guy performed. If we grant that one individual cannot be in two places at the same time, then as external observers we cannot identify both with Guy. Neither can we say that one is he but the other is only like him, for we have no way of determining which is which.

---

[22] Terence Penelhum, *Survival and Disembodied Existence* (London: Routledge & Kegan Paul, 1970), 56.
[23] That it is dependent upon *present* bodily existence is more disputable. That I now have a true memory claim is not dependent upon someone else being able to check whether I use "remember" properly or consistently, unless one contends that I cannot know for myself when I am correctly using such. Fortunately, we can avoid this problem by granting the above claim, since we are not arguing for disembodied but rather embodied future existence.
[24] Williams, 242.
[25] Ibid, 238.

So it would be best, if anything, to say that both had mysteriously become like Guy, clairvoyantly know about him, or something like this. If this would be the best description of each of the two, why would it not be the best description of Charles if Charles alone were changed?[26]

Thus, it is concluded, memory claims are not sufficient to force us to conclude that the re-created individual is identical with rather than merely similar to the deceased. Only if there were determinable bodily continuity could we guarantee that Charles and not Robert is Guy. In effect, whether or not such a person is the same is a matter of linguistic decision: it depends on whether we choose to call him the same person. We can opt for identity, but it is not logically requisite that we do so. This conventionality is purportedly fatal to the re-creationists' position, for they have failed to provide a criterion to ensure that the person in the after-life is identical with the deceased and not merely similar to him.[27]

This argument, of course, does not establish that Charles is not and cannot be Guy. That he is Guy remains logically possible. What it does indicate is that the conclusion that he really is Guy rather than merely like him (similar to him in the above-described respects) is not necessary. However, to say that it is a matter of decision is *not* to say that the decision is arbitrary. The decision that he is the same person as Guy can be made on the ground that, not only is there no good reason not to identify him with Guy (in the case where there is only one such claimant), but there is good reason to thus identify him. Of course two people could look alike, have the same character and skills, personality and memory claims, and still be merely similar. There is no way of deducing identity from these features (though of course the greater the extent of these similarities, the greater the likelihood that we are dealing with the same individual and not merely a similar one). However, two people cannot have the same memories (make true memory claims) about deeds performed only by one agent and still not be the same. Accordingly, if one holds that seriously proffered memory claims about past actions are frequently (though by no means always) right, one has good reason to say that Charles is Guy, not merely similar to him. Though this does not enable us to decide the reliability of any one particular memory claim, where a large bank of verifiable claims exists, we have good reason for claiming identity.

It might be true that if there were more than one claimant with identical features, we would have a way to determine that one rather than another is identical with the deceased, for we could not decide whose memory claims were true and whose were false. However, as we noted above, it would be impossible for God to re-create more than one individual per deceased.

A different response is suggested by Lynne Baker who, using her Constitution View of the person, appeals to a first-person perspective to determine identity. Human persons are persons because they have a first-person perspective. But one can be embodied without having a first-person perspective; all sorts of animals are bodied beings lacking this perspective. Persons, then, are not identical to but constituted by their body, and the sameness of persons between times is the sameness of their first-person perspective, not the sameness of the body.[28] Whereas the relation between me and my first-person perspective is necessary, the relation between me and a body is contingent though essential (to exist I must be embodied in some form). Given this view, suppose that God made 100 replicas of my body. Although these replicas have identically constituted bodies, they cannot have my first-person perspective, that which makes a person me. Others might not be able to distinguish me from the replicas, but I know who I am in virtue of my first-person perspective. Although sameness of first-person perspective is the criterion for

---

[26] Ibid, 239.
[27] C.B. Martin, *Religious Belief* (Ithaca, N.Y.: Cornell University Press, 1959), 106-7.
[28] Lynne Rudder Baker, "Material Persons and the Doctrine of Resurrection," *Faith and Philosophy* 18 (April 2001): 160.

sameness of person over time, there is no criterion for sameness of first-person perspective.[29] The re-created person is identical to the deceased because of this basic awareness of the self.

In short, the multiple replicas objection fails. It is logically impossible for God to make two persons identical to the deceased. Further, one might appeal to true memories or a first-person perspective to establish the identity of the re-created with the deceased.

Application to Immortality

One might wonder whether immortality understood in this fashion really is desirable. In particular, would I want to be precisely identical to the way I was at the time of my death? If I died in old age, would a future life of decrepitude or senility be meaningful or desirable? If I died of a disease that inflicted tormenting pain or irreversible debilitation, would I want to be re-created at a point where this would continue?

The re-creationist, however, is not committed to a position that requires exact similarity of the re-created to the deceased in every detail. Above we noted that what is required is that the features instantiated be substantially similar to those of the deceased. That is, the re-created person can be different in ways that do not essentially affect that person's personal identity; modification of features—physical, mental, personality—do not necessarily constitute a falsifying condition of the identity of that person with the deceased. For example, if between the time I last saw my father and the next time I see him, he loses an appreciable amount of hair, gains visible inches at the waist, or even loses one of his limbs, I would still be able to identify him as the same individual who I once called my father. Similarly with personality and mental traits: if he has become more forgetful or has changed his opinions about things, he could still be identified by me as my father.

Perhaps the discussion here is misguided, for it approaches the question of identity from the perspective of the other person: the second party point of view. Perhaps what ought to be emphasized is the appeal to a first-person perspective. As we noted above, Baker claims that a human person is a person because that person has a first-person perspective. A distinct advantage of this view is that it "allows that a person's resurrection body may be non-identical with her earthly biological body."[30] Since I am not identical with but constituted by my body, it is possible that my first-person perspective be in or from a different body, just as it was possible that Michelangelo carved his masterpiece "David" out of a different piece of marble or even wood. The particular marble he used was contingent, though "David" could not have existed without some sculpted medium. This view can well accommodate those who maintain a psychological criterion of identity of some sort and who at the same time allow that changes in the physical dimension do not destroy personal identity.

How much one can alter specific physical, mental, and personality traits before one loses one's personal identity is a difficult and perhaps ultimately irresolvable problem. The very quest for a critical threshold might itself be meaningless. What can be affirmed, however, is that some changes can occur in re-created persons without persons losing their identity. This means that the re-creationist is not committed to requiring that the re-created person be identical in all respects to the deceased, only in the essential respects. Hence, the believer in life after death need not worry about beginning the re-created life with the impediments that were associated with death.

---

[29] William Hasker argues that a first-person perspective criterion is not a criterion at all. To have a first-person perspective is to see things from the perspective of a particular person. I see things the way I do because of who I am as a distinct person. But then "to say that P_1 and P_2 have the same first-person perspective is just to say that P_1 and P_2 are the same person, and the criterion [of a first person perspective] reduces to a tautology." "The Constitution View of Persons: A Critique," unpublished paper, 16.

[30] Baker, "Material Persons and the Doctrine of Resurrection," 164.

Finally, one should be careful to distinguish what is possible under anthropological monism from what is possible under anthropological pluralism. Under traditional dualism, death of the person is not possible; immortality, literally, is provided for by the persistence of a soul-entity that is myself and does not die. Under anthropological monism survival is not possible. The individual is not literally immortal, but dies. What is possible is *life after death*. Thus, if one adopts a monistic view of humans, one should distinguish life after death from survival (or "immorality" narrowly defined as "not-dying"). Only life after death is possible under the monist view. Hence, monists should be guarded about their language, perhaps even best avoiding the term "immortality."

We have shown that the objectors fail to establish that the re-creationist's thesis is rationally incoherent. So long as the re-created person has the same or substantially similar physical, mental, and personality traits and memories to the deceased, or has the same first-person perspective, we can reasonably conclude that the re-created person can be and probably is identical with the deceased. Lack of bodily continuity is insufficient to falsify the person's claim to personal identity with the deceased. Thus, even on a monistic view of the nature of humans, life after death is possible.

Questions

1. Does Reichenbach favor Behaviourism or the Identity Theory?
2. Reichenbach responds to several objections to his Identity Theory. What are they?
3. What does Reichenbach mean by "recreationism?"
4. How does Reichenbach handle the matter of a continuing identity?
5. Which position seems more compatible with the Christian data, Reichenbach's materialism or dualism?

THE POSSIBILITY OF RESURRECTION*

Peter van Inwagen

In this essay van Inwagen argues that the Christian doctrine of the resurrection is possible. He rejects what he calls the "Aristotelian" view that bodies are reconstituted, and offers instead a recreationist account that allows for continuity and personal recognition in the resurrected state.

The real philosophical problem facing the doctrine of resurrection does not seem to me to be that there is no criterion that the men of the new age could apply to determine whether someone then alive was the same man as some man who had died before the Last Day; the problem seems to me to be that there *is* such a criterion and (given certain facts about the present age) it would, of necessity, yield the result that many men who have died in our own lifetime and earlier will not be found among those who live *after* the Last Day.

Let us consider an analogy. Suppose a certain monastery claims to have in its possession a manuscript written in St. Augustine's own hand. And suppose the monks of this monastery further claim that this manuscript was burned by Arians in the year 457. It would immediately occur to me to ask how *this* manuscript, the one I can touch, could be the very manuscript that was burned in 457. Suppose their answer to this question is that God miraculously recreated Augustine's manuscript in 458. I should respond to this answer as follows: the deed it describes seems quite impossible, even as an accomplishment of omnipotence. God certainly might have created a perfect duplicate of the original manuscript, but it would not be *that* one; its earliest moment of existence would have been after Augustine's death; it would never have known the impress of his hand; it would not have been a part of the furniture of the world when he was alive; and so on.

Now suppose our monks were to reply by simply asserting that the manuscript now in their possession *did* know the impress of Augustine's hand; that it *was* a part of the furniture of the world when the Saint was alive; that when God recreated or restored it, He (as an indispensable component of accomplishing this task) saw to it that the object He produced had all these properties.

I confess I should not know what to make of this. I should have to tell the monks that I did not see how what they believed could *possibly* be true. They might of course reply that their belief is a mystery, that God had *some* way of restoring the lost manuscript, but that the procedure surpasses human understanding. Now I am sometimes willing to accept such answers; for example, in the case of the doctrine of the Trinity. But there are cases in which I would never accept such an answer. For example, if there were a religion that claimed that God had created two adjacent mountains without thereby bringing into existence an intermediate valley, I should regard any attempt to defend this doctrine as a "mystery" as so much whistle-talk. After all, I can hardly expect to be able to understand the Divine Nature; but I do understand mountains and valleys. And I understand manuscripts, too. I understand them sufficiently well to be quite confident that the monks' story is impossible. Still, I wish to be reasonable. I admit that one can be mistaken about conceptual truth and falsehood. I know from experience that a proposition that *seems* to force itself irresistibly upon the mind as a conceptual truth can turn out to be false. (If I had been alive in 1890, I should doubtless have regarded the Galilean Law of the Addition of

---

* Reprinted from "The Possibility of Resurrection." *International Journal for Philosophy of Religion* (1978) by permission of the publisher.

Velocities and the Unrestricted Comprehension Principle in set theory as obvious conceptual truths.) Being reasonable, therefore, I am willing to listen to any *argument* the monks might have for the conclusion that what they believe is possible. Most arguments for the conclusion that a certain proposition is possible true take the form of a story that (the arguer hopes) the person to whom the argument is addressed will accept as possible, and which (the arguer attempts to show) entails the proposition whose modal status is in question.

Can such a story be told about the manuscript of Augustine? Suppose one of the monks is, in a very loose sense, an Aristotelian. He tells the following story (a version of a very popular tale): "Augustine's manuscript consisted of a certain 'parcel' of matter upon which a certain form had been impressed. It ceased to exist when this parcel of matter was radically deformed. To recreate it, God needed only to collect the matter (in modern terms, the atoms) that once composed it and reimpress that form upon it (in modern terms, cause these atoms to stand to one another in the same spatial and chemical relationships they previously stood in)."

This story is defective. The manuscript God creates in the story is not the manuscript that was destroyed, since the various atoms that compose the tracings of ink on its surface occupy their present positions not as a result of Augustine's activity but of God's. Thus what we have is not a manuscript in Augustine's hand. (Strictly speaking, it is not even a *manuscript*.) (Compare the following conversation: "Is that the house of blocks your daughter built this morning?" "No, I built this one after I accidentally knocked hers down. I put all the blocks just where she did, though. Don't tell her.")

I think the philosophical problems that arise in connection with the buried manuscript of St. Augustine are very like the problems that arise in connection with the doctrine of the Resurrection. If a man should be totally destroyed, then it is very hard to see how any man who comes into existence thereafter could be the *same* man. And I say this not because I have no criterion of identity I can employ in such cases, but because I have a criterion of identity for men and it is, or *seems* to be, violated. And the popular quasi-Aristotelian story which is often supposed to establish the conceptual possibility of God's restoring to existence a man who has been totally destroyed does not lead me to think that I have got the wrong criterion or that I am misapplying the right one. The popular story, of course, is the story according to which God collects the atoms that once composed a certain man and restores them to the positions they occupied relative to one another when that man was alive; thereby (the story-teller contends) God restores the man himself. But this story, it seems to me, does not "work." The atoms of which I am composed occupy at each instant the positions they do because of the operations of certain processes within me (those processes that, taken collectively, constitute my being alive). Even when I become a corpse—provided I decay slowly and am not, say, cremated—the atoms that compose me will occupy the positions relative to one another that they do occupy *largely* because of the processes of life that *used* to go on within me: or this will be the case for at least some short period. Thus a former corpse in which the processes of life have been "started up again" may well be the very man who was once before alive, provided the processes of dissolution did not progress too far while he was a corpse. But if a man does not simply die but is totally destroyed (as in the case of cremation) then *he* can never be reconstituted, for the causal chain has been irrevocably broken. If God collects the atoms that used to constitute that man and "reassembles" them, they will occupy the positions relative to one another they occupy because of God's miracle and not because of the operation of the natural processes that, taken collectively, were the life of that man. (I should also be willing to defend the following theses: the thing such an action of God's would produce would not be a member of our species and would not speak a language or have memories of any sort, though, of course, he—or *it*—would *appear* to have these features.)

This much is analogous to the case of the burned manuscript. Possibly no one will find what I have said very convincing unless he thinks very much like me. Let me offer three arguments against an "Aristotelian" account of the Resurrection that have no analogues in the case of the manuscript, and which will perhaps be more convincing to the generality of philosophers. Arguments (a) and (b) are *ad homines*, directed against Christians who might be inclined towards the "Aristotelian" theory. Argument (c) attempts to show that the "Artistotelian" theory has an impossible consequence.

a. The atoms of which I am composed cannot be destroyed by burning or the natural processes of decay; but they *can* be destroyed, as can atomic nuclei and even subatomic particles. (Or so it would seem: the principles for identity through time for subatomic particles are very hazy; physical theory has little if anything to say on the subject.) If, in order to raise a man on the Day of Judgment, God had to collect the "building blocks"—atoms, neutrons, or what have you—of which that man had once been composed, then a wicked man could hope to escape God's wrath by seeing to it that all his "buildings blocks" were destroyed. But according to Christian theology, such a hope is senseless. Thus, unless the nature of the ultimate constituents of matter is different from what it appears to be, the "Aristotelian" theory is inimical to a central point of Christian theology.

b. The atoms (or what have you) of which I am composed may very well have been parts of other people at some time in the past. Thus, if the "Aristotelian" theory is true, there could be a problem on the day of resurrection about *who* is resurrected. In fact, if that theory were true, a wicked man who had read his Aquinas might hope to escape punishment in the age to come by becoming a lifelong cannibal. But again, the possibility of such a hope cannot be admitted by any Christian.

c. It is possible that none of the atoms that are now parts of me were parts of me when I was ten years old. It is therefore possible that God could collect all the atoms that were parts of me when I was ten, without destroying me, and restore them to the positions they occupied relative to one another in 1952. If the "Aristotelian" theory were correct, this action would be sufficient for the creation of a boy who could truly say, "I am Peter van Inwagen." In fact, he and I could stand facing one another and each say truly to the other, "I am you." But this is conceptually impossible, and therefore, the "Aristotelian" theory is *not* correct.

No story other than our "Aristotelian" story about how it might be that a man who was totally destroyed could live again seems even superficially plausible. I conclude that my initial judgment is correct and that it is absolutely impossible, even as an accomplishment of God, that a man who has been burned to ashes or been eaten by worms should ever live again. What follows from this about the Christian hope of resurrection? Very little of any interest, I think. All that follows is that if Christianity is true, then what I earlier called "certain facts about the present age" are *not* facts.

It is part of the Christian faith that all men who share in the sin of Adam must die. What does it mean to say that I must die? Just this: that one day I shall be composed entirely of non-living matter; that is, I shall be a corpse. It is not part of the Christian faith that I must at any time be totally annihilated or disintegrate. (One might note that Christ, whose story is supposed to provide the archetype for the story of each man's resurrection, became a corpse but did not, even in His human nature, cease to exist.) It is of course true that men apparently cease to exist: those who are cremated, for example. But it contradicts nothing in the creeds to suppose that this is not what really happens, and that God preserves our corpses contrary to all appearance.... Perhaps at the moment of each man's death, God removes his corpse and replaces it with a simulacrum which is what is burned or rots. Or perhaps God is not quite so wholesale as this: perhaps He removes for "safekeeping" only the "core person"—the brain and central nervous system—or even some special part of it. These are details.

I take it that this story shows that the resurrection is a feat an almighty being *could* accomplish. I think this is the *only* way such a being could accomplish it. Perhaps I'm wrong, but that's of little importance. What *is* important is that God can accomplish it this way or some other. Of course one might wonder *why* God would go such lengths to make it look as if most people not only die but pass into complete nothingness. This is a difficult question. I think it can be given a plausible answer, but not apart from a discussion of the nature of religious belief. I will say just this. If corpses inexplicably disappeared no matter how carefully they were guarded, or inexplicably refused to decay and were miraculously resistant to the most persistent and ingenious attempts to destroy them, then we should be living in a world in which observable events that were *obviously* miraculous, *obviously* due to the intervention of a power beyond Nature, happened with monotonous regularity. In such a world we should all believe in the supernatural: its existence would be the best explanation for the observed phenomena. If Christianity is true, God wants us to believe in the supernatural. But experience shows us that, if there is a God, He does not do what He very well *could* do: provide us with a ceaseless torrent of public, undeniable evidence of a power outside the natural order. And perhaps it is not hard to think of good reasons for such a policy.

Questions

1. Peter van Inwagen sees a philosophical problem facing the doctrine of the resurrection. What is it?
2. How is the case of the buried manuscript analogous to resurrection of the body?
3. What is the "impossible consequence" of the Aristotelian theory?
4. According to van Inwagen, what does it mean to say, "I must die?"
5. What does van Inwagen think happens in the resurrection?

WHAT MAKES ME ME[*]

Richard Swinburne[1]

Swinburne argues here that persons are constituted of mind and body, but what constitutes personal identity resides in the soulish part and personal continuity also resides here. Each person has a "thisness" that is not body or physical dependent. In the final state, the soul will be reunited with the body in the resurrection, and he concludes that the soul will again be in a relationship of interaction with the resurrected body.

I seek in this paper to defend the view that each of us on Earth consists of two parts—a physical body and a non-physical soul. They interact with each other. Events in my body cause events in my soul (if you stick a needle in my arm, I feel pain), and events in my soul cause events in my body (if I decide to move my arm, my arm moves). The soul is the essential part of me. I am who I am in virtue of my soul; I go where it goes. When my body ceases to function, I die. But my soul is still there; and if there is a God—as I believe, he can cause it to function again either without a body or with a body reassembled from my bones in my grave or with an entirely new body. All of this is of course the view of Plato and Descartes. It is also the traditional Christian view, but the arguments which I shall give in its favor are ones quite independent of theological considerations.

First, let me define some technical terms. I define a *substance* as a thing, a component of the world. Thus tables, stars, and persons are substances. I define a *property* as a characteristic, which belongs to one substance (such as being yellow, or having a mass of two pounds), or is a relation between substances (such as being-taller-than or lying-between). I define an *event* as the instantiation of a property in a particular substance or substances at a particular time (such as this tie being brown at 4 pm on June 4th 2004, or Birmingham now lying between Manchester and London). A property of a substance is an essential property if necessarily that substance would not exist without that property. Thus occupying space is an essential property of my desk; it could not continue to exist and yet occupy no volume of space. The history of the world just is all the events which occur. It is this substance existing (that is having its essential properties) for a period, now acquiring this non-essential property, now losing that non-essential property, now acquiring this relation to another substance, now losing this relation, and then not existing any more. It includes for example the existence of this table for a certain period, the table being brown, then being painted red, then being six meters from that wall, then becoming only three meters from the wall; and so on until it exists no more. If you knew all the events which occurred, that is which properties were instantiated in which substances when, you would know the whole history of the world.

I shall understand by a *mental property* one to whose instantiation the substance in whom it is instantiated necessarily has privileged access on all occasions of its instantiation, and a physical property one to whose instantiation the substance concerned necessarily has no privileged access on any occasion of its instantiation. Someone has privileged access to whether

---

[*] This article printed by courtesy of Richard Swinburne.

[1] This lecture is a short presentation of views developed at length in my book *The Evolution of the Soul*, second edition, Clarendon Press, 1997. The most recent very rigorous account of these views is that in my paper 'Mental/Physical Identity and Supervenience Theories' forthcoming a volume co-edited by Peter van Inwagen and Dean Zimmerman, to be published by the Oxford University Press. The present lecture summarizes the latter paper.

a property *P* is instantiated in him in the sense that whatever ways others have of finding this out, it is logically possible that he can use, but he has a further way (by experiencing it) which it is not logically possible that others can use. A pure mental property may then be defined as one whose instantiation does not entail the instantiation of a physical property. I shall understand by a *mental event* one to whose occurrence the substance involved in it has privileged access; and by a *physical event* one to whose occurrence there is no privileged access; and by a *pure mental event* one whose occurrence does not entail the occurrence of any physical event. Mental events (normally) involve the instantiation of mental properties, pure mental events (normally) involve the instantiation only of pure mental properties, and physical events (normally) involve the instantiation only of physical properties.[2]

A mental substance is one to whose existence that substance necessarily has privileged access, and a physical substance is a substance to whose existence that substance necessarily has no privileged access, that is a public substance. It looks as if you and I are mental substances, whereas the desk is a physical substance. Since having privileged access to anything is itself a mental property, and some one who has any other mental property has that one, mental substances are just those for which some mental properties are essential. And we may define a pure mental substance as one for which only pure mental properties are essential (together with any properties entailed by the possession of pure mental properties) (Such a pure mental substance may have, contingently—that is, non-essentially—also physical properties.) I shall be arguing in due course that we, you and I, are pure mental substances.

Evidently—more evidently than anything else—there really are mental events, involving the instantiation of mental properties, as we know from our own experience. They include our perceptions (my seeing the desk) and intentional actions (my intentionally moving the desk) as well as anyone else could. For I have a way of knowing about what I am seeing and what I am doing intentionally other than the ways available to the best other student of my behavior or brain: I actually experience perceiving and intentionally acting. But neither of the two events which I have just mentioned are pure mental events, for they each include a physical component. My seeing the desk entails that the desk exists, and so does my moving the desk. But each of these mental events also includes a pure mental event as a component—my believing that there is a desk in front of me, and my trying to move the desk. Our mental lives consist of a succession of pure mental events. They include the pattern of color in my visual field, pains and thrills, beliefs, thoughts and feelings, and the intentions which I try to realize through my body or in some other way. My being in pain at midday yesterday, or having a red image in my visual field, or thinking about lunch, or forming the intention of going to London—are also such that if others could find out about them by some method, I could find out about them by the same method. Others can learn about my pains and thoughts by studying my behavior and perhaps also by studying my brain. Yet I too could study my behavior—I could watch a film of myself; I could study my brain—via a system of mirrors and microscopes—just as well as anyone else could. But, of course, I have a way of knowing about my pains, thoughts, and suchlike other than those available to the best other student of my behavior or brain: I actually experience them. But the

---

[2] My definitions of mental and physical properties have the consequence that there are some properties which are neither mental nor physical—let us call them 'neutral properties'. They include formal properties (e.g. 'being a substance') and disjunctive properties ('being in pain or weighing ten stone'). The existence of such properties leads to my including the 'normally' in my definitions of the different kinds of event. For although all events which involve only the instantiation of (pure) mental properties are (pure) mental events, there are (pure) mental events which involve the instantiation of neutral properties, e.g. the event of me being-in-pain-or-weighing-ten-stone. And analogously for physical events.

events I have just been discussing contain no other event to which there is public access. Consequently, they must be distinct from brain events, or any other bodily events. A Martian who came to earth, captured a human bring, and inspected his brain could discover everything that was happening in that brain but would still wonder 'Does this human really feel anything when I stamp on his toe?' It is a further fact beyond the occurrence of brain events that there are pains and after-images, thoughts, and intentions. You would certainly not know the whole history of world if you knew only which physical events had occurred.

In making this point, I do not of course deny that most of my pure mental events are caused by my brain events. Clearly most of the passive mental events—the ones which we find ourselves having, sensations, thoughts, beliefs and desires—are caused at least in part by brain events, themselves often caused by further bodily events; while some mental events are caused, at least in part by other mental events. My toothache is caused by a brain event caused by tooth decay. A thought that represents the conclusion of a deductive inference is caused (at least in part) by other thoughts encapsulating the premises of that inference. And in the other direction our intentions cause brain events which in turn cause further bodily events. Our embodiment consists in there being these mental-physical connections.

To know the whole history of the world you would need to know not merely which properties had been instantiated, but in which substances they had been instantiated—who had the toothache or the thought, for example which human being had them. I and my hearers are human beings, persons of a particular kind. A person would not exist unless he had a capacity for a mental life (a capacity to have sensations, thoughts etc.); and having such a capacity is itself a mental property (one to the instantiation of which in a subject he has privileged access.) Hence persons are mental substances, although as far as anything I have said so far is concerned, they might need some physical properties (e.g. those involved in having a body), as well as a mental property, in order to exist.

Now what constitutes a substance being the same substance as a previous substance? What constitutes this desk being the same desk as was here last week? First, the two substances have to belong to the same kind of substance. This desk can only be the same substance as some substance last week if that one was also a desk. This person can only be the same as that person if they are both persons. Secondly (dependent on the kind of substance involved) they have to have all or most of the same parts, or parts obtained by gradual replacement from the previous parts. Artifacts have to have most of the same parts; for this desk to be the same as the desk here last week it has to have most of the same parts. Organisms, such as plants, may over the course of time have all their parts replaced, but the replacement has to be gradual—now this part, now that part, and the new parts have to play somewhat the same role in the organism as the replaced parts did. At the other extreme, 'simple' substances which are not composed of separable parts and thus in effect have just one part, have to continue to have that part; plausibly electrons are like this.

So what constitutes the identity of a person? We have many physical parts, that is parts which are themselves physical substances—such as arms, legs, and liver. One theory is—we are the same person if we have enough of the same physical parts (or ones obtained by gradual replacement) connected with mental properties: our being a person consists in us having mental properties, our being the same person consists in us having more-or-less the same physical parts. One may think that certain parts are more important than others—a person needs the same brain, or most of the same brain in order to continue to exist. But the main point on this theory is that my continuing to exist consists in some number of particular parts of me continuing to exist, connected with mental properties. Aristotle, like many more recent philosophers, would have been happy with that answer. But it must be mistaken, because knowing what has happened to all physical bits of me (whatever your particular account of which of them are crucial), won't always tell you what has happened to me. Some particular fate for all the physical bits is compatible with me having either of two very different fates.

Let me illustrate this with the example of brain transplants. The brain consists of two hemispheres and a brain stem. There is good evidence that humans can survive and behave as conscious beings if much of one hemisphere is destroyed. Now imagine my brain (hemispheres plus brain-stem) divided into two, and each half-brain taken out of my skull and transplanted into the empty skull of a body from which a brain has just been removed; and there to be added to each half-brain from some other brain (e.g. the brain of my identical twin or a clone of me) whatever other parts (e.g. more brain-stem, and perhaps some of the other hemisphere) are necessary in order for the transplant to take and for there to be living persons with lives of conscious experiences. I cannot see that there are any insuperable theoretical difficulties standing in the way of such an operation. (Indeed that is a mild understatement—I fully expect it to be done one day.) We are, therefore, entitled to ask further question—if this operation were done and we then had two living persons, both with lives of conscious experiences, which would be me? Probably both would to some extent behave like me and claim to be me and to remember having done what I did; for behavior and speech depend, in large part, on brain-states, and there are very considerable overlaps between the 'information' carried by the two hemispheres which give rise to behavior and speech. But both persons would not be me. For if they were both identical with me, they would be the same person as each other (if a is the same as b, and b is the same as c, then a is the same as c) and they are not. They now have different experiences and lead different lives. There remain three other possibilities: that the person with my right half-brain is me, or that the person with my left half-brain is me, or that neither is me. But we cannot be certain which holds. Derek Parfit has claimed that what matters in such cases is not identity (that is, which person is me), but what he calls survival (which is for Parfit a matter of degree, and is constituted by the extent of psychological connectedness and continuity of a later person with a previous person). But, as Parfit would, I think, acknowledge, his view is counter-intuitive. The mere existence of a later person whose psychological states are in large part caused by my present psychological states is not what I hope for, when I hope to survive an operation (in the normal sense of 'survive'). It would need some very strong philosophical arguments to show that my normal hope is incoherent and so we should make do with hoping for Parfitian survival. The two such arguments normally deployed are so weak as to be hardly worth calling arguments. There is the argument that in such a situation we would never be able to discover which person was me. But if so, so what? Humans are not omniscient. Why should we expect them to be able to discover this? And then there is the argument that, if a person being me is all-or-nothing, as we took away more and more of my neurons and replacing them with neurons from elsewhere, just replacing one last neuron would make someone to cease to be me. True, but so what? Quantum theory and Chaos theory have taught us that very small causes can produce very large effects.

So to revert to the split-brain experiment—there is a crucial factual issue here, which can be shown if we imagine that I have been captured by a mad surgeon who is about to perform the split-brain operation on me. He tells me (and I have every reason to believe him) that the person to be formed from my left half-brain is to have an enjoyable life and the person to be formed from my right half-brain is to be subjected to a life of torture. Whether my future life will be happy or painful, or whether I shall survive an operation at all, are clearly factual questions. Yet, as I await the transplant and know exactly what will happen to my brain, I am in no position to know the answer to the question—what will happen to me. Maybe neither future person will be me—it may be that cutting the brain stem will destroy the original person once and for all, and that, although repairing the severed stem will create two new persons, neither of them will be me. Perhaps I will be the left-half-brain person, or maybe it will be the right-half-brain person who will be me. Even if one subsequent person resembles the earlier me more in character and memory claims than does the other, that one may not be me. Maybe I will survive the operation but be changed in character and have lost much of my memory as a result of it, in consequence of which the other subsequent person will resemble the earlier me more in his public behavior than I will.

Reflection on this thought experiment shows that, however much we know about what has happened to my brain—we might know exactly what has happened to every atom in it—and to every other physical part of me, we would not know what has happened to me. For many particular fates for all the bits of my brain are compatible with either of two very different fates happening to me. I could survive without my left-brain and not survive with it; and so the left half-brain surviving couldn't be what constituted my survival (although of course it might be evidence of it). But my surviving must consist in some part or parts of me surviving. Our ignorance about whether I have survived or not must therefore consist in ignorance about whether some non-physical part has survived. So there must be more to me than the matter of which my body and brain are made, a further essential non-physical part whose continuing in existence makes the brain (and so body) to which it is connected my brain (and body), and to this something I give the traditional name of 'soul'. I am my soul plus whatever brain (and body) it is connected to. Normally my soul goes when my brain goes, but in unusual circumstances (such as when my brain is split) it is uncertain where it goes.

Take a slightly different example. I die of a brain hemorrhage which today's doctors cannot cure, but my relatives take my corpse and put it straight into a deep freeze in California. Shortly thereafter there is an earthquake as a result of which my frozen brain is split into many parts, a few of which get lost. However, fifty years later, when medical technology has improved, my descendants take the bits of my broken corpse, warm it up and mend it, replacing the missing parts from elsewhere. The body becomes the body of a living person who behaves somewhat like me and seems to remember quite a lot of my past life. Have I come to life again, or not? Maybe, maybe not. Again there is a truth here, about whether I have survived the hemorrhage as I wanted to, and yet a truth of which we cannot be sure, however much we know about the story of my brain. Hence, my survival consists in the continuing of something else, which I call my soul, linked to my previous body; and I survive in this new body if and only if that soul is connected with it. And note that the extra truth is not a truth about what kind of mental life is connected to the brain. It is not a truth about mental properties, about what thoughts and feelings and purposes the revived person has. Rather, the extra truth, the truth about whether I have survived, is a truth about *who* the revived person is, that is in which substance those properties are instantiated. And, since mere knowledge of what has happened to every physical substance does not tell me that, it must be (at least in part) a truth about a (non-physical, that is) pure mental substance. So long as I continue to have thoughts and feelings and purposes, I have survived any operation—whatever happens to any particular physical parts of me. So my soul is an essential part of me—its survival is necessary for survival.

All that I have shown so far is that the survival of a non-physical part is necessary for my survival; but that leaves open the possibility that some physical part or other of my previous body (it does not matter which part) has to be combined with my soul in order for me to survive. But now suppose again I have a severe brain disease affecting the right brain hemisphere. The only way to keep the body functioning is to replace this hemisphere. So the doctors remove my current right-hemisphere and replace it by a right hemisphere taken from my clone or identical twin, and join it to my left hemisphere. Alas, the disease spreads to the left hemisphere, and so that too has to be replaced. Have I survived or not? Again, who can say? But clearly my survival is perfectly compatible with all the physical parts which originally composed my body being destroyed. Perhaps you may suggest that I survive if and only if the replacement of bits is done gradually, so that for example the new right hemisphere has to interact with the old left-hemisphere for at least two minutes before the latter is replaced, if I am to survive. But while that might be physically necessary for my survival, to suppose that a 2-minute as opposed to a mere 1-minute contact of new parts with old is what constitutes my survival is absurd. It's not logically necessary for my survival, though it might be evidence of it. Whether I survive is a further truth about the world additional to truths about what has happened to all the physical bits of me, and quite apart from which mental properties are associated with those physical bits.

But don't I have to have some brain or body in order to exist? Maybe, given the way things work in the world at present, that is physically necessary. Souls can exist and function only when connected to a functioning brain. But clearly this is not logically necessary. There is no logical incompatibility in supposing that I continue to exist and function without a body. I noted earlier that I have a body if and only if there is some physical substance with which I interact causally in certain ways. But there is nothing logically contradictory in supposing that these connections with a body are broken and yet I go on having thoughts and feelings; and maybe even come to have the ability to make a difference to the world and learn about it without having to do so through one particular physical substance. Nor is there any contradiction in supposing that my body could be destroyed totally at an instant (without any replacement of parts) and yet I continue to think and feel. But it could only be logically possible that that could happen to me, if I have now already another part—a non-bodily part—whose continuing in existence constitutes my continuing in existence. For a substance can only continue to exist if a part of it continues to exist. So I must now have a soul, a pure mental substance which is the essential me.

My body is only a contingent part of me. Since my having physical properties (e.g. weight and size) entails my body having these properties, and my having mental properties entails only the existence of my soul, it follows that physical properties belong to me in virtue of belonging to my body and mental properties belong to me in virtue of belonging to my soul. The full story of the world will include what happens to each of our two parts—it will record the thoughts and feelings of souls, as well as the weights and volumes of bodies.

My arguments have depended on claims that certain events are compatible with other events, e.g. me surviving is compatible with my body being destroyed; or on claims that certain events involve others, e.g. that every part of me being destroyed at an instant involves me being destroyed. How do I know which events are compatible with, and which events involve other events? In so far as events are described in ways which convey the essence of the substances, properties etc involved, it is a pure a priori exercise to detect whether the description of one event is compatible with or involves the description of another event. The compatibility is logical compatibility, the involvement is entailment. A proposition p is compatible with a proposition q, if and only if ($p\&q$) entails no contradiction. You can show that some supposition entails a contradiction by deducing the contradiction. You can show that 'A is taller than B, and B is taller than C, and C is taller than A' entails a contradiction by deducing from it '(A is taller than B) and not (A is taller than B)'. That some supposition entails no contradiction is evidenced by no one yet having drawn a contradiction out of it, and by the fact that we can apparently make sense of the world being the way the supposition supposes, that is, we can postulate a more detailed supposition which is more evidently logically possible (that is, more evidently entails no contradiction) and entails the supposition in question. To take an example far away from our present concerns, how could one show that there being more than one space is logically possible (a space is a collection of places at some distance in some direction from each other)? There would be two spaces if there are places which are not at any distance in any direction from each other. I can show that this is logically possible only by describing such a world in detail in a comprehensible way (as for example in C.S. Lewis's Narnia stories), and by trying and failing to derive a contradiction therefrom.

But there is more to the compatibility of events than logical compatibility in the stated sense, and events may involve other events without there being the kind of entailment just described. Thirty years ago Kripke[3] and Putnam[4] drew our attention to the fact that substances (properties, events etc) may be picked out by referring expressions which are rather uninformative as to the nature of what is picked out. In that case, although there may be a truth that the object picked out could or could not coexist with some other object, or involve the existence of some other object, you would need first to discover empirically (a posteriori) more fully what had been picked out before you could know this.

Consider the proposition 'Hesperus is Phosphorus' as uttered by early Greeks, where Phosphorus is 'the morning star', the bright planet (as we now know it to be) which often appears before sunrise in the morning sky, and Hesperus is 'the evening star', the bright planet which often appears after sunset in the evening sky. We know that these planets are the same planet; the early Greeks did not know this. Given what 'Hesperus' picks out and what 'Phosphorus' picks out, 'Hesperus is not Phosphorus' not merely is not, but could not be true—since a thing must be identical with itself. Hesperus could not exist without Phosphorus existing, and conversely. Yet 'Hesperus is not Phosphorus' entails no contradiction—merely understanding the proposition would not enable you to see that what it asserted could not be the case. So even if being me does not entail being embodied—an opponent may suggest— maybe it is not possible for me to exist without my body existing because the existence of me involves the existence of my body. Even though there is no logical entailment of propositions here, the nature of what is in fact picked out by 'me' and 'my body' has this consequence—it may be suggested. This would be an a posteriori metaphysical necessity, a necessity as hard as the normal a priori logical necessity.

Metaphysical a posteriori necessity arises if you can know how to use the designating expressions ('Hesperus' and 'Phosphorus') on some occasions (e.g. when the object exhibits certain features) without knowing the nature of what is picked out, and so without knowing what constitutes being the same object on other occasions and so without being able to recognize that object on other occasions. We use 'Hesperus' to pick out a planet when it has the characteristic of appearing after sunset in the evening sky; but for any planet to be that planet it has to have (roughly) the same parts, that is to be made of the same matter. But you can refer to it without having discovered of what matter it is made and so without being able to identify it on other occasions and so in ignorance of whether it is the same planet as Phosphorus. Some of the other words which we use for picking out substances or properties or substance-kinds (e.g. 'water' as used in the eighteenth century) also pick out something as of that kind in virtue of superficial properties (e.g. being the stuff in our rivers and seas), when what constitutes being of that kind is a matter of the properties which underlie the superficial ones (e.g. being made of molecules of H_2O) which may be present when the superficial ones are not. Let's call such words as 'water'

---

[3] S. Kripke, 'Identity and Necessity' in (ed.) M.K. Munitz, *Identity and Individuation*, New York University Press, 1971; and 'Naming and Necessity' in (ed.) D. Davidson and G. Harman, *Semantics of Natural Language*, D. Reidel, 1972.

[4] H. Putnam, 'The Meaning of "meaning"', republished in his *Mind, Language, and Reality, Philosophical Papers, vol. 2*, Cambridge University Press, 1975.

(as used in the eighteenth century) or 'Hesperus' (as used by early Greeks) uninformative designators.

However, most of the words we use to pick out properties (e.g. 'green' or 'square'), as opposed to substances, are not of this character. What makes a property the property of being green is what visible on the surface and not what underlies the visible; and in consequence of that we can (barring temporary illusions) recognize when some new surface is green and when it is not merely in virtue of knowing what the word 'green' means. Such words I shall call informative designators. When all our referring expressions are informative designators, we know the essence of what is being designated and hence we can identify new instances of the objects. In such cases mere a priori reflection will tell us which events are compatible with and which events involve which other events; the compatibility is the logically possibility of co occurrence, and involvement is logical entailment. Mere a priori reflection will tell us that nothing can be red and green all over, or square and round at the same time. A priori reflection is not of course infallible, but the possibility of mistake does not arise from ignorance of some recondite empirical fact, but from a lack of imagination.

Now what sort of designator is 'I' (or 'Richard Swinburne', as used by me)? These seem to be informative designators. If I know how to use these words, I can't be mistaken about when to apply them—except through a temporary illusion; and when I am considering applying them to a person in virtue of his being a subject of experience, not even temporary illusion is possible. I am in Shoemaker's phrase 'immune to error though misidentifaction'.[5] I cannot recognize that some experience (e.g. pain) is occurring and wonder whether it is mine or not, in the way that I can know how to use the word 'Hesperus', and yet wonder whether the planet at which I am looking is Hesperus. My knowledge of how to use 'I', like my knowledge of how to use 'green' and 'square' means that I know the nature of what I am talking about when I use the words. Mere a priori reflection will show what my existence involves and with what it is compatible. Hence there is no possibility that what I am picking out by 'I' has an underlying essence which requires me to be embodied. My opponent is misguided in trying to make a comparison to the Hesperus/Phosphorous situation. Hence, since my existing does not entail my body existing, it follows that my existing does not involve my body existing; I am therefore a pure mental substance, essentially a soul. And since I can exist without my body merely in virtue of being a person, other people can do the same. Each of us is a pure mental substance; we may temporarily have physical properties and so a body and it may be good for us that we do. But our existing does not as such involve our having a body. Since only physical substances can be extended and so have separable parts, souls do not have separable parts.

For me to exist, I need only to have some pure mental properties. I do not need to have any particular mental properties. I pick myself out as the subject of certain currently experienced mental properties. But I would pick out the same substance if I used less or more of the properties of which I am currently aware as co-instantiated. Thus suppose I pick out myself as the subject of two separate sensations (say, visual and tactual sensations). But if at the same time I also had two other sensations (say, auditory and gustatory), I could have picked out the same myself by means of those latter sensations. And if I had done so, the fact that I had the former (visual and tactual sensations) would have been irrelevant to who was picked out. But then the same person would have been picked out had I not had those (visual and tactual) sensations at all, the only ones I did have. So I would have been the same person if I had had quite other

---

[5] Sydney Shoemaker, 'Introspection and the Self' in (ed.) Q. Cassam, *Self-Knowledge*, Oxford University Press, 1994, p. 82.

sensations instead. And a person having all the mental and other properties which I have is not enough to guarantee that that person is me. For we can conceive of a world exactly like our world in all qualitative respects in which someone with the same life history as me lectures to people who have exactly the same life history as you, and yet you and I do not exist. You can see this if you imagine that before this world exists you are shown a film of what is going to happen in it. You would still not know—are you going to live one of the lives in this world? And if so, which one? So being me does not entail having any of the particular mental or physical properties which I have; nor does having all the mental and physical properties which I have entail being me. The 'identity of indiscernibles' does not apply to persons. Each person, and so the essential part of each person—his or her soul, has a 'thisness' a uniqueness which makes it the soul it is quite apart from the particular mental properties it has (the life it has led).

Since I am a pure mental substance, I may hope to continue to exist after the destruction of my body, and perhaps then to be given a new body. My acquiring a new body will consist in the new body (which may include any surviving parts of my former body) being brought into causal interaction with the pure mental substance which is myself. The 'resurrection of the body' of all humans at the 'last day' (the 'General Resurrection') is a central Christian doctrine. Catholics, Orthodox, and many Protestants also believe that the person continues to exist without a body in the period between death and the General Resurrection. Both these doctrines are fully compatible with the account of human nature which I have defended in this paper.

Questions

1. What makes Swinburne a dualist?

2. In what does a person's identity consist for Swinburne?

3. What sort of relationship does Swinburne see between the soul and the body?

4. What other philosopher in the history of ideas formulates a similar model of the human?

5. Do you prefer Swinburne's dualism, or some kind of materialism, and why?

Figure 10

Figure 11

Part IX
Religious Pluralism

RELIGIOUS PLURALISM AND SALVATION

John Hick

Let us approach the problems of religious pluralism through the claims of the different traditions to offer salvation—generically, the transformation of human existence from self-centeredness to Reality-centeredness. This approach leads to a recognition of the great world faiths as spheres of salvation; and so far as we can tell, more or less equally so. Their different truth-claims express (a) their differing perceptions, through different religio-cultural 'lenses,' of the one ultimate divine Reality: (b) their different answers to the boundary questions of origin and destiny, true answers to which are however not necessary for salvation, and (c) their different historical memories.

I

The fact that there is a plurality of religious traditions, each with its own distinctive beliefs, spiritual practices, ethical outlook, art forms and cultural ethos, creates an obvious problem for those of us who see them, not simply as human phenomena, but as responses to the Divine. For each presents itself, implicitly or explicitly, as in some important sense absolute and unsurpassable and as rightly claiming a total allegiance. The problem of the relationship between these different streams of religious life has often been posed in terms of their divergent belief-systems. For whilst there are various overlaps between their teachings there are also radical differences: is the divine reality (let us refer to it as the Real) personal or non-personal; if personal, is it unitary or triune; is the universe created, or emanated, or itself eternal; do we live only once on this earth or are we repeatedly reborn? and so on and so on. When the problem of understanding religious plurality is approached through these rival truth-claims it appears particularly intractable.

I want to suggest, however, that it may more profitably be approached from a different direction, in terms of the claims of the various traditions to provide, or to be effective contexts of, salvation. 'Salvation' is primarily a Christian term, though I shall use it here to include its functional analogues in the other major world traditions. In this broader sense we can say that both Christianity and these other faiths are paths of salvation. For whereas pre-axial religion was (and is) centrally concerned to keep life going on an even keel, the post-axial traditions, originating or rooted in the 'axial age' of the first millennium B.C.E.—principally Hinduism, Judaism, Buddhism, Christianity, Islam—are centrally concerned with a radical transformation of the human situation.

It is of course possible, in an alternative approach, to define salvation in such a way that it becomes a necessary truth that only one particular tradition can provide it. If, for example, from within Christianity we define salvation as being forgiven by God because of Jesus' atoning death, and so becoming part of God's redeemed community, the church, then salvation is by definition Christian salvation. If on the other hand, from within Mahayana Buddhism, we define it as the attainment of *satori* or awakening, and so becoming an ego-free manifestation of the eternal Dharmakaya, then salvation is by definition Buddhist liberation. And so on. But if we stand back from these different conceptions to compare them we can, I think, very naturally and properly see them as different forms of the more fundamental conception of a radical change from a profoundly unsatisfactory state to one that is limitlessly better because rightly related to

---

* Faith and Philosophy, Vol. 5 No. 4 October 1988. All rights reserved.

the Real. Each tradition conceptualizes in its own way the wrongness of ordinary human existence—as a state of fallenness from paradisal virtue and happiness, or as a condition of moral weakness and alienation from God, or as the fragmentation of the infinite One into false individualities, or as a self-centeredness which pervasively poisons our involvement in the world process, making it to us an experience of anxious, unhappy unfulfillment. But each at the same time proclaims a limitlessly better possibility, again conceptualized in different ways—as the joy of conforming one's life to God's law; as giving oneself to God in Christ, so that 'it is no longer I who live, but Christ who lives in me' (Galatians 2:20), leading to eternal life in God's presence; as a complete surrender *(islam)* to God, and hence peace with God, leading to the bliss of paradise; as transcending the ego and realizing oneness with the limitless being-consciousness-bliss *(satchitananda)* of Brahman; as overcoming the ego point of view and entering into the serene selflessness of nirvana. I suggest that these different conceptions of salvation are specifications of what, in a generic formula, is the transformation of human existence from self-centeredness to a new orientation, centered in the divine Reality. And in each case the good news that is proclaimed is that this limitlessly better possibility is actually available and can be entered upon, or begin to be entered upon, here and now. Each tradition sets forth the way to attain this great good: faithfulness to the Torah, discipleship to Jesus, obedient living out of the Qur'anic way of life, the Eightfold Path of the Buddhist dharma, or the three great Hindu *margas* of mystical insight, activity in the world, and self-giving devotion to God.

II

The great world religions, then, are ways of salvation. Each claims to constitute an effective context within which the transformation of human existence can and does take place from self-centeredness to Reality-centeredness. How are we to judge such claims? We cannot directly observe the inner spiritual quality of a human relationship to the Real; but we can observe how that relationship, as one's deepest and most pervasive orientation, affects the moral and spiritual quality of a human personality and of a man's or woman's relationship to others. It would seem, then, that we can only assess these salvation-projects insofar as we are able to observe their fruits in human life. The inquiry has to be, in a broad sense, empirical. For the issue is one of fact, even though hard to define and difficult to measure fact, rather than being settleable by *a priori* stipulation.

The word 'spiritual' which occurs above is notoriously vague; but I am using it to refer to a quality or, better, an orientation which we can discern in those individuals whom we call saints—a Christian term which I use here to cover such analogues as arahat, bodhisattva, jivanmukti, mahatma. In these cases the human self is variously described as becoming part of the life of God, being 'to the Eternal Goodness what his own hand is to a man'; or being permeated from within by the infinite reality of Brahman; or becoming one with the eternal Buddha nature. There is a change in their deepest orientation from centeredness in the ego to a new centering in the Real as manifested in their own tradition. One is conscious in the presence of such a person that he or she is, to a startling extent, open to the transcendent, so as to be largely free from self-centered concerns and anxieties and empowered to live as an instrument of God/Truth/Reality.

It is to be noted that there are two main patterns of such a transformation. There are saints who withdraw from the world into prayer or meditation and saints who seek to change the world—in the medieval period a contemplative Julian of Norwich and a political Joan of Arc, or in our own century a mystical Sri Aurobindo and a political Mahatma Gandhi. In our present age of sociological consciousness, when we are aware that our inherited political and economic structures can be analyzed and purposefully changed, saintliness is more likely than in earlier times to take social and political forms. But, of whichever type, the saints are not a different species from the rest of us; they are simply much more advanced in the salvific transformation.

The ethical aspect of this salvific transformation consists in observable modes of behavior. But how do we identify the kind of behavior which, to the degree that it characterizes a life, reflects a corresponding degree of reorientation to the divine Reality? Should we use Christian ethical criteria, or Buddhist, or Muslim…? The answer, I suggest, is that at the level of their most basic moral insights the great traditions use a common criterion. For they agree in giving a central and normative role to the unselfish regard for others that we call love or compassion. This is commonly expressed in the principle of valuing others as we value ourselves, and treating them accordingly. Thus in the ancient Hindu *Mahabharata* we read that 'One should never do to another that which one would regard as injurious to oneself. This, in brief, is the rule of Righteousness' *(Anushana parva,* 113:7). Again, 'He who…benefits persons of all orders, who is always devoted to the good of all beings, who does not feel aversion to anybody…succeeds in ascending to Heaven' *(Anushana parva,* 145:24). In the Buddhist *Sutta Nipata* we read, 'As a mother cares for her son, all her days, so towards all living things a man's mind should be all-embracing' (149). In the Jain scriptures we are told that one should go about 'treating all creatures in the world as he himself would be treated' *(Kitanga Sutra,* 1.ii.33). Confucius, expounding humaneness *(jen),* said, 'Do not do to others what you would not like yourself *(Analects,* xxi, 2). In a Taoist scripture we read that the good man will 'regard [others'] gains as if they were his own, and their losses in the same way' *(Thai Shang,* 3). The Zoroastrian scriptures declare, 'That nature only is good when it shall not do unto another whatever is not good for its own self *(Dadistan-i-dinik,* 94:5). We are all familiar with Jesus' teaching, 'As ye would that men should do to you, do ye also to them likewise' (Luke 6:31). In the Jewish Talmud we read 'What is hateful to yourself do not do to your fellow man. That is the whole of the Torah' *(Babylonian Talmud,* Shabbath 31 a). And in the Hadith of Islam we read Muhammad's words, 'No man is a true believer unless he desires for his brother that which he desires for himself' *(Ibn Madja,* Intro. 9). Clearly, if everyone acted on this basic principle, taught by all the major faiths, there would be no injustice, no avoidable suffering, and the human family would everywhere live in peace.

When we turn from this general principle of love/compassion to the actual behavior of people within the different traditions, wondering to what extent they live in this way, we realize how little research has been done on so important a question. We do not have much more to go on than general impressions, supplemented by travelers' tales and anecdotal reports. We observe among our neighbors within our own community a great deal of practical loving-kindness; and we are told, for example, that a remarkable degree of self-giving love is to be found among the Hindu fishing families in the mud huts along the Madras shore; and we hear various other similar accounts from other lands. We read biographies, social histories and novels of Muslim village life in Africa, Buddhist life in Thailand, Hindu life in India, Jewish life in New York, as well as Christian life around the world, both in the past and today, and we get the impression that the personal virtues (as well as vices) are basically much the same within these very different religio-cultural settings and that in all of them unselfish concern for others occurs and is highly valued. And, needless to say, as well as love and compassion we also see all-too-abundantly, and apparently spread more or less equally in every society, cruelty, greed, hatred, selfishness and malice.

All this constitutes a haphazard and impressionistic body of data. Indeed I want to stress, not how easy it is, but on the contrary how difficult it is, to make responsible judgments in this area. For not only do we lack full information, but the fragmentary information that we have has to be interpreted in the light of the varying natural conditions of human life in different periods of history and in different economic and political circumstances. And I suggest that all that we can presently arrive at is the cautious and negative conclusion that we have no good reason to believe that any one of the great religious traditions has proved itself to be more productive of love/compassion than another.

The same is true when we turn to the large-scale social outworkings of the different salvation-projects. Here the units are not individual human lives, spanning a period of decades, but religious cultures spanning many centuries. For we can no more judge a civilization than a human life by confining our attention to a single temporal cross-section. Each of the great streams of religious life has had its times of flourishing and its times of deterioration. Each has produced its own distinctive kinds of good and its own distinctive kinds of evil. But to assess either the goods or the evils cross-culturally is difficult to say the least. How do we weigh, for example, the lack of economic progress, and consequent widespread poverty, in traditional Hindu and Buddhist cultures against the endemic violence and racism of Christian civilization, culminating in the twentieth century Holocaust? How do we weigh what the west regards as the hollowness of arranged marriages against what the east regards as the hollowness of a marriage system that leads to such a high proportion of divorces and broken families? From within each culture one can see clearly enough the defects of the others. But an objective ethical comparison of such vast and complex totalities is at present an unattainable ideal. And the result is that we are not in a position to claim an over-all moral superiority for any one of the great living religious traditions.

Let us now see where we have arrived. I have suggested that if we identify the central claim of each of the great religious traditions as the claim to provide, or to be an effective context of, salvation; and if we see salvation as an actual change in human beings from self-centeredness to a new orientation centered in the ultimate divine Reality; and if this new orientation has both a more elusive 'spiritual' character and a more readily observable moral aspect—then we arrive at the modest and largely negative conclusion that, so far as we can tell, no one of the great world religions is salvifically superior to the rest.

III

If this is so, what are we to make of the often contradictory doctrines of the different traditions? In order to make progress at this point, we must distinguish various kinds and levels of doctrinal conflict.

There are, first, conceptions of the ultimate as Jahweh, or the Holy Trinity, or Allah, or Shiva, or Vishnu, or as Brahman, or the Dharmakaya, the Tao, and so on.

If salvation is taking place, and taking place to about the same extent, within the religious systems presided over by these various deities and absolutes, this suggests that they are different manifestations to humanity of a yet more ultimate ground of all salvific transformation. Let us then consider the possibility that an infinite transcendent divine reality is being differently conceived, and therefore differently experienced, and therefore differently responded to from within our different religio-cultural ways of being human. This hypothesis makes sense of the fact that the salvific transformation seems to have been occurring in all the great traditions. Such a conception is, further, readily open to philosophical support. For we are familiar today with the ways in which human experience is partly formed by the conceptual and linguistic frameworks within which it occurs. The basically Kantian insight that the mind is active in perception, and that we are always aware of our environment as it appears to a consciousness operating with our particular conceptual resources and habits, has been amply confirmed by work in cognitive psychology and the sociology of knowledge and can now be extended with some confidence to the analysis of religious awareness. If, then, we proceed inductively from the phenomenon of religious experience around the world, adopting a religious as distinguished from a naturalistic interpretation of it, we are likely to find ourselves making two moves. The first is to postulate an ultimate transcendent divine reality (which I have been referring to as the Real) which, being beyond the scope of our human concepts, cannot be directly experienced by us as it is in itself but only as it appears through our various human thought-forms. And the second is to identify the thought-and-experienced deities and absolutes as different manifestations of the Real within different historical forms of human consciousness. In Kantian terms, the divine noumenon, the Real *an sich,* is experienced through different human receptivities as a range of divine phenomena, in the formation of which religious concepts have played an essential part.

These different 'receptivities' consist of conceptual schemas within which various personal, communal and historical factors have produced yet further variations. The most basic concepts in terms of which the Real is humanly thought-and-experienced are those of (personal) deity and of the (non-personal) absolute. But the Real is not actually experienced either as deity in general or as the absolute in general. Each basic concept becomes (in Kantian terminology) schematized in more concrete form. It is at this point that individual and cultural factors enter the process. The religious tradition of which we are a part, with its history and ethos and its great exemplars, its scriptures feeding our thoughts and emotions, and perhaps above all its devotional or meditative practices, constitutes an uniquely shaped and coloured 'lens' through which we are concretely aware of the Real specifically as the personal Adonai, or as the Heavenly Father, or as Allah, or Vishnu, or Shiva...or again as the non-personal Brahman, or Dharmakaya, or the Void or the Ground...Thus, one who uses the forms of Christian prayer and sacrament is thereby led to experience the Real as the divine Thou, whereas one who practices advaitic yoga or Buddhist zazen is thereby brought to experience the Real as the infinite being-consciousness-bliss of Brahman, or as the limitless emptiness of sunyata which is at the same time the infinite fullness of immediate reality as 'wondrous being.'

Three explanatory comments at this point before turning to the next level of doctrinal disagreement. First, to suppose that the experienced deities and absolutes which are the intentional objects of worship or content of religious meditation, are appearances or manifestations of the Real, rather than each being itself the Real *an sich,* is not to suppose that they are illusions—any more than the varying ways in which a mountain may appear to a plurality of differently placed observers are illusory. That the same reality may be variously experienced and described is true even of physical objects. But in the case of the infinite, transcendent divine reality there may well be much greater scope for the use of varying human conceptual schemas producing varying modes of phenomenal experience. Whereas the concepts in terms of which we are aware of mountains and rivers and houses are largely (though by no means entirely) standard throughout the human race, the religious concepts in terms of which we become aware of the Real have developed in widely different ways within the different cultures of the earth.

As a second comment, to say that the Real is beyond the range of our human concepts is not intended to mean that it is beyond the scope of purely formal, logically generated concepts—such as the concept of being beyond the range of (other than purely formal) concepts. We would not be able to refer at all to that which cannot be conceptualized in any way, not even by the concept of being unconceptualizable! But the other than purely formal concepts by which our experience is structured must be presumed not to apply to its noumenal ground. The characteristics mapped in thought and language are those that are constitutive of human experience. We have no warrant to apply them to the noumenal ground of the phenomenal, i.e., experienced, realm. We should therefore not think of the Real *an sich* as singular or plural, substance or process, personal or non-personal, good or bad, purposive or non-purpose. This has long been a basic theme of religious thought. For example, within Christianity, Gregory of Nyssa declared that:

> The simplicity of the True Faith assumes God to be that which He is, namely, incapable of being grasped by any term, or any idea, or any other device of our apprehension, remaining beyond the reach not only of the human but of the angelic and all supramundane intelligence, unthinkable, unutterable, above all expression in words, having but one name that can represent His proper nature, the single name being "Above Every Name" *(Against Eunomius*, I, 42).

Augustine, continuing this tradition, said that 'God transcends even the mind' *(True Religion,* 36:67), and Aquinas that 'by its immensity, the divine substance surpasses every form that our intellect reaches' *(Contra Gentiles,* I, 14, 3). In Islam the Qur'an affirms that God is 'beyond what they describe' (6:101). The Upanishads declare of Brahman, 'There the eye goes not, speech goes not, nor the mind' *(Kena Up.,* 1, 3), and Shankara wrote that Brahman is that 'before which words recoil, and to which no understanding has ever attained' (Otto, *Mysticism East and West,* E. T. 1932, p. 28).

But, third, we might well ask, why postulate an ineffable and unobservable divine-reality-in-itself? If we can say virtually nothing about it, why affirm its existence? The answer is that the reality or non-reality of the postulated noumenal ground of the experienced religious phenomena constitutes the difference between a religious and a naturalistic interpretation of religion. If there is no such transcendent ground, the various forms of religious experience have to be categorized as purely human projections. If on the other hand there is such a transcendent ground, then these phenomena may be joint products of the universal presence of the Real and of the varying sets of concepts and images that have crystallized within the religious traditions of the earth. To affirm the transcendent is thus to affirm that religious experience is not solely a construction of the human imagination but is a response—though always culturally conditioned—to the Real.

Those doctrinal conflicts, then, that embody different conceptions of the ultimate arise, according to the hypothesis I am presenting, from the variations between different sets of human conceptual schema and spiritual practice. And it seems that each of these varying ways of thinking-and-experiencing the Real has been able to mediate its transforming presence to human life. For the different major concepts of the ultimate do not seem—so far as we can tell—to result in one religious totality being soteriologically more effective than another.

IV

The second level of doctrinal difference consists of metaphysical beliefs which cohere with although they are not exclusively linked to a particular conception of the ultimate. These are beliefs about the relation of the material universe to the Real: creation *ex nihilo,* emanation, an eternal universe, an unknown form of dependency...? And about human destiny: reincarnation or a single life, eternal identity or transcendence of the self...? Again, there are questions about the existence of heavens and hells and purgatories and angels and devils and many other subsidiary states and entities. Out of this mass of disputed religious issues let me pick two major examples: is the universe created ex *nihilo,* and do human beings reincarnate?

I suggest that we would do well to apply to such questions a principle that was taught by the Buddha two and a half millennia ago. He listed a series of 'undetermined questions' *(avyakata)*—whether the universe is eternal, whether it is spatially infinite, whether (putting it in modern terms) mind and brain are identical, and what the state is of a completed project of human existence (a Tathagata) after bodily death. He refused to answer these questions, saying that we do not need to have knowledge of these things in order to attain liberation or awakening (nirvana); and indeed that to regard such information as soteriologically essential would only divert us from the single-minded quest for liberation. I think that we can at this point profitable learn from the Buddha, even extending his conception of the undetermined questions further than he did—for together with almost everyone else in his own culture he regarded one of our examples, reincarnation, as a matter of assured knowledge. Let us, then, accept that we do not *know* whether, e.g., the universe was created *ex nihilo,* nor whether human beings are reincarnated; and, further, that it is not necessary for salvation to hold a correct opinion on either matter.

I am not suggesting that such issues are unimportant. On their own level they are extremely important, being both of great interest to us and also having widely ramifying implications within our belief-systems and hence for our lives. The thought of being created out of nothing can nourish a salutary sense of absolute dependence. (But other conceptions can also nurture that sense.) The idea of reincarnation can offer the hope of future spiritual progress; though, combined with the principle of karma, it can also serve to validate the present inequalities of human circumstances. (But other eschatologies also have their problems, both theoretical and practical). Thus these—and other—disputed issues do have a genuine importance. Further, it is possible that some of them may one day be settled by empirical evidence. It might become established, for example, that the 'big bang' of some fifteen billion years ago was an absolute beginning, thus ruling out the possibility that the universe is eternal. And again, it might become established, by an accumulation of evidence, that reincarnation does indeed occur in either some or all cases. On the other hand it is possible that we shall never achieve agreed knowledge in these areas. Certainly, at the present time, whilst we have theories, preferences, hunches, inherited convictions, we cannot honestly claim to have secure knowledge. And the same is true, I suggest, of the entire range of metaphysical issues about which the religions dispute. They are of intense interest, properly the subject of continuing research and discussion, but are not matters concerning which absolute dogmas are appropriate. Still less is it appropriate to maintain that salvation depends upon accepting some one particular opinion or dogma. We have seen that the transformation of human existence from self-centeredness to Reality-centeredness seems to be taking place within each of the great traditions despite their very different answers to these debated questions. It follows that a correct opinion concerning them is not required for salvation.

V

The third level of doctrinal disagreement concerns historical questions. Each of the great traditions includes a larger or smaller body of historical beliefs. In the case of Judaism these include at least the main features of the history described in the Hebrew scriptures; in the case of Christianity, these plus the main features of the life, death and resurrection of Jesus as described in the New Testament; in the case of Islam, the main features of the history described in the

Qur'an; in the case of Vaishnavite Hinduism, the historicity of Krishna; in the case of Buddhism, the historicity of Guatama and his enlightenment at Bodh Gaya; and so on. But although each tradition thus has its own records of the past, there are rather few instances of direct disagreement between these. For the strands of history that are cherished in these different historical memories do not generally overlap; and where they do overlap they do not generally involve significant differences. The overlaps are mainly within the thread of ancient near eastern history that is common to the Jewish, Christian and Muslim scriptures; and within this I can only locate two points of direct disagreement—the Torah's statement that Abraham nearly sacrificed his son Isaac at Mount Moriah (Genesis 22) versus the Muslim interpretation of the Qur'anic version (in Sura 37) that it was his other son Ishmael; and the New Testament witness that Jesus died on the cross versus the Qur'anic teaching that 'they did not slay him, neither crucified him, only a likeness of that was shown them' (Sura 4:156). (This latter however would seem to be a conflict between an historical report, in the New Testament, and a theological inference—that God would not allow so great a prophet to be killed—in the Qur'an.)

All that one can say in general about such disagreements, whether between two traditions or between any one of them and the secular historians, is that they could only properly be settled by the weight of historical evidence. However, the events in question are usually so remote in time, and the evidence so slight or so uncertain, that the question cannot be definitively settled. We have to be content with different communal memories, enriched as they are by the mythic halo that surrounds all long-lived human memories of events of transcendent significance. Once again, then, I suggest that differences of historical judgment, although having their own proper importance, do not prevent the different traditions from being effective, and so far as we can tell equally effective, contexts of salvation. It is evidently not necessary for salvation to have correct historical information. (It is likewise not necessary for salvation, we may add, to have correct scientific information.)

VI

Putting all this together, the picture that I am suggesting can be outlined as follows: our human religious experience, variously shaped as it is by our sets of religious concepts, is a cognitive response to the universal presence of the ultimate divine Reality that, in itself, exceeds human conceptuality. This Reality is however manifested to us in ways formed by a variety of human concepts, as the range of divine personae and metaphysical impersonae witnessed to in the history of religions. Each major tradition, built around its own distinctive way of thinking-and-experiencing the Real, has developed its own answers to the perennial questions of our origin and destiny, constituting more or less comprehensive and coherent cosmologies and eschatologies. These are human creations which have, by their association with living streams of religious experience, become invested with a sacred authority. However they cannot all be wholly true; quite possibly none is wholly true; perhaps all are partly true. But since the salvific process has been going on through the centuries despite this unknown distribution of truth and falsity in our cosmologies and eschatologies, it follows that it is not necessary for salvation to adopt any one of them. We would therefore do well to learn to tolerate unresolved, and at present unresolvable, differences concerning these ultimate mysteries.

One element, however, to be found in the belief-systems of most of the traditions raises a special problem, namely that which asserts the sole salvific efficacy of that tradition. I shall discuss this problem in terms of Christianity because it is particularly acute for those of us who are Christians. We are all familiar with such New Testament texts as 'There is salvation in no one else [than Jesus Christ], for there is no other name under heaven given among men by which we must be saved (Acts 4:12), and with the Catholic dogma *Extra ecclesiam nulla salus* (No salvation outside the church) and its Protestant equivalent—never formulated as an official dogma but nevertheless implicit within the 18th and 19th century Protestant missionary expansion,—no salvation outside Christianity. Such a dogma differs from other elements of Christian belief in that it is not only a statement about the potential relationship of Christians to God but at the same time about the actual relationship of non-Christians to God. It says that the latter, in virtue of being non-Christians, lack salvation. Clearly such a dogma is incompatible with the insight that the salvific transformation of human existence is going on, and so far as we can tell going on to a more or less equal extent, within all the great traditions. Insofar, then, as we accept that salvation is not confined to Christianity we must reject the old exclusivist dogma.

This has in fact now been done by most thinking Christians, though exceptions remain, mostly within the extreme Protestant fundamentalist constituencies. The *Extra ecclesiam* dogma, although not explicitly repealed, has been outflanked by the work of such influential Catholic theologians as Karl Rahner, whose new approach was in effect endorsed by Vatican II. Rahner expressed his more inclusivist outlook by suggesting that devout people of other faiths are 'anonymous Christians,' within the invisible church even without knowing it, and thus within the sphere of salvation. The present Pope, in his Encyclical *Redemptor Hominis* (1979) has expressed this thought even more comprehensively by saying that 'every man without exception has been redeemed by Christ' and 'with every man without any exception whatever Christ is in a way united, even when man in unaware of it' (para. 14). And a number of Protestant theologians have advocated a comparable position.

The feature that particularly commends this kind of inclusivism to many Christians today is that it recognizes the spiritual values of other religions, and the occurrence of salvation within them, and yet at the same time preserves their conviction of the ultimate superiority of their own religion over all others. For it maintains that salvation, wherever it occurs, is Christian salvation; and Christians are accordingly those who alone know and preach the source of salvation, namely in the atoning death of Christ.

This again, like the old exclusivism, is a statement not only about the ground of salvation for Christians but also for Jews, Muslims, Hindus, Buddhists and everyone else. But we have seen that it has to be acknowledged that the immediate ground of their transformation is the particular spiritual path along which they move. It is by living in accordance with the Torah or with the Qur'anic revelation that Jews and Muslims find a transforming peace with God; it is by one or other of their great *margas* that Hindus attain to *moksha;* it is by the Eightfold Path that Theravada Buddhists come to *nirvana*; it is by *zazen* that Zen Buddhists attain to *satori;* and so on. The Christian inclusivist is, then, by implication, declaring that these various spiritual paths are efficacious, and constitute authentic contexts of salvation, because Jesus died on the cross; and, by further implication, that if he had not died on the cross they would not be efficacious.

This is a novel and somewhat astonishing doctrine. How are we to make sense of the idea that the salvific power of the dharma taught five hundred years earlier by the Buddha is a consequence of the death of Jesus in approximately 30 C.E.? Such an apparently bizarre conception should only be affirmed for some very good reason. It was certainly not taught by Jesus or his apostles. It has emerged only in the thought of twentieth century Christians who have come to recognize that Jews are being salvifically transformed through the spirituality of Judaism, Muslims through that of Islam, Hindus and Buddhists through the paths mapped out by their respective traditions, and so on, but who nevertheless wish to retain their inherited sense of the unique superiority of Christianity. The only outlet left for this sense, when one has acknowledged the salvific efficacy of the various great spiritual ways, is the arbitrary and contrived notion of their metaphysical dependency upon the death of Christ. But the theologian who undertakes to spell out this invisible causality is not to be envied. The problem is not one of logical possibility—it only requires logical agility to cope with that—but one of religious or spiritual plausibility. It would be a better use of theological time and energy, in my opinion, to develop forms of trinitarian, christological and soteriological doctrine which are compatible with our awareness of the independent salvific authenticity of the other great world faiths. Such forms are already available in principle in conceptions of the Trinity, not as ontologically three but as three ways in which the one God is humanly thought and experienced; conceptions of Christ as a man so fully open to and inspired by God as to be, in the ancient Hebrew metaphor, a 'son of God'; and conceptions of salvation as an actual human transformation which has been powerfully elicited and shaped, among his disciples, by the influence of Jesus.

There may indeed well be a variety of ways in which Christian thought can develop in response to our acute late twentieth century awareness of the other world religions, as there were of responding to the nineteenth century awareness of the evolution of the forms of life and the historical character of the holy scriptures. And likewise there will no doubt be a variety of ways in which each of the other great traditions can rethink its inherited assumption of its own unique superiority. But it is not for us to tell people of other traditions how to do their own business. Rather, we should attend to our own.

Questions

1. What does John Hick mean when he says that "salvation" has "functional analogies in other religions?"

2. What other term does he discuss in Section II that has "functional analogies in other religions?"

3. Hick provides a general account of the picture of religious experience. What are its chief characteristics?

4. How does Hick characterize exclusivism? Inclusivism? Where does Hick go with the discussion and why?

5. On Hick's account, is there anything unique about Christianity? What, if anything?

This paper as originally delivered as the second Kegley Lecture at California State University, Bakersfield, on February 10th, 1988. For a fuller account of its proposals the reader is invited to see my *An Interpretation of Religion* (New Haven: Yale University Press and London: Macmillan, 1988).

PLANTINGA, PLURALISM AND JUSTIFIED RELIGIOUS BELIEF

David Basinger

In this paper, David Basinger shows that Plantinga is a nonevidentialist in the sense that he thinks that we need not search for propositional evidence to support our formed beliefs or the reliability of our own belief-forming faculties. He contends that, given the pluralistic challenge, the knowledgeable theist is required to look for such propositional evidence although she can justifiably continue to consider her formed beliefs properly basic even if none is found.

According to Alvin Plantinga, it has been widely held since the enlightenment that if theistic beliefs are to be considered rational, they must be based on propositional evidence. It is not enough for the theist just to refute objections. The theist "must also have something like an argument for [such a] belief, or some positive reason to think that the belief is true."[1] But this is incorrect, Plantinga argues. Basic beliefs are beliefs not based on propositional evidence; such beliefs are "properly basic in a set of circumstances" if they can be so affirmed in those circumstances "without either violating an epistemic duty or displaying some kind of noetic defect."[2] And, according to Plantinga, theistic beliefs can be properly basic. For example, he argues that "under widely realized conditions it is perfectly rational, reasonable, intellectually respectable and acceptable to believe there is such a person as God without believing it on the basis of evidence—propositional evidence vs. the kind instanced by 'the evidence of the senses'."[3]

But can a properly basic belief such as this have any epistemic credibility (warrant) if it is not conferred by other propositions whose epistemic status is not in question? Yes, Plantinga replies. There are two significantly different ways in which a proposition can acquire warrant. There is propositional warrant—warrant conferred by an evidential line of reasoning from other beliefs. However, there is also nonpropositional warrant.

> [We have] cognitive faculties designed to enable us to achieve true beliefs with respect to a wide variety of propositions—propositions about our immediate environment, about our interior lives, about the thoughts and experiences of other persons, about our universe at large, about right and wrong, about the whole realm of abstracta—numbers, properties, propositions, states of affairs, possible worlds and their like, about modality—what is necessary and possible—and about [ourselves]. These faculties work in such a way that under the appropriate circumstances we form the appropriate belief. More exactly, the appropriate belief is formed in us; in the typical case we do not decide to hold or form the belief in question, but simply find ourselves with it. Upon considering an instance of modus ponens, I find myself believing its corresponding conditional; upon being appeared to in the familiar way, I find myself holding the belief that there is a large tree before me; upon being asked what I had for breakfast, I reflect for a moment and then find myself with the belief that what I had was eggs on toast. In these and other cases I do not decide what to believe; I don't total up the evidence (I'm being appeared to redly; on most occasions when thus appeared to I am in the presence of something red; so most probably in this case I am) and make a decision as to what seems best supported; I simply find myself believing.[4]

---

* Faith and Philosophy, Vol. 8 No. 1, January 1991. All rights reserved.
[1] Alvin Plantinga, "The Foundations of Theism: A Reply," *Faith and Philosophy* 3 (July, 1986): 307.
[2] Ibid, p. 300.
[3] Alvin Plantinga, "On Taking Belief in God as Basic," Wheaton College Philosophy Conference (October 23-25, 1986), Lecture I handout, p. 1.
[4] Plantinga "Justification and Theism," *Faith and Philosophy* 4 (October, 1987): 405, 406.

And from a theistic point of view, Plantinga continues, the same is true in the religious realm. Just as it is true that when our senses or memory is functioning properly, "appropriate belief is formed in us," so it is that God has also created us with faculties which will, "when they are working in the way they were designed to work by the being who designed and created us and them," produce true theistic beliefs.[5] Moreover, if these faculties are functioning properly, a basic theistic belief thus formed "has positive epistemic status to the degree [the individual in question finds herself] inclined to accept it."[6]

But what of the alleged counterevidence to theistic beliefs? What, for example, of all the arguments which conclude that the theist has no justifiable basis for believing in God? Can they all be dismissed as irrelevant? Not immediately, answers Plantinga. We must seriously consider alleged defeaters of our basic beliefs. We must, for instance, seriously consider the claim that religious belief is mere wish fulfillment and the claim that God's existence is incompatible with (or at least improbable given) the amount of evil in the world. But to undercut such defeaters, we need not engage in positive apologetics: produce propositional evidence for mere beliefs. Only "negative apologetics"—the refutation of such arguments—"is required to defeat...defeaters."[7]

Moreover, it is Plantinga's conviction that such defeater defeaters do normally exist. With respect to belief in God's existence, for example, he maintains that "the nonpropositional warrant enjoyed by [a person's] belief in God [seems] itself sufficient to turn back the challenge offered by some alleged defeaters"—e.g., the claim that theistic belief is mere wish fulfillment. And other defeaters such as the "problem of evil," he adds, can be undercut by identifying validity or soundness problems or even by appealing to the fact that experts think it is unsound, or that the experts are evenly divided as in its soundness."[8] Thus, even considering all the seeming evidence against God's existence and other theistic beliefs, Plantinga is still inclined to believe that at least some such beliefs are properly basic for most theists—even intellectually sophisticated adult theists."[9]

There is much that Plantinga says with which I agree. His contention that many individuals simply discover theistic beliefs formed in them seems to me to be correct. Philosophers and theologians have for millennia discussed the 'evidence' for and against various theistic beliefs. But it is doubtful that many theists initially acquire theistic beliefs on the basis of such evidential discussions. Many, if not most, appear to have just found themselves with the inclination to affirm such beliefs.

And his contention that such beliefs are generated by divinely created religious belief-forming faculties which produce beliefs in a manner analogous to our visual and moral belief-forming faculties also seems acceptable. Of course, those who believe there is no God will not believe that any of our belief-forming faculties are divinely created. But Plantinga only claims that this is what he and other theists believe to be the case. Thus, in a day when a 'convincing' refutation of God's existence seems less likely than ever, Plantinga's qualified contention appears safe.

In fact, if we drop consideration of the origin of the faculties in question, Plantinga seems to be offering us a very plausible description of how certain theistic beliefs *are* in fact initially formed in many theists. Few deny that we have 'visual faculties' which receive external data—e.g., light reflected off a tree—process such data, produce in us visual images expressible by

---

[5] Ibid, p. 411.
[6] Ibid., p.410.
[7] Plantinga, "The Foundations of Theism," p. 313, n. 11.
[8] Ibid., p. 312.
[9] Ibid.

propositions such as "I am being appeared to treely," and then incline us to believe certain things—e.g., that there actually is a tree in front of us. And, analogously, it seems quite plausible to believe that many humans possess 'faculties' (whether or not they are held to be 'mental' and/or 'physical' and whether or not they are held to be divinely and/or naturally created) which receive external data—for example, encounter the starry heavens—process such data, and then produce both the religious concepts expressible by propositions such as "God exists" or "God has spoken to me" and the inclination to believe these propositions to be true.

However, I shall argue that the undeniable existence of pervasive religious pluralism places knowledgeable theists under a prima facie obligation to do more than engage in negative apologetics. It requires such theists to *attempt* to produce positive evidence for their religious beliefs. And I shall then discuss the implications of this for for Plantinga's claim that some theistic beliefs are properly basic for most theists—even intellectually sophisticated adult theists."

I

It seems to me that the essence of Plantinga's model of belief justification can be captured in what I shall label his Negative Apologetical Thesis (NAT).

> NAT: For a theist to be in a position to maintain justifiably that the basic religious beliefs formed by her religious faculties are properly basic—i.e., to be in a position to maintain justifiably that her basic formed beliefs are true even though she has no "positive reason" to think they are true—she is only obligated to defend herself against the claim that her religious faculties are not functioning properly—i.e., are not functioning as they are intended to function or are not producing true beliefs.

Or, to be even more explicit about those aspects of NAT with which this paper will be concerned, it seems to me that Plantinga is making two related, but distinct, claims about negative apologetics. He is claiming that a theist is not obligated to produce independent evidence for the beliefs that her faculties have formed. And he appears to be claiming that she is also not obligated to establish the reliability of her own religious faculties—i.e., he is claiming that she can assume the reliability of her own religious faculties until they are proven faulty.

But why accept NAT? Specifically, why should a theist assume her religious faculties are reliable until proven unreliable rather than assume such faculties are unreliable until proven reliable? The most popular argument for this aspect of NAT—and one to which Plantinga seems at times at least implicitly to be appealing—can be called the General Reliability Argument (GRA). We as humans, it is held, are naturally endowed with a considerable number of belief-forming faculties. As a result, many of us simply find ourselves believing we are 'seeing' a tree or believing that we had eggs yesterday or believing we have a headache or believing that from the conjunction of (a then b) and (a), (b) follows or believing God exists. Now, in general, we cannot prove that such formed beliefs are true and, thus, on this basis, that our faculties are reliable. Some of the greatest philosophical minds—e.g., Descartes and Hume—have tried but with a notable lack of success. But the onus is not on us to furnish such proof. We all rely on these faculties daily, and in general they serve us quite well. In fact the assumed reliability of such faculties serves as the basis for some of our most noncontroversial examples of 'knowledge'. So our basic stance toward such faculties—including our 'religious' faculties—should be to assume they are 'innocent until proven guilty'.

In short, the argument is that since we as humans can justifiably assume, without proof, that religious faculties in general are reliable, an individual theist can justifiably assume, without proof, that her own religious faculties are reliable until proven otherwise.

Now with respect to most of our human faculties—e.g., our visual faculties—GRA seems noncontroversially true. But can our 'religious faculties' be considered appropriately analogous to our other faculties in this context? Or, to put the question in its more useful form, is there any reason not to assume that religious faculties are as reliable as visual or auditory or inferential faculties?

When considering the formed beliefs of many individuals in specific, homogeneous cultural contexts, the answer to this latter question would appear to be no. For, in these contexts, all of the faculties in question appear to function in an analogous manner: they all produce consensus. That is, it is not only the case that most individuals in such cultural contexts find the same basic visual and inferential and auditory beliefs being formed in them; they also find the same basic religious beliefs being formed in them. Thus, such individuals quite justifiably assume that their religious faculties are as reliable as the others.

However, when we survey the 'world scene', a major difficulty arises. The problem, of course, is that on a world-wide scale, religious faculties consistently and pervasively produce a myriad of different, often incompatible, basic religious beliefs.

For instance, such faculties produce no common conception of God. Most theists conceive of God as a 'supreme being' in some sense. But there is little consensus on such a being's essential characteristics. While some find themselves believing in the existence of a being who is 'personal', others do not. Rather, they find themselves believing either that God is some sort of impersonal force or that God is simply the sum total of all there is. And while some find themselves believing that God is the sole, unilateral creator and controller of all, others find themselves believing that God can unilaterally create or control nothing. All reality, they maintain, is always co-creative. In fact the 'religious' faculties of some individuals produce disbelief in the existence of any sort of 'supreme being'.

Now, of course, such divergence can be explained in part by the fact that many individuals have never observed human activity outside of their own culture or have not been exposed to alternative theistic and nontheistic perspectives or have not seriously analyzed them. However, even among those knowledgeable individuals who have considered roughly the same data, nothing close to a basic consensus has emerged. Their visual faculties generally produce similar visual beliefs in similar settings. Their memories draw forth similar beliefs in similar settings. And their introspective and inferential faculties frequently produce similar beliefs in similar contexts. But their religions faculties simply do not.

In short, pervasive religious pluralism brings into serious question whether we ought to consider religious faculties to be analogous to other belief-forming faculties in the way GRA suggests. The existence of such pluralism gives us no reason to deny that religious faculties *produce* beliefs in us in a manner analogous to the way visual or auditory faculties produce beliefs. But since the reason we do not question the reliability of most of our faculties is that such faculties consistently generate similar beliefs in most individuals, the fact that religious faculties do not, in general, produce similar beliefs in similar contexts does make it much more difficult to assume they possess the same sort of reliability status. That is, this lack of consensus in the religious realm makes it difficult to assume that religious faculties, in general, produce true beliefs. And if this is so, then, of course, GRA is greatly weakened (I personally believe defeated) as a justification for affirming NAT—or, more specifically, is greatly weakened as a basis for assuming that we need only defend our religious belief-forming faculties against the claim that they are unreliable.

It will not help here, it must be explicitly noted, to move to the religious version of GRA in which Plantinga explicitly appeals: our human faculties—including our religious faculties—can be assumed innocent until proven guilty because they "have been designed, no doubt, with reliability in mind" by an all-powerful, all knowing creator.[10] This changes the 'origin' of the alleged reliability. But the same problem remains. How can religious faculties justifiably be assumed to possess the same degree of reliability as that granted other belief-forming faculties when religious faculties do not produce consensus in a manner analogous to the others?

If I am correct, where does this leave the proponent of NAT? If she is no longer in a position to assume that *her own* religious belief-forming faculties are reliable because religious faculties, in general, can justifiably be assumed to be so, must she now abandon this aspect of Plantinga's negative thesis? She might conclude that she must. That is, she might conclude that, in the absence of some helpful version of GRA, she must now do more than simply defend herself against attacks on the reliability of her own religious faculties, which is all that NAT requires. She might decide that each theist must now independently *establish* the reliability of her own religious faculties—independently identify positive reasons for believing her own faculties are reliable—before she can justifiably claim that the religious beliefs they form are properly basic.

However, in Plantinga's own words, to believe one must have "some positive reason to think" a belief is true is to be an evidentialist. Thus, although to abandon NAT in this manner is not to become an evidentialist with respect to the beliefs one's religious faculties have formed, it is to become an evidentialist with respect to the other aspect of Plantinga's negative apologetical thesis: the reliability status on one's own religious faculties.

This is not to say, it must be explicitly emphasized, that Plantinga ought not, himself, be viewed as an evidentialist in *any* sense. He does appear to view GRA (in its religious and/or natural version) as a form of evidence—as a positive reason—for holding certain opinions about our formed beliefs. Specifically he seems to see GRA as a basis for claiming that a theist can assume her religious beliefs to be 'innocent until proven guilty'—i.e., as a reason for believing each theist need not independently establish the reliability of her religious faculties. But the proponent of the line of reasoning in question, on the other hand, sees the inadequacy of GRA as a reason to believe each theist does need to establish independently the reliability of her religious faculties. Thus, this theist has now become an evidentialist in the exact sense Plantinga claims in NAT she need not.

It might be argued, however, that the proponent of NAT ought not give up so easily. The existence of pervasive religious pluralism does seriously challenge any version of GRA as a justification for the affirmation of NAT. But the burden of proof still lies with the critic. We may not have good reasons for holding that religious faculties are in general reliable. But it is still the case for any given theist that, unless it can be established that her specific religious faculties are in fact unreliable, she remains wholly justified in maintaining that her formed beliefs are properly basic—can be affirmed without positive evidence. In short, it might be argued that a theist can still justifiably affirm Plantinga's negative apologetical thesis, even if she can no longer justifiably appeal to some version of GRA.

It seems to me, though, that this line of reasoning is unacceptable. The existence of pervasive pluralism does challenge, and I think defeat, any version of GRA designed to allow us

---

[10] Plantinga, *Justification and Theism*, p. 413.

to assume the general reliability of religious faculties. But I believe that such pluralism *also* functions as a *direct* challenge to the affirmation of NAT itself—as a direct challenge to the claim that to defend the proper basicality of our formed religious beliefs, we need only *defend* ourselves against attacks on such beliefs and the faculties which have produced them. An illustration related to another type of belief-forming faculty may be helpful. Let us assume that Tom and Bill, both students in the same Introduction to Philosophy class, are discussing a forthcoming exam. What soon emerges is that, while Tom believes the exam is on Friday, Bill believes it is on the following Monday. Before their discussion neither had any reason to doubt he was correct. Both had been in class the day the exam date was announced, and neither had previously had any reason to believe his auditory faculties or memory was not functioning properly.

But what is the proper epistemological response now that a conflict has arisen? An improper response, obviously, would be for either Bill or Tom to assume immediately that his faculties had, in fact, not functioned in a reliable manner and, thus, that his formed belief ought no longer be considered true. And the same, I believe, holds in the religious realm. It is undeniably the case, for instance, that Christians or Hindus or Buddhists often find the religious beliefs formed in them to be incompatible with the religious beliefs formed in the members of other religious groups. But this fact alone is not a justifiable reason for a proponent of any given religious perspective to assume immediately that her religious faculties are, in fact unreliable and thus that the beliefs formed by such faculties ought no longer be affirmed.[11]

Does this mean, accordingly, that the knowledgeable theist who becomes aware of the pervasively pluralistic nature of religious beliefs is under no greater epistemic obligation than before? Can it be argued that since the existence of religious pluralism is not a sound reason for giving up any specific theistic belief, the theist can justifiably dismiss further consideration of this phenomenon and simply continue to assume her religious faculties are producing beliefs which are properly basic—i.e., can justifiably continue to maintain that her formed beliefs can be affirmed without positive evidence.

I do not think so. Conflicts between beliefs produced by other faculties, we all know from experience, *sometimes* occur because one of the faculties was not functioning properly. For example, two students have sometimes 'heard' different test dates because one had an ear infection or wax in his ear or was taking a prescription drug which had affected his hearing and/or memory. Moreover, we also know from experience that such conflicts can *at times* be resolved by further investigation. For example, students can usually resolve a conflict of the type under discussion simply by calling the instructor. Accordingly, *if the goal is to maximize 'truth' and minimizing 'error'*, then all parties are, I believe, under a *prima facie* obligation to attempt to resolve such conflicts.

Now, of course, students may not always be interested in determining exactly when an exam is to be given. Perhaps they have already studied or plan not to study. But most theists (and nontheists) do claim to be interested in affirming 'truth' and avoiding 'error'. Thus, the existence of pervasive pluralism—the fact that seemingly reliable religious faculties continually produce incompatible religious beliefs—does, I believe place the knowledgeable theist under the type of *prima facie* epistemic obligation in question.

---

[11] To draw such analogies is not affected by the fact that we cannot consider our religious and other belief-forming faculties to be analogous in the context of GRA. In that context, the issue is whether all can be assumed to be equally reliable. The issue here is how we ought to respond to conflicts between formed beliefs, which can (and do) arise in relation to all our belief-forming faculties.

It must be emphasized, of course, that such an obligation is *prima facie*. There may be many legitimate reasons why it cannot in fact immediately or ever be discharged. A theist, for instance, may not have the time or resources to investigate further. Moreover, I do not believe that the mere existence of this obligation need have any immediate bearing on the epistemic status of a theist's formed beliefs.[12] This is not to any, of course, that a theist who becomes aware of religious pluralism may not, in fact, find herself less inclined to affirm certain formed beliefs. And information uncovered during an attempt to resolve the conflict in question may well lead a theist to believe she is now more or less justified in affirming her formed religious beliefs than she was initially. However, the mere recognition of the existence of the obligation in question does not itself require her to modify her epistemic attitude toward her formed beliefs.

But I *am* arguing that once the theist becomes aware of the pluralistic challenge, she can no longer justifiably choose to retain a purely defensive posture. Or stated differently, *I am arguing* that the knowledgeable theist cannot justifiably claim that because the existence of pervasive pluralism does not require her to abandon her formed beliefs, she is under no obligation to consider the matter further. If she desires to determine the 'truth' of the matter to the extent possible, she is obligated, in principle, to engage in further investigation. The arena of positive apologetics must at least be entered. The game of 'negative apologetics' will no longer be enough.

Or, to put all this more explicitly into the language of NAT, the existence of pervasive pluralism is not a sufficient reason for believing that any given theist's formed beliefs are false or that her belief forming faculties are unreliable. Nor, as we shall see, is the existence of such pluralism a sufficient reason in every case to deny that our formed religious beliefs can ultimately be considered properly basic. But religious pluralism does challenge the assumption that a theist need only defend her formed beliefs and the reliability of the faculties which have produced them to preserve the proper basicality of such beliefs. The knowledgeable theist, I am arguing, is obligated to attempt to resolve the pluralistic conflict—enter the arena of positive apologetics—*before* any 'final' decision concerning the epistemic status of her formed religious beliefs can be made.

What if someone refuses to attempt to meet this obligation? This, of course, is not relevant to the question of whether formed beliefs can or cannot, in principle, be considered properly basic. But for a given theist to purposely violate the duty in question does mean, I believe, that she has forfeited her right to claim that her formed beliefs are properly basic. For, as Plantinga himself has told us, basic beliefs can only be considered properly basic if they can be affirmed without "violating an epistemic duty." And the theist in question has in essence chosen not to attempt to maximize truth and minimize error and has, thus, violated one of the basic criteria for epistemically rational behavior.[13]

II

Let us assume that I am correct. This raises two distinct, but related questions. Can the pluralistic challenge be resolved? That is, can we determine which set of formed religious beliefs is true or most worthy of affirmation? And either way, can a theist justifiably continue to maintain that her

---

[12] Since the phrase 'epistemic status' has various meanings, it is important to state explicitly that in those instances in which I inquire about the epistemic status of a theist's formed beliefs, I will be concerned with the question of whether she is within her rights in affirming the belief.

[13] See, for example, David Basinger, "The Rationality of Belief in God: Some Clarification," *The New Scholasticism* 5 (Spring, 1986), pp. 163 85.

formed beliefs are properly basic—i.e., can she justifiably continue to affirm such beliefs without possessing positive reasons for believing they are true?

We will consider potential modes of resolution first. In what ways might the theist attempt to resolve the problem posed by religious pluralism? That is, in what ways might a theist attempt to improve her epistemic position in the debate? Further exploration of our student scenario may be helpful in this respect. If Tom and Bill really do desire to determine which, if either, has correctly remembered the day of the next exam, there are two basic approaches available.

The first is to turn their attention directly to the formed beliefs in question. The most promising possibility along these lines would be to check with the instructor directly or at least see if the instructor has listed the test dates in the course syllabus. But this approach will obviously be of little value in attempting to resolve the challenge of religious pluralism. What makes this method of conflict resolution so promising in our student scenario is the fact that Tom and Bill agree on the identity of their instructor, agree that the syllabus in question was produced by this person and agree that they will be able to arrive at a mutually acceptable interpretation of what the syllabus indicates concerning this matter. However, the very basis for the problem of religious pluralism under consideration is, at least in part, the fact that we as humans cannot seem to agree on the 'identity' of the being who can justifiably be labeled 'God' (or even agree that any such being exists). Moreover, even among those who do 'believe in God', there is no agreement on which set of writings, if any, can justifiably be considered an authoritative communication from this being. And finally, even among those who affirm the same divinely inspired, written revelation, there is often little agreement on what is actually said on important issues.

There remains, however, other means by which Tom and Bill can attempt to assess their conflicting beliefs. If Tom and Bill aren't able to contact the instructor or find a syllabus, they might contact other students who had attended class on the day the date for the exam in question was announced. If all those contacted are in agreement with either Tom or Bill, then the issue will for all practical purposes be settled. But, of course, this method will also be of little value in the religious context since the pluralistic challenge only exists, at least in part, because no consensus of the requisite type has emerged.

Finally, if Tom and Bill are also not able to contact a sufficient number of class members, they might attempt to construct some sort of evidential argument intended to establish directly the correct date. For example, they might attempt to discover if all the previous exams have been given on a certain day of the week and use this as an objective evidential standard for resolving the conflict.

Now, of course, this approach has in fact often been employed in discussions of religious pluralism. Many have given serious consideration to those independent arguments for or against the 'formed' beliefs in question—e.g., those arguments for or against the existence of the Judeo-Christian God or the claim that we as humans can communicate with such a being. And this approach has, in principle, the greatest potential for objectively resolving the conflict in question. In fact historically, many theists have thought the pluralistic conflict can in this manner be resolved. That is, they have firmly believed that sound arguments do establish that the beliefs formed by the faculties of one set of religious individuals are alone true. Even today, many philosophers and theologians believe that the consideration of such arguments can help us clarify issues and possibly 'weed out' certain religious beliefs which are inconsistent or in other ways defective. However, few philosophers and theologians—especially those such as Plantinga in the analytic tradition—now believe that there exists any argument supporting a given set of specific theistic beliefs which obligates all who consider it to accept its conclusion.

However, might there not at least be some way in which a theist can justifiably establish the truth of her formed beliefs for herself? That is, might it not be the case that, although she cannot produce arguments which obligate all individuals to acknowledge that the religious beliefs which have been formed in her are more worthy of affirmation that those incompatible beliefs produced by the faculties of others, she can at least establish that *she* is justified in believing her own formed beliefs are most worthy of affirmation? One possibility along this line presents itself.

Many theists, someone might argue, believe that God has produced an external epistemic standard by which we can judge our formed beliefs. Many Judeo-Christians, for instance, believe the Bible to be the ultimate epistemic standard in relation to which believers not only can, but must, assess the 'accuracy' of their formed beliefs. Now, of course, such an evaluation tool cannot be used to resolve the pluralistic challenge in an objective, 'public' sense. But it can be used justifiably by a theist to resolve the pluralistic challenge in a personal, 'private' sense. That is, a theist who accepts the epistemic authority of this external standard can justifiably cite consistency with this standard as a basis for believing that only those formed beliefs consistent with her own are true. In one sense, this line of reasoning seems quite plausible. If we grant a theist her independent grounds for believing not only that her God exists and has created her with religious belief-forming faculties but also that this being has produced an authoritative written and/or natural epistemic standard, then there appears to be little reason, in principle, not to grant that she could justifiably use such a standard to attempt to resolve the pluralistic challenge for herself.

But this line of reasoning generates a negative response to the other question with which we are presently concerned: the question of whether, in the face of religious pluralism, a theist's formed religious beliefs can still be considered properly basic. For if the consideration of the pluralistic challenge has led a theist to believe that she must assess her 'formed beliefs' by an independent epistemic standard before she can justifiably accept them as true, then, of course, such beliefs can no longer be considered basic. Whatever positive epistemic status such beliefs *now* possess is based primarily on the theist's independent grounds for the acceptance of the assessment standard in question. In short, such a theist has now clearly become an evidentialist.

But there are, as mentioned earlier, *two* basic approaches available to those attempting to resolve epistemic conflicts of the type under consideration. One can, as we have seen, attempt to establish directly that one set of formed beliefs is true. But one can also turn one's attention to the reliability of the faculties in question. That is, one can attempt to find reasons for supposing that one's belief forming faculties are working better than one's rivals. For example, Bill and Tom might try to assess the reliability of their belief forming faculties by attempting to determine whether either had stayed up too late the night before the relevant class or had been taking some form of medication or had been talking to another student when the announcement was made.

This approach, of course, has also often been employed by those attempting to resolve the challenge of religious pluralism. Many theists have argued, for instance, that their opponents have faculties which have been damaged by 'the fall' or are under the control of some evil force or have been desensitized by too much interaction with 'worldly' concerns. But, not surprisingly, those criticized in this manner do not agree. In fact, they criticize the reliability of their opponents' faculties on exactly the same grounds. And I can see no objective, nonquestion-begging basis for determining which, if any, of the parties in this debate is correct.

But cannot the theist at least use this approach to attempt to resolve the pluralistic challenge for herself? It will, of course, not help her in this context to make any sort of appeal to the reliability of religious belief-forming faculties in general. It won't help her, for example, to argue with Plantinga that she as a theist can trust her own faculties because she has good reasons to believe they "have been designed, no doubt, with reliability in mind" by an all-powerful, all-knowing creator.[14] Such reliability, if established, only exacerbates the pluralistic challenge. For the better the reasons we have for assuming that religious faculties are, in general, reliable, the harder it becomes to make sense of the fact that such faculties generate such a wide variety of often incompatible beliefs.

But what if a theist maintains that she has what she considers to be adequate reasons for believing that the religious faculties of only a small subset of individuals (herself included) function reliably? What if she maintains, for example, that she has good reasons to believe that the 'fall' tainted the religious faculties of all but a select few (herself included), whose faculties God has chosen to reinfuse with reliability. As stated earlier, she will certainly not be able to establish this fact in an objective, public sense. But if we grant her this contention, can't she then justifiably argue that the problem of pluralism has been resolved for her personally? And, more importantly, can't she also justifiably contend that her formed religious beliefs retain their proper basicality?

I believe the answer to both questions is yes. If we grant a theist the exclusivity thesis in question, then I see no reason to deny she has justifiably resolved the pluralistic challenge for herself. And she has done so without appealing to arguments whose conclusions are the formed beliefs in question. She has done so rather by establishing the epistemic superiority of the belief-forming faculties from which the beliefs in question have come. Thus, I believe such formed beliefs can justifiably be considered *basic*—i.e., not themselves based on propositional evidence. And since she has met her obligation to attempt to resolve the pluralistic challenge, I believe these basic beliefs can be considered properly basic.

However, by approaching the pluralistic challenge in this manner, our theist has in a very important, anti-Plantingan sense again become an evidentialist. The proponent of NAT, remember, does not believe she is obligated to produce propositional evidence for her formed beliefs. Nor, more importantly, does she feel obligated to establish the reliability of her own belief-forming faculties—i.e., she believes she can justifiably assume her own religious faculties are innocent until proven guilty. But the theist in question acknowledges that the pluralistic challenge obligates her to do more than simply defend her own religious faculties. She believes she must establish the 'epistemic superiority' of her faculties. Moreover, she believes she has identified positive reasons for doing so—i.e., for maintaining that her belief-forming faculties are superior to those of her opponents. Thus, since to be an evidentialist in this context, remember, is to be someone who thinks we must have "some positive reason to think" a belief is true, our theist has again entered the evidentialist camp in a sense incompatible with one aspect of Plantinga's negative apologetic thesis.

Where, then, does all this leave the knowledgeable theist who has discovered no compelling 'public' or 'private' evidential basis for resolving the pluralistic challenge? That is, where does this leave the theist who can find no compelling public or private evidential basis for holding either that her specific beliefs alone are true or that her faculties are superior? Is there any nonevidential manner in which she can resolve the pluralistic challenge for herself while continuing to maintain justifiably that her formed beliefs are properly basic?

I believe the answer to this question is yes. If a theist who has comparatively analyzed the various competing sets of religious (and nonreligious) truth claims in an attempt to resolve the pluralistic challenge has not uncovered any compelling evidential basis for affirming hers, then I believe she is justified in resolving the conflict in her favor by an appeal to personal preference—

---

[14] Plantinga, ibid, p. 413.

a feeling (itself a basic, formed belief) that the set of basic religious truth claims she has found formed in her better organizes and explains the relevant components of reality than any other. Moreover, since she has met the relevant epistemic obligations by comparatively analyzing the competing sets of truth claims, I believe she is justified in claiming that her formed beliefs remain properly basic.

However, it is important in closing to distinguish once again between this model of 'nonevidential' religious belief justification and that proposed by Plantinga. Plantinga is a nonevidentialist in the sense that he thinks that we *need not* search for propositional evidence to support our formed beliefs' or the reliability of our own belief-forming faculties. On the other hand, it is my contention that, given the pluralistic challenge, the knowledgeable theist is required to look for such propositional evidence although she can justifiably continue to consider her formed beliefs properly basic even if none is found.

Moreover, I believe this distinction is important. If leading analytic philosophers of religion such as Plantinga were to use their considerable skills not only to defend religious beliefs but also to evaluate comparatively the 'content' of such beliefs, we could, I believe, begin to address seriously many of the theoretical and practical conflicts which differing religious perspectives generate.[15]

Questions

1. How does David Basinger show that Alvin Plantinga is a nonevidentialist?

2. What are the specifics of Plantinga's model of belief justification?

3. What are the two basic approaches available to those who are interested in resolving epistemic conficts?

4. Does Basinger think that there is a nonevidentialist route open to the theist who wants to resolve the pluralistic challenge? If so, what is it?

5. According to Basinger, why can the theist continue to think that her formed beliefs are properly basic even if no propositional evidence is available?

---

[15] I would like to thank William Alston and William Hasker for helpful comments made on earlier drafts of this paper.

PLURALISM[*]

Alvin Plantinga

Plantinga considers pluralism as a possible defeater for theism—it has the potential of counting against the rationality of faith if the objection works. The basic strategy, formed by Schellenberg, is the idea that consideration of pluralism should lead one to conclude that the probability of one's belief in Christianity, in the doctrine of the Trinity as a particular example, should lead one to see that the probability of belief in the Trinity is relatively low. This is challenged by Plantinga with the question, What is the body of evidence? A similar line is taken regarding morality and pluralism, and a similar rejoinder is offered. The conclusion drawn is, faith that God exists remains a properly basic belief.

Postmodernism, therefore, doesn't offer anything that can sensibly be thought a defeater for Christian belief. But what about the facts of religious pluralism, the fact that the world displays a bewildering and kaleidoscopic variety of religious and antireligious ways of thinking, all pursued by people of great intelligence and seriousness? There are theistic religions, but also at least some nontheistic religions (or perhaps nontheistic strands of religion) among the enormous variety of religions going under the names 'Hinduism' and 'Buddhism'. Among the theistic religions, there are Christianity, Islam, Judaism strands of Hinduism and Buddhism, American Indian religions, some African religions, and still others. All of these differ significantly from each other. Furthermore, there are those who reject all religion. Given that I know of this enormous diversity, isn't it somehow arbitrary, or irrational, or unjustified, or unwarranted (or may oppressive and imperialistic) to endorse one of them as opposed to all the others? How can it be right to select and accept just one system of religious belief from all this blooming, buzzing confusion? Won't that be in some way irrational? And don't we therefore have a defeater for Christian belief? As the sixteenth-century writer Jean Bodin put it, "each is refuted by all."[1] According to John Hick: "In the light of our accumulated knowledge of the other great world faiths, [Christian exclusivism] has become unacceptable to all except a minority of dogmatic diehards."[2]

This is the problem of pluralism, and our question is whether a knowledge of the facts of pluralism constitutes a defeater for Christian belief. The specific problem I mean to discuss can be thought of as follows. To put it in an internal and personal way, I find myself with religious beliefs, and religious beliefs that I realize aren't shared by nearly everyone else. For example, I believe both

---

[*] This article is courtesy of Oxford University Press. It appears in *Warranted Christian Belief*.
[1] *Colloquium Heptaplomeres de rerum sublimium acranis abditis*, written by 1593 but first published in 1857. English translation by Marion Kuntz (Princeton: Princeton University Press, 1975), p. 256.
[2] *God Has Many Names*, p. 27. It *is* no doubt true that Christian *exclusivism (see below* for a definition *of* that term) *is a* minority opinion in the world at large: I suppose there are no more than a *couple of* billion *or so* Christian exclusivists, with the world's population perhaps approaching three times that figure. *Of* course, these matters are not really settled by counting heads. If they were. however, it would be of some interest to note that there are perhaps a million times more of those "dogmatic diehards" than people who accept anything like Hick's pluralism.

(1) The world was created by God, an almighty, all-knowing and perfectly good personal being (the sort of being who holds beliefs, has aims and intentions, and can act to accomplish these aims)

and

(2) Human beings require salvation, and God has provided unique way of salvation through the incarnation, life, sacrificial death, and resurrection of his divine son.[3]

Now I realize there are many who do not believe these things. First, there are those who agree with me on (1) but not (2): there are non-Christian theistic religions. Second, there are those who don't accept either (1) or (2), but nonetheless do believe that there is something beyond the natural world, a something such that human wellbeing and salvation depend on standing in a right relation to it. And third, in the West and since the Enlightenment, anyway, there are people—*naturalists*, we may call them—who don't believe any of these three things. Some speak here of a *new* awareness of religious diversity, and speak of this new awareness as constituting (for us in the West) a crisis, a revolution, an intellectual development of the same magnitude as the Copernican revolution of the sixteenth century and the alleged discovery of evolution and our animal origins in the nineteenth.[4] No doubt there is at least some truth to this. Of course the fact is all along many Western Christians and Jews have known that there are other religions, and that not nearly everyone shares *their* religion. The ancient Israelites—some of the prophets, say—were clearly aware of Canaanite religion; and the apostle Paul said that he preached "Christ crucified, a stumbling block to Jews and folly to the Greeks" (1 Corinthians 1:23). Other early Christians, the Christian martyrs, say, must have suspected that not everyone believed as they did. The church fathers, in offering defenses of Christianity, were certainly apprised of this fact; Origen, indeed, wrote an eight-volume reply to Celsus, who urged an argument very similar to those urged by contemporary pluralists.[5] Aquinas, again, was clearly aware of those to whom he addressed the *Summa contra Gentiles*: and the fact that there are non-Christian religions would have come as no surprise to the Jesuit missionaries of the sixteenth and seventeenth centuries or to the Methodist missionaries of the nineteenth. Still, in recent years probably *more* Western Christians have become aware of the world's religious diversity; we have probably learned more about the people of other religious persuasions, and we have come to see more clearly that they display what looks like real piety, devoutness, and spirituality. What is new, perhaps, is a more widespread sympathy for other religions, a tendency to see them as more valuable, as containing more by way of truth, and a new feeling of solidarity with their practitioners.

---

[3] Note that it is no part of (2) to add that those—the Old Testament patriarchs, for example, as well as countless others—who haven't encountered this way of salvation cannot share in it.

[4] Thus Joseph Runzo: "Today, the impressive piety and evident rationality of the belief systems of other religious traditions, inescapably confronts Christians with a crisis—and a potential revolution" ("God, Commitment, and Other Faiths: Pluralism vs. Relativism," *Faith and Philosophy* 5, no. 4 (October 1988), pp. 343ff.

[5] See Robert Wilken's paper "Religious Pluralism and Early Christian Thought", so far unpublished. Wilken focuses on the third century; he explores Origen's respone to Celcus, and concludes that there are striking parallels between Origen's historicalsituation and ours."What is different today, I suspect, is not that Christianity has to confront other religions," he says, "but that we now call this situation 'religious pluralism'".

Now one way to react to these other religious responses to the world is to continue to believe what I have all along believed; I learn about this diversity, but continue to believe (i.e., take to be true), such propositions as (1) and (2) above, consequently taking to be false any beliefs, religious or otherwise, that are incompatible with (1) and (2). Following current practice, I shall call this *exclusivism;* the exclusivist holds that the tenets or some of the tenets of *one* religion—Christianity, let's say—are in fact true; he adds, naturally enough, that any propositions, including other religious beliefs, that are incompatible with those tenets are false. Here we need a couple of initial qualifications. First, I shall use the term 'exclusivism' in such a way that you don't count as an exclusivist unless you are rather fully aware of other faiths, have had their existence and their claims called to your attention with some force and perhaps fairly frequently, have noted that the adherents of other religions sometimes appear to display great intelligence, moral excellence, and spiritual insight, and have to some degree reflected on the problem of pluralism, asking yourself such questions as whether it is or could be really true that the Lord has revealed himself and his programs to Christians, say, in a way in which he hasn't revealed himself to those of other faiths. And second, suppose I am an exclusivist with respect to (1), for example, but reasonably believe, like Thomas Aquinas, say, that I have a knock-down drag-out argument, a demonstration or conclusive proof of the proposition that there is such a person as God; and suppose I think further that if those who don't believe (1) were to be apprised of this argument (and had the ability and training necessary to grasp it, and were to think about the argument fairly and reflectively), they too would come to believe (1). Then, obviously, the facts of religious pluralism would not furnish me with a defeater for (1). My condition would be like that of Kurt Gödel, upon his recognition that he had a proof for the incompleteness of arithmetic. True, many of his colleagues and peers didn't believe that arithmetic was incomplete, and some believed that it *was* complete; these facts did not give Gödel a defeater for his belief; he had his proof, after all. Furthermore, he wouldn't have had a defeater in these facts even if he were *mistaken* in thinking he had a proof.

Accordingly, I shall use the term 'exclusivist' in such a way that you don't count as an exclusivist if you rationally think you know of a demonstration or conclusive argument for the belief with respect to which you are an exclusivist, or even if you rationally think you know of an argument that would convince all or most intelligent and honest people of the truth of that proposition. And our question is whether it is possible to be a rational exclusivist in the above sense; our question, that is, is whether I have a defeater for my Christian belief in my knowledge of the facts of religious pluralism, coupled with my belief that I do not have a proof or argument that can be counted on to convince those who disagree with me. Must I recognize that the existence of these other ways of thinking gives me a defeater for my own?

I. A Probabilistic Defeater?

Precisely how would such a defeater work? Suppose we begin by considering a *probabilistic* antitheistic argument from pluralism. J. L. Schellenberg asks us to "Consider first the case of one who supposes there to be a number of mutually exclusive religious alternatives to a certain religious belief r having probabilities equal to the probability of r."[6] He then suggests that such a person ought to suppose that r is improbable (less likely than its denial)—at any rate if she thinks there is more than one alternative having a

---
[5] "Pluralism and Probability," *Religious Studies*, 33 no. 2 (June 1997), p. 147.

probability equal to that of r; hence she ought not believe it. Schellenberg then concedes that the typical believer will not suppose that what she believes is no more probable than alternatives to it (if she did, why would she be *believing* it?); but he thinks his argument can nonetheless be restated as follows:

> Summarizing (and allowing fur a non-uniform assignment of probabilities to alternatives), we can say quite generally that the following may be held by the critic to be a sufficient condition for the improbability of any religious belief r with an epistemic status superior to that of each of its alternatives: r is improbable if the number of times by which its probability exceeds that of each of the available mutually exclusive alternatives (or the average of their probabilities) is exceeded by the number of those alternatives.

By way of example:

> Even if a Christian were to suppose her trinitarian belief to be significantly *more* likely to be true than each of the various Jewish, Hindu, Buddhist...alternatives, the application of the approach here described could still yield the conclusion that her belief was probably false. For it might upon reflection seem intuitively obvious or at any rate very likely to the Christian that the degree of superiour probability she could credibly claim would not be sufficient to prevent the combined probability of the relevant alternatives from outweighing that of the beliefs she holds. (p. 148)

The basic idea, therefore, is that reflection on the facts of pluralism should lead the believer to think that the probability of her belief is relatively low, perhaps even less than .5. But here is the crucial question: probability with respect to *what*? What is the body of evidence with respect to which Schellenberg thinks the Christian's belief must be more probable than not, if she is not to be irrational? If it is the set of beliefs *actually accepted* by the believer, then, of course, the probability of her beliefs will be 1. After all, the believer doesn't just think it *likely* that, for example, Jesus Christ is the divine son of God; she *believes* it; it is a member of the set of propositions she believes; hence its probability with respect to that set is 1. If *that* set isn't one Schellenberg has in mind, however, which one is it? What is the body of beliefs Christian belief must be probable with respect to in order to be reasonable? Schellenberg's approach (like so many others) seems to make sense only if the believer, to be rational, must hold her Christian beliefs on the basis of their relation to *other* beliefs she has—or, at any rate, only if those Christian beliefs *are* probable with respect to those other beliefs. One of the main burdens of this however, is that the believer can be perfectly rational in accepting some of her beliefs in the *basic* way—not on the basis (probabilistic or otherwise) of other beliefs.

No doubt there are subsets S of her total set of beliefs with respect to which Christian belief is indeed improbable; perhaps, in fact, it is improbable with respect to the rest of what she believes (supposing for the moment, that there is some neat way to segregate her Christian belief from her other beliefs). But how is that relevant? The same will be true, no doubt, with respect to many other beliefs she holds in perfect rationality. She is playing bridge and is dealt all the sevens and eights. The odds against this are pretty formidable; there are many alternatives that are at least equally probable; does that mean that her belief that she was dealt all the sevens and eights is irrational? Of course not. The reason, clearly, is that this belief has a source of warrant independent of any it gets by way of its probabilistic relations to her other beliefs. The same goes for Christian belief. If there is a source of warrant for Christian belief that is independent of any it acquires by way of probabilistic relations to other beliefs, then the fact (if it is a fact) that Christian belief isn't particularly likely with respect to those others doesn't show anything of much interest. It certainly doesn't provide a defeater for Christian belief.

II. The Charge of Moral Arbitrariness

This approach, therefore, appears to be a nonstarter. Is there something else in the nearby bushes that could produce a defeater? Perhaps the most important suggestion in the neighborhood is that there is something *arbitrary* about accepting Christian belief. This arbitrariness is thought to have both a moral and an intellectual component: it is thought to be both unjustified (contrary to doxastic duty) and irrational. The moral charge is that there is a sort of egoism. perhaps pride or hubris, in accepting beliefs when one realizes both that others do not accept them and that in all likelihood one possesses no arguments that would convince those dissenters. The epistemic charge also focuses on arbitrariness: here the claim is that the exclusivist is treating similar things differently, thus falling into intellectual arbitrariness. And the idea would be that in either case, when the believer comes to see these things, then she has a defeater for her belief, a reason for giving it up or, at the least, holding it with less firmness. I shall focus on the moral charge, dealing with the charge of epistemic arbitrariness *ambulando*.

A. The Abstract Case

The moral charge is that there is a sort of self-serving arbitrariness, an arrogance or egoism, in accepting such propositions as (1) or (2); one who accepts them is guilty of some serious moral fault or flaw. According to Wilfred Cantwell Smith, "except at the cost of insensitivity or delinquency, it is morally not possible actually to go out into the world and say to devout, intelligent, fellow human beings: '...we believe that we know God and we are right; you believe that you know God, and you are totally wrong.'"[7] So what can the believer say for herself? Well, it must be conceded immediately that if she believes (1) or (2), then she must also think that those who believe something incompatible with them are mistaken and believe what is false: that's just logic. Furthermore, she must also believe that those who do not believe as she does—those

---

[7] *Religious Diversity* (New York: Harper and Row, 1976), p. 14. A similar statement from John Hick:

> Nor can we reasonably claim that our own form of religious experience. together with that of the tradition of which we are a part, is veridical whilst others are not. We can of course claim this; and indeed virtually ever religious tradition has done so, regarding alternative forms of religion either as false or as confused and inferior versions of itself.... Persons living within other traditions, then, are equally justified in trusting their own distinctive religious experience and in forming their beliefs on the basis of it...let us avoid the implausibly arbitrary dogma that religious experience is all delusorv with the single exception of the particular form enjoyed by the one who is speaking. *(An Interpretation of Religion,* p. 235).

On the topic of epistemic arrogance, see also Paul De Vries "The 'Hermeneutics' of Alvin Plantinga." *Christian Scholar's Review* (June 1989), pp. 363ff.; Lee Hardy, "The Interpretations of Alvin Plantinga," *Christian Scholar's Review* (December 1991), pp. 163ff.; my reply *"Ad De Vries," Christian Scholars Review* (December 1991). pp. 171ff.; and De Vries's reply to Hardy and myself, "Intellectual Humility and Courage: An Essential Epistemic Tension," *Christian Scholars Review* (December 1991). pp. 179ff.

who believe neither (1) nor (2), whether or not they believe their negations—*fail* to believe something that is true, deep, and important. Of course she *does* believe this truth; hence she must see herself as *privileged* with respect to those others—those others of both kinds. There is something of great value, she must think, that *she* has and *they* lack. They are ignorant of something—something of great importance—of which she has knowledge. But does this make her properly subject to the above censure?

I think the answer must be no. Or if the answer is yes, then I think we have here a genuine moral dilemma, a situation in which no matter what you do, you are wrong. Given the pluralistic facts of the matter, there is no real alternative; there is no reflective attitude that is not open to the same strictures. These charges of arrogance are a philosophical tar baby: get close enough to them to use them against the Christian believer, and you are likely to find them stuck fast to yourself. How so? As follows: as an exclusivist, while I realize that I can't convince others that they should believe as I do, I nonetheless continue to believe as I do. And the charge is that I am, as a result, arrogant or egoistical, arbitrarily preferring my way of doing things to other ways.[8] But what are my alternatives with respect to a proposition like (1) or (2)? There are three choices.[9] I can continue to hold it; I can withhold it, in Roderick Chisholm's sense, believing neither it nor its denial; or I can accept its denial. Consider the third way, way taken by those pluralists who, like John Hick, hold that such propositions as (1) and (2) and their colleagues from other faiths are literally false, although in some way still valid responses to the Real. This seems to me to be no advance at all with respect to the arrogance or egoism problem; this is not a way out. If I do this I will then be in the very same condition as I am now: I will believe many propositions others don't believe, realizing that I have no argument that will necessarily convince those others. For I will then believe the denials of (1) and (2) (as well as the denials of many other propositions explicitly accepted by those of other faiths). Many others, of course, do not believe the denials of (1) and (2), and in fact believe (1) and (2). I am therefore in the condition of believing propositions that many others do not believe; I also realize I have no demonstrations of what I believe. If, in the case of those who believe (1) and (2), that is sufficient for intellectual arrogance or egoism, the same goes for those who believe their denials. This third alternative, therefore, is no help at all with respect to the arrogance-egoism-arbitrariness problem.

So consider the second option: I can instead *withhold* the proposition in question. I can say to myself: "The right course here, given that I can't or couldn't convince these others of what *I* believe, is to believe neither these propositions nor their denials:" The pluralist objector can say that the right course is to *abstain* from believing the offending proposition, and also abstain from believing its denial: call him, therefore, 'the abstemious pluralist'. Does he thus really avoid the condition that, on the part of the exclusivist, leads to the charges of egoism and arrogance? Not really. Think, for a moment, about disagreement. Disagreement, fundamentally, is a matter of adopting conflicting attitudes with respect to a given proposition. In the simplest and most familiar case, I disagree with you if there is

---

[8] "The only reason for treating one's tradition differently from others is the very human but not very cogent reason that it is one's own!" (John Hick, *An Interpretation of Religion*, p. 235).

[9] To speak of choice here suggests that I can simply *choose* which of these three attitudes to adopt, which is wholly unrealistic. Perhaps we have very little control over our beliefs; then the moral critic of belief can't properly accuse the believer of dereliction of moral duty, but he could still argue that her stance is unhappy, regrettable, a miserable state of affairs. Even if I can't help it that I am overbearing and conceited, my being that way is a bad state of affairs.

some proposition *p* such that I believe *p* and you believe -*p*. That's just the simplest case, however; there are also others. The one that is presently of interest is this: you believe *p* and I withhold it, fail to believe it. Call the first kind of disagreement 'contradicting'; call the second 'dissenting'.

My claim is that if *contradicting* others is arrogant and egoistical, so is *dissenting*. For suppose you believe some proposition *p* that I don't believe: perhaps you believe that it is wrong to discriminate against people simply on the grounds of race, while I, recognizing that there are many people who disagree with you, do not believe this proposition. I don't disbelieve it either, of course; but in the circumstances I think the right thing to do is to abstain from belief. Then am I not implicitly condemning your attitude, your *believing* the proposition, as somehow improper—naive, perhaps, or unjustified, or unfounded, or in some other way less than optimal? I am implicitly saying that my attitude is the superior one; I think my course of action here is the right one and yours somehow wrong, inadequate, improper, in the circumstances at best second-rate. I realize that there is no question, here, of *showing* you that your attitude is wrong or improper or naive; so am I not guilty of intellectual arrogance? Of a sort of egoism, thinking I know better than you, arrogating to myself a privileged status with respect to you? The problem for the believer was that she was obliged to think she possessed a truth missed by many others; the problem for the abstemious pluralist is that he is obliged to think that he possesses a virtue others don't, or acts rightly where others don't. If one is arrogant by way of believing a proposition others don't, isn't one equally arrogant by way of withholding a proposition others don't?

Perhaps you will respond by saying that the abstemious pluralist gets into trouble, falls into arrogance, by way of implicitly saying or believing that his way of proceeding is *better* or *wiser* than other ways pursued by other people; and perhaps he can escape by abstaining from *that* view as well. Can't he escape the problem by refraining from believing that racial bigotry is wrong, and also refraining from holding the view that it is *better*, under the conditions that obtain, to withhold that proposition than to assert and believe it? Well, yes, he can; then he has no *reason* for his abstention; he doesn't believe that abstention is better or more appropriate; he simply does abstain. Does this get him off the egoistical hook? Perhaps. Of course he can't, in consistency, also hold that there is something wrong with *not* abstaining, with coming right out and *believing* that bigotry is wrong; he loses his objection to the exclusivist. Accordingly, this way out is not available for the abstemious pluralist who accuses the exclusivist of arrogance and egoism.

Indeed, I think we can see that the abstemious pluralist who brings charges of intellectual arrogance against the believer is in a familiar but perilous dialectical situation; he shoots himself in the foot, is hoist with his own petard, holds a position that in a certain way is self-referentially inconsistent in the circumstances. For he believes

(3) If *S* knows that others don't believe *p* (and, let's add, knows that he can't find arguments that will persuade them of *p*), then *S* should not believe *p*;

this or something like it is the ground of the charges he brings against the believer. The abstemious pluralist realizes, no doubt, that many do not accept (3); and I suppose he also realizes that it is unlikely that he can find arguments for (3) that will convince them. Given his acceptance of (3), therefore, the right course for him is to abstain from believing (3), to withhold or disbelieve it. Under the conditions that do in fact obtain—namely, his knowledge that others don't accept it—he can't properly accept it. So if (3) is true, nobody can believe it without being arrogant. (3) is either true or false; if the first, I fall into arrogance if I believe it; if the second, I fall into falsehood if I believe it; so I shouldn't believe it.

I am therefore inclined to think that one can't, in the circumstances, properly hold (3) or any other proposition that will do the job the objector wants done. One can't find here some principle on the basis of which to hold that the believer is doing the wrong thing, suffers from some moral fault—that is, one can't find such a principle that doesn't; as we might put it, fall victim to itself.

The abstemious pluralist is therefore self-referentially inconsistent; but even apart from this dialectical argument (which in any event some will think unduly cute), aren't the charges against the exclusivist unconvincing and implausible? I must concede that there are a variety of ways in which I can be and have been intellectually arrogant and egoistic; I have certainly fallen into this vice in the past, will no doubt fall into it in the future, and am not free of it now. Still, am I really arrogant and egoistic just by virtue of believing something I know others don't believe, where I can't show them that I am right? Suppose I think the matter over, consider the objections as carefully as I can, realize that I am finite and furthermore a sinner, certainly no better than those with whom I disagree, and indeed inferior both morally and intellectually to many who do not believe what I do. But suppose it *still* seems clear to me that the proposition in question is true: am I really immoral in continuing to believe it? I am dead sure that it is wrong to try to advance my career by telling lies about my colleagues. I realize there are those who disagree (even if they would never so much as consider lying about their colleagues, they think nothing is really right or wrong); some of these are people whom I deeply respect. I also realize that in all likelihood there is no way I can show them that they are wrong. Nonetheless, I think they are wrong. If I think this after careful reflection—if I consider the claims of those who disagree as sympathetically as I can, if I try my level best to ascertain the truth here—and it *still* seems to me sleazy, despicable, *wrong* to lie about my colleagues to advance my career, could I really be doing something immoral in continuing to believe as before? I can't see how. If, after careful reflection and thought, you find yourself convinced that the right propositional attitude to take to (1) and (2), in the face of the facts of religious pluralism, is abstention from belief, how could you properly be taxed with egoism for so abstaining? Even if you knew others did not agree with you? And won't the same hold for believing them? So I can't see how the moral charge against exclusivism can be sustained, and if it can't, this charge does not provide a defeater for Christian belief.

B. A Concrete Case: Gutting

So far we have been considering this charge of moral arbitrariness in abstraction from any actual presentation of a pluralistic case for the arbitrariness or egoism of accepting Christian belief. To remedy that defect, I propose to consider the argument Gary Gutting[10] gives for this conclusion. As we saw above, the classical foundationalist holds that there is a duty or obligation to accept only what one sees to be at least probable with respect to foundational certainties. Gutting accepts the deontology of the classical picture, but proposes a different duty. Because of "the modern phenomenon of religious

---
[10] *Religions Belief and Religious Skepticism* (Notre Dame: University of Notre Dame Press, 1982); page references to Gutting's work are to this book.

disagreement," he says, Christian and theistic belief requires justification (p. 11). Gutting means to investigate the question whether someone can justifiably, dutifully accept Christian belief, *given that there is disagreement about it* (and presumably given that she is aware of the disagreement). The question is not (as with the classical picture) whether being justified in accepting Christian belief requires evidence just as such; the question is whether being justified requires evidence or argument *once you know that others disagree with you*.

His conclusion, in brief, goes as follows. (1) We must begin by distinguishing "decisive assent" from "interim assent:" When I give decisive assent to *p*:

> I view the present case for *p* as allowing me to end the *search* for reasons for or against believing *p*. Interim assent, on the other hand, accepts *p* but without terminating inquiry into the truth of *p*. Its effect is to put me on the side of *p* in disputes about its truth. However, my endorsement of *p* is combined with a commitment to the epistemic need for continuing discussions of *p*'s truth. (105)

That is, I believe that "further discussion is needed for the project of determining the truth of *p*:" (2) A person has a right to give *decisive* assent to a proposition that she knows others don't assent to only if she has a good argument for that proposition. (3) She has a right to give *interim* assent to a proposition which others reject, even if she doesn't have good arguments for it. (4) Since there is a good argument (one from religious experience) for the existence of God, taken vaguely as "a good and powerful being, concerned about us, who has revealed himself to human beings" (p. 171), we have a right to give this proposition decisive assent. Finally, (5) there is no argument of this sort for specific Christian doctrines (for the belief, e.g., that in Christ, God was reconciling the world to himself) or for more specific beliefs about God, such as that he is all-powerful, or wholly good, or all-knowing, or the creator of the heavens and the earth.

Clearly there is much to discuss here, and much to question. I shall restrict myself to the following. (1) What does Gutting mean by justification'? And (2) *why* am I not justified in giving decisive assent to a proposition for which I don't have a good argument and about which I know people disagree? As to the first, he clearly thinks of justification in deontological terms, in terms of right and wrong, duty and obligation, being within one's epistemic rights. Someone who accepts traditional Christian belief in the face of disagreement and without having an argument for her beliefs, he charges, is not satisfying her intellectual obligations. What duty, specifically, is it that she violates? The duty to avoid epistemological egoism. *That's* the duty that is violated by the Christian who is aware of disagreement but has no good arguments:

> First believing *p* [when I don't have an argument and know that others disagree] is arbitrary in the sense that there is no reason to think that my intuition (i.e., what seems obviously true to me) is more likely to be correct than that of those *who* disagree with me. Believing *p* because its truth is supported by *my* intuition is thus an *epistemological egoism* just as arbitrary and unjustifiable as ethical egoism is generally regarded to be. (p. 86, Gutting's emphasis)

> [A] neutral epistemic observer has no intuitions pro or con about *p* and has not thought about *p* to an extent sufficient to make his not having any intuitions significant. From the point of view of such an observer, the facts are simply these (taking for simplicity the case of disagreement between two peers): (1) person A has an intuition that *p* is true; (2) person B has an intuition that *p* is false; (3) there is no reason to think that either A or B is more likely to be correct in his intuition. Surely the only proper attitude for such an observer is to withhold judgment on *p*.

> But even if I am A or B, should I not judge the situation in the same way as the neutral observer? Surely it is wrong to prefer my intuition simply because it is mine. (p. 87)

So there is a moral problem with the believer who knows others disagree with her but does not have an argument for her own views: she is being epistemically arrogant, egoistic, and self-centered in thus arbitrarily preferring the way *she* thinks things are to the way others think they are. (And perhaps, once she sees this, she will have a defeater for those beliefs.)

Here we must ask some questions. First, is it really true that if I am such a person, then I "prefer my intuition simply because it is mine"? Not really. I think it is wrong to discriminate against someone just because he's of a different race (even though I know others disagree). I am not aware of any *arguments* for my belief here, or at any rate any arguments that would convince those dissenters; the view just seems right to me. Still, it isn't the case that I accept this belief on the grounds that it is *my* belief or *my* intuition: that makes no sense. I don't accept it as the conclusion of an argument, the premise of which is that this *is* my intuition; I am not reasoning as follows: *p seems to me to be right,* therefore *p*. I don't accept it on the basis of other propositions at all. It is true that I accept it because, when I think about it, it seems right; the 'because', however, doesn't mean that the latter is my *reason,* or *argument* or *evidence* for the former.

> If Gutting's position is to have real bite, he must tell us more about those arguments the possession of which protects me from epistemological egoism when I believe something others do not believe. What kind of an argument is required? Well, such an argument, he says, must be a good argument. Fair enough; bad arguments won't do the job; but what is goodness, for an argument? In the chapter on Rorty to which I referred above (p. 431), Gutting apparently agrees with Rorty that a good argument (good 'for me') consists in reasons that are accepted by my epistemic community. If that is how the wind blows, however, there will be little problem for the Christian; after all, the Christian epistemic community may be quite prepared to accept reasons for Christian belief (e.g., that Scripture affirms it) that those outside that community will not accept. So taken, Gutting's requirement is easy to meet—trivially easy to meet.
>
> So let's suppose he has something more stringent in mind. A good argument, presumably, will be valid, and must also have some nonformal virtues: it must not be circular or beg the question against those with whom I disagree. But then what about its premises? If my argument is valid, won't the same disagreement break out with respect to the premises? If they are also propositions that wouldn't be accepted by those who disagree with me, then presumably I won't have a right to accept *them* either, unless I have a further argument for them. Of course the premises of that further argument will have to meet the same conditions: if others don't accept them, then I can't give them decisive assent unless I have a further good argument for them. The result seems to be that my duty precludes my being party to any *ultimate* disagreements, at least any *ultimate* disagreements of which I am aware, and at least as far as decisive assent goes. Can that be right? Perhaps there is no way you can find much moral common ground with a member of the Ku Klux Klan. Perhaps you can't find any premises you both accept that will serve in a good argument for your views and against his. Would it really follow that you don't have a right to give decisive assent to the proposition that racial bigotry is wrong? Hardly.

Well, perhaps it is Gutting's idea that if I don't have an argument for *p* and know that others don't believe it, then I am being egoistical. even if I don't reason in the above fashion—that is, don't believe or accept the intuition just because it is mine. But is this really true? Certainly not just as it stands. We can see this by going back to an earlier example. The police haul me in, accusing me of a serious crime: stealing your Frisian flag again. At the police station, I learn that the mayor claims to have seen me lurking around your back door at the time (yesterday midafternoon) the crime occurred; I am known to resent you (in part because I am peeved about your article in The *National Enquirer* according to which I am really an alien from outer space). I had means, motive, and opportunity; furthermore there have been other such sordid episodes in my past. However, *I* recall very clearly spending the entire afternoon on a solitary hike near Mount Baker. My belief that I was hiking there then isn't based on argument. (I don't note, e.g., that I feel a little tired, that my hiking boots are muddy, and that there is a topographical map of Mount Baker in my parka pocket, and then conclude that the best explanation of these phenomena is that I was hiking there.) Furthermore, I can't think of any argument or any other way to convince the police that I was at Mount Baker (sixty miles from the crime scene) when the theft took place. Nevertheless, I believe that's where I was. So I hold a belief for which I can't give an argument and which I know is disputed by others. Am I therefore guilty of epistemological egoism? Surely not.

Why not? Because I *remember* where I was, and *that* puts me within my rights in believing that I was off hiking, even if others disgree with me. Well, not quite; strictly speaking, it is, I suppose, my *believing* that I remember, rather than my *actually* remembering, that puts me in the right, morally speaking. I am justified, am not going contrary to duty or obligation here, because I believe, and nonculpably believe, that I have a source of knowledge or information about my movements that the police don't have: my memory. If I thought that I knew no more than they knew, and *still* held firmly to the belief that I was innocent, then, perhaps, I would be epistemically egoistical. But I think I know something they don't, and know it by way of a means to knowledge they don't have. (They know about where *they* were by memory, not about where I was.) It is because of this that I am not flouting any duties or obligations; this is what confers justification on me. It is because of this that I can't properly be accused of arbitrariness or egoism in preferring my view to theirs.

Because this is the crucial point here, let's look into it a bit further. Both rationality and epistemic duty, says the critic, requires that one treat similar cases similarly. The Christian believer, however (she says), violates this duty by arbitrarily believing (1) and (2) (above, p. 438) in the face of the plurality of conflicting religious beliefs the world presents. Well, let's suppose that rationality and epistemic duty do, indeed, require treating similar cases similarly. Clearly you do not violate this requirement if the beliefs in question are *not* on a par. And the Christian believer thinks they are *not* on a par: she thinks (1) and (2) *true* and those incompatible with either of them *false. So* they aren't relevantly similar, as she sees it, and she isn't treating similar cases differently. To make his case, therefore, the critic would have to argue that Christian belief is, in fact, false; but presumably he doesn't intend his charge of arbitrariness to depend on the assumption that Christian belief is false.

The rejoinder, of course, will be that it is not *alethic* parity (their having the same truth value) that is at issue: it is *epistemic* parity that counts. What kind of epistemic parity? Well, perhaps the critic is thinking initially of *internal* epistemic parity: parity with respect to what is internally available to the believer. What is internally available includes, for example, detectable relationships between the belief in question and other beliefs you hold; so internal parity would include parity of propositional evidence. What is internally available to the believer also includes the *phenomenology* that goes with the belief in question: the *sensuous* phenomenology, and also the nonsensuous phenomenology involved, in doxastic evidence, in the belief's just having the feel of being *right*. Once more, then, (1) and (2) are not on an internal par, for the Christian believer, with beliefs that are incompatible with them. After all, (1) and (2) *do* seem to her to be true; they do have for her the phenomenology that accompanies that seeming, and they do have doxastic evidence for her; the same cannot be said for propositions incompatible with them.

The next rejoinder: isn't it likely that those who reject (1) and (2) in favor of other beliefs have propositional evidence for their beliefs that is on a par with that of the Christian for her beliefs; and isn't it also probably true that the same or similar phenomenology accompanies their beliefs as accompanies hers? So that those beliefs really are epistemically and internally on a par with (1) and (2), and the believer is still treating like cases differently? I don't think so: I think there really are arguments available for (1), at least, that are not available for its competitors. As for similar phenomenology, this is not easy to say; it is not easy to look within the breast of another; it is hard indeed to discover this sort of thing, even with respect to someone you know really well. Still, I am prepared to stipulate both sorts of parity. Let's agree for the purpose of argument that these beliefs are on an epistemic par in the sense that those of a different religious tradition have the same sort of internally available markers—evidence, phenomenology, and the like—for their beliefs as the Christian has for (1) and (2). What follows?

Return to the case of moral belief King David saw the beautiful Bathsheba, was smitten, sent for her, slept with her, and made her pregnant. After the failure of various stratagems to get her husband, Uriah, to think he was the father of the baby, David arranged for Uriah to be killed by telling his commander to "put Uriah in the front line where the fighting is fiercest; then withdraw from him so he will be struck down and die" (2 Samuel 11:15). Then the prophet Nathan came to David and told him a story about a rich man and a poor man. The rich man had many flocks and herds; the poor man had only a single ewe lamb, which grew up with his children, "ate at his table, drank from his cup, lay in his bosom, and was like a daughter to him:" The rich man had unexpected guests. Instead of slaughtering one of his own sheep, he took the poor man's single ewe lamb, slaughtered it, and served it to his guests. David exploded in anger: "The man who did this deserves to die!" Then, in one of the most riveting passages in all the Bible, Nathan turns to David, stretches out his arm, points to him, and declares, *"You are that man!"* And then David sees what he has done.

My interest here is in David's reaction to the story. I agree with David: such injustice is utterly and despicably wrong; there are scarcely words for it. I believe that such an action is wrong, and I believe that the proposition that it *isn't* wrong—either because really *nothing* is wrong, or because even if *some* things are wrong, *this* isn't—is false. As a matter of fact, there isn't a lot I believe more strongly. I recognize, however, that plenty of people disagree with me; many believe that some actions are *better,* in one way or another, than others, but that none is really right or wrong in the full-blooded sense in which I think this action is. Once more, I doubt that I could find an argument to show them that I am correct and they incorrect. Further, for all I know, their conflicting beliefs have for them the same internally available epistemic markers, the same phenomenology, *mutatis mutandis,* as mine have for me; perhaps they have the same degree of doxastic evidence. Am I then being arbitrary, treating similar cases differently in continuing to hold, as I do, that in fact that kind of behavior is dreadfully wrong? I don't think so. Am I wrong in thinking racial bigotry despicable, even though I know that others disagree, and even if I think they have the same internal markers for their beliefs as I have for mine? Again, I don't think so. I believe in serious actualism, the view that no objects have properties in worlds in which they do not exist, not even nonexistence. Others do not believe this; I am unable to convince them; and perhaps the internal markers of their dissenting views have for them the same qualities as mine have for me. Am I being arbitrary in continuing to think as I do? I can't see how.

And the reason here is this: in each of these cases, the believer in question doesn't really think the beliefs in question *are* on a relevant epistemic par. She may agree that she and those who dissent are equally convinced of the truth of their belief, and even that they are internally on a par, that the internally available markers are similar, or relevantly similar. Still, she must think that there is an important epistemic difference: she thinks that somehow the other person has made a mistake, or has a blind spot, or hasn't been wholly attentive, or hasn't received some grace she has, or is blinded by ambition or pride or mother love or something else; she must think that she has access to a source of warranted belief the other lacks.[11] If the believer concedes that she *doesn't* have any special source of knowledge or true belief with respect to Christian belief—no *sensus divinitatis,* no internal instigation of the Holy Spirit, no teaching by a church inspired and protected from error by the Holy Spirit, nothing not available to those who disagree with her—*then,* perhaps, she can properly be charged with an arbitrary egoism, and *then,* perhaps, she will have a defeater for her Christian belief But why should she concede these things? She will ordinarily think (or at least *should* ordinarily think) that there are indeed sources of warranted belief that issue in these beliefs. (And here we have a way in which the epistemologist can be of use to the believer.)

She believes, for example, that in Christ, God was reconciling the world to himself; she may believe this on the basis of what the Bible or church teaches. She knows that others don't believe this and furthermore don't accept the Bible's (or church's) authority on this or any other point. She has an explanation: there is the testimony of the Holy Spirit (or of the divinely founded and guided church); the testimony of the Holy Spirit enables us to accept what the Scriptures teach. It is the Holy Spirit who "seals it upon our hearts, so that we may certainly know that God speaks"; it is the work of the Holy Spirit to convince our hearts that what our ears receive has come from him."[12] She therefore thinks she is in a better epistemic position with respect to this proposition than those who do not share her convictions; for she believes she has the witness of the divinely guided church, or the internal testimony of the Holy Spirit, or perhaps still another source for this knowledge. She may be *mistaken,* in so thinking, deluded, in serious and debilitating error, but she needn't be *culpable* in holding this belief. In this case, as in the Frisian flag episode, the believer nonculpably believes that she has a source of knowledge or true belief denied those who disagree with her. This protects her from epistemic egoism, as well as from the defeater that might acc awareness of it.[13]

---

[11] And of course the pluralist critic must think the same sort of thing. He thinks the thing to do when there is internal epistemic parity is to withhold judgment; he knows that there are others who don't think so (and won't be convinced by any argument he can muster), and, for all he knows, that belief has internal parity with his. If he continues in that belief, therefore, he will be in the same condition as the person he criticizes; but if he doesn't continue in this belief, he no longer has an objection.

[12] Calvin, *Commentaries on the Catholic Epistles,* tr. and ed. John Owen (Grand Rapids: Baker Book House, 1979), commentary on 1 John 2:27, p. 200.

[13] Even if she isn't egoistic in accepting Christian belief, won't she nevertheless have a defeater, here, if, in fact, Christian belief *is* on an epistemic par with its denial? Not if she doesn't believe that it is. She could perhaps be *given* such a defeater, if Gutting or someone could produce a powerful argument for the claim that there is epistemic parity here. As we saw in chapter 8, however, it is likely that Christian belief is such that if it is true, then it is warranted for those who accept it. This means that an argument for the conclusion that Christian belief is on an epistemic par with unbelief would require a previous

As a result, of course, the serious believer will not take it that we are all, believers and unbelievers alike, epistemic peers on the topic of Christian belief. She will probably feel considerable sympathy for Cardinal Newman:

> in the schools of the world, the ways towards Truth are considered high roads open to all men, however disposed, at all times. Truth is to be approached without homage. Everyone is considered on a level with his neighbor, or rather, the powers of the intellect, acuteness, sagacity, subtlety and depth, are thought the guides into Truth. Men consider that they have as full a right to discuss religious subjects, as if they were themselves religious. They will enter upon the most sacred points of Faith at the moment, at their pleasure—if it so happen, in a careless frame of mind, in their hours of recreation, over the wine cup.[14]

Newman's idea is that there is something in addition to "the powers of the intellect, acuteness, sagacity, subtlety and depth" that is needed for a proper discussion of religious subjects, or at least for a proper grasp of the truth with respect to them. Here he is echoing Jesus: "I praise you, Father, Lord of heaven and earth, because you have hidden these things from the wise and learned, and revealed them to little children" (Luke 10:21). If these things are hidden from the wise and learned, it won't be relevant to complain that the wise and learned don't accept them (adding that it is epistemically egoistic to accept what the wise and learned do not unless you have a good argument). The Christian believer will therefore think there is an important source of knowledge, here, in addition to the powers of intellect mentioned. So on this point he believes, presumably nonculpably, that those who disagree with him are really not his epistemic peers on *this* topic, even though he might be vastly inferior to them, epistemically speaking, on other topics.

The central question here, therefore, is whether the Christian's beliefs are or are not on an epistemic par with the beliefs of those who disagree with her. This is the crucial issue. If something like the extended Aquinas/Calvin (A/C) model presented in chapter 8 [*Warranted Christian Belief*] is in fact correct, then there is a significant difference between the epistemic situation of those who accept Christian belief and those who do not; the objector is therefore assuming, unjustifiably and without argument, that neither that model nor any other according to which there is a source of warranted Christian belief is in fact correct and that there is no such source for Christian belief. That assumption has nothing to be said for it; the arbitrariness charge therefore disintegrates.

> Now Gary Gutting, to be sure, claims (p. 84) that the believer does not have a right, in this context, to the view that he is better off, epistemically speaking, than the unbeliever. He gives two reasons.[15] First, the believer's view that he is the beneficiary of the *sensus divinitatis* or the internal instigation of the Holy Spirit, or the teaching of a church inspired and protected from error by the Holy Spirit or "derives from theological doctrines that presuppose theism and so cannot be legitimately called upon in a defense of the believer's epistemic right to

---

argument that Christian belief is false. But if the critic already has an argument for the falsehood of Christian belief, why is he bothering with this charge of arbitrariness?

[14] *Sermons, Chiefly on the Theory of Religious Belief, Preached before the University of Oxford* (London. Rivington, 1844), pp. 190-91.

[15] As Marie Pannier pointed out in discussion, perhaps Gutting should really have given a third, which would be to reapply his principle that one can justifiably give only interim assent to any proposition she knows is not accepted by others; for presumably the believer knows that others, such as the objector, won't agree that the believer is better off epistemically speaking, than the unbeliever.

accept theism"; and second, "there are at least some believers who themselves do not see 'God exists' as obviously properly basic; it is very hard to see how the believer can nonarbitrarily apply Calvin's views to that they are his epistemic peers."

These arguments seem mistaken. Gutting's second reason for thinking the Christian doesn't have a right to think there are such sources of warranted belief seems irrelevant: the fact that some believers do think belief in God is properly basic does not so much as slyly suggest that there are no such sources. What about the first reason, the claim that the believer is involved in some objectionable form of *circularity* if she thinks that she is the beneficiary of one of those sources of belief? But how can she be involved in circularity? She isn't putting forward an *argument* for anything; nor is she proposing a *definition*: so how does circularity so much as rear its ugly head? If she were giving an argument for theism and then proposed as a premise that she enjoyed the benefits of one of those special sources of belief, *then* her argument might be circular. But she isn't arguing for that; nor need she be arguing for anything else. Am I engaged in objectionable circularity if I appeal to physics to help explain how it is that I can perceive trees and grass—even if my knowledge of physics rests in part on observation? Not if I am not arguing for the conclusion that perception is a source of warranted belief.

But don't the realities of religious pluralism count for *anything*? Is there nothing at all to the claims of the pluralists?[16] Could that re be right? Of course not. For at least some Christian believers, an awareness of the enormous variety of human religious responses does seem to reduce the level of confidence in their own Christian belief. It doesn't or needn't do so by way of an *argument*. Indeed, there aren't any respectable arguments from the proposition that many apparently devout people around the world dissent from (1) and (2) to the conclusion that (1) and (2) are false or can be accepted only at the cost of moral or epistemic deficiency. Nevertheless, knowledge of others who think differently can reduce one's degree of belief in Christian teaching. From a Christian perspective, this situation of religious pluralism is itself a manifestation of our miserable human condition; and it may indeed deprive Christians of some of the comfort and peace the Lord has promised his followers. It can also deprive the believer of the *knowledge* that (1) and (2) are true, even if they are true and he *believes* that they are. Since degree of warrant depends in part on degree of belief, it is possible, though not necessary, that knowledge of the facts of religious pluralism should reduce his degree of belief and hence the degree of warrant (1) and (2) enjoy for him; it can therefore deprive him of knowledge of (1) and (2). He might be such that if he *hadn't* known the facts of pluralism, then he would have known (1) and (2), but now that he *does* know those facts, he doesn't know (1) and (2). In this way he may come to know less by knowing more.

Things *could* go this way, with the exclusivist. On the other hand, they *needn't* go this way. Consider once more the moral parallel. Perhaps you have always believed it deeply wrong for a counselor to use his position of trust to seduce a client. Perhaps you discover that others disagree; they think it more like a minor peccadillo, like running a red light when there's no traffic; and you realize that possibly these people have the same internal markers for their beliefs that you have for yours. You think the matter over more fully, imaginatively recreate and rehearse such situations, become more aware of just what is involved in such a situation (the breach of trust, the injustice and unfairness, the nasty irony of a situation in

---

[16] See W. P. Alston, "Religious Diversity and Perceptual Knowledge of God." *Faith und Philosophy* 5, no. 4 (October 1988), pp. 433ff.

which someone comes to a counselor seeking help but receives only hurt), and come to believe even more firmly that such an action is wrong. In this way, this belief could acquire more warrant for you by virtue of your learning and reflecting on the fact that some people do not see the matter your way. Something similar can happen in the case of religious beliefs. A fresh or heightened awareness of the facts of religious pluralism could bring about a reappraisal of one's religious life, a reawakening, a new or renewed and deepened grasp and apprehension of (1) and (2). From the perspective of the extended A/C model, it could serve as an occasion for a renewed and more powerful working of the belief-producing processes by which we come to apprehend (1) and (2). In this way knowledge of the facts of pluralism could initially serve as a defeater; in the long run, however, it can have precisely the opposite effect. The facts of religious pluralism, therefore, like historical biblical criticism and the facts of evil, do not or need not constitute a defeater for Christian belief.

Questions

1. What does Plantinga mean by somethings counting as a *defeater*?

2. How does he see pluralism counting as a possible defeater for the probability of a Christian's belief in say, the doctrine of the Trinity (as an example)?

3. How does he think of pluralism as counting as a possible defeater against a Christian's approach to morality?

4. What do you make of Plantinga's response to both charges?

5. What weaknesses, if any, do you see in Plantinga's response?

CONTRIBUTORS

1. Marilyn McCord Adams is Recigious Professor of Divinity at Oxford University and canon at Christ Church, Oxford. Before coming to Oxford, she was Horace Tracy Pitkin professor of historical theology at Yale University, and for 21 years in the philosophy department at the UCLA. Her publications include the following books: *William of Ockham* (2 vols), *Horrendous Evils and the Goodness of God*, *What Sort of Human Nature: The Metaphysics and Systemics of Christology*, and *Wrestling for Blessing*—as well as many articles on medieval and philosophical theology.
"Resources to the Rescue"

2. Robert Merrihew Adams is a senior research fellow of Mansfield College, Oxford, and visiting professor of philosophy at Oxford University. He taught philosophy for thirty-five years at the University of Michigan, UCLA, and Yale University. He works in ethics, metaphysics, and the history of modern Western philosophy, as well as the philosophy of religion. His books include *The Virtue of Faith and Other Essays in Philosophical Theology* (1987), *Leibniz: Determinist, Theist, Idealist* (1994), and *Finite and Infinite Goods: A Framework for Ethics* (1999), all from Oxford University Press.
"Kierkegaard's Arguments Against Objective Reasoning in Religion"
"Divine Commands and the Social Nature of Obligation"

3. William P. Alston, a graduate of Centenary College, he received his Ph.D. from the University of Chicago. He taught at the University of Michigan, Rutgers University, the University of Illinois, and has held visiting appointments at the University of California at Los Angeles, and Harvard University. He is Emeritus Professor of Philosophy, Syracuse University, and is author of *Philosophy of Language, Epistemic Justification: Essays in the Theory of Knowledge, Perceiving God, Divine Nature and Human Language, The Epistemology of Religious Experience, The Rationality of Sense Perception,* is editor of *Religious and Philosophical Thought* and is co-editor of *The Problems of Philosophy*, and *Reading in Twentieth-Century Philosophy*. He is co-founder of *Faith and Philosophy*, and the First President of the Society of Christian Philosophers.
"Religious Experience and Religious Belief"
"The Inductive Argument from Evil and the Human Cognitive Condition"

4. Anselm of Canterbury (1033-1109 A.D.), Benedictine monk, second Norman Archbishop of Canterbury, and philosophical theologian dubbed "the Father of Scholasticism," is famous for his "faith seeks understanding" method, his ontological argument for God's existence, the necessity of the Incarnation argument, and his satisfaction theory of the Atonement. He is the author of the *Cur Deus Homo, Monologion* and the *Proslogion*, the latter which contains his ontological argument included in this collection.
"The Ontological Argument"

5. Thomas Aquinas (1224/5-1274/5 A.D.), from Roccasecca, schooled at Monte Casino, a Dominican and the greatest medieval philosopher/theologian, is justly famous for his two classic works, the *Summa Theologiciae* (*Summation of Theology*), and the *Summa Contra Gentiles* (*On the Truth of the Catholic Faith Against the Gentiles*), and who during a Mass in 1273, had a vision and ceased writing until his death four months later. He authored commentaries on Aristotle's thought and is famous for his "five proofs" for the existence of God, three of which are cosmological. He stressed two routes to knowledge of God, the natural light of reason, and faith by which one accesses special revelation, the Word of God.
"On Faith"

6. Stephen M. Barr is professor of physics at the Bartol Research Institute, the University of Deleware, and is author of numerous articles in physics and philosophy of science, and *Modern Physics and Ancient Faith*. His areas of specialty are, physics, philosophy of science and philosophy of religion.
"Quantum Theory and Free Will"

7. David Basinger is Dean of Faculty and a professor of philosophy at Roberts Wesleyan College in Rochester, NY. While most of his teaching currently is with adult and graduate students in areas of applied ethics-bioethics, business ethics, and ethics in education-his main research remains the philosophy of religion. The author or co-author of numerous articles and a number of books on God's nature and mode of interaction with the world, he is co-author of *Reason and Religious Belief* (which appears in Russian and a forthcoming Chinese edition), author of *Divine Power*

in Process Theism: A Philosophical Critique, and co-editor of Philosophy of Religion, Selected Readings. His most recent book is Religious Diversity: A Philosophical Assessment (Ashgate, 2002).
"Planatinga, Pluralism and Justified Religious Belief"

8. Philip Clayton holds a Ph.D. in both philosophy and religious studies from Yale University. He has taught at Haverford College and Williams College. He has also held posts as Humboldt Professor and Senior Fulbright Professor at the University of Munich, and was professor and Chair of the Department of Philosophy at Sonoma State University, specializing in philosophy of science and philosophy of religion. He is presently professor of philosophy at Claremont Graduate School. He is author of forty articles in philosophy of science, philosophy of religion, and *Explanation From Physics to Theology, An Essay in Rationality and Religion* (with a German edition), *The Problem of God in Modern Thought*, and the Templeton Prize-winning, *God and Contemporary Science*. He is the first recipient of the Templeton Research Prize. He is currently Principle Investigator of the Science and Spiritual Quest Project at CTNS in Berkeley, California, a project aimed at bringing together top scientists from around the world to speak at major public events on the connections between science and spirituality.
"Science, Religion and Explanation"

9. Robin Collins, is professor of philosophy at Messiah College in Grantham, Pa. He received undergraduate degrees in mathematics and physics at Washington State University and completed two years of graduate study in theoretical physics at the University of Texas at Austin,. In 1993, he received his Ph.D. in Philosophy at the University of Notre Dame, after which he held a postdoctoral fellowship in Philosophy of Science at Northwestern University. He is widely published, with around a dozen articles and book chapters specifically addressing the argument for design from physics and cosmology. He is currently constructing a website (www.robincollins.org) and completing a book, *The Well-Tempered Universe: God, Fine-Tuning, and the Laws of Nature*, devoted to this argument.
"A Scientific Argument for God's Existence: The Fine-Tuning Design Argument"

10. William Lane Craig, served as Visiting Professor of Philosophy at the Catholic University of Luvain, and is currently professor of philosophy at Talbot Theological Seminary/Biola University. He has authored numerous articles in philosophy of religion and philosophy of science, and many books including, co-author of, *Theism, Atheism, and Big Bang Cosmology*, author of *The Kalām Cosmological Argument*, *The Only Wise God*, and *The Problem of Foreknowledge and Future Contingents from Aristotle to Suarez*.
"What Place, Then, for a Creator?: Hawking on God and Creation"

11. Peter Thomas Geach, British logician and admirer of McTaggart. He is professor of philosophy at Leeds University and author of numerous articles in philosophy and *Mental Acts* (1958), and *Reference and Generatization* (1962). A vigorous defense of Christian morality and theodicy is given in *The Virtues* (Cambridge University Press, 1977), *Providence and Evil (1977)*, and *God and the Soul*. He is the husband of Elizabeth Anscombe.
"Omnipotence and Almightiness"

12. John Hare, was professor of philosophy at Calvin College, then taught in the Department of Philosophy at Baylor University, and is currently professor of philosophy at Yale University in New Haven. He is author of numerous articles in ethics and philosophy of religion, and two books, *Ethics in International Affairs*, and *The Moral Gap*. He has been a presenter at the China Symposia. His areas of specialty include philosophy of religion, ethics, ancient philosophy and the philosophy of Immanuel Kant.
"Kant on Recognizing Our Duties as God's Commands"

13. William Hasker is professor of philosophy at Huntington College, and is author of *God, Time and Knowledge, Metaphysics: Constructing a Worldview*, co-author of *Reason and Religious Belief, The Openness of God: A Biblical Alternative to the Traditional Conception of God*, and *The Emergent Self*. He has served as Co-Chair of the China Committee, and he is currently Editor of *Faith and Philosophy*. His areas of specialty include metaphysics, epistemology, and philosophy of religion.
"Middle Knowledge"

14. John Hick is Emeritus Danforth Professor of the Philosophy of Religion at Claremont Graduate School, and was formerly H. G. Wood Professor of Theology and Fellow of the Institute for Advanced Research in the Humanities at the University of Birmingham, England, and is author of *Evil and the God of Love, Faith and Knowledge, Philosophy of Religion, Death and Eternal Life, God Has Many Names*, and other major works in modern theology. He is also editor of the *Philosophy of Religion Series* for Macmillan of London/St. Martin's of New York.

"Religious Pluralism and Salvation"

15. David Hume (1711-1776 A.D.), a Scottish philosopher, perhaps the greatest eighteenth century philosopher. While in La Flèche, France, he authored *Treatise of Human Nature, Essays: Moral and Political, Dialogues Concerning Natural Religion, Philosophical Essays Concerning Human Understanding, An Inquiry Concerning the Principles of Morals and a History of England.*
"Of Miracles"

16. Norman Kretzmann was Susan Linn Sage Professor of Philosophy at Cornell University and co-editor with Eleonore Stump of *Reasoned Faith, Hermes and Athena: Biblical Exegesis and Philosophical Theology*, and *The Cambridge Translations of Medieval Philosophical Texts* and wrote numerous articles on philosophers of the ancient and medieval periods, and in philosophy of religion. In addition to his special interest in Medieval philosophy, he wrote extensively in the area of philosophy of religion.
"Eternity"

17. Robin Le Poidevin was born in 1962, and educated at Oriel College, Oxford. He took a doctorate at Cambridge and in 1998-99 was Gifford Research Fellow at the University of St. Andrews. He joined the Leeds philosophy department in 1989, and is now Professor of Metaphysics there. He is the author of *Change, Cause and Contradiction* (Macmillan, 1991), *Arguing for Atheism, An Introduction to the Philosophy of Religion* (Routledge), and *Travels in Four Dimensions* (Oxford, 2003). *He is the co-editor* (with Murray MacBeath) *of The Philosophy of Time* (Oxford, 1993), *and editor of Questions of Time and Tense* (Oxford, 1998).
"Can the Theist Refuse to Answer the Problem of Evil?"

18. John L. Mackie (1917-81) was born in Australia, and lived an taught in Australia and New Zealand before moving to England. He was Reader in philosophy at Oxford University and Fellow of University College, Oxford. He was influential for his 'error theory' of moral values. He auhored six books including *The Cement of the Universe, Ethics: Inventing Right and Wrong, Hume's Moral Theory* and *The Miracle of Theism* and numerous journal articles in logic, philosophy of religion and ethics.
"Evil and Omnipotence"

19. Michael Martin is professor of philosophy at Boston University, and author of numerous articles in philosophy of religion, and an influential volume, *Atheism: A Philosophical Justification*. His areas of specialty include philosophy of religion, epistemology and metaphysics.
"The Argument from Miracles"

20. George I. Mavrodes is emeritus professor of philosophy at the University of Michigan, and is author of *Belief in God, A Study in the Epistemology of Religion, Revelation and Religious Belief*, and is co-editor of *Problems and Perspectives in the Philosophy of Religion*, and *Rationality and Religious Belief*. He has been a presenter at China symposia. His areas include, metaphysics, epistemology and philosophy of religion.
"Some Puzzles Concerning Omnipotence"
"Miracles and the Laws of Nature"

21. Alan Padgett was professor of theology and philosophy of science at Azusa Pacific University, then Bethel University, and is currently professor of theology and philosophy of science at Luther Theological Seminary. and is author of *God, Eternity and the Nature of Time, The Mission of the Church in Methodist Perspective*, and is editor of *Reason and the Christian Religion* (a Fetschrift to Richard Swinburne). He is past president of the Western Region of the American Academy of Religion, and founder and President of the Christian Theological Research Fellowship (CTRF).
"A New Doctrine of Eternity"

22. Alvin Plantinga holds a B.A. from Calvin College and has degrees from the University of Michigan and Yale University where he also taught. He has taught at Calvin College, and has served as visiting professor at many universities. He was Director of the Institute for Philosophy of Religion, University of Notre Dame, and John A. O'Brien Professor of Philosophy at the University of Notre Dame. He has lectured at countless universities in the U.S., Europe, China, Russia, and other former Soviet Block countries. He is author of numerous articles and *God and Other Minds, The Nature of Necessity*, and the three volume work, *Warrant: The Current Debate, Warrant and Proper Function* and *Warranted Christian Belief, Does God Have a Nature?*, edited *Faith and Philosophy*, and co-edited *Faith and Rationality, Reason and Belief in God*. He is Past President of the Society of Christian Philosophers and the American Philosophical Association. He was a recipient of a Guggenheim Fellowship, and served as a Gifford Lecturer.

"The Extended Aquinas/Calvin Model"
"The Free Will Defense"
"Pluralism"

23. Bruce Reichenbach received his Ph.D. from Northwestern University. He is professor of philosophy at Augsburg College, and is author of *The Cosmological Argument: A Reassessment, Is Man the Phoenix?, Evil and a Good God, The Law of Karma, A Philosophical Study, In Behalf of God: A Christian Ethics for Biology, Logical Reasoning,* and is co-author of *Reason and Religious Belief* and co-editor of, *Philosophy of Religion, Selected Readings.* He was a Fulbright Scholar at Daystar University, Nairobi, Kenya, and has returned to Daystar as a Visiting Philosopher. He has also been a participant in the China symposia. His areas of specialty include philosophy of religion, Eastern thought, and metaphysics.

"The Cosmological Argument"
"Monism and Immortality"

24. William Rowe is professor of philosophy at Purdue University and the author of several works in philosophy of religion, including *Philosophy of Religion: An Introduction, Religious Symbols and God: A Philosophical Study of Tillich's Theology, The Cosmological Argument, Thomas Reid on Morality and Freedom,* and co-editor of, *Philosophy of Religion: Selected Readings.*

"An Examination of The Cosmological Argument

25. Bertrand Russell (1872-1970), Third Earl Russell, British philosopher, mathematician, and Nobel Prize-winner (Literataure). One of the most influential philosophers of the contemporary periood, he taught at Cambidge University. He is co-author of the *Principia Mathematica,* author of *Our Knowledge of the External World, The Problems of Philosophy, Mathematical Logic, History of Western Philosophy, Religion and Science, Mysticism and Logic, An Inquiry into Meaning and Truth, Human Knowledge, Introduction to Mathematical Philosophy, Freedom versus Organization, Logic and Knowledge, The Analysis of Mind,* and *The Analysis of Matter.* He taught at Cambridge University.

"The Finality of Death"

26. Melville Y. Stewart did post-doctoral work at Oxford (1986). He served as a Visiting Professor of Philosophy at the University of St. Petersburg (1992-3), Russia, St. Petersburg Christian College, a Pew Scholar (1996), a Fulbright Scholar (2001) and a United Board Scholar (spring, 2004) at Peking University, Beijing, Visiting Scholar at the Central University of the Nationalities (1996), Beijing, and a United Board Scholar at Shandong University (fall, 2004), Jinan, and is Guest Professor at Wuhan University, Wuhan. He was Scholar of the Year at Bethel University (1996), and is emeritus and adjunct professor at Bethel University/Seminary and adjunct at Augsburg College/Capella University and the University of St. Thomas. In addition to receiving a Templeton Award, he has read papers at 25 universities outside the U.S. including Oxford, London, and Edinburgh. He is author of *The Greater-Good Defence, An Essay on the Rationality of Faith,* and co-author of the forthcoming, *Dictionary of Western Philosophy, English/Chinese/Pinyin,* and co-editor of and contributor to nine other books, five in Chinese, 2 in Russian, including *The Trinity, East/West Dialogue* (in English and Russian), *Philosophy of Religion, An Anthology of Contemporary Views* (in English and Chinese).

"O Felix Culpa, Redemption and the Greater-Good Defence"

27. Eleonore Stump received her B.A. in classical languages from Grinnel College (1969), and has a Ph.D. in medieval philosophy from Cornell University (1975). She has taught at Oberlin College, Virginia Tech, and the University of Notre Dame. Since 1992 she has been the Robert J. Henley Professor of Philosophy at Saint Louis University. She is Editor-in-Chief of the *Yale Library of Medieval Philosophy,* and she is section editor of the *Routledge Encyclopedia of Philosophy.* She has held grants from the American Association of University Women, the Mellen Foundation, the Pew Charitable Trusts, the National Endowment for the Humanities, the Center for the Philosophy of Religion at Notre Dame, and the National Humanitites Center. She is author of over ninety articles and fourteen books including, translator and editor of *Boethius's "In Ciceronis Topica," Boethius's "De Topics differentiis,"* and author of *Dialectic and its Place in the Development of Medieval Logic,* and is co-editor of *Reasoned Faith, Mermes and Athena: Biblical Exegesis and Philosophical Theology, The Cambridge Companion to Aquinas,* and *The Cambridge Translations of Medieval Philosophical Texts,* and co-editor of Aquinas, *Philosophy of Religion: The Big Questions,and Augustine,* She has served as President of the Society of Christian Philosophers, the American Catholic Philosophical Association, and was a Gifford Lecturer at Aberdeen University in 2003.

"Eternity"

28. Richard Swinburne, Professor of the Philosophy of the Christian Religion at Oxford University 1985-2002. He is best known for a trilogy of books on the philosophy of theism, *The Coherence of Theism* (1977, revised edition 1993), *The Existence of God* (1979, 2nd edition 2004), and *Faith and Reason* (1981, Second edition forthcoming 2005), and for a trilogy of books on the philosophy of the Christian Religion, *Responsibility and Atonement* (1989), *Revelation* (1991), *The Christian God* (1994), and *Providence and the Problem of Evil* (1998). His short book *Is There a God?* (1996) has been published in Chinese (Peking University Press, 2005). He is also author of several other books on philosophy of science, philosophy of mind and epistemology..
"What Kinds of Religious Beliefs Are Worth Having?"
"The Argument to God From Laws of Nature"
"The Problem of Evil"
"Morality and God"
"What Makes Me Me?"

29. Peter van Inwagen is a graduate of Rensselaer Polytechnic Instsitute and has a Ph.D. from the University of Rochester. He was professor of philosophy at Syracuse University from 1971-1995, and is currently the John Cardinal O'Hara Professor of Philosophy at the University of Notre Dame. He is author of *An Essay on Free Will, Material Beings, God, Knowledge and Mystery, The Possibility of Resurrection and Oher Essays in Christian Apologetics*, and *Ontology, Identity, and Modality: Essays in Metaphysics*, and numerous articles in philosophy. He delivered the Gifford Lectures at St. Andrews University.
"The Possibility of Resurrection"

30. William J. Wainwright is professor of philosophy at the University of Wisconsin-Milwaukee, and is author of numerous articles, and co-editor of, *Rationality, Religious Belief, and Moral Commitment: New Essays in the Philosophy of Religion*, and author of, *Reason and the Heart, A Prolegomenon to a Critique of Passional Reason*. He has also served as Editor of *Faith and Philosophy*, and has taken part in symposia in China.
"Jonathan Edwards and the Heart"

31. Merold Westphal holds a B.A. from Wheaton College, and a Ph.D. from Yale University, and is professor of philosophy at Fordham University. He is author of *History and Truth in Hegel's Phenomenology, God, Guilt, and Death, Suspicion and Faith: The Religious Uses of Modern Atheism.* He has also served as President of the Hegel Society of America and the Søren Kierkegaard Society, and as Executive Co-Director of the Society of Phenomenological and Existential Philosophy. He has taken part in the China symposia, and has conducted short-term lecture series in China.
"Religious Experience and Self-Transcendence"

32. Ludwig Josef Johann Wittgenstein (1889-1951 A.D.), the leading analytic philosopher of the 20th century, whose two major works altered the course of the subject, his *Tractetus Logico-Philosophicus*, and his *Philosophical Investigations*. The former is a mere 75 pages in length, but it represents one of the most important works of the period and of the first stage of his thinking, followed by his Investigations (common referred to as the *PI*). He along with G. E. Moore and Bertrand Russell taught at Cambridge University. His major contribution to philosophy falls under five headings: philosophy of language, philosophy of logic, philosophical psychology, philosophy of mathematics, and clarification of the nature and limits of philosophy itself.
"Lectures on Religious Beliefs"

33. Keith E. Yandell is professor of philosophy and South Asian Studies at the University of Wisconsin-Madison. In his, *The Epistemology of Religious Experience,* he argues against the idea that religious experience is ineffable, and traces the nature of religious experience in both Eastern and Western traditions. He is also author of, *Christianity and Philosophy,* and *Hume's "Inexplicable Mystery."* His areas of specialty include metaphysics, epistemology and philosophy of religion with a special focus on Asian thought.
"The Greater Good Defense"

34. Linda Zagzebski, formerly professor of philosophy for 20 years at Loyola Marymount University, currently holds the Kingfisher Chair in the Department of Philosophy of Religion and Ethics and is Director of Graduate Studies in the Department of Philosophy at the University of Oklahoma. She is the recipient of the national Phi Beta Kappa Society 2005-06 Romanell Professorship in Philosophy. Her publications include 60 journal articles and six books, including, *Divine Motivation Theory, Rational Faith: Catholic Responses to Reformed Epistemology*, and

The Dilemma of Freedom and Foreknowledge, which received the Oxford Best Scholarly Book Award. She is past-president of the American Catholic Philosophical Association, and is currently President of the Society of Christian Philosophers.

"The Molinist Solution"

Editors

Xing Taotao, Co-Editor with Stewart, is associate professor of philosophy at Peking University, and the author of numerous articles in logic and philosophy of religion, and was a United Board Scholar at the University of Notre Dame, 2003-04, during which time he did research and worked as a Team Director on the translation of Alvin Plantinga's book, *Warranted Christian Belief*, published by Peking University Press. Professor Xing team-taught a course on Religious Epistemology with Professor Stewart at Peking University (2001), and has presented papers at the SCP symposia. He is serving as co-author with Dr. Dai Yuanfang (Peking University Press Editor) and Stewart of, *Dictionary of Western Philosophy, English/Chinese/Pinyin*.

Melville Y. Stewart (see author profile above)

GLOSSARY

A

Absolute–the Ultimate Being, completely independent being.

a fortioiri–an asyllogistic mediate inference of the form, if B is greater than C, and A greater than B, then A is greater than C.

agnosia–being in a state of ignorance.

a priori–judgments which are true independent of experience, or concepts which are known independent of experience, for Kant, what is universal and necessary.

a posteriori–judgments which are true dependent upon experience, or concepts which are known through experience.

actualization–the act or process of bringing something into existence, *strong actualization*, a process where God alone brings something into existence, *weak actualization*, that process where God along with the agency of others–created agents–brings something into existence.

agnosticism–the view which says one does not/cannot know, and with regard to God's existence in particular, whether God exists or not.

Allah–the Muslim name for the Supreme Being.

almighty–possessing the capacity to bring about any logically possible set of states of affairs.

analogia entis–analogy of being (Thomas Aquinas).

analogia fidei–analogy of faith (Karl Barth).

analogy–a similarity or sameness between two things in circumstance, description or effect.

analytic philosophy–an Anglo-American style of doing philosophy which involves analysis of concepts, statements, arguments, values, and worldviews.

angel–a non-material agent of the spiritual realm.

anthropomorphism–the attribution of human descriptions/properties to God or non-human creatures.

apologetics–specifically, the defense of a set of religious beliefs, say Christianity, usually a discipline falling under theology.

approximation argument (Adams's portrayal of Kierkegaard's view)–the greatest attainable certainty regarding anything historical is always less than complete and hence always leaves one in a state of incompleteness regarding evidence.

aseity-God's independent existence.

atemporal eternity-the sense of God's eternity where he is viewed as outside of time and where temporal predicates cannot be applied.

atheism-the firm belief that God does not exist, and some contend that one can have evidence justifying this claim.

atonement-that notion whereby some agent, in Christianity, Christ, offers a sacrifice as a substitute for or takes an action of some kind to remove the transgression/sin/guilt of others, specifically humans.

auto-pistic-self-authenticating.

B

basic belief, properly basic–a belief that has *warrant* on its own, its warrant is not derived from another belief or from an argument, and its status of being *properly* basic is the idea that one who believes p has an *epistemic right* to do so (Alvin Plantinga).

Bayes' Theorem–a theorem concerning the probability calculus having to do with conditional probabilities such as, it is probable P (if p, then q).

behaviorism, philosophical–the view that minds or mental properties are reducible to behavior.

belief–for some a positive psychological state φ with regard to a proposition p, for others a disposition to affirm a proposition p.

best-of-all-possible worlds–(Leibniz), is a world, say W_1, that cannot be surpassed in overall positive value by any other possible world, say W_2.

Big Bang theory–the scientific theory that the universe began with an explosion and consequent expansion of an infinitesimally small piece of matter.

blik–the term introduced by R. M. Hare used to refer to ethical and religious statements which he held to be neither true nor false, but rather as ways of expressing one's way of viewing something (e.g., some value) in the world.

Brahma–in Hindu theology, the absolute, self-existent, eternal essence or spirit of the universe. Brahma is primarily seen as the Creator God.

Buddhism–a religion or philosophy (depending upon one's perspective) that had its beginnings in India and spread to China and other parts of Asia. The founder, Gautama the Buddha, was born c. 567 B.C. in Kapilavastu. He was renamed Siddhartha, and was of the Gautama clan. The knowledge had by Gautama which earned him the title the "enlightened one" is expressed in the *Four Noble Truths*: (1) Suffering, existing involves suffering; (2) the cause of suffering is desire (*tanha*); (3) how to end suffering, eliminating desire ends suffering; (4) cessation of suffering via the Noble Eightfold path, right views, right aims, right speech, right conduct, right means of livelihood, right effort, right mindfulness, right meditation. The path Gautama taught was the Middle path between self-indulgence and asceticism.

C

causa sui–literally, "cause of itself," so the idea, something which brings itself into being.

central state materialism–the view that persons are completely material, and talk about minds is just another way of talking about brains or the central nervous system.

Christian empiricism–a Christian approach to knowledge which claims that the chief source of knowledge is experience.

Christian epistemic practice (CEP, Alston)–"takes its defeaters [destructive challenges to faith] from the Bible…the…creeds and certain elements of tradition."

Christianity–a religion with three main traditions, Roman Catholicism, Protestantism, and Orthodoxy, each of which holds as central, (1) the authority of the Scriptures, (2) God is a Trinity of Persons, The Father, Son and Holy Spirit, (3) God created the heavens and the earth, (4) Christ the Son is the Incarnation of God, (5) he offered his life as a Substitutionary Atonement for those who would trust in him for their salvation, (6) Christ will come again and at his coming there will be a judgment and believers will enjoy a resurrection to everlasting life.

Christology–the study of doctrines that have to do with the person and work of Christ.

coherent–not generating a contradiction in concept or assertion.

common sense–the ordinary-meaning-of-terms approach of philosophers like G.E. Moore, or commonly shared beliefs and intuitions as to what is true, right and good.

compatibilism–for any putatively polar concepts or hypotheses, a way of affirming both without contradiction.

Confucianism–thinking derived from the most famous Chinese philosopher, Confucius (551-479 B.C.). There is no one body of doctrine as such, but there are some key ideas and principles that mark off this ancient Chinese philosophical tradition. If there is a central idea, it is the emphasis placed upon the gradual cultivation of the self in the pursuit of certain goals relating to the *tao* (*the Way*) and *te* (*virtue*, or *moral power/potency*). These two concepts are further explained in terms of *jen* (*humanity, goodness, benevolence*), *li* (*rites, ritual, propriety*) and *yi* (*rightness, duty, fittingness*). Self-cultivation was outlined in terms of the aforementioned virtues. Though they shared this common ideal, differences arose as to how the ideal was to be justified, and the sort of metaphysics invoked.

consistency strategy–an attempt to show that putatively contradictory concepts or hypotheses are really consistent/compatible.

contemplation–a process/practice which involves meditation and reflection, as in the religious contemplation of divinity.

control beliefs (Wolterstorff)–beliefs which have the function of either *generating* new beliefs, or as serving as *criteria* for testing the candidacy of new ones.

cosmological argument–for the existence of God that proceeds from observations from experience to the existence of a Supreme Being via the natural light of reason.

counterbalancing good–a good which on balance, evenly offsets the negative value of some evil.

counterfactual conditional of freedom–a conditional, which asserts, that if an agent A were but is not placed in certain circumstances C, then A would freely choose to do x. It is *counterfactual* because it is *not* (when uttered) *the case*, it is a *conditional*, because it is an *if-then statement*, and it is a *freedom* conditional, because A can freely will *to do or not do x*. Example: If Adam were placed in the Garden, he would freely choose to not eat of the fruit of the tree of the knowledge of good and evil.

Credulity Principle (or **Principle of Credulity**-Swinburne)–involves the claim that every proposition believed ("insofar as it is basic") has a probability in one's noetic structure corresponding to the strength of the belief held (*Epistemic Justification*, pp. 141-142).

critical rationalism (Mavrodes)–the view that religious beliefs are subject to rational criticism, but with the further acknowledgement that one can affirm them without requiring that they be proven.

D

de dicto **necessity**–necessity attaching to a proposition.

de re **necessity**–necessity attaching to a being or property.

decree(s)–sometimes in the plural, what God as ultimate sovereign wills.

defeater–evidence or argument that has the potential of destroying or countering a thesis or position.

deism–the view that there is a Supreme Being, but that this being is no longer in a significant causal relationship with the Creation he has brought about.

deontological–having to do with *duty*, a duty-orientated normative ethic.
design argument–the contention that since nature has a means-end ordering, there must be a conscious, non-natural creator of nature/purpose in Creation.
determinism–everything that comes about does so as a necessary result of antecedent causes and conditions.
Deus absconditus–(e.g., John Hick), the idea that God hides himself from the creature, in contrast to *Deus revelatus* which conveys the idea of God revealed..
Dharma–in Hinduism, a religious law or conformity to it, or an ancient sage. It is the teaching of the right way to live.
desire–to long for or wish for something.
divine command theory–the metaethical view that God's issuing of commands is the proper way of understanding of *good*, that is, the *good* is *what God commands*.
doxastic assurance–the conviction to a lesser or greater degree that a belief is true.
dualism–metaphysical, that there are two substances, *mind* and *body*, epistemological, that there are two things in knowing, the *object out there*, and the *content* before the mind or consciousness.
duty–having an obligation to do or perform a certain act or think a certain way (Kant).
dysteological– phenomena in which the means-end relation does not contribute to the organism's wellbeing.

E

efficient cause–the *agent* producing a certain action.
emergent dualism (Hasker)–the idea that the mind is produced by the human brain, and is *emergent* in two senses, that it *has causal powers*, and *possesses libertarian free will* (*The Emergent Self*, p. 188).
Enlightenment or **Age of Reason**–the intellectual movement beginning in the 17th century that emphasized the adequacy of Reason to address and resolve intellectual, moral, and social problems.
epistemic dilemma (Mavrodes)–a problem with regard to beliefs which may be thought contradictory. They are either *hard*, in which case they are not reconcilable, or *soft*, in which case the contradiction is only apparent.
epistemic distance (Hick)–the perception of human agents that God is distant, or not transparent to the creature in experience.
epistemic probability–probability having to do with propositions or statements.
epistemology–theory of knowledge.
eschatology–having to do with last things, or the final stage of human history or end times, in Christian thought, the doctrine of last things.
essence–the basic nature of a thing, without which it would not be what it is.
ET-simultaneity–(Stump/Kretzmann), the *contemporary* occurrence of events in God's eternity with the temporal counterpart for the creature, such that *contemporary* has a sense of *at once* for God similar to the term's application to the creature's experience.
eternal–having no beginning or ending, such as God's eternity, or eternal life.
evidentialism–an approach to belief acquisition which advocates belief only on condition of there being sufficient grounds.
evil, surd–evil that either is, or appears to be without justification/reason(s).
ex nihilo–literally, *out of nothing*, as in the Christian doctrine, God created out of nothing, no pre-existent stuff.

expanding universe–the notion in astrophysics which affirms that all elements in the universe are increasingly moving away from each other, hence the universe is ever growing outwardly.

explanation–to give a causal or rational account of a given phenomenon, to give account of why something happens.

externalism–in epistemology, the view that warrant (Plantinga) does not issue from a private internal process as with Descartes and Locke, but rather from a process that can be publicly observed and followed by others.

extrinsic–external to something.

F

facts–an actual state of affairs, or as J. R. Lucas says, "that upon which two or more disputants agree.".

fall–an event marking the decline of created agents, such as an historical Fall (Augustine), or a single failure of an individual.

falsification–to establish the falsehood of a proposition or hypothesis by appealing to observation(s).

fideism–(Kierkegaard), the view that defenses and arguments are inappropriate responses to God's call to faith, or certain doctrines or beliefs are not subject to rational justification.

fine-tuning design argument–the claim that the universe is carefully tweaked by God so as to bring about conditions incredibly suited for human existence.

finite–infinite distinction-the idea that humans have limitations, hence are finite, in contrast to God who in many ways is not thus confined, but unlimited.

first-cause argument–the argument of Aquinas, for example, that God is an Uncaused Cause which provides a sufficient explanation of all preceding caused causes.

foreknowledge–to know in advance, with *simple* foreknowledge being without the possession of middle knowledge (of all the possible choices).

foundationalism–a metaphor in theory of knowledge which usually involves the claim that there are statements the truth of which are true independent of other propositions or argumentation.

free will, libertarian–having freedom, that is, the option of choosing *x* or *y*, where *x* is *good* and *y* is *evil*.

free will defense–the strategy whereby evil is viewed as justified because God values freedom of choice, and so the creation of free creatures make evil possible.

frequency theory of probability–the view of probability that focuses on the relative frequency of events (Hans Reichenbach, Wesley Salmon).

G

gnosticism–the teachings in the 2nd-4th centuries that combined elements of Plato's *Timaeus* and *Genesis*, and which advocated a dualism of the spiritual/good world and the material/evil world.

God–a Supreme Being, in Christian, Islamic, and Jewish thought that is generally viewed as omnipotent, omniscient, and omnibenevolent.

goods–ethical values of intrinsic positive worth.

gratuitous evil–evil that is without justification.

greater-good defense–the idea that there are goods which logically require evils in order for their (the goods) realization.

H

haecceitism–that quality in terms of which an entity is a definite individual.

hard determinism–the view that everything is causally necessitated by antecedent causes and conditions, and accordingly allows for no significant sense to be given to an agent's being morally responsible.

Heisenberg's Principle of Indeterminacy–the principle that calls attention to how much "coarsening is necessary for crude joint measurement." (Bas C. Van Fraassen, *Quantum Mechanics, An Empiricist View*, p. 231) *Coarsening* is a technical term, but the idea at work is roughly, because the measuring process disturbs the atoms the result is an indeterminacy regarding measurement (some think there is a real indeterminacy).

henothism–the idea (Zhao Dunhua), that there are *many gods*, but that *one* of them evolves into a lofty being and accordingly is ascribed the title, *The Lord of Heaven*.

hermeneutics–the science of interpretation.

hiddenness of God–the notion that God absconds or is non-transparent in the world of experience.

heuristic–a device or methodology which promotes or helps produce an idea or hypothesis.

Hinduism–an Eastern religion beginning about 1700 B.C. It is a non-proselytizing religion based on the on the idea that *Reality* is *one,* but that different religious speakers describe it differently. There is a universal determinism joined with the doctrine of reincarnation of individual eternal souls. The law of karma is the principle that no suffering or pleasure/enjoyment can be undeserved hence everyone reaps what they sow.

I

identity theory–the view of the mind/body which affirms the sameness of the mind and brain, attributing differences of speech about both to the use of different language games.

image of God–the idea that there is a resemblance in some way(s) between God and the creature. Some think that Paul outlines this in terms of *knowledge*, *holiness* and *righteousness* (Ephesians 4:24, Colossians 3:10).

imitatio dei–having to do with *likeness*, rather than *image if* one takes them as having distinctly different senses as does Hick. For Hick the former has the meaning of *being created in his image*, and the latter, the sense of *growing into his likeness*.

immortality–the idea (of Plato and others), that the soul lives on after the death of the body.

immutability–unchanging in nature or essence, as in the case of the divine, God is said to be immutable or unchanging in respect to his essential nature.

imputed righteousness–a righteousness that is transferred to the creature by a divine act or investiture.

Incarnation–coming in or the adorning of flesh, in Christian doctrine, the Incarnation of God is manifest in the historical Jesus of Nazareth.

incoherent–not meaningful, as in a meaningless string of words, or inconsistent as in a proposition or set of propositions..

incomprehensibility–beyond human understanding. The doctrine that God transcends human ability to understand God's nature and ways.

inconsistency strategy–to argue that a set of beliefs is internally inconsistent, that is, not all of the beliefs can be true, because at least one is inconsistent with one or more of the other members of the set.

indexed propositions–propositions which have either temporal predicates such that their truth depends upon their corresponding to temporally indexed facts referred to in the world, or geographical predicates such that their truth depends upon their corresponding to the geographic details referred to in the world.

inductive probability–the probability of an inference from premises to a conclusion, such as, if a, then-probably b.

infallibility–not having error, or without factual mistake.

internalism (Swinburne)–an approach to epistemological theory which sees warrant or justification as issuing from an internal process of knowledge acquisition. It is a knowledge that comes from internal operations of the mind (Descartes, Locke).

Islam–one must distinguish between the philosophical side and the religion that involves belief in and the worship of Allah, one God, and which has its beginnings around 600 A.D. Followers must confess that "there is no God but God," and Muhammad is his prophet. They hold that the *Koran* (*recitation*) was revealed by the angel Gabriel to Muhammed It is the supreme revelation guiding all who wish to be obedient to God. It is a set of religious beliefs that includes God's predestination, divine creation, a Fall, a call to repentance, and the belief in a resurrection and judgment. Followers are called to a holy war (*jihad*) against unbelievers and to promote the faith. Every believer must pray to God five times a day, facing Mecca, and if possible make a pilgrimage to Mecca at least once in a lifetime.

J

Judaism–the religion of the Old Testament that involves the belief in and worship of Yahweh. Some date its beginnings around 2000 B.C. The central doctrines include the oneness of God, God as the Divine Shepherd, the doctrine of Creation, the Fall of humanity, a Messianic King which is variously interpreted, and the final Judgment. There are various rituals such as Circumcision, the Passover, the observance of the Sabbath, offerings for the Forgiveness of Sin, and the Day of Atonement.

K

Kalām argument-the cosmological argument that argues for a first cause in time (Arabic philosophers al-Kindi (c. 870), al-Ghazali (1058-111), and contemporary philosopher, William Lane Craig).

karma–the principle of Eastern thought that individuals reap what they sow, and that this works without failure in the march of nature.

kenotic Christology–the doctrine that the Incarnation of God in Christ involves an emptying of or some sort of reduction of the attributes of omnipotence, omniscience, etc. in respect to the humanity of Christ (Philippians 2).

kerygma–the kernel of the Gospel in the New Testament.

L

law, natural–principles in nature which admit of no exception. In ethics, the view that there are universally valid ethical principles known by reason alone, and hence are accessible to all.

leap of faith (Kierkegaard)–Kierkegaard held that faith must not merely transcend reason, but that it should not rely upon reason in any way. In fact, he held that faith must go against reason's deliverances, moreover the less evidence, the more virtuous the faith exercised. The leap of faith on his account involves a radical departure from rationality, most clearly in his affirmation that faith faces a paradox, the Paradox of the Incarnation, in which the Infinite becomes finite, and the Eternal becomes temporal.

lemma–a theorem proved in the course of, and for the sake of another theorem.

libertarian freedom–freedom that is contra-causally free, free of antecedent causes and conditions necessitating the choices in question.

Logos–in John's Gospel, Christ is referred to as the *Logos* (the *Word*).

M

materialism–the view that all of reality is reducible to matter alone, in respect to mind/body metaphysics, it is the view that persons are reducible to matter.

maximal perfection–having all compossible perfections (that is, having all perfections without contradiction)

Mencius (4th century B.C.)–a faithful and famous disciple of Confucius who held that human nature is basically good..

metaethics–that branch of ethics which deals with the meaning of ethical terms such as *good*, *praiseworthy*, and takes up the task of the justification of ethical principles and ethical reasoning.

metaphor–the non-literal meaning of a word used to express an idea, a literary expression used to stand for a literal substitute..

metaphysics–that area of philosophy which deals with questions and issue pertaining to reality, its components or *furniture*. It addresses questions about the existence and structure of humans, God, and nature.

meticulous providence–the view that God controls every event. Thus he has a justification for *every* evil.

middle knowledge–knowledge of counterfactual conditionals of freedom (Molinism).

miracle–an unusual or wondrous event brought about by a supernatural being; according to Hume, *a violation of natural law*.

modal–in cases of *de dicto modality*, having to do with the sort of affirmation made, whether it is *possibly true*, a *necessary* truth, or a *contingent* truth, or in cases of *de re modality*, it describes modes of being: *possible* being, *necessary* being or *contingent* being.

model–a way of looking at reality.

Molinist–one who holds that God has middle knowledge (Luis de Molina).

monotheism–the view that there is only one God.

moral argument–Kant believed that being moral is not sufficient to guarantee happiness. Being happy means that everything will follow according to one's will and desire. In order to guarantee that everything will go according to one's will and desire, one has to postulate the existence of God..

mysterium tremendum (Rudolf Otto)–the idea or sense of awe when faced with the awe-inspiring experience of the divine.

mystical–having to do with the experience of God (John Baillie). Not all religious experiences are mystical. This should perhaps be differentiated from so-called *numinous* mystical experiences, which are usually viewed as being beyond descriptions formulated in terms of rational categories (Evelyn Underhill).

mysticism–see mystical above.

N

natural theology–that knowledge of God acquired by the natural light of reason without the aid of special or supernatural revelation, the Word of God.

naturalism–the idea that the universe is fully explainable in physicalistic terms.

necessary being–a being which is such that if it exists, it cannot not exist, and if it does not exist, it cannot exist. A logically necessary being is a being whose existence cannot be denied without contradiction, and who exists in all possible worlds.

noetic–having to do with knowledge, or the cognitive capacity.

Noumena (Kant)–that which is beyond the limits of sensibility, intuition, or experience, that which transcends the phenomenal or world of appearances.

Numinous (Otto)–the experience of a mysterious Reality beyond the realm of the physical world.

O

omnibenevolent–all good or beneficent to all persons.

omnicompetent–capable of bringing about any set of states of affairs compossible with the nature of the agent in question (roughly equivalent to *omnipotent*).

omnifisicent–literally, *all creating*, the capacity of bringing about *all things* consistent with the Creator's nature.

omnipotent–capable of bringing about any logically consistent set of states of affairs compossible with the agent's nature.

omnipresent–everywhere present, or, there is no place where the agent is absent in terms of *knowledge* and *power* (Aquinas).

omniscient–all knowing, there is no truth that the agent in question does not know, consistent with his nature.

ontological argument–an argument which attempts to prove the existence of God from concepts alone. Anselm argued that God existed because he was the *greatest conceivable being*, and Descartes argued this since God is the *being with all perfections*.

orison–a method of meditation and spiritual discipline whereby the believer draws close to God (especially in Roman Catholicism).

P

panentheism (as in Process theology)–the universe is one with God, that is God is the universe, but there is some residue remaining if the universe were not to be in view.

pantheism–the view that the universe and God are identical.

paradigm–a model for viewing reality, or a proposed way of understanding and explaining data. A scientific model.

paradox–either a real or an apparent contradiction.

passion argument (Adams's account of Kierkegaard)—Adams contends that Kierkegaard argues that one should be maximally passionately committed to God, and that the degree of the passional element hinges on the degree of probability of the truth of Christianity. Increasing the probability of the truth of the Christianity, reduces the degree of passionate commitment required.

perfectly free—the state of an agent who is free to choose only between or among good alternatives. Many have held that God is only perfectly free (Anselm, Aquinas, etc.).

person-relative—a belief P (or value V) may be said to be person-relative if for example P is held by person A, but not by another B..

person-variable—a belief P (or value V) may be said to be person-variable if P is held by person A at time t_1 but not time t_2.

perturbation—an agitation or movement of the body (Russell).

phenomenology—In Husserl, the descriptive study of the essential structures of the acts and contents of consciousness, based upon reductions of the contingent and an intuitive grasp of the essences of the phenomena.

pluralism—the view that there is more than one entity in a given area of inquiry.

polytheism—the view that there is more than one God.

possibilism—the view that anything is possible, even violations of the canons of logic (Descartes, according to Plantinga in Does God Have a Nature, evidenced a limited possibilism and a universal possibilism, the former involving the claim that God is not bound by the rules of logic since he creates them, and limited possibilism, the view that God binds himself by the rules of logic once he creates them.)

possible worlds—the idea that there are possible sets of possible states of affairs which are comprehensive or all-inclusive, which combined constitute a possible world (Plantinga).

Post-modernism—a 'family resemblance term' which covers a wide variety of ideas advanced by various contemporary philosophers (Derrida, Foucault, Rorty and company). One contention is that Descartes' project to find certitudes is a misguided and hopeless task, and another, that there is no such thing as being objectively neutral. It is mainly a counter-Enlightenment way to doing of philosophy that has many interpretations.

postponement argument (Adams on Kierkegaard)—the argument Adams says Kierkegaard offers in support of his claim that the evidence required to justify faith is never forthcoming, hence one will always have to keep the door open, therefore faith can't be based on or rely upon the evidence since postponement means *never committing*.

praiseworthy—having the moral value meriting positive acclamation and affirmation.

predestination—to determine outcomes in advance without failure by willing them to happen.

presentism—the view of time which affirms that only the *present* exists, not the past or future.

prima facie—what appears to be the case at first glance.

Principle of Sufficient Reason— the view that all contingent states of affairs or beings require an explanation of their existence.

Process philosophy/theology (Whitehead, Hartshorne)—the view that reality is in process, and where the divine limits himself to allowing human agents to realize their own goals without divine intervention or coercion.

proof—an argument which is valid, and where the disputant agrees that the premises are true.

properly basic beliefs (Plantinga)–beliefs whose *warrant* does not issue from other beliefs or arguments, and hence are basic, and *properly so*, in the sense that persons who believe them have the epistemic right to do so.

Providence–that doctrine of God which claims that he sees to it that every person is provided or cared for.

Q

quantum mechanics–though there are varying *interpretations* (Bas C. Van Fraassen, *Quantum Mechanics*), this new theoretic picture of the universe offers two modal *interpretations*, one that "quantum physics describes an *indeterministic* world,...the other...the quantum theory of an isolated system which depicts its state as evolving *deterministically*." On one interpretation, it was "devised to describe only situations in which an observer is involved" (for measurement of physical phenomena). On another, a *many-worlds* interpretation, indeterminism is an illusion... " (Ibid, p. 272)

R

RT–simultaneity–is the occurrence at the same time within the reference frame of an observer.

ratio evidens–the evidence supplied by reason.

rationalism–the view (Descartes, Spinoza, Leibniz) that all knowledge comes from reason, and during the Modern period, rationalists also held that certain ideas are *innate* (such as the idea of God).

rationality–following the rules or canons (rules) of logic, good clear argumentation.

recreationism–the doctrine or belief that the Christian idea of the resurrection involves a re-creation or a remaking of the physical body or human person (Bruce Reichenbach, Peter van Inwagen).

redemption–the idea that human guilt and sin can somehow be paid for by another, for some this redemptive act is viewed as substitutionary, while others are inclined to think of it as a supreme way of demonstrating divine love.

reduction ad absurdum–the method in reasoning involving the assertion of an hypothesis, which hypothesis is then proven false by reducing it to a contradiction.

Reformed epistemology–an approach (in the tradition of Calvin, Plantinga adds Aquinas), to theory of knowledge which involves the claim that belief in God is properly basic (has warrant apart from other beliefs and argument), and that a cognitive apparatus can be operating properly when affirming such a belief.

Reincarnation (Plato)–the doctrine that when a person dies, the soul continues to live on and may inhabit another body, and this continues everlastingly into the future.

reliabilism–a view in theory of knowledge, that a person is justified in holding a belief only if the belief is exercised on the basis of a *reliable indicator* (Alston, it is noteworthy here that Alston bridges *externalism* and *internalism*, see these terms above, Alvin Plantinga, *Warrant the Current Debate*, 184, 185).

Resurrection–the Christian doctrine or belief that believers (and unbelievers) at some final future stage of history will experience the acquisition of a new body replacing the one that experienced physical death in this life.

S

satori–a level of achievement, brought about in a moment of instantaneous enlightenment, usually by means of a puzzle that is not capable of resolution by rational means, usually associated with Japanese Buddhism thought.

Scholasticism–the philosophy of the 'schools' commonly associated with the methods of thinkers of the thirteenth and fourteenth centuries, notably Anselm (the "Father of Scholasticism), Aquinas, Scotus and Ockham, all of which tried to give a rational account and defense of Christian belief.

self-transcendence (Westphal)–a desire and willingness to be myself, and letting God be God.

sempiternity–the state of being eternal.

Shangti–Chinese term for *heaven* or *God*.

significantly free–an agent that is free to choose good or evil.

simpliciter–a concept proposed or considered without qualifiers.

simultaneity–two events occurring at the same time.

sin–a moral failure or breach of a command, in Christianity, Judaism and Islam, violation of the law of God.

simple foreknowledge–knowledge of future contingents without knowledge of possible alternatives.

skepticism–the view that one cannot know.

soul–the non-material entity, which some take to be equivalent to spirit.

states of affairs–*sets* of states of affairs, or *what is the case* (Wittgenstein)

strongly actualize–the process whereby God brings about something with his agency apart from other agents.

substance–what can exist or subsist by itself.

sufficient reason–an explanation adequate to account for the set of states of affairs in question.

supererogatory–something done beyond the degree required, an especially praiseworthy act, superfluous.

supernaturalism–the view that there is something over and above the physical universe.

surd evils–unjustified evils.

symbol–something which stands for something else, such as a word.

T

Taoism–an Eastern philosophy, some take it as a religion, founded upon the doctrine of the ancient Chinese philosopher, Lao-tze (c. 550 B.C.). As a religion in China it ranks with Confucianism and Buddhism as one of the three main religions. Two basic texts are the *Chuang Tzŭ* and the *Lao Tzŭ*, both composed around the 4th-3rd centuries B.C. The basic tenet is the idea that the human world should be continuous with the natural order, and that if there is any tension, the course to follow is *wu wei* (non action), that is, go with the flow of nature.

teleological argument–the argument which proceeds from the observation that there is design in the universe, to the conclusion that this results from an intelligent designer, which is God. Various versions of the argument have been tendered of recent, notably the fine-tuning argument included in this collection (Gary Collins).

temporal eternity–that the Supreme Being, God, is eternal, but his eternity is not conceived as without temporal notions such as *past, present, future, before* and *after*.

theodicy–(a term introduced by Leibniz) an attempt to identify all of the reasons God may be viewed as having and which justify the existence of all of the evils in the world. This strategy is to be distinguished from a *defense*, which more modestly only attempts to identify a possible reason that might justify one particular kind of evil.

theonomous principle (Tillich)–the notion that the creature loves the law of God because it is *of* God (issues from him), and because God also *loves* it.

timeless–outside of time.

transcendent–beyond or above or outside of a given sphere.

transcendental (Kant)–a formal principle that is, an a priori concept or principle that has the status of being *universal* and *necessary*; that which is foundational for all else.

transworld depravity (Plantinga)–the idea that humans possibly enjoy a transworld identity regarding their *essences*, and further that their essences are possibly infected with a transworld depravity, such that in every world where they exist they make at least one choice that is evil.

transworld identity–see the first part of *transworld depravity* above.

Trinity–the doctrine of the Christian faith that God is essentially (ontologically) comprised of three Persons, the Father, Son, and Holy Spirit, all three of which are divine and eternal.

U

universal possibilism (Descartes)–see *possibilism* above.

utilitarian (Bentham, Mill)–in ethics, the normative position which says a motive/action is right which maximizes happiness/pleasure and minimizes pain for the most.

V

verification principle (a criterion of meaning of the Logical Positivists, Herbert Feigl, A. J. Ayer and company.)–the principle that a synthetic/empirical statement S is meaningful only if there are observations that can be made in actuality, or conceived in principle, which would confirm or support S.

via negativa–an approach to definition or explanation by way of negation, such as, God is a spirit, that is, he has *no body*, is *infinite, immutable* and *eternal*.

W

warrant (Plantinga)–the status which allows Plantinga to assert that a belief is properly basic, and so a person has an epistemic right in holding warranted beliefs.

weakly actualize–the process of actualization or of bringing about which involves God and the activity of the creature, in contrast to strongly actualize.

world (Wittgenstein)–*all that is the case*.

Y

yoga–in Hindu religious philosophy, union with the Supreme Being.

Z

Zen–that branch of Mahayana Buddhism that claims lineage back to Gautama (the founder). It is a form of Buddhism which features sitting meditation, and wordless, silent/noncommunicable enlightenment.

Zoroastrianism–an ancient Persian system of thought started by Zoroaster which holds to an afterlife, and a lifelong struggle of good and evil with the good eventually winning.

INDEX

A

absolute telos, 25
abstemious pluralist, 615
actualizing versus creating, 255n12
Adams, Marilyn McCord, 283-301, 312, 319
Adams, Robert Merrihew, 17-28, 356, 364, 378, 384, 390, 391, 531-540
Adam's sin, 268
Adams, Thomas, 60
Advaita, 79
a fortiori argument, 330, 344
alethic parity, 620
al-Ghāzāli (1058-1111), 119
Allah, 590, 591
almighty, 211-219, 341-351
Alston, William P., 199-206, 300, 303-326
American Civil War, 18
animism, 497
Anselm of Canterbury (1033-1109 A.D.), 98, 117-118, 138, 270, 292, 417, 425
Anselm's satisfaction theory, 289
anthropic principle, 169, 492
anthropological dualism, 557
anthropological materialism, 564
anthropological monism, 557
Approximation Argument, 17-20, 22
Aquinas, Thomas (1224/5-1274/5 A.D.), 31, 42n34, 45-58, 98, 119, 121, 128, 137, 150, 270, 345, 347, 349, 417, 445, 546, 592, 611
Aquinas/Calvin Model, 29-43
archeological evidence, 31
arguments for God's existence, 2-5
argument from laws of nature, 149-160
Aristotle (384-322 B.C.), 119, 128, 186, 348, 350, 380 420, 573
asymmetry of time, 382
atemporal life, 409-411
atheistic single universe hypothesis, 172
Athanasius (c. 296-373 A.D.), 49, 50
Atonement, 35n17
attributes of God, 7-8

Augustine (354-430 A.D.), 47, 51, 53, 57, 60, 193, 248, 268, 270, 445
Augustine *dubita*, 183
Augustine manuscript, 565, 571
Augustinians, 182
autonomy, 524
auto-pistic, 29

B

Baker, Lynn, 568
Bambi, 305, 309, 311, 314, 321, 323, 325
Banezians, 377, 380, 392
Barr, Stephen M., 503-509
Barth, Karl (1886-1968), 63n11
Basinger, David, 597-607
Bayes's Theorem, 165, 166n10
Bayesianism, 165
Beck, Lewis White, 521
Bede, St. (c. 673-735), 442
behaviourism, 558
belief as meritorious, 54-55
Bell's theorem, 491
benevolence, 77, 215
Berkeley, George (1685-1753), 59, 66n18
Berkhof, L, 272
Bertolet, Rod, 354
Bertrand paradoxes, 172
best possible world, 231
Beza, Theodore (1519-1605), 273
Big Bang Theory, 128, 129, 130, 131, 156, 482, 483
biosphere, 161
blackbody radiation, 129
Bodh Gaya, 594
Boethius, Anicius Manlius Torquatus Severinus (c. 480-524 A.D.), 399-416, 417
Bohr, Niels (1885-1962), 485
Bolton, Robert, 60
Boltzman, Ludwig, 174n20
Bonaventure, St. (1221-1274), 97, 119
Brahman, 78, 195, 557, 590
Braine, David, 426
Broad, Charles Dunbar (1887-1971), 343

Brothers Karamazov, 74
brute facts, 131
Buddha, 593
Buddhism, 587, 595
Buddhist dharma, 588
Buddhist liberation, 588
Bullough, Edward, 185
Bultmannian, 29
Burke, Edmund (1729-97), 185
Burnet, Gilbert, 71n35
Bush, George, 90
Butler, Joseph (1692-1752), 98

C

Calvin, John (1509-1564), 29-31, 38n25, 39, 40
Cambridge Platonists, 59
Camus, Albert (1913-60), 192
Cantorian mathematicians, 127
Carlyle, Thomas (1795-1881), 29n1
Carnap, Rudoph (1891-1970), 165
Carry, Bernard, 168
Cato, Marcus Porcius (234-149 B.C.), 435
C-conductive argument, 448
Chalmers, David, 504, 505
chaotic systems, 503
charismatic phenomena, 495
Chisholm, Roderick, 89n1
Christian epistemic practice (CEP), 201
Christmas, 193
C-inductive argument, 131
Clark, Samuel (1675-1729), 65n15, 119, 138
Clayton, Philip, 495-502
Cleaver, Gerald, 175n22
Clement of Alexandria (150-215), 79
closest continuer, 561
cognitive malfunction, 36
Collins, Robin, 161-179
common grace, 80
compatibilism, 224
compatibility, divine eternity/Incarnation, 415
complex universe, 132
conditional epistemic probability, 171
conditional excluded middle (CEM), 382-388
Confucius (551-479 B.C.), 589

conscience, 523
consequent absolute necessity, 270
constitutive autonomy, 514-517
contingency argument, 121-122
Copenhagen Interpretation, 485
core person, 561
cosmological argument, 119-135, 137, 137, 138, 148
cosmological constant, 103
Council of Chalcedon (451 A.D.), 271, 272
Council of Nicea (325 A.D.), 271
Council of Trent (1545-63 A.D.), 272n27
counterbalancing, 229, 270
counterfactually independent, 364
counterfactuals of freedom, 355, 357, 382-384
counter Reformation, 273
Craig, William Lane, 119, 120, 125, 127, 378, 479-493
creatio continuans, 481
creatio ex nihilo, 481
Creel, Richard, 280n4, 281n5, 294-295
Croce, Benedetto (1866-1952), 185
Crusius, Christian August (1715-75), 517-520, 522, 523
Crusius's divine command theory, 513
Cudworth, Ralph(1617-1680), 68n25
Curley, Smith, 258
curvature of space-time, 172n16

D

Damascus, St. (c. 304-84 A.D.), 51
dark energy, 130
dark matter, 130
Davies, Paul, 130, 161, 177, 479
death, 110, 553-555
death and immortality, 10, 11
de Broglie-Bohm pilot wave, 485
decree(s), 272, 273
defeater, 598, 618
defensive strategies, 5-7
deistical writers, 62
de Molina, Luis (1535-1600), 355
Dent, Arthur, 60
Denton, Michael, 164
deontological, 273
deontologically justified, 33

De Retz, Cardinal, 440
Derridean deconstruction, 183
Descartes, René (1596-1650), 242, 343, 344, 575, 599
descriptivist fallacy, 517
design argument, 161-179
deterministic non-quantum processes, 503
Dharmakaya, 590
dialectical theology, 190
different logics, 497
Dirac, Paul, 177
dispositional property, 558
divine beauty, 66-69
divine command metaethics, 531, 539
divine command theory, 544
divine good, 55
divine instigation, 32, 35
divine possibility, 292
divine Reality, 588, 589, 590, 592
Doctor Zhivago, 190
Dole, Andrew, 36n19
doxastic internalism, 90
Duns Scotus (1266-1308), 98, 121, 518, 519, 523, 527
Durkheim, Emile, 538
duties, 513-529

E

Eccles, John Carew, 507
Eddington, Sir Thomas, 487
Earman, John, 165n7
Edwards, Jonathan (1703-1758), 276n39, 31, 37, 40n29, 59-87
egoism, 615, 616
Eichman, Adolph, 537
Eightfold Path, 588
Einstein, Albert (1879-1955), 176, 177
Einsteinian concept of time, 406
ends-justifies-the-means principle (EJM), 279
enormous good, 331, 332
entropy, 129
epistemic duty, 603
epistemic justification, 200
epistemic practice, 200
epistemological probability, 171n14
E-simultaneity, 403

ESP research, 453
exchatological theodicy, 265
eternal happiness, 17, 18
eternality, 399
eternity, 399-416, 417-427
ET-simultaneity, 403-409
Eunodius, St. Magnus Felix, of Pavia (c. 473-521), 268
euthanasia, 542
Euthryphro, 520, 546
evidentialism, Edwards, 84-86
evolution, 95
exclusivism, 609
explanatory function of religious beliefs, 495
extended A/C model, 624
external rationality, 35-37
externalism, 90, 93, 95, 96
Exultet, 268

F

faith, 29-35, 45-58
faith and reason, 2-3
faith as a virtue, 56-57
faith as an object of science, 48-49
Falkner, William, 192
fatuity, 185
felix culpa, 269
Feuerbach, Ludwig Andreas (1804-72), 63n11
Feynman's sum-over-histories approach, 485, 486
Fichte, Johann Gottlieb (1762-1814), 184
Fiddes, Paul, 293, 295
fine-tuning argument, 161-179
First Sustaining Cause, 120-125
Flint, Thomas, 353
foreknowledge, 353
Foster, Michael, 349, 350
Freddoso, Alfred, 380
Freeman, Dyson, 162
free will, 503-509
free will defense, 239-265
free will solution, 216
Frei, Hans, 30n2
Freud, Sigmund (1856-1939), 63n11, 190
Fuller, Margaret, 29

G

Gadamer, Hans, 183, 188, 190
galaxy 2, 397
Galilean Law of the Addition of Velocities, 572
Gale, Richard, 120
Gandhi, Mohandas Karamchand (1869-1948), 452
Geach, Peter, 341-351
General Reliability Argument (GRA), 599, 600, 601
General Theory of Relativity (GTR), 152, 482
God as relatively timeless, 490-423
God as the Ground of time, 418
God as the Lord of time, 418-420
God as sufficient reason, 479-481
God-created universe, 158
Gödel, Kurt (1906-78), 611
God's commands, 513-529, 531-540
God's will, 523
Grand Unified Field theories, 152, 176
Grant, W. V., 447
gratuitous evil, 302, 306
great good, 331
greater good, 235, 237, 307, 329,
greater good defense, 227-238, 267-282
Gregor, Mary, 524
Gregory of Nyssa, St. (c. 330-395), 591
G-simultaneity, 403
guilt, 532, 538
Gutting, Gary, 63n10. 617=624

H

Hare, John E., 513-529
Hare, R. M., 520
Harré, Rom, 156
Harter, Donald H. 460
Hartshorne, Charles, 286, 293, 297
Hasker, William, 307n8, 353-374
Hawking, Stephen, 125, 128, 479-493
heavenly vision, 47
Hegel, Georg Wilhelm Friedrich (1770-1831), 187
Heidegger, Martin (1889-1976), 191
Heidelberg Catechism, 29

Helm, Paul, 149n1, 419, 426, 427
Heroditus, 442
Hesperus is Phospherus, 581
heteronomy, 513
Hick, John, 267, 269, 275, 500, 587-596
Hick's soul-making theodicy, 291
higher order goods, 329
Hinduism, 456, 587, 595
Hindu margas of mystical insight, 588
Hobbes, Thomas (1588-1679), 62, 341
Holland, R. F., 469
Holmes, Arthur, 497n7
horrendous evils, 294-295
Hoyle, Fred, 479
Hucheson, Francis, 70, 71, 185
human cognitive condition, 303-326
Hume, David, 62, 74, 120, 123, 138, 142, 143, 223, 263, 433-444, 451, 452, 455, 456, 457, 465, 467, 474
Humean supervenience, 153
Husserl, Edmund (1859-1938), 185

I

idealism, 77
identity, 575-583
identity theory, 559
illimitability, 401
imago dei, 234
immortality, 557-570, 571-574
impossibility of an actual infinite, 122-124
Incarnation, 35n17, 412
incomprehensibility, 61
Increase in firmness principle, 165
inductive argument from evil, 303-326
inductive probability, 89
informative designators, 582
infralapsarianism, 272
internal irrationality, 223
internal rationality, 35
internalism, 91, 94
intrinsic probability, 92n3
Irenaeus, St. (c. 130-200), 271n21
Islam, 119, 285, 587

J

James, William (1842-1910), 81, 84, 146

Index

Jastrow, Robert, 479
Jesuits, 441
Jonah, 549
Judaism, 587, 593, 595
Julian of Norwich, 289
justification, 617

K

Kaku, Michio, 175
kalām argument, 119, 120, 125-131, 482
Kane, G. Stanley, 276
Kant, First Antinomy/time, 483
Kant, Immanuel (1724-1804), 120, 124, 185 190, 194 513-529
Kantian, 591
karma, 500
kath' auto, 191, 192
Kenny, Anthony, 123, 354n2, 364, 391, 392, 394
Kierkegaard, Søren (1813-1855), 17-28, 85, 181
King of the kingdom, 516
kingdom of ends, 523
Kissinger, Henry, 241
Kline, Meredith, 275n38
Knutzen, Martin, 517
Kojève, Alexandre, 184, 185
Köningsburg, 517
Korsbaard, Christine, 513, 515, 525
Kretzmann, Norman, 399-416
Krishna, 594
Kuhn, Thomas, 63n10, 496
Kvanvig, Jonathan, 36n18, 386

L

Lady of the Grotto, 458
Last Judgement, 101, 102, 103, 104
laws of nature, 149
Lazarus, 466
leap of faith, 19, 27
Lee, Sang Hyun, 64
legislative function, 525
Leibniz, Gottfried Wilhelm (1646-1716), 98, 119, 138, 251, 254, 480 559, 560
Leibniz's Lapse, 258
Le Poidevin, Robin, 221-225

Leslie, John, 164, 169n13
levels of explanation in religion, 498-501
Levinas, Emmanuel, 187, 192, 193, 194
Levine, Robert A., 460
Lewis, Clive Staples (1893-1963), 186, 194, 449, 450, 451, 466, 581
Lewis, David, 90, 174n20, 357, 358
Lewis's kangaroos, 363
libertarian free choice, 359
life-permitting range, 167n11, 168
likelihood principle, 165
limitless being-consciousness-bliss (Brahma), 588
Lochak, Georges, 485
Locke, John (1632-1704), 59, 67, 70, 71, 74, 89n1
Lourdes, 445, 457-461
Lovejoy, Arthur, 268
Lucas, John R., 503n1
Lucian, 438
Luther, Martin (1483-1546), 242 497

M

Mackie, John L. (1917-1981), 120 211-219, 239, 242, 251, 285
Macquarrie, John, 33, 34
Madden, E. H., 150
Mahabharata, 589
Mahayana Buddhism, 79, 587
Mahomet, Mahometanism, 439
Maimonides, Moses (1135-1204), 292
Malebranch, Nicholas (1638-1715), 59, 76
many universes generator scenario, 175
many-universes hypothesis, 164, 173-177
Marcel, Gabriel (1889-1973), 182
Mariana, 442
Mars, 170
Martin, Michael, 445-463
Marty, Martin, 196
martyr's sacrifice, 319
mass-energy, 163
mature moral character (MMC), 276, 277
Mavrodes, George I., 337-339, 465-475
maxienvironment, 36
maximal word segment, 258
M-beliefs, 200
McKinnon, Alastair, 407, 408, 409, 471

McTaggart, John McTaggart Ellis (1866-1925), 341, 343, 344, 345
measured time, 421, 422
Mellor, D. H., 489
mental phenomenalism, 76
mental property, 575, 576
Merton, Thomas (1915-68), 182
metaphysical possibilities, 321
Michael, the Archangel, 281
Micheli, Vittorio, 460
middle knowledge, 353-374, 375-382
Milton, John (1608-74), 281
Minkowski, H., 490
miracles, 8, 433-444, 445-463, 465-475
Mitchel, Basil, 62n9
Moby Dick, 74
modal logic, 470
Molinism, 375-398
Moltmann Jügen, 296-298
monism, 557-570, 571-574
monotheism, 497
Moore, George Edward (1873-1958), 185
morality, 541-549
morally sufficient reason, 229
More, Henry, 59
Mt. Moriah, 594
Muhammed, 589
multiple replicas, 566-569
Murray, John, 272n25
Mussalini, Benito (1883-1945), 555
mutakallimūm, 119
Muyskens, James L., 40n32

N

naked kernel, 561
Narnia stories, 581
natural goods, 84
naturalism, 150
Nazi death camps, 285
necessary truth, 241
negataive apologetic thesis (NAT), 5999-603
Newman, Cardinal, 622
Newton, Isaac (1642-1727), 59, 176
Newtonian physics, 131
Newton's law of gravity, 162
Newton's laws, 454

Nicea, Council of (325 A.D.), 49
Nietzsche, Friedrich Wilhelm (1844-1900), 188, 554
Nixon, Richard, 407
nominalist, 547
nomological, 469, 473
non-finite universe, 129
no probability objection, 170-173
numinous, 63n11
Nyāya tradition, 119
Nyāyakusumānjali, 119

O

objective uncertainty, 18
object of faith as the First Truth, 45-46
obligation, 531-540, 544, 545
occasionalism, 76, 77
Ockham's razor, 296
Ockhamist, 380
omnipotent, 97, 211-219, 239, 242, 244, 250, 255, 257, 258, 304 327, 337-339, 341-351
omniscient, 97, 293, 304, 327
ontological argument, 117-118
Origen (c. 185-254 A.D.), 271
oscillating universe, 129
other forms of life objection, 168
Otto, Rudolph (1869-1937), 63n11, 287
overbalance, 229

P

Padgett, Alan, 417-429
Paley, William (1743-1805), 98
panentheism, 497
Paphlagonia, 438, 439
Paradise Lost, 281
paradox, 61
paradox of omnipotence, 217
Parfit, Derek, 578
Parmenides (c. 480 B.C.), 202, 402
Pascal, Blaise (1632-1662), 20
Pascal's Wager, 27
Passion Argument, 17, 22-27
passionate inwardness, 17
Paul, 98n12
Pauli-exclusion principle, 177

Index

Penelhum, Terence, 419
Penrose, Roger, 163, 164, 485, 506
perfect changing God, 424-425
perfectly free, 149
Perkins, William, 60
Perrin, Serge, 459
personal explanation, 130
Peter, 19
phenomenology, 620
phenomenology of religion, 496
Philo (c. 20 B.C.-50 A.D.), 223
Philosophical Fragments, 21
physical probability, 89
Pike, Nelson, 299-300, 413
P-inductive argument, 131, 448
Plantinga, Alvin, 29-43, 120, 239-265, 267, 300, 318, 353, 356, 364, 392, 393, 395, 597-607, 609-624
Plato (427-347 B.C.), 81n54, 119, 575
Platonic, 72n37, 38
Platonist heavens, 155
pluralism, 597-607, 609-624
Plutarch (c. 46-120 A.D.), 439, 442
Pollock, John L., 357, 358, 359,
Popper, Karl (1902-94), 492
possibility of natural theology, 61-65
possible worlds, 252
possible worlds semantics, 362
postmodern, 33
Postponement Argument, 17, 20-22
potential infinite, 127
Price, Richard, 347
primary/secondary qualities, 69
prime principle of confirmation, 167
principle guilt, 536
principle of causation, 121
Principle of Conservation of Mass-Energy, 123
Principle of Credulity, 89, 92, 94, 96
principle of excluded middle, 121
principle of sufficient reason, 120, 121, 125, 146
principle of testimony, 94, 97
Principle Principle, 90, 93n4
prior probability, 93
probability defeater, 611-613
problem of circularity, 77-78
problem of evil, 5-7, 327-333

proper basicality, 37
properly basic belief(s), 29
propositional warrant, 597
providential plan, 233
pscudo-random, 503
pure rationalist, 513
Puritan, 60, 70

Q

quanta (gravitons), 172n15
quantum indeterminacy, 503, 504, 506
quantum mechanics, 307, 483, 484
quantum physics, 125-126
quantum processes, 503
quantum theory, 152, 485 503-509
Qu'ran, 557, 594
Qu'ranic way of life, 588

R

Rahner, Karl (1904-84), 595
randomness, 503
reciprocal relationship, 497
re-creation, 562-563
Redemption, 267-282
reductionism, 560
Rees, Martin, 168
Reformation, 271, 272
Reformed epistemology, 96
Reichenbach, Bruce, 119-135, 275, 320, 557-570
Reid, Thomas (1710-1796), 37
relata, 403
relativity of simultaneity, 404
reliabilism, 90
religion and ethics, 9-10
religion and science, 8-9
religious beliefs, 89-99, 101-109, 199-206
religious experience argument, 199-206
religious explanation, 495-502
religious pluralism, 11-12, 587-596, 597-607
Rennie, Drummond, 460
repentance, 271
resurrection, 571-574
revolution of the will, 514
Ricoeur, Paul, 74, 189

Roberts, Oral, 447
Roberts, Robert, 528
Rogo, Scott, 453
Rolt, C. E., 285, 286, 292, 298
Rorty, Richard, 63n10
Ross, W. D., 72
Rous, Francis, 60
Rowe, William, 120, 123, 137-148, 304n2, 305, 309, 315, 316, 323, 325
Russell, Bertrand (1872-1970), 138 553-555
Russell, Bruce, 305
Ruth, Babe, 139

S

Sagan, Carl, 479
St. Mary's Church of Zeitoun, 445
salvation, 587-596
salvific efficacy, 595
satori, 587
Schellenberg, J. L., 612
Schleiermacher, Friedrich Daniel Ernst (1768-1834), 497
Schneewind, J. B., 513, 515, 518, 527, 528
Schopenhauer, Arthur (1788-1860), 185
scientia, 31n9
Scriptures are reliable, 65
Second Adam, 277
self-authenticating, 38, 39
self-deception, 175-198
self-forgetfulness, 189
self-transcendence, 175-198
sense of the heart, 65-66
Shaftesbury, third Earl of (1671-1713), 62, 185
Shiva, 590, 591
Sibbes, Richard, 70, 73
simulacrum, 574
simultaneity, 402
single universe hypothesis, 165-166
Sklar, Lawrence, 491
Smart, J. J. C., 170
Smith, George, 169n13
Smith, John, 72
Smith, Quentin, 120
Smith, Wilfred Cantwell, 63n10, 500 613-616
social requirements, 532-534

social theories, 532
Socinus, 271
soteriological, 596
Sovereign Pontiff, 49, 50
space-time curvature, 314
special grace, 80
Special Theory of Relativity (STR), 489
specificational "offspring," 279
Spinoza, Baruch (or Benedictus 1632-77), 346
spiritual beauty, 70, 73
spiritual cognition, 71
spiritual sensing, 70-73
split-brain experiment, 578, 579
Stalnaker, Robert C., 357
statistical probability, 89
Sterry, Peter, 60
Stewart, Melville Y., 1-12, 267-282
Stoics, 284, 285
stund in God's time, 422
Stump, Eleonore, 316, 399-416
Suárez, Francisco (1548-1617), 360
subjunctive conditionals, 384
suffering of God, 313
sufficient reason, 170
supernatural vision of God, 53
superstring theory, 175
supralapsarianism, 270, 272
Supreme Demander, 536-539
surd evils, 279
Sutta Nipata (Buddhist), 589
Swinburne, Richard, 39n28, 86, 89-99, 119, 120, 124, 130, 132 149-160, 327-333, 446, 541-549, 575-583
symbolic values, 283-284

T

Tacitus, 439
Tahquitz Rock, 361
Tao, 557, 590
Taylor, Richard, 120
Tegmark, Mark, 174n20
teleological argument, 137
temporal duration, 409, 410
Theaetetus, 347
theodicy, 328
Thomas, 34, 47

Thomas à Kempis (c. 1380-1471), 195, 196
Thomist, 380
Tillich, Paul, 497n4
Tillotson, John, 433
timeless time, 428
T-simultaneity, 403, 404
Titus, Livius, 439
Torah, 588
Tracy, Thomas F., 317n27
transcendentalist, 29
Transfer of Necessity Principle (TNP), 381
transplants, 578
transworld holy (TWH), 280
Trinity, 48, 50, 53, 54, 271 414, 571
Twain, Mark, 29

U

undefeated defeaters, 35
Uddiyāna, 119
Ultimate Observer, 486
Uncaused Cause, 119
universal history, 499
unrestricted comprehension principle, 572
Upanishads, 592

V

Van Fraassen, Bas, 173
van Inwagen, Peter, 561, 571-574
Vedas, 78
veil of soul-making, 310, 311, 312
Virgin Mary, 453
Vishnu, 590, 591

W

Wainwright, William J., 59-87
warrant, 35-37
Weatherford, Roy, 173
Weil, Simone, 287
Weinberg, Steven, 177
Westphal, Merold, 175-198
Weyl, Hermann, 507
who designed God objection, 169
wholly other, 184
Wierenga, Edward, 386

Wilde, Oscar, 185
Williams, B. A. O., 567
Wilson, Bert, 181
Wittgenstein, Ludwig Josef Johann (1889-1951), 101-109
Wolterstorff, Nicholas, 32n10
world germ, 379-380
would-probably conditionals, 370
Wykstra, Stephen, 308
Wynn, Mark, 153n8

X

Xing, Taotao, 1-12

Y

Yandell, Keith, 227-238, 276
Young, Edward J., 275n38

Z

Zagzebski, Linda, 375-398
Zen Buddhists, 595
Zeus, 456
Zoroastrianism, 589

Thomas à Kempis (c. 1380-1471), 195, 196
Thomist, 560
Tillich, Paul, 457-8
Tillotson, John, 237
timeless time, 25
Timaeus (tr.), 403, 404
Tiru, Livius, 439
Torah, 586
Tracy, Thomas F., 317n2
transcendentalism, 20
Trapnel of Necessity Principle (TNP), 38
triangulation, 579
Trisagion (holy (TWH)), 480
Trinity, 46, 50, 53-54, 391, 414-427
Twain, Mark, 29

U

undefeated defeaters, 35
Udphadana, 170
Ultimate Observer, 486
Uncaused Cause, 179
universal history, 499
unrestricted comprehension principle, 572
Upanisads, 592

V

Van Inwagen, Bas, 175
van Inwagen, Peter, 561, 571-574
Veritas, 73
veil of soul-making, 310, 311, 312
Virgin Mary, 443
Vishnu, 590, 591

W

Wainwright, William, 59-87
warrant, 35-37
Weatherford, Roy, 173
Wells, Anne, 281
Weinberg, Steven, 172
Westphal, Merold, 195-198
Werth, Horman, 307
who designed God objection, 165
wholly other, 188
Wiesner, Edward, 188

Wilde, Oscar, 185
Williams, R. A. O., 507
Wilson, Ian, 151
Wittgenstein, Ludwig Josef Johann (1889-1951), 101-109
Wolterstorff, Nicholas, 220
world, end of, 570-580
would-probably conditionals, 370
Wykstra, Stephen, 208
Wynn, Mark, 18 n6

X

King; Tropic, File

Y

Yandell, Keith, 237-238, 276
Young, Edward J., 253n8

Z

Zagzebski, Linda, 375-392
Zen Buddhism, 595
Zeus, 438
Zoroastrianism, 589